South Africa Handbook

Lizzie Williams & Francisca Kellett

> ❝❞
> Africa has her mysteries, and even a wise man
> cannot understand them, but a wise man
> respects them.
>
> *Miriam Makeba*
> *South African singer and activist*

Footprint story

It was 1921

Ireland had just been partitioned, the British miners were striking for more pay and the federation of British industry had an idea. Exports were booming in South America – how about a handbook for businessmen trading in that far away continent? The Anglo-South American Handbook was born that year, written by W Koebel, the most prolific writer on Latin America of his day.

1924

Two editions later the book was 'privatized' and in 1924, in the hands of Royal Mail, the steamship company for South America, it became The South American Handbook, subtitled 'South America in a nutshell'. This annual publication became the 'bible' for generations of travellers to South America and remains so to this day. In the early days travel was by sea and the Handbook gave all the details needed for the long voyage from Europe. What to wear for dinner; how to arrange a cricket match with the Cable & Wireless staff on the Cape Verde Islands and a full account of the journey from Liverpool up the Amazon to Manaus: 5898 miles without changing cabin!

1939

As the continent opened up, The South American Handbook reported the new Pan Am flying boat services, and the fortnightly airship service from Rio to Europe on the Graf Zeppelin. For reasons still unclear but with extraordinary determination, the annual editions continued

1970s

Many more people discovered South America and the backpacking trail started to develop. All the while the Handbook was gathering fans, including literary vagabonds such as Paul Theroux and Graham Greene (who once sent some updates addressed to "The publishers of the best travel guide in the world, Bath, England").

1990s

During the 1990s the company set about developing a new travel guide series using this legendary title as the flagship. By 1997 there were over a dozen guides in the series and the Footprint imprint was launched.

2000s

The series grew quickly and there were soon Footprint travel guides covering more than 150 countries. In 2004, Footprint launched its first thematic guide: *Surfing Europe*, packed with colour photographs, maps and charts. This was followed by further thematic guides such as *Diving the World*, *Snowboarding the World*, *Body and Soul escapes*, *Travel with Kids* and *European City Breaks*.

2008

Today we continue the traditions of the last 87 years that has served legions of travellers so well. We believe that these help to make Footprint guides different. Our policy is to use authors who are genuine experts who write for independent travellers; people possessing a spirit of adventure, looking to get off the beaten track.

South Africa is celebrated, first and foremost, for its incredible natural beauty. It has some of the most varied and extreme environments in the world, from the tropical beaches of KwaZulu Natal to the sweeping emptiness of the Kalahari Desert. Yet it is the people, a fascinating mix of cultures, religions and ethnicities, who are the beating pulse of South Africa, and who give meaning to its nickname, 'Rainbow Nation'. Many visitors come here to see the Big Five – the collective term for the big-bucks players of wildlife spotting: elephant, black rhino, buffalo, leopard and lion. While the choice of excellent game reserves virtually guarantees sightings, the country's vibrant cities are an equally compelling reason to visit. There's the fast-paced sophistication of Johannesburg and Pretoria, the steamy humidity and spicy Indian influence of Durban, or the spectacular setting and quirky beach-side hedonism of Cape Town.

Contents

A family group of cheetahs
in typical pose.

ANUP SHAH/NATUREPL.COM

Where to go

South Africa has more to offer than you could ever hope to manage in one trip. There's an expansive choice of worthwhile destinations around the country and it's a very easy place to get around. The magnificent natural beauty – South Africa's main attraction – is represented in the multitude of game reserves and national parks, which are home to a whole host of wildlife. South Africa's vibrant cities – another major draw – are characterized by the cosmopolitan populations you'd expect from the Rainbow Nation. Here there are numerous exciting urban attractions as well as the best eating and shopping opportunities on the African continent.

South Africa's history is compelling too, from the early hunter-gatherers to the arrival of the Europeans, the Boer War and the more recent breakdown of Apartheid, reflected in the cave paintings, colonial architecture, lively townships, moving battlefields and contemporary museums.

Being outdoors is also very much a way of life here and you can try hiking and surfing, or opt for one of the booming adrenaline sports such as bungee jumping or whitewater rafting. In short, the choice

of destinations, activities and itineraries is virtually inexhaustible, so careful planning is needed to make best use of your time.

South Africa's facilities, food and accommodation tend to be of a very high standard, and there's a wide range of travel options available. Independent travel is one of the most popular ways of seeing the country and South Africa's road and transport network is one of the best on the continent. Modern highways, a train network, buses and comprehensive internal flights link all the main urban centres. The best way of getting around is to hire a car. This allows the freedom to explore more remote areas and also provides independent access to national parks. There are also ever-expanding choices of organized tours, which take in the national parks and historic sites, focus on sports such as scuba diving, or are tailored to specific interests such as history or flora and fauna.

The absolute minimum time to spend in South Africa is around two weeks. Rather than cram in too much, try to arrange a visit to a specific region so you can fully appreciate what there is on offer; you can always return to another part of the country at some time in the future.

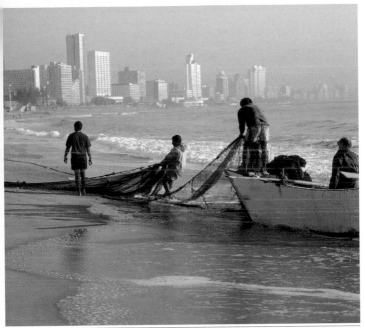

Above: Fishermen pull in their nets on Addington Beach, Durban.
Opposite left: Roasted mealies are sold from street stalls all over South Africa.
Opposite right: In Cape Town's Bo-Kaap district houses are painted in bright hues of lime, pink and blue.

As arrival in the country will probably be either via Johannesburg, Cape Town or Durban, it's best to stick to the areas accessible from these cities if you are on a shorter holiday; there are plenty of worthwhile attractions within striking distance of Jozi, the Mother City or Durbs as they are affectionately known.

The best way of getting around is to hire a car. This allows the freedom to explore more remote areas and also provides independent access to national parks.

If you have more time, venture further afield into the other provinces too, or even other countries. South Africa completely surrounds the mountain kingdom of Lesotho and most of Swaziland and these two countries, along with Namibia and Botswana, allow cars hired in South Africa to cross their borders. Another alternative would be to go on a longer organized tour which might take in several southern African countries. In short, an international flight to South Africa opens up all sorts of opportunities to visit the tip of the African continent.

None of the suggested sample itineraries overleaf are set in stone and the options are far from exhaustible; rather, they are regional suggestions for travellers wishing to explore a certain area of South Africa, or for returning visitors to travel somewhere new.

Itineraries

Two weeks

Cape Town and Western Cape

Spend a minimum of four to six days in Cape Town exploring the sights and enjoying the fine shops and restaurants. The city is home to historic buildings, museums, beautiful beaches, the botanical gardens of Kirstenbosch and the famous Constantia wine estates. Climbing to the top of Table Mountain or riding in the cable car should definitely be on the agenda, while organized and thought-provoking tours to Robben Island and the townships on the Cape Flats will offer a glimpse of South Africa's fragile past. Day trips are available to the Cape of Good Hope and Cape Point via the spectacular Cape Peninsula, the beautiful wine estates around Stellenbosch and, in flower season, to the West Coast to see the spring blooms. From Cape Town spend a week or more following the coast along the Garden Route, stopping off along the way at pretty towns such as Hermanus on the Whale Coast, Knysna or Plettenberg Bay, and at the beautiful Tsitsikamma National Park. Return to Cape Town via the tranquil back country roads surrounded by vineyards through the Western Cape interior, known locally as Route 62. Alternatively, if you have a few more days, at the end of the Garden Route in the Eastern Cape Province is the quirky surfing town of Jeffrey's Bay and the excellent Addo Elephant National Park and its neighbouring private game reserves. Again you can drive back, but there is also the option of flying back to Cape Town from Nelson Mandela Bay (Port Elizabeth).

KwaZulu Natal

Another two-week itinerary could start with a day or two in Durban where you can stroll along the beachfront and perhaps take an afternoon excursion to the Valley of 1000 Hills,

or go shopping at the massive Gateway Mall before heading north up the tropical coast road to Zululand. At least two days is needed to explore Hluhluwe-Imfolozi Game Reserve, which is home to one of the world's largest rhino populations and has been instrumental in saving this creature from extinction. The

Hiking is popular in the Table Mountain National Park. Here the trail heads towards Lion's Head.

lakes and wetlands at St Lucia warrant a day or two especially the gorgeous beach at Cape Vidal, and divers should head for the coral reefs at Sodwana Bay. Turning inland, go via the mountain reserve of Itala for one night and then on to Dundee, which is a suitable base for exploring the numerous battlefield sites relating to the Anglo-Boer and Anglo-Zulu wars. Allow a full day to do a guided tour of Isandlwana and Rorke's Drift; longer for the other sites. Then head across the Natal Midlands to the magnificent mountain chain which forms a natural border with Lesotho – the uKhahlamba-Drakensberg National Park. There are plenty of mountain resorts and country hotels to choose from and at least three or four days should be spent here to enjoy the scenery.

Northern provinces

The north is for travellers who want to see more unusual and isolated destinations, but be prepared to spend long stretches behind the wheel. Starting in Johannesburg head north to Sun City, the hedonistic casino and leisure resort next to the Pilanesberg National Park in the North West Province. To appreciate all there is on offer here stay at least two days. Then move on to one of the north's best-kept secrets, the Madikwe Game Reserve, where a number of excellent lodges offer game-watching activities. Moving on east, a long drive brings you to Kimberley in the Northern Cape where you can visit the newly vamped Kimberley Mine Museum and Big Hole to learn all about the diamond wealth that modern South Africa is founded on. Drive further north and spend three or four days in the Kgalagadi Transfrontier Park, a stunning Kalahari wilderness with a unique ecosystem, or the Ai-Ais Richtersveld Transfrontier Park where the Gariep (Orange) River winds its way towards the ocean between soaring granite cliffs. From the extreme north it's a two-day drive south to Cape Town, though there are a number of distractions along the way such as the Namakwa flowers in season, the Cederberg Wilderness Area and the west coast. Alternatively head north to explore southern Namibia and the Fish River Canyon.

Gauteng, Mpumalanga and Swaziland

Another two-week option can start with three or four days in Johannesburg or Pretoria to take informative township and city tours and visit the historic buildings and museums, such as Pretoria's Voortrekker Monument or Johannesburg's excellent Apartheid Museum and Gold Reef City. Johannesburg in particular is also known for its chic shopping malls and craft markets, varied restaurant districts and happening nightlife, and it regularly hosts major sporting events. From Gauteng head east into Mpumalanga to visit the Kruger National Park, South Africa's premier wildlife destination, which warrants at least four or five days. The area around Kruger is commonly known as the Panorama Region because of

its stunning mountain scenery. Game drives in Kruger can be combined with a visit to the Blyde River Canyon, one of the deepest canyons in the world, and the pretty mountain towns of Graskop and Sabie, as well as the historic gold-mining towns of Pilgrim's Rest and Barberton. From here you could head south into Swaziland for a couple of days' relaxation at the Mlilwane Wildlife Sanctuary or one of the lesser-known nature reserves and try some cycling, horse riding or hiking through the tranquil bush.

Three weeks

Free State and Lesotho

In addition to one of the above itineraries, visitors with another week to spare can head south from Johannesburg to the Eastern Highlands and spend a night in the scenic Golden Gate National Park in Free State. From here you can cross any of the borders into Lesotho and spend two or three days in a resort such as Malealea or Semonkong, hiking or pony trekking in the cool mountain kingdom. This is sufficient time to get a taste of Lesotho, but spend a few more days to see Lesotho's greatest attraction, which are the highlands. Until recently fairly inaccessible, new tarred roads have opened up three spectacular routes: the mountain road from Maseru to Thaba-Tseka; the new tarred road from Hlotse to Katse Dam; and the 'Roof of Africa' road between Butha Buthe and Mokhotlong. All these roads are in good enough condition during the drier months to attempt in a normal saloon car. If you have a 4WD, the last two routes can be linked in a full circle by the road between Mokhotlong and Thaba-Tseka. There's another stunning drive in the far south of the country between Moyeni (Quthing) and Qacha's Nek and, except for a short section around Sekake, it is accessible by normal car. The options from Lesotho depend on where you are and what border to cross, but both Johannesburg and Durban can be reached in a (long) day.

South Africa highlights & itineraries

See colour maps in centre of book

Two weeks

Cape Town & Western Cape

KwaZulu Natal

Northern provinces

Gauteng, Mpumalanga & Swaziland

One-week extension

Free State & Lesotho

BOTSWANA

NAMIBIA

Kalahari

Kgalagadi
Transfrontier
Park

Green Kalahari
Upington

Ai-Ais
Richtersveld
Transfrontier
Park

Diamantv

Springbok

NORTHERN CAPE

Namaqua

Atlantic Ocean

Great Karoo

Garden Route

Gorgeous beaches, pretty
forests, scenic lagoons
and a number of
attractive seaside towns,
page 301.

Winelands

World-class wines,
rolling vineyards, stark
mountains and historical
Cape Dutch estates,
page 151.

WESTERN CAPE

*Tsitsikamma
National
Park*

Cape Town   Stellenbosch   Heidelberg   Knysna

Plettenbe
Bay

Cape Town

Climb Table Mountain,
soak up the culture, shop
up a storm, or lounge on
the pristine beaches,
page 78.

Hermanus

ZIMBABWE

MOZAMBIQUE

Kruger National Park

King of the game parks, with top facilities and the chance of spotting the Big Five among many other equally interesting animals and birds, page 618.

LIMPOPO

○ Polokwane

Johannesburg

Learn South Africa's vivid history in some excellent contemporary museums such as the critically acclaimed Apartheid Museum, and the lively township of Soweto, page 562.

Blyde River Canyon

Graskop ○

● Madikwe Game Reserve

● Pilanesberg National Park

MPUMALANGA

Nelspruit ○

Sun City ○

PRETORIA □

Barberton ○

● MBABANE □

Mlilwane Wildlife Sanctuary

● Mmabatho

● Johannesburg

GAUTENG

Ermelo ○

SWAZILAND

NORTH WEST PROVINCE

Vryburg ○

Lesotho

Explore the cool mountains, steep valleys and waterfalls of the 'Kingdom in the Sky' by Basotho Pony, page 804.

Volksrust ○

● Warrenton

Harriesmith ○

○ Dundee

○ St Lucia

● Winburg ○

Golden Gate National Park ◆

Hluhluwe-Imfolozi Game Reserve

Kimberley ○

FREE STATE

KWAZULU NATAL

Bloemfontein ○

□ MASERU

LESOTHO

Durban

Famous beaches, rolling surf, a vast shopping mall and an intriguing Indian culture, page 435.

○ Semonkong

Malealea ○

● Durban

uKhahlamba-Drakensberg Park

Lofty peaks, verdant valleys, San rock art and the finest trekking in southern Africa, page 493.

EASTERN CAPE

Addo Elephant National Park

An accessible park that is home to herds of wild elephant and the unique flightless dung beetle, page 377.

Port St Johns ○

Wild Coast

Deserted windswept beaches backed by sheer cliffs and villages of isolated Xhosa kraals, page 416.

○ East London

● Nelson Mandela Bay (Port Elizabeth)

Jeffrey's Bay

Indian Ocean

N

100 km

100 miles

Game reserves

Kruger

Kruger Park is the king of South African game parks and one of the best game-viewing areas in all of Africa. The figures speak for themselves: 507 bird species, 114 reptile, 49 fish, 34 amphibian, 147 mammal and over 23,000 plant species have been recorded here. The region itself is enormous, extending from the Crocodile River in the south to the Limpopo River in the north, from the wooded foothills of the eastern escarpment to the humid plains of the lowveld. It certainly fulfils most visitors' fantasies of seeing magnificent herds of game roaming across acacia-studded stretches of savannah, and of course it is home to the Big Five.

Pilansberg

This, the fourth largest national park in South Africa, has imported animals from all over southern Africa: elephant and buffalo from Addo Elephant National Park, black and white rhino from the Natal Parks Board, eland from Namibia, Burchell's zebra and waterbuck from the Transvaal and red hartebeest from the Northern Cape and Namibia. It was also the natural habitat for a number of rare species already in existence, including brown

hyena, Cape hunting dog and sable antelope. You now have a good chance of seeing all the large animals including rhino, elephant, lion, cheetah, buffalo and even leopard.

Madikwe

Covering over 60,000 ha, this reserve has the second largest elephant population in South Africa. In the 1990s more than 10,000 animals were successfully released into the reserve. Animals now present include elephant, zebra, lion, buffalo, white rhino, spotted hyena, wild dog, steenbok, duiker, kudu, leopard and cheetah. Visitors are able to view these animals during game drives or on morning walks with a guide and experienced tracker. The introduction of community projects is allowing local communities to benefit from, and contribute to, the ecological management of Madikwe.

Addo

With the reintroduction of lion in 2003, it is now possible to see the Big Seven – elephant, rhino, lion, buffalo, leopard, whale and great white shark – in a malaria-free environment. The expansion of the park is one of the most exciting and ambitious

BOLESLAW KUBICA/SHUTTERSTOCK

conservation projects ever undertaken, and Addo, now home to the densest population of elephant on earth, has become a highlight of the Eastern Cape.

Hluhluwe-Imfolozo

This is one of the best reserves in KwaZulu Natal for seeing wildlife, and one of the finest in the world for seeing rhino. The varied landscapes of Hluhluwe-Imfolozi provide a wide range of habitats which support large numbers of big game. The Big Five are present and there are important populations of three rarely seen animals: the white rhino, the black rhino and the nyala. Despite the thriving hippo populations in nearby St Lucia, there are fewer than 20 hippo in this park because the rivers flow too fast. Over 300 species of bird, including the rare bateleur eagle, have been recorded in Hluhluwe-Imfolozi; bird lists are available from the camp offices.

66 99

It certainly fulfils most visitors' fantasies ...

the honey badger. Leopard are, as always, elusive but are seen relatively regularly in the park. You should also see giraffe, red hartebeest, Burchell's zebra and huge herds of wildebeest and springbok. The birdlife, too, is impressive. Over 200 species have been recorded in the park. The best viewing months are between February and May, especially if the rains have been good.

Kgalagadi Transfrontier

Although probably one of the least-visited national parks in the country, the Kgalagadi Transfrontier Park has some of the finest game viewing in Africa. It is remote and relatively undeveloped, with uncomfortably high summer temperatures, but few visitors begrudge the hot dusty roads once they've glimpsed their first lion. The park is famous for its predators, particularly the dark-maned Kalahari lion which can sometimes be spotted lazing in the shade of trees found along the river beds. Other predators to look out for include cheetah, wild dog, spotted hyena, bat-eared fox, black-backed jackal and

Spas and retreats

Bushman's Kloof

Set in a remote World Heritage Site renowned for its ancient rock art, and with stunning views across the Cederberg Mountains and rugged plains of the Great Karoo, Bushman's Kloof offers real luxury in the wilderness. For a pampering fix, there's a spa offering facials and Moya therapies which use aromatic, therapeutic and native South African essences to heal, nourish and soothe. Reflexology, aromatherapy, Swedish and deep-tissue massages are also available. There are plenty of hiking routes and the chance to swim in natural rock pools or three pools at the lodge, one of which is heated. Mountain biking, rock climbing and canoeing are also available, or take a game drive to spot antelope, zebra and wildebeest then watch the sun set from a nearby hilltop with a glass of wine.

Mount Grace

A favourite venue for stressed-out Gautengers set in lovely manicured grounds in the Magaliesburg Mountains, Mount Grace is a fine country house with luxury cottages spread up the hillside with their own plunge pools. The elegant thatched spa is surrounded by tumbling waterfalls and a hydrotherapy garden completely enclosed by trees. Here warm water flows through various features including a reflexology stream where you can walk over small smooth pebbles and pick them up with your feet, a large stone jacuzzi and an enormous indoor flotation pool painted in deep blue, with dim lights, underwater whale sounds and stars on the ceiling.

Lanzerac Manor

This 300-year-old traditional Cape Dutch wine estate 4 km outside Stellenbosch is an excellent luxury hotel offering gourmet food and wine and 'spafaris'. These involve numerous treatments, time in the indoor pool and hydrotherapy area, wine tasting, a walk or golf cart ride around the estate, ending with a massage and picnic under the arms of a huge willow tree. The spa

BUSHMANS KLOOF

Opposite page: Bushman's Kloof is one of the best places to see San art in South Africa.
Above: The flotation pool at Mount Grace – open to non-residents – has underwater whale sounds.
Right: The 18th-century Lanzerac estate offers spa treatments, wine tastings and cellar tours.

has saunas, steam rooms and wet rooms, and overlooks the vineyards, and there's a gazebo for outdoor treatments and a deck area on the roof for relaxing in the sunshine.

Coach House

This fine country hotel near Tzaneen in Limpopo Province is set in the picturesque Magoebaskloof Mountains and is an ideal stopover to or from Kruger. Here the Agatha Spa is centered around the Sensorium, an open-plan area incorporating a gym, heated hydro-jet pool, saunas, steam rooms and restaurant. This entire space is glass-fronted and has excellent views of the surrounding mountains and valleys. The comprehensive spa menu includes an unusual nougat body wrap and the hotel has a special kitchen dedicated to making nougat, which it sells locally.

Ulusaba

Richard Branson's super luxurious Ulusaba Private Game Reserve lies in the heart of exclusive Sabi Sands in Mpumalanga on the edge of Kruger and features stunning hilltop thatched suites with their own plunge pools. Pampering is in the temptingly named Aroma Boma, where you can try rejuvenating facials including one for the dominant male called the Lion Tamer, which also involves a close shave. After a game drive massages can be taken in the privacy of your own spacious wooden deck with magnificent views over the 13,500 ha of unspoilt, game-rich bush.

Etali Safari Lodge

In the North West Province's Madikwe Game Reserve, this luxury and intimate game lodge has suites under thatch with contemporary African furnishings, crisp white linen on the vast beds and double baths. The partially open-air spa with soothing splashes of green and beaded ethnic decor has a gym, steamroom, pool and reflexology walk; treatments include salt rubs and body wraps – the mud one is charmingly named Warthog Hour – and there's a full range of facials, manicures and pedicures.

Wineries

six of the best

Constantia Uitsig Wine Estate

Constantia Uitsig winery, hotel and restaurants are situated only 20 minutes from Cape Town's city centre, but they could be in another world. In the shadow of the Table Mountain the estate offers an exhilarating eating experience for travelling gourmets. Sixteen garden rooms have glorious views of the Constantia Valley, while a short walk through the gardens leads to the Wine Shop, where the estate's range of fine wines can be sampled. The luxuries of this hotel, its surroundings, wines, top restaurants – Constantia Uitsig, La Colombe (voted 28th Best Restaurant in the World by Restaurant Magazine 2006), and the less formal Spaanschemat River Café – make this the perfect destination for visitors with adventurous tastes.

Groot Constantia

The oldest working winery in the Cape was established in 1685 but, until recently, it was worth visiting for everything except its wine. The landmark building was undeniably interesting but the state-owned winery was underperforming woefully. A shift in philosophy and the arrival of a new winemaker have wrought huge changes, so that, today, the Gouverneur's Reserve Cabernet Sauvignon is one of the best, most subtle reds in the Cape. The Manor House contains a museum and the Cloete Cellar provides an idea of what winemaking was like here over two centuries ago. There are two restaurants: Simons and the more interesting Jonkershuis, which offers good Cape Malay cooking and estate wines.

Steenberg Vineyards

The history of Steenberg stretches back to the 1600s, when the original name of this area was Swaaneweide, meaning 'the feeding place of swans'. Today, it is spur-winged geese that are to be found here. In the mid-1800s the estate was sold to the Louw family, who owned it until 1990, when it was purchased by Johannesburg Consolidated Investments, which re-developed it into the impressive vineyard that it is today. There are around 70 ha under vine; 60% is white – mostly Sauvignon Blanc, followed by Chardonnay, Sémillon and Muscat de Frontignan – and the rest is red: a mix of Cabernet Sauvignon, Merlot, Cabernet Franc, Pinot Noir, Shiraz, plus some Nebbiolo.

CONSTANTIA UITSIG WINE ESTATE

CONSTANTIA UITSIG WINE ESTATE

Above: Steenberg Vineyards in the Constantia Valley
Opposite page left: Al fresco dining at Constantia Uitsig with views across vineyards to Table Mountain.
Opposite page right: A garden guest room at Constantia Uitsig.

Boschendal

Boschendal estate has been producing wine for 300 years and is today one of the most popular estates in the region, not least for its excellent food and pleasant wine-tasting area underneath a giant oak. The restored H-shaped manor house is one of the finest in South Africa, and is open as a museum to the public. Interestingly, a third of the estate is now owned by a black empowerment consortium. Most of the wine produced on the estate is white; their sparkling wines are highly regarded.

Saxenburg Wine Farm

The Bührer family of Switzerland took over Saxenburg in 1989 and dedicated their time to reviving the family tradition of the estate's historic past, ensuring its growth and development in future years. They also fulfilled their wish to have a sister vineyard in France, acquiring Château Capion, near Montpellier, in 1996. Saxenburg is situated on the hills above Kuils River, between the Atlantic and Indian oceans, where the vineyards enjoy ideal conditions. There are around 90 ha of vines, growing predominantly Shiraz, Cabernet Sauvignon, Sauvignon Blanc, Merlot and Pinotage. The Guinea Fowl Restaurant specializes in fresh seafood, game and a variety of exclusive guinea fowl dishes. The wines are all Saxenburg, with plenty of older vintages . There is a vine-covered terrace giving a Mediterranean feel and wonderful views of the sunsets over Table Mountain.

Spier Wine Centre

Located in a beautifully restored 17th-century barn on the main estate, the Spier Wine Centre stocks more than 200 wines. It is a haven for any wine-lover, with rare vintages, collectors' labels, and the estate's own range of wines, including their award-winning Cabernet Sauvignon and Merlot. There is also a range of wine accessories available, a delivery service, and the knowledgeable staff are always keen to help. Tastings are run every day, with the emphasis on communicating the best way to truly appreciate wine. In its passion for growth and innovation, the estate also hopes to broaden the role of the Spier brand with its diverse Programs in Education for Wine, Food and the Arts.

When to go

South Africa has a moderate climate and long sunny days for most of the year. You will only come across truly tropical conditions in the northeast corner of KwaZulu Natal around Kosi Bay and the border with Mozambique. During summer it rarely gets hotter than 30°C, though Gauteng and KwaZulu Natal get very humid, and parts of the Northern Cape experience temperatures in the region of 45°C – too hot for most people. The coast around Cape Town and the Garden Route is at its best during the spring and summer months, though the best time for whale watching is in winter. During July and August, in the middle of winter, it can get cold at night in Cape Town and the interior mountains in the Drakensberg and Eastern Cape, with frosts and snowfalls. But winter is the best time to visit the northern desert areas around Upington and the Kalahari. Most of the rain falls in the summer months and, when it does rain, there are often very heavy storms. If driving in these conditions, slow down and pull over. Also be on the lookout for flash floods, especially if you're camping.

The best time of year for game viewing is during the winter months, when vegetation cover is at a minimum and a lack of water forces animals to congregate around rivers and waterholes. Winter is also the best time for hiking, avoiding the high temperatures and frequent thunderstorms of the summer months. Despite being cooler, July and August are a popular time for visitors as they coincide with the European school holidays. December and January are by far the busiest months for South African tourism. Be sure to book your car hire and accommodation well in advance during these periods. One major disadvantage of visiting during the summer is that much of the accommodation is fully booked months in advance, and the coastal towns become horribly overcrowded. For further advice on when to go to South Africa, visit www.weathersa.co.za.

Best of the festivals

If there's one festival you have to attend, it's the National Arts Festival in Grahamstown, South Africa's oldest, biggest and best-known arts festival. It's a 10-day event which takes place in June, with hundreds of performances of theatre, music, song, dance and film. For further information, see Festivals and events, page 53.

South Africa

Activity	J	F	M	A	M	J	J	A	S	O	N	D
See the blanket of spring blooms up the West Coast								★	★	★		
Watch whales from a cliff top in Hermanus						★	★	★	★	★		
Enjoy clear sunny skies in Lesotho		★	★	★				★	★	★		
Dive in the Indian Ocean with ragged-tooth sharks			★	★	★	★	★	★	★			
Relax on glorious beaches on the KwaZulu Natal coast	★	★	★	★						★	★	★
Experience the different seasons in Kruger	★	★	★	★	★	★	★	★	★	★	★	★
Party in sunny Cape Town over the New Year	★											★

Rainfall and climate charts

Cape Town

Month	Average temperature in °C max-min	Average rainfall in mm
Jan	26 - 16	15
Feb	26 - 16	08
Mar	25 - 14	18
Apr	22 - 12	48
May	19 - 09	79
Jun	18 - 08	84
Jul	17 - 07	89
Aug	18 - 08	66
Sep	18 - 09	43
Oct	21 - 11	31
Nov	23 - 13	18
Dec	24 - 14	10

Nelson Mandela Bay

Month	Average temperature in °C max-min	Average rainfall in mm
Jan	26 - 16	31
Feb	26 - 17	33
Mar	24 - 16	48
Apr	23 - 13	46
May	22 - 10	61
Jun	20 - 07	46
Jul	19 - 07	48
Aug	20 - 08	51
Sep	20 - 10	58
Oct	21 - 12	56
Nov	22 - 14	56
Dec	24 - 15	43

Durban

Month	Average temperature in °C max-min	Average rainfall in mm
Jan	27 - 21	109
Feb	27 - 21	122
Mar	27 - 20	130
Apr	26 - 18	76
May	24 - 14	51
Jun	23 - 12	33
Jul	22 - 11	28
Aug	22 - 13	38
Sep	23 - 15	71
Oct	24 - 17	109
Nov	25 - 18	122
Dec	26 - 19	119

Johannesburg

Month	Average temperature in °C max-min	Average rainfall in mm
Jan	26 - 14	114
Feb	25 - 14	109
Mar	24 - 13	89
Apr	22 - 10	38
May	19 - 06	25
Jun	17 - 04	08
Jul	17 - 04	08
Aug	20 - 06	08
Sep	23 - 09	23
Oct	25 - 12	56
Nov	25 - 13	107
Dec	26 - 14	125

Graskop

Month	Average temperature in °C max-min	Average rainfall in mm
Jan	24 - 13	650
Feb	26 - 13	550
Mar	25 - 12	425
Apr	24 - 11	150
May	21 - 06	75
Jun	20 - 05	25
Jul	20 - 04	00
Aug	23 - 06	50
Sep	24 - 08	50
Oct	25 - 10	75
Nov	25 - 11	125
Dec	26 - 10	455

Mafiekeng

Month	Average temperature in °C max-min	Average rainfall in mm
Jan	35 - 13	90
Feb	33 - 11	80
Mar	32 - 09	83
Apr	30 - 04	30
May	27 - 11	25
Jun	24 - 10	20
Jul	24 - 09	15
Aug	27 - 11	20
Sep	32 - 02	25
Oct	34 - 07	50
Nov	34 - 08	75
Dec	35 - 10	90

Bloemfontein

Month	Average temperature in °C max-min	Average rainfall in mm
Jan	30 - 16	91
Feb	28 - 15	79
Mar	26 - 13	76
Apr	23 - 08	56
May	19 - 04	25
Jun	17 - 01	08
Jul	16 - 01	10
Aug	19 - 03	20
Sep	23 - 06	20
Oct	26 - 10	51
Nov	27 - 12	66
Dec	29 - 14	61

Springbok

Month	Average temperature in °C max-min	Average rainfall in mm
Jan	42 - 09	00
Feb	42 - 10	00
Mar	39 - 07	01
Apr	38 - 05	03
May	32 - 04	05
Jun	30 - 02	20
Jul	29 - 01	18
Aug	34 - 02	19
Sep	36 - 02	04
Oct	38 - 05	02
Nov	38 - 07	01
Dec	40 - 08	00

WILLIAM GRAY

Sport and activities

Birdwatching

ⓘ **Southern African Birding**, T031-2665948, www.sabirding.co.za. Birdwatching tours are offered by **Bird-Watch Cape**, T021-7625059, www.birdwatch.co.za, and **Safariwise**, T057-3882811, www.birdwatching.co.za.

With over 700 species of bird recorded in South Africa, birdwatching has become a popular pastime that is easily combined with game viewing. The country's incredibly diverse ecosystems, ranging from fynbos and semi-desert to rainforest, support a fascinating variety of birds, including rare species that are endemic to South Africa.

Above: Bungee jumping at Gouritz River Bridge.

Bungee jumping

ⓘ **Face Adrenaline**, T042-2811255, www.faceadrenalin.com, operates the Bloukrans and Gouritz river jumps.

The most popular location in the country is at the Bloukrans River Bridge between Plettenberg Bay and Tsitsikamma. This also claims to be the highest jump in the world, with a drop of just over 200 m. Also popular is the 60-m leap from the Gouritz River Bridge on the Cape Town side of Mossel Bay.

Diving

ⓘ For more information about dive sites and diving holidays visit www.dive southafrica.co.za. Other operators are listed in the relevant places throughout the book.

The convergence of two major ocean environments provides the South African coast with a particularly rich and diverse marine flora and fauna. The Agulhas current continually sweeps warm water down from the subtropical Indian Ocean and meets the cold nutrient-rich waters of the Atlantic. This mixing of water temperatures has created a marvellous selection of marine ecosystems, ranging from the tropical coral reefs of KwaZulu Natal to the temperate kelp forests around Cape Point. The best time of year to dive the east and southern coast is during the South African winter from April to October when the prevailing wind is from the west. Visibility is generally better and the waters are calmer. Summertime, October to March, is when you can brave the icy waters of the Atlantic for some incredible wreck and kelp dives – visibility often exceeds 20 m. If you want to get away from the crowds avoid South African holidays whenever possible. Dive schools are listed in the relevant chapters. In KwaZulu Natal Sodwana Bay, just south of the Mozambique border, is very popular with South African divers due to its warm, clear waters, tropical reefs and rare but magical whale sharks. There are common sightings of turtles, reef sharks and stingrays, along with a huge variety of hard and soft corals and colourful reef fish. Aliwal Shoal, 5 km offshore, south of Umkomaas, is famous for its ragged-tooth shark season, while Protea Banks, 8 km off Shelly Beach, is for experienced divers only and is known for its hammerheads. In the Eastern Cape, despite

Above: Non-divers can also get close to sharks and game fish at Durban's uShaka Marine World, which has the fourth largest aquarium in the world.

low visibility, the sites around Port Elizabeth are magnificent and boast coral colours more vivid than tropical waters. It is not unusual to see huge pods of dolphins, African penguins and southern right whales in the bay. Along the Garden Route the Underwater Trail at Storms River Mouth camp, Tsitsikamma National Park, is reasonably protected and there are a number of wreck and lagoon dives around Knysna. The area is notorious for great white sharks and dive briefings include rules for reducing the risk of inviting their attention. Plettenberg Bay is popular for its soft coral reefs and sheltered location. Home to dolphins and seals, the bay also acts as a nursery to the endangered southern right whales, which come to calve in winter and spring (July-December). From Cape Town, kelp diving is very popular: the sealife is prolific and the sighting of playful and inquisitive seals and shy sharks (dogfish) common. If the Cape waters are too cold, you can dive in the tanks of the aquarium, at the V&A Waterfront. The tank is surprisingly large, with inquisitive ragged-tooth sharks, stingrays, turtles and large predator fish.

Diving with sharks

Dyer Island is located 10 km off Gansbaai on Walker Bay. Populated by seals, penguins, large gamefish and birds, the area is a natural hunting ground for the protected great white sharks. Shark cage diving raises many questions about teaching sharks to associate humans with food but, for many, cage diving is a chance to witness this magnificent animal in its natural habitat safely. For non-divers there is the opportunity to snorkel at the top of the cage.

Hiking

① Details of the trails are listed in the relevant chapters.

South Africa has an enormous number of well-developed hiking trails, many passing through spectacular areas of natural beauty. These range from pleasant afternoon strolls through nature reserves to challenging hikes in wilderness areas. Hiking in South Africa does involve some forward planning and permits, but the rewards and the choice of trails are well worth the effort. Hiking

Above: The best months for hiking in the Western Cape are March to April and September to December. January and February are very hot and few people walk during these months.

opportunities begin in Cape Town on Table Mountain and the coastal trails around Cape Point, with a number of longer trails along the Garden Route. Inland, the Cederberg is an excellent and isolated hiking area, but the most popular and best-known region is the uKhahlamba-Drakensberg National Park, bordering Lesotho. This is a national park nearly 300 km long where a network of trails (some climbing to over 3000 m) offers hikers a vast mountain region with possibilities comparable to regions of the Himalayas.

Horse riding

ⓘ For information on specialist horse safari operators, contact the **African Horse Safari Association** (AHSA), www.africanhorse.com.

Horse riding is a popular activity amongst farming communities and in mountainous areas. A good place to try it is the Drakensberg, where hotels can organize anything from a short morning trot to a six-day mountain safari. Longer treks are very popular in Lesotho, where ponies are the main form of transport in rural areas. Western-style riding in the Maluti Mountains is organized by Bokpoort Farm outside Clarens in the Free

State. On the Garden Route you can ride in the ancient forests close to Knysna and on the beaches in the Western Cape.

Kloofing

ⓘ **Abseil Africa**, www.absailafrica.co.za, among other operators.

Kloofing, or canyoning, involves hiking, boulder-hopping and swimming along mountain rivers. One of the most popular kloofing trips is to the Kamikaze Kanyon in the mountains above Gordon's Bay just outside Cape Town.

Mountain biking

ⓘ **Mountain Bike South Africa**, www.mtbsa.co.za, has information on trails and events. Cape Town is also well equipped for mountain bikers; contact **Downhill Adventures**, T021-4220388, www.downhilladventures.com, who offer a number of day trips and rent out bikes.

Many nature reserves and wilderness areas have increased their accessibility for mountain bikes, with some excellent routes suitable for all levels of fitness. Some of the

Going on safari

No visit to South Africa is complete without at least one visit to a major game reserve. The game reserves here are not as crowded as the East African game parks and offer visitors the chance of seeing splendid African landscapes and wildlife including the Big Five: elephant, buffalo, rhinoceros, lion and leopard. The optimum times to go viewing are early in the morning and late in the afternoon.

The best season is during the winter months, from July to September, when dry weather forces animals to congregate around waterholes, and vegetation is lower and less dense, making it easier to spot wildlife. Summer weather, from November to January when rainfall is at its highest, also has its advantages as animals will be in good condition after feeding on the new shoots, and there are chances of seeing breeding displays and young animals. The landscape is green and lush, although the thick vegetation and the wide availability of water means that wildlife is far more widespread and difficult to spot.

South Africa's wildlife parks are well organized with good facilities for game viewing, including well-surfaced roads and hides overlooking waterholes. There are numerous safari companies operating out of Johannesburg, Durban and Cape Town, which can arrange accommodation and game-viewing trips as part of a tour. The cost varies, with companies offering everything from bargain backpacker tours to expensive luxury safaris. Organized tours can often provide more game viewing opportunities – quite simply because a group means there are more pairs of eyes on the lookout. Experienced guides will also be adept at spotting well-camouflaged animals. For malaria-free safaris, stick to the game reserves of Madikwe, Pilanesberg and the Eastern Cape; for nature on a grander scale head to Kruger – but be prepared to take precautions against malaria.

LUKA ESENKO/SHUTTERSTOCK

Organizations

▶▶ Most of the national parks and game reserves are under the jurisdiction of **South African National Parks** (SAN Parks), T012-4289111, www.sanparks.org, **Cape Nature Conservation**, T021-4260723, www.capenature.org.za, and **KZN Wildlife**, T033- 8451000, www.kznwildlife.com.

▶▶ If you are travelling independently and planning to visit a number of parks that come under the jurisdiction of SANParks, KZN Wildlife, Cape Nature, or Big Game Parks in Swaziland, then it might be well worth in investing in a **Wild Card**. You pay a set fee – currently R840 per individual, R1475 per couple and R1990 for a family of four – and the card lasts for a year and covers all entry fees into the parks and reserves. This can represent great savings, especially if you are spending a considerable amount of time in the parks, but study your itinerary carefully and compare the costs before you buy. The new **Wild Pass**, aimed at international visitors on short-term visits, is due to be launched soon. See www.wildinafrica.com.

best organized regions include De Hoop Nature Reserve in the Overberg; the Tulbagh Valley, Kamiesberg in Namaqualand, Goegap Nature Reserve outside Springbok, and the mountains around Citrusdal.

Paragliding

ⓘ For a full list of clubs offering courses and tandem glides, visit the website of the **South African Paragliding and Hang-gliding Association**, www.paragliding.co.za.

South Africa has several world-renowned paragliding locations; leaping from Lions Head in Cape Town or floating above the Kalahari are two of the most popular options. Cape Town aside, most of the action is around Kuruman in the Northern Cape and Barberton in Mpumalanga. Climatic conditions in South Africa are ideal – good thermal activity allows gliders to climb between 6 and 8 m a second and the cloud base is usually at 5000 m. The best season is between November and February.

Surfing

ⓘ For more information visit **www. wavescape.co.za**, which has everything you need to know about surfing in South Africa including SMS numbers to get the low-down on local wave action. Spike, who runs the website, is also the author of the book *Where to Surf in South Africa*.

South Africa has quickly established itself as a major surfing hotspot and has some of the best waves in the world. There are, however, two drawbacks to surfing in South Africa. Firstly, the water is cold, especially around the Cape, and full-length wetsuits are generally essential. Second, there is a small risk of shark attack – but remember that attacks on surfers are very rare. Wherever you surf, be sure to listen to local advice, vital not just for safety but also for learning about the best surf spots.

Jeffrey's Bay on the south coast of the Eastern Cape is undoubtedly South Africa's surfing hotspot, known for its consistently good surf and host to the annual Billabong surf championships in July. This is also a good place to learn to surf, with a number of courses available and areas of reliable, small breaks perfect for beginners. The whole southern coast is in fact dotted with good breaks, particularly around Port Elizabeth and East London. Cape Town, too, has an ever-expanding surfing community with some excellent, reliable breaks on the Atlantic and False Bay beaches. Surfing in the Indian Ocean at Durban and the KwaZulu Natal beaches is far warmer than the cool oceans of the Cape, though it's only permitted at designated areas due to the unpredictable currents. The Golden Mile on Durban's beachfront has good surf, well-protected by lifeguards and the presence of shark nets. Floodlit night surfing, sometimes arranged in Durban, is equally entertaining for spectators. The many backpacker hostels around the country are geared up for board rental, escorted surfaris and surfing lessons, and there are dedicated surf schools in Jeffrey's Bay, Durban and Cape Town.

Whale watching

ⓘ www.whaleroute.com has information about whales' migration routes and explanations of breaching, blowing, lobtailing and spy hopping. Contact the **Greater Hermanus Tourism Bureau**, T021-3122629, www.hermanus.co.za, for more details.

Whale Coast, along Walker Bay near Cape Town, trumpets itself as the world's best land based whale-watching spot, and with good reason. Between July and November southern right and humpback whales congregate in impressive numbers in the bay to calve. Whales can also be seen in the sheltered bays from Elands Bay on the west coast all the way round to Mossel Bay and even Ttsitsikamma on the south coast. Boat-based whale watching is also popular from points along the KwaZulu Natal coast, particularly from June to October, when southern right, mink and humpback whales travel from Mozambique to their breeding grounds at the Cape.

Whitewater rafting

ⓘ Details of the operators are listed in the relevant chapters.

There are several excellent rapids in South Africa: the Umzimkulu River in KwaZulu Natal; the Gariep (Orange) River by the Augrabies

Falls or near Kimberley in the Northern Cape; the Great Usutu River in Swaziland and the Sabie, Olifants and Blyde rivers in Mpumalanga. Details of operators are listed in the relevant chapters.

Wine tasting

ⓘ For details of all the routes, visit www.wine.co.za. Also check out Footprint's *Wine Travel Guide to the World*.

The Winelands, near Cape Town, is South Africa's oldest and most beautiful wine-producing area and the most popular tourist destination in the province after Cape Town itself. There are several wine routes criss-crossing the valleys, visiting hundreds of wine estates, which open their doors for tastings, cellar tours and sales. There are also an increasing number of wine routes around the country, such as along the Gariep (Orange) River. See pages 18 and 19.

Opposite page top: Paragliding over Hermanus.
Top right: Humpback whale.
Bottom right: Paddling on the Wild Coast.
Below: Cave Rock, near Durban, one of South Africa's classic waves

Family travel in South Africa

Give Africa a good shake, leave to stand a while and let all the best bits settle at the bottom. It's almost as if South Africa has distilled everything that is thrilling and remarkable about the continent. You might find wilder national parks in Zambia, the wildebeest migration in Tanzania or emptier roads in Namibia, but the Rainbow Nation's irresistible lure lies in its sheer diversity. You've got Cape Town – right up there with other urban beauties like Sydney and Vancouver. You've got vast swathes of wilderness, stunning wildlife, superb food, great places to stay, and, best of all for families, you've got plenty to keep you busy. Boredom simply is not an option – not in a country where, in the same day, you can stand on top of Table Mountain, swim with wild penguins and then tuck into a plate of good old-fashioned fish and chips.

Garden Route highlights

With its sandy beaches, family resorts and countless tourist attractions, the Garden Route is unashamedly the Cape's holiday hotspot. If you've driven straight from Cape Town along the N2 you will be more than

River deep …

You can abseil off Table Mountain and ride an ostrich in the Karoo, but for South Africa's greatest concentration of adventure activities head for the Drakensberg. Merely sighting the 700-m-high rampart of the Amphitheatre in Royal Natal National Park is enough to get the adrenaline pumping. Start by hiking the Sentinel Trail, a two-hour jaunt that climaxes with a short climb using chain ladders. The views are spectacular, particularly of the 3282-m Mont-aux-Sources. Next, raft the Tugela River as it pounds its way along a 22-km stretch of grade II-IV rapids with enticing names like Horrible Horace and Whiplash Smile. Tubing (drifting down-stream in large inflatable rings) is also available on calmer stretches, while the Tugela gorge is a good spot for climbing and abseiling. Mountain biking and horse riding will enable you to probe hidden corners of the Drakensberg and the family resorts have a full range of facilities like swimming pools and tennis courts and some offer canoeing, fly-fishing or clay pigeon shooting.

This page: Chapman's Peak Drive; Cable car to Table Mountain. **Opposite page**: Ostrich riding; the Drakensberg.

ready for a break at Mossel Bay, the gateway town to the Garden Route. Head to **Santos Beach** for swimming or take a one-hour boat trip to Seal Island to view the whales, dolphins, seals and seabirds that inhabit Mossel Bay. The Bartholomeu Dias Maritime Museum contains a replica of the ship used by the Portuguese navigator when he stopped here in 1488 to take on fresh water.

Wilderness National Park is a network of rivers, lakes and estuaries which supports 79 of South Africa's 95 species of water bird. Hire a canoe at Ebb & Flow South Camp and paddle through this watery maze for a spot of twitching. Two of the most popular kids' attractions lie between Knysna and Plettenberg Bay. At **Monkeyland** you can explore a 23-ha sanctuary and cross a 120-m-long rope bridge in search of no less than 14 species of free-swinging primates. Nearby, the Elephant Sanctuary and Knysna Elephant Park offer walking tours with jumbos and a chance to learn about Africa's most southerly pachyderm population. The thickly wooded hinterland of the Garden Route was once a stronghold for elephants, but now only a few survive in the wild. Older kids (14+) can try one of the route's two bungee jumps: a fairly tame 65-m one near Albertina, or a 216-m leap off the Bloukran's Bridge. Here you can also zip across the gorge on a flying fox, and in Tsitsikamma Forest you can glide through the treetops

WILLIAM GRAY

Where can I ride an ostrich?

Oudtshoorn, page 286, has been an ostrich-farming centre since 1864. Depending on their age and attitude, children will either love the ostriches at Cango Ostrich Farm or take one look at the 2-m-tall pecking machines and stick their heads in the sand, so to speak. Kids as young as four or five can ride the birds (which are 'controlled' by two handlers). Just remember that these feathered giants can reach 60 kph and kill a man with a single kick!

on a thrilling canopy tour. Other options include leisurely cruises on the Knysna Lagoon and Keurbooms River, mountain biking in Knysna Forest or a ride on the Outeniqua Choo-Tjoe, a steam train between George and Mossel Bay.

Top three beaches

KwaZulu Natal has mile after mile of glorious, sandy beaches, but take time to pick one that suits the age of your children. South of Durban, **Marina Beach** is excellent for younger children since the surf is usually restrained and there are plenty of tidal pools. North of Durban, **Willard Beach** is also popular with families. For surfing your best bet is shark-netted **Umhlanga Rocks** where you can also go whale watching and kite surfing. If you want lots to do off the beach, base yourself in Durban itself, which has Sea World and The Ushaka Marine Amusement Park.

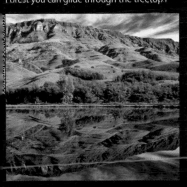

How big is your footprint?

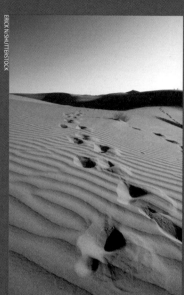

Sustainable or ecotourism has been described as "ethical, considerate or informed tourism where visitors can enjoy the natural, historical and social heritage of an area without causing adverse environmental, socio-economic or cultural impacts that compromise the long-term ability of that area and its people to provide a recreational resource for future generations and an income for themselves". South Africa is a beautiful, wild country but also a living, working landscape and a fragile, vulnerable place. By observing certain guidelines outlined in the box opposite and behaving responsibly you can help to minimize your impact and protect the natural and cultural heritage of this wonderful country.

Environmental legislation plays its part in protecting tourist destinations. CITES (Convention on International Trade in Endangered Species of Wild Fauna and Flora) aims to control the trade in live specimens of endangered plants and animals and also "recognizable parts or derivatives" of protected species. International trade in elephant ivory, sea turtle products and the skins of wild cats is illegal. Restrictions have also been imposed on trade in reptile skins, coral and certain plants and wild birds. If you feel the need to purchase souvenirs derived from wildlife, it would be prudent to check whether they are protected. Importation of CITES-protected species can lead to heavy fines, confiscation of goods and even imprisonment.

Go green: six ways to skip the flights

▸▸ Take a ferry from southern Spain to Morocco (www.trasmediterranea.es) and drive yourself to South Africa.
▸▸ Board a freight ship from the UK to Cape Town (www.strandtravel.co.uk).
▸▸ Sail in style on Cunard from Southampton to Cape Town (www.cunard.co.uk).
▸▸ Avoid internal flights and drive yourself around South Africa.
▸▸ Hop on and off the Bas Bus (www.bazbus.com) from Cape Town to Durban and on to Pretoria.
▸▸ Sit back and relax on the Shosholoza Meyl train linking major South African cities (www.spoor net.co.za).
For more ideas, see www.seat61.com.

Travelling light

» Keep on the well-marked roads and track; off-road driving is harmful because smoke, oil and destruction of the grass layer cause soil erosion.

» Do not drive through closed roads or park areas. It is mandatory to enter and exit the parks through the authorized gates.

» For your own safety, stay in your vehicle at all times. Your vehicle serves as a blind or hide since animals will not usually identify it with humans. In all the parks that are visited by car, it is forbidden to leave the vehicle except in designated places, such as picnic sites or walking trails.

» Stick to the parks' opening hours; it is usually forbidden to drive from dusk to dawn unless you are granted a special authorization. At night you are requested to stay at your lodge or campsite.

» Never harass the animals. Make as little noise as possible; do not flash lights or make sudden movements to scare them away; never try and attract the animals' attention by calling out or whistling. Never chase the animals and always give way to them; they always have right of way.

» Do not feed the animals; the food you provide might make them ill. Once animals such as elephants learn that food is available from humans they can become aggressive and dangerous when looking for more and will eventually have to be shot. If camping at night in the parks, ensure that the animals cannot gain access to any food you are carrying.

» Do not drop any litter, used matches and cigarette butts; this not only increases fire risk in the dry season, but also some animals will eat whatever they find.

» Do not disturb other visitors: they have the same right as you to enjoy nature. If you discover a stopped vehicle and want to check what they are looking at, never hinder their sight or stop within their photographic field. If there is no room for another car, wait patiently for your turn, the others will eventually leave and the animals will still be there. If there is a group of vehicles, drivers should take it in turns to occupy the prime viewing spot. Always turn the engine off when you are watching game at close range.

» Do not drive too fast; the speed limit is usually 40 kph. Speeding damages road surfaces, makes more noise and increase the risk of running over animals.

» Wild animals are dangerous; despite their beauty their reactions are unpredictable. Don't expose yourself to unnecessary risks; excessive confidence can lead to serious accidents.

South Africa on screen and page

Books to read

Probably the best known South African novelist is John Coetzee, whose books include *Dusklands*, *In the Heart of the Country*, *Waiting for the Barbarians*, *Life & Times of Michael K* (winner of the 1983 Booker Prize), *Age of Iron*, *Foe* and *The Master of Petersburg*. He won the Booker Prize again in 1999 for his novel, *Disgrace*, and was awarded the Nobel Prize for Literature in 2003, only the fourth African author to do so and the second South African after Nadine Gordimer. His style is stark and intellectual, but surprisingly accessible. He is one of the most brilliant commentators on the effects of Apartheid.

Another award-winning South African novelist is Nadine Gordimer whose books include *A Guest of Honour*, *The Conservationist* (winner of the 1974 Booker Prize), *Burger's Daughter*, *July's People*, *A Sport of Nature*, *My Son's Story*, *None to Accompany Me* and *Get a Life*. Her beautifully written work tends to concentrate on the way wider political/social events impact on individual lives, and she won the 1991 Noble Prize for Literature. For more books, see page 894.

Films to watch

Given its turbulent history, there have been a number of films made about South Africa. The epic *Zulu* (1964), starring Stanley Baker and a young Michael Caine was about the battle of Rorke's Drift, while *Zulu Dawn* (1979), with Peter O'Toole and Burt Lancaster, depicts the battle of Isandlwana. Movies covering the Apartheid regime include *Cry Freedom* (1987), the true story of black activist Stephen Biko (Denzel Washington), who mysteriously died in police custody, and whose story was taken up by white journalist Donald Woods (Kevin Klein). *Mandela & DeKlerk* (1997) covers the negotiations between the two men who broke down Apartheid and stars Sidney Poitier and Michael Caine, while *Goodbye Bafana* (2007) follows the relationship of imprisoned Mandela (Dennis Haysbert) and his Afrikaner warder (Joseph Fiennes). *Stander* (2004) is the remarkable true story of Andre Stander (Thomas Jane), a 1970s South African police captain who robbed banks during his lunch hour then returned to the scene of the crime to lead the investigation. Home-grown South African film and Best Foreign Language Film in the 2005 Academy Awards, *Tsotsi* (2005) was filmed entirely in Tsotsi-taal, a township gangster rap, and is a powerful story of life for a troubled gang member in a Soweto slum.

Contents

Essentials

Footprint features

Getting there

Air

The three main international airports in **South Africa** are OR Tambo International Airport in Johannesburg, and Cape Town and Durban International Airports. OR Tambo (renamed from Johannesburg International Airport in 2006 after the late anti-Apartheid activist Oliver Tambo) is the regional hub with numerous daily flights to Europe, North America, Asia and Australia. Although most flights arrive in Johannesburg, a fair number of carriers fly directly to Cape Town. There is a huge choice of routes and flights, but for the best fares you need to book three or four months in advance, especially over Christmas.

If you are flying through Johannesburg be sure to allow at least a couple of days to explore the attractions of Johannesburg or Pretoria at the beginning or end of your trip.

Since the liquidation of Lesotho Air several years ago, **South African Airways** (SAA), has been operating the route between Moshoeshoe I International Airport in **Lesotho** and Johannesburg's OR Tambo International Airport. There are at least three flights per day in each direction taking 1¼ hours.

From Europe

British Airways, **Virgin** and South African Airways are the main operators with daily flights between London Gatwick or Heathrow and Johannesburg or Cape Town. Flying time is 10½ hours to Johannesburg and 11 hours to Cape Town. During peak season, a direct return flight can cost as much as US$1800 but if you book several months in advance this can drop to below US$1000. **Nationwide** is a regional carrier in southern Africa but also has one daily flight between Johannesburg and London Gatwick. Other European carriers include Air France, **Air Portugal**, **Alitalia**, **Austrian Airlines**, Iberia, Lufthansa, KLM and Swiss International (LX). Indirect flights from other airlines can also be good value: Kenya Airways flies between London and Johannesburg, via Nairobi; Air Namibia flies between Frankfurt and London to Johannesburg and Cape Town via Windhoek; and Emirates flies daily to Johannesburg via Dubai from just about anywhere else in the world.

Jetlag is not an issue if flying from Europe to South Africa as there is only a minimal time difference.

From North America

Delta Airlines has code share agreement with South African Airways who run daily direct flights from Atlanta to Johannesburg, with connections to Cape Town. Flight time is around 17 hours. American Airlines has an agreement with British Airways, with flights to Johannesburg and Cape Town via London Heathrow.

From Australia, New Zealand and Asia

Qantas code shares with South African Airways, and between them they run a direct daily flight to and from Perth and Johannesburg, flying time 10 hours, with connections from across Australia. Flights run approximately four times per week and on some the same flight continues on from Perth to Sydney. Singapore Airlines offers regular flights between Sydney and Johannesburg via Singapore, and has a code sharing agreement with Air New Zealand (which means that flights from Wellington to Johannesburg have two stops). Malaysia Airlines has regular flights from Perth, Melbourne, Sydney and Darwin in Australia and Auckland in New Zealand to Kuala Lumpur, connecting with a flight to Johannesburg three times a week, which continues on to Cape Town and then Buenos Aires (Argentina). Cathay Pacific flies to/from Johannesburg from Hong Kong once a week.

From Africa and the Middle East

Johannesburg and, in some instances, Cape Town are served by a number of regional airlines that link all the major cities of Africa. These include **Air Botswana**, **Air Madagascar**, **Air Mauritius**, **Air Malawi**, **Air Namibia**, **Air Seychelles**, **Air Tanzania**, **Air Zimbabwe**, **Egypt Air**, **Ethiopian Airlines**, **Ghana Airways**, **Kenya Airways**, **Kulula.com** and **South African Airways** and its subsidiaries **SA Express** and **SA Airlink** and **Virgin Nigeria**. **Emirates** connects Johannesburg with the Middle East.

Airport information

South Africa's international airports are modern and efficient with food courts, shops, banks and ATMs, post offices, car and mobile phone rental desks, and shuttle services into the respective cities. Although there are some direct flights to Cape Town, the majority of international flights arrive in Johannesburg, and then connect on to Durban, Cape Town and the other cities. Johannesburg International Airport has undergone a major upgrade in the last few years and now has a brand new domestic terminal alongside the international terminal, which is a short walk away. Regardless of your eventual destination, immigration is done at Johannesburg, which usually means you have to pick up your luggage from the international terminal and check in again at the domestic terminal. Remember to put locks on your bags – there have been many incidents of things going missing from luggage en route through Johannesburg airport. For information on airport facilities and flight arrivals call T086-7277888 or go to www.airports.co.za.

Moshoeshoe I International Airport is 21 km south of Maseru along the Main South Road. There is a M20 departure tax on international flights when you leave Lesotho. ▸▸ *For further details, see Ins and outs, pages 78, 435, 560 and 791, and Transport, pages 129, 454, 585 and 794.*

Airlines

From the UK and Europe
Air Namibia, T0870 774 0965,
www.airnamibia.com.na.
British Airways, T0870-8509850,
www.britishairways.com.
Emirates, T0870-2432222,
www.emirates.com.
Kenya Airways, T01784-888222,
www.kenya-airways.com.
KLM, T0870-5074074, www.klm.com.
Lufthansa, T0870-8377747,
www.lufthansa.com.
Nationwide, T0129-3596658,
www.flynationwide.co.za.
South African Airways, T0870-7471111,
www.flysaa.com.
Virgin, T0870-5747747, www.virgin-atlantic.com.

From North America
Delta, T1800-2211212 (USA),
www.delta.com.
United Airlines, T1800-5382929
(USA), www.united.com.

From Australia, New Zealand and Asia
Cathay Pacific, T+852-2747 1888
(Hong Kong), www.cathaypacific.com.
Qantas, T131313 (from anywhere in
Australia), www.qantas.com.au.
Singapore Airlines, T+065-6223 8888
(Singapore), www.singaporeair.com.
Air Malaysia, T+603-7843 3000 (Malaysia),
www.malaysia-airlines.com.
Air New Zealand, T0800-737000
(New Zealand), www.airnewzealand.com.

Border crossings

There are good road connections between South Africa and Namibia, Botswana, Mozambique, Lesotho, Swaziland and Zimbabwe. In total South Africa shares 55 border crossings with neighbouring countries. They are generally open daily 0600-1800, though quieter borders will have shorter hours, while the principal border crossings on the main highways are open 24 hours.

South Africa/Botswana

Pioneer Gate and **Ramatlabana** are the main crossings and are in striking distance of Botswana's capital, Gaborone, which lies not far over the border. For those coming from the Cape and the interior of South Africa the border at Ramatlabana (6000-2000), 26 km north of Mafikeng on the R503, is the most logical (see page 699), while from Gauteng, Pioneer Gate (24 hour) is on the N4, 56 km northwest of Zeerust. **Makgobistad** (24 hour), 70 km west of Mafikeng, and **Tlokweng Gate** (6000-2200), next to Madikwe Game Reserve and 101 km north of Zeerust on the R49, are alternative border posts. Crossings are usually swift and efficient.

South Africa/Lesotho

Caledonspoort (T058-2238400, South Africa, daily 0600-2200), see page 801, is the logical border post for visitors arriving in their own transport from Gauteng or northern KwaZulu Natal. **Ficksburg/Maputsoe Bridge** (T051-9332760, South Africa, 24 hours daily), see page 729, is one of the busiest crossings. **Maseru Bridge** (T051-9244300, South Africa, 24 hours daily), page 790, is usually less crowded and is used by visitors arriving from Bloemfontein. **Van Rooyen's** (T051-5831525, South Africa, daily 0600-2200), page 811, is between Mafeteng and the small Free State town of Wepener. **Makhaleng Bridge** (T051-6731484, South Africa, daily 0800-1600), page 811, is close to Mohales Hoek and on the South African road to Zastron. **Tele Bridge** (T051-6331099, South Africa, daily 0600-2200), page 811, the southernmost border, is close to the town of Moyeni (Quthing).

There are five road crossings from the eastern mountains of Lesotho into the uKhahlamba-Drakensberg Park. **Monontsa Pass** (T058-7131600, South Africa, daily 0800-1600) is a little-used crossing between the Lesotho settlement of Libono and the South African village of Phuthaditjaba near to the Golden Gate National Park in the Free State, see page 731. This is the most northerly border crossing and can only be accessed by 4WD. **Sani Pass** (T033-7021169, South Africa, daily 0800-1600), page 802, is a well-known scenic crossing, with poor roads only passable by 4WDs, though there are plans to tar this road on the South African side (should be completed by 2009). **Qachas Nek** (T039-2564391, daily 0600-2200), page 812, is now tarred and is accessible by a normal car and traffic here is increasing. Two border crossings into the Drakensberg are totally unmanned on the Lesotho side and you can only walk or ride a horse across them: **Ongeluksnek** (T039-2567001, South Africa, daily 0800-1600) and **Nkonkoana/Bushman's Nek** (T033-7011212, South Africa, daily 0800-1600), page 813. If you enter Lesotho at either of these, you are required to present yourself at the nearest immigration office in Qachas Nek or Quthing to complete formalities.

South Africa/Mozambique

The journey between South Africa and Maputo has improved considerably since the completion of a toll road between Nelspruit and Maputo via the border at **Komatipoort/Lebombo**, page 609. There's a smaller crossing at **Ponto do Ouro**, in Maputaland, page 549, which, while being accessible by road in a normal car on the South African side, requires a 4WD in Mozambique. Visas for Mozambique are available at the border for US$25, which can also be paid in rand.

South Africa/Namibia

The main crossing point is **Vioolsdrift** (24 hours), page 778, 714 km north of Cape Town along the N7. Less frequently used borders are at **Nakop/Ariamsvlei** west of Upington, page 759, and **Rietfontein** and **Mata Mata**, page 764.

South Africa/Swaziland

The principal entry points from South Africa are **Ngwenya/Oshoek** (daily 0700-2200), page 836, is the busiest and most convenient for Gauteng; **Mahamba** (daily 0700-2200), page 832, east of Piet Retief in Mpumalanga, and **Lavumisa/Golela** (daily 0700-2200), page 832, the most convenient for Durban. Minor entry points tend to have shorter opening hours, such as **Bulembu/Josefsdal** (daily 0800-1600), page 837.

South Africa/Zimbabwe

The only border crossing is at **Beitbridge**, page 674, a notoriously slow crossing during peak periods, with long queues and thorough searches.

Swaziland/Mozambique

The **Lomahasha/Namaacha** border (0700-2000) is 98 km northeast of Manzini on the road that goes through Hlane Royal National Park and is the only crossing between Swaziland and Mozambique. Visas for Mozambique can be obtained at the border. Maputo is 75 km away on a newly tarred road. See page 831.

Discount flight agents

In the UK and Ireland
Flightbookers, T0871-2235000, www.ebookers.com.
Flight Centre, T0870-4999931, www.flightcentre.co.uk.
STA Travel, T0871-2300040, www.statravel.co.uk.
Trailfinders, T0845-0585858, www.trailfinders.com.
Travelbag, T0800-8048911, www.travelbag.co.uk.

In North America
Air Brokers International, T1800-8833273, www.airbrokers.com.
Airtech, T1212-2197000, www.airtech.com.
STA Travel, T1800-7814040, www.statravel.com.
Travel CUTS, T1866-2469762 (Canada), www.travelcuts.com.

In Australia and New Zealand
Flight Centre, T133-133 (Australia), www.flightcentre.com.au.
Skylinks, T02-9223 4277, www.skylink.com.au.
STA Travel, T134-782, www.statravel. com.au (Australia), T0800 474400, www.statravel.com.nz (New Zealand).
Travel.com.au, T1300-130482, www.travel.com.au.

Rail

There are trains between Johannesburg and Komatipoort, from where buses on the Mozambique side of the border operate services to and from Maputo. The journey to the border is 12½ hours and is overnight in both directions. Accommodation is 2 or 4-sleeper compartments and there's a restaurant car franchised to a fast food chain. Although there is a railway, trains no longer run between Zimbabwe and South Africa. The South African national railway company is **Spoornet**, T0860-008888, www.spoornet.co.za.

Namibia's railway company, **Transnamib Starline Passenger Services**, T+264 (0)61-2982175, www.transnamib.com.na, runs a service between Upington in South Africa and Windhoek twice a week. However as Namibia's trains are primarily used for freight, it is slow going with a lot of stops. Despite this the passenger compartments are comfortable with airline-like seats, videos are shown and there are vending machines for drinks and snacks.

Road

South Africa
Bus The three main coach companies cover routes across South Africa's borders and some services go as far as Malawi. All bus tickets can be booked online. **Translux**, T0861-589282 (in South Africa), T011-774333 (from overseas), www.translux.co.za, runs services from Johannesburg and Pretoria to Blantyre, Buluwayo, Harare, Lusaka, and Maputo. **Intercape**, T0861-287287 (in South Africa), T012-3804400 (from overseas), www.intercape.co.za, runs coaches from Johannesburg/Pretoria to Gaborone, Windhoek and Maputo, and from Cape Town to Livingstone in Zambia (via Namibia). **Greyhound**, T083-9159000 (in South Africa), T011-2768550 (from overseas), www.greyhound.co.za, runs coaches from Pretoria to Maputo, Harare and Bulawayo.

Car If crossing any international borders in a private car, you must have a registration document, insurance and a driving licence printed in English with a photograph. With the exception of Zimbabwe, you should be able to take a hire car into all the bordering countries, though check with the rental company first. You will need a letter of permission to take a car across a border if it is not registered in your name, and a ZA sticker (available from any AA shop). Botswana, Namibia, Lesotho, Swaziland and South Africa are all part of SADC's (Southern Africa Development Community) joint customs agreement, so if you are in your own car travelling on a carnet, you only have to produce this when crossing your first or last border to the SADC countries. ▸▸ *For border crossings, see box, page 36.*

Lesotho and Swaziland
Lesotho The most common way of entering and leaving Lesotho is by road. There is a R10 entry and departure tax on all vehicles. For driving licence and insurance requirements and for driving across international borders, see above.

Swaziland There are 13 border posts in total, 11 with South Africa and two with Mozambique. Visas for Mozambique are now issued at the border. The border posts are open every day of the year, including public holidays, and immigration and customs formalities take about 30 minutes. There is an E5 road tax on all vehicles entering Swaziland and cars hired in South Africa are usually permitted into Swaziland. ▸▸ *For further details, Transport, page 828.*

Getting around

South Africa has an efficient transport network linking its towns and cities. The road systems and flight networks are the best in Africa, making travelling the considerable distances a straightforward experience. Affordable domestic flights link the cities, a sophisticated army of private coaches criss-crosses the country, and the train system, although painfully slow, offers another way of getting from A to B. City transport, however, is a problem. South Africa's cities universally lack safe and reliable urban public transport, often making private transport the only option.

Air

South Africa

There is a far-reaching and efficient domestic service and regular daily flights connect Johannesburg with other major towns, all of which can be reached within a couple of hours' flying time. On popular routes where there is some competition, such as Durban–Johannesburg or Johannesburg–Cape Town, a single ticket is usually only a little more expensive than a bus ticket.

Airlines

By booking early online, good deals can be found with all the airlines.

British Airways Comair, T011-4418600, www.britishairways.com, has daily flights between Johannesburg and Cape Town, Durban and Port Elizabeth as well as flights between Johannesburg and Mauritius, Windhoek, Livingstone, Victoria Falls and Harare.

Kulula, T0861-585852 (in South Africa), T011-9210111 (from overseas), www.kulula.com, also owned by British Airways, is a hugely successful no-frills airline and fun to travel with (when you get off the plane the crew in their jeans and T-shirts tell you not to forget to take your husband and children with you). Daily services between Cape Town, Durban, Johannesburg, Port Elizabeth, and George. Also now flies to Mauritius, Windhoek and Harare on a code-share agreement with BA.

Mango, T0861-162646 (in South Africa), T011-3591222 (from overseas), ww5.flymango.com, is the newest of the no-frills operators with daily flights between Johannesburg, Cape Town, Durban and Bloemfontein.

Nationwide, T0861-737737 (in South Africa), T011-3053550 (from overseas), www.flynationwide.co.za. Flies daily between Johannesburg, Cape Town, Durban, Mpumalanga, Port Elizabeth, George and Livingstone in Zambia. Also worth checking out is their good-value flight from London Gatwick to Johannesburg.

One Time, T0861-345345 (in South Africa), T011-9288000 (from overseas), www.1time.co.za, is another budget carrier that flies between Johannesburg, Cape Town, Durban, George, Port Elizabeth and Bloemfontein. They have rather stylish planes with spacious leather seats, bought from a bankrupt airline.

South African Airways (SAA), central reservations T0861-359722 (in South Africa), T011-9785313 (from overseas), ww2.flysaa.com, cover most of the country as well as other southern African cities in conjunction with both **SA Airlink**, www.flyairlink.com, and **SA Express**, www.saexpress.co.za.

Rail

All the major cities are linked by rail and while this is a comfortable and relaxing way to travel, it is very slow. The trains are run by **Shosholoza Meyl**, part of the national network **Spoornet**, T0860-008888 (in South Africa), T011-7744555 (from overseas), www.spoornet.co.za. Timetables and fares can be found on the website. Shosholoza means 'to push forward' or 'to strive' and is the name of a popular traditional African song favoured particularly by hard-working men whose job it was to lay railway lines. All the trains travel overnight, the Cape Town–Durban service over two nights, so they arrive at some stations en route at inconvenient times. There are sleeping carriages, with coupés that sleep four or six people, with a wash basin, fold-away table and bunk beds. The 'sitter' carriages are not recommended for long journeys as there is only open coach seating. Always book well in advance for sleeping compartments, especially during local holidays. Refreshments are available from trolleys or dining cars, but these have been franchised to burger-type chains, so don't expect brilliant food. Note that all trains have a problem with security: if you leave your compartment, make sure a train official locks it after you. Accompanied children under four travel free; children between seven and 12 years pay half price.

Routes include: **Johannesburg–East London** (Sunday to Tuesday, Thursday and Friday in both directions, 19 hours); **Johannesburg–Musina** (Sunday to Friday in both directions, 14 hours); **Johannesburg–Komatipoort** (Sunday to Friday in both directions, 13 hours); Johannesburg–Bloemfontein (Wednesday, Friday and Saturday in both directions, 12 hours); **Johannesburg–Durban** (Sunday, Monday and Wednesday to Friday in both directions, 8 hours); **Durban–Cape Town** (Wednesday), **Cape Town–Durban** (Monday, 38 hours), **Pretoria–Cape Town** (daily in both directions, 29 hours); **Johannesburg–Port Elizabeth** (Sunday, Monday and Wednesday to Friday in both directions, 18 hours).

Spoornet also operate a more upmarket service, the **Premier Classe**, T0860-008888 (in South Africa), T011-7744555 (from overseas), www.premierclasse.co.za, between Pretoria and Cape Town once a week. The carriages are a bit nicer than the regular train, with proper food in a sit-down dining car and extras in the coupés like toiletries and dressing gowns.

There are a number of short excursions on restored vintage steam trains through amazing scenery. These are described in the relevant chapters.

Luxury trains

If the journey is more important than the destination, then experience a trip on an old-fashioned luxury train, which operate much like five-star hotels on wheels. The **Blue Train**, T021-3348459, www.bluetrain.co.za, is considered to be southern Africa's premier luxury train with 18 carriages that can accommodate 84 passengers. The wood-panelled coaches feature luxury coupés with en suite bathrooms, elegant lounge cars and fine dining in the restaurant car. It runs scheduled services between Pretoria and Cape Town, one day and one night, and occasional trips further afield to Victoria Falls. A similar luxury train experience is the **Pride of Africa**, operated by Rovos Rail, T012-3158242, www.rovos.co.za, which also runs between Pretoria and Cape Town with occasional trips to Victoria Falls. Check out the websites for routes and prices.

Metro commuter trains and high-speed rail links

Many of the larger cities such as Pretoria, Johannesburg and Cape Town have a network of metro commuter services linking the suburbs to the business districts. These should generally be avoided as there have been many cases of robbery. Avoid the metro around

Johannesburg and Pretoria at all costs. Some tourists use the Cape Town metro, www.metrorail.co.za, on selected routes; namely from the city to Simonstown on the Cape Peninsula, and experience no problems. If you do use it, stick to first class, travel only during rush hour (0600-0800, 1600-1800) and avoid it at weekends.

The **Gautrain** – a high-speed rail link between Johannesburg, Pretoria and OR Tambo International Airport – is currently being built in Gauteng. It is due to be completed by the 2010 Football World Cup. Visit www.gautrain.com for progress.

Road

South Africa

Intercity coaches **Greyhound**, T083-9159000 (in South Africa), T011-2768550 (from overseas), www.greyhound.co.za, **Intercape**, T086-1287287 (in South Africa), T012-3804400 (from overseas), www.intercape.co.za, and **Translux**, T0861-589282 (in South Africa), T011-7743333 (from overseas), www.translux.co.za, are the three major long-distance bus companies that run between towns and popular destinations, with a large number of buses on each route. All have online booking and seats can be reserved several months in advance. The coaches are air-conditioned and have a toilet; some sell refreshments and show videos. They will stop at least every three to four hours to change drivers and give the passengers a chance to stretch their legs. For long journeys, the prices are reasonable, but short routes are expensive for budget travellers. However, they are an efficient and a safe way of travelling and, on night routes, bear in mind that you will be saving the cost of a hotel room. **Note** The Intercape bus takes 10 hours to do the same route as opposed to around 24 hours on the train.

Baz Bus The **Baz Bus**, T021-4392323, www.bazbus.com, is a hop-on, hop-off bus that offers a convenient and sociable alternative to the main bus services. It is specifically designed for backpackers visiting South Africa and remains one of the most popular ways of seeing the country on a budget. One of the best aspects of the service is that the bus collects and drops off passengers at their chosen backpacker hostel. There are a few exceptions such as Hermanus, Coffee Bay and Sani Pass, where the bus will drop you off at the closest point on the main road, and the hostels will then meet you for an extra charge, though you must arrange this in advance. The Baz Bus route is Cape Town–Durban along the coast, and Durban–Pretoria on two routes via either Swaziland or the Drakensberg. Visit the website for the full timetable.

Tickets are priced per segment, for example from Cape Town to Durban. You are allowed to hop off and on the bus as many times as you like in the given segment, but must not backtrack. This is where the savings are made, since other commercial buses, such as Translux and Greyhound, charge high prices for short journeys. However, note that for long distances without stops, the mainline buses are better value. YHA and ISIC card holders are entitled to a 5% discount on Baz Bus tickets.

The Baz Bus drivers are a great source of information, both about the places of interest along the route and what to expect at each hostel. The buses are fairly cramped Mercedes vehicles, although a trailer at the back has space for rucksacks, surf boards and other luggage.

Car hire Hiring a car for part, or all, of your journey is undoubtedly the best way to see the country. The roads are generally in good condition and, away from the major urban centres, there is little traffic. South Africans are, however, notoriously bad drivers –

speeding and drink-driving are common. Do not drive at night for safety reasons. The advantage of hiring a car is that you get to explore more isolated areas, as well as seeing the national parks and nature reserves at a more leisurely pace without being tied to a tour. For budget travellers, hiring a car is ideal for carrying camping equipment and costs come down considerably if you share with three or four people. Petrol, not a major expense, is available 24 hours a day along the national highways. Driving is on the left side of the road and speed limits range from 60 kph in built-up areas to 120 kph on the main highways. The police are cracking down on drink-driving and while many locals still disregard the laws, speed traps with on-the-spot fines are employed. Also remember that if you are caught by a speed camera, the fine will go to the hire car company who have every right to deduct the amount from your credit card, even if it is some time after you have left South Africa.

It is worth asking at hostels or hotels for recommended local car hire companies, and be sure to shop around. Car hire companies have a range of vehicles, from basic hatchbacks and saloon cars, to camper vans and fully equipped 4WD vehicles. In general there are two types of deal on offer: a short weekend package including free mileage; or longer-term deals for a week or more. In the first case you can get very good rates for a Group A car, although you might want a larger vehicle for long journeys – bear in mind that during a two- to three-week holiday you're likely to clock up over 3000 km. The extra engine power and space of a Group B car will make for more comfortable and safe driving. In summer, air conditioning is also well worth the extra but make sure it works before you sign.

Tourist offices usually recommend large international organizations such as Avis or Budget, but there are a number of reliable local companies, usually with a good fleet of cars and follow-up service. Backpacker hostels are often a useful source of information and can offer competitive rates.

If you are intending to visit more remote areas, such as Maputaland, the Kalahari and the Richtersveld, consider hiring a 4WD vehicle. There are specialist companies in Cape Town and Johannesburg that hire out fully equipped safari Land Rovers or pickups with all necessary camping equipment. Fully equipped camper vans or motorhomes represent excellent value for a group or a family as money is saved on accommodation, and if self-catering, food too.

For emergency breakdown and traffic update information contact the **Automobile Association of South Africa**, T083-84322, www.aa.co.za.

Make sure you have the correct documents from the rental company if you wish to take the car into one of the neighbouring countries. See Getting there by road, page 38.

Car hire companies

All of the large firms now have toll free phone numbers which can be dialled from anywhere within South Africa, and most of them have kiosks at the airports. Be sure to book in advance though the websites for the high season. See also the Transport sections under individual towns.
Aroundabout Cars, T0860-4224022 (in South Africa), T021-4224022 (from overseas), www.around aboutcars.com, is a good national agent for local car hire and they know where to find the best deal.

Avis, T0861-021111, www.avis.co.za.
Budget, T0861-016622, www.budget.co.za.
Britz Africa, T011-3961445, www.britz.co.za. Contact for camper vans and motorhomes for travel in and beyond South Africa. Good all-inclusive deals.
Imperial/Europcar, T0800-011344, www.europcar.co.za, www.imperialcarrental.co.za.
Hertz, T0861-600136, www.hertz.co.za.
Leisuremobiles, T011-4752902, www.africanleisure.co.za. Camper vans | and fully equipped safari 4WDs.

Buying your own car If you want to stay in the country for a while, or plan a grand tour of southern Africa, buying your own car may be a sensible option. Johannesburg, Cape Town or Durban are the best places to buy or sell. Check the local press for private sales, or visit a second-hand car dealership. Alternatively consider buying a car on a buy-back scheme. There are companies that will sell you a car with a buy-back guarantee once you have finished with it. Work out the costs, though, and compare them to long-term car hire. Sometimes the price difference is minimal and with the buy-back scheme you don't get the back up of a car hire company in the case of an emergency. The following websites are useful: www.drivesouthafrica.co.za, www.drivesouthernafrica.com, www.resqrentacar.co.za.

Hitchhiking Hitchhiking is not common in South Africa and is not recommended as it can be very dangerous. Women should never hitch, under any circumstances, even in a group. If you have to hitch, say if your vehicle has broken down, be very wary of who you are accepting a lift from; a car with a family or couple in may be fine, but avoid getting into a vehicle with a group of men. In rural areas, especially so in Lesotho, you may be expected to pay if a lorry or a pickup gives you a lift.

Taxis There are few taxi ranks in South African towns so it's generally a better idea to order a taxi in advance. Any hotel, hostel or restaurant will make a booking for you. Taxis are metered and charge around R7.50 per kilometre. Larger groups should request a Toyota Venture if available as these carry nine people. Travelling by taxi, especially at night, is one of the safest ways to cross city centres when visiting a restaurant or nightclub; don't walk just to save a few cents.

Minibus taxis The majority of South Africa's population travel by minibus taxis and, in many areas, including inner cities, they are the only way of getting around. However, the accident rate of such vehicles is notoriously high, with speeding, overcrowding and lack of maintenance being the main causes. There is also the problem of possible robbery, especially at the taxi ranks, so many visitors and locals remain wary of using them.

Nevertheless, minibus taxis remain the cheapest and most extensive form of transport in the country. Many routes have experienced little or no crime, but you should exercise extreme caution and always ask people in the know before using them. In central Cape Town minibus taxis provide an efficient (and relatively safe) means of transport into the city centre from places such as Observatory, Camps Bay, Sea Point, Rondebosch and Claremont.

Lesotho
Many of Lesotho's main roads have been upgraded to tarmac in recent years (a direct result of the Lesotho Highland Project) making getting around much easier than it used to be when roads were little more than rough gravel tracks. The main route running north-south along the lowland strip is tarred and in good repair. Other tarred routes include the road from Maseru to Roma, Maseru to Mohale Dam, Leribe/Hlotso to Katse dam, and Butha-Buthe to Mokhotlong. The quality of gravel roads varies considerably: the 'mountain road' to Thaba Tseke and the road to Semonkong are both in good condition while the routes from Thaba Tseke to Mokhotlong or Qacha's Nek are very poor in parts and get very slippery in the wet.

Petrol is readily available in the lowland centres but if you are travelling into the mountains make sure you have plenty of fuel before you leave. Distances between filling stations are long and supplies are not always reliable. You will definitely need to put anti-freeze in your car radiator in the colder months as it can freeze overnight.

Car If driving yourself through Lesotho, take local advice regarding the time a journey may take, and the possible need for 4WD and chains. The tourist office in Maseru can assist with this and can give detailed instructions of the exact route to be taken. Remember that while there have been major improvements to Lesotho's roads in recent years, all road conditions deteriorate rapidly after heavy rains, they get icy in the cooler months, and some may be blocked by snow in the winter. It is worth considering carefully what time of the year to go if you are driving. It's recommended that you carry two spare wheels and a couple of spare inner tubes if possible, though many of the villages offer cheap tyre-mending services.

Road safety in Lesotho usually leaves a lot to be desired, as the death of the King in an accident in 1996 on the Main South Road indicates. Taxi drivers are often in direct competition for passengers so rush to get to stops ahead of other drivers – which often means they take huge risks. Be especially careful when driving behind taxis as they often brake sharply to pick up passengers. Drink-driving is also a problem, especially at weekends, bank holidays and at the end of the month when people have just been paid. It is probably best to avoid driving at these times. Wear your seat belt at all times, and always be wary of pedestrians, cyclists and livestock at the sides of the road.

Taxis and buses The lowland towns and villages are linked together by a regular and cheap (if hair-raising) taxi service. These consist of minibuses with about 16 seats or sometimes, in remote districts, of converted 4WDs. There is no set timetable for taxis; they simply set off when they are full. It is important to remember, however, that taxis stop running very early in the evening and it is more or less impossible to get one after sunset. There is very little space for baggage. The first passengers to arrive get the most comfortable seats next to the driver, though the downside is that you'll have a full view of Lesotho driving habits. Unlike most of South Africa, people talk to each other in taxis.

Larger buses cover the longer routes, especially over the gravel mountain roads. To most towns there is at least one bus a day to and from Maseru or another larger lowland centre. They usually leave between 0600 and 1000 depending on the distance but timetables vary with the number of passengers.

Hitching As taxis are cheap and frequent and most drivers will charge the same fare as a taxi anyway, hitchhiking in the lowlands is not usually worth the trouble. In more remote areas more or less every passing vehicle acts as a de facto taxi service – somewhat blurring the distinction between hitching and taking a taxi. There are certain routes, however, where hitchhiking is the only alternative to walking, for example over Sani Pass into KwaZulu Natal or from Qacha's Nek into the Eastern Cape. If you are hitchhiking in the mountains make sure you have a jacket or blanket (or both) to hand – most lifts will be on the back of a pickup or a truck and it can get very cold, especially on winter evenings. Although it's usually safe to hitchhike in Lesotho, remember to avoid hitchhiking alone.

Other transport Horses and ponies are the main form of transport other than foot for most Basotho in the mountains. You can hire ponies from a number of centres.

Hiking in the bush

As experienced walkers will know, good preparation is the key to a successful and enjoyable hike. It is also important to remember that, however short or easy a walk may appear to be, walking in the bush is not like going for a stroll in the park – a few basic steps should be followed. Below is a short checklist of equipment and guidelines for hiking in the bush:

Day hikes Good walking boots or shoes; sunhat; minimum of 2 litres of water per person; first-aid kit; penknife; trail snacks (peanuts, biltong, dried fruit); binoculars, camera and bird-book/gamebook; toilet paper; matches to burn paper.

Additional overnight gear Sleeping bag; fleece or equivalent top (even in summer); torch; lightweight camping stove (it is not always permitted to collect firewood); matches/lighter/ firelighters; dehydrated food (pasta, instant soups, etc).

→ Don't leave litter or throw away cigarette butts.

→ Leave everything as you find it; don't pick plants or remove fossils or rocks.

→ Stick to marked trails especially in the bush – it's easy to lose your way.

→ Camp away from waterholes so as not to frighten game away.

→ Never feed the animals.

→ Remember, in the southern hemisphere the sun goes via the north not the south.

Swaziland

The easiest way of getting around is by car and, in such a little country, everything of interest is within a couple of hours' drive. Petrol stations are frequent and are open 0700-1800. Roads are well signposted and tarred, though beware of drunk-driving in the evenings and weekends (the laws are far less stringent here than in South Africa). Note the law requires that all vehicles move to the side of the road and stop when approached by an official (usually royal) motorcade led by police escorts. Also beware of livestock on the road in the rural areas. The **Baz Bus** offers an efficient and frequent service through Swaziland. Regular minibus taxis ply the road through the Ezulwini Valley between Mbabane and Manzini.

Maps

The best map and travel guide store in the UK is **Stanfords** ⓘ *12-14 Longacre, Covent Garden, London WC2E 9LP, T020-7836 1321, www.stanfords.co.uk*, with branches in Manchester and Bristol. Within South Africa, the **Shell Road Atlas to Southern Africa**, available at all Shell service stations, is comprehensive and includes maps of major tourist areas, marking sights and some accommodation facilities, and detailed city maps. The **Automobile Association of South Africa**, www.aa.co.za, has shops in all major cities selling national, regional and touring maps. The **Map Studio**, www.mapstudio.co.za, produces a wide range of maps covering much of Africa. South African bookshops such as **Exclusive Books** and **CNA** carry a full range of maps.

Sleeping

South Africa offers a wide variety of accommodation from top-of-the-range game lodges and tented camps that charge R2000-6000 or more per couple per day, to mid-range safari lodges and hotels with self-contained air-conditioned double rooms for R750-1500, to guesthouse or B&Bs that charge R250-750 and dormitory beds or camping for under R150 a day. Generally, accommodation booked through agents in Europe will be more expensive than if you contact the hotel directly by email or book online. Make sure you keep a copy of all correspondence and reconfirm your bookings once you arrive in the country. Comprehensive accommodation information can be found on the regional tourism websites listed in each area. All accommodation in South Africa is graded a star value by the Tourism Grading Council of South Africa and the website has comprehensive lists in all categories; www.tourism grading.co.za. In the main cities, hotels often remain a practical option, although note that Cape Town and Johannesburg suffer from a shortage of hotel beds, and you should always book well in advance.

Hotels Every town has at least one hotel of two- or three-star standard but, where tourists are not expected, the service can be poor and dismissive. These hotels tend to be aimed at business travellers and may be characterless buildings with restaurants serving bland food. But there are lots of alternatives and there are some delightful family-run hotels, boutique hotels with stylish interiors and, for those who enjoy the anonymity of a large hotel, chains such as Holiday Inn and Protea.

Guesthouses Guesthouses can offer some of the most characterful accommodation in South Africa, with interesting places springing up in both cities and small towns. Standards obviously vary enormously; much of what you'll get has to do with the character of the owners and the location of the homes. Some are simple practical overnight rooms, while at the more luxurious end, rooms may be in historic homes filled with antiques, and offering impeccable service. Breakfast is almost always included and, in some, evening meals can be prepared if you phone ahead. For further information contact the Guest House Association of Southern Africa, T021-7620880, www.ghasa.co.za, or the Portfolio Collection, T021-6894020, www.portfoliocollection.com.

Bed and breakfast B&B accommodation is hugely popular in South Africa; even the smallest town will usually have one private home that rents out rooms, and B&Bs in townships are catching on fast. Local tourist offices are the best source of information for finding B&Bs. Assuming you get on with your hosts, they can offer a valuable insight into local life. In rural areas, farmhouse B&Bs are often in beautiful settings where guests will have access to a garden and swimming pool as well as to hikes and horse riding. Increasingly, some establishments are providing TVs, air-conditioning or fans, and have separate entrances for those who want more privacy away from the owners. The breakfasts are almost always good and in large enough quantities to fill you up for the day. Full English breakfasts are usually served but it is increasingly common to have a choice of continental breakfast or even a traditional South African breakfast of boerewors, mince on toast and mealie porridge.

Accommodation price codes

Hotels and guesthouses

L	over US$300	C	US$75-100
AL	US$220-300	A	US$35-75
A	US$150-220	D	US$15-35
B	US$100-150	F	under US$15

Prices refer to the cost of a double room, not including service charge or meals unless otherwise stated. See page 64 for exchange rates.

Private game reserves

L4	over US$900	L2	US$450 550
L3	US$550-900	L1	US$300-500

Prices are based on two people sharing accommodation and are inclusive of all meals and game drives.

Backpacker hostels Apart from camping, backpacker hostels are the cheapest form of accommodation, and a bed in a dormitory will cost as little as R80 a night. Some also have budget double rooms with or without bathrooms, while others have space to pitch a tent in the garden.

While hostel standards can obviously vary, stiff competition means that most hostels are clean and have good facilities. You can usually expect a self-catering kitchen, hot showers, a TV/DVD room and internet access. Many hostels also have bars and offer meals or nightly braais, plus a garden and a swimming pool. Most hostels are a good source of travel information and many act as booking agents for bus companies, budget safari tours and car hire. On the whole, hostels are very safe and security is not a problem. Your fellow travellers remains the greatest threat, especially in dormitories in the busy city hostels. The Baz Bus (see page 41) caters for backpackers and links most hostels along the coast between Cape Town and Durban, and Durban and Johannesburg via either the Drakensberg or Swaziland. For information, visit **Backpacking South Africa**, www.btsa.co.za, or **Coast to Coast**, www.coastingafrica.com, which publishes a free annual backpackers' accommodation guide and is available in all the hostels.

Camping and caravan parks Camping is the cheapest and most flexible way of seeing South Africa. Every town has a municipal campsite, many of which also have simple self-catering chalets. These vary in quality and facilities, from basic rondavels with bunks, to chalets with a couple of bedrooms and fully equipped kitchens. They can be excellent value and are often the only budget accommodation available in a town.

As camping is very popular with South Africans, sites tend to have very good facilities, although they may be fully booked months in advance, especially during the school holidays in the most popular game reserves and national parks. Even the most basic site will have a clean washblock with hot water, plus electric points and lighting. All sites have braai facilities, with charcoal, wood and firelighters available in campsite shops. Some sites also have kitchen blocks. At the most popular tourist spots, campsites are more like holiday resorts with shops, swimming pools and a restaurant – these can get very busy and are best avoided in peak season.

Camping equipment is widely available in South Africa and usually at lower prices than in the UK. If your time is limited, you should bring your own tent and sleeping bag, but if you're not on a tight schedule you may want to shop around once you've arrived. Lightweight tents, sleeping bags, ground mats, gas lights, stoves and cooking equipment can be bought at good prices in all the major cities.

Self-catering apartments Self-catering apartments are particularly popular with South African holidaymakers and there is an enormous choice, especially along the coast. Prices vary with the seasons: Christmas is the most expensive time of year, but off season many resorts are virtually empty and discounts can be negotiated. If you are travelling in a group, a flat could cost as little as R100 per person per day and these are ideal for families on a budget.

National park accommodation While the larger rest camps in Kruger have supermarkets, launderettes, post offices and banks, most camps are rather more basic. All have at least a small shop selling maps, basic food provisions and firewood. Most accommodation is self-catering, but larger camps may have restaurants. Petrol is often available at larger camps and road conditions between them are usually good. Reception is usually located within the shop or office, where you can arrange guided walks and game drives. Both are highly recommended for learning about and spotting wildlife. Some parks also offer night drives where visitors have the chance of seeing unusual nocturnal animals. National parks across the country are under the jurisdiction of **South African National Parks** (SANParks), central reservations T012-4289111, www.sanparks.org, which also has drop-in offices in Pretoria, T012-4289111, two offices in Cape Town, at the Clock Tower Centre and the V&A Waterfront, T021-4054500, or at the Cape Town tourist office on the corner of Burg and Castle streets T021-4876800, and at the Tourist Junction in Durban, T031-3044934. In the Western Cape, the game reserves are managed by **Cape Nature Conservation**, T021-6593500, www.capenature.org.za, and in KwaZulu Natal, **KZN Wildlife**, T033-8451000, www.kznwildlife.com.

The central reservations offices are a good source of advice and can help plan your trip in advance. In peak season, it's wise to book a month or two before you arrive. All bookings can be made over the telephone, by email or through the websites. Most international credit cards are accepted. If you are already staying in a park, the reception can make advance bookings for other parks.

Luxury game lodges The most famous luxury game lodges are on private game farms adjoining Kruger National Park, although there are others around the country. Their attraction is the chance to combine exclusive game viewing in prime wilderness areas, with top-class accommodation, fin dining, vintage wines and a spectacular natural setting.

The cost of staying in a luxury game lodge varies from R2000 to over R7000 per person per night. This includes all meals, drinks and game viewing trips. In order to get the most from the experience, guests tend to stay for at least two nights. The lodges are often isolated and not easily accessible by road so many reserves have their own airstrips where light aircraft can land. Charter flights save time and avoid long dusty journeys, and can be booked through the game lodge or from Johannesburg, Durban or Cape Town.
▶▶ *For details of the luxury reserves around Kruger National Park, see pages 641-645.*

Lighthousing

A relatively new initiative by South Africa's National Ports Authority is the SA Lighthouse Tourism. Due to modern technology and automation, only 15 of the 45 lighthouses along South Africa's 3700-km coastline are still manned. The authority has opened up many of the remaining 30 lighthouses as self-catering accommodation in what was once the light keepers' quarters. These lighthouses are found at Cape Columbine on the West Coast in the Saldanha Bay area, Danger Point near Gansbaai on the Atlantic side of Cape Agulhas, Cape St Blaize at Mossel Bay, Great Fish Point in Port Alfred and North Sand Bluff in Port Edward, both on the KwaZulu Natal coast.

Contact the central reservation office, T021-4492400, or visit the National Ports Authority website, www.transnetnationalportsauthority.net.

Lesotho

Hotels There is no star-grading in Lesotho and don't expect the high standards of accommodation found in South Africa. Most main centres have one or two formal and rather soulless hotels. These often look dilapidated from the outside but are usually kept reasonably clean inside. They rarely have more than a handful of guests, so you are usually able to benefit from close attention from hotel staff. Nearly all of them have restaurants and they are often the only choice for eating, but don't expect anything other than plates of basic chicken and rice or stew and pap. As these hotels are often the centre of local nightlife for local professionals it is usually best to ask for a room away from the bar area, especially at weekends. Cheaper accommodation can be found in various farming training centres, missions, or education centres. In these you'll usually get a dorm bed, a (not always hot) shower, and perhaps a simple meal. Most are very basic but nonetheless friendly and very cheap. Lesotho has a number of well run lodges in the mountains and foothills that provide excellent value accommodation, namely the **Trading Post, Semonkong Lodge, New Oxbow Lodge** and the **Malealea Lodge**. These are a much better alternative to the bland town hotels and it is in these resorts that you are going to get the most out of a visit to Lesotho as they also organize hiking and pony trekking.

Maseru has two international standard hotels (both part of the Sun International chain). Neither are outstanding, but they are comfortable with a range of facilities, though expensive. There are few budget travellers' hostels in Maseru and what are available are not very nice. For the budget traveller, it is a good idea to arrive in Maseru early in the morning, spend the day in the city before heading out to cheaper accommodation in the outlying districts, some of which is only 20-30 km away. This avoids having to pay the high prices for the city hotels. Remember that most accommodation outside Maseru only accepts cash for payment.

Camping Away from the main towns, camping is very easy if you are completely self-sufficient, but remember it can get cold, even during summer nights. You should always get permission to set up camp from the chief of the nearest village.

In the densely populated lowlands it is more difficult to find a suitable camping site and you also run the risk of losing your belongings to the crowds of children who inevitably gather. Ask around at the churches and missions for permission to camp in their grounds or at the local police station.

Eating

South Africa

Food

South African food tends to be fairly regional, although a ubiquitous love of meat unites the country. In and around Cape Town visitors will find many restaurants offering Cape Malay cuisine, a blend of sweet and spicy curries and meat dishes cooked with dried fruit. Seafood along the coast is excellent and usually very good value. KwaZulu Natal is famous for its Indian curries, especially the delicious bunny chow, served in a hollowed-out loaf of bread. Portuguese influences, thanks to neighbouring Mozambique, are strong – spicy peri-peri chicken or Mozambiquan prawns are widespread. Meat, however, is universal and South Africa offers plenty of opportunities to try an assortment of game, from popular ostrich or springbok to more acquired tastes such as crocodile or warthog. Two local meat products which travellers invariably come across are biltong and boerewors. Biltong is heavily salted and spiced sun-dried meat, usually made from beef but sometimes made from game such as ostrich, kudu or impala. Boerewors is a strongly seasoned beef sausage usually grilled on a braai. The staple diet for much of the black South African population is a stiff maize porridge known as pap, served with a stew. Pap tends to be rather bland, although the accompanying stews are often quite tasty.

Supermarkets (see page 52) usually have a similar selection of groceries to that found in Europe. Meat is generally significantly cheaper than in Europe, but fruit and vegetables are about the same. South Africa is a great source of fresh fruit, and during the summer months you should be able to get a good range of exotic fruits from the better supermarkets (Woolworth's is always a good bet). Local produce such as apples in Ceres or pineapples along the Wild Coast will always be excellent.

Drink

South Africa is a major player in the international market and produces a wide range of excellent wines. The Winelands in the Western Cape have the best-known labels (see pages 151-182) but there are a number of other wine regions dotted around the country. South Africa also produces a range of good beer. Major names include Black Label, Castle and Amstel. Windhoek, from Namibia, is also widely available and more popular than some of the South African beers. Home-brewed beer, made from sorghum or maize, is widely drunk by the African population. It has a thick head, is very potent and not very palatable to the uninitiated. Bitter is harder to come by, although a good local variety is brewed at Mitchell's Brewery in Knysna and Cape Town and can be found at outlets along the Garden Route.

No liquor may be sold on Sundays (and public holidays) except in licensed bars and restaurants. The standard shop selling alcohol is known as a bottle store, usually open Monday-Friday 0800-1800, Saturday 0830-1400 (some may stay open until 1600). Supermarkets do not sell beer or spirits, stop selling wine at 2000, and don't sell alcohol on Sundays. Note that despite drink-driving being a very serious offence, it remains a problem especially in rural areas.

Soft drinks Tap water in South African towns is chemically treated and safe to drink. Bottled mineral water and a good range of fruit juices are available at most outlets including petrol stations – the Ceres and Liquifruit brands are the best. Another popular drink is Rooibos tea, literally red bush tea. This is a caffeine-free tea with a smoky flavour, usually served with sugar or honey. The main area producing Rooibos is around Clanwilliam by the Cederberg in the Western Cape.

Eating out

Restaurants and cafés vary widely in quality and service, depending largely on where you are. Small-town hotels tend to serve bland meals focusing on standard meat-and-two-veg dishes, while town restaurants are often part of a chain. The main cities, however, have an excellent variety of restaurants and South Africa is fast gaining a reputation as a culinary hotspot. Cape Town in particular has experienced a boom in top-class restaurants, from traditional Cape Malay cooking to cordon bleu seafood, all at incredibly good prices. Johannesburg and Pretoria also have a wide selection of smart restaurants in the more affluent suburbs. Some of the best restaurants in the country are found in the Winelands around the Western Cape, many of which are part of historic wine estates. Franschhoek has a particularly good reputation, with a number of excellent French restaurants, while the Garden Route offers fresh, good-value seafood. Because of the Indian influence in KwaZulu Natal, the best curries are found in Durban and the authenticity of the dishes is better than you would expect in Europe. Meat is almost always of a high standard wherever you are, and a number of restaurants offer a variety of game such as springbok, ostrich and kudu.

Vegetarians, however, will find their choice rather limited. South Africa is a meat-loving country and menus rarely include anything but the most basic dishes for vegetarians. Away from the major cities, you'll have to make do with salads, pasta and chips. Cape Town, Pretoria and Johannesburg have a better range for vegetarians, with some trendy meat-free restaurants appearing on the scene in recent years. Self-catering is often a better option.

Eating out continues to be very good value, despite the strengthening rand. Outside the major tourist centres, people eat early and many kitchens will close around 2100, except at the weekend. Private restaurants are often closed on Sunday evenings, when hotel dining rooms or fast-food outlets may well be the only choices for eating out.

Braais

One of the first local terms you are likely to learn will be braai, which quite simply means barbecue. The braai is incredibly popular, part of the South African way of life, and every campsite, back garden and picnic spot has a braai pit. Given the excellent range of meat available, learning how to cook good food on a braai is an art that needs to be mastered quickly, especially if you are self-catering, and is part of the fun of eating in South Africa. Once you have established a core of heat using firelighters and wood or charcoal (charcoal is more eco-friendly and less smoky but wood makes for a wonderful fire), wrap up potatoes, sweet potatoes, squash, butternut, etc, in heavy-duty foil and cook them in the coals for an hour or so. Set beside a good piece of meat, with a sauce and a cold beer, and you will be living the South African dream. To check whether your braai is the right heat to cook on, hold your hand over the braai grill and count to 10. If you have to pull your hand back before 10 it's too hot, any later than 10 then it's too cold.

Lesotho

Food

Every village will have a small shop selling basic tinned and dried foods. The larger villages have small supermarkets, though more luxury items and fresh food like cheese or vegetables and fruit (other than those grown locally) can only be found in supermarkets in major towns, or should be purchased in South Africa prior to coming to Lesotho. Maize is the staple food of most Basotho. It is usually made into a stiff porridge, *pap*, and eaten with stew twice or even three times a day. It is fairly tasteless but if properly cooked and accompanied by a flavoursome stew it is enjoyable and very filling.

In the mountain areas where wheat is grown, bread forms an important part of the staple diet. The bread is baked in huge saucepans greased with mutton fat over fires – delicious.

In most towns, a profusion of street vendors can be found selling a wide variety of goods from home-made fried cakes called *makoenya* to pap and barbecued meat. Outside Maseru most restaurants serve boring but filling meals. Vegetarians will have a very limited choice. After experiencing excellent high levels of service in restaurants in South Africa, you may find the pace somewhat slower in Lesotho. Rather than complaining, try to enjoy the laid-back atmosphere.

Drink

All the major South African beers are available throughout the country and there is also a decent commercial local variety, **Maluti Beer**. Maize beer is brewed by many women as an additional source of income: a white flag (usually made from a faded maize bag) is hung outside the house when this beer is for sale. The beer has a thick, almost porridge-like head and is usually not enjoyed by visitors, though it is well worth the experience. South African wine can be purchased in Maseru and some of the larger towns but is not widely drunk by Basotho. Whisky is popular and sold at many bars.

Swaziland

Food

Basic staples include pap and stew; roasted cobs of maize are popular roadside snacks. Restaurants in Swaziland serve much the same food as those in South Africa given that all ingredients are imported from there. Like KwaZulu Natal it has the added advantage of being close to Mozambique's coastline; fresh seafood arrives daily and Mozambique's peri-peri (spicy) style of cooking is popular. There are few independent restaurants; most of the hotels feature restaurants and the best choice is along the Ezulwini Valley.

Drink

There's a full range of South African wines, beers and soft drinks. Ceremonial beer made from sorghum is reserved for special occasions and Swazi festivals. Another home-brewed concoction is marula, an intoxicating drink made from the fruit of the marula tree. Although it was banned in Swaziland in 2002 (it was thought to be responsible for a high number or road deaths caused by drunken drivers), it is still drunk surreptitiously.

Festivals and events

South African school holidays mid-December to mid-January; mid-April to early May; early August to early September. During these times prices of accommodation are often higher and most of the popular destinations become fully booked.

Festival calendar

January

Cape Town Carnival, Bo-Kaap district of Cape Town. A New Year's parade staged by the Cape coloured community in the Bo-Kaap district of Cape Town. There is a float procession, minstrel bands and dancers, culminating with a huge competition and carnival held in Green Point.

February

FNB Dance Umbrella, Johannesburg, www.at.artslink.co.za. A festival of contemporary choreography and dance from community-based dance troupes to international companies.
Prickly Pear Festival, Uitenhage, Eastern Cape, www.nmbt.co.za. A day of traditional food such as ginger beer, pancakes, *potjiekos*, home-made jam, a spit braai and fish braai, bunny chow and home-made puddings.

March

Lambert's Bay Kreeffees, Lambert's Bay, West Coast, http://kreeffees.com. Crayfish festival and rock concerts by some of South Africa's Afrikaans musicians, bungee jumping, aerial displays, a half-marathon, beer tents.
Splashy Fen, Underberg, KwaZulu Natal, www.splashyfen.co.za. A musical gathering on a farm close to Underberg. This is a mix of popular sounds and jazz bands from all walks of life, akin to the summer festivals held in Europe, with camping and fringe activities.

April

Cape Town Jazz Festival, Cape Town, www.capetownjazzfest.com. 2-day festival featuring some 40 international and African acts performing on 5 stages to an audience of 15,000.
Morija Arts and Cultural Festival, Lesotho, www.morijafest.com (see page 810).
Pink Loerie Mardi Gras, Knysna, www.pinkloerie.com. A gay festival with parade and 4 days of non-stop entertainment for anyone who enjoys a party.
Prince Albert Olive, Food and Wine Festival, Prince Albert, Western Cape, www.patourism.co.za. 2-day festival with an art exhibition, beer tents, live music, wine and olive tastings, a cycle race, an olive pip-spitting competition, and live entertainment.
Sasol Scifest, Grahamstown, Eastern Cape, www.scifest.org.za. The 7-day festival features 600 events: game drives, laser shows, robotics competitions, science olympics and a film festival. Attendance now exceeds 40,000 visitors a year, many of which are school children.

June-July

National Arts Festival, Grahamstown, Eastern Cape, www.nafest.co.za. South Africa's oldest, biggest and best-known arts festival. A 10-day event with hundreds of performances of theatre, music, song, dance and film. If there's one South African festival you have to attend, this is it.

July

Knysna Oyster Festival, Knysna, Western Cape, www.oysterfestival.co.za. Oyster braais, oyster tasting, oyster-eating competitions and other molluscular activities; there's live entertainment and lots of sporting events – cycling, running, canoeing, downhill racing and sailing.

August

Joy of Jazz, Johannesburg, www.joyofjazz.co.za. Jo'burg's biggest annual jazz festival with over 200 local and international performers at different venues across the city, particularly in Newtown.
Oppikoppi Bushveld Festival, Northam, North West, www.oppikoppi.co.za. Popular rock festival that has helped establish many South African musicians' careers. This is real bushveld: hot, dry and covered in red dust and thorn trees. Expect to shower a lot when you get home. (Oppikoppi also hosts an Easter Festival in Mar/Apr.)

September

Arts Alive, Johannesburg, www.artsalive.co.za. 4-day festival with over 600 performers in dance, visual art, poetry and music at venues in the Jo'burg inner city area; the main concert is held at the Johannesburg Stadium.
Awesome Africa Music Festival, Durban, www.awesomeafricafestival.co.za. 3 stages of non-stop music in Durban's Albert Park, with over 200 artists from more than 20 countries. The focus is on collaboration with musicians from Africa and beyond.
Hermanus Whale Festival, Hermanus, Western Cape, www.whalefestival.co.za. An entertainment-packed festival, with the best land-based whale watching in the world.
Macufe, Bloemfontein, Free State, www.macufe.co.za. 10-day African cultural festival, featuring jazz, gospel, kwaito, hip-hop, R&B, rock and classical music, as well as dance, drama, musical theatre, poetry, fine art and traditional arts and crafts. Attracts a staggering 140,000 people.

November

Woodstock, Harrismith, Free State, www.woodstock.co.za. 4-day youth-oriented music and lifestyle festival, with bands and a market of crafters and alternative lifestyle products.

December

Spier Summer Festival, Stellenbosch, www.spierarts.co.za. At the amphitheatre on the Spier Estate, four months of music, opera, dance, stand-up comedy and theatre from Dec to Mar.

Public holidays

South Africa

When a public holiday falls on a Sun, the following Mon becomes a holiday. Most business will close but shopping malls and large supermarkets in city centres remain open and public holidays are some of their busiest days – especially if a holiday week-end coincides with month-end pay day. **New Year's Day**, 1 Jan; **Human Rights' Day**, 21 Mar; **Good Friday**, Fri before Easter Sun; **Family Day**, Mon following Easter Sun; **Freedom Day**, 27 Apr; **Workers' Day**, 1 May; **Youth Day**, 16 Jun; **National Women's Day**, 9 Aug; **Heritage Day**, 24 Sep; **Day of Reconciliation**, 16 Dec; **Christmas Day**, 25 Dec; **Day of Goodwill**, 26 Dec.

Lesotho

New Year's Day, 1 Jan; **Moshoeshoe's Day**, 11 Mar; **Hero's Day**, 4 Apr; **Good Friday**; **Easter Monday**; **Workers' Day**, 1 May; **Ascension Day**, 17 May; **Heroe's Day**, 25 May; **King's Birthday**, 17 Jul; **National Independence Day**, 4 Oct; **Christmas Day**, 25 Dec; **Boxing Day**, 26 Dec.

Swaziland

New Year's Day, 1 Jan; **Good Friday**; **Easter Monday**; **National Flag Day**, 25 Apr; **Workers Day**, 1 May; **Heroe's Day**; **Public Holiday**, 22 Jul; **Umhlanga Dance**, 2-3 Sep; **Independence Day**, 6 Sep; **Christmas Day**, 25 Dec; **Incwala Day**, Dec/Jan.

Essentials A-Z

Accident and emergency

South Africa Police, 10111; **Medical**, 10177; **Fire**, 10111. All emergencies from a cell phone, 112.
Lesotho Police, 123/124; **Ambulance**, 121.
Swaziland Police, T999.

Children

Inform the airline in advance that you are travelling with a baby or toddler and check out the facilities when booking as these vary with each aircraft. Also useful is www.babygoes2.com.

South Africa is a popular family holiday destination; In Dec and Jan accommodation in the parks and along the coast is packed with South African families during the school holidays. In the main towns with supermarkets, you will find plentiful supplies of all you need to feed and look after your little ones. Hygiene throughout the country is of a good standard; stomach upsets are rare and the tap water everywhere is safe to drink. Be sure to protect your children from the sun's intense rays, and be aware of the potential dangers of wild animals, snakes and insects in the bush. Most of the accommodation options welcome families; many have either specific family rooms or adjoining rooms suitable for families, and there are plenty of family chalets or bungalows, especially in the parks. Children get significant discounts on accommodation and entry fees. South Africa has a great appeal to children: animals and safaris are very exciting for them (and their parents), especially when they catch their first glimpse of an elephant or lion. However, small children may get bored driving around a hot game reserve or national park all day if there is no animal activity. If you travel in a group, think about the long hours inside the

vehicle sharing the small space with other people. Noisy and bickering children can annoy your travel mates and scare the animals away. Many travel agencies organize family safaris that are especially designed for couples travelling with children, and there is also the option of self-drive, which is ideal for families.

Customs and duty free

The official customs allowance for visitors over 18 years includes 200 cigarettes, 50 cigars, 250 g of tobacco, 2 litres of wine, 1 litre of spirits, 50 ml of perfume and 250 ml of toilet water. Visitors are restricted to bringing in R5000 of South African rand from their home country. Tourists can reclaim the 14% VAT on purchases bought in South Africa whose total value exceeds R250. You can do this when departing, at the VAT reclaim desks at airports or border posts. Refunds are given by cheque in South African rand, which can be paid into home bank accounts. Goods need to be shown to the refund officer as proof of purchase with VAT receipts, so be sure to ask for these when you buy something, and at the airport this needs to be done before you check in your luggage. The procedure is simple enough at the airports but allow plenty of time, especially if your flight is at night. At the border crossings such as Beitbridge (Zimbabwe) or Ramotswa (Botswana) the procedure is painstakingly slow, as there are few customs officials to check goods against receipts. Expect lengthy queues. Refunds only apply to items taken out of the country and not on services rendered, such as accommodation or goods consumed or used within the country. For example, if you are buying clothes, keep the shop tags on them to prove that you haven't worn them in South Africa and you'll get the tax back. To save time at the airport or border, you can also go to one of the pre-processing offices, at the Clock Tower at Cape Town Waterfront, Sandton City shopping mall in Johannesburg, and the Riverside Mall in Nelspruit. At these offices you will be required to submit all the receipts to be checked off against goods you will be exporting from South Africa, as well as presenting your passport and air ticket. They will stamp your receipts for verification but cannot give out refunds. This still has to be done at the airport or border on departure. For more information visit www.taxrefunds.co.za.

Disabled travellers

South Africa Facilities for disabled travellers are generally of a high standard in South Africa and the 3 main airports in Johannesburg, Cape Town and Durban are fully wheelchair accessible and can provide wheelchairs for infirm travellers. Smaller domestic airports may not be so reliable. Many of the more modern hotels have specially adapted rooms and it is worth asking about these even in smaller or more remote places when enquiring about accommodation. Facilities vary from hotel to hotel and some are more accessible than others. At the best you can expect wider doors, larger bathrooms, lowered light switches and mirrors, and roll-in showers with flip-down seats and grab rails. Modern shopping malls, and many restaurants, museums and other attractions are accommodating, but as with hotels, it's always a good idea to check in advance. Safaris should not pose too much of a problem either, given that most of the time is spent in the vehicle; wheelchair-bound travellers may want to consider a camping or tented safari which provides easy access to a tent at ground level. Some tourist attractions have been developed with disabled visitors in mind, such as the Braille Trail at Kirstenbosch Botanical Gardens, or the easily accessible cable car to the top of Table Mountain. Others, such as the new museum located in the old jail at Johannesburg's Constitutional

Hill, are now fully accessible for wheelchairs via ramps and lifts. The fact that South Africa is a very car-friendly country should make getting to the major sights no problem and most places have disabled parking right by the entrance.

Lesotho Apart from the Sun hotels in Maseru, few hotels have specific facilities for disabled travellers, though it's always worth enquiring if there is a room that can be negotiated by a wheelchair. The nature of the rugged terrain means that travelers with physical impairments cannot take advantage of Lesotho's hiking or pony trekking but driving through the mountains poses no additional problems.

Swaziland Most larger modern hotels have at least 1 room that is wheelchair accessible and again it's worth phoning ahead to see if smaller places can accommodate your needs.

Useful contacts
www.eco-access.org.za A useful website promoting access to nature for disabled people in South Africa.
Endeavour Safaris, T021-5566114, www.endeavour-safaris.com. Organizes tours for not only the mobility disabled, but for those with hearing disability, visual impairment, and people on regular kidney dialysis treatment or oxygen. They can also organize equipment hire.
Epic Enabled, T021-7829575, www.epic-enabled.com. Offers an excellent range of tours for disabled travellers, using fully modified overland trucks, camp assistants and wheelchair-friendly accommodation. Not specifically for the disabled, and caters for accompanying friends and family too.
Flamingo Tours, T021-5574496, www.flamingotours.co.za. Established Western Cape tour operator specializing in disabled travel; tailor-made tours are led by a registered guide and nurse (if necessary).

Rolling SA, T033-3304214, www.rolling
sa.co.za. Organizes tours throughout South
Africa specifically for wheelchair users.
Titch Tours, T021-6865501, www.titch
tours.co.za. Custom-designed itineraries
according to travellers' needs.

Dress

Dress in South Africa tends to be casual and
most people on holiday wear shorts, sandals
and a T-shirt. If you intend to do any game
viewing, clothes in dark green, muted browns
and khaki colours are best. In general, bars
and restaurants are casual, though some
of the more upmarket establishments have
dress codes where sandals, vest and shorts
are not appreciated.

Drugs

Although marijuana, locally known as
dagga, is grown in rural areas, such as the
Wild Coast and Lesotho, and smoking it is
relatively widespread, it is illegal and strict
penalties apply. Traditionally, poor people
have smoked a lethal cocktail of mandrax
(*buttons*) and *dugga*, which will almost
instantly comatose inexperienced users.
Another highly potent drug, *tik*, or
methamphetamine, which is part of the
amphetamine group of drugs, has also more
recently become a major problem in urban
areas, especially on the Cape Flats in Cape
Town. Hard drugs such as cocaine and
heroin, along with their associated problems,
are also prevalent. Since independence there
has been an alarming growth in drug-related
crime and inner-city areas of Cape Town,
Johannesburg and, more recently, Durban
have become major transit points for drugs
en route to Europe and America.
Drink-driving is a big problem in South
Africa, and although it is illegal, the laws
are routinely ignored by locals. Be especially
wary on the roads over Christmas when the
number of road deaths soars dramatically.
Reputedly there are more deaths caused
by road accidents in Dec in South Africa,
than there are in a whole year in Australia!

Electricity

South Africa's supply is 220/230 volts AC at 50
Hz, except for Pretoria, where it is 250 volts AC.
Most plugs and appliances are 3-point round-
pin (one 10 mm and two 8 mm prongs). Hotels
usually have 2-roundpin sockets for razors.

Embassies and consulates

South Africa
Australia, Corner Rhodes Place and
State Circle, Canberra, T02-62727300,
www.sahc.org.au.
Austria, Sandgasse 33, 1190 Vienna,
T320-6493, www.saembvie.at.
Belgium, Rue de la Loi 26, Wetstraat 26,
Brussels T02-2854400, www.southafrica.be.
Canada, 15 Sussex Dr, Ottawa,
T613-7440330, www.southafrica-canada.ca.
Denmark, Gammel Vartov VEJ, No 8, 2900
Hellerup, Copenhagen, T039-180155,
www.southafrica.dk.
France, 59 Quai d'Orsay, Paris 75007,
T01-5359 2323, www.afriquesud.net.
Germany, Tiergartenstr 18, 10785 Berlin,
T030-220730, www.suedafrika.org.
Israel, Yakhin House, Top Tower, 50 Dizengoff
St, Tel Aviv 64332, T03-5252566, www.safis.co.il.
Italy, Via Tanaro 14, Rome 00198, T06-8525
4262, www.sudafrica.it.
Japan, Oriken Hirakawacho Bld,
Hirakawa-cho, Chiyoda-ku 1020093,
Tokyo, T03-3239 2990, www.rsatk.com.
Netherlands, 36 Wassenaarseweg 2596 CJ,
The Hague, T070-3105920, www.zuidafrika.nl.
Spain, Edificio Lista, Calle de Claudio
Coello 91, 28006 Madrid, T91-4363780,
www.sudafrica.com.
Sweden, Fleminggatan 20, 11226 Stockholm,
T08-6607693, www.southafricanemb.se.

Switzerland, Rue du Rhone 65, Geneva 1204, T022-8495454, http://missions.itu.int
UK, South Africa House, Trafalgar Sq, London, WC2N 5DP, T020-7451 7299, www.southafricahouse.com.
USA, 3051 Massachusetts Av NW, Washington, DC 20008, T1202-2324400, www.saembassy.org; there are also consulates in Los Angeles and New York.

Lesotho
Belgium, Boulevard General Wahis 45, Brussels, T+32 (0)2-7053976.
Denmark, Strandvejen 64H, Copenhagen, T+45 3962 4343.
Germany, Kurfursten Strasse 84, Berlin 10787, T+49 (0)30-2575720.
South Africa, 391 Anderson St, Menlo Park, Pretoria 0001, T012-460 7648.
UK, 7 Chesham Pl, Belgravia, London, T+44 (0)20 7235 5686, www.lesotholondon.org.uk.
USA, 2511 Massachussets Av, Washington DC 20008, T+1 202-797 5533, www.lesothoemb-usa.gov.ls.

Swaziland
Canada, 130 Albert St, Suite 1204, Ottawa, Ontario, T1-613-5671480, shc@direct-internet.net.
Germany, Große Präsidentenstr 5, Berlin 10178, T030-28096250, wwww.swasiland.de.
South Africa, 715 Government Av, Arcadia, Pretoria 0083, T012-3441910, www.swazihighcom.co.za.
UK, 20 Buckingham Gate, SW1E 6LB, London, T020-76306611, www.swaziland.org.uk
US, 1712 New Hampshire Av, NW Washington DC 20009, T202-2345002, www.swazilandembassyus.com.

Gay and lesbian travellers

The South African constitution is one of the most gay-friendly and progressive in the world and the government legalized same-sex marriages in Nov 2006 (at the time, the fifth country in the world to do so). Cape Town is the self-proclaimed Pink Capital of Africa and has a flourishing scene, with a yearly **Gay Pride** week, usually held in Feb, www.capetownpride.co.za. Other annual events in Cape Town are the popular gay and lesbian film festival in Aug known as **Out in Africa**, www.oia.co.za; and the annual **Mother City Queer Project**, www.mcqp.co.za, a costume dance event in Dec which is a highlight on the city's social calendar attracting local celebs and TV cameras. Up the coast, the **Pink Loerie Mardi Gras** is held in Knysna in May, www.pinkloerie.com.

The *Pink Map* of the city, available at the tourist offices, lists gay friendly/oriented accommodation, restaurants and nightlife, tour operators, and even health spas and launderettes. Away from Cape Town, Johannesburg and Durban also have burgeoning gay scenes but, away from these cities, South Africa, like **Lesotho** and **Swaziland**, remains deeply conservative. Overtly affectionate behaviour between gay and lesbian couples may elicit a disapproving response – from both black and white communities – particularly in more remote rural parts. It is wise for gay visitors to be discrete. By doing so you should encounter no problems.

Useful contacts
www.exit.co.za Leading gay and lesbian online newspaper.
www.gaynetsa.co.za Lists clubs, bars and gay-friendly accommodation around the country (and celebrity gossip).
www.mask.org.za A website dedicated to gay and lesbian affairs throughout Africa.
www.oia.co.za Out in Africa organizes annual gay film festivals in Cape Town and Johannesburg.
www.q.co.za South Africa's main gay and lesbian website with travel and entertainment news, chat rooms and a dating service.

Health

See your doctor or travel clinic at least 6 weeks before your departure for general advice on travel risks, malaria and recommended vaccinations. Make sure you have travel insurance, get a dental check (especially if you are going to be away for more than a month), know your own blood group and if you suffer a long-term condition such as diabetes or epilepsy make sure someone knows or that you have a Medic Alert bracelet/necklace with this information on it (www.medicalert.co.uk).

Vaccinations

Confirm your primary courses and boosters are up to date. Courses or boosters usually advised: diphtheria; tetanus; poliomyelitis; hepatitis A. Vaccines sometimes advised: tuberculosis; hepatitis B; rabies; cholera; typhoid. A yellow fever certificate is required if over 1 year old and entering from an infected area. If arriving in Lesotho from tropical African countries you may be asked for a yellow fever vaccination card. The final decision on all vaccinations, however, should be based on a consultation with your GP or travel clinic.

If you need to have a vaccination or buy malaria prophylactics in South Africa, visit one of the Netcare Travel Clinics in the major cities, www.travelclinic.co.za.

For further information, visit www.fitfortravel.nhs.uk.

Health risks

Altitude sickness

Acute mountain sickness can strike from about 3000 m upwards and in general is more likely to affect those who ascend rapidly (for example by plane) and those who over-exert themselves. Acute mountain sickness takes a few hours or days to come on and presents with heachache, lassitude, dizziness, loss of appetite, nausea and vomiting. Insomnia is common and often associated with a suffocating feeling when lying down in bed. You may notice that your breathing tends to wax and wane at night and your face is puffy in the mornings – this is all part of the syndrome. If the symptoms are mild, the treatment is rest and painkillers (preferably not aspirin-based) for the headaches. Should the symptoms be severe and prolonged it is best to descend to a lower altitude immediately and reascend, if necessary, slowly and in stages. The symptoms disappear quickly – even after a few hundred metres of descent. The best way of preventing acute mountain sickness is a relatively slow ascent. When trekking to high altitude, some time spent walking at medium altitude, getting fit and acclimatizing is beneficial.

Bites and stings

This is a very rare event indeed for travellers, but if you are unlucky (or careless) enough to be bitten by a venomous snake, spider, scorpion or sea creature, try to identify the culprit, without putting yourself in further danger. Snake bites in particular are very frightening, but in fact rarely poisonous – even venomous snakes bite without injecting venom. Victims should be taken to a hospital or a doctor without delay. Reassure and comfort the victim frequently, immobilize the limb with a bandage or a splint and get the patient to lie still. Do not slash the bite area and try to suck out the poison. This does more harm than good. You should apply a tourniquet in these circumstances, but only if you know how to. Do not attempt this if you are not experienced.

Certain tropical fish inject venom into bathers' feet when trodden on, which can be exceptionally painful. Wear plastic shoes if such creatures are reported. The pain can be relieved by immersing the foot in hot water (as hot as you can bear) for as long as the pain persists.

Dengue fever

This viral disease is spread by mosquitoes that tend to bite during the day. The symptoms are fever and often intense joint pains, also some people develop a rash. Symptoms last about a week but it can take a few weeks to recover fully. Dengue can be difficult to distinguish from malaria as both diseases tend to occur in the same countries. There are no effective vaccines or antiviral drugs though, fortunately, travellers rarely develop the more severe forms of the disease (these can prove fatal). Rest, plenty of fluids and paracetamol (not aspirin) is the recommended treatment.

Diarrhoea and intestinal upset

Diarrhoea can refer either to loose stools or an increased frequency of bowel movement, both of which can be a nuisance. Symptoms should be relatively short-lived but if they persist beyond 2 weeks specialist medical attention should be sought. Also seek medical help if there is blood in the stools and/or fever. Adults can use an antidiarrhoeal medication such as loperamide to control the symptoms but only for up to 24 hrs. In addition keep well hydrated by drinking plenty of fluids and eat bland foods. Oral rehydration sachets taken after each loose stool are a useful way to keep well hydrated. These should always be used when treating children and the elderly.

Bacterial traveller's diarrhoea is the most common form. Ciproxin (Ciprofloxacin) is a useful antibiotic and can be obtained by private prescription in the UK. You need to take one 500 mg tablet when the diarrhoea starts. If there are so signs of improvement after 24 hrs the diarrhoea is likely to be viral and not bacterial. If it is due to other organisms such as those causing giardia or amoebic dysentery, different antibiotics will be required.

The standard advice to prevent problems is to be careful with water and ice for drinking. If you have any doubts then boil the water or filter and treat it. Food can also transmit disease. Be wary of salads (what were they washed in, who handled them), re-heated foods or food that has been left out in the sun having been cooked earlier in the day. There is a simple adage that says wash it, peel it, boil it or forget it. Also be wary of unpasteurized dairy products as these can transmit a range of diseases.

Hepatitis

Hepatitis means inflammation of the liver. Viral causes of the disease can be acquired anywhere in the world. The most obvious symptom is a yellowing of your skin or the whites of your eyes. However, prior to this all that you may notice is itching and tiredness. Pre-travel hepatitis A vaccine is the best bet. Hepatitis B (for which there is a vaccine) is spread through blood and unprotected sexual intercourse, both of which can be avoided.

HIV/AIDS

Southern Africa has the highest rates of HIV and AIDS in the world. Efforts to stem the rate of infection have had limited success, as many of the factors that need addressing such as social change, poverty and gender inequalities are long-term processes. Visitors should be aware of the dangers of infection from unprotected sex and always use a condom. Do not inject non-prescribed drugs or share needles; avoid having a tattoo or piercing, electrolysis or acupuncture unless you're sure the equipment is sterile. If you have to have medical treatment, ensure any equipment used is taken from a sealed pack or is freshly sterilized. It may even be worth taking your own sterilized needles as part of a first-aid kit. If you have to have a blood transfusion, ask for screened blood. See also box, page 61.

Malaria

In **South Africa**, there is a seasonal (Oct-May) risk of malaria in the east of the country, particularly in Ndumu and Tembe game reserves. **Swaziland** has malaria risk in all lowland areas. For a map of malaria regions in South Africa, visit www.malaria.org.za. **Lesotho**'s high altitude makes it a healthier place than many African countries; malaria is non-existent and other tropical diseases are rare.

Removing the stigma

Lesotho has one of the highest infection rate of HIV/AIDS in the world – some 23,000-30,000 people have died of the disease each year since 2003. In 2006, the government introduced a US$12 million programme to offer free AIDS tests for everyone under the scheme called 'Know Your Status'; it's the first country in the world to offer tests to its entire population. The first person to take a public test at the launch of the programme was King Letsie III, who did so at a clinic in Maseru. Authorities hope that this gesture will go some way towards removing the stigma associated with HIV/AIDS, thus encouraging those that test positive to get the treatment they need.

Malaria can cause death within 24 hrs and can start as something just resembling an attack of flu. You may feel tired, lethargic, headachy, feverish; or more seriously, develop fits, followed by coma and then death. Have a low index of suspicion because it is very easy to write off vague symptoms, which may actually be malaria. If you have a temperature, visit a doctor as soon as you can and ask for a malaria test. On your return home, if you suffer any of these symptoms, have a test as soon as possible. Even if a previous test proved negative, this could save your life.

Treatment is with drugs and may be oral or into a vein depending on the seriousness of the infection. Remember ABCD: **Awareness** (of whether the disease is present in the area you are travelling in), **Bite avoidance**, **Chemoprophylaxis**, **Diagnosis**.

To prevent mosquito bites wear clothes that cover arms and legs, use effective insect repellents in areas with known risks of insect-spread disease and use a mosquito net treated with an insecticide. Repellents containing 30-50% DEET (Di-ethyltoluamide) are recommended when visiting malaria endemic areas; lemon eucalyptus (Mosiguard) is a reasonable alternative. The key advice is to take the correct anti-malarials and finish the recommended course. If you are popular target for insect bites or develop lumps quite soon after being bitten use antihistamine tablets and apply a cream such as hydrocortisone.

Remember that it is risky to buy medicine, and in particular anti-malarials, in some developing countries. These may be sub-standard or part of a trade in counterfeit drugs.

Rabies

Rabies is endemic throughout certain parts of the world so be aware of the dangers of the bite from any animal. Rabies vaccination before travel can be considered but if bitten always seek urgent medical attention – whether or not you have been previously vaccinated – after first cleaning the wound and treating with an iodine-base disinfectant or alcohol.

Sun

Take good heed of advice regarding protecting yourself against the sun. Overexposure can lead to sunburn and, in the longer term, skin cancers and premature skin aging. The best advice is simply to avoid exposure to the sun by covering exposed skin, wearing a hat and staying out of the sun if possible, particularly between late morning and early afternoon. Apply a high-factor sunscreen (greater than SPF15) and also make sure it screens against UVB. Be aware of sunburn at high altitudes too; it might feel cool, but the sun can be strong in the rarefied air of the mountains.

A further danger in tropical climates is heat exhaustion or more seriously heat stroke. This can be avoided by good hydration, which means drinking water past the point of simply quenching thirst. Also when first exposed to tropical heat take time to acclimatize by avoiding strenuous activity in the middle of the day. If you cannot avoid heavy exercise it is also a good idea to increase salt intake.

Tuberculosis

Tuberculosis is most commonly transmitted via droplet infection. Ensure that you have been immunized, especially those mixing closely with the local population and those at occupational risk, eg health care workers. Check with your doctor or nurse.

Underwater health

If you plan to dive make sure that you are fit do so. The **British Sub-Aqua Club** (BSAC), T01513-506200, www.bsac.com, can put you in touch with doctors who will carry out medical examinations. Check that any dive company you use is reputable and has appropriate certification from BSAC, **Professional Association of Diving Instructors** (PADI), www.padi.com, or the **National Association of Underwater Instructors** (NAUI), www.nauisa.org.

Other diseases

There are a range of other insect-borne diseases that are quite rare in travellers, but worth finding out about if going to particular destinations. Examples are sleeping sickness, river blindness and leishmaniasis. Fresh water can also be a source of diseases such as bilharzia and leptospirosis and it is worth investigating if these are a danger before bathing in lakes and streams.

Further information

Websites

Foreign and Commonwealth Office (FCO) (UK), www.fco.gov.uk.
Fit for Travel (UK), www.fitfortravel.nhs.uk.
Medical Advisory Service for Travellers Abroad (MASTA) (UK), www.masta.org.

The National Travel Health Network and Centre (NaTHNaC) www.nathnac.org.
World Health Organisation, www.who.int.

Books

Lankester T, *Travellers' Good Health Guide* (2nd edition, Sheldon Press, 2006).

Insurance

Before departure, it is vital to take out full travel insurance. There is a wide variety of policies to choose from, so shop around. At the very least, the policy should cover personal effects and medical expenses, including the possibility of medical evacuation by air ambulance to your own country. Make sure that it also covers all activities that you might do while away, trekking or skydiving for example. There is no substitute for suitable precautions against petty crime, but if you do have something stolen whilst in South Africa, report the incident to the nearest police station and ensure you get a police report and case number. You will need these to make any claim from your insurance company.

Internet

South Africa is well served by the internet and most companies, hotels, tourist offices, guesthouses and individuals have email addresses and websites. There are plenty of internet cafés in all major urban centres and many hotels, guesthouses or backpacker hostels offer email access as a service. Wireless internet is available and many internet cafés offer stations to plug in your laptop as well as a service to download digital photographs onto disc or memory stick. In the more remote regions you are unlikely to find somewhere to use the internet unless the town is served by a university or college. The Directory sections in each chapter give listings. Expect to pay around R10 per hr. In **Lesotho** internet facilities are generally only available in Maseru. In **Swaziland** wireless internet is available at the airport and the large hotels, and there are business centres and internet cafés in the shopping malls of Mbabane and Manzini.

Language

South Africa

There are 11 official languages in South Africa: English, Zulu, Xhosa, Afrikaans, Venda, Swazi, North Sotho, South Sotho, Tswana, Sindebele and Shangaan. Afrikaans is spoken by 60% of white South Africans and the majority of the Cape coloured population. In addition to this, there are 6 Asian languages spoken, mostly in KwaZulu Natal. English is widely spoken and understood and is the language used in education and business, but it is always a good idea to learn at least a couple of basic phrases in the predominant language of the area that you're travelling in – a simple 'hello' in Xhosa or 'thank you' in Afrikaans can go a long way. *Lekker* is an Afrikaans word for 'very good' or 'things are going well'.

Lesotho

Lesotho has 2 official languages, Sesotho, which is spoken everywhere, and English. Both are taught in schools from the fifth year of primary education so while English is spoken in Maseru and the bigger towns; in remote areas there will usually be somebody, often a school child, who speaks some English. See also Glossary, page 900.

Swaziland

The 2 main languages are siSwati, which is similar to the Zulu language, and English. English is the language used in education and business while parliament works with both languages. English is widely spoken and understood in urban areas; in the more isolated rural areas siSwati is prevalent. Knowing and using a couple of Siswati greetings is considered polite. See also Glossary, page 900.

Media

Magazines

There are a number of publications that travellers will find useful in South Africa. The annual *Eat Out* lists the best restaurants in the country, although it tends to concentrate on the more upmarket eateries. *Time Out Cape Town* is a useful annual magazine with good nightlife and culture listings. Similar content can be found in the monthly *Cape Etc*, which also has interesting articles on shopping, day trips, and eating out. The monthly *Getaway* is aimed at outdoorsy South Africans, but has excellent travel features and ideas, as well as reviews of accommodation alternatives and activities throughout southern Africa. *Africa Geographical* is a glossy monthly with high-quality photographs, which publishes regular articles on southern Africa's parks, reserves and wildlife. Its sister magazine, *Africa, Birds & Birding*, also monthly, is a must for anyone with an interest in birdwatching in South Africa. For inspiration before you leave home, pick up a copy of *Travel Africa*, www.travelafricamag.com.

Newspapers

The *Sunday Times* and *Sunday Independent* are weekly English-language papers with national coverage, although several editions are produced for different areas. The excellent weekly *Mail & Guardian* (with close links to the British *Guardian*) provides the most objective reporting on South African issues and has in-depth coverage of international news. Daily English-language newspapers include: *The Star* and *The Citizen* (Johannesburg); *The Daily News* and *The Natal Mercury* (Durban); *The Argus* and *The Cape Times* (Cape Town). The *Sowetan* provides a less white-oriented view of South African news and has the best coverage of international soccer. There are also a number of newspapers published in Afrikaans, Zulu and Xhosa.

Radio

Given South Africa's low literacy rate, radio is the most popular form of media in the country and even the most remote corners are reached by broadcasters. The **South African Broadcast Corporation** (SABC) has numerous national stations catering for the 11 official languages. The corporation has an agreement with the BBC, which means that listeners can hear BBC news and programmes at certain times of day. 5FM is the SABC national pop music station, while Metro FM offers R'n'B, hip-hop and Kwaito. There is also an abundance of local commercial and community radio stations, such as Good Hope FM in Cape Town, Jacaranda FM in Pretoria or Highveld FM in Johannesburg.

In Lesotho, the BBC World Service has a relay station near Maseru, and there are 6 local radio stations, 3 of which broadcast primarily in English.

Television

The **SABC** – the state broadcaster – has significantly restructured its service in the last decade to accommodate all 11 official languages. The majority of programmes are in English, followed by Afrikaans, Zulu and Xhosa. There are now 4 free channels – SABC 1, 2 and 3, and the newer e channel. The latter is the most popular and tends to have better news and entertainment programmes, although SABC 3 has live CNN broadcasts on most afternoons. The paying channel, M-Net – available in most hotels and backpacker hostels – offers a range of sport, sitcoms and movies. It is available for free from 1700-1900, known as 'open time'. Many hotels also have satellite TV, known as DSTV, with a range of sports, movie and news channels.

Lesotho TV has news and current affairs programmes that are broadcast (in Sesotho) every evening at 1730-1900. At other times South African TV channels are shown and DSTV is available at the larger hotels.

Money

Currency

Exchange rates GBP1 = R15.44; US$1 = R7.84; AUS$1 = R7.53; euro = R12.34 (June 2008). For up-to-the-minute exchange rates, visit www.xe.com.

South Africa The South African currency is the **rand** (R) which is divided into 100 cents (c). Notes are in 200, 100, 50, 20 and 10 R, and coins are in 5, 2, 1 R and 50, 20, 10 and 5 c. You can carry your funds in traveller's cheques (TCs), credit cards, rands, US dollars, euros or pounds sterling.

Visitors are restricted to bringing R5000 cash in person into the country and should change any surplus rand back into their own currency before leaving South Africa. This is most easily done at the airport; high street banks usually require proof of initial transactions. If you plan on visiting neighbouring countries, note that most of their currencies can only be purchased within South Africa and not before you leave home. However, rand can easily be exchanged in all South Africa's neigh-bouring countries and in some cases, such as Namibia and Mozambique, is used interchangeably alongside the local currency.

Lesotho The standard unit of currency is the maloti, divided into 100 lisente. It is exactly equivalent to the rand, and the 2 are interchangeable, so you can pay in either currency. Bring sufficient rand with you from South Africa, as this will considerably reduce money-changing hassles. While the rand is interchangeable with the maloti in Lesotho this is not the case in South Africa. If you are due to leave Lesotho in a few days, try to get change in rand and when you change money ask for the cash in rand.

Swaziland The standard unit of currency is the **lilangeni** (plural *emalangeni*, E) and is equivalent to the South African rand. TCs can be changed in Mbabane but the process is slow. You are better off bringing in cash in the form of South African rand. Both the rand and the emalangeni are accepted currencies just about everywhere.

Changing money
South Africa All the main high street banks offer foreign exchange services. You can also change money at branches of **Rennies Travel**, www.rennies.co.za, which acts as an agent for Thomas Cook. There are Rennies branches in all regional and tourist centres and most shopping malls. **American Express Foreign Exchange Service**, www.american express.co.za, has offices in the larger cities and offers a poste restante service to card holders. Larger hotels offer exchange facilities, but these often charge exorbitant fees.

Lesotho There are 3 main banks in Lesotho: the **First National Bank**, **Nedbank** and **Standard Bank**. All change money, although it usually involves filling out paperwork and long queues (especially on Fri). There are now several ATM machines in Maseru, which offer a hassle-free way of getting hold of local currency. Outside Maseru, most banks do not have a separate foreign exchange counter. It is illegal to change money on the black market.

Swaziland Emalangeni is not a convertible currency so make sure you change any back into rand or other currences before leaving the country. There are no restrictions on the import/export of local and foreign currency, and it is not worth changing your rand into emalangeni for just a short visit.

Credit and debit cards
Lost or stolen cards: **American Express**, T0800-990123; **Diners Club**, T0800-112017; **MasterCard**, T0800-990418; **Visa**, T0800-990475.

You can get all the way around South Africa with a credit or debit card. Not only do they offer a convenient method of covering major expenses but they offer some of the most competitive exchange rates when withdrawing cash from ATMs. They are particularly useful when hiring a car – indeed, many companies will only hire a car to foreign visitors if they have a credit card. The chip and pin system is beginning to feature. Note that credit cards are not accepted as payment for petrol, which can only be purchased with cash. ATMs are everywhere; Plus, Cirrus Visa, Mastercard, American Express and Diners' Club are all accepted. The amount you can withdraw varies between systems and cards, but you should be able to take out at least R1000 a day. Note that theft during or immediately after a withdrawal can be a problem, so never accept a stranger's help at an ATM, be aware of your surroundings and avoid using street-side ATMs. Instead, go into a bank or shopping mall, where guards are often on duty.

Lesotho Credit cards are accepted at the large international Sun hotels and can be used at ATM machines in Maseru and at the few banks in the regional towns. Some of the main branches of the banks in Maseru can advance local currency off a credit card, but this is a lengthy process.

Swaziland Major credit cards such as **Visa**, **Mastercard** and **American Express** are accepted in hotels, large town chainstores, some restaurants, and the national parks and game reserves for accommodation, though you are advised to use cash for smaller items and services. ATMs are available in Mbabane and Manzini; credit cards can be used to withdraw cash, either through the machine or from a teller.

Useful websites
www.americaexpress.com, www.mastercard.com, www.visa.com.

Traveller's cheques
The major advantage of Tcs is that if they are lost or stolen there is a relatively efficient system for replacement. Make sure you keep

a full record of the cheques' numbers and value and always keep the receipts separate from the cheques. The drawback is that replacement cheques can usually only be collected from banks in major cities. Another disadvantages is the time it takes to cash them and the commission charged, which ranges from 0.2% to 2%. The most widely accepted TCs are American Express, Thomas Cook and Visa. Thomas Cook issues South African rand TCs, which are sometimes accepted as payment in shops and hotels.

In Swaziland, TCs can be changed at **First National Bank, Nedbank, Standard Bank, Swazi Bank** and **Central Bank of Swaziland**.

Cost of travelling

South Africa is fairly good value for money for tourists spending US dollars, pounds sterling or euro. If you are travelling independently and propose to hire a car, you will need to budget R250-400 per day, depending on the season, type of vehicle and equipment included. If this is shared among a group of 4 it's the most affordable way to get around. The cost of fuel is about half of what Europeans are used to, but distances travelled can be considerable so longer holidays will run up a hefty fuel bill.

Accommodation will represent your other principal daily expense. In first-rate luxury lodges, tented camps or guest farms expect to pay in excess of R1000-2000 per night for a double, rising to R6000-7000 per person per night in the most exclusive establishments. For this you will get impeccable service, cuisine and decor in fantastic locations. If staying in simple B&Bs and hotels, budget R350-1000 per couple per night. By camping or staying in backpacker dorms, you can bring this down to R100-150 on average per person per night. See also Sleeping, page 47.

Food and drink is still good value in southern Africa and a 2-course evening meal with wine in a reasonable restaurant will cost under R300 for 2 people, and you can be pretty assured of good food and large portions. For the budget traveller there are plenty of fast-food outlets, and almost every supermarket has a superb deli counter serving hot and cold meals. Costs can be brought down by self-catering. Food in supermarkets is considerably cheaper than, say, in Europe, especially meat and fresh fruit and vegetables, and a bottle of wine and beer are an affordable R30 and R10 respectively. See also Eating, page 51.

Opening hours

South Africa Banks Mon-Fri 0900-1530, Sat 0830/0900-1030/1100. **Businesses** Mon-Fri 0830-1700, Sat 0830-1400. **Post offices** Mon-Fri 0830-1600, Sat 0800-1200, minor branches have slightly shorter hours. **Shops and supermarkets** Mon-Fri 0800-1800, Sat 0800-1300, Sun 0900-1300. Larger branches of the supermarkets stay open until late in the evening. Large shopping malls in the cities may stay open until 2100.

Lesotho Banks Mon-Fri 0900-1530, Sat 0830/0900 to 1030/1100. **Businesses** Mon-Fri 0830-1700, Sat 0830-1400. **Government offices** Mon-Fri 0830-1300 and 1400-1630. **Post offices** Mon-Fri 0830-1600, Sat 0800-1200. **Shops** Mon-Fri 0800-1800, Sat 0800-1300, Sun 0900-1300.

Swaziland Banks Mon, Tue, Thu and Fri 0830-1530, Wed 0830-1300, Sat 0830-1130. **Post offices** Mon-Fri 0800-1600, Sat 0800-1100. **Shops** Mon-Fri 0830-1700, Sat 0830-1300. Some larger supermarkets are open on Sun mornings.

Packing

A good rule of thumb is to take half the clothes you think you'll need and double the money. A backpack or travelpack (a hybrid backpack/suitcase) rather than a rigid suitcase, covers most eventualities and survives the rigours of a variety of modes of travel well. A lock for your luggage is strongly advised – there are cases of pilfering by airport baggage handlers the world over. Light cotton clothing is best, with a fleece or woollen jumper for evenings. Hikers will need comfortable walking boots that have been worn in. Those going on camping safaris will need a sleeping bag, towel and torch. Everything you could possibly need on holiday is available to buy in South Africa so you don't have to fret about leaving anything at home.

Checklist

Air tickets, cash, mobile phone and charger, contact lens solution, contraceptives, credit cards, ear plugs, electric plug adaptor, first-aid kit, insect repellent, passport, photo-copies of main documents (keep separate), small torch plus batteries, sun-glasses, sun protection cream, Swiss army knife or Leatherman, toiletries, TCs, water bottle.

Post

South Africa Both internal and international mail is generally reliable. If you are sending home souvenirs, surface mail to Europe is the cheapest method but will take at least 6 weeks. Letters to Europe and the US should take no more than a few days, although over the busy Christmas season can take longer. There is a 'speed service', but this costs significantly more. Parcels have been known to disappear en route, so it's probably best to use registered mail for more valuable items so that you can track their progress. Courier services are useful for sending heavier objects such as wooden sculptures and furniture. Contact **DHL**, T0860-345000 (in South Africa) or T011-9213666 (from overseas), for the nearest branch, or visit www.dhl.co.za.

You can send faxes from post offices and there are a number of private companies

such as Postnet, www.postnet.co.za, usually found in the shopping malls that offer fax, mail and business services.

Lesotho The main post office is on central Kingsway in Maseru, where you will spend a very long time in a queue to purchase a stamp. The international postal service is fairly quick and reliable.

Swaziland Mbabane's main post office is on Warmer St, to the east of the Swazi Plaza and there are small post offices in the regional towns. The postal service is reliable.

Safety

Send yourself an email with details of TCs, passport, driving licence, credit cards and travel insurance numbers. Someone at home should also have access to important details.

South Africa has had more than its fair share of well-publicized crime problems. In the 1980s and 90s Johannesburg was frequently dubbed the most dangerous city in the world, although crime rates are declining there today. Despite the statistics, much of the serious, violent crime is gang-based and occurs in areas that tourists are unlikely to visit, such as Mitchells Plain in Cape Town's townships, or the inner-city ghettos such as Hillbrow in Johannesburg or Point Road in Durban. Dangers facing tourists are on the whole limited to traditional mugging or, on occasion, carjacking. Guns are widely available and you should be aware that your assailant may well be armed and any form of resistance could be fatal.

Nevertheless, visitors need not worry about their safety outside the inner cities any more than they would in any foreign country. The most simple points to remember are to avoid altogether what are considered to be dangerous areas, not to walk about any urban centres at night and to avoid driving after dark. If you are going to be travelling alone in a car, it's a good idea to bring (or hire) a mobile phone; useful in any case if you break down. For specific advice for women travellers, see page 74.

Bear in mind that safety is not just a matter of avoiding crime. South Africa has a severe HIV epidemic and travellers should always take precautions, see page 60.

Problem areas

City centres Horror stories abound among travellers passing through Johannesburg. The city centre, Hillbrow, and Yoeville have the worst reputation and the crime rate remains high. There are few facilities or accommodation options in these areas, so it is feasible to avoid them altogether and visit the sights only on an organized tour. Travellers arriving at the Park City Transit Centre in Johannesburg should not walk into town. Instead, take a taxi directly to your hotel. The crime rate in Johannesburg's suburbs, where most of the hotels, hostels, nightlife, and shops are located, has improved greatly in recent years, due mainly to an increase in security measures, and you should experience few problems in these areas.

Apart from Johannesburg, city centres are generally safe during daylight hours, although listen to advice from locals about which areas to avoid. Closed-circuit cameras and private security guards have made Cape Town and Durban city centres as safe as European cities, but the likelihood of being mugged increases sharply after dark. The safest way to travel around cities at night is to take a taxi directly to and from your destination.

Townships While by no means out of bounds to tourists, it would not be wise to wander into a township by yourself. On the other hand, if you know a local or have friends living and working in South Africa who know their way around, a trip to a township market or nightclub can be an interesting and rewarding experience.

Alternatively go on a township tour which will undoubtedly give you a different picture of the way a very large number of urban South Africans live.

Carjacking This remains a problem in South Africa, although the number of incidents is constantly declining thanks to collaboration with neighbouring countries to crack down on stolen cars crossing borders. The favoured location for this crime is at red traffic lights on a junction. It is a good idea to travel with the windows closed and the doors locked. When faced with a suspicious situation at a junction, it is general practice to jump the lights and get away as fast as possible. Incidents can also happen on quiet rural roads, so be vigilant at all times. Again, it is important to remember that carjackers are almost always armed and will use their weapons when faced with resistance. Note that the insurance on hire cars in South Africa is correspondingly high.

Student travellers

Anyone in full-time education is entitled to an **International Student Identity Card** (ISIC). These are issued by student travel offices and travel agencies across the world and offer special rates on all forms of transport (including the Baz Bus) and other concessions and services. Visit www.isic.org for up-to-date information on cards and local contact details. **Youth Hostel Association** (YHA) cards also attract discounts at some of the backpacker hostels; for information visit www.hihostels.com.

Telephone

South Africa Country code: +27; international direct dialling code 00; directory enquires T1023; international operator T0009; international enquires T1025.

You must dial the full 3-digit regional code for every number in South Africa, even when you are calling from within that region.

The telephone service is very efficient. Card and coin phones are widespread and work well – even in remote national parks there are usually card phones from which one can dial direct to anywhere in the world. Note that hotels usually double the rates and even a short international call can become very expensive.

Blue call boxes are coin operated telephones but these are becoming rare as green card phones take over. Phone cards are sold for R10, R20, R50 and R100. They are available in larger supermarkets, newsagents, some chemists and Telkom vending machines. A R50 card is sufficient to make an international call to Europe for a few mins

Lesotho Country code: +266. The local telephone system is reasonable in the lowlands but there is poor coverage in the mountain areas. There are no area codes. International calls are very expensive and only possible from the larger centres. Note that some accommodation options in Lesotho have reservation telephone numbers in South Africa; if you are calling these in Lesotho, you must dial the country's access code (00) followed by the code for South Africa (27).

Swaziland Country code: +268. When making a call within the country there are no area codes. When calling from South Africa, dial the international access code 00, followed by Swaziland's country code (+268), then the telephone number. Direct dialling for international calls is possible from coin and card phones in the urban and tourist areas. All the luxury hotels have an efficient telephone system but they charge very high rates for international calls.

Mobile phones
South Africa South Africa uses the GSM system for mobile phones and overseas visitors should be able to use their mobiles,

as long as it has been arranged with their service provider prior to departure. Mobile numbers consist of 10 digits and start with 082, 083, 084 or 072 depending on the network. Mobile phones and SIM cards are available for hire at each of the 3 international airports. For anyone travelling alone by car, especially women, it is essential to hire one for emergencies.

Leotho Reception is improving steadily even in the most remote places. This is largely due to the fact that a number of mobile phone towers have been put in place in outlying areas during the Lesotho Highlands Water Project.

Swaziland If your mobile phone has international roaming it will work throughout Swaziland otherwise local SIM and top-up cards are available for the only cell phone provider, **Swazi MTN**.

Time

South Africa, Lesotho and Swaziland have only has one time zone: GMT +2 hrs, 7 hrs ahead of USA Standard Time, 1 hr ahead of Europe; 8 hrs behind Australian Eastern Standard Time. There is no daylight saving.

Tipping

Waiters, hotel porters, stewards, chambermaids and tour guides should be tipped 10-15%, according to the service. When leaving tips make sure it goes to the intended person. It is common practice to tip petrol pump attendants, depending on their service – up to R5 for a fill up, oil and water check and comprehensive windscreen clean. It is also customary to tip car guards R2-5 if parking on the street. These are usually identified by a work vest or badge. On safari you are expected to tip guides. If in any doubt, ask the company that you booked with for advice on how much to tip.

Tour operators

UK and Ireland
Abercrombie & Kent, T0845-0700600, www.abercrombiekent.co.uk.
Acacia Adventure Holidays, T020-7706 4700, www.acacia-africa.com.
Africa Explorer, T020-8987 8742, www.africa-explorer.co.uk.
Africa Travel Centre, T0845-4501520, www.africatravel.co.uk.
Africa Travel Resource, T01306-880770, www.africatravelresource.com.
Cedarberg African Travel, T020-8898 8510, www.cedarberg-travel.com.
Expert Africa, T020-8232 9777, www.expertafrica.com.
Explore, T0870-333 4001, www.explore.co.uk.
Global Village, T0844-844 2541, www.globalvillage-travel.com.
Odyssey World, T0845-370 7733, www.odyssey-world.co.uk.

Rainbow Tours, T020-7226 1004, www.rainbowtours.co.uk.
Somak, T020-84233000, www.somak.co.uk.
South African Affair, T020-7381 5222, www.southafricanaffair.com.
Steppes Africa, T01285-880980, www.steppestravel.co.uk.
Tim Best Travel, T020-7591 0300, www.timbesttravel.com.
Wildlife Worldwide, T0845-1306982, www.wildlifeworldwide.com.

Rest of Europe
Iwanowski's Individuelles Reisen GmbH, T+49 (0)21-3326030, www.afrika.de.
Jambo Tours, T+49 (0)29-3579191, www.jambotours.de.

North America
Adventure Center, T1800-2288747, www.adventure-center.com.

Africa Adventure Company,
T1800-8829453, T1954-4918877,
www.africa-adventure.com.
Bushtracks, T1707-433 0258,
www.bushtracks.com.
Maupintour, T1800-2554266,
www.maupintour.com.

Australia and New Zealand
African Wildlife Safaris, T+61-(0)3-9249
3777, www.africanwildlifesafaris.com.au.
Africa Exclusive, T+61-(0)7-5474 8160,
www.afriraexclusive.com.
Classic Safari Company, T+61-(0)2-9327
0666, www.classicsafaricompany.com.au.
Intrepid, T61 (0)39-473 2626,
www.intrepidtravel.com
Peregrine Adventure, T+61-(0)3-9662 2700,
www.peregrine.net.au.

Tourist information

South Africa
South African Tourism (SATOUR) has a
very useful website with information
on special interest travel, maps, latest
travel news, airlines, accommodation
and national parks. The website is published
in 15 languages and each version provides
specific information for people coming
from each individual country, T011 8953000,
www.southafrica.net. SATOUR also has
offices around the world (see below),
which are useful for pre-travel information.

Regional (see below) and local tourist boards
are some of the best sources of information
once in the country; even the smallest town
will have a publicity bureau with details of
local sights and accommodation. Local tourist
offices are listed under individual towns.

Tourist offices overseas
Australia Level 1, 117 York St, Sydney, NSW
2000, T02-9261 5000, bangu@southafrica.net.
France 61 Rue La Boetie, 75008 Paris,
T01-4561 0197, info.fr@southafrica.net.
Germany Friedensstr. 6-10, Frankfurt 60311,
T069-280950, info.de@southafrica.net.
Italy Via Mascheroni 19, 5th floor, 20145
Milano, T02-4391 1765, info.it@southafrica.net.
Netherlands Jozef Isralskade 48 A, 1027 SB
Amsterdam, T020-4713181,
info.nl@southafrica.net.
UK 6 Alt Grove, London SW19 4DZ,
T020-8971 9350, info.uk@southafrica.net
USA 500 5th Av, 20th floor, Suite 2040,
New York NY 10110, T1212-7302929,
newyork@southafrica.net.

Regional tourist boards
Cape Town and Western Cape Tourism,
www.tourismcapetown.co.za.
Eastern Cape Tourism,
www.ectourism.co.za.
Free State Tourism, www.dteea.fs.gov.za.
Gauteng Tourism Authority,
www.gauteng.net
Limpopo Province Tourism Board,
www.limpopotourism.org.za.

Mpumalanga Tourism Authority,
www.mpumalanga.com.
Northern Cape Tourism Authority,
www.northerncape.org.za.
North West Province,
www.tourismnorthwest.co.za.
Tourism KwaZulu Natal, www.zulu.org.za.

Useful websites

There are thousands of websites about
travel in South Africa in a number of
languages, and these days even the tiniest
dorps (villages) have their own website.
These are listed in the relevant chapters.
www.africaguide.com Everything you
need to know about African travel, also
sells holidays and reviews guidebooks.
www.exploresouthafrica.net General
overview of the main tourist attractions.
www.fco.gov.uk UK Foreign Office,
for the official advice on latest
political situations.
www.gardenroute.org Wide-reaching
website covering one of the most popular
regions in South Africa.
www.go2africa.com Accommodation
and holiday booking service, with useful
practical information and links to overland companies.
www.southafrica.co.za General information and travel advice.
www.overlandafrica.com A variety of
overland tours offered throughout Africa.
www.sanparks.org Full details of all the
national parks, including online booking.

Lesotho

Tourist Information Centre, Basotho Shield
building opposite the **Basotho Hat** building
on Kingsway in Maseru, T22312427, Mon-Fri
0800-1700, Sat 0800-1300, is extremely
helpful and stocks a range of brochures
and maps.

If you are crossing into the country
through Maseru Bridge be sure to drop in
at the **Moloti Tourist Office** in Ladybrand,
which also covers Lesotho in its jurisdiction
(see page 729).

Useful websites

www.ltdc.org.ls Lesotho Tourism
Development Corporation website
has basic information for tourists.
www.lhwp.org.ls For information about
the Lesotho Highlands Water Project; the
site also has information about the new
national parks.

Swaziland

Tourist information office, Swazi Plaza,
Mbabane, T4042531, www.welcome
toswaziland.com, Mon-Fri 0800-1700,
Sat 0830-1230.

There's a second tourist information office
at the **Ngwenya border**, T4424206, daily
0800-1700. Although this office isn't always
manned, there are useful leaflets
to pick up. You can also pick up leaflets
at the **Mantenga Craft Centre**.

Vaccinations

See under Health, page 59.

Visas and immigration

South Africa

EU nationals and citizens from the USA,
Canada, Australia and New Zealand don't
need visas to enter South Africa. On arrival,
visitors from these countries are granted
temporary **visitors' permits**, lasting up to
90 days. You must have a valid return ticket
or voucher for onward travel and at least
one completely empty page in your
passport to get a permit; without these
you maybe denied entry.

It is possible to apply for an extension
to the permit at one of the offices of the
Department of Home Affairs, Cape Town
T021-4624970; **Durban** T031-3087930;
Johannesburg T011-8363228; **Pretoria**
T012-3148109; **Nelson Mandela Bay (Port
Elizabeth)** T041-4871026; www.home-
affairs.gov.za. This can take up to 10 days

and costs R475. You will need to produce documentation to show when you are leaving the country, such as a flight ticket or tour confirmation voucher, as well as proof of funds such as a credit card or TCs. Citizens of countries other than those listed above should consult the South African embassy or consulate in their country for information on visa requirements.

Note that going to Lesotho or Swaziland and returning to South Africa is not a valid way to extend your holiday visa or permit. On re-entering South Africa, immigration officials will scan your original South African entry stamp for its date of departure. If this date has passed while you are in Lesotho or Swaziland. South African immigration will extend your visa for 2-4 weeks, during which time you are expected either to leave the country or to extend your visa. See www.home-affairs.gov.za, to find out the nearest office.

Lesotho

Holders of the following passports do not require visas for Lesotho: South Africa, Denmark, Sweden, Norway, Finland, Ireland, UK, Germany, France, Italy, Switzerland, the Netherlands, Canada, Israel and Japan. Others such as Australia, New Zealand, USA, Belgium and Austria do need visas.

People not requiring a visa will be given a one month permit with their entry stamp, although it is possible to ask for longer if you have proof of funds.

To extend your permit, go to the **Lesotho Immigration Department**, Transport Building, Assissi Rd, Maseru, T22323771. It's also worth asking at the larger border posts if they will extend it for you. Visitors who require a visa can wait until they are in South Africa and then contact the **Lesotho High Commission**, 391 Anderson St, corner of Thomas Edison St, Menlo Park, Pretoria 0001, T012-4607648, visa office Mon-Fri 0900-1200. In a few cases

you can contact the Lesotho Overseas High Commission in your own country. When applying for a visa you must fill in an application form and provide a passport photo; processing takes 24 hrs. A single entry, valid for 1 month, costs R400. Alternatively the immigration regulations allow the border officials to let you enter Lesotho, and give you 72 hrs to present yourself to the immigration office in Maseru to get a visa.

Swaziland

Nationals of the following countries do not need a visa: Austria, Belgium, Botswana, Canada, Denmark, France, Germany, Finland, Israel, Ireland, Italy, Kenya, Lesotho, Malawi, Namibia, Netherlands, New Zealand, Norway, Portugal, South Africa, Spain, Switzerland, Sweden, UK, USA, Zambia and Zimbabwe. For details of foreign embassies and consulates in Swaziland, see the Directory section for Mbabane, page 828.

Thirty-day visas are obtainable free of charge on arrival at any of the borders to nationals from Australia and all other countries not listed above.

Voltage

South Africa Voltage 220/230 volts AC at 50 Hz, except for Pretoria, where it is 250 volts AC. Most plugs and appliances are 3-point round-pin (one 10 mm and two 8 mm prongs). Hotels usually have 2-pin sockets for razors.
Lesotho Voltage 220/230 volts AC at 50 Hz.
Swaziland Voltage 220-240v.

Weights and measures

The metric system is used in South Africa, Lesotho and Swaziland

Women travellers

Although South Africa has an unusually high incidence of rape, tourists are, as a rule, not targeted and South Africa is a relatively safe country for women to travel in. However, the usual rules of not travelling alone after dark, never hitchhiking and avoiding quiet areas always apply. While women are not usually confronted with prejudice when checking into hotels or trying to be served, it is worth remembering that there is a strong macho element in most South African communities. Women may experience some unwanted attention from men, but nothing that can't be dealt with assertively. It is often a good idea to cover up in more conservative or rural areas – avoiding tight, revealing tops and short skirts should help.

Working in South Africa

There are no opportunities for travellers to obtain casual paid employment in South Africa and it is illegal for a foreigner to work without an official work permit. Most foreign workers in the country are employed through embassies, development or volunteer agencies or through foreign companies. For the most part these people will have been recruited in their countries of origin. A number of NGOs and voluntary organizations can arrange placements for volunteers, usually for periods ranging from 6 months to 2 years, visit www.volunteerafrica.org.

Contents

Footprint features

Cape Town & the Winelands

At a glance

⊕ **Getting around** Buses, taxis, car hire or day tours recommended for the Cape Peninsula and Winelands.

◉ **Time required** Minimum 3 days for central Cape Town, 1 day for Cape Peninsula, 1-2 days for the Winelands.

☀ **Weather** Chilly in July and August. Best in November and February.

✖ **When not to go** Avoid the Christmas South African school holidays.

South Africa's 'Mother City', dominated by Table Mountain and surrounded by the wild Atlantic, has unquestionably one of the most beautiful city backdrops in the world. Despite being a considerable urban hub, its surroundings are surprisingly untamed, characterized by a mountainous spine stretching between two seaboards and edged by rugged coast and dramatic beaches.

Central Cape Town with its grandiose colonial buildings and beautiful public gardens crammed up against modern skyscrapers lies in the steep-sided bowl created by Table Mountain. Atmospheric Victorian suburbs stretch around the lower slopes, while the Atlantic Seaboard with its promenade and dense crop of holiday flats and the popular V&A Waterfront development hug the coast. Further out on False Bay are the Cape Flats, their sprawling townships a lasting testimony of the Apartheid era. Beyond, in the beautiful Winelands region, the old towns of Stellenbosch, Franschhoek and Paarl nestle in a range of low mountains and scenic valleys covered by the vineyards of historic wine estates which have been cultivating grapes for some 300 years.

Cape Town's population is the most cosmopolitan in the country, with a mix of cultures, ethnicities and religions that drive the very pulse of the city. The mishmash of people, including white descendants of Dutch and British settlers, a black African population and the distinctive 'Cape Coloured' community, results in a vibrant cultural scene.

It is this mixture of environments and communities that makes Cape Town such an instantly likeable and captivating city. Few places in the world can offer mountain hiking, lazing on a beach, tasting world-class wines and drinking beer in a township shebeen all in one day. Put simply, it is a city worth crossing the world for.

Cape Town

To get the best idea of Cape Town's layout, head to the top of Table Mountain. From its summit, the city stretches below in a horseshoe formed by the mountains: Table Mountain is in the centre, with Devil's Peak to the east and Lion's Head and Signal Hill to the west. Straight ahead lies the City Bowl, the central business district backed by leafy suburbs. This is also the site of Cape Town's historical heart and where all the major museums, historical buildings and sights are. Further down is the Victoria & Alfred Waterfront, a slick development of shopping malls and restaurants. Following the coast around to the west, you come to the modern residential districts of Green Point and Sea Point which will soon be dominated by the enormous Green Point stadium currently being built for the 2010 FIFA Football World Cup. In the opposite direction the southern suburbs stretch west and south, dipping from the mountain's slopes, and here, under a blanket of trees, are Cape Town's largest mansions as well as beautiful Kirstenbosch Botanical Gardens. ▸▸ *For listings, see pages 107-131.*

Ins and outs ▸▸ *Colour map 8, B1.*

Getting there

Cape Town International Airport ⓘ *airport enquiries, T021-9371200, www.airports.co.za,* is 22 km east of the city centre, a 20-minute drive. Shuttle services run from kiosks in the arrivals hall. Alternatively you can pre-book one through your hotel, guesthouse or backpacker hostel, or directly through **Magic Bus** ⓘ *T021-5056300, www.magicbus.co.za,* that drops off at hotels and guesthouses or the **Backpacker Bus** ⓘ *T021-4397600, www.backpackerbus.co.za,* to the backpacker hostel, costing from R95 per person. Taxis running between the airport and town centre should have a special airport licence and they must use their meter by law; expect to pay around R300 to the centre of town. Within the terminal building, **Cape Town Tourism** ⓘ *daily 0700-1700,* can arrange accommodation. The **Master Currency** exchange counter remains open for international arrivals and there are ATMs. You can hire mobile phones at several outlets. Look out for joint deals between car hire companies and mobile phone companies.

The main **railway station** is in the centre of town. Next to the railway station, at Adderley Street, is where the Greyhound, Intercape and Translux **long-distance bus** services arrive. ▸▸ *For further details, see Transport, page 129.*

Getting around

Most of Cape Town's oldest buildings, museums, galleries and the commercial centre are concentrated in a relatively small area and best explored on foot. However, to

Cape Town orientation

Green Point
Victoria & Alfred Waterfront
Harbour
Sea Point
Signal Hill
Centre
N1
Woodstock
Clifton
Camps Bay
Cableway Station
Table Mountain (1066m)

N

1 km
1 mile

24 hours in Cape Town

Start the day with an early-morning jog or stroll along the wide promenade that runs the length of Mouille Point and Sea Point. Take in some fresh ocean air and admire the huge ships in Table Bay waiting to get into Cape Town's harbour. Look out for the mammoth construction site of the new Green Point Stadium that dominates Cape Town's skyline and is being built for the 2010 FIFA Football World Cup that has been awarded to South Africa (see box, page 875). Then take in the views of Table Mountain while enjoying a full English or health breakfast in the sunshine at any of the V&A Waterfront's many al fresco restaurants.

After breakfast, browse the upmarket boutiques and curio shops in the Victoria Wharf shopping mall, and look for seals splashing around in the harbour. Alternatively, spend an hour or so in the Two Oceans Aquarium, where the highlight is the giant predators' tank that is home to ragged-tooth sharks and huge eagle rays. At the Nelson Mandela Gateway board the Robben Island ferry for the 3½-hour informative excursion to the famous island prison, 12 km off shore in Table Bay. Once there, the tour includes a bus ride around the island with great views back on to Table Mountain, a guided tour of the ex-maximum security complex and a peek into Nelson Mandela's former cell.

Back at the V&A Waterfront jump on the Sightseeing Cape Town hop-on, hop-off, bright red, open-topped double-decker bus for a ride through the city bowl to the Table Mountain Lower Cableway Station. The bus stops at the excellent District Six Museum, dedicated telling the story of the forced removals in Cape Town during Apartheid, and the imposing Castle of Good Hope, the oldest colonial building in South Africa, among many other of the city centre's museums and attractions. Ride the rotating cable car to the top of Table Mountain for the dizzying views of the City Bowl, Camps Bay and Robben Island, and grab a snack or toast your ascent with a glass of champagne at the highest restaurant in Cape Town, 1073 m above the city. If you're feeling fit, set off early and walk up; this takes about three hours. Back at the Lower Cableway Station jump on the bus and continue the drive over Kloof Nek and down into the fashionable suburb of Camps Bay on the Atlantic Seaboard. Here you can join the beautiful people at any one of the bars along Victoria Road for a cocktail and admire the swathe of perfect white-sand beach and pounding waves.

In the evening dine at one of the city's popular African restaurants: **Mama Africa**, **Marco's African Place** or the **Africa Cafe** which all serve up authentic and tasty dishes such as grilled game meat and Cape Malay curries. Alternatively, opt for freshly caught Cape seafood and build your own platter at the **Cape Town Fish Market**, **The Codfather** or **Bala**, and be sure to accompany your meal with a good bottle of South African wine from Cape Town's Winelands. Those that want to see some local theatre or comedy should check out what's on at **Artscape**, the **Baxter Theatre** or the **Theatre on the Bay**. Nightcaps can be enjoyed in any of the late bars in Green Point or Camps Bay and late night revellers should head for the lively clubs at the top end of Long Street or the more sophisticated **Rhodes House** in Gardens or **Opium** in Green Point. Late-night nibbles can be found at **Mr Pickwicks** on Long Street or the **Obz Cafe** in Observatory, which are both open until 0200-0300.

explore more of the city, and to visit Table Mountain, the suburbs or the beaches, it's a good idea to rent a car. Otherwise, taxis are affordable, particularly if you use Rikki's shared taxis (see page 130).

Alternatively **Sightseeing Cape Town** ① *T021-5116000, www.citysightseeing.co.za, daily from 0930*, is a red, double-decker, open-top, hop-on hop-off bus that follows a 2¼-hour route around the city. There are two routes; the Red Route has 13 stops and a bus comes by every 30 minutes, while the Blue Route has 13 stops and buses come by every 60 minutes. The main ticket kiosk is outside the Two Oceans Aquarium at the V&A Waterfront. It's ideal if you don't want to drive and stops include the Lower Cableway Station, Camps Bay, Kirstenbosch, all the city centre museums, and as far south as Hout Bay on the peninsula. A one-day ticket costs R100, children R50, and a two-day ticket is R180/R100. The buses are wheelchair friendly.

Tourist information → *Phone code: 021. Postal code: 8000.*

Cape Town Tourism ① *The Pinnacle, corner of Burg and Castle streets, T021-4876800, www.tourismcapetown.co.za, Mon-Fri 0800-1900, Sat 0830-1400, Sun 0900-1300, closes 1 hr earlier in winter (Apr-Sep)*, the official city tourist office, can help with bookings and tours throughout the Western Cape. It is an excellent source of information and a good first stop in the city. In addition to providing practical information about Cape Town, it can help with accommodation bookings and has plenty of information on nightlife and events. It is also home to **Western Cape Tourism** (same contact details) and there is a **South Africa National Parks (SANParks)** desk ① *www.sanparks.org*, where you can make reservations for the parks. There's also a café, gift shop and internet access. There are 18 other branches/desks throughout the Cape, the most useful of which is at the **Victoria & Alfred Waterfront** ① *T021-4054500, daily 0900-2100*.

If you are planning a trip to Namibia, it is well worth picking up maps and brochures at the **Namibian Tourist Office** ① *underneath Cape Town Tourism, in the Pinnacle, T021-4223298, www.namibiatourism.com.na, Mon-Fri 0800-1700*. There's also a desk where you can pre-book accommodation in Namibia's national parks (see *Footprint Namibia*).

Background

First people
The first evidence of human inhabitants in the Cape has been dated back to nearly 30,000 years ago. Rock art found in the area was created by nomadic San people (also known as Bushmen), a hunter-gatherer group which roamed across much of Southern Africa. Some San groups survive today, mostly in Namibia and Botswana, despite continuing persecution. The original San were replaced about two thousand years ago by Khoi groups, a semi-nomadic people who settled in the Cape with herds of sheep and cattle.

First landing
António de Saldanha, a Portuguese admiral who lost his way going east, landed in Table Bay in 1503. They called the bay Aguada da Saldanha (it was renamed Table Bay in 1601 by **Joris van Spilbergen**). Saldanha and a party of the crew went ashore in search of drinking water. They followed a stream to the base of Table Mountain and then proceeded to climb to the top. From here Saldanha was able to get a clear view of the surrounding coastline and the confusion caused by the peninsula. On their return they found the crew unsuccessfully trying to barter with local indigenous Khoi for livestock. The trade quickly developed into a

row which ended in bloodshed. There was another battle between the Portuguese and the Khoi In March 1510. On this occasion the Khoi had struck back after children and cattle were stolen by the sailors. Seventy-five Portuguese were killed, including **Dom Francisco de Almeida**, who had just finished five years as the first Portuguese Viceroy to India. Few Portuguese ships landed in Table Bay after this.

The Dutch and the VOC

By the end of the 16th century British and Dutch mariners had caught up with the Portuguese and they quickly came to appreciate the importance of the Cape as a base for restocking ships with drinking water and fresh supplies as they made their long journeys to the East. Indeed, seafarers found that they were able to exchange scraps of metal for provisions to supply a whole fleet.

The first moves to settle in the Cape were made by the Dutch, and on 6 April 1652 **Jan Van Riebeeck** landed in Table Bay. His ships carried wood for building and some small cannons, the first building to be erected being a small fort at the mouth of the Fresh River. The site of the original fort is where Grand Parade in the centre of Cape Town is today. Van Riebeeck was in charge of the supply station that belonged to the Dutch East India Company (Vereenigde Oost-Indische Compagnie or VOC). After the fort was built, gardens for fruit and vegetables were laid out and pastures for cattle acquired. As the settlement slowly grew, the Khoi people were driven back into the interior. Surprisingly, the early settlers were forbidden from enslaving the Khoi; instead, slaves were imported by the VOC from Indonesia and West Africa. Although many died, these slaves were the origin of the Cape Malay community.

In 1662 Jan van Riebeeck was transferred to India. Because of rivalries in Europe, the VOC was worried about enemy ships visiting the Cape, so work started on a new stone fort in 1666. Over the next 13 years several governors came and went. During this time the French and British went to war with Holland, but the British and the Dutch East India companies joined in a treaty of friendship in March 1674, and then in July of the same year a ship arrived with the news that the British and Dutch had made peace. In October 1679 one of the most energetic governors arrived in the Cape, **Simon van der Stel**. For the next 20 years van der Stel devoted his energies to creating a new Holland in southern Africa. During his period as Governor, van der Stel paid particular attention to the growth and development of Cape Town and the surrounding farmlands. The company garden was replanted, nursery plots were created and new experimental plants were collected from around the world. North of the gardens he built a large hospital and a lodge to house VOC slaves. New streets were laid out which were straight and wide with plenty of shade. New buildings in the town were covered in white limewash, producing a smart and prosperous appearance. In 1685, in appreciation for his work, he was granted an estate by the VOC, which he named **Constantia**. During his life he used the estate as an experimental agricultural farm and to grow oak trees which were then planted throughout the Cape.

One of his more significant contributions was the founding of the settlement at Stellenbosch. He directed the design and construction of many of the town's public buildings, and then introduced a number of the crops to be grown on the new farms. For many years he experimented with vines in an effort to produce wines as good as those in Europe. He was particularly pleased when in 1688 French Protestant Huguenot refugees arrived in the Cape. He saw to it that they were all settled on excellent farmlands in what became to be known as **Franschhoek** (French glen), the upper valley of the Berg River. In 1693 he had the foresight to appoint the town's first engineer to tackle problems of a clean water supply, and the removal of rubbish. Van der Stel died in June 1712 at Constantia.

Desmond Tutu

Like Nelson Mandela, Desmond Tutu is accepted as an influential and respected figure far beyond the borders of South Africa. His powerful oration and his simple but brave defiance of the Apartheid state has impressed the world. Tutu first caught the international headlines as an outspoken secretary general of the South African Council of Churches in the late 1970s, especially with his call for the international community to stop buying South African goods. But it was the award of the Nobel Peace Prize in 1984 that really established him as an international figure.

Desmond Tutu was born on 7 October 1931 in Klerksdrop and was educated in local mission schools and the Johannes-burg Bantu High School in the Western Native township. After obtaining a BA and teaching diploma he taught at a high school in Krugersdorp before going to St Peter's Theological College to train as an Anglican priest. After being ordained he moved to London with his wife and young family, living in Golders Green, while he studied for both a BA and an MA in Theology. In 1966 he returned to South Africa.

After a spell teaching in the Eastern Cape, Tutu became a lecturer at the National University of Lesotho. He was in England again for three years in the early 1970s, before taking an appointment as the Anglican Dean of Johannesburg, but then quickly moved back to Lesotho to become Bishop. In 1978 he moved to Johannesburg once again, now as the secretary general of the South African Council of Churches. It was at about this time that the press began to take notice of Tutu's forceful anti-Apartheid statements.

In response to Tutu's comments about Apartheid the South African government took away his passport to prevent him speaking at international conferences, though he was occasionally allowed temporary travel documents and was able to address some important meetings and hold discussions with other religious leaders. Tutu made it clear that he believed that economic sanctions on South Africa were essential to make the Apartheid state introduce reforms at a faster pace. These comments obviously annoyed the South African government and Tutu was regarded as a dangerous opponent. The government was, however, always wary of treating him as cruelly as they treated many of their other opponents, as they knew that any mistreatment would lead to an enormous international outcry. This was especially so after 1984, when he was awarded the Nobel Peace Prize.

Under the British

The next period of Cape Town's history was closely related to events in Europe, particularly the French Revolution. The ideas put forward by the Revolution of Liberty, Fraternity and Equality were not welcome in colonies such as the Cape. The Dutch East India Company was seen to be a corrupt organization and a supporter of the aristocracy. When the French invaded Holland, the British decided to seize the Cape to stop it from falling into French hands. After the Battle of Muizenberg in 1795, Britain took over the Cape from the representatives of the Dutch East India Company, which was bankrupt. In the Treaty of Amiens (1803) the Cape was restored to the Batavian Republic of the Netherlands. In 1806 the British took control again at the resumption of the Anglo-French wars.

In February 1985 Tutu was made Bishop of Johannesburg and finally, in April 1986, he was elected Anglican Archbishop of Cape Town. His election was not popular with many white rank and file members of the Anglican Church who believed his calls for economic sanctions were harming their economic interests. The Anglican Church's white congregation have tended to come from the English-speaking sections of the community who regard themselves as more liberal than the Afrikaners. They did not want to be seen to oppose Tutu on grounds of race. Furthermore, it would have appeared unchristian to complain too vocally about how their privileged pockets had been affected by his stance on sanctions. Opposition was, therefore, most commonly expressed through the criticism that he was mixing religion with politics. This claim was not easy to sustain, however, as Tutu always brought a strictly moral and Christian approach to all his 'political' interventions. He often headed protest marches dressed in his Archbishop's robes, though this did not stop him being arrested on a couple of occasions and even teargassed.

Since the end of Apartheid in South Africa Tutu has continued to play a prominent, though not quite as central, public role. During 1996 he chaired the hearings of the Truth and Reconciliation Committee and argued forcibly that the policy of granting amnesty to all who admitted their crimes was an important step in healing the nation's scars. His continued espousal of a Christian philosophy of forgiveness has at times angered some of the families of the victims of Apartheid, who emphasize instead the need for justice, but few could deny the sincerity of Tutu's belief in what was undisputedly a healing process.

In recent years, Tutu has used his voice to protest against international conflicts such as those in Zimbabwe and the Gaza Strip and in 2006 was appointed head of a United Nations fact-finding mission to investigate human rights violations by Israeli military operations. In 2007, Nelson Mandela, Graça Machel and Desmond Tutu convened a group of world leaders to contribute their wisdom, independent leadership and integrity to tackle some of the world's toughest problems. This new group is known as The Elders, and Tutu is presently chairman. Nelson Mandela once said of him, "sometimes strident, often tender, never afraid and seldom without humour, Desmond Tutu's voice will always be the voice of the voiceless".

When the British took over power it was inevitable that they inherited many of the problems associated with the colony. The principal issue was how to manage European settlement. The Dutch East India Company had only encouraged settlement as a cheap and efficient means of supplying their base in Cape Town. Thereafter they were only interested in controlling the Indian Ocean and supplying ships. By the time the British arrived, the Dutch settler farmers (the Boer) had become so successful that they were producing a surplus. The only problem was high production costs due to a shortage of labour. To alleviate the situation, a policy of importing slaves was implemented. This in turn led to decreased work opportunities for the settler families. Gradually the mood changed and the Boer looked to the interior for land and work. They were not impressed by the British administration and in 1836 the Great Trek was under way.

The growth of the city and the port

Industrialization in Europe brought great change, especially when the first steamship, the *Enterprise*, arrived in Table Bay in October 1825. After considerable delay and continual loss of life and cargoes, work began on two basins and two breakwater piers. The first truckload of construction rocks was tipped by Prince Alfred, the 16-year-old son of Queen Victoria, on 17 September 1860. The Alfred Basin was completed in 1870 and a dry dock was added in 1881.

No sooner had the first basin been completed than diamonds and gold were discovered in South Africa. Over the next 40 years Cape Town and the docks were to change beyond recognition. In 1900 work began on a new breakwater which would protect an area of 27 km. After five years' work the **Victoria Basin** was opened. This new basin was able to shelter the new generation of ships using Table Bay but was unable to cope with the increase in numbers during the **Anglo-Boer War**. A third basin was created to the east of Victoria Basin in 1932 and for a while this seemed to have solved the problem, but fate was against Cape Town. In January 1936 the largest ship to visit South Africa docked with ease at B berth in the new basin. The boat, which was being used to help promote tourism in South Africa, was filled with wealthy and famous visitors. The morning on which she was due to sail, a strong southeasterly wind blew up and pressed the liner so firmly against the quay that she couldn't sail. In one morning all of the new basin's weaknesses had been exposed.

The next phase of growth was an ambitious one, and it was only completed in 1945. The project involved the dredging of Table Bay and the reclaiming of land. The spoil from the dredging provided 140 sq km of landfill, known as Foreshore. This new land extends from the present-day railway station to **Duncan Dock**. As you walk or drive around Cape Town today, remember that just over 50 years ago the sea came up to the main railway station.

▶▶ *For the best record of the vibrant community that once thrived here, visit the excellent District Six Museum, see page 92.*

Impact of the Apartheid years

The descendants of the large and diverse slave population have given Cape Town a particularly cosmopolitan atmosphere. Unfortunately Apartheid urban planning meant that many of the more vibrant areas of the city in the earlier part of this century were destroyed. The most notorious case is that of District Six, a racially mixed, low income housing area on the edge of the City Bowl. The Apartheid government could not tolerate such an area, especially so close to the centre of the city, and the residents, most of whom were classified as 'Coloured', were moved out to the soulless townships of the Cape Flats, such as Mitchell's Plain. The area was bulldozed but few new developments have taken place on the site: this accounts for the large areas of open ground in the area between the City Bowl and the suburb of Woodstock. Happily, the government recently handed over the first pocket of re-developed land to a small group of ex-residents of District Six and their descendants. What the area will become remains to be seen – the issue remains controversial as many ex-residents feel the open, barren land should remain as a poignant testimony to the forced removals.

Other reminders of the cosmopolitan history of Cape Town can be experienced in the area to the west of Buitengracht Street. This district, known as **Bo-Kaap**, is still home to a small Islamic (Cape Malay) community that somehow managed to survive the onslaught of Apartheid urban planning. The coloured population of Cape Town has historically outweighed both the white and African populations, hence the widespread use of Afrikaans in the city. This balance was maintained by Apartheid policies that prevented Africans from migrating into the Western Cape from the Eastern Cape and elsewhere. This policy was not, however, able to withstand the pressure of the poor rural Africans' desire to find opportunities in the urban economy. Over the past couple of decades there has been an enormous growth in the African population of Cape Town. Many of these new migrants have been forced to settle in squatter areas, such as the notorious Crossroads Camp next to the N2 highway. During the Apartheid era these squatter camps were frequently bulldozed and the residents evicted but as soon as they were cleared they sprang up again. Crossroads was a hotbed of resistance to the Apartheid state and much of the Cape Flats area existed in a state of near civil war throughout much of the 1980s.

Today, Cape Town remains the most cosmopolitan city in South Africa. The official colour barriers have long since disappeared and residential boundaries are shifting. The economic balance, too, is beginning to change: a black middle class has emerged in recent years, and the coloured middle class is strengthening.

Table Mountain National Park

ⓘ *www.sanparks.org. The most popular ascent of the mountain directly above the City Bowl is described below; other parts of the park are covered later in the chapter.*

Cape Town is defined, first and foremost, by Table Mountain. Rising a sheer 1073 m from the coastal plain, it dominates almost every view of the city, its sharp slopes and level top making it one of the world's best-known city backdrops. For centuries, it was the first sight of Cape Town afforded to seafarers, its looming presence visible for hundreds of kilometres. Certainly, its size continues to astonish visitors today, but it is the mountain's wilderness, bang in the middle of a bustling conurbation, that makes the biggest impression. Table Mountain sustains over 1400 species of flora, as well as baboons, dassies (large rodents) and countless birds. The Table Mountain National Park encompasses the entire peninsula stretching from here to Cape Point. Between September and March you have the additional pleasure of seeing the mountain covered in wild flowers. The most common vegetation is fynbos, of which there is an extraordinary variety, but you'll also see proteas plus the rare silver tree, *Leucadendron argenteum*.

Aerial Cableway

ⓘ *Information line T021-4248181, www.tablemountain.net; the first car up is at 0800, the last car down varies from 1800 to 2200 depending on the time of year, both the information line and the website has up-to-the-minute details of times and, given Cape Town's unpredictable weather, will tell you if the cableway is open or not (always check before going up to the Lower Cableway Station). Return ticket for adults R130, children under 18 R68, family ticket, 2 adults and 2 children R330; one-way ticket for adults R68, children under 18 R36. Note, you cannot pre-book tickets because of the weather factor and the cableway can close immediately without notice. In the summer season, Dec-Jan, this can mean considerable queues. The cableway is closed for annual maintenance for 2 weeks end Jul/beginning Aug (check the website for exact dates).*

The dizzying trip to the top in the Aerial Cableway is one of Cape Town's highlights. The first cableway was built in 1929, and since then has had three upgrades, the latest being in 1997. It's estimated to have carried up some 18 million people to date. There are two cars, each carrying up to 65 passengers, and as you ride up the floor rotates, allowing a full 360° view. Journey time is just under 10 minutes. In the base of each car is a water tank that can carry up to 4000 litres of fresh water to the top. There is a bistro restaurant and souvenir shop at the top station, as well as a self-service café that gets busy when the cableway queues are long. An extensive network of paths has been laid out from the top station, allowing walks of various lengths, leading to different lookout points with stunning views of the City Bowl, Cape Flats, Robben Island and back along the peninsula. There are also free guided walks daily at 1000 and 1200.

Hiking → *Mountain Rescue: T10177.*

The entire area is a nature reserve, and the mountain itself is protected as a national monument. There are numerous paths climbing to the top of the mountain. The most popular route starts 1.5 km beyond the Lower Cableway Station and follows a course up Platteklip Gorge; there's another path from Kirstenbosch Botanical Gardens. Both take about three hours to the top although they are both fairly tough and should not be taken lightly. Given Table Mountain's size and location, conditions can change alarmingly quickly. The weather may seem clear and calm when you set out, but fog (the famous 'Table Cloth' which flows from the top) and rain can descend without warning. Numerous people have been caught out and the mountain has claimed its fair share of lives. There have been recent muggings in Platteklip Gorge, though authorities are presently doing their best to address the problem.

Before venturing out, make sure you have suitable clothing, food and water. Take warm clothes, a windbreaker, a waterproof jacket, a hat, sunscreen, sunglasses, plenty of water (2 litres per person) and energy foods. Never climb alone and inform someone of which route you're taking and what time you should be back. A detailed map is essential – these can be purchased at the tourist office. For those wanting to spend more time on the mountain, an overnight trail – the **Hoerikwagga Trail** (meaning 'sea mountain' in Khoi) – was introduced in 2005. The six-day trek involves sleeping in renovated forester houses dotted along the top of the mountain. It starts in central Cape Town and ascends Platteklip Gorge and then follows the spine of the peninsula down to Cape Point. For full details, contact the tourist office or SANParks (see Tourist information, page 80). If you're interested in learning about the mountain's flora and fauna, take a guide or a tour (see Hiking, page 124).

Signal Hill

Signal Hill's summit offers spectacular views of the city, the Twelve Apostles (the mountainous spine stretching south from Table Mountain) and the ocean. It is possible to drive to the 350-m summit, which means that it can get pretty busy with tour groups around sunset. Nevertheless, watching the sun dip into the Atlantic from this viewpoint with a cold sundowner in hand is a highlight of a visit to Cape Town. Avoid being there after dark, as there have been reports of muggings. From the town centre, follow signs for the Lower Cableway station and take a right opposite the turning for the cableway station. The hill is home to the Noon Gun which is fired electronically at noon every day, except Sunday. There is also a *karamat* (Islamic tomb) on the hill.

Lion's Head

Halfway along the road up Signal Hill you pass Lion's Head, a popular hiking spot. The climb to the peak is fairly easy going, and takes about two hours, and the 360° views from the top are incredible. There are two routes to the top: the easier of the two winds around the mountain; the quicker one involves climbing up a couple of drops with the aid of chains. Both are signposted. Hiking to Lion's Head is especially popular at full moon, when Capetonians watch the sunset from the peak and then descend by the light of the moon. Take plenty of water and a torch, and always climb in a group.

From the Lower Cableway Station, you look out over the central residential suburbs of Tamboerskloof (Drummers' Ravine), Gardens, Oranjezicht (Orange View), and Vredehoek (Peaceful Corner), and beyond here lie the high-rise blocks of the business district. Together these form the City Bowl, a term inspired by the surrounding mountains. Closest to the mountain is **Oranjezicht**, a quiet district with a good selection of guesthouses and B&B accommodation. Up until 1900 the area was a farm of the same name. On the boundary with Gardens is the **De Waal Park** and **Molteno Reservoir**. Originally built as a main storage facility for the city in 1881, the reservoir now provides a peaceful wooded spot from where you can enjoy a view of the city. Close by, on the corner of Prince Street and Sir George Grey Street, is an **old iron pump**. Such pumps were once dotted about the city for people to draw water for domestic use.

There is nothing peaceful about **Vredehoek** today, as the De Waal Drive (M3) brings rush hour traffic into the top end of town from the southern suburbs and beyond. Most of the area has been given over to ugly high-rise apartments, though the residents benefit from some excellent views. This was the area in which many Jewish immigrants from Eastern Europe settled, and have to a large part remained.

Gardens is a lively neighbourhood with a choice of quality restaurants and comfortable guesthouses. Cape Town's best-known hotel, the **Mount Nelson**, is situated here in its own landscaped gardens. The grand gateway to the hotel was built in 1924 to welcome the Prince of Wales. From here the land slopes gently towards the Waterfront, with the commercial heart of the city laid out in between. This was the area where the Dutch East India Company first created fruit and vegetable gardens to supply the ships' crews who suffered greatly from scurvy. Across Orange Street from the entrance to the Mount Nelson Hotel is the top end of **Government Avenue**, a delightful pedestrian route past Company's Garden and many of the city's main museums. Originally sheltered by lemon trees, it is now lined with oaks and myrtle hedges, and is one of Cape Town's most popular walks. It was declared a national monument in 1937.

South Africa Museum and Planetarium

ⓘ *25 Queen Victoria St, at the top end of Company's Garden, T021-4813800, www.iziko.org.za, daily 1000-1700, R10, children R5, free on Sat. There's a shop and café in the museum.*

This, the city's most established museum, specializes in natural history, ethnography and archaeology, and is a good place to take children. There are extensive displays of the flora and fauna of southern Africa, including the popular Whale Well and interactive Shark World area, but the highlight is the 'IQe – the Power of Rock Art' exhibition. The displays of ancient San rock art have been in the museum for almost 100 years but, following a process of consultation and dialogue with Khoi-San communities, they have been re-interpreted in a far more sensitive and illuminating manner. The exhibits focus on the significance and symbolism of San rock art, with some fascinating examples including the beautifully preserved Linton panel, which depicts the trance experiences of shamans. Other themes explored include rainmaking and the significance of animal imagery; the eland, for example, appears more often than any other animal in San rock art, and it holds a central role in all major rituals, from teenage initiation to marriage and rainmaking. The whole exhibition, although short, is beautifully arranged and accompanied by the sound of San singing, a disjointed and haunting sound.

Nearby are the ethnographic galleries, offering interesting displays on the San, Khoi and Xhosa, among others, as well as the original Lydenburg Heads (see page 649). There is also a small display of pieces recovered from Great Zimbabwe that illustrate its importance as a trade centre – there are beads from Cambay, India, Chinese Celadon ware, 13th-century Persian pottery and Syrian glass from the 14th century. A recent addition to the museum is Stone Bones, en exhibition about the fossilized skeletons found in the Karoo, which date back 250 million years – predating dinosaurs. There are life-sized reproductions of the reptile-like creatures, including walk-around dioramas and examples of the actual fossils.

Next door, at the **Planetarium** ① *T021-4813900, www.iziko.org.za, show times Mon-Fri 1400, Sat and Sun, 1200, 1300, 1430, late showing on Tue 2000, R20, children R6,* presentations change every few months, but a view of the current night sky is shown and visitors receive a star map to find the constellations and planets that are visible each month. Shows last an hour and are fascinating.

Bertram House
① *Corner of Government Av and Orange St, T021-4249381, www.iziko.org.za, Tue-Thu 1000-1630, R5.*
This early 19th-century red-brick Georgian House has a distinctly English feel to it. The building houses a collection of porcelain, jewellery, silver and English furniture, the majority of which was bequeathed by Ann Lidderdale. Winifred Ann Lidderdale was an important civic figure in Cape Town in the 1950s. After her marriage to Henry Maxwell Lidderdale, she lived in England and the USA, but in 1951 the couple returned to Cape Town for their retirement. It was her desire to establish a house museum to commemorate the British contribution to life at the Cape. Downstairs the two drawing rooms contain all the trappings of a bygone elegant age – card tables, a Hepplewhite settee, a square piano and a fine harp. Three rooms have wallpaper from London, a very expensive luxury for the period.

Jewish Museum
① *88 Hatfield St, T021-4651546, www.sajewishmuseum.co.za, Sun-Thu 1000-1700, Fri 1000-1400, closed on Jewish and public holidays, R35, children R15.*
Inside this excellent, contemporary museum is a rich and rare collection of items depicting the history of the Cape Town Hebrew Congregation and other congregations in the Cape Province. The history of the community is interesting in itself: in 1841 a congregation of 17 men assembled for the first time in Cape Town to celebrate Yom Kippur. At the meeting they set about the task of raising funds to build a synagogue, and in 1862 the foundation stone was laid for the first synagogue in Southern Africa. The following year the building was completed and furnished – quite a feat for such a small community at the time. On display upstairs are bronze Sabbath oil lamps, *Chanukkah* lamps, *Bessamin* spice containers, *Torah* scrolls, *Kiddush* cups and candlesticks. There is a beautiful stained-glass window depicting the Ten Commandments in Hebrew. From here a glass corridor leads you to a newer section of the museum that is devoted to the history of Jewish immigration to the Cape, mainly from Lithuania. A lot of thought has been put into the displays, which include photographs, immigration certificates, videos and a full reconstruction of a Lithuanian *shtetl*, or village. There are special displays outlining the stories of famous Jewish South Africans, including Helen Suzman and Isie Maisels. The museum complex also houses a library, café and bookshop.

Cape Town centre

To Artscape

To ②

Jack Craig

Hertzog

Hertzog

Oswald Pirow

Long

Heerengracht

Riebeeck

Tulbagh Square

Statue

Civic Centre

Hans Strijdom

SAA

Thibault Square

Chiappini

Bree

Prestwich

Taxis

Railway Station

Somerset

Buitengracht

Riebeeck

Waterkant

Lower Burg

Adderley St

Strand

Gold of Africa Museum

Hertz

Koopmans De Wet House

CNA

Golden Acre

Castle of Good Hope

Castle St

St George's Mall

Strand

Castle

Hout

Heritage Square

Virtual Turtle

Greenmarket Square

Grand Parade

City Hall

Darling

Berg

Shortmarket St

Longmarket St

Longmarket St

Caledon

BO-KAAP

Chiappini

Fore

Bree

Church

Old Town House

Methodist Church

Groote Kerk

Church Square

St Georges Cathedral

Plein

Corporation

Parade

Albertus

District Six Museum

Bo Kaap Museum

Wale

Slave Lodge

Barrack

Harrington

Canterbury

Dorp

Slave Church Museum

South African Public Library

Houses of Parliament

Commercial

Leeuwen

Company's Garden

Upper Pepper

Pepper

Loop

Long

Parliament

St Johns

Rust en Vreugd

Roeland

Bloem

Buiten

Keerom

Queen Victoria St

Hope

Orphan

St Martin

National Gallery

Buitensingel

Baths

Vrede

Buitengracht

New Church

PadJock

Jewish Museum & Holocaust Centre

Whitford

Super Market

South African Museum & Planetarium

Mountain Club

Dunkley Square

Carlsbrook

Bertram House

Government Av

Hatfield

Rheede

Labia Cinema

School

To Lower Cableway Station for Table Mountain

Park

Kloof St

Annandale

To De Waal Drive, M3 & Southern Suburbs

Cape Town maps
1 Cape Town orientation, page 78
2 Cape Town Centre, page 89
3 Green Point, De Waterkant & Waterfront, page 96
4 Sea Point, page 98
5 Victoria & Albert Waterfront, page 100
6 Oranjezicht, Gardens & Tamboerskloof, page 105

N

200 metres
200 yards

Sleeping
Backpack 1
Cape Diamond 18
Cape Heritage 8
Cape Town Hollow 3

Cat & Moose Backpackers 5
Daddy Long Legs 16
Inn Long Street 14
Long St Backpackers 11
Metropole 12
Park Inn 10
Tudor 17
Urban Chic 19
Westin Grand Cape Town Arabella Quays 2

Eating
Africa Café 1
Biesmiellah 9
Caveau 10
Crush 8
Five Flies 3
Mama Africa 5
Marco's African Place 6
Mr Pickwicks 7
Porcini 10
Rcaffé 13
Royale 12

Savoy Cabbage 2
Simply Asia 10
Sundance 10

Bars & clubs
Chrome 14
Club Tonic 15
Deluxe 16
Jo'burg 17
Marvel 18
Zula 19

Holocaust Centre
ⓘ *88 Hatfield St, T021-4625553, www.ctholocaust.co.za, Sun-Thu 1000-1700, Fri 1000-1300, entry by donation.*

An intelligent and shocking examination of the Holocaust can be found next door at this modern museum. Exhibits follow a historical route, starting with a look at anti-Semitism in Europe in previous centuries, and then leading to the rise of Nazism in Germany, the creation of ghettos, death camps and the Final Solution, and liberation at the end of the war. Video footage, photography, examples of Nazi propaganda and personal accounts of the Holocaust produce a vividly haunting and shocking display. The exhibits cleverly acknowledge South Africa's recent emergence from Apartheid and draw parallels between both injustices, as well as looking at the link between South Africa's Greyshirts (who were later assimilated into the National Party) and the Nazis. The local context is highlighted further at the end of the exhibition, with video accounts of Jews who survived the Holocaust and moved to Cape Town.

National Gallery
ⓘ *Government Av, T021-4674660, www.iziko.org.za, Tue-Sun 1000-1700, R10, children R5.*

The National Gallery is one of the city's finest museums, housing a permanent collection but also hosting some excellent temporary exhibitions that include the best of the country's contemporary art. The original collection was bequeathed to the nation in 1871 by Thomas Butterworth Bailey, and features a collection of 18th- and 19th-century British sporting scenes, portraits and Dutch paintings. Far more interesting are the changing exhibitions of contemporary South African art. These have recently included 'Revisions – A narrative of South African Art', a brilliant private collection, with four rooms covering five decades of the country's contemporary art, including pieces by Irma Stern, fascinating lino prints by Vuminkosi Zulu and violent and humorous charcoal drawings by Dumile Feni. Snacks and light lunches are available at the **Gallery Café** and there's a good souvenir shop on site.

Rust en Vreugd
ⓘ *78 Buitenkant St, T021-4643280, Tue-Thu 0830-1630, entry by donation.*

A few hundred metres east of the National Gallery, hidden behind a high whitewashed wall, is this 18th-century mansion. It was declared a historical monument in 1940, and was subsequently restored to tis original finery. Today it houses six galleries displaying a collection of watercolours, engravings and lithographs depicting the history of the Cape. Of particular note are Schouten's watercolour of Van Riebeeck's earth fort (1658), watercolours by Thomas Baines (a British artist who travelled extensively in South Africa and Australia) of climbing Table Mountain, lithographs by Angas of Khoi and Zulus and a collection of cartoons by Cruikshank depicting the first British settlers arriving in the Cape. These are all part of the William Fehr Collection. Commercial exhibitions are held in the galleries upstairs.

Company's Garden
ⓘ *Daily 0700-1900.*

Running alongside Government Avenue is the peaceful Company's Garden, situated on the site of Jan van Riebeeck's original vegetable garden, which was created in 1652 to grow produce for settlers and ships bound for the East. It is now a small botanical garden, with lawns, a variety of labelled trees, ponds filled with Japanese koi and a small aviary, although it is not as peaceful as it might be thanks to groups of snoozing men who seem to spend their days lounging around on the lawns. The grey squirrels living amongst the oak trees were introduced by Cecil Rhodes from America. There are also a couple of statues here: opposite the South African Public Library at the lower end of the garden, is the oldest statue in Cape Town, that of Sir George Grey, governor of the Cape from 1854 to 1862. Close by is a statue of Cecil Rhodes, pointing northwards in a rather unfortunate flat-handed gesture, with an inscription reading, "Your hinterland is there", a reminder of his ambition to paint the map pink from the Cape to Cairo. There is a café in the garden, serving drinks and snacks beneath the trees.

South African Public Library
ⓘ 5 Queen Victoria St, behind St George's Cathedral, T021-4246320, www.nlsa.ac.za, Mon-Fri 0900-1700, Wed from 1000.
Adjoining the gardens is the South African Public Library, which opened in 1818. It is the country's oldest national reference library and was one of the first free libraries in the world. Today it houses an important collection of books covering South Africa's history. The building also has a bookshop and an internet café.

Houses of Parliament
ⓘ Entry via Parliament St gate, T021-4032911, public gallery tickets available during parliamentary sessions Jan-Jun, overseas visitors must present their passports, phone ahead for tours of the chambers and Constitutional Assembly.
On the other side of the avenue are the Houses of Parliament. The building was completed in 1885, and when the Union was formed in 1910 it became the seat for the national parliament. In front of the building is a marble statue of Queen Victoria, erected by public subscription in honour of her Golden Jubilee. It was unveiled in 1890.

St George's Cathedral
The last building on Government Avenue is St George's Cathedral, best known for being Archbishop Desmond Tutu's territory from 1986 until 1996 (see page 82). It is from here that he led over 30,000 people to City Hall to mark the end of Apartheid, and where he coined the now universal phrase 'Rainbow Nation'. The building was designed by Sir Herbert Baker in the early 20th century. Inside, some of the early memorial tablets have been preserved, while over the top of the stairs leading to the crypt is a memorial to Lady D'Urban, wife of Sir Benjamin D'Urban, the Governor of the Cape from 1834 to 1838. Under the archway between the choir and St John's Chapel is a bronze recumbent statue of Archbishop West Jones, the second Archbishop of Cape Town (1874-1908). The Great North window is a fine piece of stained glass depicting the pioneers of the Anglican church. There is a small café, The Crypt, open during the day for light snacks and breakfasts.

Slave Lodge
ⓘ T021-4608242, Mon-Sat 1000-1700, R7, children R2.
On the corner of Adderley and Wale streets is Slave Lodge, the second oldest building in Cape Town. The building has had a varied history, but its most significant role was as a slave lodge for the VOC (see page 81) – between 1679 and 1811 the building housed up to 1000 slaves. Local indigenous groups were protected by the VOC from being enslaved; most slaves were consequently imported from Madagascar, India and Indonesia, creating the most culturally varied slave society in the world. Conditions at the lodge were appalling and up to 20% of the slaves died every year.

It has now been developed into a museum chartering the history of the building and slavery in South Africa. At the entrance to the exhibition is a slick cinema room, with two flat-screen TVs showing a 15-minute film on the history of slavery in the Cape, highlighting the rules under which slaves lived, the conditions in which they were imported and sold, and the fundamental role slavery played in the success of Cape Town. Beyond here, the museum has a series of displays, including a model of a slave ship and images and sounds of what life was like in the lodge. The top floor houses a muddle of British and VOC weapons, household goods, furniture and money, as well as relics from Japan and ancient Rome, Greece and Egypt.

Groote Kerk
ⓘ T021-4220569, www.grootekerk.org.za, daily 1000-1900, free guided tours available.
Nearby is one of Cape Town's older corners, **Church Square**, site of the Groote Kerk. Up until 1834 the square was used as a venue for the auctioning of slaves from the Slave Lodge, which faced onto the square. All transactions took place under a tree – a concrete plaque marks the old tree's position.

The Groote Kerk was the first church of the Dutch Reformed faith to be built in South Africa (building started in 1678 and it was consecrated in 1704). The present church, built between 1836 and 1841, is a somewhat dull, grey building designed and constructed by Hermann Schutte after a fire had destroyed most of the original. Many of the old gravestones were built into the base of the church walls, the most elaborate of which is the tombstone of Baron van Rheede van Oudtshoorn. Inside, more early tombstones and family vaults are set into the floor, while on the walls are the coats of arms of early Cape families. Note the locked pews, which were rented out to wealthy families in the 19th century. Two of the Cape's early governors are buried here – Simon van der Stel (1679-1699) and Ryk Tulbagh (1751-1771).

District Six Museum
ⓘ 25A Buitenkant St, T021-4667208, www.districtsix.co.za, Mon 0900-1500, Tue-Sat 0900-1600, entry by donation. There is a small café and a bookshop in the museum.
This small museum, housed in the Methodist Church, is one of Cape Town's most powerful exhibitions and gives a fascinating glimpse of the inanity of Apartheid. District Six was once the vibrant, cosmopolitan heart of Cape Town, a largely coloured inner city suburb renowned for its jazz scene. In February 1966, P W Botha, then Minister of Community Development, formally proclaimed District Six a 'white' group area. Over the next 15 years, an estimated 60,000 people were given notice to give up their homes and moved to the new townships on the Cape Flats. The area was razed, and to this day remains largely undeveloped. Over the years there has been much talk about relocating some of those who were originally displaced to new housing in the area, but as yet there has been no progress.

The museum contains a lively collection of photographs, articles and personal accounts depicting life before and after the removals. There are usually a couple of musicians at the back, tinkering away at their guitars and tin pipes and adding immeasurably to the atmosphere of the place. Highlights include a large map covering most of the ground floor on which ex-residents have been encouraged to mark their homes and local sights. The **Namecloth** is particularly poignant: a 1.5-m-wide length of cloth has been provided for ex-residents to write down their comments, part of which hangs by the entrance. It has grown to over 1 km, and features some moving thoughts. A display in the back room looks at the forced removals from the Kirstenbosch area.

City Hall and Grand Parade

From Adderley Street, a short walk down Darling Street will take you to the City Hall and the Grand Parade. The latter is the largest open space in Cape Town and was originally used for garrison parades before the castle was completed. In 1994, after his release from prison, Nelson Mandela made his first speech from City Hall to over 100,000 people. Today the oak-lined parade is used as a car park and twice a week it is taken over by a colourful market (see page 124). The neoclassical City Hall, built to celebrate Queen Victoria's golden jubilee, overlooks the parade. Its clock tower is a half-size replica of Big Ben in London. In 1979 the municipal government moved to a new Civic Centre on the Foreshore, a dominant tower block which straddles Hertzog Boulevard. The hall is now headquarters of the Cape Town Symphony Orchestra and houses the **City Library**.

Castle of Good Hope

ⓘ *Entry from the Grand Parade side, T021-4641260, www.castleofgoodhope.co.za, daily 0930-1600, R20, children R10. Free guided tours Mon-Sat 1100, 1200 and 1400. Expect to have any bags checked since the castle is still used as the regional offices for the National Defence Force.*

Beyond the Grand Parade, on Darling Street, is the main entrance of South Africa's oldest colonial building, the Castle of Good Hope. Work was started in 1666 by Commander Zacharias Wagenaer and completed in 1679. Its original purpose was for the Dutch East India Company to defend the Cape from rival European powers, and today it is an imposing sight, albeit a rather gloomy one. Under the British, the castle served as government headquarters and since 1917 it has been the headquarters of the South African Defence Force, Western Cape.

Today the castle is home to three museums. The **William Fehr Collection** is one of South Africa's finest displays of furnishings reflecting the social and political history of the Cape. There are landscapes by John Thomas Baines and William Huggins, 17th-century Japanese porcelain and 18th-century Indonesian furniture. Upstairs is an absurdly huge dining table which seats 104, in a room still used for state dinners.

To the left of the William Fehr Collection is the **Secunde's House**. The Secunde was second in charge of the settlement at the Cape, responsible for administrative duties for the Dutch East India Company. None of the three rooms contain original furniture from the castle, but they do recreate the conditions under which an official for the Dutch East India Company would have lived in the 17th, 18th and early 19th centuries. The third museum is the **Military Museum**, a rather indifferent collection depicting the conflicts of early settlers. More absorbing are the regimental displays of uniforms and medals.

The free guided tours are informative and fun, although a little short. Tour highlights include the torture chambers, cells, views from the battlements and Dolphin Court, where Lady Anne Barnard was supposedly seen bathing in the nude by the sentries. While waiting for a tour you can enjoy coffee and cakes at a small café, or explore van der Stel's restored wine cellars, where you can taste and buy wines. There is full ceremonial changing of the guard at noon.

Adderley Street and Heerengracht

Adderley Street is one of the city's busiest shopping areas, and is sadly marred by a number of 1960s and 1970s eyesores, but it does still boast some impressive bank buildings. On the corner of Darling Street is the **Standard Bank Building** (1880), a grand structure built shortly after the diamond wealth from Kimberley began to reach Cape Town. Diagonally across is the equally impressive **Barclays Bank Building** (1933), a fine Ceres sandstone building which was the last major work by Sir Herbert Baker in South Africa. At the corner of Adderley Street and Strand Street stands a modern shopping mall complex, the **Golden Acre**. On the lower level of the complex the remains of an aqueduct and a reservoir dating from 1663 can be viewed. The line of black floor tiles close to the escalator which links the centre with the railway station mark the position of the original shoreline before any reclamation work began in Table Bay. Continuing down towards the docks, Adderley Street passes Cape Town Railway Station. At the junction with Hans Strijdom Street is a large roundabout with a central fountain and a bronze statue of **Jan van Riebeeck**, given to the city by Cecil Rhodes in 1899. At the bottom end of Adderley Street on the foreshore are statues of Bartholomew Dias and Maria van Riebeeck, donated respectively by the Portuguese and Dutch Governments in 1952 for Cape Town's tercentenary celebrations.

In front of the Medical Centre on Heerengracht is the **Scott Memorial**. What is on show is in fact a bronze replica; the original, a stone argosy, was smashed by vandals. Its location has barely changed, but when it was unveiled in 1916 it was on the approach to a pier at the foot of Adderley Street, a further indication of how much additional land has been reclaimed from Table Bay over the years. The palm trees once graced a marine promenade in this area. Up until the 1850s there was a canal running the full length of Heerengracht and Adderley streets. This was covered over as the city prospered and traffic congestion became a problem.

Greenmarket Square

A couple of blocks south of the junction of Strand Street and St George's Mall is Greenmarket Square, the old heart of Cape Town and the second oldest square in the city. It has long been a meeting place, and during the 19th century it became a vegetable market. In 1834 it took on the significant role of being the site where the declaration of the freeing of all slaves was made. Today it remains a popular meeting place, with a busy daily market selling African crafts, jewellery and clothes.

Most of the buildings around the square reflect the city's history. Dominating one side is a **Park Inn** hotel, housed in what was once the headquarters of Shell Oil – note the shell motifs on its exterior. Diagonally opposite is the **Old Town House** (1751) ① *T021-4813933, www.iziko.org.za, Mon-Fri 1000-1700, Sat 1000-1600, entry by donation*, originally built to house the town guard. It became the first town hall in 1840 when Cape Town became a municipality. Much of the exterior remains unchanged, and with its decorative plaster mouldings and fine curved fanlights, it is one of the best preserved Cape baroque exteriors in the city. The first electric light in Cape Town was switched on in the Old House on 13 April 1895. Today the white double-storeyed building houses the Michaelis Collection of Flemish and Dutch paintings, as well as the **Courtyard Café** which serves snacks. At the entrance to the house is a circle set into the floor which marks the spot from which all distances to and from Cape Town are measured. Next to the **Tudor Hotel** is the second oldest building on the square – the **Metropolitan Methodist Church** (1876). This, the only high Victorian church in Cape Town, has a tall spire decorated with an unusual series of miniature grotesques. The church was designed by Charles Freeman and is regarded as one of the finest in the country.

If you walk out of the square past the Methodist church to Church Street, you'll come to the area between Burg and Long streets, which is the venue for a daily **antiques market**.

Koopmans-De Wet House

① *Strand St, T021-4813935, Tue-Thu 0900-1600, R5.*
Just off St George's Mall, a pedestrianized road lined with shops and cafés, is the delightfully peaceful Koopmans-De Wet House. The house is named in memory of Marie

Koopmans-De Wet, a prominent figure in cultured Cape Society who lived here between 1834 and 1906. The inside has been restored to reflect the period of her grandparents who lived here in the late 18th century. All of the pieces are numbered and a small catalogue gives a brief description. Though not too cluttered, there is a fascinating collection of furnishings which gives the house a special tranquil feel. Look out for the early map of the Cape coastline at the head of the stairs, dating from 1730 – Saldanha Bay and Cape Agulhas are clearly visible. At the back of the house is a shaded courtyard and the original stables with the slave quarters above.

Gold of Africa Museum

ⓘ *96 Strand St, T021-4051540, www.goldofafrica.com, Mon-Sat 0930-1700, R20, children R10.*

A few blocks west of Koopmans-De Wit House is the **Lutheran Church**, and next door is the **Martin Melck House**, now home to the Gold of Africa Museum. Originally the house served as a clandestine Lutheran church, as in the 18th century the Dutch authorities refused to tolerate any churches other than those belonging to the Dutch Reformed Church. The present museum houses a slick display of the history of gold mining, outlining the first mining by Egyptians in 2400 BC and the subsequent development of trade networks across Africa. There are comprehensive displays of 19th- and 20th-century gold artworks from Mali, Ghana and Senegal, including jewellery, masks, hair ornaments and statuettes. It's a reasonable collection, but you need a real interest in precious metals to stay for long. Downstairs there's a café, shop and workshop where you can watch goldsmiths at work.

Long Street

One of the trendiest stretches in Cape Town, Long Street gets particularly lively at night. Lined with street cafés, fashionable shops, bars, clubs and backpacker hostels, it has a distinctly youthful feel about it, although a clutch of new boutique hotels, posh apartment complexes and upmarket restaurants is injecting the area with a new sophisticated edge. Long Street is also home to some fine old city buildings. One of Cape Town's late Victorian gems is at No 117, now an antiques shop. On the outside is an unusual cylindrical turret with curved windows; inside is a fine cast-iron spiral staircase leading to a balustraded gallery.

The **Slave Church Museum** ⓘ *No 40, T021 4236755, Mon Fri 0900 1600, free*, is the oldest mission church in South Africa, built between 1802 and 1804 as the mother church for missionary work carried out in rural areas. Fortunately the building was saved from demolition in 1977 and restored to its present fine form. Though utilized by directors and members of the South African Missionary Society, it was more commonly used for religious and literacy instruction of slaves in Cape Town; by 1960 most of its congregation had been moved to the Cape Flats. Inside are displays of missionary work throughout the Cape, and behind the pulpit are displays showing early cash accounts and receipts for transactions such as the transfer of slaves.

Heritage Square

A few blocks north of Long Street is this renovated block of 17th- and 18th-century townhouses, which include one of the city's oldest blacksmiths, but is better known for its excellent restaurants and the **Cape Heritage Hotel** (see Sleeping, page 107). In the centre is a cobbled courtyard holding the Cape's oldest living grape vine, which was planted in 1781.

Bo-Kaap and the Bo-Kaap Museum

About 600 m west along Wale Street is the Bo-Kaap, Cape Town's historical Islamic quarter and one of the city's most interesting residential areas. The area was developed in the 1760s and today feels a world away from the nearby CBD. Here the streets are cobbled and tightly woven across the slopes of Signal Hill, and the closely packed houses are painted in bright hues of lime, pink and blue. To the west, the Bo-Kaap blends into the trendy new gay area of De Waterkant.

The **Bo-Kaap Museum** ① *Wale St, T021-4813939, www.iziko.org.za, Mon-Sat 0900-1600, R5*, housed in an attractive 18th-century house, is dedicated to the Cape's Muslim community and contains the furnishings of a wealthy 19th-century Muslim family. There are antique furnishings and Islamic heirlooms such as an old Koran and *tasbeh* beads set in front of the mihrab alcove, while the back room has displays dedicated to the input that slaves had in the economy and development of Cape Town. The photos are the most interesting articles, giving a fascinating glimpse of life in the Bo-Kaap in the early 20th century. At the back is a community centre, with temporary photographic exhibitions. The house itself is one of the oldest buildings in Cape Town surviving in its original form. It

③ Green Point, De Waterkant & Waterfront

Sleeping
40 Winks Guest House 8
Atlantic Villa 10
Big Blue 7

Brenwin Guest House 2
Cape Victoria 4
De Waterkant Village 3
Graeme 9

Sunflower Stop 1
Village Lodge 5

was built by Jan de Waal for artisans in 1763 and it was here that Abu Bakr Effendi started the first Arabic school and wrote important articles on Islamic law. He originally came to Cape Town as a guest of the British government to try and settle religious differences amongst the Cape Muslims.

De Waterkant, Green Point and Sea Point

These suburbs are the closest seaside residential areas to the city, and are undergoing rapid transformation. De Waterkant – until fairly recently a run-down area of flaking bungalows – is now Cape Town's most fashionable district, with beautifully restored Victorian homes painted in bright hues crammed into a tight cobbled grid of streets, climbing up towards Signal Hill. This is the city's main gay area, with excellent nightlife and a wide choice of super-trendy restaurants and bars. About 500 m beyond is the start of Green Point, where there is a large roundabout, from which there is a turning northeast to the V&A Waterfront. To the northwest of the roundabout is the unmissable construction site of the new Green Point Stadium for the 2010 FIFA Football World Cup. It presently has an impressive cluster of a dozen cranes and completion is expected by mid-2009. As a spin off to being close to the stadium, there's presently a massive wave of development along Main Road which runs the length of Green Point and Sea Point, and the buildings are developing into a series of high-rise apartment blocks and shopping and restaurant malls. Running parallel to Main Road is Beach Road which winds its way from the V&A Waterfront and around Mouille Point, where there is another smart row of apartment blocks and the red and white candy-striped Green Point Lighthouse. This is the oldest working lighthouse on the South African coast, built by Herman Schutte (a German builder) in 1824, which was electrified in 1929. From Green Point, both Main Road and Beach Road then continue on their parallel journey through Sea Point and merge on their way to Clifton. There's a pleasant promenade the length of Beach Road, which is intercepted by short stretches of beach and has an adjoining strip of park where there are a few attractions for children such as a mini-train, mini-golf and playgrounds. Primarily it's a place where local people jog, rollerblade or walk their dogs and there are good views of Table Bay and

➡ Cape Town maps
1 Cape Town orientation, page 78
2 Cape Town Centre, page 89
3 Green Point, De Waterkant & Waterfront, page 96
4 Sea Point, page 98
5 Victoria & Albert Waterfront, page 100
6 Oranjezicht, Gardens & Tamboerskloof, page 105

Eating ⊙
Buena Vista Social Café **1**
News Café **1**
Nose **4**
Tank **4**
Wangthai **3**

some surf spots below the promenade wall. The beach is unsafe for swimming, although there are a couple of rock pools, including Graaf's Pool (men only) and Milton's Pool. The centre of Sea Point on Main Road has a bit of a scruffy reputation, but the numerous new developments are giving it a facelift and bringing in a number of upmarket shops and restaurants.

4 Sea Point

To Greenpoint, V&A Waterfront & City Centre

St Bedes
Three Anchor Bay
Fort
Catwalk
Internet
Camberwell
Glengariff
Frere
Main Dr
Rhine
Antwerp
Calais
Ocean View
Norfolk
Beach
Wisbeach
Main Rd
Oldfield
Hall
Firmount
London
Marais
Albany
Bellevue
Oliver
Graham
Clifford
Graaff's Pool
Milton
The Glen
Shell
Worcester
Arthur's
Arthur's
St Johns
Gorleston
Bordeaux

Atlantic Ocean

Pavilion
Swimming Pool
Clarens
High Level
Le Sueur
St Bartholomew
Sports Club
SEA POINT
Normandie
Protea
Disandt
Des Huguenots
Regent
Fresnaye
Le Croix
FRESNAYE
Kings
Kloof Rd
Queens
Victoria Rd
Bellwood
De Wet
Ocean View
Saunders Rocks
Beach
Bantry Bay
To Clifton, Camps Bay & Hout Bay

Signal Hill (350m)
Signal Hill

➡ Cape Town maps
1 Cape Town orientation, page 78
2 Cape Town Centre, page 89
3 Green Point, De Waterkant & Waterfront, page 96
4 Sea Point, page 98
5 Victoria & Albert Waterfront, page 100
6 Oranjezicht, Gardens & Tamboerskloof, page 105

300 metres
300 yards

Sleeping 🛏
Ashby Manor 2
Bellevue Manor 4
Blackheath Lodge 5
Clarendon 10
Glen 3

Huijs Haerlem 9
Le Vendôme 11
Olaf's 6
Villa Rosa 7
Winchester Mansions 8

Eating 🍴
Café Erté 2
La Perla 4
New York Bagels 3
Tom Yum 1

Victoria and Alfred Waterfront ●●● » pp107-131.

The V&A Waterfront, Cape Town's original Victorian harbour, is the city's most popular attraction. The whole area was completely restored in the early 1990s, and today it is a lively district packed with restaurants, bars and shops. Original buildings stand shoulder to shoulder with mock-Victorian shopping malls, museums and cinemas, all crowding along a waterside walkway with Table Mountain towering beyond. Prices are a little higher in restaurants and bars here and many have argued that the area is over-sanitized and artificial. But despite being geared towards tourists it remains a working harbour, which provides much of the area's real charm.

The choice of shops, restaurants and entertainment is unrivalled. When the main mall Victoria Wharf opened, it was similar to any other South African shopping mall and featured the usual chain stores. Over the years and with growing popularity – today it attracts 10 million visitors a year – the quality of shops has shifted upmarket. The majority of shops now sell clothes, souvenirs, jewellery and specialist items. In November 2007, a whole new extension of Victoria Wharf was opened, with 70 more shops and a fashion gallery featuring the likes of Gucci, Jimmy Choo and Burberry.

Ins and outs

There is a **tourist information office** ① T021 4054500, www.tourismcapetown.co.za, daily 0900-2100, in the Clock Tower Centre across the swing bridge from the main development. They stock a good selection of maps and guides for the whole country; there are also desks for car hire and safari companies, and a SANParks booking desk. A full list of all the shops, amenities and attractions can be found at www.waterfront.co.za.

Background

The V&A Waterfront derives its name from the two harbour basins around which it is developed. Construction began in 1860, when Prince Alfred, Queen Victoria's second son, tipped the first load of stone to start the building of the breakwater for Cape Town's harbour. Alfred Basin could not handle the increased shipping volumes and subsequently a larger basin, the Victoria Basin, was built. A number of original buildings remain around the basins and are an interesting diversion from the razzmatazz of the shops and restaurants.

Clock Tower

At the narrow entrance to the Alfred Basin, on the Berties Landing side, is the original Clock Tower, built in 1882 to house the port captain's office. This is in the form of a red octagonal Gothic-style tower and stands just in front of the Clock Tower Centre, a modern mall with a collection of shops, offices and restaurants. The Clock Tower Centre houses the Nelson Mandela Gateway to Robben Island, from where you catch the main ferry to the island. This side of the Waterfront is connected the bulk of the area by a swing bridge, which swings open every 10 minutes to allow boats to pass underneath.

Union Castle Building

Walking across the swing bridge (look out for the Cape fur seals on a landing to your right as you cross) you come to the stocky square building known as **Union Castle Building** (1919), designed by the firm of architects owned by Sir Herbert Baker. The Union Steamship Company and the Castle Line both ran monthly mail ships between Britain and South Africa in the late 19th century. In 1900 they amalgamated and from then on mail was delivered every week. The last Union Castle ship to sail to England with the mail was the *Windsor Castle* in 1977. This is now home to the **Maritime Museum** ① *T021-4052880, www.iziko.org.za, daily 1000-1700*, a collection of model ships and objects associated with the era of mail ships. It also holds an archive of over 19,000 photographs of ships that visited Cape Town from the 1920s to the 1960s. Nearby is the museum ship, the *SAS Somerset*, a boom defence vessel that is permanently moored for public viewing.

5 Victoria & Alfred Waterfront

⮕ Cape Town maps

400 metres
400 yards

N

Sleeping 🛏
Breakwater Lodge **1**   Commodore **5**   Victoria & Alfred **4**
Cape Grace **2**   Table Bay **3**

Opposite the Union Castle Building is the **Victoria and Alfred Hotel**. Now a luxury four-star hotel and shopping mall, the building was originally a coal store before being converted into Union Castle's warehouse and customs baggage store. It used to have a third floor but this was destroyed in a fire in 1939. This was the first hotel to be opened at the Waterfront and it is an important part of the success of the whole venture.

To the south of the hotel is the new **Nobel Square** ① www.nobelsquare.com, which was opened on 16 December 2006, the Day of Reconciliation, and pays tribute to four of South Africa's Nobel Peace Prize laureates – the late Nkosi Albert Luthuli (1961), Archbishop Desmond Tutu (1984) and FW de Klerk and Nelson Mandela who jointly won it in 1993. Slightly larger than life-size statues of the four formidable men stand next to each other with a backdrop of Table Mountain and, in front of the sculpture, the Laureates' preferred quotations engraved in their chosen language. In the middle of the square, the Peace and Democracy sculpture – a narrative work of a jumble of people and faces on top of each other – represents the contribution made by women and children to the attainment of peace in South Africa.

Time Ball Tower
Heading west, on the other side of Dock Road above the car park is the 1894 Time Ball Tower, its purpose was to act as an accurate reference for ships' navigators who set their clocks as the ball on the roof fell. Correct time was vital for the navigator to be able to determine precise longitude. Beside the tower is a 110-year-old dragon tree, *Dracaeno draco*, from the Canary Islands, and next to the tree is the original **harbour master's residence** (1860).

Two Oceans Aquarium
① *Entrance is on Dock Rd, by the Waterfront Craft Market, 1021-4183823, www.aquarium.co.za, daily 0930-1800, R76, children R35, under 4s free.*
Focusing on the unique Cape marine environment created by the merging of the Atlantic and Indian Ocean, this aquarium is the top attraction on the Waterfront. The display begins with a walk through the Indian Ocean, where you'll follow a route past tanks filled with a multitude of colourful fish, turtles, seahorses and octopuses. Highlights include giant spider crabs and phosphorescent jellyfish floating in a mesmerizing circular current. Then you walk past touch pools, where children can pick up spiky starfish and slimy sea slugs. Free puppet shows and face painting keep children busy at the Alpha Activity Centre in the basement. The main wall here is part of the Diving Animals Pool, and you can watch Cape fur seals dart and dive before the glass. The seals are fed at 1100 and 1400. Upstairs is a vast tank holding the Kelp Forest, an extraordinary tangle of giant kelp that sways drunkenly in the artificial tides. The highlight is the Predators exhibit, a circular tank complete with glass tunnel, holding ragged-tooth sharks, eagle rays, turtles and some impressively large hunting fish. There are daily feeds at 1530 and, with an Open Water diving certificate, you can arrange to dive with the sharks. The aquarium also has a new conservation programme, where it tags and releases ragged tooth sharks back into the sea, providing valuable data on their movements.

Cape Medical Museum
① *T021-4185663, Tue-Fri 0900-1600, entry by donation.*
Close by the Waterfront, at the City Hospital Complex on Portswood Road, the medical achievements of South Africa's doctors are celebrated in this interesting display, a must for any medical students doing their elective in Cape Town. There are turn-of-the-20th-century reconstructions of a consulting room and dispensary, dentist's room, operating theatre and hospital ward plus a collection of medical instruments.

Robben Island

Tours to the island are run by the **Robben Island Museum** ① *T021-4134200, www.robben-island.org.za*. The Nelson Mandela Gateway at the Clock Tower Centre is the embarkation and disembarkation point for the tours. The Gateway also holds a shop, the ticket office and a small museum with photographic and interactive displays on Apartheid and the rise of African nationalism, open 0730-2100. An air-conditioned catamaran completes the half-hour journey to the island. Tickets cost R150, children R75. Tours begin with a 45-minute drive around the key sites on the island, including Sobukwe's house, the lime quarry where Mandela was forced to work, the leper cemetery, and the houses of former warders. Tours around the prison are conducted by ex-political prisoners, who paint a vivid picture of prison life here. Departures are on the hour 0900-1500, and you need to allow 2½ hours on the island. You must remain with your guide throughout the tour. Be sure to book a day ahead (or three days in peak season) as tickets sell out quickly, and always phone ahead to see if the ferry is running in bad weather. Do not drink any tap water on the island.

Lying 12 km off Green Point's shores, Robben Island is best known as the notorious prison that held many of the ANC's most prominent members, including Nelson Mandela and Walter Sisulu. It was originally named by the Dutch, after the term for seals, 'rob' – actually a misnomer as none are found here. The island's history of occupation started in 1806, when John Murray was granted permission by the British to conduct whaling from the island. During this period the authorities started to use the island as a dumping ground for common convicts; these were brought back to the mainland in 1843, and their accommodation was deemed suitable only for lepers and the mentally ill. These were in turn moved to the mainland between 1913 and 1931, and the island entered a new era as a military base during the Second World War. In 1960 the military passed control of the island over to the Department of Prisons, and it remained a prison until 1996. On 1 December 1999 the island was declared a World Heritage Site by UNESCO.

Robben Island's effectiveness as a prison did not rest simply with the fact that escape was virtually impossible. The authorities anticipated that the idea of 'out of sight, out of mind' would be particularly applicable here, and to a certain extent they were correct. Certainly, its isolation did much to break the spirit of political prisoners, not least Robert Sobukwe's. Sobukwe, the leader of the Pan African Congress, was kept in solitary confinement for nine years. Other political prisoners were spared that at least, although in 1971 they were separated from common law prisoners, as they were deemed a 'bad' influence. Conditions were harsh, with forced hard labour and routine beatings. Much of the daily running of the maximum security prison was designed to reinforce racial divisions: all the wardens, and none of the prisoners, were white; black prisoners, unlike those deemed coloured, had to wear short trousers and were given smaller food rations. Contact with the outside world was virtually non-existent – visitors had to apply for permission six months in advance and were allowed to stay for just half an hour. Newspapers were banned and letters were limited to one every six months.

Yet despite these measures, the B-Section, which housed Mandela and other major political prisoners, became the international focus of the fight against Apartheid. The last political prisoners left the island in 1991.

🌙 *As a prison, the area was strictly protected allowing the fish and bird populations to flourish. There are over 100 species of bird on the island, and it is an important breeding site for African penguins.*

Southern suburbs ●❷❶ ▸▸ *pp107-131.*

Primarily encompassing the more affluent residential areas of Cape Town, the suburbs, stretching southeast from the city centre, are an interesting diversion to the usual tourist spots. Although a car is the best way to visit them, it's possible to reach all by train – the metro service between the city centre and Simon's Town runs through the suburbs, but safety can be an issue; avoid the trains when it's not busy.▸▸ *For further details, see Transport, page 129.*

Woodstock and Observatory

The first suburb, **Woodstock**, is a mixed commercial and residential area, historically a working-class coloured district. Today it is somewhat run down and depressing, although the back streets are an attractive mesh of Victorian bungalows, some of which have been taken over by fashionable bars and restaurants. **Observatory** is an appealing area of tightly packed houses, narrow streets and student hangouts. Being close to the university, there is a good range of trendy bars, cafés and restaurants catering for a mixed scene of students, bohemian types and backpackers. The observatory after which the suburb is named is where Station Road intersects Liesbeeck Parkway The first Astronomer Royal to work at the Royal Observatory was also a clergyman, the Reverand Fearon Fellowes. Aside from making astronomical observations the observatory was responsible for accurate standard time in South Africa. It has also been an important meteorological centre and has a seismograph which records earthquakes around the world. Observatory is also where you'll find the **Groot Schuur Hospital** on Main Road, the site of the world's first heart transplant performed by Professor Christiaan Barnard. A small **museum** ⓘ *T021-4045232, Mon-Fri 0900-1400, R5,* in the hospital commemorates the transplant with a restored theatre built to look as it did when the transplant took place in 1967.

Mowbray, Rosebank and Rondebosch

The next suburbs of Mowbray, Rosebank and Rondebosch lie just below the **University of Cape Town**. Again, they are popular with students and have a good selection of restaurants and shops. **Mowbray** was originally known as Driekoppen, or three heads, after the murder by three slaves of a European foreman and his wife in 1724. On their capture they were beheaded and their heads impaled on stakes at the farm entrance to act as a deterrent. **Rondebosch**, conversely, has for some time been associated with education. Aside from the university, several important schools were founded in the district. The area was also important from a practical point of view: in 1656 Van Riebeeck realized that Company's Garden was exposed to a damaging southeast wind. His first choice of a more sheltered spot was Rondebosch. This proved a success and a grain storage barn was built. Early accounts describe the area as wild country, with the farmers frequently losing livestock to hyenas, lions and leopards – an image that is hard to imagine as you sit in the evening rush hour on Rhodes Drive. Also in Rondebosch is **Groot Schuur**, the Prime Minister's official residence; **Westbrooke**, home of the State President; and the original residence of the Cape Governor over 200 years ago, **Rustenburg**.

Irma Stern Museum

ⓘ *Cecil Rd, Rosebank, T021-6855686, Tue-Sat 1000-1700, www.irmastern.co.za, R8.*
A lesser-known but fascinating attraction in the area is this museum Irma Stern was one of South Africa's pioneering artists and her lovely house displays a mixture of her own works, a collection of artefacts from across Africa, and some fine pieces of antique furniture from

overseas, including 17th-century Spanish chairs, 19th-century German oak furniture and Swiss *mardi gras* masks. Her portraits are particularly poignant and those of her close friends are superb, while her religious art is rather more disturbing. Stern's studio, complete with paint brushes and palettes, has been left as it was when she died. The most important African items were collected in the Congo and Zanzibar. Of particular note is the Buli Stool, one of only 20 known carvings by a master carver from southeast Zaire. The kitchen houses a collection of Chinese ceramics including two fine Ming celadon dishes.

Rhodes Memorial
ⓘ *T021-6899151, www.rhodesmemorial.co.za, Nov-Apr 0700-1900, May-Oct 0800-1800.*
The best-known attraction in the area is the Rhodes Memorial, off Rhodes Drive, by the Rondesbosch turning. The imposing granite memorial to Cecil John Rhodes (Cape Prime Minister from 1890 to 1896) was designed by Francis Masey and Sir Herbert Baker. Four bronze lions flank a wide flight of steps which lead up to a Greek Temple. The temple houses an immense bronze head of Rhodes, wrought by JM Swan. Above the head are the words "slave to the spirit and life work of Cecil John Rhodes who loved and served South Africa". At the base of the steps is an immense bronze mounted figure of *Physical Energy* given to South Africa by GF Watts, a well-regarded sculptor of the time; the original stands in Hyde Park, London. Other than the memorial, the great attraction here is the magnificent view of the Cape Flats and the southern suburbs. Behind the memorial are a number of popular trails leading up the slopes of Devil's Peak. Also tucked away here is an excellent little tea house set in a garden of blue hydrangeas that serves good cheesecake, sandwiches and cream teas.

South of Rondesbosch
By this point the southern suburbs have reached right around Devil's Peak and the shadowy mountains now dominating the views represent an unfamiliar view of Table Mountain. The suburb of **Newlands** backs right up to the slopes of the mountain and is probably best known for being the home to Western Province Rugby Union and the beautiful Newlands cricket Test ground. There are several good hotels and guesthouses in the area. On Boundary Road in Newlands is the **Rugby Museum** ⓘ *T021-6596700, Mon-Fri 0830-1700, free,* housed in the Sports Medical Research Institute Building. The somewhat chaotic collection commemorates the history of the sport in the country and is also home to the Currie Cup, the premier domestic competition trophy.

Also on Boundary Road, **Josephine Mill** ⓘ *T021-6864939, Mon-Fri 1000-1600, small entrance fee,* the only surviving watermill in Cape Town, has been restored as a working flour mill; note the massive waterwheel (1840). The building is in the style of a Cornish red-brick mill, built by a Swede, Jacob Letterstedt, and named in honour of his Crown Princess, Josephine. The mill is tucked away near the rugby stadium and has a brewery and a peaceful tea garden. During the summer months, concerts are held on Sundays on the banks of the tree-fringed Liesbeek River, as part of the **Nedbank Summer Concert** season.

Claremont offers little of interest. On the main road is the upmarket **Cavendish Square Complex**, another shopping mall. There are two good cinema complexes here – the Ster-Kinekor Commercial, on the second floor, shows big releases, while the Ster-Kinekor Nouveau specializes in alternative and foreign-language films.

Nearby are **Ardene Gardens** ⓘ *0800-sunset,* a Victorian park first planted in 1845 by Ralph Arderne, who was so charmed by the Cape while en route for Australia that he decided to settle here instead. He succeeded in creating a garden that would represent the flora of the world. When his son died the estate was split up but fortunately in 1927 the Cape Town Municipality bought 11 acres of the garden. Today the arboretum is probably the best collection of trees in South Africa. An obelisk marks the site from which the famous astronomer, Sir John Herschel, carried out his research from 1834 to 1838.

6 Oranjezicht, Gardens & Tamboerskloof

➡️ **Cape Town maps**

Sleeping
Alta Bay 6
Ashanti Lodge 2
Backpack 3
Cactusberry Lodge 1
Cape Cadogan 4
Cape Milner 8

Kensington
Place 12
Leeuwenvoet
House 13
Mount Nelson 15
Parker Cottage 17
Table Mountain
Lodge 18

Zebra Crossing
Backpackers 21

Eating
Arnold's 1
Aubergine 7
Green's 2
Miller's Thumb 3

Rozenhof 9
Saigon 4
Yindee's 11
Yum 6

Bars & clubs
Rafiki's 5

N
200 metres
200 yards

A little further along the main road takes you to **Wynberg**. Apart from a few curio shops, the main attraction is the group of well-preserved 19th-century homes known as **Little Chelsea**. South of Wynberg the countryside opens up. To the west lie the fertile and prosperous valleys of Constantia and Tokai; due south the road quickly brings False Bay (page 137) and the coastal resort of Muizenberg into view. To the east lie the exposed high-density suburbs on the Cape Flats – Crossroads, Guguletu, Khayelitsha, Langa and Mitchells Plain.

Kirstenbosch Botanical Gardens
① *T021-7998783, www.sanbi.org, Sep-Mar 0800-1900, Apr-Aug 0800-1800, R30, children R5. By far the easiest way of getting here is by hire car. Otherwise there are trains to the nearest station at Mowbray, 10 mins from the city centre. From here there is an erratic bus service or a very long walk. Alternatively, take a Rikki taxi – they will pick up and drop off at any time other than rush hour. Most of the organized city tours also include the gardens on their itinerary.*
Kirstenbosch, 5 km south of Rondesbosch is South Africa's oldest, largest and most exquisite botanical garden. The gardens stretch up the eastern slopes of Table Mountain, merging seamlessly with the fynbos of the steep slopes above. Cecil Rhodes bought Kirstenbosch farm in 1895 and promptly presented the site to the people of South Africa with the intention that it become a botanical garden. It was not until 1913 that it was proclaimed a National Botanical Garden – the Anglo-Boer War had caused the delay. The first director of the gardens was Professor Harold Pearson, who died just three years after the garden's creation. A granite Celtic Cross marks his grave in the Cycad garden. There is a fitting epitaph: "If ye seek his monument, look around you." The real development was under Professor RH Compton, who cared for the gardens for 34 years. The herbarium, named after him, houses over 250,000 specimens, including many rare plants.

A great deal of time and effort has been put into making the gardens accessible to the general public, ensuring they provide pleasure for both serious botanists and families enjoying a day out on the slopes of Table Mountain. In the **Fragrance Garden** herbs and flowers are set out so as to make appreciating their scents effortless. On a warm day, when the volatile oils are released by the plants, there are some rather overpowering aromas. The plaques are also in Braille. The **Dell** follows a beautifully shaded path snaking beneath ferns and along a stream. Indigenous South African herbs can be inspected in the **Medicinal Plants Garden**, each one identified and used by the Khoi and San peoples in the treatment of a variety of ailments. The plants' uses are identified on plaques, and it seems that most ailments are covered – kidney trouble, rheumatics, coughs, cancer, piles and bronchitis. For a sense of the past, it is worth visiting what is known as **Van Riebeeck's Hedge**. Back in 1660 a hedge of wild almond trees (*Brabejum stellatifolium*) was planted by Van Riebeeck as part of a physical boundary to try and prevent cattle rustling. Segments still remain today within the garden. The **Skeleton Path** can be followed all the way to the summit of Table Mountain. It starts off as a stepped path, but becomes fairly steep near the top. It involves a climb up a rocky waterfall; take special care in the wet season.

Perhaps the most enjoyable way of experiencing the gardens is at one of the Sunday sunset concerts held throughout summer (see Music, page 121). Also available for a small fee are eco-adventure tours, and tours by motorized golf cart. Just beyond the entrance is a shop and café on the courtyard terrace. The shop has the usual collection of curios, along with a good choice of books on South Africa and a selection of indigenous plants. The café serves overpriced sandwiches and cakes; better value and with far nicer views is the **Silver Tree and Fynbos Deli** inside the gardens, which serves good meals (until 2200). And, for a reasonable price, you can have a ready-made picnic with wine and join the Capetonians on the lush lawns.

⊙ Cape Town listings

Hotel and guesthouse prices
L over US$300   **AL** US$220-300   **A** US$150-220
B US$100-150   **C** US$75-100   **D** US$35-75
E US$15-35   **F** under US$15
Restaurant prices
ⵀⵀⵀ over US$30   ⵀⵀ US$15-30   ⵀ under US$15
See pages 46-51 for further information.

◉ Sleeping

If visiting Dec Jan, it's worth booking a month or so in advance as hotels get booked up quickly. Secure parking has been mentioned in the listings wherever available.

There is good choice of **backpacker** hostels in the city centre and around; all are of a similar price and most are a good source of information. Many people travelling overland from Nairobi end their journey here, so the hostels are often good places to meet people and swap travelling information. A lot of hostels also offer non-dormitory rooms at reasonable rates – usually around R200 for a double. Dorms are about R90 per person in the peak season, although if you are looking for a long-term room or bed you should be able to negotiate a discount. During peak periods, be sure to call in advance to check availability, especially around Christmas and the New Year.

Several agencies specialize in **medium-and long-term holiday lets** of private homes, self-catering flats or home swaps. These are good value for families or groups; bring reliable references with you. **Apartments and Homes**, 154 Main Rd, Sea Point, T021-4394126, www.capeholidays.co.za, have fully furnished holiday lets in apartments and family homes; **Cape Holiday Homes**, www.cape homes.co.za, is a comprehensive website listing private homes in the Peninsula and coastal area; **International Home Exchange**, www.homelinksouthafrica.org, is affiliated to HomeLink International in the UK and has a homeswap directory in over 40 countries.

City Bowl *p87, maps p89 and p105*
L Westin Grand Cape Town Arabella Quays, Convention Sq, Lower Long St, T021-4129999, www.starwoodhotels.com. Fairly new addition to the city's ultra-smart business hotels. Huge grey-glass structure overlooking the convention centre with 483 rooms, modern and minimalist style, huge beds, floor-to-ceiling windows, dark red theme, stone bathrooms, satellite TV, internet access, fax machines. Popular spa, gym, 5 restaurants and bars, swift, efficient and impressively modern service. Rated one of the top 5 hotels in Africa in the 2006 Condé Nast Traveler Readers' Choice Awards, rates are upwards of R3000 per night.

AL Cape Heritage Hotel, 90 Bree St, Heritage Sq, T021-4244646, www.cape heritage.co.za. Charming hotel set in a rambling renovated town house dating from the late 17th century. 15 huge rooms, each individually styled, with muted coloured walls (avocado, rust-red, eggshell blue), some with 4-poster beds. All have large windows and sound-proofing to protect from busy Bree St, plus newly renovated bathrooms, minibar, a/c, M-Net TV. Breakfast served under a historical vine in the courtyard, or in the airy black-and-white breakfast room. Good location close to Long St. Friendly management. Recommended.

AL Urban Chic, corner of Long and Pepper streets, T021-4266119, www.urbanchic.co.za. Italian-owned hotel in a trendy corner block. 20 rooms spread over several floors (prices rise the higher you go, as the views of the mountain improve). Beautiful, airy decor, with pale colours, modern art on the walls, large stone-clad bathrooms, some with sliding partition walls to the bedroom. Stylish bar attached, and on the 1st floor is the **Gallery Café** with a large fusion menu, for-sale art on the walls and understated, spacious seating, including in a covered balcony over Long St.

A Cape Town Hollow, 88 Queen Victoria St, T021-4231260, www.capetownhollow.co.za. Pleasant newish hotel overlooking Company's Garden. 56 rooms with fairly bland but comfortable furnishings, spotless bathrooms, fantastic views of the mountain from front-facing rooms. Small, sunny pool deck on 1st floor, some gym equipment, conference centre and spa. Smart Italian restaurant on the ground floor with adjoining bar. Pleasant all-rounder, but shame about the piped muzak in the public areas.

A Metropole, 38 Long St, T021-4247274, www.metropolehotel.co.za. Long St's first boutique hotel. 45 double rooms with understated decor, huge beds, attractive dark-wood furniture and abstract prints on the walls, some rooms rather small, though. Beautiful stone bathrooms with bath and shower. Rooftop pool, with mountain views. The **M Bar & Lounge** has become a trendy after-work drinks place, and with its red ostrich-leather chairs and subdued lighting feels more like Manhattan than South Africa. Elegant restaurant on 1st floor serves a mix of Italian and modern South African cuisine. Excellent and friendly service. Recommended.

B Cape Diamond, corner of Longmarket and Parliament streets, T021-4612519, www.capediamondhotel.co.za. In a great location just round the corner from Government Av and a short walk from Long St. 60 double rooms and 3 self-catering apartments, with contemporary decor, understated colours and the occasional splash of bright, en suite. Rooftop jacuzzi, bar, **Patat** restaurant specializing in Cape cuisine. Owner-run, good value.

B Park Inn, 10 Greenmarket Sq, T021-4232050, www.parkinn.com. City centre hotel set in the historical Shell building right on bustling Greenmarket Sq. 166 rooms with pleasant neutral decor and functional, attractive bathrooms (shower only). Small pool deck with sauna and gym with view of Table Mountain. Good steak restaurant – **The Famous Butcher's Grill** – on the ground floor

with tables overlooking the market, plus pleasant, if dark, cigar bar. Excellent service, good central location and secure parking. A practical and comfortable choice.

C Daddy Long Legs, 134 Long St, T021-4223074, www.daddylonglegs.co.za. South Africa's first art hotel with 13 rooms spread across a town house, offering funky, artistic rooms – each is individually themed and designed, with walls covered in art works. Rooms are small, but the stylish, original decor makes up for it. Breakfast is offered in the café downstairs. Good value and refreshingly different. Also offers self-catering apartments on Long St, with exposed brick walls and polished wood floors.

C Tudor Hotel, Greenmarket Sq, T021-4241335, www.tudorhotel.co.za. This historic building, right on bustling Greenmarket Sq, has 26 en suite rooms, choice of doubles and family rooms, with TV, some a/c, modern but fairly bland decor, trendy bathrooms with shower. Breakfast served in stylish downstairs café, off-street parking R60 per day. Great location, friendly staff.

D-F Cat & Moose Backpackers, 305 Long St, T021-4237638, www.catandmoose.co.za. Bright set-up and central location in an atmospheric old town house. Dorms and doubles are nicely furnished but a bit dark, those at front can be noisy, some have balconies overlooking Long St, lovely courtyard with sun deck and braai, good bar, small travel centre, TV/video lounge, breakfast available, laundry room. Laid-back, friendly atmosphere.

D-F Inn Long Street, 230 Long St, T021-4241660, www.innlongstreet.co.za. Run by young, friendly South Africans, this hostel has a great location on Long St, with a wide wrap-around balcony overlooking the goings on. 3 dorms with 6 beds, and 7 private rooms (sleeping 2-4), all with polished wooden floors, simple decor. Pleasant, airy TV lounge and bar. Self-catering kitchen and laundry room. Some rooms have views of Table Mountain. One of the friendliest on Long St.

E-F Long St Backpackers, 209 Long St, T021-4230615, www.longstreetback packers.co.za. Sociable, vaguely pretentious hostel spread around leafy courtyard, 80 beds in small dorms and doubles which feel cramped, fully equipped kitchen, TV/video lounge, pool room, internet access, travel centre, free pickup. Great mosaics in some of the bathrooms. Good security with 24-hr police camera opposite. Lively atmosphere, occasional parties organized and weekly communal braais; can be noisy.

Oranjezicht, Gardens and Tamboerskloof

L Kensington Place, 38 Kensington Gardens, Higgovale, T021-4244744, www.kensingtonplace.co.za. Cape Town's original boutique hotel in a quiet, leafy area. Small and well-run with excellent and friendly service. 8 beautiful and good-sized rooms, each individually styled with Afro-chic furnishings, big bathrooms, lots of light from the large windows, great views over the city, bar, small pool and tropical gardens, breakfast served on a leafy veranda, excellent restaurant.

L Mount Nelson, 76 Orange St, Gardens, T021-4831737, www.mountnelson hotel.co.za. Cape Town's famous colonial hotel with 131 luxurious rooms and 31 'Oasis' garden suites. Emphasis is on traditional decor – lots of floral fabrics, antique-style furniture, heavy curtains, but all in bright, airy colours. Set in beautiful landscaped parkland with heated swimming pool, tennis courts, squash court and beauty centre. Rates vary widely from R4000-16,000 depending on room and season. Celebrated **Cape Colony** restaurant serves Cape specialities and contemporary fare to live jazz. Also has the **Oasis Restaurant** (well worth visiting for the daily cream teas on the veranda) and the trendy new **Planet Champagne Bar**.

AL Alta Bay, 12 Invermark Cres, Higgovale, T021-4878800, www.altabay.com. Quiet, secluded choice in fashionable Higgovale, nestled on leafy slopes just below Table

Mountain. Beautifully designed rooms use a pale palette, beige and cream fabrics, and warm wood furniture. Each room has its own private terrace, flat-screen TVs, large stone bathrooms. Plunge pool with peaceful sun deck, huge healthy buffet breakfast served in airy room or overlooking pool. Free bar and high-ceilinged lounge area. Recommended.

AL Cape Cadogan, 5 Upper Union St, Tamboerskloof, T021-4808080, www.cape cadogan.com. Ultra-elegant 2-storey mansion with 12 rooms, spacious with grass mat flooring, private terraces, subtle lighting and decor, large 4 poster beds, interesting touches like driftwood chandeliers, fabulous bathrooms, some with enormous stone walk-in showers for 2. Shady courtyard with small pool, all-white dining room with pleasant breezes. Also has 4 self-catering mews houses.

A Table Mountain Lodge, 10a Tamboers-kloof Rd, T021-4230042, www.table mountainlodge.co.za. Characterful house with 7 beautifully decorated rooms, stripped wooden floors, white linen, large spotless bathrooms, breezy and very comfortable, small garden with even smaller pool, breakfast room, tiny bar called **Jock's Trap**, owned by the very friendly and welcoming Diana and Janne Dagh. Recommended.

B Cape Milner, 2a Milner Rd, Tamboerskloof, T021-4261101, www.capemilner.com. Fashionable business-oriented hotel, popular with media types. 57 rooms spread through a modern building on a busy road, all have neutral pale grey decor and slick dark wood furniture, plus tiled bathrooms (bath and shower), and M-Net TV. Lovely pool area, with sun deck, small infinity pool and bar, popular local meeting place, and decent restaurant serving good Capetonian cuisine. Laid-back, media-savvy choice.

B Leeuwenvoet House, 93 New Church St, Tamboerskloof, T021-4241133, www.leeuwenvoet.co.za. Pronounced Loo-en-Foot, this historical guesthouse has 12 double rooms, all en suite, traditional, attractive decor, a/c, TV, telephone, excellent breakfasts, swimming pool, off-street secure parking, close to shops and restaurants but retains a peaceful atmosphere.

B Parker Cottage, 3 Carstens St, Tamboerskloof, T021-4246445, www.parker cottage.co.za. Award-winning B&B, stylish and atmospheric set in a restored Victorian bungalow, 8 bedrooms, en suite bathrooms with claw-foot baths, polished wood floors, lots of antiques, flamboyant colours with a Victorian touch, good breakfasts, friendly service, gay-friendly. Recommended.

C Cactusberry Lodge, 30 Breda St, Oranjezicht, T021-4619787, www.cactus berry.net.ms. Friendly guesthouse in a converted Victorian cottage with Oregon pine floors and high ceilings. 6 bright and airy rooms, 2 with kitchenettes, modern decor of bright white linen and muted colours, small splash pool in the courtyard, off street parking, honesty bar, Dutch spoken.

C-E The Backpack, 74 New Church St, T021-4234530, www.backpackers.co.za. Cape Town's first hostel and today one of the most comfortable and best run in town. Set across several houses with spotless dorms, doubles and en suite doubles and singles. Polished wood floors, upmarket decor, tiled courtyard and linked gardens with pool, lovely bar with TV, meals and snacks served throughout the day, one of the best backpacker travel centres around. Recommended.

D-E Ashanti Lodge, 11 Hof St, Gardens, T021-4238721, www.ashanti.co.za. One of Cape Town's best-known and most popular hostels, not least for its party atmosphere. Medium-sized dorms and small doubles in huge old house with polished wooden floors, high ceilings, large windows and communal balconies. Some rooms surround a courtyard and small pool and there are a couple of spaces for camping. Lively bar serving good snacks, with pool table and M-Net TV. Free airport and station pickup, plus good booking centre, internet access and video room. Not to everyone's liking as it is firmly on the busy overland truck route and can be very noisy, but perfect if you're looking for people to travel or party with. Also has a guesthouse (**D**) nearby with smart en suite double rooms and spotless kitchen.

D-E Zebra Crossing Backpackers, 82 New Church St, T021-4221265, www.zebra-crossing.co.za. Quiet, friendly backpacker hostel straddling 2 Victorian bungalows, spotless dorms plus small double rooms, good views of Table Mountain, internet access and travel centre, shady courtyard café and bar serving great breakfasts, snacks and meals, helpful.

De Waterkant and Green Point *p97, map p96*

L-C De Waterkant Village, 1 Loader St, De Waterkant, T021-4304444, www.villageandlife.com. Village and Life own over 50 historical Bo-Kaap style houses and apartments in the trendy Waterkant area, each stylishly and individually decorated in either cutting-edge modern decor or traditionally with antiques, sleeping 1-6, many have delightful roof terraces. They also have **Waterkant House**, a guesthouse with 9 chic rooms with all mod cons, a splash pool, beautiful lounge and terrace. Their other main property is **The Charles**, www.thecharles.co.za, a gay-friendly guesthouse with 9 lovely bright rooms, some with Victorian bath, and good views from the spacious wooden decks. Also has a fantastic range of properties across Cape Town in stylish and historical buildings. Recommended.

A The Village Lodge, 49 Napier St, De Waterkant, T021-4211106, www.thevillage lodge.com. Relative newcomer to the area, offering 15 double rooms spread across 2 converted houses. Decor is trendy greys and white, with shimmery black stone bathrooms (shower only), some with a/c, all M-Net TV, but they feel a little cramped. Attractive restaurant, **Soho**, attached, serving Thai food in slick black surrounds. Also has a choice of cottages and apartments in the area. Good location, but overpriced.

B 40 Winks Guest House, 2 Ravenscraig Rd, Green Point, T021-4347936, www.40winks

guesthouse.co.za. Comfortable set-up in a brightly painted family house set on a quiet street above Green Point. 7 en suite rooms plus 1 self-catering cottage next door sleeping 4-6, garden with pool, pleasant dining room where cooked breakfasts are served, off-street parking, friendly management.

B Cape Victoria, 13 Torbay Rd, Green Point, T021-4397721, www.capevictoria.co.za. A mix of exclusive hotel service and the privacy of a guesthouse. 10 tastefully furnished rooms with antiques, en suite bathrooms, TV, minibar and views of the sea or Table Mountain, swimming pool, booking essential. Run by the affable Lilly. Rates drop in low season.

C Atlantic Villa, 5 Norman Rd, Green Point, T021-4343222, www.atlanticvilla.co.za. Comfortable accommodation in Victorian-style terraced house, high ceilings, airy rooms, all en suite, with beach-house feel, blue and white decor, TV, minibar, good breakfasts served. Friendly and good value, no children under 12.

C Hotel Graeme, 107 Main Rd, Green Point, T021-4349282, www.hotelgraeme.co.za. Smart hotel set on the busy Main Rd, a few mins' walk to the Waterfront. 31 en suite double rooms and 5 self-catering suites sleeping 2-6, all with TV, phone, DVD, small pool deck at back, gym, secure off-street parking, laundry, internet access, business centre. Breakfast served in a glazed courtyard; also has a bar/café and an ice cream shop facing onto the street.

C-D Brenwin Guest House, 1 Thornhill Rd, Green Point, T021-4340220, www.brenwin.co.za. Guesthouse with 13 large, well-appointed rooms with en suite bathrooms, wooden floors, simple, airy decor, shady patio overlooking tidy tropical garden with swimming pool, within easy walking distance of the Waterfront. Also rents out 3 self-catering apartments each sleeping 4.

D-E Big Blue, 7 Vesperdene Rd, Green Point, T021-4390007, www.bigblue.za.net. Spotless and airy backpacker hostel set in a gorgeous

mansion dating from 1885. 86 beds in spacious dorms with bunks, single and double rooms (en suite or shared bathrooms), all with polished yellowwood floors, high ceilings, ceiling fans, yellow and orange walls and framed pictures. The doubles have great extras such as complimentary toiletries, and some have coffee-making facilities and free chocolates. Pleasant breakfast room, bar with outdoor section leading onto small pool, internet café, travel centre, TV room, spotless kitchen. Friendly and helpful staff, refreshingly un-cliquey. Recommended.

D-E Sunflower Stop, 179 Main Rd, Green Point, T021-4346535, www.sunflower stop.co.za. Dorms with a bit more room than most, smallish doubles, clean place with a huge kitchen. Pleasant garden with swimming pool, bar, satellite TV, tours and travel advice. Good location close to restaurants and bars. Free airport and city pickup.

Sea Point *p97, map p98*
This area has a holiday resort feel but has far less character than other areas in town. It does have an excellent range of accommodation, though, and there is some good nightlife towards Green Point.

L Le Vendôme, 20 London Rd, T021-4301200, www.le-vendome.co.za. Large, well-designed luxury hotel with a French theme. Traditional and very comfortable rooms and suites with a/c, TV and internet facilities. Attractive courtyard with pool, 1 restaurant overlooks the pool and serves snacks and lunch, the other is for fine dining. Secure parking.

AL The Clarendon, 67 Kloof Rd, T021-4393224, www.clarendon.co.za. Luxurious Italian-style guesthouse with 10 spacious rooms spread across main house and garden suites, plus extra house further up the street. Rooms are large and grandly furnished with posh bathrooms, some with great views of Lion's Head. Attractive garden with large pool shaded by banana trees, breakfast served on terrace, beautiful lounge, off-street parking. Also has a similar upmarket guesthouse in Bantry Bay at 158 Kloof St.

AL Winchester Mansions, 221 Beach Rd, T021-4342351, www.winchester.co.za. A well-run family hotel. 76 rooms with TV, en suite bathroom with separate shower, some with views of the Atlantic. Pleasant pool deck and new **Ginkgo Spa**. All rooms overlook a large courtyard where meals are served beneath the palms. Also has **Harvey's** restaurant, offering fusion cuisine and jazz brunches on Sun.

A The Glen, 3 The Glen, T021-4390086, www.glenhotel.co.za. Gay boutique hotel in an Italian-style villa with views of Signal Hill. Classy decor and super-trendy stone bathrooms some of which have double showers. Tropical garden with palm trees and pool, Moroccan-themed steam room with splash pool. Secure parking. Special rates out of season.

B Blackheath Lodge, 6 Blackheath Rd, T021-4392541, www.blackheathlodge.co.za. 7 smart doubles in a Victorian mansion. Large rooms with TV and minibar, attractive decor with muted colours, off-street parking, palm-fringed patio, good-sized swimming pool, no children. Good for couples.

B Olaf's, 24 Wisbeach Rd, T021-4398943, www.olafs.co.za. Relaxed guesthouse with 8 individually decorated rooms with en suite shower, telephone, a/c and M-Net TV, mix of antiques and animal prints, breezy communal areas, breakfast served on sunny patio, small pool. Well run and friendly. German spoken.

C Ashby Manor, 242 High Level Rd, T021-4341879, www.ashbyaccommo dation.co.za. 10 self-catering apartments in a medium-sized rambling Victorian house. Secure and clean rooms with kitchen facilities, some with shared bathrooms and balconies, large communal lounge and dining area, limited off-road parking, 5-min walk from Sea Point's Main Rd.

C Bellevue Manor, 5 Bellevue Rd, T021-4340375, www.bellevuemanor.co.za. Beautiful Victorian town house that is a

National Monument with double rooms and self-catering rooms on a quiet side street. wrought-iron balconies and fine palm trees, all rooms are en suite bathrooms and have homely decor, TV and laundry.

C Huijs Haerlem, 25 Main Dr, T021-4346434, www.huijshaerlem.co.za. 2 beautifully converted neighbouring houses with 4 rooms in each, connected by well-tended gardens. All rooms are en suite and extremely comfortable, with solid antique furniture, brass beds (some 4-poster), big bathrooms, fabulous sea views. Solar-heated saltwater swimming pool. Both houses have breakfast rooms and lounge. Rates go up considerably in Dec.

C Villa Rosa, 277 High Level Rd, T021-4342768, www.villa-rosa.com. Rose-coloured Victorian villa with 8 bright and comfortable rooms, traditional, appealing furnishings, original fireplaces, new stone-tiled bathrooms, all rooms en suite with TV, some with fridges, 1 family room and 1 'flatlet'. Brilliant breakfasts served with home-made breads and jams. Off-street parking, pleasant veranda with sea views. Friendly, welcoming and relaxed place to stay. Recommended.

V&A Waterfront *p99, map p100*

Generally hotels at the V&A Waterfront are aimed at the high-spending foreign visitor, and all are expensive. For cheaper accommodation within walking distance of the Waterfront, although not at night, consider Green Point, below.

L Cape Grace, West Quay Rd, driving access is from the Clock Tower side of the Water-front, T021-4107100, www.capegrace.com. This has become one of the most luxurious hotels in Cape Town. Large development, just a short walk from the main waterfront shops and restaurants. 122 spacious, comfortable rooms with all the mod cons, traditional and plush decor, balconies have views of the waterfront or the mountain, service and food is excellent, 2 bars and the celebrated **onewaterfront** restaurant. Attractive swimming pool and deck with bar opens out from the restaurant and there's a lovely rooftop spa. Room rates start from R5000.

L The Commodore, Portswood Rd, T021-4151000, www.legacyhotels.co.za. 236 elegantly furnished rooms and suites designed for comfort, quality and luxury. Rooms are decorated in a nautical theme and are all en suite with a/c, DSTV and all mod cons. Facilities include a swimming pool, gym and steam room. The **Clipper Restaurant** offers superb breakfasts and à la carte dining in a tranquil setting.

L The Table Bay, Quay 6, Waterfront, T021-7807878, www.suninternational.co.za. Enormous luxury offering from the Sun International Group, 329 top-notch rooms, what they lack in character they make up for in facilities and comfort. Large pool and sun deck, health club and spa, bar and good restaurant. Expensive by Cape Town standards, efficient service but feels ostentatious (note the sculpture by the main entrance commemorating the stays of celebrities and politicians).

L Victoria & Alfred, Pierhead, Waterfront, T021-4196677, www.vahotel.co.za. Stylishly converted warehouse with 96 rooms, spacious with cool and comfortable furnishings, king-size beds, a/c, TV with DVD player, minibar, dramatic mountain views, large marble and stone bathrooms with separate WC, some rooms have jacuzzis on the balconies. Excellent restaurant serving seafood and steaks, fashionable, airy bar attached. Friendly and efficient service. Recommended.

B-C Breakwater Lodge, Portswood Rd, Waterfront, T021-4061911, www.protea hotels.com, www.breakwaterlodge.co.za. This hotel, managed by the **Protea** group, fills what was once the notorious Breakwater Prison (1859) and is today aimed at the tour group market. The 268 rooms are fairly small but comfortable, with functional decor. Cheaper rooms share a shower and toilet with the neighbouring room. 2 restaurants, bar, conference centre.

Overpriced for what you get but cheapest option in the Waterfront.

Southern suburbs p103

These suburbs extend east of the city, along the Eastern Blvd and around Devil's Peak towards Constantia, in the following order: Woodstock, Observatory, Mowbray, Rosebank, Rondebosch, Newlands, Claremont, Kenilworth and Wynberg. All suburbs are a short drive or train journey from the city centre. Each district has its own character and plenty of shops and restaurants close by.

Woodstock and Observatory p103

C Koornhoop Manor House, 24 London Rd, Observatory, T021-4480595, www.geocities. com/koornhoop. Converted Victorian home in a large, peaceful garden, with 8 rooms, all en suite, TV, floral and homely decor, lounge and breakfast room, off-street parking. Also has 2 huge and extremely good-value self-catering apartments with 3 bedrooms, open-plan kitchens, TV lounges, private entrance and access to garden. Run by friendly English couple Vic and Trish.

D-E The Green Elephant, 57 Milton Rd, Observatory, T021-4486359, www.hostels. co.za. A full-on backpacker joint set in an old Observatory mansion, plenty going on in the area away from the city centre, dorms plus 3 double rooms, some en suite, with rustic 4-poster beds in a separate house, also a long-stay house, garden with pool and jacuzzi, small bar, pool table, TV room, laundry facilities. Happy to organize trips to the regional sights, free collection.

South of Rondesbosch p104

L Andros, corner Phyllis and Newlands roads, Upper Claremont, T021-7979777, www.andros.co.za. Grand old Cape Dutch house built in 1908 by Herbert Baker set in neat parkland, elegant and homely ambience. 8 well-appointed rooms with TV, en suite bathrooms, under-floor heating, white and cream decor, smart breakfast room, terrace and swimming pool set in gardens, gym, sauna and beauty treatments on offer. Picnic hampers and meals arranged on request. Swiss-owned so several languages spoken.

AL The Vineyard Hotel & Spa, Colinton Rd, off Protea Rd, Newlands, T021-6574500, www.vineyard.co.za. 175 a/c rooms set around an 18th-century house; the decor is a mix of Cape Dutch with yellowwood furniture and modern. The oldest part was originally built as a country house for Lady Anne Barnard in 1799. 2 restaurants, 2 cafés, spa and gym.

AL-A Harfield Guest Villa , 26 1st Av, Claremont, T021-6837376, www.har field.co.za. Award-winning, elegant B&B with 8 individually designed rooms. All are spacious, en suite, with TV, minibar and views of Table Mountain. Lounge/bar, sun deck and swimming pool, bicycle hire, secure off-street parking. Relaxing ambience during the winter months when log fires keep guests warm. Recommended.

E-F SA's The Alternative Place, 64 St Michaels Rd, Claremont, T021-6742396, www.alternativeplace.co.za. Clean dorm sleeping 4, 1 double and 1 twin room, kitchen, garden with pool, bar and braai. A small homely set-up run by Susan and Alun who have excellent Southern and East African travel experience. A bit far from the town centre, but would appeal to travellers who don't want the large backpacker scene. Free airport pickup.

❷ Eating

Capetonians like to eat out, a fact which is reflected in its multitude of restaurants – and the extent to which they get packed out. Booking ahead is often a good idea. A great starting point for choosing a restaurant is buying the latest edition of *Eat Out*, which features South Africa's best choice of restaurants and is available at CNA and Exclusive Books. Alternatively,

www.dining-out.co.za provides hundreds of reviews and contact details of restaurants throughout the country.

City Bowl *p87, maps p89 and p105*
₦₦₦ The Africa Café, Heritage Sq, 108 Shortmarket St, T021-4220221, www.africacafe.co.za. 1830-2300. African-themed restaurant geared at tour groups, offering an excellent introduction to the continent's cuisines. The menu is a set 'feast' and includes 10 dishes from around Africa, such as Egyptian-smoked fish, Kenyan patties, Cape Malay mango chicken curry and springbok stew. The price includes as many dishes you like, as well as coffee and dessert. Excellent service, but it's pricey and very touristy.

₦₦₦ Five Flies, 14 Keerom St, T021-4244442, www.fiveflies.co.za. Mon-Fri 1200-1500, daily 1900-2300. A long-standing local favourite in a historic setting. Lovely string of dining rooms, excellent menu of traditional food with a modern slant. The preferred haunt of lawyers and judges but also attracting well-heeled media types.

₦₦₦ Savoy Cabbage, Heritage Sq, 101 Hout St, T021-4242626. Mon-Fri 1200-1430, Mon-Sat 1900-2230. Widely regarded as one of the best restaurants in Cape Town, producing its own best-selling cookbook, the **Savoy Cabbage** serves beautifully prepared contemporary South African cuisine. The menu changes daily, and includes dishes such as gemsbok carpaccio, free-range duck breast and a gorgeous soft-centred chocolate pudding. Good winelist too, especially on reds. Bookings essential.

₦₦ Mama Africa, 178 Long St, T021-4248634. Mon-Sat 1900-late. Popular restaurant and bar serving 'traditional' African dishes often with great live music. Looking a little faded around the edges, but remains popular with tourists, tasty food if overpriced and notoriously slow service. Centrepiece is a bright green carved Mamba-shaped bar. Somewhat tacky but a fun place nevertheless.

Marco's African Place, 15 Rose St, T021-4235412, www.marcosafricanplace.co.za. 1200-late. Good-value 'African' menu covering everything from slow-roasted Karoo lamb to samp and beans, plus popular Pan-African platter with assortment of grilled game. Huge place with a friendly atmosphere, tasty starters but main courses can be disappointing. Daily live music.

Porcini, Heritage Sq, T021-4221300. Mon-Sat 1200-late. Large, open-plan restaurant with tables set around an indoor courtyard and a bright red bar. High-quality fusion cuisine, modern seafood dishes and some Italian pizza and pastas. Good service, but the crowd verges on pretentious. Bookings recommended.

Biesmiellah, 2 Upper Wale St, T021-4230850. Mon-Sat 1200-1500, 1800-2200. One of the better-known and well-established Malay restaurants, serving a delicious selection of Cape Malay dishes. This is the place to come for sweet lamb and chicken curries and sticky malva pudding. There's also a kiosk for takeaways. A treat for any fan of spicy food. No alcohol.

Caveau, 92 Bree St, Heritage Sq, T021-4221367. Mon-Sat 0800-late. Laid-back, stylish deli and restaurant with stone-clad walls, comfy banquettes and tables overlooking Bree St. Menu changes daily, but includes tapas, excellent cheese and meat platters, salads and adventurous mains.

Royale, 273 Long St, T021-4224536, 1200-late. Ultra-trendy eatery specializing in gourmet burgers – try the 'Miss Piggy' with bacon and guacamole, served with sweet potato fries. Attractive decor with booths and tables spilling onto the pavement. Friendly service, popular place, expect to queue (no bookings). The **Royale Kitchen**, upstairs, has the same menu and does take bookings.

Simply Asia, Heritage Sq, T021-4263363. Outlet of a popular noodle chain, with a long list of freshly prepared stir-fries, Thai curries, noodles and sweet and spicy soups.

Tables spill outside in summer, overlooking Shortmarket St. There's another branch at the Food Court in Victoria Wharf at the V&A Waterfront.

Cafés

Crush, 100 St George's Mall, T021-4225533. 0900-1700. Lunch spot spilling onto St George's Mall serving delicious and healthy wraps, salads, soups and freshly squeezed juices. Airy, cushion-filled interior if it's colder.

Mr Pickwicks, 158 Long St, T021-4233710. Mon-Sat 0830-late. Trendy spot, a favourite with pierced and tattooed Long St locals, serving the best milkshakes in town. Excellent baguettes, toasties, quiche of the day, healthy salads, large pasta portions. Pumps out loud funk and dance tunes, licensed, gets very busy with an after work crowd, open late. Also sells tickets to Cape Town's major club nights and gigs.

Rcaffé, 138 Long St, T021-4241124. Mon-Fri 0630-1700, Sat 0830-1630. Airy, high-ceilinged café serving great Italian coffees and a delicious range of cakes and pastries baked on the premises – the double-chocolate muffins are to die for. Also serves light lunches, such as butternut quiche and feta salads. Friendly service.

Sundance, Heritage Sq, 59 Buitengracht St, T021-4241461. Bare brick walls, an airy mezzanine and brisk service make this a popular choice for stylish Capetonians after a quick caffeine fix. Great choice of coffees, and excellent sandwiches on a variety of interesting breads. Wireless hotspot.

Oranjezicht, Gardens and Tamboerskloof *map p105*

Aubergine, 39 Barnet St, Gardens, T021-4654909, www.aubergine.co.za. Tue-Fri 1200-1400, Mon-Sat 1900-2230. Sophisticated and award-winning menu, modern slants on classical European dishes such as foie gras and quail, excellent wine list. One of the best in town. Stylish shaded courtyard, lounge/bar, good service.

Cape Colony, Mount Nelson Hotel, 76 Orange St, T021-4831000. 1800-2200. One of Cape Town's finest restaurants in the impressive setting of the Mount Nelson. Dishes are a mix of traditional British (think sensible roasts) and Cape classics, such as Bo-Kaap chicken and prawn curry, plus lots of game. Impeccable service, live jazz most evenings. Also has **Oasis**, where fabulous cream teas are served every afternoon for R135 from 1430.

Miller's Thumb, 10b Kloof Nek Rd, T021-4243838. Tue-Fri 1230-1430, Mon-Sat 1830-2230. Beloved by locals, bookings essential, this place serves delicious and good value seafood, plus steaks and some veggie choices, lots of spices and a Creole or Mozambique twist on some dishes. Friendly, laid-back place, there's no written menu and hostess Jane reels off each dish in a mouth-watering way.

Rozenhof, 18 Kloof St, T021-4241968. Mon-Fri 1230-1700, Mon-Sat 1900-2200. Smart restaurant set in an attractive 18th-century town house, decorated with local artwork and chandeliers, with cool wooden floors, food to match the surrounds, look out for seasonal dishes such as asparagus and springbok, good choice for vegetarians.

Saigon, corner of Camp and Kloof streets, T021-4247670. 1200-1430, 1800-2230. Superb Vietnamese cuisine, very popular place set on a corner overlooking busy Kloof St, brilliant crystal spring rolls, barbecued duck and caramelized pork with black pepper. Book ahead. Recommended.

Yindee's, 22 Camp St, Tamboerskloof, T021-4221012. Mon-Sat 1830-2300. An excellent Thai restaurant serving authentic spicy curries, stir-fries, soups and unusual deep-fried coconut ice cream for dessert. Served in a sprawling Victorian house with traditional low tables. Service can be very slow, but the place is always popular, so book ahead.

Arnold's, 60 Kloof St, Gardens, T021-4244344, www.arnolds.co.za. 0900-2300. Popular good-value breakfast and lunch spot on busy Kloof St, good salads, pasta and more substantial meals like ostrich steak. Fast, friendly service. Happy hour 1630-1830. May have to queue for a table for breakfasts at weekends.

Green's, 9 Park Rd, Gardens, T021-4224415. Mon 0800-1700, Tue-Sat 0800-2300. Pleasant café and bar in a Victorian house with sunny tables on the patio, breakfasts and light meals during the day and a more sophisticated menu in the evening. Try the freshly baked scones and cakes, crunchy salads or quiche of the day.

Yum, 2 Deer Park Dr, Vredehoek, T021-4617607. Wed-Sun 0930-2200. Stylish deli and restaurant serving excellent sandwiches, salads and original pasta dishes, such as roast lamb tortellini or goat's cheese and roasted pepper lasagne. Good service, relaxed young crowd, delicious pickles and chutneys on sale. Arrive early if you want to try their legendary weekend brunches. Recommended.

Cafés

Vida e caffe, 34 Kloof St, T021-4260627, Gardens, T021-6837288. The original of what has become the city's most successful coffee chain. Retains its quirky atmosphere, serving excellent coffees and a choice of muffins and melting hot paninis. The minimalist interior is packed throughout the day.

De Waterkant and Green Point
p97, map p96

Tank, T021-4190007, www.the-tank.co.za, Cape Quarter, Waterkant St. 1100-late. Airy, super-fashionable seafood restaurant with attractive tables spilling out onto the piazza. Inside, tables are dotted around 2 rooms, with a huge central aquarium. Good menu with daily specials, but slightly overbearing clientele.

Buena Vista Social Café, Main Rd, T021-4330611. 1200-0200. Cuban-themed bar and restaurant in a great location with balconies overlooking Main Rd. Fashionable crowd tuck into a mix of Cuban and Tex-Mex-style dishes washed down with mojitos. Live Latin music at weekend.

The Nose, Cape Quarter, Waterkant St, T021-4252200, www.thenose.co.za. Mon-Sat 0900-late. Wine bar with tables leading onto the Waterkant piazza, serving a wide range of wines accompanied by excellent seafood (the mussels in white wine and cream are especially good), steaks and burgers. Cosy interior, dishes can be ordered in large or small portions.

Wangthai, 105 Main Rd, T021-4396164. Sun-Fri 1200-1430, 1830-2300, Sat 1800-2300. Great Thai restaurant serving mouth-watering stir-fries, well known for its spicy curries with coconut milk and lemon grass. Reservations advised.

Cafés

News Café, corner of Main and Ashtead roads, T021-4346196. Open 0700-2300. Popular café and bar serving sandwiches, salads, pub meals, stylish decor, gets busy and more alcoholic in the evenings.

Sea Point p97, map p98

La Perla, corner Church and Beach roads, T021-4349538. A long-term Sea Point favourite. Extensive Italian menu specializing in seafood. Excellent anitpasto, plenty of vegetarian options, wonderful desserts. Indifferent service, though.

Tom Yum, 72 Regent Rd, T021-4348139. Open 1200-1430, 1800-2230. Simple, popular Thai restaurant serving delicious noodle and rice dishes including great seafood and ostrich stir-fries, very spicy, great tom yum soup.

New York Bagels, 51 Regent Rd, T021-4397523. Open 0700-2230 (deli closes at 2130). Cafeteria-style deli serving a good range of food, from hearty American breakfasts and smoked salmon bagels to salads, hot dogs and fish and chips. Deli shop next door sells bagels and other Jewish tit-bits to take away.

Cafés

Café Erté, 265 Main Rd, Sea Point, T021-4346624. 1000-0400. Trendy café/bar playing loud trance and techno, good breakfasts and snacks, internet access.

V&A Waterfront p99, map p100

With over 70 restaurants and cafés, the Waterfront is one of the most popular districts in Cape Town for eating out and gets very busy. There is a wide range of places to eat but prices are steeper than elsewhere.

Baia, top floor, Victoria Wharf, T021-4210935. 1200-1500, 1900-2300. Fine seafood restaurant spread over 4 terraces with moody, stylish decor and lighting. Very smart (and expensive) venue, delicious seafood dishes following a Mozambique theme – try the spicy beer-baked prawns. Very stylish with views of Table Mountain, slightly erratic service. Book ahead.

Belthazar, Victoria Wharf, T021-4213753, www.belthazar.co.za. 1200-2300. Top-of-the-range steakhouse with tables overlooking the harbour. Excellent Karan dry- and wet-cured steaks, plus range of seafood and with a staggering 600 South African wines to choose from, including 100 wines by the glass – this claims to be the world's largest wine bar.

Cape Town Fish Market, ground floor, Victoria Wharf, T021-4135977. 1100-2300. Fish restaurant, but the reason to come here is the revolving sushi bar, serving excellent sushi and sashimi. Dishes are limited but very fresh and good value.

Den Anker, Pierhead, T021-4190249, www.denanker.co.za. Daily 0900-2300. Popular Belgian restaurant and bar with a continental feel, high ceiling flying the various duchy flags, airy bar, views across Alfred Basin of Table Mountain, civilized atmosphere. Good menu serving French and Belgian dishes, lots of seafood and an impressive selection of imported bottle beers.

Emily's, Clock Tower Centre, T021-4211133. Mon-Sat 1200-2200. Very smart restaurant serving excellent French-style cuisine, superb wine list, has won several awards, great views from balcony overlooking the Waterfront, polite service, slightly fussy but popular.

¶¶ Balducci's, Victoria Wharf, T021-4216002, www.balduccis.co.za. 0900-2230. Popular, elegant Italian restaurant with seats overlooking the harbour. Good choice of pasta dishes and mains ranging from ostrich steak and luxury lamb burgers, to confit de canard and blackened kingklip. Also has a very popular sushi bar outside the front door in the mall.

¶¶ Hildebrand, Pierhead, T021-4253385, www.hildebrand.co.za. 1100-2300. Well-established Italian seafood place right on the harbour's edge, superb handmade pasta and good antipasto platters, plus traditional Italian deserts. Good reputation, but touristy given the location.

¶¶ Quay Four, T021-4192008. 1800-2230. Popular bistro above the more relaxed pub downstairs (open all day and evening). Great views over the Waterfront, seafood is the focus but also has grills and vegetarian options. Cheaper food downstairs on the deck, calamari and fish and chips served in giant frying pans and beer on tap.

Cafés

Mugg & Bean, Victoria Wharf, T021-4196451. 0830-2330, also branches in Cavendish Sq, Claremont. Café serving mouth-watering muffins, cakes and sandwiches and good bottomless coffee. Service can be slow.

Southern suburbs *p103*

Woodstock and Observatory *p103*

¶ Don Pedro's, 113 Roodebloem Rd, Woodstock, T021-4474493. Informal, bustling restaurant serving huge portions of South African food, pasta and pizza at cheap prices. Very popular, focal point of the community, great mixed crowd, book ahead.

¶ Pancho's, Lower Main Rd, Observatory, T021-4474854. 1200-late. Mexican dishes in a lively atmosphere, all the usual tacos and fajitas, good home-made nachos, big portions, nothing fancy but a fun place. Tasty cocktails – try the strawberry margarita.

Cafés

Obz Café, 115 Lower Main Rd, Observatory, T021-4485555. 0700-2400. Popular student haunt open all day for light meals, coffee or cocktails, great salads and sandwiches, also has main meals in the evenings and occasional live music.

South of Rondesbosch *p104*

¶¶¶ Au Jardin, Vineyard Hotel, Colinton Rd, Newlands, T021-6574545, www.vineyard.co.za. Mon-Sat 1200-1400, 1900-2200. A very smart hotel restaurant with a great French menu. 6-course meals or a quick plat du jour served in a stylish setting with views of the mountain. Polite service, excellent presentation. Booking always advised.

¶¶ Barristers Grill, corner of Kildare and Main streets, Newlands, T021-6717907. Mon-Sat 0930-2300, Sun 1730-2300. A popular steakhouse that has expanded into a bistro/café during the day with plenty of alfresco tables. Great steaks and ribs, plus veggie choices. Still retains the mock-Tudor timber decor of the steakhouse.

◐ Bars and clubs

City Bowl *p87, maps p89 and p105*
The *Cape Times* and *Argus* newspapers have good listings sections, as does *Cape etc* magazine, out twice a month. Nightlife around Long St is generally fairly grungy and studenty and exercise caution on the streets after dark. The more sophisticated bars and clubs are in Green Point and Camps Bay.

Chrome, Pepper St, between Long and Loop streets, T021-7006078. Wed-Sat, doors open 0900. One of Cape Town's newest clubs, aimed firmly at the serious dance crowd, mostly hip hop and R&B, large dance floor, sophisticated lighting and sound system, VIP lounges with smoother music, over 25s.

Club Tonic, 96 Long St, T072-3237621, www.clubtonic.co.za. Wed-Sat 2200-late. Spacious club with red walls, bar and sofas, hip hop, house and R&B, casual dress, also offers salsa classes on Tue from 1930.

Deluxe, corner of Longmarket and Long streets, T021-4224832. Wed, Fri and Sat 2200-0400. Popular nightclub in the centre of town, minimalist style with cosy seating areas, large dance floor, deep house, VIP room with furry walls.

Jo'burg, 218 Long St, T021-4220142. 1500-late. Trendy bar with industrial decor serving pints and cocktails to a mixed crowd, gay-friendly, relaxed during the week but gets very busy at weekends when DJs spin funky house and drum 'n' bass. Recommended.

Mama Africa, 178 Long St, T021-4248634. Mon-Sat 1900-late. Great live music played by the large green mamba snake bar every night, usually marimba, but more popular with tourists than locals.

Marvel, 236 Long St. Another fashionable watering hole, less busy than **Jo'Burg**, with vinyl booths, a dimly lit bar and chilled out tunes. The pace picks up in the evenings, when überkool kids arrive to hang out on the pavement outside.

Zula, 194 Long St. T021-4247636, www.zulabar.co.za. Wed, Fri and Sat 2100-0200. Fashionable bar and cocktail lounge with several small rooms, big sofas, hip-hop on most nights, great balcony overlooking Long St.

Oranjezicht, Gardens and Tamboerskloof

Mercury Live & Lounge, 43 de Villiers St, T021-4652106, www.mercuryl.co.za. Mon, Wed-Fri 2100-late. Live music venue and club nights, rock and hip-hop acts play regularly, also holds weekly hip-hop parties and 'nostalgia' alternative rock nights. Cape Town's leading live music venue, lively, young crowd.

Rafiki's, 13 Kloof Nek Rd, T021-4264731. 1200-0200. Popular bar overlooking Kloof

Nek with a huge wrap-around balcony perfect for a sundowner. Relaxed atmosphere, friendly crowd, DJs and occasional live music in the evenings, simple food like pizzas and burgers.

Rhodes House, 60 Queen Victoria St, Gardens, T021-4248844, www.rhodes house.com. Fri-Sat 2100-late. Rated as one of the best nightclubs in the city. Swanky lounge with dancefloor and alfresco courtyard, super-trendy decor, frequented by models and celebs. Good music, fantastic but pricey cocktails.

Green Point p97, map p96

The area around De Waterkant and Green Point is the focus of Cape Town's gay and lesbian scene, with a number of trendy bars and clubs with mixed crowds.

Blush Lounge, 43 Somerset Rd, T021-4250295, www.blushlounge.co.za. Tue-Sun 1700-late. Recently spruced up bar and club with large windows over-looking the street, 2 bars, dance floor, cocktails and sushi, moody blue and pink lighting, couches scattered around.

Bronx, 35 Somerset Rd corner Napier St, T021-4199216, www.bronx.co.za. 2000-late. Cape Town's best known and most popular gay bar and club, gets packed out at weekends, mostly men but women welcome, live DJs spin out thumping techno every night. At the time of writing it had temporarily moved into a venue across the street, while the club was being rebuilt.

Buena Vista Social Café, Main Rd, T021-4330611, www.buenavista.co.za. Mon-Fri 1200-0200, Sat and Sun 1700-0200. Cuban-themed bar and restaurant catering to a well-heeled crowd. Latin music, live bands at weekend, tasteful decor and a relaxed atmosphere, nice balcony overlooking Main Rd, great spot for sophisticated cocktails on a hot evening.

Café Manhattan, 74 Upper Waterkant St, T021-4216666. 1000-late. Cape Town's most established gay venue in a bright red building with a wraparound balcony and long bar, popular with regulars, good varied food, especially the burgers, perfect venue to start an evening out in Green Point.

Opium, 6 Dixon St, T021-4618701, www.opium.co.za. Wed-Sat 2100-late. Great mix of stylish lounge areas and decent dance music. The main bar area is huge and long, lit by pink and red lighting and with cosy booths and sofas. Gorgeous stone courtyard, overlooked by balconies. Also has regular live music. Currently the most popular club in town; expect to queue.

Sliver, 27 Somerset Rd, T021-4215798. Fashionable lounge bar, mostly gay clientele but also very popular with a trendy, mixed crowd. Relaxed atmosphere, heats up later at night.

V&A Waterfront *p99, map p100*

Cantina Tequila, Quay 5, Victoria Wharf, T021-4190207, www.cantinatequila.com. This Mexican restaurant transforms into a packed nightclub after about 2300, mostly chart music, popular with tourists.

Den Anker, Victoria and Alfred Pierhead, T021-4190249, www.denanker.co.za. Daily 0900-2300. Belgian restaurant and bar specializing in a range of Belgian draught and bottled beers.

Ferryman's Tavern, Waterfront, T021-4197748. 1100-2300. A popular haunt with restaurant upstairs, huge outside seating area, TV continually showing sports action, the olives and feta go well with the Mitchell's Beer, a lively mixed crowd.

Quay Four, T021-4192008. 1100-2400. Large shady deck overlooking the water, popular with well-heeled locals and tourists, good meals and great draught beer, one of the more pleasant pubs on the Waterfront.

Sports Café, Victoria Wharf, T021-4195558. 2200-late. Large sports bar showing matches on big screens, can get rowdy, serves American-style snacks and meals.

Southern suburbs *p103*

Observatory is the city's alternative nightlife centre and the place to head for laid-back bars and clubs with a bohemian feel, while Rondebosch and Claremont have plenty of sports bars popular with sporty types.

A Touch of Madness, Pepper Tree Sq, Nuttal Rd, Observatory, T021-4482266. 1500-late. Flamboyant bar with series of rooms decked out with tongue-in-cheek opulence, eccentric regulars, great atmosphere, good light meals, live Irish music on Thu nights.

Café Ganesh, 46 Trill Rd, Observatory, T021-4483435, www.cafeganesh.co.za. Mon-Sat 1800-late. Lively little café and bar serving hearty Cape dishes and ice-cold beers in a leafy courtyard leading to a characterful interior. Very friendly, great place to meet local characters.

Forester's Arms, Newlands Av, T021-6895949. 1100-late. Old fashioned English-style pub, popular with weird mix of suited types on their way home from work and studenty sports jocks. A fun-loving, boozy scene with a leafy beer garden and fire inside in winter.

Independent Armchair Theatre, 135 Lower Main Rd, Observatory, T021-4471514, www.armchairtheatre.co.za. 2000-late. Dark, vibey venue set in a 1950s art deco cinema, with huge sofas to lounge in, featuring films on Mon, jazz on Thu, live bands most nights, stand-up comedy from the Cape Comedy Collective on Sun. Excellent venue, with something going on every night. Recommended.

Oblivion, corner 3rd Av and Chichester Rd, Harfied Village, between Claremont and Kenilworth, T021-6718522, www.oblivion.co.za. Daily 1130-0200. No under 23s. Laid-back wine bar and restaurant, which turns into a raucous dance venue later on. Good selection of snack platters, nachos and pizzas and an impressive wine list.

⊕ Entertainment

Cinema

The 2 major cinema groups are **Nu Metro**, www.numetro.co.za, and **Ster-Kinekor**, www.sterkinekor.com. New films are released on Fri. Evening shows are very popular, booking advised especially at weekends (this is not possible over the phone with an international credit card – you'll have to go to the cinema in person). Daily newspapers and the bi-monthly *Cape etc* have full listings. There are multi-screen cinemas at Century City, the V&A Waterfront and Cavendish Sq. The latter 2 also have a separate **Cinema Nouveau**, which screens international and art-house films.

Every year in Aug, Cape Town hosts the **Encounters Documentary Film Festival**, www.encounters.co.za, with films screened at **Cinema Nouveau** and the **Labia** (see below). There is an annual gay and lesbian film festival, known as the **Out in Africa** festival, www.oia.co.za, held every year in Nov, with screenings also at Cinema Nouveau and the Labia.
Labia on Orange, 68 Orange St, Gardens, and **Labia on Kloof**, Lifestyle Centre, Kloof St, T021-4245927, www.labia.co.za. Perhaps Cape Town's most enjoyable cinema, showing independent international films in a historic building that used to be a ballroom with a café serving good pre-movie snacks. **Labia on Kloof** is the mainstream version, with 2 screens showing Hollywood releases. Both are licensed, so you can take your glass of wine into the movie.

Music

See Bars and clubs, page 118, for live music venues such as **Dizzy Jazz Café**, **Independent Armchair Theatre**, **Mama Africa** and **Mercury Live & Lounge**.
Green Dolphin, V&A Waterfront, T021-4217471, www.greendolphin.co.za. Restaurant and jazz venue featuring top local jazz groups that play while you eat, bookings advised.

Kirstenbosch Summer Concerts, www.sanbi.org, Nov-Mar every Sun at 1700. Idyllic setting, picnics on the lawns, concerts varying from folk and jazz to classical and opera, plus Carols by Candlelight at Christmas. Recommended.
V&A Waterfront Amphitheatre, outdoor venue on the Waterfront with daily concerts and live performances, mainly jazz.

Theatre

All tickets can be purchased from **Computicket**, T011-3408000, www.computicket.com. No foreign credit cards accepted over the phone or online, but there are kiosks which do accept cards at the V&A Waterfront and Cavendish Sq and the other larger malls.
Artscape, DF Malan St, Foreshore, T021-4109800, www.artscape.co.za. Major complex offering opera, theatre and music.
Baxter, Main Rd, Rondebosch, T021-6857880, www.baxter.co.za. Long-established involvement in black theatre, good reputation for supporting community theatre, international productions and musicals.
Theatre on the Bay, Link St, Camp's Bay, T021-4833301, www.theatreonthe bay.co.za. Slightly alternative shows, licensed, interesting mix of plays, comedy and musicals.

⊗ Festivals and events

Celebrations are a serious business in Cape Town, and during the summer months you'll be hard pressed to find a free weekend. Street carnivals and festivals compete with cultural and sporting events, although publicity is often limited. See *The Cape Times* or www.tourismcapetown.co.za, for more listings.

January

Karnaval, 2 Jan, begins in the Bo-Kaap district and ends up in the Green Point Stadium. This, the city's most popular festival, includes a procession of competing minstrel bands, complete with painted faces, straw boaters and bright satin suits.

J&B Metropolitan Handicap, last Sat in Jan, www.jbmet.co.za, South Africa's major horse racing meet at Kenilworth Race Course, where everyone is expected to dress up. The 2007 theme was black, white and bling.

February/March
Cape Town Pride,
www.capetownpride.co.za. The biggest gay event in town, floats and a parade around Green Point culminating in a street party.

March
Cape Town Festival,
www.capetownfestival.co.za. Week-long arts and cultural festival held at the end of the month, various venues.

Cape Town International Jazz Festival, International Convention Centre, www.capetownjazzfest.com. 5 stages with a huge array of local and international jazz artists, last weekend in Mar.

Cape Argus Pick 'n' Pay Cycle Tour, www.cycletour.co.za. World's largest timed cycling event taking an impressive 109-km route around Table Mountain and along the shores of the peninsula. It's open to international cyclists and attracts some 40,000 participants each year.

Two Oceans Marathon, www.twooceansmarathon.org.za. 56-km race with over 9000 competitors, last weekend in Mar.

April
Start of Rugby season, at Newlands, www.wprugby.com.

June
Red Bull Big Wave, Hout Bay,
www.redbullbwa.com. Surf festival where professionals only surf waves that are at least 5 m high.

Cape Times Wine Festival, V&A Waterfront, www.waterfront.co.za. You can taste 300 wines from 85 estates, and there's a cheese hall, last weekend in Aug.

September
Hermanus Whale Festival,
www.whalefestival.co.za. Marks beginning of calving season of southern right whales, excellent viewing, last week in Sep, an easy day trip from Cape Town.

October
Cape Town Comedy Festival, Baxter
Theatre, week-long festival featuring local and international talent.

November
Cape Times/Discovery Health Big Walk,
www.bigwalk.co.za. World's largest timed walk started in 1903 attracting 25,000 on walks from 5-80 km.

December
Obz Festival, Observatory,
www.obzfestival.com, huge street party with stalls, live music and all-nights parties.

Clifton Challenge, Clifton Beach 4, www.clifton.co.za. Fitness challenge between Springbok rugby team and Clifton lifesavers, the event for beautiful people.

Kirstenbosch Summer Concerts, www.sanbi.org, every Sun until Mar. Picnics on the lawns, concerts varying from folk and jazz to classical and opera.

O Shopping

Arts, crafts and curios
African Image, 52 Burg St, T021-4238385, www.african-image.co.za. Excellent alternative to the tired souvenir shops, this gallery sells contemporary African art, such as bags made from traditional weavings, beautiful baskets, old township signs, photography, plus quirky souvenirs like coke-bottle-top bags and chickens made from colourful plastic bags. Also has an outlet in Victoria Wharf, V&A Waterfront.

Greenmarket Square Market, lively market selling crafts, textiles and clothes from across the continent. Be prepared to take part in some cheerful haggling.

Monkeybiz, Rose St, Bo-Kaap, T021-4260636, www.monkeybiz.co.za. Something of a local sensation, **Monkeybiz** creates employment for women (many of them HIV positive) in the townships of Mandela Park and Khayelitsha. The women create beautiful and quirky one-off bead works, including figures, animals and accessories.

Out of This World, V&A Waterfront, T021-4193246. One of many African arts and crafts shops at the Waterfront, better value and a more tasteful selection than many.

The Pan African Market, Long St, T021-4264478, www.panafrican.co.za. 2-storey centre set in a converted Victorian house, selling crafts from across the continent, good local crafts made from recycled material, beadwork, ceramics. Café specializing in African food, plus a book shop and holistic healing area.

Red Shed Craft Workshop, part of Victoria Wharf shopping centre. Handful of local craftsmen, goods are of suspect taste, kitsch embroidery and satin cushions, that sort of thing.

Streetwires, 77 Shortmarket St, T021-4262475, www.streetwires.co.za. Building housing a wire sculpture cooperative, useful place to browse these interesting South African craft works without feeling under pressure from the usual street vendors.

Books and maps

Bell-Roberts, 89 Bree St, T021-4221100, www.bell-roberts.com. Gallery and publishing house specializing in art books.

Clarke's Bookshop, 211 Long St, T021-4235739, www.clarkesbooks.co.za. A mass of antiquarian, 2nd-hand and new books in a muddled old shop, a must for any book lover.

CNA (Central News Agencies). A city-wide chain of shops carrying a reasonable stock of guide books, glossy coffee-table publications, some colourful maps, foreign newspapers and magazines.

Exclusive Books. A more upmarket chain with branches at the Waterfront and Cavendish Sq Mall. Good for travel and coffee-table books.

The Map Studio, www.mapstudio.co.za. Tourist maps of towns and regions as well as official survey maps. For sale in Exclusive Books.

Select Books, 232 Long St, T021-4246955, www.selectbooks.co.za. Something of a local institution, with a pleasantly ordered interior and vast range of books on the country and Southern Africa, including great contemporary choices.

Wordsworth Books, Gardens Centre, T021-4618464, and V&A Waterfront, T021-4256880. Knowledgeable staff assist in this comprehensive bookstore. They also have an outlet in the V&A Waterfront, the **Traveller's Bookshop**, completely dedicated to guide books, maps and books about South Africa.

Clothes

Long St and Kloof St in the City Bowl have become the powerhouse of Cape Town's fashion scene, and have a good choice of kooky boutiques selling one-offs and locally designed clothes and accessories. For better-known clothes chains and upmarket boutiques, head to the shopping malls. Particularly popular with the young and well-heeled are the units in Victoria Wharf, at the Waterfront, T021-4087600, www.waterfront.co.za, and Cavendish Sq, in Claremont, T021-6575620, www.cavendish.co.za. Prices here are only marginally cheaper than in Europe.

Markets

Church St Antiques Market, on Church St, between Long and Burg streets, Mon-Sat 0900-1400. Offbeat antiques, most interesting pieces shown on Fri and Sat.

Grand Parade Market, Mon-Sat 0800-1400. General market at the large parade ground in front of the old City Hall, selling clothes, fabrics and flowers.

Greenmarket Square, Mon-Sat 0900-1600. A lively arts and crafts market on a picturesque cobbled square, goods from across Africa, formerly a fruit and vegetable market, flanked by several terrace cafés.

Green Point Market, beside Green Point Stadium, Sun 0800-1700. Good mixture of curios, one lane of food stalls, plenty of buskers.

Music

CD Warehouse, www.cdwarehouse.co.za, has a massive branch at the V&A Waterfront just south of Nobel Square in its own building with a full range of CDs and DVDs. Particularly strong on African music.

Musica, www.musica.co.za, is the biggest music shop chain, selling all the latest CDs, videos and DVDs, and can be found in every shopping centre and along high streets.

The African Music Store, 134 Long St, T021-4260857, www.africanmusicstore.co.za. Stocks an excellent choice of albums by major Southern African artists as well as compilations and reggae. The staff are incredibly helpful and are happy to let you listen to any number of Cds before purchasing.

Supermarkets

Each of the suburbs has its own shopping complex with a branch of one of the major supermarket chains – **Pick 'n' Pay**, **Chequers**, **Shoprite**, **OK Bazaar** and **Spar**. For high-quality groceries head to **Woolworths** which is much the same as Marks & Spencer in Britain, with equivalent prices.

▲ Activities and tours

With its equitable climate and outdoor lifestyle, Cape Town's adventure sports scene has boomed in recent years. Most of the backpacker hostels promote a huge choice of activities, particularly the more strenuous and action-packed such as kloofing, abseiling or paragliding.

Abseiling

Abseil Africa, T021-4244760, www.abseilafrica.co.za. Operates one of the world's highest and longest commercial abseils – 112 m down Table Mountain – R395 excluding cable car fee. Also runs day trips to other abseil points around the Cape.

Cricket

In the southern suburb of Newlands is the famous **Sahara Park Cape Town Test Match Ground**, 161 Camp Ground Rd, for fixtures contact, T021-6572003, www.cricket.co.za, tickets Computicket, T011-3408000, www.computicket.com. Despite considerable redevelopment, a few of the famous old oak trees remain and it is still possible to watch a game from a grassy bank with Table Mountain as a backdrop. Some of the public seats are very exposed – wear a hat and have plenty of sun cream to hand. Since the demolition of Green Point stadium, it's also become the venue for rock concerts. (Elton John played here in early 2008.)

Fishing

The most common catches are mako shark, long-fin tuna and yellowtail, but there are strict rules governing all types of fishing. The simplest way of dealing with permits and regulations is through a charter company.

Hooked on Africa, T021-7905332, www.hookedonafrica.co.za. Deep-sea tuna trips, in-shore light tackle and fly fishing and crayfish charters. Leaves from Hout Bay. 4 boats to choose from, all gear supplied.

Nauticat Charters, T021-7907278, www.nauticatcharters.co.za. Game fishing and boat charters, also operates from Hout Bay.

Golf

For further details contact the **Western Province Golf Union**, T021-6861668, www.wpgu.co.za. Expect to pay green fees of around R200 for 18 holes. The following golf clubs are open to overseas visitors:

Milnerton Golf Club, Bridge Rd, Milnerton, T021-5521047, www.milnertongolfclub.co.za. 6011 m, par 72. This is a true links course in the shadow of Table Mountain, watch your par when the wind blows. A popular course set between the Atlantic Ocean and a river.

Mowbray Golf Club, Ratenherg Rd, Mowbray, T021-6853018, www.mowbraygolfclub.co.za. One of the oldest clubs, hosts national championships, a par-74 course with plenty of trees, bunkers and water holes.

Rondebosch Golf Club, Klipfontein, Rondebosch, T021-6894176, www.ronde bosch-golf-club.co.za. A tidy course with the Black River flowing through it.

Royal Cape Golf Club, 174 Ottery Rd, Wynberg, T021-7616551, www.royalcape golf.co.za. Length: 6174 m, par 74. An old course that has been the venue for major professional tournaments.

Simon's Town Country Club, T021-7861233, www.golf.ifm2.com/simonstown. A 9-hole, 18-tee, links course on the seafront, just by the turning for Boulders Beach. This is a narrow course and is a real test for anyone not used to playing in very windy conditions.

Hiking

Active Africa, T021-7886083, www.active-africa.com. Leading operator organizing walking tours on Table Mountain and Cape Point, plus hiking trips to the Winelands and the Garden Route. All transport, food and guides included in price.

Due South, T083-2584824 (mob), www.hikesandtours.co.za. Organizes half- and full-day walking trips up Table Mountain. Rates include transport to the start point for your hike, snacks and water, and a packed lunch on full-day hikes.

Horse riding

There are plenty of interesting riding trails around the city, and Nordhoek Beach is especially popular at sundown.

Imhoff Equestrian Centre, T082-7741191 (mob), www.horseriding.co.za.

Sleepy Hollow Horse Riding, T021-7892341, www.sleepyhollowhorseriding.co.za.

Kitesurfing

The Cape's strong winds have made it a very popular site for kitesurfing. The best spot is Dolphin Beach at Table View, north of the city centre where winds are strong and waves perfect for jumping.

Downhill Adventures, T021-4220388, www.downhilladventures.com. Offers beginners tuition from R600 per lesson and recommends 3 sessions before going alone.

Kloofing

Kloofing (canyoning) involves hiking, boulder-hopping and swimming along mountain rivers. It is very popular on and around Table Mountain; many of the tour operators listed on page 127 organize daily excursions.

Mountain biking

Downhill Adventures, T021-4220388, www.downhilladventures.com. Organizes a range of mountain-biking excursions, including the popular Table Mountain double descent (90% downhill), rides around Cape Point and the Winelands Meander. Also offers bike rentals.

Homeland, 305 Long St, T021-4260294, www.homeland.co.za. Mountain-bike rentals cost R80 for 24 hrs; cheaper rates the longer you hire. Also rents out surf boards, paddle skis and wet suits.

Paragliding

Paragliding from Lion's Head is very popular, with gliders landing by the sea between Clifton and Camps Bay. For tandem paragliding sessions contact **Para Pax**, T082-8814724 (mob), www.parapax.com.

Flights cost R850 and include pickup and drop-off, drinks and refreshments.

Rugby

International games are played at the **Western Province Rugby Football Union** ground, Boundary Rd, Newlands, T021-6594600, www.wprugby.co.za. Tickets for major games can be bought through **Computicket**, T011-3408000, www.computicket.com.

Sailing

Regattas are regularly held in Table Bay. **Royal Cape Yacht Club**, Small Craft Harbour, Duncan Rd, T021-4211354, www.rcyc.co.za. The club is for members only, but accommodates visitors if they are a member of an affiliated international club and offers visitors free rides with a member on Wed evening twilight sails.

Table Bay is not a bad place to learn to sail and **Yachtmaster**, T021-7881009, www.yachtmaster.co.za, offers a number of courses. For charters and day-trips, see Boat tours, page 128.

Sandboarding

Try the latest addition to board sports on sand dunes. It is not a very fast sport and can be frustrating if you're used to snow, but it can be a fun day out.
Downhill Adventures, T021-4220388, www.downhilladventures.com. Organizes day trips to dunes about 1 hr from Cape Town.

Scuba diving

The Cape waters are cold but are often very clear and good for wreck and kelp diving. The best season for diving is during the winter months when the weather ensures the sea is flat as the prevailing winds blow offshore. Water temperatures are between 12°C-18°C; visibility is usually between 5-10 m. When the winds change direction in the summer months visibility can be reduced to almost zero. There are a number of interesting wreck dives along the coast and most sites can be reached direct from the shore. A number of dive companies also specialize in great white shark cage dives.
Dive Action, 22 Carlisle St. Paarden Island, T021-5110800, www.scubadivecape town.co.za. Full dive shop and training centre offering a range of wreck, shore and coral dives around the Cape.
Great White Ecoventures, T021-5300470, www.white-shark-diving.com. Runs cage diving trips to see great white sharks in Gansbaai, a 2-hr drive away. Can arrange transfers from Cape Town.
Scuba Shack, 289 Long St, T021-4249368, www.scuba-shack.co.za; also in Kommetjie on the peninsula, T021-7856742. Well-run local scuba diving school. Full range of PADI-recognized instruction and equipment hire, as well as organized tours to the best dive sites and great white shark cage dives.
Table Bay Diving, Quay 5, V&A Waterfront, T021-4198822, www.tablebaydiving.com. Dive charters and full range of PADI courses, and sells scuba and snorkelling gear.

Skydiving

Skydive Cape Town, T082-8006290 (mob), www.skydivecapetown.za.net. Offers tandem jumps and static-line courses on the West Coast for R1250.

Snooker and pool

Rolling Stones, popular pool bar chain with branches on Long St, and in Observatory and Claremont. Plenty of tables, loud music, good atmosphere, open till late.

Surfing

Surfing is a serious business in Cape Town, and there are excellent breaks catering for learners right through to experienced surf rats. Some of the best breaks are on **Long Beach, Kommetjie, Noordhoek, Llandudno, Kalk Bay, Muizenberg** and **Bloubergstrand**. Daily surf report: T082-2346370.
Downhill Adventures, T021-4220388, www.downhilladventures.com. Organizes

day and multi-day courses from R595 per day as well as 'Secret Surf Spots' tours. **Homeland**, 305 Long St, T021-4260294, www.homeland.co.za, rents out surf boards and wet suits (essential) to experienced surfers.

Swimming

The beaches on the Atlantic seaboard are almost always too cold to swim in – even during the hottest months, the water temperatures rarely creep above 16°C. Camps Bay has a tidal pool and shady, grassy areas, see page 133. **Nordhoek** is too rough for swimming, but is a great place for kite-flying or a horse ride, see page 134. False Bay is always a good 5°C warmer, and is perfectly pleasant for a dip during summer. **Boulders Beach** is one of the most attractive beaches on the False Bay seaboard and is also the best place for spotting African penguins, see page 144. **Fish Hoek** has a pleasant beach with small waves and a playground, see page 142. Additionally, a number of beaches have artificial rock pools built by the water, which although rather murky can be perfect for paddling children. There are some very good municipal swimming pools in Cape Town, in Newlands, Sea Point and Woodstock. All are open air and with views of the mountain.

Tour operators

For information about a city tour in an open-top bus with **Sightseeing Cape Town**, visit www.citysightseeing.co.za or see Getting around, page 78. There are a diverse range of day tours in and around Cape Town available through the operators below. Expect to pay in the region of R300 for a half-day tour and R500 for a full day. The 3 most popular are tours of the Cape Peninsula, the Winelands and the townships. Peninsula tours generally go down the west side to Hout Bay and offer an optional boat trip to see the seals on Duiker Island, then go over Chapman's Peak Drive and into the Table Mountain National Park to Cape Point. They return to the city on the eastern side with a stop to see the penguins at Boulders Beach. Winelands tours take in about half a dozen vineyards in the Stellenbosch and Paarl regions. Township tours usually begin at the District Six Museum and continue to Langa and Khayelitsha, and companies work with the communities they visit, putting back some of the proceeds. If you want to combine a half-day township tour with the excursion to Robben Island, all operators will drop off at the ferry. For a full list of tour operators visit www.tourismcapetown.co.za.

Day tours

Andulela Experience, T021-7902590, www.andulela.com. Verry different township tours that focus on music and poetry, jazz and soccer and a day trip in Bo-Kaap that includes a walking tour, Cape Malay cookery lessons and meals.

Cape Capers, T021-4483117, www.tourcapers.co.za. Cultural tours led by Faisal Gangat who won the 'Tourist Guide of the Year' award in 2003 and 2004. Range of trips, including half-day tours looking at Cape Town's slave history, District Six and Bo-Kaap tours and the Urban Trail of Two Cities. Recommended.

Cape Rainbow Tours, T021-5515465, www.caperainbow.com. Tours run in many European languages to the townships, Winelands, Peninsula and, in season, to the West Coast to see the flowers and Hermanus for whales.

Day Trippers, T021-5114766, www.daytrippers.co.za. Peninsula tours which include 1 or 2 hrs of cycling at Cape Point, Winelands, township, Table Mountain hike and the Whale Coast. Good value and fun, popular with backpackers.

Endeavour Safaris, T021-5566114, www.endeavour-safaris.com. All Cape Town day trips for the frail and physically challenged, with specially adapted vehicles and trained guides, penisular, Robben Island and District Six, Table Mountain and Kirstenbosch, Winelands.

Downhill Adventures, T021-4220388, www.downhilladventures.com. Rents out bikes and organizes adventure tours on Table Mountain, Cape Point, along the coast and in the Winelands.

The Eco-Ist, T082-4799688 (mob), www.eco-tourisminvestments.co.za. Special interest tours with a focus on environment, flora and fauna. Trips go to Table Mountain, Kirstenbosch and the West Coast. No more than 6 people per trip.

Friends of Dorothy, T021-4651871, www.friendsofdorothytours.co.za. Gay-friendly tours, including a Four Passes tour, Peninsula, Winelands and whale-watching trips. Gay drivers and guides, max 6.

Footsteps to Freedom, T083-4521112, www.footstepstofreedom.co.za. Mon-Sat 1030-1330, R100. Starting at the tourist office this is a historical walking tour of central Cape Town which goes to the Castle, District Six Museum and Company's Garden and can be combined with a township minibus tour later in the afternoon. English and German spoken. Recommended to get the most out of the city centre's attractions.

Homeland, T021-4260294, www.homeland.co.za. Cape Point Classic tour, which includes biking, a braai lunch and transport in an open-sided overland truck.

Hylton Ross, T021-5111784, www.hyltonross.com. Full range of day tours, Cape Point with optional boat ride to see the seals from Hout Bay, winelands, township, and longer trips to the Garden Route. 10% of fees go towards the Tourism Community Development Trust, www.tcdtrust.org.za.

Tana-Baru Tours, T021-4240719, www.bokaap.co.za. Specialist tours of the Bo-Kaap lasting 2 hrs starting from the Bo-Kaap Museum, interesting and good value at R100 per person, including Cape Malay tea in a private home.

Wanderwomen, T021-7889988, www.wanderwomen.co.za. Professional tours run by and for lesbians around Cape Town and along the Garden Route.

Boat tours
See also page 102 for Robben Island Tours.
Nauticat, T021-7907278, www.nauticatcharters.co.za. Daily cruises from Hout Bay to see the seals at Duiker Island in a glass-bottomed boat.

Spirit of Just Nuisance, Simonstown T082-2577760 (mob), www.boatcompany.co.za. Short tours around the harbour area which include a special visit to the naval dockyard. Also organizes longer trips to Seal Island and Cape Point, and can be chartered for private cruises. Regular departures from the main pier.

Tigger Too, T021-7905256, www.tiggertoo.co.za. Upmarket outfit with daily departures from the Waterfront, sunset cruises and day trips, fishing can be organized, booking advised during peak periods.

Waterfront Boat Company, Quay 5, V&A Waterfront, T021-4185806, www.waterfrontboats.co.za. 6 boats to choose from including large catamaran and stylish yacht, range of boat tours including around Robben Island, whale watching, sunset and dinner cruises. Prices from R190 for 1½-hr sunset cruise, jet boat from R250, 1-hr.

Whale watching
The whale-watching season starts in Oct. Rules surrounding trips to the see the whales are very stringent, and only one boat a year is given a permit to run whale-watching cruises. These change every year, check with the helpful tourist office in Simonstown, T021-7865798, www.simonstown.com.

Windsurfing
Langebaan has the best reputation for surfable winds on the Cape; the southeasterly roars between Sep and Apr. In Mar there is a **Boardsailing Marathon** in False Bay, while **Big Bay** at Blouberg is a good spot for wave-jumping. Daily windsurf report: T082-2346324 (mob). For more information visit www.capetownwindsurf.com.

Cape Oasis Windsurfing, T076-8931274, www.windsurfingcapetown.com, offers equipment and tuition and accommodation in their own guesthouse in Table View.

⊝ Transport

Air

See also Ins and outs, page 78, for details of getting to/from the airport. Departure tax is included in the ticket price.

South African Airways (SAA) and its subsidiaries have numerous flights every day to every city in South Africa. **British Airways/Comair** has several flights/day to **Johannesburg**. Kulula flies to **Port Elizabeth, Durban** and **Johannesburg**. **Mango** has daily flights to **Bloemfontein, Johannesburg** and **Durban**. Nationwide has daily flights to **Johannesburg, George, Port Elizabeth, Durban** and **Nelspruit**. **One Time** has flights to **Bloemfontein, Johannesburg, Port Elizabeth** and **Durban**.

Airline offices

South African Airways (SAA), central reservations, T011-9781111, ww2.flysaa.com. **British Airways/Comair**, T011-4418600, www.britishairways.com. **Kulula**, T0861-585852 (in South Africa), T011-9210111 (from overseas), www.kulula.com. **Mango**, T0861-162646 (in South Africa), T011-3591222 (from overseas), ww5.flymango.com. **Nationwide**, T0861-737737, www.flynationwide.co.za. **One Time**, T0861-345345 (in South Africa), T011-9288000 (from overseas), www.1time.co.za.

Bus

Greyhound, Intercape and **Translux** all depart/arrive from Adderley St, next to Cape Town railway station. Booking offices are also here. Buses head north up the N7 to **Upington** and **Windhoek** in Namibia, east

along the N2 to **Knysna, Port Elizabeth** and **Durban**, and northeast up the N1 to **Bloemfontein, Kimberley, Johannesburg** and **Pretoria**. Full timetables can be found on the websites and tickets can be booked online.

Budget buses

The **Baz Bus** has a daily service from Cape Town to **Port Elizabeth**. The service continues from Port Elizabeth to **Durban**, the following day, for where there are 2 routes to **Johannesburg** and **Pretoria**. See page 41 for details.

Bus companies

Baz Bus, T021-4392323, www.bazbus.com, **Greyhound**, T083-9159000 (in South Africa), T011-2768550 (from overseas), www.greyhound.co.za. **Intercape**, T0861-287287 (in South Africa), T012-3804400 (from overseas), www.intercape.co.za. **Translux**, T0861-589282 (in South Africa), T011-774333 (from overseas), www.translux.co.za.

Car
Car hire

Cape Town and the surrounding Winelands are best explored in a hired car. The cheapest local car hire companies change frequently – it's a good idea to check at backpacker hostels to see which ones they recommend. See page 41 for further advice on car hire and driving.

Atlantic Car Hire, T021-9344600, www.atlanticcarhire.co.za.
Avis, T0861-021111, www.avis.co.za.
Budget, T0861-016622, www.budget.co.za.
Britz Africa, T011-3961445, www.britz.co.za. Contact for camper vans and motorhomes for travel in and beyond South Africa. Good all-inclusive deals.
Camper King, T021-5582203, www.camper king.co.za. Campers and motor homes.
Cape Car Hire, T021-3830445, www.capecarhire.co.za.
Imperial/Europcar, T0800-011344, www.europcar.co.za, www.imperialcarrental.co.za.
Hertz, T0861-600136, www.hertz.co.za.

Metro

The suburban train service, **Metrorail**, T0800-656463, www.mti.co.za, serves the suburbs. Services run as far as Simon's Town, but also go out as far as Strand. These trains are fine to use in rush hour (0700-0800 and 1600-1800), but are best avoided at quieter times due to safety issues and avoid the routes to the east, which pass through the Cape Flats.

Taxi

There are several ranks dotted around town – the most useful ones are outside the train station at Adderley St, in Greenmarket Sq, and on Long St. If you are outside the city centre, you will have to call one in advance or ask your hotel or restaurant to call one for you.

Rikki Taxis, T0861-745547, www.rikkis.co.za, can be seen buzzing around all over Cape Town. The small, shared people-carriers have now been replaced by a fleet of London black cabs. They are a cheaper alternative to regular taxis for getting around the city. You need to call one, but they pick up several people along the route, which brings down costs. They operate Mon-Thu 0630-2400 and Fri-Sun 24 hrs, and costs vary from R12-20 depending on the distance. They only operate in the City Bowl and Atlantic Seaboard as far as Camps Bay, but a few people can charter one to get to somewhere like Kirstenbosch, for example. There is also another fleet of Rikki's that operates in the Simon's Town area, T021-7862136, daily 0700-1700. Back in the city, there are now 14 **Rikki phones** at some backpacker hostels, supermarkets and petrol stations, from where you can phone a **Rikki** for free. If you happen to see one in the street, you can flag it down.

Minibus taxis

These serve all areas of the city on fixed routes, and leave from the minibus terminal accessed from the top floor of the **Sanlam Golden Acre** shopping centre on Adderley St. They can also be flagged down from the street. Minibuses to the Atlantic Seaboard usually leave from the corner of Strand and Plein St. Most trips cost around R5. Minibuses stop running at 1900. These are generally safe to use, although you'd be advised to do your best not to look like a tourist and leave all valuables at home. Avoid taking them on the highways, too, as they have high accident rates.

Train

Cape Town has one main railway station in the centre of town. Both long-distance and suburban services leave from here. Leaflets with train times and fare structure are available in the concourse. The rail network is run by **Spoornet**, www.spoor net.co.za. For more details of all train travel, including luxury services between Cape Town and Pretoria, see page 40.

ⓘ Directory

Banks

Only change money in hotels as a last resort: their exchange rates are unbelievably poor. There are plenty of 24-hr ATMs throughout the city, and most banks cash TCs. All the main branches are open Mon-Fri 0830-1530 and Sat 0800-1100.

There are 2 main bureaux de change: **American Express**, T021-4218920, lower level, Victoria Wharf V&A Waterfront, open Mon-Sat 0900-2100, who will receive and hold mail for card holders. There are also several branches of **Master Currency** at the V&A Waterfront which stay open until 2100.

Embassies and consulates

Most foreign representatives have their embassies in Pretoria, but some have consulates in Cape Town. **Canada**, Reserve Bank Building, St George's Mall, T021-

4235240. **Denmark**, 5 Tokai Rd, Tokai, T021-7157019. **France**, 78 Queen Victoria St, Gardens, T021-4231575. **Germany**, Safmarine House, 22 Riebeek St, T021-4053000. **Mozambique**, 45 Castle St, T021-4262944, visas issued within 24 hrs. **Netherlands**, 100 Strand St, T021-2156601. **UK**, 91 Parliament St, T021-4617220. **USA**, 7th Floor, Broadway Building, Foreshore, T021-4610853.

Emergencies

Fire, 10111; **Medical**, 10177; **Police**, 10111; **Sea rescue**: T021-4053500. **All emergencies from a cell phone**, 112.

Internet

Access is available at hotels and backpacker hostels, **Postnet** branches (see Telephone, below) and at the main tourist office. **Virtual Turtle** is a 24-hr internet café on the 1st floor of the Purple Turtle building, Short Market St, T021 4241037. **m@in internet café**, Lifestyle Centre, 50 Kloof St, T021-4223431, and outlet at 37 Roeland St, T021-4623248. Also has Wi-Fi for lap-top users. **Catwalk**, 251 Main Rd, Sea Point, T021-4248899 and 16 Burg St, T021-4238899. Huge internet cafés with dozens of screens, excellent value at R10 per hr, open 24 hrs and serves range of sandwiches and burgers.

There are also Internet cafes in all the shopping malls and Wi-Fi at many of the chain coffee shops and at the airport.

Medical services

Casualty facilities are available at **City Park**, Longmarket St, T021-4806111, 24 hrs; and **Cape Town Medi-clinic**, 14 Hof St, Gardens, T021-4645555. **Netcare Travel Clinic**, 11th floor, Picbel Parkade, Strand St, T021-4193172, www.travelclinic.co.za.

Newspapers

Cape Town has an English morning paper, the *Cape Times*, and an evening paper, the *Argus*. Both are good sources of what's going on in the city, with daily listings and entertainment sections. There is also a daily paper in Afrikaans, *Die Burger*.

Post office

Post offices are found in the principal shopping malls and are generally open Mon-Fri 0800-1630, Sat 0800-1200.

Radio

Radio KFM: 94.5 FM, contemporary music, mix of old classics and new hits. **Radio Good Hope FM**: 94-97 FM, teenage pop music, current hits. **Radio Lotus**: 97.8 FM, general Indian affairs and music.

Telephone

Postnet is a useful chain found throughout the city, usually in shopping malls. The main branch is in the Union Castle Building, 6 Hout St, T021-4260839, www.postnet.co.za, open Mon-Fri 0830-1700, Sat 0830-1300. Services include sending parcels, internet access, fax sending and receiving, phonecards, passport photos.

Tickets

Computicket: T011-3408000, www.computicket.com, for nationwide bus tickets, theatre, concerts and sport events.

Weather

Weather reports: T082-2339900, www.weathersa.co.za.

Wildlife and conservation

Cape Nature Conservation: T021-6593500, www.capenature.co.za.
South African National Parks (SANParks): www.sanparks.org, has a desk at the main tourist office.

The Cape Peninsula

The most popular day trip from central Cape Town is a leisurely loop around the Cape Peninsula. The stunning coast road winds its way through the city's swanky suburbs on the Atlantic Seaboard on the western side, down to Cape Point and the Cape of Good Hope at the southern tip of the peninsula, and then up again through the quaint fishing settlements on the False Bay coast on the eastern side. This can be done under your own steam and a day's hire car is an ideal way to explore at your own pace; alternatively, all the tour operators offer the excursion – some take mountain bikes too, for a spot of cycling in the Table Mountain National Park. As well as fine ocean and mountain views, there are a number attractions to stop for including the boat trip from Hout Bay to see the seals on Duiker Island, the spectacularly scenic Chapman's Peak Drive, climbing to the lighthouse at Cape Point, and the penguins at Boulders Beach. There are also ample places to stop for lunch, be it simple fish and chips or a gourmet meal, and there are many tourist shops, art galleries and roadside stalls to grab your attention along the way. ▸▸ *For listings, see pages 145-150. See also Activities and tours, page 124, and Transport, page 129.*

Atlantic Seaboard ●❷❶ ▸▸ *pp145-150. Colour map 8, B1.*

The Atlantic Seaboard refers to Cape Town's wealthy suburbs on the west side of the peninsula. Exclusive Clifton, Camps Bay and Llandudno have some of Cape Town's most sought after properties and whitewashed modern mansions and luxury apartments with their brilliantly blue swimming pools climb up the hillsides, while the pristine beaches are popular with the beautiful people. Further south the road winds its way above the rocky shoreline and below the magnificent Twelve Apostles, the spine of mountains from the back of Table Mountain, before dropping into Hout Bay and the back end of the Constantia Valley, before continuing south towards Cape Point.

Ins and out

The tour operators take the Atlantic Seaboard route on Cape Peninsula day tours, but a car is a logical option if you want to stop. Some minibus taxis from central Cape Town go beyond Green Point and Sea Point as far as the police station on the main seaside strip of Camps Bay. Golden Arrow buses also ply this route and some (roughly one an hour) continue on to Hout Bay. The Sightseeing Cape Town bus (see page 78) goes as far as Hout Bay on its Blue Route.

Clifton Beach

Cape Town's best-known beaches stretch along Clifton, and are renowned as the playground of the young and wealthy – this is the place to see and be seen. Other than being hotpots of high society, Clifton's four sheltered beaches are stunning, perfect arches of powder-soft white sand sloping gently into turquoise water. The beaches, reached be a series of winding footpaths, are divided by rocky outcrops and are unimaginatively named First, Second, Third and Fourth. Each has a distinct character – if you're bronzed and beautiful, head to First beach. More demure visitors may feel more comfortable on Fourth, which is popular with families and was awarded a Blue Flag in 2004. The sunbathing and swimming are good on all the beaches and life guards are on duty, but note that the water is very cold – usually around 12°C. Most of the relatively small-scale, high-luxury development has been behind the beaches (some impressive houses can be glimpsed from the winding steps leading down). Be warned that there is limited parking in high season, so get here early.

Camps Bay

Following the coast south, you soon skirt around a hill and come out over Camps Bay, a long arch of sand backed by the Twelve Apostles. This is one of the most beautiful (and most photographed) beaches in the world, but the calm cobalt water belies its chilliness. The sand is also less sheltered than at Clifton, and sunbathing here on a windy day can be painful. But there are other distractions; the beachfront is lined with excellent seafood restaurants, and a sundowner followed by a superb meal is quite the perfect ending to a day in Cape Town.

Cape Peninsula

The drive between Camps Bay and Hout Bay runs along the slopes of the Twelve Apostles and is beautiful. Apart from the turning to Llandudno, there is no easy access to the coast until you reach Hout Bay. **Llandudno** itself is a small, exclusive settlement with only one road in and out and no shops, and a fine beach and excellent surf.

Hout Bay

Hout Bay, a historical fishing harbour with an attractive beach, attracts swarms of South African families during peak season. Most come for the seafood restaurants and boat trips, but the best reason for heading here is for spectacular Chapman's Peak Drive (see below), which begins just outside town. As the sun sets in the summer months every pullover along the road is filled with spectators, drink in hand.

Hout Bay itself is fairly attractive, with a busy fishing harbour at the western end of the bay; at the other end is a collection of shops and popular restaurants. By the harbour is a commercial complex known as **Mariners Wharf**, a popular attraction, although looking a little wind-worn these days. It is based upon Fisherman's Wharf in San Francisco, with a whole string of fish 'n' chips restaurants, souvenir shops, boats for hire and a fish market known as **Snoekies Fresh Fish Market**, close to the harbour gates. Even if you're not intending to buy anything it is worth a quick look to see the huge variety of fish that are caught off this coast. Boats run from here to see the seals on **Duiker Island** (see Boat tours, page 128).

Back in the town, next to the **tourist office** ① *T021-7918380, www.tourism*

capetown.co.za, Mon-Fri 0830-1730, Sat-Sun 0900-1300, is the **Hout Bay Museum** ① *4 Andrews Rd, T021-7903474, Tue-Sat 1000-1630, R5,* with displays on the history of the area, aimed at visiting school groups. More popular with families is **The World of Birds** ① *Valley Rd, T021-7902730, www.worldofbirds.org.za, daily 0900-1700, R55, children R35,* with over 400 species of birds housed in impressive walk-through aviaries. There's also the **Monkey Jungle**, populated with squirrel monkeys.

Chapman's Peak Drive

It is worth hiring a car for a day just to drive along Chapman's Peak Drive, a breathtaking 9-km route with 114 curves, carved into the cliffs 600 m above the sea. The route was re-opened a couple of years ago, following extensive repairs and the rigging of giant nets to catch falling rocks. It's now a toll road, costing R24 per car. Although the road up to the toll gates is fairly busy with groups pulled over in view points, the Drive itself is remarkably quiet, allowing outstanding and uninhibited views of the craggy coastline and thrashing ocean. The best time to drive along here is close to sunset in the summer, but the views of the crescent of white sand at Hout Bay on one side, and the vast stretch of Noordhoek on the other, are recommended at any time. The Drive sometimes closes in bad weather, check its status at www.chapmanspeakdrive.co.za.

Noordhoek

The greatest attraction here is the 8-km-long deserted beach, backed by a couple of tidal lagoons which offer excellent birdwatching. There's very little to the village itself, but the **Noordhoek Farm Village** on Beach Road is a pleasant spot for a coffee or light lunch, with two family restaurants and a couple of shops selling antiques, crafts and organic produce. The beach also offers the Cape's finest setting for horse riding along the shore (see Activities, page 125).

Kommetjie → *Colour map 8, B1.*

Driving along the Atlantic side of the peninsula, you could miss Kommetjie altogether. The name means 'little basin', a reference to the natural inlet in the rocks which has been developed into a tidal pool. The settlement is small with a pub, restaurant, caravan park and little else. It is, however, a major surfing spot and Long Beach to the north is always busy with surfers, even in winter. There is also an interesting walk along Long Beach to the wreck of the *Kakapo*, offering a rare opportunity to examine a wreck at close quarters without having to don full scuba equipment. The *Kakapo* is a steamship which was beached here in May 1900 on her maiden voyage when the captain apparently mistook Chapman's Peak for Cape Point during a storm. The boiler and shell are still intact about 100 m above the high tide mark.

Scarborough

Scarborough consists of a scattering of weekend and holiday homes on the hillside overlooking the Atlantic. The beach is broad and long but swimming is not a good idea as the water is cold and there are strong currents. Just outside Scarborough, close to the entrance to Cape of Good Hope Nature Reserve, is the **Cape Point Ostrich Farm** ① *T021-7809294, www.cape pointostrichfarm.com, daily 0930-1730, R30, children R10,* which is worth visiting for its in-depth tours, describing the lifecycle of the ostrich; during breeding season you can watch eggs hatching. There's a pleasant tea garden on site.

Cape of Good Hope ›› *Colour map 8, B1.*

ⓘ *T021-7018692, www.sanparks.org, Oct-Mar 0600-1800, Apr-Sep 0700-1700, R55, children R10.*
The Cape of Good Hope Nature Reserve, now part of Table Mountain National Park, was established to protect the unique flora and fauna of this stretch of coast. In 1928 the area came under threat from developers who were looking to build more seaside resorts. Those in favour of a reserve persuaded local families to sell their land, and in 1939 the reserve came into existence. Some game animals were introduced and the land has since been left to its own devices. Today, it is a dramatically wild area of towering cliffs, stupendous ocean views, excellent hiking and beautiful, deserted beaches.

Ins and outs
Getting there Given its location at the southern tip of the peninsula, you can approach the reserve from two directions: along the False Bay shoreline via Muizenberg and Simon's Town; or by the quieter M65 via Kommetjie and Scarborough. It is about 70 km from Cape Town centre to the reserve gates. There is no public transport to the reserve.

Getting away From the entrance to the reserve take a left and follow the M65 along the edge of the reserve. After 8 km the road divides; the right turn winds over the Swartkopberge to Long Beach and Simon's Town. Known as Red Hill (M66), this is a quicker route back to Cape Town if your time is short. There are two picnic spots with braai facilities along here. The road to the left leads down to Scarborough, and then along the coast to Kommetjie, 18 km from the reserve gates. There is a craft centre just after the junction, on the right.

Getting around We strongly recommend you come with your own transport to see the reserve; alternatively, there are several companies that organize good day trips from the city. A **funicular railway** ⓘ *0800-1700; R32 return, R24 single*, takes visitors up from the main car park to the original lighthouse where there are a series of paved footpaths and viewpoints. The walk is fairly steep and takes about 20 minutes, depending on how fit you are. Next to the car park is the **Two Oceans Restaurant** ⓘ *T021-7809200, www.two-oceans.co.za, 0900-1700*, specializing in seafood but also serving steak, chicken dishes and salads. Between December and March it is advisable to book a table. There is also a takeaway cafeteria which sells hamburgers, sandwiches, cold drinks, tea and coffee, as well as an information centre, curio shop, toilets and telephones (card and coins).

Around the reserve
The Cape of Good Hope is an integral part of the Cape Floristic Kingdom, the smallest but richest of the world's six floral kingdoms. A frequently quoted statistic is that within the 7750 ha of the reserve there are as many different plant species as there are in the whole of the British Isles. In addition to all this there are several different species of antelope: eland, bontebok, springbok, cape grysbok, red hartebeest and grey rhebok, as well as the elusive cape mountain zebra, snakes, tortoises and pesky baboons.

Although the strong winds and the low-lying vegetation are not ideal for birds, over 250 species have been recorded here, of which about 100 are known to breed within the reserve. There are plenty of vantage points where you can watch open sea birds – you can expect to see the Cape gannet, shy albatross, sooty shearwater, white-chinned petrel, Sabine's gull and Cory's shearwater. In the Strandveld vegetation along the coast you can expect to see many fruit-eating birds such as the southern boubou, Cape robin and bully canary. Around Sirkels Vlei you will find some freshwater birds. Finally there are few rarities: the white-rumped sandpiper from South America, macaroni penguins from Antarctica, and the purple gallinule from the US have all been seen within the reserve. The **Vlei Museum** issues a checklist of 100 birds. Alongside each name is a code telling you the typical habitat and the bird's resident status.

Cape Point

Cape Point Lighthouse is nothing special in itself, but the climb is well worth it for spectacular views of the peninsula. On a clear day the ocean views stretching all around are incredible – as is the wind, so be sure to hold on to hats and sunglasses. You can take the funicular to the top, but the 20-minute walk allows better views of the coast. There are plenty of viewpoints, linked by a jumble of footpaths.

The first lighthouse came into service in May 1860, but it quickly became apparent that the most prominent point on a clear day was far from ideal in poor weather. It was quite often shrouded in cloud while at sea level all was clear. In 1872 the Lighthouse Commission decided on a lower site, but it was only after the Portuguese ship, the *Lusitania*, struck Bellows Rock in April 1911, that work started on a new lighthouse. This was built just 87 m above sea level, close to Diaz Rock and remains the Cape's most important lighthouse today. The current beam can be seen up to 63 km out to sea, and 18 km out there is a red lamp that warns ships that they are in the danger zone.

From the top point of the railway there are still approximately 120 steps to the old lighthouse where you get some of the finest views. If you are reasonably fit and have a good head for heights, there is a spectacular walk to the modern lighthouse at Diaz Point. From the renovated old lighthouse you can see the path running along the left side of the narrow cliff that makes up the point. The round trip takes about 30 minutes, but do not attempt it if it is windy – the winds around the Cape can reach up to 55 knots.

As you look down from the lighthouse at Cape Point it is easy to see how ships could suffer on a dark night in a storm, especially before the lighthouse was built. There are 23 wrecks in the waters around the Cape, but only five can be seen when walking in the reserve: *Thomas T Tucker* (1942); *Nolloth* (1964); *Phyllisia* (1968); *Shir Yib* (1970), at Diaz Beach and the *Tania* (1972), the most recent wreck which can be seen at Buffel's Bay. The first wreck was the *Flying Dutchman* in 1680, which has since become famous as a ghost ship. The most famous sighting was by midshipman King George V in 1881.

Diaz Beach

Apart from visiting Cape Point and the Cape of Good Hope there are a few minor attractions dotted about the reserve as well as three excellent walks, probably the best way of appreciating the splendour of the coastline. You can drive down to the Cape of Good Hope and then walk to beautiful **Diaz Beach** via Maclear's Peak, a very steep walk in parts. You can also approach Diaz Beach via a 253-step staircase. **Diaz Cross**, further inland, is a memorial to the explorer Bartholomew Diaz. Note how it is painted black on one side so that sailors can see it against the horizon.

Hiking around the Cape of Good Hope

Hiking is encouraged within the reserve. There are several marked paths and maps are available from the information centre. One of the most spectacular routes is along the coast from Rooikrans towards Buffels Bay. Look out for the wreck of *Tania* (1972). On the west side close to Olifants Bay there are a couple of walks; one to the inland lake, Sirkels

Vlei, the other along the coast where you can see the wrecks of the *Thomas Tucker* (1942) and *Nolloth* (1964). You can light a braai at one of the designated areas at Buffels Bay and Bordjiesrif, but again watch the baboons.

False Bay ●○● ➤➤ pp145-150. Colour map 8, B1.

On the eastern side of the peninsula lies False Bay, a popular stretch of coast thanks to the warmer waters – temperatures can be as much as 8°C higher. The area is also more sheltered and better developed for tourism, although some of the landscape seems almost dull after the Atlantic seaboard. Nevertheless, the area has some excellent beaches and gets busy with domestic tourists in summer. In spring, False Bay is the favoured haunt of calving whales, offering excellent opportunities to see southern right, humpback and Bryde whales. There are also some interesting fishing villages. False Bay is also known for its population of white sharks. A shark watch service operates from Muizenberg, signalling alerts when sharks come in proximity of bathers and surfers.

Ins and outs
False Bay is easily accessed from the city centre by the M3, which runs around the mountain and along the coast. There are also two routes across the mountainous spine linking the roads that hug the coast around the peninsula: you can cross from Noordhoek to Fish Hoek via the M65 and Sun Valley or, further south, take the Red Hill road from Scarborough to Simon's Town. Each route is convenient if your time is short, but the most scenic route is to follow the M65 along the coast from the Atlantic seaboard to False Bay. It is impossible to get lost as there is only one road along the shoreline.

Alternatively, the metro (for up-to-date times: T0800-656463, www.mti.co.za) continues through the southern suburbs to Simon's Town – the stretch following False Bay is spectacular. Trains go as far as Simon's Town and leave every 30 minutes, with the last trains leaving Simon's Town at around 2000. There have been some reports of crime on the trains, so it's best to avoid them at quieter times and in the evening.

Constantia
South of Kirstenbosch Botanical Gardens and the city's southern suburbs, lies the verdant area of Constantia and its winelands. This historical district was the first site of wine-making in South Africa and today it is an attractive introduction to the country's wines as well as offering some fine examples of Cape Dutch architecture. There are five estates here, of which Groot Constantia (see below) is the best known and definitely worth a visit. **Buitenverwachting** ① T021-7945190, www.buitenverwachting.co.za, is a working estate with an excellent restaurant (see page 148). **Klein Constantia** ① T021-7945188, www.kleinconstantia.com, is a beautiful hilly estate with a great tasting centre, and is famed for its dessert wine, Vin de Constance, allegedly Napoleon's favourite wine. **Constantia Uitsig** ① T021-7941810, www.constantiauitsig.co.za, has excellent wines, luxury accommodation and three restaurants (see page 146). **Steenberg** ① T021-7132222, www.steenberghotel.com, also offers superb wines as well as having luxurious lodgings, a good restaurant and a golf course (see page 146).

Groot Constantia
① T021-7945128, www.grootconstantia.co.za, 0900-1700/1800, free entrance to the main estate, museum R10. 2 restaurants: Jonkershuis has traditional Cape food; Simon's serves

burgers, salads and seafood. Wine tastings take place at the sales centre, R20 for 5 wines; cheese platters available. Cellar tours every hour on the hour.

This old wine estate has some of the finest Cape Dutch architecture in South Africa, and with its rolling, vineyard setting and wine-tasting centre is a delightful place to spend a few hours – although it does get swamped with tour buses in high season.

The main house was originally home to Cape Governor Simon van der Stel between 1699 and 1712. He named the estate after Constantia, the daughter of the company official who had granted the land to him. Before his death, van der Stel planted most of the vines, but it was not until 1778 that the estate became famous for its wines. During this period the estate was unable to meet the demands from Europe, especially France. The magnificent wine cellar behind the main house was designed by the renowned French architect, Louis Thibault. The house is now a museum full of period furniture. A booklet is available giving a brief description of the objects on show. Behind the house is a shady garden and pool overlooked by the wine cellar, with displays on brandy and wine making. There are two impressive giant oak vats each with a capacity of over 4000 litres.

Tokai Forest
① Take the M3 out of town towards the southern suburbs. Just before Muizenberg, turn right into Tokai St and follow the signs for Tokai Manor House, T021-7127471, daily during daylight hours, entry by donation.

Tokai was set up as a forest nursery in 1883 to start a programme of reforestation. Due to this, large parts of the Constantiaberg Mountains are covered in pine trees and as they are non-indigenous there is some debate on whether they should remain. Today, the forest is part of Table Mountain National Park. The arboretum contains 40 tree species – there are two walking trails, and horse riding and mountain biking are possible in the low-lying section (permits from the main gate).

Rondevlei Nature Reserve
① From Cape Town take the M5, Prince George Dr, turn left into Victoria Rd in Grassy Park, and then right into Fisherman's Walk, 17 km from the town centre, 6 km from Muizenberg, T021-7062404, www.rondevlei.co.za, 0730-1700/1900, R5, children R2.

This 220-ha reserve was originally established to protect the birdlife and the coastal fynbos vegetation. Today it is an important environmental education centre for local schools and, despite being surrounded by suburban sprawl, it is one of the best birdwatching spots around Cape Town. Only the northern shore of the lake is open to the public. A path follows the vlei's edge, along which there are two lookout towers equipped with telescopes. There are several hides along the water's edge, and cuts within the reeds allow views across the water. The best time to visit the reserve is from January to March when many European migrants can be seen. Over 230 bird species have been recorded; on a good day visitors should be able to see more than 65 species including white pelican, greater flamingo, African spoonbill and Caspian tern. There are a few small, shy mammals in the reserve, plus a small population of hippos. Inside the reserve is a small **aquarium** showing the freshwater fish that inhabit the area.

Muizenberg
Travelling out from the city centre on the M3, Muizenberg is the first settlement you reach on False Bay and as such has long been a popular local bathing spot. The Battle of Muizenberg was a small but significant military affair that began in June 1795 and ended

three months later with the (first) British occupation of the Cape. Cecil Rhodes bought a holiday cottage here in 1899. Many other wealthy people followed, building some fine Victorian and Edwardian cottages along the back streets and attracting the likes of Agatha Christie and Rudyard Kipling to its shores. Although the resort had decayed significantly over the last decade, various recent regeneration projects have meant that the area is starting to look like its old cheerful self again. The beach certainly remains beautiful: a vast stretch of powdery white sand sloping gently to the water. It is safe for swimming as there is no backwash, and it is very popular with surfers who head out to the bigger breakers. At low tide you can walk into the shallow sea for more than 300 m without having to swim.

The walk along Main Street towards St James is known locally as the **Historic Mile** and will take you past a number of interesting old buildings. Some of these are national monuments, but most are closed to the public. The first of note is the **Station building**, a fine example of art-deco architecture built in 1912. Further along on the right is **Het Post Huijs (The Post House)** ① *186 Main Rd, T021-7887972, Mon-Fri 0800-1530, Sat 0900-1300, Sun 1400-1700, entry by donation*, thought to be the oldest building in False Bay, dating back to 1742 and built by the Dutch East India Company as a toll-house to levy taxes on farmers passing by to sell their produce to ships moored in Simon's Bay. One of the early post holders was Sergeant Muys, from whom Muizenberg is thought to have got its name. The building itself is a picturesquely squat stone house, with thick whitewashed walls and a thatched roof. Inside are exhibits on the history of Muizenburg, with photos of the resort in its heyday and displays on the Battle of Muizenburg of 1795. There are original English cannonballs which the cheery curator will happily let you lift.

Rhodes Cottage ① *246 Main St, T021-7889140, daily 1000-1600, entry by donation*, is surprisingly small and austere for someone as wealthy as Cecil Rhodes. It has been restored and now contains many of his personal items including his diamond-weighing scale and the chest in which he carried his personal belongings, and there are displays on his life and achievements. It's a pleasant place to wander around, with a lovely garden around the side. This is where he died on 26 March 1902, and his body was transported by train with great ceremony to the Matobo Hills outside Bulawayo in Zimbabwe, where he was buried in a giant rock outcrop. The volunteers that keep the place open make charismatic and enthusiastic guides.

Graceland, further along Main Road, is one of the largest and most impressive mansions along the coast. It was the home of John Garlick, a well-known merchant at the turn of the 20th century. The house has a Spanish feel to it, with arched balconies and glazed clay roof tiles. Unfortunately the house is not open to the public. Just before you reach St James you pass another grand house, with palm trees in the garden, known as **Stonehenge**. Built in the style of an Italian villa this house once belonged to HP Rudd of De Beers Consolidated Mines.

St James

Just beyond Muizenberg lies the more upmarket resort of St James, an appealing village with characteristic brightly coloured bathing huts lining the tidal pool. The village is named after a Roman Catholic church which was built here in 1854 to save Catholics having to travel as far as Simon's Town to attend services – interestingly, some of the early settlers were Catholic Filipino fishermen. There is a small sheltered beach and reasonable surf off **Danger Beach** and the tidal pool is a safe place for a swim.

St James is also a suitable starting point for a hike in the excellent Silvermine section of the Table Mountain National Park. A path starts on Boyes Drive and climbs up through the

Spes Bona Forest to Tartarus Cave. The views alone are worth the hike (see page 140 for further details of hiking in the reserve).

Kalk Bay

Kalk Bay is one of the most attractive settlements on False Bay, with a bustling fishing harbour and a bohemian vibe. The town is named after the lime kilns that produced kalk from shells in the 17th century. An important local product, the lime created the white-walled appearance of many houses in the Cape, especially amongst the Bo-Kaap community. Until the arrival of the railway in 1883, the local fishermen hunted whales, seals and small fish. Today it remains a fishing harbour, worked mainly by a coloured community which somehow escaped the Group Areas Act under Apartheid. It is one of the few remaining coloured settlements on the peninsula.

Main Road is an appealing spot, lined with bric-a-brac and antiques shops and a handful of arty cafés, and the beach is sandy and safe for swimming, with a couple of tidal pools for children to explore. Between June and July the harbour is busy with the season for snoek, one of the most plentiful local fish harvests. Look out for the returning deep-sea fishing boats around the middle of the day, as there's a daily impromptu quayside auction. You can buy a variety of fresh fish at the counters and for an extra small fee get them to gut them for you too. Another attraction is **Seal Island**, an important breeding ground for birds and seals, the latter attracting hungry great white sharks. Cruises run from Simon's Town (see page 142).

You should also look out for the **Holy Trinity Church** on Main Road. It has a thatched roof, but its appeal is its windows, considered to be some of the finest in the Cape. On Quarterdeck Road is a tiny mosque built in the 1800s. If you fancy browsing for local art and antiques, take your pick from Main Road, where a dozen shops vie for custom – **Kalk Bay Gallery**, **Cape to Cairo** and **Curiosity** have the most intriguing offerings. On the other side of the road is the entrance to Kalk Bay's most popular attraction, the **Brass Bell**, a simple seafood restaurant and pub wedged between the railway tracks and the water (see Eating, page 149).

High up behind the town is **Boyes Drive**, a scenic route connecting the bay with Muizenburg. It's a spectacular route offering sweeping views of False Bay and the Atlantic, and takes just 10 minutes to complete – look out for the signs from Main Road as you head out of Kalk Bay towards Simon's Town.

Clovelly

Continuing along the main road, the next settlement you reach is Clovelly, tucked between the waters of False Bay and the mountains of the Silvermine reserve. Along the main street are several shops and places to have a snack. Anyone visiting from the west country in Britain will be interested to know that this community is named after the village in Devon. Golf enthusiasts should head a little way inland for the **Clovelly Country Club**.

Silvermine

This is a popular local reserve, now part of the Table Mountain National Park, but not often visited by overseas visitors. Table Mountain and Cape Point tend to dominate the open-air attractions, and rightly so, but this reserve is well worth a visit if you enjoy hiking, plus there are great views across False Bay and the Atlantic Ocean.

Like much of the Cape, the reserve encompasses one of the oldest floral kingdoms in the world. Over 900 rare and endangered species have been recorded in the mountains, including many types of proteas, ericas and reeds. In addition to the plants there are a couple of patches of indigenous forest in the Spes Bona and Echo valleys. Ornithologists should look out for black eagles, ground woodpeckers, orange-breasted sunbirds and rock kestrels. If you're extremely lucky, you may also come across small shy mammals such as lynx, porcupine and various species of mongoose.

Ins and outs The reserve is split into two sections by the Ou Kaapseweg Road as it crosses the Kalk Bay Mountains – the eastern sector and western sector. There is no public transport along this road. By car you can approach either from the Cape Town side or from Noordhoek and Fish Hoek. Driving out from Cape Town, follow the M3 from Newlands to its very end and then take a right. After 2 km turn left into Ou Kaapseweg Road, M64. Note that this road has one of Cape Town's highest accident rates, so take care when driving.

A variety of footpaths from Muizenberg, St James, Kalk Bay and Chapman's Peak Drive lead into the reserve and make a pleasant day trip from Cape Town. Access into the reserve is allowed between sunrise and sunset. Toilet facilities are found at Silvermine Reservoir, Hennies Pool, Bokkop Peak, and at the car park near Maiden Peak in the eastern sector of the reserve. Braais are only permitted within the Hennies Pool, Silvermine Reservoir and Bokkop picnic areas.

Around the reserve A tarred road leads from the western sector gates to the Silvermine Reservoir built in 1898 to supply Kalk Bay and Muizenberg with water until 1912. There is a shady picnic site under some pine trees close to the dam. One of the more popular walks from here is to **Noordhoek Peak** (754 m), a circuit of about 7 km from the dam. The path is marked by stone cairns. At the

Glencairn, Simon's Town & Boulders Beach

Sleeping	Rocklands **6**
Bosky Dell **2**	Roman Rock **8**
Boulders Beach Guest House & Penguin Point Café **3**	Simon's Town Backpackers **1**
British Hotel Apartments **4**	Southern Right **5**
El Mirador **7**	
Quayside & Bertha's Restaurant **12**	**Eating**
	Bon Appetit **1**
	Quarterdeck **4**
	Salty Sea Dog **3**
	Two & Sixpence **2**

summit there are spectacular views of the Sentinel and Hout Bay. Another interesting walk is from the car park to **Elephant's Eye Cave** covered with ferns and hanging plants. En route you pass the **Prinz Kasteel waterfall**. Allow about three hours for the round trip. The cave can also be reached from Tokai Manor through the Tokai Forest.

The eastern sector of the reserve has plenty of sandstone caves to explore, while the views from the peaks here are across False Bay. One of the popular trails is to **Steenberg Peak** (537 m) via the Wolfkop picnic site. If you have made your way to the top without a car, try an interesting walk which drops down to Muizenberg or St James via the **Spes Bona Valley**. Be careful if exploring any of the caves as there are dangerous deep drops.

Fish Hoek

Fish Hoek is one of the most conservative settlements on the coast, not least because the sale of alcohol is prohibited here. It does, however, have a fine beach – perhaps the best for swimming after Muizenberg – which stretches right across the Fish Hoek valley. Swimming is safe at the southern end of the bay, but avoid the northern end where a small river enters the sea, as there is the danger of quicksand. Having said that, a woman was killed by a great white shark about 20 m off the coast at Fish Hoek in 2004; however, South Africa has had fewer than 10 shark attack fatalities in the last couple of decades. From mid-August to October, there is a good chance of catching a glimpse of whales from here. The valley which stretches behind the town joins with Noordhoek beach on the Atlantic coast. In recent geological times this was flooded and all the lands towards Cape Point were in fact an island.

Glencairn

It is easy to drive through this coastal resort without realizing you've actually been here, although it does have one of the best mid-range hotels in False Bay (see Sleeping, page 147). There is a small beach by the railway station but it is exposed to the southeast winds. Be wary of the cross currents close to the inlet where a small river enters the sea. At low tide you can occasionally see the remains of a steamship, the *Clan Stuart*. She was blown aground on 20 November 1914 while the crew drank in the local hotel.

Simon's Town

ⓘ *Recommended for this area is* A Walking Guide for the Hout Bay to Simon's Town Mountains, *by Shirley Brossy. The trails are well described and the illustrations clear enough to use as a map.*

This is the most popular town on False Bay, with a pleasant atmosphere and numerous Victorian buildings lining Main Street. If you want a break from Cape Town, this makes for a good alternative base from which to explore the southern peninsula. For information, contact the helpful **tourist office** ⓘ *in the museum, T021-7865798, www.simonstown.com.*

The town is fairly quiet for most of the year but becomes very busy with families during the summer school holidays. Whenever you visit, take some time to wander up the hill away from the main road – the quiet, bougainvillea-bedecked houses and cobbled streets with their sea views are a lovely retreat from the bustling beaches. The main swimming spot is **Seaforth Beach**, not far from Boulders. To get there, turn off St George's Road into Seaforth Road after passing the navy block to the left. The beach is the second on the right, on Kleintuin Road. A little further towards Cape Point are two other popular bathing beaches, **Windmill** and **Fisherman's**. Seaforth Beach has changing and toilet facilities, snack bars, restaurants and a clean stretch of shady lawn bordering the beach with some picnic spots and bench seats. The swimming is safe, but there is no surf due to offshore rocks which protect the beach. For children there is a water slide and a wooden raft in the water. Look out for some giant pots, a legacy from whaling days, when they were used for melting whale blubber.

Simon's Town is named after Simon van der Stel, who decided that an alternative bay was needed for securing ships in the winter months as Table Bay suffered from the prevailing northwesterly. However, because of the difficult overland access, the bay was little used in the early years. It was not until 1743 that the Dutch East India Company finally built a wooden pier and some barracks here. In 1768 the town transferred into British hands, and following the end of the Napoleonic Wars in Europe, the British decided to turn Simon's Town into a naval base. It remained as such until 1957.

Just before you hit the town centre, the **Simon's Town Museum** ① *Old Residency, Court Rd, T021 7863046, Mon Fri 0900 1600, Sat 1000 1300, Sun 1100 1500, entry by donation, guided walks along the 'Historical Mile' on request*, has displays related to the town's history as a naval base for the British and South African navies. Several displays are dedicated to Just Nuisance, a great dane who became something of a local hero in the 1930s. He was officially registered as personnel aboard *HMS Afriander* and is the only dog in history to have been given a full military burial on his death. His favourite spot was to lie on the deck on the brow at the top of the gangplank. No one could easily get past him and he was loathe to move, hence the name. His image has become Simon's Town's unofficial mascot, and there's a bronze statue of him on Jubilee Square. Also of interest is the **Peoples of Simon's Town Exhibit**, a collection referring to the forcible removal of coloured families from the area in the 1960s and 1970s, photos, family trees and household goods.

Nearby, the **South Africa Naval Museum** ① *Court Rd, T021-7874686, daily 1000-1600, entry by donation*, includes a collection of model ships, gunnery displays, information on mine-sweeping, a modern submarine control room plus relics from the Martello Tower.

In the centre of town, the **Quayside Centre** is a smart development on Wharf Street, next to Jubilee Square in the centre of town, which has greatly enhanced the seafront. Above the shops and restaurants is a comfortable new hotel, the **Quayside Lodge**. Cruises in the harbour can be booked here.

Just round the corner from Jubilee Square, and worth a quick peek, is the **Warrior Toy Museum** ① *St George's St, T021-7861395, daily 1000 1600, entry by donation*, a tiny museum with an impressive collection of model cars, trains, dolls and toy soldiers. This is a great little place and definitely worth a stop – nostalgic for adults and fun for kids. New and old model cars are also for sale.

The nearby **Heritage Museum** ① *Amlay House, King George's Way, T021-7862302, Tue-Fri 1100-1600, Sat 1100-1300, entry by donation*, faithfully charts the history of the Muslim community in Simon's Town. The town was designated a 'white' area during the Group Area Act and over 7000 people classified as coloured were relocated. The Amlay family were the last to be forcibly removed from Simon's Town in 1975 and were the first to return in 1995 – today the Muslim community has all but disappeared here, although there is still an attractive working mosque up behind Main Road. The exhibition consists mainly of pictures and artefacts dating back to the turn of the 20th century. There is a traditional bridal chamber, with wedding clothes and a display in the Hadj room. Zainab Davidson is the co-founder of the Nourul Islam Historical Society and began the museum.

Mineral World ① *Dido Valley Rd, T021-7862020, Mon-Fri 0830-1645, Sat and Sun 0900-1730*, is an important gemstone factory where you can watch the different stages of polishing and buy the finished product. There is also the 'Scratch Patch', a large landscaped yard covered with a deep layer of polished stones.

Boulders Beach

About 2 km south of Simon's Town is a lovely series of little sandy coves surrounded by huge boulders (hence the name). It is a peaceful spot, safe for swimming and gently shelving, making it good for children.

The real attraction here, however, is the colony of African penguins that live and nest between the boulders. **Boulders Coastal Park** ① *T021-7862329, www.sanparks.org, R25, children R5, Apr-Sep 0800-1700, Oct-Mar 0700-1900*, has been created to protect the little creatures, and their numbers have flourished. Bizarrely, they take little notice of their sunbathing neighbours and happily go about their business of swimming, waddling and braying (their characteristic braying was the reason they were, until recently, known as Jackass penguins). This is one of two colonies on mainland Africa, the other being in Betty's Bay (see page 240). The best time to see large numbers of penguins is just before sunset, when they return from a day's feeding at sea. The beach is a protected area, and the admission charge is well worth it to get close to the penguins – but be sure to avoid the nesting areas. A new information centre has been built telling you all you need to know about penguins. Note that the first cove gets very busy with families at weekends and during school holidays. Walk along the boardwalk or crawl under the rocks on one side of the beach to get to a more peaceful spot.

Miller's Point

This is the last easy access to the sea on this side of the peninsula. Beyond **Partridge Point** the main road cuts into the hillside, and access to the beach is via steep footpaths. Miller's Point is one of the few remaining beaches to levy a small entrance fee. Gates close at 2000. There is a large caravan site here plus a picnic area and a good restaurant, the **Black Marlin** (see Eating, page 150), which is a popular lunch stop for coach tours of the Cape Peninsula. The road climbs above the sea before rounding the mountains by **Smitswinkel Bay**. On a clear day you can look back to a perfect view of the cliffs plunging into the sea. A short distance from the shore is the Cape of Good Hope Nature Reserve entrance (see page 135).

Beyond Miller's Point be on the lookout for baboons. They are not shy and will approach cars. Wind windows up and remember they can be vicious.

A number of **boat trips** to the Cape of Good Hope originate from Simon's Town harbour. Taking a trip from here allows views of the spectacular coastline and its hinterland from a different angle. In addition to straightforward sightseeing tours, there are several options for viewing bird life, seals and whales during the right season.
▶▶ *For Tour operators, see page 128.*

⊙ The Cape Peninsula listings

Hotel and guesthouse prices
L over US$300 **AL** US$220-300 **A** US$150-220
B US$100-150 **C** US$75-100 **D** US$35-75
E US$15-35 **F** under US$15
Restaurant prices
¶¶¶ over US$30 ¶¶ US$15 30 ¶ under US$15
See pages 46-51 for further information.

⊖ Sleeping

Camps Bay p133

L The Bay, Victoria Rd, T021-4384444, www.thebay.co.za. Set just across the road from the beach, member of the Small Luxury Hotels of the World, with 70 modern de luxe a/c rooms all with views across the bay, pleasant contemporary feel, large pool with deck and beach facing restaurant with a good reputation. Excellent service, a well known place for the rich and famous.

AL Bay Atlantic, 3 Berkley Rd, T021-4384341, www.thebayatlantic.com. Family-run guesthouse with some of the best views in Cape Town. 6 individually decorated en suite rooms, TV, light and airy with terracotta tiles and white linen, some with private balcony. Quiet garden with good-sized pool, breakfast served on balcony overlooking the bay, relaxed atmosphere. Run by welcoming Smith family.

B Whale Cottage Guesthouse, 57 Camps Bay Dr, T021-4383840, www.whalecottage.com. Small tasteful place with marine decor, 10 sunny double rooms with en suite bathrooms, breakfast deck overlooking the beach, good views of the Twelve Apostles, satellite TV and internet access, 5 mins' walk to the restaurants and beach. Also has properties in Hermanus, Franschoek and Plettenberg Bay.

Hout Bay p133

B Chapmans Peak Hotel, Main Rd, T021-7901036, www.chapmanspeakhotel.co.za. This traditional hotel has 10 en suite double rooms, with simple, contemporary decor, large windows, some with sea views. Good restaurant which is well known for its excellent calamari and popular bar with seating on

veranda, great location just across from the beach and close to Chapman's Peak Drive. 21 rooms opening in a new block mid-2008.

B Froggs Leap, 15 Baviaans Cl, T021-7902590, www.froggsleap.co.za. Converted 'plantation' house with stunning veranda overlooking the bay. 3 double rooms with en suite bathroom, TV, minibars and airy decor with a seaside feel, wicker furniture. Good breakfasts served on veranda. Also arrange trips on their catamaran.

B Sorgh Vliet Lodge, 3060 Valley Rd, T021-7902767, www.sorghvlietlodge.com. 2 self-catering cottages and 1 B&B cottage set in peaceful gardens with mountain views. Bright and comfortable with wooden floors, cane furniture, open-plan kitchens, access to gardens, patio and pool, small terraces at back. Breakfast on request. Run by friendly Mike and Lindy.

Noordhoek p134

A Monkey Valley, Mountain Rd, T021-7891391, www.monkeyvalleyresort.com. Luxurious resort with self-catering thatched log cottages set in woodland overlooking Noordhoek Bay. Each sleeps 4-8, with 2 or 3 bedrooms, kitchen, lounge and bathroom, log fires, plus secluded veranda with superb views.

A-C Goose Green Lodge, Briony Close, T021-7892933, www.goosegreen.co.za. B&B accommodation in main house, also has 5 self-catering cottages in converted family homes dotted around pretty gardens, sleeping up to 8, very comfortably furnished, close to Chapman's Peak and the beach.

E-F Chapman's Peak Caravan Farm, Dassenheuwel, T021-7891225. 5 caravans with hot water and power points, space for tents, swimming pool, peaceful rural setting at the end of Chapman's Peak Drive. Lots of animals.

Kommetjie p134

L The Long Beach Villa, 1 Kirsten Av, T021-7996561, www.thelongbeach.com. 6 modern luxury suites with views over Long Beach, spacious airy decor in pale blues and pinks, internet access, a/c and DSTV, lunch and dinner on request, stunning swimming pool right on the sand dunes, bar, rates include all drinks, spa treatments.

D-E Imhoff Caravan Park, Wireless Rd, T021-7831634, www.imhoff.co.za. Large site with 100 camping and caravanning sites, all grass, electric points, well lit, 2 brick self-catering chalets sleeping up to 6, laundry, games room, TV lounge, 500 m from beach, aimed at families.

Constantia p137

The original Cape Dutch homestead and vineyard that gave the area its name is today surrounded by one of Cape Town's most exclusive suburbs, dotted with luxury hotels.

L The Cellars-Hohenhort Hotel, 93 Brommersulei Rd, 15 mins from Cape Town centre, T021-7942137, www.cellars-hohenort.com. Part of the **Relais & Chateaux** group. One of the most luxurious hotels in Cape Town, set in 2 converted manor houses on a wine estate, with 13 spacious suites and 33 individually decorated double rooms, plus the Madiba Presidential Suite, a 2-storey house with private pool, and the Dove Cote suite overlooking the golf green. 2 excellent restaurants (see Eating, page 149). 2 swimming pools, tennis court, golf course, set in 3½ ha of mature gardens which overlook False Bay, impeccable service.

L Constantia Uitsig, Spaanschemat, River Rd, T021-7946500, www.constantiauitsig.co.za. On the well-known wine estate, with 16 luxurious and spacious cottages set in neat gardens with views across vineyards to the mountain. Plush furnishings, private verandas, activities include horse riding and vineyard walks and there's a new spa. 2 excellent restaurants.

L Steenberg Country Hotel, 20 km from Cape Town in the Constantia Valley, T021-7132222, www.steenberghotel.com. Luxurious country hotel with 30 elegant, traditional rooms furnished with beautiful antiques, in converted farm buildings overlooking manicured gardens and working vineyards. Swimming pool, gym, spa and steam room, horse riding and 18-hole golf course. **Catharina Restaurant** has an excellent reputation. Relaxed and friendly atmosphere.

L-AL Alphen Hotel, Alphen Dr, 20 mins' drive from the city centre, at the head of Constantia Valley, T021-7945011, www.alphen.co.za. 21 spacious rooms on elegant 18th-century Cape Dutch estate. Suites and rooms decorated with fine antiques, polished floors and log fires. Lunches in the pub or in the gardens during the summer, popular restaurant in the manor house, swimming pool.

Muizenburg p138

D Sonstraal Guest House, 4 Axminster Rd, T021-7881611, www.sonstraalguest house.com. Pleasant, old-fashioned guesthouse a short walk from the beach and seafront. 7 rooms in the main house, 5 of which are en suite, plus self-catering cottages sleeping 4-6 and studios sleeping 2. Simple decor, spotless rooms and bathrooms, sunny breakfast room, plant-filled courtyard, pool.

Kalk Bay p140

B The Inn at Castle Hill, 37 Gatesville Rd, T021-7882554, www.castlehill.co.za. Elegant restored Edwardian house with wrought-iron balconies and veranda offering fine sea views. 6 comfortable en suite rooms with white linen and fresh flowers, guest lounge and breakfast room, veranda is the most pleasant part of the house and perfect for whale watching during the season. Secure parking, well run.

Fish Hoek p142

B-C Tudor House by the Sea, 43 Simon's Town Rd, T021-7826238, www.tudor house.co.za. 5 comfortable self-catering apartments with 1-3 bedrooms, friendly and very reasonably priced. Apartments have all mod cons, serviced daily, secure parking, secluded gardens, ideal for a longer break for those wishing to explore the area, very popular in season, advance reservations necessary.

C Sunny Cove Manor, 72 Simon's Town Rd, T021-7822274, www.sunnycovemanor.com. Friendly, family-run B&B in a solid old manor house overlooking False Bay. 4 en suite rooms, comfortably furnished in green and white or floral fabrics, some have wide ocean views, breakfast room and lounge. Well run and welcoming. Recommended for families.

Glencairn *p142, map p141*
B Southern Right, 12-14 Glen Rd, T021-7820314, www.southernright.info. Delightful hotel in turn-of-the-20th-century building set a short walk from the sea. 8 double and twin en suite rooms with high ceilings, dark polished wood floors, subtle decor, some with 4-poster beds and baths only, others with shower and bath. Stylish bar and restaurant serving pub meals, seafood and grills and 3 boules pistes in front of the hotel with regular matches on Fri and Sun afternoons (guests can join in). Fashionable place but family friendly. Recommended.

Simon's Town *p142, map p141*
L British Hotel Apartments, 90 St George St, T021-7862214, www.britishhotelapartments.co.za. Despite the unpromising name, this is one of the best places to stay in False Bay. Converted characterful Victorian hotel with 4 elegant self-catering apartments. Each apartment is enormous, stretching over 2 open-plan floors, with 3 bedrooms, all en suite with delightful Victorian bathrooms. Polished wood floors throughout, attractive mix of maritime antiques, art deco and stylish modern furnishings, open-plan kitchen and lounge, separate TV room, great views of the bay from magnificent balconies, breakfasts available on request. Highly recommended.
B Quayside Hotel, Jubilee Centre, St George's St, on the seafront, T021-7863838, www.quayside.co.za. A smart, modern development in a great central location overlooking the harbour. 26 spacious double rooms, comfortable marine blue and white decor, bright and sunny with good views. Book well in advance for visits during local holidays. Good restaurant attached. A harbour cruise and entrance to the penguins at Boulders are included in the rates.

C El Mirador, 15 Victory Way, T021-7861066, dennisla@iafrica.com. Self-catering apartment set high above the town with spectacular views of False Bay. Sleeps up to 5 in 2 bedrooms (1 double, 1 twin), both en suite, small open-plan kitchen and eating area, lounge, pleasant decor with terracotta floors, great private terrace overlooking the sea, friendly owner. Good value.
C-D Roman Rock, 21 Dorries Dr, past Simon's Town on way to Cape Point, T021-7863431, www.simonstown-accommodation.com. Comfortable and modern self-catering apartments sleeping 2-6, in a secluded setting overlooking the beach and sea, cool tiled interiors, large balconies, braai facilities, 3 mins' walk to beach, parking.
D Rocklands, 25 Rocklands Rd, Murdoch Valley South, T021-7863158, www.rocklandsbnb.com. Cool and comfortable B&B, airy tiled rooms with TV and balconies overlooking the sea, simple furnishings, sunny breakfast room, short walk to the beach. Also offer self-catering apartments and holiday homes.
E-F Simon's Town Backpackers, 66 St George's St, T021-7861964, www.capepax.co.za. 38-bed backpacker joint spread across cramped dorms and fairly pleasant doubles, brightly painted walls and bush-camp-style furniture, small kitchen, honesty bar, braai on balcony overlooking the main street and harbour, bikes for hire and can organize sea kayaking.

Boulders Beach *p144, map p141*
B Bosky Dell, 5 Grant Av, near Boulders Beach, T021-7863906, www.boskyonboulders.co.za. Peaceful cluster of converted houses overlooking Boulders Beach, in fact so close that penguins are known to wander into the reception area, choice of 5 self-contained self-catering units with 1-3 bedrooms. Clean and tidy, each with TV, private garden and braai area, serviced daily, secure parking and direct access down to beach. Advance booking essential during local holidays.

B Boulders Beach Guest House, 4 Boulders Place, T021-7861758, www.boulders beach.co.za. One of the most relaxing places you could stay in the area. This friendly, well-run beachside guesthouse is a firm favourite. 12 double rooms with en suite bathrooms, most arranged around a paved yard without sea view, good-sized beds and baths, simple, refreshing design. Also has 2 self-catering apartments. At night you're likely to see penguins exploring the grounds after everyone has gone home. Good restaurant. Recommended.

⊘ Eating

Clifton *p132*
♥♥ Clifton Beach House, 4th Beach, T021-4381955. Open 1100-2200. Breakfast, lunch and dinner overlooking Clifton's beautiful beach, good seafood plus some Thai dishes, relaxed during the day but smarter in the evening. Pleasant, bustling atmosphere, good cocktails.

Camps Bay *p133*
♥♥♥ Blues, Victoria Rd, T021-4382040, www.blues.co.za. 1200-late. Popular and well-known seafood place with superb views, Californian-style seafood menu served to a beautiful crowd. Good, stylish food, famous seafood and oyster platters, but you pay for the restaurant's reputation.
♥♥♥ The Codfather, corner of Geneva Dr and The Drive, T021-4380782. 1200-2300. One of the best seafood restaurants in Cape Town, stylish laid-back place offering a range of superbly fresh seafood. No menu – the waiter takes you to a counter and you pick and choose whatever you like the look of. Also has an excellent sushi bar. Highly recommended.
♥♥ Ocean Blue, Victoria Rd, T021-4389838. 1000-late. Friendly seafood restaurant on Camps Bay trendy strip overlooking the beach. Good fresh seafood, especially daily specials, superb grilled prawns and butterfish kebabs. Less pretentious than many of the restaurants in the area. Recommended.

♥♥ Tuscany Beach, 41 Victoria Rd, T021-4381213, www.tuscanybeach restaurant.com. 1000-late. Italian seafood place overlooking the beach. Delicious seafood specials – don't miss the kingclip kebabs served on a dangling sword. Also serves wood-fired pizzas, salads, burgers and steaks. Trendy place, gets very busy for sundowners.

Cafés
No 16, Shop 16, The Promenade, Camps Bay, T021-4382322. 0700-1900, stays open later in season. Smart 1st-floor café overlooking Camps Bay beach, serving sandwiches, pastries, muffins and cakes as well a fine selection of bistro-style light lunches.

Hout Bay *p133 and p134*
♥♥ Chapman's Restaurant, Chapman's Peak Hotel, T021-7901036. 1100-2200. A lively restaurant and bar with wood panelled interior, serving good seafood dishes in frying pans, also grills and pub fare. The outside terrace gets packed in summer. Be sure to book ahead.
♥♥ Dunes, Hout Bay Beach, T021-7901876. 0900-late. Sprawling restaurant overlooking the dunes behind the beach, very popular with families, large menu, quick service but the food can disappoint – stick to the tasty fish and chips. Book ahead at weekends or you'll be stuck in the hot courtyard instead of the breezy balcony tables.
♥ Fish on the Rocks, Harbour Rd (beyond Snoekies Market), T021-7901153. 1000-1900. Simple and delicious fresh fish and chips, deep-fried calamari and prawns, overlooking harbour. No frills, and getting popular with big tour groups.

Constantia *p137*
♥♥♥ Buitenverwachting, Klein Constantia Rd, T021-7945190, www.buitenverwacht ing.co.za. Mon-Sat 1200-1330, 1900-2100. The main restaurant serves a cosmopolitan menu with flawless Italian, French and South African dishes. Good service, upmarket, prices reflect the quality of the food.

†††† Catharina's, Steenberg Country Hotel, Spaanschemat River Rd, T021-7132222. 0700-2130. The principal restaurant in a 5-star hotel (see Sleeping, page 107). Breakfast is served in the conservatory, lunch and dinner under the oaks or at tables set in cosy alcoves created from old wine vats. Elegant hotel restaurant serving excellent South African fare such as West Coast mussels, Knynsa oysters and springbok loin on polenta. Fine wine list.

†††† The Greenhouse, The Cellars-Hohenort Hotel, 93 Brommersvlei Rd, T021-7942137, www.cellars-hohenort.com. 0730-2200. One of 2 highly rated restaurants at this 5-star hotel (see Sleeping, page 146), set in a pretty conservatory with white wicker furniture. The Michelin-trained chef produces top-quality fare – mostly modern South African, so expect fresh fish and game, and divine desserts. Excellent wine list to match. One of the finest restaurants in the area.

†††† La Colombe, Constantia Uitsig, T021-7942390, www.constantiauitsig.co.za. Mon-Sat 1200-1430, 1930-2130. Regarded as one of the finest restaurants in the Cape. Excellent French menu with strong Provençal flavours. Delicious fresh fish and a range of meat and duck dishes, with emphasis on rich sauces. In fine weather you can sit outside overlooking gardens and a pool. Also here is the **Constantia Uitsig Restaurant** and the **River Café**.

†† Silver Tree, Kirstenbosch Botanical Gardens, T021-7629585, www.kirstenbosch restaurant.com. 0830-2200. Lovely terrace with views of the gardens and mountain looming behind. Decent Cape menu, including a great sweet and spicy bobotie, butternut ravioli, ostrich burgers, plus sandwiches and salads. Also offers a picnic hamper service.

Muizenburg p138

†† Gaylords, 65 Main Rd, T021-7885470. Wed-Sun 1200-1430, Wed-Mon 1830-2200. Unpretentious, bustling Indian restaurant set in a Victorian cottage with tacky decor and good value, highly rated north and south Indians curries, recommended for vegetarian dishes.

† Balmoral On Beach, Beach Rd, T021-7886441. Wed-Mon 0900-1700. Despite the grand name, this is little more than a stylish café serving healthy breakfasts and surfer-friendly fry-ups as well as light lunches such as butternut risotto cakes.

† Empire Café, 11 York Rd, T021-7881250. Tue-Sat 0700-2100, Sun and Mon 0700-1600. Hip eatery serving eclectic breakfasts and lunchtime fare, including interesting salads and omelettes (try the famous bacon, banana and honey) and some seafood specials. Popular with local surfers and trendy day-trippers.

Kalk Bay p140

†† Cape to Cuba, Main Rd, T021-7881566. 1100-2300. Atmospheric Cuban restaurant and cocktail bar serving good-value seafood with Caribbean flavours. Great setting on water's edge with tables overlooking the harbour, funky decor, Cuban music, good cocktails and cigars for sale. Bar open till 0200.

† Brass Bell, by the railway station, T021-7885455. Mon-Fri 1100-2300. A well-known and very popular pub and restaurant in a great location. Simple set-up serving pub meals and good pizzas and fish and chips. Downstairs gets packed with a young crowd, very busy around sunset, great for a cool beer outside close to the waves. More expensive restaurant upstairs serves fresh fish and steak.

† Olympia Café & Deli, 134 Main Rd, T021-7886396. 0700-2100. Another Kalk Bay institution, this laid-back café serves some of the freshest bread on the peninsula, plus light lunches, fabulous cakes and fresh daily specials. Great atmosphere and good service, but expect to queue at weekends.

† Sirocco, 82 Main Rd, T021-7881881. Stylish restaurant set right on the main road, with blue and white tables on a shady terrace with lots of plants and an area to relax on cushions. Seafood, steaks, good spot for coffee and all-day breakfasts, try the salmon omelette.

† The Timeless Way, 106 Main Rd, T021-7885619. Mon-Fri 1200-1600, 1800-2230, Sat and Sun from 0900. An excellent, old-fashioned restaurant serving Cape cuisine, steaks and seafood. The bobotie is good, as is the pasta.

Simon's Town *p142, map p141*

¶¶¶ **Bon Appetit**, 90 St George's St, T021-7862412. Tue-Sat 1200-1400, 1830-2200. One of the finest restaurants on the peninsula specializing in top-notch French cuisine – the chef is Michelin-trained. Excellent set menus and imaginative main meals such as ravioli of rabbit plus French staples like confit de canard. Popular and quite small. Book ahead.

¶¶ **Bertha's**, Jubilee Sq, Wharf Rd, T021-7862138. 0700-2130. A seafood grill in a prime location overlooking the yacht harbour. During the day the outside terrace is a good place to enjoy good fresh seafood and watch the goings on in the harbour. Inside is a dining area perfect for large family meals. Great selection of fresh seafood dishes, good value.

¶¶ **Black Marlin**, Miller's Point, 2 km from Simon's Town, T021-7861621, www.black marlin.co.za. Mon-Sat 1200-1600, 1800-2100, Sun lunch only. Set in an old whaling station, this place is well known for its excellent seafood and is a good lunch stop on the way to or from Cape Point. Fabulous sea views and wide range of fresh seafood, delicious crayfish and kingclip skewers, also good-value evening menu. Great wine list. Recommended, but it can get busy with tour buses in summer.

¶¶ **Quarterdeck**, Jubilee Sq, T021-7863825. Open 0800-1900, Fri till 2300. Simple café with great views over the harbour, serving sandwiches, burgers and interesting salads like avocado with smoked chicken and biltong. Also has a **Cape Malay** buffet on Fri evenings.

¶ **Salty Sea Dog**, next to Quayside Centre, T021-7861918. Mon-Sat 1000-2100, Sun 1000-1630. Cheap and cheerful place serving fresh fish and chips with seats overlooking the harbour. Good value, friendly and swift service. Popular with groups.

¶ **The Two and Sixpence**, 88 St George's St, next to the **British Hotel**, T021-7865735. 1000-2400. Local British-style pub serving standard bar food such as burgers, bangers and mash, ploughman's, plus Yorkshire pudding specials, Sun roasts and curry nights. Also has pool tables and occasional live music.

Boulders Beach *p144, map p141*

¶¶ **Penguin Point Café**, Boulders Beach Guest House, T021-7861758, www.boulders beach.co.za. Great family restaurant with bar and sun deck, gets busy with day-trippers. Good English breakfasts, cocktails (including Pickled Penguins), delicious seafood platters and daily specials, plus salads for a light meal.

⊙ Bars and clubs

Clifton *p132*

La Med, Glen Country Club, Victoria Rd, T021-4385600, www.lamed.co.za. 1100-late. Something of a Cape Town institution, hugely popular meeting place for locals, busy bar over-looking the sea, good pub food, great for a sundowner when you'll be hard pressed to find a seat, turns into a raucous club later on. Also a venue for watching rugby matches on giant TVs and is well known for its New Year's Eve party.

Camps Bay *p133*

Café Caprice, Victoria Rd, T021-4388315. 0900-late. Popular café and bar with outdoor seats, great fresh fruit cocktails, gets packed and very noisy around sunset, loud house music played until late by a DJ every night in season and at the weekends in winter.

Dizzy Jazz Café, 41 The Drive, T021-4382686. 1130-late. Busy bar and music venue, popular at the weekend, mostly jazz but has everything from funk to rock, comfortable couches, low tables, food includes sushi and pizza.

Ignite, Victoria Rd, T021-4387717. Thu-Sun 1800-0200, Wed in season. Lounge bar with terrace overlooking the beach, minimalist all-white interior, cubed seating, raised dance floor, fashionable place to be seen at sunset, great but relatively pricey cocktails. Robbie Williams and Colin Farrell have been here.

Sandbar, 31 Victoria Rd, T021-4388336, www.sandbar.co.za. Popular for sundowners at one of the shady tables looking onto the beach. Small place so get here early if you want to secure a table, menu includes wraps, sandwiches and nachos.

The Winelands

The Winelands is South Africa's oldest and most beautiful wine-producing area, a fertile series of valleys quite unlike the rest of the Western Cape. It is the Cape's biggest attraction after Cape Town, and its appeal is simple: it offers the chance to sample several hundred different wines in a historical and wonderfully scenic setting.

This was the first region after Cape Town to be settled, and the towns of Stellenbosch, Paarl and Franschhoek are some of the oldest in South Africa. Today, their streets are lined with beautiful Cape Dutch and Georgian houses, although the real architectural gems are the manor houses on the wine estates. While the wine industry flourished during the 18th and 19th centuries, the farmers built grand homesteads with cool wine cellars next to their vines. Most of these have been lovingly restored and today can be visited as part of a Winelands tour – a few have even been converted into gourmet restaurants or luxury hotels. ▸▸ *For listings, see pages 171-182.*

Ins and outs

Getting there The N2 highway goes past Cape Town International airport, 22 km east of the city, and then continues along the northern fringes of the Cape Flats, home to the sprawling townships of Mitchells Plain, Nyanga and Khayelitsha. Beyond these the R310 left turning is the quickest route to Stellenbosch, the heart of the Winelands, 16 km from the N2. The N2 continues east splitting the towns of Strand and Somerset West before climbing over the Hottentots Holland Mountains into the Overberg via Sir Lowry's Pass (see page 163). The R44 is an alternative route from Strand to Stellenbosch. Paarl and Wellington are best accessed by the N1 from Cape Town, and Franschhoek by either route. The wine estates in the region are far too numerous to list in full, but on an organized tour (see page 181) or a self-drive trip, there is ample opportunity to visit several estates in one day.

Tourist information Tourist offices in Cape Town (see page 80) can provide brochures and maps; also visit www.tourismcapewinelands.co.za. For a list of tour operators offering day tours to the Winelands from Cape Town, see page 127. Wine estates charge a small tasting fee of about R5-20, which often includes a free wine glass.

Background

The Cape's wine industry was started in earnest by Simon van der Stel in 1679. Previously, vines had been grown by Van Riebeeck in Company's Garden and in the area known today as Wynberg. The first wine was produced in 1652, and there was soon a great demand from the crews of ships when they arrived in Table Bay after months at sea. As the early settlers moved inland and farms were opened up in the sheltered valleys, more vines were planted. Every farmer had a few plants growing alongside the homestead, and by chance the soils and climate proved to be ideal. Van der Stel produced the first quality wines on Constantia estate, with the help of Hendrik Cloete. These were mostly sweet wines made from a blend of white and red Muscadel grapes, known locally as *Hanepoot* grapes. The industry received a boost in 1806 when the English, at war with France, started to import South African wines. However, under Apartheid, sanctions hindered exports and the Kooperatieve Wijnbouwers Vereniging (KWV) controlled prices and production quotas. Since the lifting of sanctions, the KWV has lost much of its power, allowing the industry to experiment and expand.

Today, all major wine grape varieties are grown in South Africa, plus the fruity red Pinotage, a variety produced in Stellenbosch in 1925 by crossing Pinot Noir and Cinsault. Wine is now produced as far north as the Orange River Valley in the Northern Cape.

Strand and around 🏨🍴🅿️🛍️ ›› pp171-182. Colour map 8, B1.

Although principally an industrial area, Strand is a popular seaside resort and commuter town with an excellent 5-km white-sand beach. It mainly caters for domestic tourists and, despite its proximity to Cape Town, the Winelands and the Whale Coast, it holds little appeal. Further inland, **Somerset West** is a prosperous town and again a major commuter centre. It has a beautiful location on the slopes of the Helderberg Mountains, with unimpeded views of False Bay and, occasionally, Cape Point.

1 Winelands

➡ **Winelands maps**
1 Winelands, page 152
2 Franschhoek Valley, page 162
3 Paarl Winelands, page 166
4 Wellington district, page 168

Willem van der Stel

Two of the farms on the banks of the Lourens River, Parelvallei and Vergelegen, belonged to two sons of Simon van der Stel, Governor of the Cape. When the governor retired, he went to live on his estate of Constantia. The directors of the Dutch East India Company honoured his works in the Cape by appointing his son, Willem Adriaan, as his successor to the governorship. This proved to be a disaster since Willem principally devoted his energies to building up his estate, Vergelegen. Over the next six years he acquired most of the land in the valley and used the Cape's resources to improve the estate. He was not unskilled at farming and, before he was found out, Vergelegen was regarded as one of the most gracious and successful country estates in the Cape.

However, in 1707 the Dutch East India Company was made aware of the corrupt nature of Willem's dealings and he was recalled to the Netherlands. Vergelegen was confiscated, divided into four farms and sold. Since Simon van der Stel died at Constantia on 24 June 1712 there have been no Van der Stels in the Cape.

Vergelegen Estate

① *T021-8471334, www.vergelegen.co.za, daily 0930-1600. From Somerset West take the R44, turn right at the traffic lights and after 1 km turn left into Lourensford Rd; the estate is 4 km on the right. There is a shop, displays on the history of the estate, a smart wine-tasting room and 2 restaurants: Lady Phillips Restaurant is à la carte, teas and coffees are served 1000-1145 and 1430-1600, lunch 1200-1430, booking essential for lunch T021-8471346; the Rose Terrace is an open-air light lunch spot, Nov-Apr 1000-1600. There is also a picnic hamper service.*

This is one of the Cape's finest estates and the highlight is a visit to the magnificent manor house filled with beautiful period furniture and historical paintings, similar to the collection at Groot Constantia. At the front of the house are five **Chinese camphor trees** that were planted by Willem van der Stel between 1700 and 1706. They are the oldest living documented trees in South Africa and are now a national monument. Behind the house is a walled octagonal garden – many of the plants were planted here by Lady Phillips (wife of Sir Lionel Phillips, owner for 25 years from 1917), who wished to recreate a typical English garden, complete with herbaceous border. Look out for the collection of roses next to the main house. The surrounding parkland, much of it similar to an English country estate, is also open for exploration.

Stellenbosch ☺❷❶❸❀❀O▲❸❶ » pp171-182. Colour map 8, B1.

Stellenbosch, the centre of the Winelands, is the oldest and most attractive town in the region, with a large university giving it a liveliness which is lacking in other nearby towns. The centre has a pleasing mix of architectural styles: Cape Dutch, Georgian, Regency and Victorian houses line broad streets, dappled with shade from centuries-old oak trees, and furrowed with water ditches which still carry water to the gardens. It's a fairly large place but, with its handful of good museums and fun nightlife, is a perfect base for visiting the wine estates.

Ins and outs

The town is served by the suburban Metro railway from Cape Town. But for safety reasons, this is best avoided. Hiring a car is the best way of getting here as you then have the freedom to explore the surrounding wine estates. The trip from Cape Town takes about an hour, either along the N1 or the N2. Stellenbosch itself is perfect for exploring on foot as many of the interesting sights are concentrated in a small area along Church, Dorp and Drostdy streets. **Stellenbosch Tourist Office** ① *36 Market St, T021-8833584, www.stellenboschtourism.co.za, Mon-Fri 0800-1800, Sat 0900-1700, Sun 1000-1600 (in Jun and Aug the office opens 1 hr later and closes 1 hr earlier)*, is a professional and helpful office that provides maps and can help with accommodation bookings, tour information and wine routes. **Stellenbosch On Foot** ① *T021-8879150, or book at the tourist office*, offers 90-minute guided walks that leave from the tourist office every day, 1100 and 1500, R70.

Background

In November 1679 Simon van der Stel left Cape Town with a party of soldiers in order to explore the hinterland. There was already a great need for additional land to be brought

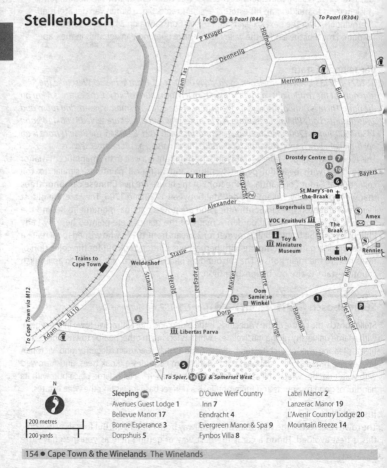

Stellenbosch

Sleeping 🛏
Avenues Guest Lodge **1**
Bellevue Manor **17**
Bonne Esperance **3**
Dorpshuis **5**

D'Ouwe Werf Country
Inn **7**
Eendracht **4**
Evergreen Manor & Spa **9**
Fynbos Villa **8**

Labri Manor **2**
Lanzerac Manor **19**
L'Avenir Country Lodge **20**
Mountain Breeze **14**

under cultivation to supply both Cape Town and passing ships calling for fresh supplies. On the first night the group camped beside a stream they named the Kuilsrivier. The stream turned out to be a tributary of a much larger river, the Eersterivier. As they followed the Eersterivier towards the mountains they found themselves in a fertile alluvial valley. There was no sign of human habitation, the waters were cool and clean and everything seemed to grow in abundance – exactly the type of land Van der Stel had been sent to discover. Several days after entering the valley the group camped under a large tree on an island formed by two branches of the Eersterivier. The camp was named Van der Stel se Bosch (Van der Stel's Wood).

Six months later, in May 1680, eight families from Cape Town moved into the area, tempted by the offer of as much free land as they could cultivate, and by the summer of 1681 Stellenbosch was a thriving agricultural community. This became the first European settlement in the interior of southern Africa. By the end of 1683 more than 30 families had

Ryneveld Country	Eating 🍴	Dros 6	Bars & clubs 🍸
Lodge 10	Blue Orange 1	Fishmonger 8	Bohemia Pub 12
Stellenbosch 11	Brazen Head 9	Volkskombuis 5	Fandango 7
Stumble Inn 12	Café Nouveau 2	Wijnhuis 13	Mexican Kitchen 10
Wilfra Court 21	Coachman 3		Tollie's 11

settled in the valley, a school had been built and a *landdrost* (magistrate) had been appointed. Throughout his life, Simon van der Stel maintained a close interest in the development of the town. One of his greatest legacies was to order the planting of oak trees along the sides of every street. Canals were also built to bring water to the town gardens. Today, a number of the original oaks are still standing and some have been proclaimed national monuments.

It is difficult to picture it today, but at the end of the 17th century this new settlement was a frontier town. For the next 100 years the magistracy had dealings with the explorers, hunters, adventurers and nomadic peoples who lived beyond the Cape, and the authority extended over 250,000 sq km. In the meantime, the town prospered as an agricultural centre and also emerged as a place of learning. In 1859 the Dutch Reformed Church started a Seminary which in 1866 became the Stellenbosch Gymnasium, renamed Victoria College in 1887. After the creation of the Union of South Africa in 1910, there was pressure on the new government to establish a single national university. By this stage Victoria College had emerged as a respected Afrikaner school, and Stellenbosch itself was regarded as an important centre of Afrikaner culture. In 1915 a local farmer, Johannes Marais died and left £100,000 towards higher education in Stellenbosch. This bequest finally persuaded the government to yield to public pressure and in April 1918 the Victoria College became the University of Stellenbosch.

Sights
Stellenbosch offers two approaches to sightseeing: walking around the town centre viewing public buildings, oak-lined streets and stately homes; or going on a wine tour, visiting any number of the roughly 100 wineries and private cellars. Spend a couple of days in Stellenbosch and you'll get to do both. No other town in South Africa has such an impressive concentration of early Cape architecture. However, like Swellendam (see page 264), many of the earliest buildings were lost to fires in the 18th and 19th centuries; what you see today is a collection of perfectly restored buildings. Following each fire, the destroyed buildings were recreated with the help of photographs, original plans and sketches, although the technology and materials of the day were used. This is perhaps why they appear to have survived in such good condition. This restoration process is not unusual: the town of Tulbagh in the Breede River Valley was completely destroyed by an earthquake in 1969, but today it has the look and feel of an unspoilt quaint Victorian village.

Dorp Street, which runs east-west in the southern part of town, has all the classic features – an avenue of oak trees, running water in open furrows and carefully restored white-walled buildings. A walk from the **Libertas Parva** building to the Theological College takes you through the oldest parts of town and past some of the best-preserved old buildings. Libertas Parva is a beautifully restored classic H-shaped manor house built in 1783. Today it serves as an **art gallery** ① *Mon-Fri 0900-1245, 1400-1700, Sat 1000-1300, 1400-1700*, with pictures of Cape Town. The cellar behind the house has a small wine and cork museum. Continue east along Dorp Street, where you'll pass the famous **Oom Samie se Winkel** (No 82), a Victorian-style general store that is still functioning as a shop today. Of particular note are the town houses just past the junction with Helderberg Street. **Hauptfleisch House** (No 153), **Bakker House** (No 155), **Loubser House** (No 157), and **Saxenhof** (No 159), are regarded as the best-preserved street façades in old Stellenbosch.

Branching off from Dorp Street is Drostdy Street, dominated by a building with a tall tower. Also in this street is the town church, the **Moederkerk**; its current steeple church was designed by Carl Otto Hagen and built in 1862. Inside, it is worth admiring the pulpit and the unusually thick stained-glass windows.

Western Cape brandy route

South Africans consume over 45 million litres of brandy each year. There are a dozen or so cellars on the Western Cape brandy route around Stellenbosch, Wellington and Worcester. For more information visit www.sabrandy.co.za.

Van Ryn Brandy Cellar, Vlottenburg, 8 km from Stellenbosch, T021-8813875, www.vanryn.co.za, tours Mon-Fri 1000, 1130 and 1500, Sat 1000, 1130. This is the oldest working cellar in the Cape, where you can view the distillation process and the workshop where the coopers make the maturation barrels from French oak.

Tokara, at the top of the Helshoogte Pass (R310), 5 km from Stellenbosch, T021-8085900, www.tokara.co.za, Mon-Fri 0900-1700, Sat-Sun 1000-1500. A wine estate that produces a five-year-old brandy matured in French oak vats.

Avontuur Estate, R44, 3 km from Somerset West, T021-8553450, www.avontuurestate.com, Mon-Fri 0830-1700, Sat-Sun 0830-1600. Produces a five-year-old copper-distilled brandy and a 10-year-old limited edition made from Chenin Blanc grapes.

Louiesenhof, R304, 4 km outside Stellenbosch towards the N1, T021-8652630, www.louiesenhof.co.za, Mon-Fri 0900-1700, Sat-Sun 1000-1700. Produces alambic-distilled 16-year-old blend brandies made using an antique distilling kettle that was built in Stuttgart in 1930.

Uitkyk, R44 towards Paarl from Stellenbosch, T021-8844416, Mon-Fri 0900-1700, Sat-Sun 1000-1600. Produces one of South Africa's finest 10-year-old estate brandies in a lovely setting on the slopes of the Simonsberg Mountain.

Backsberg, R44 towards Paarl, T021-8755141, www.backsberg.co.za, Mon-Fri 0800-1700, Sat 0930-1400, Sun 1030-1630. A well-known wine estate producing brandies in a state-of-the-art still imported from the Cognac region of France.

Turn right at the top of Drostdy Street into Van Riebeeck Street, then left into Neethling Street to reach the **Botanical Gardens** ① *Mon-Fri 0900-1630, Sat 0900-1100.* These are part of the University of Stellenbosch, with a fine collection of ferns, orchids and bonsai trees. One of the more unusual plants to look out for is the *Welwitschis* from the Namib Desert.

Heading west back along Van Riebeeck Street brings you to Ryneveld Street, where you'll find the entrance to the engaging **Village Museum** ① *T021-8872902, www.museums. org.za/stellmus, Mon-Sat 0930-1700, Sun 1400-1700, R20, children R5.* The complex currently spreads over two blocks in the oldest part of town. If you follow the guide numbers you will be taken through four houses, each representing a different period of the town's history. The oldest of these is **Schreuderhuis** (1709), one of the earliest houses to be built in Stellenbosch. The simple furniture and collection of household objects are all of the same period. The house was built by Sebastian Schreuder, a German. **Blettermanhuis** (1789) is a perfect example of what has come to be regarded as a typical H-shaped Cape Dutch home. The furnishings are those of a wealthy household between 1750 and 1780. The house was built by Hendrik Lodewyk Bletterman, the last *landdrost* to be appointed by the Dutch East India Company. Notice the contrast in furnishings between Schreuder the messenger and Bletterman the magistrate. The third building in the museum to have been restored is **Grosvenor House** (1803), in Drostdy Street. This is an excellent example of the two-storeyed town houses that once dominated the streets of Cape Town. The home was built by Christian Ludolph Neethling, a successful farmer, in 1782. The fourth and final house is the fussy **OM Bergh House** (1870), which once had a thatched roof. All four houses are set in neat kitchen gardens which have been recreated to reflect the popular plants of each period. Guides dressed in period clothes are at hand answer any questions and point out interesting details.

Midway along Church Street is the **D'Ouwe Werf Country Inn** (see Sleeping, page 171), which stands on the site of the first church. The present structure dates from 1802 and the current owners have preserved the foundations and they can be viewed in the cellar of the garden coffee house. As you look back towards the church, the steeple is perfectly framed by grand old oak trees.

Much of the town's activity today takes place around the **Braak**, at the western end of Church Street. This is the original village green, and one-time military parade ground. On the western edge by Market Street is the **VOC Kruithuis** ① *T021-8872902, Mon-Fri 0930-1300, small entry fee,* or Powder House, built in 1777 as a weapons store. Today it is a military museum. A short distance north, on the corner of Alexander Street, is the **Burgerhuis** ① *T021-8870339, www.museums.org.za/burgerhuisstel, Mon-Fri 0800-1630, Sat 1000-1300, 1400-1600, free,* a classic H-shaped Cape Dutch homestead built by Antonie Fick in 1797, that is now decorated to represent the house of a well-to-do Stellenboscher in the Victorian era.

Two churches overlook the Braak, **Rhenish Church**, built in 1832 as a training school for coloured people and slaves, which has a very fine pulpit, and **St Mary's-on-the-Braak**, an Anglican church completed in 1852. A little to the west, on Market Street just behind the tourist office, is the **Toy and Miniature Museum** ① *T021-8879433, Mon-Sat 0930-1700, Sun 1400-1700, minimal entry fee,* a small but fairly diverting collection of antique toys including a working model of the Blue Train, and a set of rooms devoted to miniatures. Most interesting is the small workshop where you can observe the painstaking work of an on-site craftsman producing tiny replicas of furniture, clothes and household items.

Stellenbosch wine route

① *Maps and brochures on the wine route can be picked up at the tourist offices in Stellenbosch and Cape Town or visit www.wineroute.co.za. Remember the drink-drive laws in South Africa. When wine tasting, you may be offered up to 15 different wines to sample at each estate, so make sure one of you stays sober.*

This was the first wine route to open in South Africa, in April 1971. It was the idea of three local farmers: Neil Joubert, Frans Malan and Spatz Sperling. It has been hugely successful, attracting tens of thousands of visitors every year, and today the membership comprises around 100 private cellars. It's possible to taste and buy wines at all of them, and the cellars can arrange for wine to be delivered internationally. Many of the estates have excellent restaurants as well as providing very popular picnic lunches – at weekends it is advisable to book in advance.

Delaire ① *T021-8851756, www.delairewinery.co.za, sales and tastings: Mon-Fri 0900-1700, Sat 1000-1700, Sun 1000-1600.* This small estate has some of the best views in the valley, and has produced some very high-standard wines. Their flagship Merlot is very popular, while the Chardonnay remains a favourite export label. The **Green Door** restaurant serves lunch Tuesday to Sunday; picnic hampers are available. On a clear day visitors are rewarded with views of the Simonsberg Mountains. **Note** Delaire was closed for renovations at the time of writing but should reopen by the time you read this.

Delheim ① *T021-8884600, www.delheim.com, sales and tastings: Mon-Fri 0900-1700, Sat 0900-1600, Sun 1030-1600 (Oct-Apr only), cellar tours: Mon-Fri 1030 and 1430, Sat 1030, restaurant: Mon-Sat 0930-16300, Sun (Oct-Apr only) 0930-1630.* This is one of the more commercially oriented estates and may seem a little too impersonal. However, the restaurant has a beautiful setting with views towards Cape Town and Table Mountain and serves breakfasts, lunches and teas. Tastings are conducted in a cool downstairs cellar.

Eikendal ① *T021-8551422, www.eikendal.com, sales and tastings: Oct-Apr, Mon-Sat 0900-1630, Sun 1000-1600, May-Sep, 1000-1600; cellar tours: Oct-Apr, Mon-Fri, 1000 and 1430, May-Sep, on request.* The microclimate on the western slopes of the mountain is ideal for viticulture, and there is a wide selection of both whites and reds. Lunch is served in the wine-tasting room or the gardens; Swiss owned so expect unusual European dishes on the menu.

Hartenberg ① *T021-8652541, www.hartenbergestate.com, sales and tastings: Mon-Fri 0900-1715, Sat 0900-1500, lunches: 1200-1400.* This privately owned old estate, founded in 1692, is off the Bottelary Road, 10 km north of Stellenbosch. During the summer, lunches are served in the shade and peace of the gardens; come winter the tasting room doubles up as a restaurant with warming log fires. A number of red and white wines are produced, but their reds seem the most successful – past award winners include their 2003 Shiraz and Pinotage.

Neethlingshof ① *T021-8838988, www.neethlingshof.co.za, sales and tastings: Mon-Fri 0900-1700, Sat-Sun 1000-1600, cellar and vineyard tours: by appointment, meals are served in 2 restaurants, Lord Neethling and Palm Terrace, 0900-2100.* With its fine restaurants, Cape Dutch buildings and grand pine avenue (which now features on the labels of the estate wines), this estate is a very pleasant one to visit. The first vines were planted here in 1692 by a German, Barend Lubbe, and the manor house was built in 1814 in traditional Cape Dutch H-style. Today this has been converted into the Lord Neethling restaurant renowned for its venison and veal. Neethlingshof has won a clutch of awards – the Lord Neethling Pinotage is a consistent trophy winner.

Saxenburg ① *T021-9036113, www.saxenburg.co.za, sales and tastings: Mon-Fri 0900-1700, Sat 1000-1700, Sun 1000-1600 (Sep-May only). The Guinea Fowl restaurant is open Wed-Mon for lunch and Wed-Sat for dinner.* Saxenberg has a long history, starting in 1693 when Simon van der Stel granted land to a freeburgher, Jochem Sax. Sax planted the first vines and built the manor house in 1701, and the estate has been producing ever since. It produces a small number of cases each year; its Private Collection of red wines is very good. The restaurant attracts most of the visitors.

Spier ① *Welcome Centre, T021-8091100, www.spier.co.za, sales and tastings: daily 1000-1630. Meals are available throughout the day and evening at 4 on-site restaurants (book several days ahead); picnics and a deli are also available. Accommodation is in The Village at Spier (see Sleeping, page 171).* This is the Winelands' most commercial wine estate, offering a vast array of activities and wine tastings – of both Spier's own wines and those of other Stellenbosch estates. Spier wines are well regarded, and their Private Collection Chenin Blanc 2001 is especially good. As well as wine tasting, there is a cheetah outreach programme (although the creatures seem rather lacklustre) and a birds of prey area, plus horse riding, fishing, an 18-hole golf course and the Camelot spa. There are four superb restaurants on site including a riverside pub, the outdoor 'African' Moyo BBQ, and the Jonkershuis, which has superb (if expensive) Cape Malay buffets. These are hugely popular with tourists and are listed separately under eating. An annual music and arts festival is held at the open-air amphitheatre during the summer months.

Simonsig ① T021-8884900, www.simonsig.co.za, sales and tastings: Mon-Fri 0830-1700, Sat 0830-1600, cellar tours: Mon-Fri 1000 and 1500, Sat 1000. This large estate has been in the Malan family for 10 generations, and in recent years has produced some exceptionally fine wines. There is an attractive outdoor tasting area with beautiful views out over the mountains. One wine worth looking out for is the Kaapse Vonkel, a sparkling white considered the best of its kind in South Africa. Their Chardonnay is consistently very good and not badly priced too.

Villiera ① T021-8652002-3, www.villiera.co.za, sales and tastings: Mon-Fri 0830-1700, Sat 0830-1300. Villiera is highly regarded and produces some of the best wines in the Cape. There are plenty of classic wines to choose from, including their Merlot and Sauvignon Blanc. They no longer conduct cellar tours, but allow self-guided tours.

Franschhoek Valley ●❶❶▲ ›› pp171-182. Colour map 8, B2.

Franschhoek
This is the most pleasant of the Wineland villages, with a compact centre of Victorian whitewashed houses backed by rolling vineyards and the soaring slopes of the Franschhoek Mountains. It does, however, have an artificial feel to it as most of the attractions here have been created to serve the tourist industry. The outlying wine estates all have their individual appeal, but the village itself is made up of restaurants and touristy craft shops. Nevertheless, Franschhoek is famed for its cuisine and dubs itself the 'gastronomical capital of the Western Cape', so a visit here should guarantee an excellent meal accompanied by a fine glass of wine.

Franschhoek

Sleeping
Ashbourne Guesthouse 10
Auberge Bligny 1
Auberge Chanteclair 2
Auberge La Dauphine 3
Bo La Motte 5
Franschhoek Country House 6
Huguenot 7
La Cabrière 8
La Fontaine 9
Le Ballon Rouge 11
Le Quartier Français 4
Mont Rochelle 12
Plumwood Inn 13
Résidence Klein Oliphants Hoek 14

Eating
Chamonix 9
French Connection Bistro 2
Grapevine 4
La Fromagerie at La Grange 1
La Petite Ferme 8
Le Bon Vivant 3

Ins and outs Franschhoek is 71 km from Cape Town (via the N1), 26 km from Paarl and 31 km from Stellenbosch. There is no regular public transport so you will need a car. Most of the tour operators offering Winelands tours don't usually include Franschhoek. The **tourist office** ① *29a Huguenot Rd, T021-8763603, www.franschhoek.org.za, Mon-Fri 0900-1800, Sat 1000-1700, Sun 1000-1600,* has helpful staff with a good knowledge of accommodation and restaurants. The office also has a wine estates' desk and a wine and cheese tasting area, and there's a plant nursery at the back.

Background Although the first Huguenots arrived at the Cape in 1688, the village of Franschhoek only took shape in 1837 after the church and the manse had been built. The first immigrants settled on farms granted to them by Simon van der Stel along the Drakenstein Valley at Oliphantshoek in 1694. Franschhoek is built on parts of La Motte and Cabrière farms. The village became the focal point of the valley but the oldest and most interesting buildings are to be found on the original Huguenot farms and estates.

Sights The **Huguenot Memorial Museum** ① *T021-8762532, Mon-Sat 0900-1700, Sun 1400-1700, R5,* is housed in two buildings either side of Lambrecht Street. The main building, to the left of the Huguenot Monument, is modelled on a house designed by the French architect, Louis Michel Thibault, built in 1791 at Kloof Street, Cape Town. The displays inside trace the history of the Huguenots in South Africa. There are some fine collections of furniture, silverware and family bibles, but the most interesting displays are the family trees providing a record of families over the past 250 years. One of the roles of the museum today is to maintain an up-to-date register of families, so that future generations will be able to trace their ancestors.

Next door to the museum is the rather stark and unattractive **Huguenot Monument**, a highly symbolic memorial built to mark 250 years since the first Huguenots settled in the Cape. It is set in a peaceful rose garden with the rugged Franschhoek Mountains providing a contrasting background. The three arches represent the Trinity, and the golden sun and cross on top are the Sun of Righteousness and the Cross of Christian Faith. In front of the arches, a statue of a woman with a bible in her right hand and a broken chain in her left symbolizes freedom from religious oppression. If you look closely at the globe you can see objects carved into the southern tip of Africa: a bible, harp, spinning wheel, sheaf of corn and a vine. These represent different aspects of the Huguenots' life, respectively their faith, their art and culture, their industry and their agriculture. The final piece of the memorial, the curved colonnade, represents tranquillity and spiritual peace after the problems they had faced in France.

Franschhoek wine route

All the vineyards lie along the Franschhoek Valley, making it one of the most compact wine routes in the region. What makes this such a rewarding route is that many estates have opened their own excellent restaurants and several also offer luxury accommodation. There are now 26 wine estates on the route, with more being added every year. All the valley's wine can be tasted at the **Franschhoek Vineyards Cooperative** ① *T021-8762086, www.franschhoek-vineyards.co.za, Mon-Fri 0930-1700, Sat 1000-1600, Sun 1100-1500,* on the right just before you enter the village when approaching from Stellenbosch. There is a restaurant, and information on all the estates is available here.

Allée Bleue ① *T021-8741021, www.alleebleue.com, sales and tastings: daily 1000-1600.* This estate is a good place to drop in for some quick wine tasting if you haven't the time to see a whole vineyard. There is a small, fashionable restaurant and deli set just off the R45 towards Franschhoek at the entrance, serving light meals 0900-1700. Tastings include four wines accompanied by four cheeses to offset the flavours. There is also a nursery here that sells, amongst other things, mushrooms and organic herbs.

Boschendal ① *T021-8704272, www.boschendal.com, sales and tastings: daily 0830-1630, vineyard tours: 1030 and 1130, by appointment. The cellar restaurant, Boschendal, serves an excellent buffet lunch; between Nov-Apr Le Pique Nique offers picnic hampers in the gardens. Le Café is open daily for snacks and afternoon teas.* Boschendal estate has been producing wine for 300 years and is today one of the most popular estates in the region, not least for its excellent food and pleasant wine-tasting area underneath a giant oak. The estate started life as two farms in 1687, and was bought in 1715 by Abraham de Villiers. The restored H-shaped manor house (1812) is one of the finest in South Africa, and is open as a museum to the public. Interestingly, a third of the estate is now owned by a black empowerment consortium. Most of the wine produced on the estate is white; their sparkling wines are highly regarded. In 2004 Boschendal was named South African Wine Producer of the Year.

Cape Chamonix ① *T021-8762494, www.chamonix.co.za, sales and tastings: daily 0930-1630, cellar tours: by appointment.* This is one of the largest farms in the valley, with an underground cellar providing pleasantly cool tours at the height of summer. Wine tastings are held in the Blacksmith's Cottage; you can also try their fruit schnapps or the Chamonix

2 Franschhoek Valley

3 Platberg (748m)

To Paarl
R45
Berg River
To Paarl (11 km)
R303
Wemershoek Dam
Tafelberg (1748m)
Olifants River
Perdekop (1122m)
R310
La Motte
Wemmershoekberge
Allée Bleue
Cape Chamonix
To Stellenbosch
L'Ormarins
Boschendal
R310
Roberts River
Middenberg (663m)
Franschhoek
Franschhoek Pass
Drakensteinberge
Mont Rochelle
Paradise Stables
Joubertsgat Bridge
R45
To Villiersdorp & N2
Dewdale Fly Fishing
Olifantsberg
Assegaaibos Dam

➡ **Winelands maps**
1 Winelands, page 152
2 Franschhoek Valley, page 162
3 Paarl Winelands, page 166
4 Wellington district, page 168

N

3 km
3 miles

Sleeping 🛏
Lekkerwijn 3

Four Passes

One of the popular recommended day drives from Cape Town is known as the Four Passes route. This takes you through the heart of the Winelands, and, as the name suggests, over four mountain passes. It is a wonderful day out from Cape Town, especially if combined with fine wine and gourmet food in Franschhoek. The first stop on the drive is Stellenbosch. From here you take the R310 towards Franschhoek. Driving up out of Stellenbosch you cross the first pass – **Helshoogte Pass**. After 17 km you reach a T-junction with the R45: a left turn would take you to Paarl, 12 km, but the route continues to the right. This is a pleasant drive up into the Franschhoek Valley. The road follows a railway line and part of the Berg River. After passing through Franschhoek, take a left in front of the Huguenot Monument and climb out of the valley via the **Franschhoek Pass**. This pass was built along the tracks formed by migrating herds of game centuries earlier, and was originally known as the Olifantspad (elephant's path). One of the more surprising aspects of this drive is the change in vegetation once you cross the lip of the pass, 520 m above the level of Franschhoek.

As the road winds down towards Theewaterskloof Dam, you pass through a dry valley full of scrub vegetation and fynbos – gone are the fertile fruit farms and vineyards.

Take a right across the dam on the R321 towards Grabouw and Elgin. An alternative but much longer route back to Cape Town is to take a left here, onto the R43. This is the road to Worcester, 50 km, the principal town in the Breede River Valley (see page 211). From Worcester follow the N1 back to Cape Town.

The Four Passes Route continues across the Theewaterskloof Dam and then climbs **Viljoens Pass**, the third of four. To the right lies the Hottentots Holland Nature Reserve, a popular hiking region. The country around here is an important apple-growing region. At the N2 highway turn right and follow the road back into Cape Town. The fourth and most spectacular pass is **Sir Lowry's Pass**, which crosses the Hottentots Holland Mountains. From the viewpoint at the top you will be rewarded with a fine view of the Cape Flats with the brooding Cape Peninsula behind.

mineral water. The **Chamonix** restaurant (see Eating, page 176) is family friendly and highly rated. Food is prepared on a stove built in Paris in 1908. Accommodation is also available in seven comfortable whitewashed self-catering cottages (**D**).

Mont Rochelle ⓘ *T021-8763000, www.montrochelle.co.za, sales and tastings: daily 1000-1800, cellar tours: Mon-Fri 1100, 1230, 1500.* This estate has one of the most attractive settings in the region with beautiful views of the valley. Owner Miko Rwayitare has doubled the area under vines in the last few years and completely redeveloped the estate, now offering two white and three red wines. Tastings are informal and friendly and picnic baskets are available. The estate is also home to a hotel and restaurant (see page 173).

La Motte ⓘ *T021-8763119, www.la-motte.co.za, sales and tastings: Mon-Fri 0900-1630, Sat 1000-1500, cellar tours: by appointment, light lunches served in summer.* The original manor house was built in 1752 and the grand old cellars, worth a visit in themselves, are now used as a classical concert venue in the evenings. Wine tasting takes place in a smart tasting centre overlooking the cellars. As a relatively small producer, only 15,000 cases a year, the estate has managed to create some excellent wines. The La Motte Millennium Claret blend remains their most popular wine.

L'Ormarins ① *T021-8741026, www.lormarins.co.za, sales and tastings: Mon-Fri 0900-1630, Sat 1000-1430, cellar tours: by appointment*. This vineyard has a beautiful setting on the slopes of the Drakensteinberge, above the Bellingham estate (excellent, but no longer open to visitors). The original land was granted to the Huguenot, Jean Roi, in 1694, who named the farm after his village in the South of France. The present homestead was built in 1811 – from its grand marble halls and staircases you look out across an ornamental pond and neat gardens. The other notable attraction is the original wine cellar; this has been carefully restored and now houses a set of giant wine vats. On offer is the classic range of wines, plus the Italian varietal range, Terra del Capo. Cheeseboards are available during summer.

Paarl Winelands ●❷▲● ⏵⏵ *pp171-182. Colour map 8, A1.*

Paarl

While Paarl is home to two of South Africa's better-known wine estates, KWV and Nederburg (see page 167), the town itself is not as interesting as Stellenbosch or as fashionable as Franschhoek. All of the attractions and restaurants are strung out along Main Street at the base of Paarl Mountain. When the first European arrival, Abraham Gabbema, saw this mountain in October 1657 it had just rained; the granite domes sparkled in the sunlight and he named the mountains *paarl* (pearl) and *diamandt* (diamond). The first settlers arrived in 'Paarlvallei' in 1687 and, shortly afterwards, the French Huguenots settled on four farms, **Laborie**, **Goede Hoop**, **La Concorde** and **Picardie**. The town grew in a random fashion along an important wagon route to Cape Town. Several old buildings survive, but they are spread out rather than concentrated in a few blocks as in Stellenbosch. There is a helpful **tourist office** ① *corner of Plantasie and Main St, at the turn-off to the Grande Roche Hotel, T021-8634937, www.paarlonline.com, Mon-Fri 0800-1700, Sat 0900-1400, Sun 1000-1400.*

Sights The 1-km walk along Main Street will take you past some of the finest architecture in Paarl. Here you'll find one of the oldest buildings, the **Paarl Museum** ① *303 Main St, T021-8762651, www.museums.org.za/paarlmuseum, Mon-Fri 0900-1700, Sat 0900-1300, R5.* This 18th-century U-shaped Cape Dutch former parsonage houses a reasonably diverting collection of Cape Dutch furniture and kitchen copperware plus some more delicate silver. There is also a small section outlining Paarl during Apartheid, although the fact that Nelson Mandela spent his final years in prison near Paarl is barely mentioned. Only a few hundred metres away, in Gideon Malherbe House, the **Afrikaans Language Museum** ① *Pastorie St, T021-8723441, www.taalmuseum.co.za, Mon-Fri 0900-1600, Sat 0900-1300, R10*, gives a detailed chronicle of the development of the Afrikaans language and the people involved. Between the two museums is **Zeederberg Square**, a 19th-century square with a fine mix of restored buildings and lively restaurants. Further south on Main Street is the **Strooidakkerk**, a thatched church consecrated in 1805 and still in use.

On the east bank of the Berg River is a 31-ha **arboretum** ① *open during daylight hours.* From the tourist office, go down Market Street and cross the river; the arboretum is on the right. It was created in 1957 to mark the tercentenary of the discovery of the Berg River Valley. To help establish the parkland the town treasurer asked other municipalities in

Paarl

To Rheboksloof Wine Estate

To Nederburg Wine Estate, Wellington, Ceres & Tulbagh

EK Green

Jan Van Riebeeck

Huguenot Bypass

Malan
Olyven
Botha
Napier
R45 Main
Du Plessis
Stirling
Navarre
Rhone
Congony
Berg River Blvd
Plein
Hospital
Breda
Distillery

Plein
Reyneke
Alexander
Loule
Ottawa
Bethel
Fabriek
Dorp
De Villiers
Vester
Synagogue
Swartvlei
Castle
Waterkant

Vintage Cape Tours
Mill
Nantes
Upper Lady
Lady Grey
New

Kloof
Myburgh
Victoria
Zeederberg Square
Paarl Museum
Loop
Van der Lingen
Matherbe
Afrikaans Language Museum
Pastorie
Deoken
Thom
Du Toit
Breda
Thesen
Moni
Textile
Eiland

Durr
Timber
pietra
Orange
Hour
Van

Faure
Civic Centre
Helpmekaar
Market
Arboretum
R101 Langenhoven

City Hall
Market
Bernhardi
Devine
Auret
Berea
Protea
Falaise
Pontac
Zion
1st
2ad
3rd
4th
Patriot

High
Roze
Templier

Klein Reservoir
Haarlem
Rabie
Strooidakkerk

Berg
Bosman
Elisabet
Brug
Bultekant
Stakel
Elba
Treurnich
Rosendal

Plantasie
Paarl Vintners
Constantia
Enslin

To Bretagne Rock & Paarl Nature Reserve
To "Jan Philips Mountain Drive"
To Stellenbosch & Cape Town

Berg River Blvd
Roodeburg
R45
Cecilia

To Paarl Station & KWV Winery

Berg River

To Franschhoek 26 km (R301)
R301
To Du Toitskloof Wine Cellar

Huguenot Station
Van der Merwe
Ambagsvallei
Kelsey
Fairview
Muscadel
Aurora

To Du Toitskloof Wine Cellar

Sleeping
Amberg Guest Farm **7**
Berg River Resort **11**
De Oude Paarl **8**
Eben Haëzer Country House **12**
Grande Roche & Bosman's Restaurant **2**
Lemoenkloof Guest House **3**
Nantes-Vue **5**
Oak Tree Lodge **6**
Pontac Manor **4**
Zomerlust **13**

Eating
De Malle Madonna **6**
Dros **1**
Kosinrichting **2**
Laborie **3**

N

300 metres
300 yards

South Africa to contribute trees and shrubs from their region. The response was excellent and when the arboretum was inaugurated there were trees from 61 different regions. Today there are over 700 different species and around 4000 trees.

Nelson Mandela spent his final years in prison near Paarl. His first steps of freedom were from Victor Verster Prison, 9 km south of town on the road to Franschhoek.

Parl Mountain Nature Reserve
ⓘ *Daily 0700-1900 in summer, 0700-1800 in winter. There is a small entrance fee to the reserve, but you do not need to obtain further permits for hiking. The tourist office should be able to give you a clear colour map which has details of access roads and footpaths. There are several car parks with toilets and braai spots. If you wish to fish in one of the dams you need to go to the municipality for a permit.*

Paarl runs along the eastern base of Paarl Mountain, a giant granite massif, which in 1970 was declared the Paarl Mountain Nature Reserve. To get there go south along Main Street and follow the Jan Phillips Mountain Drive out of town to the west, Within the 1900-ha reserve is a network of footpaths, a circular drive and a couple of dams. The vegetation differs from the surrounding countryside because of the bedrock – the granite mass is not as susceptible to veld fires and many of the fynbos species grow exceptionally tall.

The domed summit is easy to climb, and near the top is an old cannon dating from the early days of the Cape Colony. On the summit are three giant granite rocks. The highest point is 729 m and there is a chain to help you up the last steep incline. Nearby is **Gordon's Rock**, named after Colonel Robert Jacob Gordon who commanded the British troops at the Cape from 1780 to 1795. This rock is dangerous and should only be tackled by experienced climbers. The third rock is known as **Paarl Rock**. Just below the summit a mountain stream flows through the **Meulwater Wild Flower Reserve**. This garden was created in 1931, and contains specimens of the majority of flowers found around Paarl Mountain including 15 species of proteas.

Set high on the slopes of Paarl Mountain amongst granite boulders and indigenous trees stands the controversial **Afrikaanse Taalmonument** ⓘ *daily 0800-1700*, three concrete columns linked by a low curved wall. This is the Afrikaans Language Monument, inaugurated in October 1975 and designed by Jan van Wijk. Built to celebrate 100 years of Afrikaans being declared as a different language from Dutch, it is thought to be on the only monument in

3 **Paarl Winelands** 4

Winelands maps
1 Winelands, page 152
2 Franschhoek Valley, page 162
3 **Paarl Winelands, page 166**
4 Wellington district, page 168

Sleeping
Berg River Resort 1
Palmiet Valley Estate 3
Roggeland Country House 4

2 km
2 miles

the world dedicated to a language. Each column represents different influences in the language. The relative heights of each column and the negative connotations associated with them have been the subject of criticism in recent years. The **coffee shop** ⓘ *Mon 0830-1700, Tue-Sun 0830-2200*, has excellent views across the Berg River Valley.

The best views of the surrounding countryside are from Bretagne Rock; on a clear day you can see False Bay, Table Mountain and all the vineyards.

Those with children in tow may wish to visit **Butterfly World** ⓘ *Klapmuts, T021-8755628, daily 0900-1700, R28, children R15*, the largest such park in South Africa, with butterflies flying freely in colourful landscaped gardens. There is a craft shop and the **Jungle Leaf Café** on site.

Paarl wine route
ⓘ *The wine route information office can be found at Paarl Vintners at 86 Main Rd, T021-8634886, www.paarlwine.co.za.*
The route was set up in 1984 by local producers to help promote their wines and attract tourists into the area. The programme has been a great success and some of the estates have opened their own restaurants. All of the estates have tastings and wine sales on a daily basis. Today there are 35 members, but only the largest estates conduct regular cellar tours. Below is a short selection.

Boland ⓘ *T021-8626190, www.bolandwines.co.za, sales and tastings: Mon-Fri 0800-1700, Sat 0900-1400, cellar tours: by appointment.* The estate has an excellent wine cellar, and offers one of the most interesting cellar tours. Their Boland Cellar Reserve No 1 Shiraz 2005 won the 2007 Paarl Shiraz Challenge. Picnics and cheese platters are on offer.

Fairview ⓘ *T021-8632450, www.fairview.co.za, wine and cheese sales and tastings: Mon-Fri 0830-1700, Sat 0830-1600, Sun 0930-1600.* This popular estate has a rather unusual attraction in the form of a goat tower, a spiral structure which is home to two pairs of goats. In addition to a variety of good wines (look out for the popular Goats do Roam and Bored Doe blends – a humorous dig at French wines) visitors can taste delicious and award-winning goat and Jersey milk cheeses. The goats are milked each afternoon from 1530.

The Laborie ⓘ *T021-8073390, www.laborie.co.za, sales and tastings: daily 0900-1700, closed Sun from May-Sep, cellar tours: by appointment.* Part of KWV (see below), this is a beautifully restored original Cape Dutch homestead – in many ways the archetypal wine estate, and developed with tourism firmly in mind. It's an attractive spot, with a tasting area overlooking rolling lawns and vineyards, and a highly rated restaurant.

KWV ⓘ *T021-8073007, www.kwvwineemporium.co.za, sales and tastings: Mon-Sat 0900-1600, Sun 1100-1600, cellar tours: Mon-Sat 1000, 1015 (in German), 1030, 1415.* A short distance from the Laborie estate is the famous **KWV Cellar Complex** which contains the five largest vats in the world. The Ko-operative Wijnbouwers Vereniging van Zuid-Afrika (Cooperative Wine Growers' Association) was established in Paarl in 1918 and is responsible for exporting many of South Africa's best-known wines. They are also well known for their brandy and tastings are served with Belgium chocolates.

Nederburg ⓘ *T021-8623104, www.nederburg.co.za, sales and tastings: Mon-Fri 0830-1700, Sat 1000-1600, Sun 1100-1600, cellar tours are available in English, German and*

French but must be booked in advance; picnic lunches are available (vegetarian and children's menu available) or enjoy a 2-hr 3-course lunch where the food is matched to a selection of 6 wines. This is one of the largest and best-known estates in South Africa. Their annual production is in excess of 650,000 cases. As such a large concern they are involved in much of the research in South Africa to improve the quality of the grape and vine. Every April the annual Nederburg Auction attracts buyers from all over the world and is considered one of the top five wine auctions in the world. The homestead was built in 1800, but throughout the 19th century the wines were not considered to be anything special. This all changed in 1937 when Johann George Graue bought the estate. Riesling and Cabernet Sauvignon vines were planted, and the cellars completely modernized. Today their wines win countless annual awards. To get there from the centre of Paarl, cross the Berg River and take the R303 towards Wellington as you leave town, the estate is signposted to the right.

Nelson's Creek ① *T021-8698453, www.nelsonscreek.co.za, sales and tastings: Mon-Fri 0800-1800, Sat 0900-1400, restaurant is open during the summer months, picnic baskets also available for lunches on the estate.* This is a very pleasant estate to spend the afternoon exploring. Its most recent owner, Alan Nelson, has been successfully producing wines since 1987. In 1996, he donated part of his estate to his farm labourers who now produce wines under the 'New Beginnings' label. A farmers' market is held here on the first Saturday morning of the month.

Rhebokskloof ① *T021-8698386, www.rhebokskloof.co.za, sales and tastings: daily 0900-1700, the Victorian Restaurant serves breakfast, lunches and teas and dinner Fri-Sun.* This old estate is now a thoroughly modern outfit, informal tastings are accompanied by

4 Wellington district

To Porterville
Berg River
R44
Groenberg
Kromme River
Wellington Wine Cellar
Wamakersvallei
To Malmesbury
Bovlei
R301
Wellington
Blouvlei
Berg
R45
To Paarl
R303
To Paarl
To
N
3
Witt River
To Ceres & Tulbagh via Bain's Kloof Pass

1 km
1 mile

➡ **Winelands maps**
1 Winelands, page 152
2 Franschhoek Valley, page 162
3 Paarl Winelands, page 166
4 Wellington district, page 168

Sleeping 🛌
5 Mountains Lodge 1
Augusta Kleinbosch
Guest Farm 2

Diemersfontein Wine
& Country Estate 4
Klein Rhebokskloof 7

cheese and biscuits, or pre-booked formal guided tastings by a variety of snacks to bring out the flavours of the wines and a cellar tour. The terrace café is popular with tour groups. One of their best wines is the 2001 Cabernet Sauvignon.

Wellington district ⊖❷❷ ▸▸ pp171-182. Colour map 8, A1.

Wellington

Wellington, like the other Winelands towns, is surrounded by beautiful countryside and has a number of fine historic buildings, with the added bonus of far fewer tourists thronging the streets. Nevertheless, there is little in the town to keep visitors for long – there are a few wine estates in the surrounding area, but the town is best known for its dried fruit. (The other important fruit centres, Ceres and Tulbagh, are on the eastern side of the Limietberg. They can be visited via the magnificent Bain's Kloof Pass, see page 170). To the north, the countryside opens up into the rolling Swartland, an important wheat region. A short drive to the south reveals steep hills where all the farmland is given over to vines. The staff at **Wellington Tourism Bureau** ⓘ *104 Main St, housed in the Old Market Building next to the Dutch Reformed Church, T021-8734604, www.wellington.co.za, Mon-Fri 0800-1700, Sat 0900-1400, Sun 1000-1300,* are helpful and well organized and there is a good selection of local wines on sale.

The Murray Jubilee Hall and Samuel House were once an institute for training Dutch Reformed Church missionaries; they are now part of **Huguenot College**. The shady **Victoria Park** in Church Street is notable for its roses. Look out for the archway which was built to commemorate the coronation of King Edward VII in 1902. The fountain in **Joubert Square** was unveiled in 1939 as a memorial to the Huguenot settlers in the valley. The **Wellington Museum** ⓘ *Church St, T021-8734710, www.wellingtonmuseum.org, Mon-Fri 0900-1700, R5,* has a small collection on the history of the town and the Huguenot farms in the district. The archives of the Huguenot Seminary are kept here.

Wellington wine route

This is one of the smallest routes in the area, with only 25 members. Much of the farmland in the district is devoted to the production of wheat, and grapes used for dried fruit. The following is a selection of winemakers who open their doors to the public.

Bovlei ⓘ *T021 8731567, www.bovlei.co.za, sales and tasting: Mon-Fri 0800-1700, Sat 0830-1230, out of town on the R301 towards Bain's Kloof Pass.* Established in 1907 and with a completely modernized cellar, Bovlei produces mainly white wines and the Chenin Blanc won a gold award in 2004.

Wamakersvallei ⓘ *T021-8731582, www.wamakersvallei.co.za, sales and tasting: Mon-Fri 0800-1700, Sat 0830-1230, north of town on the R44.* This is one of the largest wine producers on the Wellington route. It has won several awards in recent years, for its Cabernet Sauvignon and Pinotage varieties amongst others.

Wellington ⓘ *T021-8731163, www.wellingtoncellar.co.za, sales and tasting: Mon-Fri 0800-1300, 1400-1700, cellar tours by appointment, close to the railway station.* This is another award-winning cellar; Chenin Blanc is their most important white cultivar, and the Pinotage is the most popular red. It's worth a visit to see some of the most advanced wine-making technology in the region.

Bain's Kloof Pass

No matter which direction you take when leaving the Cape by road you will at some stage have to cross the mountains via a spectacular pass. Bain's Kloof is regarded as one of the greatest passes; as you drive through, enjoy the views but also take note of its construction history. The pass was a tremendous feat of engineering and the route has not changed since it was built; the only change made in 154 years of use was to tar the road in 1934.

In 1846 Andrew Geddes Bain, the inspector of roads, noticed a gap in the mountain range in the direction of Wellington while working in the Breede River Valley. A few months later, he traversed the mountains via the 'gap' and put forward a proposal for a new pass. John Montagu, the colonial secretary, gave his full backing to the project, but work did not start until 1849.

This was the greatest period of road building in the Cape, but these ambitious projects could only be afforded by using convict labour. On his arrival in the Cape, John Montagu had been shocked by the conditions on Robben Island, where convicts were incarcerated. In 1847, Ordinance 7 was promulgated, for the "discipline and safe custody of convicts employed on public roads". This was Montagu's plan to reform prison conditions and ways of punishment. The first pass to be constructed under the new system was Mitchell's Pass in 1846. From then until 1888 all the major roads and passes were built using the convict system. It was considered a great success, but the labour was hard and the prisoners wore chains. The only tools available were picks, shovels, sledgehammers, rock drills and gunpowder.

Before work could start at Bain's Kloof, neat stone barracks were built to house over 200 convicts. Conditions were better than in prison and local farmers were contracted to supply fresh straw for palliasses on a weekly basis. The total cost of Bain's Kloof Pass was £50,000; the convicts were paid 60 pence per month, but the cost of their daily rations, seven pence, was deducted from this; Bains was paid an annual salary of £300; the head warders and chaplains were paid £100 per annum, while the ordinary warders received £12 per annum plus rations. The cost of gunpowder used was £1223 – over 10 km of rock had to be blasted out.

The pass took 1608 days to complete, a considerable achievement considering the terrain and the tools available. Most of the labour was unskilled (at the outset) and yet retaining walls, culverts, aqueducts and drains were built – all using drystone masonry techniques. What's more, all these features are still in place and in use today. The pass was opened by Petrus Borchardus Borcherds, chairman of the Central Roads Board, Cape Town, on 14 September 1853, amidst great celebrations. The new route between Cape Town and Worcester was 57 km shorter and it saved two days' travel.

In total, Andrew Geddes Bain built eight passes in South Africa during the first half of the 1800s. His son Thomas Charles John Bain built another 24 major mountain roads and passes in the Cape during the second half of the 1800s. These include Prince Alfred's Pass from Knysna to Uniondale (1865), Seven Passes road from George to Knysna (1882) and Swartberg Pass from Oudtshoorn to Prince Albert (1888).

◉ Winelands listings

◉ Sleeping

Strand and around *p152*

A Willowbrook Lodge, Morgenster Av, Somerset West, T021-8513759, www.willowbrook.co.za. Homely country lodge set in a beautiful garden, 12 large, well-appointed rooms with a/c, TV, private patio, good restaurant, beautician, swimming pool, pleasant setting on outskirts of Somerset West.

B Die Ou Pastorie, 41 Lourens St, Somerset West, T021-8501660, www.dieoupastorie.com. Restored parsonage originally built in 1819. 16 luxurious rooms with comfortable, traditional furnishings, TV, some rooms in separate complex, mature Victorian gardens, swimming pool. Attached restaurant is popular and has won national awards for its food and wine list (see Eating, page 176).

B Zandberg Guest House, 96 Winery Rd, just out of Somerset West towards Stellenbosch, T021-8422945, www.zandberg.co.za. Guesthouse on a working wine estate, 11 luxury cottages set in immaculate gardens, some have fireplaces, all have private terraces and contemporary decor. Swimming pool, braai, fine restaurant, beauty treatments. Recommended. Rates drop considerably in winter.

Stellenbosch *p153, map p154*

The Winelands has a fine selection of accommodation, much of it in historic buildings furnished with antiques, but room rates are very high. However Stellenbosch has an excellent backpacker hostel, which enables budget travellers to explore this region on an overnight stay.

In town

A Dorpshuis, 22 Dorp St, T021-8839881, www.dorpshuis.co.za. A very smart Victorian townhouse with 22 a/c rooms, some of which are suites, all have TV, marble-clad bathrooms, heavy fabrics and dark furniture, private patios, antiques, large breakfasts with plenty of choice, neat gardens, swimming pool.

A D'Ouwe Werf Country Inn, 30 Church St, T021-8874608, www.ouwewerf.com. Converted Georgian house with 31 a/c rooms, all individually decorated with antique furnishings and polished floors. Off-street parking, good-sized pool, beauty salon and vine-shaded terrace where breakfast and lunch are served. Restaurant **1802** offers traditional Cape cooking in smart surroundings, and has had good reports. Recommended as a treat.

A-B Evergreen Manor & Spa, 29 van Riebeeck St, T021-8866343, www.evergreenmanor.co.za. Stylishly converted corner house with 5 attractive a/c double rooms in the main building, and 4 in garden units, individually decorated, some with 4-poster beds, big sofas, antiques, free-standing baths, TV, lovely sunny courtyard. Close to botanical gardens and town centre. The spa offers a full range of treatments. Welcoming place to stay. Recommended.

A-B Eendracht, 161 Dorp St, T021-8838843, www.eendracht-hotel.com. Housed in a reconstruction of what was one of Stellenbosch's oldest houses, this boutique hotel has 12 rooms with modern understated decor and luxuries like silk-filled duvets, a/c, DSTV, wireless internet, pool, bar, lounge. The small restaurant serves traditional South African dishes such as waterblommetjiebredie.

A-B Fynbos Villa, 14 Neethling St, T021-8838670, www.fynbosguesthouse.co.za. Converted family home with garden extension. 13 a/c rooms, all with TV, en suite bathroom and kettle. 1 self-catering cottage sleeping up to 4. Large courtyard, pool, private parking, friendly, homely feel, though rather fussy decor. Short walk to town centre. German spoken.

A-B Stellenbosch Hotel, 162 Dorp St, T021-8873644, www.stellenbosch.co.za/hotel. Central hotel with 27 a/c rooms and 2 apartments in a national monument building. Each room has TV, minibar and pleasant bathroom, although the decor could do with an update. Friendly bar popular with locals, bright dining room with tables on terrace overlooking the street, serving game and seafood (see Eating, page 177).

B Labri Manor, 71 Victoria St, T021-8865652, www.labrimanor.co.za. 10 luxury rooms with beautiful decor, polished wooden floors, huge 4-poster beds, subtle yellow walls and dark wood antiques. Spacious Victorian-style en suite bathrooms, TV lounge, cobbled court-yard, dinner and picnic baskets on request, extras include fresh flowers and a glass of port, a fine Victorian house. Recommended.

B Ryneveld Country Lodge, 67 Ryneveld St, T021-8874469, www.ryneveldlodge.co.za. B&B in a smart Victorian house with 15 a/c rooms (some in more expensive cottages). Beautiful house full of antiques with breakfast room, shady terrace, small pool, secure parking.

C Avenues Guest Lodge, 32 The Avenue, T021-8871843, www.theavenues.co.za. 8 en suite rooms, some non-smoking, wooden floors and bright, simple furnishings. The garden-facing room (No 5) is the nicest, with original fittings in the bathroom. TV lounge, small pool, secluded gardens (can be noisy from traffic), huge breakfasts served.

C Bonne Esperance, 17 Van Riebeeck St, T021-8870225, www.bonneesperance.com. Appealingly rambling Victorian townhouse with wrap-around veranda, opposite the botanical gardens. 15 comfortable en suite rooms with high ceilings and an English feel to the decor, sunny and spacious dining room, lovely garden with small swimming pool.

E-F Stumble Inn, 12 Market St, T021-8874049, www.jump.to/stumble. Popular hostel in 2 separate Victorian bungalows. Spacious double rooms, cramped dorms and camping. Original house has attractive garden, bar, TV room, kitchen, hammocks, shady cushion banks; other house has small pool, kitchen. Very relaxed and friendly place. Excellent value **Easy Rider Wine Tours** (see page 181), bicycles to hire, remains by far the best budget option in town.

Out of town

L Lanzerac Manor, 2 km from town centre towards Jonkershoek Reserve, Jonkershoek Rd, T021-8871132, www.lanzerac.co.za. Very expensive but fittingly luxurious hotel set around an 18th-century Cape Dutch manor house on a wine estate, tastings and cellar tours on offer. 48 suites, some around a patio and swimming pool, spacious and plush with all mod cons. 2 restaurants: the formal **Governor's Hall**, which is rather fussy with slow service; and the relaxed and more enjoyable **Lanzerac Terrace** for al fresco dining during summer. New addition is an extensive wellbeing centre and beauty spa with a separate pool overlooking the vines.

AL The Spier Hotel, Spier Wine Estate on the R44, T021-8091100, www.spier.co.za. Probably the Winelands' most commercial wine estate, but a thoroughly enjoyable place to stay. Accommodation is in condo-style buildings set around courtyards with private pools for each section. The 155 rooms are enormous and very comfortable, with neutral, stylish decor, trendy polished concrete floors, huge beds, lots of windows, TV, minibar, beautiful bathrooms stocked with aroma-therapy products. 4 restaurants on site. See page 177 for details on the wines and all the activities on offer. Recommended if you only have a day in the Winelands.

AL Wedgeview Country House and Spa, The Bonniemile, 5 km south of town, T021-8813525, www.wedgeview.co.za. Attractive thatched farmhouse, converted family home with 11 garden-based thatched luxury suites and 1 family cottage, main house has snooker room, bar, drawing room, dining room, all set in 1.5 ha of attractive gardens surrounded by vineyards, 2 swimming pools, jacuzzi and wellness and beauty spa.

B Bellevue Manor, 5 km south of Stellenbosch on Strand Rd (R44), T021-8801086, www.bellevuestellenbosch.co.za. Purpose-built a/c cottages in Cape Dutch style with thatched roofs, pleasant country-style furnishings, TV, fireplace, bathroom, honesty bar fridge, private terrace, good-sized pool with braai area, close to 2 golf courses. Rates drop in winter. Debi, the onsite therapist offers de-stress treatments such as reiki and reflexology.

B L'Avenir Country Lodge, 5 km north of Stellenbosch off the R44 towards the N1 and Paarl, T021-8895001, www.lavenir.co.za. A peaceful setting on a smart wine farm with 9 luxury en suite bedrooms with contemporary African decor, 5 in the main house and 4 pool-side rooms, flat screen TVs, a/c, Wi-Fi, honeymoon suite has private heated splash pool. Price includes breakfast and wine tasting, meals arranged on request. Substantial discounts are available off season. Well-run, peaceful and elegant place to experience the Winelands. Recommended.

C Wilfra Court, 16 Hlne St, approximately 3 km from town centre, turn left off the R44 road to Paarl at the Welgevonden Estate, T021-8896091. Spotless and comfortable, 2 double rooms with shared bathroom, choice of continental or English breakfast, secure parking. Run by William and Frances, a very friendly couple. Anyone with an interest in South African political affairs should stay here, as this was the first guesthouse in the region run by coloured people. The affable William was an MP for more than 30 years and is an ex-mayor of Stellenbosch. Strongly recommended.

D-F Mountain Breeze, 6 km south of town on R44, T/F021-8800200, mountainbreezeresort@adept.co.za. Caravan and camping site in forest setting, 3 fully equipped self-catering chalets, hot water, electric points, swimming pool. Popular with South African family groups.

Franschhoek *p160, map p160*

L Le Quartier Français, 16 Huguenot Rd, T021-8762151, www.lequartier.co.za. An elegant country house with 17 enormous en suite rooms all with fireplaces, beautiful bathrooms, plush furnishings and views over the gardens. Small central swimming pool and peaceful, shady courtyard. The attached restaurant (see Eating, page 176) is rated as one of the best in the Western Cape. A superb hotel with impeccable service, child-friendly, listed in the 'Top 100 hotels In the world' by the US's *Travel & Leisure* magazine in 2007. Recommended.

L-A Mont Rochelle, Dassenberg Rd, T021-8762770, www.montrochelle.co.za. 24 luxury suites and rooms set in the main manor house or in garden units, elegantly decorated with enormous bathrooms, superb award-winning restaurant (see Eating, page 178) cigar bar, swimming pool, gym and sauna, attentive service, good mountain views and pleasant rolling gardens. Rates vary considerably depending on room and season.

AL Franschhoek Country House, Main Rd, T021-8763386, www.fch.co.za. Very elegant boutique hotel with 14 rooms and 12 suites, some with fireplace, underfloor heating, private verandas, the new suites are 100 sq m and very luxurious, French style furniture, dramatic drapes and candelabra, 2 swimming pools, lovely fountains in the grounds, excellent restaurant.

A Ashbourne Guesthouse, 47 Huguenot Rd, T021-8762146, www.ashbourne.co.za. Beautifully restored Victorian town house with sunny wooden deck around a swimming pool, 6 spacious double rooms with en suite bathrooms, tiled floors, neutral decor. Set on main road just a brief walk from the shops and restaurants. No children.

A Auberge Chanteclair, 500 m behind the Huguenot Monument on Middagkrans Rd, T021-8763685, www.chanteclair.co.za. 6 beautiful, spacious rooms with en suite bathrooms and old-fashioned decor, in a Victorian farmhouse. Comfortable lounge, swimming pool, secluded gardens set among

30 ha of orchards and vineyards. A superior B&B with attentive service to match. Recommended.

A La Cabrière, Middagkrans Rd, T021-8764780, www.lacabriere.co.za. Small luxurious and stylish guesthouse set just outside town in formal lavender and herb gardens. 6 a/c rooms with Provençal decor, limed-wood furniture, grass matting floors and large stone en suite bathrooms, some rooms have fireplaces and views of vineyards and mountains, swimming pool.

A La Fontaine, 21 Dirkie Uys St, T021-8762112, www.lafontainefranschhoek.co.za. One of the finest guesthouses in Franschhoek, with 12 rooms set in a Victorian house near the village centre, elegant decor with antiques and fine wooden floors, some rooms set in garden around pool with tasteful ethnic decor. Friendly, efficient and a beautiful place to stay. Highly recommended.

A-B Auberge Bligny, 28 Van Wijk St, T021-8763767, www.bligny.co.za. A beautifully restored house dating from 1861, with 9 en suite double rooms, including a special honeymoon suite which opens onto a shaded veranda, and 1 wheelchair-friendly room. TV, lounge with a small library and open fire in winter, neat gardens, swimming pool, friendly management, German spoken.

A-B Plumwood Inn, 11 Cabrière St, T021-8763883, www.plumwoodinn.com. 7 individually styled en suite bedrooms, each with private entrance, TV, country-style furniture and brightly painted walls, breakfast served in the well-kept garden by a small swimming pool, dinner available on Mon, Wed and Fri. No children.

B Auberge La Dauphine, at La Dauphine Wine Estate off Excelsior Rd, T021-8762606, www.ladauphine.co.za. One of the most peaceful locations in the valley. 6 luxury en suite, a/c rooms each with a spacious lounge and patio in a carefully restored and converted wine store, surrounded by beautiful gardens and vineyards. There is a large swimming pool, guided tours of the farm available, plus mountain bike trails and horse riding in the nearby mountains.

B Bo La Motte, Middagkrans Rd, T021-8763067, www.bolamotte.com. 4 fully equipped cottages with fireplaces, braais, shared pool, great views of the mountains. English-run. Peaceful spot on a working wine farm just outside the village. Fly-fishing also available on the farm's dams.

B Le Ballon Rouge, 7 Reservoir St, T021-8762651, www.ballon-rouge.co.za. 8 double rooms set in a converted Victorian bungalow with wrap-around shady veranda offering private entrances to the rooms, which are small but nicely and individually decorated, swimming pool, no children under 12.

B Résidence Klein Oliphants Hoek, 14 Akademie St, T021-8762566, www.klein oliphantshoek.com. A very fine guesthouse close to the centre of Franschhoek which was built originally as a missionary hall in 1888. 6 comfortable and old-fashioned en suite a/c double rooms with TV (M-Net). The vast, high-ceilinged lounge, once the original meeting hall, is filled with antiques, big sofas and has a fireplace. Good-sized pool. Restaurants are within walking distance. Recommended.

C Lekkerwijn, T021-8741122, www.lekker wijn.com. 10 mins' drive from the centre of Franschhoek, heading towards Paarl, just before the junction with the R310 to Stellenbosch. A fine B&B in an old Cape Dutch homestead close to Boschendal wine estate, in fine park-like gardens with peacocks and guinea fowl. 3 double rooms and 1 single, plus a cottage suitable for a family of 4. The bedroom wing was designed by Herbert Baker and is arranged around a private pillared courtyard, tastefully furnished lounge and swimming pool.

D Huguenot, 34 Huguenot Rd, T021-8762092, atielouw@mweb.co.za. 8 spacious and good-value self-catering apartments set on the main road, each sleeping 2-3. Simple bedrooms, lounge and kitchen, en suite bathrooms, some rooms have mountain views. Excellent location right in the village centre.

Paarl Winelands *p164, map p165*

One of the most luxurious hotels in the valley, Santé Winelands, is presently closed as the company that owned it went bankrupt in 2007. It's currently on the market and Richard Branson of Virgin fame is rumoured to be interested. The hotel is laid out in extensive grounds, and has 90 luxury suits and what was the best spa in the country.

L Grande Roche, Plantasie St, T021-8635100, www.granderoche.co.za. An 18th-century manor which has established itself as one of the top hotels in South Africa. The 34 luxury a/c suites, non-smoking rooms, are set in a collection of restored farm buildings that stand in peaceful gardens, surrounded by vineyards, 2 floodlit tennis courts, 2 swimming pools, gym. **Bosman's** restaurant is regarded as one of the best in the country (see Eating, page 179). Will collect from Cape Town airport.

L-A Palmiet Valley Estate, T021-8627741, www.palmiet.co.za. A restored 1642 historic Cape Dutch homestead located on a wine estate to the east of the town centre, surrounded by vines and giant oak trees. 10 spacious en suite doubles and 1 honeymoon suite with TV, CD player, each decorated with antiques, private balconies or terraces, neat garden, swimming pool, very good food served in the dining room or terrace. Very popular wedding venue.

A Roggeland Country House, Roggeland Rd, Dal Josafat, T021-8682501, www.roggeland.co.za. A fine Cape Dutch farmhouse (declared a national monument) with 10 spacious luxury rooms, large en suite bathrooms, Cape-style furnishings, mature gardens, swimming pool. Highlight of a stay here is the excellent cuisine: lodging prices include 4-course dinner, bed and breakfast.

AL-A Pontac Manor Hotel, 16 Zion St, T021-8720445, www.pontac.com. Elegant fully restored Victorian manor house with manicured gardens full of oak trees that are home to an army of squirrels. 22 spacious individually decorated rooms, one is wheelchair accessible, TV and a/c, a mix of African and antique decor, the 5 rooms in the pool annexe also have microwave and fridge and there's a 5-bed cottage with kitchenette. Smart bar, lounges with fat armchairs and very good restaurant (see Eating, page 179).

B De Oude Paarl, 132 Main St, T021-721002, www.deoudepaarl.com. Swanky hotel in a set of national monument buildings dating back to 1700 on the main road, with 26 individually designed rooms, rather dark but comfortable with a nod at 'boutique' hotel style, fine stone bathrooms. Excellent restaurant (see Eating, page 179), wine boutique and bar, Belgian chocolate deli, friendly and efficient service.

B Lemoenkloof Guest House, 396a Main St, T021-8723782, www.lemoenkloof.co.za. Luxurious converted country house on northern edge of town. 20 a/c rooms and a family unit grouped in several buildings set around gardens and palm-shaded pool. Each room has TV, minibar, floral fabrics, fresh flowers in vases, black-and-white tiled bathrooms, separate entrance. Large breakfasts, evening meals on request for large groups, friendly owners. Recommended.

B Eben-Haëzer Country House, Sonstraal Rd, T021-8627420, www.eben-haezer.co.za. Original Cape Dutch homestead, 7 large and very comfortable double rooms, individually decorated with antiques and with Victorian-style bathrooms, 1 self-catering cottage, swimming pool, breakfast served under oak trees in the tea garden or in the 18th-century dining room, beautiful whitewashed chapel for weddings. Friendly management, also offers fishing in the dam.

B Zomerlust, 193 Main St, T021-8722117, www.zomerlust.co.za. 14 rooms in a restored historic country house in the centre of town. All rooms are en suite, with TV, fireplaces and decked out in antiques. Some rooms are in converted stables. Courtyard, terrace, swimming pool, library and cellar pub. Check for winter discounts. Recommended.

C Amberg Guest Farm, Klein Drakenstein, T021-8620982, www.amberg.co.za. Good budget option on farm with spectacular setting. 5 self-catering cottages sleeping 2-6 with a/c and TV, gardens, large pool, braai facilities, friendly Swiss owners (German and French spoken).

C Nantes-Vue, 56 Mill St, T021-8727311, www.nantes-paarl.co.za. Elegant B&B set in a Victorian house in the centre of town. 4 double rooms and 1-bedroom cottage in garden, all with high ceilings and TV, understated decor, iron bedheads, enormous showers and free-standing baths, breakfast room has country farm feel to it, splash pool. Good value. Recommended.

C Oak Tree Lodge, 32 Main St, T021-8632631, www.oaktreelodge.co.za. 18 modern en suite rooms with TV, set in a large family home, underfloor heating, children well catered for, rather twee decorations, sunny breakfast room, garden, large pool, secure parking, central location.

D-F Berg River Resort, 5 km out of town towards Franschhoek (R45), south side of the N1, T021-8631650, www.bergriver resort.co.za. Self-catering chalets of varying comfort sleeping 2-6, caravan and camping space available (first-come, first-served basis), hot water, electric points, swimming pool, mini-golf, kiosk for snacks and drinks, nice spot next to the river but lock everything up as theft has been a problem here in the past.

Wellington district p169, map p168
A 5 Mountains Lodge, east of town on the R301 towards Bain's Kloof, T021-8643409, www.exclusiveescapes.com/5mountains. Mix of luxurious garden cottages and suites in original homestead, stylish bedrooms with 4-poster beds, en suite bathrooms, private deck with beautiful views, breakfast served by the pool or in an attractive dining room, meals on request. Very friendly, family-run, excellent choice for a relaxing night. Recommended.

A-B Augusta Kleinbosch Guest Farm, south of the town off the R303 (close to Paarl), T021-8682481, www.kleinbosch.de. German-run guesthouse in a fine Cape Dutch homestead and converted Afrikaans school set among orchards on a working wine and guava

farm. 9 en suite rooms, spacious and elegant, with mini-fridges, CD players, some with TV, 4-poster beds, à la carte restaurant, swimming pool, walks around the vineyards possible.

B Diemersfontein Wine and Country Estate, Van Riebeck Dr, off the R303, T021-8645050, www.diemersfontein.co.za. A classic luxury country house set in beautifully tended gardens on a wine estate. 17 rooms, either in the main house or in garden annexe, traditional, plush furnishings, elegant teak-panelled lounge, grand veranda, swimming pool, very good restaurant and horse riding. Wine tasting daily 1000-1700.

C Klein Rhebokskloof, 4 km out of town, off Berg St, T021-8734115, www.wine-estate-hildenbrand.co.za. Old country guesthouse set on an olive and wine farm. 4 double rooms, simple and comfortable with TV, ceiling fans, private terrace, plus 2 self-catering apartments, shared lounge, restaurant, swimming pool with sun deck and beautiful garden, children will enjoy the farm animals.

C Soete Huys, 1 Stadsig, T021-8643442, www.soetehuys.com. Beautiful converted family house, 4 en suite double rooms, and 2 4-bed family units, pleasant furnishings with wrought-iron beds, terracotta-tiled floors, good breakfasts served, garden and pool, quiet location on the outskirts of town.

🍴 Eating

Strand and around p152

¶¶¶ Die Ou Pastorie, 41 Lourens St, Somerset West, T021-8522120, www.dieoupastorie.com. Tue-Sat 1200-1400, Mon-Sat 1900-2130. Award-winning French restaurant set in a luxury lodge in a gracious Victorian parsonage. Changing menu of traditional French cuisine, also has good vegetarian options and makes good use of game. Silver service, award-winning wine list. Booking advised.

¶¶ 96 Winery Road, Zandberg Wine Estate, 96 Winery Rd, just out of Somerset West on the Stellenbosch road, T021-8422020, www.zandberg.co.za, www.96winery

road.co.za. Mon-Sat 1200-1500, 1900-late, Sun closed in the evening. An excellent award-winning restaurant in an informal farmhouse setting. Very good grills, and some fish such as Norwegian salmon, and specials like guinea fowl or duck and cherry pie. Also has luxury overnight cottages on the estate (see Sleeping, page 171). Recommended.

Stellenbosch p153, map p154

As well as restaurants in town, most of the wine estates on the Stellenbosch wine route also have restaurants that are especially nice for lazy lunches in a picturesque setting. Recommended for the overseas visitor are the restaurants at **Spier Estate**, which are a very special dining experience. You may even want to consider making a reservation before your arrival in South Africa.

₸₸₸ Jan Cats, 162 Dorp St, T021-8872644. 0700-2200. Part of the **Stellenbosch Hotel** and well known for its game dishes. Just about everything from the African bush is served up, from crocodile kebabs to kudu steaks. Also has specials like ostrich cottage pie or warthog ribs, plus some seafood including excellent fresh crayfish. Cheaper pub lunches available.

₸₸₸ Jonkershuis, Spier Estate, on the R44, T021-8091159. 1230-1530, 1830-2230. Atmospheric Cape Malay restaurant set in restored farmhouse decorated with fine antiques, outside tables in the shade of oak trees, spicy bredies, curries, seafood, home-made breads and soups, baked puddings and biscuits, huge variety of food buffet style – a good opportunity to try all of South Africa's unique recipes. Recommended but book well in advance.

₸₸₸ Moyo, Spier Estate, on the R44, T021-8091133, www.moyo.co.za. 1200-1600, 1800-2300. Consistently fully booked so make a reservation at least a week ahead. Superb restaurant in a beautiful location and a highlight of a trip to South Africa. Arranged in Bedouin tents with outside tables in delightful tree houses or wrought-iron gazebos lit by candles. The vast buffet has just about everything imaginable from hot mussels to fine cheese and pan-African food. As well as wine and food, each table is entertained by women who decorate your face with traditional Xhosa white paint, Zimbabwean musicians, jazz bands and township opera singers. Allow extra time to browse in the superb souvenir shop. Touristy yes, but the atmosphere is unbeatable. A magical experience and highly recommended. Other branches in Johannesburg and Durban.

₸₸ Brazen Head, 62 Andringa St, T021-8829672. 1100-late. Friendly, informal Irish themed pub and restaurant with beer garden, Guinness and Kilkenny on tap, Irish whiskies, long varied menu including a 1-kg steak, seafood platter and traditional Irish stew, children's menu and a roast at Sun lunch.

₸₸ The Coachman, Ryneveld St next to the Village Museum, T021-8832230. 1200-2400. Cobbled courtyard with a beer garden feel, serving light meals and Cape specialities such as bobotie, springbok stew and lamb chops. Convenient location but can get very busy with tour groups.

₸₸ Dros, corner of Bird and Alexander streets, T021-8864856. 0800-2200. A large bar-cum-restaurant with outdoor seating in a lively square. Popular chain serving standard pub fare such as burgers, steaks, ribs, pizza. Good value, but portions are on the small side.

₸₸ Fishmonger, corner of Plein and Ryneveld streets, T021-8877835, www.fishmonger.co.za. 1200-2200. Portuguese-style seafood restaurant serving a great choice of fresh Cape seafood – kingclip, calamari, tiger prawns, oysters and the like – including taster platters for those who can't decide. Also has a sushi chef, and a choice of vegetarian dishes. Good service, booking essential. Recommended.

₸₸ Volkskombuis, Aan de Wagen Rd, T021-8872121, www.volkskombuis.co.za. 1200-1430, 1830-2130, closed Sun during winter. High standards of food and service, with a focus on traditional Cape cooking. Try the home-made oxtail or springbok pies. Housed in a characterful building – a restored

Herbert Baker Cape Dutch homestead, with views across the Eerste River. A sensibly priced treat.

♥♥ Wijnhuis, Andringa St, T021-8875844, www.wijnhuis.co.za. 0800-late. Bustling wine bar and wine shop, pretty outside eating in a courtyard, full of steak, some seafood, and venison, delicately presented, over 20 wines available by the glass.

♥ Blue Orange, 77-79 Dorp St, T021-8872052. Mon-Sat 0700-1800, Sun 0830-1700. Delicious range of breakfasts, good-value snacks and sandwiches plus light lunches such as quiche and pasta. Interesting mix of students, well-coiffed locals and backpackers. Also has an attached deli selling local produce such as jams, bread, fruit and veg.

♥ Café Nouveau, corner of Plein and Ryneveld streets, T021-8875627. 0700-1700. Lovely old-fashioned café with gilt mirrors and tightly packed tables serving sandwiches, light meals, coffee and cakes throughout the day.

Franschhoek *p160, map p160*

Franschhoek is dubbed 'gourmet capital of South Africa', and for good reason. There are some superb restaurants here. Booking ahead, especially at the weekends, is advised.

♥♥♥ Chamonix, 1 Uitkyk St, T021-8762393, www.chamonix-restaurant.co.za. Lunch daily 1200-1600, dinner Fri and Sat only 1830-2100. Highly rated upmarket country-style restaurant set on a wine estate (see page 162). Ideal for a long lazy lunch with a fine selection of South African and international dishes including a vegetarian menu. Better equipped than most to take families, with an on-site jungle gym and children's menu.

♥♥♥ Ici at Le Quartier Français, 16 Huguenot Rd, T021-8762151, www.lequartier.co.za. 0730-1030, 1200-1530, 1800-late. Rated as one of the best restaurants in the Western Cape with a chef trained in New York. French and South African dishes, best known for their lamb burgers and slow-roasted pork with sage mash, plus rabbit and duck. Nice decor with bright orange walls, expensive but a place for a treat.

♥♥♥ Mange Tout, Dassenberg Rd, T021-8762770, www.montrochelle.co.za. 1200-1500, 1900-2130. Small, formal restaurant based at the ultra-smart **Mont Rochelle Hotel** and wine estate. Perfect setting overlooking the vineyards, excellent gourmet menu with separate vegetarian section, light lunches are proving popular, also arranges picnics and offers 5-course dinners, long wine list. A pianist plays a white baby grand piano.

♥♥♥ Monneaux, Franschhoek Country House, Main Rd, T021-8763386, www.fch.co.za. 0800-1000, 1200-1430, 1900-2100. Highly rated restaurant serving contemporary fusion cuisine, more up-to-date than many restaurants in Franschhoek, attractive outdoor terrace and cosy dining room. Lots of game and fish with strong spicing; to whet your appetite consider confit of guinea fowl and beef in vanilla bean béarnaise or smoked duck breast with watermelon and feta salad. Good local wine list.

♥♥ The French Connection Bistro, 48 Huguenot Rd, T021-8764056. 1200-1530, 1830-2100. French bistro serving refreshingly unfussy food such as steamed mussels, steak-frites or Toulouse sausages and mash. Children have their own menu. Pleasant bustling atmosphere and you can watch the chef at work in the kitchen behind glass.

♥♥ The Grapevine, Huguenot Rd, T021-8762520. 0800-2100. Family restaurant serving big breakfasts, light lunches (try the tasty butternut soup) and steaks and pizzas in the evening. Also some good Cape Malay dishes like the ever-popular bobotie, and warming hot chocolate with a shot of brandy in it.

♥♥ La Fromagerie at La Grange, 13 Daniel Hugo St, T021-8763420. Daily for lunch 1200-1600. Excellent deli specializing in cheese with 40 varieties for sale, set up in a 200-year-old barn, salads and quiches, soups and all things cheesy such as soufflé and pasta, recommended is the Camembert with caramelized pears. The owner is a jazz pianist who plays here occasionally.

La Petite Ferme, on Franschhoek Pass Rd, T021-8763016. Daily for lunch 1200-1600. Spectacular views over the Franschhoek Valley from this smart 'boutique' winery. The restaurant is well known for its wholesome country fare as well as delicate fusion dishes like smoked salmon on sweet potato and coconut mash, or hearty French cassoulet. Good desserts and wine list, too.

Le Bon Vivant, 22 Dirkie Uys St, T021-8762717. Thu Tue 1200-1500, 1830-2100. Small garden restaurant with tables set in dappled shade, serving delicious light lunches (don't miss the local smoked trout sandwich) and a 5-course dinner which has had excellent reports. Good value, friendly service. Recommended.

Paarl Winelands p164, map p165

Bosman's, Grande Roche Hotel, Plantasie St, T021-8632727, www.granderoche.co.za. 0700-1030, 1200-1400, 1900-2100, closed mid-May to 31 Jul. Award-winning international cuisine of the highest standard in a grand vineyard-fringed setting. Popular 3-course set lunch, but the real treat is the celebrated 5-course 'Flavours of the Cape' menu (R380), offering superbly created examples of Cape cuisine. Good choice of vegetarian dishes, award-winning wine list. Regarded as one of the finest restaurants in South Africa and it is Africa's only Relais Gourmands (Relais & Chateax) establishment.

Gabbemas/Café Cuba at the De Oude Paarl Hotel (see Sleeping, page 175), 132 Main St, T021-8721002, www.deoude paarl.com. Mon-Sat. Fashionable, moodily lit restaurant, light lunches served in the **Café Cuba** (1200-2300) courtyard, or formal suppers indoors in the **Gabbemas** restaurant (1900-2300). Lots of modern twists on traditional dishes, with Moroccan, Indian and Cape Malay influences, try the lamb shank on roasted butternut or the venison wrapped in parma ham with chocolate and whisky sauce. Good wine list.

Dros, Main Rd, T021-8630350. 0900-late. Outlet of pub-style chain serving steaks, ribs and pasta dishes in a cellar atmosphere. Also has a good choice of beers at the bar.

Laborie, Taillefer St, T021-8073095. 1000-1700. Lunchtime restaurant on wine estate with pleasant seating under giant oak trees. Delicious Cape and Mediterranean dishes, lots of contemporary choices such as kudu fillet in bacon-wrapped figs, as well as Cape specialities like bobotie and some vegetarian options. Smart but relaxed atmosphere, good service. Recommended.

Pontac, Pontac Manor Hotel, 16 Zion St, T021-8720445, www.pontac.com. 1200-1400, 1900-2200. Informal and friendly restaurant in a cosy setting in a 17th century manor house, serving traditional dishes (lots of game), weekly specials and imaginative vegetarian options, everything on the menu is available in full or half portions. Good service.

Victorian Restaurant and Terrace, Rhebokskloof Estate, T021-8698606, www.rhebokskloof.co.za. Daily 0800-1700, also open for dinner Thu-Mon. Wonderful views from the terrace over farmland and giant oaks, where light lunches are served. The club sandwiches and salads are good, as is the Sun starter buffet. Old-fashioned interior is the setting for a heavier international evening menu.

Wilderer's, Wilderer's distillery, 3 km outside Paarl on R45, T021-8633555. Tue-Sun 1100-1700. Relaxed French restaurant in a schnapps distillery, speciality is *lammkuchen*, a type of pizza from Strasbourg. Finish off with a shot of their pear or fynbos schnapps. Live jazz on the 1st Sun of the month.

De Malle Madonna, 127 Main Rd, T021-8633925. Tue-Sun 0830-1730. Cool and kooky café serving creamy quiches, huge sandwiches, burgers and wraps, plus towering cakes and muffins in the afternoon. Refreshingly modern spot for a snack.

Kosinrichting, 19 Pastorie Av, T021-8711353. Mon-Fri 0800-1600, Sat 0900-1400. Coffee shop serving light meals, sandwiches and coffee and cakes, pancakes with sweet and savoury fillings, tables outside on the veranda at the front are in the dappled shade of oak trees, while there's a pretty garden and stoep out back.

Wellington district *p169, map p168*
Oude Wellington, R303, Bain's Kloof Pass, 5 km south of town, T021-8731008. Lunch Wed-Sun 1230-1430, dinner Tue-Sat 1830-2130. Lovely spot in an old white-washed farmstead with 2 fireplaces, outside seating in the grounds with dogs, peacocks and ostriches roaming around, good country-style cooking, home-made bread, pasta and ice cream, also a wine estate.
D'Olives Restaurant and Tea Garden, 41 Church St, T021-8643762. Mon-Sat 0800-2200, Sun 0900-1500. Pleasant restaurant with cool terracotta-tiled floor and wrought-iron furniture, short but good menu of salads, pasta, grills and fish, best known for their waffles and pancakes.
Perfect Place, 66 Church St, T021-8736620. Mon-Fri 0800-1700, Sat 0800-1500. Charming old-world coffee shop in a Victorian house with corrugated-tin roof and decorated with lace, sweet and savoury stuffed pancakes, try the pear, nuts and caramel one, also serves wine and sells antiques.

Bars and clubs

Stellenbosch *p153, map p154*
Bohemia Pub, corner of Andringa and Victoria streets, T021-8828375, www.bohemia.co.za. 1000-late. One of the main student haunts with an eccentric brightly coloured interior and attractive wrap-around veranda. This popular bar gets very busy with a young clientele who come for the cold beers, relaxed atmosphere and occasional live music.

Dros, corner of Bird and Alexander streets, T021-8864856. 0800-2400. The restaurant turns into a noisy bar later at night. Tables spill out onto the square and get crowded with backpackers and students.
Fandango, Shop 11, Drostdy Centre, T021-8877506, www.fandango.co.za. 0900-0100. Café and bar offering internet access with tables outside on the square, popular for after-work cocktails, occasional live music.
Mexican Kitchen, 25 Bird St, T021-8829997, www.mexicankitchen.co.za. 1100-2400. Lively cantina-style restaurant and bar serving huge portions of nachos, bean soup, fajitas, tacos and steaks. Relaxed setting with inventive decor – some of the seats are swings. Also hosts salsa sessions and serves good shooters and cocktails including excellent margaritas.
Tollie's, Drostdy Centre, Bird St, T021-8865497. Open 2100-late. Popular nightclub, packed with students on weekend nights, dance and pop music, occasional live bands.

Entertainment

Stellenbosch *p153, map p154*
Theatre
Dorp Street Theatre, T021-8866107, www.dorpstraat.co.za. Local productions, plays in Afrikaans, and jazz on Sun.
Endler Hall, at the university, T021-8082340, www.sun.ac.za/music. Classical music concerts and university productions.
Oude Libertas Amphitheatre, on a wine estate just to the west of the centre off the R306, T021-8087473, www.oudelibertas.co.za. Outdoor events from Nov-Mar.
Spier Amphitheatre, T021-8091100, www.spier.co.za. Open-air summer concerts, jazz events, plays and comedy on the wine estate. The open-air amphitheatre here is a great venue.

☺ Festivals and events

Stellenbosch *p153, map p154*
Aug The **Stellenbosch Wine Festival**, in the first week of Aug, is an annual event to promote local award-winning wines along with traditional rural cuisine, and music and arts, www.wineroute.co.za.

O Shopping

Stellenbosch *p153, map p154*
Oom Samie se Winkel (Uncle Sammy's Shop), 84 Dorp St. Has been trading since 1791. The first owner, Pieter Gerhard Wium, traded in meat, but the shop became famous between 1904 and 1944 when the store was owned and run by Samuel Johannes Volsteedt. He stocked virtually everything you could need, and was known throughout the town. Today the shop still sells a wide range of goods and it has retained its pre-war character with items hanging from all corners, and old cabinets full of bits and pieces. It has all the makings of a tourist trap, but unlike many others it is genuine.

Franschhoek *p160, map p160*
Bordeaux Street Gallery, Huguenot Rd, T021-8762165, bordeauxgallery@saol.com. Series of rooms selling local arts and crafts, including antique furniture, Massai jewellery, woven baskets, fabrics and batiks.

▲ Activities and tours

Stellenbosch *p153, map p154*
Bicycle hire
Adventure Centre, next to the tourist office, T021-8828112, www.adventureshop.co.za.
Stumble Inn, 12 Mark St, T021-8874049, www.jump.to/stumble, good advice.

Horse riding
Spier Horse Trails, T021-8813683. Expect to pay R160 per hr. The horses are well trained

and can take complete novices. Pony rides for children and carriage rides for non-riders are also on offer.

Wine tours
As well as those listed below, many Cape Town tour operators organize day trips to the Winelands, see page 127.
Easy Rider Wine Tours, T021-8864651, stumble@iafrica.com. Hugely popular day-long wine tour aimed at backpackers organized by the **Stumble Inn** (see Sleeping, page 171). Tours take in 4 estates, with several tastings in each, restaurant, lunch and cheese tasting included, good value (R250 all inclusive) although they seem to take too many people, making it rather chaotic.
Vine Hopper, T021-8828112, or book through the Adventure Centre (above). A useful hop-on, hop-off bus that tours between 6 estates and the tourist office in town, costing R135 per person. Farms on the route are Vredenheim, Van Ryn Brandy Cellar, Spier, Dombeya, Bilton and Kleine Zalze.

Franschhoek *p160, map p160*
Bike hire
Manic Cycles, La Gare Centre, Huguenot St, T021-8764956, www.maniccycles.co.za. Mountain bike hire for self tours of the village and wine farms, or guided tours with lunch from R400.

Fly-fishing
Dewdale Fly Fishing, off the Robertsvlei Rd, 7 km from Franschhoek, T021-8762755, www.dewdale.co.za. Specializes in rainbow and brown trout, and American steelhead trout, lovely setting in the mountains. Rods can be hired and tuition can be arranged.

Horse riding
Paradise Stables, outside the village on the Robertsvlei Rd, T021-8762160, www.paradisestables.co.za. Guided trails through the vineyards with stops at 2 estates for wine tasting.

Tour operators

Winelands Experience, T083-2344038 (mob), www.winelands-experience.co.za. Daily scheduled food and wine tours.

Paarl Winelands *p164, map p165*
Bike hire
Bike Point, T021-8633901, www.bikepoint.org. Organizes fun rides in the regions, as well as renting out bikes and providing route maps.

Tour operators

Vintage Cape Tours, T082-6563994, www.vintagecape.co.za. Specialist wine tours, historical walking tours and hiking. More suited to the older client.

⊖ Transport

Strand and around *p152*
Somerset West is 50 km from central Cape Town and 31 km from Cape Town International Airport along the N2.

Stellenbosch *p153, map p154*
Taxi
Let's Go Taxis, T021-8525835.

Paarl Winelands *p164, map p165*
Taxi
Paarl Radio Taxis, T021-8725671.

Train
Huguenot station is across the river from Lady Grey St and is on the Cape Town–Pretoria via Bloemfontein and the Cape Town–Durban via Bloemfontein routes. **Spoornet**, T0860-008888, www.spoornet.co.za.

Wellington district *p169, map p168*
72 km to **Cape Town**, 131 km to **Saldanha**, 49 km to **Stellenbosch**. To return to **Cape Town** take the R44 around Paarl Mountain, and turn right after 20 km onto the N1. The R45 to Malmesbury continues west towards Saldanha Bay and the Atlantic. Alternatively, travel north on the R44 to Porterville and join with the N7 before it starts to climb Grey's Pass. From the top of the pass you descend into the Olifants River Valley.

Train
The daily service between **Cape Town** and **Durban** stops in Wellington. This is the best option for travel to Cape Town. Departs Wellington 1350 for **Cape Town** (80 mins), and departs Cape Town at 1000. See www.spoornet.co.za for timetables.

⊙ Directory

Stellenbosch *p153, map p154*
Banks All the main South African banks are found here, all with ATMs. The following **Bureaux de Change** are open Mon-Fri 0830-1700, Sat 0900-1200: **Rennies Foreign Exchange** (local representatives of Thomas Cook), Mill St, T021-8865259; **American Express**, 4 Plein St, T021-8870818. **Internet** Fandango, Shop 11, Drostdy Centre, T021-8877506, www.fandango.co.za, 0900-0100, café and bar offering internet access; you can also check your email at the **tourist office** on Market St. **Medical services** 24-hr private Medi-Clinic, corner Saffraan and Rokewood Aves, T021-8838571, www.stellenboschmc.co.za. **Post office** Main post office, Plein St.

Contents

Footprint features

Western Cape

At a glance

⊖ **Getting around** Buses on major routes, car hire.

◉ **Time required** At least 1 week for major sites.

☼ **Weather** Chilly in July and August. Best in November and February.

⊗ **When not to go** The Karoo gets very cold in winter, June-August.

Indian
Ocean

WESTERN CAPE

NORTHERN CAPE

Great Karoo

Great Karoo

Atlantic
Ocean

★ Don't miss ...

1 West Coast fishing villages, page 186.

2 Whale watching around Hermanus, page 241.

3 Cape Agulhas, page 249.

4 Shark spotting near Gansbaai, page 261.

5 Oudtshoorn ostrich farms, page 286.

6 Vineyards and orchards on Route 62, page 292.

N

50 km

50 miles

The Western Cape is arguably the most beautiful and varied of South Africa's nine provinces. It has just about everything that the entire country can offer, from endless beaches and indigenous forests to historic wine estates and scorched semi-desert.

The Breede River Valley is best known for its farming, with isolated settlements tucked away along the banks of its river. It's dotted with vineyards and fruit orchards and the peaceful country roads make a pleasant alternative to the N2 highway en route to the famed Garden Route. Further east lie the parched plains of the Karoo, their endless shimmering horizons peppered with craggy mountains and lonely farm-steads. Hemmed in by impressive mountain ranges crossed by spectacular mountain passes, the Little Karoo offers hiking, the popular Cango Caves and, of course, ostriches, who peer over every fence around Oudtshoorn. The southern coast begins with Walker Bay, which claims to have the best land-based whale watching in the world; in season, sightings are almost guaranteed from the clifftops in Hermanus. Further south the waters around Gansbaai are home to seals, penguins and great white sharks, while the lighthouse at Cape Agulhas marks the most southerly point of Africa.

Far less visited is the west coast, north of Cape Town: a wild area of fynbos-covered sand dunes, sun-bleached beaches and remote fishing villages. Inland, the undulating landscape of wheat fields and low grassy hills are tinged with colour during flower season, while the higher mountains attract snow (and curious Capetonians) during winter. Further north the Ceder-berg Mountains are a rugged range with ancient San rock art and some of the best hiking in the country.

West Coast

The West Coast is vastly different from the more-visited Garden Route – a wild, bleak stretch lashed by the icy Atlantic and backed by rolling dunes covered in coastal fynbos; it's far removed from the lush green landscape full of rivers and waterfalls found in the south. It has now become a standard fixture for tourists, who are attracted by both the sun-bleached coast and the spectacular flowers that blanket the area in spring. The cold Benguella of the Atlantic also brings with it some of the most nutrient-rich waters found on the planet. This fertile sea supports an enormous wealth of marine life; the fishing is superb and the coast is famous for its excellent seafood. Inland lies a fertile farming region, the Swartland, known for its grain and wine. Further north, the N7 highway passes along the magnificent Cederberg, a wilderness area with some of the best hiking in South Africa.
▶▶ *For listings, see pages 194-199.*

Ins and outs

Getting there Driving out of Cape Town, follow the N1 through Durbanville and the northern suburbs for the West Coast. If time is not an issue, turn off the N1 at the Maitland junction, signposted Milnerton M5, and follow the signs for the R27. This is the old coast road which runs all the way north to Velddrif, north of the West Coast National Park. If you are pressed for time, take a left at Acacia Park and follow signs for the N7. This is the main highway from Cape Town to Namibia, which runs up the west coast through the Northern Cape Province.

Tourist information For information on the West Coast visit www.capewestcoast.org.

Best time to visit While the sea may be too cold for swimming, the region's climate is very favourable. As you travel north from Cape Town the summer temperatures are higher, and the rainfall is less. The air is dry and, even in winter, providing the winds aren't blowing, it can be very warm. Most of the rain falls between June and September. Whales start arriving along the West Coast around May and the mating pairs and family pods remain until December.

Cape Town to Vanrhynsdorp via the coast 😊🙂 ▶▶ *pp194-199.*

Darling → *Colour map 8, A1.*

Less than an hour's drive north of Cape town, the first settlement of note is Darling, a small, thriving town, named after a Lieutenant Governor of the Cape, Sir Charles Henry Darling. It's the sort of town where it's not unusual to see a gaggle of geese waddling down the streets. Reflecting the prosperity of the surrounding area, it is in typical **Swartland** country, surrounded by vast expanses of wheat fields and lush irrigated pastures for dairy herds. Few visitors will spend much time here, except during the spring months of August and September, when the wild flowers on the veld are blooming – a **Wild Flower Show** has been held here during the third weekend of September since 1917. The most common flowers found in the area include daisies, nemesias, vygies and lilies. There are four vineyards in the Darling region which are all open for tastings and sales. The **tourist information office** ① *in the museum on Pastorie St, T022-4923361, www.darlingtourism.co.za, or www.tourismdarling.co.za, Mon-Sat 0900-1200*, is a good source of local information especially when the wild flowers are in bloom. The **museum** has a typical small-town collection devoted to depicting the region's history. The slightly unusual display traces the history of the butter industry in Darling. Staff at the museum will direct you to local farms which are open for viewing wild flowers during spring.

More recently, Darling has become well known as the home of Evita Bezuidenhout, a sort of Afrikaans Dame Edna created by comedian Pieter Dirk-Uys. Evita is something of a South African gay institution, and hosts lively cabaret shows at her **Evita se Perron** café-theatre in the tiny old railway station (see Eating, page 197).

At Kraalbosdam farm, 6 km to the north, stands the **Hildebrand Memorial**. This commemorates the southernmost confrontation of the Anglo-Boer War (1899-1902). There is a memorial and the gravestone of Hildebrand, a Boer Commando who was killed here. The local farm, Oudepost, is famous for its orchid nursery, the largest in South Africa. These amazing blooms are available locally, but the majority are for the export market.

Yzerfontein → Colour map 8, A1.

Driving north from Cape Town (85 km) on the R27, Yzerfontein is the first settlement of any size along the West Coast, still with distant views of Table Mountain in clear weather. It is named after a local spring rising from an ironstone formation. The village sits on the edge of an exposed rocky headland which in turn forms a sheltered bay. The harbour has a slipway suitable for the launching of small fishing boats, popular for the abundant shoaling snoek found off the coast. At times it may be possible to see whales sheltering in the bay, although there are better spots along this coast for whale watching. To the south of the village is an excellent sandy beach which is safe for swimming, although the water is always cold. A further attraction is the strong swell in the bay which makes it great for surfing. For information, contact the Yzerfontein **Tourism Bureau** ① 46 Main Rd, T022-4512366, www.tourismyzerfontein.co.za, Mon-Fri 0730-1230, 1300-1500, weekends in season 1000-1400. Many of the local holiday homes stand empty and the town can be very quiet out of season. Most of the local amenities are concentrated around the petrol station.

Dassen Island

If you have access to a boat, **Dassen Island**, 9 km to the southwest, makes for an interesting day trip. The island, the largest along the west coast, is the peak of an underwater mountain. When Jan van Riebeeck first visited here in 1654, the island was home to hundreds of seals. These have long since been hunted out, but there remain large cormorant and African penguin breeding populations. A caretaker lives on the island to monitor and protect the only breeding ground in the Cape for the great white pelican. Closer to the shore is a smaller island, **Meeurots**, which has become home for cormorants and gulls.

Langebaan ●●●▲● → pp194-199. Colour map 6, B1.

A little more than an hour by road from Cape Town (125 km), this is a very popular family resort which has been all but spoilt by heavy development. Situated on the sheltered waters of the beautiful **Langebaan Lagoon**, it is an ideal centre for watersports – sailing conditions are reputedly the best along the Western Cape coastline. The beach is also good and sheltered so it's not too cold for swimming. The **Langebaan Tourism Bureau** ① corner of Breë and Oostewal streets, T022-7721515, www.langebaaninfo.com, Mon-Fri 0900-1700, Sat 0900-1300, is in the municipality.

Today it is impossible to picture the town's origins as a small fishing village in the 1880s. The hillside is a mosaic of new houses and vacant plots waiting for the next

West Coast National Park birdwatching

The main attraction in the park is the varied and impressive birdlife, and there are a number of hides allowing good viewing. Almost 250 species of bird have been recorded: flamingos from the Etosha Pan in Namibia; an estimated 50% of the world's population of swift terns during season; 25% of the world's Cape gannets, and a sizeable population of rare African black oystercatchers. Other rare species to look out for are the black harrier, great-crested grebe and the silver gull. Each year over 65,000 waders visit the lagoon – many of these birds started life in the Siberian marshlands. The greatest influx occurs between September and April. It takes the birds about six weeks to complete the 15,000-km journey from Siberia to Langebaan. It is vital that the habitat of the lagoon is protected; otherwise it is uncertain where these birds could or would migrate to.

building to obstruct the view of an earlier speculator. The town is dominated by the hideous-looking **Club Mykonos** timeshare complex and hotel, a collection of elaborate pastel-coloured town houses built to look like so-called Greek tavernas where holidaymakers from Cape Town spend their allotted two weeks of time share, parking their ski boats in the little harbour, and gambling in the on-site 24-hour casino. In October the annual Langebaan Mussel Festival includes good food, wine tasting and arts and crafts stalls.

The first Europeans to visit the region were French whale and seal hunters in the 17th century who stored their booty – whale oil and seal skins – on an island in the lagoon known as Isle la Biche. This was renamed by the first Dutch settlers as **Schaapen Island**. It was not until 1870 that a village began to take shape. Prior to this, Langebaan was put on the map by Lord Charles Somerset, Governor of the Cape in the 1820s, who built a hunting lodge on a private farm overlooking the lagoon. The growth of the village was slow due to a shortage of fresh water, a problem which was only solved after the Second World War when a pipeline was built to bring water from the Berg River to the northeast.

The lagoon is an important feature of the region. The northern part, opening onto the Atlantic Ocean, is known as **Saldanha Bay** and is the deepest and safest natural harbour in South Africa. Not surprisingly, it has been fully utilized by the South African navy. More recently, mining interests have built a large iron-ore wharf and steel mill on the bay, a real eyesore which is visible from all angles. In contrast, the southern shores and waters are part of the fascinating **West Coast National Park** (see below) – a rather precarious situation, as heavy ore carriers and naval boats frequenting the lagoon threaten the fragile marine environment.

West Coast National Park ⬤❼ ▸▸ *pp194-199. Colour map 8, A1.*

ⓘ *Jun-Sep 0700-1830, Oct-Apr 0600-2000, R60 in flower season, R20 otherwise.*
Although it may not seem very remarkable at first sight, this park remains unmatched in South Africa. Covering 30,000 ha, it was established in 1985 to protect the rich marine life in the lagoon and the rare coastal wetlands. It extends from just north of Yzerfontein to Saldanha Bay, and includes the Postberg Nature Reserve, Langebaan Lagoon and the islands – Malgas, Jutten, Marcus and Schaapen. The diversity of species here is impressive, but the main attraction is the excellent variety of birdlife.

Ins and outs

Getting there You can enter the park from two directions: from the south (look out for the signs along the R27); or by driving south out of Langebaan town. If you don't mind paying the small entrance fee, it is a pleasant alternative to drive through the park when travelling between Langebaan and Cape Town. All the roads are surfaced.

Tourist information SANParks ① *T022-7722144, www.sanparks.org.* The main **information centre** ① *just before the entrance to the park (follow the signs from Langebaan centre),* has maps and information on the area. Within the park, a beautiful farmstead dating from 1860 has been fully restored and turned into an environmental centre and tea rooms. This is found at the southern end of the lagoon and is known as the **Geelbek**

Saldanha Bay & West Coast National Park

To Paternoster, Stompneusbani & St Helena Bay

To Velddrift & Lamberts Bay

R45

Saldanha

Harbour

Danger Bay

Ore Terminal

R27

To Hopefield & Moorreesberg

North Head

Malgas Island

Marcus Island

Saldanha Bay

Jutten Island

Military

Schaapen Island

Langebaan

South Head

Military Area

Postberg Nature Reserve

Entrance

West Coast National Park

Stony Head

Kraalbaai

Vondeling Island

Langebaan Lagoon

Atlantic Ocean

Geelbek Homestead

Sand Dunes

Sixteen Mile Beach

Entrance

R27

Yzerfontein

To Cape Town

N

3 km
3 miles

Sleeping 🛏
Houseboat **2**
Joanne's Beach Cottage **1**

Sishen–Saldanha railway

Anyone driving north from Saldanha Bay is likely to follow a route close to the Sishen–Saldanha railway. This was purpose-built between 1973 and 1976 to transport high-grade iron ore from the Northern Cape to a new deep-water harbour in Saldanha Bay. The line is 861 km long and only has three bends. It has earned a place in the Guinness Book of Records. In 1989 a world record was set when the longest and heaviest train covered the route. It was 7.3 km long, had 660 loaded trucks weighing 71,210 metric tonnes and was pulled by 16 locomotives. You can see segments of a train in the marshalling yards just outside the harbour. When there is a waiting train the road to Langebaan is diverted.

Homestead. Most visitors, including tour groups, stop here. Apart from the attraction of a pot of tea or toasted sandwich, there are some interesting displays on the different ecosystems found in the park. Several walks start from here, leading to simple hides in amongst the reed beds and the mud flats.

Postberg Nature Reserve

Apart from the prolific birdlife in the park the other major attraction is its wild flowers which bloom after the first spring rains. Because of the variety of soil types, you can see many different flowers within a small area. The most colourful spreads are frequently found in Postberg Nature Reserve. Since 1987, this private nature reserve has been administered by the national park, while the actual lands remain the property of farmers. Three farms make up the reserve: Nieuwland, Kreeftebaai and Oude Post. Between 1838 and 1966 the land was used as winter grazing for cattle. In 1969 it was declared a private nature reserve which would be open during the flower season. It is found at the tip of the peninsula that forms the western shore of the lagoon. It is still only open from August to September, but during the spring it is one of the best places to see wild flowers. The land has also been stocked with eland, zebra, hartebeest, kudu and wildebeest. There are three picnic sites with toilets. Allow sufficient time to exit the park at the end of the day as it is a long drive all the way round the lagoon.

Langebaan Lagoon

The beautiful lagoon, a wide expanse of sparkling turquoise water, is an important and integral part of the park. It is rich in nutrients – twice a day the tides replenish the lagoon with cold plankton-rich water – and home to thousands of birds. Every year between 50,000 and 70,000 birds fly more than 15,000 km from northern Russia to spend the summer feeding on Langebaan lagoon. Looking down from a high vantage point helps you appreciate how exceptionally clear the waters are. This has been attributed to colonies of mussels which filter the microscopic particles brought in by the tide.

Saldanha → *Colour map 6, B1.*

At the northern end of Langebaan Lagoon, Saldanha is the largest town in the area and is certainly the less appealing part of the lagoon. Large numbers of fishing vessels offload their harvests here to be processed in one of three factories. The greatest blight on the area, however, is the massive steel mill, the long iron ore jetty and the bulk ships which sit complacently in the bay waiting to transport the ore. Aquaculture in the lagoon has grown into a very important local industry. The first harvest was in 1984, and the quality was exceptional – surprising perhaps, considering the vicinity of the jetty. The main crop is the Mediterranean blue mussel, along with Japanese oysters and local clams. Saldanha is also the location of a South African naval base and is home to the South African Military Academy. Some of the northern reaches of the West Coast National Park are closed to the public.

Saldanha is also an important tourist centre for the thousands of South Africans who descend on the lagoon every summer. Conditions are safe and ideal for watersports, which means that the lagoon gets its fair share of boats and jet skis zipping up and down the otherwise peaceful waters. **Tourist office** ① *Van Riebeeck St, T022-/142088, www.saldanhabay.co.za, Mon-Fri 0830-1630, Sat 0900-1200.*

Coastal fishing villages ●● ▶▶ *pp194-199. Colour map 6, B1.*

Running in a clockwise direction to the north of Vredenburg are the small fishing communities of Paternoster, Stompneusbaai, St Helena Bay, Laalplek and Dwarskersbos. None of these have much to keep visitors in the area for long, but offer a view of quiet coastal life. This may change soon, though, given that it is an easy drive from Cape Town; the land along this region of the West Coast is being snapped up by property developers with plans for large holiday resorts and timeshare complexes.

Paternoster
Paternoster is a typical fishing village 15 km northwest of Vredenburg along a gravel road. It's very pretty with whitewashed homes with bright red and blue roofs and a wide expanse of sandy beach. At the waterfront is a fairly new development where you can buy fresh fish and seafood or traditional fish and chips. The fishing community is supported by a thriving Cape lobster export business. The name means 'Our Father' in Afrikaans and it is believed that this stretch of coast was the first place in Africa that the Lord's Prayer was uttered by Vasco de Gama and his sailors. At the south end of Paternoster Bay is a working lighthouse built in 1936 marking the treacherous **Cape Columbine**, which has wrecked many ships. *Columbine* was in fact a barque wrecked in 1829. You can visit the lighthouse You can visit the **lighthouse** ① *T022-7522/05, May-Sep Mon-Fri, Oct-Apr daily 1000 1500*, and now you can also sleep in it (see box, page 49). The lands around here make up the **Columbine Nature Reserve** ① *T022-7522718, 0700-1900, minimal entrance charge.* This area of protected coastline has a rich mix of wild flowers in the spring, also Karoo succulents and nesting seabirds, and there is a simple beach camp here (see Sleeping, page 196).

Stompneusbaai
Stompneusbaai is a similar coastal village. The presence of a fish-processing factory detracts somewhat from the attractive local fishermen's cottages, but it is an important source of income for the village. This is also the area where Vasco da Gama landed in 1497 after three months at sea, the first voyage he had made this far south. The modern monument commemorating this is hardly worthy of his feat.

St Helena Bay
A surfaced road links Stompneusbaai with St Helena Bay, an important centre of South Africa's commercial fishing industry, especially for lobster. Remember it is illegal to buy lobster directly from the fishermen. The bay was named by Vasco da Gama who anchored here with four vessels on 7 November 1497, St Helena Day. A granite monument commemorating this event stands on the shore near Sandy Point.

Rocherpan Nature Reserve → *Colour map 6, A1.*

ⓘ *Daily, Sep-Apr 0700-1800, May-Aug 0800-1700, T022-9521727, www.capenature.org.za.*
There are no staff at the small interpretive centre next to the gate, but visitors should sign in and drop their fee (R22) into the honesty box. You can also pick up an excellent bird checklist with map from here. The reserve office is another 100 m into the reserve. There are 2 sturdy bird hides beside the freshwater lake. Behind the car park a footpath leads across the dunes to the desolate beach.

This important and rarely visited bird sanctuary is 12 km beyond Dwarskersbos. More often than not, you'll have it to yourself with an endless beach and only the sound of thousands of feeding birds. The 914-ha reserve was established in 1967 around a seasonal *vlei*. In 1988 the boundaries were extended to include all the area up to the shore of the Atlantic Ocean. When fully flooded the *vlei*, fed by the Papkuils River, is nearly 3 km long, although it is unable to drain into the sea because of the sand dunes. The reserve maybe closed to the public when this happens. This mix of protected habitats provides excellent breeding and feeding conditions for over 180 bird species. Nearly 70 varieties of waterbirds have been recorded, including some endangered species. If you are lucky you might spot the African black oystercatcher, one of the rarest endemic breeding coastal birds in South Africa. During its breeding season (November to March), listen out for its high-pitched call, designed to startle intruders. It usually feeds at low tide, looking for mussels and limpets. White pelicans, Cape shovellers and flamingos are often seen here. There is also the chance of spotting a few of the resident small mammals such as steenbok, duiker, water mongoose and the shy African wild cat.

Elands Bay → *Colour map 6, A1.*

There are three very good reasons for visiting this small and isolated coastal community, which makes it all the more surprising to find that tourism has barely made its mark. First, it is a good location for whale watching – this is about the furthest north that southern right and humpback whales can be seen from the shore. Second, it is well known for its good surfing conditions. Finally, it lies at the mouth of **Verlorenvlei**, a stream with marshlands that support a large, varied aquatic bird population. Over 240 species have been recorded in the area. There's an interesting walk out to Baboon Point with good views of the bay. Ask for directions to the cave which has some San paintings. All activities are concentrated around an open square by the **Eland Hotel**, which also acts as the local **tourist information office**. There is a post office, bottle shop, supermarket and a cheap café.

Nearby, on the way to Lambert's Bay, is **Wadrif Salt Pan**. After rains there are a couple of shallow ponds here, providing an excellent chance of seeing flamingos. Take a left by the railway bridge and follow the line to Lambert's Bay. Wadrif Salt Pan is by the railway line.

Lambert's Bay 🌐🚭🏕🅘 ▸▸ *pp194-199. Colour map 6, A1.*

Once a small fishing village, Lambert's Bay is now a popular holiday town and gets very busy in summer. Between July and November you have a good chance of seeing the southern right whale migrating north. The excellent **Muisbosskerm** restaurant (see page 198) played an important role in drawing visitors to the region, but the bay has appeared on maps for many years – it was the last point at which Bartholomeu Dias went ashore before sailing around the Cape in 1487. The village is named after the British admiral, Sir Robert Lambert, who produced detailed charts of this coastline between 1826 and 1840. In 1918 Axel Lindstrom established the **Lambert's Bay Canning Co** and the future of the fishing community was assured. **Lambert's Bay Tourism Bureau** ⓘ *Main St, T027-4321000, www.lamberts bay.info, Mon-Fri 0900-1300, 1400-1700, Sat 0900-1230 (open Sun during the flower season).*

The town itself is modern and rather unattractive, although it has one absorbing, if pungent, attraction – **Bird Island**. No longer an island, this 3-ha rock outcrop is now joined to the land by a concrete jetty. It is an important breeding ground for Cape gannets and, to a lesser extent, cormorants, and it attracts Cape fur seals. Although the birds make for interesting viewing, their cantankerous screeching and overpowering smell leaves a rather longer-lasting impression. Quite unexpectedly during the 2005 gannet breeding period, seals began to attack gannets on the island (although not unheard of, it's very unusual for seals to attack birds on dry land). Cape Nature estimated that they found over 2000 gannet carcasses and the gannets all but abandoned the island, their nests and eggs. In an attempt to entice them back, the Lamberts Bay Bird Island Action Committee commissioned 50 plaster of paris decoys from local artist Gerrit Burger – these are sort of half-moon-shaped protective shelters under which the birds can build their nests. Within an hour of placing the decoys the gannets started coming back. From the end of the jetty there are good views of the fishing fleet and more sea birds. Note that around high tide, breakers crash across the jetty as you walk out to the island. Wear shoes with grip, as the surface is very slippery and uneven. The **Bird Island Interpretation Centre** ① *T022-9312900*, daily 0800-1700, has exhibits on the birds and a feature on the history of collecting guano, traditionally used as fertilizer, plus a mini aquarium, and a rather sad-looking penguin pool. There's also a hide to watch the gannets from a little further inland.

Lambert's Bay to Vredendal
Doring Bay is a small fishing village based around a crayfish factory. The rocky coastline and deep coastal waters make this an ideal spot for crayfish to live in. Diamond boats can sometimes be seen around the jetty. There is a good restaurant here, the **Cabin**, on the seafront which is worth a visit (see Eating, page 199).

About 8 km further on is the northernmost village on the coast, **Strandfontein**. This is a delightful settlement built on the slopes of a small basin. The coastline is quite rocky and mountainous along here with a clean white-sand beach with excellent surfing conditions. Although usually quiet, the village is very popular during the school holidays when there are full-time lifeguards present on the beach. There are strong cross currents so only swim in front of the town where there is a tidal pool for children. The earliest residents got their drinking water from a spring on the beach, and Strandfontein means beach fountain.

Papendorp, close to the estuary of the Olifants River, is more of a cluster of fishermen's cottages than a village. There is a small island in the middle of the river mouth, and at low tide there are thousands of waterbirds on the mud flats. As an important wetland reserve, it is being considered as a future world RAMSAR site. From this point the road turns inland towards Lutzville (20 km from Strandfontein), a small farming village, and on to Vredendal.

Vredendal → *Colour map 6, A1.*
Despite the fact that it is some distance west of the main N7, Vredendal is the main commercial centre in the northwestern Cape. It is a modern town which owes its existence entirely to the Olifants River irrigation scheme. The first settlers came to the region as early as 1732 when the Dutch East India Company granted a farm to Pieter van Zyl, but it was only when the Bulshoek Dam was built that new farmers were attracted to the area. In 1925 a bridge was built across the Olifants River and the town grew rapidly into its present form. The region is also home to several quarries which extract dolomite and limestone. For tourist information contact the **Vredendal Information Office** ① *11 Church St, T027-2013376, www.tourismvredendal.co.za, Mon-Fri 0800-1300, 1400-1700, Sat 0830-1300.*

West Coast listings

Sleeping

Darling p186

C Trinity Guest Lodge, 19 Long St, T022-4923430, www.trinitylodge.co.za. Beautifully converted family home, with 4 stylish, understated bedrooms, each with their own entrance, goose-down duvets and hand-embroidered linen, old-fashioned Victorian bathrooms, lovely bright restaurant also open to non-guests, swimming pool, friendly owners Shaun and Debbie.
C-D Darling Lodge, 22 Pastorie St, T022-4923062, www.darlinglodge.co.za. A comfortable, restored 19th-century town house with a stream running through the garden. 5 en suite double rooms with shared lounge with TV and fridge, 1 self-catering unit in the garden, swimming pool, generous breakfasts.

Yzerfontein p187

C-D Kaijaiki Guest House and Restaurant, 36 Park Rd, T022-4512858, www.kaijaiki.co.za. Comfortable, homely guesthouse. Each of the 5 en suite rooms has its own fire-place and separate entrance, decorated with old photos and antiques, good restaurant attached serving West Coast traditional food. German, Dutch and French spoken. Recommended.
D Emmaus on Sea, 30 Versveld St, T022-4512650, www.emmaus.co.za. B&B or self-catering, upstairs family unit with 2 double rooms and 1 bathroom, downstairs 3 double rooms, 2 en suite, 1 with private bathroom, enclosed terrace and pub offers sea views without the wind.

D Caravan Park, Park St, T022-4512211. Good facilities, next to the dunes on the main beach with sweeping ocean views, bungalows and caravans for hire, but camping not allowed.

Langebaan p187

There are plenty of options, given the town's popularity on the domestic holiday front, but many of these choices are for a minimum period of a week and are closed in the winter. Nevertheless, visitors have considerable bargaining power in the winter months. As with all South African coastal resorts advance booking is necessary during the school holidays, especially Dec and Jan.
B Club Mykonos, T022-7077000, www.clubmykonos.co.za. Dominating the whole village, this is an enormous Greek-style resort with over 330 *kalivas* – 1- to 3-bedroom villas, most self-catering, arranged in a village with views of the ocean or the lagoon. Facilities include several swimming pools, casino and restaurant complex, and watersports can be arranged. A lot of the units are timeshare and, whilst comfortable, the resort has a very impersonal feel about it.
B-C Falcon's Rest, 21a Zeeland St, T022-7721112, www.falconsrest.co.za. Large converted family home with 12 en suite double rooms with TV, several lounges, panoramic views from the garden, large pool, sun deck. Attentive service.
B-C The Farmhouse, 5 Egret St, T022-7722062, www.thefarmhouse langebaan.co.za. A smart and cosy converted Cape Dutch farmhouse. 18 rooms, some with fireplace, en suite bathroom or shower, TV, good restaurant with pine furnishings and a crackling fire open to non-guests, provides picnic baskets, swimming pool, overlooks Langebaan Lagoon, library, no young children. Recommended.

C Langebaan Beach House, 44 Beach Rd, T022-7722625, www.langebaanbeach house.com. Small guesthouse in idyllic setting right on beach overlooking the lagoon. 4 tastefully furnished rooms, understated with terracotta-tiled floors, white linen, en suite, TV, private lounge or veranda overlooking beach, cooked breakfasts served on terrace, neat gardens and pool, no children under 12. Recommended.

C-E Oliphantskop Farm Inn, opposite turning for **Club Mykonos**, T022-7722326. Set in converted farm buildings, 17 en suite rooms plus some self-contained chalets, sleeping 2-6, set around a lovely swimming pool designed to look like a rock pool. In the low season backpackers are put in main rooms for budget rates, making it extraordinarily good value. Stables on the farm specialize in horse trails. Candlelit restaurant set in long barn with log fires, choice of good-value seafood and steaks, beer garden.

West Coast National Park *p188, map p189*
SANParks run a couple of options within the park's boundaries. Reservations through **SANParks** Pretoria office, T012 4289111, www.sanparks.org. Bookings can also be made in person at the offices in Cape Town and Durban (see page 48). For cancellations or reservations under 72 hrs in advance contact the park directly, T022-7722144.
B Houseboat Permanently moored in the lagoon, can accommodate 4 adults and 2 small children, with gas-operated kitchen, shower, flush toilet, braai and parking. There's also a larger houseboat that sleeps 22 but this is more suited to corporate groups than holidaymakers. These have their own website, www.houseboating.co.za.
B Joanne's Beach Cottage Churchaven, within walking distance of the lagoon. 8-bed fully equipped self-catering cottage, no electricity but solar lighting and gas appliances. Linen, towels and all cooking equipment provided, you just need to bring food and firewood.

Saldanha *p190, map p189*
B Blouwaterbaai (Bluewater Bay) Hotel and Resort, Henry Wicht Av, T022-7141177, www.blouwaterbaai.com. 20 1- to 3-bed fully equipped, self-catering cottages with TV, simple furnishings but big views from the large windows, patio and lawn in front leading to the beach, 16 more luxurious rooms in the whitewashed hotel, swimming pool, tennis, windsurfing, full range of beauty treatments on offer, restaurant and bar overlooking Saldanha Lagoon. Check there's not a large conference on.
C Jane's Guest House and Coffee Shop, 8 Beach Rd, T022 7143605, www.janes.co.za. A selection of luxury en suite rooms, self-catering units or a family town house all overlooking the beach. Decorated to a very high standard with either private veranda or balcony, B&B available. Coffee shop serves light meals all day on a terrace overlooking the ocean.
C Protea Hotel Saldanha Bay, 51 Main Rd, T022-7141264, www.proteahotels.co.za. Standard chain hotel in centre of town, 58 rooms, some non-smoking, TV, restaurant, swimming pool, secure parking. One of the less characterful Proteas but reasonable value.
D-E Saldanha Holiday Resort, Camp St, T022-7142247. Large, grassy camping and caravan site close to the beach, plus 48 simple self-catering chalets sleeping 4-6 people in bunk beds, with bathroom and kitchen with hotplate, microwave, fridge, kettle and basic utensils. Gets very busy over Christmas with families.

Paternoster *p191*
There are a number of holiday cottages in the village, contact **Paternoster Properties**, T022-7522087, www.paternosterprop.co.za.
C Paternoster Hotel, St Augustine St, T022-7522703, www.paternosterhotel.co.za. 10 spacious en suite rooms, with 1 double and 1 single bed, DSTV, 4 have balconies with sea view, great pub with crackling fire,

restaurant open to all serving good range of seafood including crayfish. Also lets out a number of self-catering cottages in the village, which are good for families.
E Beach Camp, Cape Columbine Nature Reserve, T082-9262267, www.ratrace.co.za. A-frame huts and tents with beds, you'll need to bring your own sleeping bag, lovely setting in the nature reserve, hot communal showers, self-catering facilities, *lapa* area, also serves seafood dinners and can arrange sea kayaking and boat trips. Excellent budget option.

St Helena Bay *p191*
B Oystercatcher Lodge, 1st Av, T022-7421202, www.oystercatcherlodge.co.za. An upmarket B&B, all the rooms have panoramic views of the bay, with stylish all-white decor, underfloor heating for chilly winter nights, terrace and swimming pool with sun loungers, bar, comfortable lounge with fireplace and DSTV, a good base for exploring the region.
E-F Laingville Caravan Park, Strand St, T022-7361684. Standard holiday park with 7 very basic and bare self-catering chalets (no bedding) and caravan and camping sites and ablution block. Quiet until the school holidays, when it gets far too crowded.

Elands Bay *p192*
D-F Eland Bay Hotel, Beachfront, T022-9721640, www.elandsbay.co.za/hotel.htm. Comfortable en suite rooms with sea views, large and airy seafood restaurant, TV lounge, braai facilities, the principal building in the village, cheap backpacker beds are in an annexe with shared bathrooms.
E Elands Bay Caravan Park, T022-9721736. Small municipal site right on beachfront in the village centre, windy but low thick hedges provide some shelter, it's an ideal spot for surfers and a short walk from the Eland Bay Hotel.

Lambert's Bay *p192*
C Lambert's Bay Hotel, Voortrekker St, T027-4321126, www.lambertsbayhotel.co.za. 47 large rooms with marine decor, front upstairs rooms have a mixed view of the scenic harbour and ugly fish-processing factory – do NOT open your windows when the factory is working. Popular **Waves** restaurant specializes in fresh, quality seafood, lively bar, within walking distance of shops plus Bird Island, ask about whale-watching boat trips.
E-F Lambert's Bay Caravan and Camping Park, T027-4322238. Overlooks the main beach, a bit exposed, very busy in peak season, communal laundry and kitchen facilities, a kid's playground and kiosk.

Lambert's Bay to Vredendal *p193*
C Die Anker, Doring Bay, T027-2151016, www.doringbaai.com. Main local hotel, mix of accommodation including B&B rooms in the main house, self-catering units and some camping space, all with sea views, walking distance to beach, fully licensed restaurant serving a good selection of seafood and meat dishes.
C-E Strandfontein Resort, Kreef Rd, Strandfontein, T027-2151169. A well-equipped park which is a bit hectic when all 150 stands are occupied during the holidays. At quieter times, this is a relaxing spot to have a break. It is situated next to the beach, with 4- and 6-bed self-catering chalets, power points, tidal swimming pool, café open all year plus a small kiosk (open in peak season).

Vredendal *p193*
B-C Tharrakamma Guesthouse, 18 Tuin St, T027-2135709, www.tharrakamma.co.za. 5 double rooms, 2 family self-catering chalets, a/c, TV, non-smoking available, lovely wooden African furniture, beautiful house with wide verandas, pretty garden full of palms, meals on request, award-winning guesthouse. Recommended.

D Vredendal Hotel, 11 Voortrekker St, T027-2131064, www.vredendalhotel.co.za. Main hotel in town, 2-storey brick building with 51 a/c rooms with TV, **Saddles Steak Ranch** restaurant, bar with pool table, swimming pool.

⊘ Eating

Darling *p186*
♈♈ Evita se Perron, in the old railway station, T022-4922831, www.evita.co.za. Open for breakfast and lunch, Tue-Sun 1000-1600 and dinner when performances are on – check out the website. A range of entertainments set in the old railway building, including a restaurant, coffee shop and famous cabaret shows performed by Evita Bezuidenhout (see page 187). Good range of South African dishes such as bobotles and bredies and excellent entertainment.
♈♈ Trinity, at the Trinity Guest Lodge (see Sleeping, page 194), dinner by arrangement only. A Victorian building with outside tables next to the pool, home-cooked food using produce from their own garden, variable and innovative menu depending on what's in season. Debbie the chef is especially well known for her pear and chocolate tart. Occasional wine-tasting evenings are held.
♈ Marmalade Cat, 19 Main Rd, 0800-1630. A small decor shop with a café serving simple country fare such as chicken pie, savoury tarts, salads and apple pie.

Yzerfontein *p187*
♈♈♈ Die Strandkombuis, T082-5759683. Closed Jun-Aug, otherwise open for lunch daily at 1300, and dinner by arrangement only, also weather dependent so phone first. Open-air seafood braai, one of many beach seafood set-ups popular on the west coast. Start with seafood soup, and move on to smoked snoek, mussels and crayfish all cooked over hot coals. If it's a little chilly you can hire heaters.

♈♈♈ Beaches, corner of Beach Rd and Ninth St, T022-4512200. Lunch Tue-Sun 1200-1530. À la carte restaurant specializing in seafood, also serves steaks and some vegetarian dishes, both the seafood curry and seafood *potjie* are worth a try, also has lite bites and pizzas in the bar, all with ocean views.

Langebaan *p187*
♈♈♈ Boesmanland Plaaskombuis, on the beach at Club Mykonos, T082-7730646. 1200-1500, 1900-2200. Another open-air buffet restaurant on the beach, although this is covered, tables strewn out on the sand lit by paraffin lamps in the evening. As well as crayfish, prawns, snoek and mussels, there's farm-style roast lamb and chicken, and South African desserts like melktart and koeksisters.
♈♈♈ Strandloper, T022 7722490. Open 1200-2100, again weather dependent, phone first. Follow signs for **Club Mykonos**, on the beach, casual, romantic surroundings with wooden tables under sunshades, cooking is done in a central fire pit. Excellent seafood buffet, award winning, booking advised at weekends, light guitar music in the evenings. Lunch begins at noon and dinner at 1800. Mussels are served for starters, then the empty mussel shells are used as cutlery for about 10 courses of fish served in the West Coast tradition with home-made bread and apricot jam. The final course is half a crayfish. Expect to pay approximately R150 per head for an all-you-can-eat meal. Discounts for children. Charming, one of the best eating experiences in South Africa. Highly recommended.
♈♈ The Farmhouse, in the guesthouse (see Sleeping, page 194), 5 Egret St, T022-7722062. 0700-2300. Good lamb steaks, fresh seafood, quality food, vegetarian menu, Sun roasts, views across the bay from an 1860s farmstead, crackling fires in winter. The pub has a cheaper menu of sandwiches, fish and chips and lasagne.

¶¶ **La Taverna**, 1 Breë St, T022-7722870.
Closed Mon and Tue out of season.
Good-value seafood, pizza and pasta, and a
menu with Austrian overtones, schnitzel,
sauerkraut and eisbein, very popular during
holiday season.

¶¶ **Pearly's** and **Driftwood Restaurant**, 46
Beach Rd, T022-7722734. 0930-late. Sister
restaurants right next to the beach, fresh
seafood and spare ribs, very popular, be
prepared to wait during busy periods since
all the dishes are freshly prepared, relaxing
views across the lagoon. Recommended.

¶ **Lagoon Fisheries**, Breë St. Fast-food
joint dishing out tasty fish and chips.

Saldanha p190, map p189

¶¶¶ **Blouwaterbaai**, restaurant in the
holiday resort (see Sleeping, page 195),
T022-7141177. 0700-2200. Stylish dining
room serving up some surprising dishes
for such a remote location, Moroccan lamb
with chorizo sausage, truffles, and duck,
very popular with people from Cape Town,
booking essential.

¶¶ **Mussel Cracker**, 51 Main Rd,
T022-7141264. 0630-1030, 1230-1430,
1900-2200. Part of **Protea Hotel**, smart
seafood restaurant with views across bay,
good fresh fish, crayfish and mussels, also
steak combos such as rump with calamari.
There's a good seafood buffet on Sat night
and a carvery on Sun lunchtime.

¶¶ **Slipway**, Main Harbour, T022-7144235.
0900-2100, closes at 1600 in the winter.
Seafood, vegetarian and pasta dishes, steak
and seafood combos are recommended,
as are the unusual mussels in coconut
cream, all overlooking the yachts at
the jetty.

Paternoster

¶¶ **The Noisy Oyster**, 62 St Augustine Rd,
T022-7522196. Daily 1200-1500, Wed-Sat
1800-2100. Cosy restaurant with an outside
courtyard beneath trees lit with fairy lights
serving West Coast fare such as oysters,
spicy calamari and freshly caught linefish.

St Helena Bay p191

¶¶ **Cattle Baron Oystercatcher**, First Av,
Shelley Point, T022-7421042. High season
1200-1430, 1800-2200, low season closes
2100, closed Sun evening and all day Mon.
Great views and the restaurant is perched
right on the rocks, lots of choice of steaks
and sauces, the brandy sauce is especially
good with a melt-in-your-mouth fillet,
also a full range of seafood.

Lambert's Bay p192

¶¶¶ **Die Kreefhuis**, T027-4322235. Mon-Sat.
An excellent seafood restaurant opposite
the entrance to Bird Island. Quality shellfish –
you can select your own crayfish from the
tank. Good selection of wines, light easy-
going atmosphere, high standard of service,
a must if you are in the area, booking
advised during peak periods. Acts as a coffee
shop in the mornings and after lunch when
home-made cakes and breads are served.
Very limited for vegetarians, though.

¶¶ **Bosduifklip**, 4 km out of town towards
Clanwilliam, T027-4322735. Opening
times depend on weather and number
of customers; call in advance to check.
Set outside amongst some rock formations
on Albina farm. Another popular open-air
restaurant serving buffet meals in West
Coast style, bar or bring your own drink,
booking essential at weekends and in
holidays. Enjoy a tasty selection of seafood
dishes including mussels, crayfish, smoked
snoek and pickled fish, and farm cuisine
such as lamb on the spit and venison stew.
The salads are slightly unusual, but go well
with the home-made breads and butter.

¶¶ **Muisbosskerm**, 5 km towards Elands Bay,
T027-4321017. Summer, lunch 1300, dinner
1900, winter open at weekends depending
on weather. Several years ago a new style
of restaurant evolved on the outskirts of
Lambert's Bay – an open-air, no-frills
seafood braai. Today there are several
such places along the coast, but the first
was the Muisbosskerm. For a fixed price
(approximately R140) you have a wide

choice of seafood dishes cooked over a braai, baked and smoked, eat as much as you like, meals last about 3 hrs, bring your own drink, small corkage fee, book even out of season. During peak periods there can be more than 150 people eating here – it can become a bit of a scrum around the braais.

Lambert's Bay to Vredendal *p193*
¶¶ The Cabin, on the edge of Doring Bay village, T027-2151016. Open 1200-1300, 1800-2100. Run by a family team, the outside tables are on a mock-up of a boat hull; inside you can sip sherry by a roaring fire in a decor of fishing nets and life belts. Well known for its fish soup and calamari and, for meat eaters, the spare ribs are good. There's a separate pub with pool table, dart board and TV.

○ Shopping

Langebaan *p187*
Freeport is a large shopping and accommodation development with a supermarket, bakery, bottle store and café. All other shops and restaurants are in Breë St, close to the town hall. Here you will find a bookshop, launderette, **Standard Bank** and curio shops.

▲ Activities and tours

Langebaan *p187*
Golf
Langebaan Country Club, Oostewal Rd, T022-7722112. There's currently an 18-hole golf course being developed on the edge of the lagoon.

Mountain bikes
Cape Sports, on the beach on the northern reaches of town, T022-7721114, www.capesport.co.za. Bikes available for hire. Also organizes windsurfing, kitesurfing and watersports with full instruction per hr or per day. Also rents out surfboards.

Lambert's Bay *p192*
Fishing
Game fishing is very popular along this stretch of coast, as is collecting crayfish. Fishing permits are issued by the post office.

Tour operators
Lambert's Bay Boat Charters, office at the harbour, T027-4321230, www.lamberts bay.info/boattrips.html. A strongly recommended boat trip to see dolphins, seals, whales (and sharks if you're lucky), and excellent for birdwatchers, expect to pay in the region of R350 per person.

● Directory

Langebaan *p187*
Emergencies Police, T022-7722111; Sea rescue, T082-9905966. **Medical services** West Coast Private Hospital, T022 7191030.

Lambert's Bay *p192*
Emergencies Police, T027-4321122. **Banks** Standard Bank in Church St is the best place to change money, with an ATM.

The N7 to the Northern Cape

If your time is short or you want to get to the Northern Cape, the quickest way out of Cape Town is to take the N7 highway. The first part of the route passes through rolling wheat country known as the Swartland, or 'Black Country', named after the dark hue of the rhinoceros bush, which once covered the area. Most of the towns in the region are small, prosperous farming communities, with little in terms of sights, despite their long history. The principal centres of the wheat industry are Malmesbury and Moorreesburg. Around this region and clearly signposted, are the vineyards that are part of the Swartland wine route (www.swartlandwineroute.co.za). Further north the eastern boundary of the Olifants River valley is made up of the spectacular Cederberg Mountains, a striking wilderness area offering some of the best hiking in South Africa. Both Citrusdal and Clanwilliam are a two- to three-hour drive from Cape Town and make good bases for exploring the area, their irrigated valleys providing a powerful contrast to the seemingly barren Cederberg. ‣‣ *For listings, see pages 207-210.*

Malmesbury → *Colour map 8, A1.*
About 50 km north of Cape Town the N7 passes Malmesbury, the centre of the surrounding wheat industry and the principal settlement in the Swartland. The sleepy town lies in a shallow valley close to the Diep River. For information visit the **Malmesbury Tourism Bureau** ① *1 Church St, T022-4872989, www.tourismswartland.co.za. Mon-Fri 0900-1600.*

The town was given its current name in 1829 when the British Governor, Sir Lowry Cole, visited and renamed it in honour of his father-in-law, the Earl of Malmesbury. Today the skyline is dominated by the unsightly grain silos and huge flour mills. **Swartland Cellars**, 4 km outside town, produces a full-bodied red wine and the famous Hanepoot, with its strong honey flavour, is popular as a dessert wine. The winery has won a number of awards, despite the fact that experts claim local climatic conditions are far from ideal. One of the grandest buildings in town is the **Dutch Reformed Church** on Church Street, opposite the city hall. Although the original building was completed in 1751, the present form dates from around 1899 when the church was enlarged by building the existing transepts. The magnificent heavy church bell isn't rung for fear of the vibrations damaging the structure – instead, a recording is played at services.

Moorreesburg → *Colour map 8, A1.*
Further north on the main N7, 102 km north of Cape Town, is this important farming and railway centre in the heart of the Swartland. Like Malmesbury, the surrounding area is devoted to wheat fields and sheep farming. Close to the railway are enormous grain silos and flour mills – wheat has been grown in the area since 1752. The settlement was founded in 1879 as a church centre, on a farm called **Hooikraal**. The town was named after the Reverend HA Moorrees. For information contact the **tourist office** ① *Municipality building, corner of Plein and Retief streets, T022-4331072, www.tourismmoorreesburg.co.za. Mon-Fri 0900-1600.*

The **Wheat Industry Museum** ① *Main Rd, T022-4331093, Mon-Thu 0800-1600, Fri 0800-1700, small entrance fee,* proudly proclaims that it is one of only three in the world and has a fairly diverting collection that traces the history of the crop. Before the cultivation of the area, the dominant vegetation was rhinoceros bush, a dark shrub found throughout the Swartland, which first gave it its name. Some of the early harvesting and threshing machines are well worth a look; they are reminiscent of kit models, which in many ways is what they are, having been shipped out from England in pieces.

Piketberg → *Colour map 6, B2.*

After 31 km the N7 passes the turning for Velddrif and the small town of Piketberg. The Piketberg hills rise as a large massif to the east as the road heads across the plains to the Olifants River Mountains. Before the road starts to climb, you pass the turning on the right for Porterville. This is the R44 and takes you back towards Paarl and Cape Town. Piketberg is another typical agricultural town, with a few old buildings and churches in the centre surrounded by modern suburbs, which in turn give way to rolling wheat fields. Look out for an old cannon in the grounds of the high school. There was once a series of cannons along the mountain slopes all the way to Cape Town, which were fired to let farmers know when a new ship was arriving in Table Bay to take on board fresh supplies. The cannon was also used to warn of the approach of Khoi-San people. The name of the town dates back to 1792 when a lookout post was set up on Honigberg Farm to protect the local farmers from looting by the Khoi-San. The actual word is derived from the French word *picquet*, referring to a small group of soldiers on the lookout. For information, contact the local **tourist office** ① *Kerk St, T022-9132063, www.piketberg.com, Mon-Fri 0830-1630.*

Like most of the small towns in the region, the dominant building is the **Dutch Reformed Church**, built 1880-1882. It is a striking building, neo-Gothic in style with plenty of turrets and plastered panels. There is an obelisk in its grounds commemorating the 1838 Great Trek. In 1938 the building was declared a national monument. There is a small **museum** housing antiquities donated by the community.

Olifants River Valley ⊜⊘▲ ↦ *pp207-210.*

As you drop down from the Piekenierskloof Pass, the scenery changes significantly with the arrival of the Olifants River. Although not one of South Africa's largest rivers, it is of vital importance to the region, irrigating over 12,000 ha of farmland. This is most immediately obvious in the brilliant green citrus farms interspersed with vineyards. Marking the east of the valley are the stark and magnificent Cederberg Mountains.

Citrusdal → *Colour map 6, A2.*

As the name implies, this modern rural town is the centre of the local citrus industry, nestling in a valley filled with citrus farms. During spring, the air is heavy with the scent of orange blossom and from May hundreds of thousands of oranges are packed up and exported. Even more striking is the town's setting at the southern edge of the Cederberg Mountains. Along with Clanwilliam, Citrusdal makes an ideal base for exploring the wilderness of the mountains, though there are no roads from Citrusdal into the Cederberg; from here you will have to continue along the N7 to the turning to Algeria. The **tourist office** ① *39 Voortrekker St, T022-9213210, www.citrusdal.info,* is housed in a recently built example of a typical Sandveld dwelling.

Many of the surrounding farms are now growing grapes, and the region is known for its excellent Goue Valley wines. There is a **Goue Valley shop** ① *Voortrekker St, near the tourist office, T022-9212233, www.gouevallei.co.za, Mon-Fri 0900-1700, Sat 0900-1230,* with sales and tastings.

Just out of town, by the turning for The Baths (see Sleeping, page 207), is **Die Sandveldhuise**, a historic thatched building and one of the first in the area. It houses a small country **museum** ① *T082-7349467, Mon-Fri 0900-1630, Sat 0900-1400,* outlining local history, but its main appeal is as a farm stall offering good light meals and wine tasting.

Clanwilliam, lying at the northern edges of the Cederberg, is a peaceful agricultural centre and one of the oldest towns in South Africa. During the spring, the profusion of wild flowers that blanket the area attract a large number of visitors, many of whom travel up from Cape Town (240 km). Just off the N7, Clanwilliam is a good base for exploring the Cederberg, and more peaceful and picturesque than Citrusdal. **Clanwilliam Tourism Bureau** ① *Main Rd, just to the left of the Old Jail, T027-4822024, www.clanwilliam.info, Mon-Fri 0830-1700, Sat 0830-1230 (longer hrs during flower season)*, a very helpful, friendly office, is worth a visit, although for more detailed advice on hiking in the area, you'll have to go to the office in Algeria in the Cederberg Wilderness Area (see page 208).

Background

The entire area of the Cederberg was populated by nomadic San people for over 20,000 years, and a profusion of rock art bears testament to their presence and displacement from the area. The land was first settled by white farmers in 1726; Jan Dissels started one of the first farms here, building a homestead close to the wagon track route from Table Bay. At the time, this spot was referred to as *Aan de Renoster Hoek*, literally, 'By the Rhinoceros Corner'. Similar names in the region refer to *olifants* and *seekoei*, elephant and hippopotamus, providing further evidence of the wildlife that once roamed the area.

In 1808 a garrison was constructed to try to deal with the problem of cattle rustling by Khoi people. The hot and arid farming conditions further dissuaded families from settling here, and the first British settlers were in fact brought here by the British government to create a human buffer in a grand scheme to stabilize the border from further tribal incursions. Only six families remained and, when the village was renamed in 1814, there were only 16 families living in the area. The new name was given by Sir John Cradock, the Governor of the Cape, in honour of his father-in-law, the Earl of Clanwilliam. Despite being a strong Afrikaner region, the name has stuck.

Sights

The majority of South Africans come to Clanwilliam to make use of the sporting facilities on and around the beautifully situated **Clanwilliam Dam**, though there are a couple of sights worth seeing in town. The **Old Jail** ① *Mon-Fri 0800-1300*, built in 1808, is a stocky white fort-like building overlooking the main street. The first part of the museum is devoted to the works of Clanwilliam's two famous residents: Dr P le Fras Nortier, who worked on citrus and the rooibos bush; and Louis Leipoldt, a well-known nature poet. There are also some displays on the rooibos (red bush) and cedar industries. At the back of the museum is an incredible giant threshing machine which was shipped out to South Africa in parts from Ipswich, England.

The road to the right of the Old Jail leads to the **Rooibos Tea Factory** ① *T027-4822155*. The industry originally flourished during the Second World War when teas from the Far East were difficult to obtain in Europe. After the war the market collapsed, but in recent times it has grown in popularity since it is caffeine-free and low in tannin. Today it is the biggest industry in the area and the tea is a refreshing, if acquired, taste. For a cup of tea and a video show contact the factory. Further along the same road is the **Clanwilliam Dam Resort**, part of which is the **Ramskop Nature Reserve** ① *mid-Jul to Oct*, worth visiting in season to view its magnificent wild flowers in bloom, of which there are over 400 species. There are well-laid-out paths through the reserve to the dam wall with good views of the mountains.

Cederberg Wilderness Area ● ➤➤ pp207-210. Colour map 6, A2.

The Cederberg is famous for its rugged scenery, stunning rock formations and ancient rock art, all of which make it fantastic walking country. There are over 250 km of paths in the mountains, passing streams and waterfalls and bizarre mountain flora. The highest peaks are Snow Peak (2028 m) and Table Peak (1969 m), while the most notable sandstone features include the **Wolfberg Arch**, the **Maltese Cross**, the **Wolfberg Cracks**, **Lot's Wife**, the **Town Hall** and the **Valley of the Red Gods**.

Ins and outs

Getting there and around All of the roads into the Cederberg Mountains are gravel, with steep and twisting sections, although some of the steeper parts have been covered with tarmac. The principal administrative centre for the wilderness is Algeria. Approaching from Citrusdal, the quickest route to Algeria is north along the N7; after 27 km take a right, signposted Kriedouwkrans and Algeria. You will cross the Olifants River via a low-level bridge and then descend into Algeria via Nieuwoudt Pass. The bridge crossing is sometimes flooded during winter. Contact the Algeria office to enquire about road conditions before setting off.

Best time to visit Climate is an important factor to bear in mind when planning a hike. During the summer months daytime temperatures are high, most streams and pools are dry, and you will need to carry plenty of water. Conversely, in the winter there can be heavy snowfalls, so you must carry the appropriate equipment. The best months for hiking are March to April and September to December. January and February are very hot and few people walk during these months; between June and August you can expect to encounter snow on the high ground.

Tourist information Cape Nature Conservation office ① *T027-4822403, www.cape nature.co.za*, in Algeria, is the best source of information and issues hiking permits and maps. The region is divided into three areas and 50 people are allowed in each area per day, but you shouldn't have to book permits in advance, even in peak season.

Hiking

As an officially declared wilderness, you are allowed to walk and camp anywhere in the mountains. There are, however, important rules to observe. No fires are allowed, so gas or paraffin stoves must be carried on overnight hikes. All waste material must be taken away – if you come across other people's rubbish, don't ignore it but carry it with you. Finally, while you are allowed to swim in the streams and pools, **do not wash with any form of soap** in the waters. The idea behind a wilderness is that the entire watershed is left to its own devices with minimal interference from man. There are few areas, even in South Africa, where you can wander so freely, so enjoy it and respect the rules. While there are recognized trails, these are not always easy to follow. Anyone planning a hike of more than one day should buy the excellent Cederberg map available at the Cape Nature Conservation office, and always carry a compass.

Warning There are 16 species of snake found in the mountains. Hikers may encounter a snake sunning itself on a path and although they are not aggressive it's best to wear strong hiking boots; also check your camp at night. The most harmful species are the puff adder

Cederberg Wilderness Area

To Calvinia & Route 27

To Vanrhynsdorp, Springbok & Namibian border

Biedou River

Sevilla Trail

Pakhuis Pass
Pakhuis

Cederberg Mountains

Clanwilliam

Ramskop Nature Reserve

Clanwilliam Dam

Tra-tra River

Wuppertal

Nieuwoudt Pass

Kriedouwkrans

Algeria

Uitkyk Pass

Wolfberg Arch

Wolfberg Cracks
Red Gods

Snow Peak (2028m)

Maltese Cross

Cederberg (Dwarsriver)

Uitsig

Citrusdal

Piekenierskloof Pass
To Piketberg, Malmesbury & Cape Town

To Prince Alfred Hamlet & Ceres

N

4 km
4 miles

Sleeping
Algeria Camp **10**
Baths **2**
Bushman's Kloof **1**
Cederberg Oasis **3**

Clanwilliam Dam
 Public Resort **6**
Elephant Leisure Resort **7**
Gekko Backpackers **8**

Karukareb Wilderness
 Lodge **9**
Sanddrif **4**

and berg adder, both of which can be sluggish but are highly venomous. Beware, too, of baboons stealing food at night from your camp.

Vegetation and wildlife

Although once covered in cedar trees, the vegetation that remains is predominantly mountain fynbos. There are few trees found along the major hikes – shade and shelter is usually provided by rock overhangs. In the wetter gullies and valleys you will find yellowwoods, hard pears and the Cape beech. The rare endemic snow protea, *Protea cryophila*, grows above the snowline. It is only found in a few locations but these are kept a secret. There are some photos of the flowers in the Clanwilliam museum.

The most common antelope found here include klipspringers, duiker and grey rhebok, but it is unlikely that you'll see any of these during a hike. Since 1988 there has been a programme to protect the leopard population, and apparently there are plenty in the mountains, although it is virtually impossible to see them. Due to the lack of vegetation at higher altitudes, the birdlife is not very varied, but look out for grey-wing francolin, Cape siskin, Cape sugarbird and Victorin's warbler.

Rock art

The Cederberg is literally riddled with ancient San rock art, and peeking underneath a rocky ledge or in a cave will often reveal the faint markings of worn away images. Some of the better-preserved sites have become major tourist attractions, and seeing these ancient paintings in such a stunning setting is a real highlight.

One of the best ways of seeing a good selection of San art is by walking the **Sevilla Trail**, an 8-km hike on private land. The walk is fairly easy going and crosses a rocky plain, passing along a 4-km stretch of rocky overhangs, outcrops and caves. There are 10 sites in total, ranging from simple hand prints to extraordinary images of hunters, processions of women, running antelope and elephants. The highlight of the hike is Site Five, a rocky overhang covered with images in various stages of erosion, with a beautifully clear hunter carrying a bow, and a painting of a zebra foal, perfectly embodying its first uncertain steps. Even those with just a passing interest in San art will find this walk thoroughly absorbing. The stunning rock formations, silent bush and shimmering mountains add to the atmosphere. The trail begins at **Traveller's Rest Farm** ① *34 km from Clanwilliam on Wupperthal Rd, over the Pakhuis Pass, T027-4821824, www.travellersrest.co.za*. Permits are issued at the farm and there are also 12 self-catering cottages. If your interest in rock art isn't satiated and you've got plenty of cash, spend a day or two at **Bushman's Kloof** (see Sleeping, page 209).

North of Cederberg ⊖**⊙** » *pp207-210*.

Calvinia → *Colour map 6, A2*.

Although Calvinia is actually in the Northern Cape, it is relatively far from most sights in the north, and therefore usually visited as part of the Western Cape. It is a typical hot, sleepy Karoo town that most people just pass through, perhaps stopping for petrol and a cool drink. It has a beautiful setting though, at the foot of the Hantams Mountains. It's also an important sheep-farming centre, though, given the vast size of the farms, chances are you won't see any sheep. It also has clear star-filled skies at night 80% of the time, and attracts many South African astronomers.

Your first port of call should be **Hantem House**, the oldest surviving building in town, which started life as a homestead in 1854 and today houses the **tourist office** ⓘ *44 Hoop St, T027-3411606, www.calvinia.co.za*, and a smart café and gift shop. The **Calvinia Museum** ⓘ *Church St, T027-3418500, Mon-Fri 0800-1300, 1400-1700, Sat 0800-1200*, relates to the early history of the region, made up of photographs and farming implements. In the garden is a Class 24 steam locomotive from England and a horsemill. These are still in use on farms in the depths of the Karoo.

Vanrhynsdorp → *Colour map 6, A1.*

This town is known as the gateway to arid Namakwa region (see the Northern Cape chapter). North from here the countryside seems a thousand miles from the fertile Cape. The town is named after Petrus Benjamin van Rhyn, the first representative for Namaqualand to sit in the old Cape Legislative Council. Although the region was first visited by Pieter Crythoff in 1662 it was only settled in the 1740s. The town itself first took shape in 1887 with the building of a church. The **tourist office** ⓘ *Van Riebeeck St, T027-2191552, www.tourismvanrhynsdorp.co.za, Mon-Fri 0800-1230, 1500-1600, sometimes Sat in flower season*, is near the old jail.

The green-fingered may want to visit the **Kokerboom Succulent Nursery** ⓘ *74 Voortrekker St, T027-2191062, Mon-Fri 0800-1700, small entrance charge*, on the outskirts of town. Gardeners come here from afar, and it's worth a visit if you're here out of the flower season. It claims to be the largest such nursery for the distinct kokerboom (aloe) trees in South Africa. **Latsky Radio Museum** ⓘ *close to the post office on Church St, T027-2091032, Mon-Sat 0900-1200, 1400-1700*, is a private collection of over 200 domestic radios covering the period 1915-1965.

● The N7 to the Northern Cape listings

Hotel and guesthouse prices
L over US$300 AL US$220-300 A US$150-220
B US$100-150 C US$75-100 D US$35-75
E US$15-35 F under US$15
Private game reserves
L4 over US$900 L3 US$550-900
L2 US$450-550 L1 US$300-500
Restaurant prices
††† over US$30 †† US$15-30 † under US$15
See pages 46-51 for further information.

● Sleeping

Malmesbury p200

C-E Caravan & Chalet Park, Piketberg Rd, T022-4873266. Chalets sleeping 4-6 and shady caravan stands, laundry, telephone, swimming pool, a small, well-run site.
D Bergzicht, 43 Bergzicht St, T022 4824274, www.bergzichtlodgings.co.za. Comfortable B&B with 4 double rooms and 4 garden self-catering units sleeping 2-4, next to the swimming pool, pretty courtyard with a fountain, full English breakfasts.

Moorreesburg p200

C Kolskoot Guest House, 10 km from the town centre, T022-4332528, info@kolskoot.com. This building was constructed during the Second World War by Italian POWs as a chicken coop. Today it has 6 en suite doubles and a family room, each decorated with rustic furniture and paintings by a local artist. Activities include mountain biking, horse riding and clay-pigeon shooting, and South African dinners can be arranged. Recommended. Booking is essential.
D Samoa Hotel, Royal St, T022-4331201, www.samoahotel.co.za. Friendly rural hotel with comfortable a/c rooms, popular **Oscar's Bar and Diner** with a good range of meals for a small town including black-board specials and pizza oven, bar, swimming pool, secure parking.

Piketberg p201

B-C Dunn's Castle, T022-9132470, www.dunnscastle.co.za. Dunn's Castle was built in the 1890s for George Dunn and was designed by Sir Herbert Baker. 5 pretty double rooms in the castle with Victorian finishes, country decor, fireplaces and free-standing bathtubs; self-catering cottages in the grounds, swimming pool, restaurant and bar.

Citrusdal p201

Plenty of farms in the region provide accommodation, convenient for hiking. Full lists are available from the tourist office.
C Cedarberg Lodge, 67 Voortrekker St, T022-9218026, www.cedarberglodge.co.za. This is a family-run town hotel with 26 a/c rooms, TV with M-Net, swimming pool, full-size billiard table, gardens and gym. **Tangelo's** restaurant has a good reputation, mix of usual steaks with country cooking, pub with big-screen TV showing sports.
C Elephant Leisure Resort, 7 km from Citrusdal in the shadow of the Cederberg Mountains, T021-9212884, www.elephant leisure.co.za. 10 well-equipped cottages on a private nature reserve with views of the valley and nearby dam. Each cottage sleeps 4, with a/c, TV, fridge, cooking facilities (including microwave), fireplace, braai area and veranda. Rather unusually each has a 4-seater jacuzzi and there's a swimming pool.
C-F The Baths, 18 km to the south of Citrusdal, the well signposted turning is between the N7 and the town, T022-9218026, www.thebaths.co.za. A popular and long-established site at a natural hot-water spring surrounded by citrus groves, the first resort was established here in 1739 and the main Victorian stone buildings survive. 16 well-equipped chalets, 12 flats and 15 camping pitches, all self-catering, bring bedding and towels, shop on site but buy fresh groceries in Citrusdal, restaurant and bar, hot and cold swimming pools, tennis courts, mountain

biking, hiking trails, individual spa baths/ jacuzzis, all set in a tract of indigenous woodland. A lovely peaceful spot, no TVs or cell phone reception. Recommended.
E-F Gekko Backpackers, 20 km north of Citrusdal on the N7, turning to left is signposted, T022-9213721, www.gekko.co.za. Excellent backpacker lodge on a citrus farm. Double rooms, dorms, camping, if you don't have a sleeping bag, bedding can be hired, brightly painted bathrooms, large kitchen, bar, meals on request, table-tennis room, small lounge, hammocks strung underneath trees for relaxing on the lawns. Access to swimming holes in river and added bonus of San rock art on the farm. Popular with overlanders, so can be lively, but usually very peaceful. Will pick up from the Intercape bus in Citrusdal by prior arrangement. Highly recommended.

Clanwilliam *p202*

A Karukareb Wilderness Lodge, 13 km from Clanwilliam in the Cederberg, T027-4821675, www.karukareb.co.za. 5 colonial-style rooms or 5 luxury permanent safari tents with claw foot baths, very stylish with a/c, wooden floors, lovely restaurant and bar in a thatched *lapa*, swimming pool, lots of activities from hiking trails to horse riding and mountain biking. An excellent base to explore the Cederberg, but no children permitted.
C Clanwilliam Hotel, Main St, T027-4821101, www.clanwilliamhotel.co.za. Friendly and homely standard 3-star town hotel, large comfortable rooms, en suite, a/c, TV, good restaurant and tea room, swimming pool, sauna, good value and excellent service. Across the road from **Reinhold's Restaurant**.
C Blommenberg, 1 Graafwater Rd, T027-4821851, www.blommenberg.co.za. Comfortable set of 12 units, 4 of which are self-catering, en suite, M-Net TV, minibar, breakfasts served in a dining room full of antiques, lovely gardens, braai areas, pool, hard to miss on the right-hand side just before town.

D-F Clanwilliam Dam Public Resort, 1 km out of town beside the dam, T027-4828000. Huge resort with 180 grassy caravan and tent stands on tiers up the hillside, modern but plain self-catering chalets, plenty of trees offering shade, electric and gas points, gets very busy and noisy in season when you should watch security. Out of season you should be able to turn up on the day and find space. No restaurant, bar or shop.

Cederberg Wilderness Area *p203, map p204*

Outside Citrusdal and Clanwilliam are a host of private farms. The list includes those closest to the mountains. If you are self-catering, stock up in advance. Basic groceries can be bought at a shop just before Algeria.
C-E Algeria Camp, run by **Cape Nature Conservation**, reservations through their Cape Town office, T021-6593500, www.capenature.co.za. Take the N7 27 km north of Citrusdal, turn right on Algeria Rd; it is 18 km to the camp on a dirt road. The camp is in a beautiful setting on the edge of a pine forest by a mountain stream and swimming hole. It is exceptionally clean, well run and very popular; book in advance especially for school holidays. Self-catering stone cottages sleep 4-8, all fully equipped, plus 48 shady camping spots, some with electric points.

At the foot of Uitkyk Pass, 5 km to the south of Algeria, are 2 more **cottages**, sleeping 4-6. These are very basic, with solar electricity, although there is a gas-run fridge and stove, and hot water. You'll need to bring bedding, towels and extra candles with you. The helpful information office and camp reception is open 0730-1600; you must arrive before 1600 to collect keys for accommodation. It also issues hiking permits and maps for some of the longer trails in the Cederberg Mountains starting from the camp. There is a card and coin phone next to reception and firewood is available. Guests can swim in the nearby river. Note that accommodation is more expensive at the weekend and on public holidays.

C-F Sanddrif, 25 km south of Algeria, T027-4822825, www.cederbergwine.com. 15 chalets, a choice of standard self-catering chalets, luxury chalets or a grassy and shady campsite, bring bedding and towels. The standard chalets have no shade but views of the mountains, and all are close to the river. 20 mins' walk downstream is Maalgat, an 8-m-deep pool popular with divers. There are power points at the campsite, and campers can use the deep freeze in the office at Dwarsriver. The farm sells fresh milk, butter and their own wine. The advantage of staying here is that you can easily visit the Maltese Cross, Wolfberg Cracks and the Wolfberg Arch on a day's walk from the camp without having to drive anywhere, and hiking permits are available from the office. Recommended.

E-F Cederberg Oasis, 30 km south of Algeria and 67 km from the turn-off for Algeria on the N7, T027-4822819, www.cederberg-oasis.co.za. A well-placed backpacker hostel for many of the major hikes, and is part of the Cederberg conservancy. Good-value cottages, some with dorms, self-catering, camping, restaurant, bar, swimming pool and internet access. Maps and information available. A good friendly family-run set-up.

Private lodges and camps

L2 Bushman's Kloof, Wupperthal Rd over the Pakhuis Pass, central reservations, T021 6852598 (Cape Town), www.bushmanskloof.co.za. This private reserve claims to have the 'world's largest open-air art gallery', and it certainly is one of the best places to see San art in South Africa with over 130 sites, dating back as far as 10,000 years. Animals present include Cape mountain zebra, klipspringer, baboon and smaller mammals. Accommodation is in luxurious cottages and in the main building. All rooms are a/c, with en suite bathrooms, 4-poster beds, tasteful decor, log fires and wooden decks overlooking a lake. There are 4 swimming pools, sauna, beauty spa, excellent restaurant with outdoor terrace, gift shop,

library, billiard room, and wine cellar. An overnight itinerary begins with check-in at 1400, followed by afternoon tea, an evening game drive and dinner; the next morning is an excursion to the rock art followed by lunch and check out at 1200. Prices include all meals, game drives and tours but at almost R5000 per night for 2 people the experience does not come cheap; ask about specials Apr-Jun. Air and road transfers can be arranged from Cape Town.

Calvinia p205

B Hantem House, 44 Hoop St, T027-3411606, www.calvinia.co.za. Several converted Victorian houses in the village, with luxury en suite rooms, wooden floors, antique furniture, cosy traditional kitchens, full of old world charm and no TVs, the only modern amenities are the electric blankets on the beds. Overall very smart and of a high standard. Light meals can be arranged in the house kitchens or eat at the main restaurant at **Hantem House** (♥♥). Restored 19th-century homestead, the best place to try traditional Karoo cuisine, excellent breakfasts. Recommended.

D Hantam Hotel, Kerk St, T027-3411512, www.hantamhotel.co.za. A large solid building with great shady verandas, 16 en suite rooms with a/c or fans, **Busibee** restaurant serving predominantly steaks, bar popular with local farmers, the principal town hotel but with far less character than the Victorian houses above.

Vanrhynsdorp p206

D Namaqualand Country Lodge, Voortrekker St, T027-2191633, www.namaqualodge.co.za. Some old rooms plus new rooms in block at back, comfortable TV lounge and open central courtyard decorated with wood carvings, used by tour groups, steakhouse style restaurant, small bar, swimming pool, the smart external appearance is let down by ordinary faded rooms.

D Van Rhyn Guest House, Van Riebeeck St, T027-2191429, www.vanrhyngh.co.za. 11 comfortable en suite rooms, non-smoking, in a pleasant old Victorian 1-storey house built in 1916 in gardens full of trees, fully licensed and offers wine from the Olifants River region, dinner on request.

● Eating

Malmesbury *p200*
¶¶ **Die Herehuis**, 1 Loedolf St, T022-4871771. 0730-1400, 1800-2100, closed Sun evening. Enormous choice on the à la carte menu, 4-course set menu at Sun lunchtime includes a local roast with fresh vegetables. Friendly service, garden setting, oil lamps and roaring fires in winter. Recommended.

Moorreesburg *p200*
¶¶ **Oscar's Bar and Diner**, Samoa Hotel, Royal St, T022-4331201. 1000-2200. Good-value country fare, with an extensive menu of steaks, pasta and pizza. Sun roasts are a grand affair, popular with the townsfolk after church.

Citrusdal *p201*
¶¶ **Hebron**, on Piekenierskloof Pass, before you descend into the Citrusdal Valley, T022-9212595. Lovely terrace setting and good gourmet breakfasts and lunches for this remote location. Freshly ground coffee, home-made bread and rolls, fresh vegetables, chickpea stew or beef with couscous, and lots of sticky puddings.
¶¶ **Patrick's**, 77 Voortrekker St, T022-9213062. Mon 1830-2200, Tue-Sat 1230-1500, 1830-2200. Friendly restaurant with an Irish theme, excellent ostrich steak, also good grilled line fish and wide range of steaks, good value. There's a separate pub.

Clanwilliam *p202*
¶¶ **Olifantshuis Pizzeria**, Main St, T027-9822301. Mon-Sat 1800-late. Popular and informal pub serving steaks and good pizzas. Garden tables and friendly atmosphere.

¶¶ **Reinhold's**, T027-4821101. Tue-Sat 1900-2100. Smart à la carte opposite **Clanwilliam Hotel**, dinner only, small bar and cosy atmosphere, good range of steaks, fish and pasta, the best option in the area.
¶ **Nancy's Tearoom**, Main St, T027-4821101. Daily 0900-1600. Coffee shop set in beautiful gardens. Good sandwiches and cakes.

▲ Activities and tours

Clanwilliam *p202*
Tour operators
Blue Yonder, T083-2324306, www.blueyonder.co.za. Adventure trips using 4WD and 'Xumbugs', small 4WD go-carts, into the Cederberg mountains.
Cederberg Travel, T027-4822444, www.cedarberg-travel.com. Day tours in the mountains, adventure trips, hikes, also organize trips from Cape Town.

● Transport

Bus
Intercape, T0861-287287, www.intercape.co.za. There is a daily service in both directions between **Cape Town** and **Namibia** along the length of the N7. The bus stops in **Malmesbury** outside Malmesbury Motors, **Moorreesburg** outside Swartland Motors, **Citrusdal** outside Sonop Motors, **Clanwilliam** outide Cedar Inn, **Vanrhynsdorp** outside Turck's Garage at the junction with the N7, and then on to **Springbok** and **Windhoek**. There is another service between **Cape Town** and **Upington** – the bus turns off the N7 at **Calvinia** where it arrives and departs in the middle of the night.

● Directory

Calvinia *p205*
Banks Standard, 21 Hoop St; ABSA, 25 Hoop St.

Breede River Valley

Only 310 km long, the Breede River (also known as the Breë, meaning 'broad') is one of the most important rivers in the Cape, and its valley is a beautiful boundary zone. Fed by streams from the mountains, the river is a major source of water for a large number of orchards and vineyards. Leaving the mountains behind at Ceres, the river passes through the Bontebok National Park and then flows across an undulating coastal terrace, meandering through the wheat fields of the Overberg before entering the Indian Ocean at St Sebastian Bay.

Worcester is the principal town of the region. Along the broad valley are important farming centres such as Ceres, Prince Alfred Hamlet, Ashton and Bonnievale and the picturesque villages of Tulbagh, McGregor and Montagu. These old settlements are surrounded by vineyards and fruit farms that undergo beautiful colour changes through the seasons. Behind the farms are mountains rising to 2000 m with challenging hiking trails and hidden valleys, their peaks capped with snow in the winter. The valley acts very much as the dividing line between two contrasting regions of South Africa. To the southwest are the verdant Winelands and populous Cape Town, both very fertile and prosperous districts. To the northeast is the start of the Karoo, a vast expanse of semi-desert, dotted with the odd sheep farm or isolated Victorian town. ▸▸ *For listings, see pages 229-238.*

Ins and outs

Since the opening of the Huguenot Toll Tunnel in 1988 it has been possible to drive to Worcester from Cape Town in less than an hour. Worcester lies just to the south of the N1, and is the largest town in the Breede Valley. From here you can continue your journey in three different directions. Firstly, the main N1 highway continues for another 1300 km to Johannesburg. Locals regard this road as dull and something to be got over with as quickly as possible. The road passes through the southern margin of the Great Karoo, known as the Koup. While most people only pause here to refuel or stay overnight, this is a wonderful region to explore with a couple of beautiful Victorian towns as well as the superb Karoo National Park outside Beaufort West.

Heading north from Worcester along the R43, you quickly reach the N7 highway. The N7 is the main road between Cape Town and Namibia, running up the West Coast. This route will take you to the upper reaches of the Breede River Valley and the agricultural centres of Tulbagh and Ceres.

The final direction you could take when leaving Worcester is to follow the R60 along the Breede River Valley as far as Swellendam in the Overberg and then head east along the N2 highway to the Garden Route and Port Elizabeth.

The 3.9-km-long Huguenot tunnel reduces the journey through the mountains by 11 km. As you emerge on the Cape Town side, the road is perched high on a viaduct with superb views of Paarl Mountain, its hillsides covered with ordered vineyards – a sharp contrast to the countryside at the other end of the tunnel.

Worcester and around ●●●▲●● ▸▸ *pp229-238. Colour map 8, A2.*

This medium-sized farming centre is the capital of the Breede River Valley, a prosperous town with many interesting historic buildings and a fine collection of museums. The excellent Karoo National Botanical Garden is well worth visiting, particularly during the flowering months of August to October, and there's a wine route to explore.

Ins and outs

Tourist information Worcester Wine and Tourism ① *25 Baring St, T023-3482795, www.worcestertourism.com, Mon-Fri 0800-1700, Sat 0830-1230*, provides a walking-tour booklet that can also be downloaded from the website.

Background

The first Europeans to settle in the region were farmers, and when it became necessary to build a settlement, their land had to be acquired. The streets were laid out and the first plots were sold in 1820; the new settlement was named after the Marquess of Worcester, the eldest brother of the Governor of the Cape, Lord Charles Somerset. One of the first buildings to emerge was the local *drostdy* (magistracy), which was one of the finest Cape buildings in South Africa. Today it is part of the Drostdy Technical High School. The wealth in the region is almost entirely derived from agriculture, a fact that is easy to appreciate while travelling past the numerous vineyards and orchards of the valley. Many of the neat farms visible from the roadside depend upon irrigated waters. The highly fertile neighbouring Hex River Valley is in effect the last of the productive Cape farmlands. In contrast, driving east from the valley one quickly comes to the dry and arid Karoo.

Worcester

Sleeping
Church Street Lodge **3**
Habit Guesthouse **1**
Protea Cumberland **4**
Wykeham Lodge **6**

Eating
Barn **1**

Pear Tree **7**
Saddles **5**
San Diego Spur **6**

Sights

If time permits, a short walk around the centre is very pleasant. The main sights are central and close together, and the grid street pattern makes it easy to find your way about. There are some fine Victorian town buildings, although the main road is made up of mostly modern shops and fast-food outlets. Many of the old buildings are along **Church Street**, most of which were built between 1840 and 1855. Also in Church Street is the **Congregational Church**, housing some fine original examples of wooden church furnishings and standing in a well-kept garden. The **Dutch Reformed Church** dates from 1832, a Gothic-style building which dominates the town skyline. Its spire has an interesting history: the original was considered to be too squat and was replaced by a cheap tin version in 1899. The current spire was built in 1927 after the tin one had twice been blown down by the summer gales from the southeast.

Next to Church Square is a **Garden of Remembrance** which contains some monuments commemorating local residents. It was designed by one of the town's more famous citizens, the artist Hugo Naudé. Each Saturday morning a **Flea Market** is held on Church Square.

Worcester is well known throughout South Africa as being the home of two important institutes for the disabled set up by the Dutch Reformed church. In 1881 an **Institute for the Blind** (www.blind-institute.org.za) was opened, and a few years later an **Institute for the Deaf** (http://deafnet.co.za) was founded in De la Bat Street. Each institute has opened a shop in the town centre selling crafts made by members (see Shopping, page 237). The institutes are also open to visitors who wish to learn more about the pioneering work undertaken with blind and deaf people. Unlike most South African towns, the pedestrian crossings in Worcester emit sounds for the blind.

On the corner of Baring and Church streets is **Beck House** ① *T023-3420936, Mon-Fri 0830-1300, 1330-1630, small entrance fee*, built in 1841 in typical Cape Dutch style. It has an interesting display depicting the town life of an important Worcester citizen, Cornelius Beck. There are some excellent examples of late 19th-century furnishings – the quality of the yellowwood and stinkwood furniture is regarded as some of the best in South Africa. Look out for the bath house, the delightful herb garden and the Cape cart in the old coach house. Today it is home to the **Pear Tree** restaurant and gift shop.

The interesting **Hugo Naudé & Jean Welz Gallery** ① *115 Russell St, T023-3425802, Mon-Fri 0830-1630, Sat 0900-1200*, is home to a mixed collection of works by prominent South African artists. The first collection is of sculptures by Bill Davis, displayed in the garden. Inside are paintings by Jean Welz, Paul de Toit and Hugo Naudé. Hugo Naudé was a pioneer painter who also designed this large two-storey building and had it built as his home in 1904. He lived and worked here until his death in 1941.

There are 18 cooperative wine cellars, three wine estates, and several brandy distilleries in the Worcester region. **KWV Brandy Cellar** ① *Church St, T023-3420255, www.kwv.co.za, Mon-Fri 0800-1630 for tastings, guided tours of the distillery in English Mon-Fri at 1000 and 1400, tours in other languages organized on request*, is the largest in the world under a single roof. There are 120 copper pot stills producing 10- and 20-year-old brandies.

Look out for the Braille labels on some of the local wine – these are the only Braille wine labels in the world.

Kleinplasie Open-air Museum

ⓘ *Robertson Rd, T023-3422226, www.kleinplasie.co.za, Mon-Sat 0900-1630, small entry fee.*
Kleinplasie is an open-air museum depicting the lifestyle of the early pioneer farmers. The collection is a series of old farm buildings, many with traditional skills on show such as tobacco rolling. There is also an indoor collection of smaller tools and implements as well as an excellent restaurant. Kleinplasie is also the home of **Worcester Winelands** ⓘ *T023-3428710, www.worcesterwinelands.co.za,* which is very helpful in giving information on the surrounding winelands, as well as offering tastings and sales of local wines. Allow at least two hours to look around all the exhibits. The first part of the display comprises 26 buildings which have been furnished or equipped in the styles of the period 1690-1900. Only the tobacco shed is an original structure, dating from 1900; all the other buildings are reconstructions, but good ones. Several rural skills are demonstrated using traditional methods and tools. You can watch an ironmonger at work, or view the grinding of flour and baking of bread, plus cheese- and candle-making. Walking around the buildings gives one the feel of being on an old working farm: there are horses, cattle, pigs and geese in pens, not to mention all the farmyard smells and sounds. The second part of the collection is indoors and equally interesting. Most of the displays are of old farm implements and home industry pieces. All are clearly displayed and well labelled. A couple of items worth a closer look include the early example of a fruit grader, and a mean-looking self raker from the 1860s which was used in the wheat industry. The painted Voortrekker wagon near the entrance illustrates what the living conditions were like.

Beyond the outdoor section is a collection of buildings that can be viewed from a toy train which starts from close to the dipping kraal. Most of these buildings are from a rural village, including a post office, a general dealer and a cartwright's shop.

There is a craft shop at the entrance with a small selection of books. Just before the main entrance on the right is the **Kleinplasie Restaurant**. It is excellent value, serving fresh healthy meals. This is also a good place to sample local wines. There is a cheaper cafeteria inside the main building where snacks and cool drinks are sold. Behind the farm buildings is a picnic site.

Karoo Desert National Botanical Garden

ⓘ *Off Roux St beyond the golf club on the north side of the N1, T023-3470785, www.nbi.ac.za, daily 0700-1800, free, small entry fee in the flower season, Aug-Oct. Plant shop and tea garden.*
This garden, hidden away from the commercial centre of town, combines 144 ha of natural semi-desert plants and 10 ha of landscaped gardens filled with plants from similar arid regions within South Africa. The collection was originally started at Whitehill near Matjiesfontein in 1921, but moved to Worcester in 1946 to make the gardens more accessible to visitors from Cape Town.

Visiting during a time of year when many of the species are in flower allows you to appreciate how colourful deserts can be when it rains. August, September and October are good months to go, assuming the rains have been good. Stapelias bloom from the New Year through to mid-March, and June is the ideal period to see the exotic aloes in flower. In the formal gardens there are a few greenhouses which display a collection, world-famous among botanists, of stone plants, *conophytum*. Two common plants of the region to look out for are the Namibian wild grape, *Cyphostemma juttae*, and the Karoo bush, *Pteronia paniculata*. Given that the collection comprises over 400 species of flowering plants (*aloes, lampranthus, lithops, conophytum*) it is not surprising to find that the local birdlife is exceptionally rich. Over 70 species have been recorded in the gardens. There are also several short trails, including an excellent 1-km-long Braille Trail. Children will especially enjoy the porkwood plant maze.

Worcester wine route

There are 21 estates listed as part of the Worcester wine route. All are fairly local, and some of them offer tastings, tours and sales to visitors. Unlike many of the more visited wineries around Stellenbosch, most of the cellars here were founded in the 1940s – the farm buildings therefore lack much of the history and beauty found elsewhere. Furthermore, the countryside is not as dramatic as that around Paarl, and none of the cellars yet offers the excellent meals available on the Franschhoek Valley estates. That's not to say that the route is not worth visiting – one major advantage it has is that it is far less commercial than the Winelands and, by comparison, relatively tourist-free.

Listed below are some of the more interesting cellars. The **Worcester Winelands office** in the Kleinplasie Open-air Museum (see opposite page) is a good starting point. They can provide you with additional information on other members of the wine route and also offer tastings and sales of the area's best wines.

Botha Wine Cellar ① *T023-3551740, sales and tastings: Mon-Fri 0730-1730, Sat 0900-1300, cellar tours: by prior arrangement, 20 km along the R43 towards Ceres.* This is a pleasant cooperative with a neat tasting centre beside a colourful rose garden. The cellar is known for its Chardonnay, Hanepoort Jerepiko and port. Several varieties are on sale including some dessert wines and very good grape juice.

Worcester wine route

Sleeping		
ATKV Goudini Spa **5**	Merwida Country Lodge **2**	Nuy Valley Guest House **6**
	Nekkies Holiday Resort **3**	

Bergsig Estate ① *T023-3551603, www.bergsig.co.za, sales and tastings: Mon-Fri 0800-1700, Sat 0900-1700, cellar tours and lunches: by prior arrangement, 40 km along the R43 towards Ceres.* This is the oldest estate in the region and Bergsig has belonged to the Lategan family for six generations – the first vine was planted in 1843. It is a friendly estate with some good off-dry and semi-sweet whites.

Du Toitskloof Wine Cellar ① *20 km from Worcester along the N1 towards Cape Town, T023-3491601, www.dutoitskloof.com, sales and tastings: Mon-Fri 0900-1800, Sat 0900-1700, cellar tours: Mon-Fri by appointment.* Some of the best award-winning local wines are produced here, on one of the most progressive estates in the country. It has a mixture of red wines, semi-sweet whites, dessert wines and grape juices.

Merwida Riverstone Wine Cellar ① *T023-3491144, www.merwida.com, sales and tastings: Mon-Fri 0830-1230, 1330-1700, Sat 0900-1300. Cellar tours: by appointment, 10 km from Worcester off the road to Rawsonville.* Despite being a small and relatively young cellar, Merwida produces some excellent wines, including an award-winning Ruby Cabernet and an excellent white.

Nuy Winery ① *T023-3470272, www.nuywinery.co.za, sales and tastings: Mon-Fri 0830-1630, Sat 0830-1230, no cellar tours, 22 km from Worcester along the R60 towards Robertson.* This excellent small cellar is well known for its award-winning dessert wines and is situated in the lee of the Langeberg Mountains. The office and shop are welcoming and there is a restaurant.

Overhex Wine Cellar ① *T023-3476838, www.overhex.com, sales and tastings: Mon-Fri 0800-1700, cellar tours: by appointment, 6 km from Worcester along the Robertson Rd.* A smart, modern cellar, Overhex offers a range of wines from muscadets to sparkling whites plus some sweet grape juices.

Waboomsrivier Wine Cellar ① *T023-3551730, sales and tastings: Mon-Fri 0800-1700, Sat 0800-1000, cellar tours: Mon-Fri, only by appointment, 25 km from Worcester on the Ceres road.* This cellar has a good tradition of wine makers. There are 47 members who farm from the banks of the Breede River to the slopes of the Mostertskop. Their whites include a Chenin Blanc, Riesling, and Perlé. The reds on sale are a Ruby Cabernet, Pinotage and Cinsaut.

Hex River Valley → *Colour map 8, A2.*
① *For more information visit www.hexrivervalley.co.za.*
No matter the time of year you visit, this is one of the most beautiful valleys in South Africa. Approaching from the arid landscapes of the east, this is the first glimpse one gets of the fertility and splendour of the Cape. The soils are naturally productive and this has for a long time been an important grape-growing region. Over 60 of the table wines grown for export originate from here, and there are an estimated eight million vines growing in the valley and on the mountain slopes. This multitude of vines provides a colourful backdrop: verdant green in summer, rich bronzes and reds in autumn, beautiful snow-capped peaks against the leafless plants in winter.

De Doorns → *Colour map 8, A2.*

Heading towards the interior, 32 km along the N1 from Worcester, is this small settlement lying in the centre of a major grape-producing region. The name meaning 'the thorns' in Afrikaans refers to the local Acacia thorn bush. Information is available from the **tourist office** ① *Voortrekker St, T023-3562041, www.tourismdedoorns.co.za.*

De Doorns Wine Cellar ① *T023-3562100, Mon-Fri 0800-1300, 1400-1800, Sat 0800-1200, tours Feb-May only, next to the N1,* is a large co-op in an old Cape Dutch building. In addition to producing a popular Hanepoort Jerepigo, there are refreshing red or white grape juices for sale, plus sherries and an alcohol-free sparkling wine. This is also a good stop for tourist information as there are many brochures on display. Nearby are a couple of farm stalls selling a good range of fresh local produce including table grapes in season. From De Doors the N1 continues northeast through the Hex River Pass to Touws River and the Aquila Private Game Reserve (see page 276).

North from Worcester ⊜⊘⊛▲ → *pp229-238.*

The R43 follows the Breede River Valley to Wolseley and the major fruit-producing regions. Most of the farms can be visited on a day visit from Worcester, but there is a greater variety of choice in places to stay on the farms around Tulbagh and Ceres. The road follows the Breede River flows as it flows through the vineyards towards its source.

Wolseley → *Colour map 8, A2.*

This small town is in a unique position on the watershed of two rivers, one flowing into the Atlantic Ocean, the other into the Indian Ocean. Given the beauty of the surrounding countryside and the variety of tourist sights in Tulbagh and Worcester, there is no reason to spend much time here aside from a lunchtime meal. The few interesting old buildings that had survived through time were destroyed in the same earthquake that caused much of the damage in Tulbagh in 1969.

Tulbagh → *Colour map 8, A2.*

Tucked away in the Tulbagh Valley, surrounded by the Winterhoekberg, Witsenberg and Saronsberg Mountains, is this small village with a beautifully preserved centre of traditional Cape buildings. Along with Swellendam in the Overberg, it rates as one of the best examples of a rural Victorian settlement in South Africa. Like Swellendam, however, the state of the buildings is somewhat artificial because much of the settlement was destroyed by a sudden earthquake on 29 September 1969. This was a significant local tragedy: nine people died and considerable damage was done to property. However, the earthquake gave rise to the largest restoration project in South Africa's history. Many of the old buildings had been in a bad state of repair and some were practically derelict, but the village underwent massive restoration and became the fine settlement you see today.

The original name of the valley was Land van Waveren, an outpost of the Dutch East India Company dating from 1699. In the early days of Dutch rule the western hinterland, stretching as far north as present-day Piketberg and Porterville, was known as Waveren. The first settlers arrived in the valley on 31 July 1700 but it was another 40 years before permanent structures appeared and a village took shape. As with many settlements in the Cape, Tulbagh is named after a former Governor of the Cape, Ryk Tulbagh (1751-1771). Today Tulbagh is a prosperous and peaceful settlement, isolated from Cape Town by several intervening mountain ranges. North of the town, the upper valley of the Little

Berg River is a centre for some small wine estates and fruit farms. Sheep and wheat farming are also important to the local economy.

The **tourist office** ⓘ *4 Church St, T023-2301348, www.tulbaghtourism.org.za, Mon-Fri 0900-1700, Sat 1000-1600, Sun 1100-1600*, is enthusiastic and friendly, with some interesting and useful leaflets covering the area. There is an attached restaurant and coffee shop with outdoor seating overlooking beautiful Church Street. The office is in one of the houses which is part of the museum; tickets for all the museum buildings are sold here.

Sights in the town The main attraction is the delightful tree-lined **Church Street**; 32 of its original buildings were restored after the earthquake, and the whole street feels like a living museum. The majority of the buildings are in private ownership, but three are part of

Tulbagh Valley

Sleeping
Hunter's Retreat
Guest Farm **1**

Rijk's Country Hotel **4**
Schalkenbosch Farm **5**
Villa Tarentaal **6**

Wild Olive Farm **8**

the town museum (see below) and a couple have been converted into B&Bs. The old slave lodge is now the **Paddagang** ('frog passage') **Restaurant**, overlooking lush lawns. In complete contrast, the main commercial centre, Van der Stel Street, is a straight line of dull modern buildings saved by a colourful municipal garden.

If your time is short, the one place to visit in Tulbagh is the **Oude Kerk Volksmuseum** ① *2 Church St, T023-2301041, Mon-Fri 0900-1700, Sat 0900-1600, Sun 1100-1600, small entrance charge*, which has one of the most interesting collections of Victorian furniture and objects in the Cape. The high ceiling and good light of the church makes it an ideal display case and it's a popular venue for weddings. There is also interesting information about the 1969 earthquake.

Sights outside the town The **Old Drostdy Museum** ① *T023-2300203, Mon-Sat 1000-1230, 1400-1630, Sun 1430-1630, small entrance charge*, is built on one of the early settler farms, Rietvlei, 4 km out of town. Designed by Louis Thibault, it has been restored and now houses a fine collection of sherry vats in the cellars, plus a museum devoted to antique furniture upstairs. Nearby are the Drostdy wine cellars where local wines and sherries are made (see below). The old Drostdy building appears on their wine labels. Their fortified wines can be tasted in the atmospheric, candle-lit cellars.

Wine route
This area is in fact better known for its fruit production – Ceres, the centre of the fruit industry, is only 35 km away. **Drostdy Wine Cellar** ① *T023-2301086, www.drostdy wines.co.za, sales and tastings: Mon-Fri 0830-1200, 1315-1700, Sat 0830-1200, cellar tours: Mon-Fri 1100 and 1500* (see above), is due north of the village, beyond the signs for Kliprivier Park. North of Tulbagh is **Theuniskraal Estate** ① *T023-2300688, www.theuniskraal.co.za, sales and tastings: Mon-Fri 0900-1700, Sat 1000-1200, tours by appointment only*, which has been in the hands of the Jordaan family since 1927. Their white wines have won several awards. Their Riesling, with John Platter's seal of approval, is highly acclaimed. **Twee Jonge Gezellen** ① *T023-2300680, www.tjwines.co.za, sales and tastings: Mon-Fri 0900-1600, Sat 1000-1400, cellar tours: Mon-Fri 1100 and 1500, Sat 1100*, has the only underground champagne cellar in South Africa and there's a restaurant open during peak season. To get there take a left turn at the north end of Church Street. The tourist office can provide all the details of other estates in the valley.

Ceres → *Colour map 8, A2.*
Anyone travelling for some time in South Africa will undoubtedly try one of two brands of fruit juice – **Liquifruit** or **Ceres**, both of which are packed in Ceres. This is the most important fruit-growing centre in the country, and all types of soft fruits are grown and processed in the valley. Surrounded by the harsh and rugged Skurweberg Mountains, this attractive farming centre was founded in 1854 and aptly named after the Roman goddess of agriculture. During the winter months there can be heavy snowfalls in the mountains, enough at times for some limited winter sports. Snow is such a novelty in South Africa that when there is snow on the ground, curious Capetonians visit here in droves: cars line the country roads and the local farmers' fields are trampled by thousands of people. When the snows melt, the Dwars, Koekedouw and Titus rivers become the perfect environment for trout fishing. For information visit **Ceres Tourism** ① *Owen St, T023-3161287, www.ceres.org.za*, in the town library.

One of the town's first magistrates, JA Munnik, was responsible for planting numerous trees around the town to provide shade. Fortunately, this tradition has been maintained and, as a result, there are plenty of mature trees lining the roads and the banks of the Dwars River, which flows through the town centre and the gardens of the **Belmont Hotel**.

Togryers' Museum (Transport Riders' Museum) ① *8 Oranje St, T023-3122045, Mon-Fri 0930-1300, 1400-1700, Sat 0900-1200 in summer, small entrance charge*, houses a fine collection of horse-drawn vehicles. All types of wagons and carriages are on show, celebrating the town's past importance as a centre for making these vehicles. Before the railways arrived, the fruit produced here had to be transported to the Cape in such wagons. Some excellent photographs capture the spirit of the time.

The following fruit packhouses and factories allow visitors to look around on tours – a sort of 'fruit route', if you like. It is surprisingly interesting to see how life starts for a peach or a potato that is going to end up on a local or even international supermarket shelf. Note that most of the factories insist on visitors wearing closed shoes and long trousers for hygiene purposes. **Ceres Fruit Growers (CFG)** is worth visiting to see its vast cold-storage facilities. This is one of the larger cooperatives specializing in deciduous fruits. **Ceres Fruit Juices (CFJ)** is home to the award-winning juices found on supermarket shelves around South Africa. **Ceres Potatoes** is a similar operation but with a crop of onions and potatoes. Tours run twice a day Monday to Friday at 1000 and 1400 depending on demand but they must be booked in advance through Ceres Tourism (see page 219); two-hour tours cost

Ceres

To Prince Alfred Hamlet & Citrusdal (R303)

To Calvinia, Touws River & Inverdoorn Game Reserve

To Ceres Fruit Growers & Ceres Fruit Juices

Lover's Bridge

Togryers' Museum

Victoria Park

To Tulbagh

N

400 metres
400 yards

Sleeping ⊜
Pine Forest 6
Village Guesthouse & Restaurant 1

R60 per person. During the fruit season, December to March, they can also organize tours to working fruit farms or drying yards in the Ceres region.

Prince Alfred Hamlet → Colour map 8, A2.

This small village is the second most important farming centre in the Warm Bokkeveld Valley. It was named after the second son of Queen Victoria, who was the first member of the British royal family to visit South Africa. In 1865 he went on a hunting expedition in this region. North from here the road skirts along the western fringes of the arid Karoo for over 100 km, without passing through any settlements of note. The farmlands in this area are very productive, so much so that a rail link was specially built from Ceres to transport fruits and vegetables. Apples, peaches, plums, nectarines and pears are grown in the valley, and the short drive north from Ceres (R303) is particularly enjoyable during the spring when the orchards are in full blossom. Popular activities include fruit tours and trout fishing. Continuing north towards the Cederberg Mountains and Citrusdal, the road

Ceres Valley

Sleeping
Bergstroom Farm Cottage 1
Bushmen Lodge 5
Houdenbek Farm Cottages 3

Inverdoorn Game Reserve 4
Klondyke Cherry Farm 6

leaves the valley through **Gydo Pass**, R303. This is yet another pass built by Andrew Bain, this time while he was also working on the more important Michell's Pass. It was completed in 1848, and remained as a gravel road until the 1950s. The settlement is also the junction to the **Swartberg Pass** or R328 to 'The Hell', Oudtshoorn and the Cango Caves (see page 289). This is a good place to stop for a cool drink before climbing the scenic mountain pass. For local tourist information you're best off contacting the Ceres office, as Prince Alfred falls under their control.

Kagga Kamma Private Game Reserve
ⓘ *Off the R303 north of Prince Alfred Hamlet, T021-8724343, www.kaggakamma.co.za.*
Kagga Kamma Private Game Reserve is 90 minutes' drive from Ceres, on the fringe of the Cederberg Mountains. It is a nature reserve devoted to the history of the San people who lived here, the remarkable rocky landscape dotted with their ancient rock art. The reserve did have a resident San village within its boundaries, but the villagers have moved back to their ancestral lands in the Kalahari. They drop in periodically to sell traditional wares. The area is one of outstanding natural beauty and the best way of exploring it is on foot. Resident anthropologists accompany visitors to rock art sites to explain their meaning, and are also very knowledgeable about the traditions, lifestyle and beliefs of the San.

It is possible to go on game drives in the reserve, which has a good variety of antelope including eland, gemsbok, bontebok, springbok and kudu. There are also lynx, caracal and leopard, but these are very elusive. If you're in a hurry and have money to burn, you can fly the 260 km from Cape Town in just 40 minutes. Access to the reserve is by overnight stays at the lodge (see Sleeping, page 232) or day trips can be arranged for R700. Visit the website for package deals.

Inverdoorn Game Reserve
ⓘ *T021-4344639, www.inverdoorn.com.*
Inverdoorn Game Reserve is 55 km from Ceres. Follow the R46 for Touws River and the N1. Take the R355 turning for Calvinia and almost immediately after join the R356 for Sutherland. The entrance is on the left. This is a private 3500-ha game reserve specializing in 4WD game safaris to view its range of wildlife, which includes rhino, buffalo, giraffe, zebra, wildebeest, eland, kudu and impala. A pair of lions and seven cheetahs were introduced a few years ago. The area is a typical Karoo landscape and quite beautiful to drive around. Other activities on offer include hikes to San rock art, birdwatching, fishing and mountain biking. There are a few options here: the first is a fully guided game drive for R550 per person, R690 with lunch. Alternatively, the overnight stays at the lodge also include one or two game drives (see page 232), or again, check out the website for packages.

South from Worcester ⚫🏃🏠⚫🚌🚶 ▶ *pp229-238.*

As the Breede River meanders south from Worcester, the valley starts to broaden out and the level lands are given over to agriculture. As you drive along the R60 towards Robertson, the Langeberg mountains run parallel to the north. When the crops are maturing this is a beautiful drive through landscapes of contrasting colours. Along the roadside are farm shops selling fresh produce and several of the wine estates are open for wine tastings and sales. Both Worcester and Robertson have their own organized wine routes. After Robertson the R60 divides; the R317 runs close to the river as far as Bonnievale, while the R60 continues towards Ashton, Montagu and Swellendam.

Robertson → *Colour map 8, B2.*

This small, prosperous town has a vaguely time-warped feel to it, with tidy jacaranda-lined streets, orderly church squares and neat rose gardens. It is the centre of the largest area of irrigated vineyards in the Cape with over 20 wineries, many of which have won awards. The high-quality dessert wines and liqueurs produced here have ensured the town's continued prosperity, as has the large brandy distillery. The town itself was founded in 1852 as a new parish to cope with the growing population of Swellendam further down the Breede River Valley. Conditions are ideal for agriculture as there is an abundant water supply from the Langeberg Mountains to the north and the Riviersonderend hills to the south. The lime-rich soil here provides good grazing for horses and there are a number of stud farms in the region. While there isn't a great deal to see in town, it is a pleasant place to spend a day exploring the sleepy centre and nearby vineyards. **Robertson Tourism Bureau** ① *T023-6264437, www.robertsonr62.com, Mon-Fri 0900-1700, Sat and Sun 0900-1400*, is on the corner of Reitz and Voortrekker streets.

Robertson Museum ① *50 Paul Kruger St, T023-6263681, Mon-Sat 0900-1200, free*, or 'Druids Lodge', remained in the hands of the same family for nearly 100 years. The original house was built circa 1860, only a few years after the grid pattern for the town had been first laid out. In 1883 the resident magistrate, Mr WHD English, bought the house and it remained the property of the family until 1976, when the last living member, Miss Violet English, died. The municipality bought the house and set up a museum. Most of the collection is devoted to the lives of William Henry Dutton English and his offspring, as well as the history of Robertson and the area. Of particular note is a beautiful collection of lace. Here you can pick up a useful guide for a historical walk around the village that takes in the villas built during the ostrich feather boom.

Robertson

200 metres
200 yards

N

To ⑤, Ashton, Montagu & Swellendam (R60)
To ⑥ ⑨, Vrolijkheid Nature Reserve, Breede River & McGregor

Sleeping 🛏	Grand 2	Pat Busch Private Nature	Eating 🍴
Ballinderry 1	Hanepoot Huisies 7	Reserve 9	Branewynsdraai 1
Fraai Uitzicht 5	Little France 8	Robertson Backpackers 3	Café Rosa 2
Goedereede Guest Farm 6			

Robertson Valley wine route

① T023-6263167, www.robertsonwinevalley.co.za.

The Robertson Valley is home to 10% of South Africa's vineyards, and produces excellent Chardonnays and several good Muscadets. Ask about the Food and Wine Festival held every October; it's an excellent chance to sample the region's varied fresh produce.

This wine route follows the Breede River Valley and embraces the districts of Robertson, McGregor, Bonnievale and Ashton. In total there are 46 cooperatives and estates open to the public. The greatest concentration is found along the R317 as it follows the Breede River between Robertson and Bonnievale.

One of the most welcoming estates along the wine route is **Van Loveren** ① T023-6151505, www.vanloveren.co.za, Mon-Fri 0930-1700, Sat 0930-1500. Try their Blanc de Noir wines. Tastings are conducted in a restored rondavel set in the middle of a colourful garden. Guests are allowed to taste the full range and someone is always close at hand to assist with any queries.

The **Bon Courage Estate** ① 9 km from Robertson along the R317, T023-6264178, Mon-Fri 0930-1700, Sat 0930-1500, is best known for their award-winning Chardonnays and wine tasting is in an old Cape Dutch whitewashed building or on the lawns and the Café Maude is open for lunch. **Robertson** ① T023-6263059, www.robertsonwinery.co.za, Mon-Thu 0800-1700, Fri 0800-1800, Sat-Sun 0900-1500, is the oldest winery in the area. The shop and processing plant are located on Constitution Road. During the harvest time you can see tractor loads of grapes being delivered to the town.

McGregor → Colour map 8, B2.

This picturesque village lies off the beaten track in the lee of the Riviersonderend Mountains. The village is made up of a collection of perfectly preserved, whitewashed thatched cottages which radiate out from a **Dutch Reformed Church** which is in turn surrounded by a neat, colourful garden. Originally, McGregor was known as Lady Grey, after the wife of Sir George Grey, a former governor of the Cape Colony. In 1903 it was renamed, as there was another town in the province with the same name. The new name came from the Reverend Andrew McGregor, a Scottish minister who had worked in the district during the formative years of the village. Dr Mary Cooke, a local historian, described McGregor as "easily the best-preserved and most complete example of mid-19th-century townscape in the Cape Province". Today the village has a good choice of accommodation, as well as a range of shops and a couple of restaurants. In recent years, McGregor has attracted a creative population and there are a number of artists, potters and craftsmen living in the small cottages. The village surrounded by olive groves and vineyards remains far from spoilt, however, and is a beautiful, peaceful spot from which to explore the Breede River Valley. The **McGregor Tourism Bureau** ① T023-6251954, www.tourismmcgregor.co.za, www.mcgregor.org.za, Mon-Fri 0900-1300, 1400-1630, Sat 0900-1300, is on the corner of Church and Voortrekker Street.

Boesmanskloof Trail

① Contact the tourist office. There is no official accommodation along the trail and camping is not allowed. Follow the yellow footprints.

This 16-km trail links McGregor with the village of **Greyton** on the northern side of the Riviersonderend Mountains. The path requires a reasonable level of fitness. In summer it's hot and you should carry drinking water. In winter, conditions are cold and wet. The trail follows forested valleys rich in protea and erica species. Antelope can sometimes be seen. In the spring this area is covered with a beautiful display of wild flowers.

Each direction can easily be completed in a day – the problem lies with transport. There is no easy way to travel quickly between the two towns. As hiking permits are only available from the **McGregor Tourism Office**, the logical option is to hike from McGregor to Greyton, stay overnight, and then hike back the next day. This is a popular trail and numbers are restricted to 50 people per day. It is advisable to book in advance during the local holidays. Rangers do patrol and check for permits.

Vorlijkheid Nature Reserve

① *Enquiries T021-6593500, www.capenature.co.za.*

Vorlijkheid Nature Reserve lies 15 km south of Robertson on the McGregor road. The landscape is rugged and strikingly scenic, with sandstone and underlying shale formations. Small mammals such as klipspringer, grysbok and springbok are fairly common, and if you are very lucky you may see a caracal, a type of wildcat. The terrain lends itself to raptors and there are often buzzards or goshawks circling the arid landscape during the summer months. Despite the fact that the reserve lies in an area a good distance to the west of the Karoo, many of the plants and trees are identical to those growing there. Grasses are scarce on the rocky lands, but there are plenty of succulents, and during September the land is covered with a colourful blanket of wild flowers, assuming the spring rains have been good enough.

Two hiking trails have been clearly marked out, known as the **Heron Trail** and the **Rooikat Trail**. The Heron Trail is a simple 3-km walk to a couple of dams where there are some bird hides. Waterbirds can always be seen on the lakes. A rare attraction for enthusiastic herpetologists is the Robertson dwarf chameleon. The office at the gate has species lists and can help you with suggestions of what to look out for, and where. The Rooikat Trail is a much more strenuous 19 km and requires you to carry at least two litres of water per person (none is available en route). The terrain is rocky in parts and proper hiking boots should be worn. This is a circular walk through the Elandsberg Mountains, taking in a few peaks of over 500 m with views of the Langeberg and Riviersonderend Mountains. Allow at least eight hours. From November to March temperatures are high and precautions should be taken against sunstroke. Wear a hat and drink plenty of fluids before and during the walk. A pamphlet available at the gate contains a good scale map with contours shown, which will help you plan your day.

Bonnievale → *Colour map 8, B2.*

This small town is known for its wines and cheese, and is the site of the main Parmalat dairy factory, a brand that becomes very familiar to visitors in South Africa. The settlement was founded by one of the first farmers to appreciate fully the agricultural potential of the area, Christopher Rigg, who arrived in the valley and immediately set about building an ingenious system of canals to irrigate it. Most of the land is devoted to grape and wine production today, but you will also find several fruit orchards, including peaches, navel oranges, clementines and apricots. The **Bonnievale Tourism Office** ① *Main St, T023-6163563, www.bonnievale.co.za, Mon-Fri 0800-1700*, is a well-organized and helpful office covering the whole Breede River region.

In the town itself the only real tourist attraction is the **Myrtle Rigg Memorial Church**, which is kept locked but keys can be obtained from the tourist office during working hours. This church has a rather sad story behind it. Two of the Rigg's children died when they were still very young, and their third child, Myrtle, died at the age of seven, in 1911. Before her untimely death, Myrtle asked that her parents build a small church to remember her by. This little Gothic-style building was constructed using the finest materials from around the world, including roof tiles from Italy and a fine carved door from Zanzibar. It was consecrated in 1921, but fell quickly into disrepair after the Riggs' deaths. Fortunately the municipality saw fit to restore it in 1977, and today it is a museum. The **Parmalat cheese factory**, which produces 40 tonnes of gouda and cheddar each day, is another legacy of Mr Rigg and today many Parmalat dairy products are found on South African supermarket shelves. The shop sells cheese, butter, milk, yoghurt and cottage cheese.

Bonnievale wine cellars
The following is a small selection of wine estates close to Bonnievale, open for tastings and purchases. They are all members of the Robertson Valley wine route (see page 224 for further details).

De Wetshof ① *T023-6151853, www.dewetshof.co.za, Mon-Fri 0830-1630, Sat 0930-1300, cellar tours by prior arrangement*, a well-known export label, is a short drive from the town on the far side of the Breede River. This was the first registered wine estate in the region and is known for its excellent white wines, especially its award-winning Chardonnay. **Langverwacht** ① *T023-6162815, Mon-Fri 0800-1230, 1330-1700*, has good Riesling and Colombard. **Viljoensdrift** ① *T023-6151901, www.viljoensdrift.co.za, Mon-Fri 0830-1700*, is a relatively new member of the wine route which resumed producing wine after a 30-year gap. In addition to wine tastings you can enjoy a one-hour cruise on a raft on the river that departs at 1200 and make up a picnic from their deli to take with you. **Weltevrede Estate** ① *T023-6162141, www.weltevrede.com, Mon-Fri 0830-1700, Sat 0900-1530*, has a restaurant and self-catering cottages (see Sleeping, page 233 and Eating, page 236).

Ashton and around → *Colour map 8, B2.*
The small settlement of Ashton is rather an odd place, dominated as it is by two major canning factories. Pass through here on a weekday, and it seems that the entire population of the town is dressed in either green or blue uniforms, depending upon which factory they work in. There is little of interest in town, although there are a couple of wine cooperatives. The **Tourism Bureau** ① *Main Rd, T023-6142471, www.montagu-ashton.info, Mon-Sat 0900-1700, Sun 0930-1230*, is next door to a finely preserved steam locomotive built in 1919, and used on the Worcester–Mossel Bay line until 1983.

A large proportion of local wine production is handled by the **Ashton Wine Cooperative Wine Cellar** ① *T023-6151135, sales and tastings: Mon-Fri 0800-1230, 1330-1700, Sat 0900-1300, guided tours by prior arrangement*, who are also well known for their excellent grape juice. If you are keen on your wines, the pleasant **Zandvliet Estate** ① *T023-6151146, Mon-Fri 0900-1700, Sat 0930-1300*, on the banks of Cogmans River, is well worth a visit. Although the cellar's first wine, a Shiraz, was initially produced as recently as 1975 it has won many prizes and is highly regarded in wine-producing circles. The estate has invested heavily in the latest techniques to help grow and produce quality wines. The estate house is a fine example of a traditional thatched Cape Dutch homestead.

If you have taken the main road, the R60, between Robertson and Ashton you will pass **Sheilam Cactus Farm/Nursery** ① *T023-6264133, www.sheilamnursery.com, Mon-Sat 0900-1700, small entry fee*, or 'Little Mexico', as it is now known, where you can admire some of the 3000 cactus plants and succulents. It rates itself as the biggest cactus nursery in the southern hemisphere. Plants and seeds can be bought here and sent back home.

Montagu and around → *Colour map 8, B2.*

Although Montagu is very much a Karoo town, it is usually visited by people exploring the Breede River Valley. It is 245 km from Oudtshoorn, the administrative centre for the Little Karoo, and only 15 minutes' drive from Ashton and the Breede River. It is a delightful place in a stunning setting, its long streets lined with oak trees and whitewashed Cape Dutch houses, sitting humbly beneath jagged mountain peaks. Founded in 1851, the settlement was named after John Montagu who, as the colonial secretary from 1843 to 1853, had been responsible for the first major road-building programme in the Cape. The greatly improved road network enabled previously remote settlements such as Montagu to thrive and grow. From its early days the region was recognized as ideal for fruit and wine production. The valley was fertile and the climate ideal for vines. In 1940 the Langeberg Co-op was formed, which proved to be the necessary boost for the local economy. Within 10 years, local production of apples and pears had doubled, while over a period of 16 years the wine produced increased by fivefold.

The exceptionally helpful and enthusiastic **Montagu Tourism Bureau** ① *24 Bath St, T023-6142471, www.montagu-ashton.info, www.tourismmontagu.co.za, Mon-Sat 0900-1700, Sun 0930-1230, 1500-1700,* has several useful leaflets including one about the historic homes in the area. The **Montagu Market** ① *Bath St, opposite the tourist office, Sat 0900-1300,* is good for for crafts, food and collectables.

Montagu

N
400 metres (approx)
400 yards (approx)

Sleeping 🛏
7 Church St **1**
Avalon Springs & Da Vinci's Restaurant **2**
Caravan Park **3**
Cynthia's Cottages **4**

John Montagu **6**
Kingna Lodge **7**
Mimosa Lodge **8**
Montagu Country Hotel **9**

Eating 🍴
Bistro **1**
Jessica's **4**
Prestons & Thomas Baines Pub **5**
Templeton's @ Four Oaks **3**

Joubert House ① *25 Long St, T023-6141774, museum: Mon-Fri 0900-1300, 1400-1630, Sat 1030-1230, garden: Mon-Fri 0900-1300, 1400-1700, small entrance fee*, the oldest building in the town, is now part of the museum (housed further along Long Street). The house has a collection of late 19th-century furnishings and ornaments and part of the garden has been turned into an indigenous medicinal plant collection.

Long Street, a popular attraction, has 14 national monuments along its length. With so many well-preserved buildings, it is easy to get a vivid impression of how the settlement would have looked in its early days.

The **Montagu Nature Garden** ① *Van Riebeeck St, T023-6142590, daily, small entrance fee, teas served on Tue and the first Sat of the month, May-Nov, the best time to visit is spring (Aug-Oct)*, on the south side of the Kinga River off Van Riebeeck Street, has the largest collection of mesembryanthemums in the country.

Just 3 km from the town centre are the hot mineral springs at the **Avalon Springs Resort** ① *T023-6141150, R25, R18 child, see Sleeping, page 234, for resort details*, which have been used for over 200 years for their healing powers. There are two indoor pools and five outdoor pools, all at different temperatures. At the weekends and holidays it gets very busy so try to go early in the morning or in the evening when it's cooler. The waters are radioactive and have a steady temperature of 48°C. In 1980 Montagu suffered a tragic setback when continued heavy rains in the Langeberg resulted in a flash flood down the Keisie River. It was a local catastrophe and 13 people were killed. The hotel was filled with several metres of sand and debris and the hot springs were covered with mud, but the town itself was barely touched.

Tractor rides ① *R60, R25 child, trips usually go Wed and Sat 1000 and 1400 if there are enough takers, for reservations, contact the tourist office*, to the top of the Langeberg mountains are on offer from Neil Burger, a local farmer; the trip leaves from his farm in the **Koo Valley**. There are impressive views across the Karoo and down into the Breede River Valley from the summit. For an extra R60 (R25 for children) you get an excellent meal of *potjie*, home-baked bread and a drink. Note that the tractor does not operate in October. Wear warm clothes. To get there from Montagu, take the R318 towards Matroosberg, after 30 km the road descends the Burger Pass into the Koo Valley.

Montagu wine route

The Montagu cellars are best known for producing white wines with the Muscadel grape, which tend to be fairly sweet, fortified dessert wines. There are several wineries in the district which can be visited for tastings and sales. Cellar tours are by appointment only. For further information visit www.kleinkaroowines.co.za.

Montagu Co-op Wine Cellar ① *T023-6141125, www.montaguwines.co.za, sales: Mon-Fri 0800-1230, 1330-1700, Sat 0900-1200*, is next to the golf course, heading out of town via Bath Street. **Rietrivier Wine Cellar** ① *T023-6141705, www.rietrivier.co.za, sales: Mon-Thu 0800-1700, Fri 0800-1500*, is 20 km east of Montagu on the Barrydale road. **Uitvlucht Winery** ① *T023-6141340, www.uitvlucht-wines.co.za, sales: Mon-Fri 0800-1730, Sat 0830-1330*, is just off the main road not far from the police station.

⊙ Breede River Valley listings

Hotel and guesthouse prices
L over US$300 **AL** US$220-300 **A** US$150-220
B US$100-150 **C** US$75-100 **D** US$35-75
E US$15-35 **F** under US$15
Restaurant prices
†††† over US$30 †† US$15-30 † under US$15
See pages 46-51 for further information.

⊜ Sleeping

Worcester and around *p211, maps p212 and p215*

There are few hotels in the town itself; most of the private accommodation is on farms in the surrounding valleys. These are all very pleasant and in most cases good value.

In town

B-C Protea Hotel Cumberland, 2 Stockenstroom St, T023-3472641, www.cumberland.co.za. 55 comfortable a/c rooms, breakfast extra, smart à la carte **Gallery** restaurant, plus a daytime coffee shop and poolside cocktail bar, immaculate swimming pool, health complex including a gym, sauna, spa bath, squash courts and a tennis court. Check for special offers.
C Church Street Lodge, 36 Church St, T023-3425194, www.churchst.co.za. A modern guesthouse with 21 en suite bedrooms with extras such as coffee facilities, fridge and satellite TV, comfortable lounge areas with fat leather sofas, swimming pool set in peaceful grounds with fountains.
C Habit Guesthouse, 6 Porter St, T021-3423538, www.tiscover.co.za/the habitguesthouse. Quaint historic home built in 1837 with wraparound veranda, polished wooden floors and lovely established gardens with swimming pool, 6 en suite rooms, guest lounge with honesty bar.
C Wykeham Lodge, 168 Church St, T023-3473467, www.theguesthouse.ch A pleasant B&B set in a lovely thatched 1835 homestead at the quieter end of Church St on the edge of town overlooking open parkland. 7 double rooms with en suite bathroom, TV, private balconies, secure off-street parking, small bistro restaurant for guests, pretty gardens.

Out of town

A Merwida Country Lodge, 3 km from Rawsonville, 13 km from Worcester, T023-3491435, www.capeweddings.co.za. An elegant luxury lodge built in the style of an American colonial mansion, set on a wine estate. The façade is dominated by tall columns and a balcony. Inside, the reception hall contains a giant marble staircase that leads up to the 7 bedrooms. Some suites have private balconies overlooking the mountains. Downstairs are 2 spacious lounges with open log fireplaces, a billiard room, restaurant, breakfast room and a pub. The back of the house opens onto a shaded terrace and crystal-clear swimming pool. The grounds are surrounded by vineyards and mountains. As the website suggests, it's a popular place for country weddings. Booking essential. Recommended.
B-C Nekkies Holiday Resort, 4.5 km from Worcester on Lake Marais, T023-3432909, nekkies@breedevallei.gov.za. 14 self-catering log chalets built on stilts overlooking the lake, with 2 bedrooms and 2 bathrooms, fully equipped kitchen, balcony and fireplace, good for families.
B-E ATKV Goudini Spa, 22 km from the town centre just off the N1 at Rawsonville, T023-3443013, www.goudinispa.co.za. A very popular family resort and warm mineral water spa. It has 154 fully equipped self-catering rondavels and duplex flats with 2-8 beds, 53 camping and caravan pitches, plus excellent facilities, outdoor pools, tennis courts, mini-golf and jacuzzis, in beautiful setting in the lee of Slanghoek Mountains, surrounded by vineyards. Rates are higher at the weekends.

D-E Nuy Valley Guest House, 19 km
from town off the R60 towards Robertson,
T023-3421258, www.nuyvallei.co.za. A large,
well-kept guesthouse in an 1871 Cape Dutch
building close to the river on a wine estate
in the countryside. 27 en suite rooms, à la
carte restaurant, self-catering kitchen,
swimming pool, neat gardens with rose
trees and ornamental ponds. A walk will
take you to a refreshing waterfall. Call
ahead to check if a wedding or conference
is on. The wine cellar, nearby, has been
converted into cheaper rooms for backpackers with shared bathrooms. Outstanding
value, recommended.

Hex River Valley *p216*

Given the excellent choice of places to
stay in the valley, De Doorns is usually
only visited when driving through.
C De Vlei Country Inn, 5 km out of town
on Voortrekker Rd, T023-3563281, devlei
countryinn@telkomsa.net. A well-restored
CapeDutch coach house, peaceful location,
5 well-appointed double chalets with underfloor heating in pretty gardens surrounded
by vines, good restaurant and bar, worth
stopping for a meal here, French spoken.
D-E Arbeid Adelt Guest House, Voortrekker
Rd, T023-3562204, www.arbeidadelt.co.za.
Late 18th-century Victorian house on a grape
farm, 5 en suite double rooms, 1 self-catering
cottage sleeping 6, 3 caravan/camping
pitches, B&B, dinner on request, tea garden
with lawns and ornamental fountain, pretty
veranda to take in the mountain views.

Wolseley *p217*

C White Bridge Farm, 9 km from Wolseley
towards Ceres, take the R46 and turn right
on to the R43, T023-2310705, www.white
bridge.co.za. Farm accommodation in
1 B&B double room or 3 attractive
self-catering cabins sleeping 4-6 built from
natural materials such as stone, reeds and
bamboo, swim in the pool or in the river
among orchards of citrus fruits, pears
and plums.

Tulbagh *p217, map p218*
In town
C De Oude Herberg, 6 Church St,
T023-2300260, www.deoudeherberg.co.za.
4 en suite rooms with French windows onto
the pretty veranda in a national monument
Cape Dutch building, TV, ideal for walking
to main town attractions, restaurant (closed
Mon), sheltered sunny courtyard, swimming
pool, laundry service, can arrange sundowner
trips to the mountains.
C Tulbagh Country House, 24 Church St,
T023-2301171, www.tulbaghguest
house.co.za. Delightful renovated 1809 Cape
Dutch house, complete with thatched roof
and neat flower garden. 5 attractive,
comfortable en suite rooms with polished
wood floors and antique furnishings, huge
breakfasts are served up in an appealing
dining room. Also acts as an art gallery.
Perfect for a night in a historic Tulbagh
home. Recommended. Also rents out a
house nearby with 4 double rooms.
D-F Klipriver Park Holiday Resort, Van der
Stel St, T023-2300506. Large caravan park
with excellent amenities, one of the prettiest
in the Cape, also has 18 self-catering chalets
with 2 bedrooms, hot water, electric points,
shop, restaurant, swimming pool, set among
trees close to river dam with fine mountain
views, chalet prices lower out of season.

Out of town
Some of the rates are per cottage – if there are
4 or more of you staying, they're good value.
B Rijk's Country Hotel, Tulbagh,
T023-2301006, www.rijks.co.za. Luxury
development on a wine estate on the
outskirts of town. 12 suites in a stunning,
thatched Cape-style house, 3 self-catering
cottages, overlooking vineyards and a dam.
Swimming pool, excellent restaurant, bar,
extensive gardens, wine tasting and cellar
tours, another popular country wedding
venue. Recommended.
C Hunter's Retreat Guest Farm, 2 km from
Tulbagh, T023-2300582, http://hunters
retreat.lando.co.za. On Ruimte farm, 4 en suite

double rooms in an original labourer's cottage, shared lounge, plus 2 luxury suites with Victorian bathrooms, B&B, swimming pool surrounded by lawns and gardens full of rose bushes. Chapel on the farm for weddings.

C Villa Tarentaal, 1 km from town, T023-2300868. With 2 attractive self-contained 2-bedroom cottages set on farm, open-plan kitchen, lounge, bathroom, veranda and beautiful mountain views, braai area, breakfast available on request. Professional beautician Christine offers aromatherapy massages, reflexology and facial treatments.

C-D Schalkenbosch Farm, 8 km east of Tulbagh in the lee of the Witsenberg Mountains, T023-2300654, www.schalken bosch.co.za. Historic manor house (1792) on a wine farm, declared a national monument, 3 B&B rooms and 3 luxury self-catering cottages, swimming pool, billiard room, views across Tulbagh Valley. No young children.

C-F Wild Olive Farm, 7 km south of Tulbagh turn-off on the R46, T023-2301160, www.wildolivefarm.com. 6 self-contained cottages, each with a different configuration, ranging from a basic room with hot plate to 2-bedroom cottage with kitchen, lounge, TV and fireplace. Also 10 caravan sites and 15 camping pitches with shared ablution block and use of gas braais and a fridge/freezer. The whole set-up is on a working farm with lovely mountain views.

Ceres *p219, maps p220 and p221*
There is a surprisingly small choice of accommodation or restaurants in the town, and the **Belmont Hotel** has recently been demolished, but there are several excellent places in the surrounding countryside.

In town

D Village Guesthouse and Restaurant, 64 Vos St, T023-3162035, www.ceres.org.za/VillageGuest. Comfortable guesthouse with 7 spacious individually decorated rooms with private entrances set around a courtyard, swimming pool, bar and simple meals in

the restaurant including some traditional South African dishes.

D-F Pine Forest, Carson St, 1 km from town centre, T023-3161882, pineforest@ceres.co.za. Large caravan park with some self-catering rondavels, camping permitted on request. A well-organized municipal site in a great setting beneath towering pine trees, swimming pool, squash courts, mini-golf, table tennis and pool table, boats can be hired on nearby dam, trout fishing. Book ahead during the school holidays.

Out of town

B-D Houdenbek Farm Cottages, 55 km from Ceres, follow the R303 towards Citrusdal up the Gydo Pass, turn right in the village of Op-Die-Berg (the road is surfaced as far as Sand River, but the last few kilometres are gravel), T023-3170749, www.houdenbek.co.za. 2 fully equipped self-catering cottages each sleeping 4, and 1 fully equipped house sleeping 11, rates average R150 per person per night, B&B and evening meals available on weekdays, and breakfast baskets available at the weekend. A beautiful and remote spot on the Môrester Estate, a working fruit and vegetable farm. Worth spending a few days here walking in the mountains, can also organize trout fishing and canoeing.

B-E Bergstroom Farm Cottage, 57 km from Ceres, off the Citrusdal Rd (R303), T023-3170678, jooschristae@lantic.net. 2 pleasant self-catering cottages in the mountains of the Koue Bokkeveld sleeping 4 and 12 with kitchen, lounge, large fireplace, rates are R150 per person per night. Good base for hiking trails, and there's a lovely waterfall with natural rock pools for swimming on the farm. Popular in winter with South Africans for the novelty of seeing snow.

C-F Klondyke Cherry Farm, T023-3121521, www.cherryfarm.co.za. 3 homely self-catering cottages sleeping 2, 4 and 8 on farm with superb views of the mountains, camping also possible under pine trees with ablution block. Ideal for keen walkers, bass fishing in the farm dams, cherry picking mid-Nov to early Jan. Again be prepared for snow in winter.

Prince Alfred Hamlet p221
There is only 1 hotel here, but there are several farms between here and Ceres that offer accommodation. See above for details.
D Hamlet Country Lodge, Voortrekker St, T023-3133070, hamletcountrylodge@telkomsa.net. Typical old town hotel, 6 spacious old-fashioned rooms, some with a/c or fans and coffee-making machines, bar and **Taylor's Grill** restaurant, permits and gate keys issued from the hotel to those wishing to go trout fishing on Lakenvlei Dam.

Kagga Kamma Private Game Reserve p222
AL Bushmen Lodge, T021-8724343 (Cape Town), www.kaggakamma.co.za. 18 chalets built into caves in the rock, or free-standing. Voted one of the world's best honeymoon lodges, with stunning views, a pool, open-air boma restaurant and bar, rates include all meals, game drives, a visit to the rock art, and sundowners at a 500-m-deep canyon. Rates drop significantly in low season; May-Aug.

Inverdoorn Game Reserve p222
A Luxury chalets, T023-3161264, www.inverdoorn.com. 7 a/c chalets with fireplace, and 2 100-year-old farmhouses with 2 bedrooms for families, all sumptuously decorated. Excellent restaurant on site serving French cuisine, several lounges, pool and deck, library, mini-gym, curio shop, all rates include meals and game drives, and there is a landing strip and helipad for those who want to arrive in style.

Robertson p223, map p223
In town
B Ballinderry, 8 Le Roux St, T023-6265365, www.ballinderryguesthouse.com. Smart villa with 6 spacious a/c rooms with stylish modern decor, fireplaces and wooden floors, champagne breakfast, 3-course dinners, pool, internet and bar. Run by a friendly Belgium couple.

D The Grand, 68 Barry St, T023-6263272, www.grandhotel.co.za. Reasonable, if not a little faded, Victorian old-style town hotel on a corner of leafy White St. 9 double rooms with en suite bathrooms and TV. Good restaurant, bar with an L-shaped pool table, swimming pool, helpful staff. 4 cheaper rooms in the house next door.
E-F Robertson Backpackers, 4 Dordrecht St, T023-6261280, www.robertsonbackpackers.co.za. Located in an old 1880s Victorian house, with pretty garden full of chill-out hammocks to enjoy the mountain views, dorms and doubles with huge duvets or camping on the lawn. 3 meals a day or self-catering in the kitchen, can organize local activities including wine tours and boat trips on the Breede River.

Out of town
B Fraai Uitzicht, 13 km from Robertson on the Ashton road, T023-6266156, www.fraaiuitzicht.com. Restored farm cottages on a wine estate, luxurious decor but rooms on the small side, with embroidered linen and nice works of art, beautiful spot surrounded by orchards and vines, excellent award-winning restaurant (see Eating, page 235) that occasionally hosts live music. Several languages spoken.
C-D Hanepoot Huisies, 9 km from Robertson off the Worcester road, T023-6264139, www.hanepoothuisies.co.za. 3 restored old farm cottages set on a 190-ha farm, hidden away among vines and fruit trees. Each is self-catering and sleeps up to 5. Plenty of activities can be organized including boat trips and fishing. Recommended.
D Goedereede Guest Farm, T023-6264173, karlp@intekom.co.za. Converted farm buildings just out of town on a fruit farm through which the Breede River flows, 3 cottages with 2, 4, or 6 beds overlooking a picturesque dam, good farm breakfasts, TV lounge, self-catering, swimming, hiking.
D Little France, 5 km from Robertson on the Worcester Rd, T023-6264174, www.littlefrance.co.za. Attractive modern

building with stylish furnishings, 5 en suite rooms, tasteful and comfortable with polished wooden floors, brass beds with bright white linen. Dining room, lounge, large pool and deck, good breakfasts served by pool or log fire in dining room, dinner on request. Recommended.

D Pat Busch Private Nature Reserve, 15 km from Robertson, off the R60 heading towards Ashton, T023-6262033, www.patbusch.co.za. Self-catering accommodation in 3 cottages, Peach, Fig and Oak, plus 2 simple farm houses located in the foothills of the Langeberg Mountains. There is a 40-km network of circular walks which follow the kloofs between the hills. The vegetation consists of a mix of proteas and ericas, with lilies and ferns along the streams. This is an excellent spot for birdwatching and a few small antelope have been introduced. A peaceful place to really get away from it all.

McGregor p224

C Green Gables Country Inn, Voortrekker Rd, T023-6251626, www.tourismmcgregor. co.za/greengables.htm. A delightful old town house that was once a trading store. 8 en suite double rooms in the garden with separate entrances, B&B. Also has a splash pool, small lounge and good restaurant (see Eating, page 236). Recommended.
C Old Mill Lodge, Mill St, T023-6251841, www.oldmilllodge.co.za. This beautifully restored 1860s lodge is at the far end of the village among vineyards and fruit orchards. Accommodation is in 4 cottages, each with 2 bedrooms and en suite bathrooms. The central building has a comfortable lounge with an open fireplace, much needed during the winter, and a bar and dining room looking out over the vineyard. There's a swimming pool tucked away and beauty treatments are also on offer. The restaurant, which is open to non-guests, is excellent value and the evening meals take on a French twist. There's an old watermill in the grounds. Recommended.

C Whipstock Guest Farm, 8 km from the village on the far side from the Robertson Rd, T023-6251733, www.whipstock.za.net. Choice of 4 cottages, each with a different style. **Rietvlei Cottage**, which sleeps 6, is the oldest building. There is no electricity, but oil lamps and candles help create a peaceful atmosphere in the evenings. Hot water for the bathroom comes from a gas geyser. **Long lands**, which sleeps 8, is a Cape Georgian house tastefully furnished with rural antiques. **The Barn** sleeps 6, and **Winterfield Cottage** can also sleep 6, with en suite bathrooms. Excellent wholesome farm breakfasts and dinners are included in the rate and lunch packs are available for hikers – don't miss the home-made bread. An excellent place to bring children as this is a working farm with plenty to see and do each day.
D McGregor Country House, Voortrekker St, T023-6251656, mcgcountry@telkomsa.net. 3 double rooms and 1 family room with small kitchenette, shared TV lounge, swimming pool, decorated in a Georgian theme, good value. Located in the same building as the local pub, **The Overdraught**.

Bonnievale p225

There are several places within the town centre, although staying on one of the many farms along the banks of the Breede River is more enjoyable. On most farms the river flows through the land, and there are often boats available for hire to explore this beautiful stretch as it winds its way through vineyards, orchards and stud farms.
C Merwenstein Guest Farm, 6 km from town centre off the Swellendam Rd, T028-6162806, www.merwenstein.co.za. An old fruit and vegetable farm with the Breede River running through. 3 double rooms with en suite bathrooms, smart restaurant , offering hearty home-made meals, swimming pool, birdwatching trips on the river. German spoken. Recommended.
C Weltevrede Wine Estate, T023-6262141, www.weltevrede.com. A beautiful and peaceful location on the wine estate 5 km

to the east of the town; follow signs to Robertson. 2 self-catering cottages between the vines, fully equipped, sleep 2-4, swimming pool, rose gardens, small art gallery selling work by local artists, estate restaurant open for lunch Mon-Fri, excellent value, evening meals on request.

C-D Toy Cottages, 6 km from town centre off R60, T023-6162735, www.bonnie vale.co.za/toycottages.htm. 2 a/c self-catering cottages with modern interiors, each sleeps up to 6 people so price depends on size of group, DSTV, swimming pool, fishing, canoe hire, set among vineyards right on the banks of the Breede River. A tranquil spot.

D Bonnies B&B, Van Zyl St, T023-6162251, www.bonniesb-b.co.za. 5 rooms with en suite bathrooms and rather flowery decor, DSTV, separate entrances leading into the garden with swimming pool. Evening meals available on request, healthy breakfasts served with freshly baked bread. Bicycles for hire, braai facilities. Good value. German-speaking hosts.

Montagu and around *p227, map p227*
Ask at the tourist office for details of budget accommodation suitable for hikers on surrounding farms.

A Kingna Lodge, 11 Bath St, T023-6141066, www.kingnalodge.co.za. 7 rooms in an 1898 Victorian house, some with private patio, TV, non-smoking lounge with collection of art and books, 5-course dinners on request served in an elegant black and gold dining room, swimming pool and jacuzzi in private gardens. Presidents Mandela and de Klerk both once stayed here. Recommended for its service and food.

A-B Montagu Country Hotel, 27 Bath St, T023-6143125, www.montagucountry hotel.co.za. A well-established central hotel in a 1920s art deco building, with 22 large rooms, a/c, TV, 4 suites, a smart dining room with open log fires during the winter, swimming pool, heated mineral pool, beauty treatments, secure parking. Recommended.

B Mimosa Lodge, Church St, T023-6142351, www.mimosa.co.za. Excellent local hotel

owned by a Swiss-German chef with 9 rooms (those upstairs have balconies), 7 garden suites, 3 guest lounges, library, very stylish decor with original 1920s art deco items, neat gardens, restaurant, bar, heated swimming pool. The restaurant menu reflects the wide variety of locally grown fresh produce, rates are half board. Recommended.

B-C Avalon Springs, 3 km from town centre, Uitvlucht St, T023-6141150, www.avalon springs.co.za. A well-developed resort centred on the hot springs including 30 self-catering apartments and 14 en suite hotel rooms, conference facilities and a health spa, 3 restaurants – **Da Vinci's** serves good pasta – bar, shops, several hot and cold swimming pools, 60-m water slide, jacuzzis and spa baths, gym and sauna, tennis courts. Comfortable and in a peaceful spot, but inconvenient for those wishing to explore the town. Check their website for out-of-season special rates.

B-C Cynthia's Cottages, 3 Krom St, T023-6142760, www.cynthias-cottages.co.za. Delightful restored country cottages with thatched roofs. Brass beds add to the homely atmosphere. Suitable for 2-6 people, self-catering. Each with own garden and braai, some have fireplaces and outdoor spa pool.

C 7 Church St, T023-6141186, www.7church street.co.za. Beautiful views from this stylish, friendly guesthouse, 3 large en suite family rooms and 2 garden suites with TV and extras such as embroidered linen and fresh flowers, large lounge, good English breakfast, rose and herb garden, off-road parking, swimming pool. Recommended.

C The John Montagu, 30 Joubert St, T023-6141331, www.johnmontagu.co.za. 5 taste-fully decorated rooms, antique furnishings, small pool and bar in the gardens at the back, off-street parking. The perfect place to relax after exploring the area. Recommended.

D-F Caravan Park, west end of Bath St, across the Keissies River, T023-6143034. Camping and caravan sites, budget 4-bed log cabins with fridge and oven, shared ablution blocks, swimming pool, boating and fishing on the dam. Short walk into the town centre.

Eating

Worcester and around p211, maps p212 and p215

Surprisingly for a town with a reasonable population, Worcester has few restaurants, apart from the usual takeaways and family steakhouses: both ¶ **Saddles**, T023-3427779, and the ¶ **San Diego Spur**, are on High St.

¶¶¶ **The Pear Tree**, 75 Church St, T023-3420947. Mon-Sat 0830-2300, Sun 0900-1600. A fairly new restaurant in the historic Beck House, fine dining and an excellent selection of Breede River wines. French country cooking and excellent service, intimate dining rooms with fireplaces or eat outside under the vines; very unusual dishes on the menu for a small South African town such as blue cheese, biltong and grilled pear salad. Recommended for a treat.

¶¶ **The Barn**, 170 Church St, T023-3428136. Sun and Mon 0900-1700, Tue-Fri 0900-late, Sat 0900-1400, 1830-late. There is an interesting collection of hand-blown glass objects here, with demonstrations by the master glass-blower, David Reede. The shop and restaurant are situated in a renovated wine cellar, unusual and delicious menu, such as mushroom filo parcels or butternut risotto, and lots of dishes using fresh herbs. A lighter and cheaper menu during the day and wine and olive tastings are offered.

Wolseley p217

¶¶ **Mill & Oaks**, 7 km from Tulbagh, take the R46 and turn right onto the R43, T023-2310860. Sun-Tue for lunch. Serves some beautifully presented food on a patio with mountain views, try the oven-roasted duck or mushroom risotto followed by the crème brûlée for dessert. Also has 3 B&B rooms, and dinner is available on request.

¶ **Traders**, on the main road 1 km from Wolseley towards Worcester. This old-fashioned general store and coffee shop sells local crafts and produce and serves good home-cooked meals. Try the refreshing home-made ginger beer.

Tulbagh p217, map p218

¶¶ **Ballotina**, 43 Church St, T023-2310427. Dinner Tue-Sat summer, Fri-Sat winter, lunch Sun. Set in an 1817 building with red and white checked tablecloths this has an Italian edge and pasta lovers and vegetarians are well looked after. The Sun lunch is very popular: antipasti followed by a traditional carvery.

¶¶ **Paddagang**, 23 Church St, T082-3244463. Daily 0900-1630. Set in well-kept tranquil gardens with tables under vines. Good for late breakfasts, quality fresh Cape cuisine, the chocolate cake is to die for, selection of Tulbagh wines, very popular, well worth a visit, also conducts wine tastings of all the local wines. Recommended.

¶¶ **Readers**, 12 Church St, T023-2300087. Wed-Sun 1230-1500, 1900-2130. Quality home cooking in a pleasant old dining room in the oldest house in Tulbagh (1754), decorated with colourful exhibits from the local art school. Varied and interesting menu with tempting specials on the blackboard, and in summer there is a rather unusual range of home-made ice cream with sweet and also savoury flavours – cumin, sesame or garlic.

¶¶ **Rijk's Ridge**, north of town at **Rijk's Country Hotel**, T023-2301006. Open 0730-2230. Very smart country hotel set on wine estate, excellent restaurant and wine cellar, the usual steaks, salads and pasta and more unusual offerings such as pork fillet with blue cheese and cider sauce and crêpes suzettes for dessert. Delicious food in a stylish environment and in summer you can pre-order picnics to enjoy on the lawns. Recommended.

¶ **Shamrock & Thistle**, 22 Van der Stel St, T023-2300071. Daily 1100-late. Jovial traditional Irish pub and restaurant set in an old hotel, good home-cooked meals, popular local drinking hole with crackling fire, large range of malt whiskies.

Robertson p223, map p223

The town lacks a good choice of restaurants – only a handful are worth trying:

¶¶ **Fraai Uitzicht 1798**, Klaasvoods East, on the Ashton road, T023-6266156. Open 1200-

1500, 1800-2030. Award-winning restaurant set on the historic wine estate in beautiful herb, bamboo and rose gardens. Very good food, choose the 6-course set menu with accompanying wines, or individual dishes such as salmon in champagne or rabbit in white wine sauce and desserts made from Belgian chocolate, good service.

♥♥ **Branewynsdraai**, 1 Kromhout St, T023-6263202. Mon-Sat 0900-1700. Light meals at lunchtime with a good choice of wine, during summer you can sit outside in the neat gardens as long as the traffic is not too heavy – the restaurant is right next to the main road. In winter a blazing log fire greatly adds to the atmosphere. Also sells over 150 wine labels.

♥♥ **Grand Hotel**, 68 Barry St, T023-6263272. Very faded and old fashioned decor, but exceptionally large and popular country food, popular carvery on Sun when all the townsfolk seem to eat out after church, good-value set-menu lunches, there's a pub next door to the restaurant.

♥ **Café Rosa**, Robertson Nursery, 9 Voortrekker Rd, T023-6265403. Mon-Fri 0800-1730. Nice setting among the plants in the nursery, serving tea, coffee, wine, light lunches and home-made cakes, friendly service.

McGregor p224

The popularity of the village as a day-trip destination is reflected in the choice of a few good places to grab a meal or have afternoon teas in. Most overnight guests will take their evening meal at their guesthouse or self-cater.

♥♥ **Green Gables**, at **Green Gables Country Inn**, Voortrekker St, T023-6251626. 0900-late. Popular family-run local restaurant serving light lunches and teas and good country fare such as roast dinners or steak and kidney pie in the evenings. Eat in the cosy pub or on the candle-lit garden terrace. Recommended.

♥ **Café Temenos**, corner of Bree and Voortrekker streets, T023-6251115. Tue-Sun 0900-1630, for lunches and afternoon tea. Espresso, ciabatta, bruschetta, pasta, all

things Italian, in a lovely garden setting with a duck pond.

♥ **Villagers**, corner of Tindall and Voortrekker streets, T023-6251951. Daily 0930-1700 except Sun. A typical all-purpose village shop selling curios and local crafts, as well as serving home-made food, fresh fruit juices including prune, pear and plum, and good cups of coffee in the garden or on the terrace.

Bonnievale p225

♥♥ **Under the Vines**, at the **Weltevrede Wine Estate** on the R317, T023-6262141, www.weltevredegf.com. Mon-Sat 0900-1500. Pleasant country setting, wine available, daily blackboard specials, game pies, thick soups, salads and good cheese platters served with fresh farm bread.

Montagu and around p227, map p227

Montagu has a surprisingly large number of good restaurants, with a fine variation of cuisines – not just the usual steaks and pizzas.

♥♥♥ **Templeton's @ Four Oaks**, 46 Long St, T023-6142778. Mon-Sat 1230-1430, 0700-2200, open on Sun in season. Good local cuisine and Mediterranean deli items in the historic setting of an 1855 farmhouse, slow-cooked oxtail, lamb curry and good home-made burgers, lovely garden and tables in a courtyard under 100-year-old pear trees, cosy bar serving bubbly and oysters, chef used to work at the **Mount Nelson Hotel** in Cape Town. It's possible to stay as there are 4 rooms next door (**C**).

♥♥ **Jessica's**, 47 Bath St, T023-6141805. 1830-late. A slightly off-beat place with bright pink walls and decorated with loads of pictures and ceramic statues of dogs. A good opportunity to sample the best of South African ingredients washed down with good local wines. Known for their rich creamy sauces, try springbok in mushroom sauce, and finish with fruit and white chocolate sauce. Recommended.

♥♥ **Prestons & Thomas Baines Pub**, 17 Bath St, T023-6143013. Daily 1030-1430, 1730-late. Popular à la carte menu, tasteful decor with a small outside courtyard, friendly hosts. Try the Prestons platter or the Karoo lamb, all served with excellent salads. The pub, which has a cosy wood bar and tables and outside terrace for warm days, stays open after the kitchen closes. Recommended.

Wild Apricot, at the **Montagu Country Hotel**, 27 Bath St, T023-6143125. Open 0730-2200. Excellent Sun lunch of roast meat and veg, traditional South African bobotie, cheeses and desserts. À la carte menu of local dishes such as tomato bredie and Karoo lamb chops, all set in the bright pink art deco hotel.

The Bistro, 20 Bath St, T023-6143108. Wed-Mon 0900-1800. New daytime bistro and café, serving good snacks, sandwiches and salads. Internet access.

● Bars and clubs

McGregor *p224*
Overdraught Pub, Voortrekker St, T023-6251656. A tiny, old-fashioned bar with an English pub feel that can only accommodate about a dozen people. Serves a selection of draught beers including Guinness and Caffery's imported from Ireland and a number of British bitters, but no food.

⊛ Festivals and events

Tulbagh *p217, map p218*
Jun The **Christmas in Winter** is held along Church St, which is decorated in Christmas decorations with craft and food stalls. Christmas dinners are served in the restaurants.
Sep The local **Agricultural Show** is held on the banks of the Kliprivier. This is the oldest of its kind in South Africa.
Oct The **Visual Arts Show** sees many of the historic houses on Church St open up as art and craft galleries.

○ Shopping

Worcester and around *p211, maps p212 and p215*
Curios
Blind Shop, 126 Church St. Furniture, woodwork and woven products made by the visually impaired and sold from this outlet. Visits to the workshop are possible.
Deaf Shop, De la Bat St. Handicrafts such as ceramics, cane work and art curios – some excellent pieces at very reasonable prices. Again it is possible to visit the workshop.

Shopping malls
Mountain Mill Shopping Mall, on the N1 at the turn-off to town. Mon-Sat 0900-1800, Sun 1000-1600. The largest mall in the region and a good place to stock up if self-catering in cottages along the Breede River, with 117 shops, including chain stores and supermarkets, and a NuMetro cinema.

▲ Activities and tours

Worcester *p211, map p212*
Canoeing
African Water Wanderers, based in nearby Rawsonville, T082-3456878, www.africanwaterwanderers.co.za. Full-day river rafting trips on the Breede River (Oct-Mar).

Golf
Worcester Golf Club, 3 km north of town across the N1, T023-3427482, www.worcestergolfclub.co.za. The club was founded in 1895. The present 18-hole course designed by the Gary Player Group is over 10 years old and has some large greens of tournament standard. The mountains are a perfect backdrop. The large modern club-house has good restaurant facilities.

Ceres
Sky diving
Skydive Ceres, T021-4625666, www.skydive.co.za. Offers tandem jumps from 10,000 ft with a 35-second freefall for R1100, from a nearby farm.

Robertson *p223, map p223*
Viljoensdrift, T023-6151901, www.viljoensdrift.co.za. Wine estate 12 km from Robertson on the Bonnievale road on the banks of the Breede River. Relaxed cruises on their river boat. You can pick up a picnic basket and a bottle of wine from their shop.

Bonnievale *p225*
Boat trips
The *Breede River Goose*, a 2-storey pontoon with a tender boat for fishing, runs daily trips on the river with additional braais; book in advance, T023-6162175.

Montagu and around *p227, map p227*
Mountain biking
Dusty Sprocket, Cottage Coffee Shop, 78 Bath St, T023-6141932, www.montagu.org.za/mtbtrails.htm. Bikes for hire and Ron Brunings will guide cyclists along trails in the region ranging from 16 km to 55 km.

⊖ Transport

Worcester and around *p211, map p212*
Worcester is 112 km from **Cape Town**, 60 km from **Ceres**, 50 km from **Paarl**, and 117 km from **Swellendam**.

Bus
All services arrive/depart from the Breede Valley Shell Ultra City on the N1 and the railway station. Each of the major long-distance luxury bus services stop here as they head inland from the Cape to **Bloemfontein**

(11 hrs), **Johannesburg** and **Pretoria** (16 hrs), but they do not offer good value for the 2-hr journey to/from **Cape Town**.

Bus companies Greyhound, T083-9159000, www.greyhound.co.za. **Intercape**, T0861-287287, www.intercape.co.za. **Translux**, T086-1589282, www.translux.co.za.

Train
The station is off Tulbagh St to the north of the centre. Central reservations, T0860-008888, www.spoornet.co.za, timetables and fares are published on the website. To **Cape Town** (3 hrs) daily; to **Durban** (33 hrs) via **Bloemfontein** (20 hrs) and **Harrismith** (25 hrs); to **Pretoria** (24 hrs) daily via **Kimberley** (15 hrs) and **Johannesburg** (22 hrs).

Robertson *p223, map p223*
48 km to **Worcester**, 67 km to **Swellendam**.

Bus
Robertson has surprisingly poor transport connections and at the time of writing was only accessible by **Translux** bus. **Cape Town** (2½ hrs): daily, via **Worcester** (45 mins). **Port Elizabeth** (9 hrs) daily via **Swellendam** and the **Garden Route**.

Bus companies Translux, T086-1589282, www.translux.co.za.

⊕ Directory

Worcester *p211, map p212*
Medical services Medi-Clinic, Russell St, T023-3481500, www.worcestermc.co.za.

Montagu and around *p227, map p227*
Banks Standard is on Market St and ABSA is on Bath St, both with ATMs.
Medical services Hospital, Hospital St, T023-6141133.

Overberg and the Whale Coast

The evocatively named Whale Coast lives up to its title from July to November, when large numbers of whales seek out the sheltered bays along the coast for breeding. Whales can be seen close to the shore from False Bay all the way east to Mossel Bay, but by far the best place for whale spotting is Hermanus as the whales favour the sheltered Walker Bay, and daily sightings are guaranteed in August and September. Elsewhere along the coast there are opportunities to see the fearsome great white shark. There are seaside towns with miles of sandy beaches and rock pools, plus the southernmost point in South Africa, Cape Agulhas.

More than 120 ships have been wrecked along this coast (the first recorded wreck dates from 1673); there are hazardous reefs, headlands and rocks all the way to Cape Infanta and the Breede River estuary. A museum in Bredasdorp traces the misfortunes of the wrecked ships. In addition to whale watching, this coast offers some of the best fishing in South Africa and an opportunity to dive historic shipwrecks. ▸▸ *For listings, see pages 253-261.*

Gordon's Bay to Hermanus ⬤❼ ▸▸ *pp253-261.*

The most beautiful and exhilarating stretch of the coast is between Gordon's Bay and Hermanus, where the mountains plunge into the ocean forming a coastline of steep cliffs, sandy coves, dangerous headlands and natural harbours. This is an area of much beauty and also botanical significance and in 1998 it was the first UNESCO-declared Biosphere Reserve in southern Africa and is now known as the Kogelberg Nature Reserve. It's known for its fynbos and over 1700 species of plant has been recorded here. This route is often compared to the spectacular Chapman's Peak Drive on the Cape Peninsula, and rightly so.

Whale Coast

Sleeping ⬤
Mosaic Farm 1

Gordon's Bay, Rooiels and Pringle Bay → *Colour map 8, B1.*

Set in the lee of the Hottentots Holland Mountains at the eastern end of False Bay, away from the more glamorous beaches of Cape Town, is the popular family seaside resort of Gordon's Bay. There are two sandy beaches, **Bikini** and **Main**, both of which are safe for swimmers. The rocky shoreline, a short walk from the seafront, is popular for fishing. The most likely catch includes mackerel, steenbras and kabeljou. The beach road is lined with a number of seafood restaurants and this is a popular lunch spot at the weekends for people from Cape Town.

Following the R44 south, the first small coastal resort after Gordon's Bay is **Rooiels** (19 km), a cluster of holiday homes at the mouth of a small river. The beach has a strong backwash, so be wary if children are swimming. Continuing towards Hermanus, the road leaves its precipitous course and climbs the hills inland. After 5 km turn right to **Pringle Bay**, which is dominated by a large rock outcrop known as the Hangklip, 454 m. This is the rock you see when standing by the lighthouse at Cape Point looking across False Bay. The gravel loop road around **Cape Hangklip** is a scenic distraction; another track leads to Hangklip. The road rejoins the R44 just before Silver Sands.

Betty's Bay → *Colour map 8, C1.*

This small holiday village, midway between Strand and Hermanus, is known for its penguin colony and botanical garden. The community was named after Betty Youlden, the daughter of a local businessman who had plans to develop the Cape Hangklip area in the 1930s. Fortunately little came of the idea and today the village remains an untidy collection of holiday homes in a beautiful location. At Stoney Point there is a **reserve** ⓘ *0900-1700, R5,* to protect a small breeding colony of African jackass penguins, one of the few places where you are guaranteed to see these birds breeding on the mainland. A boardwalk has been constructed to allow visitors good views of the penguins without disturbing them. Also here are the remains of a whaling station plus the hulk of a whaler, the *Balena*. Behind the village are the well-known **Harold Porter Botanic Gardens**, worth a visit if time permits. Along the main beach is another area of protected land, the **HF Verwoerd Coastal Reserve**. There is safe swimming close to the kelp beds, and the dunes above Silver Sands are a popular spot for sandboarding. For sandboarding operators, see Cape Town chapter, page 126.

 African jackass penguins mate for life and return to the same nest each year to breed.

Harold Porter Botanic Gardens

ⓘ *T028-2729311, www.sanbi.org, Mon-Fri 0800-1630, Sat-Sun 0800-1700, small entrance fee, the garden is signposted from the main road, just outside Betty's Bay. There is the pleasant Sugarbird Tearoom and a gift shop by the entrance gate, 0900-1630. To the left of the entrance is a picnic site and toilets. Guided tours should be arranged in advance.*

This garden, lying between mountains and coast, was originally acquired in 1938 by Harold Porter, a keen conservationist. In his will he bequeathed the grounds to the nation. There are 10 ha of cultivated fynbos garden and a further 191 ha of natural fynbos which has been allowed to flourish undisturbed. [Fynbos is the term given to a type of vegetation that is dominated by shrubs and comprises species unique to South Africa's southwestern and southern Cape.] The reserve incorporates the whole catchment area of the Dawidskraal River. The garden has many fynbos species, including proteas, ericas, legumes, buchus and brunias. Another draw is the chance of seeing red disa flowering in its natural habitat – this usually occurs from late December to late January. More than 88 species of bird have been identified; of special interest are the orange-breasted sunbird and the rare protea canary, which is only seen in fynbos environments. The best time to visit is from September to November, although it can still be cool and windy at this time.

There are three longer paths which lead from the formal grounds into the surrounding mountains. Disa Kloof has a small dam and a waterfall; Leopard's Kloof takes you several kilometres into the Kogelberg; and a contour path starts by the Harold Porter memorial stone, from which there are excellent views of the ocean and the gardens. Fire prevention is an important issue, especially from January to March when the terrain is dry and the wind prevails from the southeast. Fynbos contains resin and oils which are highly flammable.

Kleinmond, Vermont and Onrus → Colour map 8, B1/C2.

Kleinmond is a popular summer resort in Sandown Bay that has been frequented by the wheat farmers of the interior since 1861 and is today a sizeable resort. Exercise caution when swimming at Kleinmond as the sandy beach is steep; children should be watched at all times. The name Kleinmond refers to the 'small mouth' of the Bot River lagoon. The settlement is overlooked by the magnificent Kogelberg Mountains which in the spring are full of flowering proteas. Information is available from the helpful **Hangklip-Kleinmond Bureau** ① signposted, just off the R44, T028-2715657, www.ecoscape.org.zu, Mon-Fri 0830-1700, Sat 0900-1400, Sun 1000-1400. The Harbour Road area has an intriguing collection of shops. To the east of the town is the Bot River Lagoon, a popular sailing and canoeing area. Where the Bot River meets the sea is a large marsh which is home to thousands of waterfowl. This is a birdwatchers' paradise, especially at low tide. The more common species are spoonbills, herons, pelicans, gulls, terns, kingfishers and geese and a pair of fish eagles breed at the lagoon. There is also a small herd of wild horses that roam the marshlands; after several attempts to cull them in the 1950s, they are now protected.

After Kleinmond the R44 joins the R43, which then continues along the coast to the next sizeable settlements of **Vermont** and **Onrus**, these days more or less suburbs of Hermanus, before arriving in Hermanus proper. Vermont, named after the American state, was founded by CJ Krige who became the first speaker of the South African parliament. The beach here is sheltered by high dunes and is safe for children. Onrus, meaning 'restless', lying on the east bank of the mouth of the Onrus River, was named by the first European settlers because of the perpetual noise made by the waves along the rocky coastline. The Onrus River forms a small lagoon with a short sandy beach which is also safe for children to swim from. The beach is popular with surfers too.

Hermanus and around ●❼❀○▲❶❻ ›› pp253-261. Colour map 8, C2.

Hermanus has grown from a rustic fishing village to a much-visited tourist resort famed for its superb whale watching. It is the self-proclaimed world's best land-based whale-watching site, and indeed Walker Bay is host to impressive numbers during the calving season (July to November). However, don't expect any private viewings – Hermanus is very popular and has a steady flow of binocular-clutching visitors. While this means it can get very busy, there is also a good range of accommodation and restaurants, making it a great base for exploring the quieter reaches of the Overberg and, while you may find it far too crowded at Christmas, at other times it reverts to its small-town calm. Alternatively, being only a few hours from Cape Town, Hermanus is an easy day trip from the city.

Ins and outs

Hermanus is 120 km from Cape Town (via N2). Despite being a popular destination, none of the three major coach companies runs a service via Hermanus. One of the easiest ways to visit, if you don't have a car, is to travel on the **Baz Bus** from Cape Town to Bot Rivier on the N2, which is 23 km from Hermanus. From here you can arrange to be collected by your hosts for a small fee, but this must be arranged in advance. **Splash Shuttle and Tours** ① *T082-6585375 (mob), splash@hermanus.co.za*, can arrange a car shuttle service to and from Cape Town.

The **Greater Hermanus Tourism Bureau** ① *Old Station Building, Mitchell St, T028-3122629, www.hermanus.co.za, Mon-Fri 0800-1800, Sat 0900-1700, Sun 0900-1500 (shorter hours in winter)*, is extremely helpful and has lots of information on the surrounding area, plus an accommodation booking service.

Background

The town is named after Hermanus Pieters, an old soldier who set up camp in the bay while looking for better pastures for his animals during the hot summer months. The presence of a freshwater spring persuaded him to spend the summer here. Soon other farmers arrived with their families from the interior. Almost by accident it became a holiday destination – the herds required little attention, so the men turned their attention to fishing while the women and children enjoyed themselves on the sandy beaches. When the farmers returned inland to the winter pastures, it was the fishermen who remained and settled here.

Hermanus

Sleeping		Eating
Auberge Burgundy 1	Misty Waves 11	Annie se Kombuis 6
Forty Five Marine Drive 4	Mitchell St Village 12	Bientang's Cave 1
Hermanus Backpackers 13	Moby's 8	Burgundy 2
Hermanus Esplanade 14	Whale Rock Lodge 9	Fisherman's Cottage 4
Hortensia Lodge 5	Windsor 10	Marimba Café 5
Livesey Lodge 2	Zoete Inval 3	Prince of Whales 9
Marine 7		Zebra Crossing 3

In the 1920s the town gained a reputation as an excellent location for convalescing, and even doctors from Harley Street in London were recommending the 'champagne air' of Hermanus. As it became popular with the gentry, so suitably smart hotels were built to accommodate them. After the Second World War the construction of a new harbour stimulated the expansion of the fishing industry and there are now three canning factories in Walker Bay.

Sights

The **Old Harbour** is a national monument and a focal point for tourist activities. A ramp leads down the cliff to the attractive old jetty and a group of restored fishermen's cottages, including the **museum** ⓘ *T028-3121475, Mon-Sat 0900-1300, 1400-1700, small entry fee*. The displays are based on the local fishing industry and include models of fish, a whale skeleton, some shark jaws, fish tanks and early fishing equipment. One of the most interesting features is the recordings of calls between whales. There are also telescopes to watch the whales further out. An information plaque helps identify what you see. Outside the museum on the harbour ramp is a collection of small restored fishing boats, the earliest dating from 1855. Also on show are the drying racks for small fish and cement tables which were once used for gutting fish.

The **De Wet's Huis Photo Museum** ⓘ *Market Sq, T028-3130418, Mon-Fri 0900-1300, 1400-1700, Sat 0800-1300, 1400-1600, small entry fee*, houses an interesting collection of photography depicting the historical development of Hermanus.

Outside the old harbour is a memorial to those who died in the First World War. Set in the stonework is a barometer and the words "to help to protect the lives of present and future fishermen". Either side of the beehive-shaped monument are two ship's cannons. The new harbour, to the west of the old harbour in Westcliff, is still a busy fishing port. It's a great idea to head down to the dockside to buy fresh crayfish, mussels or linefish from the fish shop. The staff will be happy to advise you on how best to cook your selection.

Walks around Hermanus

The excellent **Cliff Path** starts at the new harbour in Westcliff and follows the shore all the way round Walker Bay to Grotto Beach, a distance of just over 15 km. Between cliffs the path goes through stands of milkwood trees and takes you around the sandy beaches. The most popular viewpoints are Dreunkrans, Fick's Pool, Gearing's Point, the Old Harbour, Die Gang, Siever's Punt, Kwaaiwater and Platbank. On an ideal day allow at least a morning for the walk. Bench seats are provided at the prime viewpoints, which make them good spots for a picnic.

Beaches

There are some good beaches a short distance in either direction from the town centre. The best beaches to the west are found at Onrus and Vermont (see page 241). Heading east towards Stanford and Gansbaai, there are long, open beaches or secluded coves with patches of sand and rock pools. **Grotto Beach** is the largest, best developed and most popular for swimming and is one of South Africa's 20 Blue Flag beaches. The fine white sands stretch beyond the Klein River Lagoon, and there are changing facilities, a restaurant and a beach shop. Slightly closer to the town centre is **Voëlklip Beach**, a little run down, but with well kept lawns behind the sand. Conditions are good for swimming and surfing. The most popular spot for surfers is **Kammabaai** next door to Voëlklip beach. There are braai facilities under the shade of some milkwood trees, an ideal setting for beach parties.

Whale watching

The WWF acknowledges Hermanus as one of the 12 best places in the world to view whales. It is the ideal destination if you wish to see whales from land without bobbing around in a boat. The town promotes itself as the 'heart of the Whale Coast', and during the season most visitors should not be disappointed. The town's advantage is that whales can come very close to the shore. The combination of low cliffs and deep water at the base of the cliffs means that you are able to look down from above into clear water and see the outlines of whales from as close as 10 m.

To add to the excitement there is a whale crier who between 1000 and 1600 during September and October strolls around the town centre blowing a kelp horn to announce the arrival of each whale in Walker Bay. The whale crier is easily identified: he wears a giant Bavarian-style hat and carries a sandwich board which records the daily sightings of whales from different vantage points around Walker Bay. You can phone him directly on his cell phone, T079-3014665 to ask if there are whales in the bay.

The first southern right whales start to appear in Walker Bay from June onwards. By the end of December most have returned to the southern oceans. The whales migrate north to escape heavy winter storms in the oceans around Antarctica. In August and September most of the calves are born in the calm sheltered bays, where the cows then stay with their young for a further two months. They can travel up to 2000 km to and from Antarctica on this continuous annual cycle. Out of an estimated world population of only 7000 southern right whales, up to 80 have been recorded mating and calving in Walker Bay. The best months are September and October when daily sightings are almost guaranteed. You would be unlucky not to see some sign of whale action during this period, though of course they are just as likely to be in the middle of the bay as up close to one of the vantage points along the cliff path.

The southern right whale is distinguished from other whales by its V-shaped 'blow', produced by a pair of blowholes, and callosities which appear randomly on and around the oval head. The callosities are growths of tough skin in patterns which help to identify individuals. Southern right whales are basically black with occasional streaks of grey or white on the back. Their flippers are short, broad and almost square. They are thought to live for up to 100 years, and a fully grown adult can weigh as much as 80 metric tonnes.

They are so-named because they were regarded as the 'right' whale to catch. The carcass yielded large quantities of oil and baleen, and the task of collecting the booty was made all the more easy by the fact that the whale floated in the water when killed. The northern right whale is virtually extinct, and the southern right has shown only a slight increase in numbers since international legislation was introduced to protect the species. The South African coastline is the most likely place in the world to see them in coastal waters.

Fernkloof Nature Reserve

① *T028-3138100, www.fernkloof.com, 24 hrs, free. Reservation for the 4-berth overnight hut, T028-3122985. The visitors' centre, 500 m from the entrance, has a display of the most common plants you are likely to see when walking in the reserve. All the hiking trails start from here.*

Set in the hills behind Hermanus, the reserve has a 60-km network of trails through an area rich in protea and coastal fynbos. Access is from the east end of Hermanus – just before the Main Road crosses Mossel River, turn up Fir Street. The reserve gates are just beyond the botanical society buildings. The diversity of plants in the reserve is due to the long period it has been under protection, plus its range of elevation from 60 to 850 m. With such a diverse plant population, there is also a wide range of bird and animal species including mongoose, dassie and baboon. Higher up in the mountains, look out for breeding black eagles. Small patches of indigenous forest remain in some of the moist ravines.

Hermanus wine route

Hidden away in the **Hemel-en-Aarde Valley** behind Hermanus are a few vineyards producing some surprisingly good wines, mostly Burgundy varieties based around Pinot Noir and Chardonnay grapes. Rarely crowded, three vineyards are open to the public and have tastings in their cellars. **Hamilton Russell Vineyards** ⓘ *T028-3123595, www.hamiltonrussellvineyards.com, tastings: Mon-Fri, 0900-1700, Sat-Sun 0900-1300*, is the oldest and one of the more picturesque estates and dubs itself the most southerly wine estate in Africa. The cellar and tasting room are set beside a small trout lake. Follow the R43 out of Hermanus towards Cape Town, after 2 km take a right turn marked Caledon, R320; there is a signpost and right turn 5 km along this gravel road.

Whalehaven Wines ⓘ *T028-3161633, www.whalehavenwines.co.za, tastings: Mon-Fri 0930-1700, Sat-Sun 1030-1430*, is one of the newest vineyards in the valley, so all their wines are quite young – the Pinot Noir is their flagship wine. The cellars and production rooms are open to visitors. Take the R320 turning for Caledon, as above. The winery is almost immediately on the right after turning off the R43.

Bouchard Finlayson Wines ⓘ *T028-3123515, www.bouchardfinlayson.co.za, tastings: Mon-Fri 0900-1700, Sat 1930-1230, closed Sun*, on the Caledon road 1 km beyond the Hamilton Russell Vineyard, has won several awards.

Stanford and around ⊖❷▲ ›› *pp253-261. Colour map 8, C2.*

Stanford, the next town along the R43 17 km east of Hermanus, is a peaceful Victorian village set inland from the Atlantic, which has become a popular centre for artists and craftsmen. It is an attractive spot, with some well-restored Victorian thatched cottages and a beautiful setting on the Klein River. This is also the nearest village to the small **Salmonsdam Nature Reserve**. The **Stanford Tourism Bureau** ⓘ*T028-3410340, www.stanfordinfo.co.za*, is next to the library on Queen Victoria Street. Information can also be found at www.stanfordvillage.co.za.

Sights

The **Birkenhead Micro-Brewery** ⓘ *T028-3410183, www.birkenhead.co.za, 1100-1600*, is just out of the village off the R326 towards Caledon and is the most popular sight in the area. Six beers are brewed and sold, of which the tastiest is Birkenhead Premium Lager, a slow-brewed beer using rich malted two-rowed barley and aromatic Hallertau and Saaz hop cones. Many of the ingredients are grown on the site and you can take a tour of the hop garden before going inside the modern buildings. Wine is also on sale and can be tasted. The restaurant and pub on the site is open for lunch daily and dinner at the weekends in high season.

The crucial whale lexicon

Blowing This is the sight we are all familiar with, the spout of water vapour accompanied by an echoing sound as air is expelled from the whale's lungs through the blowhole. Seasoned whale watchers will be able to identify the species from the shape of the spout. The vapour is created by condensation when the warm breath comes in contact with the cooler outside air.

Breaching Probably the most spectacular sight, this is when whales lift their entire body out of the water in an effortless arc, creating a huge splash as they fall back into the sea. Not an isolated event, a whale will often leap several times so keep your binoculars trained. The experts have yet to agree on why the whale does this, and the whales aren't giving much away.

Grunting Just a loud grunting sound which carries a long way over water, a moving noise when heard on a calm moonlit night. No translations available. Lobtailing The action of the whale slapping the surface with its tail producing a loud clap. This can be seen repeatedly over a long period. Interpreted as some form of warning or social communication.

Sailing The whale lifts its tail clear of the water for long periods. There are several theories about this action: to use the wind to 'sail' through the water (dubious), to feed on the sea-floor, or as a means of temperature control. Diehard watchers reckon the whales are just showing off.

Spyhopping When the whale lifts its head and part of its body above the water vertically. This gives the whale a 360° view of the sea.

Another popular place to stop is **Klein River Cheese** ① *T028-3410693, Mon-Fri 0900-1700, Sat 0900-1300*, a factory specializing in Gruyère and other cheeses using Jersey and Friesland milk. Visitors can watch cheese being made, taste the produce in the shop, or enjoy a delicious picnic lunch on the banks of the Klein River. Baskets are filled with home-made breads, crackers, pâtés, pickles, cold meats, salads and a selection of cheese. To get there from the R43, take the left turn onto the R326 opposite the turning to Stanford and follow the signposts.

Walker Bay Nature Reserve
① *T028-3140062, www.capenature.co.za, open to day visitors 0700-1900, R20.*
Driving out of Hermanus to the east you pass through the suburb known as **Voëlklip**. If you are planning to visit the Walker Bay Nature Reserve you must collect your entry permit from the **office** ① *corner of 7th St and 17th Av, Voëlklip, Mon-Fri 0800-1600*. The reserve stretches from the Klein River estuary to De Kelders just before Gansbaai and covers about 1000 ha with a coastline of 17 km. It features a long beach, known as **Die Plaat**, with white sands and rocky limestone outcrops to the east. Most of the mammals in the reserve are shy, but the tracks of Cape clawless otter, bushbuck, duiker, grysbok and steenbok are occasionally seen. Offshore, whales can be spotted in season and the reserve is home to numerous species of seabirds, including the striking African black oystercatcher. Visitors can explore the coast on hikes though swimming is not recommended as the sea can be rough. There is no overnight accommodation in the reserve. There are two entrances, one to the west of Stanford on a back road, and one further south off the R43 just north of De Kelders.

Salmonsdam Nature Reserve

ⓘ *T028-3140062, www.capenature.co.za, open to day visitors 0700-1800, R24. There are 3 basic cabins and a campsite (see Sleeping, page 255). The reserve is 33 km from Hermanus and 16 km from Stanford. It can easily be visited as a day trip from either of these towns. On reaching Stanford, turn right on to the R326. A few kilometres up this road turn right onto a gravel road. The reserve is clearly signposted.*

This small reserve was established in 1962 and was named after Captain Robert Salmon of the ill-fated *HMS Birkenhead*, which sank at Danger Point in 1852 with a loss of 454 lives. It covers 834 ha of the mountains which form part of the catchment area for the Paardenberg River. The main attraction here is the opportunity to view how the Overberg region would have appeared before much of it was cleared by farmers. As you either drive or walk up to the main viewpoint, **Ravenshill**, you pass by several deep, lush valleys which retain a number of indigenous trees. An added attraction is several waterfalls, best viewed after the rains. There are three distinct vegetation zones to look out for, each of which hosts different bird species. The high areas are covered with mountain fynbos – disas, waboom and ground proteas. Around the campsite and in the low-lying, flooded vleis are reeds, water heath and fountain bush. Between the high and low areas, stands of lush indigenous forest fill the kloofs formed by streams running off the mountains. These forested areas are the most rewarding parts to walk in (there are three short trails of 3, 4 and 7 km, which start behind the camping area. Look out for small antelope such as steenbok, grey duiker, grey rhebuck, klipspringer and bontebok.

Gansbaai and around ⊖❼▲ ⇥ *pp253-261. Colour map 8, C2.*

The R43 reaches Gansbaai 22 km south of Stanford. The history of this popular fishing centre dates back over a century to when a local youth from Hermanus decided to make his home here. The story goes that in 1881 Johannes Cornelis Wessels walked across the sand dunes between Stanford and Gansgat. He found the fishing to be very good and the natural cove provided a safe and sheltered landing spot for the small fishing vessels in use at the time.

The bay was named by fishermen who used it for protection against large storms. The name *gansgat* refers to the colony of Egyptian geese, *kolganse*, which used to nest in the reeds that surrounded a natural spring in the bay. These days the village is a prosperous fishing harbour with a modern deep-water wharf and several fish-canning factories. It has, however, managed to retain the character of a small community and busy fishing harbour, albeit with strong ties to the tourist industry. A number of Capetonians have second houses along this coast.

Ask at **Gansbaai Tourism Bureau** ⓘ *corner of Berg and Main streets, T028-3841439*, for details of the best operators for shark diving. The office also produces some good maps of the coastline showing the area's walking routes.

Sights

Like Hermanus at the other end of Walker Bay, there are some excellent vantage points for whale watching. The southern right whales come close inshore to the sheltered deep waters to calve between June and November each year. A couple of kilometres up the coast at **De Kelders** are tall cliffs which quickly give way to a large white-sand beach. The local lighthouse is 9 km away at **Danger Point**. It's 18 m tall and on weekdays from 1000 to 1500, the lighthouse keeper will give you a tour. In May 1852 the *HMS Birkenhead* sank here with a loss of 445 lives, though every woman and child on the ship escaped unharmed in the lifeboats and this is where the phrase 'women and children first' was thought to be originated. It took the sinking of a further 20 ships before a lighthouse came into operation in 1895.

Dyer Island is named after Samson Dyer, a black American who lived on the island collecting guano around 1806. Today the island is an important breeding spot for African penguins. On nearby **Geyser Island** there is a breeding seal population thought to number 60,000. Both can be visited on boat tours (see Activities and tours, page 261) The area between the two islands is known as Shark Alley, as great white sharks are attracted to the breeding seals. For details of great white shark cage diving see page 261.

South from Gansbaai

From Gansbaai the R43 continues southeast along the coast, passing through the small resorts of Kleinbaai, Franskraal, Pearly Beach and on to Die Dam at Sandbaai. Few visitors venture this far into the Overberg, although it is the area's relative isolation that is much of its appeal. From Sandbaai, the road turns inland and cuts across wild countryside that remains virtually untouched. During the spring the fields are full of wild flowers, and throughout the year the area is rich in varieties of fynbos. Follow signs for Wolvengat, formerly known as Viljoenshof, and continue on to Elim.

Elim → *Colour map 8, C2.*

Founded by German missionaries in 1824, this is one of the best-known Moravian mission stations in South Africa. The settlement is named after the spot where, in Exodus 15:27, the Israelites rested after crossing the Red Sea. To live here you must be a member of the local Moravian church and your livelihood must come from the earth. A new industry has emerged in recent years, based upon two long-lasting species of wild flower – helipterum and helichrysum – which are now successful export crops. Once dried, they are very popular for wreaths in Germany, keeping the historical connections alive today.

The whole village has been declared a national monument, so it is not surprising that there is a variety of quaint old buildings still standing and in use. One attraction is a restored **watermill** dating from 1833. It has a huge Burmese-teak wheel, which replaced the original stone wheels. The mill was reopened in 1990 to produce wholewheat flour. The **Old Mill Tea Room** serves delicious Elim biscuits and other items made from the mill's flour. Two other old buildings worth looking out for are the **parsonage** and the original **mission church**, which has a thatched roof and a clock. The church has a clock that dates back 235 years and still keeps good time. It was acquired for Elim in 1914 but has been working since 1764 when it was built in Germany for a church in Herrenhut.

Bredasdorp and around ⊝🖸▲ → *pp253-261. Colour map 8, C2.*

This is South Africa's first *dorp*, founded in 1837 by Michiel van Breda, an important local figure. From his farm, Zoetendalsvlei, he played an active role in the development of the Merino sheep industry throughout South Africa and was the first mayor of Cape Town in 1840. The old farmstead can be visited by prior arrangement. For tourist information, head to the regional **Cape Agulhas Tourism Bureau** ① *Dowling Building, Long St, T028-4242584, www.capeagulhas.info, Mon-Fri 0800-1700, Sat 0900-1300.*

Sights

Despite its age, there is little to keep you in town for long. Worth a peek is the **Shipwreck Museum** ① *Independent St, T028-4241240, Mon-Fri 0900-1645, Sat-Sun 1100-1545, small entry fee*, which houses a collection of odd bits and pieces salvaged from along the coast, 24 km away. The whole display is greatly enhanced by the sound effects. In the Shipwreck Hall you hear the distinct shrieks of seagulls and the thunderous sound of waves on a stormy night. Four wrecks are featured: the *Queen of the Thames*, HMS *Birkenhead*, the *Oriental Pioneer* and HMS *Ariston*. In the coach house are some old horse-drawn carts and an fire engine.

South from Bredasdorp

Driving south on the R319 for a further 36 km takes you to **Cape Agulhas**. Before reaching the coast, the road runs close to some large *vleis* (marshes): Karsrivier and Soetendals. These are important breeding grounds for aquatic birds, and there is a good chance of seeing flamingos. At the coast the road passes through **Struisbaai** before ending at a lighthouse and some retirement homes. A second road going south from Bredasdorp, the R316, ends at Waenhuiskrans.

Malgas

This small settlement on the banks of the Breede River was a vital point in the transport route in the mid-19th century of the famous Overberg tycoon, Joseph Barry. Until the roads east from Cape Town were improved and the many mountain passes negotiated, the majority of goods were brought into the Overberg region through Malgas. The Barry family had a 158-ton vessel, *Kadie*, especially built to transfer goods from Cape Town to Port Beaufort. From here the cargo was transferred to river boats and taken upstream as far as Malgas, before the final stage of transportation was completed by ox wagon. Today the settlement is famous for having the last manually operated pontoon in South Africa. Cars are carried across the river during daylight hours.

Struisbaai and L'Agulhas

This attractive fishing village has a collection of holiday homes, good spear-fishing, safe swimming in the bay, and a 14-km white-sand beach. L'Agulhas just to the south and at the end of the road is a rather wind-blown settlement of a few houses and shops. The principal attraction in this region is nearby **Cape Agulhas**. This is the southernmost point in Africa, but it is rather disappointing and lacks the grandeur one might hope for. Aside from the lighthouse, the surroundings are rather dull and the beach is very rocky, although it's excellent for fishing. This is where the warm waters of the Indian Ocean meet the cooler waters of the Atlantic Ocean, although most visitors seem to think they meet at Cape Point. However it doesn't happen in a straight line and the warm waters of the Indian Ocean do reach as far west as False Bay.

The **Cape Agulhas Lighthouse**, 1 km east of the tip of Africa, was built in 1848. It was modelled on the Egyptian pharaohs' light in Alexandria and now houses a pleasant tea room, decorated with antiques and museum pieces, which serves breakfast and light lunches. If you climb up the stairs there are good views over the unforgiving ocean that has claimed many ships and lives.

🌙 *The official position of the southernmost tip of Africa is 34°49'58" south and 20°00'12" east and is found approximately 1 km west of the Cape Agulhas Lighthouse. The location is marked by a simple cairn.*

Agulhas National Park

ⓘ *For information contact T028-4356222, www.sanparks.org, free entry.*

The park encompasses a large area of coastland centred around Cape Agulhas, and it was created to help protect the rugged coastline and the immediate hinterland, known as the Agulhas Plain, which forms the southernmost area of Africa. The Agulhas Plain is home to almost 2000 species of indigenous plants, of which 100 are endemic to the area. A large part of the area is taken up by a variety of wetlands which attract more than 21,000 migrant and resident birds annually. The park also protects a couple of islands found just offshore which are home to seals and seabirds, as well as the whales which frequent this part of the coastline in spring and early summer. Finally, the area is important in archaeological terms, and several ancient habitation sites have already been discovered. At present, there are limited tourist facilities in the park (a couple of toilets and little else), but there are plans by SANParks to build a 60-bed accommodation facility by 2009. The quickest route from Cape Town (230 km) is to take the N2 highway as far as Caledon and then turn onto the R406 for Bredasdorp. From Bredasdorp follow the signs for either Struisbaai or L'Agulhas. At present these are the two closest settlements to the park with accommodation facilities.

Arniston (Waenhuiskrans)

This tranquil fishing village, which is known to locals by its Afrikaans name, Waenhuiskrans (wagon house cliff), is made up of a jumble of whitewashed, thatched cottages. Some of these are the homes of poor fishermen who put their brightly painted boats (chukkies) to sea early each morning, while others have been renovated into smart holiday homes. The appeal of the place is its beaches – the water is noticeably warm and turquoise here on the Indian Ocean side, and is backed by bone-white dunes making the effect all the more startling. Just to the west of the village is **Waenhuiskrans Cave**, a huge cavern overlooking the sea, which can be explored at low tide. The cavern goes back into the cliffs and is named after the ox wagons which it once held.

The town's other name is derived from the wreck of the *Arniston* (1815), which lies about 1 km from the slipway. Items salvaged from the wreck are on display in the **Bredasdorp Shipwreck Museum**. The wreck can be dived, but there is a heavy swell. There is a monument to the deceased near the beach; only six of the 378 passengers survived. There are two beaches, **Slipway** in front of the **Arniston Hotel**, and **Bikini Beach**. The waters are warm and bright blue, with some good snorkelling. At low tide a couple of rock pools are exposed on Bikini Beach, and are fun for children to explore. A few shops in the village stock the basics for self-catering. You can only reach here in your own vehicle; there is no public transport.

De Mond Nature Reserve

ⓘ *The gates are open daily 0700-1600. Vehicles are not allowed in the reserve. There is a car park next to the office by the main gate from where the Sterna Trail begins, and a 3-bedroom cottage to rent (see Sleeping). Further information: T028-4242170, www.capenature.co.za. The best time to visit is Oct-Mar.*

This pleasant small reserve is centred around the mouth of the Heuningnes River, 26 km south of Bredasdorp. Two former farms were designated as a nature reserve in 1986. About 10 km of the shoreline is also protected, although most of the land remains inaccessible to the public. A 7-km hike known as the Sterna Trail starts from the office, following the beach for several kilometres. This is an easy path that winds through a range of different coastal habitats, including dune forest, stabilized dunes, riverine vegetation and some salt marshes.

De Hoop Nature Reserve ● ⟶ pp253-261. Colour map 8, C3.

① *Reserve gates and office Sat-Thu 0700-1800, Fri 0700-1900, R25. There is a small entrance fee per person/vehicle. An additional cycling fee per person/day applies if you intend to use the mountain-bike trail in the eastern sector. Information and reservations for accommodation in the reserve (see Sleeping, page 257) T028-5421253, www.capenature.co.za.*

This is an important coastal reserve which extends 5 km out to sea, protecting the shoreline and marine life. It is divided into two sectors. The **western region** is for hiking, game viewing and birdwatching while the **eastern section** is for mountain biking. The region enjoys a Mediterranean climate with mild winters and warm summers. August is the wettest month, with some morning fogs. The sea has strong currents and can be dangerous for swimming. Consult the reserve office for advice on safe spots to swim.

The reserve covers an exceptionally varied and rich environment – seven different ecosystems are found within the 34,000 ha reserve. De Hoop is a large freshwater *vlei* surrounded by marshlands which stretch for 15 km. The coastline is a mix of sandy beaches, rocky headlands and cliffs with wave-cut platforms. Further inland are giant sand dunes, some as high as 90 m, and behind these are limestone hills and the Potberg Mountains. The higher ground is clearly divided by kloofs covered with indigenous vegetation. It has been estimated that over 1500 plant species grow here, of which 34 are endemic to the reserve, including rare lowland fynbos species. Details of the rarer plants are displayed at the environmental education centres and the reserve offices at De Hoop and Potberg.

Ins and outs

Getting there Coming from Bredasdorp, follow the R319 towards Swellendam. After 8 km is a signposted right turn onto a gravel road. After 40 km you reach **Ouplaas** – take a right for the western section or continue straight on for another 10 km for the entrance to the eastern section. The office and car park are at Potberg. Approaching from the N2, the quickest route is to take the Witsand (see also page 268) turning 12 km east of Swellendam. After 23 km turn right for Malgas and then follow the signs. Both entrances are about 20 km from Malgas. The last 50 km or so on both of these routes is on gravel roads.

Tourist information Cycling on the service tracks within the western sector is free. In the eastern sector cars are left at the Potberg Environmental Education Centre. It is 11 km from here to the accommodation at Cupidoskraal. Allow about one hour with a loaded bike. There are information displays at De Hoop and Potberg offices introducing the visitor to the environment and the diversity of species to be found in the reserve. The closest shops and petrol are in Ouplaas, 15 km from the De Hoop office.

Wildlife

With such a variety of terrain in a relatively small area, the region supports a diverse range of wildlife. Over 250 species of bird have been recorded here, while elusive leopard, bontebok and Cape mountain zebra roam around, along with the more common eland, grey rhebok, baboon and klipspringer. The last known breeding colony of the Cape vulture in the southwestern Cape is close to Potberg, and you may glimpse them circling high in the skies. The **Windhoek Cave** is home to a large colony of bats which have attracted their fair share of research interest. Other rare species that you might see include black oystercatchers, which forage amongst the dunes. Finally, there is a chance of seeing southern right whales, which calve in the shallow waters and can be seen between July and December (see page 244). Although the whales found here are often in larger concentrations than elsewhere, they are difficult to see as they remain beyond the breakers.

Hiking and mountain biking

The reserve is traversed by a number of self-guided hiking trails, as well as a popular mountain-biking route. There is also an 11-km circular drive for vehicles in the middle of the reserve and another 15-km drive along the coast. Driving gives you the opportunity to appreciate quickly the diversity of the landscape and explore all corners, although it can detract from viewing wildlife – a quieter approach on foot is more rewarding.

Hiking Trails have been designed for all levels of fitness and with different interests in mind. There are four one-day walks close to the camps and car parks and the **Vlei Trail** follows the banks of the De Hoop Vlei where you'll find masses of waterbirds. A new five-day **Whale Trail** follows the coast and simple overnight huts are found at suitable intervals. This trail needs to be pre-booked at the office.

Mountain biking Cyclists are permitted to use any of the management roads in the western sector of the reserve. There is also the **De Hoop Mountain Bike Trail** laid out in the eastern sector (bookings essential). A hut at **Cupidoskraal** is used as an overnight base for cyclists on the trail. The trail varies in difficulty and cyclists will need to allow two to three days to complete it. Numbers are limited to 12 cyclists per day. The hut provides comfortable overnight accommodation for 12 people, with storage space for bicycles, gas, fireplace, no bedding. The only drinking water available is by the overnight hut, so make sure you carry enough for each day. Beware of dehydration and cramp when cycling in the heat. Always carry a rudimentary first-aid kit; you will quickly appreciate how isolated you are in the reserve.

⊙ Overberg and the Whale Coast listings

Hotel and guesthouse prices
L over US$300 **AL** US$220-300 **A** US$150-220
B US$100-150 **C** US$75-100 **D** US$35-75
E US$15-35 **F** under US$15
Restaurant prices
TTT over US$30 **TT** US$15-30 **T** under US$15
See pages 46-51 for further information.

⊜ Sleeping

Gordon's Bay *p240*
A Berg en Zee, 131 Beach Rd, T021-8563095, www.bergenzee.co.za. Stylish, intimate guesthouse in a whitewashed house with wooden floors, 6 rooms and 1 honeymoon suite with white furnishings and bedding, terrace, splash pool, bar, within walking distance of restaurants, beauty treatments on offer, and the host, a registered guide, offers local day tours.
B Celtic Manor, 22 Suikerbossie Dr, T021-8561907, www.celticmanor.co.za. High up on the hill above Gordon's Bay with sweeping views of False Bay, this boutique guesthouse has 6 rooms and 1 self-catering apartment sleeping 4 arranged around the hillside. Guests share dinner around a large dining table, there is a comfortable lounge and bar, swimming pool and separate spa with 2 therapists.

Pringle Bay *p240*
B Moonstruck on Pringle Bay, 764 Hangklip Rd, T028-2738162, www.moonstruck.co.za. Intimate guesthouse with large windows overlooking the ocean and mountains, 4 spacious rooms, stylish decor, balconies and fireplaces, pool with wooden deck, 100 m from the beach reached by a private path through the fynbos.

Betty's Bay *p240*
C Buçaco Sud, Clarence Dr, T028-2729750, www.bucacosud.co.za. Spanish-style villa with 6 tastefully decorated en suite rooms, terracotta tiles, fireplaces in public areas, all rooms have either mountain or coastal views, breakfast served in attractive courtyard with pool, no children under 10.

D Waterlilly Lodge, on the R44, Porter and Angler Dr, T028-2729378, www.waterlilly lodge.co.za. 6 stylish rooms with bright white bedding, some with wooden floors, pretty garden and patio with sea and mountain views, attentive host who's an ex South African Airways steward, good wholesome breakfasts.

Vermont and Onrus *p241*
B On the Vermont Guest House, 21 Tiptol Cres, T028-3162873, www.hermanus-onrus-accommodation.co.za. Smart modern lodge in a Tuscan-style villa with 4 comfortable rooms, 1 completely wheelchair accessible with lift and roll in shower, balconies, DSTV, swimming pool and patio.
D Flick's Places, 8 Beach Rd and 69 Atlantic Dr, Onrus, T028-3162998, www.flicks place.co.za. This is actually 2 B&Bs, owned by a well-known local caterer. 1 property is based right on the beach, the other a few mins' walk away. Both have comfortable en suite double rooms, private entrances, satellite TV. Also self-catering units. Delicious meals on request, excellent breakfasts.

Hermanus *p241, map p242*
There are hundreds of accommodation options in Hermanus and we only have room to list a few examples. For a full listing visit www.hermanus.co.za or visit the tourist office on arrival. Be sure to book well ahead during whale season and school holidays.
L The Marine, Marine Dr, T028-3131000, www.marine-hermanus.co.za. Part of the Relais & Chateaux group, a historic hotel and one of the finest in the country. 42 luxurious rooms, some with stunning ocean views, all with exceptionally fine furnishings – silk curtains, plush carpets, pale suede armchairs and marble bathrooms. A/c, satellite TV, fresh flowers, 4-poster beds, some have his 'n' hers bathrooms. Rates drop significantly in winter. Also has a spa, heated swimming pool, shop, internet and 2 restaurants; the seafood restaurant has won many awards (see Eating,

page 257). Impeccable service. Highly recommended for a treat.

B Auberge Burgundy, 16 Harbour Rd, T028-3131201, www.auberge.co.za. Provençal-style villa in the heart of Hermanus, 17 rooms, a mix of luxury doubles and suites, the penthouse can sleep 6, all set around a sumptuous inner courtyard with a swimming pool, private terraces or balconies, some with fine views across Walker Bay. Also owns the **Burgundy** restaurant, opposite (see Eating, page 257). Good reports from some readers.

B Misty Waves, T028-3138460, www.hermanusmistybeach.co.za. 2 luxurious properties manged together under the Misty Waves brand: the **Misty Waves Boutique Hotel** and **Hermanus Guest House**, both on Marine Dr. The hotel is a spacious modern building on 2 levels with ample decks and roof terraces, suites have ocean views, spa baths, swimming pool, restaurant, whilst the guesthouse offers elegant B&B accommodation with 4-poster beds and chandeliers in smart white blocks, in rooms that have all the mod cons.

B-C Mitchell St Village, 56-60 Mitchell St, T028-3124560, www.56.co.za. 12 rooms, all very differently designed (the owner is an interior decorator), some have private courtyards or balconies and fireplaces, 2 swimming pools, attractive lounge and breakfast rooms and crayfish dinners can be arranged in season.

C Hortensia Lodge, 66 Mitchell St, T028-3124358, www.hortensialodge.co.za. Small comfortable guesthouse set in neat gardens with swimming pool. 5 rooms, en suite with TV and views of the garden, simple decor. German, French, and Hungarian spoken, no children under 14.

C Livesey Lodge, 13 Main Rd, T028-3130026, www.liveseylodge.co.za. Friendly guesthouse with 6 en suite double rooms set around garden with good-sized pool. Spacious and bright, all have separate entrances, individual decor, TV, mini-fridge, huge beds, nice touches like books in all the rooms. Off-street parking. Location a little outside town is a drawback, but otherwise it's a good value, attractive and well-run place. Recommended.

C Windsor Hotel, 49 Marine Dr, T028-3123727, www.windsor-hotel.com. Large and popular, this is Hermanus's oldest hotel built in 1896, set on cliffs overlooking the ocean. 60 en suite rooms with TV, some have sea views. Excellent views across Walker Bay from the glazed lounge. Slightly plain restaurant. Frequently used by tour groups, small boat hire service.

C-D Whale Rock Lodge, 26 Springfield Rd, T028-3130014, www.whalerock.co.za. Well-appointed B&B with 11 double rooms, en suite, TV, set in a thatched building decorated with antiques and oil paintings, close to the new harbour and a short walk from the cliff path. Garden with pool, lounge, no children under 6.

D Forty Five Marine Drive, and **Hermanus Esplanade**, 45 and 63 Marine Dr, T028-3123610, www.45marinehermanus.com. Jointly managed self-catering accommodation in large white blocks in a commanding position above the rocks and waves, 2- to 3-bedroom fully equipped apartments with kitchen and lounge, underfloor heating, TV, lock-up garages, not very stylish but modern and functional with great views and good value for families.

D-E Moby's, 9 Mitchell St, T028-3132361, www.mobys.co.za. Backpacker joint offering a good range of rooms: doubles, dorms sleeping 6-8, family rooms, all are en suite. Pub with DSTV, large garden with pool, daily braais, internet access, TV lounge, fully equipped kitchen. Friendly and laid-back place, can book Baz Bus pickups for small fee. Also organizes cheap shark dives, wine tasting, sandboarding and the usual excursions.

D-E Zoete Inval, 23 Main Rd, T028-3121242, www.zoeteinval.co.za. Excellent budget choice with 7 double B&B rooms, and another double, 1 family rooms, and 2 dorms in a converted loft, which has self-catering facilities. Pleasant TV lounge, laundry, sunny deck, internet access, secure parking. Will meet the Baz Bus at **Bot River Hotel** for a small fee. Friendly and good value.

E-F Hermanus Backpackers, 26 Flower St, T028-3124293, www.hermanusbackpackers.co.za. Well positioned behind Main Rd, dorms, doubles/twins with or without bathrooms, vibey atmosphere, bar with pool table, TV lounge with DVD library, nightly braai, pickup from Baz Bus for a small fee, will book all activities and give out maps of the area.

Stanford and around p245

AL Mosaic Farm, 11 km west of Stanford on the edge of the Klein River Lagoon, T028-3132814, www.mosaicfarm.net. Luxury accommodation in 5 chalets made from canvas and thatch with stunning views of the mountains and lagoon, large bathtubs, outdoor showers, wooden decks, swimming pool. Rates are all-inclusive of meals and activities such as sundowner drives and kayaking.

C De Kleine Rivers Valley House, 14 Church St, T028 3410048. Beautiful B&B in one of the oldest houses in Stanford, dating from 1785. 2 doubles and 1 single en suite room, decked out with English furnishings and antiques, huge Victorian bathrooms, excellent value, run by affable British couple. Recommended.

C Galashiels Lodge, 10 King St, T028-3410181, gslodge@hermanus.com. A family-run guesthouse with 4 en suite doubles and 2 suites, traditional Victorian plush furnishings, vague Scottish theme, cosy lounge with log fire, bar, evening meals on request, peaceful garden.

C-D Springfontein, T028-3410651, www.springfontein.co.za. A collection of comfortable self-catering cottages, sleeping 2-6, some of them thatched, on a working farm 4 km from Stanford. Excellent value for families, with pool, gardens, beautiful setting surrounded by farmland and a small vineyard.

D Stanford Hotel, Queen Victoria St, T028-3410900, www.stanfordvillage.co.za. Attractive historic inn set in the heart of Stanford. Recently renovated, with 6 rooms of varying sizes, all en suite with wooden floors, wicker furniture, brass beds, simple and comfortable. Popular pub attached serving evening meals Wed and Thu weekend braais. Good value. Recommended.

Salmonsdam Nature Reserve p247

D-F Salmonsdam Cabins, T028-3410018, www.capenature.co.za. 3 basic overnight cabins, 1 sleeps 8 with 3 rooms, living area,

kitchen and bathroom, the other 2 sleep 4 in bunk beds, shared ablution block, suitable for hikers, no electricity but gas fridge, stove, cooking and eating utensils, visitors need to bring bedding and food. There are also 10 camping sites (**F**) and a small cement swimming pool.

Gansbaai and around p247

B Gansbaai Guesthouse, 9 Slabber Rd, Klipfontein, just south of Gansbaai, T021-4341385 (Cape Town), www.casablanca.co.za. Lovely 2 storey guesthouse with wrap-around balconies, great views and completely surrounded by fynbos, very stylish interiors, everything is bright white with some interesting African art and scented candles, 6 rooms, candlelit baths have sea views, dinner on request, usually seafood or fish braais.

B Klein Paradijs Guest Farm, T028-3819760, www.kleinparadijs.co.za. Follow the main road south out of Gansbaai, direction Pearly Beach, 21 km. A pleasant farm just inland from the beautiful white-sand beach. 5 individually decorated rooms, newly refurbished, with thatched ceilings, elegant table d'hôte dining room, superb food from a Swiss-trained chef. Also has 5 much cheaper self-catering cottages dotted about the farm (**D**) and guests can still eat in the restaurant. Recommended.

B Marebella Seafront Guesthouse, De Kelders, T028-3842665, www.marebella.co.za. 3 km along Walker Bay towards Hermanus from Gansbaai. Smart and comfortable B&B with 3 en suite rooms, shared lounge with satellite TV, breakfast and dinner served on large deck overlooking the sea, private garden leads down to the water. Stunning location perched high up on the cliff, the perfect location for whale watching in the bay Jun-Nov.

C The Great White House, 5 Geelbek St, T028-3843273, www.white-house.co.za. Popular thatched house with 3 'fishermen's cottages' with fireplaces, wood floors, en suite, pleasant African-themed decor, range of activities including whale watching and shark diving arranged, restaurant popular with divers, good location close to the harbour.

D-F Uilenkraalsmond Caravan Park, T028-3880200, 5 km along the coast, south towards Pearly Beach. A vast modern campsite with 40 self-catering family chalets, wash blocks, grassy, limited shade, sea breeze can be a problem at times. Plenty of facilities for children, supertube, trampoline, crazy golf, swimming in the lagoon. Very busy during local school holidays, but for the rest of the year it is quiet.

Bredasdorp *p248*

B Earl of Clarendon, corner of Dirkie Uys and Clarendon streets, T028-4251420. Historic building with 4 elegant rooms, all with wood floors, en suite with Victorian baths, 4-poster beds, antiques, crisp white linen. Restaurant, bistro and curio shop on site. Recommended.

C Firlane Guesthouse, 5 Fir Lane, T028-4251192. Historic 1926 mansion with gleaming wooden floors and high ceilings with scrolled cornices, 8 double rooms, some en suite, individually decorated, spacious and luxurious bathrooms, breakfast served in smart dining room or in garden.

D-F Suikerbossie Caravan Park, T028-4251919. Muncipal camping ground with 117 caravan stands and 22 good-value but very simple self-catering chalets sleeping 4-5, bedding is extra.

Struisbaai *p249*

C Harbour Lights, 5 Kusweg, T028-4356053, www.capeagulhas.co.za. Smart bright-yellow B&B within walking distance of the harbour with 5 comfortable rooms with fans, TV, fridge and electric blankets, bar, evening meals available, no children under 12.

D-F Struisbaai Caravan Park, Main Rd, T028-4356820. Camping and 16 self-catering chalets, good shade, laundry, shop and café in walking distance, overlooks the sea, short walk to lighthouse. All ablution facilities have been modernized.

L'Agulhas *p249*

A-B Agulhas Country Lodge, Main Rd, T028-4357650, www.agulhascountry lodge.com. An unusual building made of

limestone set amongst the rocks with broad ocean views, 8 rooms with balconies and complimentary sherry, some with jacuzzis, restaurant, bar with nautical and aviation theme, cigar bar. Rates drop in winter months.

B Villa@Cape Agulhas, 17 Golf St, T028-4356917, www.villacapeagulhas.co.za. Very stylish upmarket B&B with views of the lighthouse, the walls in the communal areas are painted bright orange, pink and lime green, funky furniture, fireplaces, rooms have TV, sea views and fridge. Jacuzzi, no smoking or credit cards.

Arniston *p250*

A Arniston Spa Hotel, Beach Rd, T028-4459000, www.arnistonhotel.com. An elegant seaside hotel, 40 rooms, thoughtfully decorated, small bathrooms, TV, sea-facing rooms have private balconies but are more expensive than the pool/courtyard-facing rooms, restful reception rooms with fireplaces. Good restaurant, bar built around a fish tank, swimming pool, sheltered garden. The newest addition is the spa, which has a long menu of treatments and spa packages are on offer.

C Arniston Lodge, 23 Main Rd, T028-4459175, www.arnistonlodge.co.za. An appealing thatched cottage which blends in well with the traditional fishermen's cottages. 4 double en-suite rooms, characterful upstairs rooms have thatched ceiling and views across the beach, sheltered swimming pool, lounge with log fireplace, evening meals can be arranged, a welcome peaceful retreat, German spoken.

D Arniston Seaside Cottages, Huxham St, T028-4459772, www.arniston-online.co.za. Compact development set among the dunes with 20 whitewashed thatched cottages, self-catering, log fireplaces, reed ceilings, pine furnishings, most with sea views from private balcony, cottages are serviced every day, all facilities close by, fresh fish from the boats as they land. Recommended.

E South of Africa Backpackers Resort, T028-4459240, www.southofafrica.co.za. A smart backpacker hostel, set in the wing of **Die Herberg Hotel**. No more expensive than other hostels, but infinitely more comfortable. No dorms – singles, doubles and triples with TV, kitchen, chill-out room, TV room, breakfasts served in hotel restaurant and included in price, full access to hotel's facilities including indoor pool, gym and squash courts.

De Mond Nature Reserve *p250*
C De Mond Cottage, T021-6593500 (Cape Town), www.capenature.co.za. The cottage is located near the entrance to the reserve among milkwood trees and coastal fynbos and has ocean views. Self-catering with 3 bedrooms, 2 single beds in each, electricity, hot water, shower, braai, stove, fridge, toaster and kettle, bring food and bedding.

De Hoop Nature Reserve *p251*
A variety of accommodation is within the reserve; below is a selection. All are managed by **Cape Nature Conservation**, T021-6593500 (Cape Town), www.capenature.co.za.
AL Lekkerwater, is a farmhouse situated right by the beach with wonderful ocean views, it sleeps 10 people in 5 rooms, gas powered stove, fridge and geysers but no electricity, lighting is by paraffin lights and candles, fully equipped kitchen. It takes a minimum of 6 people (**A**), and while these rates seem high, per person it's just over R300.
C-E Cottages and camping, 12 self-catering cottages sleeping from 4-8 people with fridge and stove. Some have bedding, but it's a good idea to bring your own, and kitchen utensils. The setting is perfect, right on the edge of the vlei. The campsite has basic facilities, with views over the vlei and set under milkwood trees. There are no electric points. Firewood is available from the De Hoop office. The **Vlei Trail** starts in the camp and 2 paths follow a route around the freshwater lake.

🍴 Eating

Gordon's Bay *p240*
🍴 **Bertie's Moorings**, Harbour Island, T021-8563343, www.berties.co.za. 1000-2400.

Lively pub serving light meals and good seafood on the waterfront. Also venue for stand-up comedy and live bands at the weekends. The furniture and the bar were hand crafted from wine barrels by owner Bertie Reed.
🍴 **Harbour Lights**, Gordon's Bay Harbour, T021-8561830. Tue-Sun 1200-1500, 1800-2200. Excellent seafood and good views of the yacht basin at night. Popular place, especially with families in the holidays, serving daily specials, linefish and seafood platters, plus a good wine list and a collection of rare whiskies.
🍴 **Indigo**, 33 Beach Rd, T021-8562460. Daily 1000-2200. Pleasant spot with outside wooden deck with umbrellas, overlooking the beach, light snacks and well-priced seafood including a generous platter. Next door in the blue building is **Trawlers** for takeaway seafood.

Pringle Bay *p240*
🍴 **Hook, Line & Sinker**, T028-2738688. Daily for lunch from 1200, dinner at 1900. Lunch is hake and chips wrapped in newspaper for R25, while dinners and Sun lunch is an ever-changing chalkboard menu cooked by owner and chef Stephan in the open-plan kitchen. Most nights it's seafood, but on Wed and Sun nights he also cooks steak, and there's a single dessert of crème brûlée, which is finished off by blow torch at your table.
🍴 **Miems**, Hangklip Rd, T028-2738764. Wed-Sun 1130-1500, Tue-Sat 1800-2100. Cosy village pub serving good-value seafood and pub grub, hearty portions, a good place to hole up on a cold day.

Kleinmond *p241*
🍴 **Europa**, 1 Harbour Rd, T028-2715107. 0800-2200. Large seafront restaurant and coffee shop, good views from the deck, light meals like open sandwiches and freshly baked cakes, plus seafood, spare ribs and steaks, long wine and spirit menu.
🍴 **Potters Garden**, 14 Harbour Rd, T028-2715505. Open 0800-1700. Look out for the giant blue teapot in front. Light meals, coffees and snacks, big breakfast served all day, Sun lunch popular with the local people.

Vermont and Onrus *p241*

¶¶ Milkwood, Beach Rd, Onrus Beach, T028-3161516. 0900-2230. Standard breakfast and lunch menu, tea cakes in the afternoon followed by more upmarket dinners, good seafood including fresh grilled calamari and linefish plus venison and steaks, good views of the beach.

¶ What the Dickens, Onrus Trading Post, Main St, T028-3163946. 1000-late. Well-known and good-value pub lunches with a full menu in the evenings.

Hermanus and around *p241, map p242*
The tourist trade in Hermanus supports an enormous number of restaurants and cafés, far too many to list. It's just a case of wandering around town until you find something that takes your fancy, though it's advisable to book ahead in season.

¶¶¶ Seafood at the Marine, Marine Dr, T028-3131000, www.marine-hermanus.co.za. 1200-1400, 1900-2100. This superb award-winning establishment serves the freshest seafood in stylish surrounds. The menu is refreshingly unfussy, and includes a crayfish platter, seafood bunny chow, 'Rich man's' fish and chips and gorgeous prawn and leek ravioli with lobster bisque. The wine list is excellent and the service friendly and fast. Highly recommended. There is also the cheaper **Seafood Express** in the hotel that is open for lunch only (1200-1600).

¶¶ Annie se Kombuis, Warrington Arcade, Harbour Rd, T028-3131350. Tue-Sun 1000-late. Unusual menu of South African dishes such as waterblommetjies, babotie, oxtail, chicken pie, ostrich, venison and seafood, served up in a homely atmosphere.

¶¶ Bientang's Cave, T028-3123454, www.bientangscave.com. 1130-1600, Fri and Sat 1900-2130, out of season, only open Fri-Sat for dinner. The name doesn't lie – the venue is an actual cave with an extended deck overlooking the waves. Superb spot for whale watching during season. Excellent seafood buffets and famous bouillabaisse soup, simple wood benches and long tables,

very popular, book ahead. Access is via steps from the car park on Marine Dr, between the village square and **Marine Hotel** – look out for the Bientang Seaworld sign.

¶¶ The Burgundy, Market Sq, Marine Dr, T028-3122800. 0830-1700, 1900-2000, closed for dinner in winter. Restored rural cottage set back from the old harbour. One of the top restaurants in town but relaxed and good value, with tables spilling onto a shady terrace outside. Excellent seafood including superb grilled crayfish. Recommended.

¶¶ Fisherman's Cottage, Old Harbour, T028-3123642. 1100-1500, 1800-2200. Tiny place set in an old thatched cottage serving excellent seafood, simple dishes such as seafood *potjie*, half and full portions available, charming setting. Choose a veranda table in good weather. Known as the smallest pub in town. No credit cards.

¶¶ Marimba Café, 9 Royal Lane, off Main Rd, T028-3122148. 1100-late, closed Sun out of season. Fun 'African' restaurant with dishes from across the continent, including good seafood gumbo, Moroccan lamb shanks and Cape Malay curries. Also has daily specials and occasional live music.

¶¶ Mogg's Country Cookhouse, Hemel-en-Aarde Valley, 12 km from Hermanus centre, take R43 out of town for Cape Town, after 2 km turn onto the R320 for Caledon, T028-3124321. Wed-Sun 1230-1400, Sat 1930-2100. Farm restaurant in an old farm labourer's cottage with a seasonal menu. From the bread to the ice cream, every dish is home-made and freshly prepared and served in a lovely rustic setting. Likely dishes include lamb shank, seafood risotto or ostrich fillet. Recommended.

¶ Prince of Whales, Astoria Village, T028-3130725. Mon-Fri 0815-1700, Sat 0815-1330. Excellent breakfasts, filled pancakes, sandwiches, cakes and fresh croissants.

¶ Zebra Crossing, corner of Long St and Main Rd, T028-3123906. Mon-Sat 0900-0200, Sun 1000-0200. Lively pub with zebra-print theme, serving burgers, steaks, salads and ploughman's lunches. Turns into a popular drinking haunt later at night.

Stanford and around *p245*

Blue Gum Estate, on R326, T028-3410116, www.bluegum.co.za. 1200-1500, also Fri and Sat 1900-2200. Smart restaurant set on a luxurious country estate, stylish dining room and beautiful terrace, delicious local cuisine that is delicately and lovingly presented and good wine list.

Havercrofts, 1 km from Stanford off the Hermanus road, T028-3410603. Lunch Sat and Sun, dinner Thu-Sat. No credit cards. Lovely setting with terrace overlooking the mountains, or inside next to a roaring fire, simple country menu, changes according to what is seasonally available, full wine list.

Mariana's Home Deli and Bistro, 12 Du Toit St, T028-3410272. Fri-Sun 0900-1600. Deli stocked with local products, cheeses, stuffed olives and chutneys. Also serves bistro-style meals on the vine-shaded terrace. The mussels are particularly good. Much of the produce is grown in the back garden.

Gansbaai *p247*

The Great White House, 5 Geelbek St, T028-3843273, www.white-house.co.za. At the lodge of the same name (see Sleeping). 0730-1600. Daytime restaurant serving filling breakfasts, light lunches and snacks. The pan-fried calamari is very good. At Sun lunch the menu expands to include steaks. This is where cage shark divers warm up in front of the fireplace after their excursion.

Bredasdorp *p248*

Blue Parrot, Dirkie Uys St, T028-4251023. Mon-Fri 1130-1400, 1830-late, Sat 1830-late. Popular family restaurant, cosy candlelit tables, reliable food with standard steaks, pasta and salads, and local wine list.

Julian's, 22 All Saints St, T028-4251201. Mon-Sat 0900-late. Unusual purple and orange building next door to a ceramics factory that is worth a browse, the crockery is used and sold in the restaurant. Grills and seafood, sandwiches, pancakes and burgers, plenty of choice for vegetarians. Best known for their baked chocolate cheesecake.

Struisbaai and L'Agulhas *p249*

Agulhas Country Lodge, Main Rd, T028-4357650, www.agulhascountry lodge.com. Lunch 1200-1500, dinner 1900. Elegant restaurant set in a guesthouse which serves excellent fresh seafood – crayfish is a speciality. Also well known for its local lamb. Dinner is a formal 4-course affair.

⊛ Festivals and events

Hermanus and around *p241, map p242*
Aug Hermanus Food and Wine Festival, www.hermanuswineandfood.co.za. Wine tasting from over 40 vineyards, plus cheese, olives and sushi.
Sep Whale Festival, T028-3130928, www.whalefestival.co.za. Primarily an arts festival which attracts theatre and singing acts along with children's events and a craft market, and also the best time of the year to spot whales in Walker Bay. A **Wild Flower Festival** http://fernkloof.com/festival, is also held in Sep in Fernkloof Nature Reserve

⊙ Shopping

Hermanus and around *p241, map p242*
As befits a popular tourist town there are plenty of curio shops and speciality boutiques. **Market Sq** has a small, daily craft, curio and clothes market. A popular shopping mall is the **Village Square**. To the west of the town centre is the larger **Gateway Centre**. This has all the high-street shops as well as restaurants and amusements for children.

Wine

Wine Village, at the entrance to the Hemel-en-Aarde Valley, corner of the R43 and the R320 on the way into town, T028-3163988, www.wine-village.co.za. Mon-Fri 0900-1800, Sat 0900-1700, Sun 1000-1500. This advertises itself as the biggest wine shop in South Africa and sells wine from over 600 estates. Can also organize international shipping.

▲ Activities and tours

Hermanus and around p241, map p242
Diving
Scuba Africa, New Harbour, T028-3162362, www.scubaafrica.com. Equipment hire, dive courses (NAUI) and daily organized dives. In addition to coral reef and kelp forest dives, there are 3 stimulating wreck dives between here and Arniston. In Walker Bay, the most rewarding dives close to the shore are at Tamatiebank, which has been recommended for snorkelling, and The Haksteen, a pinnacle with steep drop-offs, 26 m. A short boat trip from the new harbour is Whale Rock, or Table Top. Conditions are quite calm, maximum depth is 40 m. Expect to see seafans and corals. From the high-tide mark to 500 m out to sea is a marine reserve. No marine animals may be collected or disturbed. **Warning** Do not attempt to dive when whales are in the bay. If you come within 300 m of a whale, either in a boat or the water, there are heavy fines, and visitors will be deported. Enjoy them from the cliff vantage points instead. For shark cage diving see under Gansbaai, page 261.

Fishing
For many local visitors the principal reason for coming to Hermanus is the excellent sea fishing. There are strict regulations concerning what you can catch, the bait you use and the actual season. Permits are available from any post office for R50. Most of the coastline in front of the town centre is a marine reserve so, although angling is allowed, nothing else may be removed from the sea in this area. Chartered fishing trips start from the new harbour; check with the tourist office for which charters are operating. Rock angling is popular with local fishermen; steenbras, cob, red roman, silver fish, red stumpnose and John Brown are often caught. Deep-sea angling is more popular with foreign tourists, who hope to catch tuna, the local snoek and Cape salmon. Crayfish and perlemoen are a big draw for divers, but are subject to stringent regulations due to a problem with poaching.

Golf
Hermanus Golf Club, Main Rd, T028-3121954, www.hermanusgolfclub.com. This is a beautiful par-73 course in the lee of the mountains with heather-lined fairways, some holes have sea views, visitors welcome.

Hiking
There is a 10-km cliff path marked around Walker Bay that starts in the New Harbour and ends at Grotto Beach, with plenty of benches at potential whale-viewing spots. There are also well-maintained trails in Fernkloof Nature Reserve.

Swimming
On a calm summer day Walker Bay looks cool and inviting from the cliff paths, but it has its dangers. There are strong undercurrents, so look out for warnings and advice, especially at spring tides. During the holidays all the popular swimming beaches have lifeguards on duty. Don't swim alone in isolated coves. There are several tidal pools which offer safe bathing for children and a fun place to snorkel for the first time. Below the Marine Hotel is the **Marine Tidal Pool** (*Bietang se Baaigat*), which always has plenty of sealife and fish. Along Westcliff Rd is a smaller pool known as **Fick's Pool**. This is a sheltered spot and has the bonus of a sandy bottom. There are toilets and changing rooms close by. Out of town there is a tidal pool at the Onrus River campsite which is open to day visitors.

Tour operators
Hermanus Whale Cruises, office in the New Harbour, T028-3132722, www.hermanus-whale-cruises.co.za. Daily whale-watching cruises in season.
Southern Right Charters, office in the New Harbour, T028-3163154, seascapes@hermanus.co.za. Boat-based whale watching with a hydrophone on board allowing you to listen to the whales too.
Walker Bay Adventures, just out of town towards Gansbaai at Prawn Flats, T028-3140925, www.walkerbayadventures.co.za.

Daily cruises on the lagoon, weather permitting, for larger groups and canoe and sea-kayaking trips.

Stanford and around *p245*
Boat cruises up the Klein River are a great way of enjoying the birdlife on the banks – there are around 130 species.
Klein River Cruises, T082-7811704 (mob), www.stanfordvillage.co.za.

Gansbaai *p247*
Great white shark cage diving
One of the most popular activities here is cage diving to see great white sharks. Several companies offer trips to view the sharks, and people with a diving certificate can see them from an underwater cage. Non-divers can still do it, but they first have to spend a day doing a course. The boats used are motorized catamarans and trips last 3-7 hrs. Alternatively you can go on a long shark-diving day trip from Cape Town. This has become one of South Africa's booming tourist industries and viewing a great white at such close quarters is certainly an amazing experience. However, conservationists argue that these trips can be harmful to the sharks as they interfere with their natural eating patterns, and can encourage them to equate humans with food (contrary to popular belief, we do not feature on their standard menu). If you are considering viewing the sharks off Dyer Island, check with the tourist offices in Cape Town or locally to find out which is currently the best company running trips, and try to choose one which is taking part in conservation and research into the species.
Shark Diving Unlimited, Gansbaai, T028-3842787, www.sharkdivingunlimited.com.
Shark Lady, Kleinbaai, T028-3123287, www.sharklady.co.za.

White Shark Adventures, 13 Main Rd, Gansbaai, T028-3841380, www.white sharkdiving.com.
White Shark Diving Co, Kleinbaai, T021-4611583 (Cape Town), www.sharkcagediving.co.za.

Tour operators
Dyer Island Cruises, T028-3840406, www.dyer-island-cruises.co.za. Boat trips to Dyer Island to see penguins and seals. All cruises depart from Kleinbaai harbour near Gansbaai and, during the season, whales and sharks may be spotted too.

L'Agulhas *p249*
Eco Quad, 612 Main Rd, T082-8545078, www.ecoquad.co.za. Guided nature trails on quad bikes in the Agulhas National Park.

⊖ Transport

Hermanus *p241, map p242*
Hermanus is 120 km from Cape Town (via N2). None of the 3 major coach companies runs a service via Hermanus. For transport options to and from Hermanus, see Ins and outs, page 242.

⊕ Directory

Hermanus *p241, map p242*
Banks Standard Bank, 99 Main Rd; ABSA, 67 Main Rd; there are also ATMs in all the shopping centres and arcades. **Internet Great White Internet Shop**, 2 Harbour Rd, T028-3130215. **Medical services Hermanus Private Hospital**, Hospital St, T028-3130168.

Overberg interior

While most South Africans can tell you where the Overberg is, they might have difficulty defining its limits. It is a vague term which generally refers to the area to the east of the Hottentots Holland Mountains extending as far as Mossel Bay. To the north are the Langeberg Mountains and to the south the ocean.

Having climbed the spectacular Sir Lowry's Pass from Somerset West, the N2 highway cuts east across the interior of the Overberg towards Mossel Bay and George. The landscape is immediately very different on this side of the mountains – the road passes through forested hills before opening onto the endless dry, orange plains of the Overberg. To the north lie the Langeberg Mountains, their smooth foothills and sharp peaks providing a serene backdrop to the route. Most of the towns en route are quiet farming centres, and were some of the first areas settled by white farmers as they ventured east of Cape Town in search of new farmlands.

Most visitors choose to stick to the main road, and it is easy to pass quickly through the region without taking much in. If you are keen to get to the Garden Route, George can be reached in three hours, but there are several sights worth lingering over on the way. One centre that deserves a stopover is Swellendam, the third-oldest town in the Cape. Nearby are a couple of nature reserves, and the town has some well-preserved examples of early Cape architecture.

In February 2006 there was the biggest fire in the Overberg for more than a century. During five long days the fire burnt an 80-km-long trail from Elim all the way to the fringes of Stanford (see pages 248 and 245), swallowing over 40,000 ha of farmland, fynbos fields and forestry plantation. Now the vegetation has largely recovered. ▸▸ For listings, see pages 270-274.

East to Caledon on the N2

Ten kilometres from Sir Lowry's Pass is a turning signposted Villiersdorp, R321. This takes you back into the heart of the Winelands, or north to the Breede River Valley. A short loop takes you to the undistinguished twin towns of **Grabouw** and **Elgin**. Regional information is available from **Elgin Valley and Grabouw Tourism** ① *T021-8591398, www.tourismelginvalley.co.za, daily 0900-1700,* at the Peregrine Farm Stall on the N2. (Grabouw is the centre of South Africa's apple industry and is where the popular fizzy drink Appletizer is made.) Continuing east, the N2 crosses the Houhoek Pass where there is a famous watering hole, the **Houw Hoek Inn**, always worth a stop (see Sleeping, page 270). At Bot River is the turning for Hermanus. It is a further 23 km on the N2 to the regional capital of the Overberg, Caledon.

Hottentots Holland Nature Reserve → *Colour map 8, B1.*

① *The entrance to the reserve is at Nuweberg, high in Viljoen's Pass between Grabouw and Villiersdorp. To get there turn left at Elgin, on to the R321. After about 10 km, at the bottom of Viljoens Pass past Nuweberg Dam, turn left to the Nuweberg Forest Station and reserve office. Reserve information: www.capenature.co.za, enquiries: T021-6593500. There is an information centre in the car park.*

The Hottentots Holland Mountains are the southern end of a continuous mountainous chain which extends inland as far as Ceres and beyond, effectively cutting the Cape off from the rest of South Africa, and overlooking False Bay. The 42,000-ha reserve stretches from Elgin in the south to beyond Villiersdorp in the north, and from the Stellenbosch Mountains in the west, eastwards to the Groenland Mountains. It's an important conservation area for mountain fynbos: over 1300 species have been recorded here, including some rare and endemic plants. There are also small populations of rhebuck, klipspringer, duiker and grysbok.

Being so close to Cape Town makes this an important and popular hiking region. Various restrictions are in force to help protect the flora and fauna as well as the physical landscape. The main trail in the reserve is the **Boland Hiking Trail**. The full circuit is 50 km and takes three days to cover. The shorter hikes are known as the **Nuweberg Circuit** and the **Riviersonderend Canyon**. Due to flooding, all hiking trails are closed from July to the end of August. There are also two mountain bike trails; the 6 km **Hottentants Holland Trail** is fairly easy and family orientated, while the 22 km **Groenlandberg Trail** is a little more challenging.

☾ *In the early days of settlement, people would refer to the area beyond the Hottentots Holland as 'over the berg'. It was not until the construction of Sir Lowry's Pass that the region began to be cultivated.*

Caledon and around ●●❀▲● ➠ *pp270-274. Colour map 8, B2.*

The regional capital of the Overberg, 120 km from Cape Town, lies just off the N2 at the foot of the Swartberg Mountains. It is a typical rural town – small and quiet, with a couple of sights, but only really worth an hour or two; it's best to press on to Swellendam for an overnight stay. The town is famous for its six naturally occurring hot springs, which produce over 800,000 litres per day. The water has a high ferrous carbonate content. Not surprisingly the first European settler, Ferdinandus Appel, sought to develop the springs. He was granted an 18-ha freehold, on the condition that he built baths and accommodation. Word of the water's healing powers spread quickly, and distinguished guests from the Dutch East India Company frequented the springs. At the turn of the 20th century the Caledon Mineral Baths and Sanatorium was built to cash in fully on their popularity. For 40 years they continued to be an attraction until a fire destroyed the complex in 1946. It was only in 1990 that a new hotel, **The Caledon** (see Sleeping, page 270), was built. Day visitors can use the spa's facilities which includes a waterfall and a series of pools. The one at the top is the hottest with water temperatures averaging 40°C. There are additional saunas, gym, cold pool, steam room, and treatments such as massages and facials are available.

Today the prosperity of the town and the region is based on agriculture. Caledon was the centre of a major development in wool production with a new breed of sheep, the merino. For information, visit **Cape Overberg Tourism Association** ⓘ *22 Plein St, T028-2141466, www.tourismcapeoverberg.co.za, Mon-Fri 0830-1600, Sat 0830-1230.*

The **Caledon House Museum** ⓘ *11 Constitution St, T028-2121511, Mon-Fri 0800-1700, small entrance fee*, is based in a Victorian house that was originally the Freemasons' Lodge. It has displays on local history, domestic items and crafts. There is a working kitchen where bread is baked every few days. For a small fee the curator will show you around and make the items on display a bit more interesting. The museum shop in Donkin Square is full of local farm produce and curios. **Mill Street** has a collection of historic buildings which have been declared national monuments. The Holy Trinity Church on Prince Alfred Drive is a small, neat church dating from 1855. Outings to local wetlands and the nearby nature reserves can be arranged for bird enthusiasts; contact the tourist office for details. Look out for the endangered blue crane which is found in the area on open farmland. Due to their vulnerable status, an Overberg Crane Group was created in 1991 by Cape Nature Conservation to devise a protection programme. (75% of South Africa's blue cranes, the national bird, are found in the Overberg.)

Caledon Nature Reserve

This small reserve, 214 ha, is just on the edge of town. Since 1892 the annual wild flower show has been held in the grounds, usually in September. Part of the reserve was turned into the **Victoria Wild Flower Garden** ① *0700-1700*, by Cecil Young and CW Meiring in 1927, local enthusiasts who had the foresight to protect the amazingly rich local flora. Of the 630 known species of *erica* in the world, over 200 grow in the Caledon district. This may not be everyone's cup of tea (56 ha of the reserve were converted into formal gardens with ponds, shaded paths and picnic spots) but for the botanist it is a fascinating attraction. Within the reserve there is a 10-km walk, the **Meiring Trail**, a good chance to appreciate the many species of fynbos and birds of the area. There is no shelter and hikers must bring all their drinking water. Allow up to five hours for the full circuit. A leaflet from the tourist office has a simple map of the hiking trail.

Greyton → *Colour map 8, B2.*

Just a short drive north of the main N2 highway, the quiet village of Greyton is a popular place to retire and attracts many artists. The mixture of restored old buildings and streets, lined with oaks, have helped create a low-key and peaceful atmosphere. When the first streets were laid out in 1854, the settlement was named after Sir George Grey, who had served two periods as governor of the Cape Colony. To the north lie the **Riviersonderend Mountains**, which in winter often have snow on their peaks – Kanonberg (1466 m) is the tallest peak overlooking the village. The **Greyton Nature Reserve** is at the edge of town on the southern slopes of the Sonderend Mountains. The best time to visit is from September to November. There is a short 20-minute walk to the **Noupoort Gorge**, which can be followed close to the Kanonberg summit. There are a number of streams running off the hills through forested valleys, with the occasional waterfall which can be reached by paths. Greyton is at the end of the well-known **Boesmankloof Hiking Trail**. This 16-km trail links Greyton with the village of **McGregor** on the northern side of the Riviersonderend Mountains (see page 224 for further details). For tourist information, contact **Greyton Tourism** ① *29 Main St, T028-2549564, www.greyton.net, Tue-Fri 1000-1630, Sat 1000-1600*.

Swellendam and around ⊜🕜🔺⊝🕒 ₩ *pp270-274. Colour map 8, B3.*

Founded in 1745, Swellendam is the third oldest European town in South Africa, and it is also one of its most picturesque. The main centre bears witness to its age with an avenue of mature oak trees and whitewashed Cape Dutch homesteads. Unfortunately, before the town fully appreciated their inherent charm and tourist potential, many of the trees and older buildings were knocked down in 1974 to widen the main street. Nevertheless, the town is very pretty and has an appealing, quiet atmosphere, which, combined with the rural setting and beautiful views, makes it a very pleasant spot to spend a day or two. Swellendam also acts as an important base for exploring the region, with the Breede River Valley, the Little Karoo and the coast all within easy reach, and it is roughly halfway between Cape Town and the Garden Route.

Tourist information is available at **Swellendam Tourism** ① *Oefeningshuis, Voortrek St, T028-5142770, www.swellendamtourism.co.za, Mon-Fri 0900-1300, 1400-1700, Sat 0900-1200*. This office produces a leaflet called *Swellendam Treasures* which outlines the interesting Cape Dutch buildings still standing today.

Background

Swellendam started as a trading outpost for the Dutch East India Company. The new settlement was named after Governor Hendrik Swellengrebel and his wife, Ten Damme. Once established, all sorts of characters passed through looking for their fortunes or more land. One of the most successful was Joseph Barry who, in the 1800s, had a virtual monopoly on all trade between Cape Town and the new settlements in the Overberg and Little Karoo.

In 1795 a particularly strange event took place. Just at the point when British soldiers were bringing an end to Dutch rule in the Cape, the burghers of Swellendam declared themselves to be an independent republic, in a reaction to the mal-administration and corruption of the Dutch East India Company. Hermanus Steyn was president from 17 June to 4 November 1795 but, once the British had set up a new regime in Cape Town, the republic was quietly forgotten about. During the 19th century the town prospered and grew as the agricultural sector gradually expanded. This came to an abrupt halt in May 1865, when a fire that started in a baker's destroyed 40 of the town's finest old buildings. Even greater harm was caused by a prolonged drought and when, in 1866, the influential Barry Empire was declared bankrupt the whole region's fortunes declined. Today the town is a prosperous community, and many of the old buildings are still standing, or have been restored.

Sights

Of all the old Cape buildings in town the **Drostdy Museum** ① *18 Swellengrebel St, T028-5141138, www.drostdymuseum.com, Mon-Fri 0900-1645, Sat and Sun 1000-1545, small entrance fee*, is the most impressive and is often described as one of the country's great architectural treasures. The main building dates from 1747, built as the official residence and seat for the local magistrate or *landdrost*. Originally built in the shape of a T, the addition of two wings changed the form to an H. Inside, some of the floors have been preserved; what was the lounge has a lime-sand floor, while the kitchen floor is made from cow dung, which helps keep the room cool. The museum concentrates on local history, with a well-preserved collection of 18th- and 19th-century furniture. Within the grounds is a restored Victorian cottage, **Mayville**, which has an antique rose garden plus the original gazebo and is today home to a coffee shop.

Close by is an open-air display, on the Crafts Green, of many of the early farm tools, charcoal burners, wagons and a horse-driven mill complete with threshing floor. Opposite the museum is the **Old Gaol building** ① *T028-5143847*, which housed both prisoners and local government officials, including the jailer who was also the postmaster. In the middle of all the cells was one without windows, known as the 'black hole'. Today, this is a local arts and crafts centre, with a good café (see Eating, page 273).

Not far from the town centre are more restored buildings from the town's early days. The **Oefeningshuis** (1838) first served as a place for the religious instruction of freed slaves; it now houses the tourist office. Note the painted plaster clock face, which reads 1215, set above a working clock. This was designed for illiterate church goers – if the painted face was the same as the clock's, it was time for service. Worth a look is the fine, domineering **Dutch Reformed Church**. This large whitewashed building has a tall central clock tower and a mix of architectural styles. Just next to the church, on **Church Square**, are some fine examples of early two-storey town houses built by wealthy farmers who used to visit the town for holy communion. The square had to be large enough to hold their ox wagons. Another grand town house is the **Auld House** dating from 1802 which for many years was the family home for the Overberg trader, Joseph Barry. Inside is some furniture, originally fitted on a steamer which used to sail between Cape Town and Port Beaufort. Also worth a visit is the small **Church of St Luke** built in 1865. Finally, look out for the shop **Buirski & Co**, built in 1880. It has one of the finest examples of Victorian wrought-iron balconies and fittings in the town.

Swellendam is an ideal base for exploring this part of the Overberg. Close by is the small Bontebok National Park, and the larger Marloth Nature Reserve. They have only simple accommodation and both can easily be visited on a day trip. **Suurbraak** (sour marsh) 25 km towards Tradouw Pass, is a small village established by the London Missionary Society in 1812. Many of the buildings have been restored to their original forms, and it is very much a living museum. This is one of the few places in South Africa, where whites were required to move out during Apartheid. The village is well known for its handmade wooden chairs.

Bontebok National Park → *Colour map 8, B3.*
Although this is one of South Africa's 20 national parks, it has less of interest than other parks. Nevertheless, it is a good place to spot several species of antelope, and has a pleasant riverside setting. Most of the park is accessible by car, and there are two 2-km self-guided nature trails which you can walk at any time without a permit or booking. Guided walks are organized when there is sufficient demand. Swimming and fishing are both possible in the Breede River, but only within the confines of the campsite. An angling licence must be shown.

Ins and outs The park is 238 km from Cape Town and 6 km from Swellendam. The turning off the N2 is clearly signposted, on the George side of Swellendam. There is a 5-km gravel road from the highway to the entrance. Information is available at the **SANParks office** ① *T028-5142735, www.sanparks.org, Oct-Apr 0700-1900, May-Sep 0700-1800, R60.* There is a camp here, which SANParks is currently revamping.

Background At the beginning of the 20th century the bontebok was the rarest species of antelope in Africa. It had been hunted and driven off its natural habitat by the settler farmers in the Overberg. Fortunately, something even scarcer came to their rescue – a group of local conservation-minded farmers, who recognized the need to set up a protected area to save the remaining animals. In 1931 the first reserve was established, but it was not until the herd was moved to a more suitable environment beside the Breede River in 1960 that the numbers started to recover significantly. This has proved to be a success but, although no longer endangered, there are still not many places where the bontebok can be seen in the wild. Today, other antelope indigenous to the Overberg have been introduced to the reserve including red hartebeest, steenbok and duiker plus the rare Cape mountain zebra.

Marloth Nature Reserve → *Colour map 8, B3.*
This mountain reserve encompasses a number of the peaks and forested valleys of the Langeberg Mountains. Looking at the peaks from the centre of Swellendam, locals claim to be able to tell the time between 0700 and 1300 by the shadows cast by seven of the **Clock Peaks**. There is a variety of hiking trails, including a rewarding six-day route. Small stands of indigenous forest have been preserved. These are very important when you consider that the mountains were once forested all the way along this coast from Cape Town to Port Elizabeth and beyond. Today, only a few small pockets of forest remain.

Some of the more common indigenous trees which can be seen in the reserve include yellowwood, red alder, hard pear, spoon wood, Cape beech and cherrywood. The wildlife is confined to mountain species – look out for klipspringer standing on rock outcrops, and if you're lucky you may glimpse bushbuck in the cooler, darker patches of forest. The colourful Cape sugarbird is a common sight on flowering aloes and ericas.

Ins and outs

Follow the signs to the forest station, 3 km to the north of Swellendam. The ideal time to visit is in the spring (September and October) when the flowers are at their best. The wettest months are March and October. Permits for the six-day walk or climbing the peaks are issued from the **park office** ① *T028-5141410, www.capenature.co.za, Mon-Fri 0800-1600.* Check availability at weekends, as numbers are limited. The only accommodation within the reserve is in basic huts (see Sleeping, page 272).

Hiking The **Swellendam Trail** is the principal hiking trail in and around Marloth Reserve. The complete circular route is 74 km long and hikers are advised to allow six days for the full circuit. This was the first trail designed in the Cape to return hikers to their starting point without having to backtrack. Hiking conditions require a medium level of fitness, as there are strenuous segments when the trail goes around several peaks. Each day's walking passes through montane forest as well as open fynbos terrain. Be wary of the sun and carry plenty of water. The six overnight huts are fitted out with bunks, toilets and drinking water. Do not walk in heavy rain or misty conditions.

Shorter day walks are possible in the vicinity of the entrance gate by the forest station. Six trails have been defined, ranging from an easy stroll to the picnic site in a sheltered valley known as the **Hermitage**, to an all-day trail taking in two of the peaks closest to Swellendam. The most difficult day walk climbs from the car park to the **Tienuurkop peak** (1195 m), along a ridge to **Twaalfuurkop** (1428 m), and then zigzags back down to the entrance. The walk is 9 km and takes at least eight hours. The other day walks are on the lower slopes and most can be completed in less than three hours. Day walks do not require permits or pre-booking.

Heidelberg to Albertina ● ⇒ *pp270-274. Colour map 7, B1.*

Continuing east from Swellendam along the N2 highway, the road bypasses several small agricultural towns which have little of interest to detain most tourists. One of these settlements is **Heidelberg**, which is dominated by its Dutch Reformed church on the banks of the Duivenhoks River. The first settlers arrived in the valley in 1725, and in 1855 it was named Heidelberg after the city in Germany. To the north in the Langeberg Mountains is the Grootvadersbosch Nature Reserve (see below). The Anglican church, St Barnabas, has some wood sculptures of note and particularly fine rose windows. **Tourist information** ① *25 Van Riebeeck St, T028-7222700, www.heidelberginfo.co.za.*

Grootvadersbosch Nature Reserve → *Colour map 8, B3.*

① *All advance details and reservations are made through the manager, T028-4255020, or www.capenature.co.za. Permits are available in the reserve on arrival, but note that the trails have a limit of 12 people so it is a good idea to pre-book.*

This 250 ha of preserved forest is the finest remaining cover of indigenous forest in the southwestern Cape. There is an excellent hiking trail (see below) and paths which provide easy access to the forest. The early settlers in the Overberg managed to satisfy the huge demand for hardwoods at the turn of the 20th century throughout South Africa, but in doing so almost totally destroyed the unique forests in the Cape. Grootvadersbosch was established to preserve the area and restore it to its former beauty. Between 1896 and 1913 alien trees such as ash, bluegum, Californian redwood, Australian blackwood and camphor were planted on the slopes which had been cleared of indigenous forest. Efforts are now being made to reclaim these areas. The wilderness areas remain untouched and this is reflected in the richness of wildlife and birdlife one encounters while walking here. There is a good chance of seeing the shy bushbuck in the forest.

Ins and outs The reserve is 22 km northwest of Heidelberg on the R322 towards Tradouw Pass. Coming from Swellendam, take the R324 turning for Suurbraak then keep heading in the direction of Heidelberg – the left turning for the reserve is 27 km further on. There is a simple campsite by the entrance gates with 10 camping pitches and two cottages, communal ablution block and thatched braai area with fridge. Look out for a bird hide 500 m into the reserve. The nearest comfortable accommodation is in Swellendam, 40 km away.

Hiking The **Bushbuck Trail** is a series of paths allowing you to choose a route between 2 km and 10 km without having to backtrack too often. The paths weave between the moist and dry forest of the slopes of the Langeberg Mountains. The best periods for walking are May to July and December to January.

Witsand → *Colour map 8, B3.*

Just outside Swellendam is the R324 turning to Witsand, a quiet, picturesque seaside town at the mouth of the Breede River. The area is best known for its land-based whale watching and its excellent fishing, but there is little other reason to come here. The town is small and peaceful and as such attracts mainly older couples wanting to escape the bustle of larger resorts. From June to November southern right whales come to the bay to calve and rear their young and the town is frequently dubbed the 'whale nursery' by the regional tourist boards. In 2005 a count by helicopter recorded 94 whales including 43 calves in the bay on one day during the season. In town, one building of note is the wool store built for the Barry family business. The neighbouring settlement of **Port Beaufort** was built by Joseph Barry, a businessman from Swellendam who, for a period, dominated all forms of trade in the Overberg (see page 265). Large boats from Cape Town unloaded their cargo here, which was then transferred to river boats and taken upstream as far as Malgas. The Barry family built a church in the village in 1859, which is now a national monument. For tourist information contact the **Witsand Tourism Bureau** ① *T028-5371010, www.witsandtourism.co.za, on the main street.*

Riversdale → *Colour map 8, B3.*

Riversdale is a small farming centre based around wheat, wool and potatoes. There is little in town for visitors other than fuel and food, although there is the small **Julius Gordon Africana Museum** ① *Long St, Mon-Fri 0800-1300*, which outlines the lives of several local characters and is home to some paintings by Thomas Baines and Peter Wenning. Around the town are no fewer than 15 stone churches, the oldest being the St Matthew's Anglican Church, built in 1856. The district is well known for the growing of Agathosma shrubs which emit a very strong aroma. For anyone with an interest in wild flowers the **Van Riebeeck Garden** has a superb collection of aloes and vygies. The best time to visit is in May and June when the flowers are in full bloom. The **Werner Frehse Nature Reserve** outside the town has a few small antelope. The road to Ladismith in the north crosses the spectacular Garcia Pass before entering the Little Karoo. The **tourist office** ① *corner of Mitchell and Hudson streets, T028-7131996, www.tourismriversdale.co.za, Mon-Fri 0830-1600*, is not very used to drop-in visitors.

Still Bay → *Colour map 8, B3.*

This small fishing village is in a beautiful spot straddling both sides of the Kafferkuils River. On the west bank is a fishing harbour, while the east bank holds a cluster of holiday cottages and shops. The beach is sandy and safe for swimmers. Surfers speak of good waves here, while the river is ideal for small pleasure boats. The bridge joining the two settlements was opened in 1955, replacing a pontoon that had been in use since 1930. Like many South African seaside towns, Still Bay remains eerily quiet for much of the year, but during the school summer holidays the place comes alive with families. Next to the **tourist office** ① *on the east bank, T028-7542602, www.stilbaaitourism.com*, there's a fountain where eels are fed Monday to Saturday at 1100.

Albertina → *Colour map 7, B1.*

Being only a few hours from Cape Town and tantalizingly close to the Garden Route, few people stop here. The predominant business is still wheat and sheep farming, although the local economy was able to diversify following the discovery in the 1920s of large ochre deposits. Another unusual product collected around Albertina is the juice from aloe plants, *Aloe ferox*, which is an important ingredient in medicine and cosmetics. You can visit the **Alcare Aloe Factory** ① *T028-7351454, www.alcare.co.za*, just outside town. They conduct free daily tours and sell a variety of aloe skincare products and there's a coffee shop.

Garden Route Game Lodge ① *7 km east of Albertina off the N2, T028-7351200, www.grgamelodge.co.za*, is a private game lodge that has been stocked with a number of species of large game including giraffe, white rhino, lion, elephant, kudu, zebra, wildebeest and buffalo. It's a popular overnight stay from Cape Town and one of the nearest places to the city for wildlife viewing. Transfers from Cape Town can be arranged. There is luxurious accommodation at the lodge but day visitors are also welcome for game drives and lunch, which must be pre-booked. As well as morning and evening game drives, tours of the reptile centre are on offer where the resident herpetologist (reptile man) will share his knowledge of snakes, crocodiles and other cold-blooded creatures. You can also visit the cheetah-breeding centre and there is a variety of programmes for children including bush survival skills, children's game drives and guided bush and insect walks. ▶ *See also Sleeping, page 272.*

On the N2 10 km out of Albertina and 40 km before Mossel Bay you'll see a crowd of people gathered at the Gouritz River bridge. This is a popular **bungee jump** ① *daily 0900-1700, T044-6977001, www.faceadrenalin.com, bungee R170 single, R220 tandem*, from the road bridge into the 65-m-deep river gorge. Booking isn't necessary, just pitch up and jump. It's fun but with a drop of only around 60 m, it pales in comparison to the 216-m Bloukrans Bridge Bungee further up the Garden Route, which is the longest in the world.

Overberg interior listings

Sleeping

East to Caledon on the N2 p262
B Villa Exner, 11 Essenhout Av, Grabouw,
T021-8593596, www.villaexner.com. Country
retreat with 4 suites in the main whitewashed
manor house and 2 garden units, elegantly
furnished with art and designer pieces, 2
lounges with fireplaces, library and dining
rooms, swimming pool in rolling lawns, close
to the Hottentots Holland Nature Reserve.
C Houw Hoek Inn, off N2 12 km past Grabouw,
T021-2849646, www.houwhoekinn.co.za.
The oldest licensed hotel in South Africa.
50 a/c rooms in an elegant country hotel, the
oldest section dates from 1779, the upstairs
was built in 1860, while there's a newer block
of modern rooms. All the rooms have en
suite bathrooms, the dining room is in a
converted farm building, and is very popular
at weekends when dinner dances are held on
Sat night and there's a traditional roast Sun
lunch. The gardens are dominated by large
old oak and blue gum trees, swimming pool.
C Wildekrans Country House, Houw Hoek
Farm, turn left at **Houw Hoek Inn** sign, follow
road round to left, the farm is on your right,
T021-2849827, www.wildekrans.co.za. 6 B&B
rooms, or self-catering cottages with TV and log
fires, dinner on request, swimming pool, wild
farm gardens with lots of rose bushes, national
monument, quiet setting on a working farm.

Hottentots Holland Nature Reserve p262
There are 2 overnight huts in the reserve:
F Keurkieboom Chalet and **Rusbos**,
sleeping 2, and up to 6, respectively. There is
no accommodation at the reserve entrance,

Nuweberg, but there are some toilets and
shower facilities. Each hut is equipped with
bunks, mattresses, basic cooking facilities
and water. **Keurkieboom** has solar panels
to provide electricity. Fires are only allowed
at braai sites as there is a high risk of veld fires.

Caledon and around p263
B The Caledon Hotel, Spa & Casino,
1 Nerina Av, T028-2145100, www.the
caledon.co.za, 1 km out of town just off the
N2. Unattractive modern complex based
at the historic springs, with a flashy casino,
95 a/c rooms and 3 restaurants, including
an Italian one. There is a pub with log fires,
extensive gardens, a number of hot and
cold pools, a beauty clinic, mountain bikes
for hire, full-size snooker tables, 18-hole
putting golf and the excellent Victorian
hot-spring baths enclosed by a pavilion.
Most people come here for the brash casino.

Greyton p264
B The Post House, 42 Main Rd,
T028-2549995, www.theposthouse.co.za.
A high-quality country guesthouse,
13 rooms with a Beatrix Potter theme, the
honeymoon suite is called Two Bad Mice.
Each room has an open fire and a private
veranda. The oldest parts of the building,
which was once a post office, date back
to 1860. Good food and service, picnic
baskets prepared to order, colourful
gardens, swimming pool, quiet setting,
easy access to the village. There's an
adjoining coffee and hand-made
chocolate shop. Recommended.
C Greyton Lodge, 46 Main Rd, T028-2549876,
www.greytonlodge.com. 15 en suite rooms,
some with 4-poster beds, in a renovated
1882 trading store that has also served as
a police station, excellent restaurant open
to non-guests from 0800-late, swimming
pool, gardens, comfortable country lodge
feel, a neat whitewashed building with a
corrugated-iron roof and small veranda.

Swellendam and around *p264*

B De Kloof, 8 Weltevreden St, T028-5141303, www.dekloof.co.za. Elegant and luxurious thatched Cape Dutch homestead (1801) set in a neat garden, 6 double rooms with en suite bathroom, contemporary African and Asian decor, TV lounge, library and cigar bar, gym with mountain views, garden, swimming pool, champagne breakfasts included in the rate, evening meals available, very friendly. Recommended.

B C Adin & Sharon's Hideaway, 10 Hermanus Steyn St, T028-5143316, www.adinbb.co.za. Award-winning B&B in the centre of town. 5 spacious, comfortable en suite rooms with a/c, in a Victorian cottage, overlooking a neat, shady garden with 600 rose bushes and a splash pool. Excellent breakfasts, very friendly hosts. Recommended.

B-C Old Mill Guest House & Restaurant, 241 and 243 Voortrek St, T028-5142790, www.oldmill.co.za. En suite rooms in a beautiful listed building set in a spacious garden with a stream flowing through, superb meals served in the restaurant which is well known for its Belgian pancakes and waffles. Slightly overpriced, but still recommended.

B-C Klippe River Country House, from the N2 take the R60, left at crossroads, 2 km, T028-5143341, www.klipperivier.com. 6 double rooms in and around a restored Cape Dutch homestead (1820), declared a national monument. Large rooms with brass beds, gleaming wooden floors, some with cosy fireplaces and under thatch, private balconies, superb restaurant (see Eating, page 273), swimming pool, a peaceful and superior location, look out for owls in the oak trees, family owned and managed, no children under 8. Recommended.

C Coachman Guesthouse, 14 Drostdy St, T028-5142294, www.coachman.co.za. Lovely whitewashed converted historic homestead with 3 en suite double rooms with separate entrances, plus 2 thatched garden cottages with log fires. TV lounge, laundry, evening meals available, swimming pool.

C Klein Drostdy, 12 Drostdy St, T028-5141542. An old home full of beautiful antiques and 6 rooms with en suite bathroom. Good breakfasts, swimming pool, billiard room, large leafy gardens, near the museum.

C Swellengrebel, 91 Voortrek St, T028-5141144, www.swellengrebel hotel.co.za. Large, bland and modern hotel set on the main road, with 48 rooms, some with mountain views, restaurant with good food, swimming pool, pool room, jacuzzi, sauna and gym, noisy public bar. Comfortable, but seems a shame to stay somewhere so characterless compared to most of the B&Bs in town. Ask about weekend discounts.

C-E Swellendam Caravan Park, Glen Barry Rd, T028-5142705. Caravan park with 20 fully equipped thatched chalets, 4 beds, bring your own linen, 100 well-grassed and shady tent and caravan stands. A beautiful and peaceful setting with good mountain views within walking distance of town centre, popular during school holidays.

D Moolmanshof, 217 Voortrek St, T028-5143258, www.moolmanshof. homestead.com. A homestead built in 1798 and full of character with 3 en suite rooms, furnished with antiques, guest lounge with TV, swimming pool, mature gardens, extra beds available for children. Recommended.

E-F Swellendam Backpackers, 5 Lichtenstein St, T028-5142648, www.swellendambackpackers.co.za. An excellent hostel with a small dorm in the main house, plus individual Wendy houses (no electricity but paraffin lamps) in secluded corners around the garden, lots of camping space, internet, well-organized kitchen, home-cooked breakfasts and dinners. Can arrange local tours, hiking in the mountains and visits to the nearby Bontebok National Park. The Baz Bus calls here twice a day.

Marloth Nature Reserve *p266*
For reservations contact T021-6593500,
www.capenature.co.za.
C Cottages 2 basic self-catering cottages,
1 sleeping 8, the other 5, good value for
families or groups, fully equipped kitchens
with microwave, stove, fridge and all utensils,
bedding and towels provided, comfortable
option especially for the night before
tackling the Swellendam Hiking Trail.
E Hiking huts 6 basic huts equipped with
bunks, bush toilets and drinking water,
which can accommodate 22 hikers. If you
stay in these huts bring all your provisions,
they only provide a roof and a mattress.
Firewood is only provided at 2 of the huts,
Koloniesbos and Wolfkloof, but you are
not permitted to light fires elsewhere in
the reserve. Bring a gas stove for cooking.

Witsand *p268*
B-C Breede River Lodge, T028-5371631,
www.breederiverlodge.co.za. Comfortable
en suite lodges and hotel cabins overlooking
the river, well furnished, some with dining
area and kitchenette, great views, bar,
restaurant serves fresh seafood. Boats and
fishing tackle for hire for trips up the river.
C Big Cob Chalets, 104 Main Rd, T028-
5371942. Neat gardens around 4 self-catering
chalets with 3 rooms, each room has twin
beds, fully equipped, thatched roof, braai
area, secure parking.

Riversdale *p268*
D Sleeping Beauty, 3 Long St, T028-7131651,
www.sleepingbeautyguesthouse.com.
A Victorian guesthouse built as a parsonage
in 1880 with 6 double rooms, home-made
breads for breakfast, lush gardens and
double-storey veranda.

Still Bay *p269*
C Papillon, corner of Perlemoen and Seebreis
St, T082-7748381, www.papillonstilbaai.co.za.
Beachfront cottage sleeping 6 and a separate
flat that sleeps 2, both with fully equipped
kitchens, bright and airy decor, gardens

rolling down to beach, views of the bay,
braai area, TV and video, internet, wheelchair friendly.

Albertina *p269*
AL Garden Route Game Lodge, 7 km east
of Albertina off the N2, transfers from Cape
Town can be arranged, T028-7351200,
www.grgamelodge.co.za. Accommodation
in main lodge or in secluded thatched
chalets, decorated with an African theme,
superb restaurant serving local dishes,
comfortable bar, swimming pool, rates
include game drives and meals, special
activities for children, horse riding and
quad-biking also on offer.
D Albertina Country Hotel, Main St,
T028-7351030, info@albertinahotel.co.za.
Comfortable town hotel with friendly
service, 16 en suite rooms with TV, good
traditional restaurant, rates are for B&B.
If you are not staying the pub lunches are
recommended on your way through.

🍴 Eating

East to Caledon on the N2 *p262*
🍴 **Houw Hoek Farm Stall**, by the
Houw Hoek Inn, T021-2849015, see
Sleeping, page 270. A full-blown shop
and café serving light lunches, coffee
and picnic hampers, and
it's open on Fri nights for dinner.
  Several other local farms in this region
have small stalls selling a variety of fresh
fruit juices and other fruit products.

Caledon and around *p263*
🍴🍴 **Dassiesfontein**, on the N2 between
Caledon and Bot River, T028-2141475.
0830-1730. Country restaurant and farm
stall selling home-made bread, cheese
and biltong, tables in the cottage decorated
with antiques, local dishes such as bobotie
and bredie, good chicken and game pies,
for breakfast try the fried slice of bread
with apricot jam.

Greyton p264

Greyton-on-Main, 31 Main St, T028-2549722. Daily 0800-1100, 1900-late, Thu-Sun also open for lunch 1200-1500. Housed in an old trading store with a lovely bar and blue porcelain on the tables, à la carte or set menu, unusual European dishes such as eisbein, sauerkraut and mash, plus a fine cheeseboard and the chef's special Belgium chocolate mousse.

Swellendam and around p264

Most local restaurants are closed Sun evening; be prepared to eat by 2100.

Klippe Rivier Country House, see Sleeping, page 271, T028-5143341. Open for breakfast and dinner, booking essential. Popular restaurant, delicious Cape haute cuisine served in a classic Cape Dutch manor with manicured gardens, good wine list. Recommended.

The Connection, 132 Voortrek St, T028-5141988. 1200-2100, closed Wed and Sun afternoon. Pleasant restaurant serving light lunches, and meatier dinners such as venison, hearty soups, some Italian dishes, outdoor tables on terrace.

Herberg Roosjie van de Kaap, 5 Drostdy St, T028-5143001. Breakfast 0800-1000, dinner Tue-Sun 1900-2130. Local word has this down as the best place to eat in town. Booking essential for dinner. Cosy atmosphere in a candlelit room with thick walls and a low roof. Superb gourmet pizzas plus hearty South African fare, good steaks and seafood, fine wines. Recommended.

Koornlands, 5 Voortrek St, T028-5143567. Open Wed-Mon for lunch and dinner. A historic Cape Dutch cottage serving local food such as crocodile steaks, ostrich fillets, loin of kudu, guinea fowl and freshwater trout, washed down with local wines. Recommended.

La Belle Alliance, Swellengrebel St, T028-5142252. 0800-1700, closed evenings. Good place for a lazy lunch in a lovely setting under the trees by the stream. Popular giant breakfasts, good sandwiches, fully licensed.

Mattsen's Steak House, Voortrek St, T028-5142715. Open 1200-2130. Busy restaurant serving excellent, good-value steaks, popular with tour groups. Recommended. Close to the *Oefeningshuis* (tourist office).

Old Mill Restaurant and Tea Garden, 241 Voortrek St, T028-5142790, see Sleeping. Open 0700-late. Good afternoon teas, syrupy waffles and cinnamon pancakes, outside tables in pretty gardens with chickens pecking around, romantic candlelit tables inside for dinner, South African dishes such as Karoo lamb or local curries.

Zanddrift at Stromsvlei, off the N2 between Swellendam and Riviersonderend in the direction of Bonnievale on the R317, T028-2611167. Fri-Wed 0830-1700. Breakfast and dinner, closed evenings, country cooking and a changing menu of steaks, pasta and salads, local wines, a good place to sample a typical large South African breakfast, good value. Recommended.

Coffee Shop at the Old Gaol, Drostdy Museum, T028-514384/, www.oldgaol restaurant.co.za. Daytime licensed café serving light meals, coffee and cakes, home-made lemonade, and local specialities such as melktert.

⊛ Festivals and events

Caledon p263

Mar A sort of harvest festival, the rather unusual **Beer and Bread Festival** is held in a large marquee near the Wild Flower Garden. Live music is laid on in the evenings, and plenty of local farm produce is available. **Sep** To coincide with the annual bloom of wild flowers, Caledon holds a **Wild Flower Festival**. It is an excellent opportunity to see the plants which make up the Cape fynbos, including protea, erica, gladioli and iridaceae. The principal display hall is in Hope St, a short walk from the town museum, and tractor rides are on offer to see flowers on local farms.

▲ Activities and tours

Caledon and around *p263*
Mountain biking
The Klein Swartberg is a popular venue for mountain biking and an annual rally is held here. Contact the tourist office for details.

Swellendam and around *p264*
Golf
9-hole 72-par course, Andrew Whyte St, in the lee of the Langeberg Mountains, T028-5141026, www.swellendamgolfcourse.co.za.

Tour operators
Bontebok Tours, 23 Swellengrebel St, T028-5143650, www.bontebok.co.za. Excellent local travel agent, organizes a range of local tours plus trips to Bontebok and Marloth parks, bird-watching trips, township and walking tours. Also acts as local information office and has internet access.
Breede River Dream Cruises, T028-5421049, www.rivercruises.co.za. A range of houseboats with onboard sleeping, aimed at fishermen, can negotiate 50 km of the river.
Felix Unite River Adventures, T021-4041830 (Cape Town office), www.felixunite.co.za. Professional outfit that runs trips from Cape Town to the Breede River, with overnight stays in bush camps, restored Voortrekker ox wagons, or A-frame houses.
Umkulu, T021-8537952 (Cape Town), www.umkulu.co.za. Another operator that will take you to the Breede River from Cape Town for a day's float, some wine tasting, and an overnight at a local lodge.

⊖ Transport

Caledon and around *p263*
Bus
Greyhound, **Intercape** and **Translux** serve Caledon and **Swellendam**. Buses stop at the Caledon Hotel and Spa and the Swellengrebel Hotel in Swellendam and run daily to **Cape Town** (2 hrs); and **Durban** (24 hrs) via **Port Elizabeth** (9 hrs).
Bus companies Greyhound, T083-9159000, www.grey-hound.co.za; **Intercape**, T086-1287287, www.inter cape.co.za; **Translux**, T086-1589282, www.translux.co.za.

Car
Continuing east from Caledon, the N2 passes through rolling wheat fields towards **Mossel Bay**. From Caledon you can also deviate inland to the villages of **Genadendal** and **McGregor**; the R406 makes a convenient loop. Alternatively take the R316 south towards **Bredasdorp** into the heart of Overberg country. The R319 rejoins the N2 just before **Swellendam**.

Swellendam and around *p264*
240 km to **Cape Town**, 225 km to **George**, 560 km to **Port Elizabeth**, 270 km to **Knysna**.

Bus
The Baz Bus, T021-4392323, www.bazbus. com, stops daily in Swellendam and can take you as far as **Port Elizabeth** in a day. From **Cape Town** it arrives about 1200 allowing plenty of time to see the sights in the afternoon. From **Port Elizabeth** it arrives around 1800.

⊕ Directory

Swellendam *p264*
Banks Standard Bank, 32a Voortrek St; ABSA, 14 Voortrek St. **Medical services** Hospital, Drostdy St, T028-5141140.

Great Karoo → www.centralkaroo.co.za.

From Cape Town the N1 heads northeast through the Great Karoo, a vast, ancient plateau that covers nearly a third of the total area of the country. It is a beautiful and extraordinary region, as much for its history as for its remarkable emptiness. Today, the landscape is a parched expanse of baked red earth inhabited by tough merino sheep and their even tougher owners. Endless plains stretch between stark mountain ranges, with little but the characteristic steel windmills peppering the horizons. Hundreds of millions of years ago, however, this was an enormous swamp inhabited by dinosaurs, making it a key palaeontological site. More recently, the region has played a significant historical role, as the Voortrekkers penetrated the interior with their ox wagons, evidence of which can be seen in a handful of perfectly preserved Victorian settlements. The name Karoo comes from karusa, a Khoi word which means dry, barren, thirstland.
▶▶ *For listings, see pages 282-284.*

The Koup ☺ ▶▶ *pp282-284.*

The 'Koup' refers to the southern districts of the Great Karoo, traversed by the N1 highway between Cape Town and Johannesburg. Travelling east from the Hex River Valley, the countryside quickly becomes arid and seemingly barren, with vast stretches of uninhabited semi-desert stretching to all horizons. Despite the area's arid appearance there is a surprisingly abundant supply of underground water, brought to the surface by the windmills which dot the plains. The most common vegetation is the Karoo bush which forms the staple diet of the merino sheep bred here. Most of the farms are used for sheep, although more and more are being converted into game farms for game viewing and hunting. The sheer scale of the area is remarkable – the average farm size is over 20,000 ha, which makes popping round to the neighbours an arduous task. The isolated Karoo towns have a great sense of history, with many preserved 19th-century buildings, as well as a delightfully slow pace of life. Although rather off the beaten track, visitors often end up spending the night in one of these towns while en route to Cape Town or Johannesburg. None of them warrant a special visit, but have an hour or two's worth of distractions if you want to take a break from driving. Note that if you arrive in South Africa in either Johannesburg or Cape Town and tour the country, the likely route back to your starting point (to meet return or onward flights) will be along the N1. If you don't want to fly, you can negotiate this route by returning a hire car or travelling by mainline bus.

Climate

The dry summer months are oppressively hot. During and after the rains, however, the countryside takes on an entirely different appearance. The first rains arrive in the winter months, although centres such as Graaff-Reinet and Colesberg receive their rains in late summer. If you plan to hike in the region remember that summer daytime temperatures frequently exceed 40°C, while in the winter the nights get very cold and snow can fall on the mountain peaks.

Touws River → *Colour map 8, A2.*

As the railways moved further inland from Cape Town, this became an important depot for locomotives, bringing about the growth of the town in the 1870s. However, since electrification its importance as a railway centre has all but vanished. The area has become a graveyard for old **steam engines** – an impressive if somewhat eerie open-air museum. In its early days the station was known as Montagu Road; its present name was adopted in 1883. In addition to the steam engines, look out for a pair of concrete pillars behind the town hotel, the Loganda. They were used to mount astronomical instruments to view the transit of **Venus**. On 6 December 1882 a British astronomer took readings to help calculate the distance between the sun and earth.

Aquila Private Game Reserve
① *Off the R46 south of Touws River, T021-4054513 (Cape Town), www.aquilasafari.com.*
In the last few years this private game reserve has had a rather staggering R25 million spent on it, mostly through the relocation of large animals. It's also the closest game reserve to Cape Town (less than two hours' drive) with lion, giraffe and rhino. It is set among 4500 ha of mountains, rivers, valleys and kloofs which make up the southern Karoo highlands and is now home to a wide range of species, many of which were relocated from other parts of the country. As well as the above, there are buffalo, black and blue wildebeest, zebra, a variety of antelope, bat-eared fox, mountain leopard, crocodile, ostrich, black-backed jackal and hippo. It has the largest breeding herd of white rhino in the Cape and, in February 2005, the first white rhino was born at the reserve, thought to be the first rhino born in the Cape for over 200 years. Aquila also has a huge natural wetland, which is home to 172 species of bird including several breeding pairs of the rare and endangered black eagle. There is luxury accommodation on the reserve (see Sleeping, page 282) but you can also visit for the day for a safari and lunch, for around R1500 per person, less if you're in your own car.

Before the arrival of Aquila, the unemployment rate in Touws River was 97%. Today the reserve is the single biggest employer in the region and provides for around 180 families. It also sponsors the local cricket team, school teachers and helped establish Touws River's supermarket and coordinates regular fundraising activities in Cape Town to provide blankets, clothes and basic necessities for the people of Touws River.

Matjiesfontein → *Colour map 8, A3.*
In 1975 the entire village of Matjiesfontein was declared a national monument – small surprise considering the excellent state of repair of its Victorian houses. There is little to the town itself, other than a couple of dusty streets lined with perfectly preserved period houses, the highlight of which is the famous **Lord Milner Hotel**, resplendent with turrets and adorned balconies. The history of the settlement is a reflection of the life of a young Scot, Jimmy Logan, an official on the Cape Government Railways in the 1890s. He originally came here hoping that the dry air would cure a chest complaint. He found the climate so beneficial that he decided to settle permanently. As an ex-railwayman he quickly saw the opportunity to supply water to steam trains from his farm. While the engines took on water, he served the passengers cool drinks and meals as back then the trains had no dining cars. Today, the luxurious **Blue Train** still stops here for lunch. So successful was his business that he built the fashionable **Lord Milner Hotel**, attracting rich and influential guests who suffered from lung complaints. These included Cecil Rhodes and the Sultan of Zanzibar. During the Anglo-Boer War the town became a military headquarters and a marshalling ground for troops. Logan financed a regiment and served in the war – the hotel's turrets were used as lookout posts. Jimmy Logan lived here until his death in July 1920. Another famous resident was the writer and feminist Olive Schriener, whose first novel *The Story of an African Farm* was set in the Karoo. She lived in a

Matjiesfontein cottage from where she corresponded with friends including George Bernard Shaw and William Gladstone.

Today the town is a popular stopover for travellers between the Cape and Johannesburg. There is a small town museum, the **Marie Rawdon Museum**, in the old jail under the railway station, and a newer shed displaying some vintage cars, train carriages and a penny farthing bicycle just to the east of the hotel. The **cemetery**, 11 km to the west, has some interesting monuments and tombstones dating from the 1900s. Visit the hotel for **tourist information** ① *T023-5613011, www.matjiesfontein.com.*

Laingsburg → *Colour map 6, B3.*

Laingsburg, another small town on the N1, started life as a staging post for coaches on a farm belonging to Stephanus Greeff. When the railway arrived, plans for a town were drawn up and in 1879 it was named Laingsburg after the John Laing, a Cape government official. Sadly, little of the original centre remains after a huge flood in 1981 washed away most of the town, though the magistrate's court and the old post office survived. The library contains a collection of photographs taken after the flood. The town hosts an 80-km ultra-marathon through the Karoo in September. For information visit the **Municipality offices** ① *Van Riebeeck St, T023-5511019, www.centralkaroo.co.za/laingsburgdistrict.*

N1 northeast

After crossing the Dwyka River, you reach the small settlement of **Prince Albert Road**. Turning south on the R328 takes you to Prince Albert (45 km), over the **Swartberg Pass**, and to the secluded **Gamkaskloof Valley**, known as 'The Hell' (see page 291). The next settlement of note along the N1 is **Leeu-Gamka**. The name means 'lion', a sad reminder that the last Cape Lion was shot here in 1857, making the species extinct.

Beaufort West ⬤🄵🄾🄾 ▶ *pp282-284. Colour map 7, A2.*

This is the largest and oldest of the Central Karoo towns, but despite its history it is an unattractive place. Most of its energies seem devoted to servicing those travelling from Johannesburg to Cape Town – the N1 passes right through town, lined with petrol stations and fast-food joints. It is known as the 'oasis' town, hard to believe when you see hot, dusty streets but, thanks to the presence of the Nuweveld Mountains to the north, its 150 mm annual rainfall is far higher than other towns in the Karoo. Beaufort West was named after the fifth Duke of Beaufort, father of the Cape governor, Lord Charles Somerset. It was established in 1818 to try and control gun smuggling and general lawlessness in the region. In 1837 it became South Africa's first municipality. Before the railway reached the town in 1880, all of the locally produced merino wool had to be transported to the coast by wagon across the Swartberg Mountains. The earliest route was via Meiringspoort Pass (see page 294), one of several magnificent passes which link the Great Karoo with the Little Karoo.

The country around Beaufort West is home to the largest variety of succulents in the world. In the town itself, there are more different species than in all of Great Britain. Pear trees – some of which date back to the 1830s – provide welcome shade as you walk along the pavements. The **Beaufort West Tourism Bureau** ① *57 Donkin St, T023-4151488, www.beaufortwestsa.co.za, Mon-Fri 0900-1700, Sat 0900-1200,* is an efficient, well-run office and they have prepared some useful material on the region and its major sights.

Sights

The tourist office provides a *Stroll Through Our Town* leaflet that takes about an hour and covers the main sights. The old Town Hall (1867) on Donkin Street houses the **Beaufort West Museum** ① *T023-4152308, Mon-Fri 0830-1245, 1345-1645, Sat 0900-1200, R5.* This has a couple of above-average collections relating to two of the town's most famous past residents – Dr Christiaan Barnard and Dr Eric Louw. Dr Louw was the MP for Beaufort West for many years and rose through the government's ranks to become South Africa's Foreign Minister between 1957 and 1963. The late Dr Barnard is known throughout the world for his pioneering work with heart transplants. He performed the world's first at Groot Schuur hospital in Cape Town in 1967. The displays include awards and trophies given to each, along with some of their personal effects. There is also a replica of Dr Barnard's heart transplant theatre. Next door is the **Dutch Reformed Mission Church** and the **parsonage** in which Dr Barnard spent his childhood. After his death in 2001, his ashes were scattered in the garden. In the next street are some fine examples of Karoo Victorian single-storey houses. These are all private homes; similar buildings can be seen in Matjiesfontein and other Karoo towns. In the **cemetery** is the grave of Stefanus Marais, a member of a group of Voortrekkers from Beaufort West who fought in the 1838 Battle of Blood River in Natal, as well as the graves of several British soldiers killed during the Anglo-Boer War.

Karoo National Park ◑ ►► *pp282-284. Colour map 7, A2.*

Only 5 km from Beaufort West, this national park was created to conserve a representative area of the unique Karoo environment. There are two other conservation areas in the Karoo, each preserving a slightly different ecosystem: the Karoo Nature Reserve near Graaff-Reinet, and the Karoo Mountain Zebra Park at Cradock. Despite limited human presence the environment of the Great Karoo has undergone radical change during the past 150 years and the protected areas are now recognized as important conservation centres as well as popular tourist destinations. Springbok are present in large numbers – a reminder of the once-massive herds that could stretch for several kilometres, which used to cross the Karoo on annual migrations.

Ins and outs

Getting there The main entrance is signposted off the N1 highway 5 km southwest of Beaufort West. The entrance gate is beside the highway and the road takes visitors straight to the park office and accommodation facilities. The gates are open 0500-2200; it is 7 km from the main entrance to the reception office, T023-4152828, which is open 0730-1900. The daily conservation fee per person, which also covers the vehicle, is R60, R30 children. Next to the office is the **Rest Camp** (see Sleeping page 283), which has a restaurant open for breakfast and dinner 0700-1000, 1800-2100, and shop open 0730-2000, selling frozen meat, firewood and booze. The office has trail and park maps as well as pamphlets detailing the main attractions within the park, and every evening except Sunday there is a slideshow. There is a bird hide near the dam close to the camp.

Climate The Karoo is semi-desert, which means extremes – very hot days in summer (average for January is 32°C) with temperatures often reaching over 35°C, and warm days in winter but very cold nights (from June to August frost is common, and snow falls on the mountain peaks). March and April are regarded as the wet months, although the rainfall only averages 250 mm annually.

Background

The 70,000-ha national park was proclaimed in September 1979 after a lengthy and concerted effort by local residents to conserve the Karoo environment before farming practices totally destroyed it. The success of the campaign was primarily due to the efforts of a local farmer, William Quinton. The municipality donated over 7000 ha, and funds raised by the Nature Foundation were used to purchase two farms, Stolshoek and Puttersvlei. The success of the park is attributed to the efforts of the first warden, Bruce Bryden and his wife Helena. Between 1977 and 1980 they saw to the removal of all the old farm fences and ripped out as much alien vegetation as possible. This was not without opposition; local farmers feared the reserve would become a protected breeding ground for predators which would then prey upon their sheep. The numbers of caracal and jackal have increased, but so too have the smaller mammals they traditionally prey on, so they now have less need to hunt the farmers' sheep. The park has modern chalets and camp sites in a scenically situated camp.

The current boundaries of the park encompass an area of Karoo plains, which merge into mountain slopes and a high plateau. The **Nuweveld Mountains** in the north of the park are nearly 2000 m high. The vegetation in the low-lying areas is a mixture of grasses and shrubs such as honey-thorn and the common acacia karroo. On the steep slopes a sourgrass known as renosterbos (*Elytropappus rhinocerotis*) and harpuis flourish. The flora can be studied along the specially laid out Bossie Trail (see below). Note the difference in vegetation cover between areas within the park and the neighbouring farms. The over-grazed farms have little grass cover and small, unpalatable shrubs.

Wildlife

There is a surprisingly diverse range of game and smaller wildlife in the park. Records list 174 species of birdlife, 38 species of reptile, 37 types of gecko and lizard, and five different species of tortoise (this is the largest number in a conservation area in the world). In another effort to help restore the area to its previous state, antelope such as eland, black wildebeest, gemsbok, Cape mountain zebra, springbok and red hartebeest have been moved into the park. The reserve is also home to two endangered species: the **black rhino** and the **riverine rabbit**. While the statistics are impressive, actually spotting most of these animals requires a degree of patience, effort and, of course, luck. Look out for the tent tortoise; it is well camouflaged and looks like an inverted egg box.

Hiking in the park

There are three short day walks known as the **Fossil Trail**, 400 m, the **Pointer's Hiking Trail**, 10 km, and the **Bossie Trail**, 800 m. Each of these explores a different aspect of the park. The most interesting is the the Fossil Trail along which you can see fossils in situ. It has been adapted for the blind as well as people in wheelchairs: Braille boards tell the 250-million-year tale of the region. The trails all start from near the environmental educational centre where further information about the park is on display.

Driving in the park

Visitors in 4WDs are allowed on certain short tracks in the park. The park also has its own vehicle for hire, and day trips with a nature guide and lunch included can be organized. Other trips on offer include night drives and overnight tours. The trails are rough, slippery and steep in parts and previous experience with a 4WD is essential. There are a few rough roads open for game viewing, but given the mountainous conditions you cannot go too far. Walking remains the best way to enjoy the park.

The N1 to Johannesburg

The N1 covers the distance between Cape Town and Johannesburg via Bloemfontein in just over 1400 km, the majority of which runs through the Great Karoo. With a couple of drivers the journey can be made in one very long day but you need to leave early to arrive in either Cape Town or Johannesburg before dark. Alternatively, many people break their journey in one of the regional towns in either the Free State or Western Cape that have no shortage of accommodation for motorists on this route. Recommended overnight stays are Beaufort West (roughly a third of the way from Cape Town), Colesberg (approximately halfway), or Kimberley and Bloemfontein (almost two-thirds of the distance from the Cape to Gauteng). The road is long and straight, and much of the Karoo scenery is featureless – be wary of getting tired behind the wheel and take frequent breaks. The towns have large petrol stations with toilets, shops and a restaurant such as Wimpy, but remember there are some big distances between the centres so fill up with fuel when you can. The road is heavily used by trucks and mainline buses and at times can be very busy – over the few days at the beginning of the Christmas holidays some 500 cars an hour leave Jo'burg with Gauteng families bound for the Cape. Finally, if you are driving through the 'boring' Karoo – pull over to the side of the road, switch off the engine of your car and take a moment before the next truck comes rumbling by. The space and silence is deafening.

East to Colesberg ☻ ⟫ pp282-284. Colour map 7, A2/3.

This tiny settlement of **Three Sisters** is 78 km north of Beaufort West and there's nothing here except an Ultra City for petrol and refreshments. It is however the junction of the N1 and N12. The N1 continues to Johannesburg via Bloemfontein whilst the N12 goes to Johannesburg via Kimberley. The N1 is slightly shorter as far as mileage is concerned. If you want to break the journey by exploring one of these two cities, it is at Three Sisters that you will have to choose which road to follow.

If you decide to continue on the N1 via Bloemfontein, then **Hanover** is the midway point between Cape Town and Johannesburg, and there is a sign marking its geographical importance. Once you have reached here during a long day on the road, remember it is another 700 km in either direction.

Colesberg ☻☻ ⟫ pp282-284. Colour map 4, B2.

Colesberg actually lies in the Northern Cape but for ease of reference it is included here. The town is situated at the base of a distinctive landmark, **Cole's Kop** (1700 m), visible from 40 km away. This rounded rock outcrop was a very important landmark for early settlers, who moved inland across a largely featureless region. In those days it was called Toringberg – Towering Mountain – although some insist it meant Magic Mountain. The town was then named after Sir Lowry Cole, Cape Governor in 1830.

The town is an important junction between the N9, which heads south towards Port Elizabeth and George, and the N1, which cuts right through the centre of town. Many of the town's oldest buildings are found along here, and turning off the N1 takes you to further clusters of Victorian houses tucked between a couple of picturesque hills. In its early days, this was a classic frontier town with illicit trade in a wide range of commodities, especially gunpowder and liquor. During the Anglo-Boer War it was close to the front and several battles were fought in the vicinity. The surrounding hills are named after the British regiments who held them: Suffolk, New Zealand, Worcester and Gibraltar. The town itself was captured by the Boers and for four months was part of the Free State territory.

Today Colesberg is the centre of two very successful businesses: horse breeding and sheep farming. Many champion racehorses have been bred around the town, due mainly to the soil type which yields high-quality grasses and other fodder. The legendary golfer Gary Player owns a nearby stud farm. The majority of visitors are just passing through along the N1 – the town springs to life in the early evening as people arrive, there is a burst of action as bills are settled and fuel tanks filled in the morning, and then Colesberg reverts to a peaceful farming town for the rest of the day. The **tourist office** ① *T051-7530678, www.colesberginfo.co.za*, is on Murray Street.

Sights
There are a few historic buildings mainly along **Bell Street**. The flat-roofed cottages which line the street were built between 1860 and 1870, and have today been attractively restored. There is also an old flour mill which was operated by horses and was the country's last working horse mill until it was turned into a pub a few years ago. The street is named after Charles Bell, a surveyor who is known in philatelic circles for designing a rare Cape Triangular stamp issued in September 1853. There are four churches around town. The most interesting is the **Church of the Province** (1848), designed by the wife of the first Bishop of Cape Town, Lady Grey. She had intended it to be a cathedral, but only the chancel was built. The **Dutch Reformed Church** (1866) is a characteristically grand, whitewashed building.

The **Colesberg Kemper Museum** on Bank Square is a short walk from the Central Hotel, and contains an interesting photo collection, objects relating to the Anglo-Boer War and a 19th-century toy collection. It is a fine, solid two-storey structure built in 1862 to house the Colesberg District Bank, later absorbed by the Standard Bank. Look out for the pane of glass in the museum on which the letters 'DP' have been scratched. In 1866 John O'Reilly, a diamond trader and transport rider from the Northern Cape diamond fields, brought a stone to the Colesberg magistrate, Lorenzo Boyes, who told O'Reilly that the scratching seemed to confirm that the stone was indeed a diamond. This was the first recognized stone to be found in South Africa. The diamond was 21.25 carats, and was bought for £500 by the Cape's governor, Sir Philip Wodehouse.

From Colesburg, the N1 enters the Free State and heads north to Bloemfontein.

Hotel and guesthouse prices
L over US$300   AL US$220-300   A US$150-220
B US$100-150   C US$75-100   D US$35-75
E US$15-35   F under US$15
Restaurant prices
††† over US$30   †† US$15-30   † under US$15
See pages 46-51 for further information.

● Sleeping

Touws River p275

L Aquila Game Lodge, Aquila Private Game Reserve, off the R46 west of Touws River, T021-4054513 (Cape Town), www.aquila safari.com. Tastefully decorated luxury cottages with en suite bathrooms, outdoor showers, ceiling fans, fireplaces, and minibars. Raw materials such as rock, river pebbles, natural wood, reeds and thatch have been used wherever possible to maintain a natural look. There is the **Cigar Bar** and **Boma Restaurant**, and horseback safaris or traditional game drives are included in the price, check the website for details of packages.

D Loganda, T023-3851130, www.loganda lodge.com. The main town hotel, in a 1960s dreary-looking block, but with 15 fairly comfortable rooms, some with a/c, a restaurant, beer garden, pub with DSTV and swimming pool.

Matjiesfontein p276

C Lord Milner, T023-5613011, www.matjies fontein.com. The original old Victorian town hotel is very much part of the town's history. The 53 large rooms are filled with antiques, as is the lounge and entertainingly old-fashioned dining room, which serves good-value meals. There are cheaper rooms in the garden. Don't miss the wonderfully atmospheric old bar. Recommended.

Beaufort West p277

All the best-value lodges and hotels are fully booked months in advance by families from Gauteng, especially at the beginning and end of the long Christmas holidays. For the rest of the year trade is much quieter, although there is a continual flow of people driving between the Cape and Gauteng. Room rates increase during school holidays.

C Lemoenfontein Game Lodge, 2 km north of Beaufort West and 4.5 km off the N1 on the De Jager's Pass road, T023-4152847, www.lemoenfontein.co.za. A luxury lodge with 13 en suite rooms with modern decor, swimming pool, country cooking in the dining room on a wooden deck, game drives and hiking on the farm where giraffe and zebra are present as well as a number of antelope.

C-D Beaufort Manor, 13 Bird St, T023-4152175, www.beaufortmanor.co.za. 16 modern and attractive en suite rooms with private entrances opening onto a courtyard where there is a swimming pool, 5 open-plan self-catering cottages with a/c sleeping up to 4 which are good value for a family, located next to a pond with ducks and swans, very good restaurant and bar, 3-course Karoo dinners, famous for their lamb.

C-D Matoppo Inn, corner of Meintjies and Bird streets, T023-4151055, www.matoppo inn.co.za. Set in a quiet residential street, this was originally the 1834 *drostdy* (magistrate's house), now converted into a luxury guesthouse with high ceilings, beautiful yellowwood floors, comfortable rooms furnished with antiques, traditional Karoo candlelit dinners, neat garden with swimming pool. Cecil Rhodes stayed here on the way to what was then Rhodesia. Recommended.

C-E Wagon Wheel Country Lodge, 500 m north of town centre on the N1, T023-4142145, www.wagonwheel.co.za. Friendly country motel with simple rooms to suit most groups and some camping pitches with a kitchen block, TV, bar, cheap restaurant with filling meals, swimming pool, disabled facilities, laundry service. Booking essential as it's a popular and good-value stopover for motorists on the N1.

D The Flight Deck, based in Beaufort West's old airport terminal building, 12 km north on the N1, T023-4143444, www.theflight deck.co.za. 4 rooms, 3 en suite, 1 with private bathroom, with fans and heaters. Enjoy sundowners and breakfast in the control tower with great views over the Karoo. Simple accommodation but something different. Dinner is available but it must be pre-booked. The airport is still operational for private planes.

D Formula 1, 144 Donkin St, T023-4152421, www.hotelformula1.co.za. Clean, modern, cheap option, characterless, 52 small rooms, drive in late, sleep, and drive out early.

D Young's Budget Accommodation, 56 Donkin St, T023-4143878, www.wagon wheel.co.za/youngs. 36 en suite budget rooms sleeping up to 5 people decorated in country style, with TV, coffee-making facilities, fans and heaters, 24-hr security and reception, safe parking, big swimming pool, braai facilities and excellent **Mac Young's Restaurant**, see Eating. Recommended.

Karoo National Park *p278*

B Cottages, 36 spacious self-catering thatched cottages (Cape Dutch style) grouped around the swimming pool, sleeping 2-6 people, kitchen, lounge with highly unusual furnishings for parks accommodation – ornate clocks on the wall, Persian rugs, bellows and coal scuttles by the fireplace! One cottage is wheelchair-friendly and is also kitted out for visually impaired visitors.

B-E Rest Camp, reservations through **SANParks** Pretoria office, T012-4289111, www.sanparks.org. Bookings can also be made in person at the offices in Cape Town and Durban (see page 48). For cancellations and bookings under 72 hrs, for campsite reservations, and for general enquiries, phone the camp reception direct, T023-4152828. The camp is at the entrance gate to the park where there is a shop selling basic groceries, an à la carte restaurant, laundry and a stunning bright-blue swimming pool. The accommodation here is superb, even by **SANParks** standards.

E Campsite, 24 grassy caravan and camping sites, good clean ablution blocks, kitchen unit, power points, maximum of 6 per site.

Hanover *p280*

C-D Hanover Lodge, corner of Queen and Mark streets, T053-6430019. Excellent family-run hotel and guesthouse, good-sized rooms, secure parking, children under 15 free, restaurant serves good bar meals even for late arrivals, discounts available out of season.

Colesberg *p280*

C The Lighthouse, 40 Church St, T051-7530043, www.karoolighthouse.co.za. Popular good-value guesthouse with 1 self-catering cottage and 10 comfortable en suite rooms, furnished with antique farm furniture, well managed, good reports, booking essential, swap driving tales in the communal lounge.

D Colesberg Lodge, 32 Church St, T051-7530731, www.colesberglodge.co.za. A large old town hotel with 52 en suite double or family rooms with a/c or fan, rather faded and old fashioned but adequate, restaurant serving standard but filling meat and veggie dishes, swimming pool.

D-F Van Zylsvlei, on the Philippolis road 6 km north of town, T051-7530589. Roadside motel with 19 rooms in rondavels, hearty farm breakfasts and dinner on request, swimming pool and bar, 4 stands for caravans or tents, grassy and shady, electric points, shops at nearby petrol station.

E Caravan Park, Church St, T051-7530149. Not very shady, quite a lot of sand, reservations needed for holiday period, good washblocks, easy walk to all shops and services.

E-F Colesberg Backpackers, 39 Church St, T/F051-7530582. Friendly hostel with dorms and doubles plus camping space. Kitchen, meals on request, laundry, splash pool, veranda perfect for a cold beer at the end of a hot day's driving. A welcome budget stopover on the long road from Johannesburg to Cape Town.

❷ Eating

Town hotels have restaurants and welcome non-residents for evening meals. Most of the guesthouses offer dinner given sufficient notice.

Beaufort West *p277*
King Pie, **Wimpy** and **Kentucky Fried Chicken** are along the main street
♦♦ Mac Young's, 156 Donkin St, T023-4144068. Bustling restaurant decorated in tartan, including the carpet, serving steaks from a charcoal grill, plus pizza, pasta and seafood. One of their more unusual dishes is haggis, the last dish you'd expect to find in the middle of the Karoo.
♦♦ Wagon Wheel Country Lodge (see Sleeping, page 282), T023-4142145. Light lunches, bar snacks and quality à la carte evening meals, huge menu, big portions and great value. The bar has a fireplace and TV, good place to wind down after a day's driving.

❸ Transport

Beaufort West *p277*
Bus
Greyhound, **Intercape** and **Translux** all stop at Beaufort West (and the other Karoo towns along the N1) on the Cape Town–Johannesburg route, though they often arrive and depart at awkward times during the night. The town is surprisingly quiet from as early as 2100, it is unlikely anyone will be around to help if you haven't reserved a seat. Buses stop at the **Engen Garage**. **Cape Town** (6 hrs) daily via **Worcester** (4 hrs). **Johannesburg** and **Pretoria** (12 hrs) daily via **Bloemfontein** (6 hrs) or via **Kimberley** (6 hrs).

Bus companies Greyhound, T083-9159000, www.grey hound.co.za; **Intercape**, T0861-287287, www.intercape.co.za; **Translux**, T086-1589282, www.translux.co.za.

Train
Spoornet, T0860-008888, www.spoornet.co.za. Daily to **Cape Town** (9 hrs), Tue to **Durban** (27 hrs) via **Bloemfontein** and **Harrismith**. Daily to **Pretoria** (17 hrs) via **Kimberley** (7½ hrs). Trains stop here for almost 30 mins.

Colesberg *p280*
It's 778 km to **Cape Town**, 226 km to **Bloemfontein**, 625 km to **Johannesburg**.

Bus
Many services depart at awkward times in the middle of the night. Buses arrive in Colesburg 4 hrs after leaving Beaufort West and stop at the Shell Ultra City for 20 mins.

Train
Spoornet, T0860-008888, www.spoornet.co.za. There is a daily service between **Johannesburg** and **Port Elizabeth**. Change at Bloemfontein for other train services to **Durban**, **Kimberley** and **Cape Town**. **Johannesburg** (10 hrs) via **Bloemfontein** (6 hrs) and **Port Elizabeth** (7 hrs).

Little Karoo → www.tourismlittlekaroo.co.za and www.route62.co.za.

Unlike the Great Karoo to the north, the Little Karoo is not a flat, dry and empty landscape; instead, it is made up of a series of parallel fertile valleys, enclosed by the Swartberg Mountains to the north and the Langeberg and Outeniqua Mountains to the south. It is an especially rewarding region to explore and much of it is hardly visited by tourists. The Cango Caves are a big attraction, as are the ostrich farms, which are often visited as a detour off the Garden Route, but further afield lies spectacular and peaceful countryside, dotted with a multitude of small, historic villages. Here are some of the most dramatic kloofs and passes in South Africa (there are 14 in all) with excellent hiking and the springtime allure of bright patches of flowers.

The majority of the passes, constructed in the late 19th century, were surveyed and built by Thomas Bain, a truly remarkable engineer. Perhaps the greatest testament to his work is that almost every pass he constructed is still in use today along almost identical lines. A fairly new tourist initiative is 'Route 62', a beautiful stretch of road following the R62 from Uniondale in the east to Montagu in the west and passing a few wine estates on the way – it is marketed as the longest wine route in the world ▶▶ *For listings, see pages 295-299.*

Climate

The climate of the Little Karoo is markedly different from that of the coastal Garden Route, and yet it is no more than 30 km further inland. The principal reason for this is the mountains which act as a barrier to the weather moving inland. In the summer it is hot and dry and daytime temperatures of 40°C are not uncommon. During the winter you can expect to see snow on top of the Swartberg Mountains. Average annual rainfall is about 300 mm; water has to be carefully managed and farmers need to irrigate crops.

Vegetation and wildlife

There are several nature reserves managed by Cape Nature Conservation in the region, including Anysberg, Towerkop, and Swartberg. For the botanist, it is one of the best environments in the world for succulents. There are many fascinating small plants which have adapted to the scorching hot sunshine, erratic limited rainfall and rocky shallow soils. Aloes, lilies, geraniums and fynbos vegetation dot the landscape. A rare red variety of protea (*Aristata protea*) grows only in the Seweweekspoort Valley. The guided tours in Gamkaberg Nature Reserve are some of the most informative outings, and will leave you with a greater appreciation of the unique nature of the Karoo landscape.

Around Oudtshoorn, you'll see ostrich peering at you over fences everywhere you turn. When explorers from the Cape first came to the valley, they found it to be teeming with buffalo, elephant, rhino, lion, hippo, kudu and the now-extinct quagga. Today only a few leopard remain in the remote hills; the more common antelope can be found in the reserves. The **Gamkaberg Nature Reserve** is home to the rare Cape mountain zebra, as well as antelope such as steenbok and klipspringer. Antelope can also be seen in the **Swartberg Nature Reserve**.

Oudtshoorn ⊜⨀🅰️▲⊖⊙ ⇢ *pp295-299. Colour map 7, B2.*

By far the largest settlement in the Little Karoo, this is a pleasant administrative centre which still retains much of the calm of its early days. It is a major tourist centre thanks to the nearby Cango Caves and the countless ostrich farms surrounding the town. Oudtshoorn itself is appealing, with broad streets, smart sandstone Victorian houses, many of which are now B&Bs, and a good choice of restaurants.

Oudtshoorn Tourist Bureau ⓘ *Baron van Rheede St, T044-2792532, www.oudtshoorn.com, Mon-Fri 0800-1800, Sat 0830-1300,* has a well-informed, enthusiastic and helpful team and is worth a visit for details on accommodation and the less well-known sights of the Karoo.

Background

In 1838 a small church was inaugurated on the Hartebeestrivier Farm to serve the farmers who had settled along the banks of the Olifants and Grobbelaars rivers. Nine years later the village of Oudtshoorn was founded when land was subdivided and sold by the

Oudtshoorn

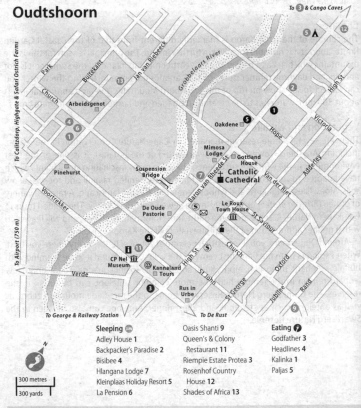

Sleeping ⊜	Oasis Shanti **9**	Eating 🍴
Adley House **1**	Queen's & Colony	Godfather **3**
Backpacker's Paradise **2**	Restaurant **11**	Headlines **4**
Bisibee **4**	Riempie Estate Protea **3**	Kalinka **1**
Hlangana Lodge **7**	Rosenhof Country	Paljas **5**
Kleinplaas Holiday Resort **5**	House **12**	
La Pension **6**	Shades of Africa **13**	

surveyor J Ford. The town was named after Baron Van Rheede van Oudtshoorn, who died on his way to the Cape to take up the post of governor in 1773. In 1858 the first group of British immigrants settled in the village.

When visiting during the dry season it is easy to see how for many years the supply of water to the new settlement restricted its growth. A severe drought in 1865 persuaded many established farmers to move on and most made the long trek to the Transvaal. In its early days, water was brought to the town in barrels and then sold to households at sixpence a bucket. But the local farmers learnt to cope with this handicap and many of South Africa's early irrigation experts came from the region. When you cross the Grobbelaars River in the centre of town during the dry season, all the bridges and culverts seem redundant but they provide ample evidence of how much water can pass through when it rains. If you have time, walk across the Victorian **Suspension Bridge** where Church Street crosses the river; this is now a protected national monument.

It was the advent of two ostrich-feather booms (1865-1870 and 1900-1914) that truly established the town, and led to the erection of the fine sandstone buildings and 'ostrich palaces' that now line Oudtshoorn's streets. For a period of almost 40 years it was the most important settlement east of Cape Town. At the peak of its fortunes, ostrich feathers were selling for more than their weight in gold – little wonder that so many birds were bred. The boom attracted a large Jewish community, most of which had emigrated from Lithuania to escape the Tsarist pogroms. But when the good years finished, few chose to remain. While ostrich farming no longer brings in as much wealth, it remains an important business in the Karoo. Today, it is the production of specialized agricultural seed which contributes most to the region's wealth.

Sights

The two major reasons for coming here are the ostrich farms and the superb Cango Caves. There are also several nature reserves and scenic drives, which are introductions to the diversity of the landscape.

Within the town limits there is little to see aside from appreciating the sandstone Victorian buildings. There are several **ostrich palaces** in town, which unfortunately are not open to the public. They are still worth a look from the outside since their ornate exteriors were very much part of their design. Most examples are in the old part of town on the west bank of the Grobbelaars River. Look out for **Pinehurst**, on St John Street, designed by a Dutch architect, and **Gottland House**, built in 1903 with an octagonal tower. Other buildings of note include **Mimosa Lodge**, **Oakdene** and **Rus in Urbe**. Unfortunately, many fine Victorian buildings were demolished in the 1950s.

The **Catholic Cathedral**, on Baron von Rheede Street, is a fascinating modern cruciform building with splendid stained-glass windows and a chapel beneath the main altar. The cathedral houses two notable works of art: the first is a painting given by Princess Eugenie in memory of her brother – the last of the Bonapartes, who died fighting with the British against the Boers. The second is a replica of a Polish icon incorporating childhood items from refugee children sent to Oudtshoorn during the Second World War; the children returned bearing the gift to celebrate the 50th anniversary of their evacuation.

In the centre of town, next to the old Queen's Hotel on Baron van Rheede Street, is the **CP Nel Museum** ⓘ *T044-2727306, www.cpnelmuseum.co.za, Mon-Fri 0800-1700, Sat-Sun 0900-1700, small entrance fee.* This fine sandstone building with its prominent clock tower was originally built as a boys' high school. The masons who designed the building had been brought to Oudtshoorn by the 'feather barons' to build their grand mansions. The

Ostrich trivia

→ The ostrich (*Struthio camelus*) has been around since the Pliocene period, and has changed little in the intervening eight million years.

→ A giant ostrich-feather fan was discovered in Tutankhamen's tomb.

→ The Oudtshoorn area has 97% of the world's ostrich population.

→ The shell of an ostrich egg can withstand the weight of a human adult.

→ Incubation, 42 days, is carried out by both birds; the male sits at night, the female during the day.

→ Each egg can weigh more than 1 kg, they make good omelettes, and can feed 20 people in one go.

→ It takes two years for the chick to mature.

→ The best-quality feathers are produced by birds aged between three and 12 years.

→ Plucking occurs every nine months: about 1 kg of feathers is removed.

→ Over 80% of the feathers are exported.

→ Their skin makes excellent handbags and wallets.

→ The meat once used only for biltong is now popular in Europe and America because it is almost fat free.

→ The male bird has a vicious kick and a sharp toenail – beware!

displays include a reconstructed trading store, synagogue and chemist, plus an interesting section on the history of the ostrich boom and the characters involved. The rest of the collection of historic objects was bequeathed to the town by CP Nel, a local businessman. A short walk away is **Le Roux Town House**, at 146 High Street, which is part of the CP Nel Museum. This classic town house was built in 1908 and provides a real feel for how the wealthy lived in the fine ostrich palaces of Oudtshoorn. The interior and furnishings are in art nouveau style and the furniture was shipped from Europe between 1900 and 1920. During the summer, teas are served in the garden. **Arbeidsgenot**, Jan van Riebeeck Road, is the former home of Senator Cornelius Langenhoven, a leading figure in the history of the Afrikaans language who wrote the old national anthem of South Africa.

Around Oudtshoorn

Visiting an ostrich farm in the area can be great fun, although the appeal of riding ostriches, feeding ostriches, buying ostrich eggs and leather, or eating ostrich-egg omelette can fade quickly. To keep visitors for longer, some farms have introduced different species. Visiting the farms or the Cango Caves without your own transport can be surprisingly tricky. There are no longer any tour companies that organize daily trips, although it is possible to find a guide through the tourist office. Otherwise, you might want to hire a car for the day.

Cango Ostrich Farm ⓘ *T044-2724623, www.cangoostrich.co.za, daily 0800-1700, R45 R18 children, tours every 20 mins, duration 45 mins*, in the Shoemanshoek Valley 14 km from Oudtshoorn, is particularly convenient as it is on the way to and from the Cango Caves. The farm attractions are also within walking distance of each other. You can interact directly with the birds, sit on or ride them, buy local curios and sample Karoo wines and cheeses.

Wilgewandel Holiday Farm ⓘ *T044-2720878, www.wilgewandel.co.za, daily 0800-1500*, is also in the Shoemanshoek Valley, 2 km before the Cango Caves. It offers you the chance to ride a camel around the farm, R20, R12 children – a pleasant change from a those ostriches. There are also lots of attractions for children such as farmyard animals, a pet area, trampolines, bumper boats, donkey cart rides, and a restaurant serving anything from tea and scones to crocodile and ostrich steaks.

Highgate Ostrich Farm ① *T044-2727115, www.highgate.co.za, daily 0800-1700, R40, children R26, tours every 15 mins, duration 1½ hrs*, is 10 km from Oudtshoorn off the R328 towards Mossel Bay. This very popular show farm, named after the London suburb of Highgate, has been owned by the Hooper family since the 1850s. It has won prizes in the last few years for its high standards, and is very well run and better organized than other farms. You will learn everything there is to know about the bird, and can then try your hand at riding (or even racing!) them. Snacks and drinks are served on the porch of the homestead. As well as English, guides speak German and Dutch.

Safari Ostrich Farm ① *T044-2727311, www.safariostrich.co.za, daily 0730-1700, adults R46, children R24, tours depart every 30 mins, duration 1 hr*, 6 km from Oudtshoorn on the Mossel Bay road, has the usual array of ostrich rides, educational exhibits and curio shops. There is also a smart homestead known as Welgeluk. The house was built in 1910, and is a perfectly preserved example of an ostrich palace. There are roof tiles from Belgium, teak from Burma and expanses of marble floors, proof of the wealth and influence the short-lived boom brought to Oudtshoorn families. Unfortunately, the house is closed to visitors; the closest you can get is the main gate.

Cango Wildlife Ranch ① *T044-2725593, www.cango.co.za, daily 0800-1700, R80, children R50, tours every 40 mins, duration 1 hr*, is 3 km along the R328 towards Cango Caves and is a popular stop for tour groups. There are mixed opinions on this place since it is, in effect, a zoo which stocks animals including white lions, leopards, cheetahs and, oddly, jaguars, pumas and two rare white Bengal tigers that produced three cubs in 2003. There is even an albino python. However the ranch is a leading player in conservation and breeding, particularly with cheetah and wild dog, and the enclosures are very spacious. After walking safely above the animals, you have the choice of paying a little more to pet a cheetah, or you can visit the restaurant. A new attraction here is the Valley of the Ancients, a well-forested string of lakes and enclosures connected by boardwalks that are home a number of unusual animals. The pools are home to Nile crocodiles, pygmy hippos, monitor lizards and otters, while birds include flamingos and marabou storks. You can watch the crocodiles being fed by hand and this is probably the only place in the world that offers cage-diving with crocodiles (children must be over 12).

North of Oudtshoorn
Following the R328 north, the road passes several ostrich farms and then follows the Grobbelaars River Valley towards the Cango Caves (see below). The little village of **Schoemanshoek**, 15 km from Oudtshoorn, is in a lush valley with small farms and homesteads and has some good places to stay.

Cango Caves ›› *Colour map 7, B2.*

Tucked away in the foothills of the Swartberg Mountains 28 km from Oudtshoorn, the Cango Caves are a magnificent network of calcite caves, recognized as among the world's finest dripstone caverns. In 1938 they were made a national monument. Despite being seriously hyped and very touristy, they are well worth a visit. Allow a morning for a round trip if based locally; if you have a car it is possible to visit them and Oudtshoorn on a day trip from towns along the Garden Route such as Mossel Bay, George and Wilderness.

Ins and outs

The caves are 28 km north of Oudtshoorn along the R328, clearly signposted from the centre of town. The road goes straight to the caves; you have to turn left for the Swartberg Pass and Prince Albert. A range of facilities has been developed in the middle of this sparsely inhabited wilderness. There is a restaurant, a crèche, several curio shops and a small money exchange. The caves are usually around 20°C, so a T-shirt and shorts will be fine. Wear shoes with reasonable grip, as after rain the floors can become a little slippery. It is a criminal offence to touch or take anything from inside the caves. Please adhere to these rules and be careful not to touch the rock formations – the acidity of the human sweat that is left from by wandering hands has already caused considerable damage. Eating, drinking and smoking are also forbidden inside. The caves are open daily 0900-1700; you can only enter on a tour (see Oudtshoorn Activities and tours, page 299) – these run until 1600. During the holidays it gets very crowded and nearly 200,000 people pass through the caves each year. Each tour has a maximum number of people, so you may have to wait an hour or more. It's a good idea to get here early in the morning to avoid queues.

Cave tours

ⓘ *T044-2727410, www.cangocaves.co.za. There are 2 tour options: the standard tour starting every hour from 0900, with the last tour at 1600, 1 hr, R52, R28 children, and the adventure tour starting at half past every hour 0930-1530, 1½ hrs, R66, R43 children.*

The only access to the caves is on a guided tour: the short tour takes in two chambers and provides a brief insight into the cave complex; the most popular tour takes in six caves, while the adventure tour follows narrow corridors and involves some crawling. During the tours, each section is lit up and the guide points out interesting formations and their given names. Although one small chamber is still lit in gaudy colours, the rest are illuminated with white light to best show off the formations. These are turned off behind you as you progress further into the system as research has shown that continued exposure to light causes damage to the caves.

The caverns are not just a beautiful series of bizarre formations, but represent over a million years of slow chemical processes. The Cango cave system is known as a phreatic system, the term given to caves which have been chemically eroded by underground water. Once the caves had been exposed to air, the first deposits started to form – these now make up the incredible stalagmites, stalactites and flowstones visitors can see. The timescale of some of the formations is mind-boggling; many of the pillars took hundreds of thousands of years to form, while the oldest flowstone is over a million years old.

The standard one-hour tour is a good introduction to the caves and allows you to see the most impressive formations. It is, however, aimed at tour groups, so visitors with a special interest may find it rather simplistic. The adventure tour lasts for 1½ hours, is over 1 km long and there are over 400 stairs. This can be disturbing for some people, since it involves crawling along narrow tunnels, and at the very end climbing up the Devil's Chimney, a narrow vertical shaft. It leads up for 3½ m and is only 45 cm wide in parts – definitely not for broad people. If at any stage you feel you can't go on, inform the guide who will arrange for you to be led out. Although strenuous, this tour allows you to see the most of the caves, and gives a real feeling of exploration.

Swartberg Nature Reserve ● ▶▶ pp295-299.

Just before the Cango Caves is the turning for the Swartberg Pass and Prince Albert that travels through the Swartberg Nature Reserve. The reserve encompasses 1,291,000 ha of mostly state-owned land and includes the area around Swartberg Pass and the Gamkaskloof Valley (see below). The main attractions here are the mountain fynbos and a varied birdlife. Animals likely to be spotted include kudu, baboon, klipspringer, and dassie. Leopard and caracal also occur in the region but are rarely seen. The mountains behind the Cango Caves are 2000-3000 m high and have a maze of trails snaking through them. The longest trail, the **Swartberg Hiking Trail**, is 60 km long and takes five days. There are three overnight huts at Ou Tol, Bothashoek and Gouekrans, with bunks, showers and braai facilities. Permits and maps are issued by the **Cape Nature Conservation** ⓘ *George, 1021-6593500, www.capenature.co.za*. Water has to be carried between huts during the day.

Swartberg Pass → *Colour map 7, B1.*

One of the most spectacular passes in South Africa, the Swartberg Pass is a national monument in recognition of the engineering genius of Thomas Bain (see page 285). Following severe floods in 1875 which closed Meiringspoort and Seven Weeks Poort and washed away parts of the road, farmers in the region petitioned the government in Cape Town to build a reliable road across the Swartberg. After the first contractor went bankrupt Bain finished the job. It was built between 1881 and 1888 using convict labourers. The route is 24 km long; the top of the pass is 1585 m and the summit is often closed in winter due to snow. The road today follows much the same route and care must be taken. It is very steep, climbing 1000 m within 12 km, and there are very sharp, blind hairpins. As you descend towards Prince Albert there are plenty of shaded picnic sites to pause at and enjoy the views.

Gamkaskloof Valley: 'The Hell'

ⓘ 3 km past the summit of Swartberg Pass, coming from Oudtshoorn, is a gravel road to the left signposted 'The Hell' in the Gamkaskloof Valley. The Otto du Plessis road is suitable for a saloon car but be sure to take care driving here. The road is narrow and steep in parts and there are many blind bends. In all, it is 58 km to the start of the valley; allow at least 1½ hrs each way. Note that there are no shops or fuel.

Gamkaskloof Valley is 16 km long with two seasonal rivers criss-crossing the road. This is one of the more unusual places to visit in South Africa. It is an isolated valley, which is hidden away in the mountains, and whose residents have managed to avoid the change going on all around them. For more than 50 years these European immigrants were the forgotten people. They paid no taxes, had no schoolteachers and made their own clothes. It was only in 1963, 126 years after the first Europeans built their homes here, that a road was built connecting the valley to the outside world. Prior to this all provisions had been brought in by pack donkeys from Prince Albert.

It was during the Great Trek that farmers searching for a place free of the influence and interference of British officials decided to settle in the kloof. Amongst the last people to leave the valley were their descendants. The last farmer, Piet Swanepoel, left the valley in 1991. An account written in 1955 in Karoo, by L G Green, relates an accurate image of conditions in the valley: "Calitzdorp is the nearest village, but 'The Hell' can be reached in comfort only by helicopter. It has no road, nothing but a track for pack-donkeys. As there are only about 20 families living in the kloof, the road-makers have by-passed this solitude. You must leave your car at Matjiesvlei farm and struggle along the Gamka River banks on foot for two or three hours, sometimes knee-deep in water, to meet white people who have never seen the outside world."

Prince Albert → *Colour map 7, B1.*

This old village lies on the edge of the Swartberg Mountains and only 2 km from the start of the scenic Swartberg Pass. Canals from these hills bring water to the gardens, helping to give an oasis feel to the settlement. There is an old watermill on the edge of town. A few minutes walking about the village quickly gives one an impression of life at the turn of the 20th century during the hot summers of the Karoo. Fortunately, many of the homes from this period have survived in a good state of repair. Reflecting the richness of the landscape is the **Frans Pienaar** collection of fossils, one of the largest in the world, housed in the local **museum** ① *Mon-Fri 0900-1230, 1400-1700, Sat 0900-1200, Sun 0900-1030.* There is also an excellent display of Victorian items, including a fully made-up bedroom of furniture, and information about the building of the Swartberg Pass. Tourist information for the area can be found next door to the **Frans Pienaar Museum** ① *Church St, T023-5411366, www.patourism.co.za.* There is a supermarket, general shops, an excellent market next to the museum on Saturday mornings selling home-made cheese, pickles, olives, dried fruit, bread and cakes, plus a couple of restaurants. Some of the original cottages in the valley have been restored as accommodation by Cape Nature, see Sleeping, page 297. The town holds the annual Olive Food and Wine Festival on the last weekend of April with a street market, music, a half marathon, cycle races, a strongman competition and an olive spitting contest.

West of Oudtshoorn ●② ⟩ *pp295-299.*

The main road through the Little Karoo to the west of Oudtshoorn is the R62, a beautiful stretch which is now marketed as **Route 62**. After 52 km you reach Calitzdorp, a small farming centre. Take the old road which follows the Olifants River to visit the **Gamkaberg Nature Reserve** and **Calitzdorp Spa**. North from Calitzdorp is a gravel road to Groenfontein along the Nels River Valley. This route is narrow and full of tight bends, and should not be travelled after heavy rains in an ordinary road vehicle. Eventually it joins up with the R328, Oudtshoorn–Prince Albert road. A loop back to Oudtshoorn via the Cango Caves is a possible circuit. Continuing west from Calitzdorp, the R62 crosses the Dwyka River. After 24 km is a turning north to Seven Weeks Poort. Soon after this you pass the mission stations of Amalienstein and Zoar. It is another 21 km to Ladismith. The area around Ladismith is good for hiking.

Calitzdorp → *Colour map 7, B1.*

Until the branch line from Oudtshoorn arrived in 1924, this settlement remained a small service stop for farmers. The village is now a successful agricultural centre and an important area for port production in South Africa. It is possible to visit a couple of port farms, and a **port festival** is held every July. At harvest time, fresh fruits are sold along the wide roads of the village. The village is also known for the warm healing waters at **Calitzdorp Spa**, 22 km towards Oudtshoorn on the old cement road (see above). When the first farms were established in the area, the surrounding plains were full of game. Sadly today only the early farm names survive as a reminder. The helpful **tourist office**

Anysberg Horse Trail

This is a gentle two-day circular horse trail through the Anysberg Nature Reserve, suitable for inexperienced riders. At first glance the horses appear to be feral as they spend their days grazing on the mountainside, but a whistle from a staff member will soon have them reporting to the tack room for duty. This is a unique experience. The trail goes through traditional Karoo countryside with the ever-present backdrop of the looming mountains. In the relative silence of clipping hooves, you are likely to get close to mammals and the big raptors that inhabit the reserve. At the overnight spot, where water is available and meals are cooked over an open fire, you sleep on a mattress under the stars in a makeshift camp next to your mount. Cooking equipment, mattresses and firewood are included in the price but you bring your own food. Everyone is responsible for their own horse, including cleaning and feeding it. Riders are restricted to a body weight of 95 kg and 5 kg of luggage. The ride is limited to six riders and costs R600 per person. Reservations through T021-6593500, www.capenature.co.za.

① *Voortrekker St, T044-2133775, www.calitzdorp.co.za*, has some good leaflets on the area as well as information about the wineries.

Anysberg Nature Reserve

This is one of the newer reserves in the region, reflecting the need to protect the Karoo. Created in 1988, the area covers 34,000 ha and has a rich and varied fauna and flora along with some well-preserved Khoisan paintings in the Anysberg hills. The further you explore into the wilderness, the more likely you are to see elusive wildlife such as scrub hare, black-backed jackal and the caracal. There are some spectacular gorges which are home for birds such as the black eagle and the pale chanting goshawk. During dry periods the dams provide a focal point for animals and birds. Walking is allowed but no trails have been marked out.

Ins and outs The reserve is on the northern fringe of the Little Karoo. There are two possible routes to the campsite and offices. From the north, travelling along the N1 highway between Touws River and Beaufort West, take the turning at Laingsburg. For the first 25 km the road is surfaced. Take a right turning onto a good dirt road (signposted Ladismith). After another 25 km another right turning takes you into the hills towards the nature reserve. The camp is 23 km from here. From Calitzdorp it is about 120 km to the reserve via the small settlement of Ladismith on the R323 dirt road. This is a beautiful drive as the road climbs up into the Swartberg Mountains over the Seven Weeks Poort and Garcia passes.

Barrydale → *Colour map 8, B3.*

This is the centre of a small farming community set in a fertile valley between the Little Karoo and the Breede River Valley. It's a quiet rural town where the odd cow or sheep can occasionally be seen munching on someone's garden lawn. The surrounding farmland is a colourful mix of vineyards and wild flowers and in the spring the hillsides are covered with mesembryanthemums. The area also produces peaches, apricots, apples and brandy. The local wine cooperative has been a great success and any meal eaten in the locality should be accompanied by their Chardonnay. For tastings visit the **Barrydale Wine Cellar** ① *on the R62 towards Montagu, T028-5721012, www.barrydalewines.co.za, Mon-Fri 0800-1700, Sat 0900-1300*. For information contact the **Barrydale Information Office** ① *1 Van Riebeeck St, T028-5721572, www.barrydale.co.za*.

Tradouw Pass

Running parallel to the Langeberg Mountains, the R62, or Route 62, continues west along the course of the Kingna River to Montagu, 66 km. To the south, the R324 passes over the spectacular Tradouw Pass through the Langeberg Mountains to join the N2 11 km west of Swellendam. When opened in 1873, the pass provided an important trade link for the farmers of the Little Karoo with Port Beaufort at the mouth of the Breede River. As with many civil engineering projects of the time, convict labour was used to build the road, under the direction of road engineer Thomas Bain (Bain built 13 road passes in the southern Cape in the 1800s. Halfway up the remains of the prisoners' camp can still be seen.

East of Oudtshoorn ⬤❼ ▸▸ *pp295-299.*

De Rust → *Colour map 7, B2.*
This well-preserved village 35 km from Oudtshoorn along the N12 has a number of classic Karoo homes. Surprisingly it is world renowned for its rare pelargoniums from which geraniums were first grown. If you have time, the wine farm **Domein Doornkraal** ① *T044-2516715*, has tastings and sales. Information is available from the **tourist office** ① *2 Schoeman St, T044-2412109, www.derust.org.za*, which also a curio shop and internet café.

Continuing along the N12, the road through the **Meiringspoort Pass** in the Swartberg Mountains is worth the petrol; so too is the 60-m **Meiringspoort waterfall**. This can be reached via a short path from the car park. The road through the mountains was built by AG de Smidt, the son-in-law of the famous road builder Thomas Bain. It was opened in 1857, but because it more or less followed the course of the River Groot, it suffered considerable damage during the rains and by 1885 had been completely washed away. Funds collected at the toll gate were never sufficient to pay for repairs. The tar road still survives today along the base of the gorge, and crosses the river 30 times. The 17-km drive is one to be savoured as the vast sandstone cliffs loom above you. After the pass, the road splits; the N12 continues to Beaufort West approximately 120 km away, and the R407 eventually ends up at **Prince Albert**, 90 km away. You can then return to Oudtshoorn (72 km) via the scenic Swartberg Pass along the R328.

◉ Little Karoo listings

Hotel and guesthouse prices
L over US$300 **AL** US$220-300 **A** US$150-220
B US$100-150 **C** US$75-100 **D** US$35-75
E US$15-35 **F** under US$15
Restaurant prices
††† over US$30 †† US$15-30 † under US$15
See pages 46-51 for further information.

● Sleeping

Oudtshoorn *p286, map p286*

For a town slightly off the main tourist trail, Oudtshoorn has a good and varied choice of accommodation. However, if you plan to stay at a guesthouse or B&B, book in advance. If you are interested in staying as a guest in someone's home in a township, this can be arranged through the tourist office.

AL-A Rosenhof Country House, 264 Baron van Rheede St, T044-2722232, www.rosenhof.co.za. 12 a/c rooms with DSTV, swimming pool, beautiful rose garden, beauty spa, gym, jacuzzi, sauna, and there's fine food in the restaurant. Great thought and care has gone into choosing the furnishings of this restored Victorian house, and the fabrics and the ornaments create a comfortable homely atmosphere. For total privacy the 2 executive suites are 100 m from the main house and have their own swimming pools. Recommended.

B Adley House, 209 Jan van Riebeeck Rd, T044-2724533, www.adleyhouse.co.za. A comfortable B&B in a fully restored 1905 house built during the ostrich boom, set in large grounds a short distance from the town centre. 14 rooms, all with en suite bathroom, M-Net TV, minibar, heaters in winter. Home-made bread at breakfast and excellent 4-course evening meals available, 2 swimming pools. Recommended.

B Queen's Hotel, 5 Baron van Rheede St (next to CP Nel Museum), T044-2722101, www.queenshotel.co.za Historic hotel set in tidy gardens in the centre of town. 60 a/c rooms, en suite, stylish and comfortable.

Good restaurant on 1st floor with balcony, serves a buffet lunch on Sun and some interesting South African dishes. Has a swimming pool, tennis courts, curio shop, laundry service and secure parking. A comfortable and friendly hotel which is owned and run by the Barrow family. Good value with discounts during quiet periods. Recommended.

C Hlangana Lodge, 51 North St, T044-2722299, www.hlangana.co.za. An excellent lodge with 19 rooms in a pretty, low building surrounded by palm-filled gardens, a/c, TV, safe, minibar, saltwater pool, mountain bikes for hire, attentive and friendly hosts. The expansive breakfast buffets will keep you going all day. Recommended.

C La Pension, 169 Church St, T044-2792445, www.lapension.co.za. A well-furnished B&B set in large garden with shady fruit trees. 7 rooms in the Cape Dutch-style house built in 1914, TV, sauna, swimming pool.

C Riempie Estate Protea, Baron van Rheede St, 3 km from town centre, T044-2726161, www.proteahotels.co.za. Mix of thatched rondavels and double a/c rooms surrounded by farmland. 40 a/c rooms, 2 non-smoking rooms. The restaurant offers tasty country cuisine. Swimming pool, horse riding, mature shady gardens.

C Shades of Africa, 238 Jan van Riebeeck Rd, T044-2726430, www.shades.co.za. A new building which has been decorated with some fine examples of African art and textiles. 5 very stylish en suite double rooms by the swimming pool set in indigenous gardens, a/c, TV, country or vegetarian breakfasts, use of the kitchen, bar, no children under 12.

D Bisibee, 171 Church St, T044-2724784. Large colonial home with 5 rooms, all with en suite bathroom, B&B, swimming pool. Popular with Europeans, and one of the friendliest welcomes you will receive in South Africa. Breakfast will keep you going all day, outstanding evening meals.

D-E Backpacker's Paradise, 148 Baron van Rheede St, T044-2723436, www.back packersparadise.hostel.com. Spotless lodge set over 4 houses, with a mix of dorms and en suite doubles, camping, volleyball court, well-stocked kitchen, pub with pool table, nightly ostrich braais, splash pool, email facilities, within walking distance of shops, free town pickup, and a daily pickup from the Baz Bus in George. Plenty of activities can be organized from here. Recommended.

D-E Kleinplaas Holiday Resort, 171 Baron van Rheede St, T044-2725811, www.klein plaas.co.za. 56 simple brick-built fully equipped self-catering chalets sleeping 2-6 people, each with M-Net TV, own braai and carport. Caravan and camping pitches with plenty of shade (**E**), electric points, swimming pool, shop, laundry.

E-F Oasis Shanti, 3 Church St, T044-2791163, www.oasisshanti.com. Clean and quiet hostel with a good range of rooms, including singles, doubles, triples and uncrowded dorms as well as some space for camping. Swimming pool with braai area, ostrich-egg breakfasts, nightly ostrich braais and also vegetarian meals, TV lounge, bicycle hire, good travel advice especially about hiking in the region.

North of Oudtshoorn p289

A Altes Landhaus, 13 km north of Oudtshoorn towards the Cango Caves, T044-2726112, www.alteslandhaus.co.za. Award-winning guesthouse in a Cape Dutch homestead, 10 en suite double rooms, some with a/c and TV. Each room is decorated with antiques and has its own special character, evening meals with fine wines available on request, salt pool in garden with pool bar, German spoken. Recommended.

B De Opstal, 12 km north of Oudtshoorn off the road to Cango Caves, T044-2792954, www.deopstal.co.za. A working ostrich farm that offers tours, with 20 en suite double rooms, some of which are converted farm buildings and stables circa 1830 with plenty

of character, some have a/c and/or fire-places, swimming pool with sun loungers, restaurant and bar. Check first there's not a wedding on.

C Oue Werf, 13 km north of Oudtshoorn, T044-2728712, www.ouewerf.co.za. Old 1857 farmhouse with 6 comfortable en suite rooms and 2 self-contained cottages in the grounds, with swimming pool, plus boating on farm dam, 4-course evening meals on request; an ideal base from which to explore the area.

C-E Cango Mountain Resort, 7 km before Cango Caves is a turning off the R328, the resort is 3 km down the road (the road follows the Oude Murasie Valley and can be followed all the way to De Rust, see page 294), T044-2724506, www.cango mountainresort.co.za. A large resort with 21 fully equipped self-catering 4-6 bed chalets with TV, 70 caravan and 40 camping sites, electric points, shop and 3 swimming pools, one of which is suitable for children. A peaceful spot next to the Koos Rauben-heimer Dam, where there are some pleasant braai spots among the oak trees.

Swartberg Nature Reserve p291

Efforts have been made by **Cape Nature Conservation** to restore some of the houses scattered throughout the Gamkaskloof Valley, also known as 'The Hell'. Reservations, T021-6593500, www.capenature.co.za.

C Self-catering cottages, sleeping 4-8 are very good value for families or groups. For a detailed description of each cottage, and a little bit of history about the individual former residents, check out the website. Each has solar lighting, gas stoves and fridges but no electricity. Bedding and cooking and eating equipment are provided but you need to bring food and towels. Rates are higher at the weekends.

E Camping. There are 10 camping sites with a braai and cold showers, tents only, caravans cannot access here. You can swim in the Gamka River. All-round recommended for a rustic and remote few days.

Prince Albert *p292*

Although there is little choice, this is an ideal base for the many hiking trails in the area.

C Dennehof, 5 mins from the village on the R328, T023-5411227, www.dennehof.co.za. Large garden with views of the Swartberg, swimming in the summer months in a country dam. The main house, a well-preserved Cape Dutch farmhouse, the oldest in the village, has 3 en suite rooms, there's 2 garden cottages and the farm's wagon shed has been converted into the honeymoon suite, evening meals on request. The friendly and helpful hosts, who are also tour guides, can arrange tours to 'The Hell'. Recommended.

C Saxe-Coburg Lodge, 60 Church St, T023-5411267, www.saxecoburg.co.za. A well preserved Victorian house with 4 a/c rooms and 5 cottages in the garden, honeymoon room has spa bath and swimming pool. The pub lounge is a relaxing place to end the day by the fire. Richard and Regina can offer advice on hiking. French and German spoken.

C Swartberg Hotel, 77 Church St, T023-5411332, www.swartberg.co.za. 13 rooms plus 5 garden rondavels, delightful restored Victorian home, over 150 years old, with antiques, restaurant, South African dishes a speciality, bar with roaring fire in the winter, swimming pool. Recommended.

Calitzdorp *p292*

C Port Wine Guest House, 7 Queen St, T044-2133131, www.portwine.net. A smart guesthouse in a historic Cape thatched building from the 1830s surrounded by vines. 8 en suite double rooms with a complimentary decanter of port, 4-poster beds and open fires, swimming pool, evening meals available on request taken under the vines. The owners can tell you all you need to know about the region. If you have the time, try to arrange a visit to their ostrich farm. Recommended.

D Welgevonden Guest House, St Helena Rd, T044-2133642, www.welgevonden guesthouse.co.za. A peaceful country guesthouse. 4 rooms with chintzy furnishings and en suite bathrooms, communal lounge and kitchenette. Lush gardens, swimming pool, part of a Chardonnay farm, enjoy the comfort of a family home, evening meals by arrangement.

Anysberg Nature Reserve *p293*

E Anysberg Cottages, reservations through Cape Nature Conservation T021-6593500, www.capenature.co.za. 5 restored labourers cottages with no electricity, light is from candles and lamps, gas fridge, basic kitchen, braai, and communal ablution block, bring bedding, towels and food. This is where the Anysberg horse trails start.

F Camping. A grassy area under the shade of eucalyptus trees near the office has 2 caravan/camping sites with ablution block.

Barrydale *p293*

C Rietfontein Guest Farm, off the R62 between Barrydale and Ladismith, 12 km from the main road, T028-5512128, www.rietfontein.co.za. Lovely rural retreat set in the foothills of the Touwsberg Mountains on a working apricot, port wine, almond and olive farm, 5 self-catering cottages sleeping 5-6, well furnished and equipped, just bring food and drink, the swimming pool pump is powered by solar energy.

D Dandelion Guest House, 12 Van Riebeeck St, T028-5721539, jberry@mweb.co.za. Delightful Cape Dutch-style thatched cottage with outside wooden stairs to rooms in the roof, 2 comfortable but tiny en suite rooms with lots of character, 1 garden rondavel, swimming pool, B&B, evening meals on request.

De Rust *p294*

C De Gat, 7 km from De Rust on the R341, T044-2412406, www.diegat.co.za. B&B with 5 en suite rooms in garden units separate from the main house, which is a lovely farm homestead dating back to around 1800 and a national monument. It's also possible to sleep overnight in the ox wagon. Traditional Karoo dinners on request. There's a swimming pool and Anton can take guests out on the farm by landrover for a bush braai.

D Olivier's Rust, 9 Schoeman St, T044-2412258, www.derust.org.za. 8 self-catering, fully equipped modern brick chalets sleeping 2-4, garden, pool, braai area, attached **Herrie's** coffee shop where you can get a light meal until 2100 and home-made bread.

● Eating

Oudtshoorn *p286, map p286*
Most of the hotels have their own bar and restaurant, which tend to stay open a little later than the restaurants in town.
Colony, Queen's Hotel, 5 Baron van Rheede St, T044-2792414. Open 1800-2300. Excellent restaurant set in this historic hotel. Menu has a very wide range of local dishes, such as Karoo lamb, springbok steak and ostrich. Balcony overlooking the main street, good atmosphere and service, crisp white linen. Recommended.
The Godfather, 61 Voortrekker Rd, T044-2725404. Mon-Sat 1800-2300. Good game menu with springbok steaks and ostrich, plus pizza and good Italian fare, tasty meals but a little more expensive than elsewhere. The bar here is also a good place for a nightcap.
Headlines, Baron van Rheede St, T044-2723434. Mon-Sat 0830-1500, 1745-2300, Sun 1100-1500. Coffee shop and restaurant specializing in ostrich dishes of all kinds from ostrich-egg omelettes to ostrich-liver pâté. The Bushmen kebab is a favourite, with ostrich, venison, crocodile, pork/beef fillet and chicken all on one skewer.
Kalinka, 93 Baron van Rheede St, T044-2792596. Daily for dinner 1800-late.

A fine menu served in a cosy converted sandstone town house. Variety of ostrich dishes including good steaks, plus dishes with a Russian twist like caviar pancakes.
Paljas, 109 Baron van Rheede St, T044-2720982. Open 1700-2300. Pan-African cuisine, a good selection of Cape Malay curries, Karoo roasts, West Coast seafood, and a few unusual Zulu and Xhosa dishes, extensive wine list, a good place to try a 3-course meal with a lot of different flavours.

Calitzdorp *p292*
Rose of the Karoo, 21 Voortrekker Rd, T044-2133133, www.roseofthekaroo.co.za. Mon-Sat 0700-2200. A group of buildings surrounding a vine-covered courtyard with a cosy restaurant with fireplace open all day until 2200 for freshly home-cooked food and famous for their chicken pie and rosemary lamb. Pick up home-made preserves and dried fruit in the delicatessen, and there's a curio shop, and 2 overnight family en suite rooms sleeping 4 (**C**) with fridge and kettle.

Barrydale *p293*
Jam Tarts, on the R62 as it goes through town, T028-5721173. Attached to an eccentric gift shop, **Jam Tarts** sells home-made jams and deli products including chilli jam and olive bread. The varied menu includes Spanish omelettes, Moroccan dishes and organic salads.

De Rust *p294*
The Plough, corner Schoeman and Burger streets, T044-2412020. Tue-Sat 0800-1100, 1200-1500, 1800-2100, Sun 0800-1100, 1200-1500. A good spot for Karoo lamb and traditional dishes, fresh salads and vegetables, old-fashioned sticky desserts and excellent farm-style breakfasts from a full English to a bowl of highland oats with brown sugar, fresh cream and a tot of whiskey!

O Shopping

Oudtshoorn *p286, map p286*
Baron van Rheede St is lined with curio shops selling every ostrich by-product imaginable, from expensive leather purses to feather dusters and tacky enamelled eggs. One such emporium is **Kuriopik**, on the High St. For arts and crafts try **De Oude Pastorie**, 43 Baron van Rheede St.

▲ Activities and tours

Oudtshoorn *p286, map p286*
Backpacker's Paradise, 148 Baron van Rheede St, T044-2723436, www.back packersparadise.hostel.com. Plenty of activities can be organized from this backpacker hostel. Mountain biking to the Swartberg Pass leaves daily at 0830: you are driven to the top and enjoy the long ride downhill. On the way back to Oudtshoorn, you can stop at the Cango Caves and all the other attractions along the R328. They can also organize overnight trips to the 'The Hell', wine tastings and cave trips.
Swartberg Adventures, 56 St Saviour St, T082-9269389, www.swartberg adventures.co.za. Local company that can arrange a number of activities in the Swartberg region, including quad-biking through the Swartberg Pass, abseiling, hiking and kloofing.

☉ Transport

Oudtshoorn *p286, map p286*
It's 172 km to **Beaufort West**, 510 km to **Cape Town**, 60 km to **George**, 245 km to **Montagu**, 93 km to **Mossel Bay**.

Bus

Translux buses depart from the Queen's Riverside Mall. Daily to **Knysna** (2 hrs), **Johannesburg** and **Pretoria** (14 hrs) via **Kimberley** (7 hrs) or via **Bloemfontein** (5 hrs). **Intercape** run a daily service to **Johannesburg** and **Pretoria** (14 hrs) via **Kimberley** (7 hrs) or via **Bloemfontein** (5 hrs).
  Bus companies Translux, T086-1589282, www.translux.co.za; **Intercape**, T0861-287287, www.intercape.co.za

☉ Directory

Oudtshoorn *p286, map p286*
Banks Branches of the major banks are along High St or Baron van Rheede St. **Medical services** Private hospital, Medi-Clinic, T044-2720111.

Contents

Footprint features

Garden Route

At a glance

⊛ **Getting around** Buses and Baz Bus on major routes, car hire, tours start and finish in Cape Town.

◉ **Time required** 3-5 days.

☀ **Weather** Chilly July and August, reasonably pleasant rest of the year.

✖ **When not to go** Christmas and Easter South African school holidays.

WESTERN CAPE

Indian Ocean

Tsitsikamma Mountains

To Nelson Mandela Bay (Port Elizabeth)

Storms River
Storms River Bridge
Storms River Mouth
Tsitsikamma National Park

Langkloofberg

Louterwater

Misgund

Avontuur

Uniondale

To Willowmore

R62

N9

Prince Alfred's Pass
Die Vlug

Ysternek Nature Reserve

Keurbooms River Nature Reserve

Keurbooms
Keurbooms River

The Crags

Monkeyland Nature's Valley
Keurboomsrivier
Lookout Beach
Plettenberg Bay
Cape Seal
Robberg Peninsula Nature Reserve

Bloukrans Pass
Groot River Pass
Toll
Groot Bridge
Bloukrans

Palmiet
Groot

Otter Trail

Diepwalle Forest
Elephant Trail

Uplands

Bitou

Knysna
Elephant Park

N2

Knysna Forests

Millwood

Goudveld Forest

Rheenendal
Homtini

Outeniqua Trail

Sedgefield

Swartvlei

Seven Passes Road

Groenvlei

Goukamma Nature Reserve

Buffalo Bay

Brenton on-Sea
Knysna Lagoon
Featherbed
Knysna
Noetzie
Brenton Nature Reserve

R339

Outeniqua Mountains

Kommanassie

Daskop

Beervlei
Kleinplaat
Touw

Herold
Montagu Pass

George
Wilderness National Park
Wilderness
Victoria Bay

Pacaltsdorp

Herolds Bay

N9

N2

Brak

Holgate
Outeniqua Pass

Jonkersberg

Gannakraal

Mossel Bay

Hartenbos
Cape St Blaize
St Blaize Trail
Dana Bay

Robinson Pass

Botlierskop Private Game Reserve

Mossel Bos

R328

Dysseldorp

To Cango Caves

Oudtshoorn

Kammanassie Dam

N12

To Heidelberg

N

10 km
10 miles

★ Don't miss ...
1 Wilderness National Park, page 313.
2 Knysna Lagoon, page 316.
3 Knysna Elephant Park, page 319.
4 Monkeyland, page 323.
5 Tsitsikamma National Park, page 325.

The Garden Route is probably South Africa's most celebrated area, a stretch of coast heralded as one of the country's highlights. The publicity it receives has made it hugely popular and few visitors to Cape Town miss it. The area is undeniably beautiful: a 200-km stretch of rugged coast backed by mountains, with long stretches of sand, nature reserves, leafy forests and tourist-friendly seaside towns. Officially the route runs from Heidelberg in the west to the Tsitsikamma National Park in the east, though the most popular stretch is the coast from Mossel Bay to Storms River in Tsitsikamma National Park. The region is separated from the interior by the Tsitsikamma and Outeniqua mountain ranges. In contrast to the dry and treeless area of the Karoo on the interior side of the mountains, rain falls all year round on the Garden Route, and the ocean-facing mountain slopes are covered with luxuriant forests. It is this dramatic change in landscape, which occurs over a distance of no more than 20 km, that prompted people to refer to the area as the Garden Route.

The larger towns, such as Plettenberg Bay and Knysna, are highly developed tourist resorts, while other areas offer untouched wilderness and wonderful hikes, including one of the most famous in the country, the Otter Trail. This runs along the coast in Tsitsikamma National Park, one of the most popular national parks in South Africa. There is a second national park, Wilderness, which is also very popular. If hiking isn't your scene, the beaches are stunning, offering a mix of peaceful seaside villages and livelier surfer spots, and there are various attractions hugging the N2 to distract the motorist. Finally, the Garden Route is coming into its own as an adventure destination and there are numerous activities on offer from bungee jumping to mountain biking.

Ins and outs

Getting there
The most direct route from Cape Town to the Garden Route is along the N2. It's an easy 365-km drive and you may break your journey in the attractive town of Swellendam or at the Gouritz River bridge bungee jump, 10 km out of Albertina. Alternatively, there is the option of travelling from Cape Town away from the N2 via either the Whale Route or Breede River Valley/Route 62 if you have the extra time. See the Western Cape chapter for details.

Getting around
To get the most out of the Garden Route you really need a car, and whilst it's quite easy to drive the full length of the Garden Route in a day, most visitors either choose a base for exploring the area, or spend a day or two in several places of interest along the way. Many of the attractions are in between the major resorts so it's good to have the flexibility to stop when you want. ➤➤ *For touring the Garden Route on public transport, see box, page 305, and Transport, page 346.*

Best time to visit
The area's popularity means that good-value accommodation is difficult to find, and gets booked up months in advance, especially during peak season. It is advisable to avoid the area during the two weeks over Christmas and the New Year, and at Easter. For the rest of the school holidays most of the self-catering accommodation will still be fully booked, but bed and breakfasts or hostels should have a free room – call in advance to be sure. For more information about the Garden Route visit www.gardenroute.co.za or www.gardenroute.org.za. ➤➤ *For listings, see pages 329-348.*

Background

Travelling along the coast, the vegetation is lush and green compared to the interior, but this hides the fact that the majority of the Knysna and Tsitsikamma forest was completely destroyed by the early settlers. What remains today is only a small fraction of the indigenous forest, and this is threatened by the encroachment of alien species. The recent history of the region is closely linked with the search for timber for the growing population in the Cape. It only took a few years for the small patches of forest in Hout Bay, Rondebosch, Newlands and Kirstenbosch to be depleted, and the first white colonists to reach Mossel Bay in 1711 came looking for wood. During the 1850s the forests around the Humansdorp area were exploited, but it was not until a road was cut through to the Keurbooms River in 1867 that the Tsitsikamma forest came under threat.

In 1880, Comte De Vasselot de Regne, a French forestry scientist of international repute, introduced the idea of preserving the indigenous forest. However, it wasn't until 1938, when all remaining woodcutters were pensioned off, that over-exploitation ceased to be a problem. The first exotic species were planted in 1891; red gum and cluster pine were planted near Bloukrans to replace sections of the forest damaged by the great fire. The supply of timber for the industry is now based entirely upon fast-growing exotic species such as slash pine, monterey pine, karri gum and Australian blackwood. However, these species are having a negative effect on indigenous species – their fast water absorption has starved other trees, in effect suffocating indigenous species. Some areas have started to remove the exotic aliens in order to control the problem. Today only

Touring the Garden Route

If you don't want to self drive, there are a number of other options for exploring the Garden Route. The **Baz Bus**, T021-4392323, www.bazbus.com, offers a very adequate service and drops and picks up at Garden Route hostels every day. Mainline buses also operate a daily service, but most departures and arrivals are in the middle of the night and it's not as economical as the Baz Bus. For those on a budget and short of time, the **Bok Bus**, T082-3201979, www.bokbus.com, is a comprehensive award-winning five day tour of all the major attractions along the Garden Route starting and finishing in Cape Town. The tour visits most of the adventure activities (optional extras) and accommodation is in hostels or you can upgrade to guesthouses. Prices start at R3750 and include breakfasts, most dinners and entrance fees. There are numerous other coach and minibus operators running short tours from Cape Town along the Garden Route that appeal to a wide range of age groups and offer a variety of accommodation alternatives. These include: **African Eagle**, T021-4644266, www.daytours.co.za. **Cape Rainbow**, T021-5515465, www.caperainbow.com. **Eco-Tours**, T021-7885741, www.ecotours sa.co.za. **Springbok Atlas**, T021-4604700, www.springbokatlas.co.za.

65,000 ha of the original forest remain along the Garden Route, most of which is in Tsitsikamma National Park and around Knysna.

Mossel Bay ⬤⬤⬤⬤⬤⬤ » pp329-348. Colour map 7, B2.

Built along a rocky peninsula which provides sheltered swimming and mooring in the bay, Mossel Bay is one of the larger and less appealing seaside towns along the Garden Route. During the school holidays the town is packed – it receives one million domestic visitors in December alone – but for the rest of the year it is just another dull coastal town. A fact often overlooked in promotional literature is that since the discovery of offshore oil deposits, Mossel Bay is also the home of the ugly Mossgas natural gas refinery and a multitude of oil storage tanks. The town has a number of Portuguese flags and names dotted around, thanks to the first European to anchor in the bay Bartolomeu Dias, who landed in February 1488. His efforts to communicate with local herdsmen were met with stone throwing, but Vasco da Gama, who moored in the bay in 1497, had more luck; he managed to establish trading relations with them. The bay's safe anchorage and freshwater spring ensured that it became a regular stopping-off point for other seafarers. The town was named by a Dutch trader, Cornelis de Houtman, who in 1595 found a pile of mussel shells in a cave below the present lighthouse.

Ins and outs
Mossel Bay Tourism Bureau ⓘ *corner of Church and Market streets, T044-6912202, www.visitmosselbay.co.za, Mon-Fri 0800-1800, Sat and Sun 0900-1700*, provides information and acts as a central reservations office for accommodation. Cage diving to see great white sharks is possible in Mossel Bay; see page 343.

Sights

Many of the local attractions relate to the sea and reflect the bay's importance to early Portuguese navigators and Dutch explorers. All the museums are on one site known as the **Bartolomeu Dias Museum Complex** ① *T044-6911067, www.diasmuseum.co.za, Mon-Fri 0900-1645, Sat-Sun 0900-1545*. Here you'll find the Culture Museum, the Shell Museum, an Aquarium, the Maritime Museum, some Malay graves, and the original freshwater spring that attracted the early sailors and which still flows into a small dam. There's also a tea shop on site in a restored 1830s cottage. The displays in the Maritime Museum are arranged around a full-size replica of Bartolomeu Dias's caravel. Also here is a tree with a fascinating past, the **Post Office Tree**, a giant milkwood situated close to the freshwater spring. History relates that in 1500 a letter was left under the tree by a ship's captain. A year later it was retrieved by the commander of the Third East India Fleet en route to India. Messages were also left carved in rocks and left in old boots tied to the branches. The tree has been declared a national monument and it is still possible to send a postcard home from here – all mail dispatched from the Post Office Tree is franked with a special commemorative stamp and makes a great souvenir.

In the middle of the bay is **Seal Island** which can be visited by cruises departing from the harbour. The island is inhabited by colonies of African penguins and Cape fur seals (the best month to see seal pups is November). It's also possible to see great white sharks and small hammerhead sharks which prey upon the seals. Between September and

Mossel Bay

Sleeping		
Allemans Dorpshuis **1**	Mossel Bay Backpackers **4**	Santos Express Train Lodge **8**
Diaz Strand **2**	Mossel Bay Guesthouse **5**	The Point **9**
Huijs te Marquette **4**	Protea Mossel Bay **6**	
	Santos Caravan Park **7**	

November the warm waters of the bay are often visited by southern right, humpback and brydes whales while calving. Another vantage point for viewing whales and dolphins is **The Point** at the end of Marsh Street. Close by is the 20-m high **St Blaize Lighthouse** ① *Mon-Fri 1000-1200, 1230-1500*, built in 1864, one of only two remaining continuously manned lighthouses in South Africa.

St Blaize Trail

The St Blaize Trail is a perfect introduction to the stunning coastline that you are likely to encounter along the Garden Route. This is a 13.5-km walk along the cliffs and rocky coast west from Mossel Bay. The official trail starts from Bats Cave, just below the lighthouse; the path is marked by the white image of a bird in flight. As you walk further from the town the scenery becomes more and more spectacular. You can leave the coast at Pinnacle Point, and follow a path inland to Essenhout Street. This cuts about 5 km off the walk. The path ends by a group of houses in Dana Bay. From here you will have to organize your own transport back into town, so it helps to have a mobile phone to call a taxi from Mossel Bay. A helpful map is available from the tourism office. You are rightly warned to be careful in places during strong winds, as there are some precipitous and unprotected drops from the cliff tops. Some years ago Khoi-San articles dating back 80,000 years were discovered in **Cape St Blaize Cave**, also known as Bats Cave, which are now in the museum. You can visit the cave, where this a boardwalk, some reproduction Khoi-San huts, and restaurant with open deck.

Eating ⑦
Café Gannet **4**
Jazzbury's **5**
Kingfisher & Delfino's **6**
Pampeon **9**
Pavilion **7**
Tidals **6**

Botlierskop Private Game Reserve

① *T044-6966055, www.botlierskop.co.za. To get there turn off the N2 on to the R401 to the northeast of Mossel Bay, the Klein Brakrivier turn-off, and follow signs for 25 km.*

This private reserve is situated on a 2400-ha game farm, which is home to 24 different species of animals and a wide variety of birds. A former farm, Botlierskop was bought in 1996, and the new owners saw the opportunity to reintroduce wildlife in this area. After four years of recovering from domestic farming, it was opened in 2000. The land has been restocked and wildlife includes the rare black impala, rhino, elephant, lion, buffalo, giraffe, mountain zebra and eland. Activities include game drives, quad biking, nature walks, picnics and helicopter flips (rides). The most exciting activity is elephant riding (this is the only place elephant rides are offered on the Garden Route). Expect to pay in the region of R550, no children under six. The two elephants are orphans who survived a culling program in the Zambezi Valley in Zimbabwe. There is luxurious accommodation available (see Sleeping, page 330) or you can visit for the day, though booking is essential. Check out the website for prices and programmes.

George and around ⊜❶❷❸▲❸❶ ›› *pp329-348. Colour map 7, B2.*

Often referred to as the gateway to, or the capital of, the Garden Route, George owes its status to the fact that it has an airport. It is also an important junction between the N2 coastal highway and the N9 passing through the Outeniqua Pass into the Karoo. It lies in the shadow of the Outeniqua Mountains, but unlike the majority of towns along the Garden Route, it is not by the sea. The town itself is a mostly modern grid of streets interspersed with some attractive old buildings and churches. While it is pleasant enough, it has little appeal compared to other towns along the coast; the main reason overseas visitors come here is to play golf. George has several outstanding golf courses and received worldwide attention in November 2003 when it hosted the President's Cup Golf Tournament. More recently it hosted the inaugural Women's World Cup of Golf.

Ins and outs

There's a very helpful **Tourism Bureau** ⓘ *124 York St, T044-8019295, www.tourismgeorge.co.za, Mon-Fri 0800-1700, Sat 0900-1200*, with a wide range of information on the Garden Route. But, like many offices along the Garden Route, they only promote accommodation which pays a fee to the office.

Sleeping ⊜	Outeniqua Backpackers **12**	Conservatory at Meade
Far Hills Country **11**	Pine Lodge **10**	House **8**
George Tourist Resort **9**	Protea King George **5**	Kingfisher **7**
Hawthorndene Country		Mei Ling **3**
Inn **7**	**Eating** ❼	Old Town House **2**
Loerie Guest Lodge **6**	Capannina **1**	Reel & Rustic **12**
Oakhurst Manor House **8**		Zanzibar's **6**

The milkwood tree

Four white milkwood (*Sideroxylon inerme*) trees in South Africa have been proclaimed as national monuments. All milkwoods are protected to such an extent that a permit is required before an individual can even prune a tree on his or her land. Their name is derived from the milky latex found in the fruit and the bark. The flowers have a very distinctive smell which attracts insects, which in turn attract birds. The trees also bear fruit which, when ripe, turns a purple colour and is eaten by birds and baboons. These beautiful shade trees are found all along the Pacific coast in many shapes and sizes. In the harshest of conditions they may only grow into a shrub-like bush; the largest tree is on a farm near Bredasdorp: it has a spread of 20 m, a trunk girth of over 3 m, and is thought to be over 1000 years old. The most famous specimen is the Post Office Tree in Mossel Bay which must be at least 500 years old. Milkwoods were one of the species that early settlers singled out for commercial use: their wood is hard and durable and was used for building boats, bridges and homes. These days the threat to their survival comes from alien vegetation in the forests. During a bush fire, alien plants burn fiercely and any milkwoods close by may die as a result of the intensity of the heat. Thick alien growth also prevents the germination of milkwood seeds and the growth of the saplings.

Background

The first settlement appeared here in 1778 as a forestry post to process wood from the surrounding forests. In 1811 it was formally declared a town, and named after King George III. It was at this time that its wide tree-lined streets – Courtenay, York and Meade – were laid out. For the next 80 years the town remained the centre for a voracious timber industry. Much of the indigenous forest was destroyed supplying wood for wagons, railway sleepers and mine props. Some of the trees, which are endemic to South Africa, came to be known as **stinkwoods** because of their odour when freshly cut. Few remain today, although they are slow growing back.

Sights

Within the town itself there are only a few sights of interest. On the corner of Cathedral and York streets, **St Mark's Cathedral**, consecrated in 1850, has an unusually large number of stained-glass windows for its size; many were designed by overseas artists of limited fame. In 1911 a bible and royal prayer book were given to the church by King George V. The interior of the **Dutch Reformed Mother Church** at the north end of Meade Street reflects the town's early history as a centre for the timber industry. The pulpit is carved out of stinkwood and took over a year to create. The ceiling was built from yellowwood, and six yellowwood trunks were used as pillars. The mountains create an impressive backdrop to the church when viewed from the corner of Courtenay and Meade streets.

In front of the tourist office, housed in the King Edward VII library, is an ancient oak tree known as the **Slave Tree**. It is one of the original trees planted by Adrianus van Kervel in the early 1800s and has been declared a national monument. The tree acquired its name because of the chain embedded in the trunk with a lock attached to it. The story of the chain can be traced back to when a public tennis court was in use next to the library (now the information office), and the court roller was secured to the tree to prevent playful

Outeniqua Choo-Tjoe

Until recently, the most enjoyable way to travel between George and Knysna was on the Outeniqua Choo-Tjoe, a historic steam train. This picturesque branch line was opened in 1928 and the 67-km journey gave passengers an extraordinary view of some spectacular coastal scenery and forests, passing through Wilderness National Park and along the Goukamma Valley. The journey ended by crossing Knysna Lagoon via a long bridge. Unfortunately after landslides during bad weather in August 2006, the line has been damaged beyond repair and has closed. However, the train still runs but on an alternative line. Since November 2006 the Outeniqua Choo-Tjoe resumed operations between George and Hartenbos, a scenic route traversing the farmlands outside George with the Outeniqua Mountain in the background before descending to the Indian Ocean. Then, in April 2007, the service was extended and it now ends at the Dias Museum Complex in Mossel Bay. It runs every day except Sunday and departs from the Railway Museum in George at 1200, gets to Mossel Bay at 1200, leaves again at 1415 and arrives back in George at 1615; return R100, children under 16 R60, children under 6 free; one-way R85, children under 16 R50, children under 6 free. Reservations and information, George Railway Museum, T044-8018288.

children from rolling it down the street. Housed in the old Drostdy, the **George Museum** ⓘ *Courtenay St, T044-8735343, Mon-Fri 0900-1630, Sat 0900-1230, coffee shop*, has displays on the timber industry as well as musical instruments and a collection of old printing presses. In the Sayer's Wing is an exhibition devoted to former President PW Botha, who was a member of parliament for George for 38 years. The **Outeniqua Transport Museum** ⓘ *2 Mission Rd, just off Knysna Rd, T044-8018288, Mon-Sat 0800-1700*, has an interesting display outlining the history of steam train travel including 13 steam locomotives, a 1947 Royal Mail coach, and a room dedicated to model railways, as well as a collection of vintage cars and flight memorabilia. It is adjacent to the new platform from which the **Outeniqua steam train** departs (see box, page 310).

Victoria Bay → *Colour map 7, B2.*

If you are based in George and wish to spend a quiet day by the sea, this small resort is only 9 km or 15 minutes' drive away. Victoria Bay, 2 km off the N2, is an excellent place to surf during the winter. It has a narrow cove with a broad sandy beach, a grassy sunbathing area, and a safe tidal pool for children. There's only one row of houses with some of the best-positioned guesthouses in the region.

Little Karoo and Montagu Pass

The N2 continues from George to Wilderness, but if you have been travelling along the coast from Cape Town, a short diversion into the Little Karoo is well worth the effort. Starting in George, the most direct route is the N9 via the **Outeniqua Pass**. Having reached the summit (799 m) it quickly becomes apparent why the narrow coastal belt is referred to as the Garden Route. The dry, undulating terrain is in stark contrast to the lush coastal region, no more than 15 km away. From the top of the pass it is 35 km to **Oudtshoorn**, the capital of the Little Karoo, known for its ostrich farms and the **Cango Caves** (see page 289).

Returning from Oudtshoorn, an alternative and scenic route through the mountains is via **Montagu Pass**, the fourth pass over the Outeniqua range. It was opened in 1847 and took over four years to complete. Travelling on the N12 from Oudtshoorn, look out for a left turn just before the road starts to climb up to Outeniqua Pass. This is the N9 and will be signposted to Uniondale and Willowmore. After several kilometres, look out for a right turn for Herold and Montagu Pass. Before the road starts to climb it goes through a fertile valley full of hops and fruit trees. The area is ideal for hop growing since it is sheltered from strong winds and rarely has hail. Harvest time is during February and March. This road is gravel so take care after rain. For much of the route there is a low stone wall along the side of the road, and several stretches are single track. Fortunately, very little local traffic uses this road. Near the summit the road passes under a narrow bridge – the railway line linking George with Oudtshoorn – an amazing engineering feat when you look out across the valley below. Halfway along the road are the ruins of a blacksmith's shop and, before the road links up with the N12 back into George, you'll see the old toll house.

Seven Passes Road
One of the most enjoyable drives in the region, the Seven Passes Road (or the Old Passes Road), is the name given to the original route between George and Knysna. It starts 3 km out of George, just before Pine Lodge. The route was surveyed and built by Thomas Bain in 1867 and, like so many of his engineering projects, is still in use today. Much of the road follows the foothills of the Outeniqua Mountains. When it was built the engineers had to cut their way through dense forest and negotiate the fast-flowing rivers coming out of the mountains. The seven passes which give the road its name are: the Swart River, Kaaimans, Touw River, Hoogekraal, Karatara, Homtini and Phantom. At each pass the road winds down the gorges to a narrow bridge at the bottom. The stone bridges over the Silver and Kaaimans rivers have been declared national monuments.

After crossing the Swart River, which flows out of the Garden Route dam, the road rises through the forest onto a plateau. Some 5 km from the turning is the entrance to **Saasveld**, a college of forestry founded in 1905. The descent to the Kaaimans River was a major obstacle for Bain in 1867. Loaded wagons slid on their brake shoes to the bottom before being hauled up by 32 oxen on the other side, the ground so soft that the wheels were gouged out 3-m-deep channels. Shortly after the road crosses the Silver River, there is a junction with White Road for **Wilderness**. After crossing the fourth river, Touw, the road reaches turnings to Woodville, Bergplaas and Kleinplaat forest stations. Just before Woodville there is a turning north leading to a giant yellowwood tree which is thought to be more than 800 years old. It is 31 m high and has a girth of 9 m. A picnic site and a short trail into the forest have been laid out close by. At Bergplaas there is a right turning which leads down to the lakes, **Langvlei** and **Rondevlei**, before joining the N2 outside Sedgefield.

The next two passes are the **Hoogekraal** and **Karatara**. The village of Karatara was established in 1941 as a centre for woodcutters who could no longer practice their skills as attitudes towards the forests and trees changed. The **Homtini Pass** is a beautiful wooded valley which ends by the turning for the village of Rheenendal. After another kilometre there is a left turning signposted for Millwood, Goldfields and Bibby's Hoek. The rest of this route into Knysna is described in the West of Knysna section (see page 317).

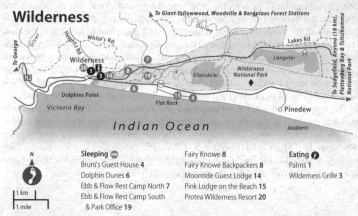
This appealing little town is an ideal base for exploring the Garden Route and has a superb swathe of sandy beach. Check locally for demarcated areas for swimming and surfing. Children should be supervised in the sea as there are strong rip currents. One of the safest spots for swimming is in the Touw River mouth. Except for the few hectic weeks at Christmas and New Year, Wilderness is generally very relaxed and has an excellent range of accommodation. The advantage of staying here is that you are also within a day's drive of all the interesting sights of the Little Karoo. The highlight, however, is Wilderness National Park, a quiet, well-managed park, with three levels of self-catering accommodation and a campsite.

The town itself doesn't have much of a centre, but stretches instead up the lush foothills of the Outeniqua Mountains and along leafy streets by the lake and river. The supermarket, restaurants, post office and tourist office are by the petrol station, where the N2 crosses the Serpentine channel.

Ins and outs
Wilderness Tourism Bureau ⓘ *Leila's Lane, turn left by the post office, T044-8770045, www.tourismwilderness.co.za, Mon-Fri 0800-1800, Sat 0800-1300, Sun 1500-1700,* is a very helpful office, especially when it comes to finding good-value accommodation during the peak season.

Background
The first European to settle in the district was a farmer, Van der Bergh, who built himself a simple farmhouse in the 1850s. It was in 1877 that the name was first used, when a young man from Cape Town, George Bennet, was granted the hand of his sweetheart only on condition that he took her to live in the wilderness. He purchased some land where the present-day **Wilderness Hotel** stands and promptly named it 'wilderness' (of dense bush and forest) to appease his new father-in-law. At this time the only road access was from the Seven Passes Road between George and Knysna. Bennet cut a track from this road to his new farmhouse. In 1905 Montagu White bought the homestead from Bennet and

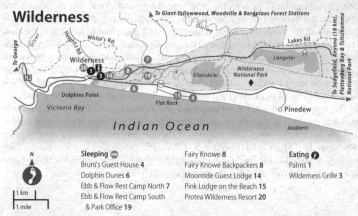

Wilderness

To Giant Yellowwood, Woodville & Bergplaas Forest Stations

To George · Silver · Heights Rd · White's Rd · Wilderness · Duiwe · Lakes Rd · Langvlei · Eilandvlei · Wilderness National Park · To Sedgefield, Knysna (18 km), Plettenberg Bay & Tsitsikamma National Park

N2 · Dolphins Point · Victoria Bay · Flat Rock · Pinedew · Jouberts

Indian Ocean

N · 1 km · 1 mile

Sleeping 🛌
Bruni's Guest House **4**
Dolphin Dunes **6**
Ebb & Flow Rest Camp North **7**
Ebb & Flow Rest Camp South & Park Office **19**

Fairy Knowe **8**
Fairy Knowe Backpackers **8**
Moontide Guest Lodge **14**
Pink Lodge on the Beach **15**
Protea Wilderness Resort **20**

Eating 🍴
Palms **1**
Wilderness Grille **3**

converted it into a boarding house. It wasn't a great success: the area was undoubtedly beautiful, but the swimming was dangerous and access was still a problem. When the property changed hands in 1921 the farmhouse/boarding house underwent further alterations and the Wilderness Hotel came into being. In 1907 the railway line from Mossel Bay reached George and six years later, Oudtshoorn. It wasn't until 1928 that the link between George and Knysna was completed. By 1928 a second hotel, now known as the **Fairy Knowe Hotel**, had been built by the river. In 1985 the original Wilderness Hotel was destroyed in a fire – the new building is the smart four-star hotel of the same name.

Wilderness National Park → *Colour map 7, B2.*
ⓘ *The camp reception, T044-8771197, www.sanparks.org, 0700-2000, has a map of the camp and useful information on the surrounding countryside. The daily conservation fee is R60, R30 for children. The nearest supermarkets and restaurants are in Wilderness.*

Since the accommodation is provided by SANParks it is excellent value, especially for four or more people, and this is one of the most relaxing places to stay along the Garden Route. The main attraction is the water and the birdlife in the reed beds but there are some excellent hikes and a beautiful sandy beach. Each of the accommodation units has a folder with maps and details of all the possible hikes and routes in the park.

Four kilometres east of Wilderness, off the N2, a gravel road drops down the edge of the hill to the main camp next to a river. The park covers 2612 ha and incorporates five rivers and four lakes as well as a 28-km stretch of the coastline. The series of freshwater lakes is situated between the Outeniqua foothills and sand dunes which back onto a beautiful, long sandy beach. As this is such a stunning and unique ecosystem, the land around the national park is also protected by SANParks – this area is referred to as the National Lake Area. The four lakes are known as Island, Langvlei, Rondevlei and Swartvlei. There are bird hides on Langvlei and Rondevlei.

There are two ways in which to enjoy the beauty of the surroundings, on foot or in a canoe. You can cover more ground by walking, but canoeing is ideal for seeing birds. There are five trails in the park. The **Pied Kingfisher Trail**, a 10-km circular route, can be completed in four hours. It follows the river in one direction and the beach on your return. The other walks are also forest walks, except for the 3-km **Dune Molerat Trail** which takes you through dune fynbos where you may see proteas in flower in season.

The main camp has canoes and pedalos for hire – these should be arranged through **Eden Adventures** (see page 344). One of the more interesting short routes is to continue up the Touw River past the Ebb and Flow Camps. This quickly becomes a narrow stream and you have to leave your canoe. A path continues along the bank of the stream through some beautiful riverine forest. Eden Adventures also have mountain bikes, some with child seats, to rent out for use on the trails in the park.

Sedgefield and around ⊖⊖ ⟫ *pp329-348. Colour map 7, B2.*
Unless you turn off the N2, all that can be seen of Sedgefield is a collection of curio shops, supermarkets and snack bars. Between the main road and the beach is the **Swartvlei Lagoon**, South Africa's largest natural inland saltwater lake, most of which lies on the inland side of the N2. The lake is a popular spot for watersports and birdwatching, although the two pastimes don't always go well together. Around Sedgefield's lakes and forests look out for the secretive starred robin, the blue mantle flycatcher, the difficult-to-see Victorian warbler and the rare African finfoot.

The village itself is of little interest, but the country around the lakes is spectacular and very peaceful. On the Knysna side of Sedgefield is another lake, **Groenvlei**, a freshwater lake lying within the Goukamma Nature Reserve. **Sedgefield Tourism Bureau** ① *30 Main Rd, T044-3432007, www.tourismsedgefield.co.za, Mon-Fri 0800-1700, Sat 0830-1100*, has good information on accommodation.

Goukamma Nature Reserve

① *Gates open 0800-1800, T044-8025310, www.capenature.org.za, entry for day visitors R25.*
The reserve was established to protect 2230 ha of the hinterland between Sedgefield and Buffalo Bay. This includes Groenvlei or Lake Pleasant, a large freshwater lake, and a 13-km sandy beach with some magnificent sand dunes covered in fynbos and patches of forest containing milkwood trees. The **Goukamma River** estuary in the eastern part of the reserve has been cut off from the sea by the large sand dunes. The lake is now fed by natural drainage and springs, and is surrounded by reed beds which are excellent for birdwatching; more than 75 species have been identified. However, because of extensive flood damage in 2006, the estuary and Buffalo Bay on the eastern side are no longer accessible to visitors and are closed off indefinitely. Cape Nature accommodation on the eastern side has been closed but there are still bush camps in the western region of the park (see Sleeping, page 332). To get there, look out for the turning for the Lake Pleasant Hotel, just east of Sedgefield. Beyond the hotel the road divides; take the left turning by the dunes to the bushcamp and the Groenvlei office. A 4-km hiking trail starts close by which runs along the lake shore.

Knysna and around ⊜❺❼❻❿⚠❻ⓖ ➠ *pp329-348. Colour map 7, B2.*

Knysna (the 'K' is silent) is the self-proclaimed heart of the Garden Route. It is no longer the sleepy lagoon-side village it once was – far from it – but is nevertheless a pleasant spot to spend a day or two. The town itself is fully geared up for tourists, which means a lot of choice in accommodation and restaurants, as well as overcrowding and high prices. It remains quite an arty place, though, and many of the craftspeople who have gravitated to the region display their products in craft shops and galleries. Nevertheless, development is booming, with a slick waterfront complex, complete with souvenir shops and fast-food outlets, setting the pace. If you're trying to choose between Knysna and Plettenberg Bay as a base, Knysna offers more amenities and activities, while Plett is far more relaxed and has the better beach. Both get very busy during high season.

Ins and outs

Getting there and around Knysna can easily be accessed by road as it lies on the N2 between Cape Town (500 km) and Port Elizabeth (260 km). **Baz Bus** has a daily service between Cape Town and Port Elizabeth, from where it continues to Durban five times a week. Mainline buses stop at Knysna daily on the route between Cape Town and Durban. **Translux** has a service between Knysna and Johannesburg and Pretoria via Bloemfontein. The centre of town is compact and it is easy to find your way about, although you'll need transport to see the sights. ➠ *For further details see Transport, page 348.*

Tourist information **Knysna Tourism** ① *40 Main St, T044-3825510, www.visitknysna.com, www.tourismknysna.co.za, Mon-Fri 0800-1700, Sat 0830-1300*, can make reservations for accommodation, tours and public transport. It's a helpful and professional office, well clued-up on the region. For more information on Knysna, visit www.knysna.org.

Background

The Hottentots named a local river in the area by a word that sounded like Knysna to the early Europeans, and it's generally believed to mean a place of wood or leaves. In 1804 George Rex, a timber merchant, purchased the farm Melkhoutkraal, effectively taking ownership of all the land surrounding the lagoon. It was rumoured he was the first and illegitimate son of England's King George III. By 1817 the Knysna Lagoon was being used by ships to bring in supplies, and later to take away timber. The vast, indigenous forests just outside Knysna became an invaluable source of timber for buildings, ships and wagons. In 1870, Arnt Leonard Thesen and his family moved from Norway to Knysna and set up the first trading store and counting house, and by 1881 the settlements of Melville and Newhaven united to form the new town of Knysna. The timber industry continued well into the 20th century and unfortunately wiped out much of the natural forest on the coast, so whilst there are still tracts of Knysna forest, the region undoubtedly looks very different to what it did 150 years ago.

1 Knysna

➡**Knysna maps**

1 Knysna, page 315
2 Knysna lagoon, page 316

Sleeping 🛏
Aesta's B&B **2**
Falcon's View Manor **5**
Gallery Guest House **4**
Highfield Backpackers **6**
Knysna Manor House **7**
Overlander's Lodge **10**

Protea Knysna Quays **3**
Wayside Inn **13**
Yellowwood Lodge **14**

Eating 🍴
34' South **9**
Anchorage **1**

Cruise Café **4**
Drydock Food Co **6**
Oyster Catcher **7**

Bars & clubs 🍸
Tin Roof **3**
Zanzibar's **2**

Sights

Although there are a couple of sights and museums in the town, Knysna's highlights are its natural attractions. The main feature of the town is the **lagoon**, around which much of Knysna life revolves. **The Heads**, the rocky promontories that lead from the lagoon to the open sea, are quite stunning. The **Knysna National Lakes**, over 15,000 ha of protected area, are also wonderful to explore, comprising islands, seashore and beach. This fragile ecosystem is bound to suffer from the ever-expanding tourist industry; of particular concern is the rich variety of aquatic life in the lagoon. This has not been helped by the construction of large retirement residential suburbs, such as Belvidere Estate, Thesen Island and Leisure Island – the latter two should never have been built upon. One of the striking features of Knysna is the location of the sprawling township, which is at the top of the hills above the town. From a boat trip on the lagoon you can look back at the town; all the sleek modern and luxurious development in the foreground and, quite by contrast, the tight cluster of shacks at the very top of the hill.

The **Knysna Museum** ① *Queen St, T044-3026300, Mon-Fri 0930-1630, Sat 0930-1200, small entrance fee*, is housed in the Old Gaol – the first public building erected by the

2 Knysna Lagoon

To Terblans Walk & Gouna Forest
To Wilderness & George
To ❶ ❸, Seven Passes Road, Phantom Pass & Millwood Goldfields
White Bridge
Salt River
Old Cape Rd
Welbedacht Rd
Knysna River
Belvidere
The Point
Knysna Lagoon
Brenton
Brenton-on-Sea
Knysna
Fitchat
Main St
Long
Jetty
Thesen's Island
Leisure Isle
George Rex Dr
To Diepwalle Forest & Ysternek Nature Reserve
Bokmakerrie
Vigilance
Barracuda
Howard
Knysna Private Hospital
Knysna Golf Club
Wilson
Marr
The Heads Adventure Centre
Knysna Heads
Featherbed Nature Reserve
The Heads
Indian Ocean

➡Knysna maps
1 Knysna, page 315
2 Knysna lagoon, page 316

N
1 km
1 mile

Sleeping 🛏
Ashmead Resort **4**
Belvidere Manor **2**
Forest Edge **3**
Heron Water Lodge **5**
Isolabella **7**

Knysna Belle **9**
Leisure Isle Boutique Lodge **6**
Phantom Forest Eco-Reserve **1**
Under Milkwood **10**

Eating 🍴
Crabs Creek **1**
Ile de Pain Bread & Café **5**
Knysna Oyster Co **4**
O'Pescador **2**
Paquitas **3**

colonial government in the 1870s. Most of the collection focuses on fishing methods used along the coast, with a variety of nets and tackle on display. Unless you are a devoted angler this is not going to take up too much of your time. The highlight is in fact a fish, or to be more precise, a *Coelacanth*. This is a prehistoric fish that was believed to be extinct, but a live specimen was famously caught by a fisherman in 1938. There is also an art gallery, tearoom and gift shop.

Millwood House ① *Mon-Fri 0930-1630, Sat 0930-1230*, is a single-storey wooden building similar to those that once made up the gold-mining community of Millwood (see page 318). The house was originally built in sections and re-erected here. It is now a national monument and houses the local history museum, including a display depicting the goldrush days. Next door is **Parkes Cottage**, a similar wooden house, which was moved three times before arriving at its present site. Originally erected in Millwood village, it was moved into Knysna when the gold ran out. In 1905 it was moved to Rawson Street, and then finally in 1992 it was moved to its present site.

There are two **St George's Churches** in Knysna, the old and the new. Both ran into financial difficulties during construction. To complete the old church the Bishop of the Cape Colony, Robert Gray, persuaded six local businessmen to come up with the necessary £150. The church was consecrated in October 1855. The interior has a timbered ceiling and a fine yellowwood floor. In the 1920s it was decided that a second church needed to be built to accommodate the local congregation. It was 11 years between the foundation stone being laid and the church being consecrated by Bishop Gwyer of George in April 1937. Construction had been delayed due to lack of funds. The community was very proud of the fact that all the materials used in the construction were local – the stone for the walls was quarried from the other side of the lagoon in the Brenton hills. Most of the interior fittings are made from stinkwood, and commemorate local worthies.

Featherbed Nature Reserve ① *T044-3821693, www.knysnafeatherbed.com, daily 1000, 1115, 1230, R300 adults, R150 children*, is the unspoilt western side of the **Knysna Heads**. This is a private nature reserve that can only be reached by the **Featherbed Co** ferry which runs from the John Benn Jetty, at the Knysna Quays. The reserve is home to South Africa's largest breeding herd of blue duiker (*Cephalophus monticola*), an endangered species. Also of interest is a cave once inhabited by the Khoi, which has been declared a national heritage site. This four-hour excursion includes return ferry trip, 4WD vehicle ride up the western promontory of the Knysna Heads and an optional 2 km guided nature walk through the forest, onto the cliffs, into the caves and along the spectacular coastline. It ends with a buffet lunch under some Milkwood trees before returning to Knysna. This is an excellent family excursion. The Featherbed Co also offers two-hour cruises around the lagoon with lunch or dinner on a paddle cruiser, R295 adults, R150 children. In addition, they run the **Cruise Café** at the boat departure point at the Knysna Quays (see Eating, page 341).

West of Knysna ● ›› *pp329-348*.

Belvidere, Brenton and Brenton-on-Sea
These villages, 12-14 km from town on the western shores of the lagoon, are in many ways really smart suburbs of Knysna. Brenton has the great attraction of having the nearest sandy beach (Brenton-on-Sea), making it very popular during the school holidays. There is a fine hotel and a limited selection of seaside cottages. Belvidere is

primarily a leafy residential suburb along the banks of the river where it enters the lagoon. A large proportion of the village is made up of the relatively new Belvidere Estate, a prestigious development on 67 ha, made up of large houses and gardens.

The small village church, **Belvidere Church**, is a popular attraction in the area and is a miniature replica of a Norman church. It was built in 1855 from local stone and timber, with picturesque stained-glass windows and stinkwood fittings. The rose window on the west side was installed in 1955. Further along the road is the seaside resort of Brenton-on-Sea.

> *Some of the glass in the window of Belvidere Church is from the bombed ruins of Coventry Cathedral in England.*

Knysna Forest and Millwood Goldfields

On the southern slopes of the Outeniqua Mountains, behind Knysna, are the remnants of the grand forests that first attracted white settlers to the region. No longer a single expanse, the patches go under a variety of names which can be confusing: Diepwalle Forest, Ysternek Reserve, Goudveld State Forest, and Millwood Creek (and Jubilee Creek) Nature Reserve. As a whole, these state forests are often referred to as the **Knysna Indigenous Forests**. The indigenous forests are noteworthy for the variety of birdlife and their magnificent trees. Species of special interest include the yellowwood, assegai, stinkwood, red alder, white alder and the Cape chestnut. A variety of short walks has been laid out in the forests. In some areas horse riding and mountain biking is allowed. The tourist office produces a good trail map.

About 25 km from Knysna, in the **Goudveld State Forest**, are the remains of an old mining town, **Millwood** ① *sunrise-sunset*. This was the site of a minor goldrush in the 1880s, just before the gold was discovered at Pilgrim's Rest and Johannesburg. The first gold was discovered here in 1876 when a local farmer picked up a nugget in the Karatara River. This triggered the usual manic influx, and by 1887 Millwood had a court building, three banks, 32 stores, six hotels and three newspapers. By 1900 most people had left as the reefs became too difficult to mine. Today only one building survives, along with some mining machinery which has remained untouched for over 60 years. To reach the mine, take the Phantom Pass road out of Knysna, just before the village of Rheenendal take a right turn, signposted for Millwood, Goldfields and Bibby's Hoek.

Further up the slope is the shaft and a short Co-Co Pan rail track. In addition to the mine buildings, there are a few picnic spots and short paths leading into the forest; you only have to walk a few metres before being completely enveloped by trees.

East of Knysna ● ›› pp329-348.

Diepwalle Forest and Elephant Trail

① *Before setting out you must sign in at the forest station where maps are on offer. There is no charge but the hike is only open 0600-1800.*

Starting from the Diepwalle forest station is the 20-km Elephant Walk, an easy-going, level hike that gives a clear insight into the forest environment. The trail is marked by elephant silhouettes and takes around seven hours to complete. The hike is made up of three loops, but it is possible to shorten the walk by completing only one or two loops. The three paths are simply known as Routes I, II and III, and are 9-, 8- and 6-km long, respectively. Apart from the (very slim) possibility of spying the rare Knysna elephant (see box, page 322), of which there are three on record at present, the main attractions are the giant forest trees, particularly the Outeniqua yellowwood. There are eight such trees along the full trail – the largest, at 46 m, is known as the **King Edward VII Tree**, and stands just off the R339 by the Diepwalle picnic spot at the end of Route I and the start of Route II. The end of the **Outeniqua Trail** meets with Route III.

To get there from Knysna, follow the N2 towards Plettenburg Bay. After 7 km turn onto the R339 and the Diepwalle forest station is about 16 km on a gravel road. The R339 passes through the middle of the forest en route to Uniondale via the Prince Alfred's Pass.

Noetzie and Brackenhill Falls

Noetzie is a small village on the coast with an outlandish collection of holiday homes built to look like castles from medieval Europe, complete with towers and battlements. On the curiosity scale they rate quite high, but unfortunately you can only see them from the outside, as they are all private homes. A further 5 km beyond the Noetzie turning is another turning to the right; a gravel road passes through a eucalyptus and pine plantation to a picnic spot which overlooks the Brackenhill Falls. This is where the Noetzie River plunges into a narrow gorge with flourishing plants growing in the spray on the steep sides.

Knysna Elephant Park

ⓘ *T044-5327732, www.knysnaelephantpark.co.za, daily, tours every half hour, 0830-1630, R130 adults, R65 children, bookings not required; elephant riding R495 adults, R275 children, booking essential.*

On the N2, 20 km from Knysna and 10 km before Plettenburg Bay, this small park is a refuge for orphaned elephants. Visitors are taken on tours around the forest area and are allowed to touch and play with the little elephants. Although the animals are 'free range' they are very used to human contact, making it a wonderful experience for children. Longer walks with the elephants can also be arranged and the newest option here is elephant riding, which is a two-hour excursion through the bush ending with refreshments. Sleeping with the elephants is also on offer, and a large self-catering flat has been built above the elephants' boma where they sleep at night (see Sleeping, page 335). This is also the only realistic chance you'll have of seeing elephants in the area — the fabled indigenous ones are far too elusive.

Plettenberg Bay ⬤⬤⬤⬤⬤⬤ ⤻ *pp329-348. Colour map 7, B2.*

Plettenberg Bay, or 'Plett', as it is commonly known, is one of the most appealing resorts on the Garden Route. Although it is modern and has little of historical interest, the compact centre is attractive and the main beach beautiful. Plett has now become fashionable and, during the Christmas season, the town is transformed. Wealthy families descend from Johannesburg and the pace can get quite frenetic – expect busy beaches and long queues for restaurant tables. For the rest of the year the pace is calmer and the resort becomes just another sleepy seaside town. There are three beaches that are good for swimming, but the coastline is spoilt by a multi-storey hotel built without much thought on a sandbar between two of the three beaches.

Plettenberg Bay

To Polo Field & Main Road - N2 for Nature's
Valley & Tsitsikamma National Park (55 km)

◆ Keurboom
Nature Reserve

Keurbooms
River Lagoon

Indian
Ocean

Lookout
Viewpoint

Lookout
Beach

Milkwood
Trail

Lookout

San Gonzalez
(1630)

Hobie Beach

Central
Beach

Old
Whaling
Station

Footbridge

Beacon
Island

Robberg
Beach

Piesangs River

To Robberg Peninsula Nature Reserve

N

200 metres
200 yards

Sleeping 🛏
Albergo For Backpackers **1**
A Room with a View **8**
Beacon **2**
Coral Tree Cottages **3**
Cottage Pie **6**

Hunter's Country House **7**
Nothando Backpackers **4**
Plettenberg **5**
Stone Cottages **9**

Eating 🍴
57 Kloof **2**
Blue Bay **1**
Lookout **5**
Med Seafood & Grill **4**
San Francisco **2**

South African Wildlife

Introduction

A large proportion of people who visit South Africa do so to see its spectacular wildlife. This colour section is a quick photographic guide to some of the more fascinating mammals you may encounter. We give you pictures and information about habitat, habits and characteristic appearance to help you when you are on safari. It is by no means a comprehensive survey and some of the animals listed may not be found throughout the whole country. For further information about South Africa's mammals, birds, reptiles and other wildlife, see the Land and environment section of the Background chapter.

The Big Nine

It is fortunate that many of the large and spectacular animals of Africa are also, on the whole, fairly common. They are often known as the 'Big Five'. This term was originally coined by hunters who wanted to take home trophies of their safari. Thus it was, that, in hunting parlance, the Big Five were elephant, black rhino, buffalo, lion and leopard. Nowadays the hippopotamus is usually considered one of the Big Five for those who shoot with their cameras, whereas the buffalo is far less of a 'trophy'. Equally photogenic and worthy of being included are the zebra, giraffe and cheetah. But whether they are the Big Five or the Big Nine, these are the animals that most people come to Africa to see and, with the possible exception of the leopard and the black rhino, ii you have an excellent chance of seeing them all.

Hippopotamus *Hippopotamus amphibius*. Prefers shallow water, grazes on land over a wide area at night, so can be found quite a distance from water, and has a strong sense of territory, which it protects aggressively. Lives in large family groups known as 'schools'.

Black rhinoceros *Diceros bicornis*. Long, hooked upper lip distinguishes it from white rhino rather than colour. Prefers dry bush and thorn scrub habitat and in the past was found in mountain uplands. Males usually solitary. Females seen in small groups with their calves (very rarely more than four), sometimes with two generations. Mother always walks in front of offspring, unlike the white rhino, where the mother walks behind, guiding calf with her horn. Their distribution has been massively reduced by poaching and work continues to save both the black and the white rhino from extinction. You might be lucky and see the black rhino in Kruger, Shamwari and Pilansberg national parks and private reserves like Mala Mala and Londolozi.

White rhinoceros *Diceros simus*. Square muzzle and bulkier than the black rhino, they are grazers rather than browsers, hence the different lip. Found in open grassland, they are more sociable and can be seen in groups of five or more. More common in Southern Africa due to a successful breeding program in Hluhluwe/Umfolozi National Park.

Opposite page:
Leopard with a kill.
Above left: Black rhinocerous.
Above right: White rhinocerous.
Right:
Hippopotamas.

■ **Reticulated giraffe** *Giraffa reticulata*. Reddish-brown coat and a network of distinct, pale, narrow lines. The patches tend to be much larger than those found in East Africa and have well-defined outlines, although giraffes found in the desert margins of Namibia are very pale in colour and less tall – probably due to a poor diet lacking in minerals.

■ **Leopard** *Panthera pardus*. Found in varied habitats ranging from forest to open savannah. They are generally nocturnal, hunting at night or before the sun comes up to avoid the heat. You may see them resting during the day in the lower branches of trees (**see picture page ii**).

■ **Common zebra (Burchell's)** *Equus burchelli*. Generally has broad stripes (some with lighter shadow stripes next to the dark ones) which cross the top of the hind leg in unbroken lines. The true species is probably extinct but there are many varying subspecies found in different locations across Africa, including Chapman's (Etosha National Park, Namibia, east across Southern Africa to Kruger National Park).

■ **Common/Masai giraffe** *Giraffa camelopardis*. Yellowish-buff with patch-work of brownish marks and jagged edges, usually two different horns, sometimes three. Found throughout Africa in several differing subspecies.

■ **Cheetah** *Acinonyx jubatus*. Often seen in family groups walking across plains or resting in the shade. The black 'tear' mark is usually obvious through binoculars. Can reach speeds of 90 kph over short distances. Found in open, semi-arid savannah, never in forested country. Endangered in some parts of Africa, Namibia is believed to have the largest free-roaming population on the continent. More commonly seen than the leopard, they are not as widespread as the lion *Panthera leo*.

Opposite page left:
Common giraffe.
Opposite page right:
Reticulated giraffe.
Top left: Burchell's zebra.
Top right: Grevy's zebra.
Above: Cheetah.
Right: Leopard.

v

■ **Lion** *Panthera leo* (**page i**). The largest (adult males can weigh up to 450 pounds) of the big cats in Africa and also the most common, lions are found on open savannah all over the continent. They are often not at all disturbed by the presence of humans and so it is possible to get quite close to them. They are sociable animals living in prides or permanent family groups of up to around 30 animals and are the only felid to do so. The females do most of the hunting (usually ungulates like zebra and antelopes).

■ **Buffalo** *Syncerus caffer* (**top**). Were considered by hunters to be the most dangerous of the big game and the most difficult to track and, therefore, the biggest trophy. Generally found on open plains but also at home in dense forest, they are fairly common in most African national parks but, like the elephant, they need a large area to roam in, so they are not usually found in the smaller parks.

■ **Elephant** *Loxodonta africana* (**above and page xvi**). Commonly seen, even on short safaris, elephants have suffered from the activities of war and from ivory poachers. However overall numbers have recovered to around 18,000 leading to problems of over population. As a result culling programmes are being considered by the South Africa government.

Gemsbok *Oryx gazella* 122 cm (**below**). Unmistakable, with black line down spine and black stripe between coloured body and white underparts. Horns (both sexes) straight, long and look -shaped (seen face-on). Only found in arid, semi-desert country. ■ **Nyala** *Tragelaphus angasi* 110 cm (**bottom left**). Slender frame, shaggy, dark brown coat with mauve tinge (males). Horns (male only) single open curve. The female is a different chestnut colour. They like dense bush and are usually found close to water. Gather in herds of up to 30 but smaller groups more likely. Found in Kruger National Park and across Zimbabwe and Malawi. ■ **Common** *Kobus ellipsiprymnus* and **Defassa** *Kobus defassa* **waterbuck** 122-137 cm (**bottom right**). Very similar with shaggy coats and white marking on buttocks. On the common variety, this is a clear half ring on rump and around tails; on Defassa, the ring is a filled-in solid white area. Both species occur in small herds in grassy areas, often near water.

■ **Sable antelope** *Hippotragus niger*
140–145 cm (**below**) and **Roan antelope**
Hippotragus equinus 127–137 cm. Both
similar shape, with ringed horns curving
backwards (both sexes), longer in the
sable. Female sables are reddish brown
and can be mistaken for the roan. Males
are very dark with a white underbelly. The
roan has distinct tufts of hair at the tips of
its long ears. Sable prefers wooded areas
and the roan is generally only seen near
water. Both species live in herds.

■ **Greater kudu** *Tragelaphus strepsiceros*
140–153 cm (**above**). Colour varies from
greyish to fawn with several vertical white
stripes down the sides of the body. Horns
long and spreading, with two or three twists
(male only). Distinctive thick fringe of hair
running from the chin down the neck.
Found in fairly thick bush, sometimes in
quite dry areas. Usually live in family groups
of up to six, but occasionally larger herds of
up to about 30.

■ **Topi** *Damaliscus korrigum* 122–127 cm
(**below**). Very rich dark rufous, with dark
patches on the tops of the legs and more
ordinary looking, lyre-shaped horns.

■ **Hartebeest** In the hartebeest the horns arise from a bony protuberance on the top of the head and curve outwards and back- wards. There are three sub-species: **Coke's hartebeest** *Alcephalus buselaphus* 122 cm is a drab pale brown with a paler rump; **Lichtenstein's hartebeest** *Alcephalus lichtensteinii* 127-132 cm is also fawn in general colouration, with a rufous wash over the back and dark marks on the front of the legs and often a dark patch near shoulder; and the **red hartebeest** *Alcephalus caama* (**right**). All are found in herds, sometimes they mix with other plain dwellers such as zebra.

■ **Brindled** or **blue wildebeest** or **gnu** *Connochaetes taurinus* (**top**) 132 cm is found only in southern Africa and is often seen grazing with zebra.

■ **Eland** *Taurotragus oryx* 175-183 cm (**left**). The largest of the antelope, it has a noticeable dewlap and shortish spiral horns (both sexes). Greyish to fawn, sometimes with rufous tinge and narrow white stripes down side of body. Occurs in groups of up to 30 in grassy habitats.

Smaller antelope

■ **Bushbuck** *Tragelaphus scriptus* 76-92 cm (**top**). Shaggy coat with variable pattern of white spots and stripes on the side and back and two white, crescent-shaped marks on front of neck. Short horns (male only) slightly spiral. High rump gives characteristic crouch. White underside of tail is noticeable when running. Occurs in thick bush, especially near water. Either seen in pairs or singly.

■ **Steenbok** *Raphicerus campestris* 58 cm (**top right**). An even, rufous brown colour with clean white underside and white ring around eye. Small dark patch at the tip of the nose and long broad ears. The horns (male only) are slightly longer than the ears: they are sharp, have a smooth surface and curve slightly forward. Generally seen alone, prefers open plains, often found in more arid regions. A slight creature which usually runs off very quickly on being spotted.

■ **Bohor reedbuck** *Redunca redunca* 71-76 cm (**bottom left**). Horns (males only) sharply hooked forwards at the tip, distinguishing them from the oribi (see next page). It is reddish fawn with white underparts and has a short bushy tail. They usually live in pairs or otherwise in small family groups. Often seen with Oribi, in bushed grassland and always near water.

■ **Klipspringer** *Oreotragus oreotragus* 56 cm (**bottom right**). Brownish-yellow with grey speckles and white chin and underparts with a short tail. Has distinctive, blunt hoof tips and short horns (male only). Likes dry, stony hills and mountains.

■ **Common (Grimm's) duiker** *Sylvicapra grimmia* 58 cm (**below**). Grey-fawn colour with darker rump and pale colour on the underside. Its dark muzzle and prominent ears are divided by straight, upright, narrow pointed horns. This particular species is the only duiker found in open grasslands. Usually the duiker is associated with a forested environment. It's difficult to see because it is shy and will quickly disappear into the bush.

■ **Oribi** *Ourebia ourebi* 61 cm (**bottom left**). Slender and delicate looking with a longish neck and a sandy to brownish-fawn coat. It has oval-shaped ears and short, straight horns with a few rings at their base (male only). Like the reedbuck (see above) it has a patch of bare skin just below each ear. They live in small groups or as a pair and are never far from water.

Suni *Nesotragus moschatus* 37 cm (**bottom right**). Dark chestnut to grey-fawn in colour with slight speckles along the back, its head and neck are slightly paler and the throat is white. It has a distinct bushy tail with a white tip. Its longish horns (male only) are thick, ribbed and slope backwards. This, one of the smallest antelope, lives alone and prefers dense bush cover and reed beds.

Springbuck *Antidorcas marsupialis* or **springbok**, 76-84 cm (**below**). The upper part of the body is fawn, and this is separated from the white underparts by a dark brown lateral stripe. It is distinguished by a dark stripe which runs between the base of the horns and the mouth, passing through the eye. This is the only type of gazelle found south of the Zambezi River and you will not see this animal further north. You no longer see the giant herds the animal was famous for, but you will see them along the roadside as you drive between Cape Town and Bloemfontein. They get their name from their habit of leaping stiff-legged and high into the air.

Impala *Aepyceros melampus* 92-107 cm (**bottom**). One of the largest of the smaller antelope, the impala is a bright rufous colour on its back and has a white abdomen, a white 'eyebrow' and chin and white hair inside its ears. From behind, the white rump with black stripes on each side is characteristic and makes it easy to identify. It has long lyre-shaped horns (male only). Above the heels of the hind legs is a tuft of thick black bristles (unique to impala) which are easy to see when the animal runs. There's also a black mark on the side of abdomen, just in front of the back leg. Found in herds of 15 to 20, it likes open grassland or sometimes the cover of partially wooded areas and is usually close to water.

Other mammals

There are many other fascinating mammals worth keeping an eye out for. This is a selection of some of the more interesting or particularly common ones.

■ **African wild dog** or **hunting dog** *Lycacon pictus* (**right**). Easy to identify since they have all the features of a large mongrel dog: a large head and slender body. Their coat is a mixed pattern of dark shapes and white and yellow patches and no two dogs are quite alike. They are very rarely seen and are seriously threatened with extinction (there may be as few as 6000 left). Found on the open plains around dead animals, they are not in fact scavengers but effective pack hunters.

■ **Brown hyena** *Hyaena brunnea* (**above**). High shoulders and low back give the hyena its characteristic appearance. The spotted variety, larger and brownish with dark spots, has a large head and rounded ears. The brown hyena, slightly smaller, has pointed ears and a shaggy coat, and is more noctural. Although sometimes shy animals, they have been know to wander around campsites stealing food from humans.

■ **Warthog** *Phacochoerus aethiopicus* (**left**). The warthog is almost hairless and grey with a very large head, tusks and wart-like growths on its face. It frequently occurs in family parties and when startled will run away at speed with its tail held straight up in the air. They are often seen near water caking themselves in thick mud which helps to keep them both cool and free of ticks and flies.

■ **Chacma baboon** *Papio ursinus* (**opposite page, bottom**). An adult male baboon is slender and weighs about 40 kg. Their general colour is a brownish grey, with lighter undersides. Usually seen in trees, but rocks can also provide sufficient protection, they occur in large family troops and have a reputation for being aggressive where they have become used to man's presence.

■ **Rock hyrax** *procavia capensis* (**above**). The nocturnal rock hyrax lives in colonies amongst boulders and on rocky hillsides, protecting themselves from predators like eagle, caracal and leopard by darting into the rock crevices.

■ **Caracal** *felis caracal* (**right**). Also known as the African lynx, it is twice the weight of a domestic cat, with reddish sandy colour fur and paler underparts. Distinctive black stripe from eye to nose and tufts on ears. Generally nocturnal and with similar habits to the leopard. They are not commonly seen, but are found in hilly country.

Ins and outs

Getting there For short trips to other towns along the Garden Route the **Baz Bus** represents the best value and most convenient schedule and has a daily service in either direction between Cape Town and Port Elizabeth. Mainline buses stop at the Shell Ultra City out of town on the N2. ▸▸ *For further details, see Transport, page 348.*

Best time to visit Avoid Plett on the last week of November and the first week of December. This is the end of Matric (final school exams) in South Africa, when thousands of young people descend on the resort to celebrate – known locally as 'The Plett Student Rage'.

Tourist information **Plettenburg Bay Tourism** ① *in the Melville's Corner shopping centre on Main St, T044-5334065, www.plettenbergbay.co.za, Mon-Fri 0900-1700, Sat 0900-1300, slightly longer hours during the peak summer season,* is a helpful office with quite a detailed website.

Background

In 1630 a Portuguese vessel, the **San Gonzalez**, was wrecked in the bay. This was 20 years before Jan van Riebeeck's arrival at the Cape. The survivors stayed here for eight months, during which time they built two smaller boats out of the wreckage, and one of the boats managed to sail up the coast to Mozambique. The survivors were eventually returned home to Lisbon, but they left behind a sandstone plaque on which they had inscribed the name *Baia Formosa*. Today a replica can be seen in Plett in the same place that the first was left by the sailors. (The original is now on show in the South African Museum in Cape Town.) The Portuguese had a number of names for the bay, but none stuck for very long. Later the Dutch also gave the bay several different names, such as Content Bay and Pisang River Bay; it was only in 1778 when Governor Joachim van Plettenberg opened a timber post on the shores of the bay, and named it after himself, that a name stuck.

Plettenberg remained an important timber port until the early 1800s when the Dutch decided to move operations to Knysna since it was a safer harbour. For a period the bay became famous as a whaling station but all that remains is a blubber cauldron and slipway. Most of the buildings were destroyed in a fire in 1914.

Sights

The tourist office gamely tries to promote some sights to visit but the attraction of this area is the sea and the outdoors. Aside from the three beaches, **Robberg**, **Central** and **Lookout**, there is excellent deep-sea fishing and, in season, good opportunities to spot whales and dolphins, particularly southern right whales from June to October. Plett climbs up a fairly steep hill; there are many elevated land-based vantage points as well as regular boat tours offering closer encounters with the marine life. The nearby **Keurbooms River lagoon** (see page 323) is a safe area for bathing and other watersports, and the dunes around the lagoon are now part of the **Keurboom River Nature Reserve**. In town itself, the main streets are just a collection of modern shopping malls and restaurants, but there are a few old buildings still standing which represent a little of the town's earlier history: St Andrew's Chapel, the remains of the Old Timber Store (1787), the Old Rectory (1776), the Forest Hall (1864) and the Dutch Reformed Church (1834). Also look out for the polo field with its lush grass and stylish white pavilion.

Invisible elephants

No guide to Knysna would be complete without a mention of the Knysna elephants. They have come to represent the last stand of wildlife against man in the region. The elephants live deep in the forest and few people have ever seen them. Little is known about their numbers or their characteristics. They belong to the same species as the savanna elephant but as a result of living in the forest their lifestyle and habits have changed, and they are thought to now resemble the forest elephant found in the equatorial jungle of Central Africa. In 1876, several hundred elephants were recorded in the region, but under heavy pressure of ivory hunters they were reduced to 20 to 30 individuals by 1908. In 1970 the Knysna elephant population was estimated at 11, and by 1994, only one Knysna elephant was known to survive, an elderly female. In the same year, three young elephants from the Kruger National Park were introduced into the range of the elderly female in an effort to increase numbers. Unfortunately, one of them died of stress-related complications soon after release. The remaining two elephants joined up with the elderly female for only short periods before choosing to spend 80% of their time in mountainous fynbos habitat beyond the Knysna forest. In 1999 they were then recaptured and relocated to the Shamwari Private Game Reserve in the Eastern Cape. Then, after a study in 2007, conservation geneticists from the US University of Missouri-Columbia announced that there could be several elephants in Knysna Forest. By extracting DNA samples from dung, they established that there were five individual females and at least one bull, and possibly a calf was born recently. They also established that these were not related to the reintroduced Kruger elephants. Happy hiking – you may just see more than the Knysna lourie.

Hiking

Milkwood is a 3- or 5-km trail in and around the town. Follow the yellow footprints. The walk starts from the car park off Marine Drive and takes you via Piesangs River lagoon, Central beach, and Lookout beach. At this point the shorter route turns back through the centre of town via some of the historic buildings, while the longer route continues via Keurbooms Lagoon and round the back of town.

There are some recommended walks in the **Robberg Peninsula Nature Reserve** ① *8 km south from Plett on the old airport road, T044-5332125, www.capenature.org.za, Feb-Nov 0700-1700, Dec and Jan 0700-2000. Permits are available at the entrance gate, R25, R12 child.* There are three possibilities ranging from 2-9 km on this loop along the peninsula which forms the western boundary of Plettenberg Bay. Follow the 'seal' markers. Walking is easy thanks to boardwalks, and there are plenty of prominent viewpoints from which it is possible to see whales, seals and dolphins in the bay, but beware of freak waves along the coastal paths. Allow at least four hours for the full route. If you want to go on a guided walk of Robberg, contact **Robberg Guided Walks** ① *T044- 5332632, www.robbergwalks.homestead.com.*

The N2 continues east from Plettenberg Bay, but don't expect to travel too fast as there are a number of attractions and sights in rapid succession that are worth stopping for.

Keurbooms River Nature Reserve

ⓘ *7 km east of Plett, T044 5332125, www.capenature.co.za, 0800-1800, R25 adults, R12 children.*

First up is Keurbooms River Nature Reserve. Taking a sailing trip upstream on the **Keurbooms River Ferry** (see Activities and tours, page 346, for further details) is a great way to spend a few hours. You are ferried 5 km along the river through a spectacular gorge overhung by indigenous trees and other flora. At the furthest point from the jetty there is an optional 30-minute walk, with a professional guide, through the forest. This is the ultimate eco-experience and a relaxing way of being introduced to the plants, sights and sounds of the forest. Make sure you are wearing sturdy footwear if you intend to join the walk.

The Keurbooms River is also a safe designated area for canoeing and waterskiing and it is possible to hire canoes from the **Cape Nature office** ⓘ *on the east side of the Keurbooms River Bridge on the N2, T044-5332125, a double canoe costs R75 per day, if you just want to picnic next to the Keurbooms River it's R5 per person.* Alternatively, you can go on an overnight trail up the river. This is a 14-km round journey through a pretty gorge where you've got a good chance of spotting kingfishers and fish eagles. As the gorge narrows further up the river, you leave behind the pleasure boats and waterskiers and reach a section of river that is seldom used by other boaters. You overnight at the **Whiskey Creek Hut**, a stilted log cabin (see Sleeping, page 337, for further details).

Monkeyland and Birds of Eden

ⓘ *T044-5348906, www.monkeyland.co.za, www.birdsofeden.co.za, daily 0830-1700, a guided tour for each attraction costs R100, children under 12 R50; a combo ticket for both is R160, children R80. To get there, turn off at the signpost on the N2 at the Forest Hall turning, Monkeyland and Birds of Eden are a further 2 km down the road.*

At the settlement known as The Crags 16 km east of Plettenburg Bay (just after the BP filling station) is the well-signposted turning to Monkeyland. As the name suggests, this is a primate reserve with lemurs, apes and monkeys from several continents where the attractions are free to move about in the living indigenous forest. Most are rescued pets. Visitors are advised to join a guided walk which takes in various waterholes in the forest Guides have a keen eye for spotting animals. One of the highlights here is the Indiana Jones-style rope bridge that spans 118 m across a canyon, offering glimpses of species that spend their entire lives in the upper reaches of the forest. The primates themselves also use this bridge (supposedly the longest of its kind in the southern hemisphere). If you don't wish to join a tour, the day centre has a good viewpoint and the restaurant serves a tasty lunch. Great for kids. **Birds of Eden**, is a 2.3-ha mesh dome spanning more of the same forest with 1.2 km of walkways, 900 m of which is elevated, that go past waterfalls and dams. Along the same principle as Monkeyland, previously caged birds have been released into a natural environment and visitors, who are permitted to wander around without a guide, can get a bird's eye view of macaws, cockatoos, parrots and louries.

If you are in a hurry, stay on the N2 – this is a good stretch of road, although there is a toll of around R10. The more spectacular route is via the village of Nature's Valley along the old R102, a beautifully forested road that branches off the N2 just after The Crags. Look out for ververt monkeys in the trees.

Nature's Valley → *Colour map 7, B3.*

This small village has one of the most beautiful settings along the Garden Route. Since the N2 toll road was opened in 1984, most traffic bypasses this sleepy community. The village is surrounded on three sides by the western section of the **Tsitsikamma National Park** (see page 325). The approach by road is particularly spectacular. The R102, dropping 223 m to sea level via the narrow Kalanderkloof Gorge, twists and turns through lush green coastal forest. At the bottom is a lagoon formed by the sand dunes blocking the estuary of the **Groot River**. A right turn leads into the village, made up of a collection of holiday cottages and one shop that is an all-in-one restaurant, bar and **tourist information bureau** ⓘ *T044-5316835, www.natures-valley.com.* Note that there are no banks in Nature's Valley. There are several braai spots on the sandy beach, but be warned that swimming in the sea is not safe. Canoes, rowing boats and yachts can all be used on the Groot River and lagoon, but powerboats are prohibited.

Groot River and Bloukrans Passes

As the road starts to climb out of the Groot Valley it passes the **Nature's Valley Rest Camp** on the right. This is the only camp at the western end of the Tsitsikamma National Park (see page 337 for booking details). Many visitors will end up here because it is one end of two of the Garden Route's most spectacular hiking trails, the **Tsitsikamma Trail** and the **Otter Trail**. From the top of the Groot River Pass the road continues for 6 km before crossing a second river valley, the Bloukrans Pass. Here it descends 183 m into the narrow gorge before crossing the river and climbing up again. The R102 rejoins the N2 highway 10 km further on and crosses the **Bloukrans River Bridge**. Just after the bridge is a turning to the left that leads to a viewpoint at the top of the Bloukrans Gorge. The bridge is apparently the highest in Africa, and the drop into the gorge is quite spectacular. But the main reason for stopping is the **Bloukrans Bungee Jump** ⓘ *T042-2811458, www.faceadrenalin.com, daily from 0900-1700, booking not essential but recommended, bungee jump R580 which includes the bridge walk.* At 216 m it is the highest commercial bungee in the world. The first rebound is longer than the previous holder of the record, the 111-m bungee jump at Victoria Falls. It's a hugely exhilarating experience and the free fall once you've leapt from the bridge lasts seven seconds, travelling over 170 kph before you reach the maximum length of the bungee cord. The new event at Bloukrans is the Flying Fox, R150, a 200-m cable slide from a platform on land to the centre of the bridge arch. If you cannot muster up the courage to do either of these, than you can go on a guided bridge walk for R50. This involves walking out to the bungee platform along the caged walkway underneath the bridge where a guide tells you how the bridge was built and a little bit about the surrounding area. This is not for anyone who suffers from vertigo, but if you want to support a mate that's doing a jump, it's a great way to feel some of the fear they are experiencing when standing on the lip of the bungee platform. Also at the top of the gorge is the Tsitsikamma Forest Village, a fairly new sustainable initiative to help local people make and sell curios to the very many passing tourists. Shops are in a collection of attractive reed Khosian huts, and you can buy items such as candles or home-made paper.

Storms River Bridge → *Colour map 7, B3.*

Storms River Bridge is a further 5 km along the N2 from Bloukrans. There is a viewing platform to look down into the river gorge. Next to the bridge is the **Petro-Total Village**, a popular stopover with petrol pumps, curio shops, a restaurant, small museum and the **Tsitsikamma Information office** ① *T042-2803561, www.tsitsikamma.info, daily 0830-1630.* It is worth stopping briefly here to pick up some local tourist leaflets, especially if you have plans to hike in the region. It is a helpful office and can provide information and local bookings for a whole variety of adventure activities. This is also an official stop for the mainline buses that travel along the Garden Route. **Note**: Storms River Village is a further 8 km along the N2, not to be confused with Storms River Mouth which is in the Tsitsikamma National Park.

Tsitsikamma National Park ⊕▲↠ *pp329-348. Colour map 7, B3.*

This is one of the most popular national parks in the country, second only to Kruger. It consists of a beautiful 80-km stretch of lush coastal forest and is known for its excellent birdlife. Not only is the forest protected, but the park boundaries reach out to sea for 5.5 km in the eastern sector. No boats are allowed in this area, nor is spearfishing permitted and no shells (even dead ones) may be removed or disturbed.

Ins and outs

Getting there There are two access points into the park depending in which restcamp you are staying in, though generally day visitors enter the Storms River Mouth entrance, where there are better facilities for those on day trips. The turn-off for **Storms River Restcamp** is on a straight stretch of the N2, about 4 km after the Storms River Bridge, easy to miss if driving fast. A surfaced road leads down to the reception centre on the coast. The last part of this drive is a beautiful, steep descent through lush rainforest, a marked contrast to the coniferous plantations along the N2 toll road. If you are travelling along the R102, the turning is just beyond the sawmill at Boskor. If you are approaching from the Port Elizabeth side, the turning is 4 km after the small village of Storms River.

The **Nature's Valley Restcamp** is 40 km west of Storms River Mouth and can only be reached from the R102; when approaching from Knysna take the Nature's Valley turning at Kurland (R102). If you miss this turning you cannot turn off the N2 toll road until it meets with the other end of the R102, at which point you are only 8 km from the turning for Storms River camp. When approaching from Port Elizabeth look out for signs for Nature's Valley, R102. Nature's Valley Restcamp is clearly signposted 3 km outside the village of the same name.

Best time to visit The best time to visit is between November and February. Bear in mind that, although this is midsummer, you can expect rain at any time. Annual rainfall is in excess of 1200 mm; June and July are the driest months, while May and October are the wettest.

Park information Gates open 0700-1900, office hours 0730-1800, T042-2811607. The daily conservation fee including vehicles R80, children R40. At the Storms River Restcamp is a shop open daily 0800-1800 that stocks gift items as well as groceries, wine and beer. **Tiger's Eye Restaurant** is open 0730-1000, 1200-1500 and 1800-1930, but you must make reservations for evening meals by 1700. Other facilities include a swimming pool, card telephone and occasional film shows on the park ecology.

Background
The park stretches 80 km along the coast between Nature's Valley and Oubosstrand. For most of its length it is no more than 500 m wide on the landward side. At the western end, where the Otter Trail reaches the Groot River estuary, the park boundary extends 3 km inland. It was established on 4 December 1964 in response to an appeal for the creation of more marine parks and reserves, made during the First World Conference on National Parks in Seattle in 1962. The main administrative office is at Storms River Restcamp, which is almost the midpoint of the park. The park is the location for the famous 42-km **Otter Hiking Trail** (see box, page 327), which follows the coastline between Storms River Restcamp and Nature's Valley Restcamp. The trail can be hiked in either direction.

Vegetation and wildlife
A cross-section of the coastlands would reveal the Tsitsikamma Mountains (900-1600 m), whose slopes level off into a coastal plain or plateau at about 230 m, and then the forested cliffs which plunge 230 m into the ocean. The slope is only precipitous in a few places; elsewhere along the coast it is still very steep, but there is enough soil to support the rainforest which the park was in part created to protect. The rainforest is the last remnant of a forest which was once found right along this coast between the ocean and the mountains. The canopy ranges between 18 m and 30 m and is closed, which makes the paths nice and shady. The most common species of trees are milkwood, real yellowwood, stinkwood, Cape blackwood, forest elder, white pear and candlewood, plus the famous Outeniqua yellowwood, a forest giant. All are magnificent trees which combine with climbers such as wild grape, red saffron and milky rope to create an outstandingly beautiful forest.

In the forest itself 35 different bird species have been recorded, while in the park as a whole over 220 species have been identified. The most colourful bird in the forest is the **Knysna lourie** (*Touraco corythaix*). Its call is a korr korr korr, and in flight it has a flash of deep red in its wings, with a green body and distinctive crest. In the vicinity of the Storms River campsite and the Groot River estuary you will see an entirely different selection of birds: over 40 species of seabird have been recorded here. The most satisfying sighting is the rare **African black oystercatcher**, with its black plumage and red eyes, beak and legs.

With such steep slopes and dense forest you will only come across a few small mammals. The species that do occur include caracal, bushbuck, blue duiker, grysbok, bushpig and the Cape clawless otter. The **blue duiker** is the smallest antelope in South Africa -- the adult male stands less than 30 cm high and weighs about 4 kg, although the female is slightly bigger. They live in forest and thick bush along the coast, feeding on forest fruits and flowers that are dropped from the canopy by feeding monkeys, or birds such as the Knysna lourie or rameron pigeons. Each animal lives alone in a territory of about 6 ha in extent. The most likely time to see them is at dawn or dusk in an open clearing -- ask the park rangers about recent sightings. The **Cape clawless otter** is also very rare and considered an endangered species. It feeds on fish and sea crabs, emerging from its den in the early evening. You will be very lucky to catch a glimpse of either of these mammals.

Hiking in the park
Nature's Valley Rest Camp Across the Groot River from the camp are six trails in the Grootkloof Forest. There are a number of large trees here and the birdlife is excellent, although there's the usual problem of catching sight of them in the first place. The best spots are in clearings and along streams. Note that there are a large number of streams in the forest which can be difficult to cross after heavy rains. South of the camp the river

The Otter Trail

This is one of South Africa's best hiking trails, managed by South African National Parks (SANParks), and it was also the first of its kind to be laid out. The 42.5-km trail is unidirectional; it runs between Storms River Mouth restcamp in the Tsitsikamma National Park and the village of Nature's Valley at the western end of the national park. It takes five days and four nights to complete, and closely follows the coast – care should be taken near the cliffs. None of the sectors are that long, but it is still fairly strenuous in parts since you have to cross 11 rivers and there are steep ascents and descents at each river crossing. Apart from the natural beauty and the birdlife, the trail passes some fine waterfalls and Strandloper caves. Look out for the fine large old hardwood trees which have escaped the dreaded axe.

This is a very popular hike and booking opens 13 months in advance, though it's always worth asking about cancellations. Permits are available from SANParks, Pretoria, T012-4265111, www.sanparks.org. Bookings can also be made in person at the offices in Cape Town (see page 48) and Durban. The offices also provide excellent maps which are packed full of background information and advice to help make your experience an enjoyable one. The route is marked with painted otter footprints.

Distances: **Day 1** = 4.8 km (± 2 hours); **Day 2** = 7.9 km (± 4 hours); **Day 3** = 7.7 km (± 4 hours); **Day 4** = 13.8 km (± 6 hours); **Day 5** = 6.8 km (± 3 hours). **Total distance** = 42.5 km. Only 12 people can start the trail each day; groups should consist of a minimum of four. It costs R525 per person, which includes four nights in the hiking huts as well as the permit.

The four overnight camps are Ngubu, Scott, Oakhurst and André. At each site there are two log huts, each sleeping six people in bunk beds; mattresses and firewood are provided. Each hut has a braai place with a sturdy steel grill but hikers need to provide their own pots for cooking. There are numerous streams and springs throughout the length of the Otter Trail that are suitable for drinking. However, it may be wise to use purification tablets especially if you are not used to this water and where streams/rivers pass through communities such as the Coldstream/Witels River (3.6 km mark of Day 4) and the Lottering River (7.5 km mark of Day 4). There are rainwater tanks at each overnight hut that may also be used. The Bloukrans River crossing presents the most problems. Check tide tables; you will at least have to wade, or even swim across. Waterproofing for your rucksack is vital. If you are unable to cross the river, you can take the escape route, which branches to the right of the trail, where it climbs steeply to the top of the plateau and leads to the N2. Take time to enjoy the trail, relish the scenery and the solitude, respect the environment and leave with positive and happy memories.

estuary broadens into a lagoon which is a popular spot for watersports. Fortunately no powerboats are allowed on the water, and exploring the limits by canoe is great fun.

Storms River Camp There are four different trails in the vicinity of the camp. The most popular, and strongly recommended, is a 1-km walk along a raised boardwalk from the restaurant block to the mouth of the Storms River. The last part of the walk involves a steep descent – there is a solid handrail, but the wooden steps can be slippery after rains, as can other parts of the walk. At the bottom is the suspension bridge which appears in many pictures promoting the Garden Route. The views from this point are excellent, especially at midday when there is a clear view of the narrow river gorge extending back inland. The path continues on the other side of the bridge, and from here you can climb the hill for superb views; there are over 300 steps and the path is narrow and steep. Look out for identification labels on the trees as the path winds through the forest. This is a great opportunity to see the trees which a century ago were in great demand for household furniture and building projects – much of the reason for the extensive deforestation in the area. Allow at least an hour for the walk to the bridge and back.

The other trails close to the camp are the **Lourie Trail**, 1 km through the forested slopes behind the camp; the **Blue Duiker Trail**, 3.7 km further into the forest; and the **Waterfall Trail**, a 3-km walk along the first part of the Otter Trail (see page 327); hikers without a permit have to turn back at the waterfall.

The latest addition to the park is the **Dolphin Trail** ① *information and reservations T042-2803588, www.dolphintrail.co.za*, a three-day guided trail to the east of Storms River Restcamp and in the opposite direction to the Otter Trail. This is a far more upmarket hike – luggage is transported from one night stop to the next, accommodation is in luxurious lodges, all meals are included (with pre-packed picnics for lunch), and the entire hike is professionally guided. This trail is also much more expensive, at R3300 per person for three days.

Behind the restaurant is the rather unusual **Underwater Trail**, which can be completed with scuba equipment or a mask and snorkel. You can see a good cross-section of the marine life found along the south coast, but conditions are not ideal, so few people complete the trail. If you do want to give it a go, the best time of year is in the summer, although conditions are rough for most of the year and visibility is rarely more than 10 m. The water is fairly cold, so be sure to wear a wetsuit.

Storms River Village → *Colour map 7, B3.*

Storms River Village lies 8 km east of the Storms River Bridge, 4 km from the entrance to Tsitsikamma National Park, and 1 km south of the N2. Administratively, this is the first settlement in the Eastern Cape Province, but it is also regarded as the first and last town along the Garden Route, hence its inclusion here. This small village of around 40 houses has several accommodation options catering for visitors to the park and hikers wishing to head for the inland mountains. It's also a stop-off for the **Baz Bus** and the starting point for many of the adventure activities in the region. The small supermarket and liquor store are useful for those self-catering at Tsitsikamma. Note that the village is nowhere near the sea.

● Garden Route listings

Hotel and guesthouse prices
L over US$300 **AL** US$220-300 **A** US$150-220
B US$100-150 **C** US$75-100 **D** US$35-75
E US$15-35 **F** under US$15
Private game reserves
L4 over US$900 **L3** US$550-900
L2 US$450-550 **L1** US$300-500
Restaurant prices
¶¶¶ over US$30 ¶¶ US$15-30 ¶ under US$15
See pages 46-51 for further information.

● Sleeping

Mossel Bay *p305, map p306*
During busy periods, contact the **Mossel Bay Tourism Bureau**, T044-6912202, to confirm overnight accommodation. It acts as a central reservations office for registered members. In Dec it's essential to pre-book.
AL Diaz Strand, Santos Beach, T044-6928400, www.diazbeach.co.za. Luxury hotel opened in 2004 in a commanding position on Santos Beach overlooking the waves, 86 spacious rooms in a modern block all with ocean views. Facilities include outdoor rim-flow pool, indoor heated Olympic-sized pool and wellness centre, a water theme park with tubes and a lazy river, live entertainment and the highly regarded Bahia Dos Vaqueiros restaurant (see Eating, page 339).
B The Point, Point Rd, T044-6913512, www.pointhotel.co.za. Large, ugly construction but in an unbeatable location, right on the rocks below the lighthouse. All 48 rooms are en suite and have satellite TV, sea views and private balconies. **The Lighthouse** restaurant and bar caters for most. There is a rock pool just outside which is good for swimming.
B Protea Hotel Mossel Bay, corner of Church and Market St, T044-6913738, www.oldposttree.co.za, www.proteahotels.com. This is part of the museum complex and was formerly known as the **Old Post Office Tree Manor**. Comfortable hotel rooms and self-catering suites in a smart manor house which is the 3rd-oldest building in Mossel

Bay. Outdoor dining area with views across bay, swimming pool, popular and always recommended by visitors, check for seasonal discounts.
C Huijs te Marquette, 1 Marsh St, T/F044-6913182, www.marquette.co.za. A comfortable house which has been very thoughtfully decorated, 12 en suite rooms, relaxed atmosphere, small snug bar and lounge with fireplace, evening meals on request, swimming pool, secure parking, wheelchair friendly. Recommended.
C Mossel Bay Guesthouse, 61 Bruns Rd, T044-6912000, www.mosselbaygh.co.za. Friendly guesthouse with 4 en suite double rooms with sea views and M-Net TV. Heated pool and wooden deck with ocean views where breakfast is served in summer, and small pub. The house is tucked back from the town centre up the hill.
D Allemans Dorpshuis, 94 Montagu St, T044-6903621, allemans@telkomsa.net. In the heart of town, lovely old-fashioned hotel in a fine restored Victorian town house with the original iron balcony at the front. 6 beautifully furnished rooms with en suite showers and polished wooden floors. French and German spoken, very good value out of season.
D-F Mossel Bay Backpackers, 1 Marsh St, T044-6913182, www.gardenroute adventures.com. Part of Huijs te Marquette, dorms and double rooms, some camping space for small 2-man tents only, TV room, breakfasts and dinners available, self-catering kitchen, convenient location 300 m from the beach and close to some bars, travel centre can organize activities, popular.
D-F Santos Caravan Park, on the George road 2 km from town centre, T044-6912915. Large well-grassed park with 54 camping and caravan sites, limited shade, some self-catering chalets, not the place to stay when full, but fine at the quiet time of year, right on the beach.

E Santos Express Train Lodge,
T044-6911995, www.santosexpress.co.za.
Converted train carriages set 30 m from the
sea on Santos beach with tiny cabins sleeping
4, shared hot showers, sun deck and an
onboard pub and restaurant serving seafood,
lamb on the spit and braais. Baz Bus stop.

Botlierskop Private Game Reserve *p307*
Private lodges and camps
L1 Botlierskop Private Game Reserve,
T044-6966055, www.botlierskop.co.za. 19
luxury tented suites on wooden platforms,
good views over river and mountains, some
have private jetties for fishing, decorated in a
colonial theme with 4-poster beds swathed
in mosquito nets. Rates include game drives,
walks and all meals. An all-round safari
experience close to the Garden Route.

George *p308, map p308*
L Fancourt Hotel and Country Club,
6 km from George airport, T044-8040000,
www.fancourt.com. This is an exclusive
upmarket resort and thanks to the
President's Cup being hosted here in
Nov 2003, it is one of the world's leading
golf destinations. Set on more than 500 ha
of land, Fancourt encompasses 4 outstanding 18-hole golf courses, 2 of which
were designed by Gary Player. There are
rooms in the 19th-century manor house or
garden suites and studios overlooking the
golf courses. Health spa, gym, tennis courts,
2 outdoor pools, 1 indoor heated pool,
5 superb restaurants. Golf open to members
and guests only. Special packages are
sometimes published on the website.
Golfer Ernie Els sponsors a golf academy
here for talented young South Africans
who could not under normal circumstances
afford to participate in the sport. Room
rates drop significantly in low season
(1 Apr-31 Aug).
A Far Hills Country Hotel, off the N2
towards Wilderness, T044-8890000,
www.farhillscountryhotel.co.uk. A large
comfortable country hotel in the lee of

the Outeniqua Mountains. 51 tastefully
decorated rooms with fireplace and balcony,
some with superb views across the forest,
but a bit cramped. Café, **Country Cuisine**
restaurant with – rather surprisingly –
a sushi bar, open terrace, lounge, bar
and swimming pool. Very attentive service
for such a big hotel.
A-D George Tourist Resort, York St,
T044-8745205, www.george-tourist-
resort.co.za. Huge complex with self-catering
chalets sleeping up to 8, smaller rondavels
and caravans. Shady sites with power and
water, indoor pool and outdoor heated pool,
gym, sauna, tennis courts, crazy golf, shop,
laundry, room for 300 caravans! Double
the price during peak season.
B-C Oakhurst Manor House, corner of
Meade and Cathedral streets, T044-8747130,
www.oakhursthotel.co.za. Luxury town inn
in the design of a classic Cape Dutch house
with thatched roof, 25 smart, individually
decorated en suite rooms, large restaurant,
lounge, ladies' bar and swimming pool.
Professionally run but aimed at the
business traveller.
C Loerie Guest Lodge, 91 Davidson Rd,
T044-8744740, www.loerielodge.co.za.
Modern buildings with 22 large and
comfortable en suite rooms, a neat garden
with a swimming pool and sun deck, pub
on the first floor with a deck for good views
of the mountains. Alright for an overnight
stop, but predominantly a conference venue.
Also rents out a 5-bedroom house nearby.
C Protea Hotel King George, King George
Dr, T044-8747659, www.proteahotels.com.
Smart Victorian hotel situated close to the
11th fairway of the George Golf Course,
60 comfortable rooms, good restaurant,
pub, 2 swimming pools, the usual quality
of service expected in a Protea.
C-D Pine Lodge, Knysna Rd, close to Pick
'n' Pay, T044-8711974, www.pinelodge
george.co.za. Large resort close to Victoria
Bay, suitable for families with 46 self-catering
chalets with 1-3 bedrooms, M-Net TV,
telephone and braai area. Restaurant, the

Courtyard Grill, bar, tennis courts and swimming pool. There are a few budget rooms without kitchens.

D Hawthorndene Country Inn, Langenhoven Rd, T044-8744160, www.hawthorndene.co.za. Family-run country inn with 26 en suite rooms, pool, a good restaurant and bar with log walls and crackling fire, big TV screen and live music at the weekends.

D-F Outeniqua Backpackers, 115 Merriman St, T082-2167720, www.outeniqua-back packers.com. Newish hostel with 20 dorm beds and a couple of doubles, bright and airy, some with mountain views, braai area, breakfasts, DSTV and internet. Only backpacker option in town. Baz Bus stop. You can hire bikes and they'll drop you off at the top of Montagu Pass for the ride back down.

Victoria Bay p310

A The Waves, 6 Beach Rd, T044-8890166, thewaves@intekom.co.za. A superior B&B right on the beach, 3 double rooms with en suite bathroom, balconies and sea views, 1906 historic building, friendly, low-key place, a more pleasant location than the centre of George, 2 separate family cottages available (B&B or self-catering). Recommended.

B Lands End, The Point, T044-8890123, www.vicbay.com. 2 double en suite rooms with TV, 3 self-contained apartments with sun deck, self-catering, or breakfasts served on an open veranda only 6 m from the ocean, beautiful location, fishing and surf equipment hired out, golf at Fancourt can be arranged, extras such as laundry, wine cellar, and a glass of sherry on arrival, ask for Rod or Shanell.

B-C Sea Breeze, 300-m walk to the beach, T044-8890098, www.seabreezecabanas.co.za. 36 units, modern development of self-catering flats and chalets with M-Net TV, bedding supplied but you have to bring your own towels and dishcloths. The beach has a safe tidal pool, good for families.

Wilderness p312, map p312

A Dolphin Dunes, Buxton Close, approaching from George, turn right off the N2, 2.5 km after the Caltex petrol station T044-8770204, www.dolphindunes.co.za. A fine upmarket purpose-built guesthouse with 8 tasteful, double en suite rooms, some with wheelchair access, fridge, TV, telephone, splash pool, private access to the beach. Also rents out a fully equipped modern holiday villa sleeping 8-10.

A Protea Wilderness Resort, T044-8771110, www.proteahotels.com. Smartest hotel in the area, large with over 155 stylish en suite rooms with TV, restaurant, beauty spa, 2 swimming pools, bowling green, giant chess board in the grounds, great views all round. If you are not staying here, pop in for the very good-value Sun lunch from 1230-1500.

D Moontide Guest Lodge, Southside Rd, T044-8770361, www.moontide.co.za. 8 en suite thatched cottages, one of them a honeymoon suite, set under milkwood trees in a beautiful garden overlooking the lagoon. Each cottage has been tastefully decorated with kilims and fine furniture. Easy access to the hiking trails in the national park, a short walk from the beach and a good spot for birdwatchers. A well-appointed and well-run guesthouse. Recommended.

B The Pink Lodge on the Beach, 45 die Duin, T044-8770263, www.pinklodge.co.za. B&B or self-catering in a great position right on the beach, 7 spacious, a/c, en suite rooms, 1 with self-catering facilities, all facing the ocean, spot whales or dolphins from your bed, rolling lawns, a very relaxing spot. Shame about the hideous bright pink colour.

B-C Fairy Knowe, Dumbleton Rd, T044-8771100, www.fairyknowe.co.za. 42 rooms, some thatched rondavels, peaceful forested location on Touw River, close to Wilderness National Park, bird watchers will enjoy regular visits by the Knysna lourie and there are a couple of resident Cape spotted eagle owls, restaurant, bar, canoes, pedalos and tennis.

C Bruni's Guest House, 937 8th Av, Wilderness East, T044-8770551, www.brunis.co.za. 4 en suite double rooms in a thatched house perched on the dunes with sweeping views of the ocean from the glassed-in breakfast room. German spoken, no children under 12.

D-F Fairy Knowe Backpackers, Dumbleton Rd, just off Waterside Rd, T044-8771285, www.fairyknowe.com. A great set-up in 2 farmhouses surrounded by gardens and milkwood trees, clean attractive rooms, dorms and doubles, camping space in the garden, bar, great breakfasts, nightly camp fires and braais. Also has a travel desk. A very relaxing place to rest up for a few days. Baz Bus stops here. Recommended.

Wilderness National Park *p313, map p312*
Accommodation is laid out in 2 camps divided by the railway and the Serpentine River channel: **Ebb & Flow Rest Camp, North** and **Ebb & Flow Rest Camp, South**. All the park's accommodation must be vacated by 0900. Arriving visitors can have access from 1200. Reservations through **SANParks** Pretoria office, T012-4289111, www.sanparks.org. Bookings can also be made in person at the offices in Cape Town and Durban (see page 48). For reservations under 72 hrs or cancellations contact the park reception directly, T044-8771197.

C-E Ebb and Flow Rest Camp, South, on the Touw River close to Wilderness village, has 34 units in total:

C Cottages, 2 bedrooms and sofa bed, bathroom, partially equipped kitchen, lounge, modern bungalows with no appeal when you compare them with the log cabins.

C Log Cabins, self-catering cabins on stilts, all have views across the river and the reed beds, 2 bedrooms, bathroom, kitchen, comfortable lounge area and a veranda, lots of character. Good value for 4 people especially with a seasonal discount.

D Forest cabins, sleeping 2 or 4, fairly basic but with en suite bathroom and partially equipped kitchen, communal kitchen also available.

E Campsite, in thick grass with patches of good shade on the banks of the river, beautiful setting and good facilities, an excellent campsite with 59 caravan and camping sites, full of character as long as it is not too full.

E Ebb & Flow Rest Camp, North, a short walk from the office, this is a smaller camp beside the Touw River where it emerges from the hills. A beautiful and peaceful spot but its geography means that cold air collects in the narrow valley and the sun only reaches the camp for a few hours.

E Huts 12 1-room rondavels with 2 single beds, 2-plate electric stove, fridge, cooking equipment, plus a shower, for 2 people, or a cheaper option with no en suite shower.

E Camping 45 caravan and camping sites on the banks of the Touw River, plenty of grass and shade, wash block, no communal kitchen but braais, some sites with electric points.

Sedgefield and around *p313*
As with all villages along this stretch of coast, prices are considerably higher at Christmas and rooms need to be booked well in advance. There is a choice of overnight stops and holiday cottages in the village and around the lakes.

A Lake Pleasant, east of Sedgefield on the edge of Groenvlei, T044-3492400, www.lakepleasanthotel.com. This comfortable 5-star hotel has had a major overhaul and now belongs to the South African Mantis chain of luxury hotels. Set right on the lake, with 36 rooms with en suite bathroom, opening onto gardens, all with lake views. Smart lounge furnished with antiques, library, cigar bar, restaurant with a menu to match the setting – great lunch stop if you're passing through. Swimming pool, tennis court, gym, health spa. Perfect for birdwatchers with some hides by the lake, rowing boats for hire. Recommended.

B-D Sedgefield Arms, Pelican Lane, off the N2 in the village centre, T044-3431417, www.sedgefieldarms.co.za. A comfortable mix of self-catering cottages suitable for 2-6 people with patio and braai, or B&B. Attached restaurant and lively English theme pub, good spot for lunch on the lawn, bar with big sports screen, swimming pool, all set in leafy gardens, good value and fun atmosphere. Rates drop significantly out of season.

C Groenvlei & Muvubu Bushcamps, reservations, T021-6593500, www.cape nature.org.za. In the western side of the reserve, hidden away in the milkwood forest, are 2 thatched family en suite houses sleeping 8-9, with living area and kitchen linked by boardwalks, furnishings made from wood or reeds. Both a short walk to the lake where you can swim and watch the sun set. Bring all your own food and bedding. A beautiful setting with particular attention paid to the environment. Recommended and good value for 4 or more.

D-F Landfall Resort, 1/T044-3431804. Well-maintained campsite with plenty of shade and grass. Fully equipped 2-bedroom self-catering cottages that sleep 6 people are also available. This is an excellent campsite right on the estuary, a short distance from the beach. A good, cheap option.

Knysna *p314, maps p315 and p316*
It is difficult to find accommodation during the Christmas and New Year period unless you book 6 months in advance. As one of the most popular holiday centres along the Garden Route, there is plenty of choice of accommodation, both in type and location, but it's generally more expensive than in other towns along the Garden Route. The list below is far from comprehensive. Remember you'll be paying a premium to stay over school holiday periods. The centre of Knysna is on the northern margin of the lagoon. To the east of town, George Rex Dr leads to Leisure Island and the Knysna Heads. Along and off this road are a number of guesthouses and B&Bs. For something different, and especially recommended for families, **self-catering houseboats (A)** are available for hire on the Knysna Lagoon. All eating and sleeping equipment is

included, and you do not need to have any nautical experience. They are very easy to operate and allow you to explore the lagoon at leisure. Contact **Lightleys Holiday Houseboats**, T044-3860007, www.houseboats.co.za.

AL-A Falcon's View Manor, 2 Thesen Hill, T044-3826767, www.falconsview.com. Small upmarket hotel in a classic Victorian house with 9 spacious en suite double rooms (non-smoking) with DSTV, tastefully decorated and furnished to an exceptional level of comfort. There's a relaxing veranda overlooking the lagoon, swimming pool, neat gardens and intimate bar. Recommended. You can book online through the African Pride hotel group; www.africanpridehotels.com.

A Isolabella, Cearn Dr, Leisure Isle, T044-3840049, www.isolabella.co.za. Italian-run villa with wrap-around balconies in a commanding position overlooking the lagoon, with 3 en suite rooms decorated in luxurious cream carpets, walls and bedding and fresh flowers. Breakfast served on the balcony or in your private lounge.

A Leisure Isle Boutique Lodge, 87 Bayswater Dr, Leisure Isle, T044-3840462, www.leisureislelodge.co.za. Award-winning guesthouse with spacious rooms, comfortable lounge and bar, heated swimming pool, views across bay, gardens stretch to waterfront, no children under 12, superb food in the elegant restaurant, spa for massages and treatments a short drive from Knysna Heads.

A Under Milkwood, T044-3840745, www.milkwood.co.za. 16 self-catering log chalets at Knysna Heads set in a grove of milkwood trees, can sleep 6 people, excellent kitchen facilities. Not all have views of the lagoon. Plenty of light, relaxing sun deck, recommended if you plan to spend a week in the district. Out of the town, but still close to all the amenities. Avoid Dec-Jan when rates take a significant hike.

B Gallery Guest House, 10 Hill St West, T044-3822510, www.galleryguesthouse.co.za. 2 double and 2 twin rooms in an old house overlooking the lagoon. Breakfast is served on the peaceful balcony overlooking the swimming pool. Owner Lolly is an artist.

B Knysna Belle, 75 Bayswater Dr, Leisure Isle, T044-3840511, www.knysnabelle.co.za. 7 very stylish individually decorated en suite rooms, 1 with a Victorian bath tub, very good breakfasts, swimming pool, lovely balconies to relax and enjoy the views of the lagoon, mountain bikes and a rowing boat available to rent out, no children under 6.

B Knysna Manor House, 19 Fitchat St, T044-3825440, www.knysnamanor.co.za. A peaceful Victorian stone house with good views of the lagoon, a short walk from town centre, 13 en suite rooms with TV but decor is a bit frilly.

B Protea Knysna Quays, Waterfront Dr, T044-3825005, www.proteahotels.com. Usual large state-of-the-art hotel, with 123 comfortable a/c rooms, restaurant, cocktail bar, lounge, attractive swimming pool and Wi-Fi internet. Great location next to the Waterfront.

B Yellowwood Lodge, 18 Handel St, T044-3825906, www.yellowwoodlodge.co.za. Lovely guesthouse in one of Knysna's older houses with 10 thoughtfully decorated rooms. Ask for an upstairs room – they have relaxing balconies with views of the lagoon and Heads. Delicious buffet breakfasts, immaculate garden, swimming pool, strictly non-smoking household, no children under 10. Loses some of its appeal when full, look out for the flagpole.

B-C Ashmead Resort, George Rex Dr, T044-3841166, www.ashmeadresort.co.za. 61 log cabins and modern brick cottages set in mature gardens overlooking lagoon, B&B or self-catering, bright lobby and lounge, stark restaurant, bar, miniature golf, swimming pool, popular domestic family holiday venue.

C Wayside Inn, 48 Main St, T044-3826011, www.waysideinn.co.za. Smart set-up in the centre of town with a Victorian theme. 15 luxury rooms with iron beds and sisal carpets, fans, fine African art on show, private

balconies, wicker furniture, TV, superior picnic hampers can be made to order. Several readers have commented on the lack of a lounge area and breakfast is served in the rooms or on the patio, weather permitting. Friendly staff.

D Aesta's B&B, 21 Fitchat St, T044-3824849, www.aestas.co.za. Nice views from several spacious and attractive rooms, swimming pool, walking distance from the tourist office and shops and restaurants on the main road, well-run medium-sized B&B, children under 6 sharing with parents free.

D Heron Water Lodge, 33 Cearn Dr, Leisure Isle, T044-3840624, www.garden route.co.za/knysna/heron. A friendly and comfortable B&B just 20 m from the lagoon with 4 spacious en suite double rooms, 2 of the rooms overlook the lagoon in a separate wing. Sun deck, bar, swimming pool, generous filling breakfasts, mountain bikes available to rent. Recommended.

E-F Highfield Backpackers, 2 Graham St, T044-3826266, www.highfieldsback packers.co.za. Quiet backpacker hostel set in 2 town houses, dorms and doubles, shared bathrooms, bar with pool table, kitchen, courtyard with pool, travel centre. A bit of a rabbit warren but the new owners have done much to spruce up the place. Baz Bus stop.

E-F Overlander's Lodge, 11 Nelson St, T044-3825920, www.overlanders.co.za. Large dorms, clean bathrooms, TV room, small swimming pool, well-stocked kitchen, pool table, good for camping, scooter and bike hire. There are much quieter doubles and twins and another 2 kitchens in the house next door. Fun atmosphere but not to everyone's liking – the parties can be raucous. Baz Bus stop.

West of Knysna *p317*

AL Belvidere Manor, Duthie Dr, Belvidere, T044-3871055, www.belvidere.co.za. 34 smart cottages arranged around a swimming pool in shady gardens, private verandas with views across the lagoon, sleeping 2-4 people, kitchens, DSTV and DVD players. Some have a study; all are individually furnished and have log fires. The manor house, from 1834, houses the reception and the elegant dining room. **The Bell** pub is housed in an old farm cottage and the highlight here is seeing the wine cellar underneath the glass floor. Friendly and attentive staff.

Knysna Forest *p318, map p316*
L Phantom Forest Eco-Reserve,
T044-3860046, www.phantomforest.com.
Signposted from the Phantom Pass road.
This lodge offers ultra-stylish accommodation in a superb collection of 14 luxurious and eco-friendly 'tree suites' set in the forest high above the lagoon. Each has a private terrace and luxurious bathroom – the showers are open to the forest. Individual houses are connected by walkways to the excellent restaurant, bar, lookout points, beauty spa, and stunning pool on the edge of a wooden deck. Attentive, helpful staff, the perfect place to experience the forest. Highly recommended.
C-D Forest Edge, just past the Rheenendal Post Office, turn right at the Bibby's Hoek sign. At the entrance to the state forest, turn left for 1.5 km, the lodge is the last property on this road, T082-4561338, www.forestedge.co.za. 3 holiday cottages with delightful names – Field Mouse, Froggy Pond and Fire Fly, self-contained and fully equipped, sleeping 4-5 people, overlooking a picturesque dam. Linen and towels are provided and there is a fireplace, telephone, braai facilities and outdoor hot shower. Mountain bikes available for hire, you can walk straight into the forest from here.

Knysna Elephant Park *p319*
B-D Elephant Boma, T044-5327732, www.knysnaelephantpark.co.za. 5 newly refurbished twin en suite rooms and 1 large family flat sleeping 6 over the *boma* where the elephants sleep, so you can fall asleep to their nightly sounds (and smells!), and see them when they are out and about. Modern

and comfortable with DSTV and large picture windows.

Plettenberg Bay *p319, map p320*
During Christmas it is difficult to find a bed unless you have booked well in advance. Along with Knysna, there is an unbelievable transformation here during the midsummer holiday rush. For the rest of the year, hotels and B&Bs cry out for guests. In an effort to attract visitors during the winter months, discounts are offered so it's worth checking these out when choosing somewhere to stay.
L The Plettenberg, 40 Church St, Lookout Rocks, T044 5332030, www.plettenberg.com.
40 a/c rooms, lounge and dining rooms furnished with antiques, superb food and wine, swimming pool, beauty spa, smartest in area, another Relais & Chateaux property, everything you would expect in a small, exclusive top-class, 5-star hotel, but very expensive. Request a room with ocean views, some of them look over the car park. Rates double in high season.
L-AL Hunter's Country House, 10 km towards Knysna, T044-5327818, www.hunterhotels.com. 21 luxury individually decorated thatched suites with fireplace, antique furnishings and private patio, 2 swimming pools, conservatory, antique shop, forest chapel for weddings, child care service, one of South Africa's top country hotels and part of the Relais & Chateaux group, which has won awards for food and service, a special place to treat yourself to. Recommended.
AL Beacon Island, Beacon Island Cres, T044-5331120, www.southernsun.com.
Multi-storey building dominating the bay, right on the water between 2 beaches, 200 rooms, 4 excellent restaurants, swimming pool, tennis, also a timeshare resort. A superb location but an eyesore on Plett's sweeping beach.
A Stone Cottages, corner of Harker and Odland streets, T044-5331331, www.stonecottage.co.za. Beautifully restored 19th-century cottage, tastefully

decorated rooms with high ceilings and gleaming wooden floors, antiques and old photographs, fully equipped for self-catering, sleeps 5 in 3 bedrooms, panoramic views of the ocean, deck with jacuzzi overlooking the main beach. Close by is a smaller modern, cheaper self-catering cottage for 2, with TV and DVD in the lounge, decor in the same theme as the older cottage. A good option for families or friends travelling together, and price per person is reasonable.

B A Room with a View, 5 Julia Av, T044-5331836, www.roomwithaview.co.za. Near the beach with, as the name suggests, good views, an unusual building arranged in blocks up the hill with 3 en suite rooms and 1 suite with extra kitchen, with TV, fridge, heater and fan, special touches like fruit bowls and glasses of sherry, lovely garden terraces where you can take breakfast.

B Cottage Pie, 16 Tarbet Ness Av, T044-5330369, www.cottagepie.co.za. Homely but upmarket guesthouse offering 8 well-appointed rooms, very comfortable and cosy with TV and minibar. Pool, bougainvillea-bedecked terrace. Slightly out of town, but only 100 m to Robberg Beach. Healthy or full English breakfasts served, evening meals on request. Recommended, though pricey in the height of season when rates double.

B-C Coral Tree Cottages, off the N2 11 km from Plett towards Knysna, T044-5327822, www.coraltree.net. Good self-catering option if you have a car, 6 spacious and nicely furnished thatched cottages with 1 or 2 bedrooms, satellite TV, fully equipped kitchen, patio and braai area, set in lovely green woodlands full of flowers, breakfast on request. Good as a base for a few days as Knysna is only 25 km away.

D-F Albergo For Backpackers, 8 Church St, T044-5334434, www.albergo.co.za. Centrally located hostel with sea views. Dorms, double rooms and camping area, garden with hammocks and bonfires, 2 kitchens, travel centre, TV room, bar and pool table, surfboards for hire. Baz Bus stop.

D-F Nothando Backpackers, 5 Wilder St, T044-5330220, www.nothando.co.za. Camping, dorms, double rooms, B&B, in a central location. Clean, cheap and friendly, with extras like hairdryers in the bathrooms, plus offering plenty of activities with discounts. Beds have duvets, some rooms are en suite. Small kitchen, large TV lounge, kitchen, bar with braai and pool table. Baz Bus stop.

East of Plettenberg Bay *p323*

L Hog Hollow Country Lodge, 18 km east of Plettenberg Bay at the Crags off the N2 main road, T044-5348879, www.hog-hollow.com. Closed Jun. One of the finest lodges along the Garden Route set in a private nature reserve, with 15 suites, all with ceiling fans, minibar decorated with locally made wall hangings and woodcarvings, each with its own wooden deck with hammock over-looking the Matjies River gorge and Tsitsi-kamma Mountains. There is a spacious lounge with open fireplace for log fires in the winter months. Good evening meals are served around a communal table in a relaxed manner. Swimming pool with stunning views, library/lounge in the main house. Special touches include a glass of milk and gingerbread man for children at bedtime. The lodge also organizes 3-hr boat trips around the bay to view whales and dolphins, and there are a number of walking trails through the forest surround-ing the lodge which are very popular with birdwatchers. Recommended.

B-C Protea Hotel Keurbooms River, on the Keurbooms River 8.5 km east from Plett, T044-5359300, www.proteahotels.com. Modern and functional but very comfortable hotel set in indigenous gardens, 61 en suite rooms with TV and kettles, swimming pool, bar and restaurant with charming wooden deck with outstanding river views.

C-F Forever Resorts Plettenberg, 6 km east of Plett on the Keurbooms River, T044-5359309, www.foreversa.co.za. 30 neat wooden self-catering chalets nestled along the riverbank, plus 112 camping and caravan spots with excellent facilities, though can get very crowded in season. Swimming pool, canoes and pedalos for hire, tennis and volleyball courts, good all-round family option.

D Whiskey Creek hut, Keurbooms River Nature Reserve, T044-8023300, www.cape nature.org.za. R480 per night midweek, R600 per night weekends, for 1-4 people and includes canoe hire. The stilted log cabin has 10 basic bunks, hot water, flush toilets, bedding on request, and a fully equipped kitchen with outside braai facilities. There's no electricity but solar energy fuels the fridge and lights. The hut is only accessible by canoe and it's a delightfully isolated spot.

Nature's Valley *p324*
Surprisingly Nature's Valley has hardly any accommodation and sleeping is limited to only 2 establishments.

A-B Tranquility Lodge, 130 St Michaels Av, next to the Nature's Valley shop and pub, T044-5316663, www.tranquilitylodge.co.za. Fairly new and already readers have recommended it. Lovely reed-and-timber lodge in pretty gardens, 7 en suite rooms, 1 of which is a honeymoon suite with spa bath, double shower and fireplace, very nicely decorated throughout with lots of lounging areas. The owner is also a chef and meals can be taken together with other guests in the dining room, or alone in a tree house. There's a swimming pool, outside hot pool, each room gets its own double kayak to explore the lagoon, a complimentary bridge walk at the nearby Bloukrans Bridge is included in the price, and finally it's registered with BirdLife as a birder-friendly establishment.

C-D Hiker's Haven, 411 St Patrick's St, T044-5316805, www.hikershaven.co.za. A large stone guesthouse with thatched roof, 7 comfortable individually decorated rooms, 5 en suite and 2 share a bathroom, TV lounge, pool table, beach and lagoon a 200-m walk away. Operates a shuttle service to take hikers back to their cars at the opposite ends of the Tsitsikamma and Otter trails and provides

hearty breakfasts for hikers starting these trails from Nature's Valley.

Groot River and Bloukrans Passes *p324*
C-D Tsitsikamma Forest Village, off the N2 next to the Bloukrans bungee jump, T042-2811450, www.tsitsikamma.org.za. 16 self-catering log chalets, some on stilts with kitchen, braai area, lounge and veranda, suitable for families. Also here is the **E-F Bloukrans Backpackers Lodge**, offering a good range of accommodation including 2 dorms sleeping 8, and some double rooms, modern and comfortable communal kitchen and lounge area with DSTV and a pool table, while the **E-F Caravan Park**, has electrified points and shared ablutions. The Baz Bus stops at this site, though a car is a necessity as there are no amenities in the vicinity and only a coffee shop on site. Despite being comfortable inside the chalets and backpacker lodge, this is a bleak spot in winter.

Tsitsikamma National Park *p325*
This is a very popular national park, particularly with South Africans, so during the school holidays it is almost impossible to find accommodation here. Reservations must be made up to 12 months in advance. Fortunately there is plenty of accommodation along the Garden Route. If you're staying in Knysna, for example, the park can still be reached within a 1-hr drive. There are also several private lodges close to the main entrance (see below).

All of the park's accommodation must be vacated by 0900. Arriving visitors have access from 1200. There are 2 rest camps in the park: **Storms River Mouth**, the main camp with a full range of facilities, and **Nature's Valley**, a very basic camp close to the settlement of the same name. Reservations, through the **SANParks** office in Pretoria, T012-4289111, www.sanparks.org. Bookings can also be made in person at the offices in Cape Town and Durban (see page 48). For cancellations and reservations under 72 hrs contact the

Storms River Mouth camp directly, T042-2811607. Credit card bookings are accepted over the phone. Seasonal discounts apply to all forms of accommodation in May-Aug.

Storms River Mouth

On a narrow strip of land between ocean and forested hills, this is one of the most beautiful settings of all the national parks.
B Log Cabins, with 2 bedrooms sleeping a maximum of 6 people, fully equipped kitchen with fridge and stove, bedding provided, bathroom, lounge area.
C Oceanettes, with 2 bedrooms, fully equipped kitchen, bathroom, lounge, a little less smart and comfortable, but ideal when you are likely to spend most of the day outdoors.
C-D Forest Cabins, sleeping 2, very basic but self-contained with bathroom and kitchen facilities. Generally, these can only be booked on a nightly basis as they are used for accommodation on the Dolphin Trail (see page 328) but enquire with SANParks when booking.
D Forest Huts, sleeping 2, very basic, shared ablution block.
E Camping, terraced lawns in a beautiful location right on the shoreline, but exposed when the wind blows. There are a few shady trees, and it is a real thrill to peer out of your tent at dawn and watch the waves crashing on the rocks right in front of you. There are twice as many places for caravans as for tents, braai sites but no electric points, laundry and central wash blocks.

Nature's Valley Rest Camp

This camping and caravan site is 40 km west of Storms River Mouth. The site is set in an indigenous forest on the banks of the Groot River, and in recent years has been upgraded. On top of the accommodation rates, there is a daily conservation fee of R80, R40 for children to enter this section of the park. Accommodation is in **D Forest huts**, which are very basic with 2 beds and electricity, or **E Campsites**. Both of these share the wash block, hot water, laundry, no electricity, no shop or restaurant, all supplies can be bought in Nature's Valley village, 3 km away.

Storms River Village p328

A Tsitsikamma Lodge, 2 km east of the village along the N2, T042-2803802, www.tsitsikamma.com. Luxurious selection of 32 timber log cabins, including several honeymoon suites. Each log cabin has an en suite bathroom with spa bath, TV, telephone. Set in forested grounds and colourful gardens, cosy restaurant serving buffet lunches, swimming pool. The short 'strip-tease' trail into the forest brings you to some enticing cool pools. The whole complex is of a high standard and well run, the ideal base from which to start the Otter Trail as the management will transport you to the start and collect you at the end after 4-5 days for a small fee, a very useful service. Special offers in low season.
A-B The Armagh, T042-2811512, www.thearmagh.com. Comfortable guesthouse with 7 double rooms including a free-standing cottage, all with en suite facilities and private patios, guest lounge, craft shop and pool. Views and walks from the lodge are good and the garden is full of birds. Attached **Rafters** restaurant has a good local reputation with tasty buffets.
E-F Tube 'n Axe, corner of Darnell and Saffron streets, T042-2811757, www.tubenaxe.co.za. 4-bed dorms, doubles and some pre-erected tents on wooden platforms, set in a forested garden with plenty of room for camping and overland vehicles. The rustic bar has a pool table and braai pit. Breakfast and dinner available or self-catering kitchen. Shuttles to the Bloukrans Bridge Bungee, and they rent out quad bikes and mountain bikes. The **Stormsriver Adventures** office is a stone's throw away so there's plenty to keep the adventurer occupied for a couple of days. Baz Bus stop, picks up from mainline buses at the Petro-Total Village at Storms River Bridge.

❶ Eating

Mossel Bay *p305, map p306*

¶¶¶ Admirals, in the **Garden Route Casino** at Pinnacle Point south of Mossel Bay off the N2, T044-6933900, www.admirals.co.za. 1200-1500, 1800-2300. Great-value buffet in the main casino restaurant, over 120 dishes, plus Mongolian stir-fry bar where you make up your own plate of food before the chef cooks it in front of you, plenty of seafood and roasts, cold meat and cheese platters, and desserts including home-made ice cream. Recommended for the very hungry.

¶¶¶ Bahia Dos Vaqueiros, in the Diaz Strand Hotel, T044-6928400. Open 1900-2200. Dominated by a giant frieze on the ceiling of the Portuguese landing on the coast and sweeping ocean views, an upmarket spot with cigar bar, walk-in wine cellar and attentive service. Interesting combinations of taste such as pork medallions with red cabbage and blue cheese.

¶¶ Café Gannet, Bartholomeu Dias Museum Complex, Market St, T044-6911885. Open 0700-2300. A well-established seafood restaurant, popular all year round since the tour buses stop here, seafood grills and pizza from a wood oven, enjoyable bay views from a shady outdoor terrace, mixed reports on quality of the food but efficient and prompt service.

¶¶ Jazzbury's, 11 Marsh St, T044-6911923. 1800-2300. A popular restaurant serving good-value traditional meals such as *potjes* and *bredies*, ostrich steaks, seafood and a delectable dessert trolley. Eat at tables on the patio or inside the cosy bar. Decor is a striking bright orange and deep purple. Recommended.

¶¶ Kingfisher, The Point, T044-6906390, www.thekingfisher.co.za. 1030-2300. Modern development overlooking the beach, seafood platters and combos, good grilled fish served with rice and chips, some meat dishes, indifferent service. **Delfino's**, T044-6905247, is an attached pizza and pasta restaurant downstairs that also does sandwiches during the day.

¶¶ Pampeon, 3 Powrie St, T044-6911177. Mon-Sat 1200-2300, Sun 1130-1500. Pasta and seafood, recommended for line fish, one of the best in town. Outside tables in the garden.

¶¶ Pavilion, Santos Beach, T044-6904567. 1000-2300. The ideal spot for lunch, just stroll up straight from the beach onto the old wooden veranda and enjoy a steak, burger, pizza or light lunch while watching the boats sailing in the bay. Bustling atmosphere.

¶¶ Tidals, The Point. Seafront tavern built on the rocks overlooking the ocean, cool rooms with high ceilings and plenty of light. Previous complaints from readers about the food (frozen burgers and fish). But currently being revamped by new owners.

George *p308, map p308*

As well as the town restaurants, **Fancourt Hotel and Country Club** has several superb top-range restaurants open to non-guests.

¶¶¶ Reel and Rustic, corner of York and Courtenay streets, T044-8840707. Open 1230-1430, 1830-late, closed Sat lunch. Popular seafood restaurant with smart decor of velvet drapes and candelabras in a historical building serving good fresh cajun and creole dishes and unusual stuffed fish dishes and decadent desserts. Limited menu for vegetarians. Award-winning wine list.

¶¶ Capannina, York Rd near the tourist office, T044-8745313. Mon-Fri 1100-1400, 1800-2200, Sat-Sun 1800-2200. Popular and homely Italian with local art on the walls and some outside tables, long menu of pizza, pasta, grills and fish and daily specials such as veal masala or marinated tuna.

¶¶ Kingfisher, 1 Courtenay St, T044-8733127, www.thekingfisher.co.za. 1200-2230. Fresh seafood dishes, renowned for prawns and fish and chips, some meat dishes including good ostrich, also has a fine selection of pasta and pizzas and a sushi bar. Good range of wine and whiskies.

¶¶ Mei Ling, 69 Fichat St, T044-8840088. Oct-Feb daily 1130-1400, 1730-2130,

Mar-Sep closed Sun. Over 70 authentic Taiwanese and Chinese dishes, some exotic seafood dishes, good-value set menus, cheaper snacks such as won ton or shrimp chips.

ŶŶ Old Town House, corner of Market and York streets, T044-8743663. Mon-Fri 1200-1500, 1800-late, Sat dinner only. Housed in one of George's oldest buildings, local specialities such as lamb shank and venison pie, plus steak, seafood and grills, and very good home-made desserts, good-value wine list.

ŶŶ The Conservatory at Meade House, 91 Meade St, T044-8741938. Mon-Fri 0800-1600, Sat 0830-1500, Wed-Sat 1830-2200, Sun 1200-1500. Quality restaurant set in one of the oldest homes in George, dine in the conservatory or in the pretty gardens, very extensive à la carte from cakes and muffins to full meals of steak and grilled fish. Open for breakfast, lunch, afternoon teas, and dinner on some nights, also has a well-stocked shop of gifts and books.

Ŷ Zanzibar's, 70 Courtenay St, near the museum, T044-8732052. Mon-Sat 0900-late. Grill house serving good pub meals in 2 old train carriages, also with outside seating which is a good place to watch the world go by, and stays open late for serious drinking.

Wilderness *p312, map p312*

Wilderness does not have a large choice of restaurants but most hotels and hostels offer meals. The majority of domestic visitors will self-cater.

ŶŶŶ The Palms, corner of George and Owen Grant roads, Central location off the N2, T044-8771420. Open daily for set 4-course dinners from 1900, reservations essential, tables in the thatched restaurant or under umbrellas, wine is matched to the food. The menu changes daily but there is a choice from 2 starters and 2 mains which are finished off by the likes of petit fours and cheese. Aimed at people who want a change from self-catering accommodation in Wilderness.

ŶŶŶ Wilderness Grille, George Rd, T044-8770808. Open 0800-2200. Seafood, steaks and pizza, good breakfasts, outdoor leafy terrace, pop in throughout the day and you'll get something substantial to eat, though service is somewhat slow.

Knysna *p314, maps p315 and p316*

Knysna is well known for its seafood, especially its excellent oysters which are cultivated in the lagoon. During the peak season, it is not uncommon to wait an hour or more before getting a table – be sure to book ahead at the better-known restaurants.

ŶŶŶ O'Pescador, Brenton Rd, T044-3860036. Mon-Sat 1830-late. Long-established and popular Portuguese restaurant, traditional cosy decor, Mozambique prawns or try the spicy fish dishes, peri peri chicken or grilled sardines. Portuguese wines. Booking advised in season. Recommended.

ŶŶ 34' South, Knysna Quays, T044-3827268. Open 0830-2330. Snacks and meals daily in a deli-style seafood restaurant, try the seafood platter or paella, make up a meal from the packed fridges or buy takeaway items including cook books, wine and home-made goodies, laid-back sunny deck overlooking the quays. Recommended.

ŶŶ Anchorage, T044-3822230, 11 Grey St. 1830-late, from 1200 in season. Seafood platters, prawns, oysters and steaks all washed down with excellent draught Mitchell's beer and a good choice for vegetarians too, some outside tables on the patio.

ŶŶ Crabs Creek, 8 km from Knysna, 200 m off the N2 on the Belvidere road, T044-3860011. Open 1100-late. A mock-Tudor building beside Knysna River, secluded country pub in a garden of oak trees, pleasant outdoor terrace overlooking the river, sensible prices, good selection of wines and several beers on tap, mostly seafood, Sat is popular to watch sport on the giant TV screens in the afternoon and there's live music in the evening. Poor reports of the food recently from readers.

Cruise Café, 400 m west of the Knysna Quays, T044-3821693. Mon-Sat 0800-2200, Sun 0800-1700. Great views of fishing boats on the lagoon, best known for seafood, plus good breakfasts and simple lunches like ploughman's platters and fish and chips; more sophisticated menu in the evening, long wine and cocktail list.

Drydock Food Co, Knysna Quays, at the Waterfront, T044-3827310. Open 1130-2200. Modern restaurant with good views from the 2nd floor, mostly seafood but steaks and vegetarian options too, oysters, fish with pickles, slightly different twists on standard dishes, try west coast mussels with white wine or the kingklip espetada.

Knysna Oyster Co, Thesen's Island, T044-3826942. Open 0900-1700, until 2100 in high season. This restaurant is right next to the oyster farm that has been in operation since 1949; you need to drive across the causeway to get there from town. Once on the island, take a left just after the timber factory. The seafood restaurant is perhaps the best place to try a dozen of Knysna's famous raw or cooked oysters washed down with a glass of champagne. It's one of Kynsna's must-dos but unfortunately the service is dire. Despite this, it's recommended.

Oyster Catcher, Knysna Quays, T044-3829995. Another place to try oysters, at working quays with a backdrop of busy boats coming and going. If oysters aren't your thing, try the tapas or nachos. Good cocktails and vegetarian choices.

Paquitas, George Rex Dr, Knysna Heads, T044-3840408. Open 1200-2200. Relaxed family restaurant and vibey pub, burgers, pizza, pasta, seafood and steaks, but the main reason for coming here is for the stunning views of the Knysna Heads and the long beach where kids can play.

Ile de Pain Bread & Café, The Boatshed, Thesen's Island, T044-3025707. Tue-Fri 0700-1700, Sat 0700-1500, Sun 0900-1330. Superb bakery and coffee shop emitting lovely warm smells of freshly baked goodies, such as croissants and pastries. The bakers

live upstairs and start baking at 0200. Good coffee, fresh fruit salad, cheeses and olives, good spot for a light brunch or lunch.

Plettenberg Bay p319, map p320
All the hotels have their own restaurants and bars and you can pre-order meals at the backpacker hostels.

Hunter's Country House (see Sleeping, page 335), off the N2 10 km towards Knysna, T044-5327818. Excellent food served in a rambling thatched house, 3 dining rooms with silverware and china on the tables, pricey but worth it, recommended for special occasions, booking essential. Tea on the veranda is quite special.

57 Kloof, Melville Shopping Centre, corner of Main St and Marine Dr, T044-5335626. Open 0830-late. Modern decor and floor-to ceiling windows highlighting great views, good range of meat and fish dishes, some with an Asian slant, large fresh salads, unusual breakfasts such as eggs hollandaise, and excellent vegetarian menu.

The Lookout, perched on the rocks above Lookout Beach, T044-5331379. Open 0900-2300. Popular family seafood restaurant, perfect location, excellent seafood, soups, salads and steak, also has a busy bar, lively, bustling atmosphere. From the terrace you can watch surfers share a wave with a dolphin. Recommended.

The Med Seafood and Grill, Village Sq, T044-5333102, www.med-seafood bistro.co.za. Mon-Fri 1230-1500, Mon-Sat 1800-late, open 7 days in high season. Established 20-year-old European-style bistro with alfresco dining on the leafy patio. À la carte seafood, good light lunches, huge seafood platters, excellent duck with orange sauce and slow-cooked lamb shanks, plus the odd vegetarian dish. Nice ambience.

Blue Bay, Lookout Centre, Main St, T044-5331390. Daily 0800-2200 in high season, Mon-Sat lunch and dinner only in low season. Seafood, pasta and sandwiches, light deli lunches, good coffee. Try the roasted beef fillet with parmesan or the crusted seared tuna with sesame seeds. The **Blue Bay Ice** bar overlooking the shady courtyard serves ice cream during the day and cocktails in the evening. Helpful and knowledgeable waiters complement a vibey ambience.

† **San Francisco**, Melville Shopping Centre, corner of Main St and Marine Dr. Coffee shop and restaurant serving excellent breakfasts, sandwiches and salads, good coffee, shady seating on outdoor terrace overlooking the bustle of Marine Dr.

🄾 Bars and clubs

Knysna *p314, maps p316 and p315*
Tin Roof, corner of Main and St George's roads. Cavernous upstairs drinking joint, with a few bar snacks available early in the evening, live bands at the weekends and during holiday season, long wooden bar, pool tables, outside balconies for conversation, rocks to the early hours.
Zanzibar's, Main Rd, T044-3820386. Terraces overlooking Main Rd, dance floor and pool tables. Tue-Sat 1900-0200 in season, tribal decor, occasional DJs and live music, upstairs quieter cocktail lounge.

🄴 Entertainment

Knysna *p314, maps p316 and p315*
Cinema
Knysna Movie House, Pledge Square, 50 Main St, T044-3827813. Daily shows of new releases on 2 screens.

🄾 Shopping

Mossel Bay *p305, map p306*
Arts and crafts
Craft Art Workshop, Market St, next to the tourist office. Mon-Fri 0900-1700, Sat 0900-1500. Sells African curios from all over the continent and you can watch artists at work.

The Goods Shed Indoor Fleamarket, 68 Bland St, T044-6912104, www.thegoods shed.co.za. Mon-Fri 0900-1700, Sat 0900-1500, also Sun in high season 1000-1600. Sells a variety of items including clothes, jewellery, arts and crafts, home-made food and hand-crafted furniture in an interesting historical railway goods shed built in 1902.

Shopping malls
The **Liberty Shopping Centre** on Bland St contains most of the shops you'll need including chemists, bookshops, a wine store and a **Pick 'n' Pay** supermarket.

George *p308, map p308*
Arts and crafts
Strydom Gallery, Marklaan Centre, 79 Market St, T044-8744027. Mon-Sat 0900-1700. An art shop with interesting exhibits as well as pieces for sale from a cross section of South African artists and sculptors, organizes delivery worldwide.

Shopping malls
Marklaan, between Market and Meade streets. Mall in converted store rooms arranged around 2 open squares. There is a coffee shop plus a couple of curio shops. A **farmers' market** is held in the square Fri 0700-1000.
Garden Route Mall, www.gardenroutemall.co.za, is out of town on the junction with the N2. A new R400-million, 125-store mall with all the usual South African chain stores, restaurants, multi-screen Ster-Kinekor cinema and exhibition space.
St George's Mall, at the southern end of York St, new slick mall with the usual clothes and food shops, Ster-Kinekor cinema and restaurants.

Sedgefield *p313*
Arts and crafts
Scarab Art and Craft Village, on the N2 next to the Engin petrol station, T044-3432455. Well worth a stop for the interesting craft

shops and stalls including one that demonstrates making handmade paper, the **Num Num Café** and a nursery.

Knysna *p314, maps p315 and p316*
Keeping in tune with Knysna's reputation as a cultural arts and crafts centre are a number of galleries and craft shops. Check at the tourist office for special exhibitions. There is a good **African craft market** on the side of the road as you enter Knysna on the N2 from George, with an extensive range of carvings, baskets, drums and curios. There is also a cluster of expensive curio shops and a daily fleamarket at the **Knysna Quays**.
Birds of Africa, 12 Waenhout St, T044-3825660 www.birdsofafrica.co.za. Unusual carved wooden birds.
Bitou Craft, Woodmill Lane Centre, Main St, T044-3823251. Local arts and crafts. There's another branch at Knysna Quays.
Metamorphosis, 12 Main Rd, T044-3825889. Interesting selection of items made from recycled cans and other materials, mostly by artists from Knysna's townships.
Model Shipyard, Knysna Quays, T044-6911531. Hand-crafted model ships and maritime antiques. There's another branch at the Waterfront in Cape Town.

Shopping malls
Woodmill Lane Centre, corner Main and Long streets, www.woodmillane.co.za. Mon-Fri 0900-1800, Sat 0830-1300. An open-air shopping centre constructed around a restored Victorian timber mill built in 1919, with 75 shops, fountains and trees in the squares, and regular performing artists and buskers. There are several boutiques and arts and crafts shops and a branch of **Pick 'n' Pay** supermarket here.

Plettenberg Bay *p319, map p320*
There is a wide range of souvenir shops reflecting the town's popularity with domestic visitors. The only products which could be regarded as a speciality of the area are those made from wood and paintings.

The Art House, 1 Melville's Corner, Main St, T044-5331673. Locally made crafts, fabrics and pottery.
Lookout Art Gallery, Main St, T044-5332210. Antiques and artwork.
Old Nick's, on the N2 3 km outside Plettenberg Bay going east, T044-5331395, www.oldnick village.co.za. Group of galleries, craft workshops and studios, with a weaving museum, shops and a restaurant. Look out for the ceramics and Zimbabwean sculpture at the **Porcupine**.

▲ Activities and tours

Mossel Bay *p305, map p306*
Diving
The best time for diving is between Dec and the end of Apr. During this period the sea is at its calmest and conditions in the bay are clear and safe. Close to Santos Beach are 4 recognized dive sites but none could be considered spectacular. All can be reached from the shore. For experienced divers, the **Windvogel Reef**, 800 m off Cape St Blaize, is highly recommended. The reef is fully exposed to the ocean and should therefore only be dived when the sea is calm. There are dropoffs and a few caves. Soft corals and colourful sponges are plentiful. The maximum depth is 27 m. (See also Essentials, page 63.)
Electro Dive, T044-6981976, www.electrodive.co.za. Equipment hire and boat charters, also offer PADI courses.

Shark cage diving
Shark Africa, corner Market and Church streets, T044-6913796, www.shark africa.co.za. Cage diving or to view from the boat R800. Offers cage diving and snorkelling in pursuit of a great white shark on a 15-m catamaran aptly named *Shark*. The trip is 4-5 hrs long and includes lunch and drinks.

Tour operators

Romonza, T044-6903101, www.mosselbay.
co.za/romonza. Runs daily pleasure cruises
from Vincent Quay in the harbour off Bland
St. Look out for the blue tent. The most
popular outings are to Seal Island (see page
306), a boat carrying up to 50 people leaves
on the hour 0100-1600, advanced booking
is advised. The sunset cruise lasts 2 hrs and
there's a cash bar. **Romonza** also offers the
only licensed boat-based whale watching
in Mossel Bay, Jun-Oct.

George p308, map p308
Golf

Fancourt Hotel and Country Club,
T044-8040030, www.fancourt.com. 4 gold
courses including the par 71, 5935-m,
championship links course designed by
Gary Player, open to members and hotel
guests only. This was the location of the
President's Cup tournament in 2003.
George Golf Club, Langenhoven St,
T044-8736116, www.georgegolfclub.co.za.
Par 72, 18 holes, 5852-m course surrounded
by trees. Visitors welcome.

Hiking

There are over 20 recognized hiking trails
around George and Wilderness, many
on private farmland. Check out
www.tourismgeorge.co.za for contact details.

Tour operators

Outeniqua Adventure Tours,
T044-8711470, www.outeniquatours.co.za.
Minibus tours to sights along the Garden
Route or Klein Karoo, can also organize
cycling tours.
South Cape Travel, 111 York St,
T044-8746930, www.southcapetravel.co.za.
Very helpful local travel agent. Book flights,
bus seats, local tours.

Wilderness National Park p313, map p312
Eden Adventures, T044-8770179,
www.eden.co.za. A good-value adventure
tour operator that organizes daily trips to the
national park. Activities on offer include
kayaking, kloofing, mountain biking,
abseiling, rock climbing and walking tours.
The guides are very knowledgeable about
the environment and are happy to answer
endless questions. Recommended.
Windmaster Paragliding, T072-1526093,
www.paraglidingsa.com. Around Sedgefield
and Wilderness are many thermic sites,
perfect for paragliding. Best conditions are
Oct-Jun, though training conditions are
best Jan-Apr. This company offers
introductory courses, tandem flights and
the full pilot's course that takes 2 weeks.
They can arrange accommodation.

Knysna p314, maps p315 and p316
Golf

Knysna Golf Club, George Rex Dr,
T044-3841150, www.knysnagolfclub.com.
18-hole, par 73 course. Visitors welcome
but booking advised.

Tour operators

Deep South Eco Adventures,
T044-3822010, www.deepsoutheco.com.
Arrange half-day mountain bike tours from
12-14 km in the forests around Knysna.
The Heads Adventure Centre, George Rex
Dr, T044-3840831, www.headsadventure
centre.co.za. PADI courses from their dive
centre at Knysna Heads, equipment rental,
daily trips to reefs and to the *Paquita* wreck
in the lagoon. Also, amongst many other
activities, abseiling at the Knysna Heads,
paintball, canoeing and kayaking on the
Knysna River and a tour of Knysna's
townships. A very professional company.
Knysna Forest Tours, T044-3826130,
www.knysnaforesttours.co.za. Half- and
full-day guided hikes, or overnight trails
along the coast or in local nature reserves.
For the less active they offer a short guided
drive into Knysna forest to see the Big Tree,
a 650-year-old yellowwood.
Mountain Biking Africa, bookings in the
Knysna Railway Station, T044-3820260,
www.mountainbikingafrica.co.za. Guided

mountain-bike trails around the forest in the area, easy rides, lots of downhills, bikes and refreshments included.

SEAL Adventures, office next to the **Protea Hotel** at Knysna Quays, T044-3825599, www.sealadventures.co.za. Stands for sea, earth, air and land. Adventure operator that offers abseiling and rap jumping at the Knysna Heads, canoeing on the lagoon, and quad-bike trails through the forests. Or do all of the above in 1 exhilarating day as the Awesome Foursome. No under 16s, no-one over 110 kg.

Springtide Charters, Knysna Quays, South Jetty, T082-470 6022 (mob), www.springtide.co.za. 3-hr sunset cruises on a 50-ft sailing boat including a stop for a swim. Departs Dec-Jan 1700, Feb-Apr and Sep-Nov 1600, R490 including sushi and seafood snacks and champagne. Maximum of 12 people per trip. Also available for charter overnight for honeymooners to stay in the lovely master cabin.

Plettenberg Bay *p319, map p320*
Diving and snorkelling
Conditions are best for diving during the winter months of Sep and Oct. The average water temperature is 16-18°C with visibility 5-10 m. There are not many tropical fish but due to an abundance of planktonic matter there is a colourful reef life. One of the more exciting dive sites is **Groot Bank**, about 12 km northeast of Hobie Beach. The reef is 35 m offshore and is best reached by boat. The maximum depth is 25 m and there is a whole variety of rock formations to explore, including tunnels and caves. There is a good chance of seeing parrotfish, ragged-tooth sharks and steenbras. At the southern end of Plettenberg Bay is the wreck of the *MFV Athina*, a Greek trawler sunk in 1967. It should only be dived in the calmest of conditions. For those who enjoy snorkelling, there is a popular spot in front of the Beacon Isle Hotel known as **Deep Blinders**; behind the reef is a sandy area where you might see stingrays.

The Heads Adventure Centre, T044-5331158, www.headsadventure centre.co.za, in the **Beacon Island Hotel**. Runs daily dives and rents equipment.

Fishing
There are several good rock-angling sites along the coast – Beacon Island, Robberg Beach, Lookout Rocks and Nature's Valley. Elf, galjoen and steenbras are the most frequent catch. Deep-sea fishing is also possible.
Coastal Fishing Charters, T082-4287439. www.coastalfishingcharters.co.za. Deep-sea and river fishing.

Golf
Goose Valley Golf Estate, T044-5335082, www.goosevalley.net. A challenging 72 par, 6000-m, 18-hole golf course on the banks of Keurbooms Lagoon designed by Gary Player with good ocean views.
Plettenberg Bay Country Club, T044-5332132, www.plettgolf.co.za. Lush 18-hole course in the middle of a private nature reserve, Piesang Valley. Tennis and bowls also available. The Knysna loerie and woodpeckers are often seen on the course. Priority bookings for members Dec-Jan, visitors welcome the rest of the year.

Horse riding
Equitrailing, Wittedrift Rd, T044-5330599. Lessons as well as trails through the forest from 1 hr to overnight. Note horse riding is not permitted on the beaches around Plett.

Whale and dolphin watching
There are several companies who organize whale- and dolphin-watching trips in season. Trips are about 2 hrs and cost R400-500 per person. Some of them can also arrange sea-kayaking.
Ocean Blue Adventures, T044-5334897, www.oceanadventures.co.za.
Ocean Safaris, T044-5334963, www.oceansafaris.co.za.

East of Plettenberg Bay p323
Boat Trip

Keurbooms River Ferries, T044-5327876, www.ferry.co.za. Daily summer trips, 1100 and 1400, boat trip plus walk and swim lasts for 2½ hrs, adults R85, children R30, breakfast, lunch or picnic baskets can be organized in advance and there's a cash bar, the ferry departs from the jetty on the east side of the Keurbooms River Bridge on the N2, each ferry can carry up to 30 people, they are shaded and have a toilet on board, highly recommended for nature lovers.

Bungee jumping

Bloukrans Bungee Jump, see page 324 for details.

Storms River Village p328
Tour operators

Tsitsikamma Canopy Tour, T042-2811836, www.tsitsikammacanopytour.co.za. A fantastic way to see the forest from a new angle, which involves climbing up into the trees and gliding between 10 different platforms on a steel rope, the longest of which is 80 m, giving extraordinary views from high above the ground. Excellent for birdwatching, and the Knysna loerie may be spotted. Departure times are every 45 mins 0800-1545 in summer and 0830-1445 in winter, the excursion lasts around 3 hrs and costs R395 and includes light refreshments. For the less active, 4WD tours of the forest are available.

⊖ Transport

Mossel Bay p305, map p306
It's 394 km to **Cape Town**, 55 km to **George**, 116 km to **Knysna**, 80 km to **Oudtshoorn**, 206 km to **Tsitsikamma**, 375 km to **Port Elizabeth**. The N2 bypasses Mossel Bay, almost halfway between Cape Town and Port Elizabeth.

Bus

All mainline buses stop at the Shell Truck Stop at Voorbaai, on the N2 7 km from Mossel Bay. The **Baz Bus** is the only service that goes right into town.

Greyhound, **Intercape**, and **Translux** all stop here daily on the Cape Town–Durban route. **Cape Town** (6 hrs), **Durban** (19 hrs) via **Port Elizabeth** and **East London** (13 hrs).

Intercape and **Translux**, also have a daily service between Mossel Bay and **Johannesburg** and **Pretoria** (16 hrs).

Towards **Cape Town** the Baz Bus arrives in Mossel Bay 1500-1600, towards **Port Elizabeth**, 1330-1430.

Bus companies Baz Bus, T021-4392323, www.bazbus.com; **Greyhound**, T083-9159000, www.greyhound.co.za; **Intercape**, T0861-287287, www.intercape.co.za; **Translux**, T086-1589282, www.translux.co.za.

George p308, map p308
It's 420 km to **Cape Town**, 320 km to **Port Elizabeth**, 61 km to **Knysna**, 55 km to Mossel Bay, 93 km to **Plettenberg Bay**, 151 km to **Tsitsikamma**, 60 km to **Oudtshoorn**.

Air

George airport is 10 km from the town centre, T044-8769310, www.airports.co.za. You'll need to take a taxi, **George Taxis**, T044-8708146. If you wish to leave your car at the airport there are a few lock-up garages available.

SAA have daily flights between George and **Cape Town** (1 hr), **Durban** (2½ hrs), and **Johannesburg** (1 hr 45 mins).

Nationwide and the budget no-frills airlines **Kulula** and **One Time** have daily flights between George and **Johannesburg** (1 hr 45 mins).

Airline offices SAA, reservations T011-9785313, ww2.flysaa.com; **Nationwide**, reservations T0861-737737 (in South Africa), T011-3053550 (from

overseas), www.flynationwide.co.za;
Kulula, T0861-585852 (in South Africa),
T011-9210111 (from overseas),
www.kulula.com; and **One Time**,
T0861-345345 (in South Africa),
T011-9288000 (from overseas).

Bus
All buses stop in St Mark's Sq. **Greyhound**,
Intercape and **Translux** run daily to **Cape
Town** (6 hrs) and **Durban** (18 hrs) via
Knysna (1 hr), **East London** (9 hrs) and
Port Elizabeth (4 hrs).

 Translux and **Intercape** also have a
daily service between George and
Johannesburg (14 hrs) and **Pretoria**
(16 hrs) via **Bloemfontein** (9 hrs).

 Baz Bus runs a daily service in both
directions between **Cape Town** and
Port Elizabeth. Drops off at McDonalds.
Towards Cape Town it arrives around
1500-1600, and towards Port Elizabeth
1430-1530.

 Bus companies Baz Bus,
T021-4392323, www.bazbus.com;
Greyhound, T083-9159000, www.grey
hound.co.za; **Intercape**, T0861-287287,
www.intercape.co.za; **Translux**,
T086-1589282, www.translux.co.za.

Car hire
The car hire companies all have desks at the
airport. **Avis**, T044-8769314, www.avis.co.za,
Budget, T044-8769204, www.budget.co.za,
Europcar, T044-8769070, **Hertz**,
T044-8014700, www.hertz.co.za.

Taxi
George Taxis, T044-8708146.

Train
The railway station is in the centre of town
at the east end of Market St. The **Outeniqua
Choo-Tjoe** runs between George and
Mossel Bay, T044-8018288 (see page 310
for further details).

Wilderness *p312, map p312*
Bus
Translux, **Greyhound** and **Intercape** all
stop at Wilderness, 20 mins before or after
George. The daily **Baz Bus**, T021-4392323,
www.bazbus.com, will collect and drop off
at **Fairy Knowe Backpackers**. From **Port
Elizabeth** it arrives 1345-1415 and from
Cape Town 1500-1600.

Sedgefield *p313*
Bus
Greyhound, **Intercape** and **Translux** services
stop at the Shell garage, 15 mins to **Knysna**.
See Knysna transport, below, for timetable
and contact details. The **Baz Bus**, T021
4392332, www.bazbus.com, will stop
in Sedgefield if requested in advance.
See Knysna transport for details.

Knysna *p314, maps p315 and p316*
It's 932 km to **Bloemfontein**, 500 km to
Cape Town, 61 km to **George**, 1350 km
to **Johannesburg**, 100 km to **Mossel Bay**,
120 km to **Outdshoorn**, 32 km to
Plettenberg Bay, 244 km to **Port Elizabeth**,
90 km to **Tsitsikamma National Park**.

Bus
All buses stop outside the railway station
near the Knysna Quays. **Greyhound**,
Intercape and **Translux** all run daily to **Cape
Town** (8 hrs), **Port Elizabeth** (3½ hrs), and
Durban (18 hrs). **Intercape** and **Translux**
also have a daily service between Knysna
and **Pretoria** and **Johannesburg** (14 hrs),
via **Bloemfontein** (11 hrs).

 Baz Bus runs a daily service in either
direction between **Cape Town** and **Port
Elizabeth**. Heading towards Cape Town
expect to be picked up around 1230-1330,
towards Port Elizabeth 1630-1730. Drops
and picks up at all the hostels.

 Bus companies Baz Bus, T021-4392323,
www.bazbus.com; **Greyhound**, T083-
9159000, www.greyhound.co.za; **Intercape**,
T0861-287287, www.intercape.co.za;
Translux, T086-1589282, www.translux.co.za.

Taxi
Crown Cabs, T044-3821890.

Train
The **Outeniqua Choo-Tjoe** steam train between Knysna and **George** (2½ hrs) is no longer running due to landslides destroying part of the line in 2006 (see page 310). In the event it starts up again, the station is on Remembrance Av close to the lagoon.

Plettenberg Bay *p319, map p320*
It's 525 km to **Cape Town**, 93 km to **George**, 32 km to **Knysna**, 171 km to **Mossel Bay**, 236 km to **Port Elizabeth**, 55 km to **Tsitsikamma National Park**.

Air
There used to be daily flights between Johannesburg and Plettenberg Bay, and the airport is 10 km from town. However, these were suspended by **SAA** as the airport was considered too small for their aircraft. The airport is still open to private air traffic.

Bus
Mainline buses depart from the Shell Ultra City on the N2 out of town. You will have to arrange a taxi with your hotel, but remember that some of the buses pass through in the early hours of the morning.

Greyhound, Intercape and **Translux** all stop here daily on the Cape Town–Durban route. **Cape Town** (8½ hrs) daily, **Durban** (17½ hrs) daily via **Port Elizabeth** (3½ hrs).

Intercape has a service between Plettenberg Bay and **Pretoria** and **Johannesburg** (14 hrs) daily via **Oudtshoorn** (2 hrs), and **Bloemfontein** (11 hrs).

Baz Bus has a service towards Cape Town, expect to be picked up 1200-1300, and to Port Elizabeth, 1730-1800.

Bus companies Baz Bus, T021-4392323, www.bazbus.com; **Greyhound**, T083-9159000, www.greyhound.co.za; **Intercape**, T0861-287287,

www.intercape.co.za; **Translux**, T086-1589282, www.translux.co.za,

❶ Directory

Mossel Bay *p305, map p306*
Emergencies Sea Rescue: T082-9905954 (mob). **Medical services** **Bayview Private hospital**, corner Alhof and Ryk Tulbach streets, T044-6913718, www.bayviewprivatehospital.com.

George *p308, map p308*
Banks All the principal banks, **First National, Nedbank, Standard** and **ABSA Bank** are in York St and the shopping malls. **Internet** J & D Internet Kafee, corner of Cradock and Courtenay streets, T044-8740008, internet café with full range of digital services. **Medical services** Medi Clinic, corner Gloucester and York streets, T044-8032000, www.georgemc.co.za. **Post office** York St.

Knysna *p314, maps p316 and p315*
Banks All the banks have branches on Main St and ATMs can be found in the Knysna Quays and other shopping centres. **Emergencies** Police, T10111, T044-3026600; Sea rescue, T044-3840211. **Internet** Internet access can be found at a few spots around town including the tourist office, the Knysna Movie House, at the Knysna Quays and at all the backpacker hostels and hotels. **Medical services** Knysna Private Hospital, Hunters Dr, T044-3841083, with a casualty department.

Plettenberg Bay *p319, map p320*
Banks First National, 22 Main St. **Nedbank**, Nedbank Pl, Main Rd. **Standard**, 17 Main St. **Internet** There is an Internet Café, just next to the Melville Shopping Centre, on Main Rd. **Post office** Plettenberg St, by police station.

Contents

Footprint features

Eastern Cape

At a glance

⊖ **Getting around** Buses and Baz
Bus on major routes, car hire.

◉ **Time required** Minimum
3-5 days to do the coastal route,
extra time to head inland.

☀ **Weather** Chilly July and
August, best for beaches
November-February.

✗ **When not to go** Traffic can
be heavy on the N2 over Christmas
when many people return home
from Cape Town.

★ Don't miss ...
1 Surfing at Jeffrey's Bay, page 371.
2 Addo Elephant National Park, page 377.
3 Shamwari Game Reserve, page 380.
4 National Festival of Arts in Grahamstown, page 394.
5 Valley of Desolation, page 400.
6 Wild Coast by landrover, bike and canoe, page 416.
7 Nelson Mandela Museum, page 423.

The Eastern Cape, although far less visited than many parts of South Africa, is a fascinating region of wild, empty beaches, forested mountains and the sun-baked plains of the Karoo. Nelson Mandela Bay (Port Elizabeth), a major industrial centre, has surprisingly good beaches, and acts as a gateway to the Garden Route, the lush coast stretching towards Cape Town, and Tsitsikamma National Park. A short drive from here is Jeffrey's Bay, where the long beach and perfect waves attract surfers from around the world.

To the north is a variety of game reserves and national parks, including the extended Addo Elephant National Park, the third largest game reserve in the country, where lions have been introduced among its famously large herds of elephant. It's now the only place in South Africa where you can see the Big Seven – elephant, lion, rhino, buffalo, leopard, whale and shark. Nearby, a clutch of newly created private game reserves have been restocked with animals not seen in the region for more than 150 years. Further inland lie the mystical landscapes of the Amatola Mountains and the Mountain Zebra National Park, which is a haven for the endangered mountain zebra. In the north is the sharply contrasting Karoo, with its surreal semi-desert conditions and quirky 19th-century towns.

During the Apartheid era the eastern region was referred to as the Transkei, the former homeland for the Xhosa people. These days the area is known as the Wild Coast because of its rugged, virtually deserted coastline. The area is far less developed than much of South Africa's coast, and most of the people live in rural settlements and work on the land. Instead of full-blown resorts, there are small seaside villages backed by protected stretches of verdant coastal forest and windswept dunes.

Getting around

Compared to the other provinces in South Africa, a little planning ahead is needed if you are travelling around the Eastern Cape by public transport. The Eastern Cape is bisected neatly by the N2, which runs closely along the coast on its route from the Western Cape to KwaZulu Natal. At most it is only 100 km from the coastal resorts. For years, the black homelands of the Wild Coast and Transkei were not awarded the pristine tarred roads that the rest of the country was. There are still many gravel and dirt roads in the province though many of these are in the process of being upgraded. Try to avoid driving along the N2 at night as facilities such as service stations are sparse and domestic animals on the road can cause accidents. You will need a car if you want to visit the more remote villages in the Karoo as there is no public transport – the **Owl House Backpackers** in Nieu Bethesda sums it up very eloquently in their advertising material: 'No street lights. No Baz Bus. No crime'. The **Baz Bus** runs along the N2 five days a week between Nelson Mandela Bay (Port Elizabeth) and Durban. It picks up and drops off at the most convenient hostels along this route; for the more out of the way backpacker hostels, you should be able to arrange shuttles from Baz Bus stops but you must book ahead. The mainline buses all stick to the N2. Many hotels also offer shuttle services but again these need to be pre-arranged.

Best time to visit

The coastal area of the Eastern Cape is a further extension of the subtropical Western Cape that rises inland to the plains of the Great Karoo, a mountainous semi-desert. The two experience very different climates. In the northeast, along the Wild Coast, towns like Port St Johns have long, hot summer months and moderate winters, while up towards the Free State, at towns such as Lady Grey and Aliwal North, the rise in altitude causes the lowering of temperatures and conditions here are favoured more by skiers than sunbathers. In general, the weather along the coast is kind to visitors. Nelson Mandela Bay (Port Elizabeth) enjoys a daily average of seven hours of sunshine annually and the region rightly earns its title as the Sunshine Coast. It's only in the Karoo regions that the weather reaches extremes, from the height of the harsh Karoo summer to the icy winters.

Tourist information

There are plenty of sources of tourism information for the Eastern Cape. Search on the internet and you will find a whole bunch of websites, many of which we have listed under the relevant destinations. The official government **Eastern Cape Tourism Board** ⓘ *Tourism Centre, corner of Longfellow and Aquarium roads, Quigney, T043-7019600, www.ectourism.co.za*, is based in East London, with other branches in Nelson Mandela Bay (Port Elizabeth) and Mthatha. Their website is a good source of information before you leave home.

Nelson Mandela Bay (Port Elizabeth)

→ *Phone code: 041. Colour map 7, B4.*

Nelson Mandela Bay – until recently Port Elizabeth – is a major port and industrial centre, the biggest coastal city between Cape Town and Durban. The centre of town, known as 'Central', is an attractive grid of Victorian houses and green spaces (burnt brown in summer) but the rest of the city – a modern sprawl of shopping malls, office blocks and apartments – is less aesthetically pleasing. The main tourist area is along the long beaches of Algoa Bay, and although the endless soft-sand beaches are enticing, the holiday flats and apartment blocks creeping onto the flat land behind them are less so. Nevertheless, Nelson Mandela Bay is celebrated for its long hours of sunshine and the warm waters of the bay, making it a good place to try some watersports.

The city's other great draw is its proximity to a number of game reserves. The most popular, open for game viewing, are the Addo Elephant National Park and the Shamwari Game Reserve. These offer the opportunity to see the Big Five without having to worry about malaria. Although Shamwari is a private reserve only open to guests at the very smart camps, there are other similar private game reserves nearby that open to the public for day visits as long as you book in advance (see page 367). Combine this with the fact that you can fly back to Cape Town in less than an hour and it becomes obvious why Nelson Mandela Bay is rapidly growing as a popular tourist destination. ►► *For listings, see pages 360-369.*

Ins and outs

Getting there

Nelson Mandela Bay (Port Elizabeth) Airport, 4 km from the city centre along Alister Miller Drive, receives several flights daily from major South African cities. Visitors staying at Humewood Beach and Summerstrand can reach the airport without having to negotiate the city centre by way of an elaborate ring road and flyover system. There is no public transport from the airport into town but most major hotels provide a courtesy bus; alternatively, there are taxis and airport shuttle services to any hotel at the airport. The mainline **railway station** is on the edge of the town centre on Station Street, by the harbour. Nelson Mandela Bay (Port Elizabeth) is served by **Greyhound**, **Intercape** and **Translux** buses, and it is the overnight spot for the **Baz Bus** on the route between Cape Town and Durban, which calls in at most of the backpacker hostels. ►► *For further details, see Transport, page 368.*

Getting around

Local buses depart from **Market Square Bus Station**, beneath the Norwich Union Centre Building on Strand Street. The **Algoa Bus Company** ① *T080-1421444 (toll free)*, operates a regular service between the beachfront, city centre, St George's Park, Rink Street, Greenacres and the Bridge Shopping Complex – Route O.

Best time to visit

Southern right whales visit the bay from June to November, while humpback whales calve and feed their young between May and December.

Tourist information

Nelson Mandela Bay Tourism ① *Donkin Lighthouse Building, Belmont Terr, T041-5858884, www.nmbt.co.za, Mon-Fri 0800-1630, Sat-Sun 0930-1530 (there is also an office in the Boardwalk, T041-5832030),* is a useful office that can book accommodation and advise on nightlife, tours and travel throughout the Eastern Cape. **Eastern Cape Tourist Board** ① *also in the Boardwalk, T041-5857761, www.ectourism.co.za,* has excellent regional information and their website is very informative. **Eas'capism.com** ① *Boardwalk Centre, beach entrance, T041-5077912, www.eascapism.com, daily 0800-2200,* is a private tourism information service with an **Avis** car hire desk on site. It has a very comprehensive website and can book tours, transfers and accommodation.

◐ *Nelson Mandela Bay, is fondly referred to as 'Ibhayi' by Xhosa speakers, 'Die Baai 'by Afrikaners and 'The Bay' by English speakers.*

Background

In 1497, Vasco da Gama noted the 'Bay' on one of his voyages. It was later named Baia de Lagoa, referring to the lagoon situated at the mouth of the Baakens River. For hundreds of years, however, Nelson Mandela Bay (Port Elizabeth) was referred to on navigational

1 Nelson Mandela Bay (Port Elizabeth)

Sleeping
Backpackers Base Camp **3**
Jikeleza Lodge **4**
Millbrook House **5**
Port Elizabeth Backpackers **6**

Protea Edward **2**

Eating
Royal Delhi **3**
Sabatino's **2**

charts only as "a landing place with fresh water". The city was established in 1820 when the first British settlers arrived. The town became a port and a trading centre catering for the early settlers who were gradually moving inland. During the first half of the 20th century, Port Elizabeth expanded and became an important trading and manufacturing city. The main exports were mineral ores, citrus fruits and wool. Ford General Motors opened its first assembly plants here in the 1920s. Today, with a population of around 1.3 million, it is South Africa's fifth largest city, and one that is currently reinventing itself as 'Nelson Mandela Bay', which is its new formal name. As an industrial city it is understandable that tourists don't want to spend a great deal of time here. However, with the massive growth in tourism along the Garden Route, the city has become a convenient point for visitors to start or finish their journey.

Sights

Central Nelson Mandela Bay

The 5-km **Donkin Heritage Trail** has been created to show visitors the most important monuments, buildings, gardens and churches around the city centre. An excellent guidebook, available from the information office, contains 47 places of historical interest.

➡Nelson Mandela Bay maps
1 Nelson Mandela Bay (Port Elizabeth)
2 Humewood and Summerstrand

A few of the more interesting buildings are mentioned below – they are not in the order you might come across them on the trail. The trail starts in Market Square opposite the City Hall, simply follow the useful signs.

Market Square is probably Port Elizabeth's most attractive corner, with a couple of fine buildings and the beginning of bustling Govan Mbeki Avenue. **City Hall** was built between 1858 and 1862; the clock tower was added in 1883. While part of the hall is still used by the council, it is also now a lecture and concert hall for public performances. Look out for a replica of the Diaz Cross in Market Square. This was donated by the Portuguese Government to commemorate the arrival of Bartholomeu Diaz in Algoa Bay in 1488. The **Main Public Library** ① *T041-5858133, Mon-Fri 0900-1700*, dominates the northwestern corner of Market. Stlt is worth noting that the Namibian dollar is interchangeable with the South African Rand and both are accepted throughout Namibia, so you do not need to change money. is worth noting that the Namibian dollar is interchangeable with the South African Rand and both are accepted throughout Namibia, so you do not need to change money.quare. This fine early Victorian building, with its terracotta façade shipped out from the UK, dates from 1835 and started life as a courthouse. It was not until 1902 that it was officially opened as the public library. Outside by the road is a fine marble statue of Queen Victoria, erected in 1903. Once inside, visitors have the opportunity to view some beautiful early books.

The **Prester John Memorial** stands in Fleming Square, behind City Hall. It is dedicated to the mythical king-priest and the Portuguese explorers who discovered South Africa. It was unveiled in 1886 and is thought to be the only monument in the world depicting Prester John. The monument is in the form of a large Coptic cross.

The **Campanile** ⓘ *Strand St, Tue-Sun 0900-1230, 1330-1400*, is a 53-m bell-tower on close to the docks down by the railway station. It was built to commemorate the landing of the 1820 settlers and was once the highest structure in Port Elizabeth. The views of the city and harbour remain impressive though, and if you're fit you can climb up 204 stairs to the observation room at the top. It contains the largest carillon of bells in the country as well as a chiming clock, and the tower is a useful reference point on the coast. Note this is in a rough area and it's advised to visit in a group.

South of City Hall, near the Translux bus station, is the **Wezandla Gallery and Craft Centre** ⓘ *27 Baakens St, T041-5851185, www.wezandla.com, Mon-Fri 0900-1700, Sat 0900-1300*, hard to miss with its brightly painted exterior. This is an interesting collection of African art: wire and wood sculptures, woven baskets, pottery, crafts and curios. Many of the items are the work of local craftsmen and there are a reputed 25,000 items for sale.

Donkin Reserve is a public park in Central, high up on a hill with views of Govan Mbeki Avenue and the harbour. On the inland side of the park is the fine façade of the **Edward Hotel**; on the other side is a lighthouse and an unusual pyramid. The lighthouse dates from 1861 and is today home to the **Nelson Mandela Bay tourist office**. The rest of the lighthouse building can be opened on request. The odd-looking pyramid is actually a memorial erected by Sir Rufane Donkin in memory of his wife, Elizabeth, after whom the city was named. Local folklore is rather more sinister and suggests that her heart was buried in

② Humewood & Summerstrand

Sleeping
Beach 1
Brighton Lodge 2
Conifer Beach House 6
Fifth Avenue Beach House 4

Formula 1 5
Humewood 7
Kingfisher Guest House 9
King's Beach
Backpackers 10

King's Tide 11
Lungile Backpackers 12
Protea Marine 13
Summerstrand Inn 16
Willows Resort 17

the pyramid. Rufane Donkin, a British colonialist and former Cape Governor, was sent to administer Port Elizabeth in the late 19th century, but his wife Elizabeth never saw the town.

South of Donkin Reserve, **Castle Hill Museum** ① *7 Castle Hill Rd, T041-5822515, Mon-Fri 0900-1300, 1400-1600, small entrance fee*, is housed in one of the oldest buildings in the city. It was built in 1827 for the Reverend Francis McCleland as the Rectory. The cottage has been restored to look like an early-Victorian home, complete with a slate roof, yellowwood floors and 19th century furniture and household goods.

Continuing south on Belmont Terrace, is **Fort Frederick** ① *daily, sunrise to sunset, free*. This was the first stone building in the Eastern Cape, completed in 1799. From its high point it overlooks the mouth of the Baakens River. It was built to stop any French troops from landing in the rivermouth but had the effect of helping the rebels at Graaff-Reinet. No shot has ever been fired from, or at, the fort.

Running through the town is the Baakens River Gorge which is surrounded by the well-kept, 54-ha **Settlers Park** – not what you would expect to find in the middle of South Africa's fifth largest city. The valley runs for 7 km and is full of interesting birds, plants and even some small buck. Unfortunately, despite the tranquil setting, there are occasional muggings, so don't come alone. The park has three entrances: How Avenue, just off Park Drive; Chelmsford Avenue, just off Target Kloof; and Third Avenue, Walmer. Look out for the recommended walks by each entrance, such as the 8-km **Guinea Fowl Trail**, which starts in the car park at Third Avenue. **Birdlife Eastern Cape** ① *T041-3793201*, meet here at 0800 on the first Saturday and third Thursday of each month for birdwatching walks; visitors are welcome.

On the western fringes of the city centre is **Nelson Mandela Metropolitan Art Museum** ① *1 Park Dr, T041-5861030, www.artmuseum.co.za, Mon and Wed-Fri 0900-1700, Tue, Sat and Sun 1400-1700, 1st Sun of every month 0900-1400, free*. Formerly the King George VI Art Gallery, most of the collection on display is of 19th- and 20th-century British art, but there are also some good monthly contemporary exhibitions, accompanied by films and lectures. Other displays include a collection of oriental miniatures as well as pottery and sculpture.

➡**Nelson Mandela Bay maps**
1 Nelson Mandela Bay (Port Elizabeth)
2 Humewood and Summerstrand

Eating ❼
Dizzy Dolphins Café **1**
Up the Khyber **5**

All other restaurants are in the large entertainment centres, marked on the map

The **Horse Memorial** standing on the corner of Russell and Cape roads was created after the Boer War. Between 1899 and 1902 thousands of horses died, more often through fatigue and starvation than from being slain in battle. The inscription on the memorial reads: "The greatness of a nation consists not so much in the number of its people or the extent of its territory as in the extent and justice of its compassion." The statue shows a man kneeling in front of a horse with a bucket in his hands making as if to feed or quench the horse's thirst.

Outside Central

Most visitors head for Nelson Mandela Bay (Port Elizabeth)'s beaches which lie to the east of the city centre in the suburbs of **Humewood** and **Summerstrand**, where there are a number of typical seaside attractions and facilities. There are also other beaches and a couple of game reserves within striking distance of the city.

In Humewood, **Bayworld** ① *off Marine Dr, T041-5860650, www.bayworld.co.za*, comprises the Main Museum, Oceanarium and Snake Park. The **Main Museum** ① *daily 0900-1630, small entrance fee*, is a mix of natural and cultural history. Look out for the southern right whale skeleton and the fully rigged models of early sailing ships. There is also a collection of objects collected from wrecks in and around Algoa Bay. The rest of the collection focuses on fossils and early man. The **Oceanarium** ① *0900-1245, 1345-1700, R35, children R17, dolphin and seal shows daily 1100 and 1500*, has over 40 species of fish, as well as a ragged tooth shark tank, rays, turtles and African penguins. The most interesting part of the complex is the dolphin research centre, with seal and dolphin presentations which children will enjoy.

Also in Humewood is the **South End Museum** ① *corner of Humewood Rd and Walmer Blvd, T041-5823325, www.southendmuseum.co.za, Mon-Fri 0900-1600, Sat-Sun 1000-1500*. This museum is dedicated to the South End suburb, which was destroyed when the Group Areas Act in 1950 led to the forcible removal of the cosmopolitan population of the area. South End was one of the prime areas of the city because it was close to the centre of town, the beachfront and the harbour. During Apartheid, not only the blacks, Indians and coloureds were forcibly relocated from the city, but the Chinese too.

Midway between Humewood and Summserstrand on Marine Drive opposite Shark Rock Pier is the **Boardwalk Casino and Entertainment World**, also known as the **Boardwalk Centre** ① *T031-5661802, www.suninternational.com/resorts/boardwalk*, which has added a whole new dimension to leisure in the city. The complex is set around a series of man-made lakes and beautiful gardens lit by some 40,000 lights after dark. There are numerous entertainment venues in the centre, including the Tsitsikamma Conference Centre, the Supersport Arena and the Boardwalk Amphitheatre. The casino offers 700 slot machines and 20 gaming tables, and there's a selection of restaurants (see Eating, page 363), specialist shops and a five-screen cinema.

Townships

The townships around Nelson Mandela Bay (Port Elizabeth) can be visited on a tour (see page 367). The New Brighton township has been in existence since the region was mostly farmland. In 1903, land 8 km north of Port Elizabeth was earmarked for the establishment of a large 'model native settlement'. The outbreak of bubonic plague in 1901 was used as an excuse to gain government assistance for forced removals to this new 'location'. Over time New Brighton became known as the **Red Location** and takes its name from a series of corrugated-iron barracks, brought down here from a defunct concentration camp at Uitenhage as well as the Imperial Yeomanry Hospital at de Aar. Both had been used in the South African War of 1899-1902. In time, these sheds eventually rusted and turned deep red. After the ANC's armed wing Umkhonto we Sizwe went underground in 1960, Red Location was used for hiding political fugitives. Well-hidden cells were erected between shack floors and the ground where these fugitives could hide from the security police. Today the township is home to the new **Red Location Museum** ① *corner Olof Palme and Singaphi streets, T041-4088400, www.freewebs.com/redlocationmuseum, Tue-Fri 1000-1700, Sat-Sun 0900-1500, R10*. Opened in 2006, the striking, industrial warehouse-styled complex uses space, corrugated iron, wood and steel to echo its shanty town surrounds and has already won three major international architectural awards including the Royal Institute of British Architects' inaugural Lubetkin Prize for the most outstanding work of architecture

Sunshine Coast beaches

A combination of natural conditions and man-made developments means that the Algoa Bay beaches around Nelson Mandela Bay (Port Elizabeth) form one of the most popular stretches of coast in South Africa. The water is clean, warm and calm for most of the year, making it an ideal spot for watersports.

The two main northern beaches are **New Brighton** – good for swimming and fishing, with changing rooms, lifeguards and a promenade – and **Bluewater Bay** – a long stretch of white sand with good swimming, but the lifeguards are only present during summer. To get to there by car, take the N2 towards Grahamstown and follow the signs.

The southern beaches come right up to the city centre. **King's Beach** is the closest, lying between the harbour and Humewood. Being so close to the city it can get very busy, but the swimming is safe, boogie-boarding is allowed and there

are lifeguards and changing facilities. This is probably the best beach for families as there is a go-kart track, mini-golf, children's playground, swimming-pool complex, and plenty of kiosks and snack bars. In contrast, **Humewood** is a quieter beach, which has been awarded the Blue Flag, the swimming is good and there is plenty of shade. The next stretch, **Hobie Beach**, is marked by Shark Rock Pier. In the evenings this is a busy area due to the presence of The Boardwalk, an entertainment centre (see Bars and clubs, page 364). The swimming is safe and throughout the year there are local body surfing, beach volleyball and boardsailing competitions. Next up, **Pollock Beach** is one of the better surfing spots. Beyond the lighthouse at Cape Recife, **Sardinia Bay** is the most beautiful beach near the city and a marine reserve popular for snorkelling and scuba diving. Dolphins are often seen close to the shore on this stretch of coastline.

outside the UK and Europe. It tells the history of the township and its part in the struggle, and includes a series of 'memory boxes' or galleries of photos and exhibits. There's a museum shop and café, and outside is a vast space for public events.

Other townships surrounding the city are **Swartkops**, **Kwa-Zakhele** (meaning 'place to build yourself' in Xhosa) and **Motherwell** on the road to Addo, which is reputedly the largest township in the Eastern Cape with its origins from the 1980s when the city's population swelled with people looking for work.

❶ *In 2006, at the opening of the museum there was a reburial ceremony of anti-Apartheid activists Raymond Mhlaba and Govan Mbeki. They are now laid to rest in the mausoleum within the museum complex.*

Game parks

Kragga Kamma Game Park ① *T041-3794195, www.kraggakamma.com, 0800-1700, self-drive R35, R15 children*, is a 15-minute drive from Nelson Mandela Bay on the Kragga Kamma road off the N2. This private game reserve is in a lush tract of coastal forest where all the animals roam free. These animals include rhino, buffalo, giraffe, zebra, cheetah and a number of antelope, including the shy nyala. The resident bird of prey is the jackal buzzard and other species include fish eagles, yellow-billed kites and Knysna loeries. You can drive around the small network of gravel roads in your own car or alternatively take a two-hour guided game drive on offer for R200 pp. There's a café and some picnic sites and accommodation in the way of safari tents and log cabins.

A 25 km drive west of Nelson Mandela Bay, **Seaview Game and Lion Park** ① *T041-3781702, www.seaviewgamepark.co.za. 0900-1700, lion feeding 1200 Sun, R33, R14 children*, is a wildlife park with around 40 species of animal including giraffe, zebra, wildebeest, impala, duiker and monkeys. But it is the lions that most people come to see. In total there are 55, all hand reared, including three white lion and, for an extra fee, visitors can get close up to a lion cub and possibly cuddle one. Except for the lions, many of the animals arrive at the park as orphans or have been injured and wherever possible are rehabilitated and returned to the wild. There are nature trails and self game drives, a restaurant and curio shop and a few stands for caravans and tents. To get there, turn off the N2 at the Seaview sign and the park is 7.5 km towards the sea.

⊚ Nelson Mandela Bay (Port Elizabeth) listings

Hotel and guesthouse prices
L over US$300 AL US$220-300 A US$150-220
B US$100-150 C US$75-100 D US$35-75
E US$15-35 F under US$15
Restaurant prices
††† over US$30 †† US$15-30 † under US$15
See pages 46-51 for further information.

⊜ Sleeping

During the last few years Nelson Mandela Bay (Port Elizabeth) has experienced a rapid expansion in tourist accommodation. Much of this has been in the seaside suburbs of Humewood and Summerstrand, and if you're looking for something close to the beach, it's perfect. The seafront area, however, is a modern and ugly stretch of high-rise blocks and shopping malls. The centre, around the Donkin Reserve, has more character and is far more appealing with a number of quiet back streets lined with some finely restored Victorian houses.

Central *p355, map p354*
B Protea Hotel Edward, Belmont Terr, T041-5862056, www.proteahotels.com. This building is a fine example of late 19th-century architecture and is one of Nelson Mandela Bay (Port Elizabeth)'s famous landmarks, its elegant façade bordering the Donkin Reserve. There are 110 comfortable double rooms with en suite bathroom, telephone and TV, some with good city views. The restaurant is rather fussy but, nevertheless, an excellent

carvery. There is also a bar, lounge, laundry service and secure covered parking. Despite its faded charm, the surrounding streets have become fairly seedy in recent years.
C Millbrook House, 2 Havelok Sq, T041-5823774, www.millbrookhouse.co.za. A delightful B&B in a leafy square in the centre of town. Victorian house with wrought-iron balconies, peaceful setting, perfect for seeing the sights. Family-run with 4 charming en suite rooms, with ceiling fans, TV with M-Net, clean, bright and airy. Small garden with splash pool, lounge, the owners are very friendly and welcoming. Recommended.
E-F Backpackers Base Camp, 58 Western Rd, T041-5823285, pebasecamp@yahoo.com. Large, functional backpacker place in a good location in the centre of town. Double-storey Victorian building with Oregon floors and a fireplace in the dorm. Range of rooms with shared bathrooms and doubles with en suite bath or shower, TV, telephone, decent furnishings. Clean and practical place, good buffet breakfasts, kitchen, bar, and pool table. On the Baz Bus route and can provide free pickup and drop-off from the airport.
E-F Jikeleza Lodge, 44 Cuyler St, T041-5863721, www.highwinds.co.za/jikeleza.htm. Double rooms, dorms, 1 family room, kitchen, pleasant backyard, internet access, free pickup across town, close to shops and some restaurants. Helpful set-up, keen to organize transport and tours, Baz Bus stop.
E-F Port Elizabeth Backpackers, 7 Prospect Hill, T041-5860697,

www.pebackpackers.za.org. Attractive old Victorian building with bright and airy dorms, some doubles, well-equipped kitchen, meals available, spacious lounge with fireplace, good location, small backyard, good travel centre, Baz Bus stop.

Outside Central *p357, maps p354 and p356*
Walmer and Mill Park
The leafy suburb of Walmer is on the far side of St George's Park and southwest of the centre and is convenient for the airport, but not for the beach.

L Hacklewood Hill Country House, 152 Prospect Rd, Walmer, T041-5811300, www.hacklewood.co.za. Luxurious guest-house housed in a late-Victorian manor house full of antiques and paintings, 8 a/c tasteful double rooms, each with massive en suite bathrooms and DSTV. In the beautiful gardens is a swimming pool and tennis court, plus secure covered parking. Elegant dining room where you'll need to brush up on the use of silverware, and some special touches which make this a fine choice: guests, for example, are encouraged to select their wine from the impressive cellar. Advance booking essential during the peak season. No children under 14.

C King George Guesthouse, 2 King George Rd, Mill Park, close to the cricket ground in St George's Park, T041-3741825, www.king george.co.za. A mock-Tudor family home built in 1915 with plenty of space for guests. 8 double rooms with en suite bathroom, mini-bar and TV. There is also a study and a lounge, plus sizeable gardens with a swimming pool. Extra meals available on request.

D Oak Tree Cottages, 112 Church Rd, Walmer, T041-5813611, www.oaktree-accommodation.co.za. A well-run B&B with 5 good-value double rooms set in the garden with private entrances with en suite bathroom, TV, kettle, fridge, and microwave, swimming pool, shady gardens, laundry, secure parking.

E-F Lemon Tree, 14 Mill Park Rd, Mill Park, T041-3734103, www.lemontreelake.co.za.

A little bit off the beaten track but convenient for the shopping centres. Homely award-winning guesthouse with spacious rooms decorated with antiques and opening up on to the gardens, DSTV, wireless internet, minibar, swimming pool, German spoken.

Humewood and Summerstrand
A The Beach, Marine Dr, Summerstrand, T041-5832161, wwwpehotels.co.za. Luxurious, low-rise hotel right on the beach. 58 well-appointed rooms, 3 good restaurants, bar with ocean views from the patio, golf, large pool, laundry, secure parking, tidy gardens, good service, just across the road from Shark Rock pier and adjacent to the Boardwalk Centre, a short drive from the centre.

A King's Tide, 16 Tenth Av, Summerstrand, T041-5836023, www.kingstide.co.za. PE's first luxury boutique hotel, very stylish with 10 beautifully decorated suites, extravagant bathrooms, MNet TV, internet access, good gourmet breakfasts, dinner on request, bar, comfortable and friendly.

A Protea Hotel Marine, Marine Dr, Summerstrand, T041-5832101, www.proteahotels.com. Large, unattractive high-rise block just across from the beach. 98 a/c rooms with DSTV, comfortable and recently refurbished, some of the 34 rooms in the loft extension have upstairs bedrooms and additional kitchenettes and lounges downstairs, 2 swimming pools, one on the roof with great views of Pollock Beach and Algoa Bay. The **Connaught** restaurant has a good local reputation.

B Humewood, 33 Marine Dr, T041-5858961, www.humewoodhotel.co.za. Attractive old-fashioned seaside building right on King's Beach. 91 plain but adequate rooms, most of which are sea-facing with small private balconies. Restaurant, bar, the morning coffee shop has a pleasant ambience and some seats on a terrace overlooking the street, though lacks a proper garden for children to enjoy.

C Brighton Lodge, 21 Brighton Dr, Summerstrand, T041-5834576, www.brighton lodge.co.za. A very comfortable guesthouse where each of the 11 bedrooms has been decorated from a different period, all have en suite bathrooms, microwave, fridge, DSTV and a private entrance, swimming pool, walking distance from the Boardwalk and the beach. Recommended.

C Conifer Beach House, 39 Windermere Rd, Humewood, T041-5855959, www.conifer.co.za. Pretty house and garden with 4 self-catering units with private entrances and patios, wood floors, white linen, stylish furniture, TV, breakfast available, friendly hosts, recommended by readers. German and Dutch spoken.

C Kingfisher Guest House, 73 Brighton Dr, Summerstrand, T041-5832150, www.kingfisherpe.co.za. Family-run B&B close to the beach, with 8 individually decorated double rooms with en suite bathrooms, private entrance and patio, TV, fridge, microwave and toaster, lounge, disabled facilities, laundry, swimming pool and peaceful garden to relax in.

C Summerstrand Inn, Marine Dr, Summerstrand, T041-5833131, www.hotsummer.co.za. Large hotel with 237 spacious but dreary and dimly lit rooms, with a/c and TV, 126 of them are singles aimed at conference delegates, views of Humewood Golf Course, leafy gardens offer privacy around the pool area. **Palm Grill** restaurant serves buffet meals, cosy **Boodles** bar, courtesy bus offered. Good location but in need of refurbishment.

C-D Fifth Avenue Beach House, 3 5th Av, Summerstrand, T041-5832441, www.fifthave.co.za. Guests can stay in the main house or in a neat complex with a balcony overlooking 2 palm-fringed swimming pools. 10 double rooms with TV, garden has a tropical feel with several mature palm trees, 200 m from the beach. A friendly and good-value set-up. Recommended.

D Formula 1, Marine Dr, next to the Oceanarium, Spur restaurant and McDonalds, T041-5856380, www.formule1.co.za. Soulless basic modern accommodation units where the shower and loo are in a sort of cubicle in the corner, but clean and good value in an

emergency. 88 basic rooms, same price for 1-3 people, breakfast packs can be bought in the lobby.

D-E Willows Resort, Marine Dr, Schoen makerskop, T041-3661717, www.willows. madibabayresorts.co.za. A large, self-contained complex with more than 70 caravan sites, and 70 sea-facing self-catering chalets and rondavels with TV. Café serves snacks on the site during the day, plenty of extras for children: tidal pool, trampolines, mini-golf, children's playground, rock fishing, tractor rides, quad bikes, tennis courts and, in season, a crèche. Very popular in summer.

E-F King's Beach Backpackers, 41 Windermere Rd, Humewood, T041-5858113, kingsb@agnet.co.za. Set 2 blocks back from the beach and close to restaurants, bars and clubs. Comfortable dorms, slightly cramped double rooms set in individual buildings in the garden, and camping space on the lawn. Excellent kitchen facilities, TV and video lounge, internet access, laid-back bar, travel centre, Baz Bus stop.

E-F Lungile Backpackers, 12 La Roche Dr, Humewood, T041-5822042, www.lungile backpackers.co.za. Lively lodge set in a fine modern house about 10 mins' walk from Humewood Beach and the beachfront nightlife. Camping space, dorms in the main house and double rooms in separate wooden cabins at the back, some with TV. Also has a garden with pool, TV and video lounge, bar, pool table, laundry, and a clean kitchen. Free use of surfboards. Great value. Recommended.

Game parks p359

D Kragga Kamma Game Park, 15-min drive from PE on the Kragga Kamma road off the N2, T041-3794195, www.kraggakamma.com. Self-catering thatched lodges and chalets, with lounge, kitchen and undercover braai area, good for families. Also cheaper pre-erected tents on platforms also with self-catering facilities. All scattered around a pretty forest area where overnight guests are likely to encounter animal activity during the night.

🍴 Eating

Nelson Mandela Bay (Port Elizabeth) claims to have the highest per capita ratio of restaurants in South Africa, which for tourists means a wide choice without the inflated prices of Cape Town or Johannesburg. There are 2 purpose-built entertainment centres, **Brooke's Hill Pavilion** and **The Boardwalk**, where you will find a wide selection of restaurants and bars under one roof. These are similar to modern shopping malls – there is ample parking and visitors can feel more secure than they would wandering the streets at night. Away from these centres, most of the restaurants are either in the old city centre or close to the seafront in the suburbs of Humewood and Summerstrand.

Central p355, map p354

Old Austria, 24 Westbourne Rd, T041-3730299. Mon-Sat 1200-1500, 1800-2230. Set in a restored Victorian whitewashed rectory, with chandeliers, polished wooden floors and grandfather clocks, the menu features seafood and Austrian fare such as schnitzels and apple strudel.

Royal Delhi, 10 Burgess St, T041-3738216. Open 1200-2330, closed Sun and Sat lunchtime. A very popular local curry house serving a full range of Indian dishes, famous for its messy crab curry and home-made samosas and fish cakes. Large groups can eat in their own separate dining room.

Sabatino's, 35 Westbourne Rd, T041-3731707. Open 1200-1500, 1800-2200. Italian option where the quality of the food is matched by the ambience and attentive service. Recommended.

Outside Central p357, maps p354 and p356

Hacklewood Hill Country House, 152 Prospect Rd, Walmer, T041-5811300. Elegant dining room in a luxury guesthouse, open all day for breakfast, lunch, and dinner, candlelit 4- to 5-course dinners (you'll need to know how to use the silverware), with wine suggestions for each course and waiters wearing white gloves. Very romantic and intimate. Recommended as a special treat for couples.

Kyoto, 56 Boardwalk Centre, T041-5831160. Wed-Sun 1200-1400, 1800-2200, Mon-Tue 1800-2200 only. PE's only upmarket Japanese restaurant, with Japanese-inspired decor. Sit in a tatami – low tables in booths with cushions on the floor – or eat at the sushi bar, comprehensive menu and excellent service.

34' South, 29 Boardwalk Centre, T041-5831085. Open 1000-2130. Fabulous deli and sister branch to the one at the Knysna Waterfront, with all sorts of treats from olives to cookery books. Chrome and glass decor, you can make up meals from the counters or choose a selection of tapas and seafood snacks, tables outside on the wooden deck.

The Cannaught, Protea Hotel Marine, Marine Dr, Summerstrand, T041-5832101. A quality hotel restaurant with nice ocean views serving good seafood and meat dishes. Excellent all-you-can-eat carvery at Sun lunch.

Lai Kung, Boardwalk, Summerstrand, T041-5831123. Open 1130-2300. Large Chinese restaurant specializing in Cantonese cuisine with a huge range of good-value dishes, plenty for vegetarians, quick service.

Mauro's, McArthur Baths Centre, Humewood, T041-5824910. Mon-Fri 1100-1500, Mon-Sat 1800-late. Fashionable seafood restaurant overlooking the beach, modern airy decor, good grilled fish, calamari, baked crab and giant prawns, also pasta and some meat dishes, lighter lunches served on the spacious deck with outdoor tables and bar, good service.

Piccolo Blackbeards, Brookes Hill Pavilion, corner of Marine Dr and Brookes Hill Dr, Summerstrand, T041-5855567. Open Mon-Sat for dinner only, reservations advised. An à la carte seafood restaurant which has been run by the same family for 3 generations. Great ocean views and impressive fish tank displays, extensive range of seafood, steak, Italian, vegetarian and poultry dishes. Recommended.

♔ **Zorba's**, Dolphin's Leap, 9 Marine Dr, T041-5863804. Open 1800-late. Greek restaurant specializing in mezze and seafood. Romantic interior, good food, bar stays open after the restaurant has closed, non-smokers are advised to book as they get the smaller area.

♔ **Dizzy Dolphins Café**, 1 Shark Rock Pier, T041-5834536. Trendy cocktail bar and restaurant serving seafood, steaks and salads. Popular with a young, lively crowd.

♔ **Up the Khyber**, McArthur Baths complex, King's Beach, T041-5822200. Mon-Sat 1000-2200. Cheap curries, burgers and steaks in a great setting right above the beach with casual wooden tables on the veranda. Try the rather unusual oxtail curry.

Cafés

Café Dulce, Boardwalk, Summerstrand, T041-5831193. Great coffee shop open 0900-2200, selling tasty sandwiches, salads, milkshakes, ice creams; gets more alcoholic as the day gets longer.

🌙 Bars and clubs

Nelson Mandela Bay (Port Elizabeth)
p353, map p354 and p356

Nelson Mandela Bay (Port Elizabeth) has a good choice of late-night bars and clubs, often offering meals in the early evening and live music or DJs later. As in all cities, clubs change regularly – for up-to-date information about which is the happening venue, ask at one of the backpacker hostels or the waiters at **Tapas al Sol**. Some places have dress codes – this usually means no shorts, vests or sandals.

Most of the nightlife is focused at 2 major entertainment centres, **The Boardwalk**, on Marine Dr by Shark Rock Pier, and **Brookes Hill Pavilion**, on the corner of Beach Rd and Brooke's Hill Dr in Summerstrand. These areas are safe to walk about at night,

which is much of their appeal. In Central, the busiest area is along **Parliament St**, where there are a number of informal Kwaito clubs, but expect to attract quite a bit of attention if you're white and be wary of walking here at night – stick to taxis.

Barney's Tavern, The Boardwalk, T041-5834500. Atmospheric bar with live music every night as well as on Sat-Sun afternoons on 'The Deck'.

Tapas al Sol, Brookes Hill Pavilion, T041-5862159, www.tapas.co.za. Tapas bar and pub with extended happy hour on Thu, DJs on Fri and Sat, sometimes live SA rock bands.

🎭 Entertainment

Nelson Mandela Bay (Port Elizabeth)
p353, map p354 and p356
Cinema
All the latest releases from Europe and the US are shown, check the local newspapers for screenings. The main cinemas are:
Cinema Starz, Boardwalk Complex, T041-5832000, www.starz.co.za; **Nu-Metro**, Walmer Park Shopping Complex, T041-3671102, www.numetro.co.za; and **Ster-Kinekor**, The Bridge Mall, Cape Rd, T041-3630577, www.sterkinekor.com.

Theatre
There are regular concerts and plays performed by local musical and performance groups. Check out the press for details or contact the Computicket call centre, T041-5863177, www.computicket.co.za. The most popular venues in the city are: **The Feather Market Centre**, Baakens St, Central, T041-5855514; **The Opera House and Barn**, Whites Rd, Central, T041-5862256; and the **Vodacom Amphitheatre**, at the Boardwalk Centre, Marine Dr, Summerstrand, T041-5077777.

⊛ Festivals and events

Nelson Mandela Bay (Port Elizabeth)
p353, map pp354 and p356
Feb Shakespearian Festival, a selection of plays are put on at the Mannville Open-Air Theatre in St George's Park. The theatre is named after the late Helen and Bruce Mann, who instituted the festival in 1970. A most enjoyable way to pass a summer's evening.
Prickly Pear Festival, in Uitenhage, 34 km northwest of Nelson Mandela Bay (Port Elizabeth). With over 250 products on sale, crowds of over 25,000 turn up each year to enjoy food such as pancakes, ginger beer, *potjiekos*, jam, spitbraais, fish braais, curry bunnies and home-made pudding.
Easter Splash Festival, 4-day beach festival over the Easter weekend with watersports, surfing competitions, live music and fireworks. Very popular annual event that attracts 200,000 daily and fundraiser for the Community Chest.
Oct Addo Rose Show, www.addorose.co.za, a massive display with over 25,000 blooms on show, including new varieties. An enjoyable day out for anyone keen on gardens.
Dec Opening of the Summer Entertainment Programme, very much for families. The mayor gets the show rolling by turning on the Christmas lights and there is a firework display on the beach. There is also a 4-day ski-boat race from Nelson Mandela Bay (Port Elizabeth) to East London.

O Shopping

Nelson Mandela Bay (Port Elizabeth)
p353, map p354 and p356
Flea markets
Art in the Park, St George's Park, located along Park Dr. An open-air exhibition of craft stalls and local art on 1st Sun of every month.
Humewood Beachfront, between the King's Beach parking area and McArthur's Baths, Sat and Sun but everyday over school holiday periods.

Shopping malls
Like all South African cities, Nelson Mandela Bay (Port Elizabeth) has its share of modern shopping malls where not just shops but banks and post offices are located. Most well-known chain stores have relocated from the city centre to these malls. Shops are open Mon-Fri 0900-1800, and longer over the weekend, restaurants and cinemas until 2200-2300.
Bridge Shopping and Entertainment Centre, Langenhoven Dr, Greenacres, is a giant upmarket centre, built over a main road with great views from its elevated position. There are 8 cinemas, ATMs, restaurants, coffee shops and fast food outlets, plus a smart fashion mall for those with spare cash.
 Other shopping centres include:
Greenacres Shopping Centre, adjacent to Bridge Shopping Centre; **Pier 14 Shopping Centre**, 444 Govan Mbeki Av, North End, a central location but more downmarket than the others; and **Walmer Park Shopping Centre**, Main Rd, Walmer.

▲ Activities and tours

Nelson Mandela Bay (Port Elizabeth)
p353, map p354 and p356
Nelson Mandela Bay (Port Elizabeth) has excellent facilities catering for sports, especially watersports, golf, tennis, yachting and athletics. It is also a great city in which to watch sport and is often dubbed by locals as 'SPort Elizabeth'.

Boat trips
Algoa Bay is world renowned in sailing circles and the prestigious yacht club in the city, the **Algoa Bay Yacht Club**, www.abyc.org.za, is based at the harbour. There are 2 prevailing winds which produce either very rough and choppy conditions or calm and flat conditions. Southern right whales mate and calve between Jul and Oct in the bay, humpback whales pass by during Jun-Jul, and again in Nov-Dec, and the sardine-eating

Bryde's whale is present throughout most of the year. Also be on the lookout for Cape fur seals, penguins, bottlenose dolphins, gannets and cormorants.

Polani Ocean Cruises, T041-5832141. Offers breakfast and sunset cruises from the Boardwalk Centre on an 65-ft schooner.

Raggy Charters, based at the harbour, T041-3782528, www.raggycharters.co.za. Runs marine life-watching trips into the Algoa Bay and to islands that form the marine section of the Addo National Park, beachfront cruises from 1½-3 hrs, and half-or full-day fishing trips using a variety of craft.

Cricket

Nelson Mandela Bay (Port Elizabeth) is home to the **Eastern Province Cricket Board**. Matches are played at **St George's Park Sahara Oval**, also now known as the 'Crusaders Ground', ticket enquiries, T041-5851646, www.epcricket.co.za. The first Test match played here was between South Africa and England on 12 Feb 1889, which was also the first Test match to be played in Africa. St George's is a pleasant old stadium with a capacity for 22,000 and an enjoyable venue to watch cricket. The 2 ends are known as the Duckpond End and the Park Drive End. There has been a cricket club here since 1843. There is some interesting cricket memorabilia on display in glass cases in the Khaya Majola Room in the Centenary Pavilion at St George's. Semi-final matches were played here during the 2003 Cricket World Cup.

Football

Between Feb and Oct there are afternoon games every weekend. There is a fundamental sporting division in South Africa: rugby and cricket is for whites; soccer is for blacks. These ridiculous divisions mean that local whites often discourage white visitors who want to see a match – ignore them, but contact the tourist office about safety issues for visitors. The principal venues are the Gelvandale Stadium in Liebenberg Rd, and the **Westbourne Oval** in Westbourne Rd.

For match details contact **The South African Football Association (SAFA) Eastern Cape**, T041-4513716. A new 50,000 stadium is presently being built for the 2010 FIFA Football World Cup.

Golf

There are several golf courses in and around the city, but the best bet for visitors are: **Port Elizabeth Golf Club**, T041-3743140, www.pegolf.co.za, accessed from Westview Dr, Mill Park, a 100-year-old beautifully maintained 18-hole/par 72 course. **Humewood Golf Club**, T041-5832137, www.humewoodgolf.co.za, Marine Dr, Summerstrand, a challenging links course and rated as one of the top 10 courses in the country, 18 holes/72 par with a very elegant clubhouse.

Horse racing

There are 2 major racecourses, **Arlington**, Schoenmakerskop Rd, Walmer, T041-3661666, and **Fairview**, Draaifontein Rd, Greenbushes, T041-3721859. Both are managed by Phumelela, www.phumelela.com. There are races every Fri afternoon at both of the 2 courses throughout the year.

Mountain biking

There are a number of mountain bike trails around the city. The **Baakens River Trail** is a 23-km circuit in a valley right in the middle of Nelson Mandela Bay (Port Elizabeth); although surrounded by an urban environment, it has plenty of examples of indigenous vegetation. The trail starts from the car park at Dodds Farm, off 9th Av, Walmer, and ends at Abelia Cres in Sunridge Park. Concrete bollards with a bicycle painted on them mark the trail. The **Swartkops Trail** is a 22-km circular route in the Swartkops Valley Nature Reserve, an 850-ha reserve on the northern outskirts of town. The reserve was created in 1993 to protect an area of threatened valley bushveld as well as local bird-breeding colonies. This is a much more difficult trail with sections where some riders are likely to push their bikes up the escarpment. You will need to wear a helmet and have a full puncture repair kit – do not ride this trail alone. The route is marked by a blue arrow and bicycle motif on concrete bollards; the start is at the Corobrik brick factory next to the Bramlin-Markman Highway.

Surfing

Good waves on this stretch of coast aren't restricted to **Jeffrey's Bay**. The Pipe in **Algoa Bay** is one of the most popular spots, as is **Millars Point** further to the west. One drawback of the waves closer to town is the crowded beaches and the industrial backdrop.

Swimming

The beaches around Nelson Mandela Bay (Port Elizabeth) are very clean, but the sea temperature rarely gets above 21°C. Away from the large hotels there are a couple of excellent municipal swimming pools.
McArthur Baths, King's Beach Promenade, T041-5863412. Sep-Apr daily 0700-1700. Tidal pool, children's water-chute, splash pool, freshwater pool, permanent lifeguard, restaurants and snack bar.
St George's Park Baths, St George's Park, T041-5857751. Sep-Apr Mon-Fri 0700-2100, Sat 0900-1800, Sun 1030-1800. Olympic-size pool with diving facilities, children's pool, restaurant, snack bar.

Tour operators

In general, there are 3 types of tours on offer: historical town tours which may involve walking; township tours, which are growing in popularity; and wildlife tours, with visits to one or more of the local game reserves such as Addo Elephant National Park. For a full list of tour operators and to book a tour, contact the tourist office, see page 353.
Calabash Tours, 8 Dollery St, Central, T041-5856162, www.calabashtours.co.za. Excellent city tours, including visits to various townships, visits to local artists and self-help projects, and evening shebeen

tours. Also runs tours to Addo Elephant National Park and visits to the beaches. Minimum 2 people. Good value, highly recommended, this company was joint winner of the 2004 Responsible Tourism Award at the World Travel Market in London.
East Cape Tours, T041-5816260, www.eastcapetours.com. Day tours around Nelson Mandela Bay including half-day township visits and good-value full-day tours of Addo for R600 including lunch and entrance fees
Fundani Cultural Tours, 72 Ferguson Rd, New Brighton, T/F041-4542064. Cultural tours of the townships, which generally involve visits to places of historical and cultural importance including the new Red Location Museum, viewings of local art and a stop at a shebeen for a drink and a meal. Travel is by minibus taxi, and they now have their own township B&B in New Brighton for overnight stays.
Highwind Tours, T041-5863721, www.highwinds.co.za. 3-hr city tours for R290, can also guide visitors around the city's Donkin Heritage Trail, plus townships and night-time shebeen visits.
Shield Tours, 1082-3810235, www.shieldtours.co.za. Historical city tours and trips to the game parks.

Windsurfing

Experienced windsurfers have the opportunity to go out at Noordhoek, where they are totally exposed to the ocean swell, but it is important to check the tides. There are excellent reef breaks and cross-shore conditions when the southwest wind blows. Off Hobie Beach the conditions are much calmer, particularly when there is a southwest wind. Be careful at all times to avoid the designated public bathing areas. The Swartkop River Mouth is a good area for beginners as the conditions are calm. Some of the hotels on the beach front in Summerstrand and Humewood have equipment to rent out to residents.

⊖ Transport

Nelson Mandela Bay (Port Elizabeth)
p353, map p354 and p356

It's 72 km to **Addo Elephant National Park**; 643 km to **Bloemfontein**; 763 km to **Cape Town**; 295 km to **East London**; 124 km to **Grahamstown**; 246 km to **Graaff-Reinet**; 79 km to **Jeffrey's Bay**; 1050 km to **Johannesburg**; 150 km to **Port Alfred**; 74 km to **Shamwari Game Reserve**.

Air

Nelson Mandela Bay (Port Elizabeth) airport is 4 km from the city on Alister Miller Dr, T041-5077319, www.airports.co.za. The airport has restaurants, ATMs and a tourist information desk in arrivals. There are several daily connections with the other major cities on **South African Airways (SAA), Kulula, Comair, Nationwide** and **One Time** (see page 39 for contact details). Your hotel may be able to offer a pre-arranged pickup or there are plenty of taxis at the airport. Several car hire groups have a desk in the terminal, see below for contact numbers.

Bus

Baz Bus provides the best budget bus travel service along the coast between Cape Town and Durban. Nelson Mandela Bay (Port Elizabeth) is the midway point where the bus stays overnight. In other words, if you start the day in Cape Town and are heading towards Durban, Nelson Mandela Bay (Port Elizabeth) is the furthest you can get in a single day. There is a daily service to and from **Cape Town** and it runs 5 days a week to and from **Durban**. The Baz Bus arrives in Nelson Mandela Bay (Port Elizabeth) from both Cape Town and Durban 2130-2230 and departs 0645-0715.

The 3 mainline bus companies have daily departures linking the other major cities. Reservations can be booked through the **Computicket**, call centre, T041-5863177, www.computicket.co.za.

Bus companies Baz Bus, T021-4392323, www.bazbus.com. **Greyhound**, T041-3634555, www.greyhound.co.za. Coaches arrive/depart from the rear car park, 107 Govan Mbeki Av, and in front of Edgars at the Greenacres Shopping Centre. **Intercape**, T041-5861165, www.intercape.co.za. Coaches arrive/depart from the office in the Flemming Building behind the Old Post Office, corner of Flemming and North Union streets. **Translux**, T041-3921333, www.translux.co.za. Coaches start/finish their journey by the railway station in the centre of town, then stop at the office, Ernst and Young Building, Ring Rd, Greenacres. If arriving by bus check with your hotel which is the most convenient stop for their location.

Car hire

Avis, airport T041-5814291, toll free T0861-021111, www.avis.co.za. **Budget**, airport T041-5814242, toll free T0861-016622, www.budget.co.za. **Dollar Thrifty**, airport T041-5814774, toll free T0861-002111, www.thrifty.co.za. **Imperial**, airport T041-5814214, toll free T0861-131000, www.imperialcarrental.co.za. **Tempest/Sixt Car Hire**, airport T041-5811256, toll free T0861-8367378, www.tempestcarhire.com.

Taxi

Hurters Radio Cabs, T041-5855500. Local company that rather astonishingly has been operating in Port Elizabeth for 75 years.

Train

The railway station is in the town centre on Station St, just off Strand St which runs parallel to Govan Mbeki Av. Information T041-5072662, reservations T0860-008888, www.spoornet.co.za. There are services between Port Elizabeth and **Johannesburg** and **Bloemfontein**. Train schedules and fares are published on the website.

Diving in Nelson Mandela Bay

There are a number of good dive sites around Nelson Mandela Bay (Port Elizabeth) and the best time for diving is during the winter months of May to September when average visibility is 8-15 m. There are a variety of dive sites from colourful reefs and drop-offs to shipwrecks and soft corals. The best diving in the area is around **St Croix Islands**, 20 km from Nelson Mandela Bay (Port Elizabeth) harbour. The average dive is along a slope with a maximum depth of 30 m, where there are a few caves and gullies. The islands and the surrounding waters are protected: fishing and spearfishing are not permitted and it is forbidden to land on the islands. A consequence of this has been a flourishing population of African jackass penguins, gulls, terns and cormorants on land, while the surrounding waters are rich in marine life, providing a plentiful diet for the birds. Other popular local dives are **Thunderbolt Reef, Sardinia Bay, Devil's Reef, Roman Rock** and **Philip's Reef**. There are also some good wreck dives at the **Pati**, on Thunderbolt Reef; the **Inchcape Rock** wreck (this steel hull from 1902 suffers from poor visibility); the **Western Knight** wreck (experienced wreck divers only); and the **Haerlem** wreck (a navy vessel sunk in 1987 to 21 m specifically for divers). The following dive operators can organize daily trips. **Ocean Divers International**, 10 Albert Rd, Walmer, T041-5815121, www.odipe.co.za. **Pro Dive**, Main Rd, Walmer, opposite the Walmer Park Shopping Mall, T041-5811144, www.prodive.co.za. Pro Dive can also organize cage diving in the shark tank at the Oceanarium.

❶ Directory

Nelson Mandela Bay (Port Elizabeth)
p353, map p354 and p356
Banks American Express Boardwalk Centre, T041-5832025. **Embassies and consulates** Germany, 11 Uitenhage Rd, T041-4872840, Mon-Fri 0830-1230. **UK**, 5th floor, First Bowring House, 66 Ring Rd, Greenacres, T041-3638841, Mon-Fri 0900-1230. **Emergencies** Surf and Sea Rescue, T041-5073911. **Internet** You can access the internet at all the backpacker lodges and hotels. Otherwise, there is **Boardwalk Internet Café** at the Boardwalk Centre, T041-5834725. **Medical** services Netcare Greenacres Hospital, Ring Rd, Greenacres, T041-3907000, private hospital. St George's Hospital, Park Dr, Central, T041-3926111. **Post** office Main Post Office, 259 Govan Mbeki Av, T041-5084039, Mon-Fri 0800-1700, Sat 0830-1300. **Useful contacts** Immigration: corner of Stone and Lavinia streets, T041-4871026, for visa extensions, Mon-Fri 0800-1500.

West of Nelson Mandela Bay

From Nelson Mandela Bay (Port Elizabeth) the N2 heads west for around 190 km to Storms River and the Tsitsikamma National Park at the eastern end of the Garden Route. Although Tsitsikamma is officially in the Eastern Cape and Storms River marks the provincial boundary, we deal with it in the Western Cape chapter along with the rest of the Garden Route. This stretch of road is nowhere near as scenic as the Garden Route itself, though there are a few attractions if you veer off the N2. These include the modern town of Jeffery's Bay, internationally famous for its good surf, a few interesting nature reserves, and the tranquil village of St Francis Bay and its neighbour, the upmarket resort of Cape St Francis. **»** *For listings, see pages 373-376.*

Van Stadens Wild Flower Reserve

ⓘ *The reserve has a visitor centre, nursery and a picnic site, 0800-1700. For more information contact the reserve manager, T041-9560155.*

The N2 from Nelson Mandela Bay (Port Elizabeth) to Humansdorp passes directly through the middle of the wild flower reserve. The turning into the reserve is 35 km from Nelson Mandela Bay (Port Elizabeth). Established to protect and propagate indigenous flora, the area is also worth visiting for its butterflies and birds. The best time to visit is between February and August when many of the plants are in bloom. Plants to look out for include ground orchids and proteas. The southern part of the reserve is an interesting area of forest with ironwood and wild pomegranate trees, as well as a rare tree species, the Cape star-chestnut.

There are two short walks through the different ecosystems of the reserve: the **River Walk**, 4 km, passes the nursery and follows the course of the Van Stadens River; the **Forest Walk**, 6 km, enters an area that has been replanted with proteas. From the highest point of the walk there are views of riverine forest in the valleys and gorge below.

Langkloof

Three mountain ranges lie to the north of the N2 and Jeffrey's Bay: the **Kouga**, the **Baviaanskloof** and the **Grootwinterhoek**, known collectively as the 'Langkloof'. At 270,000 ha, the Langkloof is the third largest wilderness region in South Africa. It became the meeting point of the Khoisan – San hunter-gatherers and Khoi pastoralists. Their rock art in overhangs and caves throughout the area stands testament to their existence.

One of the most fascinating routes to take through the Langkloof is to follow the N2 for 92 km west of Nelson Mandela Bay (Port Elizabeth) to Thornhill, and then the R331 and R332 along the Baviaanskloof River Valley between Patensie and Willowmore. However, it is a narrow, steep, gravel-surfaced, winding road and the distance to Willowmore is approximately 200 km, which can take aobut six to eight hours. A 4WD vehicle is preferable. There are also no shops or fuel in the valley. The road meanders through a landscape dominated by the red sandstone hills on either side. The hills are rich in proteas, ericas, orchids and the 'drie-bessie-bos', an endemic plant which can only be seen in this area. As the road climbs further up the river valley, the scenery becomes more rugged with the mountains rising to over 1600 m. The mountains are a maze of cliffs and ravines inhabited by baboons and tortoises; the trails here pass through thick areas of woodland where you can see the unique Baviaanskloof cedar. From the top of the mountains there are views over the acacia woodland to the fruit farms in the valleys below. Eland and Cape mountain zebra have now been reintroduced, and kudu, bushbuck, klipspringer and baboon are present.

This region offers some of the wildest areas for hiking in the Eastern Cape; hikes here are strenuous and involve some long climbs. Summers here are too hot for long hikes so it makes sense simply to drive through the area. March to November is cooler and more suitable for hiking. For information check out www.baviaans.co.za, www.baviaans.net or www.baviaanskloof.net, or go to the **Tolbos Country Shop and Restaurant** ① T042-2830437, on the R331 in the Gamtoos Valley, roughly 30 km north of the N2.

Jeffrey's Bay ⊖⊜▲⊜ ↠ pp373-376. Colour map 7, B4.

Jeffrey's Bay, or 'J-Bay' as it's known locally, is surf central. Home to the 'perfect wave', this is an internationally acclaimed surfing spot and a major playground for self-respecting surf rats. In the evenings, the local bars buzz with talk of supertubes and perfect breaks. Waves can get big, sometimes as high as 3 m giving rides of over three minutes, but J-Bay is surprisingly renowned for its safety. Unsurprisingly, it attracts more than its fair share of long-term resident travellers but, away from the beach, there's little going on in town. There are numerous surf shops selling a wide range of boards and wetsuits, as well as Billabong and Quiksilver factory outlets, but when surf's up don't be surprised to find many of the local businesses closed.

Ins and outs

Getting there If you don't have a car the J-Bay Cabs, T083-6111003, will bring you here on request from Nelson Mandela Bay (Port Elizabeth). The town is served by the **Baz Bus** (for further details, see Transport, page 376). The nearest drop-off for the mainline buses (**Greyhound** and **Translux**) is in Humansdorp.

Tourist information **Jeffrey's Bay Tourism** ① corner of Da Gama and Darommedaris roads in the Shell Museum complex, 1042-2932923, www.jeffreysbay tourism.org, Mon-Fri 0830-1700, Sat 0900-1200, are helpful and enthusiastic, although back-packer hostels offer the best practical information about surfing. For hourly information on surfing conditions, swell maps, satellite images, moon and tide data, weather forecasts and wave graphics, visit www.jbaytv.co.za.

Background

The origins of Jeffrey's Bay date to 1894, when a trading post was established here by Joseph Avent Jeffrey, a whaler from the island of St Helena. The trading post received goods by sea and supplied

Jeffrey's Bay

Indian Ocean

Main Beach

N

200 metres
200 yards

Sleeping 💤
Beach Cabanas 3
Diaz 15 House on the Beach 1
Guesthouse 8
Island Vibe 9
Jeffrey's Bay
Backpackers 2
Stratos 7
Supertubes 4

Eating 🍴
De Viswijf 2
Die Walskipper 6
Kitchen Windows 1
Le Grotto 3
Sunflower Café 5

settlers living inland in the Langkloof. Little of the original settlement remains and today Jeffrey's Bay is a sprawl of unattractive bungalows and holiday homes. Out of season in summer, when most of the coast is at its liveliest, the resort is a quiet and desolate place and there's little of the surfing scene or nightlife you might expect. In winter, however, when the waves are at their best, the town comes back to life. July is also when the **Billabong Pro J-Bay** surf competition (www.billabongpro.com) is held – with prize money amounting to US$250,000 which draws surfers from across the globe and the town gets packed out. This is a major surfing event, and you'll get to see some of the best surfers in the world compete.

Sights

The waves here are definitely the main attraction, but as an alternative, the **Shell Museum** ① *T042-2931945, Mon-Sat 0900-1600, Sun 0900-1300*, makes for an interesting visit. The collection is incredibly large and has many rare examples of Indo-Pacific and southern Cape shells found on nearby beaches. The position of Jeffrey's Bay along the coast happens to coincide with the meeting point of two opposing ocean currents, which explains why so many unusual shells have been found on the local beaches. Some shells have been carried all the way down the western coast of Africa. The collection was put together over a 30-year period and left to the town by Charlotte Kritzinger.

Aston Bay, Paradise Beach and the Kabeljous River Estuary are only a short drive away and make a pleasant change from the main beach in Jeffrey's Bay.

St Francis Bay and Cape St Francis 🏖🏄 ▸▸ *pp373-376. Colour map 7, B4.*

The adjoining villages of St Francis Bay and Cape St Francis are 20 km from Humansdorp, just off the R330. Less than 40 years ago there was nothing here except fine, white-sand beaches and a mule track which ran from Humansdorp to the lighthouse at Cape St Francis. These days a prosperous collection of whitewashed, thatched holiday homes line the beach just south of the Krom River Mouth, alongside an 18-hole golf course and a shopping centre.

A modern marina development, **The Canals**, is constructed around the largest man-made web of canals in the country. The only privately owned harbour in South Africa, it is full of smart yachts and *chokka* (calamari) fishing boats. A highlight of any visit is eating fresh calamari on the quayside. The nearby dam, the Churchill, supplies Nelson Mandela Bay (Port Elizabeth) with much of its water.

The **Cape St Francis lighthouse** was built in 1878 and, at a height of 27.75 m, is the tallest stonework tower on the South African coast. You can go on a tour of the lighthouse, where there is also a small **coffee shop** ① *T042-2980428, daily 0900-1630, which also opens for dinner Wed-Sat*. Also based at the lighthouse is an **African penguin rehabilitation centre** ① *www.penguin-rescue.org.za, donations welcome*, run by Ajubatus Marine and Wildlife Rescue, which treats and re-releases sick and injured penguins and cleans up those damaged by oil slicks. They have a small centre with a penguin pool and visitors can look through the large windows. All marine birds are extremely vulnerable to oil pollution, but penguins even more so than flying birds. Once oiled, their insulation becomes severely compromised and they cannot enter the sea to hunt, and as a result slowly starve to death or die of exposure/hypothermia.

The bay, with its 16-km beach, is famous for its waves and attracts surfers from all over the world. In 1963 the surfing movie *Endless Summer* was filmed here, as well as the remake *Endless Summer II* in 1992. For information, contact **St Francis Bay Tourism** ⓘ *corner of Lime Rd South and St Francis Dr, T042-2940076, www.stfrancistourism.co.za.*

🌙 *St Francis Bay was named after the patron saint of sailors by the Portuguese explorer Manuel Perestrelo in 1575.*

Maitland Nature Reserve

Facing St Francis Bay, the reserve is a small strip of coastal forest near the estuary of the Maitland River. This was the site of a number of lead mines in the 19th century but as these were abandoned so was the whole area, giving the forest a chance to recover. The reserve is now renowned for its birdlife and is an excellent place for seeing paradise flycatchers and Knysna louries. One of the best months to visit is October, when many of the forest plants are either flowering or in fruit.

The 3-km **Sir Peregrine Maitland Trail** is a leisurely walk through forest along an old wagon trail; the 9-km **De Stades Trail** covers the length and breadth of the reserve, passing through small areas of dune forest and open grassland.

⊚ West of Nelson Mandela Bay listings

⊜ Sleeping

Jeffrey's Bay *p371, map p371*
As the best-known surfing spot in South Africa, Jeffrey's Bay attracts large numbers of surfers from all over the world. Consequently, there is a good range of budget accommodation here. Each backpacker place has its own scene and you're bound to come across people who are staying there for the whole season.
AL Diaz 15 House on the Beach,
15 Diaz Rd, T042-2931779, www.diaz 15.co.za. 8 luxury self-catering apartments with 2 or 3 bedrooms, fully equipped kitchens with microwave, large lounge with open balcony overlooking the beach, 2 bathrooms, TV with M-Net, breakfasts available, rim-flow pool, perfect for families looking for a high standard of comfort } right on the beach, walking distance to the shops and restaurants. Very popular,

so you'll need to book several months in advance.
A Stratos, 11 Uys St, T082-5651732, www.stratos-za.com. A modern brick house on the seafront set in a quiet residential district. 7 luxury double rooms with en suite shower/bath and TV, 4 have sea views, non-smoking room, solar-heated swimming pool. Swiss owners, Italian, French and German spoken.
B Supertubes, 6, 10-12 Pepper St, T042-2932957, www.supertubesguesthouse.co.za. Laid-back B&B set 30 m from the beach and supertubes wave, 14 en suite double rooms with balcony, or more luxurious suites with extras like a/c and heated towel rail, set across 4 houses. Meals are available on request or there's a kitchen and dining area for guests' use, as well as hanging space for wetsuits and boards for surfers.
C The Guesthouse, 17 Flame Cres, Wave-crest, T042-2931878, theguesthouse@ eastcape.net. Variety of accommodation available: a self-contained thatched cottage which can sleep up to 4, with a fully equipped kitchen and TV; a honeymoon suite with an oval bath and champagne on arrival in your room; plus 3 other double rooms with bathrooms. Set in a secure walled garden, close to the beach and a shopping centre.

The owner offers excellent advice, information and hospitality. Recommended.

D Beach Cabanas,118 Da Gama Rd, T042-2932820, www.beachcabanas.co.za. Located 150 m from the beach, small attractive swimming pool surrounded by palms, 16 smart modern flats on 2 storeys with kitchenette, heater, fan and TV, good breakfasts, motel-style parking. One reader reports excellent service and friendly and helpful owners.

D-E Jeffrey's Bay Backpackers, 12 Jeffrey St, T042-2931379, www.jeffreysbayback packers.co.za. This was the first backpacker place to open in Jeffrey's Bay. It is well run and popular, and is in a good location in the centre of town, close to Main Beach, small dorms, 5 double rooms, camping in garden, off-street parking, reductions can be negotiated for long stays, well-stocked and clean kitchen, bedding provided, hires out surfboards and bikes. Baz Bus stop and pickups can be arranged from Humansdorp.

D-F Island Vibe, 10 Dageraad St, T042-2931625, www.islandvibe.co.za. This hostel has an excellent location at the top end of Jeffrey's Bay, perched high up with views across 2 beaches and steps down to the beach. Dorms, doubles and camping, kitchen, bar, café serving set evening meals and good breakfasts. The place has a big surfer scene, so don't expect to get much sleep. Music from the bar pumps out through the night. Very popular and perfect for a couple of day's partying. The new and quieter **Beach House** has en suite doubles and open-plan kitchen and lounge with great sea views. Rents out bikes, canoes, fishing rods and, of course surfboards. A new activity is a walking tour to the local township. Also has a good travel centre and internet access, and is the location of **Jeffrey's Bay Surf School** (see Activities and tours, below). If you stay here you get 10% off in the Billabong factory shop. Offers a free pickup from buses in Humansdorp and is a Baz Bus stop. All in all, recommended to get a genuine feel of what J-Bay is all about.

St Francis Bay and Cape St Francis *p372*
AL The Beach House, 4 Frank Rd, T042-2941225, www.stfrancisbay.co.za/ thebeachhouse. Beautiful guesthouse set right on the beach. 4 luxurious and stylish rooms under thatch, 2 with ocean views, 2 overlooking the pool, excellent breakfasts, also evening meals by prior arrangement, attentive unfussy service. Recommended.

AL The Sands @ St Francis, 8 Frank Rd, T/F042-2941888, www.thesands.co.za. Smart, comfortable guesthouse just a few mins from the beach. Attractive thatched house with 5 en suite a/c rooms, bathrooms have jacuzzi bath tubs and separate showers, each with its own timber deck overlooking the beach, some with private outside shower and jacuzzi. Swimming pool, sun deck, steam room, beauty therapies on request, breakfast and gourmet dinners served in a very unusual octagonal restaurant with thatched roof and glass walls with a 360° view. Recommended, but pricey.

AL-A Cape St Francis Resort, Da Gama Rd, Cape St Francis, T042-2980054, www.capestfrancis.co.za. Good-value holiday village with a range of accommodation, 3 luxury villas perched on the dunes sleeping up to 12, superior thatched cottages with 3 bedrooms, kitchen and lounge, and en suite apartments with 1 bedroom and kitchen around the swimming pool, **Park Off Pub** and **Joe Fish Restaurant**. The on-site adventure centre can organize a number of activities from boat rides to deep-sea fishing.

B-C Thatchwood, 63 Lyme Rd, T042-2940082, www.stfrancisbay-accommodation.co.za. Smart and comfortable thatched guesthouse overlooking the local golf course with private access across the fairways to the beach. 7 double rooms with en suite bathroom and TV, meals served on the lawn or from an open dining room, bar.

C Port View Place, Leighton Hullet Dr, Port St Francis, T042-2941553, www.portviewplace.co.za. Towards the back of the marina development, small B&B with 4 tastefully decorated en suite rooms, a

2-bedroom apartment, spacious lounge, breakfast on balcony with harbour views.

D St Francis Bay Lodge, St Francis Bay, T0846-701131. Situated behind the Police Station, this lovely B&B is 10 mins' walk from the sea. Several clean, airy and spacious 2- and 3-bedroom apartments. The couple that run the lodge are very friendly and make the stay very enjoyable. An honesty bar is open in the evenings around a log fire. Try the delicious home-made biltong.

D Seal Point Backpackers, Da Gama Rd, Cape St Francis, T0, www.seals.co.za. Great-value upmarket backpacker lodge (no dorms) 400 m from the beach, with well-kept self-catering apartments, each with TV, en suite bathrooms and open-plan kitchen, plus balconies with sea views. Good restaurant and bar downstairs serving cheap meals, braai area, pool, popular with surfers. Organize booze cruises on the canal. Will pick up from the Baz Bus at Humansdorp by prior arrangement.

● Eating

Jeffrey's Bay p371, map p371

⟨ De Viswijf, 55 Diaz Rd, T042-2933921. 1100-1500, 1700-late, closed Sun evenings. Enclosed deck overlooking the surf and fishing boats, wide selection of seafood and steaks, and specials such as *potjies*, unusual dishes such as curried tripe and occasional game meat.

⟨ Die Walskipper, Marina Martinique Harbour, out of town towards St Francis Bay, T042-2920005. Tue-Sat 1200-2100, Sun 1200-1600. As befits a popular surfing venue, this open-air restaurant with a corrugated-iron roof and shade cloth attracts a fun crowd on the beach. During the winter months the owners bring coal stoves to the beach. The menu consists of good local dishes with fresh ingredients and home-made breads. Steaming seafood platters with plenty of 'white gold' (calamari) is the go, served up on enamel plates, and

drinks are distributed in tin mugs. Recommended.

⟨ Kitchen Windows, 23 Diaz St, T042-2934230. Tue-Sun 1130-1400, 1800-late. Informal spot with chunky wooden furnishings and terracotta floors, ocean views from the deck, good seafood including kingklip with oysters and shrimps baked in the pizza oven, steaks and sauces, pasta, long menu.

⟨ Le Grotto, Jeffrey's St, T042-2932612. Open 1100-late. Popular corner restaurant serving fresh seafood, steaks and burgers, good catch of the day, famous for its 1-kg steaks.

⟨ Sunflower Café, 20 Da Gama Rd, T042-2931602. Daily 0800-2300. Café and restaurant serving great range of light meals, including plenty for vegetarians. Delicious milkshakes and home-made cakes, good evening meals such as grilled calamari or pasta. Internet access and local artwork on permanent display. Recommended.

St Francis Bay and Cape St Francis p372

There are several coffee shops and restaurants in the **Village Shopping Centre** on St Francis Dr in the middle of St Francis Bay.

⟨ Big Time Taverna, 10 Mayotte Circle, T042 2941309. Tue-Sun 1200-1500, 1830-late. Overlooking the Kromme River and canals, this restaurant is aimed at wealthy Johannesburg holiday-makers, traditional Greek blue and white decor, excellent service and renowned for its seafood.

⟨ Joe Fish, pub and restaurant at the **Cape St Francis Resort** (see Sleeping, page 374), T042-2980054. Open 1130-late. Excellent seafood, especially the calamari steaks, or try the spare ribs, alfresco terrace around the swimming pool or cosy pub with fireplace.

⟨ Trattoria San Francesco, Village Centre, St Francis Dr, T042-2940819. Tue-Sun 1200-1430, 1800-2200. Affordable trattoria-style Italian on the 2nd floor of the shopping centre, good range of pasta and rich sauces, and crisp wood-fired pizzas.

▲ Activities and tours

Jeffrey's Bay *p371, map p371*
Horse riding
Papiesfontein Beach Rides, on the farm of the same name 10 km to the east of Jeffery's Bay off the R102, T082-5749396 (mob), beachrides@mweb.co.za. Suitable for novices and instruction is given, rides depart daily at 0900 and 1500, R150, booking advised. A 13-km circular trail goes to the Gamtoos River and then leads over the picturesque dunes at the Gamtoos River mouth to the beach. From here, there's 6 km of coastline for galloping or splashing through the waves. There's also a 5-bedroomed self-catering house on the farm that sleeps 12 (**C**).

Sandboarding
JayBay Sandboarding, T042-2962974, or book through the tourist office. There are some big dunes around Jeffrey's Bay – perfect for sandboarding. Trips run daily and include boards and tuition.

Surfing
Jeffrey's Bay Surf School, based at **Island Vibe Backpackers**, T042-2931625, www.islandvibe.co.za. Beginner lessons run daily year-round and include wetsuits, beginners' boards and tuition, advanced lessons using video sessions to see what you did right or wrong, ask about the 7-day learn to surf packages which include accommodation and meals.

◎ Transport

Jeffrey's Bay *p371, map p371*
It's 78 km to **Nelson Mandela Bay** (**Port Elizabeth**), 20 km to **Cape St Francis**, 20 km to **Humansdorp** (N2), 206 km to **Knysna**, 1062 km to **Durban**.

Bus
Baz Bus, T021-4392323, www.bazbus.com. Backpackers' budget service that calls in at hostels to collect/drop off. They should have room to carry your surfing equipment but let them know in advance. Coming from Cape Town, Jeffrey's Bay is the last drop-off, arriving 2030-2100, before the bus crew spend the night in Nelson Mandela Bay (Port Elizabeth). If you want to travel further east than Nelson Mandela Bay (Port Elizabeth), you'll have to depart from there the next morning. Travelling from Jeffrey's Bay to **Cape Town** the **Baz Bus** picks up 0830-0900 and arrives in Cape Town later that night.

   Greyhound and **Translux** pick up and drop off at **Humansdorp**, 20 km from Jeffrey's Bay on the N2 on the service between **Cape Town** and **Durban**. From here, you have to hitch or take a local taxi. **J-Bay Cabs**, T083-6111003. It may be possible to arrange for your accommodation to collect you for a small charge but remember some of the departure and arrival times are either late at night or in the early hours of the morning.

Nelson Mandela Bay to East London

There are two routes to East London from Nelson Mandela Bay (Port Elizabeth). The quickest is on the N2 via Grahamstown. An alternative route is to take the R72 coastal road, but there are three very compelling reasons for following the N2: to explore the wonderful Addo Elephant National Park; to visit the string of new private game reserves, including the superb Shamwari Game Reserve; and to see the old colonial town of Grahamstown.» *For listings, see pages 388-395.*

Addo Elephant National Park ⊜▲» *pp388-395. Colour map 7, B4.*

The original elephant sector of the Addo Elephant National Park, proclaimed in 1931, covered 12,000 ha, when only 11 elephants remained in the area. Since 2000, the park has been undergoing a process of expansion. New land purchase has been made possible by funds from the government and overseas donors. This process, as well as the rehabilitation and fencing of the new land, is still underway. When the expansion is finished, the park will cover 292,000 ha and it will be the third largest conservation area in South Africa. The park now encompasses five neighbouring game reserves and wilderness areas and stretches from the Indian Ocean to the Little Karoo and incorporates five different habitat biospheres.

At the coast is a belt of coastal dunefields and forest. The 200-m Alexandria Dunefield, the largest active dunefields in the world after the Namib Desert, now falls within the park and the 120,000-ha marine reserve adjoining Addo includes many islands that are home to the largest population of African gannets and the second largest population of penguins. With the reintroduction of lion in 2003, it is now possible to see the Big Seven – elephant, rhino, lion, buffalo, leopard, whale and great white shark – in a malaria-free environment. This expansion of the park is one of the most exciting and ambitious conservation projects ever undertaken, and Addo, now home to the densest population of elephant on earth, has become a highlight of the Eastern Cape.

Today this finely tuned ecosystem is sanctuary to a breeding herd of over 420 elephants, 450 Cape buffalo, 40 black rhino, hippo, cheetah, leopard, lion, a variety of antelope species, as well as the flightless dung beetle – unique to the park and found wherever there's elephant dung. Over 185 species of bird have been recorded here. The relative flatness of the bush and the large number of elephant mean that they are easily seen. To add to this, there are a couple of waterholes which can be accessed by car. Visitors will often see several herds drinking at one time – this can mean watching over 100 elephant – a magnificent experience. Although you'll see them at any time of year, one of the best times to visit is in January and February, when many of the females will have recently calved.

Ins and outs

Getting there Most visitors head for the area where the elephants are found which is south of the main camp at the main park entrance, 72 km from Nelson Mandela Bay (Port Elizabeth). It can be reached by taking the R335, which is well signposted off the N2 from Nelson Mandela Bay (Port Elizabeth) to Grahamstown. A new access road into the park has been constructed that feeds off the N2 highway near Colchester, and goes through the new Matyholweni Gate and Camp in the new southern block of the park before joining up with the existing network of tourist roads in the park. To get there from Nelson

Mandela Bay, take the N2 highway towards Grahamstown, and after 40 km where the road crosses the Sundays River Bridge, turn left at the 'Camp Matyholweni' sign. Follow this road for about 3 km until you enter Matyholweni Gate at Camp Matyholweni. Follow the southern access road inside the park for 36 km to Addo's main camp. Coming from the Grahamstown direction, either take this new southern route, or from the N2 turn on to the N10 towards Cradock/Cookhouse, 80 km east of Grahamstown. Then, after 22 km, take the R342 to the left when you get to the intersection with Paterson on your right, which leads into the park and continues on to the main camp. Within the park there is a network of good gravel roads if you are in your own car or you can book day and night drives, game walks, and horse rides through reception. Booking ahead is essential. The coastal section and Alexandria Dunefield is south of the N2, and there are access points to the beach off the R72. The northern section is best visited from the **Darlington Lake Lodge**, see page 389.

Addo & around

Sleeping
Africanos Inn **2**
Darlington Lake
 Lodge **3**
Elephant House **4**
Elephants Footprint
 Lodge **5**
Gorah Elephant
 Camp **6**
Intsomi Forest
 Lodge **7**
Main Camp **1**
Matyholweni
 Camp **8**
Narina Bush Camp **9**
Protea Addo **10**

N

10 km
10 miles

Best time to visit The weather here is usually warm and dry and visits to the park are enjoyable all year round.

Park information T042-2330556, www.sanparks.org, R80, R40 children. Entrance gates open daily 0700-1900; the wildlife viewing area is open 0600-1800 in summer and 0700-1730 in winter, though times vary according to season so check with reception; office 0700-2000; restaurant 0800-2100, serves light snacks and meals; shop 0800-1900, sells a selection of groceries, meat, bread and wines; petrol (no diesel) 0730-1700; laundry, telephone and postal services are also available. There is a swimming pool and tennis court at the main camp and a hide at a game-viewing waterhole that is floodlit at night. The park's other hide tends to be busier as it is near the restaurant, but it overlooks a small dam and is good for birdwatching. **Note** In the elephant-watching area it is illegal to leave your vehicle anywhere other than at signposted climb-out points.

Alexandria Trail

ⓘ *Permits for the Alexandria Trail are available through SANParks, www.sanparks.org. Alternatively, contact the main reception office at Matyholweni Rest Camp, T042-2338621. Maximum 12 people; it's a popular trail over weekends. Take precautions against ticks.*

On the coast to the south of Alexandria between the Bushman's River and the Sundays River mouths is the part of the park that is dunes and coastal forest. There are many easy trails passing along the beach and into the forest. The longest hike, for which permits are necessary, is the Alexandria Trail. It is 36 km long and is a marked two-day circular track – be warned that the markers can be blown over in strong wind and get buried in the sand. The trail starts at the Woody Cape offices of the park, near the town of Alexandria. Turn right out of the park entrance towards Paterson. At the Paterson intersection, turn right towards Nelson Mandela Bay (Port Elizabeth). Once you reach the N2, take the R72 to Port Alfred. Just before entering the town of Alexandria, take the gravel road to the right, marked with the park signboard, to the office, T046-6530601.

There is no large game here but this is the habitat of the hairy-footed gerbil which is endemic to this area. The forests are good for birdwatching and along the coast it is possible to see dolphins and the Damara tern. The first day takes you from the base camp at Langebos through forest down to the coastal dunefield which extends for 120 km up the coast. The hiking can be tough along the windy dunes but worth it for the fine isolated beaches. One night is spent in the hut at Woody Cape. In the morning the trail then heads back across farmland in the Langevlakte Valley and back to Langebos.

◗ *The Alexandria dunes are the tallest sand dunes south of the Namib Desert and in some places reach heights of 150 m.*

East of Addo ● ➥ *pp388-395.*

Schotia Safaris
① *T042-2351436, www.schotia.com.*
To the east of Addo, 55 km from Nelson Mandela Bay (Port Elizabeth), and just north of the junction of the N2 and N10, is **Schotia Safaris**. This is a private game reserve on the edge of Addo with 15 types of antelope, several smaller species such as warthog, monkeys and genets, and lion, hippo, giraffe and rhino. Schotia is also known for its huge open-air dining *lapa* – reputedly the largest in South Africa – built of reed and thatch, which is supported by several large Schotia trees. The lodge here has three double units (see Sleeping, page 389) and if you are staying overnight all game activities are included; day and night game drives into Addo are also available. It is also possible to visit as a day visitor between 1500-2200 and the package includes afternoon and evening game drives and a buffet dinner and drinks for R600. Alternatively, you could combine the above day visit with a morning safari to Addo and pickups can be arranged from Nelson Mandela Bay (Port Elizabeth) if you don't have a car. Check out the website for options.

Shamwari Game Reserve → *Colour map 7, B5.*
① *From Nelson Mandela Bay (Port Elizabeth), follow the N2 towards Grahamstown. After 65 km take a left turn, signposted Shamwari. This gravel road is the R342; after 7 km take a right turn. It is then a further 2 km to the entrance. From Grahamstown, the R342 turning is about 58 km along the N2, T042-2031111, www.shamwari.com.*
This is a privately owned 20,000-ha reserve which in many aspects resembles the reserves of Mpumalanga along the boundary of Kruger National Park. In 1990 Adrian Gardiner, a successful businessman from Port Elizabeth, bought the property and read up on historical accounts of the Eastern Cape, which described the region as one of the richest wildlife zones in Africa. Reports dating back to the 18th century indicate a time when vast herds of Cape buffalo and zebra, wildebeest, black rhino, leopard and lion freely roamed the hills and valleys. However, by 1853 early settlers had wiped out most of the game and cleared vast areas of forest for farmland. When Gardiner bought the property all that remained was a dry, eroded dust bowl, but in the last decade natural grasses and bush flora have been planted and many species of game reintroduced. Once decimated by overgrazing and drought, the landscape has been transformed into big game country. Today the park has been well stocked with game from all over the region including black rhino, elephant, buffalo, leopard, lion and antelope of all sizes. Wild dog, last seen in the area over 200 years ago, have also been reintroduced. Day visitors are not permitted, but there are six super-luxurious lodges within the reserve and overnight packages include all meals and game activities (see Sleeping, page 390).

Amakhala Game Reserve

ⓘ *Off the N2 approximately opposite the turning for Shamwari Game Reserve (see above); the road is well signposted, T046-6362750, www.amakhala.co.za.*

This is another of the Eastern Cape's successful new game reserves. The 6000-ha reserve was created in 1999 as a joint conservation venture between neighbouring farms and today has six independently owned lodges. All are owner-managed by the descendants of the original families who arrived here as British settlers from 1820. The lodges offer various styles of accommodation: there are two colonial homesteads, two classic bush lodges, a historic inn and a settler farmhouse (see Sleeping, page 390, for details). The reserve has been stocked with rhino, elephant, cheetah, buffalo, giraffe, black wildebeest, zebra and over 16 antelope species. These can be seen on day and night drives and on game walks arranged from the lodges for overnight guests. There is also the opportunity to go on a cruise or canoe trip on the Bushman's River. Day visitors are welcome and safaris commence in the early afternoon with a two-hour game drive followed by a sunset cruise on the Bushman's River with cheese and wine; a four-course dinner is served in a bush *lapa*, and the excursion ends with a short night game drive, all for just under R720 per person. The day visit is not recommended for children under 12 due to the long programme.

⬤ *Amakhala means aloe in Xhosa, named after the vibrant orange flower that is common in the area.*

Lalibela Game Reserve

ⓘ *22 km from Shamwari and 24 km east of Grahamstown off the N2, T041-5818170, www.lalibela.co.za.*

This is a another private game reserve covering 7500 ha and spanning four ecosystems that are home to the Big Five as well as cheetah, hyena, hippo, giraffe, zebra, warthog and numerous species of antelope. Wild dog were released here in 2006. Day visitors are not permitted but there are three luxury lodges (see Sleeping, page 391).

Grahamstown ⬤⬤⬤▲⬤⬤ ➤➤ pp388-395 Colour map 7, B5.

Grahamstown is first and foremost a student town. At the top end of the high street is one of the country's major centres of learning, **Rhodes University**, which has 70 major buildings on a 195-ha campus with approximately 3200 students and 1800 staff. The presence of the university has a significant impact on this small town and during term time the pubs and bars are packed with students. It is a pleasant enough place to wander around and there are a number of interesting little shops along the high street.

Despite the English feel to the town centre the other side of the valley is dominated by a poor, dusty and badly serviced township where the majority of the African residents live. The proximity of the two sides of town makes the contrast more apparent than in some of the bigger towns and cities where the townships are some distance from the centre.

Ins and outs

Getting there The town has fairly good transport links and is served by some mainline buses on the route between Nelson Mandela Bay (Port Elizabeth) and Durban. The **Baz Bus** does not stop here, though, as it deviates off the N2 after Nelson Mandela Bay (Port Elizabeth) and goes via Port Alfred on the coast. ➤➤ *For further details, see Transport, page 395.*

Tourist information **Grahamstown Tourism** ① *63 High St, T046-6223241, www.grahams town.co.za, Mon-Fri 0830-1700, Sat 0900-1300*, is a well-organized centre with accommodation-booking facilities for the entire region. The staff can arrange and book a variety of local tours. There is also a **Translux** desk. A worthwhile local scheme is 'Step-On Guides' under which locally registered guides join you in your own vehicle and show you around the various sights.

Background

Grahamstown was established around a fort which had been built here after the Fourth Frontier War. It was founded in 1812 and named after Colonel Graham. Within two years it was a busy border settlement. The 1820 settlers began to arrive after the end of the Fifth Frontier War, during which Grahamstown had been besieged by Xhosa warriors. Despite the continual threat of armed conflict and problems of security, the town had evolved into the second largest settlement in the whole of southern Africa by 1836.

Grahamstown

Sleeping ⬛	Makana Municipal	Eating ❼
137 High Street **1**	Caravan Park **5**	Café Dulce **1**
Aucklands Country House **9**	Oak Lodge **6**	Calabash **3**
Cock House **2**	Old Gaol Backpackers **7**	Ginos **2**
Evelyn House **3**	Protea Grahamstown **4**	Henry Ate **2**
Hermitage **8**		Rat & Parrot **5**
		Redwood Spur **6**

One factor behind the town's rapid growth was that the majority of the 1820 settlers were ill-prepared to be farmers, let alone in an environment of which they had no knowledge. As soon as they realized farming was not going to bring them wealth and security they gave it up and returned to the town to take up the jobs they were trained to do. Grahamstown quickly established a thriving industry based around blacksmiths, carpenters, millers and gunsmiths. Having settled back in the town, the skilled settlers quickly built a series of elegant stone buildings which remain grand specimens of the era's architecture today. Of particular note are the buildings around Church Square, but elsewhere there are churches and fine private homes. The culmination of all this is a smart town centre with a distinctly English atmosphere.

Sights

When you look at a map or walk about the town centre you quickly come across a variety of different museums: the Observatory Museum, Natural Science Museum and the History Museum, along with Fort Selwyn and the Provost. These displays are all part of one museum, the **Albany Museum** ① *1046-6222312, Tue-Fri 0900-1300, 1400-1700, Sat 1000-1400, Observatory Museum also open Mon; entry to each is about R5-8*, which celebrated its 150-year anniversary in 2005. The collection has grown as the town developed and presents a fairly complete picture of its history.

The **Observatory Museum** ① *on the right hand side of Bathurst St, as you look up towards the City Hall*, is a unusual building. It contains a collection of Victorian furniture, household goods and silver, but the highlight is the entertaining camera obscura (a rare specimen, claimed to be the only Victorian camera obscura in the southern hemisphere), which projects an image of Grahamstown onto a screen. Visitors are led up a tiny spiral staircase to a small room on the roof, where an enthusiastic guide pivots the camera to show a 360° view, pointing out major sights. There is also an observatory and a meridian room, from which astronomical time can be calculated. The clock is a miniature of one that was made in 1883 for the Royal Courts of Justice in London. The painting on the pendulum of *Father Time* is by the well-known Frontier Artist, Frederick Timpson I'Ons. The building, which itself is loosely connected with the drawn-out identification of the *Eureka* diamond back in 1869 (see page 743), has a magnificent presence. There are three floors of balconies, each with ornately carved arches and railings, enough to give a hint of how it would have looked in its heyday.

At the **Natural Science Museum** ① *Somerset St*, most of the displays are aimed at children. Some of the more interesting exhibits include a large iron meteorite which came down in a shower in Namibia, a Foucault pendulum and some dinosaur fossils. There are regular temporary exhibitions, and this is one of the main venues for the Scifest, a science and technology festival held in March. There is a café in a courtyard at the back.

The **History Museum** ① *Somerset St, opposite the Natural Science Museum*, houses an interesting collection outlining the area's history, including beadwork displays from the Eastern Cape, traditional Xhosa dress, 1820 settler history and some art galleries, with regularly changing contemporary exhibitions.

The **Provost** ① *off Somerset St, at the western end of town in the botanical gardens*, is a quadrangle building with a double-storeyed tower at its apex. It was built in 1837 by the Royal Engineers to act as a military prison; their actual instructions were to build a "fortified barrack establishment". A lot of thought went into the overall design of the complex as the architects of the time sought to come up with a design where, from the central tower, it would be possible to view as many prisoners as possible with minimal manpower. In January 1838 the first 20 convicts were brought here. They were mutineers, and after they had shot one of their officers, Ensign Crowe, they were executed on the parade grounds. The building was proclaimed a national monument in 1937.

Fort Selwyn ① *Fort Selwyn Dr, open by prior appointment only*, is at the western end of town close to the Settlers Monument. During the sixth Frontier War in 1834 parliament decided that it would be necessary to protect the barracks. The Royal Engineers who built the fort were commanded by Major Charles Jasper Selwyn. Between 1841 and 1868 the fort was used as an artillery barracks and a semaphore link – a mast was erected in the northeast corner – but then the army gave up using the building in 1870. During the Anglo-Boer War the fort served in the defence of Grahamstown, but by the 1920s it had once more been left to become run down and overgrown. It was not until the 1970s, when it was proclaimed a national monument, that the building finally got the restoration work it deserved. Although it stands on the property of the Department of Nature and Environmental Conservation, it was given to the Albany Museum to use as exhibition space to further promote the history of Grahamstown.

The **1820 Settlers Monument** is, oddly, a large modern office block with rather a totalitarian feel to it. There is a series of rooms which includes a conference hall, theatre and a restaurant. It overlooks the city and completely dominates its surrounds on Gunfire Hill. It was opened in July 1974, but in 1994 disaster struck and fire gutted the whole complex. The memorial is surrounded by the **Makana Botanical Gardens** ① *daily 0800-1630*, which were laid out in 1853 with displays of indigenous plants. The botanical garden has a recreation of a nostalgic old English garden, but more interestingly there is a huge collection of aloes, cycads, proteas and tree ferns. Assuming you're not afraid of ghosts, try to catch a glimpse of Lady Juana Smith, the Spanish wife of Sir Harry Smith who reputedly haunts the gardens.

Part of the university, the **International Library of African Music (ILAM)** ① *Prince Alfred St, T046-6038557, www.ilam.ru.ac.za, by appointment only, Mon-Fri 0830-1245, 1400-1700*, is a research centre for traditional African music, and houses a fascinating collection, with over 200 traditional African instruments from across the continent. To get there, follow signs from the gate opposite Rhodes University Theatre.

The **Cathedral of St Michael and St George** occupies its rightful position in the centre of town on Church Square. The style of this building is early English Gothic, a 13th-century style which the Victorians chose to revive in the late 19th century. Like similar buildings in Europe, the cathedral took generations to complete. Work started in 1824 and the first usable form was opened in 1830 as a single-room church. In 1952 the Lady Chapel was completed and so the cathedral had taken 128 years to build. Look out for the memorial tablets which together provide a vivid history of Grahamstown as the frontier of the empire.

The **Priest's House**, on Beaufort Street, was built as a residence for the bishop and the clergy of the Catholic church. It is one of the finer buildings in Grahamstown and like the Observatory Museum has a connection with the identification of the *Eureka* diamond (see page 743). Because of this connection, the De Beers Group rescued the house in 1981, helped to partially restore the building and then oversaw the establishment of the **National English Literary Museum** ① *T046-6227042, Mon-Fri 0900-1230, 1430-1630*. These days the research carried out behind the scenes is proving to be an important component in the understanding of the role of English as a national language of South Africa. There is a comprehensive collection of scholarly books, articles and press-clippings as well as a good bookshop. A small display gallery presents temporary exhibitions focusing on a particular writer, literary period or theme. The house is also of interest. The façade is typical of the Cape during the 1800s – flat, with a colonnaded neo-Georgian portico.

The **Shaw Hall** is behind the Observatory Museum, but still in the High Street. It was inaugurated in 1832 as a Methodist Church, with three galleries and room for over 800 members. Once the Commemoration Church had been completed in 1850, the first building was turned over for use as a meeting hall. The Reverend William Shaw was a local missionary worker. The most important role the building played was on 25 April 1864 when the Governor of the Cape Colony, Sir Philip Wodehouse, convened a session of parliament in the hall. This was part of a programme of tacit support for a movement that was trying to break away from the western part of the province and set up an independent government. Although nothing ever came of the idea, it was a clear indication of how serious the government took the threats of secession, since this was the only time that the Cape parliament ever sat outside of Cape Town.

Thomas Baines Nature Reserve

ⓘ *12 km from town off the N2 towards Nelson Mandela Bay (Port Elizabeth), T046-6227216.*
The Thomas Baines Nature Reserve offers canoeing, fishing, sailing and windsurfing at Settlers Dam. The reserve is named after the famous 19th-century artist who left a valuable record of the rich diversity of fauna and flora in the region, including the now-extinct quagga. There are 15 km of dirt tracks which pass through fynbos and bushveld inhabited by bontebok, black wildebeest, an impressive herd of 45 buffalo, eland, impala and one white rhino called Tom. There's a short drive around the reserve and picnic sites with braai facilities and toilets are provided at Settlers Dam.

Port Alfred to King William's Town ⊙❻▲⊝❻ ≫ *pp388 395. Colour map 7, B5-B6.*

Port Alfred

Port Alfred can be reached along the R72 coast road from Nelson Mandela Bay (Port Elizabeth) or on the R67 from Grahamstown. It consists almost entirely of holiday homes and bungalows nestling into dunes. It is one of the largest holiday resorts on this stretch of coastline and overlooks large expanses of water in all directions: the Kowie River, the lagoon and the smart Royal Alfred Marina, where many local people keep their powerboats. The town's history is closely linked to the 1820 settlers and there is a small **Methodist Church** 1 km out of town whose cemetery makes for an interesting visit. Many of the names on the gravestones are those of original settlers.

The weather on this coast is mild all year round and Port Alfred has a wide range of facilities to offer tourists. Walks through the dune forests are always pleasant but for the more intrepid, there is a scuba-diving school which organizes trips to nearby reefs, as well as facilities for canoeing and game fishing. The **Fish River Casino** and **St Francis Spa** are both nearby and are popular excursions from town. For information contact **Port Alfred Tourism Information Centre** ⓘ *Causeway St, T046-6241235, www.portalfred.co.za, Mon-Fri 0800-1630, Sat 0830-1200.* This is a very helpful and brightly painted office which also offers internet access and sells crafts. Port Alfred gets fairly busy at the weekends during term time when students from Grahamstown University come to the coast to play.

Occasionally there are trips on the *Kowie Chu Chu* from Post Alfred Station 16 km inland to Bathurst. The short, three-carriage, brightly coloured mini-train stops in Bathurst long enough for lunch at the local **Pig and Whistle** pub before returning to Port Alfred. The excursion includes lunch and costs R140, children R70. Enquire at the tour office or phone the station, T046-6249090.

Huberta the hippo

Huberta the hippo is one of the most famous wild animals in South African history. She was born in the Mhlatuze Lagoon near the modern-day port of Richard's Bay in Zululand, and in 1928 inexplicably decided to head off on an 800-km trek down the coast. This incredible journey took three years and her story was followed by newspapers around the world. She walked through the middle of Durban, looking into shop windows while pedestrians dived for cover, and astounded holidaymakers when she walked on to Durban's beach and swam in the sea. She continued south down what is today the Wild Coast and arrived in Port St Johns in March 1930. She

seemed to like it – she stayed for six months and lived in the river. Despite its name (Mzimvubu, meaning 'home of the hippo') none of her ilk had been seen in the river for years. It was a lively six months for the residents of the town as Huberta wandered through gardens, grazed on lawns, upset a few boats, and things only calmed down after her departure in September. There was national mourning at the end of the year when news flashed around the world that a pair of trigger-happy farmers had shot Huberta in a river in the Eastern Cape. Her remains can be seen at the Amathole Museum in King William's Town. There has never been another hippo in the Mzimvubu River.

Also just outside Bathurst is the **World's Biggest Pineapple** ① *off the R67, 15 km north of Port Alfred, T046-6250515, 0900-1700*. This is a copy of the giant pineapple on Australia's Sunshine Coast in Queensland but at 16.7 m high it's 70 cm taller than the original. It comes as quite a surprise to discover a giant yellow pineapple, topped with a bright green stalk standing in the middle of a field. Made of fibreglass, on the three floors inside you'll learn everything imaginable about pineapples. On the ground floor is a gift shop selling among other pineapple-related items, home-made jams and chutneys, on the second floor is information about growing, canning and selling pineapples, while on the third floor a continuous DVD explains about the Eastern Cape pineapple industry. If nothing else, it's worth climbing to for unbeatable views of the rolling fields and the Indian Ocean.

Kowie Nature Reserve

① *Permits for the Kowie Canoe Trail and overnight hut are available from the tourist office. Only 12 people are allowed on the trail at any one time. The trail is very popular and can get fully booked up to 6 months in advance, especially over weekends. However, it is always worth checking to see if there have been any last minute cancellations or no shows. R25 per person, including the hire of a 2-person canoe.*

This reserve lies along the banks of the Kowie River, about 5 km from Port Alfred on the Bathurst road. It passes through a thickly forested canyon and offers walking trails and a well-run canoe trail, which has turned this into one of the most popular nature reserves in the region.

The **Kowie Canoe Trail** is about 24 km in total and takes two days to complete. The first day is spent paddling 22 km up the Kowie River from Port Alfred to the forests of the Kowie Nature Reserve where you then spend the night in the reserve hut. On the second day you can attempt the 8-km walking trail, following yellow 'footprints' followed by canoeing back to Port Alfred. Make a note of when the tide will be coming in and going out and try to plan your trip to coincide with the flow each time. This will make the journey far more fun and less tiring. One of the more popular parts of the hike is a steep climb up the escarpment from where you are rewarded with a perfect view of the horseshoe bend in the river below. Look out for the small mammals found here, such as duiker and bushbuck; both are very shy and well camouflaged. There are plenty of shorter walks across the gentle hills and through the forests along with a number of picnic sites, braai facilities and toilets.

King William's Town → *Colour map 7, B6.*

King William's Town, more commonly known simply as King, is 56 km northeast of East London. The London Missionary Society established a mission station here in 1826 and over the years the town has grown into an important commercial centre. The town is best known as the birth and burial place of Apartheid activist Steven Biko who was put under house arrest in the town between 1974 and 1977 before he was arrested at a road block near Grahamstown, outside his restricted area. After his arrest he was taken to Nelson Mandela Bay (Port Elizabeth) and intensively interrogated until he died of a brain haemorrhage in police custody on 12 October 1977. The police first claimed he had starved himself to death while on a hunger strike. They later changed their story to say Biko had hit his head against a wall in a scuffle. Finally, 20 years later, the police admitted before the Truth and Reconciliation Commission that they had killed Biko. Diplomats from 13 counties joined mourners at his funeral in King William's Town but not a single South African was made accountable for his death. His grave with a lovingly tended polished tombstone lies in the **Steve Biko Remembrance Garden** on the edge of town on the road to Nelson Mandela Bay (Port Elizabeth). To reach the grave, follow Cathcart Street south of King William's Town and turn left down a dirt track that is signposted to the garden. It's a moving place and the grave is much humbler than expected for such an important figure in South African history. The **Amathole Museum** ① *Alexander St, Mon-Fri 0900-1630, Sat 0900-1300, small entry fee, T043-6424506, www.museum.za.net*, is a good place to get a feel for Xhosa history with displays on how the British crushed the Xhosa during the various frontier wars. There's also some contemporary art including bus, bikes and cars made from wire, and some dusty old stuffed mammals including Huberta the hippo (see box, page 386).

Hotel and guesthouse prices
L over US$300 AL US$220-300 A US$150-220
B US$100-150 C US$75-100 D US$35-75
E US$15-35 F under US$15
Private game reserves
L4 over US$900 L3 US$550-900
L2 US$450-550 L1 US$300-500
Restaurant prices
₮₮₮over US$30 ₮₮ US$15-30 ₮ under US$15
See pages 46-51 for further information.

⦿ Sleeping

Addo Elephant National Park *p377*
Some of the accommodation is run by
SANParks while others are private
concessions within or at the edge of
the park.

SANParks accommodation
Reservations through **SANParks**,
T012-4289111, www.sanparks.org, see page
48 for details. Bookings need to be made
well in advance, especially during school
holidays. For late bookings or cancellations
less than 72 hrs phone Addo reception
direct, T042-2330556.
AL-E Main Camp, next to the main entrance
gate and park reception. There are 61 units
in total each fully equipped for self-catering;
some have a/c and braai facilities.
Guest cottages (AL), have 6-beds with
2 en suite a/c bedrooms, fully equipped
kitchen and a living room. There are only
2 such cottages, known as **Hapoor**
and **Domkrag**.
Bungalows (C), are suitable for
4 people, bathroom plus a kitchen.
2-bed huts (D) are simple units with
a shower, fridge and toilet. There is a
fully equipped communal kitchen.
2-bed Safari Tents (D) 5 tents with
bedding, towels, fan, fridge and braai,
use of communal ablutions and kitchen.
Camping (E), a maximum of 6 people can
occupy any 1 campsite. The grounds are
well grassed and there is plenty of shade.

Communal kitchens have hot plates,
power points and hot water.
C Narina Bush Camp, is next to the Witriver
in the Zuurberg Mountains approximately
22 km (gravel road, 40 mins' driving) from
the main rest camp and park reception.
This is a tented camp with 4 tents (2-bed)
and must be booked as 1 unit, towels and
bedding are provided, open lapa/braai area,
kitchen with gas stove, fridge, paraffin lamps,
cutlery, crockery and cooking utensils,
1 shower with hot water from a paraffin
cylinder geyser, and 1 toilet. Because of no
electricity the guests have to arrive at least
2 hrs before sunset but no later than 1800
as they still have to carry their food and
clothing to the camp from the car park,
crossing a river and walking 400-500 m
through the forest. A torch is essential.
The camp can also be reached on horseback on Basuto pony/Boerperd crossbreeds.
All the necessary equipment is provided,
but it is important to book in advance
through reception at the park entrance,
T042-2330556. If you want to go on horse
back, departure time is no later than 1100
from the top of the Zuurberg Mountain,
approximately 16-km gravel road from
the main rest camp (25 mins' driving).
C Matyholweni Camp, in the south of the
park, 3 km from the N2 at the Sundays River
Mouth, and accessed through Matyholweni
Gate, T042-2338621. Nearest shops,
restaurants and fuel are in Colchester.
Small camp with 12 brand new SANParks
en suite cottages sleeping 2, some have
extra sofa bed suitable for children only,
open plan with kitchenette, braai facilities.
E Alexandria Hiking Huts, there are
2 huts on the Alexandria Trail (see
page 379), both sleeping 12 people on
bunks and mattresses; the hut at base
camp has toilets and cold showers; at
the overnight hiking hut at Woody
Cape you'll be using rainwater to
wash with.

Private lodges and camps

L4 Gorah Elephant Camp, central reservations T044-5327818, www.relais chateaux.com. This luxurious camp is a Relais & Chateaux property and has a private concession covering 4500 ha but can also access the rest of the park. Accommodation is in 11 huge, luxurious tents with a colonial theme, complete with 4-poster beds, en suite bathrooms and terraces overlooking the park. Relaxing boma area with rock swimming pool, meals are served in a superbly renovated coach house, overlooking a waterhole frequented by elephant, buffalo and antelope. The price includes all meals, guided game drives and night drives.

L1 Intsomi Forest Lodge, in the Alexandria Forest at Woody Cape, T046-6538903, www.intsomi.com. All-inclusive luxury lodge with 8 suites, open walls, African decor, opulent bathrooms, swimming pool, wellness centre, large deck overlooking a waterhole where antelope and zebra drink, the staff will put on dancing, game drives take in the sweeping views of the Alexandria Dunefield and ocean.

Private accommodation

L Elephant House, on the left of the R335, 5 km before Addo's main gate, T042-2332462, www.elephanthouse.co.za. Exclusive 9-room lodge decorated with the owner's private collection of antiques and Persian rugs, good food, qualified guides conduct excellent daily game drives into the park on open Land Cruisers as well as day visits to the various private game reserves in the area.

A Darlington Lake Lodge, situated next to Darlington Dam in the northern tip of Addo, 180 km north of Nelson Mandela Bay (Port Elizabeth) on the R75 to Graaff Reinet, T/F042-2433673. 5 double rooms and 5 safari tents with en suite facilities furnished in colonial style, meals are served outdoors in a traditional boma. Wide range of activities on offer around the dam, walking trail, horse rides, 4WD game-viewing trips, fishing and

boat cruises. A tranquil spot to enjoy the little-visited furthest reaches of the new part of the park.

B Elephants Footprint Lodge, 1 Riverside Dr, Colchester, 2 km from Matyholweni Gate, T041-4680499, www.elephantsfoot print.co.za. 12 spacious en suite rooms under thatch, additional outdoor shower, crisp white linen, muted cream and brown decor, large communal lounge with leather furniture, log fire and TV, swimming pool and wooden deck with sun loungers.

B Protea Hotel Addo, 32 km north of the main entrance on the Zuurberg Mountain Pass, access on the R335, T042-2330583, www.proteahotels.com. There are 36 double rooms; some are in the original 1850s manor house while the rest are delightful individual spacious lodges under traditional thatch in the Zuurberg Village. Restaurant and pub with magnificent views, swimming pool, tennis, conference centre, chapel for weddings.

C Africanos Inn, corner of Main and Zuurberg roads, Addo, 10-min drive from the park gate, T042-2330605, www.africanos-inn.co.za. An excellent fairly new spot to stay if you cannot get accommodation in the park, 10 very spacious and modern motel-style rooms, each with lounge area, tea tray and DSTV, the barn is used for weddings and some times live music, great restaurant and bar with a long menu, swimming pool, can organize day and night drives into the park. Recommended.

Schotia Safaris p380

Private lodges and camps

L1 Schotia Safaris Private Game Reserve, east of Addo National Park, 55 km from Nelson Mandela Bay (Port Elizabeth), just north of the junction of the N2 and N10, T042-2351436, www.schotia.com. 2 double en suite chalets with fireplaces, hidden in the bush so very private and aimed at honeymooners, a third chalet has 4 beds suitable for families, all meals and game drives included in the price, transfers from

Nelson Mandela Bay (Port Elizabeth) can be arranged. No electricity, but lamps will be lit for you in the evening.

Shamwari Game Reserve *p380*
Private lodges and camps

There are 6 luxury camps within the reserve – all are expensive. Each is completely self-contained and independent of the others. Rates are all-inclusive of meals, morning and evening game drives, walking safaris with an armed guard, and visits to the Shamwari/Born Free Conservation Centre. Current rates per person are R2500-R6800 depending on season. Reservations: T042-2031111, www.shamwari.com.

L4 Lobengula Lodge, at the northern extremity of the reserve, the most luxurious of the 6 complexes, with thatched roof and decorated to the highest standard. 6 rooms and a maximum of 12 guests can stay here. 5 rooms have en suite bathroom and outside shower plus a/c and underfloor heating; the 6th room is the most expensive option in the whole reserve – the Pretorius Suite. It has a separate lounge with super a/c and fan, plus underfloor heating, private plunge pool, and outside shower. The swimming pool has a sunken cocktail bar and there's a small gym, beauty spa and steam bath.

L3 Bushman's River Lodge, a small lodge at the centre of the reserve. The 4 double rooms are beautifully decorated in an ethnic theme and set in restored settlers' cottages. Plunge pool and a personal ranger service.

L3 Eagles Cragg Lodge, the most central of the 6 camps. This is a restored settler's cottage which has been divided into 9 suites with twin beds and an en suite bathroom, private deck and plunge pool. Lodge facilities include a dining area, library, business centre, lounge, bar, and beauty spa.

L3 Long Lee Manor, the Edwardian manor house near the main entrance on the western side of the reserve. Largest of the 6 camps, although it never feels crowded. The 30 rooms here are in the Manor House, Palm Court or Sidbury Suites, with underfloor heating, ceiling fans, a/c, TV, telephone. Facilities include 2 swimming pools, a floodlit tennis court, a beauty spa and, down by the Bushman's River at a point known as the hippo pool, is a covered *lapa* where guests can watch the animals drink while they enjoy a meal.

L3 Riverdene Lodge, the latest addition to Shamwari, has 9 a/c en suite rooms, with separate lounges. The lodge has elegantly furnished lounges, a sunroom, a rim flow swimming pool with sun deck and poolside bar, the dining room opens onto a spacious outdoor barbecue area.

L2 Bayethe Tented Lodge, stone-walled and thatch-roofed main lodge with viewing deck and dining boma, accommodation is 9 double, a/c, tented suites, with en suite bathroom, outside shower, private plunge pool and deck.

Amakhala Game Reserve *p381*
Private lodges and camps

Game activities such as walks, drives or cruises are included in the price at the more expensive lodges, and are available at extra cost at the less expensive ones. All rates are full board and in most you eat with the host families. All of them have swimming pools. Reservations for all the lodges T046-6362750, www.amakhala.co.za.

L3 Leeuwenbosch Country Lodge, built in 1908 and set in its own lovely garden, traditional country house with 4 en suite doubles and 1 suite, cellar pub with full-size antique billiards table.

L3 Safari Lodge, intimate thatched lodge with stylish safari decor, luxurious huts with double baths and outdoor showers, outside terraces with open fire in the evening, rim flow pool.

L2 Shearers Lodge, set in the grounds of **Leeuwenbosch**, originally built in 1930 and used for shearing and classing wool, and now beautifully converted into 4 luxury en suite bedrooms, one with a private lounge. All the rooms open on to a wide colonial veranda overlooking the gardens and chapel.

L2 Woodbury Lodge, 4 modern stone and thatched cottages designed to blend in with the natural surroundings, good views from the wooden decks, central dining room and braai area, lounge and bar.

L1 Cararvon Lodge, an 1857 farm where guests are accommodated in the historic farmhouse or the elegantly restored Edwardian cottage, rooms with wrought-iron beds, some with fireplaces, private lounges, farm-style meals.

L1 Reed Valley Inn, 4 en suite rooms in historic buildings that once were the rest stop for the mail wagon in the 19th century, set on a working farm, farm-style breakfasts and 3-course dinners in the main dining room, babysitting can be arranged.

Lalibela Game Reserve *p381*
Private lodges and camps
Rates for all the 3 luxurious lodges in the reserve are all-inclusive of meals, drinks and game drives. Each lodge has a large lounge, viewing deck, swimming pool, and an outdoor dining 'boma' and indoor dining area. There are special arrangements for children who are kept entertained by childminders whilst parents go on game drives and are offered their own 'kiddie's' game drives. Reservations T041-5818170, www.lalibela.co.za.

L4 Mark's Camp, thatched and stone cottages, sleeps 20 in 4 doubles and 3 family units, private decks overlooking a waterhole, swimming pool, a fire is lit at the outside boma to sit around with drinks after dinner.

L4 Tree Tops, 5 luxury safari tents perched high on thatched platforms at 'tree top' level, joined by raised walkways with fantastic views, really feels as if you are staying in a treehouse, open-air dining deck overlooking a small waterhole, swimming pool.

L3 Lentaba Lodge, 8 thatched chalets with large beds with white linen, safari decor and antique African art throughout, good views from the hilltop location, the outdoor eating boma overlooks a waterhole that has a spotlight at night.

Grahamstown *p381, map p382*
Some residents in Grahamstown township offer overnight accommodation in their homes (**D**). Most is in brick houses with a hospitable Xhosa family. The tourist office can arrange this.

A Evelyn House, 115 High St, T046-6222366, www.albanyhotels.co.za. A very fine guest house in a local landmark building dating from the 1800s. 4 double rooms, 2 luxury suites, 1 with jacuzzi, a/c, laundry service, M-Net TV, swimming pool, sauna, gym, secure off-street parking. Well-appointed accommodation. Recommended.

B Protea Hotel Grahamstown, 123 High St, T046-6222324, www.proteahotels.com. Rather unattractive building but in a good location. 27 rooms with en suite bathrooms, TV, lounge. **Calabash** restaurant has a good local reputation, cocktail bar with pool table and darts, laundry service, secure parking, comfortable town hotel within a short walk of the shops and sights.

C 137 High Street, 137 High St, T046-6223242, www.137highstreet.co.za. Stylish hotel in a good location close to restaurants and sights, with 8 luxurious rooms, en suite bath or shower, good service, attractive old building, restaurant downstairs serving excellent breakfasts and freshly made cakes and scones, as well as more substantial meals for dinner.

C Aucklands Country House, 8 km from the town centre off the N2 towards Nelson Mandela Bay (Port Elizabeth), T046-6222401, www.aucklands.co.za. A fine country house with 6 spacious rooms and en suite bath-rooms, set in 14 ha of beautiful grounds with a swimming pool, tennis court, croquet lawn, and resident herd of blesbok. Horse riding and hikes nearby. Excellent gourmet meals, friendly owners. An extremely well-run establishment.

C The Cock House, 10 Market St, T046-6361287, www.cockhouse.co.za. Beautifully restored 1820s national monument with 9 double rooms with en suite bathrooms, 4 self-catering flats, special touches include electric blanket and home-made biscuits. Luxurious guesthouse with a good à la carte restaurant attached with a comfortable lounge and library. Peter and Belinda have clearly made a good impression – Nelson Mandela has stayed here 3 times and famous South African author Andre Brink was a former resident. The 1st-floor veranda is a particularly fine feature. Affordable and recommended.

C Oak Lodge Hotel, 95 Bathurst St, T046-6229123, www.albanyhotels.co.za. Large old building with 23 rooms, TV lounge, gardens, swimming pool, braai area, bar, secure parking. Tours arranged. A short walk from the town centre.

D The Hermitage, 14 Henry St, T046-6361503. Beautifully restored house, a fine example of a villa built in the 1820s by an early British settler. 1 elegant double suite with en suite bathroom and sitting room with TV and private entrance. The neat gardens complement the house, breakfasts served on a veranda. Good value, recommended.

E-F Old Gaol Backpackers, Somerset St, opposite the Albany Museum, T046-6361001, www.oldgaol.co.za. An unusual and excellent place to stay. This is the only backpacker place in Grahamstown, and is housed in an old Victorian jail. Double rooms are in individual cells, complete with thick stone walls, domed ceilings, and tiny barred windows. The dorms are housed in the communal cells. There is also a lounge with kitchen, TV room, the **Gallows** pub and restaurant, and you can sunbathe in the old exercise yard. The building is listed, so no work can be done on the original structure. While this gives the place a run-down (and rather too authentic) feel with original prisoners' graffiti on the walls, the cells are spotless and the beds comfortable. Highly recommended as an atmospheric and unique backpackers.

Camping

Makana Municipal Caravan Park, Grey St, on the outskirts of town on the N2 heading towards Nelson Mandela Bay (Port Elizabeth), T046-6036072. An easy walk to town, with sites for tents or caravans, and family chalets and rondavels. It is currently closed for refurbishment and landscaping but should reopen by the end of 2008.

Port Alfred *p385*

AL Halyards, Royal Alfred Marina, off Albany Rd, T046-6043300, www.riverhotels.co.za. Smartest hotel in Port Alfred, provides luxury accommodation in a nautical theme for the wealthy set during peak holiday periods. During quiet periods, however, you should find bargain room rates on offer. 49 spacious a/c rooms with all mod-cons, good views of the marina. 2 restaurants, bar, swimming pool, spa, gym, wooden decks, pleasant grounds.

C The Residency, 11 Vroom Rd, T046-6245382, www.theresidency.co.za. Turn-of-the-20th-century settler's house, with wooden floors and ball and claw baths, 4 en suite rooms furnished with cottage-type items, breakfasts are taken on the wrap-around veranda, German spoken.

C Royal St Andrews Lodge, 19 St Andrews Rd, T046-6241379, www.royalstandrews lodge.co.za. Across the road from the golf course, Tudor mock exterior with 14 bright and modern rooms, doubles and family rooms, and self-catering chalets, swimming pool with wooden deck, the **Thistle** restaurant and **Highlander** pub, good-value small, friendly hotel. Entertained the Prince of Wales in 1925, hence the royal title.

D-E Medolino Caravan Park, 23 Stewart Rd, T/F046-6241651, www.caravanparks.co.za/medolino. This is a medium-sized park with 48 sites, well grassed and plenty of shade, electric points, electric lights, well-equipped laundry and 2 heated pools. 5 self-catering log cabins sleeping 2-4, tents are allowed and you can hire a caravan, disabled access.

D-F Station Backpackers, 1 Pascoe St, T046-6245869, www.thestation.co.za. A fairly new backpacker place housed in Port Alfred's old station, now a national monument. Doubles, dorms, **The Station** restaurant and bar which is very popular locally, internet access, the Baz Bus will drop you here.

Kowie Nature Reserve *p386*
E Horseshoe Reserve Hut, a simple hut sleeping up to 12 people. You'll need to bring bedding and all camping supplies; the only cooking facilities are a braai area. Book through the tourist office in Port St Alfred.

King William's Town *p387*
C Dreamers Guest House, 29 Gorden St, Hospital Hill, T043-6423012, www.dreamers guesthouse.com. Neat house on a quiet street, colourful gardens, 4 en suite rooms and 1 family unit, lunch and dinner on request, large pool and patio area. The lounge has antiques wood floors and an organ dating from 1867.
C-D Grosvenor Lodge, 48 Taylor St, T046-6047200, www.grosvenor.co.za. Modern business hotel with 19 plain rooms, extras include a/c and satellite TV, restaurant, **Kings Head** pub. Very average but one of the only options in town.

🍴 Eating

Grahamstown *p381, map p382*
Many of the quality restaurants in town are in the main hotels. There are also plenty of cheap cafés and takeaways catering to the large student population and the town features the usual **Wimpy** and **KFC**.
Ψ Calabash, 123 High St, T046-6222324. Open 0700-2300. Popular traditional South African restaurant specializing in Xhosa hotpots, various South African dishes and a regular menu of seafood, steaks and venison. Generous breakfasts and daily specials at lunchtime.
Ψ Ginos, 8 New St, entrance is from the car park behind on Hill St, T046-6227208. Mon-Fri 0700-2100, Sat and Sun 0800-2200. 20-year-old family-run restaurant with Tuscan murals on the walls, good selection of pizza and pasta dishes, and some meat dishes and regular specials, very popular, especially with students.
Ψ Henry Ate, adjoining **Ginos** (see above) 8 New St, T046-6227208. Mon-Sat 1700-2300.

Dark wood furniture, medieval theme with a large portrait of Henry VIII, large portions of steaks, burgers, ribs, some vegetarian dishes and a children's 'jester' menu, separate ladies bar.
Ψ Norden's, The Cock House, 10 Market St, T046-6361287. Open 1200-1430, 1900-late, closed Mon lunch. Excellent restaurant which is part of a smart town guesthouse (see Sleeping, page 391). Plenty of attention is given to presentation and quality of the country cuisine. If you don't fancy eating then enjoy a beer in the cosy yellowwood bar with a light snack. One of the most popular spots in town so booking advised.
Ψ Redwood Spur, 97 High St, T046-6222629. Daily 1100-2300. Predictable steak, ribs, Tex Mex, chain restaurant, one of the few options open Sun. Good service from clean-cut students working here part time.
Ψ Café Dulce, 112 High St. Tue-Sun 0800-2200, Mon 0800-1700. Café and ice cream parlour, excellent sandwiches made to order, ice cream sundaes, milkshakes and salads.
Ψ Rat & Parrot, 59 New St. Mon-Sat 1100-late. A popular bar which is big with students on Wed and Sat nights, gets quite rowdy once a few rounds of shooters have been passed around, wide range of beers and alcoholic drinks, big-screen TV for major sports, bar snacks including good *potjies*.

Port Alfred *p385*
Ψ Buck & Hunter, 9 Main St, T046-6245960. Mon-Sat 1230-late. Relaxed pub/restaurant serving good seafood, steaks and pub lunches in wildlife-themed decor, the odd special dish such as duck, gammon and game, and good vegetarian options like butternut bake.
Ψ Butlers Riverside Restaurant, 25 Van der Riet St, T046-6243464. Wed-Mon 1100-late. Restaurant-cum-pub with a lively atmosphere. Pub snack menu served on the open deck overlooking the river, or eat inside in a slightly more formal setting with a more expensive menu. The fresh fish is excellent, menu and blackboard items change according to the whim of the chef.

� The Charthouse, **Halyards Hotel**, Royal Alfred Marina, T046-6043300. A smart option with nautical decor, good-value all-you-can-eat buffets for lunch and dinner. Fri evening is a braai on the deck, Sat night a seafood buffet, and Sun lunch a full carvery with roasts, vegetables and a gooey selection of desserts, good service and views across the marina.
♫ Guido's on the Beach, West Beach Dr, T046-6245264. Open 1100-2200. The restaurant serves great pizzas and pasta dishes along with seafood and steaks, children's menu and play area. Busy and boozy bar upstairs with views across the waves.

⊛ Festivals and events

Grahamstown *p381, map p382*
Check with the local tourist office for the exact dates and programme details.
Mar The town hosts a large **Scifest**, www.scifest.org.za, which features some 600 events: lectures, game drives, laser shows, robotics competitions, science olympics, interactive exhibitions and a film festival. Attendance now exceeds 35,000 visitors a year, many of them school children.
Jun-Jul The famous 10-day **National Festival of Arts**, T046-66031103, www.nafest.co.za, is one of the top cultural events in the country. Over 50,000 visitors are attracted to the town to watch a range of shows, which include theatre, dance, fine art, films, music, opera and an increasing variety of traditional crafts and art, plus a huge range of fringe shows. There's something for everyone from techno raves to medieval banquets. The centre of the festival is the 1820 Settlers Monument. During this period accommodation gets booked very quickly, so make reservations several months ahead, or phone the tourist office to check if any private homes are letting out rooms. During the festival the whole atmosphere of the town changes, so if you are in the country at this time it is well worth a visit.

▲ Activities and tours

Addo Elephant National Park *p377*
Addo Elephant Back Safaris, in the north of the Addo Elephant National Park in the Zuurberg Mountains, on the Toevlugt Farm. 1.5 km before Addo's main gate, turn left at the Zuurburg sign. The farm is 34 km from this turn-off. T042-2351400, www.addo elephantbacksafaris.co.za, R650 per person. Here there is the opportunity to walk with 3 tame elephants through the bush and forest. The walk is at an enjoyable pace and not strenuous and allows visitors to observe the elephants' habits close up and in their natural surroundings. After the walk you can ride the elephants to the waterhole, where you can watch them swim. Snacks or lunch are provided.

Grahamstown *p381, map p382*
There are several local registered guides who will take you on historical tours, bird-watching or game viewing, on foot or in your own vehicle. Contact the tourist office for recommendations.
Alan Weyer Tours, T046-6227896, www.alanweyerstours.co.za. Acclaimed SATOUR registered guide who won South Africa's Tour Guide of the Year in 2005. Anyone with an interest in the history of the Eastern Cape could do no better that spend a day listening to his entertaining tales. Half-day historical tours in and around Grahamstown start from R525.
Frontier Country, T046-6228054, www.frontiercountry.co.za. 1- to 4-day trips in the Eastern Cape starting from Grahams town or Nelson Mandela Bay (Port Elizabeth), half-day tour of the town and township, frontier village tour, Addo, can also arrange abseiling and horse riding in the region.
Umthathi Training Project, at the Spoornet Station Building, T082-7841458, hadeda@ imaginet.co.za. Organizes half-day tours to the large township in Grahamstown which is known as **Rhini**, or Grahamstown East, and lies to the east of the town across the river.

Not surprisingly, most local whites will never have visited this part of their town and will know very little of it. Tourists, however, are offered a choice of township tours, with visits to a 'traditional' Xhosa family for a meal, as well as visiting craft centres and shebeens.

Port Alfred p385
Diving
Keryn's Dive School, small boat harbour, T046-6244432, keryn@keryndiveschool.com. Fishing charters and dive courses available, plus daily dives for certified divers. The nearby reef has some fine corals and there are some popular wreck dives, but the water is not warm, nor is the visibility that good.

Golf
The **Royal Port Alfred Golf Course**, T046-6244796, www.rpagc.co.za, has a magnificent view of the sea. This 18-hole, 72 par course was laid out between 1907 and 1915 and was given royal status from King George V.

Horse riding
The roads that access the most beautiful and remote beaches and river valleys are poor, which means that horses are often the best mode of transport. If you have never ridden before, this is a good place to learn.

Rufanes Rides and Hikes, T046-6241669, T082-6971297 (mob). Trails through rolling hills, milkwoods, dunes and along beaches. Experienced guides, can pace to any level including children. They also have hiking trails on their farm.

Three Sisters Farm, 15 km along the R72 towards East London, T046-6751269. Beach trails, forest dune trails, family outings, as well as 2- to 3-day safaris with game viewing on horseback.

Transport

Grahamstown p381, map p382
Bus
Greyhound and **Translux** coaches depart from outside the Frontier Hotel, Bathurst St. The town tourist office acts as a local booking agent. Buses stop in Grahamstown on the **Cape Town–Durban** route.

Bus companies **Greyhound**, T083-9159000, www.greyhound.co.za, and **Translux**, T0861-589282, www.translux.co.za.

Port Alfred p385
Bus
The **Baz Bus** stops at Station Backpackers 5 times a week.

King William's Town p387
Bus
Greyhound coaches depart from the Engen One Stop (Wimpy), Cathcart St. **Translux** coaches depart from the BP service station on Alexander Rd. Buses stop in King William's Town on the **Cape Town–Durban** route.

Bus companies **Greyhound**, T083-915000 www.greyhound.co.za. **Translux**, T0861-589282, www.translux.co.za.

Directory

Grahamstown p381, map p382
Banks and internet All the major banks have branches in the **Pepper Grove Mall** on African St, where there are also internet cafés.

Port Alfred p385
Banks **Standard Bank** and **First National**, both in Govan Mbeki Av.

Eastern Cape Karoo

The surreal Karoo landscape, clear air and desert sunsets are evocative of the very heart of South Africa. The archaic scenery, created from sedimentary rock around 250 million years ago, is rich in fossils and San paintings. This is an area of vast open spaces studded with scrub and cacti, craggy mountains looming in the distance. Despite its barren appearance, this is mainly a farming area, known for its sheep, cattle, angora goats and horses. The most beautiful place to experience the Karoo is in the Valley of Desolation next to the historic town of Graaff-Reinet. The fastest route north into the Karoo is via the N2 from Nelson Mandela Bay (Port Elizabeth) past Addo, which connects with the N10 heading to Cradock and Middelburg. The R63 leaves the N10 at Cookhouse and heads west to Somerset East and Graaff-Reinet. For more information on the region visit www.karooheartland.co.za. ➤➤ *For listings, see pages 401-403.*

North of Nelson Mandela Bay ◙♟▲◙ ➤➤ *pp401-403.*

Somerset East → *Phone code: 042. Colour map 7, A4.*

Somerset East, a neat agricultural town typical of the Karoo, is 180 km north of Nelson Mandela Bay (Port Elizabeth). It was founded on a farm that produced horse fodder for the cavalry on the frontline of the many skirmishes going on at the time, and was and named after Lord Charles Somerset, Governor of the Cape in 1815. The town has a few historical buildings and faces the Bosberg Mountains. The **Somerset Museum** ① *Mon-Fri 0800-1700, small entry fee*, recreates the atmosphere and lifestyle of a Victorian parsonage. It is set among beautiful rose gardens and the rose petals are used to make jam which is on sale in the museum shop. The **Walter Battiss Art Museum** ① *Mon-Fri 1000-1600*, is also here and has the world's largest collection of work by this South African artist, who was a friend of Pablo Picasso. For information contact **Blue Crane Tourism** ① *88 Njoli Rd, T042-2431333, www.somerseteast.co.za.*

Cradock → *Phone code: 048. Colour map 7, A4.*

This small Karoo town is made up of an attractive grid of wide roads lined with Victorian bungalows. It was once a frontier town and has three Victorian churches. The **Dutch Reformed Church** on Stockenstroom Street was opened in 1868 and is based upon London's St Martin in the Fields, on Trafalgar Square. Cradock is now better known for its connections with the author Olive Schreiner who wrote *The Story of an African Farm*. The **Olive Schreiner House** ① *9 Cross St, T048-8815251, Mon-Fri 0800-1245, 1400-1630, small entrance fee*, illustrates aspects of her life.

The **Great Fish River Museum** ① *behind the town hall, T048-8812390, Tue-Fri 0800-1300, 1400-1600, Sat 0800-1200, small entrance fee*, is located in a restored parsonage built in 1849, which is today a national monument. It depicts early pioneer history and on display are old ox wagons and horse carts including a hearse. **Cradock Spa** ① *4 km from Cradock on the Marlow road, T048-8812709, 0645-1930, R7*, is a series of indoor and outdoor pools set around natural sulphurous springs. From here, there are also two short circular hiking trails. The 10-km **Fish River Trail** follows the Fish River into town, crossing over the bridge and returning on the opposite bank. The **Eerstekrantz Trail**, 4.5 km, is a hike up the mountain opposite the spa resort. Note the ubiquitous silver windmills, a distinguishing feature of the Karoo, on the surrounding farmland.

For information contact **Cradock Tourism** ① *municipality building, Stockenstroom Rd, T048-8812383, www.cradock.co.za, Mon-Fri 0830-1230, 1400-1600.* The office is very helpful and has a good collection of maps and accommodation listings.

◑ *The Cradock Library is home to a copy of an 1869 first edition Encyclopaedia Britannica.*

Mountain Zebra National Park → *Colour map 7, A4.*

① *T048-8812427, www.sanparks.org, gates open Oct-Apr 0700-1900, May-Sep 0700-1800, R60, R30 children. The park is 280 km from Nelson Mandela Bay (Port Elizabeth) and 25 km west of Cradock in the foothills of the Bankberg. The reserve is signposted from the Cradock to Middelburg road.*

The plains and mountains of this Karoo landscape support a wide variety of mammals including black wildebeest, kudu, eland, mountain zebra, red hartebeest, springbok, buffalo, black rhino and caracal. The Rooiplat Plateau is a particularly good area for seeing the zebra. Over 200 species of bird have been recorded here including many raptors and the endangered blue crane. Less appealingly, this is also the home of the giant earthworm. Buffalo were introduced in 1998 and black rhino in 2001, which put a stop to hiking in the reserve. Game viewing can be done by car during the day on the 37 km of tracks which cross the reserve.

The national park was established in 1937, when the mountain zebra was facing extinction and there were only five left on 65 sq km of land, four of which were male. There are now over 300 of them here, making it the largest herd of mountain zebra in the world. After breeding, many are relocated to other parks in South Africa.

There is a park camp with a fully licensed à la carte restaurant (open 0700-1900), which also serves snacks; and a shop, 0700-1900, which sells a good range of groceries, wines, curios, books and firewood. The camp also has a swimming pool (resident guests only), post office, telephones and petrol. For accommodation details see Sleeping, page 401.

Nieu Bethesda → *Colour map 7, A3.*

Nieu Bethesda was founded in 1874 on a farm, Uitkyk, by a group of farmers who wanted a church that was closer than the one at Graaff-Reinet, several hours' ride away on horseback. Uitkyk belonged to BJ Pienaar – on his gravestone is engraved *De ouers van de dorp* (the parents of the town). Even today, many people in and around Nieu Bethesda carry the same surname. The first church services were held in a wagon shed, until the Dutch Reformed Church was built in 1905. Even today, this is still lit by gas chandeliers that pre-date the arrival of electricity to the village, and has an imposing white steeple with a clock that chimes accurately on the hour.

This small village has become best known through the work of Helen Martins and her **Owl House** ① *T049-8411603, www.owlhouse.co.za, daily, May-Oct 0900-1700, Nov-Apr 0800-1800, R26.* Helen was a local eccentric who lived a hermit-like existence, devoting her time to her art and the study of Eastern philosophies. She was born in the house in 1898, and when she reached her fifties and when her parents died, she embarked on an extraordinary 25-year transformation of the house. Then in old age with crippling arthritis and poor eyesight – and considering her decoration of her house complete – she took her own life in 1971. Most of the surfaces on the inside of the house are decorated with finely ground glass of many colours, and in the pantry are rows of jars of crushed glass that Helen carefully graded by colour and weight. The light and colour of the glass is highlighted further by the many candles, lamps and strangely shaped mirrors. At the back of the house is an enclosed area known as the Camel Yard, filled with hundreds of sphinxes, camels and other figures made from cement and glass. Her remarkable house and its grounds, along with much of her art is now a museum, which attracts some 13,000 visitors a year.

The village has a collection of other artists' galleries, one shop, two restaurants, and no street lights. If you are self-catering it is better to stock up elsewhere and there is no petrol available here. There are a couple of good accommodation options or, as it is only 50 km from Graaff-Reinet, it can easily be visited in a day though you'll need to have your own transport. There is an **information office** ① *T049-8411401, www.nieubethesda.co.za.*

🌙 *Traffic was once so infrequent in Nieu Bethsda that certain streets were allowed to be used for growing potatoes.*

Graaff-Reinet 😊🍴🏕️😊 ▸▸ *pp401-403. Colour map 7, A3.*

Founded in 1786, Graaff-Reinet, the oldest town of the Eastern Cape, lies between the Sneuberg Mountains and the Sundays River. The town was originally described as "nothing more than a collection of mud huts", but years of prosperity from farming are reflected in the local architecture – over 220 of the town's historical buildings have been declared national monuments. Today it is surprisingly smart, with row upon row of perfectly restored houses, leafy streets and a quiet, bustling atmosphere. Nevertheless, Graaff-Reinet remains a small provincial town in deep Karoo country, so don't expect much in the form of entertainment.

The town was originally established as an administrative centre to control the frontier districts for the government in the Cape. Mauritz Woeke was sent as governor or landrost in 1785. He chose the site of Graaff-Reinet because of its water supplies and fertile soils. The town grew to become an important trading centre on the new frontier and there was a boom in sheep farming during the 1850s, when English settlers first brought merino sheep to the region. The **Graaff-Reinet Publicity Association** can provide **tourist information** ① *7 Church St, T049-8924248, www.graaffreinet.co.za, Mon-Fri 0800-1700, Sat 0900-1200, Sun 1000-1200.*

Sights
① *All of the town's museums are open Mon-Fri 0900-13030, 1400-1700, Sat-Sun 0900-1200, unless otherwise stated. All the sights can easily be explored by foot.*
The earliest surviving historic buildings, mostly square and originally thatched but now roofed with corrugated iron, are on **Cradock Street**. The buildings are typical of Karoo architecture and were designed to be cool during the blistering summer heat. They have thick whitewashed walls and shuttered windows.

A walk down Parsonage Street and Church Street passes many of Graaff-Reinet's most interesting historical buildings. The **Drostdy Hotel** is a fine example of classical Cape architecture designed by Louis Thibault. It was built in 1806 and was the site of the local council for 40 years. In 1855 it was bought by Captain Charles Lennox Stretch and converted into a hotel. The modern Drostdy Hotel was restored in 1977.

Reinet House on Parsonage Street was completed in 1812 and became the parsonage for the Dutch Reformed Church. It was opened to the public as a historic museum in 1956. It is still decorated with original yellowwood and stinkwood furniture and boasts the world's largest vine, planted in 1870. The most recent addition to the complex is a brandy still, built in 1990, now used to demonstrate the distillation of *withond*, a local brand of fire-water from the early settler days.

Opposite is the **Old Residency Museum** ① *open Mon-Sat*, which was originally a townhouse built early in the 19th century. It became the magistrate's residence in 1916.

Today it houses the Jan Felix Lategan Memorial collection of sporting rifles as well as Middellandse Regiment memorabilia. On the same street, the **John Rupert Little Theatre** was originally the church of the London Missionary Society. It became an art gallery during the 1970s and is now a theatre.

On Church Street, the **Old Library Museum** was built in 1847 and has displays of period costumes and a collection of fossils, and quite by contrast, an exhibition dedicated to the life and work of Robert Sobukwe, founder of the Pan Africanist Congress. The tourist

Graaff-Reinet

To Camdeboo National Park & Murraysburg (90 km)

To Airfield & Cradock

Union Monument

Magazine Hill

Sundays River

Queen

Rothman

Sports Field

Park

Cradock

Stockenstrom

Donkin

Ryneveld Square

Hope

North

Church Square

Town Hall

Graaff Reinet Pharmacy

Caledon

Muller

3

Dutch Reformed Church

1

Market Square

Khartoum

4

Hester Rupert Art Museum & Old Library Museum

Kitchener

Cemetery

Jansen

Somerset

Parliament

Drostdy

Stretch's Courts

Parsonage

5

John Rupert Little Theatre

Reinet House

Old Residency Museum

Kruger

11

1

Caroline

Bourke

Cradock

Jail

Middle

Plaster

Middle

Conlock

West

River

Sundays River

Murray

7

College Rd

Show Ground

Church

Industrial Estate

To Beaufort West & Nelson Mandela Bay (Port Elizabeth) (251 km)

N

200 metres

200 yards

Sleeping	Eating
Andries Stockenström Guest House **1**	Cypress Cottages **7**
Camdeboo Cottages **3**	Drostdy **5**
	Urquhart Caravan Park **2**
	Villa Reinet **11**

Eating
Coral Tree **1**
Die Kliphuis **4**
Number 8 **3**

information office is also here. Next door, the **Hester Rupert Art Museum** makes a pleasant change from the nostalgia of other museums. The art gallery has a collection of South African contemporary art.

The **Graaff-Reinet Pharmacy** on Caledon Street is a Victorian chemist's shop which still has many of its original fittings. There are a number of Victorian chemists which have been converted into tourist attractions in South Africa, but this one is considered to be among the finest.

Around Graaff-Reinet

Camdeboo National Park → *Colour map 7, A3.*
ⓘ *Daily 0600-2000, T049-8923453, R30. The Driekoppe Trail must be booked in advance through SANParks, T012-4289111, www.sanparks.org. Information on the trails can be found at www.graaffreinet.co.za.*

Formerly the Karoo Nature Reserve, the Camdeboo National Park is now administered by SANParks and covers 14,500 ha and virtually surrounds Graaff-Reinet. The landscape is typical of the Karoo, with spectacular rock formations, peculiar desert flora and interesting game and birdlife. There are three main areas within the reserve: the Valley of Desolation to the west; a game drive area to the north; and the eastern hiking area. To reach the park, take the road towards Murraysburg past the 1000-ha dam, which has picnic sites and is a popular place to sail and windsurf.

The **Valley of Desolation** is a national monument within the Camdeboo National Park. The bizarre rock formations were formed millions of years ago by weather erosion. Sheer cliffs and precariously balanced columns of dolerite rise 120 m from the valley floor. From the entrance to the valley, drive up to the first viewpoint which has fabulous views of the Karoo in all directions to the horizon. Looking out over the harsh landscape gives you a good idea of the overwhelming obstacles that the Voortrekkers managed to overcome. If you continue up the road, you come to a car park and a short 1.5-km hike, with stunning views of the mountains and the chance of seeing black eagles and dassies. Back down off the main road, is the 19-km game drive, where you may see Cape buffalo, kudu, mountain zebra and springbok. The **Eerstefontein Day Walks** start at the Spandau Kop Gate. There is a choice of three walks of 4 km, 11 km or 14 km. The walks pass through a wilderness area where you can see black wildebeest, kudu and springbok. Permits are required and can be bought at the gate; the trails are marked by lizard emblems. The **Driekoppe Trail** is an overnight trail that passes through the mountainous eastern area of the reserve. This area is rich in wildlife, and hikers can see klipspringers, kudu, mountain reedbuck and mountain zebra. The overnight hut sleeps eight hikers. The trail must be booked in advance through SANParks.

Kalkkop Impact Crater
ⓘ *Follow the N9 towards Aberdeen for about 30 km; at Aberdeen, turn left onto the R338 until you reach a right-hand turn marked as Aberdeen Rd. From here there is a dirt track that leads to the crater, follow the signs.*

A short distance from Graaff-Reinet are the weathered remains of a giant crater created by a meteorite more than 200,000 years ago. Research has shown the original hole to have been several hundred metres deep. Over time the crater has been filled with limestone deposits, but the circular ridge, with a diameter of 640 m, is still visible.

Eastern Cape Karoo listings

Sleeping

Somerset East p396

D Glen Avon Farm, 12 km from Somerset East, off the R63 towards Cookhouse, T042-2433628, www.glenavonfarm.co.za. Lovely picturesque farm offering hikes to streams and interaction with the farm animals for children, 2 comfortable guest rooms in the main farmhouse, 2 self-catering cottages (3-bed) with yellowwood floors, wrought-iron beds, **Hart Cottage** is a restored 1817 thatched, wattle-and-daub building. Swimming pool, tennis court, fresh farm produce for breakfast or for sale to self-caterers. A peaceful country retreat.

D Somerset Hotel, 83 Nojoli St, T/F042-2430557, www.somerseteast.co.za/somersethotel. Simple town hotel built in the 1800s with tin roof, plain but good-value doubles and singles with TV, cheaper rooms without bathrooms, friendly pub where you can meet the Karoo farmers, adequate restaurant on site.

Cradock p396

C Die Tuishuise, 36 Market St, T048-8811322, www.tuishuise.co.za. Characterful guesthouse based in a series of historical buildings on Market St, each restored and decorated to reflect the British and Dutch settlers' lifestyles a century ago. All of the houses have a fully equipped kitchen and lounge and are ideal for families or 2 couples travelling together. All rooms have en suite bathrooms and the staff are very friendly and helpful. Delicious, huge breakfasts are served in a Victorian dining room. A good evening

meal can be had in the **Victoria Manor Hotel** (see below) at the end of the street. Has won numerous awards, recommended, almost worth a detour alone.

C Heritage House, 45 Bree St, T048-8813210, www.heritagehousecradock.com. Delightful 170-year-old farmhouse with 7 comfortable en suite rooms in the main house or in garden cottages set on wide lawns, TV, electric blankets and heaters. Good breakfasts, friendly owners, the perfect spot to relax and soak up the Karoo atmosphere.

C Victoria Manor Hotel, corner of Market and Voortrekker streets, T048 8811650, reservations also through www.tuishuise.co.za. Lovely old town inn set in a 3-storey white-washed Victorian building built in 1840. Full of character, with old-fashioned furnishings, a very good restaurant serving Karoo dinners, bar, tea room and attached curio shop.

D Palm House, 26 Market St, T048-8814229, metcalf@eastcape.net. Victorian bungalow with 3 rooms, en suite, no smoking, old-style furnishings, high ceilings, log fires in winter, lovely old dining room, TV lounge, good breakfasts, very friendly owners.

Mountain Zebra National Park p397
Reservations through **SANParks**, T012-4289111, www.sanparks.org. See page 48 for details. For late bookings or cancellations within 72 hrs of arrival, phone the reception direct on T048-8812427.

B Doornhoek Guest House, a restored Victorian farmhouse built in 1836, registered as a national monument. The house sleeps up to 6 people in 2 cast-iron double beds and 2 single beds; all en suite. The house is decorated in a Victorian style, with pine floors, stained-glass windows, open fireplaces, fully equipped kitchen. To complete the feeling of isolated luxury, the house is set in its own valley.

D Cottages, these 19 self-catering cottages are rather more functional. Each has 2 bedrooms, a bathroom, living room and a partially equipped kitchen.

E Campsite, has 20 caravan and camping sites set amongst good shade trees. There is a communal wash block and kitchen facilities. A maximum of 6 people are allowed on each site. Some sites have power points.

Nieu Bethesda p397
D House Number One, 1 Cloete St, T049-8411700. Attractive old-style fully equipped self-catering house, 3 very comfortable spacious rooms sleeping 7 in total, with antique furnishings, polished wooden floors, 2 bathrooms, lounge with a full-size snooker table, kitchen, dining room, and veranda with braai. At R160 per person per nigh, it's good value for a group.
D-F Owl House Backpackers, Martin St, T049-8411642, www.owlhouse.info. Pleasant budget alternative with creatively decorated dorms and double rooms, cottage, camping, kitchen, bar and home-cooked meals. The friendly owners can organize tours to the Valley of Desolation and the Mountain Zebra National Park, and for a small fee they will pick you up and drop you off in Graaff-Reniet.

Graaff-Reinet p398, map p399
A Andries Stockenström Guest House, 100 Cradock St, T049-8924575, www.stockenstrom.co.za. This guesthouse was originally built in 1819 and has been restored and lavishly decorated. 6 en suite, a/c double rooms, swimming pool, and a superb dining room (residents only, closed Sun, ₩₩₩) serving an imaginative selection of haute cuisine Karoo meals including kudu, springbok, ostrich and guinea fowl with a French twist. The chef was trained at the **Ritz** in Paris.
A-B Drostdy Hotel, 30 Church St, T049-8922161, www.drostdy.co.za. Beautifully restored building designed by Louis Thibault in 1804. There are 51 rooms, all en suite and with a/c, the rooms at the back of the main house are in an appealing complex of 19th-century cottages known as **Stretch's Courts**, originally the homes of emancipated slaves. The public areas are decorated with antiques and paintings. The **Camdebo** and the **Court Room** restaurants have a good reputation

(see Eating, below). There's a secluded garden where you can have pre-dinner drinks, a pool and secure, off-street parking. Recommended.
B Villa Reinet, 83 Somerset St, T049-8925525, info@villareinet.co.za. A guesthouse set in an old church hall (national monument) with high ceilings and comfy furnishings. There are 2 a/c double rooms with en suite bathroom and large French doors leading onto a garden and splash pool, and 6 a/c garden cottages with hammocks. Breakfast is served in the cosy kitchen or under a pear tree in the garden.
C Camdeboo Cottages, 16 Parliament St, T049-8923180, www.camdeboocottages.co.za. A group of national monument 19th-century buildings which have been converted into 8 self-catering cottages built around a courtyard with a swimming pool and braai; meals available on request. Hot-water bottles provided in winter, coffee shop on the premises. Central.
C Cypress Cottages, 80 Donkin St, T049-8923965, www.cypresscottage.co.za. 2 whitewashed Karoo single-storey cottages, 3 en suite bedrooms in each, communal lounge and dining room full of antiques, large garden, good for families, B&B.
D-E Urquhart Caravan Park, at the edge of town next to the Camdeboo National Park, T049-8922136. Large park with clean, modern facilities for campers and caravans. There are a couple of chalets next to the Sundays River, some with kitchen, and very simple but excellent value rondavels, though you need to bring your own bedding and towels.

🍴 Eating

Cradock p396
Cradock has its fair share of chain restaurants. Alternatively, you can eat in the lovely dining room of the **Victoria Manor Hotel** (see page 401), part of the Die Tuishuise Guesthouse, to sample traditional Karoo cuisine.

Nieu Bethesda p397
₩ Die Waenhuis Pub & Grub, corner of Hudson and Martin streets, T049-8411627.

Mon-Thu 1100-1430, 1700-late, Fri-Sat 1100-late. Cosy pub with fireplace, stews and pies, hearty country cooking and big portions, large TV screen for important sports matches.

¶ **The Brewery and Two Goats Deli**, Pienaar St, T049-8411602. Open 1100-1500. Simple rustic café with wooden benches, known for its home-brewed beer and fresh goat's cheese, excellent ploughman's platters with pickles, cheese and cold meat, eat in or take away.

Graaff-Reinet p398, map p399

One of the best restaurants is at the **Andries Stockenström Guest House** (see Sleeping, page 401), but you have to staying there to eat.
¶¶¶ **Die Kliphuis**, 46 Bourke St, T049-0922345, kliphuis@elink.co.za. Daily for breakfast and dinner. One of Graaff-Reinet's most beautiful historical buildings (1857), serves dinners of Karoo lamb or springbok in a traditionally decorated dining room with a roaring fire. They grow their own vegetables and herbs. There are also 2 rooms here (**B**), with Victorian bathrooms, overlooking a Karoo garden with fruit trees and a pomegranate hedge.
¶¶¶ **Drostdy**, 28 Church St, T049-8922161. The historical **Drostdy Hotel** has 2 excellent, romantic and elegant restaurants. Beautiful setting with high ceilings, polished wooden floors and candle light. Great nightly buffets with a fine range of local Karoo dishes, the à la carte menu is much more expensive but superb. Need to dress up a bit or there is a light more casual menu in the garden.
¶¶ **Coral Tree**, 3 Church St, T049-8925947. Mon-Sat, closed for a couple of hrs each afternoon. Great location opposite the church. Very popular restaurant serving a good range of typical Karoo dishes – try the Karoo lamb or kudu steaks. Recommended.
¶¶ **Number 8**, 8 Church St, T049-8924464. Mon-Sat 12-late. Very popular pub and grill house in a Victorian building, good simple steaks, fish and chips, and more adventurous Mozambique prawns or Portuguese *espetadas*, TV showing sports, special kids' room with toys, busy local watering hole.

▲ Activities and tours

Nieu Bethesda p397
Tour operators
Ganora Excursions, T049-8411302, www.ganora.co.za. Excellent small operator that specializes in trips to view ancient San rock art, as well as walking trails and fossil walks on their farm 7 km from Nieu Bethesda towards Middleburg. They also rent out a large stone cottage that sleeps 6. Recommended.

Graaff-Reinet p398, map p399
Tour operators
Karoo Connections, 7 Church St, T049-8923978, www.karooconnections.co.za. Well-organized local tour operator offering a wide range of trips, including guided historical town walks, township tours, trips to San rock art, and Karoo farms. Also hires out mountain bikes.

⊖ Transport

Cradock p396
Bus
Intercape, T0861-287287, www.inter cape.co.za, and **Translux**, T0861-589282, www.translux.co.za. Cradock is on the **Nelson Mandela Bay–Johannesburg** route.

Train
Spoornet, T0860-00888, www.spoornet.co.za. Cradock is on the **Nelson Mandela Bay (Port Elizabeth)–Johannesburg** train route.

Graaff-Reinet p398, map p399
It's 251 km to **Nelson Mandela Bay (Port Elizabeth)**, 90 km to **Murraysburg**.

Bus
Intercape and **Translux** buses stop in Graaff-Reinet daily on the **Cape Town–Queenstown – East London** route. Buses stop at the Engen garage on Church St. **Bus companies** Intercape, T0861-287287, www.intercape.co.za; Translux, T0861-589282, www.translux.co.za.

Cape Midlands and East London

From King William's Town the N2 heads back to the coast and East London. To the north of the city is the mountainous region lying between Stutterheim and Fort Beaufort, which is a beautiful area of rolling hills, lush indigenous forests and waterfalls. These are the Amatola Mountains and the region is referred to as the Cape Midlands. Sadly, some areas have now been replaced with pine plantations. Nevertheless, there remains an abundance of unharmed forest, criss-crossed with trails and perfect for hiking. The principal centre of the region is the coastal city of East London. It's predominantly an industrial city, though useful for stocking up on provisions before travelling up the Wild Coast. ▸▸ *For listings, see pages 411-415.*

Ins and outs

Getting there From King William's Town to Queenstown there are two routes. The first follows the R63 west to Fort Beaufort and then heads north along the R67 to Queenstown. The second route heads north via Stutterheim and Cathcart via the N6. The Amatola Mountains can be reached from both sides. Further south the N2 runs through East London on its way to the Wild Coast. East London and Queenstown are connected by bus services running inland along the N6 from East London to Bloemfontein and Johannesburg. ▸▸ *For further details, see Transport, page 414.*

Best time to visit The mountains are at their best in spring or autumn; in winter it can get very cold and it is not unusual to have snow in May. Most of the rain tends to fall during the summer months. On the coast the climate is mild and sunny all year round.

Hogsback ●❷❸▲❹ ▸▸ *pp411-415. Colour map 7, A5.*

→ *Altitude: 1200 m.*

The quiet village of Hogsback lies in the centre of the Amatola Mountains, surrounded by rolling hills covered in forest reserves. The beautiful surroundings and slow pace of life make it a delightful spot to rest up for a few days and explore the forests. The village itself has no real centre, but is made up of a string of cottages, hotels, tea gardens and craft shops dotted along several kilometres of gravel road. Tucked away down the side lanes are some beautiful gardens, more reminiscent of rural England than inland Africa. Among the early settlers was Thomas Summerton, a market gardener from Oxford, and his attempts to recreate the English countryside can still be seen in apple orchards, avenues lined with hazelnut, berry fruits and the flowering plants that have spread throughout the area. It's one of the few places in South Africa where berries thrive: red, white and black currents, blackberries, raspberries, loganberries, strawberries and English gooseberries. As you can imagine the local people have gone into bottling overdrive and there are some delicious jams for sale in Hogsback's crafts shops. The Hogsback Spring Festival is held over two weekends in September when there's a craft market and many residents open their gardens to visitors.

Look out for **Oak Avenue**, an avenue of grand oak trees planted in the 1880s, which are still used for church services at Easter and Christmas when worshippers are seated on logs placed across the road. A new attraction in Hogsback is the labyrinth at **The Edge** (see Sleeping, page 411), which is an 11-circuit labyrinth, similar in design to the labyrinth at Chartres Cathedral in France. The total distance of the walk to the centre of the maze and

out is 1.4 km and the circumference is 91 m. There is a helpful **tourist office**
ⓘ *Stormhaven Crafts, Main Rd, T045-9621050, www.hogsbackinfo.co.za, Mon-Fri
1030-1230, 1500-1700, Sat 1030-1230.*

There are several theories as to how the area got its name. One is that a peak in the
Hogsback range resembles the back of a hog when viewed from a particular angle. The other
is that the founder was a Captain Hogg who had been based at Fort Mitchell. The Xhosa name
for the peaks is *Belekazana* (to carry on the back), as another view from a different angle
resembles a woman carrying a child on her back. Three peaks can be seen from the village,
Hog One (1836 m), **Hog Two** (1824 m) and **Hog Three** (1937 m). The highest peak in the
region lies to the north of Hogsback and is known as **Elandsberg** (2019 m).

Local hikes

The spectacular waterfalls are a highlight in the surrounding forests. The most popular falls
are known as Madonna and Child, Kettle Spout and the 39 Steps. The **Madonna and Child**
falls are a 30-minute walk from a car park on Wolfridge Road, 5 km from the village centre.
The easiest falls to visit are the **39 Steps**, which are 10 minutes' walk from the end of Oak
Avenue. Look out for a green pig with a red triangle. If you're staying at **Away with the
Fairies** (see Sleeping, page 411), there's a good one-hour walk to the **Swallowtail Falls**,
where you'll pass an impressive 'big tree' and see plenty of vervet monkeys and birdlife.

A short distance from the centre of the village is the church of **St Patrick on the Hill**.
The original chapel dates from 1935. Just beyond the church is a track off to the right,

Hogsback

Sleeping ⬤		Eating ❼
Arminel Mountain Lodge 1	Hogsback Inn & Spa 3	High-on-the-Hog 1
Away with the Fairies 2	King's Lodge 5	
	The Edge 6	

Gaika Road, which leads up to the viewpoint **Gaika Kop** (1963 m). The path is not very easy to follow – get a local map from one of the hotels before you set off.

Some of the finest views are from **Tor Doone** (1565 m), weather permitting. The easiest path follows the fire break at the end of Oak Avenue. Look out for markers with a yellow pig and a single green stripe; the contour path is marked with a green pig and yellow dot. Allow a minimum of two hours to get to the top.

Note that if you are here during the winter months the weather gets very cold at night. Even in summer, the nights are cold and a warm clear morning can quickly develop into low cloud and thunderstorms which may take a day or two to clear. If in doubt, check with local people who should be able to interpret the vagaries of the weather.

Queenstown → *Colour map 7, A5.*

Queenstown, the largest town in the Cape Midlands, was named after Queen Victoria. Like many settlements in the area, it only started to thrive once the Frontier Wars had ended. However, the central square in the town was designed with defence in mind. Known today as the Hexagon, the square has six main streets radiating off it like spokes on a wheel. The idea was that defenders would have a clear line of fire to the outskirts of town from the fortified central square. There are several fine buildings in and around the square including the town hall, court house and public offices and the Anglican church of St Michael. Many of the streets are lined with oaks and blue gums. The small **Frontier Museum** ⓘ *Mon-Fri 0800-1245, 1400-1600*, is devoted to the achievements of the early settlers and the Frontier Wars.

Witteberge Mountains ●❶❷❸ ⟩⟩ *pp411-415.*

The Witteberge Mountains are rather grandly known as the 'Switzerland of South Africa', forming part of the southernmost limits of the Drakensberg. It is the location of South Africa's only ski resort. The road heading into the Witteberge from Queenstown passes through the small towns of Elliot, Lady Grey and Rhodes.

Elliot → *Colour map 7, A6.*

This small mountain town is handily placed for visiting the 32-m-long gallery of Khoisan paintings on **Denorbin Farm**, on the road to Barkly East. It is literally at the bottom of the garden behind the farm house and the paintings are finely detailed, but are difficult to see at certain times of the day as the background rock is dark. Contact Denis Small, T045-9312232. **Thompson Dam** is a popular local picnic spot.

Barkly East → *Colour map 4, C4. Altitude: 1183 m.*

Barkly East is nestled among the southern Drakensberg foothills. It's very close to Tiffindell, South Africa's only ski resort (see below), and there are snowfalls on the mountains here most winters. This area attracts skiers in winter and fly fishermen in the summer. The small **Barkly East Musuem** ⓘ *White St, T045-9710724, Mon-Fri 0900-1200, 1500-1630, www.barklyeast.co.za*, has a collection of exhibits of the early settlement of the region, and displays on the Boer War. The museum also provides tourist information.

Rhodes → *Colour map 4, C5.*

Rhodes is a peaceful little mountain village overlooked by **Ben MacDhui** (3000 m), with a stone school house designed by Herbert Baker, a Victorian hotel, a general store and one pay phone. If you arrive here in winter bring lots of warm clothes – while electricity did arrive a few years ago, there is still no central heating, though hotels will provide electric blankets. The road from Barkly East to Rhodes is gravel, and although usually in good condition, drive with care as there are many hairpin bends. In heavy rains or snow it can become treacherous, so always phone hotels in Rhodes ahead to check on weather and road conditions. For information contact the **Rhodes Hotel** (see Sleeping, page 412). Mountain bikers arrive here every October to compete in the 87-km **Rhodes Mountain Challenge**.

Originally known as Rossville, the village was renamed by town leaders after the mining magnet and imperialist, Cecil John Rhodes, in the hope that he would make a substantial contribution to the town's finances. He obliged by donating a wagonload of pine trees that still decorate the streets, and £500 which promptly disappeared at the same time as the town clerk.

Tiffendell

Tiffendell is located on the slopes of the highest mountain in the Eastern Cape, the 3001-m Ben Mc Dhui on the border with Lesotho. The village is a one-hour drive from the ski resort at Tiffendell, the only ski resort in South Africa, but the skiing is not up to much compared to other places in the world and the main slope is only 650 m long. The drive to Tiffendell through some scenic mountain passes is only accessible to 4WD, though ask at the **Rhodes Hotel** (see Sleeping, page 412) about transfers. There is a ski lift, snow-making machines and ski hire. Depending on the snow the resort is usually open from the end of May to the beginning of September. The **Snow Festival** ① *T011-4654370, www.snow.co.za*, takes place in at the end of July when there are skiing and snowboarding races. For information contact. Accommodation is available at the resort, and three- and four-night packages are inclusive of bed, breakfast, ski and snowboard equipment hire and ski pass, as well as emergency medical assistance and resort entertainment. Instruction is also available for beginners. see Sleeping, page 412. The resort is also popular during the summer for fly fishing, mountain biking, horse riding, grass skiing and hiking, all of which can be arranged at the resort's reception the day before.

Lady Grey → Colour map 4, B4.

Lady Grey lies in a forested sandstone valley surrounded by the high peaks of the Witteberge, often covered with snow in winter. The town dam is used for picnics, swimming and trout fishing. Tourist information is available at the **Home Coffee Shop** ① *T051-6030176, www.ladygreytourism.co.za*. The **Karringmelkspruit Vulture Reserve** is 12 km south of Lady Grey on the road to Barkly East. Over 500 Cape vultures breed on the cliffs of this reserve.

Aliwal North → Colour map 4, B4.

Aliwal North, on the south bank of the Orange River, was founded by Sir Harry Smith, governor of the Cape, in 1849 and named after his victory over the Sikhs at Aliwal in India. The 'north' bit was added, as at one time Mossel Bay on the coast was to be named Aliwal South. It marks the border between the Eastern Cape and the Free State on the other side of the river. In the south of the town is a **Concentration Camp Memorial** commemorating the 715 Afrikaner people (mostly children) who died in terrible conditions in the camps set up by the British during the Boer War. The town is also known for its hot springs and the rather pungent waters are supposedly therapeutic for rheumatism and arthritis. They are presently housed in a faded 1960s resort to the east of town but, along with the adjoining **Buffelspruit Nature Reserve**, which has a limited number of game animals, these are not functioning as the local municipality is trying to sell them off to private investors for refurbishment.

◖ *Aliwal North is on the site of what was a strategic ford on the Orange River used by the Voortrekkers on their great trek north from the Cape. This was upgraded with a pontoon in 1872 and, much later, by a bridge.*

East London ◉◕◑◒▲◓◒◉ ➤ *pp411-415. Colour map 7, B6.*

East London is South Africa's only river port and a major industrial centre, with an economy based on motor assembly plants, textile and electronics industries. Nevertheless, the city centre has a handful of attractive historical buildings, and there are some good beaches which surprisingly get very busy with domestic tourists over Christmas. Nahoon Beach is best known for its excellent surfing, and the city has attracted a real surfing community in recent years. Despite this, it's not a very attractive city and most travellers only pass through on their way to other coastal resorts or to the Amatola Mountains.

Ins and outs

Getting there **East London Airport** is 11 km from the city centre, T043-7060306, www.airports.co.za. It's nowhere near as busy as the other regional airports (although it is a busy hub for the exportation of Eastern Cape pineapples). Check with all of South Africa's airlines as services to East London are routinely started up (and dropped again) depending on demand. **East London Bus Shuttles** ⓘ *T082-5693599 (mob), www.elbusshuttle.com*, operates an airport shuttle service to the centre of town. **East Coast Shuttle** ⓘ *T043-7403060*, operates from the airport to the resorts from Gonubie to Kobb Inn on the Wild Coast. The larger car hire companies have desks at the airport. The **train station** ⓘ *T043-7002129*, is on Station Street. There are bus services to most South African cities with **Greyhound**, **Intercape**, and **Translux**. The **Baz Bus** also stops here. ➤ *For further details, see Transport page 415.*

Tourist information The main tourist office covers the region from East London to King William's Town and is known as **Buffalo City Tourism** ⓘ *King's Entertainment Centre, Esplanade, T043-7226015, www.visitbuffalocity.co.za, Mon-Fri 0815-1630, Sat 0900-1400, Sun 0900-1300*. The main office of **Eastern Cape Tourism Board** ⓘ*T043-7019600, www.ectourism.co.za*, is also located here.

Background

East London was originally founded as a military camp on the banks of the Buffalo River in 1847 and its strategic position as a port was soon recognized. Sir Harry Smith, the British governor, ambitiously named it London, and its two main thoroughfares are still Fleet Street and Oxford Street. Later it was renamed the Port of East London, and then simply as East London – not after London's East End but because the port was on the eastern bank of the river.

Sights

The town centre is a modern, bustling place, but there are several historical monuments: the Colonial Division Memorial is in front of the City Hall; the German Settler Memorial is on the Esplanade; and there are War Memorials on Oxford Street.

The **Ann Bryant Art Gallery** ⓘ *St Marks Rd off Oxford St, T043-7224044, Mon-Fri 0900-1700, Sat 0930-1200, free,* is in an interesting Edwardian building dating from 1905. The collection was originally mostly of British artists but now has many fine contemporary South African works. An arts and crafts fair is held here on the first and second Sunday of each month.

The **East London Museum** ⓘ *Upper Oxford St, T043-7430686, Mon-Fri 0930-1700, Sat 1400-1700, Sun and public holidays 1100-1600, small entry fee, coffee shop,* has a surprisingly interesting range of natural history exhibits. The highlights of the museum include the world's only dodo egg, and the coelacanth that was trawled up off the Chalumna River in 1938. The coelacanth, known as the fossil fish, was thought to have been extinct for 80 million years until it was 'rediscovered' earlier this century (see box, page 410). The museum also has some good displays on Xhosa culture and customs, as well as a section devoted to Nguni beadwork.

East London

To ⑪ ①, Umtata, Durban, N2 & Beacon Bay
Buffalo Park (Cricket)
To ⑩ ⑩ & Nahoon Beach

To Ann Bryant Art Gallery, East London, Museum, Vincent & Nelson Mandela Bay (Port Elizabeth), N2

Indian Ocean

To West Bank Village

N

200 metres
200 yards

Sleeping 🛏
Blue Lagoon **1**
Esplanade **2**
Garden Court **3**
Kennaway **4**
Loerie Hide **10**

Niki-Nana Backpackers **7**
Premier King David **5**
Sugar Shack **9**

Eating 🍴
Al Mare **1**

Buccaneers **2**
Ernst's Chalet Suisse **3**
Le Petit **10**
Quarterdeck **8**
Strandloper Café **11**

Coelacanth – back from the dead

The discovery of a living coelacanth off the coast of East London in 1938 provided scientists with a link to prehistoric times. At first it was thought that they shared a common connection with lungfish and land vertebrates; on closer examination it became obvious that the fish had hardly changed since the Devonian period, 350 million years ago. It had been assumed that it had become extinct after some 290 million years. The fact that a living specimen was trawled from the deep destroyed this theory but the fish became known as a living fossil.

Named *Latimeria chalumnae*, this lobe-finned fish grows to about 1.5 m and can weigh 68 kg. It is bright blue and produces large quantities of oil and slime. Its four fins resemble legs and these have some rotating movement which allows them to crawl along the seabed. They have very powerful jaws.

More of these fish have been found near the Comoros Islands, to the north of the Mozambique Channel between Madagascar and mainland Africa. After all the excitement, it turned out that the Comores had been eating coelacanth for years. So much for coming back from the dead!

Also on Oxford Street, the **City Hall** dates from 1897, and the design of the clock on **Victoria Tower** was modelled after London's Big Ben. Inside, the marble staircase was constructed from marble directly imported from Carrar in Italy. Outside, is a monument to honour **Steven Bantu Biko**, which was unveiled by Nelson Mandela on 12 September 1997 to mark the 20th anniversary of his death while in police custody.

Gately House ⓘ *1 Park Gates Rd, T043-7222141, Mon, Wed-Fri 0930-1630, Sat 1100-1600, small entry fee*, was built in 1876 by John Gately, one of East London's first mayors. The house was donated to the city in 1966 and is now a town house museum decorated with original Victorian furnishings.

On the Esplanade is the **Aquarium** ⓘ *T043-7052637, 0900-1700, R25*. This is the oldest aquarium in the country with over 400 freshwater and marine species on display. There's a seal show twice daily at 1130 and 1530 and feeding times are half an hour before. There's also a whale deck with a telescope – a blue flag flies when whales are sighted.

The **Lock Street Gaol Shopping Complex** is on Fleet Street. Built in the 1800s, this was South Africa's first women's jail, whose most famous inmates were Winnie Madikizela-Mandela (ex-wife of Nelson Mandela) and Daisy de Melker, who was accused of poisoning two husbands and a son. The original gallows can still be seen. It now houses shops and offices; check out the African curios shop for a good selection of items to take home.

West Bank Village

West Bank Village is the oldest surviving area of East London with some interesting old buildings on Bank Street and near the entrance to the harbour. **Hood Point Lighthouse** ⓘ *T043-7003056, Mon, Wed, Fri 1400-1600, Sat 0900-1100, small entry fee*, was built in 1895 and is a typical Victorian lighthouse with a steel upper gallery and keyhole windows. **Fort Glamorgan** is a vaulted brick building on Bank Street, closed to the general public though devotees of Victorian military architecture can get permission to visit the fort through Major Du Toit, T043-7311610. The fort was built in 1847 during the Seventh Frontier War to defend the supplies that were being sent to the inland garrisons from the Buffalo River Mouth.

Hotel and guesthouse prices
L over US$300 AL US$220-300 A US$150-220
B US$100-150 C US$75-100 D US$35-75
E US$15-35 F under US$15
Restaurant prices
₹₹₹ over US$30 ₹₹ US$15-30 ₹ under US$15
See pages 46-51 for further information.

Sleeping

Hogsback *p404, map p405*
In addition to the options listed below there are more than 20 different self-catering establishments. If you plan to hike in the region, these may be more convenient than staying in a lodge or hotel where meal times are fixed. Contact the local tourist office for further details. Be sure to book ahead during local school holidays.

B-C Arminel Mountain Lodge, Main Rd, T045-9621005, www.arminelhogsback.co.za. 23 log cabins with en suite facilities, excellent restaurant serving meals based on local fresh produce. Room rates include breakfast and evening meals. Extensive gardens with great mountain views, swimming pool, tennis. The management is very friendly and keen to further promote this beautiful area which few overseas travellers visit. Recommended.

B-C Hogsback Inn & Spa, Main Rd, T045 9621006, www.hogsbackinn.co.za. Old-fashioned rural retreat with 28 comfortable (if chintzy) rooms and 2 self-catering family cabins. There is a good restaurant and a cosy, traditional pub, swimming pool, tennis court and spa facilities such as jacuzzi, massage and hairdresser, all set in 7 ha of grounds with the Tyume River flowing through. Log fires greatly add to the ambience. Very friendly and a good place to meet local folk.

C-D The Edge, off Woodside Rd, T045-9621159, www.theedge-hogsback.co.za. 12 self-catering rondavels and 4 B&B rooms with log fires and feather duvets in a stunning setting perched on a cliff with spectacular views, surrounded by waterfalls and meadows filled with mushrooms and butterflies. If not staying, visit the **Tea Thyme** tea room to enjoy home-made goodies and the mountain views. Recommended.

D King's Lodge, Main Rd, T045-9621024, www.kingslodge.co.za. 22 rooms with en suite bathroom, popular restaurant and bar for light meals or opt for the excellent 4-course table d'hôte dinners, fine wood-panelled lounge and reception area. Large garden with a swimming pool and tennis court. Self-catering rooms available in the garden sleeping 2-6.

D-F Away with the Fairies, Ambleside Close, T045-9621031, www.awaywiththe fairies.co.za. A friendly, relaxed and well-run place, with well-kept, brightly painted dorms, en suite double rooms, well-equipped kitchen, clean bathrooms and cosy lounge with fireplace. The rooms are named after characters in *Lord of the Rings*. The surrounding gardens are beautiful and a nesting ground for the Cape parrot – of which there are only 300 left in the wild – with plenty of camping space and a gate that leads to forest trails. There's a lively bar, great breakfasts and evening meals, daily guided walks and sun-downer trips, regular shuttles to East London and Chintsa most days of the week, which get to East London in time to hook up with buses. Everyone feels very welcome and there's always plenty to do from rock climbing to mountain biking. Recommended.

Queenstown *p406*
C Carthews Corner, 1 Park Av, Blue Rise (a suburb above the railway line), T/F045-8381885. Very smart B&B, with 8 rooms in garden cottages, swimming pool, secure parking, braai facilities, ask for Linda or Bridget.

D Hazelmere Country Lodge, off the N6, 57 km towards Aliwal North, 4 km south of the Penhoek Pass, T045-9669622. Comfortable B&B en suite rooms in a farmhouse on a sheep farm, lounge with TV, dinner (but needs to be prearranged), tennis court, swimming pool and croquet lawn.

Witteberge Mountains *p406*
B-D Tiffindell Ski Resort, T045-9749004/5, www.snow.co.za. 180 guests are accommodated in centrally heated rooms within 100 m of the ski slope and the main restaurant and bar. There is a choice of private chalets, en suite rooms, budget rooms with shared ablution facilities, or luxury self-catering accommodation in wooden cabins sleeping 6. Packages include all meals and skiing in winter.

C Mountain View Country Inn, 36 Botha St, Lady Grey, T051-6030421, www.lady grey.co.za. A pleasant rural retreat in a Victorian building with a lovely view over the town towards the mountains. 12 family and double rooms with en suite bathroom, nicely decorated with antiques, excellent home-made food, especially the scones and marmalade, and friendly pub to meet the locals.

C Rhodes Hotel, corner of Miller and Sauer streets, Rhodes, T045-9749305, www.rhodes village.co.za/hotel.htm. Charming old-style hotel restored to resemble the original hotel of more than a century ago, 9 en suite rooms with antiques and electric blankets, rates include breakfast and dinner in the **Partridge Pot** restaurant and pub, good home cooking, tennis court, local tours, fly-fishing and horse riding organized.

C Siskin's B&B, 43 Graham St, Barkly East, T045-9749900. A rambling old home with wood floors, high ceilings, fireplace, rooms with shared bathroom in the house or 2 en suite rooms in a restored outbuilding, TV lounge, good food as owner is a cordon bleu chef, rates include dinner. Also offers self-catering accommodation in a nearby farmhouse and cottage.

C Umtali Country Inn, 47 Dan Pienaar Av, Aliwal North, T/F051-6332400. Smart lodge with 33 newly renovated rooms with a/c, underfloor heating and DSTV, lovely swimming pool, generous meals served in the restaurant with fireplace.

C Walkerbouts Inn, 1 Vorster St, Rhodes, T045-9749290, www.walkerbouts.co.za.

6 comfortable and spacious en suite rooms with electric blankets, B&B, cosy pub with the only satellite TV in the village, 2 pizza ovens and local beer on tap. Can organize trout fishing.

East London *p408, map p408*
There is not a great deal of interesting accommodation in East London and most is in old beachside block hotels. The majority of backpackers staying in East London are here for the surf. Others tend to move on to the far nicer Chintsa, 38 km up the coast.

A-B Premier King David Hotel, 27 Inverleith Terr, T043-7223174, www.premierhotels.co.za. Comfortable city-centre option aimed at business travellers. 80 rooms, some more luxurious and thus more expensive, DSTV. **Motombo** restaurant serves table d'hôte dishes and a good-value Sun carvery lunch, also **East London** restaurant for coffee and light lunches, 3 bars, secure covered parking.

B Blue Lagoon, Blue Bend Place, Beacon Bay, T043-7484821, www.bluelagoonhotel.co.za. 76 en suite rooms in what used be a time-share resort on the Beacon Bay headland overlooking the sea and estuary with stunning views. Some 2-bedroom apartments and 3-bedroom townhouses with kitchenette and lounge set in large grounds full of palms, 2 restaurants and bars, swimming pool, squash and tennis courts.

B Kennaway Hotel, Esplanade, T043-7225531, www.kennawayhotel.co.za. A large, modern block overlooking Orient Beach, with 103 rooms, non-smoking room available, restaurants, bar, lounge, a bit impersonal and avoid if there's a conference on but fine ocean views.

C Esplanade, 6 Clifford St, Beachfront, T043-7222518, www.eastlondonsa.com/hotels/esplanade. 74 rooms, family holiday-style hotel, dated building, but completely refurbished inside, standard facilities but a little dull though in a good location with undercover parking.

C Garden Court, corner of Esplanade and Moore streets, T043-7227260, www.southern

sun.com. This was a **Holiday Inn** which has been rebranded. Modern block set back from the beach, 173 standard a/c rooms, with balcony, some have views of the beach, restaurant, bar, swimming pool, curio shop, secure parking, on the seafront.

C Loerie Hide, 2b Sheerness Rd, Bonnie Doon, T043-7353206, www.loeriehide.co.za. B&B (1 room) in the main house with antique bathroom, and 3 thatched cottages for 2 with fridge, TV, and a safari look complete with leopard-skin bedspread, tucked away in a beautiful garden, . The grounds border the Nahoon riverine forest, swimming pool, close to the beaches, a short drive from city centre.

E-F Niki-Nana Backpackers, 4 lillview Rd, T043-7228509, www.nikinana.co.za. Friendly set-up with dorms and doubles and camping in the garden, swimming pool, bar, internet, spacious self-catering kitchen, the whole place is decorated in a zebra theme, including the roof which is painted with unmissable zebra stripes. The Baz Bus stops here.

E-F Sugar Shack, Esplanade Rd, Eastern Beach, T043-7228240, www.sugarshack.co.za. The best backpacker place in East London in a lively location by the beach. Always popular and parties most nights. Dorms, double rooms, some en suite, well-stocked kitchen, free town pickup, free surf and boogie boards, 20 m away from a whale- and dolphin-watching tower, good value daily adrenaline-fuelled activities organized. Ideal location with a number of local pubs and clubs in walking distance. Recommended. Baz Bus stop.

❼ Eating

Hogsback *p404, map p405*
The main hotels include dinner in their room rate, so there is not much of a choice for eating out at night. If staying at a guesthouse, check if evening meals are available.

High-on-the-Hog, Main Rd. The only local restaurant, with good nightly specials. Great soups (don't miss the creamed butternut), steaks and pasta dishes, and friendly bar.

Kings Lodge, Main Rd. Simple pub serving hearty lunch and dinner, focus on steaks and burgers, and 4-course table d'hôte dinners, which must be pre-booked, popular local drinking hole.

Tea Thyme, at the Edge off Woodside Rd, T045-9621159. Informal tea garden with stunning views, serving breakfasts, light lunches, home-made cakes and scones with fresh farm cream. On cold days offers hot chocolate and gluhwein inside in front of the fire.

Queenstown *p406*
The usual chain restaurants are in the **Pick 'n' Mall** on Cathcart St, near the tourist office.

East London *p408, map p408*
East London has a fair smattering of good places to eat and, thanks to the youthful edge the surfers bring to town, many places double up as restaurants during the early evening and then bars, some with live music, as the night wears on.

Ernst's Chalet Suisse, Orient Beach, T043-7221840. Mon-Fri 1200-1430, 1800-2300, Sat dinner only, Sun lunch only. Probably the best food in town, friendly and efficient service in a 30-year-old East London institution. Local fish and traditional Swiss dishes available, daytime views of the pier and harbour at Orient Beach, romantic night-time dining overlooking a floodlit tropical garden, good-value Sun lunch buffet

Le Petit, 54 Beach Rd, Nahoon, T043-7353685. Mon-Fri 1200-1430, 1800-2230, Sat 1800-2230. A formal Swiss-themed restaurant, with Swiss and French dishes, pub lunches including ostrich and crocodile (and frogs' legs). À la carte or good-value 3-course set menu. It's fun watching the chef prepare flambé dishes.

Al Mare, at the aquarium complex, T043-7220287. Mon-Sat 1200-1500, 1800-late. New spot that has already gained a good reputation, modern decor and good ocean views, daily specials, Mediterranean-influenced dishes, pizza and pasta. For dieters, there are calorie-controlled 'skinny' options.

Buccaneers, Eastern Beach, Esplanade,
T043-7435171, www.buccaneers.co.za.
1100-late. Popular pub and grill house serving
steaks, seafood and salads, the mood at lunchtime is more business-orientated then it gets
very lively at night with live music on 2 stages,
inside and out, and a thumping bar. Very
popular venue for surfers and backpackers,
on the beach close to the **Sugar Shack**.

Quarterdeck, Orient Pavilion, Esplanade,
T043-7431840. Mon-Fri 1200-1430, 1800-2300,
Sat 1800-2300. A busy seafood dining room
and bar with German beer on tap and live music
Wed, Fri and Sat. Shares a kitchen with the
more upmarket **Ernst Chalet Suisse**. Great if
you're on a tight budget but want to eat well.

Strandloper Café, 95 Old Transkei Rd,
T043-7354570. Mon-Sat 1830 for dinner.
A small, quiet and unremarkable restaurant
serving surprisingly good seafood such as
imported New Zealand green-lipped mussels
and Norwegian salmon. This is the place to
go for seasonal oysters and crayfish.

⊙ Shopping

Hogsback *p404, map p405*
There is a supermarket, a bottle store and a
petrol station in town (but no banks). Otherwise, there are several craft shops which sell
gifts as well as delicious locally made jams.
When you first arrive in the village you are
likely to be greeted by local Xhosas selling
their crafts. Look out for the clay animals: kudu,
horses and hogs are the most common. These
items are not found elsewhere in South Africa.

East London *p408, map p408*
Vincent Park Centre, Devreux Av, 5 km from
the city centre, follow Oxford St and turn right
onto Devreux Av just after the museum. This
is a modern South African shopping mall where
you will find a full complement of shops, plus
banks, post office, multi-screen cinema
showing the latest blockbuster releases, and
restaurants. It holds an arts and crafts market
every Sun 0900-1300.

▲ Activities and tours

Hogsback *p404, map p405*
Trout fishing is popular in the dams and rivers
belonging to the Wild Trout Association, 50
farmers in the region who allow access to their
land for fishing. Fly fishing can be arranged
through a day-permit system run from **Walkerbouts Inn**, T045-9749290, www.wildtrout.co.za.

East London *p408, map p408*
Cricket
The East London cricket ground, **Buffalo Park**,
is South Africa's newest international venue.
It is a short distance from the beach and is the
smallest of the current Test match grounds in
the country, with a capacity of 28,000. Ticket
enquiries T043-7437757, ticket sales through
Computicket, www.computicket.com.

Surfing
The best-known surf break is **Nahoon Reef**,
with a reputation for having the most
consistent break in the country. **Easterns**, in
front of the Sugar Shack backpackers, is the
most consistent beach break in the area, with
regular tubes. The best surf information is to
be found at the Sugar Shack and the other
backpacker hostels, most of which will hire
out surfboards and offer lessons to beginners.

Tour operators
Imonti Tours, T043-7413884, www.imon
titours.co.za. Half-day city and township tours.
Can also arrange tours to the Nelson Mandela
Museum at Qunu, up the N2 (see page 423).

⊖ Transport

Queenstown *p406*
Bus
Buses depart from Shell Ultra City on Cathcart
St. Queenstown is on the **Johannesburg–
East London** route. **Bus companies**
Greyhound, T0861-287287, www.grey
hound.co.za. **Translux**, T0861-589282,
www.translux.co.za.

Train
Spoornet, T0860-008888, www.spoornet. co.za. Queenstown is on the **Johannesburg–East London** route, daily except Wed and Sat. For timetables and fares see the website.

Witteberge Mountains *p406*
Bus
Buses depart from Balmoral Hotel on Somerset St in **Aliwal North**. Contact details for **Greyhound**, and **Translux**, same as for Queenstown, above. Aliwal North is on the **Johannesburg–East London** route.

East London *p408 map p408*
From East London it is 584 km to **Bloemfontein**, 1099 km to **Cape Town**, 674 km to **Durban**, 395 km to **Graaff-Reinet**, 1002 km to **Johannesburg**, 310 km to **Nelson Mandela Bay (PE)**, 207 km to **Queenstown**, 235 km to **Mthatha**.

Air
One Time flies daily between East London and **Johannesburg** (1 hr 45 mins) and **Cape Town** (1 hr 35 mins). **SAA** flies daily between East London and **Durban** (1 hr 10 mins), **Johannesburg** (1 hr 45 mins), **Nelson Mandela Bay (PE)** (50 mins), and **Cape Town** (1 hr 35 mins).

Airline offices One Time, T0861-345345, www.1time.aero; SAA, reservations, T011-9781111, ww3.flysaa.com.

Bus
Baz Bus runs a hop-on, hop-off service for backpackers between **Nelson Mandela Bay (PE)** and **Durban** 5 days a week. The bus will collect and drop off at any of the local backpacker hostels. From Nelson Mandela Bay (PE) it arrives around 1100-1130 and from Durban around 1800-1830.

All the long-distance buses depart from Windmill Park on Moore St. **Greyhound** and **Translux** both have services to **Durban** (9 hrs) daily via **Mthatha**, **Kokstad** and **Port Shepstone**, to **Cape Town** (14 hrs) daily via **Nelson Mandela Bay (PE)** and **Knysna**; and

to **Johannesburg** and **Pretoria** (14½ hrs) daily via **Bloemfontein** (7 hrs). **Intercape** has a service to **Cape Town** (14 hrs) via **Nelson Mandela Bay (PE)** (4 hrs). There is no direct service to **Johannesburg/Pretoria** but you can change buses in Nelson Mandela Bay (PE).

Bus companies Baz Bus, T021-4392323, www.bazbus.com; **Greyhound**, T043-7439284, www.greyhound.co.za; **Translux**, T043-7437893, www.translux.co.za; **Intercape**, T0861-287287, www.intercape.co.za.

Car hire
Avis, airport T043-7361344, toll free T0861-021111, www.avis.co.za. **Budget**, airport T043-7362364, toll free T0861-016622, www.budget.co.za. **Hertz**, 165 Jan Smuts Av, Greenfields, T043-7025700, toll free T0861-600136, www.hertz.com. **Imperial**, airport T043-7362230, toll free T0861 131000, www.imperialcarrental.co.za.

Taxi
Border Taxi, T043-7223946.

Train
The railway station is in the town centre on Station St, which runs parallel to Oxford St. Information T043-7002719, reservations T0860-008888, www.spoornet.co.za. There are services between East London and **Johannesburg** (20 hrs), via **Queenstown** (4½ hrs) and **Bloemfontein** (13 hrs). Fares and schedules are published on the website.

❻ Directory

East London *p408, map p408*
Banks Branches of **Standard Bank**, **First National** and **ABSA** have ATMs and exchange facilities along Oxford St and in the shopping malls. On the Wild Coast there are no banks in small resort towns. **Internet** There are a few spots around town or try **Cyber Lounge**, 58 Beach Rd, **Nahoon** or the backpacker hostels. **Medical services** East London Private Hospital, 32 Albany St, T043-7223128.

Wild Coast

The coastline region that stretches roughly 280 km from East London to the Umtamvuna Nature Reserve next to Port Edward in KwaZulu Natal was once the former Transkei independent homeland during the Apartheid years. These days it is known as the Wild Coast and is a largely rural area of rolling grasslands wedged between the Great Kei River in the south and the Umtamvuna River in the north. Its inland borders are the Drakensberg and the Stormberg mountains, and dotted between are small villages, brightly painted kraals and endless communal pastureland. It remains a traditional area populated by the Xhosa, who still practise customs such as dowry payments and initiation ceremonies. The Great Kei River was originally the border between South Africa and the Transkei and, as the N2 crosses the Kei River 65 km north of East London, the difference in the standard of living between the two areas is striking. Years of overpopulation and under-investment have taken their toll in the former Transkei. The landscape is deforested and seriously eroded and, away from the N2, the roads are in poor condition compared to the rest of the country. There are few tourist amenities here and you will get a more realistic picture of the poverty that still blights South Africa. Nevertheless it is a beautiful region and the coastline itself is rugged and peaceful, with a number of caves, beaches, cliffs and shipwrecks to explore. ▸▸ *For listings, see pages 425-429.*

Ins and outs

Getting there and around The N2, the Wild Coast's main road, is well surfaced. However, it doesn't run along the coast but rather from East London up to 100 km inland until it meets the coast again at Port Shepstone in KwaZulu Natal, from where it heads north to Durban. The towns along the N2 have thriving economies based around transport. There are abundant petrol stations, basic supermarkets and one or two small hotels, but these are mainly for commercial clientele so there are very few frills. Consequently the towns along the N2 are utilitarian and scruffy and always thronged with traffic. The long-distance buses stick to the N2, and the **Baz Bus** only deviates to Port St Johns. The coast itself is the area's main attraction and there is a fine selection of isolated seaside accommodation between East London and Port St Johns. A number of roads lead from the N2 to the coastal resorts, often by way of ramshackle villages, and although there has been a lot of road resurfacing going on in the Eastern Cape in the last few years, many of these are gravel. If driving, it is always a good idea to check on the latest state of the road, as the region is prone to seasonal flooding. **Note** Before heading for the coast from the N2, remember to stock up on petrol, food, cash and everything you think you will need – the nearest shop or bank could be 100 km away.

Tourist information Arriving at a resort without a reservation is not a good idea as they are often at the end of long and difficult roads. Remember most resorts are fully booked during the holiday season. All towns along the N2 have public telephones, so even with a last-minute decision it is possible to phone ahead and to check on the condition of the road. For more information visit www.wildcoast.org.za.

Wild Coast Holiday Reservations ① *T043-7436181, www.wildcoastholidays.co.za*, is an excellent central reservations service that can provide advice on accommodation. This can be very useful when trying to find out about some of the more remote hotels. An excellent way of seeing the most inaccessible areas of the Wild Coast is by doing a tour of the rural regions. ▸▸ *For further details, see Activities and tours, page 429.*

The Wild Coast

To Durban

Port Shepstone
Oribi Gorge Nature Reserve
To Ixopo & Pietermaritzburg

R56

Franklin
To Underberg & Sani Pass (Lesotho)

Harding
Mount Currie Nature Reserve

KWAZULU NATAL

Mtamvuna

N2

Port Edward

Kokstad

Brooks Nek
Bizana

R61

Amadiba Trails

Magusheni

Mkambati Nature Reserve

Mzimvubu

Mt Ayliff

Mzimhlava

Port Grosvenor
Grosvenor 1782

Flagstaff

To Qacha's Neck & Lesotho

Mt Frere

Embotyi

R61

Lusikisiki

Tina

Tsitsa

Qumbu

Mzimvubu

Port St Johns
Silaka Nature Reserve

R390

Tsolo

R61

Libode

Inxu

Hluleka Nature Reserve

Mtata Dam

Mthatha

Coffee Bay
Hole in the Wall

Viedgesville

Mtuvi

Dick King Memorial

Santo Alberto 1593

Mqanduli

Qunu

Ngqungqu

Coghlan

R61

Elliotdale

Alderley

Mbashe River Mouth

Engcobo

R393

Xuka

N2

Mbashe

Idutywa

Frontier III 1939

Willowvale

Qhorha Mouth
Mazeppa Bay

R364

Nxaxo Mouth
Jacaranda 1971
Qholorha Mouth

Tsomo

Butterworth

Kentani

R366

Kei Mouth
Strandloper Trail
Morgan's Bay

Cofimvaba
To Queenstown & Bloemfontein (N6)

Great Kei

Haga-Haga

Tsomo

R61

Komga

R349

Nyara Forest

Mooiplaas

Cefane Mouth

R63

Inkwenkwezi Game Reserve

Chintsa

20 km
20 miles

To Bisho (R63)

To East London

The coast immediately to the north of East London has been named the 'Romantic Coast' by the local tourist board, and its relative wildness makes the statement ring true. Although the coast is being developed for tourism there are still considerable stretches of the coastline which are protected nature reserves. There are thick dune forests and windswept open beaches stretching to wild waves. The coastal resorts nearest to East London can get crowded during the South African school holidays, but for the rest of the year it is quite surprising how isolated and quiet this coast really is. **Note** Do not drive through the former Transkei (roughly East London to Port Shepstone) after nightfall. Some of the roads are rough and even on the N2 there is the danger of hitting a stray animal.

Ins and outs

Getting around The resorts of Gonubie, Chintsa, Haga-Haga, Morgan's Bay and Kei Mouth are all within an hour's drive of East London. Public transport to these resorts is virtually non-existent, but as the hoteliers on the coast regularly visit East London to collect supplies, you can often get a lift to the coast by telephoning ahead. The **East Coast Shuttle** ① *T043-7403060*, runs a service from East London to the coastal resorts as far as Kobb Inn but requires a minimum of six passengers.

Gonubie → *Colour map 7, B6.*

This tourist resort overlooks the Qunube (Gonubie) River and the lagoon. It is only 20 km northeast of East London and 8 km off the N2 and has become a popular suburb with commuters. The beach here has large dunes, is safe for swimming in the sea and in the tidal pool, and it's possible to spot dolphins and whales from the 500 m boardwalk overlooking the beach. For information contact **Buffalo City Tourism** in East London, see page 408.

Kwelera Nature Reserve lies 10 km to the north of Gonubie and is an area of sand dunes and dune forest facing the sea. The highest dune here rises just over 250 m above sea level. The forests are inhabited by vervet monkeys, bushbuck and numerous forest birds. There is a small picnic site which is popular with local visitors who come here to fish and surf. This nature reserve is part of the Strandloper Trail, see page 419.

Inkwenkwezi Game Reserve

① *T043-7343234, www.inkwenkwezi.com, 33 km from East London. Take the N2 towards Mthatha and after 25 km out of East London, turn right at the Inkwenkwezi/Chintsa signpost, the reserve is 8 km on the right.*

This private 100-sq-km coastal game reserve has a combination of forest dunes and bushveld, and is home to an impressive range of imported game, including rhino, elephant, lion, wildebeest, giraffe, warthog, Eastern Cape kudu and an abundance of birdlife. The best time of year for spotting birds is from September to November; the wild flowers are best from August to September. Visitors leave their cars at the entrance and are transported around the reserve by 4WD. A range of trips can be organized, including night drives, horse riding and walking trails. Day visitors can expect to pay around R500 for a four-hour game drive with lunch, and R600 for a four-hour night drive with dinner. Meals are served in a restaurant with a terrace overlooking the reserve and accommodation is available (see Sleeping, page 425).

Strandloper Trail

The term Strandloper derives from the Dutch *strand*, meaning beach, and *loper*, meaning walker. This is a popular five-day, 55-km hike along the coast from Kei Mouth to Gonubie, overnighting in huts. It's an ideal walk for anyone looking for a peaceful but energetic few days along the coast and the trail passes through Kwelera Nature Reserve so there is a good chance of seeing some wildlife.

The trail runs in one direction and starts at the manager's station at Cape Morgan at Kei Mouth where you are issued with a permit. The trail is clearly marked with painted yellow footprints and can be walked at any time of year, though the best weather is between February and May, which have warm windless days. Hikers are issued with a tide table to assist in crossing the Quko, Kwenxura, Kwelera and Gonubie rivers.

You need to take strong watertight bags and rope in your pack.

The four huts along the trail; Beacon Valley, Cape Henderson, Pumphouse and Double Mouth, have water and ablution facilities. All have braai places except at Cape Henderson which is in a state forest and no fires are permitted. Take all necessary equipment. The huts are included in the cost of the trail, but there is the option to upgrade and stay in resorts at Morgan's Bay and Haga-Haga, or at the backpacker hostel in Chintsa.

The trail is limited to 12 people and the cost is R400 per person. It is managed by the **Strandloper Ecotourism Board**, T043 8411046, www.strandloper trails.org.za, and bookings can be made online. There are several other hikes along the Wild Coast; visit www.wildcoast.org.za for more information.

Chintsa → *Colour map 7, B6.*

The combined villages of Chintsa East and Chintsa West nestle on lush hills rolling down to a lagoon and a wide stretch of deserted beach. (It takes about 10 minutes to walk from Chintsa West to Chintsa East along the beach, but nearly 30 minutes to drive between them around the lagoon.) Although popular during the Christmas holidays, the resort is blessedly isolated for the rest of the year and offers relaxing outdoor activities such as canoeing and horse riding, though the main appeal here is lazily exploring the shell-strewn beach, forests and tranquil lagoon. Construction of the large Chintsa River Golfing Estate on the west bank is underway and the project is to include an 18-hole golf course, 650 holiday/time-share homes and a large hotel. Time will tell how it will change the face of this peaceful coastal settlement.

Haga-Haga → *Colour map 7, A6.*

Further along the coast lies this tiny seaside resort, 72 km from East London and 27 km from the N2. The road travels through fields of pineapples. There are two theories on how it got its name. One is that it is derived from the sound the waves make as they wash the shoreline. The other is that the village was started in the early 1920s when farmers from the hinterland would bring their livestock here for winter grazing, the smaller animals by ox wagon. To cross the beach they would unspan one team of oxen and hook them onto the other team, hence the word *haka haka* which is isiXhosa for 'hook on'. The rocky coastline, good beaches and lagoon to swim in make it ideal for hiking and fishing and, with only one shop and a hotel, this is a peaceful spot to spend a few days and lose track of time.

Morgan's Bay → *Colour map 7, A6.*

This is a perfect resort 90 km from East London for a peaceful beach break and a taste of the Wild Coast. The village itself is tiny and somewhat isolated and has little more than a hotel with pub and restaurant, the local store, a bottle shop, a couple of curio shops and a petrol pump. The surrounding countryside is a nature reserve and is a great place for hiking along the cliffs or strolling along the miles of white sandy beach where deep currents wash up unusual shells. The bay is regarded as one of the most beautiful in the country. Called Double Mouth, it consists of a lagoon formed by two small rivers backed by a line of sandstone cliffs. The beach with a lighthouse here was voted in the top 10 beach walks of South Africa by the South African outdoor magazine *Getaway*.

Kei Mouth → *Colour map 7, A6.*

This quiet seaside resort has a couple of supermarkets, some curio shops, a butcher, two bottle stores and a petrol station. Nearby are some municipal tennis courts and a golf course. There was one hotel here, but it is currently closed for renovation as a timeshare resort.

The **Kei River** used to be the border between the two former homelands of Ciskei and Transkei, now all part of the Eastern Cape. The river is navigable upstream for a short distance by boat or canoe, although sandbanks make it difficult at times. A popular river trip is to **Picnic Rock**, about 8 km upstream. The journey passes a private game reserve where it is possible to spot game. The cliffs around **Cob Hole** on the eastern side of the river are quite dramatic and the patches of forest further on are rich in birdlife. There is a spot on the eastern bank of the river with a small creek and a landing stage. The path from here climbs up a riverbed through forest and at the end of the trail is a deep pool with two waterfalls where you can swim – this is Picnic Rock.

North from Kei Mouth ⬤ ⏭ *pp425-429.*

There are two possible routes leading on from Kei Mouth. The Pont is a **car ferry** ① *0630-1730, R30 per car*, which crosses the Kei River. After crossing on the Pont, the R366 heads uphill for 9 km where it joins the R48/1 at Kentani. The road then divides, heading inland to Butterworth or seawards to Qholorha Mouth. All these roads have been tarred and are in excellent condition.

Kentani

Kentani itself is a tiny settlement but it has a huge history. It was the site of the final battle of the Frontier Wars between the Xhosa and the settlers in 1878. The Xhosa warriors had been told by their witchdoctor that he had made them impervious to bullets. Therefore they stormed a fort of colonial troops but were mown down by heavy fire. Three hundred warriors died, with a loss of only two of the English forces.

Butterworth → *Colour map 7, A6.*

This is the first town that the N2 passes on its way through the old Transkei. It is a hectic and unappealing stretch of supermarkets and discount stores, and has little to keep you there for long. Founded as a Wesleyan mission station in 1827, it is the oldest town in the Transkei, although little of its history is evident today. At the end of the Frontier Wars in 1878, traders began to settle here and the town has grown to become a small industrial centre. Just outside of town, there is one attraction worth stopping for: the **Bawa Falls** on the Qholorha River are spectacular after the rains when the water drops over 100 m. From Butterworth, the N2 continues north to Mthatha, 135 km.

Qholorha Mouth → *Colour map 7, A6.*

Qholorha Mouth has a private airstrip and is accessible by light aircraft. The alternative is to travel the 16 km from the *Pont* over the Kei River or come directly from Butterworth. There are two holiday resorts here on a beautiful stretch of headland overlooking a spacious beach and the Qholorha Lagoon where the Qholorha River widens before spilling into the sea. There is a hike up the **Gxara River Heads**, 4 km inland, to the pool where Nongqawuse, a young Xhosa girl, saw visions and communed with her ancestral spirits. She heard voices telling her that the dead would rise and destroy the European invaders if the Xhosa destroyed all their cattle and crops. This disastrous prophesy lead to the deaths of thousands of people through starvation, and Nongqawuse had to spend the rest of her life in hiding. She is buried on a farm near Alexandria.

Nxaxo Mouth → *Colour map 1, C5.*

The road heading north from Kentani goes to Nxaxo Mouth, which lies at the confluence of the Nxaxo and Nqusi rivers. The area has a lagoon and is dotted with swamps and islands. The estuary is rich in birdlife and there are hiking trails through a small strip of coastal forest to a colony of crowned cranes. Listen for the distinctive calls of groups of trumpeter hornbills which inhabit the forest.

Mazeppa Bay → *Colour map 4, C5.*

This small holiday resort is named after the *Mazeppa*, a coastal trading ship that ran aground here in 1842 on its way from Port Natal. There is a suspension footbridge to the island from where you can see Clan Lindsay Rocks, the site where the *Clan Lindsay* was wrecked in 1898. **First Beach** is good for swimming, and the waves on this stretch of coast attract local surfers. Just back from the beach are the shell middens left by strandlopers. August is a busy month when many people come here for the shark fishing. The nearby **Manubi Forest** has 7 km of trails passing through patches of yellowwood and sneezewood trees. A 4-km hike north along the coast leads to the grounded wreck of the *Jacaranda*, a 2000-ton Greek ship that ran aground in 1971.

Qhorha Mouth → *Colour map 4, C5.*

The N2 highway continues north from Butterworth until it reaches Idutywa. There is a turning at Idutywa to Willowvale, 32 km, from where there is a road which passes the village of Nyokana and leads to Qhorha Mouth, 66 km from Idutywa. This road is tarred. Despite what some maps say, there is no road from Mazeppa to Qhorha Mouth. To get between the two, you have to go via the N2. Qhorha Mouth is a small collection of houses, hardly large enough to be called a village, and is known for its kob fishing. The rivermouth here marks the ecological boundary between the sundu palms whose habitat lies to the south of the river and are characteristic to KwaZulu Natal, and the lala palms which only grow to the north. At the mouth of the river is a lagoon and a fine swathe of beach.

Coffee Bay → *Colour map 4, C6.*

At the mouth of the Nenqa River, Coffee Bay is easily accessible on a tarred road and is well known for its good surf, making it a major stop on many backpacker routes. Nevertheless, development has been low key and it remains a quiet and laid-back place. The name

isiXhosa

Most of the Eastern Cape is populated by the Xhosa and the predominant language is isiXhosa. In the Wild Coast region, the former Transkei homeland during the Apartheid years, isiXhosa is spoken by approximately 7.9 million people, about 18% of the South African population. Several letters of the language are represented by a click and even the word *isiXhosa* has a click in it. There are three main clicks; the first is the dental click, which is made with the tongue on the back of the teeth, the second is the lateral alveolar click, which is made by the tongue at the sides of the mouth, and the third is the postalveolar click, which is made with the body of the tongue on the roof of the mouth.

The spelling of place names in South Africa, especially in the more remote areas, can sometimes be inconsistent. Place names are derived from so many languages, which then have often become corrupted or Anglicized. It is not unusual to find the same place having slight variations in spelling in different books or maps and on signposts. Also, in the Eastern Cape some places have reverted to their isiXhosa spellings, though this may take a while to reflect on road signs and maps. Cintsa is now spelt Chintsa, Qolora Mouth and Qolora River is now Qholorha, Qora is now Qhorha, and Umtata is now spelt Mthatha. While on the Wild Coast, and especially off the beaten track, you will invariably encounter the Xhosa people. They will be most delighted if you try out a few words of isiXhosa.

English	isiXhosa
Hello	Molo
Good morning	Intsasa emnandi
Good night	Ubusuku obumnandi
How are you?	Unjani?
Good-bye	Sala kakuhle
Please	Enkosi
Thank you	Enkosi kakhulu
Yes	Ewe
No	Hayi

Coffee Bay comes from the coffee trees which grew here briefly in the 1860s after a ship ran aground with a cargo of coffee beans. The **Hole In The Wall** is a famous natural feature and well worth a visit. An enormous tunnel has been eroded by the sea through a cliff which lies just offshore. The local Xhosa call it *izi Khaleni*, which means 'place of thunder'. At high tide the sound of the waves clapping can be heard throughout the valley. A small holiday resort has sprung up by the beach here.

Mthatha ●●● ►► *pp425-429. Colour map 4, C5.*

It is believed that a clan of the Tembu tribe had a custom interring their dead by casting them into the river with the entreaty *'mThate Bawo'* (Take him, Father) and that this was the origin of the name of the river on which Mthatha was founded. Today Mthatha is a sprawling, unattractive modern town full of cheap supermarkets and discount liquor stores with a small grid of historical buildings at its core. Founded in 1871, it was the capital of Transkei from 1976 to 1994 and has grown to be a busy administrative centre. The N2 passes through the city centre where some of the oldest buildings are located, including the City Hall built in 1908 and the Bhunga (parliament) Building dating from 1927. The latter is now home to the **Nelson Mandela Museum**, the latest addition to the city's (limited) sights, but definitely worth a stop for an understanding of how homelands such as the Transkei were created under the Apartheid system, and to learn more about the formidable man

Sights

The former site of the Transkei parliament, is the **Nelson Mandela Museum** ⓘ *Bhunga Building, Owen St, T047-5325110, www.nelsonmandelamuseum.org.za, Mon-Fri 0900-1600, Sat 0900-1230, free.* It was officially opened by the great man himself on 11 February 2000, to coincide with the 10th anniversary of his release from prison. The displays provide a moving insight into Mandela's life and his struggle against Apartheid, focusing on his autobiography, *Long Walk to Freedom*. There are extracts of the book complemented by photography, personal items, letters and video footage, including a short excerpt from an interview he gave in 1961. Other displays include international awards and honorary degrees that he received, portraits and sculptures of him and diplomatic gifts he received during his term of office. There's even a boxing glove signed by Mohammed Ali and George Foreman (Mandela used to box in his youth).

Other components of the museum are Mandela's primary school and birthplace. The school consists of two rondavels and a hut in the tiny rural village of **Qunu**, where Mandela lived as a youth. The graves of his parents and his son and daughter are also here, along with his new house, which can be photographed from the outside but not visited. Today the rondavels form the **Community Museum and Cultural Centre** Mandela's **birthplace** at the former Transkei village of **Mvezo** is on the other side of the N2. There are remains of the homestead where he was born and some photographs on display, including one of Mandela burning his pass book. The staff at Mthatha are very enthusiastic about the museum and are happy to answer questions. If you don't have your own transport, they will also arrange a tour from Mthatha to Qunu and Mvezo, a short drive south on the N2. A recommended experience.

Port St Johns ●● ❯❯ *pp425-429. Colour map 4, C6.*

This small, peaceful town on the banks of the Mzimvubu River has a laid-back atmosphere which may have something to do with the fact this is a major cannabis-growing area. Its bohemian feel has attracted many artists and, more recently, backpackers. Consequently, there's a good selection of budget accommodation here, much of which is self-catering. There aren't many restaurants but local produce such as papaya, avocado pears, pecans, macadamia nuts and fresh fish is sold on the beach.

Portuguese ships stopped here to pick up water on their journeys up the coast and the town itself is named after the *São João*, which was wrecked here in 1552. A trading post was built in 1846, and in 1878 the British established a military outpost here and built Fort Harrison. When the Transkei was an independent homeland, much of Port St John's 'green gold' (cannabis) was sent to the gold mines of Johannesburg.

Second Beach is the most attractive beach: a beautiful stretch of soft sand, backed by smooth, forested hills. As a pleasant contrast to most beaches visited by tourists, the majority of sunbathers and swimmers here are black. There are two nature reserves within easy reach of town: Silaka (see below) and **Mount Thesiger**, which has a small herd of wildebeest belonging to an unusual sub-species which has no mane. The warm, sulphurous springs at Isinuka are just outside town.

The **tourist office** ⓘ *T047-5641187, www.portstjohns.org.za*, is on Town Entrance Square, just to the right as you enter the town.

Silaka Nature Reserve → *Colour map 4, C6.*
ⓘ *Open to day visitors 0600-1800. For overnight stays, see Sleeping, page 428.*
This reserve is on a gravel road 6 km south from Port St Johns and lies in a forested valley that stretches from Second Beach to Sugarloaf Rock. Although the reserve is small, the tropical atmosphere of the trails weaving through the tangle of thick forest is unmissable. Blesbuck, blue wildebeest and Burchell's zebra have been reintroduced. There is a beautiful stretch of rugged coastline and just off the beach is Bird Island, a breeding colony for sea birds. Interesting rock pools occur on the shore surrounding the island, which may be reached at low tide. At the estuary opposite Bird Island, an attractive pebble beach is surrounded by driftwood and aloes, which grow almost to the sea.

Hluleka Nature Reserve → *Colour map 4, C6.*
ⓘ *Open to day visitors 0600-1800.*
Some 30 km south of Port St Johns, on a good dirt road, this reserve covers 772 ha of evergreen forest, lagoon, saltmarsh and rocky seashore. The Hluleka River flows through and out of the forest into an open area where large coral trees, quinine trees and Natal figs grow along its banks. A network of paths has been laid out from which you can see wildlife, including blesbuck, blue wildebeest, Burchell's zebra, which have been introduced, and Cape clawless otter and monitor lizards. The birdlife here is particularly rich and the African jacana, black duck, Cape batis, dabchick, green pigeon, long-crested eagle, olive bushshrike and yellow-throated longclaw have all been seen here. The 12 self-catering chalets within the reserve are currently closed for repair. To check on their status, contact **Eastern Cape Parks** ⓘ *T043-7424450, www.ecparks.co.za.*

North to Port Edward and Durban ◉ ➤➤ *pp425-429.*

Mkambati Nature Reserve → *Colour map 5, C1.*
ⓘ *Sunrise to sunset, small entry fee, for overnight stays see Sleeping, page 424.*
The coastal reserve covers an area of 8000 ha between the Msikaba and Mtentu rivers. The grasslands here are known for their gladioli, ground orchids and watsonias. Large numbers of grazing herbivores such as eland, red hartebeest, blue wildebeest, blesbuck and gemsbok, have been introduced into the reserve, although only the first two species are indigenous to the area. Of the many streams running through the reserve, the Mkambati is perhaps the most beautiful with its crystal-clear pools and series of spectacular waterfalls, the impressive **Horseshoe Falls** drop down several metres into the ocean. The forested ravines along the Msikaba River are lined with thick riverine forest and the unique Pondo coconut or Mkambati palm. This is the only place in the world where it grows. Cape vultures nest on the cliffs above the Msikaba River gorge. Gurney's sugarbird, the greater double collared sunbird, the red-shouldered widow and many other woodland birds can be seen here. Canoe trips, horse riding and hiking are the best way to see this area of forested ravines and coastal grasslands.

The reserve lies on the coast and is accessed off the R61 between Port St Johns and Port Edward. The road from Port St Johns passes through the villages of Lusikisiki, Flagstaff and Holy Cross. There are plans to surface the road to Mkambati, but until that happens it is best to do the journey in a 4WD.

Wild Coast listings

Sleeping

Gonubie *p418*

C Amanda's B&B, 2 Hart St, T043-7404691, daphneb@mweb.co.za. 5 luxury sea-facing en suite rooms with floor-to-ceiling windows and spacious balcony or terrace, bright white decor, fresh flowers, swimming pool, braai, modern set-up overlooking the beach.

C-F PSA Holiday Resort, T043-7321022, www.psaresort.co.za. 105 caravan and camping sites set in forested dunes full of birds, a few mins' walk from the beach, ablution blocks and kitchen units, 5 fully equipped self-catering chalets that offer a bit more than the usual caravan park chalets with cushions, tablecloths and TV overlooking the Quenera rivermouth, swimming pool.

Inkwenkwezi Game Reserve *p418*
Private lodges and camps
L1-L2 Inkwenkwezi Tented Camp, T043-7343234, www.inkwenkwezi.com. Luxury tents or chalets, some with fireplaces and fridges, bathrooms set in a cave-like environment with showers to look and feel like a waterfall, rates include meals and game drives. The **Emthombeni** restaurant and bar serves Eastern Cape cuisine overlooking the river valley.

Chintsa *p419*
B Cintsa Lodge, 684 Fish Eagle Dr, Chintsa East, T043-7385146, www.cintsalodge.com. Attractive, modern complex with picture windows, smart swimming pool and terraces and balconies with ocean views, private

walkway to the beach. 5 bright and spacious doubles in the main house, and 2 family chalets in the gardens, breakfast included, dinner on request.

D-F Buccaneer's Backpackers, T043-7343012, www.cintsa.com. Superb backpacker lodge set in forests overlooking the lagoon and beach. A 2-km dirt track leads to the secluded site, with a choice of dorms, doubles, fully equipped self-catering cottages and camping on platforms beneath trees. There is a lively bar, pool, kitchen, volleyball court, climbing wall, horse riding on the beach, beauty treatments and massages, free canoes and surfboards, excellent home-cooked evening meals and free daily activities. Also home to **African Heartland Journeys**, an ecotourism initiative for exploring the Wild Coast (see Activities and tours, page 429). Very relaxing spot in a beautiful setting and well run. Recommended. Baz Bus stop.

Haga-Haga *p419*
B-C Haga-Haga Hotel and Cabanas, 155 Mariner's Way, T043-8411670, www.haga hagahotel.co.za. A large family-run complex situated on a rocky headland. 15 twin or double hotel rooms, 30 self-catering cabanas sleeping 4, seafood restaurant, bar with pub grub, TV lounge, swimming pool, tennis, fishing, safe tidal pools. Good rates are for full board and a recommended family option.

Morgan's Bay *p420*
B Morgan's Bay Hotel, Beach Rd, T043-8411062, www.morganbay.co.za. This is a family-run hotel which markets itself as an affordable family resort, great if you are travelling with kids, it was voted in the top 10 family holidays by the South African outdoor magazine *Getaway*. There are 33 good-value rooms; prices vary with the tourist season but the service maintains its high standard throughout the year and off-season is excellent value. Swimming pool, views across the bay, gardens which extend down

to the beach. Inside there is a comfortable lounge, a quiet reading room, a dining room with an extensive breakfast buffet and an à la carte menu in the evenings, both inclusive in the rates. Travellers with children have the option of a separate dining room and child minders. There is also a caravan and camping park (**E**) with 31 sites.

C-D Mitford Lodge, follow the beach road past the **Morgan's Bay Hotel**, T043-8411510, www.morgansbay.co.za. Excellent choice of comfortable en suite rooms and self-catering chalets, sleeping 2-6, to suit most budgets. **Krans Kombuis Bar and Restaurant**, home-cooked meals, speciality burgers and seafood, pub, outside deck and internet access.

Qholorha Mouth *p421*
A-B Trennery's, T047-4980004, www.tren nerys.co.za. 45 thatched chalets set in large shady gardens full of mature trees, seafood restaurant, swimming pool, canoeing, golf, boating, tennis, fishing, bowls, snooker table and a small shop. Excellent value given that all meals are included in the rates and there are good-value weekly specials. An all-round holiday resort in one of the finest settings along this stretch of coast. Recommended.
B Seagulls Beach Hotel, T047-4980044, www.seagulls.co.za. Beachfront hotel with 29 double rooms with en suite bathroom, TV, private patio, some with sea views. The rooms are in small, single-storey units dotted around the grounds. Restaurant, bar, swimming pool, direct access to a sandy beach. The central reception block houses a TV lounge, snooker table and the **Anchor Inn** bar. Guests can enjoy canoeing, windsurfing and fishing in the nearby lagoon. Further afield it is possible to go horse riding and play golf. Rates are inclusive of breakfast and dinner, or ask about 7-day packages.

Nxaxo Mouth *p421*
A-B Wavecrest, T047-4980022, www.ho quality.com/Wavecrest. An excellent family resort in a beautiful setting on the edge of a lagoon, with 35 thatched bungalows, bar,

seafood restaurant, tennis, watersports, deep-sea fishing, private airstrip. Off-season full-board packages start from around R460 per person, good value, recommended.

Mazeppa Bay *p421*
C-D Mazeppa Bay Hotel, T047-4980033, www.mazeppabay.co.za. Accommodation is a mix of doubles, family rooms and rondavels, all with sea views and private surrounds. The central building has a restaurant, the **Red Blanket** bar which serves snacks, a TV lounge, snooker table and terrace. The whole complex sits on a green ridge covered with tropical vegetation, overlooking a broad sandy beach. Also prides itself on having its own island, accessible by an ancient swing bridge. Anglers have a choice of rock, lagoon or river fishing. Fairly basic but cheaper than some of the other Wild Coast resorts.

Qhorha Mouth *p421*
B Kob Inn, T047-4990011, www.kobinn. co.za. Isolated, comfortable hotel set on rocks above the sea. Accommodation is in 10 thatched cottages with 1 or 2 bedrooms and en suite bathroom. There is a restaurant specializing in seafood, and a bar. The swimming pool is perched on rocks over-looking the ocean, and the extensive gardens are surrounded by coastal forest. There are a couple of shady beaches nearby plus the Qhorha River which is ideal for canoeing. Deep-sea fishing trips can be organized from the hotel. Substantial discounts for children.

Coffee Bay *p421*
A-E Hole In The Wall Hotel and Holiday Village, T047-5750009, www.holeinthe wall.co.za. Set by the beach, this large resort has a selection of accommodation to suit all budgets, 26 en suite double rooms in garden thatched rondavels, 28 self-catering white-washed units with 2 bedrooms sleeping up to 8, 10 campsites and a backpacker lodge with 9 cheaper doubles and 3 dorms further up the hill (backpackers/campers can use hotel facilities). Swimming pool, bar, restaurant,

pool tables, volley ball court, TV lounge, nightly seafood braais. With notice will pick up from the Baz Bus stop at Shell Ultra City in Mthatha. A good all-round option on the Wild Coast and can organize plenty of activities.

B Ocean View Hotel, T047-5752005, www.oceanview.co.za. Comfortable set-up perched on a headland above the main beach, 29 double rooms with terraces and sun loungers, 50 m from the beach, swimming pool, bar, restaurant, rates include breakfast and dinner. Golf and horse riding nearby, deep-sea fishing charters. Trips can be arranged to a traditional Xhosa village.

D-F The Coffee Shack, T047-5752048, www.coffeeshack.co.za. Daily shuttle to Shell Ultra City in Mthatha to hook up with the mainline buses and Baz Bus. Popular party place set right on the beach. Mix of dorms and doubles, some en suite, in thatched rondavels, camping, good kitchen facilities, **Bablaza** pub which gets very noisy at night, great seafood and African suppers and big breakfasts, plenty of activities on offer, free surfing lessons. Great spot for a couple of wild days by the beach. Recommended.

E-F Bomvu Paradise, T047-5752073, www.bomvubackpackers.com. Another party lodge set in tropical gardens with decks and hammocks. There are dorms, double rooms and campsites, a restaurant and a bar, be wary of the space cakes. An alternative place, with yoga lessons, drum sessions, monthly full-moon parties and Xhosa song and dance performances. Strong emphasis on surfing.

Mthatha *p422*
It is far preferable to stay in nearby Coffee Bay or Port St Johns and visit Mthatha when passing through. There is no backpacker accommodation here and the centre of town is not particularly safe at night.

B-C Garden Court Mthatha (part of the **Holiday Inn** chain), 3 km north on the N2, T047-5370181, www.southersun.com. 117 a/c rooms, TV, swimming pool, restaurant, bar, slot machines, comfortable but unremarkable 2-storey concrete block.

Port St Johns *p423*
Backpackers will find plenty of accommodation and things to do in Port St Johns.

A Umngazi River Bungalows and Spa, about 25 km west of the town, off the R61 back towards Mthatha, T047-5641115, www.umngazi.co.za. Thatched luxury bungalows facing the estuary surrounded by mangrove forest, restaurant, bar, dine in the wine cellar, shop, swimming pool, wide range of watersports including sunset cruises up the river and night fishing, conference centre, beauty spa, fly-in packages, award-winning resort, good value for families, full-board rates.

C-F The Jetty, 5 km from the town centre by the river, T047-5641072, www.thejetty.co.za. A small, peaceful guesthouse with 4 double rooms, 3 self-catering units and 2 campsites each with their own ablution block, all set in beautiful gardens on a bank of the Umzimvuba River full of avocado and lychee trees where the rare Cape parrot feeds. B&B or self-catering possible in a communal kitchen, no bar. Perfect location for a few relaxing days, and the owners can organize fishing. Recommended.

C-D Outspan Inn, Main Rd, T047-5641057, www.outspaninn.co.za. A local favourite with 9 double rooms, 4 self-catering units and a backpacker dorm room, at the mouth of the Umzimvubu River. The restaurant and pub has a good reputation and is worth visiting, and there's a swimming pool. Reception also act as an unofficial local information centre.

D Gwyneth's Barn, First Beach, T/F047-5641506. Short walk from the beach. Self-catering units in 1 cottage and 1 tree house for 4-8 people. Well equipped with all mod cons, including satellite TV for sports junkies. The units are set in wild gardens with private terraces and a braai area. Great atmosphere.

D-F Ikaya Le Intlabati, Second Beach, T047-5641266, ikaya@telkomsa.net. A fine, small guesthouse-cum-backpackers, one of the last places at the end of the dirt road on

Second Beach, the name means house on the beach in isiXhosa. The building is surrounded by tropical indigenous bush, and the gardens extend down to the beach. A mix of singles, doubles and triples, 1 cottage sleeping 4, and camping, self-catering or meals, pre-book a pickup from Mthatha. Next door is a hand-dyed clothing workshop – **Jakotz Clothing**. Worth a visit if you're planning on spending some time in PSJ. Secure parking.

D-F Jungle Monkey and Island Backpackers, 340-1 Berea Rd, First Beach, T047-5641517, www.junglemonkey.co.za. 2 backpacker places next door to each other sharing the same facilities. The **Jungle** has dorms and camping, bar, restaurant with pizza oven, TV room, bright murals and rambling garden with hammocks and swings, pool with wooden deck. **The Island** has quieter en suite double log cabins perched on the hillside. Baz Bus stop.

F The Kraal, Mpande, T082-8714964, www.thekraal-backpackers.co.za. Sign-posted from road to Port St Johns. The Kraal is a 20-km drive along a bad dirt road, but is well worth the trip. Set on an isolated hill above a beach and lagoon, the lodge is made up of 3 traditional Xhosa rondavels with dirt floors, no electricity and 'eco-loos'. Accommodation is in dorms, or there is space for camping. Communal kitchen where you can buy all your supplies, superb meals served, hot showers, wonderful views over the sea. The Kraal built the local school which often needs volunteer teachers, call them if you're interested. A genuine retreat and perfect for experiencing village life in the old Transkei. Recommended.

Silaka Nature Reserve *p424*
Reservations are made through Eastern Cape Parks, T043-7424450, www.ecparks. co.za. 14 very simple self-catering, thatched **bungalows (D)** with 2 bedrooms, kitchen, bathroom, an easy stroll to the beach. You will have to book in advance to stay here.

Mkambati Nature Reserve *p424*
A Wild Coast Sun, accessed from the R61 north of the reserve, near Port Edward, T039-3059111, www.sun-international.com. Modern, brash, luxury hotel with 245 rooms, pool, casino, cabaret, cinema, championship golf course, beach and watersports, at an undeniably good location with miles of sweeping beach. Once part of the Transkei and only 90 mins' drive from Durban, this used to be the place gamblers from KwaZulu Natal would come when gaming was only legal in the homelands.

B-D Cottages and Rondavels reservations through Eastern Cape Parks, T043-7424450, www.ecparks.co.za. The better option are the 6 stone, prefab cottages sleeping up to 6, with fully equipped kitchens and modern furnishings, located in the forest near the reception office, while the 6 rondavels, sleeping 2, are older and simpler with basic self-catering facilities but are in a good position overlooking the beach. There are also 2 larger houses in the reserve, sleeping groups of 10 or 20, more suited to groups of fishermen.

Eating

Most eating along the Wild Coast is in the hotels and resorts. There is the usual range of chicken and burger chain restaurants in Mthatha and Butterworth but not much else. Most of the petrol stations along the N2 have restaurants such as **Wimpy** attached. If you are self-catering along the coast, the supermarkets in East London or in Port Shepstone in KwaZulu Natal are the best places to stock up on provisions.

Chintsa *p419*
††† **Michaela's**, Steenbras Dr, Chintsa East, T043-7385139, www.michaelas.co.za. Wed-Sun 1130-1430, 1830-2130, Mon 1130-1430 only. This is a remarkable restaurant perched on the top of Chintsa's biggest sand dune, reached by a short funicular train ride. If you are not fit, call

ahead to check this is operating. The thatched restaurant has 2 levels with large windows and outside decks overlooking the ocean, the seafood is excellent as are the salads that make good use of seasonal fruits and vegetables. The gut-busting Sun lunch buffet is recommended.

Port St Johns *p423*
¶¶ **Gecko Moon**, First Beach, T047-5641221. Open 1100-2000. Excellent German cook, specializes in fish menus, plus good wood-fired pizza.

▲ Activities and tours

Chintsa *p419*
African Heartland Journeys, based at Buccaneer's Backpackers in Chintsa (see Sleeping, page 425), 1043-7343012, www.ahj.co.za. Sensitively run camping tours by 4WD, bike and canoe that go right into the heartland of the Wild Coast to places you could never get to otherwise. Overnight accommodation is in Xhosa villages, which is an excellent way to see how people live without roads, electricity or cars. Highly recommended.

North to Port Edward *p424*
Amadiba Adventures, trails start at the office at the Mzamba Craft Village, 6 km south of Port Edward opposite the **Wild Coast Sun**, T/F039-3056455, www.amadiba adventures.co.za. This is part of a govern-ment tourism development programme funded by the European Union, where coastal communities run and own the tourism initiatives. Accommodation is in mobile camps with eco-toilets and hot bush showers, and prices include 3 meals per day. There are plenty of activities available, such as hiking and swimming beneath waterfalls, and excellent 4- to 6-day horse or hiking trails up the coast and inland. Local guides are very knowledgeable about the area and much of the tour involves contact with local people.

All proceeds go back into local community. Reports have been excellent and it is an organization worthy of support.

⊖ Transport

Baz Bus
From East London the **Baz Bus**, T021-4392323, www.bazbus.com, runs along the N2, stopping at **Chintsa** before turning off at **Mthatha** to the coast and **Port St Johns**, from where it goes back on to the N2 and continues on to **Port Edward** in KwaZulu Natal. It runs the same route in reverse. For the 100-km or so journey to Coffee Bay hostels will collect backpackers from the **Baz Bus** at the Shell Ultra City on the N2 outside Mthatha for a small fee and by prior arrangement. Hotels may also pick up guests by prior arrangement. Minibus taxis also run to both resorts, and leave from Circus Triangle in town. It is not advisable to try and hitch this route. Avoid driving here after dark, as there have been violent incidents.

Mthatha *p422*
Bus
Greyhound, **Intercape** and **Translux** buses all stick to the N2 and Mthatha is on the Cape Town–Durban route. **Cape Town** (18½ hrs) via **Nelson Mandela Bay** (**Port Elizabeth**) (7 hrs) and **East London** (3 hrs). **Durban** (6 hrs) via **Port Shepstone** (4½ hrs).
   Bus companies Greyhound, T083-9159000, www.greyhound.co.za; **Intercape**, T0861-287287, www.inter cape.co.za; **Translux**, T0861-589282, www.translux.co.za.

⊕ Directory

Mthatha *p422*
Medical services St Mary's Private Hospital, 30 Durham St, T047-5312911. 24-hr service.

Contents

Footprint features

At a glance

⊖ **Getting around** Buses and Baz Bus on major routes, car hire, tours start and finish in Durban.

◎ **Time required** Minimum 1-2 weeks to cover in depth.

☽ **Weather** Good all year around, though humid June-August.

⊗ **When not to go** Christmas and Easter school holidays.

★ **Don't miss ...**
1 **Durban nightlife**, page 451.
2 **Gateway Shopping Mall**, page 452.
3 **Battlefields tour**, page 481.
4 **Hiking in uKhahlamba-Drakensberg Park**, page 493.
5 **Hluhluwe-Imfolozi Game Reserve**, page 527.
6 **Greater St Lucia Wetland Park**, page 530.
7 **Diving in Sodwana Bay**, page 547.

N

30 km

30 miles

KwaZulu Natal manages to squash the country's greatest diversity into a wedge of land between the towering Drakensberg Mountains and the long sweep of sub-tropical coastline. Here, visitors can go on safari, hike through dramatic wilderness, surf the country's best beaches and experience South Africa's strongest African culture. The mountains in the uKhahlamba-Drakensberg Park soar to over 3000 m, offering the country's finest hiking on an extensive network of remote trails. Zululand, rich in history and evocative landscapes, draws visitors both for its traditional Zulu lifestyles, and the superb game reserves, some of the finest in South Africa. Hluhluwe-Imfolozi Game Reserve is the best known and has become famous for its rhino conservation programme, which has brought the rhino back from the brink of extinction. Maputaland, lying to the north of Zululand, is an extraordinary area of undisturbed African wilderness, with remote game parks and pristine coastlines, far off the usual tourist trail. The variety of wildlife experiences on offer here is on a par with Kruger – but without the crowds. The landscape of the central region, dotted with small industrial towns and rolling farmland, makes up in history what it lacks in scenic drama. This area, better known as the Battlefields, still bears the scars of the Zulu Wars: the Zulu-Boer War, the Anglo-Zulu War and the Boer War. There are dozens of battlefield sites, but the most evocative are those at Isandlwana, Rorke's Drift and Blood River. For a more light-hearted alternative, KwaZulu Natal's beaches are some of the most beautiful in the country. While those around Durban and to the south are heavily developed, the coastline extending from the north towards Maputaland is relatively wild, with long empty sweeps of white sand backed by thick tropical dune forests – an excellent place for interesting wildlife encounters.

Ins and outs

Getting around

Travel within KwaZulu Natal is uncomplicated; the main areas of interest are connected by either the N2 or the N3. The **N2** runs along most of the coast from Port Shepstone in the south, through to Durban, Zululand and Maputaland in the north, before heading inland north to Mpumalanga, past Swaziland. The **N3** heads inland from Durban towards Pietermaritzburg, skirting the Battlefield Route to the east and the uKhahlamba-Drakensberg National Park in the west, eventually reaching Gauteng. The **Baz Bus** is convenient for exploring the province as it runs all the way along the coast as far as Mkuzi before heading inland to Swaziland. A second service runs from Durban towards Gauteng through the Drakensberg. All the main centres are linked by mainline bus services, so KwaZulu Natal can quite feasibly be visited by local transport, though you may want to consider a hire car for some of the national parks and game reserves. To the north, the roads in Maputaland are gradually being surfaced but there are still vast tracts of wilderness which are best explored in a 4WD. The most accessible reserve is Sodwana Bay where the colourful tropical reefs have become South Africa's most popular diving destination. The battlefield sites in the centre of the province are isolated and best experienced on a guided historical tour (see page 492).

Tourist information

Tourism KwaZulu-Natal ① *T031-3667500, www.zulu.org.za, Mon-Fri 0800-1630, Sat 0900-1400, Sun 0900-1300*, also known as the Kingdom of the Zulu, is the regional tourist office and is based at **Tourist Junction** in Durban (see page 436). This is an excellent office with a huge range of information on the province, as well as an attractive curio shop.

    KZN Wildlife ① *PO Box 13053, Cascades 3202, Pietermaritzburg, T033-8451000, www.kznwildlife.com,* is the central reservations office for all the accommodation within the various nature reserves and conservation areas throughout the KwaZulu Natal. This includes many of the Drakensberg resorts, as well as excellent wildlife reserves such as Itala and Hluhluwe-Imfolozi. All the parks' offices are open October to March 0800-1900 and April to September 0800-1800. Reservations can be made six months in advance and some of the popular camps are fully booked during the local school holidays. Credit card and online bookings are accepted. Note that accommodation in huts must be booked through KZN Wildlife whereas campsites are booked directly through the campsite manager or reception by phone. (Do not confuse KZN Wildlife with SANParks (see page 48). SANParks is responsible for parks such as Kruger, Tsitsikamma and Addo Elephant Park.)

Durban → Phone code: 031. Colour map 5, B2.

The sprawling conurbation of Durban is Africa's largest port and although its appeal is not immediately apparent – few original buildings survive and it can feel hectic and overcrowded – it boasts wide beaches, an extensive beachfront and a steamy tropical climate. The city also has one of the country's most interesting cultural mixes – it is home to substantial Zulu and white communities and South Africa's largest Indian population. Away from the Central Business District (CBD) are attractive suburbs, where tropical foliage spills from ornate balconies and the fast pace of city life is all but forgotten. ▶▶ *For listings, see pages 447-455.*

Ins and outs

Getting there A limited number of international flights fly direct into **Durban International Airport** ① *T031-4516758, www.airports.co.za*, and there are numerous and regular domestic flights. Car hire desks can be found in both the domestic and international terminals. There is a **tourist information office** ① *T031-4081000, daily 0630-2100*, in the domestic arrivals hall, and several mobile phone rental shops. The airport is 16 km from the city centre and transport into Durban takes about 30 minutes. Many hotels and backpacker hostels offer free airport collection/transfer service.

1 Greater Durban

➡**Durban maps**
1 Greater Durban, page 435
2 Durban centre, page 438
3 Durban beachfront, page 442

24 hours in Durban

Head down to the Golden Mile in the early morning; except for the few early-rising surf fanatics and muscular lifeguards limbering up, you will have the wide promenade, sandy beaches and crashing waves to yourself, before the crowds, holiday-resort tackiness and humidity set in. Breakfast at one of the small cafés where the surfers congregate to swap wave stories.

Explore the Indian shopping district off Grey Street, an exotic, cross-cultural, shopping experience, where the tangy aroma of eastern spices mingles with the colourful fabrics, trinkets and jewellery in the courtyard bazaars. When entering the Juma Masjid Mosque on Grey Street, the largest in the southern hemisphere, make sure you remove your shoes. Relish the cool tranquillity here before heading back on to Durban's hectic streets. Enjoy an African shopping experience at Victoria Market, where curios and souvenirs can be haggled over, and sample a famous Durban bunny chow at one the traditional food stalls.

Afterwards, catch the bird show at Umgeni River Bird Park, the only one of its kind in the world. Some of South Africa's largest and rarest birds, including the blue crane, are on display in this innovative show.

Sink a couple of cold Castle lagers and watch the sun go down on the deck of the **Bat Café** in the small craft harbour. If you're lucky you may catch some township jazz here before heading to one of Durban's top Indian restaurants to sample a fine Durban curry. The best are the **Jewel of India**, with cushions and low tables where you can kick off your shoes and relax, and **Ulundi**, where days of colonial Natal are echoed through turbaned waiters and rattan furniture.

Florida Road in Morningside and Musgrave Road in Musgrave are Durban's current hip and happening café-lined streets. Take your pick of fashionable late-night bars, pubs, open-air restaurants and live music venues, all conveniently located along these two suburban streets.

Alternatively, there are several private companies providing airport transfer services departing from the departure terminal such as **Airport Shuttle**, T031-4651606. Behind Durban railway station on NMR Avenue (M12) is the Motorcoach Terminal for major long-distance coaches run by **Translux**, **Intercape** and **Greyhound**. ▸▸ *For more detailed information, see Transport, page 454.*

Getting around   Durban has developed into South Africa's largest sea port and is also one of its main tourist centres. The approach to Durban passes through coastal tourist resorts, industrial areas, townships and eventually reaches the CBD. The extensive beachfront and the most important landmarks are within easy walking distance in the city centre. **Mynah**, T031-3073503, is a frequent local bus service that runs between the city centre, the beachfront and Berea and Morningside, R3; it's very useful if you want to get to town from the suburbs, or from the north or south of the city centre. Timetables are free and can be obtained from the city centre bus terminal, opposite the Workshop Shopping Mall on Commercial Road.

Tourist information Durban Africa ① *Tourist Junction, Station Building, 160 Pine St, T031-3044934, www.durban.kzn.org.za, www.bookabedahead.co.za, Mon-Fri 0800-1630,*

Sat 0900-1400, Sun 0900-1300, is the city tourist information service, which is very helpful and produces a range of brochures, including accommodation, restaurant and events guides. It also offers hotel and tour bookings, coach and rail bookings, foreign exchange, a curio shop, a café and runs extremely good city tours.

Safety Safety has been a long-standing issue in downtown Durban. Although safety standards plummeted in the late 1990s, a number of initiatives in recent years, such as the development of the waterfront and upgrading of local housing, has improved the situation a great deal. Nevertheless, it's sensible to keep your wits about you – stick to busy areas, don't carry valuables and avoid looking like a tourist. Most importantly, avoid walking around downtown after dark. The suburbs are safe to walk around.

Background

The area around the bay was once covered with mangroves and inhabited by pelicans, flamingos and hippos. The earliest inhabitants were members of the Lala tribe who fished in the estuary, and hunted and grew crops in the fertile tropical forests along the coast. The first Europeans to land here were Portuguese explorers en route to the east. On 25 December 1497, Vasco da Gama sighted land and called it Natal, though this was probably off the coast of present-day Eastern Cape. The Portuguese cartographer Manuel Perestrello mapped the coast of Natal in 1576, but it was nearly 200 years after the earliest European sighting that the first trading ships arrived. In 1684 the *Francis* began a new era when she sailed to Natal to buy ivory.

After the relative success of the first trading expedition, the Dutch East India Company planned to open a trading post here (after buying land off Chief Inyangesi for 1000 guilders worth of beads, copper rings and iron). But after a few technical hitches involving the estuary's sandbars, trade was never really developed and in 1730 the Dutch established an alternative trading station at Delagoa Bay.

The first British traders arrived in 1823 on the *Salisbury*, spurred on by news of Shaka, the powerful chief of the Zulus and his Empire. Lieutenant Francis and George Farewell arrived in the Bay of Natal and were blown over the sandbars in a storm. They returned in May 1824, with Henry Francis Fynn and a group of other adventurers, and set up their first camp in what is now known as Farewell Square. Henry Fynn was the first European trader to make contact with Shaka. Fynn and the other adventurers claimed (falsely) to be envoys of King George and were well received. Fynn became a favourite of the royal household after he helped Shaka recover from a stab wound sustained during a battle. In thanks Shaka granted Fynn a huge tract of land, over 9000 sq km.

Fynn and his young colleague Nathaniel Issacs ran this area as their own personal fiefdom, taking many Zulu wives and fathering dozens of children. Fynn declared himself King of Natal and wielded power in the same brutal manner as his infamous neighbour, Shaka. Even though Fynn and his men broke many Zulu laws, including the prohibition on all but the king from trading in ivory, they were treated with great respect by Shaka (though the chiefs they bought the ivory from were invariably executed).

The area remained undeveloped, however, with just a few dozen European settlers, and the British refused to annex the region. It was not until the establishment of the Voortrekker republic of Natalia in 1838 that the British felt their interests to be under threat. The capital of Natalia was in Pietermaritzburg, but settlements had also been established at Weenen and Durban, giving the Voortrekkers access to the sea. The possibility of a viable independent Voortrekker republic wasn't acceptable to the Cape

Colony and an expeditionary force was sent from the Cape in 1842. Although they were besieged by the Voortrekkers on their arrival, by June of that year the parliament in Pietermaritzburg had accepted British rule. The Cape Colony annexed Natal in 1844, and the security given by becoming part of the Cape Colony encouraged many new settlers in search of land to come to Durban.

The development of the sugarcane industry in the 1860s encouraged the growth of Durban as a port and gave the city one of its most unique characteristics. Initially the sugarcane industry suffered from a lack of cheap labour, so the planters imported a large number of indentured labourers from India, who lived in conditions not dissimilar to slavery. After working off their five-year indenture contracts some returned home, but a number remained in Natal. Many continued farming and eventually came to dominate the local fruit and vegetable market. Others established small businesses and gradually built up important trade connections with India. These ex-indentured labourers were joined by a number of more affluent traders, mainly from Gujarat, who arrived direct from India to set up a business.

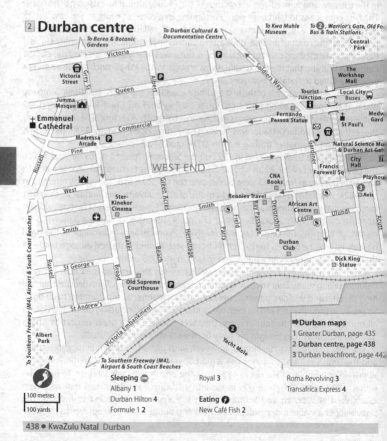

2 Durban centre

Durban maps
1 Greater Durban, page 435
2 Durban centre, page 438
3 Durban beachfront, page 442

Sleeping		Eating	
Albany 1	Royal 3	New Café Fish 2	Roma Revolving 3
Durban Hilton 4			Transafrica Express 4
Formule 1 2			

With the development of the Golden Mile in the 1970s, Durban was promoted as a seaside resort for white holidaymakers, particularly for families from Gauteng. During Apartheid, the extensive beach was split according to colour – black people were permitted to walk the length of the whole beach but, on the whites-only Addington Beach, they were not allowed to sit down or go into the sea. The late 1980s, however, saw a huge influx of workers from Zululand, transforming the fabric of the city. With the end of Apartheid came another influx: that of black holidaymakers, which gave the city the tag of 'Soweto-on-Sea' – a phrase used by both whites and blacks. However, divisions still remain: far fewer white people holiday in Durban, while the city centre has taken on a distinctly African feel.

Sights

The main areas of interest to tourists are the **city centre** around Farewell Square, the **Indian district** around Queen and Grey streets, and the beachfront **Golden Mile**. The best way of seeing the major sights in the city centre is on one of the guided tours run by the tourist office.

City centre

The small area surrounding City Hall between Commercial Road and Smith Street in central Durban is one of the city's more interesting spots. The colonial buildings and gardens offer a striking contrast between Durban's past and the present. High-rise office blocks tower over the remains of Durban's colonial history, where pastel-coloured art deco buildings are dwarfed by mirrored skyscrapers. The city centre's eclectic mixture of architectural styles is the responsibility of Lord Holford, the town planner who developed the city centre during the 1970s. Lord Holford was originally from South Africa but became one of England's most notorious town planners when he created many of the soulless city centres built in England during the 1960s. He returned to South Africa to help redesign city centres as part of the Apartheid programme; his work destroyed the bustling Indian atmosphere of the city centre when thousands of Indians were moved out. The original plans for the new centre involved the demolition of the City Hall and the old railway station, but vociferous protests by conservationists prevented this.

Francis Farewell Square is the hub of this area and is named after the first British settler who built his home here out of wattle and daub in 1824. Today the square has a busy street market, but at night it resembles, rather incongruously, a Victorian cemetery as this is where most of Durban's commemorative statues have been placed. There is a cenotaph to those who died in both world wars, a memorial to the dead of the Boer War and statues of Queen Victoria, in commemoration of her diamond jubilee, and Natal's first two prime ministers.

The **City Hall**, on Smith Street, faces directly onto the Francis Farewell Square. This is one of Durban's most impressive buildings and reflects the town's municipal might at the turn of the 20th century. The neo-baroque building was completed in 1910 and in its day was one of the British Empire's finest city halls in the southern hemisphere. The main entrance is on Farewell Square and the hall inside is decorated with an interesting collection of portraits of Durban's mayors. What is particularly appealing about the building are the palms lining the street outside. You will also find the Natural Science Museum and Durban Art Gallery here.

The **Natural Science Museum** ① *T031-3112256, Mon-Fri 0830-1600, Sat 0830-1200, Sun 1100-1600, free entry, gift shop and coffee shop*, has a grand colonial entrance adorned with palm trees. Inside is an assortment of scientific displays, including a huge gallery of stuffed African mammals. More interestingly, the museum also houses an extremely rare Dodo skeleton and South Africa's only Egyptian mummy. The **KwaZuzulwazi Science Centre** has an excellent series of displays dedicated to the Zulu culture.

The **Durban Art Gallery** ① *T031-3112265, Mon-Sat 0830-1600, Sun 1100-1600, free*, on the upper floor of City Hall, has a superb collection of work by South African artists dating from the beginning of this century. This was one of the first galleries in South Africa to collect black art, and it remains an important cultural centre. It also hosts regularly changing exhibitions of contemporary art and handicrafts, and the Durban RedEye arts festival takes place here several times a year.

The Playhouse is directly opposite the Smith Street entrance to the City Hall. It was built in 1935 and was originally used as a bioscope, which seated 1900 people. The lounge bar became popular with visiting sailors during the 1970s and was notorious for its heavy drinking sessions and occasional fights. The cinema was eventually forced to close after a fire and has now been restored and converted into an arts complex with five theatres (see Entertainment, page 452).

St Paul's Church was originally built in 1853, and was rebuilt in 1906 after a fire. The church is purely British in architectural style and inside there are commemorative plaques to Durban's early settlers. The chapel of St Nicholas on the left side of the aisle was part of the Mission to Seamen between 1899 and 1989. Reverend Wade, who was rector of the church between 1952 and 1961, was the father of tennis one-hit-wonder Virginia Wade, who won the ladies singles title at Wimbledon in 1977.

The **post office**, built in 1885, was originally Durban's first town hall. There is a plaque on the southern corner of the building, which commemorates Winston Churchill's speech after his escape during the Boer War.

The grand structure that is now home to **Tourist Junction** is Durban's old railway station. The building, modelled on a traditional British Victorian railway station, was completed in 1899 and is one of the few left standing in South Africa.

The **Fernando Pessoa Statue** is directly opposite Tourist Junction on the other side of Gardiner Street. The bronze statue commemorates Fernando Pessoa who lived in Durban during the early years of his life between 1896 and 1906. On his return to Portugal he lived in poverty while teaching English in Lisbon but went on to become Portugal's most celebrated and complex modern poet.

The Workshop, also on Commercial Road, lies directly behind the old railway station and is an enormous shopping mall that has been built inside the old train sheds. With the transition of major shops to the Pavilion and Gateway malls in the suburbs, the Workshop has suffered a decline in recent years and is starting to look shabby.

Around 500 m north of the Workshop, on Ordnance Road, near Warrior's Gate, is the **Kwa Muhle Museum** ① *T031-3112223, Mon-Fri, 0800-1600, Sat 0800-1100, free*, housed in the Old Pass Office. It's a fascinating and moving exhibition of what it was like to be an African under the old regime and is also known locally as the **Apartheid Museum**. There is a collection of waxwork figures in hostels along with a series of photographs of incidents and riots of the past 25 years. Another display features the Indian merchants of Grey Street; here you can learn more about the first trade union, the Grey Street mosque, Victoria Street beer hall, the Bantu Social Centre and bunny chow (see page 451). One of the exhibits is on the 'Durban System', a method for Durban's city council to raise revenue to finance the administration of African affairs during Apartheid without using a penny of white taxpayers' money. they gave themselves the monopoly on brewing sorghum beer, which they sold for a fine profit in African-only public beer houses.

The **Warrior's Gate Moth Museum** ① *Old Fort Rd, T031 3073337, Tue-Sun 1100-1500, free*, has a large collection of military memorabilia from the First and Second World Wars and battlefield relics from the Anglo-Boer and Zulu wars.

Indian district

The area around Victoria Street, Queen Street and Grey Street is one of the oldest areas of Durban still standing. It is a good 20-minute walk west from the centre down Commercial Road or Pine Street, or take a taxi to Victoria Street. The pastel-coloured shopping arcades were built in the 1920s and 1930s by Indian traders. Originally they were designed so families could have their homes over their shops. In 1973, however, legislation was introduced which prohibited Indians from living in the area, though not from trading. Family labour living above the shops was seen as integral to their success and the legislation was deliberately introduced in an effort to reduce their competition with white-owned businesses. With the new legislation, much of the residential population was forced to move out to Chatsworth or Phoenix; the wealthier traders moved to Westville.

Thankfully the new residential rules did not succeed in destroying the Indian-owned businesses and many have continued to prosper. A number of original shops are still here, selling spices, saris and other goods from India, but it is now very much a commercial, rather than residential, area.

Durban Cultural and Documentation Centre ① *corner of Epsom Rd and Derby St, T031-3097559, Mon-Fri 0830-1530*, is well worth a visit if you're interested in the history of the Indian Community in South Africa. There are displays on the indentured Indian community, Gandhi in South Africa, culinary art and traditional clothing.

Victoria Street Market ① *T031-3064021, Mon-Sat 0600-1800, Sun 1000-1600*, is on the corner of Queen Street and Victoria Street. The original market was destroyed in 1973 by fire and has been replaced by a modern market. The new concrete building is rather dingy, but there are over 170 stalls inside selling curios, leather goods, fabrics, copper and spices. The main attraction of the stalls here are the spices and dried beans imported from India. Upstairs are a variety of food stalls serving up delicious snacks such as bunny chow,

To Snake Park, Flea Market, Battery Beach,
Suncoast Casino & Entertainment World

➡ **Durban maps**
1 Greater Durban, page 435
2 Durban centre, page 438
3 Durban beachfront, page 442

Bay of Plenty

Surfing

Bay of Plenty Pier

Amphitheatre

Playfair

Snell Parade

Lower Marine Parade

Pavilion

Swimming

North Beach

Moth Museum of Military History

Old Fort

North Beach Pier

Gresham

Frobisher

Foster

Bowling Greens

Ordnance

Dairy Beach

Brickhill

North

Boscombe

Central Beach Pools

Dairy Beach Pier

John Milne

Morrison

West

Hunter

East

Milne

South

Victoria Park

Surfing

Wedge Beach

Library

Sea View

Commercial St

Kearsney

Pine St

Palmer

Beachview Mall

Cinema

Toilets

Swimming

Addington Beach

Farepark

Daynite Pharmacy

West St Mall

Prince Alfred

West St

Peck St

Tyzack

Farewell

Smith St

Brighton

uShaka Marine World

Timber

Gull

Beatty

Cato

Creek

Roy

Map Centre

Fisher

Point Rd

Gillespie

Marine Parade

The Wheel

To Tourist Junction

To Kingsmead Stadium & Old Fort

N

100 metres
100 yards

Sleeping 😴
Bluewaters 3
Protea Edward 2
Tropicana 1

Eating 🍴
Cargo Hold 2
Jewel of India 1
Joe Kools 3

samosas and Durban curries. It gets extremely busy, so beware of pickpockets and don't take anything valuable with you.

The entrance to the **Madressa Arcade** is on Grey Street. The bazaar-like arcade was built in 1927 and houses shops selling luggage, CDs and Indian fabrics.

The **Juma Masjid Mosque** ① *corner of Queen St and Grey St, T031-3060026, open to all Mon-Fri 0900-1600 but not during prayer times*, was also built in 1927 and claims to be the largest mosque in the southern hemisphere, despite the fact that Muslims are a minority in Durban, which is largely Hindu. It sports gilt-domed minarets and a peaceful marble hall. The dress code must be adhered to: no shorts for men and women should wear long skirts or trousers and cover their shoulders; leave your shoes at the door.

Victoria Embankment
The Victoria Embankment was originally built in 1897 and was a grand and desirable residential area facing a beautiful stretch of beach. Very little of this remains today, and at first glance the Embankment seems like any other busy road lined with skyscrapers. There are still a few sights worth seeking out, though. At the eastern end of the Embankment is the ornate **Da Gama Clock**. A good example of late-Victorian design, this large cast-iron clock was erected to commemorate the 400th anniversary of Vasco da Gama's discovery of the sea route to India in 1487.

A short walk further on at the junction of Gardiner Street and the Victoria Embankment is the **Dick King Statue** which commemorates Dick King's epic 10-day ride to Grahamstown in 1842 whilst Durban was under siege. The **Durban Club** is on the opposite side of the embankment and was built in 1904. This is one of the few original buildings left on the Victoria Embankment, a grand edifice which gives an inkling of what the Victoria Embankment once looked like.

Wilson's Wharf is a modern development overlooking the harbour, home to a couple of cafés, a fish market and three boats which house the **Natal Maritime Museum** ① *entrance is on the docks opposite the junction of Aliwal St and the Victoria Embankment, T031-3112230, Mon-Sat 0830-1600, Sun 1100-1600, small entry fee.* Visitors can walk through the minesweeper, the *SAS Durban*, and the two tugs, the *Ulundi* and the *JR More*.

Just beyond the Maritime Museum is the excellent non-profit making **BAT (Bartle Arts Trust) Centre** ① *on the harbour front, T031-3320451, www.batcentre.co.za.* This is a popular arts centre with a concert hall and a bar and restaurant, as well as several little shops selling excellent contemporary Zulu weavings, wood-cut prints and handmade shoes. Above the **Trans Africa Express** restaurant is a gallery which hosts cutting-edge exhibitions, such as the one by local cartoonist Themba Siwela. The centre also features nightly events, from live jazz to poetry readings.

Beachfront
The most popular seafront area extends along the length of Marine Parade. Traditionally known as the **Golden Mile**, it's a favourite with South African holiday-makers. The beachfront is lined with high-rise hotels, gardens and a promenade; behind is a built-up urban area which had become distinctly insalubrious. Developments over the last few years, however, have upgraded housing, brought in investment and improved safety here, although it's still best avoided at night. There's a police station on the promenade and a high police presence.

The beaches, all of which are impressive stretches of long, golden sand, are divided into areas designated for surfing, boogy boarding and swimming. All are protected with shark nets and lifeguards are on patrol daily 0800-1700. At the northern end of the Lower Marine Parade is a **flea market**, a hive of activity at weekends, with stalls selling Indian snacks and curios.

The promenade along Lower Marine Parade and Snell Parade has numerous tourist attractions. Running from north to south, the entertainment starts with the flea market and the **Snake Park** ① *0900-1630, small entry fee*. The park has a large collection of snakes from around the world with daily snake-handling demonstrations several times daily and feedings at weekends. Nearby are several stands where extravagantly dressed rickshaw drivers wait for tourists. The options are either a quick and painless photograph with the driver, or a photograph and ride up and down Marine Parade, usually costing around R20.

The leading attraction here, however, is **uShaka Marine World** ① *1 Bell St, T031-3288000, www.ushakamarineworld.co.za, 0900-1800, Wet 'n' Wild closed Mon-Tue Apr-Oct, Wet 'n' Wild R70, SeaWorld R92, combined ticket R135; free entry to Village Walk*. This enormous waterpark is the largest in Africa, and has the fourth largest aquarium in the world. The park is split into three areas: SeaWorld is an impressive underground aquarium; Wet 'n' Wild has a huge choice of impressive waterslides and rides; and Village Walk is a retail village filled with shops and restaurants. The highlight in SeaWorld is the phantom ship, where visitors walk through glass tunnels surrounded by ragged-tooth sharks and game fish. Each corridor has a different theme, and there is a range of presentations in pools surrounding the ship throughout the day. There's also a dolphinarium, a seal pool, dive tank and a snorkel reef. Another free zone is the uShaka Beach, which hosts a variety of activities such as beach volleyball and surfing, and has 24-hour security.

A new waterfront housing and leisure development to be known as The Point is currently under construction at the entrance of the harbour at the end of Point Road.

Battery Beach

Heading 1 km north of Snell Parade and the Golden Mile, Battery Beach is perhaps the most attractive of Durban's beaches, with good swimming and fewer crowds. It's also the location of the **Suncoast Casino and Entertainment World**, with slot machines, cinemas, a selection of bars, takeaway joints, themed restaurants and a car park for 2000 vehicles. There's a boardwalk linking the complex to the beach where you can sunbathe or rollerblade on the sundeck.

Durban suburbs

Berea

This residential district, to the west of the city centre, is one of Durban's oldest and most attractive. Fine whitewashed mansions and Victorian bungalows line the quiet streets, and this is one of the best places to head for restaurants and nightlife. On Sydenham Road, in Upper Berea, are the **Botanic Gardens** ① *T031-2011303, daily 0730-1715, until 1745 in summer, free entry. A free tour leaves from the information centre on the last Sun of every month at 0930.* The gardens were founded in 1849, making them, supposedly, the oldest botanical gardens in Africa, and they cover almost 15 ha. There are some impressive avenues of palms crossing the park, an ornamental lake, an orchid house and an information centre. The tea garden, open 0930-1615, is a pleasant place to relax. The KwaZulu Natal Philharmonic Orchestra performs by the lake on Sundays during summer.

Three other smaller parks are **Mitchell Park**, at the end of Musgrave Road, which are public gardens with an open-air café, aviaries and a few small animals and reptiles; the adjoining **Jameson Park**, with extensive rose gardens and a good view of Durban from the top; and the **Japanese Gardens**, on Prospect Hall Road in Durban North.

The **Campbell Collection** ① *220 Marriott Rd, T031-2073432, main house open to the public by appointment only Mon-Fri 0830-1630, free entry*, is a museum and African library in a Cape Dutch house built in 1914, which still has most of its original decorations. There are some fine examples of Cape furniture and early South African oil paintings, displays of African sculpture, weapons, musical instruments and a rare collection of paintings by Barbara Tyrrell. Most of the paintings are of Africans dressed in traditional clothes from the 19th century; the paintings form part of a unique record of what people wore before contact with European settlers.

Chatsworth

Reached from the N2 south of the centre, the **Hare Krishna Temple of Understanding** ① *south of the centre on Ambassador Rd, T031-4033328, daily, free entry*, opened as an ashram in 1969, but the futuristic marble temple set in extensive ornamental gardens was only opened to the public in 1975. There is a good vegetarian restaurant here serving everything from light snacks to large curries.

Nature reserves

① *Information centres at the reserves stock maps and guides detailing walking trails.*

Durban's suburbs hold a number of natures reserves, most with walking trails which provide a welcome respite from the bustle of the city. **Burman Bush Nature Reserve** ① *Windermere Rd, Morningside, T031-3124466*, is a relatively small reserve, with an important patch of dense coastal bush and a large population of vervet monkeys. There are several walks from 500 m to 2 km, which are marked by coloured arrows at ground level. On the opposite side of the Umgeni River is the **Umgeni River Bird Park** ① *T031-5794600, www.umgeniriverbirdpark.co.za, daily 0900-1700, R25*, which has over 3000 exotic and indigenous birds, from flamingos to macaws. There is a free flight show (1100 and 1400), where large birds such as owls, raptures and vultures fly over the heads of the audience to perches at the top of the open-air auditorium. **Kenneth Stainbank Nature Reserve** ① *96 Coedmore Av, Yellowwood Park, T031-4692807, daily 0600-1800, small entrance fee*, is a fairly large area of woodland and grassland next to a dam with an impressive array of game including impala, zebra, duiker and bushbuck. There is a mountain bike trail and 13 km of walking trails including a 500-m trail for the physically disabled and sight-impaired.

Around Durban

Durban's motorway network opens up a range of day trips within driving distance of the city centre, although good public transport connections are limited to the south coast, Pietermaritzburg and Umhlanga.

To the north, inland along the N3, is the Valley of 1000 Hills, Pietermaritzburg, the Natal Midlands and the Battlefields. To the south on the N2 are the surfing beaches and tourist resorts heading to Port Shepstone and Margate. To the north along the N2 lies Umhlanga and the coastal resorts of the north coast, whilst just inland from the N2 is the historical Zulu town of Eshowe.

Valley of 1000 Hills

The Valley of 1000 Hills, a peaceful area named after the dozens of hills which fold down towards the Umgeni River, is an easy 35-km drive from Durban. Follow the N3 north out of the city and leave at the Westville/Pavilion Mall exit. Join the old Pietermaritzburg road (R103) and drive through the suburbs of Kloof and Hillcrest. Here you will pick up signs for the Valley of 1000 Hills Meander which runs through the villages of Botha's Hill, Drummond, Monteseel and Inchanga. The **Comrades Marathon**, a gruelling 90 km between Pietermaritzburg and Durban, follows this route in June. For information contact **1000 Hills Tourism** ① *Old Main Rd, Botha's Hill, T031-7771874, www.1000hills.kzn.org.za.*

Two excellent nature reserves are located in this area. **Krantzkloof Nature Reserve** ① *152 Kloof Falls Rd, T031-7643515, daily 0600-1800*, has a forested gorge and three waterfalls, 20 km of trails and is home to antelope such as impala and grey and blue duiker. **Shongweni Reserve** ① *Shongweni Dam, T031-7691283, daily 0600-1800 winter, 0500-1900 summer*, is a good place to see birds with over 200 species on record. Mammals include wildebeest, giraffe, warthog and kudu; both white rhino and buffalo have been reintroduced. There are 15 km of self-guiding hiking trails, and activities include morning and evening game drives, horse riding and canoeing.

Between Durban and Pietermaritzburg the landscape quickly climbs some 700 m over a series of rolling hills characteristic of the suburbs around the two cities. From Botha's Rest, there are many viewpoints on the R103 from where you can see the valley unfold. The fertile hills are dotted with villages, farms and encroaching townships closer to Durban. The valley has historically been a Zulu stronghold and, in the early 19th century, was a refuge for dispossessed Zulus who had lost their farmland through battle further north.

The R103 runs along the lip of the valley; tourism has gone into overdrive along this route, with a variety of craft shops, restaurants, B&Bs, guesthouses, farm stalls and several Zulu cultural villages. The most popular of these is **PheZulu Safari Park** ① *5 Old Main Rd, Botha's Hill, T031-7771000, www.phezulusafaripark.co.za, several Zulu shows daily*. There are commanding views of the valley from here, a reptile farm, a small game park with zebra and antelope, curio shops, the **Crocokraal** restaurant which specializes in croc steaks, and the **Mbizo** restaurant, which serves traditional *potjies* (stews), open Sundays only. The main attraction here is the Zulu show, where visitors are taken into traditional beehive-shaped huts and Zulu beliefs, rituals and artefacts are explained. There follows an impressive dancing display.

The Umgeni Steam Railway's **1000 Hills Choo-Choo** ① *T082-3536003 (mob), www.umgenisteamrailway.co.za, 2 daily departures on the 1st and last Sun of each month, 0845 and 1230, tickets from Kloof Station, R100 per person return*, is a vintage 1912 steam train that runs along a line built 1877-1880. On departure days there are two round trips, between Kloof Station and Inchanga, and it's a leisurely way to enjoy the scenery.

> ● *The Valley of 1000 Hills was supposedly named by the writer Mark Twain on a visit to South Africa at the end of the 19th century.*

⊙ Durban listings

⊖ Sleeping

Central Durban and the beachfront have a
wide selection of accommodation, although
safety issues have caused a decline in tourist
numbers in recent years. Current measures
mean that it's much safer now, but it's best
to avoid walking around the centre after dark.
Safer, more attractive and with a wider range
of restaurants are the suburbs of Morningside
and Berea. Contact the **Accommodation
Reservation Service**, Tourist Junction, 160 Pine
St, T031-3043868, www.bookabead.co.za.

The **Baz Bus** collects and drops off from
all backpacker hostels 5 times a week.

City centre and the beachfront p439 and
p443, maps p438 and p442
L Royal Hotel, 267 Smith St, T031-3336000,
www.theroyal.co.za. The hotel originally built
on this site in 1842 was made of wattle and
daub, it now has luxurious 5 star service,
251 rooms, a/c, DSTV, pleasant decor, an
attractive outdoor pool, and 6 restaurants
including an excellent Indian restaurant, a
grill and a theatre supper club (see Eating,
page 449).
AL Durban Hilton, 12-14 Walnut St, next
to the International Conference Centre,
T031-3368100, www1.hilton.com. All the
trappings you'd expect from a modern 5-star
'name' city hotel. Popular with conference
delegates. 327 rooms, restaurant, bar,
gym, pool, curio shop.
B Protea Hotel Edward, 149 Marine Park,
T031-3373681, www.proteahotels.com. Large
luxury hotel on the Golden Mile, with 100 a/c
rooms, en suite with M-Net and minibar,

2 restaurants, bar, pool and deck, secure
covered parking, one of the most luxurious
of the beachfront hotels.
C Bluewaters, 175 Snell Parade, North Beach
T31-3277000, www.bluewatershotel.co.za.
250 rooms, standard modern beachfront
hotel, rooms have DSTV, en suite bathrooms,
a/c, plus excellent views of the beach.
Restaurant, indoor pool, hairdressing salon.
C Tropicana, 85 Marine Park, T031-
3774222, www.goodersonleisure.co.za/
tropicana.html. 168 a/c rooms, fairy spacious
but with uninspiring decor, all are en suite
and have DSTV and internet access. Large
pool area, 2 restaurants, plus the popular
Clippers Café Bar which serves light meals
on the terrace. Swimming pool, secure
covered parking.
C-D Albany, 225 Smith St, T031-3044381,
www.albanyhotel.co.za. Classic art deco
hotel in a big pink block, 72 simple, functional
rooms, en suite, a/c, M-Net TV, rooms have
views over gardens. Restaurant, 2 bars, central
location opposite City Hall and Playhouse.
D Formule 1, next to the railway station and
long-distance coach station, T031-3011551,
www.formule1.co.za. Modern, clean, budget
rooms for up to 3, ideal for late arrivals but
nothing to keep you there other than
sleeping. Book to guarantee a room as
there are few budget options in the centre.

Durban suburbs p444
The suburbs are far more appealing
than the centre, both for their attractive,
historical architecture and the wide choice
of restaurants and bars, all within safe
walking distance of each other.
AL Riverside Hotel & Spa, Northway,
T031-5630600, www.threecities.co.za.
Large modern hotel overlooking the river,
with spacious rooms, a/c, DSTV, dark wood
furniture, beauty and wellness spa. Friendly
service and a great restaurant and popular
bar, secure parking. Some noise from traffic,
very popular with tour groups.

A Quarters, 101 Florida Rd, Morningside, T031-3035246, www.quarters.co.za. 4 historic homes have been converted to create this boutique hotel. Refreshingly modern feel, 25 bedrooms, cool white walls and dark red fabrics, black and white photographs on the walls. Excellent on-site brasserie serves meals throughout the day, shaded courtyard, modern bar. Some of the rooms have a small veranda overlooking palm-shaded gardens, but some are slightly cramped, and are set on a busy corner. Good location close to restaurants.

B 164, 164 St Thomas Rd, Musgrave, T031-2014493, www.164.co.za. Stylish boutique hotel in the centre of Musgrave. Luxurious rooms with polished wooden floors, fashionable decor, simple colour palette, Victorian bathrooms, DSTV. Secure parking, swimming pool set in gardens, delicious cooked-to-order breakfasts, attractive bar with ocean liner decor. Low-key, friendly service, excellent value for what is one of the best guesthouses in Durban. Recommended.

B Beside Still Waters, 30 Braemar Av, La Lucia, T031-5727797, www.besidestill waters.co.za. 14 a/c self-catering units with DSTV and Wi-Fi, in a lovely tract of tropical gardens with fish ponds and a swimming pool, very friendly management, breakfast available, stylish bright decor. Recommended by readers.

B Westville, 124 Jan Hofmeyr Rd, Westville T031-2666326, www.threecities.co.za. Luxury hotel aimed at business travellers and tour groups, 42 a/c rooms, TV, the **Sage** restaurant (renowned for its good Mediterranean cuisine), swimming pool, squash courts, big Irish themed sports bar.

C Elephant House, 745 Ridge Rd, Berea, T031-2089580, elephanthouse@mweb.co.za. The building housing this small B&B is said to be one of the oldest in Durban, and got its name from once having come under attack from elephants. Peaceful and friendly, 2 double rooms, a/c, en suite, TV. Guest lounge, laundry and attractive, quiet tropical gardens. Meals available on request.

C Ridgeview Lodge, 17 Loudoun Rd, Berea, T031-2029777, www.ridgeview.co.za. 7 double rooms each with a/c, en suite bathrooms, TV, phone with email connection and private patios. An elegant house with excellent guest facilities. Secluded lush gardens with swimming pool and good views. Close to restaurants and shops. Airport transfer can be arranged.

C Rosetta House, 126 Rosetta Rd, Morning side, T031-3036180, www.rosettahouse.com. 4 luxury a/c double rooms, cool tiled or wood floors, country inn-style furnishings, en suite, TV, some rooms have separate entrance. Secure parking, a fine old Edwardian town house set in tranquil gardens. Good value and close to the restaurants on Florida Rd.

C-D Bali on the Ridge, 268 South Ridge Rd, Glenwood, T031-2619574, www.baliridge.co.za. Close to the University of Natal, spectacular views of the city and harbour, elegantly furnished with pieces from Bali, attractive polished wooden floors, stylish a/c rooms, TV, bar fridge, pool.

C-D Triple Five, 555 Essenwood Rd, Berea, T031-2096787, www.triplefive.co.za. 2 2-bed a/c separate apartments, extremely comfortable, with well-equipped kitchens, lounges, balconies and DSTV. Garden with jacuzzi, dining area, B&B or self-catering, secure off-street parking.

C-E On the Beach, 17 Promenade, Glenashley, T031-5621591, www.durban backpackers.com. Great location on the beach, north of the city centre and with easy access to the Gateway Mall. Smart set up with mix of guesthouse-type en suite doubles with TV and self-catering dorms. Most rooms have floor-to-ceiling glass windows with ocean views. Prices include breakfast. Lively bar, home-cooked meals, comprehensive travel centre, pool, internet, DSTV, secure parking. To get here follow the M4 through Durban North; after Virginia Airport take the Aubery Dr exit to the beach. Recommended.

D-F Anstey's, 477 Marine Dr, Bluff, T031-4671192, www.ansteysbeach.co.za. The Bluff is the section to the south of Durban that sticks out to sea on the opposite side of the entrance to the port. Another beachside hostel, with dorms, self-catering apartments sleeping 4, bar with pool table, meals. Family-run but with a surf vibe, so lively. Can arrange city tours of Durban, horse rides along the beach and surfing lessons. The lodge is opposite the cave rock, thought to be the most hollow wave in South Africa – surfers should head here.

E-F Hippo Hide, 2 Jesmond Rd, Berea, T031-2074366, www.hippohide.co.za. A small, upmarket backpacker place set in a pretty tropical garden, double rooms, some en suite with TV, one en suite dorm with attached self-catering kitchen, relaxed atmosphere, rock pool, outside bar and pleasant deck, close to shopping centres and restaurants on Musgrove Rd. Good information desk which can help with tours and bookings.

E-F Nomads, 70 Essenwood Rd, Berea, T031-2029709, www.durban.co.za/nomads. Spacious dorms and doubles, self-catering facilities, **Bambooza** bar, swimming pool, pool table. Friendly backpacker place in a safe area within easy walking distance of shops, bars and restaurants. The owners can offer travel advice and are knowledgeable about the area.

E-F Tekweni Backpackers, 169 Ninth Av, Morningside, T031-3031433, www.tekwenibackpackers.co.za. One of the liveliest, most popular hostels in Durban, 2 km from the beach, bus station and town. Dorms and double rooms, small swimming pool and bar out front, space for a couple of tents, laundry facilities, internet access. Often in a party mood, quieter doubles next door. The excellent **Tekweni Ecotours**, T031-4629017, www.tekweniecotours.co.za, is based here.

Eating

A wide choice of restaurants, bars and cinemas can be found in the Gateway shopping mall, see page 452.

City centre *p439, map p438*

$$$ New Café Fish, Yacht Mole, Victoria Embankment, T031-3055062. Open 1200-1500, 1830-2200. Set right on the water with yachts moored within arms reach, upstairs bar great for a sundowner, a basket of calamari and view of the working harbour. Downstairs is the more formal restaurant, seafood a speciality, very popular, outdoor deck in summer.

$$$ Royal Grill, Royal Hotel, 267 Smith St, T031-3336000. Mon-Sat 1830-2300. One of 6 restaurants in this upmarket hotel. This is the hotel's 70-year-old flagship restaurant, serving excellent steaks in an opulent setting with chandeliers, grand piano, soaring ceilings and potted palms. An elegant, colonial dining experience. Save room for something from the dessert trolley.

$$$ Ulundi, Royal Hotel, 267 Smith St, T031-3336000. 1200-1430, 1800-2230, closed Sat lunch. Also based in the **Royal Hotel**, this is regarded as one of the best Indian restaurants in town. Top-end curries with a feel of colonial Natal, turbaned waiters, rattan furniture, ceiling fans, tandoori grills and traditional Durban curries. Good choice for vegetarians.

$$$ Roma Revolving, John Ross House, Victoria Embankment, T031-3682275, www.roma.co.za. Mon-Sat 1200-1430, 1800-2230. Old-fashioned and kitsch concept, this long-running Italian restaurant is set on the 32nd floor, with a revolving floor offering excellent city views. Italian dishes, seafood and pasta, heavily laden dessert trolley, good value 3-course set meals, unparalleled views

$ Transafrica Express, in the BAT Centre, Victoria Embankment, T031-3320804. Relaxed, trendy venue with a deck overlooking the harbour. African menu, including Congo crocodile curry and 'funky chow' – a bunny chow served in warm olive bread. Fashionable, arty crowd, gets very busy in the evenings when there's live music on in the auditorium. Also has jazz on the deck on Fri and Sun afternoons.

Beachfront *p443, map p442*

Cargo Hold, uShaka Marine World, T031-3288065, www.ushakamarine world.co.za. Open 1200-1500, 1800-2230. Great location, popular with families, spread over 3 floors in the phantom ship, with a glass wall looking into the shark tank, with ragged tooth sharks sidling by as you eat. Impressive menu, including good seafood, steaks, warm salads and Mediterranean starters. Reservations essential.

Jewel of India, Holiday Inn Elangeni, 63 Snell Parade, T031-3378168. Large restaurant with traditional Indian decor. Attractive side room with cushions and low tables where you can kick off your shoes and relax with a drink. Tasty North Indian dishes served with tandoori breads.

Joe Kools, North Beach, T031-3329698, www.joecools.co.za. Tue-Sun 1100-late. Superb views of North Beach, large restaurant and pub with a set of wooden decks overlooking the sand. Standard pub fare, range of burgers, pizza, pasta, fried seafood (calamari and fish and chips) and club sandwiches. Perfect for people-watching, turns into a lively bar at night.

Durban suburbs *pp444, map p435*

Durban's most popular night time hubs are Florida Rd in Morningside and Musgrave Rd in Berea, both lined with bars and restaurants.

9th Avenue Bistro & Bar, Avonmore Centre, 9th Av, Morningside, T031-3129134, Tue-Fri 1200-1430, Mon-Sat 1800-2200. Classic bistro atmosphere with a smart, traditional setting, award-winning wine list, good oxtail and roast duck, and luxurious seared tuna and lobster bisque. Plenty of loyal local regulars.

Christina's, 134 Florida Rd, Morningside, T031-3032111. Open for dinner Wed-Sat, breakfast, teas and lunch Tue-Sat. This restaurant is linked to a chef's training school, offering a weekly changing menu. Excellent standard of French cuisine in the evenings, international, themed buffets at lunch and superb breakfasts. Superb cheese board, good deserts and interesting wine list. Outdoor shaded patio is pleasant in the summer.

Bean Bag Bohemia, 18 Windermere Rd, Greyville, T031-3096019. Open 1000-2400. Hugely popular set-up, with a vibey bar on the ground floor and smarter tatty-chic restaurant upstairs, in an old converted Durban town house. Quirky decor, great menu with a Mediterranean bias, mezze platters, pasta and steak. Popular cocktail evenings on Weds. Recommended.

Café 1999, corner of Silverton and Vasue roads, Berea, T031-2023406. Mon-Fri 1230-1430, Mon-Sat 1830-1030. Sheltered outdoor eating area and relaxed, stylish interior. Modern European food, excellent salads, Italian-style mains, great coffees and cakes, too. Young, well-dressed crowd.

Indian Connection, 485 Windermere Rd, Mornigside,T031-3121440. 1100-1500, 1730-1030. Traditional suburban home which has been converted into a modern, stylish Indian restaurant. Refreshingly free of the usual curry house decor, the interior is pure white with wooden floors. Mix of north and south Indian dishes, choice of tandooris, tikkas and biriyanis, plus local coconut prawn curries, friendly service and a trendy, urban crowd.

Mykonos, 156 Essenwood Rd, Berea, T031-2025636, open daily for 3 sittings, 1200-1500, 1730-2000, 2015-2300. Lively atmosphere with Greek music and dancing. Simple decor, excellent value eat-as-much-as-you-can buffet with an extensive selection of dishes, including great roast lamb and grilled prawns. Booking advised.

Bunny chow

One of the more popular and delicious takeaway meals in Durban is bunny chow: a quarter, half or whole loaf of bread with the middle scooped out and filled with curry. The scooped-out bread is then used instead of a spoon to soak up the sauce. There are lots of theories about where it got its name but it's generally thought the dish was originally created for Indian caddies, known as bunnies, at the Royal Durban Golf Course In the 1940s. They were unable to get off from work for long enough to nip into Grey Street for a curry at lunchtime, so the story goes that they got their friends to go and buy the curry for them and that it was brought back to the golf course in hollowed-out loaves of bread because there were no disposable food containers at the time. There's quite an art to eating a bunny; after eating the scooped out piece of bread, you tear pieces off of the side of the loaf and dip them into the curry. The trick here is to avoid tearing off pieces of loaf which are below the current gravy line otherwise you end up with a steaming-hot mass in your lap. You should also check whether your bunny chow was made from the end of a loaf or whether it is a *funny bunny* made from the middle and, hence, without a crust at the bottom.

---

†† Thunder Road Rock Diner, 136 Florida Rd, Morningside, T031-3033440. Themed American rock and roll restaurant with a menu of salads, smoked meats, seafood and no fewer than 10 types of excellent nachos. Run by music industry people, it's best known for promoting local musicians on the small stage.

†† Vestige, 225 Musgrave Rd, corner of St Thomas St, Morningside, T031-2017767. Fashionable, low-key restaurant on a street corner with tables on the veranda outside or in the funky, white and airy interior. Long menu, with good specials such as grilled crayfish or Durban prawn curry, and delicious salads, pasta and open sandwiches – the spicy butternut salad is excellent. Laid-back, friendly service, good value. Recommended.

† Blue Zoo Restaurant and Tea Garden, in Mitchell Park, Musgrave Rd, T031-3129134, Mon-Sun 0800-1700, Tue-Sat 1800-2230. Pleasant spot in the picturesque park with outside tables, simple and cheap build-your-own breakfasts, sandwiches, salads, and light meals like fish and chips or bangers and mash, also dinner menu on some evenings.

† Legends Café, Musgrave Centre, Musgrave Rd, T031-2010733. Simple café serving a mix of stirfries and Mexican dishes, the inside is decorated with posters of movie stars, bar and kitchen open late.

❶ Bars and clubs

Bean Bag Bohemia, 18 Windermere Rd, Greyville, T031-3096019. The trendy bar on the ground floor is one of the most popular in the area. Great cocktail menu including a long list of martinis, popular cocktail nights on Weds. Arty, stylish crowd.

Café Vacca Matta, Suncoast Casino and Entertainment World, T031-3686535, www.vaccamatta.co.za. Fri-Sat 1900-late. This super-sleek bar and club features enormous interiors, ultra-chic decor, lounge areas and bar-dancers. Strictly over 25s and smart dress code, varied music including house, hip-hop and R&B.

Jazzy Rainbow, 93 Goble Rd, Morningside, T031-3038398. Open from 1900. Upmarket jazz venue with African-style decor, bar and snacks, cover charge R50, live jazz most nights until 2300, a DJ follows on weekend nights.

Joe Kools, North Beach, TT031-3329698, www.joecools.co.za. Tue-Sun. Right on the beach opposite one of the most popular surf sites, outside terraces which liven up with live DJs at night, very popular bar with the surfing fraternity.

Roman Lounge, 201 Florida Rd, Morningside, T031-3039022. Gay bar, with a fashionable, mixed clientele. Packed at weekends, good music.

Society, Hollis House, 178 Florida Rd, Morningside, T031-3123213. Converted historical house, now home to an ultra-stylish lounge bar, popular with well-heeled fashion types. Good cocktails, light meals, the place to go for a bout of posing.

⚙ Entertainment

Durban p435, maps p438 and p442
Cinema
The following are multi-screen cinemas.
Nu Metro, www.numetro.co.za, at Suncoast Entertainment World, Snell Parade, T031-3283333, and the Pavilion mall in Westville, T031-2650001.
Ster-Kinekor, Musgrave Centre, Musgrave Rd, Berea, www.sterkinekor.co.za.

Theatre
Catalina Theatre, Wilson's Wharf, Victoria Embankment, T031-3056889, www.catalinatheatre.co.za. 175-seater venue for comedy, theatre and music with new productions every 2-3 weeks.
The Playhouse, 231 Smith St, T031-3699596, www.playhousecompany.com. Shows regular performances in 5 auditoriums: the Opera, Loft, Drama, Studio and Cellar Supper Theatre. An eclectic range of shows ranging from Shakespeare to contemporary political satire and modern dance.
The Royal Backstage, Royal Hotel, 267 Smith St, T031-3336000, www.theroyal.co.za. A cabaret venue and supper theatre offering 3-course meals and various shows. Wed-Sat from 1900.

⊙ Shopping

Durban p435, maps p438 and p442
African Art Centre, 94 Florida Rd, Morningside, T031-3123804, www.afriart.org.za. This is one of the best places in Durban to buy Zulu beadwork, baskets and ceramics, at slightly marked-up prices, but excellent quality. The shop is a non-profit making outlet for rural craftspeople.

Antiques and Bygones, 437 Windermere Rd, Morningside, T031-3038880, www.antiquesandbygones.co.za. Sells a range of silver jewellery and European antiques.

BAT Centre, Victoria Embankment, T031-3320451, www.batcentre.co.za. Superb arts and crafts shops selling a variety of goods, from contemporary Zulu art and jewellery to traditional wood cut prints or handmade shoes.

Matombo Art Gallery, Tourist Junction, T031-3049963. Good quality but expensive stone sculptures from Zimbabwe.

Victoria Street Market, corner of Queen and Victoria streets, T031-3064021. This modern, rather dingy market is crammed with over 170 stalls selling African curios, leather goods, fabrics, copper and spices. The main attractions are the spices and dried beans imported from India.

Village Walk, uShaka Marine World, 1 Bell St, T031-3288000, www.ushaka marineworld.co.za. The shopping arm of this huge marine park, with a wide range of shops, including chain stores and independent boutiques, surf shops and a mix of fast-food outlets.

Suburban shopping malls
Gateway, north out of town in Umhlanga Rocks, T031-5662332, www.gateway world.co.za. This vast complex is supposedly the largest shopping mall in the southern hemisphere – easily believable once you step inside and you can easily spend a day here. There's a huge variety of shops and restaurants, 18-screen cinema, IMAX theatre,

impressive climbing and abseiling wall, an artificial surf wave and the world's only man-made double point break (for those who understand surf jargon), plus a championship skateboard park.

Musgrave Centre, 115 Musgrave Rd, Berea, T031-2015129. Over 110 shops with a mix of trendy boutiques and national chain stores. A craft and curio market is held on level 5 of the car park on Sun 0900-1600.

Pavillion, accessed from the N3, Westville, T031-2650558, www.thepav.co.za. 320 shops and restaurants, and a multi screen cinema. It's always busy – an estimated 1.7 million people visit this mall each month.

▲ Activities and tours

Durban *p435, maps p438 and p442*
Cricket
Kingsmead, T031 3329703, information and tickets from www.sacrickettickets.co.za. Home to the KwaZulu Natal provincial cricket team, Kingsmead is a modern stadium with large grandstands. All of Durban's big matches are played at this popular venue. The weather for matches is generally good but being close to the sea there is always a chance of rain or poor visibility.

Diving
Operators dive from Durban or can arrange trips to other sites such as Sodwana Bay or the Aliwal Shoal. Visibility is at its best during the winter months.
Meridian Dive Centre, 45 Danville Av, Durban North, T031-5732190, www.scubadivesouthafrica.co.za. PADI courses and single dives.

Golf
Windsor Park Municipal Golf Course, next to the Umgeni River just north of Durban, T031-3122245. 18 holes, phone for teeing off times for visitors as competitions are held here regularly, equipment can be hired here by the day or by the week. There are also a number of newer golf courses further north or south along the coast.

Horse racing
Race meetings are held at one of Durban's racecourses operated by the Golden Circle Turf Club: **Greyville**, 150 Avondale Rd, Greyville, T031-3141500; and **Clairwood Park**, 89 Barrier Lane, Merewent, T031-4691020. Each has regular stands and an indoor buffet restaurant overlooking the course for which you will need to dress up a bit. Night racing is held at Greyville only. Phone ahead for times.

Surfing
There are several designated surfing and boogie-boarding beaches along the seafront, and a number of surf shops on the South Beach promenade have boards for hire.
Surf Zone, Ocean Sports Centre, North Beach, T031 3685818. Rents out surf- and body boards by the hr (R40), half-day (R70) or full-day (R100), and organizes surf lessons from R180 per hr.

Tour operators
Durban Africa, Tourist Junction, T031-3044934. The tourist office runs a range of walking tours through the city Mon-Fri, from R75 per person. The 3-hr tours must be booked a day in advance and are a good, safe way of getting to know the city. There's a choice of an Oriental/Indian or a history theme.
Durban Ferry Services, T031-3011953, seamarine@mweb.co.za. Sundowner cruises and harbour tours.
Catchet Tours, T031-2057502, www.cachet tours.co.za. Good range of half- and full-day tours including Durban city, Valley of the 1000 Hills, overnight trips to St Lucia and the Drakensberg.
Islamic Propagation Centre, T031-3060026. Guided tours of the mosque on Queen St.
Jikeleza Tours, T031-7021189, www.jikelezatours.co.za. Township tour

starting at the Kwa-Muhle Museum to understand the nature of Apartheid, before visiting the Umlazi or Nanda township. Also evening trips with local guides for drinks at the township shebeens, plus wider city tours.

Strelitzia Tours, T031-2672252, www.strelitziatours.com. A comprehensive range of tours in the province 1-3 days with regular departures. City tours and day trips to townships, Valley of 1000 hills.

Tekweni Ecotours, at Tekweni Backpackers, 169 Ninth Av, Morningside, T031-4629107, www.tekweniecotours.co.za. Budget tour operator offering a huge range of tours. Regular tours to Hluhluwe-Umfolozi and St Lucia game parks, scuba-diving trips, tailor-made bird trips, and city, Valley of 1000 Hills and township day tours. There are also a number of cultural day and overnight trips to Zululand. Consistently good reports.

Watersports
Durban Charter Boat Association, Fuelling Jetty, Yacht Mole, T031-3011115, www.charterboats.co.za. Offers a wide range of boats, for small speed boat diving trips and deep-sea shark fishing to luxury booze cruises.

⊖ Transport

Durban *p435, maps p438 and p442*
Air
Comair/British Airways has daily flights to and from **Johannesburg**. **South African Airways** (SAA) has a number of daily flights to **Cape Town** and **Johannesburg**, as well as to other principal South African cities. **Mango** has daily flights between Durban and **Cape Town** and **Johannesburg**. **Nationwide** flies from Durban to **Port Elizabeth**, **Cape Town** and **Johannesburg**. **Kulula** flies to **Johannesburg**, **Port Elizabeth** and **Cape Town**. **One Time** flies to **Johannesburg** and **Cape Town**.

Airline offices **Comair/British Airways**, T011-4418600, www.british airways.com. **Kulula**, T0861-585852 (in South Africa), T011-9210111 (from overseas), www.kulula.com. **Mango**, T0861-162646 (in South Africa), T011-3591222 (from overseas), ww5.flymango.com. **Nationwide**, T0861-737737 (in South Africa), T011-3053550 (from overseas), www.flynationwide.co.za. **One Time**, T0861-345345 (in South Africa), T011-9288000 (from overseas), www.1time.co.za. **South African Airways** (SAA), central reservations T0861-359722 (in South Africa), T011-9785313 (from overseas), ww2.flysaa.com

Bus
Greyhound, **Intercape** and **Translux** all run regular buses to **Cape Town** via Mthatha, East London, Port Elizabeth, Knysna and Swellendam, or via Harrismith, Bloemfontein and Beaufort West; **Pretoria** and **Johannesburg** on the N3 or via **Richards Bay** and the N2.

Margate Mini Coach departs Durban Station, advance booking essential, to the **Wild Coast Sun** (3 hrs 15 mins) in the Eastern Cape (see page 428). There are up to 3 services in each direction via Durban Airport, Scottburgh, Hibberdene, Port Shepstone, Margate; expect to pay R160 for the full one-way trip.

Baz Bus has services to **Port Elizabeth**, and **Johannesburg** and **Pretoria**, via Northern Drakensberg, or via Zululand and Swaziland.

Bus companies Baz Bus, T021-4392323, www.bazbus.com. **Grey hound**, T083-9159000 (in South Africa), T011-2768550 (from overseas), www.greyhound.co.za. **Intercape**, T086-1287287 (in South Africa), T012-3804400 (from overseas), www.intercape.co.za. **Margate Mini Coach**, T039-3121406, after hours T082-4559736

(mob), www.margate.co.za/minicoach.htm.
Translux, T0861-589282 (in South Africa),
T011-7743333 (from overseas),
www.translux.co.za.

Car hire
For the nearest location in Durban of the
main companies, visit the websites or phone
the toll-free numbers listed on page 42.
Avis, www.avis.co.za, airport, T031-4081777.
Berea Car & Bakkie Hire, 597 Berea Rd,
T031-2023333, www.bcrea.co.za. **Budget**,
www.budget.co.za, airport T031-4081888.
Hertz, www.hertz.com; airport, T031-
4694247. **Imperial**, www.imperial
carrental.co.za; airport T031-4690066.

Taxi
Taxis must be booked in advance:
Mozzie Cabs, T031-2630467;
Zippy Cabs, T031-2027067.

Train
Trains for Durban arrive at the **Durban
Station**, NMR Av, T0860-008888,
www.spoornet.co.za. The country's longest
route, from Durban to **Cape Town** (36 hrs),
leaves weekly, and runs via **Bloemfontein**
and **Kimberley**. The route to **Johannesburg**
(13 hrs), via **Pietermaritzburg** (2 hrs) and
Ladysmith (6 hrs), leaves Sun, Mon and
Wed-Fri.

Directory

Durban *p435, maps p438 and p442*
Banks
American Express, Pavilion Mall, T031-
2651455/6; 213 Musgrave Rd, T031-2028733,
Mon-Fri 0800-1700, Sat 0830-1200.
Rennies, foreign exchange and Thomas
Cook representative, 163 Windermere Rd,
Morningside, T031-3122707, The Pavilion,
Westville, T031-2650751.

Consulates
Belgium, 18 Ross Gardens, Morningside,
T031-3032840. **Germany**, 9 Kensington Dr,
Westville, T031-2663920,
www.germanconsulatekzn.co.za. **Italy**,
14th floor, Embassy House, 199 Smith St,
T031-3684388/9, www.consdurban.esteri.it.
Mozambique, 5th floor, 320 West St,
T031-3040200. **Netherlands**, 8th floor,
Standard Bank Building, 135 Musgrave Rd,
Berea, T031-2020461. **Sweden and Norway**,
17 Overpoort Dr, Berea, T031-2076900.
United Kingdom, 124 Davenport Rd,
Glenwood, T031-2026823. **USA**, 31st floor,
Old Mutual Building, 303 West St,
T031-3057600.

Emergencies
Police Tourism Unit T031-3682207.
Sea Rescue T082 911.

Internet
The **Freedom NetCentre**, 385 Smith St,
T031-3073461, has 65 terminals and is open
0800-2400. **Durban Online**, Ushaka Village
Walk, T031-3371818, has numerous outlets
in the shopping malls and most of the
backpacker hostels offer internet access.

Medical services
Addington Hospital (Principal State
Hospital), Erskine Terrace, South Beach,
T031-3272000. **Entabeni Private Hospital**,
148 South Ridge Rd, T031-2041300. **North
Beach Medical Centre**, 37 Sol Harris Cres,
T031-3326060. The **Travel Doctor**, 45
Ordnance Rd, International Convention
Centre, T031-3601122. Vaccination centre
and a good place to pick up anti-malarials.
Pharmacies Emergency pharmacy
T031-2073946.

Useful contacts
Weather T082-2311603.

KwaZulu Natal coast

The stretch of coast directly north of Durban is a mix of built-up holiday resort and city suburbs. To the south, the coastal resorts have more of a holiday feel. Much of this stretch has undergone considerable development and is extremely popular with domestic tourists. ›› *For listings, see pages 464-469.*

South of Durban ⊜❷❼▲ ›› pp464-469.

The landscape south of Durban includes a fertile subtropical region stretching from the southern tip of the Drakensberg Mountain Range to the Indian Ocean. The Umzimkulu, the Umkomaas and the Elands rivers wind their way from the Drakensberg escarpment through the rolling hills of KwaZulu Natal to the sea. This was one of the first areas to be settled by the British during the 19th century and continuous agricultural development has left its mark on the landscape. Some of South Africa's largest pine and eucalyptus plantations extend for mile after mile around Harding, while, nearer to the coast, sugarcane and banana plantations dominate the scenery. A strip of subtropical forest runs down the coast bordering onto the beach. Excellent roads also make the Strelitzia and Hibiscus coastlines among South Africa's most popular holiday destinations.

Dolphin watching and scuba diving on the Aliwal Shoal and on the reefs south of Port Shepstone thrill an ever-growing number of enthusiasts. A wide range of sporting facilities, including numerous golf courses and tennis courts, are available at the resorts. The main attractions inland are the nature reserves at Oribi Gorge and Umtamvuna.

Amanzimtoti → *Colour map 5, B2.*

The Srtrelitzia Coast is one of the more built-up areas south of Durban. Driving down the N2, the road passes Durban's international airport and goes through an extensive industrial belt. Amanzimtoti, or 'toti', only 22 km south of Durban, is effectively a suburb, a huge built-up holiday resort with little to keep you in town. The Zulu name translates as 'sweet waters', as described by Shaka. Thousands of locals spend their annual holiday here, swimming, soaking up the sun and partying. A wide range of holiday accommodation is available among the high-rise flats and holiday homes facing the beach. **Inyoni Rocks** and **Pipeline Beach** are the two main beaches for swimmers and sunbathers, behind which is a busy main road. On the outskirts of town is a large chemical factory and an explosives factory. However, the lagoons beyond Amanzimtoti have been spared the relentless pace of development and these havens of tropical vegetation are sanctuaries for the coast's prolific birdlife.

Kingsburgh to Scottburgh → *Colour map 5, B1.*

Between Amanzimtoti and Umgababa are a series of coastal resorts and beaches known collectively as Kingsburgh. The 8-km stretch is known for its good beaches and is popular with surfers and jet-skiers. Travelling down the coast from Amanzimtoti, the first beach you reach is **Doonside**; across the Little Manzimtoti River is **Warner Beach**. **Winkelspruit** is one of the more developed parts of the area. Across the Lovu River is **Illovo** beach, which is backed by a lagoon at the mouth of the river. **Karridene** is at the mouth of another river, the Msimbazi. **Umkomaas** is the last resort in this area, next to the **Empisini Nature Reserve**, where a small dam has been built on the river which attracts an interesting variety of birdlife. The reserve can be reached by taking the Umkomaas and Widenham exit off the N2.

Scottburgh → *Colour map 5, B1.*

Scottburgh, 58 km south of Durban, is one of the busiest resorts on the Strelitzia coast. The popular beach by the estuary of the Mpambanyoni is protected by shark nets. The beaches are connected by a miniature seafront railway. There is a **tourist office** ⓘ *library centre, Scott St, T039-9761364, www.scottburgh.co.za.*

South Coast

The **Aliwal Shoal** lies just north of Scottburgh, and after Sodwana Bay is one of South Africa's most popular diving areas (see page 468). The shoal is a haven for marine life and offers a good selection of dives on wrecks and on the reef. The caves attract ragged-tooth sharks each winter.

Hibiscus Coast
▶▶ *pp464-469.*

There is less industrial development along this coast, which stretches from Scottburgh to Port Edward, but the overall impression as you drive down the coast is of a long line of caravan parks and holiday homes, set in a lush subtropical strip of forest. The ocean is the highlight here. During the warm winter months billions of sardines travel close to the beaches, attracting dolphins, sharks, game fish and birds, and the ocean teams with life.

Vernon Crookes Nature Reserve
ⓘ *sunrise to sunset, R10.*
From the N2, the R612 heads inland towards Ixopo. After passing Umzinto (8 km), there is a signpost to the Vernon Crookes Nature Reserve. The road passes through eucalyptus and sugarcane plantations as it heads towards a typical African landscape of grassland and thornveld, which supports 56 species of mammals.

This is one of the best reserves to see blue wildebeest, eland, impala, nyala, oribi, reedbuck and zebra near to the south coast. The wide range of habitats here supports over 300 species of bird. The best time of year to see the reserve's wild flowers is during the spring in September and October – there are some magnificent displays of orchids, lobelias and watsonias. A network of dirt roads crosses the park and there are picnic sites, a dam and viewpoints.

Umzumbe Village

This small, pleasant village 100 km south of Durban has a great backpackers' place to chill out at by the sea. It's also a good spot for dolphin watching and scuba diving. From Durban, turn off the N2 at Hibberdene and follow the R102. Turn right at the sign for Umzumbe Fairview Mission and look out for the sign after about 1 km. It's also on the Baz Bus route.

Port Shepstone → *128 km from Durban. Colour map 5, C1.*

Located at the mouth of the Umzimkulu River, Port Shepstone is the largest town on the south coast and is more of an industrial centre than a tourist resort. **Hibiscus Coast Tourism** ① *Princess Elizabeth Dr, T039-6822455, www.hibiscuscoast.kzn.org.za.*

South of Port Shepstone

The towns and villages on this southernmost stretch of coast are the last of the chain of resorts that feel like seaside holiday camps before the R620 enters the Wild Coast (see page 416). Hiking in Umtamvuna Nature Reserve, diving on Protea Banks and the reefs off Shelly Beach, and whale and dolphin watching are the highlights of this region.

Shelly Beach is 5 km south of Port Shepstone on the R620. It is quite a large suburb with one of the region's biggest shopping malls and has a wide variety of shops, restaurants and a cinema. The beach here is popular as a launch site for various fishing and diving charters.

Uvongo, 12 km south of Port Shepstone, is built on cliffs looking out to sea and is one of the more pleasant resorts on the south coast. The beach, protected by shark nets, is safe for swimming and surfing. The waterfall at the nearby **Uvongo River Nature Reserve**, open from sunrise to sunset, is a pleasant place for a picnic. The 23-m-high waterfall tumbling over cliffs into the beachside lagoon is the reserve's main feature. At the rear of the beach are some steps to a viewpoint overlooking the falls.

Margate → *Colour map 5, C1.*

Originally a palm-fringed stretch of sand, the town began to be developed in 1919 and is now a highly developed family resort, popular with holidaymakers from Gauteng. The beach is excellent and was awarded the Blue Flag a few years ago. From the junction with the South Coast Toll Road, the link road immediately enters the tourist zone passing the mini-golf and holiday homes on the way into town. In the centre, high-rise flats are crammed in towards the beachfront, which gets very crowded during school holidays. For information contact **Hibiscus Coast Publicity Association** ① *Panorama Parade, Margate Beachfront, T039-3122322, www.hibiscuscoast.kzn.org.za.*

Ramsgate is 2 km south of Margate and is now practically a suburb, but the beach here is a little quieter and has shark nets so is popular for surfing. It has a tidal pool for swimming, with pedalos and canoes for hire.

Southbroom

Southbroom is a popular resort with subtropical trees coming down to the beach. It consists mainly of private holiday homes belonging to wealthy Gautengers and can feel deserted out of season. There is safe swimming in a tidal pool just down the coast at Marina Beach, a beautiful 5-km stretch of sand and rolling dunes.

The **Riverbend Crocodile Farm and Art Gallery** ① *Old National Rd, T039-3166204, www.crocodilecrazy.co.za, daily 0900-1630, feeding time Sun 1500, small entry fee*, breeds around 200 Nile crocodiles. There is also a snake house, with snake handling demos every day at 1430. This tourist complex has a tea garden, a restaurant, farm stall and an art gallery.

Mpenjati Nature Reserve ① *sunrise to sunset, R10*, is 12 km south of Southbroom and is popular with windsurfers, canoeists and fishermen. The reserve covers a small area of coastal forest and wetlands along the edge of the lagoon and is good for spotting wetland and woodland birds including a resident pair of breeding fish eagles. There are some leisurely walking trails along the Mpenjati River and around the lagoon, with two picnic spots.

Port Edward → *Colour map 5, C1.*

This small tourist resort has a large palm-fringed beach backing onto tropical forest. There are shark nets here and good swimming and surfing. It is a convenient place to stay when visiting Umthamvuna Nature Reserve.

Umtamvuna Nature Reserve

① *8 km north of Port Edward towards Izingolweni, T039-3132383, sunrise to sunset, R10.*
This is the southernmost and one of the lesser visited reserves in KwaZulu Natal, but has some of the finest hiking in the region. The sheer walls of lichen-covered rock, dropping down into thick rainforest at the bottom of the gorge, are the centre of this dramatic landscape. There is no big game here but the reserve is known for its displays of wild flowers in the spring and its colony of Cape vultures. It's also regarded as one of the world's top plant spots with over 330 species of woody plants and 80 herbaceous plants, of which 30 are endemic to South Africa. One shrub, *Raspalia trigyna*, is very rare and only found in this reserve. It is usually fairly easy to spot bushbuck, blue and common duiker, and the ubiquitous chacma baboons. Shy Cape clawless otters inhabit the reserve but the most visitors ever see of them are the white calcareous droppings found along river banks. There are two entrances to the reserve: the first turning, off the Izingolweni road, leads to the southern gate; the second turning, 5 km further on, leads to the northern gate. A simple map, bird checklist and some ecology information leaflets are available at the entrance.

Towards the Wild Coast

The Wild Coast lies to the south of Port Edward, on the other side of the former border over the River Umtamvuna. This used to be part of the former homeland of Transkei but since the abolishment of the homelands it is now part of Eastern Cape (see page 416). The contrast between the former homeland and KwaZulu Natal could hardly be more marked – crossing the old border is like crossing into another, much poorer, country. Road conditions deteriorate immediately and this is not a good route for access to the Wild Coast unless you have a 4WD. The alternative route to the Wild Coast is along the N2 via Kokstad and Mthatha to Port St Johns on a tarred road. It is dangerous to drive at night because of the goats, cattle and stray dogs that wander across the roads.

West from Port Shepstone

The road heading inland from Port Shepstone to the Oribi Gorge Nature Reserve passes through an extensive agricultural area of sugarcane fields, eucalyptus plantations and cattle pastures, crowded with Zulu huts and smallholdings. The contrast between the outlying farmland and the untouched African bush in the gorge is striking. There are two routes to Oribi Gorge (21 km). The fastest route is to follow the N2; just past Oribi Flats East there is a signpost to the park on the right-hand side of the road. The alternative route is slightly longer and involves turning off the N2 onto a minor road 7 km outside of Port Shepstone. This road leads to Oribi Flats (21 km) and to the Oribi Gorge Hotel. The road passes through some rugged scenery along the Umzimkulweni River Valley.

Oribi Gorge Nature Reserve → *Colour map 5, B1.*

ⓘ *21 km west of Port Shepstone via the N2, T039-6791644, www.kznwildlife.com, 0630-1930, R10.*

Established in 1950 to protect this area of thick woodland and towering cliffs where the Umzimkulu and Umzimkulweni rivers meet, the Oribi Gorge Nature Reserve is 24 km long and 5 km wide. The views from the top of the sandstone cliffs, some of which are up to 280 m high, look out over the forest, which clings to the sides of the ravines below. The cliffs provide nesting sites for birds of prey, and the forest, home to the African python, is so thick that although leopard live here they are never seen. One of their prey, the Samango monkey, can sometimes be seen in small groups. Favouring dense, evergreen jungle, the Samango has a dark brown face and longish hair. Birdlife here is prolific, with over 250 species present, including Knysna louries, narina trogons, trumpeter hornbills and five kingfisher species. Ironically, oribi are not common and are very rarely seen.

Samango Falls, **Hoopoe Falls** and **Lehr's Falls** are the most spectacular waterfalls in the gorge and are best seen after heavy rain when vast quantities of water come crashing down into the ravines below. There are several clearly marked hikes, from 1 km to 9 km. A series of tracks lead to viewpoints over the gorge. There are stunning views from **Oribi Heads**, **Horseshoe Rock**, **Camel Rock** and the **Overhanging Rock**.

A tarred road winds down 4 km from the hutted camp to a picnic spot next to the bridge crossing the Umzimkulweni River. There are some impressive views of the gorge. The Umzimkulweni River is not safe to swim in as it is infected with bilharzia but there is a pleasant swimming pool in the camp. The camp shop sells wildlife books, souvenirs, charcoal, firewood and a limited range of food. Fresh meat, vegetables and cheese are available from a farm shop just by the entrance to the reserve. The nearest petrol station is 4 km away in Paddock.

Don't leave valuables in your car when you walk to the edge of the gorge as cases of petty theft have been reported.

North of Durban (Dolphin Coast) ⊖❷🅞🅐🅖🅒 ⇝ *pp464-469.*

The area north of Durban, between Umhlanga and Tugela Mouth, is known as the Dolphin Coast, thanks to the bottlenose dolphins that frolic in the waves year-round. It is also known as the Sugar Coast, thanks to the rolling sugar plantations backing the sea. Like the coastline to the south of Durban it is possible to miss many of the sights and small coastal settlements if you remain on the N2 highway. The inland towns of Verulam, Tongaat and Stanger/KwaDukuza, tucked between vast rolling sugar plantations, have large resident Indian populations and are processing centres for the area's industry, with few attractions for tourists.

The old coast road, however, runs parallel to the sea passing through the beach resorts of Umhlanga Rocks, Ballito and Salt Rock, attracting vast crowds of holidaying South Africans in summer. After Umhlanga Rocks, most of the resorts are far smaller than those found on the south coast and appeal to more upmarket holidaymakers, but the area is developing quickly. Nevertheless, it feels more relaxed and far less developed than the south coast, with crowds thinning out the further you get from Durban. The beaches are beautifully wild stretches of soft sand, pounded by impressive waves (but remember to check if they're protected by shark nets before going for a dip). Away from the water, locals flock to the impressive golf courses, although a quieter choice are the numerous tropical nature reserves; seldom overrun with visitors, these well-run protected areas provide some fine birdwatching opportunities.

Dolphin Coast

Map showing Dolphin Coast with labels including: To St Lucia & Hluhluwe, Enselini Nature Reserve, Richards Bay, Empangeni, R34, N2, Umhlatuzi Lagoon, Mtunzini, Umlalazi, Umlalazi Nature Reserve, Gingindlovu, aMatikulu, Amatikulu Nature Reserve, R102, Mandini, Tugela Mouth, Harold Johnson Nature Reserve, Fort Pearson, Darnall, Shakaland, Zinkwazi Beach, Stanger/KwaDukuza, Shaka's Memorial, Blythdale Beach, Salt Rock, Shaka's Rock, Ballito, Crocodile Creek, Tongaat, Umhloti Beach, Verulam, Umhlanga Rocks, Sharks Board, Gateway Shopping Mall, Virginia Airport, Durban, To South Coast. Side labels: To Melmoth & Ulundi, To Ulundi, Eshowe & Vryheid, To Greytown & Ladysmith, To Pietermaritzburg. Scale: 10 km / 10 miles.

Umhlanga Rocks → *Colour map 5, B2.*

Sugar Coast Tourism Association
① *Chartwell Dr, T031-5613978, www.sugar coast.kzn.org.za, Mon-Fri 0800-1630, Sat 0900-1200,* arranges accommodation and provides advice on visiting the nature reserves. It also has maps and brochures.

The upmarket holiday resort of Umhlanga Rocks is a short drive north of Durban – these days it is virtually a suburb of the city, although its sprawl of concrete highrises makes it feel more like a Spanish costa. The main attraction here away from the beach is **Gateway**, South Africa's premier shopping mall, allegedly the largest in the southern hemisphere (see page 452).

Umhlanga Rocks beach is a beautiful stretch of wave-lashed sand, although day visitors have little chance of seeing it, thanks to the belt of highrises stretching along its length. Access to the water is almost exclusively through resort complexes and hotels, and there's no beachfront area. Nevertheless, South Africans flock to the hotels and condominiums, and the area has a buzzing atmosphere in high season. **Umhlanga Lagoon** lies just to the north of town, where there are beautiful expanses of wetland, forest and an unspoilt, open beach yet to be concreted over by the developers.

The town's name means 'Place of Reeds' in Zulu after the reeds that are washed down the river to the north and onto the pristine beaches. The area was once covered with dune forest; today, only small pockets of original vegetation have been preserved in surrounding nature reserves. In the 19th century, the land was part of a large sugar estate, Natal Estates Ltd, owned by Sir Marshall Campbell. The estate was managed from Mount Edgecombe in the interior; a track was built from here to the coast and local farmers began to lease small plots on the beach and build holiday cottages. The first cottage was built in 1869 and was known as the Oyster Box, today the **Oyster Box Hotel**, which is presently being refurbished.

A popular local landmark is the **Umhlanga Lighthouse**. The distinct red and white circular concrete tower stands 21 m above the beach and acts as a fixed point to help ships waiting to dock in Durban harbour confirm their exact position in the outer anchorage. The lighthouse tower has stood here since November 1954, occupying the centre point on the beach, right in front of the **Oyster Box Hotel**. The lighthouse has never had a keeper; instead it is operated by the owner of the **Oyster Box Hotel** from controls in the hotel office.

The **Sharks Board** ⓘ *Herrwood Dr, T031-5660400, www.shark.co.za, display hall and curio shop Mon-Fri 0800-1600, tour and video Tue-Thu 0900 and 1400, Sun 1400, R20*, set inland from the resort, studies the life cycles of the sharks that inhabit the sea off the coast of KwaZulu Natal and investigates how best to protect bathers with various forms of netting. Umhlanga Rocks became the first beach to erect shark nets in 1962, following a series of attacks along the whole coast in December 1957. Today the Sharks Board is responsible for looking after more than 400 nets, which protect nearly 50 beaches. Tours at the Sharks Board begin with a 25-minute multimedia video show on the biology of sharks and their role as top predators in the marine food chain. This is followed by a stomach-churning shark dissection. The display hall has a variety of replicas of sharks, fish and rays, including that of an 892-kg shark. It is also possible to accompany researchers on the Sharks Board boat as they go about their daily servicing of the shark nets off Durban's Golden Mile (R200). The boat goes from Wilson's Wharf back in Durban at 0630.

Hawaan Nature Reserve is 4 km north of Umhlanga Rocks at the end of Newlands Drive. During the 1920s, William Alfred Campbell, son of Sir Marshall who had founded the sugar estates, used to stage an annual hunt in this unique forest environment. It was not until 1980 that 60 ha were protected as part of the nature reserve. Within the reserve there are 4 km of leisurely guided walks through an unusual area of mature coastal forest. The trails are not open to the public but walks can be organized with the **Wildlife Society** ⓘ *T031-5612030*. The area is rich in birdlife and you can also see bushbuck, duiker and vervet monkeys.

Crocodile Creek ⓘ *T032-9443845, daily 0930-1700, small entry fee*, is between Umhlanga and Ballito; turn off the Old Main Road (R102) close to Maidstone Golf Course. This crocodile centre has regular hands-on guided tours viewing its population of over 9000 crocodiles, as well as snakes, tortoises and small monkeys. Between December and March, it is possible to see baby crocs hatching. The curio shop sells goods made from the skins and the coffee shop has crocodile on the menu.

Ballito and around → *Colour map 5, B2.*

The small-scale, largely low-rise resort of Ballito is far more attractive than Umhlanga, with easy access to the long beach and attractive accommodation nestled in lush vegetation stretching up the hillside. At the entrance of town, just off the coast road, is the **Sangweni Tourism Centre** ⓘ *T032-9461997, www.thedolphincoast.co.za, Mon-Fri 0830-1700, Sat 0900-1300*, a useful stop-off with information on the Dolphin Coast area. Most visitors to Ballito are South African holidaymakers, who settle in for a bucket-and-spade holiday every summer. If you're passing through, it's a pleasant enough spot for a day or two by the beach, but stick to the southern, less developed end.

North of Ballito, **Salt Rock** is named after a rock where the Zulus used to collect salt, and is similar to Ballito, while nearby **Shaka's Rock**, also developing fast, is named after the cliff from which Shaka is said to have thrown his enemies to their foamy deaths. There is good snorkelling at Tiffany's Reef and Sheffield Reef, but neither resort holds much appeal other than for those after a sand and sea holiday.

Tongaat, Verulam and Stanger/KwaDukuza

Inland from Umhlanga Rocks, the R102 passes through the towns of Verulam, Tongaat and Stanger/KwaDukuza, which collectively form the heart of KwaZulu Natal's sugar processing industry. The descendants of the indentured labourers, who were brought here from India in the 1860s, give the region a distinct Indian atmosphere and, although the towns are now predominantly industrial centres, the Hindu temples and Indian markets are interesting. Accommodation is available here, but the beach resorts on the coast are more pleasant places to stay.

In Tongaat, the **Juggernath Puri Temple** is 23 m high and can be seen from miles away. There are no windows in the tower, but inside, as the eye adjusts to the darkness, the Vishnu statue gradually becomes visible. **Shri Gopalal Temple** is just outside of Verulam on the road to the Packo food factory. The temple was opened by Gandhi in 1912, and catered for wealthier and more educated Gujurati immigrants. **Subramanyar Alayam Temple** is set in a beautiful tropical garden just north of town as you reach the railway bridge. A good time to experience the atmosphere of the temple is at weekends when many weddings are held. It is customary to remove your shoes before entering the temple buildings.

Stanger/KwaDukuza is a busy commercial centre surrounded by extensive sugar plantations. It is currently undergoing a name change to KwaDukuza, which was the original settlement here that was founded by Shaka as his capital. At its height there were up to 2000 beehive huts surrounding Shaka's royal kraal. Shaka was murdered here by his half-brothers Dingaan and Umhlangana on 22 September 1828. A monument was erected in Shaka's memory in 1932, which today has become the focus point for the small **KwaDukuza Visitor Centre** ① T032-5527210, 0830-1600, free. Here, visitors can watch a short audio-visual display on Shaka's life, and have a nose around his memorial garden and tea room. For further information on Shaka, see page 846.

)) *Albert Luthuli, who won the Nobel Peace Prize in 1960, was restricted to living in Stanger as punishment for his political activities with the ANC. He died here in 1967.*

Harold Johnson Nature Reserve

① T031-4861574, daily 0600-1800.

Just over 20 km north of Stanger/KwaDukuza on the N2, a signposted dirt track leads through sugar plantations up to the entrance of this 100-ha reserve, where there is a parking area and a picnic site. In the reserve are the remains of **Fort Pearson**, which was used as a base from which British troops invaded Zululand in 1879. The **Ultimatum Tree**, the other attraction here, was where Shepstone read out the ultimatum to Cetshwayo's *izindunas* (warriors) giving them 20 days to disband their armies, pay fines in cattle and conform to the coronation vows that Shepstone had imposed. These demands and others were totally unreasonable to the Zulus but non-compliance with the ultimatum was used by the colonial authorities as an excuse for war.

In the reserve, wildlife includes red and grey duiker, bushbuck, impala, vervet monkey and over 110 species of butterfly, which can be sought out on 7 km of walking trails. The **Muthi Trail** gives an interesting insight into the medicinal uses of various traditional plants used by the Zulu people; a booklet can be bought at the entrance. At the picnic site there's a small cultural **museum** ① R10, portraying traditional Zulu dress and culture.

Hotel and guesthouse prices
L over US$300   AL US$220-300   A US$150-220
B US$100-150   C US$75-100   D US$35-75
E US$15-35   F under US$15
Restaurant prices
♥♥♥ over US$30   ♥♥ US$15-30   ♥ under US$15
See pages 46-51 for further information.

Sleeping

Kingsburgh p456
E-F Angle Rock Backpackers, 5 Ellcock Rd, Warner Beach, T031-9167007, www.anglerock.co.za. Smart backpackers' place in a great beachside location, with octagonal-shaped dorms and double rooms. Also has camping, excellent kitchen, laundry facilities, snooker table, swimming pool in a private garden full of palm trees and a great tropical feel. Owners organize diving at the Aliwal Shoal, free use of surfboards and fishing rods, recommended as the place to stay south of Durban, call in advance for pickups from Durban stations and airport.

Scottburgh p457
C Blue Marlin Resort, 180 Scott St, T039-9783361, www.bluemarlin.co.za. Large resort on a hill overlooking the beach, pool, gardens, games room, 2 bars, inclusive of buffet meals, 120 spacious and functional rooms, has weekly specials for senior citizens so, as you can imagine, activities lean towards bingo, bowls and bridge.
C Cutty Sark, beachfront, T039-9761230, www.cuttysark.co.za. Modern, slightly dated hotel in a lovely beachside location. 55 rooms, TV, 2 restaurants, bar, swimming pool, tennis and squash courts, gym, in 6 ha of well-kept tropical gardens. Horse riding on the beach and diving can be arranged from here. Popular family hotel.
D-E Scottburgh Caravan Park, seafront, T039-9760291, www.scottburghcaravan park.co.za. Giant caravan park, over 300 sites

stretching along 1 km of beach, designed to cater for families during school holidays. The park has several swimming pools and has good sports facilities. Gets very busy during school holidays, but is a great setting out of season.

Umzumbe Village p458
E-F Mantis & Moon, Station Rd, T039-6846256, www.mantisandmoon.net. Rustic backpackers set in lush jungle, with dorms, doubles and camping dotted between wild banana trees, also has newer tree house, with double rooms. Pool table, candle-lit bar, great music, home-cooked food, free use of surf boards, courtyard with a wild garden, outdoor hot tub, rooftop deck. Recommended.

Port Shepstone p458
B Kapenta Bay, 11-12 Princess Elizabeth Dr, T039-6825528, www.kapentabay.co.za. 50 units, all 3 room self-catering suites with 2 bathrooms, bland modern block over-looking the beach, large swimming pool, secure parking, typical resort set-up and popular conference venue.
D-F Pepper Pots, 60 Commercial Rd, T039-6950852, pepperpots@telkomsa.net. Family-run set-up, smaller and less sprawling as the usual beachside resorts. Self-catering chalets, backpackers dorm, caravan and campsites, bar, restaurant, TV lounge, walking distance to the beach.

South of Port Shepstone p458
C Ayton Manor, 2.5 km inland from Shelly Beach, after driving under the N2, take the first right, T039-6850777, www.ayton manor.co.za. B&B and self-catering guest lodge with 6 rooms and 2 family suites set in a fine country house on a sugar estate, rather over-the-top decor (frills, heavy curtains), private balconies and separate entrances, TV, fridge, microwave, bar, pool, children will like the working farmyard.

D Greyfare, 38 Frere Rd, Shelly Beach, T039-3157446, www.greyfare.co.za. 6 modern spacious flats for 1-6 people, private balconies or secluded patios, fully equipped, TV, lovely small pool and garden, breakfast available on request, walking distance to beach, shops and cinema, cheap rates, good value for money.

Margate *p458*

B Margate Hotel, 71 Marine Dr, T039-3121410, www.margate.co.za/ margatehotel.htm. 69 a/c en suite rooms, TV, **Keg** pub and restaurant, swimming pool, tennis, comfortable but run-of-the-mill family hotel set in mature gardens overlooking the beach. Discounts in low season.

B Wailana Beach Lodge, 436 Ashmead Rd, T039-3144606, www.wailana.co.za. Luxury guesthouse located 1 km to both Ramsgate and Margate centres, easy walking distance to all amenities, nice gardens with hammocks and pool, B&B, 5 stylish en suite rooms, TV, fan, lovely private sun decks with ocean views, evening meals on request, much more friendly than the standard holiday flats.

C Beach Lodge Hotel, Marine Dr, T039-3121483, www.beachlodge.org.za. 35 a/c rooms, TV, plus modern self-catering units, all with well-equipped kitchens, dining area, TV, DVD player. Restaurant serving buffet breakfast, bar, large swimming pool, secure parking, Dutch spoken.

C-D Dumela Holiday Resort, St Patrick's Rd, T039-3173301, www.dumelamargate.co.za. Simple self-catering cabanas overlooking Margate's Blue Flag beach, 2 bed, 2 bath, kitchen, balcony with braai, DSTV, café and takeaway, pool, thatched bar, good value for groups/families up to 6, especially out of season.

Southbroom *p458*

B Nature's Cottage, Churchill Rd, T039-3168533, www.naturescottage.co.za. Charming log buildings encircled by large verandas and raised decks with cane furniture, set in a patch of indigenous forest and competition-winning gardens. 3 guest rooms, 2 self-catering cottages, 1 of which is built on stilts, TV, video and CD player, 2 swimming pools. No under 13s. Recommended.

Port Edward *p459*

A Estuary Country Hotel, 1 km before Port Edward on the N2, clearly signposted, T039-3132675, www.estuaryhotel.co.za. 24 en suite a/c rooms in a restored Cape Dutch manor house, most with balcony overlooking the estuary, TV, bar, pool, health and beauty spa, close to a safe swimming beach. The **Fish Eagle Restaurant** is open to non-residents, ownership by an Austrian family, interesting and varied South African and European menu.

D-E Ku-Boboyi River Lodge and Backpackers, 4 km north of Port Edward in Leisure Beach on the R61, T039-3191371, www.kuboboyi.co.za. A bright hilltop lodge with good views over the ocean and beach. Singles and doubles with en suites or shared bathrooms, decorated in an African theme, plenty of space for camping, pool, sunny veranda, B&B. The owner, Eric, is a chef and cooks exceptionally good value gourmet meals each night.

Oribi Gorge Nature Reserve *p460*

B-D Oribi Gorge Camp, reservations through **KZN Wildlife**, T033-8451000, www.kznwildlife.com. 6 huts with 2 beds in each, a 7-bed chalet and a 10-bed chalet, plus 3 tent sites. The huts and chalet are equipped with fridge, kettle, toaster, crockery and cutlery but no cooker. Bring all food and drinks with you. There's also a communal braai area, lounge with satellite TV and a swimming pool with sundeck for use by all guests and campers.

C Oribi Gorge Hotel, T039-6870253, www.oribigorge.co.za. Small family hotel with 18 comfortable rooms, restaurant, snooker, gym, country pub, curio shop, swimming pool. The hotel, built in the 1870s, is a colonial building encircled by a veranda. The restaurant serves burgers, steaks, pies and pub food. There is a pleasant beer garden where you can eat outside under the trees. The gorge can be seen from viewpoints on farmland adjoining the hotel, which is only 17 km from the hutted camp. A number of activities can be arranged from here with **Wild 5 Adventures** (see page 468). Follow the scenic route through the gorge and, on leaving the reserve, head towards Port Shepstone. The hotel is on the northern side of the gorge and is clearly signposted.

Umhlanga Rocks p461

The **Oyster Box**, Lighthouse Rd, T031-5612233, www.oysterbox.co.za, was the area's 1st hotel dating back to the 1940s and was always popular with British travellers visiting the colonies, in a spectacular setting behind the dunes, the beach and the lighthouse. It's presently undergoing refurbishment but should be open by the end of 2008. In addition to hotels and B&Bs, there is a large selection of holiday apartments, most of which are rented out by the week. During the off season it may be possible to organize shorter lets in the middle of the week. **Umhlanga & Coastal Letting**, at the Caltex service station on Lighthouse Rd, T031-5615838, www.getcoastal.co.za, offers short and long term lets as well as time share. Contact well in advance if you are planning on renting a family-size apartment during any local school holidays.

L Beverly Hills Hotel, Lighthouse Rd, T031-5612211, www.southernsun.com. 90 rooms in a smart luxury hotel overlooking the beach, a/c, TV, choice of top-end restaurants including the **Sugar Club** and **Elements** cocktail bar, swimming pool, fitness centre, tennis and squash courts, afternoon tea served daily.

AL Teremok Marine, 49 Marine Dr, T031-5615848, www.teremok.co.za. A boutique lodge set in a tropical garden, contemporary and stylish decor and design, 8 luxury suites with a/c, stand-alone baths, rain showers, home entertainment systems, Wi-Fi, spacious lounge, pool, wellness spa, lovely breakfast room with picture windows

opening on to a giant milkwood tree. Recommended.

C Cathy's Place, 18 Stanley Grace Cres, T031-5613286, www.cathysplace.co.za. Homely B&B run by the affable Irish Cathy, with en suite doubles and singles in modern bungalow and 1 self-catering family cottage in the garden, TV, swimming pool. 5 mins' walk from the beach and shops, can arrange airport pickups.

C Honey Pot, 11 Hilken Dr, T031-5613795, sugarfld@iafrica.com. Set in a restored farm manager's house surrounded by mango and avocado trees, 5 smart B&B rooms with private entrances and patios, Mnet TV, fridge, bar, communal lounge in the old ox wagon shed, swimming pool. Child and dog friendly.

D Jessica's, 35 Portland Dr, T031-5613369, www.jessicaskzn.co.za. Close the beach and shops, 3 self-catering comfortable cottages in the tropical garden sleeping 2-4, with M-Net, overlooking the pool.

Ballito and around p462

L Zimbali Lodge, just off the coast road, south of Ballito, T032-5381007, www.sun-international.com. Luxurious lodge set in the grounds of a country club and golf course, stretching along the coast. Golf carts ferry guests around the estate, between the sport facilities, spa, posh restaurants and opulent rooms, which have polished wooden floors, huge beds, balconies and all mod cons. All set in beautiful tropical forest. Stunning pool area and direct access to the beach.

A Boathouse, 33 Compensation Beach Rd, Ballito, T032-9460300, www.boathouse.co.za. Luxury guesthouse right on the beach, 22 beautifully decorated rooms, the floor-to-ceiling windows have a boat rail with life rings attached, TV, phone, a/c, the bar is a great place to have a sundowner and spot dolphins, lovely pool on a wooden deck. Recommended.

B Salt Rock, Basil Hluett Dr, Salt Rock, T032-5255025, www.saltrockbeach.co.za. A big block overlooking the beach but a friendly hotel with a beautiful location, restaurant, bar and swimming pool, all rooms are sea facing and have DSTV, fridge. Caravan and camping park attached (**E**).

C Beach House, 3 Osborne Dr, Salt Rock, T/F084-5815573. Mediterranean-style villa with 6 double rooms with spacious en suite facilities, TV, internet access, garden, swimming pool, sundeck overlooks the beach, secure parking.

C-E Dolphin Holiday Resort, Ballito, T032-9462187, www.dolphinholiday resort.co.za. Pleasant caravan park with shady campsites and 10 self-catering log cabins sleeping 2-6, pool, games room, kiosk, trampolines for kids and volley ball court. You can't see the sea from here but it's only a couple of mins' walk to the beach.

Harold Johnson Nature Reserve *p463*
There are 6 shady sites for tents or caravans with a tap, braai pit and ablution block. Come fully prepared as there are no other facilities. Reservations are made directly with the campsite office, 1032-4861574.

🍴 Eating

Amanzimtoti *p456*
🍴 **Butcher Boys**, 417 Kingsway, T031-9037390. Open 1200-1500, 1800-2200. A lively pub atmosphere serving a wide range of food including steaks with a selection of sauces, seafood, chicken, burgers and a children's menu. Good setting in an old house with sea views.
🍴 **Clearwaters Spur**, 97 Beach Rd, T031-9038813. Busy Western-style saloon bar with enormous steaks, roast chicken and beer.

South of Port Shepstone *p458*
🍴 **Stephward Estate**, 17 Peter St, Uvongo, T039-3155926. Part of a guesthouse with a tea garden open for light lunches and cakes, and upmarket restaurant serving à la carte dinners in the elegant dining room or al fresco on Wed, Fri and Sat evening, booking essential. The menu changes, but expect the likes of duck and seafood.

Margate *p458*
🍴 **The Bistro**, 2450 Marine Dr, Ramsgate, T039-3144128 www.thebistro.co.za. Closed Sun lunch out of season. Friendly restaurant serving traditional cuisine, such as a good rack of lamb, roast duck, as well as grilled seafood and curries. Comprehensive wine list.
🍴 **Eat & Meet**, Granada Building, Marine Dr, T039-3122213. Open 1800-late. Seafood restaurant, vast menu and large portions, including good fresh grilled seafood, and occasional buffets.
🍴 **La Capannina**, 206 Marine Dr, T039-3171078. Authentic Italian restaurant with Italian chef, known for slow roast lamb and tripe stew, plus good fried prawns. Tue-Sun lunch and dinner, closed Sat lunch.
🍴 **7 Seas**, William O'Connor Dr, T039-3174349. Beachfront restaurant and bar with live music. Good spot for a sundowner.
🍴 **Larry's**, corner of O'Connor Dr and Panorama, beachfront, T039-3172277. Pizza restaurant with a long menu, some salads and pasta choices, with seating on a busy terrace overlooking the beach.
🍴 **The Waffle House**, Marine Dr, Ramsgate, T039-3149424. Open 0900-1700. Sweet and savoury authentic Belgium waffles on a terrace next to Ramsgate Lagoon, breakfast waffles until 1100, beers and wine by the glass, next door is the Gaze Gallery exhibiting the work of local artists.

Umhlanga Rocks *p461*
🍴 **Razzmatazz**, Cabana Beach Hotel, 10 Lagoon Dr, T031-5615847. Open 1230-1530, 1830-2200. 5-star prices in a 5-star hotel serving excellent food, unusual game and seafood dishes, such as lemongrass-steamed langoustines, and a great setting on an outdoor deck overlooking the ocean.
🍴 **Sugar Club**, Beverly Hills Hotel, Lighthouse Rd, T031-5612211. Open 1200-1430, 1830-1030. Pricey but lovely colonial theme restaurant with ocean views, terrace and downstairs cocktail bar,

2-, 3- or 4-course options at lunch, dinner is à la carte, seafood platters, curries, steaks, and a breakfast buffet on Sun morning. Long wine list includes French champagne.

Ψ Al Firenze, 21 Ray Paul Dr, T031-5725559. Tue-Sun 1100-2230. Home-made pasta, wood-fired pizzas and seafood. Specials could include quail, duck or oxtail. There's a lively terrace or else takeaways are available.

Ψ Cottonfields, 2 Lagoon Dr, T031-5612744. Mon-Sat. Popular bistro and bar, freshly cooked seafood and meat dishes cooked in *potjiekos*, traditional cast-iron pots, large-screen TVs to watch sport, occasional live bands and karaoke.

Ψ Lord Prawn, Umhlanga Plaza, T031-5611133. Open 1130-1430, 1730-2200. Recommended for its good-value seafood dishes, including surf 'n' turf combos, fish and chips, and very good Durban prawn curries.

Ballito *p462*

ΨΨΨ Mariner's, Valenti Centre, Compensation Beach Rd, T032-9461858. Excellent but pricey seafood, with good prawn curries and fresh linefish, served in a mall setting. Non-smoking.

❸ Entertainment

Margate *p458*

Funworld, Marine Dr, T039-3120741. 3-screen cinema, bowling alley, pool tables, arcade games.

❍ Shopping

Umhlanga Rocks *p461*

The enormous **Gateway** shopping mall lies uphill from the coast in Umhlanga (see page 452). The other malls in the area are far smaller and more manageable, such as **Granada Centre**, on Chartwell Dr, and **La Lucia Mall**, on Armstrong Rd. In town, there is a small selection of craft and souvenir shops.

▲ Activities and tours

Scottburgh *p457*

Aliwal Dive Centre, 2 Moodie St, Umkosaas, T039-9732233, www.aliwalshoal.co.za. PADI 5-star dive centre, boat dives and courses, snorkelling and whale- and dolphin-watching boat trips; also offers good-value accommodation above the dive centre with dorms, en suite doubles and meals for divers. Check out the website for packages.

Margate *p458*

Being the main tourist centre on the south coast, Margate is a good place from which to organize activities. Fishing is allowed off the pier and off Margate Rocks and there are plenty of tackle shops in town. Designated surfing and boogie-boarding areas are on Main Beach and at Lucien Point. Boards can be hired from a number of shops in town. Main Beach is shark-protected and therefore the safest and most popular for swimming.

African Dive Adventures, T039-3171483, www.africandiveadventures.co.za. Offers a wide range of diving courses, and specializes in shark dives. Dives take place at the Protea Banks where schools of hammerhead and Zambezi sharks are regularly seen.

Margate Country Club, T039-3120571, www.margategolf.co.za. Tue-Sat 0800-1700, Sun 1400-1700. 18-hole golf course, visitors welcome. Green fees R225.

Oribi Gorge Nature Reserve *p460*

In addition to its hiking trails, Oribi Gorge is also the ideal location for adventure sports.

Wild 5 Adventures, T039-6870253, www.oribigorge.co.za, based at the **Oribi Gorge Hotel** (see page 465) offers white-water rafting in conventional rafts or large inner tubes on the Umzimkulu River, and abseiling from Lehr's Waterfall, the last 66 m being a free abseil during which you can feel the spray of the falls on your back. Also has the Wild Swing, a 75-m freefall and a 100-m outward swing over the falls, and the Wild Slide, a 120-m steel cable slide over Lehr's.

Umhlanga Rocks *p461*
Diving
There are 2 interesting wreck dives at the *T-Barge* and the *Fontao*. Both sites are at around 20 m deep where visibility is good. The boats were sunk to create artificial reefs and provide habitats for tropical fish.
36 Degrees, at the ski boat launch ramp on the beach in Umhlanga Rocks, T082-5532834 (mob), www.36degrees.co.za. PADI and NAUI, equipment rental and sales, courses, single dives, 2-hr dolphin-watching boat trips, and exciting speed boat trips.

Golf
Zimbali Country Course, just off coast road, south of Ballito, T032-5381007, www.zimbali.org/golf_course.htm. 18-hole championship course designed by Tom Weiskopf. Green fees for visitors R210-300, depending on day/season.

Ballito and around *p462*
La Mercy Microlight Flights, La Mercy Airfield, T084-2663359 (mob), www.comefly.co.za. Short flights over Umhlanga Lagoon from R200 for 12 mins, ideal for whale spotting; lessons also available.

⊙ Transport

South of Durban *p456, map p457*
Air
Margate Municipal Airport is 2 km from the town centre, T039-3120560. The only scheduled service is operated by **SA Airlink**, central reservations, T011-9781111, ww2.flysaa.com, to **Johannesburg**, operating most days.

Bus
The **Baz Bus**, T021-4392323, www.bazbus.com, runs between **Durban** and **Port Elizabeth** in 1 day before continuing on to **Cape Town** the next day. It drops off at the backpackers' hotels along the south coast. **Greyhound** and **Translux** (see Durban, page 454, for contact details) run between **Durban** and **Cape Town** and stop in the resorts along the N2. **Margate Mini Coach**, reservations T039-3121406, after hours T082-4559736 (mob), www.margate.co.za/minicoach.htm, runs between **Durban** and the **Wild Coast Sun** in the Eastern Cape (see page 428). There are up to 3 daily services in each direction via Durban Airport, Scottburgh, Hibberdene, Port Shepstone and Margate.

North of Durban *p460, map p461*
Bus
Greyhound, T083-9159000 (in South Africa), T011-2768550 (from overseas), www.greyhound.co.za, has a regular service between **Durban** and **Pretoria** via Richards Bay, Vryheid, Piet Retief and Evander.

Taxi
Dolphin Coast Taxis, T032-5259449.

Pietermaritzburg and the Natal Midlands

→ *Colour map 5, B1. Altitude: 647 m.*

This attractive city, the capital of the Colony of Natal in the late 19th century, was named after the Voortrekker leaders Gert Maritz and Piet Reteif, who settled here in 1838 after the Battle of Blood River; today it is the legislative capital of KwaZulu Natal. It markets itself as a distinctly English city and, despite its largely African population and bustling street life, its red-brick buildings do give it a strikingly similar look to a provincial English town centre. An important trading centre for the local farming industry, Pietermaritzburg is also home to the University of Natal and a number of technical colleges, giving it a young, student feel during term time, with a decent selection of nightlife.
▶▶ *For listings, see pages 477-480.*

Ins and outs

Getting there Pietermaritzburg is only 80 km from Durban on the N3 and can easily be visited in a day. **Durban International Airport** (see page 435) is 45 minutes' drive from Pietermaritzburg. **Peitermaritzburg/Msunduzi Airport** is 6 km from the centre of town and has daily domestic flights to Johannesburg operated by **SA Airlink**. The **railway station** is on the corner of Church and Pine streets. This is a rough part of town, so arrange to be collected in advance if you're arriving by train. Long-distance **buses** stop here on the route between Durban and Johannesburg. Pietermaritzburg lies on the Durban–Johannesburg **Baz Bus** route, via the Northern Drakensberg; **Sani Pass Carriers** runs regular shuttles to the Southern Drakensberg.

Best time to visit The climate is subtropical with heavy rainfall from December to February. The rest of the year tends to be warm and dry and makes a pleasant change from the humidity in Durban.

Tourist offices Pietermaritzburg Tourism ① *Publicity House, 177 Chief Albert Luthuli (Commercial) Rd, T033-3451348, www.pmbtourism.co.za, Mon-Fri 0800-1700, Sat 0800-1300,* is conveniently situated and has a comprehensive range of maps and leaflets as well as an accommodation and mainline bus booking service. Staff are helpful, friendly and keen to promote their city. The original building was completed in 1884 and used to be the local police station.

Pietermaritzburg is the location of the central office of **KZN Wildlife** ① *T033-8451000, www.kznwildlife.com.* To get here, follow Commercial Street out of town towards Hilton, and follow signs for the Cascades shopping mall. The KZN offices are next to the mall in the Queen Elizabeth Park Nature Reserve.

Background

Pietermaritzburg was founded as the capital of Natalia in 1838. Originally, the town was laid out in the same way as Cape Dutch towns, with thatched houses, wide streets, large gardens and irrigation channels running down the streets. The small rural capital was a trading centre for farmers and game hunters and later became a stopover for wagon trains heading for the interior.

The republic of Natalia only lasted a few years; the British arrived in 1843 and established a garrison here, and the safety provided by the garrison encouraged other settlers to arrive from Britain and Germany. Pietermaritzburg became a prosperous

Victorian town and many of its most attractive buildings date from this period. The administrative buildings of the Colony of Natal are in the city centre, but it is the quiet side streets, lined with fine Victorian houses built by wealthy merchants, which make the town so pretty. Here, the mix of bungalows and two-storey red-brick houses retain their original verandas, decorated with cast-iron lattice work, hardwood windows and brass fittings, all shaded by huge, arching jacaranda trees.

Pietermaritzburg

The city centre has Pietermaritzburg's most imposing Victorian buildings, civic gardens and war memorials. The old buildings are not all open to the public but it is possible to walk around most of the sites in a morning. Dominating the centre is the grand **City Hall**, which looms on the corner of Chief Albert Luthuli (Commercial) Road and Church Street. Built on the site of the Volksraadsaal (people's council) in 1900, it is supposedly the largest all-brick building in the southern hemisphere and is decorated with stained-glass windows.

Tatham Art Gallery

ⓘ *60 Chief Albert Luthuli (Commercial) Rd, T033-3422801, www.tatham.org.za, Tue-Sun 1000-1800, free.*

Opposite the City Hall is a similarly imposing red-brick structure, completed in 1879 and used as a post office until 1906, when it became the site of the Supreme Court. Renovation work started during the late 1980s and, in 1990, it was inaugurated as the new home for the Tatham Art Gallery.

Inside is a fairly ramshackle selection of modern and Victorian art; the original collections are of French and British Victorian art, and although the landscapes are fairly pleasant there is nothing particularly striking about them. But the gallery does have some interesting and unusual works, including a Stanley Spencer landscape called *Near Nareta, Bosnia*, and paintings by Degas, Renoir, Braque and Picasso. There is a large, highly ornate ormolu late-Victorian clock at the top of the stairs on the first floor which is worth seeing. During chiming, a screen is raised to reveal a clockwork blacksmith and some bellringers moving in time to the chimes. The South African Gallery is perhaps the most interesting, with a collection of contemporary art including beadwork of Zulu and Xhosa origins. These eclectic works are a refreshing change from the worthy but somewhat staid collections of Victoriana. There is a tea room on the first floor, overlooking the gardens.

Voortrekker Museum

ⓘ *351 Langalibalele (Longmarket) St, T033-3946834, www.voortrekkermuseum.co.za, Mon-Fri 0900-1600, Sat 0900-1300, R5.*

This museum is on the site of the original Church of the Vow and has a collection of period farm machinery, furniture and Voortrekker relics, as well as some more up-to-date exhibits. There is an interesting display that ponders the subject of Kruger's war chest, which disappeared en route to Lorenço Marques (known today as Maputo – the capital of Mozambique) and has never been recovered. Another item to look out for is a pair of enormous Voortrekker trousers. The former Longmarket Street Girls' School building has been incorporated into the site, and now houses more culturally significant exhibitions on Zulu heritage, including a reproduction of a traditional Zulu home, filled with household goods. There is also a display on the life of Prince Imperial of France, Louis Napoleon, who stayed in Pietermaritzburg before being killed by a Zulu ambush near

Ulundi during the Anglo-Boer war. His death in South Africa ended the Bonaparte dynasty. In the garden is a replica of a Hindu Shiva temple.

Welverdient House, the thatched house opposite the Voortrekker Museum, was moved from Edendale, a farm outside the city, in 1981. It used to be the house of Andries Pretorius, the victor at the battle of Blood River, and gives a good idea of the spartan conditions in which the early Voortrekkers lived.

Supreme Court Gardens

The Supreme Court Gardens are opposite the City Hall on the corner of Church and Commercial streets and are the site of several war memorials. The **Memorial Arch** is flanked by two field guns captured from the Germans by South African forces in

Pietermaritzburg

Sleeping 🛏	Redlands Lodge **5**	Jailbreak Café **5**
Ascot Inn **4**	Tockwith B&B **2**	Saki **6**
City Royal **1**	Umphiti Backpackers **8**	Turtle Bay **1**
Gables **6**		
Imperial **3**	Eating 🍴	Bars & clubs 🍷
Prince's Gate **7**	Els Amics **4**	Crowded House **2**

Southwest Africa in 1915. The **Zulu War Memorial** has a cannon next to it which was cast in Scotland in 1812 and used to be fired to let the citizens of Pietermaritzburg know that the mail had arrived. The **statue of Gandhi**, commemorating the centenary of his arrival in South Africa (1893), is just below the gardens on Church Street, and across the street is the old **Colonial Building**, built in 1899, decorated with Natal's coat of arms, featuring a wildebeest and Pietermaritzburg's coat of arms, featuring an elephant. From the Gandhi statue continue down Church Street on the same side and you'll reach the **Presbyterian Church** built in 1852, the first British church in Pietermaritzburg.

The Lanes

The Lanes are a network of alleyways between Langalibalele (Longmarket) and Church streets. They were originally the site of Pietermaritzburg's legal and financial centre and used to be private rights of way to the small offices behind the Supreme Court. Today they are lined with small shops and cafés and administrative buildings dating from the turn of the 20th century. From Church Street, enter the Lanes on Timber Street where you can see **Harwin's Arcade**. The arcade was built in 1904 and has a skylight running through it, illuminating the second-hand bookshops.

Timber Street leads into Langalibalele (Longmarket) Street; turn left here and return to Chief Albert Luthuli (Commercial) Road. This route passes the impressive **General Post Office**, opened in 1903, and the offices of the *Natal Witness*, South Africa's oldest newspaper established in 1846. The **Old Legislative Assembly** and the **Old Legislative Council** are on the left-hand side. On the right is Witness Lane which leads to the Natal Museum.

Natal Museum

ⓘ *237 Jabu Ndlova (Loop) St, T033-3451404, www.nmsa.org.za, Mon-Fri 0900-1630, Sat 1000-1600, Sun 1100-1500, R5.*
The Natal Museum has a more diverse collection than many other South African museums. The natural history gallery has a considerable collection of stuffed creatures that date from the foundation of the museum. The last wild elephant shot in Natal in 1911 is on display, as are two specimens of the black and white rhino. The first treasure chest of the Colony of Natal can be found here; it is an old iron chest that used to travel around the colony by wagon and was used to collect the Native Hut Tax. The colony's finances were at times so desperate that the chest held less than a pound.

Upstairs is the relatively new **Origins** gallery, with anthropology displays including a fascinating section on the Ashanti people of the Gold Coast. There is a wooden stool decorated with strips of gold, a sacred object which was demanded by the British as a token of surrender. The collection of brass weights is particularly beautiful; they were used for weighing gold and were moulded from natural objects such as snails, ground nuts and grasshoppers. There are also a number of archaeological displays, with examples of San rock art in a reconstructed cave, and recreations of Stone Age life. The final gallery focuses on Portuguese shipwrecks.

South of the Lanes

At the other end of Langalibalele (Longmarket) Street is **St Peter's Church**, a museum with displays of European stained glass. The church was built in 1857 after Colenso split with the Church of England. Bishop Colenso is buried in front of the altar. From here, turn left into Peter Kerchhoff (Chapel) Street, then right into Jabu Ndlova (Loop) Street. At No 11 is the **Macrorie House Museum** ⓘ *T033-3942161, Mon 1100-1600, Tue-Thu 0900-1300,*

Mahatma Gandhi in South Africa

Gandhi was asked by a journalist when he was on a visit to Europe what he thought of Western civilization. He paused and then replied: "It would be very nice, wouldn't it". The answer illustrated just one facet of his extraordinarily complex character. A Westernized, English-educated lawyer, who practised law in South Africa from 1893 to 1914, he preached the general acceptance of some of the doctrines he had grown to respect in his childhood, which stemmed from deep Indian traditions – notably *ahimsa*, or non-violence. From 1921 he gave up his Western style of dress and adopted the hand-spun *dhoti* worn by poor Indian villagers, giving rise to Churchill's jibe that he was a 'naked fakir' (holy man). Yet, if he was a thorn in the British side, he was also fiercely critical of many aspects of traditional Hindu society. He preached against the iniquities of the caste system, which still dominated life for the overwhelming majority of Hindus. Through the 1920s much of his work was based on writing for the weekly newspaper *Young India*, which became *The Harijan* in 1932. The change in name symbolized his commitment to improving the status of the outcastes, Harijan (person of God) being coined to replace the term outcaste. Often despised by the British in India, he succeeded in gaining the reluctant respect and ultimately outright admiration of many.

Gandhi arrived in South Africa in 1893 but soon became involved in South African politics after being a victim of racial prejudice himself when he was forcibly removed from a whites-only train carriage in Pietermaritzburg. He founded the Natal Indian Congress in 1894 to fight for the freedom of the indentured Indian labourers that were working in the docks, sugar plantations and railways. He moved to a farm just outside Durban with his family and followers in 1903, to produce a resistance magazine called *Indian Opinion*, and his fame as an opponent to the rising racial prejudice saw him negotiating with General Jan Smuts in person. Thousands of indentured workers went on strike when the government passed a law to ban Indians entering the Transvaal in 1907, which led to the Indian Relief Bill in 1914 that finally emancipated the Indians. With the fight over, Gandhi returned to England in July 1914 and never saw South Africa again.

His death at the hands of an extreme Hindu chauvinist in January 1948 was a final testimony to the ambiguity of his achievements: successful in contributing so much to achieving India's Independence, yet failing to resolve some of the bitter communal legacies which he gave his life to overcome.

closed Fri-Sun, small entry fee, where Bishop Macrorie lived from 1870 to 1892. The house is decorated with period furniture and houses a collection of Victorian costumes.

Beyond the city centre

Butterflies for Africa ① *Willowton Rd, T033-3871356, www.butterflies.co.za, Tue-Fri 0900-1630, Sat 0930-1530, Sun 1030-1530, R24,* is clearly signposted from the N3 towards Durban. It incorporates a large enclosed butterfly house, a butterfly garden and nursery with a maze, a craft and coffee shop, an art gallery and museum, and audio-visual presentations on the life of a butterfly. There's a new monkey house, with examples of small monkeys and a walk-through path.

Alexandra Park lies to the south of the city centre and can be reached by following Chief Albert Luthuli (Commercial) Road past the Voortrekker Cemetery. The park was founded in 1863 and has large public gardens with a beautiful old cricket pavilion built in 1898. Two other interesting features here are the Victorian bandstand and a cast-iron water trough for horses. An open-air art show is held here every May.

World's View lies to the west of town and you can get to it by following the Old Howick Road (R103), past the Country Club golf course and into World's View Road. A plaque at World's View, next to the Voortrekker Road, marks the route taken by the early Voortrekkers. The short trails follow the path of an old railway line and pass through pine and wattle plantations where it is possible to see interesting birdlife and some small buck. There are magnificent views of Pietermaritzburg from the top of the hill.

KwaZulu Natal Botanical Gardens ① *2 Swartkops Rd, Mayors Walk, T033-3443585, www.nbi.ac.za, daily 0800-1730, restaurant closed Mon, R10*, were founded in 1870 and following a fine Victorian tradition have a collection of plants from all over the world. The most interesting feature in the gardens is the **Zulu Muthi Garden**, created with the help of local healers and including a traditional beehive-shaped healer's hut. This is a 'living display' to inform visitors about traditional plant-use and associated conservation issues but it is also designed as a centre where healers can attend courses on the sustainable use of traditional medicine plants. It is an ideal place for a leisurely stroll or afternoon tea next to the ornamental lake.

Queen Elizabeth Park Nature Reserve ① *off the Howick road on the outskirts of Pietermaritzburg, free*, is small but has a network of short walking trails from which you can see blesbock, impala and zebra. The flora here is particularly interesting; the park has been a wild flower reserve since 1960 and has stunning displays of colour in the spring. The headquarters of **KZN Wildlife** (see page 470) are located within the park.

Trainspotters will be interested in the **KwaZulu Natal Railway Museum** ① *Hilton Station, T033-3431857, www.umgenisteamrailway.co.za, daily 0800-1600, small entry fee*, which is part of Umgeni Steam Railway and run by volunteers. The museum has a fine display of railway memorabilia and a number of coaches and locomotives dating from the 1930s. Some of the highlights of the museum include a sleeper coach from 1903, a bullion coach from 1937 and a 36-ton steam crane.

Natal Midlands ●● ⤳ pp477-480. Colour map 5, B1.

The Midlands cover the region between Greytown and Richmond, Pietermaritzburg and Estcourt. The many rivers flowing off the Drakensberg escarpment have created a well-watered, fertile landscape that originally supported a large population of Zulu cattle herders and farmers in the lowlands. San migrated between here and the Drakensberg, following the herds of eland according to the changes of the seasons. Later the fertile territory attracted first the Voortrekkers and then British immigrants in the 1850s, all of whom fought for control of the land.

Today, the farms here cultivate wattle for tanning and paper pulp, and there are large horse-breeding studs, cattle and sheep ranches. The N3 bisects the Midlands and the majority of traffic passes through on its way between Gauteng and Durban. However, by taking the alternative R103, the Midlands towns and countryside can be explored by following the Midlands Meander route, a tourist initiative highlighting the multitude of craft outlets, country restaurants and rural retreats, popular with South African tourists.

Ins and outs

There is an excellent map and brochure available in the region's tourist information offices promoting a series of routes for visiting the Midlands by car. The 'meander' is reminiscent of a Sunday afternoon drive through English countryside and is one of South Africa's local tourism success stories. Over 400 places are marked on the map and include a selection of bed and breakfasts, craft shops and restaurants. The antique shops, potteries and weavers are good places to buy gifts. Information is available from **Midlands Meander Association** ① *T033-3307260, www.midlandsmeander.co.za.*

Howick → *Colour map 5, B1.*

The small and quiet town of Howick has grown up around what was originally a fording point across the Umgeni River on the wagon route to the interior. The original settlement was named by the colonial secretary Earl Grey after his English home of Howick in Northumberland. More recently, Howick was the location where Nelson Mandela was arrested in 1962 before being sent to jail for 27 years. The actual spot where the police arrested him is just outside of town on the R103, on a road heading towards Tweedie Junction. He was disguised as a driver for a white friend and it is thought the police stopped the car because of a tip off. There is a memorial, unveiled by Mandela himself in 1996, marking this otherwise unassuming spot in a field next to the road.

The 95-m-high **Howick Falls** are popular with South African tourists, who stop off here for a break while travelling on the N3. In 1951 they were proclaimed a national monument. To the Zulu people the waterfall is known as kwaNogqaza, 'the place of the tall one'. There is a path to the bottom of the falls but beware of the slippery rocks. Above the falls is an open-air café.

The **Howick Museum** ① *T033-3306124, Tue-Fri 0930-1530, Sat and Sun 1000-1300, small entry fee,* is just next to the falls and has a display of Victorian furniture and farm machinery. There is also an interesting collection of military badges. Next door is the Old Agricultural Hall, now home to an excellent craft and curio shop, **Craft Southern Africa**, T033-3305859. The hall was built in 1899 and is well worth a look.

Midmar Nature Reserve

① *From Howick the R617 crosses the N3 and passes Midmar Public Resort Nature Reserve (7 km) en route to Bulwer (90 km) and Underberg (120 km). Reserve open 24 hrs, R15.*

This attractive dam is a hugely popular holiday resort with numerous sporting facilities on offer including power boating, jet-skiing, windsurfing and yachting. Sunset cruises can be organized with advance notice. There is a small shop open at weekends and peak periods where bikes, windsurfs and canoes can be hired. Day visitors are permitted. The Midmar Mile swimming contest is held here every February and attracts around 10,000 entrants. It's now the world's largest inland swimming race.

Towards Estcourt

The fastest route north from Howick to Mooi River (37 km), Estcourt (60 km), Spioenkop (92 km) and the Free State is on the N3. An alternative scenic route is to take the R103 through Nottingham Road (29 km) to Mooi River (48 km).

The Nottingham Regiment gave their name to the small farming settlement of **Nottingham Road** after being stationed near here in the 1870s. This is a quiet, rural area, known for its trout fishing and holiday farms. The **Nottingham Road Brewery Company** ① *Old Main Rd, Rawdons Estate, T033-2666728, www.rawdons.co.za, tastings and shop* *daily 0800-1700*, is a rustic brewery with enticingly named beers that are hand-brewed using spring water: Tiddly Toad Lager, Pie-eyed Possum Pilsner, Pickled Pig Porter. From Nottingham Road, the R27 heads west towards the Drakensberg reserves at Kamberg (48 km; see page 508) and Lotheni (70 km; see page 512). This road is a rough dirt track which can become impassable after rain; check on road conditions before starting out.

Further northwest, the **Mooi River** flows through a small farming community en route from the Drakensberg Mountains to the Tugela River. The area around Mooi River is well known for stud farming; it's smaller than the Cape but has produced a higher proportion of winners. The Drakensberg reserves at Kamberg (42 km) and Giant's Castle (see page 506) are well signposted from here.

Estcourt → *Colour map 5, B1.*

Estcourt is a thriving industrial town, site of South Africa's largest sausage factory and a Nestlé factory, both of which can be visited on a factory tour, if you're that way inclined. Factories aside, there's no reason to stop in Estcourt other than to stock up if you're on the way to self-catering accommodation in the Drakensberg.

Bushman's River Tourism ① *Old Civic Building, Upper Harding St, T/F033-3526253, Mon-Fri 0900-1600*, is an excellent tourist office, stacked full of brochures from all over the country. Well worth a stop if you are passing through town, it also has internet facilities and a craft shop. Greyhound and Translux buses stop outside.

Fort Durnford ① *T033-3523000, daily 0900-1200, 1300-1600*, has interesting displays on military history, a good section on fossils and, rather oddly, one of Africa's most complete bird egg collections, donated by a local collector. In the grounds you can look around a reconstructed Amangwane Zulu kraal. The fort itself was built in 1874 in order to protect local residents from feared Zulu attacks.

⊚ Pietermaritzburg and the Natal Midlands listings

Hotel and guesthouse prices
L over US$300 AL US$220-300 A US$150-220
B US$100-150 C US$75-100 D US$35-75
E US$15-35 F under US$15
Restaurant prices
♥♥♥ over US$30 ♥♥ US$15-30 ♥ under US$15
See pages 46-51 for further information.

⊜ Sleeping

Pietermaritzburg *p470, map p472*
There are lots more B&Bs in town; check with the tourist office for details.
B Imperial, 224 Jabu Ndlova (Loop) St, T033-3426551, www.imperialhotel.co.za. Historical building with 70 comfortable rooms with DSTV, a/c, room service, secure parking, restaurant and bar, the restaurant is recommended for its game dishes, oldest hotel in town and recently refurbished but feels a little impersonal. The Imperial Crown Prince of France, Louis Napoleon, stayed here during the Anglo-Boer War.
B Redlands Lodge and Hotel, 1 George Mcfarlane Lane (off the Old Hilton Rd), T033-3943333, redlands@mweb.co.za. A luxury hotel set in a slightly surreal gated development, in a quiet suburb. Country-style pastel-coloured rooms with private balconies, bar and mediocre restaurant. Popular with business people. Comfortable with friendly service, but feels isolated.
C Ascot Inn, 210 Woodhouse Rd, Scottsville, T033-3862226, www.ascot-inn.co.za. B&B or self-catering cottages set in a large garden with 2 swimming pools. Simple, cosy decor and friendly bar and grill restaurant on site. Has become a popular conference venue.
C City Royal, 301 Burger St, T033-3947072, www.cityroyalhotel.co.za. Slightly run down

but fairly spacious double rooms, with a/c, en suite facilities and TV, set in a modern, run-of-the-mill town hotel. Restaurant serving traditional food in a rather dark setting, bar, plus an open-air terrace for drinks. Secure parking.

C Gables, 216 Woodhouse Rd, Scottsville, T033-3460792, www.thegables.co.za. Comfortable B&B or self-catering units in converted stables of a former racehorse stud, with rooms set around a small garden. All units have TV. Small restaurant and bar with set meals each night.

D Prince's Gate, 227 Prince Alfred St, Scottsville, T033-3450159. 12 simple self-catering units with open-plan kitchen/lounge, TV, a/c, set around a small garden. Good value, central location.

D Tockwith B&B, 208 Peter Kerchhoff (Chapel) St, T033-3425802. A small cottage with a veranda, sleeps 4, TV, swimming pool and garden, plus 2 double B&B rooms in the main house. Ask for Megan.

E-F Umphiti Backpackers, 317 Bulwer St, T033-3943490, www.umphiti.co.za. Backpacker's hostel housed in a Victorian home bang in the centre of town, with a pleasant veranda and small, lush garden with pool. Lounge with DVDs, meals available, accommodation in dorms and doubles and space for camping. Adventure tours can be arranged. Baz Bus stop.

Howick p476

A Old Halliwell Country Inn, 10 km north of Howick on Curry's Post Rd, T033-3302602, halliwell@mweb.co.za. A traditional English-style country hotel and restaurant built in 1830 as a wagon stop. Each double en suite room has a fireplace, honeymoon suites with jacuzzis, underfloor heating. Cosy pub, swimming pool and golf driving range.

A-B Shafton Grange, 12 km from Howick towards Rietvlei, T033-3302386, www.shaftongrange.co.za. A fine old farmhouse built in 1852, 5 rooms with en suite facilities, lounge, country meals, swimming pool. The attraction here is horse riding or polo on the 52-ha farm, there are 21 stables and people from Johannesburg bring their horses here on holiday.

B Penny Lane Guest House, 11 km from Howick on the R103 towards Lidgetton, T033-2344332, www.pennylane.co.za. 8 spacious rooms, decor varies from twee to tasteful, fan-cooled and heaters for the winter months. The guest lounge has a log fire, DSTV and a bar with a rustic African feel, traditional meals served. Swimming pool and tennis court.

D Howick Falls Hotel, 2 Main St, T033-3302809. 19 simple rooms in one of Howick's oldest buildings, built in 1872. Former guests include Mark Twain and Cecil Rhodes. Don't expect too much but it's cheap, full of atmosphere and the rooms have been renovated, quite a good Greek restaurant on site.

Midmar Nature Reserve p476

B-E Midmar Camp, KZN Wildlife, T033-8451000, www.kznwildlife.com. Range of rustic cabins, en suite self-catering units, chalets and campsites, some set on the shoreline, including a 6-bed chalet equipped for the disabled, shared ablution blocks for units without bathrooms. The campsites get very crowded during the school holidays, and have shared ablution blocks. Some have electricity.

Towards Estcourt p476

B The Bend, 14 km from Nottingham Rd towards Kamburg on the R103, T033-2666441, www.thebend.co.za. Smart lodge set in a nature reserve with a variety of lodge rooms and cottages, spacious with attractive decor and antique furniture, country meals, indoor swimming pool, horse riding and hiking, 5 km of the Mooi River runs through this reserve, trout fishing on 6 dams. Has its own chapel for country weddings.

B Rawdons, Old Main Rd (R103), T033-2636044, www.rawdons.co.za. A luxurious, thatched English-style country hotel in a 195-ha estate. 25 double rooms,

light, airy decor, en suite bathroom, TV, restaurant, swimming pool, bowls, tennis, 7 trout dams for fishing, also location of the **Nottingham Road Brewery** (see page 476).
B Thatchings, 12 km from Nottingham Rd on the Curry Post Rd on the other side of the N3, T033-2666275, www.thatchings.co.za. Rural guesthouse set in a huge garden. 7 en suite rooms with TV, country-style decor, fresh flowers. À la carte evening meals. Bar with snooker table, golf course nearby as well as trout fishing on the farm.
C E Sierra Ranch, on the R622 or Old Greytown Rd, 16 km from Mooi River, T033-2631073, www.sierraranch.co.za. Huge Western-themed resort with restaurant, swimming pool, offers a wide range of sporting activities including tennis, bowls, river tubing, horseriding. Accommodation is in chalets, rondavels, en suite doubles or the bunkhouse.

Estcourt p477
B Blue Haze Country Lodge, 6 km from Estcourt, T036-3525772, www.bluehaze.co.za. Thatched lodge located on the way to the Battlefields and mountains, overlooking a peaceful lake. 23 comfortable garden suites, swimming pool fringed by palms, cosy pub serving meals. Game trails, horse riding and river rafting can be organized.
E-F Wagendrift Public Resort Nature Reserve, KZN Wildlife, T033-8451000, www.kznwildlife.com. Wagendrift Dam is 5 km from the town centre on the road to Ntabamhlopem. There are 2 campsites with a total of 39 sites, ablution blocks. Also has a 4-bed self-catering chalet. The reserve is a popular holiday resort and has facilities for power boats and fishing, canoes are available for hire. There are some short walking trails and a feeding site for vultures. The remains of trenches dug during the Boer War can still be seen.

🍴 Eating

Pietermaritzburg p470, map p472
🍴🍴🍴 **Turtle Bay**, Cascades Centre, T033-3471555. Mon-Sat 1100-2200, Sun 1100-1600. Fine-dining choice in the Cascades Centre, with lovely terrace. Traditional dishes, fresh seafood such as crayfish and tiger prawns, plus roast duck and delicious pies. Popular afternoon teas.
🍴🍴 **Els Amics**, 380 Langalibalele (Longmarket) St, T033-3456574. Tue-Fri 1200-1430, Tue-Sat 1800-late. Long-running restaurant set in a large Victorian house serving Catalan and Mediterranean food, delicious gazpacho and fish dishes, and decent wine list, plus tasty Italian desserts.
🍴🍴 **Saki**, 157 Victoria Rd, T033-3426999, 1200-late. Asian-themed restaurant in the Victoria Centre mall, informal atmosphere at long wooden tables, family orientated, a wide selection of affordable Thai, Indian, Japanese and Chinese food, something for everyone, Singapore and Indian beer to drink and, of course, saki.
🍴 **Jailbreak Café**, corner of Burger St and Pine St, T033-3945342. Mon-Fri 0800-1630, Sat 0800-1400. Located in the old prison that is a national monument, slightly musty but friendly café and tea garden, breakfasts, cakes, lunches, surrounded by number of excellent African craft shops, open 0800-1600.

🍸 Bars and clubs

Pietermaritzburg p470, map p472
Crowded House, Chief Albert Luthuli (Commercial) Rd, T033-3455977, www.crowdedhouse.co.za. Tue, Thu and Sat from 2000. Long-running dance club in town. Popular with the students from the university. Alternative live music and DJs playing R'n'B, kwaito and house music.

🎭 Entertainment

Pietermaritzburg *p470, map p472*
Club Lanes, Club Lane, T033-3428220.
10-pin bowling.
Numetro, Cascades Centre near the
new Grey's Hospital. 8-screen cinema.

⛰ Activities and tours

Pietermaritzburg *p470, map p472*
The tourist office has a full list of registered
guides for tours of the city, Drakensberg
and the Battlefields.
Countryside Tours, T083-3868753,
sheph@worldonline.co.za. Local guide Dennis
Shepard organizes a number of day tours
around the Natal Midlands area, as well as
longer tours into the Drakensberg or around
the Battlefields. Minimum 2, from R220 per
person for 3 hrs. The **Pietermaritzburg Tour**
(3 hrs) visits the city centre, botanical gardens
and parks; **Valley of 1000 Hills Tour** (3 hrs)
takes in a crocodile park and Zulu dancing;
Midlands Meander (8 hrs) includes a visit to
Howick Falls and a drive around the Midlands
with views of the Drakensberg.
Meet us in Africa, T033-2394607,
www.meetusinafrica.co.za. Interesting tours
to some of the lesser visited nature reserves
near Pietermaritzburg, plus flower trips to
Drakensberg. Informative company run by
Carolyn and Derek McDonald who are
specialist field guides and can arrange birding
and flower tours to the Drakensberg.

🚌 Transport

Pietermaritzburg *p470, map p472*
Air
Durban International Airport is a 45-min
drive from Pietermaritzburg. There is also a
small town airport, 6 km from the centre, on
the Oribi Rd from where **SA Airlink**, central
reservations, T011-9781111, ww2.flysaa.com,
runs services to **Johannesburg**.

Car hire
Budget, Imperial Hotel, T033-3428433,
www.budget.co.za.

Bus
The **Baz Bus** stops in Pietermaritzburg 3 times
a week. **Greyhound**, **Intercape** and **Translux**
stop in Pietermaritzburg on the route between
Durban, and **Johannesburg** and **Pretoria**.
   Sani Pass Carriers has a service Mon-Sat,
to **Underberg**, useful if you wish to get
close to the Drakensberg Mountains without
your own transport. The bus picks up and
drops off at the Imperial Hotel mid-morning.
   Bus companies Baz Bus, T021-4392323,
www.bazbus.com. **Greyhound**, T083-9159000
(South Africa), T011-2768550 (from overseas),
www.greyhound.co.za. **Intercape**, T086-
1287287 (in South Africa), T012-3804400 (from
overseas), www.intercape.co.za. **Sani Pass
Carriers**, T033-7011017. **Translux**,
T0861-589282 (in South Africa), T011-7743333
(from overseas), www.translux.co.za.

Taxi
Yellow Cabs, T033-3971910.

Train
The railway station is on the corner of Church
and Pine streets, www.spoornet.co.za. Trains
running between Durban and Johannesburg
stop here daily except Tue and Sat.

Estcourt *p477*
Greyhound (see Pietermaritzburg transport
for details), stops in Estcourt between
Durban, **Johannesburg** and **Pretoria**.

🛈 Directory

Pietermaritzburg *p470, map p472*
Banks Rennies Foreign Exchange, Park Lane
Centre, Chief Albert Luthuli (Commercial) Rd,
T033-3943968. **Internet** Hive Media Café,
Nedbank Centre, 50 Durban Rd, Scottsville,
T033-3428988. **Medical services**
Mediclinic, 90 Payne St, T033-8453700.

Battlefields Route

The vast, open landscapes of northern KwaZulu Natal are as evocative as one would hope, with rolling plains and savannah grasslands stretching to the horizons and studded with flat-topped acacias, mysterious rock formations and granite koppies. This landscape forms the stage upon which three major wars have been fought, and the battlefields of the clashes between Boers, Britons and Zulus can all be visited. Don't expect self-explanatory sights, however – many of the battlefields are marked by little more than small commemorative plaques, and you'll need a good guide to really bring the history of the region to life. This area also provides an eye-opening glimpse into the lives of rural Zulus, the roads passing numerous traditional subsistence kraals, with their thatched rondavals, herds of goats and waving children. The poverty of these remote areas can be striking after the affluence of the coastal resorts.

The best way to appreciate the history of the battles is to go on an organized tour; with a decent guide it can be surprisingly moving. The major sites can be visited in a day. Two of the best museums are the Siege Museum in Ladysmith and the Talana Museum in Dundee. Of the wars fought between the Voortrekkers and the Zulus, the most interesting battlefield site is Blood River, east of Dundee. Two of the most interesting historical sites of the Anglo-Zulu War are Isandlwana and Rorke's Drift; the latter has a good museum, making it the best site to visit without a guide. The most interesting Boer War sites to visit are Talana, the Siege of Ladysmith and Spioenkop. ➤➤ *For more information visit www.battlefields.kzn.org.za. For listings, see pages 490-492.*

Ladysmith and around ⬤🅕🔺⬤🅖 ➤➤ pp490-492. Colour map 4, A6.

Ladysmith is a quiet rural town surrounded by cattle and sheep ranches, with little more than a run-down shopping complex, a handful of Victorian buildings and the Siege Museum – a good place from which to start a visit to the Battlefields Route. In recent years, the town centre has undergone something of a transformation, and today has a vibrant African feel to it, although it remains an unattractive place to stay. The siege aside, Ladysmith is perhaps best known as being home to Ladysmith Black Mambazo band, the phenomenally popular South Africa band. The region lying to the south of Ladysmith is where many of the Boer War Battlefields are located. The Siege Museum in Ladysmith will help to arrange tours or provide a detailed map of the battlesites.

🌙 *One of Ladysmith's first industries was a lard factory set up by two Scotsmen who culled the region's vast herds of zebra and melted down their fat.*

Ins and outs

Getting there Ladysmith is on the N11 and is well connected to the highway network. The N11 heads north to Newcastle (100 km), Volksrust (153 km) and into Mpumalanga. Some 26 km south of Ladysmith, the N11 connects with the N3, which in turn leads north into the Free State and south to Durban. The N11 also connects at this junction with the R616 leading to the Northern Drakensberg.

Tourist information **Ladysmith Tourist Information Office** ⓘ *Siege Museum, Murchison St, T036-6372992, www.ladysmith.kzn.org.za, Mon-Fri 0900-1600, Sat 0900-1300,* has a good selection of maps and leaflets on the battlefields. The bureau is also very helpful with accommodation suggestions and advising on battlefield tours.

Background

The Voortrekkers first arrived in 1847 and established a small republican settlement on the banks of the Klip River. However, it was only a matter of months before the area fell under the British sphere of influence. British settlers began to arrive during the 1850s to farm in the area. Ladysmith grew in importance as a trading centre because it was on the trail connecting the diamond and gold mines of the interior, Kimberley and Barberton, with Port Natal on the coast. Ladysmith is most famous for being besieged by General Piet Joubert for 118 days during the Boer War (see box, page 483). The British garrison of 12,500 men was cut off from the outside world for the duration of the siege.

Sights

Ladysmith's historical monuments are on the main square by the town hall on Murchison Street. The **town hall**, on the corner of Murchison and Queen streets, is a classic Victorian municipal building which was completed in 1893. During the siege, it was converted into a hospital until the clock tower was hit by a six-inch shell. The town hall was repaired in 1901 after the end of the siege. There is a small **museum** ① *Mon-Fri 0900-1600*, with a gallery of photographs illustrating Ladysmith's history up to the present day. The **Siege Museum** ① *Murchison St, T036-63722231, Mon-Fri 0900-1600, Sat 0900-1300, small entry fee*, is next to the town hall. This is a fascinating museum, with one of the country's largest collections of South African military memorabilia, including reconstructions of scenes from the Siege of Ladysmith and the Boer War. There are displays of weapons, uniforms and household goods that were used during the siege, with explanations in English, Afrikaans and Zulu.

Ladysmith

Sleeping	Peaches & Cream 2	Eating
Bonnie Highlands 4	Rietkuil Country Cottages 6	Guinea Fowl Steakhouse 1
Bullers Rest Lodge 1	Royal 3	
Naunton Guest House 5		

The siege of Ladysmith

The siege of the British in Ladysmith by Boer forces lasted from early in the Anglo-Boer War, October 1899, until February 1900 – 118 days in total. The British forces in northern Natal, under General White, had been forced to withdraw into Ladysmith after a series of defeats at the hands of Boers from both the Free State and Transvaal. The Boer forces had taken up positions in approximately a six-mile radius around the town but made few attempts to defeat decisively the 10,000 remaining British troops.

The Boers, under the command of Piet Joubert (ably assisted by his tactically minded wife), did make one major assault on the British defences at Bester's Ridge on 6 January 1900. The British were, however, able to repulse the Boer attack, although it succeeded in placing a further strain on their already stretched resources.

The Boer forces decided to concentrate on starving out the British or shelling them into submission while they held off any British attempts to relieve the town from the south by establishing secure defensive positions in the hills overlooking the Tugela River.

For the besieged British troops the defence of Ladysmith required patience and organization rather than heroics. In December 1899 General White had been ordered to try to break-out and join up with the British forces under Buller attempting an advance through Colenso – but details of when the advance was to take place were never relayed to him and the first he knew of the attack was when he heard the artillery fire. After the losses sustained in the defence of Bester's Ridge in January 1900, White was unable to offer any support to General Buller's forces in their attempts to relieve Ladysmith and all his troops could do was sit tight and survive the bombardment as best they possibly could.

Conditions for the town's inhabitants, whether military or civilian, were harsh. Food and other provisions were in short supply and what was available became exceptionally expensive. Tins of condensed milk, for example, could fetch up to a pound and bottles of whisky seven pounds. One source of comfort for the civilians and wounded was that the Boer commanders allowed them to set up a camp and hospital at Intombi, some four miles southeast of the town, so that they were spared the heavy artillery bombardment of the town centre. News of Buller's numerous blunders at Colenso, Spion Kop and other battles along the Tugela did nothing for morale, however, and many inhabitants felt it was only a matter of time before they had to give in to the Boers.

In February 1900 Buller's substantial army at last had some success in assaults on the Boer positions along the Tugela. On 27 February the British succeeded in taking Pieter's Railway and Terrace Hills overlooking the railway crossing of the Tugela at Colenso and the Boer forces surrounding Ladysmith rapidly lost morale. As news of the decisive defeat of General Conje's forces in the northern Cape filtered through to the Boer military lines, their resolve snapped and they fell back towards Elandslaagte, many in fact returning home, leaving the path clear for Buller's troops to at last relieve the beleaguered troops and citizens at Ladysmith.

There are four field guns on Murchison Street just outside the museum: **Castor** and **Pollux** are the two guns sent from Cape Town at the outbreak of the Boer War for the defence of the town; **Long Tom** is a replica of the Creussot Fortress Guns, which were used by the Transvaal Republic to bombard Ladysmith from the surrounding hills. The Boers destroyed the original gun at Haenertsburg when Kitchener's Fighting Scouts threatened to capture it. The last gun is a German **Feldkanonne**, which was captured in German Southwest Africa and sent back as a war trophy.

Walking south down Murchison Street will take you past two historical hotels which are still in use. The **Royal Hotel** was built before the siege during the gold and diamond rushes of the interior. During the siege it was used by the press corps as a base. The **Crown Hotel** is the site of Ladysmith's first hotel, which was built of wattle and daub. The earliest battlefield tours, on horseback, could be booked here in 1904. Further down Murchison Street, on the corner with Princess Street, is the **Old Toll House** where wagon drivers paid a toll before entering town.

Walking north up Murchison Street to the junction with Albert Street, visitors can see what is left of the old Indian district. Before the introduction of the Group Areas Act this used to be a thriving trading area. **Surat's House**, **Seedat's** and **Asmal's Stores** were all magnificent buildings in the 1920s. These fell into disrepair when the Indian traders were forcibly relocated to the 'Oriental Plaza'. Next door are two buildings from the same period: the **NGR Institute**, a magnificent structure built in 1903 to house railway workers, and the **Central Mosque**, completed in 1922, with its beautiful fountain and courtyard surrounded by palm trees.

A refreshingly non-historical site is the **Cultural Centre** ① *Old Railway Institute Building, 316 Murchison St, T036-6354231, Mon-Fri 0900-1600, small entry fee*. There is a collection of cultural and natural history exhibits, a township shack and a tribute to the Drakensberg Boys' Choir. There is also a hall dedicated to **Ladysmith Black Mambazo** – the world-renowned group that became South Africa's most successful band (see box, page 485). The music-filled hall contains the footprints of the members of the band eternalized in concrete, and life-size cut outs of the band on a mock-up stage. The curio shops sells the band's CDs.

Colenso

An easy excursion from Ladysmith, the town was named after John William Colenso, the Anglican Bishop of Natal from 1853 to 1883. The first advance by British troops trying to break the siege at Ladysmith was foiled here by General Louis Botha in a battle fought along the Tugela River. It was to be a further two months before Ladysmith was relieved. The small **RE Stevenson Museum** ① *Sir George St, T036-6372992, open on request, ask at the municipal offices next door for the key*, concentrates on the Battle of Colenso, with exhibits of weapons, medals and photographs. There are also two vintage steam engines and a steam tractor.

Weenen Game Reserve

① *20 km south of Colenso on the R74. From Durban take the N3 to the Estcourt junction and follow the R74 to the reserve, 25 km. From Ladysmith follow the R74 to Colenso and then on to Weenen. Oct-Mar 0500-1900, Apr-Sep 0600-1800.*

The 6500-ha reserve is the core area of the much larger **Thukela Biosphere Reserve**. The reserve has been hailed as a conservation success as it has succeeded in converting heavily eroded farmland into an area where the flora and fauna indigenous to the Natal Midlands have been re-established. The vegetation is mostly grassland, interspersed with

Ladysmith Black Mambazo

Ladysmith Black Mambazo is one of the best known South African musical groups of all time, outselling both the Beatles and Michael Jackson in their homeland. Over the years their music has been traditionally based on *isicathamiya* music and dance that was born in the gold mines of Johannesburg at the turn of the 20th century. The word itself does not have a literal translation; it is derived from the Zulu verb *cathama*, which means walk softly, or tread carefully. Back then, blacks went to the mines from all over southern Africa as migrant workers, leaving their homes and families for 11 months a year. Poorly housed in overcrowded hostels, they would entertain themselves after a six day week by singing songs into the early hours every Sunday morning, with dance steps that were choreographed softly so as not to disturb the hostel security guards.

As a child, founding member Joseph Shabalala worked as a simple herd boy in the Ladysmith area. In 1961 he formed the group Ladysmith Black Mambazo, meaning the black axe of Ladysmith. At their first concert in Soweto the band became an immediate hit and each member received the princely sum of R5.28.

Internationally Ladysmith Black Mambazo were relatively unknown until Paul Simon 'discovered' the band on a visit to Johannesburg in the mid-1980s. They collaborated with him on his album *Graceland*, released in 1986, which sold millions of copies worldwide and brought them instant fame. Joseph gave Paul Simon the Zulu nickname *Vulindlela*, 'he who has opened the gate'. To date, the band has rather astonishingly been going strong for over 45 years. For more information visit www.mambazo.com.

---

acacia woodland. One of the great attractions are the black and white rhino. Other more common species include giraffe, red hartebeest, eland, zebra, kudu, ostrich and common reedbuck. This is a good reserve for birdwatchers; more than 250 species have been recorded including korhaans, blue crane and the scimitarbilled woodhoopoe. Thukela has short walking trails, picnic sites, a 47-km network of game viewing dirt roads, 4WD trails and the Isipho Hide, which can be rented at night for game viewing.

Dundee and around ⊖❼❼▲ ≫ *pp490-492. Colour map 5, A1.*

The R602 leaves the N11 26 km north of Ladysmith and shortly passes the village of **Elandslaagte**, where there is a signpost leading to the site of the Battle of Elandslaagte. On 21 October 1899, British forces abandoned the village and the railway station. They had kept it open to enable the Dundee garrison to retreat to Ladysmith. The R602 continues to Dundee through a vast treeless plain with plateaux rising up in the distance. The small mining and farming town of **Glencoe**, just before Dundee, is named after the town in the Highlands of Scotland, from where some of the first miners originated.

The modern town of Dundee grew up around the coal mining deposits which were first exploited here on a large scale in the 1880s. The town centre unfortunately fell victim to South Africa's town planners, and is today a rather dull grid of modern streets lined with sleepy shops. Although it provides a convenient base from which to explore the battlefield sites at **Isandlwana**, **Rorke's Drift** and **Blood River**, it might be preferable to stay at one of the more remote lodges away from town.

Ins and outs

Tourist information Tourism Dundee ⓘ *Civic Gardens, Victoria St, T034-2122121, www.tourdundee.co.za, Mon-Fri 0900-1630*, is a helpful office with information on accommodation and excellent advice on how best to view the battlefields depending upon your time, budget and level of interest. Ask about personal tour guides.

Sights

The **MOTH Museum** ⓘ *corner of Beaconsfield and Wilson streets, open by appointment through the tourist office*, is one of the best private collections of military memorabilia in South Africa and includes pieces from the Anglo-Zulu War. The museum can usually only be visited on an organized tour. MOTH stands for Memorable Order of Tin Hats and refers to the British ex-serviceman of the Anglo-Boer War.

The **Talana Museum** ⓘ *1 km north of town on the R33, T034-2122654, www.talana.co.za, Mon-Fri 0800-1630, Sat and Sun 1000-1630, R15*, has been built on the site of the Battle of Talana Hill, which took place on 20 October 1899 and was the first major battle of the Boer War. British forces had been sent to Dundee to protect the coal field from the advancing Boers. General Lucas Meyer, moving down from the Transvaal, took the hill and began bombarding the British. The counter attack succeeded in forcing the Boers off the hill but only at great cost to the British, who lost 255 soldiers including their commanding officer General Penn Symons. A self-guided trail visits the remains of two British forts and the Boer gun emplacements, passing a cairn where General Penn Symons was wounded.

The main building is a modern museum with good displays on the Zulu Wars and the Anglo-Boer War. The industrial section includes the **Consol Glass Museum**, which has an extensive display of glass products, which were once produced here, illustrating the changes in taste from highly decorative Victorian vases to the crisp designer products of today. The **Chamber of Mines Coal Museum** has re-created scenes of early mining in Dundee with many of the original tools on display. The **Miner's Rest** restaurant and curio shop is housed in a typical miner's cottage of the 1920s in the gardens behind the new building.

Dundee

Sleeping 🛏	Fugitive's Drift Lodge **4**	Penny Farthing **5**
Battlefields Country	Isandlwana Lodge **3**	Royal Country Inn **1**
Lodge **2**	Lennox Cottage **6**	

Many of the outlying buildings are original. The **Peter Smith Cottage** has been restored and decorated with period furniture, while the workshop and stables outside have a collection of original blacksmith's tools and several wagons. **Talana House** has historical displays on the lifestyles of the Zulus and the early settlers in Dundee, with interesting bead collections. Both these buildings were used as dressing stations during the Battle of Talana Hill.

Battlefield excursions

The battlefield sites around Dundee can easily be visited on day trips. The major sites are clearly signposted and can be reached from Dundee or Ulundi. However, the sites themselves are often little more than a war memorial in a windswept field; they are isolated and accessed along dirt roads. Allow enough time to return in daylight as the bad roads and wandering cattle make it dangerous to drive at night. The best way to appreciate the sites and the epic events that took place in this region is to take a guided tour with a qualified historian. ▸▸ *For further details, see Activities and tours, page 492.*

Ncome-Blood River ① *48 km from Dundee, T034-2718121, www.ncomemuseum.co.za, 0900-1600, free,* is the site of a replica *laager* that commemorates the dreadful battle between the Zulus and the Boers on 16 December 1838. The 64 wagons are made of bronze and include replica bronze spades, lamps and buckets, all slightly larger than life-size, and there is a small museum, the **Ncome Museum**, on site. There is also a café serving drinks, snacks and selling a selection of historical leaflets. To get to the site, take the R33 northeast as far as Dejagersdrif, where there is a turning on the right leading to Blood River. The last section of the journey is on a dirt road.

Isandlwana ① *80 km southeast of Dundee, T034-2718165, Mon-Fri 0800-1600, Sat and Sun 0900-1600, R15,* is where the 24th Regiment were defeated by 25,000 Zulu warriors on the 22 January 1879. This is perhaps the most epic of the great Zulu War stories, where the Zulu army sat silently in a valley out of sight of a small British regiment (which thought the Zulu were elsewhere), waiting for the signal to attack. A British patrol stumbled across them, upon which the Impis leapt to their feet and stormed over the lip of the hill, descending upon the small regiment in the characteristic 'horns of the buffalo' manoeuvre. Within just two hours, 1329 and 1700 British soldiers were dead. Today, it is an atmospheric spot, with white-painted cairns marking the places where British soldiers were buried, and a self-guided trail taking in the memorials, starting with the relatively new memorial to the Zulu dead, represented by a giant bronze replica of a Zulu victory necklace. To reach the site, take the R68 west, passing through Vant's Drift and Nqutu; the dirt road leading to Isandlwana is clearly signposted south of Nqutu.

Rorke's Drift ① *42 km from southeast of Dundee, T034-6421687, daily 0900-1600, R15,* is clearly signposted off the R68 between Dundee and Nqutu. Made famous by Michael Caine and his memorable performance in the movie *Zulu*, this site was a Swedish Mission next to a ford over the Buffalo River. In 1879, the mission consisted of two small stone buildings, a house and a storeroom, which was also used as a church, and these were commandeered by the British at the start of the war and converted into a hospital and a supply depot. Only 110 men were stationed there on 23 January 1879, when two survivors of Isandlwana arrived warning about an imminent attack. Four thousand Zulus arrived 1½ hours later and launched the assault on the mission station. The British refused to surrender, and succeeded in defending the mission from behind a makeshift barricade of grain bags and biscuit boxes. The ferocious attack was resisted for 12 hours before the Zulu impis withdrew, losing around 400 men; 17 British officers were killed. The mission station has been converted into a fascinating little **museum** which illustrates scenes from the battle and outlines the lives of the men who were awarded the Victoria Cross. Just beyond the museum there is a cemetery and a memorial to those who died.

> The defence of Rorke's Drift is one of the epic tales of British military history. No fewer than 11 Victoria Crosses were awarded here, the most ever awarded at a single battle.

Newcastle and around ●●◐◑ ›› pp490-492. Colour map 5, A1.

This major industrial town is supported by surrounding coal and steel mines. It was established in 1864 by a Dr Sutherland from Newcastle in England who was trapped on the swollen banks of the Ncandu River during his honeymoon. To pass the time he planned a township for the site, named streets after the then government, and filed his plan on return to Pietermaritzburg. There is little in this modern town to attract tourists, although the nearby mountain range, which rises to over 2000 m, has become a popular destination for South African hikers.

Ins and outs

Newcastle is well connected by road and rail and local taxis will take hikers out to the farms that organize private hiking trails. **Tourism Newcastle** ⓘ *Town Hall, Scott St, T034-3153318, www.tourismnewcastle.co.za, Mon-Fri 0900-1600, Sat 0930-1530*, has a useful range of brochures and information on hiking and birdwatching.

Sights

Fort Amiel ⓘ *Memel Rd, Mon-Fri 1000-1600*, was built in 1876 and used for military operations until 1902. It was built by a detachment of the Staffordshire Volunteers (80th regiment) and named after their commander Major Charles Frederick Amiel. It was used as a hospital during both Anglo-Boer wars. After the original plans for the fort were found in a London m useum in 1985 the fort was completely rebuilt. The museum houses displays on the Boer War and has an interesting section on Rider Haggard world famous writer of novels such as *King Solomon's Mines*, *She*, *Jess* and several others. There is a Boer War cemetery just outside.

Majuba Battlefield is 43 km from Newcastle on the N11 to Volksrust. The site is signposted from the highway. A 2-km dirt road leads to the battlefield where there is a caravan park, a youth hostel and a small museum. Majuba is the site where the British were defeated by the Boers in 1881. There is a short trail (45 minutes) heading up Majuba Mountain from where there are spectacular views of Volksrust, Newcastle and the surrounding countryside. The N11 continues north from here into Volksrust and Mpumalanga Province.

Blood River

The year 1838 had been a difficult one for the Voortrekkers in Natal. In February their leader Piet Retief was beaten to death at the Zulu king Dingane's kraal and shortly afterwards about 500 members of a Voortrekker party at Bloukrans River were killed in a Zulu ambush. The majority of the dead were in fact 'coloured' servants but subsequent generations of Boers honoured the defeat by naming the site *Weenen* meaning 'weeping'. Voortrekker attempts at reprisals against the Zulus similarly failed and in a battle near the Buffalo River Piet Uys, another Voortrekker leader, was killed. It was only with the arrival later in the year of Andries Pretorius and a party of 60 experienced commandos that Voortrekker fortunes began to take a turn for the better.

On 9 December Pretorius set out with 468 men and three cannon to confront Dingane's army. Before setting out he reportedly stood on a gun carriage and made the famous vow that if God gave them victory "we would note the date of victory to make it known even to our latest posterity in order that it might be celebrated to the honour of God". Many historians doubt if the vow was ever really made; certainly it was not commemorated until many years after the event. Nevertheless the vow has taken on an important place in Afrikaner traditions.

On 15 December Pretorius' scouts reported a heavy Zulu presence nearby and he ordered the column to move their wagons into the tried and tested Voortrekker defensive *laager*. The method involved lashing all the wagons together into a ring and protecting all cattle, horses and stores in the centre. This allowed trekkers to hide in and under the wagons and fire out at any approaching attackers. Pretorius had formed his *laager* on the banks of the Ncome River with a deep gully to the rear and an open plain to the front. He placed the three cannon at points along the perimeter of the *laager* to give them a clear line of fire across the open ground. Early in the morning of 16 December the Zulu army, estimated at about 10,000, began its attack.

Wave upon wave of Zulu soldiers charged the *laager* but their short spears, so effective in hand to hand combat, were useless against the trekkers' rifles and the grapeshot from the cannons. Finally the Zulu attack faltered and Pretorius sent out a party of mounted commandos to pursue the shattered Zulus. The trekkers were merciless and shot every Zulu in sight, including more than 400 hiding in a small ravine. No prisoners were taken and around 3000 people were killed. No trekkers had been killed and only three were injured – including Pretorius who was stabbed in the hand. So many Zulu soldiers were shot whilst trying to flee back across the Ncome River the waters ran red – hence the name Blood River.

◉ Battlefields Route listings

Hotel and guesthouse prices
L over US$300   AL US$220-300   A US$150-220
B US$100-150   C US$75-100   D US$35-75
E US$15-35   F under US$15
Restaurant prices
††† over US$30   †† US$15-30   † under US$15
See pages 46-51 for further information.

◉ Sleeping

Ladysmith p481, map p482

B Bullers Rest Lodge, 61 Cove Cres,
T036-6376154, www.bullersrestlodge.co.za.
B&B accommodation in a family-run lodge,
set in a thatched house with fine views of the
mountains. Chalets with double and single
rooms, with en suite facilities. The **Boer War
Pub** on site has a fine collection of battlefield
artefacts. Located near the site of the Naval
Gun Shield. Recommended.

C Royal Hotel, 140 Murchison St,
T036-6372176, www.royalhotel.co.za.
A busy central hotel with an interesting
history, but the 71 en suite rooms, are
well overdue for refurbishment, TV, a/c,
grill restaurants, and the **Tipsy Trooper**
pub, swimming pool and garden.

D Bonnie Highlands, 10 Tozer St,
T036-6378390. A fine old town house with
good views of the surrounding area and
5 double rooms. The homely rooms are set
along a shady veranda. Evening meals on
request. The peaceful gardens are the
perfect place to relax after a day exploring
the Battlefields.

D Naunton Guest House, 4 km from town
centre off the Newcastle Rd (N11),
T036-6313307, www.nauntons.co.za.
6 double rooms with en suite facilities
in a farmhouse, DSTV, cosy pub with pool
table, evening meals available on request,
swimming pool. A pleasant alternative
to suburban B&Bs.

D Peaches & Cream, 4 Berea Rd,
T036-6310954, pc.bb@mweb.co.za. Centrally
located old-fashioned B&B, family-run, with

8 en suite rooms with TV. Small pool, dinner
served on request, friendly management.

D Rietkuil Country Cottages, 12 km out
of town off the Newcastle Rd (N11),
T036-6319021. All 4 self-catering cottages,
sleeping up to 6, are fully equipped and
have private patio, braai facilities and are
set in fine gardens with mountain views
and swimming pool, undercover parking.
Evening meals available on request.

Weenen Game Reserve p484

D Cottage, reservations through KZN
Wildlife, T033-8451000, www.kznwildlife.com.
5-bed self-catering cottage, 2 bedrooms,
fully equipped modern bungalow. Also has
12 pitches for tents and caravans near the
entrance gate, 7 with electricity points,
shared ablution block. There's also a game-
viewing hide overlooking a waterhole.

Dundee and around p485, map p486

L Isandlwana Lodge, Islandlwana, 74 km
southeast of Dundee, accessed off the R68,
T034-2718301, www.isandlwana.co.za.
Superbly constructed luxury lodge with
awesome views over Isandlwana and the
rolling grasslands. The stunning wood,
thatch and stone double-storey building
sensitively blends in with the landscape
and is built into the rock that the Zulu
commander stood on the start of the
Isandlwana battle. 13 tastefully decorated
rooms, with huge beds, stylish mirrors and
fashionable stone bathrooms, plus private
balconies with views over the battle site.
The smart dining room, also with brilliant
views, has Zulu chefs. Rob Gerrard is the
resident historian, offering excellent
battlefield tours – his storytelling will
provide a startlingly moving insight to
the battles (R350 per person). Rates
include all meals. Recommended.

AL Fugitive's Drift Lodge, approximately
50 km south of Dundee towards Greytown on the R33, T034-6421843,

www.fugitivesdrift.com. Home to the Rattray family, this lodge offers traditional accommodation and excellent guided tours. Bedrooms are stylish and comfortable and have private verandas. There are also rooms in an annex cottage. The lounge and dining room is filled with Battlefields memorabilia. Very sadly, the Battlefields finest historian David Rattray died in 2007 but prodigies Rob Caskie and Joseph Ndima now take tours. The original Battlefields experience. Recommended.

B Battlefields Country Lodge, overlooking Talana Hill battlefield site, T034-2181641, www.battlefieldslodge.co.za. 30 en suite rooms in quiet double storey circular bungalows, plus camping (**E**), **Warriors Arms** pub where 3-course country evening meals are served. Can organize battlefield tours in English, French or German, or alternatively take a tour with a Zulu guide for a different perspective.

B Penny Farthing, Greytown Rd, T034-6421925, www.pennyf.co.za. This farmhouse is 31 km south of Dundee on the R33, with a choice of rooms in either the old fort, the colonial sandstone farmhouse or the garden cottage. Luxury B&B catering for up to 14 guests and offering battlefield tours with resident guide, plus hiking, swimming pool. Reservations essential.

C Lennox Cottage, a few kilometres out of town off the R68 towards Nqutu, T034-2182201, www.battlefieldsaccommodation.co.za. A comfortable spacious guest house with 10 doubles with en suite bathrooms. Plenty to keep yourself occupied in the gardens, a swimming pool, tennis court, plus a snooker room, some wildlife on the farm including eland and giraffe. Owned by a former Springbok rugby player. This has been recommended as an ideal base for exploring the battlefields.

C Royal Country Inn, 61 Victoria St, T034-2122147, www.royalcountryinn.com. 21 a/c en suite double rooms and 5 cheaper rooms with shared bathrooms in a mock-Tudor building over 100 years old, with well-preserved pressed iron ceilings and wrought-iron fittings, opening onto a peaceful garden. Decent meals served in the à la carte restaurant, a bar decorated with Zulu and Boer War memorabilia, and a tea garden.

Newcastle and around *p488*
Many of the farms offering hiking trails have camping facilities and overnight huts.

C Haggard's Hilldrop, 15 Hilldrop Rd, 3 km out of town, T034-3152098, www.haggardshilldrop.co.za. Beautiful house which used to be the home of Sir Rider Haggard, whose novel *Jess* (1887) was based on his experiences at Hilldrop. The house is now a national monument set in 3 ha of indigenous forest and gardens. 30 en suite double rooms, stylish decor, some rooms under thatch, TV, pub, log fires, large pool, evening meals on request. Ask for the forest rooms, which have private balconies and separate entrances. Recommended.

C Majuba Lodge, 27 Victoria St, T034-3155011, www.majubalodge.co.za. Self-catering chalets, fully equipped, DSTV, kitchen facilities, set around a main building where meals are served, swimming pool, gym and a driving range for golfers, friendly set-up, but avoid if there is a big conference going on.

D Cannon Lodge, Allen St, T034-3152307, www.thecannon.co.za. 22 double rooms with en suite facilities, motel-style set-up, all rooms have phone, a/c, TV, room service, basic decor. Attached to **The Cannon** pub and restaurant, very popular with locals, and next door to a gym.

❼ Eating

Ladysmith *p481, map p482*
♔ Guinea Fowl Steakhouse, Shop 13, Marco Centre, Francis Rd, T036-6378163. Steakhouse, known for their excellent ribs. Good value and friendly, with outdoor tables spilling onto the pavement.

♥-♥ Royal Hotel, 140 Murchison St, T036-6372176. An old-fashioned carvery restaurant, serving a selection of steaks, pub lunches, and with the occasional large, good-value buffet dinner. Friendly, laid-back staff.

♥ Santa Catalina Spur, Oval Shopping Centre, T036-6311260. The usual family chain restaurant serving reliable if uninspiring portions of steak, ribs and chicken, plus a salad bar and baked potatoes.

Dundee and around *p485, map p486*
♥♥ Royal Country Inn, 61 Victoria St, T034-2122147, www.royalcountryinn.com. 1200-1400, 1600-2200. The best place to eat in town is at the principal hotel, which has 2 dining rooms, tables outside in a courtyard and the Garrulous Griffin Pub, named after the 24th Welsh Regiment who fought at Rorkes Drift.

Newcastle and around *p488*
♥♥ The Cannon, Allen St. Bar and restaurant attached to a hotel, large menu and portions. Outside terrace. Busy at the weekend, open late, very popular with local families.

O Shopping

Dundee and around *p485, map p486*
ELC Craft Centre, Rorke's Drift museum. Sells locally produced Zulu crafts: baskets, ceramics and dyed cloth as well as replica spears. Mon-Fri 0800-1730, Sat and Sun 1000-1600.

▲ Activities and tours

Battlefield tours can be organized from the tourist offices in Ladysmith, page 481 and at the Talana Museum in Dundee. Expect to pay around R700-900 for a full-day tour with a guide in your own vehicle.

Dundee and around *p485, map p486*
Battlefield tours
Mike Nel, T034-2122601, mike@dundee kzn.co.za, battlefields and Zulu culture tours.
Paul Garner, T034-2121931, garner@ xsinet.co.za. Enjoyable tales of the San paintings found in the area.
PMB Heritage Tours, T034-2124040, www.battleguide.co.za. One of the leading operators visiting the **Battlefields Route**, Evan Jones is a member of the British Guild of Battlefield Guides, tours are tailor made. Recommended.
Rob Gerrard, T034-2718301, www.isan dlwana.com. Based at **Isandlwana Lodge**, offering excellent tours of Isandlwana, Rorke's Drift and walks between the 2, known as the **Fugitive's Trail**, providing a nail-biting account of the area's history. Recommended.

⊖ Transport

Ladysmith *p481, map p482*
Train
www.spoornet.co.za. Trains from **Johannesburg** and **Pretoria** most days, en route to **Durban**.

Newcastle *p488*
Train
www.spoornet.co.za, trains to **Durban** and **Johannesburg**.

❸ Directory

Ladysmith *p481, map p482*
Medical services La Verna Private Hospital, T036-6310065.

uKhahlamba-Drakensberg Park

The Drakensberg Mountains, which rise to 3000 m and extend 180 km along the western edge of KwaZulu Natal, form the backbone of the uKhahlamba-Drakensberg Park, and determine the border with Lesotho. This formidable mountain range is one of South Africa's most staggeringly beautiful destinations, and in 2001 it was awarded the status of a World Heritage Site by UNESCO, both for its diverse flora and fauna and its impressive San rock paintings. The greater uKhahlamba-Drakensberg Park extends from the Royal Natal National Park in the north to Sehlabathebe National Park, part of Lesotho, in the south. The protected area is 180 km long and up to 20 km wide. Almost the entire range falls within protected reserves managed by KZN Wildlife (see page 434). Despite going through a series of name changes over the years, this conservation body has looked after the region's natural heritage for decades and succeeded in striking a balance between protecting the fragile resources and giving visitors an opportunity to appreciate all the mountains have to offer. There are numerous points from which to explore the Berg, ranging from fully equipped holiday resorts and luxury hotels to campsites, mountain huts and isolated caves. ▸▸ *For listings, see pages 514-522*

Ins and outs → *Colour map 4, B6.*

Getting there Baz Bus ① *T021-4392323, www.bazbus.com*, runs through the Drakensberg three times a week en route between Johannesburg and Durban, stopping at Oliviershoek Pass and Winterton. In the southern Drakensberg **Sani Pass Carriers** ① *T033-7011017*, run to and from Underberg/Sani Pass and Pietermaritzburg.

Getting around There is little in the way of public transport, so the best way of exploring the area is by car. The most popular resorts are within two to three hours' drive of Johannesburg, Pretoria or Durban, accessed from the N3 and then a network of minor roads heading west into the mountains. The popular sights and resorts are well signposted. Those in the far south are best approached via Underberg on the R617 from Pietermaritzburg, or the R626 from Kokstad. The Central Drakensberg resorts, and the reserves around Monk's Cowl and Cathedral Peak, are signposted from Winterton and Bergville, off the N3, along the R74 and then onto the R600. The Northern Drakensberg resorts can be reached by taking the N3 as far as the Northern Berg turning. From here the R74 goes through Winterton and Bergville, and on to the Royal Natal National Park. The Battlefields Route lies to the northeast (see page 481). ▸▸ *For further details, see Transport, page 522.*

Best time to visit The weather in the Drakensberg can be divided into two main seasons: summer and winter. Although the weather tends to be pleasant all year round, the altitude and the mountain climate shouldn't be underestimated. Climatic conditions can change rapidly and snow, fog, rain and thunderstorms can develop within minutes, enveloping hikers on exposed hillsides.

Winter (May to August) is the driest time of the year and also the coolest. There will always be some rain during the winter months which, when it's cold enough, will occasionally fall as snow. Daytime temperatures can be as high as 15°C, while at night temperatures will often fall below 0°C. Despite the risk of snow, this the best season for hiking.

Summer (November to February) is the wettest time. The mornings tend to be warm and bright, but as the heat builds up clouds begin to collect in the afternoon. The violence of the thunderstorms when they break is quite spectacular, usually accompanied by short bursts of torrential rain. Daytime temperatures average around 20°C and the nights are generally mild with temperatures not falling much below 10°C. The summer is a less popular season for hiking, although the landscape is greener and the wildlife more abundant.

Tourist information There are a number of information offices in the area. The **Drakensberg Tourism Association** ① *Municipal Building, Thatham Rd, Bergville, T036-4481296, www.drakensberg.kzn.org.za, Mon-Fri 0900-1700*, provides information on the whole region. The accommodation office can be contacted on T036-4481557, www.drakensberg.org.za. The **Central Drakensberg Information Centre** ① *Thokozisa, on the R600, 13 km west of Winterton, T036-4881207, www.cdic.co.za, daily 0900-1700*, is an arts, crafts and tourist centre, which has a coffee shop and restaurant and stocks useful maps and brochures. It can also help arrange accommodation.

Safety There have been a number of carjacking incidents in the Drakensberg. Beware when driving down isolated roads and always take local advice.

Entry fees An entry fee, which includes a community levy and an emergency rescue levy, is payable each time you enter a protected area administered by **KZN Wildlife**. This fee is included in the cost of accommodation within the parks so only day visitors pay an entry fee at the gate. Current rates for day visitors are R20-25 adults, R10-15 children depending on the park.

Background
San The earliest human inhabitants of the Drakensberg were the San who lived here as hunter-gatherers. Evidence of their time here is the rock art which can be seen in numerous caves and rock shelters throughout the range. It is thought that groups of San would gather at certain points in the year at these sites to exchange goods, arrange marriages and carry out shamanic ceremonies.

For the rest of the year they dispersed into smaller family groups moving slowly in search of food. The women gathered edible plants and looked after children while the men hunted. Part of the reason for the success of their lifestyle was its relative simplicity. The few goods that they needed could be made from local materials – hides for clothing, bones, flint and wood for tools, and hunting poison from crushed insects and plants.

Anthropological studies of modern hunter gatherers in Australia and the Amazon estimate that they only spend about 20 hours a week collecting enough food to survive. Considering the relative abundance of food, it is thought likely that the Drakensberg San had a similar working week, dedicating much of the rest of their time to rock painting, singing and dancing.

The San came under increasing pressure towards the middle of the 19th century as new settlers established themselves on their land. Opportunities for hunting decreased as European immigrants shot such large numbers of game, and gradually the San were forced to adapt. They were driven further and further into the mountains, and eventually abandoned their stone tools and hunting poisons in favour of horses and guns and became cattle rustlers. Their raids on farms in Natal were so successful that the raiders were often hunted down and shot.

Attitudes of Europeans towards the San during 19th century couldn't be more different from the rather romantic view in which they are held today. They were seen, at best, as pests, were often shot on sight and were captured and forced into slavery. The last records of San being seen in the Drakensberg date from 1878 just before the Natal government began auctioning plots of land at the base of the mountains themselves.

Originally the Nguni people called the mountains uKhalamba (Barrier of Spears), an apt description of the escarpment that rises sharply from the rolling hills of Natal.

Colonial The first Europeans to see the Drakensberg were a group of Portuguese sailors whose ship was wrecked on the Transkei coast in 1593. They had decided to head inland on their way back to Lourenço Marques and reported having seen snow-covered mountains in the distance.

Almost 250 years later the first hunters, missionaries and farmers began to arrive. The Voortrekkers arrived from the north, moving down into Natal through what was later to be called Oliviershoek Pass while the settlers from the Eastern Cape moved up from the south. As the land gradually fell under their control, the Drakensberg's natural resources were subject to the settler's rapacious exploitation. The timber and sheep farming industries were particularly successful in the short term, but their effects on the delicate ecosystem of the Drakensberg were eventually to lead to the creation of the national park.

Modern The first area of the park to receive protection was the Giant's Castle Game Reserve in 1903. Over the years more land was acquired and given protected status.

One of the main reasons for creating a national park here is that the Drakensberg escarpment is the source of many of the rivers which flow through Natal. The Tugela, the Mkhomazi and the Mzimkhulu are three of the most important sources of water in Natal. During the 1950s, damage caused by deforestation and overgrazing was proved to be affecting the water supply. The indigenous vegetation of the Drakensberg was shown to play an essential role in holding water from torrential seasonal rain and preventing flash floods. The root systems in the soil release the water gradually throughout the year providing Natal with a regular water supply. The park now protects a unique area of Afro-montane and Afro-alpine vegetation and access to this delicate ecosystem is restricted in order to prevent further damage. In 2001 UNESCO named the park a World Heritage Site, in recognition of its universal environmental value to mankind. Presently, the Maloti-Drakensberg Transfrontier Conservation Area initiative is underway. This links the Sehlaba-Thebe National Park in Lesotho and the uKhahlamba-Drakensberg Park, which covers 8113 sq km in total. The main objectives of the project are to conserve the globally significant biodiversity in the Maloti and the Drakensberg Mountains.

Landscape

The Drakensberg are divided into two areas known as the High Berg and the Little Berg. The **High Berg**, covering the area which rises steeply up to the plateau, is the more interesting of the two with its spectacular scenery of high peaks and cliffs. The top of the escarpment averages an altitude of around 3000 m and forms the western boundary of the park along the watershed between Natal and Lesotho. The **Little Berg** lies at lower altitude and consists of the spurs of sandstone which stretch out towards the plains of Natal. The landscape here is of rolling hills and grassland divided by forested ravines. The Little Berg is the most popular area for hiking and many of the KZN Wildlife resorts are located here.

Drakensberg snakes

There are only two deadly poisonous snakes in the Drakensberg, the puff adder and the *rinkhals* or ring-necked spitting cobra. Both are extremely rare and mostly live at lower altitudes in the low-lying farmlands and, as they are both brightly coloured, are fairly easy to see. At higher altitudes, the Berg adder, which is poisonous but not life-threatening, is more common and is endemic to the area. Several other species of non-poisonous snake occur in the Berg, although again they are rarely encountered. The largest of these is the brown water snake, which frequents river banks and can grow to over 2 m in length.

Most snakes will be terrified at your approach and will try to make a quick getaway. If you are walking in single file, this gives them an almost 360° choice of route. Both the puff adder and Berg adder adopt a defensive coiled posture if they feel they cannot escape in time, while the cobra will rear up and flatten its hood. The adders can strike at an alarming speed, straightening one or more of their coils in the process and thus extending their reach. Never approach a coiled snake. As terrifying as it sounds, if you get almost to within striking distance of an adder or cobra, it's best to freeze. Neither snake really wants to bite you; they prefer to keep their venom for catching food, and in any case have poor vision and are best at detecting movement. In the unfortunate event of a snake bite get to a hospital as soon as possible (for further advice see Health, page 59).

Wildlife and vegetation

The different wildlife habitats in the Drakensberg vary according to altitude, which can range from the subtropical at around 1000 m to the Afro-alpine at over 3000 m. The wealth of plantlife in the Drakensberg is quite staggering: over 1500 plant species have been identified here, among which 350 are endemic. By far the best time of year to see the veldt is during the spring, when the grass is green and lush and many of the orchids, irises and lilies are in flower. Plants on the high plateau are hardy, small alpine plants consisting mostly of grasses, shrubs and succulents.

The **wildlife** is not as easy to spot as in some of South Africa's other wildlife reserves. Numbers are relatively low, and viewing wildlife is more the preserve of enthusiastic naturalists rather than casual observers. The large mammals you might see include eland, baboon, and some of the small antelope such as klipspringer and duiker. Red hartebeest, blesbok, bushbuck and oribi are present but are seen less often as they only inhabit certain areas. Leopard, lynx, serval, aardvark, aardwolf and porcupine are thought to be present but are almost never seen, even by park staff or regular hikers.

Birdlife in the Drakensberg is particularly rich, as it is possible to visit several different ecosystems within a relatively small area. Over 300 species have been recorded here, most of which live below 2000 m. The best time to see the birds is during the summer when they are courting and nesting. This is their most active time of year and their most colourful, as the birds will be in their breeding plumage.

The rarest birds live at higher altitudes on the summit plateau, and include the orange-breasted rockjumper, the Drakensberg siskin, the bald ibis, the Cape vulture and the lammergeyer. Conditions are so harsh in this environment that only 54 species have been recorded here. The environment in the Little Berg is less extreme and many species of bird common to other parts of KwaZulu Natal can be seen here.

To Lesotho via the Drakensberg escarpment

The border between South Africa and Lesotho follows the watershed along the top edge of the Drakensberg escarpment. It is essential to carry your passport with you at all times.

Hiking

Trails vary between short, well-marked strolls to challenging hikes at high altitude, lasting several days. The majority of visitors to the Drakensberg prefer to complete a number of day hikes and stay overnight in KZN Wildlife camps.

Experienced hikers have compared some of the longer trails to hiking in the Himalayas, where several days are spent in isolated wilderness areas at altitudes of up to 3000 m. Some of the longer hiking trails can last up to 10 days crossing through isolated and challenging mountain passes such as the Mnweni and Ifidi, which are among the wildest and most beautiful trails along the Northern Berg. Planning ahead is essential for longer hikes as overnight caves and mountain huts have to be booked in advance. It is recommended that all overnight hikers read KZN Wildlife's brochure *It's Tough at the Top – Hiking Safely in the Drakensberg*.

Permits Permits are necessary on all longer walks and are available from camp offices for a small fee. Maximum group size is 12 people and the minimum size is three. Hikers intending to stay overnight in the mountains must fill in the **Mountain Rescue Register**, carry detailed maps and be equipped to deal with extreme weather. Mountain registers are located at all the trail heads and should be filled in even for short day walks.

Hazards The most common problems to watch out for are the effects of intense sunlight at high altitudes. Sunstroke and dehydration are best avoided by wearing a sun hat, using a high protection factor suncream and by carrying enough water. It's worth considering going on a guided hike, as registered guides will be well versed in mountain safety. Contact any of the tourist offices in the Drakensberg region who will be able to arrange a guided hike

Equipment and supplies See page 45 for a full list of recommended hiking equipment. Note that **camping stoves** are essential for overnight hikes as fires are not allowed in the park. Petrol is available for multi-fuel stoves from some of the larger resorts. **Camping gas** and other fuels should be bought in advance from a camping shop in a large urban centre such as Durban or Pietermaritzburg. It is better to buy meths from a pharmacy than a supermarket, as it is much better quality.

Resort shops and the local stores up in the mountains have a limited selection of tinned **food**. It's best to bring lightweight dry food from Durban or Johannesburg. Fresh produce can be bought in the towns en route to the mountains.

Some hikers choose not to carry a tent if they have booked accommodation in caves or mountain huts. However, these are not always marked accurately on maps and they can be difficult to find, so it's sensible to have a tent as a backup in case you get caught out at nightfall. On overnight hikes a **trowel** or a spade is necessary for digging toilets to prevent litter and pollution. Dig a hole at least 30 m away from streams and make sure everything is properly buried.

The most exciting Drakensberg hikes are the ones up to the summit plateau. The **clothing** you carry with you should protect you from the weather you are likely to encounter over 3000 m. An anorak made from waterproof breathable fabrics like Goretex will be useful all year round, while in winter layers of thermal underwear, fleece, a woolly hat and gloves should prepare you for sub-zero temperatures. Even on short day hikes in the Little Berg a waterproof jacket and a sweater are invaluable.

Maps A map, a compass and a good knowledge of map reading are essential for hiking in the Drakensberg. **KZN Wildlife** produce a series of six comprehensive 1:50,000 maps, which usefully also cover the Lesotho side of the mountains. Contact KZN Wildlife in advance.

Activities and tours

Hiking, horse riding and mountaineering are the traditional Drakensberg sports but newer activities like mountain biking and hang-gliding are becoming very popular. Many of the larger resort hotels also offer a wide range of sporting facilities such as tennis, squash, golf and swimming. ▶▶ *For further details, see Activities and tours, page 521.*

Staying in the park

There is a huge choice in the area, including within **KZN Wildlife** accommodation and in private establishments on the fringes of the park. KZN Wildlife offers a wide range of facilities, from luxury lodges and chalets through to campsites, mountain huts and caves. All of the KZN Wildlife camps are basically self-catering and although there are some camp shops which sell food, the choice is limited. It is far better to come prepared and buy your food beforehand in the nearest large town.

The area bordering the national park is increasingly being developed for tourism and a number of self-contained holiday resorts and timeshares have sprung up. These tend to offer numerous sporting and entertainment facilities but they are sometimes rather distant from the Drakensberg Mountains themselves. There is also a good selection of B&Bs, which can offer better value.

Reservations for **KZN Wildlife** ① *T033-8451000, www.kznwildlife.com*. Bookings can be made by telephone or online; camping reservations must be made directly with the officer in charge of the campsite, see individual areas for details.

Northern Drakensberg ●●●▲●● ▶▶ *pp514-522.*

The scenery of the Northern Berg is exceptional in its grandeur, and is perhaps the most photographed section of the range. The Royal Natal National Park is the most popular of all the resorts in the Drakensberg, and although there are some good hikes outside the park, they don't really compare with the sheer majesty of those within its boundaries.

Ins and outs

From Royal Natal National Park the R74 heads east to Bergville (41 km) and Winterton (62 km). The R615 heads north off the R74, 14 km from the park gates. After 11 km it reaches the top of Oliviershoek Pass from where it is a further 37 km to Harrismith.

Royal Natal National Park

The highlight of a visit to the park is the first view of the massive rock walls that form the **Amphitheatre**. The **Eastern Buttress** (3009 m) is the southernmost peak of the 4-km of cliff face, which arcs northwards towards the **Sentinel** (3165 m) forming an impressive barrier. On the plateau directly behind the Amphitheatre is **Mont-aux-Sources** (3299 m) named by French missionaries in 1836. This mountain is the source of five rivers: the **Elands** which flows into the Vaal; the **Khudeda** and the **Singu** leading into the Orange/Gariep River in the Free State; and the **Tugela** and the **Bilanjil** which lead into Natal.

The most impressive of these is the Tugela which plunges over the edge of the Amphitheatre wall, dropping around 800 m through a series of five falls. The gorge created by the waters of the Tugela is a steep-sided tangle of boulders and trees which at a point near the Devil's Tooth Gully has bored straight through the sandstone to form what appears to be a tunnel around 40 m long.

The national park was established in 1916 when farms around the Amphitheatre were bought by the government to protect the land. Tourism started around this time and the park has been popular since then. Queen Elizabeth II visited the park in 1947, five years before she became queen; since then, the national park and the (now closed) hotel are prefixed by the word 'Royal' in memory of this visit.

🌙 *Michael Caine and the film crew stayed at the Royal Natal National Park Hotel, now closed, during the filming of Zulu in the early 1960s. The film set was close to the Amphitheatre.*

Royal Natal National Park

Sleeping 🛌
Mahai **1**
Rugged Glen **2**
Thendele Camp **3**

N

1 km
1 mile

Cannibal Cave

This large cave overlooking a quiet valley is accessible on foot either from Mahai Campsite or Rugged Glen. The remains of some San paintings can still be seen.

During the Zulu wars, refugees escaped into the mountains and lived in the caves. Times were so turbulent that people were unable to plant crops and, as game became scarcer, the refugees were forced to eat passing travellers or even their own children. Rumour has it that the bodies were hung from the cave roof to keep them fresh.

The cannibals lived here for around 20 years, eventually becoming such a threat that they were hunted and killed by the Zulus.

Ins and outs The park can be reached on tarred roads from Harrismith (60 km) or Bergville (40 km). The route is well signposted from the N3. Note that the number of day visitors is controlled to prevent overcrowding in the park; however, this only tends to be a problem at weekends and on holidays. The **visitor centre** ① *T036-4386303, daily 0800-1630, R25 per person*, has a gift shop that sells a good selection of books, T-shirts, a very limited range of tinned goods, curios, alcoholic and soft drinks, maps and sometimes fresh trout. Petrol is also available here.

Hiking There are over 130 km of walking trails around the Royal Natal National Park, many of which are easy half-day strolls. Even the hikes that don't climb up to the top of the escarpment wind through beautiful countryside of grassland dotted with patches of yellowwood forest and proteas set against the stunning backdrop of the Amphitheatre. The visitor centre sells hiking maps and a leaflet describing the many possible walks around the park. Permits are also available here. Soil erosion has increasingly become a problem as more and more hikers visit the park. In an attempt to control erosion some paths may be closed to hikers.

The 20-km hike up to **Mont-aux-Sources** (3299 m) can be completed in a strenuous day's walk. The path starts at **Mahai Campsite** and heads steadily uphill following the course of the Mahai River. The path climbs steeply around the eastern flank of the Sentinel (3165 m). Just after the Sentinel Caves is the notorious chain ladder, built in 1930, which takes you up a 30-m cliff face. Once on top, Mont-aux-Sources is only 3 km away and involves no more serious climbing. The views from the top of the escarpment are splendid as they stretch out over KwaZulu Natal. The hike up to Mont-aux-Sources is restricted to 100 people per day because it is so popular.

The walk up the **Tugela Gorge** is a 14-km round trip which begins at the car park below Tendele Camp. The path heads up the gorge and follows the Tugela River passing through shady patches of yellowwood forest. Higher up along the valley there are rock pools which are ideal for swimming in. After around 6 km at the entrance to the gorge there is a chain ladder; from here you can either wade through the gorge or climb up the ladder and walk along the top. There are magnificent views here of the Devil's Tooth, the Eastern Buttress and Tugela Falls. Beware of heavy rain on this walk as flash flooding through the gorge is extremely dangerous.

The 8-km trail to **Cannibal Cave** (see box, above) heads north from the road leading to **Mahai Campsite**. The route follows the Goldie River for 1 km before crossing over and following the ridge north again until it passes close to Sunday Falls. The path then rises over Surprise Ridge and on to the Cannibal Cave. The walks from the **Rugged Glen**

Campsite are over rolling hills and although there are some good views of the Amphitheatre, they don't compare with the hikes from the Thendele and Mahai camps.

Oliviershoek Pass

Oliviershoek Pass was named after Adriaan Olivier who was one of the first Voortrekkers to descend from the Orange Free State in the 1830s. He claimed a farm for himself at the foot of the pass. As the R615 ascends to the top of the pass it begins to climb through pine forests. Although the mountains here aren't as spectacular as Mont-aux-Sources, they do have their own quiet charm and it is worth stopping off at one of the few restaurants on this road. The pass isn't as crowded as the national park and at 1730 m it is higher than the other resorts and does have a wilder feel to it. Once over the pass, the road circles Sterkfontein Dam and then descends to Harrismith.

Bergville → *Colour map 4, A6.*

This quiet country town is in the centre of a maize and dairy farming area. Most visitors will either be passing through en route to the resorts in the Northern Drakensberg or be heading northeast towards Ladysmith and the Battlefields. The main reason for stopping is to visit the helpful **Drakensberg Tourism Association** (see page 494).

Central Drakensberg ⊖🔊⊕⊙🛆⊙ ⚬ *pp514-522.*

The Giant's Castle Nature Reserve is the most spectacular of the Central Berg resorts. It has two camps: Giant's Castle and Injisuthi. Here, the basalt cliff faces rise up to 3000 m and stretch out to the north and south for over 30 km. Further north, the road to Monk's Cowl, with its string of resorts, curio villages and golf courses, is one of the most heavily developed areas of the Drakensberg. While you may see more tourists in this region, the scenery is no less spectacular and access is easier than in other areas of the park. This is also home to the internationally famous Drakensberg Boys' Choir.

Ins and outs

Two roads from Winterton lead towards the central Drakensberg resorts: heading north the R74 goes via Bergville, 22 km, to the **Royal Natal National Park**, 62 km. Two kilometres south of Winterton on the R600 there is a signposted turning to **Cathedral Peak**, 43 km. The R600 continues on to **Monk's Cowl** (Champagne Valley), 35 km. To reach **Injisuthi**, take the turning to Loskop off the R600, before reaching Loskop there is a dirt road on the right. Follow the signposts to Injisuthi from here. Heading southeast, the R74 crosses the N3 to **Estcourt**, 43 km.

Winterton → *Colour map 4, A/B6.*

This village is an important centre for dairy farms as well as being the last place to stock up on supplies for visitors to Cathedral Peak or Monk's Cowl. It's worth stopping here for a look around its pleasant tree-lined streets and small museum, and to gather some local information. The petrol station and the supermarket are on the junction of the R74 with the road leading into the centre of village. Nearby in Thokosiza is the **Central Drakensberg Information Centre**, a major arts, crafts and tourist centre, see page 494.

Spioenkop Dam Nature Reserve → *Colour map 4, A6.*

ⓘ *14 km north of Winterton on the R600. Office T036-4881578. Oct-Mar 0600-1900, Apr-Sep 0600-1800, R20.*

This 6000-ha game park is a popular tourist resort for boating and fishing. Almost all the game here has been reintroduced and there is a good chance of seeing white rhino and buffalo. With this in mind visitors must be careful when walking in the open around their campsite. Other animals you can expect to see include giraffe, kudu, mountain reedbuck, waterbuck, blesbok, impala, zebra, eland, duiker and steenbok. The area is particularly rich in birdlife and more than 270 species have been recorded here. Anglers can fish the reservoir from the dam or from the shore.

The **Battle of Spion Kop**, 24 January 1890, was yet another embarrassing defeat for the British at the hands of the Boers and had a marked impact upon British public opinion. In order to relieve the beleaguered British troops at Ladysmith (see page 483), General

1 Northern & central Drakensberg

10 km
10 miles

Sleeping
Alpine Heath **1**
Amphitheatre Backpackers **13**
Bingelela Lodge **21**
Caterpillar & Catfish **15**

Cathedral Peak **2**
Cavern **11**
Didima Camp **23**
Drakensville Berg Resort **16**
Iphika Tented Bush Camp **7**

Lilac Lodge **3**
Little Switzerland **8**
Montusi Mountain Lodge **4**
Sandford Park Resort **9**
Spionkop Lodge **10**
Swallow's Nest **5**

Warren attempted a direct assault on the Rangeworthy Hills to dislodge the Boer positions. He decided to occupy the highest peak on the ridge – Spion Kop. However, this meant that the shallow British defences were exposed to Boer gunfire from all sides and soon suffered heavy losses. A brigade under General Lyttelton came to Warren's assistance but General Buller disastrously reversed the decision, ordering all British forces to retreat down from Spion Kop and back across the Tugela. Some 1750 British troops were either killed, wounded or captured at Spion Kop compared to about 300 Boers. The famous battlefield overlooks the dam and is clearly visible from the reserve. It can be reached on one of the self-guided trails.

🌙 *In 1906 Liverpool Football Club named the home stands at Anfield 'Spionkop' in memory of those who died here during the Boer War. The stands are still called 'the Kop' to this day.*

Cathedral Peak → *Colour map 4, B6.*

ⓘ *T036-4888000, reception, shop and information office daily 0700-1900. R20 per person, vehicles to Mike's Pass R35. Signposted from Bergville and Winterton. The road is tarred and is usually passable even after rain*

Cathedral Peak is the main point of access to some of the wildest areas of the central Drakensberg, and provides some of the most spectacular scenery for hikers. Driving into the area, the road passes traditional Zulu villages and dips through leafy valleys, with the views gradually opening up as you get closer to the park. The park itself is ringed by dramatic peaks with views of the Cathedral Spur and Cathedral Peak (3004 m), the Inner and Outer Horns (3005 m), and the Bell (2930 m). An alternative to hiking round the peaks is to drive up Mike's Pass, suitable for saloon cars (although it says 4WD only), from where there are spectacular views of the Little Berg (R35 per car).

The sheltered valleys in this area are thought to have been one of the last refuges of the San in the Drakensberg. This is one of the best places to see a large number of San cave paintings found in the Drankensberg; the Rock Art Centre at Didimi makes a good starting point. Leopard's Cave and Poacher's Cave in the Ndedema Gorge have especially good galleries of paintings.

An earlier name for Cathedral Peak was Zikhali's Horn, named after Zikhali who escaped to Swaziland after his father was killed by Dingaan. During the years that he and his tribe spent in Swaziland they assimilated many aspects of Swazi culture. Swazi influences can still be seen today in the way that traditional huts are built in this region.

Hiking The Cathedral Peak area is growing in popularity with hikers. There is a good network of paths heading up the Mlambonja Valley to the escarpment from where there are trails heading south to Monk's Cowl and Injisuthi or heading north to Royal Natal National Park. The campsite at Mike's Pass or the **Cathedral Peak Hotel** are good bases from which to set out exploring the area on a series of day walks. Maps are available in the information office and show a number of walks departing from the hotel. For keen hikers there are designated caves and mountain huts on the longer trails. The 10-km hike to the top of **Cathedral Peak** (3004 m) is one of the most exciting and strenuous hikes in this part of the Drakensberg, and the views from the top of the Drakensberg stretching out to the north and south are unforgettable.

Cave paintings An excellent introduction to San rock art in the area is just past the entrance to the park, at the **Rock Art Centre** ⓘ *Didima Camp, T036-4888025, 0800-1300, 1400 1600, small entry fee, coffee shop and craft centre.* The stylish thatched building holds a series of displays

Cave paintings

The sandstone caves of the Drakensberg are one of the best places in the world to see rock art. Most of the surviving paintings are on the walls of rock shelters. There are traces of paintings on exposed rocks but they have been heavily weathered. The paintings tend to be quite recent and are probably only 200 to 300 years old, but they do form part of a long-standing tradition. The earliest cave paintings in Southern Africa date from 28,000 years ago.

The pigments used by the San were made from natural ochre mixed with blood, fat or milk. Artists would carry their pigments in antelope horns hanging from their belts. The San here were particularly prolific and there are hundreds of caves throughout these mountains which are covered with layer upon layer of paintings. Some of the most beautiful of South Africa's cave paintings can be found in the Drakensberg.

There have been numerous attempts at interpreting the meaning of these paintings. One of the more outlandish theories held by European archaeologists at the beginning of the last century was that they had been drawn with the help of migrating Carthaginians.

Other more recent theories hold that the paintings are either little more than well-executed graffitos illustrating scenes from daily life or that they were used in sympathetic magic.

The most recent research has drawn from ethnographic records from the end of the last century and interviews with the remaining San people in this century. The eland features largely in San mythology and is one of the most frequently painted subjects. It seems unlikely that the eland were painted as part of a hunting ritual using sympathetic magic as the eland is not often found in food debris from archaeological excavations. It is thought that the eland in some way represented god.

The most prevalent current theory holds that the paintings of human figures dancing which show people with nose bleeds hallucinating geometric patterns, are people taking part in shamanic rituals who are in a state of trance.

There are also other paintings which seem to deal with more mundane matters. The scenes of San collecting wild honey, hunting pigs or being chased by a leopard reveal aspects of a way of life which has now disappeared.

terpreting the art found in the surrounding mountains. A key thread in the museum is the eland, a vital aspect in San mythology and culture, with some life-size replicas in the entrance. The museum begins with an introduction to the culture and lifestyle of the San, with a look at archaeological finds, quotes from some of the last San descendants, and descriptions of the symbolic meaning of some of the most famous paintings. At the back of the museum is a replica of an open-topped cave, complete with starry sky and fake camp fire, where recordings of San folklore stories are played. This leads to the auditorium, an impressive structure built to look like a rock overhang, where you can watch an interesting 15-minute audio-visual show on the history of the San and their cave paintings.in

There are several caves within walking distance of the **Cathedral Peak Hotel** (accessible with a guide only; call the hotel to book, see page 516). **Mushroom Hill** has two particularly interesting scenes, one of two mythical human figures with animal heads and hooves holding what are thought to be early musical instruments, and the other depicting a more lighthearted scene of some San scrambling away from an irate leopard. **Xeni Shelter**, 2 km beyond Mushroom Rock and also easily reached from the hotel, shows a group of people and a few antelope. **Ladder Shelter** shows San ladders with a small picture of a man climbing up the rock face. **Junction Shelter** has a number of interesting scenes of men crossing on a rope bridge, a baboon hunt and some human figures dancing. **Eland Cave** is a large cave with many splendid paintings; more mysteriously, a San hunting kit was found here in the 1920s, which can now be seen at the Rock Art Centre.

Monk's Cowl → *Colour map 4, B6. See also map below.*

① *T036-4681103. Park gates Oct-Mar 0700-2000, Apr-Sep 0600-1800. Camp office daily 0800-1230, 1400-1630. R25 per person. The nearest shop to Monk's Cowl is opposite the Champagne Sports Resort (9 km).*

The road to Monk's Cowl passes through one of the most developed areas of the Drakensberg. Looking down from Monk's Cowl the view of KwaZulu Natal is dotted with hotels, golf courses and timeshare developments and the area is locally dubbed 'Champagne Valley'. However, **Champagne Castle**, **Monk's Cowl** and **Cathkin Peak** are still impressive features in this landscape and several interesting long-distance hikes begin from here.

The **Drakensberg Boys' Choir School** is on the right of the R600 towards Monk's Cowl and is one of the most beautiful locations for a school in the whole of South Africa.

Monk's Cowl

Drakensberg maps
1 Northern and central Drakensberg, page 502
2 **Monk's Cowl, page 505**
3 Giant's Castle Reserve, page 507

Sleeping ⌂
Ardmore Guest Farm 1
Cathkin Cottage 2
Champagne Castle 4
Champagne Sports Resort 5

Dragon Peaks 6
Inkosana Lodge 9
National Parks Campsite 10
Nest 11

The school is highly accredited in its own right, but is most famous for the choir that has performed all over the world over the last three decades. Boys aged between nine and 15 have performed in front of the Pope and 25,000 people at the Vatican City, sung with the Vienna Boys' Choir in Austria, and have been proclaimed top choir three times at the World Festival of Choirs. The choir has even received a special award at Disney's Magic Kingdom. Most audiences expect only classical choral renditions but the boys sing anything from Beethoven to Freddy Mercury. ▶ *For further details, see Entertainment, page 520.*

Just before the **Champagne Castle Hotel**, turn off the R600 to reach **Falcon Ridge** ① *T082-7746398 (mob), bird shows Sat-Thu at 1030*, a rehabilitation centre for rescued birds of prey, mostly injured through flying into power lines. The daily show is a big attraction, and you can don a glove and have your photo taken with a large raptor.

Hiking The short hikes around Monk's Cowl get busy as so many tourists visit here for the day. A map is available from the office and the paths are clear and well signposted. Places to visit include **Nandi's Falls** (5 km), **Sterkspruit Falls** (2 km), and **The Sphinx** (3 km). The paths cross areas of proteas and some woodland.

The hike up to **Champagne Castle** (3377 m) is a 20-km, two-day hike which involves a steady slog uphill, but no climbing skills are needed. From the camp, the trail rises up and follows the Mhlawazini Valley circling around Cathkin Peak and Monk's Cowl. There is a campsite just below Gray's Pass. A path winds steeply up the pass for 2 km to the top of the escarpment. From here it is possible to walk to the top of Champagne Castle or to visit the cliffs at Vulture's Retreat where a colony of Cape vultures breed.

Giant's Castle Reserve → *Colour map 4, B6.*

This reserve was established in 1903 when there were only 200 eland left in the whole of KwaZulu Natal. Over the years, the reserve has successfully helped the eland population in the Drakensberg to recover and at present there are around 600 in the reserve. Blesbok, mountain reedbuck and oribi are some of the other mammals you are likely to see. Rolling hills of sourveld grasslands dominate the landscape of the reserve, with the Drakensberg escarpment towering over the main camp. A wall of basalt cliffs rise up to over 3000 m and the peaks of **Giant's Castle** (3314 m), **Champagne Castle** (3248 m) and **Cathkin Peak** (3149 m) can be seen on the skyline. The grasslands below the cliffs roll out in a series of massive hills, which give rise to the Bushman's River and the Little Tugela River. On the drive to the main camp from the park gates, the road passes through a cutting which exposes layers of brown, red, yellow and purple rock. These are the **Molteno Beds**, layers of sandstone deposited 200 million years ago where plant and dinosaur fossils have been found.

Ins and outs The road to Giant's Castle is signposted from Mooi River (64 km) and Estcourt (65 km) on the N3. The road from Estcourt is tarred for most of the way while the mostly dirt road from Mooi River should be avoided in wet weather. From Mooi River take the road to Ncibidwana Store, 46 km, and then follow the signs. Petrol is for sale by the main gate.

Giant's Castle camp and around ① *T036-3533718. Park gates Oct-Mar 0500-1900, Apr-Sep 0600-1800. Camp office Mon-Fri 0800-1800, Sun 0800-1600, R20.* The area around the camp has a network of short paths through riverine forest and wetlands which supports many species of bird. The malachite kingfisher, Gurney's sugarbird and the various sunbirds are often spotted here and grey duiker can sometimes be seen walking around the camp.

There are numerous interconnected hikes crossing the reserve. The shorter walks explore the forests and river valleys within a few kilometres of the camp, whilst the longer ones take up to three days and can reach areas as far afield as Injisuthi. A comprehensive leaflet detailing the hiking choices is available from the camp office.

The **Main Cave** is half an hour's walk from the camp and has a large wall covered in paintings and a simple display on the archaeology of the cave and the San who lived there. The cave must be visited with a guide; book at the main office, T036-3533718.

The 7-km hike up to **World's View** (1842 m) follows a path north along a ridge overlooking the Bushman's River. The climb up to the top is not too strenuous and the views looking over Wildebeest Plateau to Giant's Castle and Cathkin Peak are well worth the effort. The best time to see the peaks of the mountains is early in the morning as clouds tend to descend in the afternoon.

③ Giant's Castle Reserve

➡ **Drakensberg maps**
1 Northern and central Drakensberg, page 502
2 Monk's Cowl, page 505
3 Giant's Castle Reserve, page 507

Sleeping 🛏
Giant's Castle Camp **2**
Injisuthi Camp **5**

White Mountain Resort **3**

The more challenging walks to **Langalibalele Pass**, 12 km, **Bannerman Pass**, 20 km, and **Giant's Castle** involve a long uphill struggle to reach the top of the escarpment. The hike up to Giant's Castle at 3314 m takes three days and means using Giant's Hut as a base camp for two nights. The second day's hike from the hut up to Giant's Castle Pass, 12 km, rises up through scree slopes and loose rubble. From the top of the pass it is a further 1 km to the peak. Giant's Hut is 10 km from the main camp and there are several well-marked paths which lead to it.

Injisuthi camp and around ① *Signposted from Winterton and Loskop, the last 30 km of the journey are on a poor dirt road. T036-4317848. Gates Oct-Mar 0500-1900, Apr-Sep 0600-1800. Office daily 0800-1230, 1400-1630. R20 per person.* Injisuthi is an isolated camp high up in the Giant's Castle Nature Reserve. The valley is covered with large areas of yellowwood forest and grassland, and looming over the camp are the awe-inspiring mountain peaks of**Champagne Castle** (3248 m), **Monk's Cowl** (3234 m) and **Cathkin Peak** (3149 m). **Mafadi** (3446 m), **Injisuthi Dome** (3410 m), the **Injisuthi Triplets** – Eastern Triplet (3134 m), Western Triplet (3187 m), Injisuthi Buttress (3202 m) – are some of the highest peaks in South Africa and have become magnets to South Africa's climbers. The game in Injisuthi Valley used to be abundant and the Zulu word *Injisuthi* actually means 'well-fed dog' as hunting parties here were often so successful. San also thrived here and left many cave paintings.

There is a selection of trails for day hikes beginning at the campsite and following the Injisuthi Stream to the southwest. Poacher's Stream is a tributary of the Injisuthi and this path leads off Boundary Pool (3 km) where it is possible to swim. Following the Injisuthi further up the valley are Battle Cave (5 km), Junction Cave (8 km) and Lower Injisuthi Cave (8 km). There is a daily guided walk, 7 km, to **Battle Cave** and other San sites, which should be booked the day before. Battle Cave is named after one its cave paintings, which shows two groups of San attacking each other. Figures are shown running into the fight with arrows flying between them. There are hundreds of other paintings on the cave walls of animals that used to live here, including lions, eland, rhebok, an elephant and an antbear.

Giant's Castle is a three-day hike from Injisuthi following the contour path south. The trail can be exhausting but it does pass through spectacular mountain scenery including Popple Peak. Reservations for sleeping at Lower Injisuthi Cave and Bannerman Hut have to be made beforehand.

Kamberg Nature Reserve
① *48 km from Nottingham Rd travelling via Rosetta; the route is well signposted and only the last 19 km are on dirt roads. If travelling from Mooi River (42 km) on the N3, take the turning to Rosetta, T033-2637312. Gates Oct-Mar 0500-1900, Apr-Sep 0600-1800. Office daily 0800-1130, 1400-1530. All visitors must report to the office on arrival. R20.*
The reserve was established on farmland in 1951. The scenery is not as spectacular as at some of the other resorts, however, the Clarens Sandstone around Kamberg does have its own special appeal, and there is some good San rock art within the reserve. The reserve is at relatively low altitude, the highest point being **Gladstone's Nose** at 2265 m, and is therefore known for its birdlife with over 200 species recorded here.

Kamberg is probably best known for its trout fishing; there is a hatchery open to the public and several dams stocked with brown and rainbow trout which can be fished all year round. The Mooi River can only be fished during the season between September and April. Food and petrol are not for sale at the camp. The nearest shops and petrol station are 42 km away in Rosetta.

The trails around Kamberg are quite leisurely and involve no steep climbs. The **Mooi River Trail**, 4 km, has been designed with wheelchair access in mind, and is a relaxing stroll past willows and eucalyptus trees along the banks of the Mooi River. Longer trails, such as the hike up to **Emeweni Falls**, are detailed in a booklet available in the camp office.

There are several rock art sites in the reserve, but the two main sites worth visiting for the variety and quality of the paintings are Game Pass Shelter and The Kranses. The sheer number of paintings at **Game Pass Shelter** (about a 7 km walk from Kamberg) is impressive. Among the many scenes on the rock wall is one of a human with hooves instead of feet holding the tail of a dying eland. This is thought to have shamanic meaning and to be connected to a trance-like state. Just outside the shelter there are some fossilized dinosaur footprints. An impressive **San Rock Art Interpretation Centre** ① *T033-2637312, daily 0800, 1100, 1230 and 1330, R40 per person, book in advance*, provides visitors with an insight into the lifestyle of the San hunter-gatherers. There's an audio-visual presentation followed by a guided walk to the Game Pass Shelter that takes about 2½ hours. The centre also has a small restaurant.

The walk to the **Kranses** group of caves is a 12-km round trip. Apart from these there are also several other interesting caves to visit. The Kranses has a long sheltered rock wall covered in paintings of eland. Among these are some smaller scenes showing a group of people, some of whom are carrying shields. It is known that the San didn't use shields so they must be paintings of cattle herders, possibly the Amazizi, who moved up into the Drakensberg and lived peacefully with the San.

Southern Drakensberg ⊖⊘⊗⊙▲ ⧼ *pp514-522.*

The southern section of the Drakensberg is the least visited part of the mountain range, although the scenery here is no less spectacular, and offers some excellent walks – particularly around Cobham. The area is best known for the Sani Pass, a spectacular track crossing over to the mountains to Lesotho, reaching 3000 m at its highest point. The main towns in the south are Underberg and Himeville – both are convenient stop-off points for stocking up on supplies.

Ins and outs
Underberg is the main access point to the Southern Drakensberg resorts. Both Underberg and Himeville are sleepy farming villages but have a good variety of pubs, restaurants and shops, and are convenient stop-offs for provisions en route to the KZN Wildlife camps or the Sani Pass. Despite its relative isolation, **Sani Pass Carriers** offers transport to/from Underberg, which helps make this beautiful area of the Drakensberg accessible for budget travellers.

Southern Berg Escape ① *7 Clock Tower Centre, Main Rd, Underberg, T033-7011471, www.drakensberg.org*, produces a leaflet with information on activities and accommo-dation in the Southern Drakensberg, and can book accommodation.

Always make sure you have warm clothing as conditions can change very quickly in this area. Try and hike in groups of three or more people.

Towards Underberg
Bulwer is a small village in the foothills of the Drakensberg set among pine plantations. There is little of interest for tourists here but it is one of the few centres for paragliding and hang-gliding in the Drakensberg and was host to the national champlonships in 2002. ⧼ *For further details, see Activities and tours, page 521.*

Lammergeyers

Lammergeyers are one of the world's rarest vultures, living mainly in isolated high mountain areas in the Pyrenees, the Atlas Mountains of Morocco and the Middle East. However, there are around 200 pairs of lammergeyers in the Drakensberg and Lesotho, and a visit to the hide at Giant's Castle is one of the best ways to see them.

They live on a diet of dried bones, waiting for a carcass to be cleaned by other vultures before they will start to feed. The lammergeyer flies off with bones from the carcass and drops them onto rocks below. The bones crack open enabling the bird to feed on the bone marrow inside.

The lammergeyer is a rare and endangered species, under threat from local farmers, who leave poisoned carcasses out in the wild to kill jackals. The carcasses attract vultures who, in their turn, are poisoned.

The lammergeyer hide is a popular attraction and advance booking is necessary. Up to six people are driven up to the hide in the early morning but must make their own way back to the camp on foot. In addition to the lammergeyer you can expect to see the lanner falcon, jackal buzzard, Cape vulture and the black eagle. ① *T036-3533718, May-Sep Sat and Sun only, R150 per person, minimum per party R480.*

From here the R617 begins to climb, offering spectacular views of the mountains in the distance. Twenty kilometres beyond Bulwer towards Underberg, a sign marks the turning to the **Reichenau Mission**. This old Catholic mission station was originally run by Trappist monks; the highlight here is the Zulu Mass held every Sunday. The church has no organ so all the hymns are purely choral and the singing is amazing. Most of the people here are Zulu speakers and only the local nuns and priests speak English. Guides are available for the local rock art sites and fishing is permitted in the trout dam.

Underberg → *Colour map 4, B6.*
This small market town was founded in 1886 and is still very much the main service centre for this part of the Drakensberg. The junction with the road to Himeville is where the banks, supermarkets and the tourist information office can all be found.

Himeville → *Colour map 4, B6.*
Founded in 1893, Himeville is a small prosperous village reminiscent of England. Arbuckle Street runs through the village centre where there is a supermarket, post office, museum, hotel and petrol station. **Himeville Arms** is the main hotel; its distinctive Tudor architecture wouldn't be out of place in an English village. There is a small **museum** ① *T033-7021184, Tue-Sun 0930-1230*, in the old fort and prison. It is an early sandstone building with exhibits on settler history and one of the better displays on San.

Himeville Nature Reserve ① *0600-1800, day visitors R15,* is set on the outskirts of Himeville, where there are two dams surrounded by grassland. The 105-ha protected area is a home for waterbirds and the occasional blesbok and black wildebeest; look out for three different species of crane which have been bred here in captivity.

Cobham

ⓘ *T033-7020831. Park gates Oct-Mar 0500-1900, Apr-Sep 0600-1800. Office daily 0730-1300, 1400-1630. R20. There is a curio shop at Cobham; otherwise plan on being totally self sufficient. The nearest shops and supermarkets are in Underberg.*

On the road between Underberg and Himeville, a signposted turning leads down a dirt road (D7) to Cobham (14 km). This is a fascinating wilderness area and is an ideal base for many exciting hikes. The land rising up towards the escarpment has been gouged with steep-sided gorges filled with thick yellowwood forest. The view above the cliffs of the escarpment is of the Giant's Cup, lying between Hodgson's Peaks, and the Drakensberg stretching out to the north and south. The Mzimkulu River rises here and flows to Port Shepstone. This area is relatively undisturbed by human activity and the clean waters of the high Drakensberg streams are a sanctuary for Cape clawless otters and spotted necked otters. People rarely see them, as they are very shy animals, but they tend to be active at dusk and dawn. White droppings on riverbanks are a sign of their presence; the distinctive colour comes from the calcium of the crab shells that make up a large proportion of their diet.

Hiking There are five hikes of various lengths in the reserve, most of which leave from the campsite, including the **Gxalingenwa River Trail**, **Ouhout Trail**, **Troutbeck Loop**, **Emerald Stream Trail** and the **Pholela River Trail**. The camp office has full information on all hikes available. Most notable is the Giant's Cup Hiking Trail, a 60-km five-day trail.

Note that hiking permits for the Sani Pass area (see below) including the Giant's Cup Hiking Trail are available from Cobham. Caves should also be reserved here. For your own safety, a mountain rescue register must be filled in. Nights at Cobham are cold all year round, so it is a good idea to bring some warm clothing.

Sani Pass → *Colour map 4, B6.*

The road from Himeville to Sani Pass (15 km) rises steadily through rolling hills covered in grassland and patches of pine plantation until it passes the **Sani Top Chalet** and the 3000 m peaks on the escarpment come into view. **Hodgson's Peaks**, at 3256 m and 3229 m, the **Twelve Apostles** and **Sani Pass**, at 2874 m, are at their most beautiful after snow. Flora and fauna have adapted to this harsh environment and some of the Drakensberg's rarest species can be found here. The road is one of the most dramatic in Africa and is the only route leading into Lesotho on its eastern border with South Africa.

Sani Pass was originally used by traders transporting goods by mule into Basutoland. A trading post was opened in the 1920s at Good Hope Farm at the bottom of the pass, which was the closest store to Mokhotlong in Lesotho. Then the Sani Pass was little more than a bridle path, but it was upgraded to a road in 1955 after the first 4WD Land Rover managed to complete the ascent. Maize and trade goods, including a fair number of guns, were taken up, while wool and hides were taken down. Trade still continues on this route, although these days most traders supplying shops in Lesotho have their own 4WDs and prefer to drive to the larger warehouses in Pietermaritzburg to stock up on goods. The Good Hope trading post closed in 1990 but the remains of the buildings can still be seen at the bottom of the pass. The provincial government of KwaZulu Natal has recently decided to have the Sani Pass road tarred, and the project should be completed by 2009. It might be a loss for adventure tourism as it's a thrilling ride up by 4WD, but for the poor rural people of Lesotho, economically completely dependent on South Africa, it would definitely mean progress.

Tours and hikes The pass is a popular attraction with tourists, and organized trips to the top of the pass and over the border to Lesotho are available from Underberg, the **Sani Pass Hotel** and **Sani Lodge**. Travellers are taken up by Land Rover; the road is terrifyingly steep and winding but the views are outstanding. The tours are a good way to discover local history and wildlife and include a visit to a Basotho village to see sheep shearing, maize cultivation or beer making. A picnic lunch in the Black Mountains or lunch at the **Sani Top Chalet** is included; don't miss a glass of warming mulled wine at the pub at the Sani Top Chalet – at 2874 m it is the highest pub in Africa.

Hiking permits for the Sani Pass area are available from Cobham (see page 511). For your own safety, a mountain rescue register must be filled in. The most rewarding hike in this area is the day hike up to the top of Sani Pass at 2874 m. There is a car park at the South African border post from where it is a further 14-km hike to the top. The trail is quite straightforward and just involves following the road. A number of shorter walks visit **Gxalingwena**, **Kaula** and **Ikanti Shelter**. These cave-like dwellings are home to a number of San rock paintings. New regulations stipulate that for the protection of the paintings, they must only be visited with a registered guide. These can be arranged from the **Sani Pass Hotel** or **Sani Lodge**, where survey maps are also available for a deposit of R50.

Mkhomazi Wilderness Area ›› *Colour map 4, B6.*

Vergelegen
① *T033-7020712, entry fee R20, overnight hiking permits R30.*
Vergelegen is one of the most remote reserves in the Drakensberg National Park and as such receives fewer visitors than most other reserves. Thaba Ntlenyana on the Lesotho side of the border is the highest mountain in Southern Africa at 3482 m and can be seen from the top of the escarpment in the reserve. The rugged mountain terrain here makes this an ideal base from which to explore the mountains on some of the most inaccessible and demanding hiking trails in the Drakensberg. Permits are needed for hikes which leave from Vergelegen. Hikers can register at the camp office. **Note** Facilities such as petrol or basic food supplies are not available at Vergelegen; visitors should be completely self-sufficient.

Lotheni
① *T033-7020540. Park gates Oct-Mar, 0500-1900, Apr-Sep, 0600-1800. Office daily 0800-1230, 1400-1630. R20.*
The reserve can be reached either from Himeville or from Nottingham Road; both access routes are along rough dirt tracks which can become impassable during heavy rains. The most popular route is the signposted dirt track from Himeville which heads north for 45 km towards **Lotheni Store** and the reserve. The Nottingham Road track heads southeast for 60 km to **Lotheni Store**, from where there is a signposted turning for the last 10 km to the reserve. There is a camp shop here which sells hiking maps and permits; otherwise the nearest shop is **Lotheni Store**, 14 km from the entrance to the camp. Petrol is not available here.

The landscape at Lotheni is mainly rolling grassland rising up towards the High Berg and Redi Peak at 3298 m. The grassland is interspersed with patches of protea woodland, tree ferns and the rare Berg bamboo. The demand for timber in the first half of this century resulted in most of the indigenous woodland being cut down leaving large areas of grassland. The land was then used for grazing and as farmland until the 1950s when it was bought by the **KwaZulu Natal Parks Board**.

To Lesotho via Sani Pass

Until the road is tarred (completion expected in 2009) access to the pass is restricted to 4WD vehicles, motorbikes, mountain bikes and pedestrians. In spite of its isolation you should expect full border formalities at Sani Pass. The South African border is at the bottom and the Lesotho post is at the top and both are normally quick and easy. These are likely to be moved closer together when the road is tarred. The road is so rough that saloon cars are not allowed past the border post. If you are hiking, the walk between the two border posts takes about three hours.

Border opening hours South African border post daily 0800-1600; Lesotho border post daily 0700-1700.

Customs and immigration Interestingly, there are no customs and immigration officials at this border and all formalities are conducted by the police. This could be due in some part to the high incidence of *dagga* (marijuana) smuggling. Some overnight hikers on the KZN Wildlife trails have reported coming across Lesotho smugglers with great bags of *dagga* hiding in the mountains so they can cross into South Africa undetected by night. For Sleeping, see page 518.

Streams cutting down through the rock have formed narrow wooded gorges, which have been stocked with brown trout. The trout season lasts from September to April and during these months accommodation at weekends can be fully booked. Spring is also a popular time for visitors who come to see the magnificent wild flowers. There are three leisurely day hikes and two overnight trails in the reserve, for which maps can be bought in the camp shop. During hot weather it is worth remembering that it is safe to swim in the Lotheni River when it is not in flood. There are some natural pools a short walk from the camp although the water flowing straight off the mountains can be icy.

Garden Castle

ⓘ *Entrances at Drakensberg Garden (34 km from Underberg) and Bushmen's Nek (45 km from Underberg), both signposted off the R626, T033-7011823. Park gates Oct-Mar 0500-1900, Apr-Sep 0600-1800. Office daily 0800-1300, 1400-1600. R20. Overnight hiking fee R30. There are plenty of huts and caves to spend the night in, but no fires are allowed anywhere within the Garden Castle Reserve.*

Garden Castle is the southernmost reserve in the Drakensberg Park, a wild area with few visitors, home to eland, grey rhebok and reedbuck. The landscape consists mostly of grassland with patches of proteas and tree ferns. There are many tarns in this part of the Drakensberg where waterbirds and wildlife can be seen. There are magnificent views up into the mountains on a clear day, with the mountain peaks of **Walker**, at 3322 m, **Wilson**, at 3342 m, and the **Rhino**, at 3051 m, towering over the reserve.

Overnight hikers must complete the Mountain Rescue Register before starting their hike and make sure they sign in on return. The office has a small shop which sells basic supplies, permits and hiking maps, otherwise the nearest shops are in Underberg. Petrol is not available here.

The highest peaks in this area, which can be hiked in a day via a strenuous 11-km trail, are **Mashai Pass** (peak 3313 m) and **Rhino Peak** at 3051 m. **Engagement Cave** and **Sleeping Beauty Cave** are only 4 km from the KWS office and are easily visited in a morning. There are many options for day hikes around Bushman's Nek to various caves.

⊙ uKhahlamba-Drakensberg Park listings

Hotel and guesthouse prices
L over US$300 **AL** US$220-300 **A** US$150-220
B US$100-150 **C** US$75-100 **D** US$35-75
E US$15-35 **F** under US$15
Restaurant prices
††† over US$30 †† US$15-30 † under US$15
See pages 46-51 for further information.

● Sleeping

Royal Natal National Park p498, map p499
A-C Thendele Camp, camp office open daily
0800-1600, advance bookings on T033-
8451000, www.kznwildlife.com. Stunning
location with unrivalled views of the Amphitheatre from a cluster of chalets, cottages and
a lodge sleeping 4-12. The cottages and
lodge have cooks who prepare food supplied
by the guests, while the chalets are self-
catering with fully equipped kitchens, a coal
fire, a private terrace and braai overlooking
the Amphitheatre. The camp's setting makes
it one of the most popular in the entire
Drakensberg, so must be booked months in
advance. There is also a curio shop here selling
books, T-shirts, jackets, boots and souvenirs.

Camping
F Mahai, T036-4386310. The spacious campsite has pleasant lawns and is bordered by
large pine trees and a stream. 120 sites, most
with power points, 5 modern ablution blocks,
washing machines, good views of the
Drakensberg and footpaths leading straight up
into the hills make this campsite very popular
(it can be crowded and noisy at weekends).
F Rugged Glen, T036-4386303. Small
campsite to the north of the park, with
20 sites shaded by pine trees and a central
ablution block, some with power points.
There are no other facilities here.

Oliviershoek Pass p501, map p502
AL Little Switzerland, look out for the
signposted turning off the R74 next to the
petrol station, just below Oliviershoek Pass,

T036-4386220, www.lsh.co.za. 66 thatched
cottages and self-catering chalets set in a
2000-ha reserve, this large luxury resort offers
a choice of sporting facilities including riding,
fishing, canoeing, tennis and swimming.
Recent additions include indoor heated
pool, health and beauty centre, and gym.
Geared towards South African families.
AL Montusi Mountain Lodge, follow signs
along R74 towards Royal Natal National Park,
T036-4386243, www.montusi.za.net.
Attractive series of luxury chalets, with large
bedrooms and plush sitting rooms with large
TVs, fridge, private terrace with staggering
views towards the Amphitheatre. The chalets
are surrounded by lawns, and there's a good
restaurant and small bar on site. The owners
run a choice of daily guided walks to the
Royal Natal Park, including San rock art walks.
Fly-fishing, horse riding, pool, cycling, flying
trapeze on attached grounds. Unlike some of
the other resorts, it's not family orientated.
A The Cavern, 10 km, follow the signs heading
off the R74 towards the Royal Natal National
Park, T036-4386270, www.cavern.co.za. The
resort is a large complex set among gardens
and woodland offering accommodation in 55
luxury thatched cottages. A wide range of
activities are on offer including horse riding,
bowls, swimming and a weekend disco. Rates
include all meals and guided hikes. A superb
location, with well-kept mature gardens and
an overall friendly and welcoming atmosphere; good choice for families.
A-B Alpine Heath, below Oliviershoek Pass,
follow signs along the R74 (Cavern Berg Rd),
T036-4386484, www.threecities.co.za. A fully
self-contained and well-established resort,
with a large conference village, and offering
a range of activities. 100 self-catering chalets
with 3-bedrooms, lounge, 2 bathrooms, and
private patio, TV. Facilities include 2 pools,
gym, sauna, tennis, squash, restaurant.
B Caterpillar & Catfish, at the top of
Oliviershoek Pass, T036-4386130,
www.cookhouse.co.za. A pine-panelled

mountain lodge in a restored trading post, tucked under large pine trees with great views. Decorated with African antiques, stripped pine and handmade furniture. 9 comfortable and stylish en suite bedrooms, huge buffet breakfasts, guided hikes to some fascinating rock art, fishing in a well-stocked trout dam. Beautifully decorated piano bar and 24-seater restaurant specializing in trout and fusion cooking. Popular with groups from Gauteng for Sun lunch, gaining a fast-growing reputation. Recommended.

B-C Drakensville Berg Resort, from Oliviershoek Pass, the turning is on the left towards Jagersrust, T036-4386287, www.drakensville.co.za. A large all purpose holiday camp with 70 self-catering chalets for couples, plus family units and more upmarket B&B rooms. Sporting facilities include water-skiing, fishing, riding, tennis, squash and mini-golf. There's also a camping and caravan park (**E**) set under big shady trees.

E-F Amphitheatre Backpackers, 21 km northwest of Bergville on the R74, T036-4386675, www.amphibackpackers.co.za. Excellent backpackers. The main building is a converted sandstone house with log fires, dorms, doubles and camping, hearty home-cooked meals, packed lunches to take with you on over 30 hikes in the area. On the Baz Bus route. Recommended.

Bergville *p501, map p502*

A-B Sandford Park Resort, R616 to Lady-smith, T036-4481001, www.sandford.co.za. One of the finest lodges in the region, this resort has grown up around a hotel dating back to 1852. There are 50 charming en suite rooms, some in separate rondavels, with tasteful furnishings. Neat gardens around the house, large swimming pool, horse riding, hiking and canoeing, plus a popular restaurant and bar. Rates are for dinner, B&B. Good base from which to explore both the Drakensberg and the battlefields.

D Bingelela Lodge, a short drive out of town towards Woodstock Dam, T036-4481336, www.bingelela.co.za. 10 units in comfortable,

rustic, thatched cottages, a honeymoon suite with spa bath, swimming pool, attached à la carte restaurant and friendly pub serving good standards of South African cuisine.

E-F Bergville Caravan Park, T036-4481273, bergcarav@xsinetco.za, on the R74 just south of town. There are 10 bungalows, 2 rondavels and a campsite next to the Tugela River, in the low season and during the week the resort offers large discounts on accommodation, the river is popular for canoeing.

Winterton *p501*

D Lilac Lodge, Springfield Rd, T036-4881025, purple@futurenet.co.za. Homely B&B with 2 garden cottages, sleeping 2-10, all with en suite bathrooms and TV. Braai area, small pool, trampoline and children's play area. Meals served in the **Purple House** restaurant.

D Swallow's Nest, 1 Bergview Dr, T035-4881009, swallowsnest@telkomsa.net. Double rooms, with fans and heaters, shared bathroom, separate toilet. There's also a garden cottage that can sleep 4, with a fridge and microwave, and a family room sleeping 4. TV lounge for communal use, breakfasts served in the homely dining room. All set in a landscaped garden. A short walk from the **Bridge Lodge** restaurant for evening meals. Good value, recommended.

Spioenkop Dam Nature Reserve *p502*

B Spionkop Lodge, on the R600 between Winterton and Ladysmith, T036-4881404, www.spionkop.co.za. This delightful country lodge makes an excellent base from which to explore the surroundings. 15 comfortable double rooms, fully inclusive, on a farm close to Spioenkop. Owner Raymond Heron is a vivid story teller and excellent guide to the area. Can also arrange canoe rides on the nearby Tugela River, birdwatching trips to Spioenkop Dam and horse riding (including Battlefield tours on horseback). Recommended.

D Iphika Tented Bush Camp, KZN Wildlife, T033-8451000, www.kznwildlife.com. Can sleep up to 4 in 2 large 2-bed tents and also has a stone and thatch lounge area with fireplace and kitchen. It is set on the slopes of Spioenkop Mountain overlooking a small waterhole and it is possible to go on game walks from here; Spioenkop battlefield is a short walk away, up a steep slope.

D-E Bungalows, KZN Wildlife, T033-8451000, www.kznwildlife.com. 3 chalets, each with 3 twin bedrooms and fully equipped kitchen. Visitors need to bring their own food and drink. The closest shops are in Winterton, 14 km away.

Camping

E Next to the dam are 30 sites with power points, slip ways for launching of boats, popular with anglers. Reservations direct with the officer, T036-4881578.

Cathedral Peak *p503, map p502*

A Cathedral Peak Hotel, at the end of the road past the entry gates, T036-4881888, www.cathedralpeak.co.za. An all-round resort, popular for weddings in its own stone chapel, traditionally used as a base by hikers and climbers because of its stunning location close to the high peaks of the Drakensberg. 90 luxurious double rooms, several restaurants and bars, 3 swimming pools, 9-hole floodlit golf course, horse riding, squash, jogging and mountain bike trail, 10-m climbing tower, gym, beauty spa, and tennis. It is one of South Africa's most popular destinations and booking in advance is essential all year.

B-C Didima Camp, on the road leading into Cathedral Peak, just before **Cathedral Peak Hotel**, KZN Wildlife, T033-8451000, www.kznwildlife.com. The camp is themed around the art of the San people and the thatched chalets have been designed to look like caves. 63 2-bed self-catering units built back to back so can be converted into 4-bed units using a connecting door, 1 6-bed chalet and a honeymoon suite. All have satellite TV and fireplace, and there's a central restaurant, bar and small shop. The conference centre/ wedding chapel has a full height glass wall framing a view of Cathedral Peak. Also the location of the **Rock Art Centre** (see page 503).

Camping

There are 21 sites opposite the information office. This is a secluded campsite up in the mountains with a quiet, tranquil feel to it. The facilities here are simple: there is only an ablution block for campers. The campsite is popular so it is advisable to book up to a month in advance. Camp gates are open daily from 0600-1800, and until 2100 on Fri. There are also at least 15 caves near here in which hikers can camp. They should be booked well in advance. Reservations through the officer in charge, T036-4888000.

Monk's Cowl *p505, map p505*

All the accommodation listed below is outside the park and signposted off the R600. The distances shown are from each hotel to the entrance to Monk's Cowl.

AL Champagne Sports Resort, 9 km, T036-4688000, www.champagnesports resort.com. Large sporty resort with beautiful views, attracting weekenders from Gauteng and Durban. 62 newly refurbished rooms with bright furnishings, stylish bathrooms and private balconies. Impressive 18-hole golf course, large buffet restaurant, sports bar, 4 swimming pools, tennis, squash, horse riding, gym and beauty salon. Also has timeshare bungalows. Pleasant, typically South African family resort. Rates include all meals.

A Champagne Castle, 2 km, T036-4681063, www.champagnecastle.co.za. Traditional Drakensberg resort in a spectacular mountain setting, with 47 luxurious rooms, rates include all meals, plus some self-catering cottages, set in the main lodge and annexes with thatched roofs, surrounded by attractive leafy grounds. Restaurant, horse riding, tennis, swimming pool, spa.

A The Nest, 13 km, T036-4681068, www.thenest.co.za. 55 guestrooms in thatched rondavels with private verandas and views of the mountains, bright furnishings and wood furniture. Restaurant, bar, guest lounges, swimming pool, bowls, horse riding. Rates include all meals as well as afternoon tea; good base for exploring the area.

B Ardmore Guest Farm, 12 km, T036-4681314, www.ardmore.co.za. Superb views with lovely gardens overlooking a dam. Mix of B&B, full board or self-catering in 8 double en suite rooms. Popular with anglers for the dam fishing, where you can also canoe. Good local reputation for home-cooked meals, 4-course dinners are taken at a long table with hosts and other guests, also known for its ceramic art studio – worth a visit, with a tea garden on site. Recommended by several readers.

C Cathkin Cottage, 13 km, after the **Drakensberg Sun** hotel, turn right into Yellowood Dr, T036-4681513, www.cathkincottage.co.za. Simple double rooms and family units with en suite facilities and private entrances. Some rooms have fridge and TV, small pool and pretty garden. Good breakfasts served. Secure parking. Val and Ian can organize guided walks.

C-D Dragon Peaks, 4 km, T036-4681031, www.dragonpeaks.com. Mix of B&B and self-catering chalets with TV, plus a camp and caravan site. Popular restaurant with outdoor lapa area. Good facilities for families, including 2 swimming pools, tennis, and horse riding, plus a wide range of organized entertainment. There is a small supermarket here with an ATM and a petrol pump.

D-F Inkosana Lodge, 7 km, easy access via a good surfaced road, T036-4681202, www.inkosana.co.za. Simple lodge with fine views towards the mountains, set in a large garden with a swimming pool. 4 small dorms, double rooms, some en suite, rondavels and camping. Large dining area with hearty home-made meals on request, kitchen available for self-catering. Tours, email access, laundry, horse riding, evening meals, large modern bungalow. Guided hikes lasting up to several days can be organized from here. Free collection from the Baz Bus in Winterton.

Camping

There are 15 pitches, some with electric points, and an ablution block bordered with indigenous trees and shrubs next to the camp office. Reservations for this campsite should be made through the officer in charge, T036-4681103. At the office is a tea garden, open 0800-1600 for light meals that also provide hiker's picnics in backpacks with cutlery. Order these the day before.

Giant's Castle Reserve *p506, map p507*
B-C Giant's Castle camp, KZN Wildlife, T033-8451000, www.kznwildlife.com. Revamped camp, 44 chalets with between 2 and 6 beds, lounge and dining area and fully equipped kitchen. Self-catering or fully catered. Shop sells a wide range of books and curios but only a limited selection of dried and frozen food. The camp is popular all year and accommodation tends to be full at weekends. **Izimbali** restaurant and pub, Rock Lodge conference centre and wellness spa. Swimming in summer is permitted in the Bushmen's River below the camp.

B-D White Mountain Resort, on the road to Giant's Castle from Estcourt, T036 3533437, www.whitemountain.co.za. Family holiday camp, full-board rooms, self-catering chalets sleeping 2-6, camping and caravan sites, pool, bar, restaurant. The resort is self-contained and offers a wide range of organized activities, but is a long distance from the higher parts of the Drakensberg. There is a small supermarket and petrol is also available.

C-F Injisuthi camp, KZN Wildlife, T033-8451000, www.kznwildlife.com. 16 6-bed chalets, fully equipped for self-catering with gas stove and fridge, no plug points. Also basic 8-bed dormitory cabins. Electricity between 1730 and 2200 only. Coffee bar, TV room, there is no shop here so visitors need to bring all supplies with them.

Camping

There are 20 sites at Injisuthi camp that can accommodate 120 people, 3 2-bed pre-erected tents, and shared ablution blocks. Reservations direct, T036-4317848.
Lower Injisuthi Cave, **Upper Injisuthi Cave** and **Grindstone Cave**, can all be used by hikers for overnight stops but should be reserved in advance. No fires allowed, very

basic facilities. Come well-equipped.
Reservations T036-4317848.

Mountain huts
There are 4 mountain huts about 4-5 hrs walk
from Giant's Castle camp: Giant's Hut, Centenary Hut and Bannerman Hut sleep 8 people
each, and Meander Hut sleeps 4. All the huts
are at an altitude of around 2000 m and can
get very cold at night. Bunks and mattresses
are provided. Reservations through **KZN
Wildlife**, T033-8451000, www.kznwildlife.com.

Kamberg Nature Reserve p508
It is possible to camp on overnight hikes
but you need to be fully equipped.
C Main Camp, KZN Wildlife, T033-8451000,
www.kznwildlife.com. 7 self-catering chalets
with 2-6 beds. Kitchenettes and a communal
lounge area.
C Stillerus Rustic Cottage, 8 km from the
main camp, KZN Wildlife, T033-8451000,
www.kznwildlife.com. 1 cottage with 8 beds,
for a minimum of 6. Self-catering and fully
equipped with a gas stove, a fridge and
gas lighting. Bring your own bedding.
**E-F Drakensberg International
Backpackers Lodge**, T033-2637241,
wildchild@telkomsa.net. The actual address
is 'Grace Valley Farm' on the Highmoor Rd;
there are signposts but call for directions if
you don't have a good road map. 18 dorm
beds, 2 double rooms, camping, TV lounge,
kitchen, bar, email facility, laundry service,
horse riding, evening meals provided. Lovely
farm surrounded by mountains. Owned by
Lionel who runs local tours, pickup from the
Baz Bus at Mooi River Wimpy, also offers
shuttle service to Durban for groups.

Underberg p510
C Elgin, Bushman's Nek Valley, 7 km from
Underberg towards Swartberg, T033-7011918,
www.elginholidayfarm.co.za. 4 luxurious suites
set in wings attached to a farmhouse, en suite,
TV, attractive decor. Also has a self-catering log
cabin sleeping 10, all set on a working farm,
with organic dairy and vegetables for sale.

C Rocky Mountain Lodge, off the Swartberg
Rd, T033-7011676, www.rockylodge.com. 4
self-catering log cabins sleeping 2-12 people,
B&B also an option. Magnificently positioned
on a mountain plateau, with beautiful views
and a peaceful setting overlooking the
Mzimkulu River. Private feel with cosy log fires.

Himeville p510
C-D Ripon Country Cottage, T033-7021154,
www.riponcottage.com. Self-catering
accommodation in a cottage on a rose and
cherry farm north of Himeville, sleeps up to
10, popular with 4WD owners.
C-E Himeville Arms, Arbuckle St,
T033-7021305, www.himevillehotel.co.za.
Old-fashioned, 100-year-old hotel. Rooms can
be rather gloomy in summer, but are cosy in
winter thanks to well-stocked log fires.
Cheaper backpacker beds available in shared
rooms. Good lunchtime bar menu in the
excellent **Arms Pub** with home-brewed real
ale, plus 2 restaurants, swimming pool.

Cobham p511
Reservations for campsites, trail huts and
caves should be made through the Cobham
officer in charge, T033-7020831. The
campsite here is very basic with an open area
for setting up tents and you need to be totally
self-sufficient. Basic toilets and hot showers
and campers may swim in the river below the
campsite if it's not too cold.

Sani Pass p511
A Sani Pass Hotel, Sani Pass Rd, 22 km
from Underberg, T033-7021320,
www.sanipasshotel.co.za. A large resort hotel
offering accommodation either in the hotel
building or in luxury cottages in the gardens.
Sporting facilities include squash, fly-fishing,
tennis, bowls, riding and swimming. The
restaurant has a reasonably priced set menu.
Beautiful location, but slightly overpriced.
C-E Sani Top Chalet, top of the pass, next to
the Lesotho border post, T033-7021158 or
T082-7151131 (mob), www.sanitopchalet.co.za.
A combination of double rooms in the main

building or in stone en suite rondavels out back, plus backpacker rooms with dorms and shared bathrooms in a converted store in the nearby village – bring warm bedding for these. You can camp but you'll need thermals. The hotel has a licensed pub (the highest in Africa) and dining room warmed by roaring wood fires, overlooking the dramatic road below. Fantastic hikes and pony trekking to some awe-inspiring viewpoints along the escarpment. When it does snow it is possible to hire skis from the hotel.

D-E Sani Lodge, 19 km from Underberg on the Sani Pass road, call for collection from Underberg, T033-7020330, www.sani lodge.co.za. If you are coming from Pieter maritzburg, travel with Sani Pass Carriers, see page 522 for details, who drop off here. There are 4 small dorms, 5 large double rooms with pine ceilings and good insulation, 2 private rondavels, a 22-bed dorm, and plenty of space to pitch a tent, outside hot shower with tremendous views of the mountains. Large kitchen, comfortable lounge with open fire for the winter months when it can get very cold, and a veranda with a superb uninterrupted view of the Drakensberg escarpment. Run by Russell and Simone who are experts on hiking in Lesotho and organize several tours and guided hikes, which are excellent but have had poor reports about food here recently.

Mkhomazi Wilderness Area *p512*
Reservations for all accommodation are made through **KZN Wildlife**, T033-8451000, www.kznwildlife.com.
C Lotheni, 2 self-catering cottages with 6 beds, and 12 self-catering bungalows, with 2 or 3 beds. All the accommodation is fully equipped; there are 2 freezers in the camp kitchen which can be used by guests, electricity from 1700-2200 only.
C Simes Rustic Cottage, sleeps 10, although the minimum charge is for 6 people. The small dam nearby has been stocked with brown trout and is exclusively for the use of visitors staying at the cottage. The cottage has a gas supply but visitors are expected to

bring their own bedding, gas lamps and torches.

Camping
The 10 sites at **Lotheni**, T033-7020540, are a secluded 2 km from the hutted camp and it's a beautiful spot. The only facility is an ablution block with hot and cold water. It is possible to camp overnight within the **Verlegen** reserve on long-distance hikes.

Garden Castle *p513*
There are 3 rustic huts on the Giant's Cup Hiking Trail. Each can accommodate up to 30 people. During the winter months hikers are strongly advised to stay in these huts as there can be heavy snowfalls and very cold conditions. There are 10 camping sites and an ablution block near to the park entrance as well as 12 caves in the park available to hikers Campsites, caves and huts should be booked in advance through the camp office T033-7011823.
A-D Penwarn Country Lodge, T033-7011417, www.penwarn.com. 2 luxury lodges close to Bushman's Nek, 25 km from Underberg. Choice of en suite bedrooms or simple self-catering log cabins. This is a comfortable mountain farm offering a wide range of activities: canoeing, fly fishing, clay pigeon shooting, archery, mountain biking and hiking. Excellent food served in a colonial-style restaurant, and a homely atmosphere during the winter months.

🍴 Eating

All the large mountain resorts have restaurants and bars on site. Much of the other accommodation is self-catering; as a result there is a lack of choice for eating out in the region.

Winterton *p501*
♦ **Purple House**, 10 Springfield St, T036-4881025. The restaurant attached to **Lilac Cottage** (see Sleeping, page 515).

South African home-cooked meals, light lunches, afternoon teas and cool drinks.

¶ **Thokosiza Centre**, T036-4881273, on the R100, 13 km west of Winterton. Coffee shop and restaurant in this cultural/craft/tourist centre, popular spot for a light lunch or mid-afternoon tea, with pleasant wooden tables on a shady deck. Closed evenings.

Underberg *p510*

¶¶ **Underberg Pub**, **Underberg Hotel**, Main Rd. Pub grub and bar meals just like a pub in England. This is where the local farmers come to drink, there's sport on the satellite TV, rock music and plenty of beer, for a good meal try the freshly grilled trout.

¶ **Lemon Tree Bistro**, White Cottage Shopping Centre, T033-7011589. Open 0820-1645, Fri-Sat 1800-2045. Well worth a stop for light lunches, coffee, good produce in the deli and winery during the day, also open Fri and Sat evening, phone ahead, with a bistro-style menu.

Himeville *p510*

¶¶ **Moorcroft Manor**, Sani Rd, T033-7021967. Open 0730-2130. Restaurant within a luxury lodge, stylish dining room with beautiful terrace, breakfasts, light lunches like ploughman's platter, upmarket menu with a French feel for dinner. Bookings are essential.

Entertainment

Monk's Cowl *p505, map p505*

Drakensberg Boys' Choir, T036-4681012, www.dbchoir.info. During term-time, the choir performs on Wed at 1530 in the school's impressive auditorium. Bookings are essential.

Festivals and events

Underberg *p510*

Easter weekend Splashy Fen Festival, www.splashyfen.co.za. A popular music festival held on Splashy Fen Farm. Over the years it has increased in size and it now attracts a broad selection of modern musicians as well as South Africa's folk crowd.

Shopping

Bergville *p501*

There are several supermarkets in town to stock up in before heading into the reserves. The shops at the campsites stock only the most basic supplies. Outside the centre, look out for farms selling fresh produce.

Tevreden Cheese, take the R74 out of the village towards the Northern Berg, take a left turn after approximately 7 km, T036-4481840, 1000-1500. Cheesemaking farm with tastings, a good spot to stock up before a hike.

Winterton *p501*

There are several craft shops along the R600 to Champagne Valley and Monk's Cowl.

Cheesery, 6 Springfield Rd, T036-4881296. Farm shop specializing in various cheeses, free tastings.

KwaZulu Weavers, 12 km west of Winterton on the R600, T036-4881098, www.kwazulu weavers.com. Colourful handwoven rugs made from wool and mohair. Attached is a popular handmade candle shop.

Rainbow Room, off the R600 just after the **Nest Hotel**, heading towards Monk's Cowl, T036-4681801. An unusual selection of handmade crafts; unfortunately, the larger pieces are a bit too big to take home for overseas visitors but they can arrange shipping. Run by Inger.

Thokozisa, on the R600, 13 km west of Winterton, T036-4881207. A one-stop tourist centre (the **Central Drakensberg Information Centre** is here) with shops selling arts and crafts and wines, and a coffee shop.

Cathedral Peak *p503, map p502*

The shop at Mike's Pass sells a limited range of basic groceries, otherwise the nearest supermarket is at Winterton. Petrol can be bought at the **Cathedral Peak Hotel**.

Giant's Castle Reserve p506, p507
Petrol is for sale by the main gate. There's a farm shop next to the park gates selling fresh and smoked trout, otherwise the nearest supermarket is in Estcourt.

Underberg p510
There are a number of craft shops and a coffee shop in the **White Cottage Shopping Centre**, a rather twee mini shopping mall.

▲▲ Activities and tours

uKhahlamba-Drakensberg Park p493
Climbing
The Drakensberg is a relatively undiscovered mountain range – due largely to the sports boycott imposed on South Africa during the Apartheid era. Today, the mountains are becoming increasingly accessible and present challenging climbing.
Mountain Club of South Africa, www.kzn. mcsa.org.za. A useful source of information.

Fishing
Trout were introduced into the rivers of the Drakensberg around the turn of the last century and over the years fly-fishing has become popular. Fishing licences are available from **KZN Wildlife**, T033 8451000, www.kznwildlife.com.

Golf
In good weather, the backdrop for each is spectacular. Green fees are very reasonable; call in advance to check on availability of equipment hire. There are courses at the **Cathedral Peak Hotel**, T036-4881888, 9 holes; **Monk's Cowl Country Club**, T036-4681300, 9 holes; and the **Champagne Sports Resort**, T036-4688000, 18 holes. The **Amphitheatre Golf Club**, T036-4386308, 9 holes, is in Royal Natal National Park.

Hang-gliding and paragliding
Wildsky Adventures, Bulwer, 50 km west of Pietermaritzburg, T082-7488637, www.wildsky.co.za. Courses or one-off tandem glides. Also offers a number of other activities, including abseiling, horse riding or fishing, and has simple accommodation in log cabins available to those who are undertaking paragliding courses.

Helicopter flights
There is an airfield opposite the **Champagne Sports Resort** (see page 516) from where you can take short helicopter flights over the mountains. Bookings can be made at the **Cathedral Peak Hotel**, or the **Champagne Sports Resort**, or call **Westline Aviation**, T036-4681104. A 20-min scenic flight should cost R450 per person; book at hotel reception.

Horse riding
The full length of the Berg is negotiable on horseback, by way of trails and bridleways. Riding is available in the KZN Wildlife parks of **Rugged Glen** and **Spioenkop** and can be arranged at the parks offices. Trips into the mountains of the **Royal Natal National Park** are available from Rugged Glen and cost roughly R50 per hr. The rides are very popular during the holiday period and it is best to book in advance at the stables, T036-4386303. Day trips on horseback are also available from the hotels at **Sani Pass**, **Drakensberg Gardens**, **Bushman's Nek** and **Coleford Nature Reserve**. In the **Royal Natal National Park**, trips from many of the large resort hotels on the boundaries of the national park offer riding as an activity, and several include overnight adventure rides for groups of 5 or more into the parks. Contact the local tourist office or ask the people where you are staying to point you in the direction of the nearest operator, of which there are many.
Khotso Horse Trails, Bergvlei Farm, 10 km from Underberg towards Drakensberg Gardens, T033-7011502, www.khotsotrails.co.za. Mountain rides for beginners and advanced riders, specialist adventure rides and cattle round-ups. Accommodation is available in dorms in a log cabin with shared kitchen and bathroom or in self-catering thatched chalets.

Ice climbing

In winter, there is the possibility of ice climbing the **Lotheni Falls**, which are usually frozen from mid-Jun to mid-Aug. This is strictly for experienced mountaineers only, with full equipment, including an ice pick. Contact one of the regional tourism offices, or specialist ice climber Gavin Raubenheimer at **Peak High**, T033-3433168, www.peakhigh.co.za, for details.

Mountain biking

Mountain biking has become hugely popular in recent years. 3 areas of the Drakensberg have designated biking trails: **Cathedral Peak**, **Champagne Valley** and **Underberg**. There are 70 km of dirt roads in the Cathedral Peak area which can be used by mountain bikers. The routes are by no means extreme but they pass through some spectacular scenery. The views from the top of Mike's Pass are as exhilarating as the 5-km ride back down.

The route from Underberg to **Sani Pass** and back is one of South Africa's epic mountain bike rides. The 20-km climb up to the Lesotho border is a challenging ascent along a trail cut out of the rock. The altitude at the highest point of the trail is around 2800 m from where there are spectacular views over the sheer cliffs and gorges of the Mkhomazana Valley. There are also a number of more sedate rides around Underberg itself.

A 75-km Mountain Bike Challenge is held at **Giant's Castle** annually on the last Sun in Apr. Check www.ultimatemtb.org.za for further details.

Tour operators

Most of the Drakensberg National Park is more or less inaccessible to travellers who have not hired a car. Based in Underberg, **Major Adventures**, T033-7011628, www.majoradventures.com, **Sani Pass Tours**, T033-7011064, www.sanitours.co.za, and **Thaba Tours**, T033-7012888, www.thabatours.co.za, all offer daily 4WD day trips to the top of Sani Pass.

Drakensberg Adventures, Sani Pass Lodge, T033-7020330, www.sanilodge.co.za. Great selection of tours in area, including an overnight trip into Lesotho. Russell is a formidable guide for the Sani Pass excursion and local hikes. On offer are 4WD tours, hikes to San rock art, horse riding and visits to local Zulu families where you can spend the night. Guided climbs of Thabana Ntlenyana (Africa's second tallest mountain) also organized.

⊖ Transport

Northern Drakensberg p498, map p502
Baz Bus, T021-4392323, www.bazbus.com, runs from **Ampitheatre Backpackers** in Oliviershoek Pass to **Johannesburg** and **Durban**.

Central Drakensberg p501, map p502
Baz Bus, T021-4392323, www.bazbus.com, runs in both directions between **Johannesburg** and **Durban**, drops off and picks up outside of the First National Bank in Winterton.

Southern Drakensberg p509
Sani Pass Carriers, bookings T033-7011017, runs between **Underberg**, **Himeville**, **Sani Pass** and **Pietermaritzburg**. The minibuses pick up from **Sani Lodge**, **Sani Pass Hotel**, the **Himeville Arms** and the **Underberg Hotel**, every morning, and drop off and pick up from the **Imperial Hotel** in Pietermaritzburg. They arrive back in Underberg early the same afternoon.

❶ Directory

Bergville p501
Banks First National Bank, South St. **Emergencies** Mountain Rescue Service T031-3077744/084-6291647. **Medical services** Bergville Medical Centre, T036-4482507.

Zululand

Zululand, homeland of Shaka and one of the most evocative regions of South Africa, will forever be associated with the classic movie starring Michael Caine as the redoubtable British officer fighting Zulu warriors. Today, this region – extending from the northern bank of the Tugela River up to Mkhuze and Maputaland – is rather more peaceful and offers long, unspoilt beaches, excellent game reserves and a chance to experience traditional Zulu culture. Gone are the vast herds of migrating elephant, wildebeest and springbok, victim in part to the many battles fought over this wealthy province. Despite being one of the more traditional areas of South Africa, it has thriving industrial cities and vast areas of sugarcane and eucalyptus plantations. However, game reserves at St Lucia and Hluhluwe-Umfolozi are still natural magnets for tourists and around six per cent of KwaZulu Natal is managed by KZN Wildlife as conservation areas. ▸▸ For listings, see pages 537-543.

Elephant Coast ◐ ▸▸ pp537-543.

Ins and outs
The route into the Zulu heartland follows the N2 north from Stanger/KwaDukuza to the village of Gingindlovu. From here the R68 goes inland to Eshowe (26 km), Ulundi and the Battlefield sites (see page 481), while the N2 continues up the coast to Mtunzini, Empangeni, Richards Bay, Hluhluwe-Umfolozi, St Lucia and Maputaland. This is the most popular area of Zululand, and was recently renamed the Elephant Coast – thanks to the reintroduction of elephant in sections of the Greater St Lucia Wetland Park. There are a number game farms in the area offering luxury accommodation, while scuba diving and deep-sea fishing are available in the coastal resorts. The region has a subtropical climate; it is hot and humid from December to March and warm and dry from April to November. ▸▸ For more information on the region visit www.zululand.kzn.org.za.

Gingindlovu and around → Colour map 5, B2.
Gingindlovu was originally a military kraal established by Cetshwayo after the Battle of Ndondakusuka where he defeated his half-brother Mbulazi and gained control of the Zulu Kingdom. Today Gingindlovu is a small commercial centre surrounded by farmland and sugarcane plantations.

Six kilometres from Gingindhlovu on the coast is the entrance to **Amatigulu Nature Reserve** ① T032-4530155, open sunrise to sunset, R10. The reserve is 100 km from Durban and covers approximately 2000 ha of forested dunes overlooking the sea and is a beautiful place to combine game watching with a beach holiday. Unlike the other small reserves in this area, Amatigulu does have some big game since giraffe, zebra and waterbuck have been reintroduced; it is the one of the few places to see animals grazing close to the sea. Bush baby and large-spotted genet are frequently seen around the camp at night and the Nyoni River attracts the elusive African finfoot and other unusual waterbirds. There are game drives and walking trails but the most interesting way to see the reserve is by canoeing up the Amatigulu River; canoes can be hired from the camp office. A newer addition in the reserve is a whale-watching tower built on the dunes.

◗ Gingindlovu means 'the swallower of the elephant', although the British used to call it 'Gin-Gin-I-love-you'.

ⓘ *The northern KwaZulu Natal coast is a low-risk malarial area.*

Eshowe is a historical inland town named after the sound of a breeze passing through bushes. Situated on a hill, the town has pleasant views over Dlinza forest and is an administrative centre for the surrounding sugarcane growing region. Although there's little within town for visitors, this makes a good base for taking a cultural tour of Zululand. The historical origins of Eshowe are based around a kraal called Eziqwaqweni which was established here by Cetshwayo. In 1860 the Norwegian missionary, Reverend Oftebro, was allowed to open a mission station here which was occupied by the British in 1879 while they planned an attack on Ulundi. The Zulus briefly gained the upper hand here when they laid siege to the garrison for 10 weeks. Eshowe was relieved by Lord Chelmsford in April 1879, but not before the Zulus had managed to burn the mission station down.

Dlinza Forest ⓘ *T035-4744029, www.zbr.co.za/boardwalk, Sep-Apr daily 0600-1800, May-Aug daily 0800-1700, R25 includes guide*, is next to the municipal caravan park. It is a 250-ha area of dense hardwood forest, ferns and creepers where Shaka supposedly hid his wives and children during attacks. There are two short walking trails here through orchids, wild plum and milkwood trees, and knarled vines that are clearly labelled, which in turn attract a number of birds and butterflies. Dhlinza is great for birdwatchers, with 65 species recorded in the forest, including the endangered spotted thrush and Delegorgue's pigeon. A recent addition, and the first of its kind in South Africa, is a 125-m wheelchair-accessible aerial timber boardwalk, which takes you through the treeline to the 20-m viewing platform that overlooks the canopy of the forest.

On Fort Nongqai Road is the **Zululand Historical Museum** ⓘ *daily 0900-1600, R20*. Fort Nongqai was built in 1883 and served as a residence for the Natal Native Police who acted as bodyguards for Sir Melmoth Osborn, the Resident for British Zululand. It is a square fort with high towers on each corner. The museum has displays on John Dunn and his 49 wives and on the Bambata rebellion, as well as a number of Zulu items. John Dunn was the first European settler in what is now KwaZulu Natal. He became an honorary chief and was granted land by the Zulus, ruled at the time by Cetshwayo. His 49 wives gave him 117 children. Given this statistic, not surprisingly the surname Dunn is still very common in this region.

Vukani Collection Museum ⓘ *T035-4745274, daily 0900-1600, small donation*, is housed in a purpose-built centre in the grounds of Fort Nongqayi. While there are antique items on display, this is actually an exhibition of the Vukani Association – a body of over 1000 Zulu craftspeople run and owned by the crafters themselves to manage the pricing and quality of their products. It is quite probably the largest display of Zulu art in existence with some 3000 to 4000 pieces on display. Some of the exhibits are by award-winning artists and include carvings, pottery, colourful basketry and the famous Zulu beadwork.

North of Eshowe

From Eshowe the R66 heads north through the **Nkwalini Valley** to **Melmoth** (52 km). **Shakaland** ⓘ *signposted off the R66, 14 km north of Eshowe, T035-4600912, www.shakaland.com, 3-hr tours at 1100 and 1200, R210*, is a very popular Zulu theme park with daily cultural shows, which include Zulu dancing and tours of a traditional village where tribal customs such as spearmaking, the beer ceremony and Sangoma rituals are explained. This is a reconstruction of a 19th-century village but it doesn't give a very authentic insight into how the Zulu people live today. However, the food isn't bad and a lunch in the **Shisa Nyama Restaurant** is included.

The Protea Simunye Zulu Lodge is about 30 km out of Eshowe; look out for a left turning, marked with a wagon wheel and a large 'S', on to the D256. This road will take you to another popular Zululand stop, a lodge hosted by the Biyela clan, offering a marginally more authentic introduction to Zulu culture. Follow the gravel road for 12 km until you reach an old trading store. This is the assembly point for guests before they are taken down to the lodge on horseback (for accommodation, see page 537). West of Melmouth, Central Zululand is famous for its rich cultural heritage. The museums and battlefield sites are the main attractions and are the best way to gain an insight into the region's history. ▶▶ For further details, see pages 481-492.

Zululand game reserves

Sleeping 🛏
Bushlands Game Lodge **2**
Cape Vidal Camp **6**
Gazebo Safari Lodge **5**

Hluhluwe **11**
Hluhluwe River Lodge **9**
Isinkwe Backpackers **4**
Maphelana Camp **7**

Sand Forest Lodge **8**
Wendy's Country Lodge **3**
Zulu Nyala **10**

Note The R66 north of Eshowe is notorious for having one of the highest rates of carjacking in KwaZulu Natal province.

Mtunzini and around ⊜ ⧐ pp537-543. Colour map 5, B2.

Mtunzini means 'the shady place' and is a pleasant town at the mouth of the Umlalazi River facing the lagoon, 18 km from Gingindhlovu, set in an area of coastal forest and mangrove swamps. John Dunn, who had become a Zulu chief in his own right and was one of Cetshwayo's advisors, lived here with his 49 wives and 117 children.

Umlalazi Nature Reserve
① *132 km north of Durban, 1 km east of Mtunzini, daily 0500-2200, R10.*
Signposted from the N2, this is a small nature reserve but it is popular with South African tourists and, when full, can accommodate at least 300 people, who come here for fishing, windsurfing and the beaches. There are no shark nets. The natural ambience of the 1028-ha reserve is best felt when it is less crowded and it is easier to appreciate the long tropical beaches and walks along the banks of the lagoon and mangrove swamps. There's good fishing in the lagoon and Mlalazi River but crocodiles and sharks are present. Other wildlife includes red, grey and blue duiker, and bushbuck.

Empangeni and around ⊜⊕⊕⊜⊕ ⧐ pp537-543. Colour map 5, A2.

Empangeni is named after the Zulu word of *pangaed* meaning grabbed – due to many people being taken by crocs on the banks of the Mpangeni River, on which the town is situated. King Shaka grew up in this area before the Norwegian Missionary Society mission station opened in 1851. The town has developed into a busy industrial centre and has been pulping wood since the first eucalyptus plantations were established in 1905. While many visitors pass through on their way between St Lucia and the Battlefields, there is nothing to merit a stop. Nor is there any reason to follow the R34 east from Empangeni, crossing the N2, towards Richards Bay (18 km), although those using Richards Bay airport might pass through this flat plantation landscape, loomed over by clusters of pylons and the ugly chimneys of industrial complexes. The N2, meanwhile, allows a quick escape north to St Lucia (80 km), and Hluhluwe-Umfolozi (106 km).

Ins and outs
This area is undergoing a series of name changes. Officially Empangeni and Richards Bay, 18 km away (as well as Esikhawini, Vulindlela, Felixton, Nseleni and Ngwelezane, and the rural areas under Amakhosi Dube, Mkhwanazi, Khoza, Mbuyzai and Zungu), have now joined together as one municipal area, referred to jointly as the city of **uMhlathuze**. It will be some time before this change is reflected on maps or signposts and in reality they are still some distance from one another, so, for the purposes of this guide, the old names are used, despite the fact that the towns share many of the same facilities.

Game reserves
West of Empangeni and north of the small village of Heatonville, **Thula Thula Private Game Reserve** ① *T035-7928322, www.thulathula.com*, makes for an excellent stopover for those who have missed the larger parks further north. Day visitors are welcome for game drives and either breakfast, lunch or dinner from R375 (check out the website for

options). To get there, take the R34 for 8 km before turning onto the road to Heatonville, which is a further 10 km. Thula Thula is signposted down a gravel road from Heatonville. The reserve is a large private game reserve in the Enselini Valley, originally part of King Shaka's hunting ground. It was converted from farmland in 1964, and the present owners offer exclusive accommodation, game drives and bush walks through rolling, acacia-covered thornveld. Some of the larger mammals you can expect to see are white rhino, elephant, cheetah, giraffe, kudu, nyala and other antelopes and, if you're lucky, a leopard. There are plans to take down the fences between here and Hluhluwe-Impfolozi Game Reserve, creating a huge wildlife area, and bringing the Big Five to Thula Thula.

Enselini Nature Reserve ① *17 km north of Empangeni on the N2, T035-7920034, sunrise to sunset, free*, is a small, 293-ha reserve on the banks of the Enselini River, run by KZN Wildlife. The **Nkonikini Trail**, 7 km, passes along raised platforms over the swamp and through grasslands where game has been reintroduced. Here you can see hippo, crocodile, giraffe, nyala, waterbuck, wildebeest and zebra. The shorter **Mvuvu Trail** passes through similar terrain. This is an interesting reserve to visit and a good chance to break the monotony of driving through the vast plantations that line the N2. At the reception centre there is a picnic site, where maps and information leaflets are available.

🌙 *Thula Thula's owner, Lawrence Anthony, was instrumental in the rehabilitation and rescue of animals at Iraq's Baghdad Zoo in 2004.*

Richards Bay → *Colour map 5, B2.*

Richards Bay, a modern rash of a town, focuses entirely on its enormous industrial port, soon to be the largest in Southern Africa. The port exports mineral ores and coal, and massive tankers arrive here to discharge oil for Gauteng through the oil pipeline; this is the first port of call for ships coming from Asia and Suez. Characterized by a series of vast industrial plants and featureless highways (albeit skirting around a pretty series of canals and a lagoon), the only reason for coming here is to use the small airport (see page 543), and then hire a car to speed up the coast to the parks

Hluhluwe Imfolozi Game Reserve ⊜🄵🄸🄾▲» *pp537-543. Colour map 5, A2.*

This is one of Africa's oldest game reserves and one of the few parks in KwaZulu Natal where you can see the Big Five. What were traditionally two reserves have been joined into one national park. Hluhluwe is named after the umHluhluwe or 'thorny rope', a climber which is found in the forests of this area. The aerial roots hanging from the sycamore figs where the Black Umfolozi and the White Umfolozi rivers meet give the area its name. Imfolozi is named after 'uMfula walosi' or the 'river of fibres'. The park has a variety of landscapes – thick forests, dry bushveld and open savannah – that are home to a number of species of game, including healthy populations of rhino and the rare nyala. What is unusual about the park is the hilly terrain, which provides a great vantage point for game viewing.

Ins and outs

Getting there Hluhluwe-Imfolozi is 280 km north of Durban just off the N2. There is a turning at Mtubatuba leading west on the R618 (50 km) to the **Imfolozi sector** ① *Oct-Mar 0500-1900, Apr-Sep 0600-1800, office daily 0800-1230, 1400-1630, conservation levy (per day) R80*, and a turning opposite the exit to Hluhluwe village, which leads (14 km) to the northern Memorial Gate entrance to the **Hluhluwe sector** ① *same hours and levies as* *above, camp reception at Hilltop daily 0700-1930.* This is an easy park to visit on a day trip if you are staying in the Maputaland or St Lucia regions.

Best time to visit The best time to see the park is between March and November. The park's vegetation is lush during the summer months, when the weather is hot and humid, but this makes it more difficult to see the game. During the winter months the climate is cool and dry and you might even need a sweater in the evenings. Animals congregate at the waterholes and rivers at this time of year and the lack of vegetation makes it easier to see them.

Background

The confluence of the Black and White Umfolozi rivers is where Zulu King Shaka dug his hunting pits. Once a year game was driven into the area and would fall into the pits, where it was speared by young warriors eager to prove their courage. Consequently, Hluhluwe-Umfolozi was established as a protected area as long ago as 1895. Since then the park has suffered a number of setbacks, such as temporary de-proclamation and the massive slaughter of thousands of game animals in a campaign to eliminate tsetse fly. Aerial spraying of the chemical DDT eventually eliminated the tsetse fly but at great cost

Hluhluwe-Imfolozi Game Reserve

Sleeping
Gqoyeni Bush Lodge **1**
Hilltop Camp **2**
Hlathikhulu **9**

Masinda Lodge **3**
Mpila Camp **5**
Mtwazi Lodge **2**
Muntulu Bush Camp **6**

Munyawaneni **7**
Nselweni **8**

to the environment. In 1947 the newly formed **Natal Parks, Game and Fish Preservation Board** took control of the park and reintroduced locally extinct species such as lion, elephant, rhino and giraffe.

Wildlife

This is one of the best reserves in KwaZulu Natal for seeing wildlife, and one of the finest in the world for seeing rhino. The varied landscapes of Hluhluwe-Imfolozi provide a wide range of habitats which support large numbers of big game. The Big Five are present and there are large populations of three rarely seen animals: the white rhino, the black rhino and the nyala. Despite the thriving hippo populations in nearby St Lucia, there are fewer than 20 hippo in this park because the rivers flow too fast. Over 300 species of bird, including the rare bateleur eagle, have been recorded in Hluhluwe-Imfolozi; bird lists are available from the camp offices.

Hluhluwe is the northern sector of the reserve and has a hilly and wooded landscape; elephant are often seen in the area around the Hluhluwe Dam, where the thick forests are inhabited by the rare samango monkey. There are some areas of savanna in this sector where white rhino and giraffe can be seen feeding.

Imfolozi, in the south, is characterized by thornveld and semi-desert; the grasslands here support large populations of impala, kudu, waterbuck, giraffe, blue wildebeest and zebra. Predators are rarely seen but cheetah, lion, leopard and wild dog are all present.

An extensive network of dirt roads crosses the reserve which can easily be negotiated in a saloon car. There are hides at Mphafa waterhole and Thiyeni waterhole but much of the best game viewing can be done from a car. Good areas for viewing game are the Sontuli Loop, the corridor connecting Imfolozi to Hluhluwe and the areas around the Hluhluwe River.

Wilderness trails

One of the most exciting ways to see wildlife here is on foot. Although this experience is not always as spectacular as viewing from a car, it tends to be more intense; there is little that can compare with the excitement of tracking rhino through the wilderness. **Guided walks** must be booked well in advance at the camp offices, which run through the wilderness in the southern section of the park. The area used to be part of traditional royal Zulu hunting grounds and is now totally undisturbed by man – there are no roads and access is only allowed on foot; you must be accompanied by a game ranger. Three **wilderness trails** cross the wilderness area, with guided walks running from mid-March to December. They are limited to a maximum of eight people and are extremely popular, so should be booked well in advance. Food, drinks, water bottles, cutlery and cooking equipment, bedding, towels, day packs, backpacks and donkey bags are all provided by KZN Wildlife. The trails cover about 15 km per day and cost from R16000 to R27000 per person for up to three nights (accommodation is in tented camps in the wilderness area). There are also three self-guided walks in the Imfolozi sector. Reservations for all accommodation and wilderness trails within the park can be made up to six months in advance through **KZN Wildlife** ① *T033-8451000, www.kznwildlife.com*.

Hluhluwe → *Colour map 5, A3.*

Hluhluwe is a small village in an area surrounded by large luxury game farms. It is a good base to explore the region as it is within easy reach of many of the local game parks and is only 15 km from St Lucia's False Bay. An international game auction is held here annually

Saving the rhino

The biggest conservation success story for Hluhluwe-Imfolozi is the white rhino, which has been brought back from the brink of extinction. It is estimated that in the late 1800s when the reserve was proclaimed, the entire world population of southern white rhinos was only 20, all of them living in this area. Southern Africa is the genetic home for the white rhino and all populations in the world have their origins here.

The rhino's early protection from hunting allowed numbers to grow to such an extent that, since the 1950s, surplus rhino have been transferred to other areas as part of the internationally famous 'Operation Rhino'. As a result, the population of white rhino in South Africa has grown from around 500 in the 1950s to 6000 today, and the global population is put at about 13,000.

Hluhluwe-Imfolozi is now focusing on saving the black rhino, whose numbers in Africa over the last decade have dwindled from 14,000 to a mere 1550. KZN Wildlife is currently working with the World Wildlife Fund (WWF) on the Black Rhino Range Expansion Project, which identifies and helps to stock suitable conservation areas with surplus black rhinos from KZN Wildlife reserves. At least a quarter of the world's population of black and white rhino are found in Hluhluwe-Imfolozi.

by KZN Wildlife. There are a couple of craft villages in the area; **Dumazulu Traditional Village**, a short drive from Hluhluwe, is one of the better ones, with displays of Zulu dancing, spear making and basket weaving.

The **Hluhluwe Tourism Association** ① *next to the Engen garage, Main St, T035-5620353, www.hluhluwe.net, Mon-Fri 0800-1700, Sat 0900-1300*, acts as a booking agent for the area.

Greater St Lucia Wetland Park ●❷❷○▲❸❶ ➤➤ pp537-543. Colour map 5, A3.

The Greater St Lucia Wetland Park was declared a World Heritage Site in 1999, the first place in South Africa to be awarded this status. It's presently going under a name change to **iSimangaliso Wetland Park** – iSimangaliso is isiZulu for 'miracle'. The protected area is the largest estuarine lake system in Africa, with a variety of flora and fauna which compares favourably with the Okavango Delta or Kruger National Park. The birdlife is outstanding, with a staggering 420 species recorded here. But despite drawing a huge number of visitors throughout the year, the town remains small and low-key, with an appealingly languid, tropical atmosphere.

Ins and outs

Getting there and around The area now known as the Greater St Lucia Wetland Park consists of a number of formerly separate nature reserves and state forests. These are still referred to locally under a bewildering array of old and new names, but the greater area is considered to be South Africa's third largest park. The entire 328,000-ha reserve starts south of the St Lucia Estuary and stretches north to the border with Mozambique, and is about 280 km in length. The terrestrial section of the park varies from 1 km to 24 km wide, and the marine section extends 5 km out to sea, protecting 155 km of coastline.

In the southern region, accessible from St Lucia, the park falls into three main areas: **St Lucia Public Resort and Estuary National Park**, which is a good area to see crocodile, hippo, impala, waterbuck, wildebeest and zebra; the coastline up to **Cape Vidal**, 32 km north of St Lucia, with the beautiful Cape beach; and the **western shore** of the lake, which is much quieter than the other two and affords the opportunity to explore the lake by boat.

The Greater St Lucia Wetland Park also encompasses **Maphelana** to the south (see page 534), accessed from Kwambonambi, and all the coastal parks to the north, from Sodwana Bay to Kosi Bay Nature Reserve on the border of Mozambique. ▸▸ *For further details, see Maputaland, page 544.*

Best time to visit Each season in the wetlands has its own attraction. From November to February there tends to be more rain, making the vegetation greener. June to August is the best time for birdwatching as this is the breeding season. The best months for walking are March to November when it is less hot and humid. The school holidays are always a popular time for South African tourists to visit and accommodation at these times should be booked well in advance.

Tourist information For information about the Greater St Lucia Wetland Park, visit the St Lucia office of **KZN Wildlife** ① *Pelikan Rd, near Eden Park campsite, T035-5901340, www.kznwildlife.com, daily 0800-1630.* It has a small selection of brochures and can help with accommodation and trail information; reservations should be made well in advance, though (see below).

Staying in the park Reservations for all self-catering accommodation and wilderness trails within the park can be made up to 12 months in advance through **KZN Wildlife Reservations** ① *T033-8451000, www.kznwildlife.com.* There are only limited supplies available in the camp shops so it is essential to bring your own food. The nearest supermarket is in St Lucia, unless you are staying at Charters Creek or one the camps around False Bay, in which case the nearest shops are in Hluhluwe. ▸▸ *For further details, see Sleeping, page 540.*

Safety When hiking around the lake, watch out for hippos – they kill more people than any other mammal in Africa. If you come across one on land, retreat and, if possible, try and climb a tree. Also keep an eye out for snakes and crocodiles; avoid the water's edge. When swimming in the sea, stay well away from the estuary, which is inhabited by crocodiles and Zambezi sharks. Note that most self-guided trails in the area have been closed following the reintroduction of elephant. St Lucia is a malarial area and prophylactics should be taken.

Background

The land now occupied by the park has had human inhabitants since the Early Iron Age. Archaeological excavations have uncovered the remains of settlements and middens, and large areas of forest and dunes are thought to have been cleared to provide charcoal for iron smelting. St Lucia was named by the Portuguese explorer Manuel Perestrello in 1575, although European influence in the area was minimal until the 1850s. Up to that time the area was inhabited by a relatively large population of Thongas and Zulus who herded cattle and cultivated the land.

Professional hunters began visiting the lake in the 1850s in search of ivory, hides and horns which were at one point the Colony of Natal's main source of income. So successful were these hunters that within 50 years the last elephant in this region had been shot.

Amongst the big game hunters here were William Baldwin, Robert Briggs Struthers, 'Elephant' White and John Dunn who recorded having shot 23 seacows in one morning and a total of 203 seacows in the following three months. Hunting parties would kill hundreds of elephants, crocodiles and hippos on each expedition.

During the 1880s the British government annexed St Lucia in a move which would foil the Boers from the New Republic in their search for access to the sea. It was after this that land was distributed to settlers and that missions were founded at Mount Tabor, Cape Vidal and Ozabeni.

St Lucia Lake, along with Hluhluwe-Umfolozi, was one of the first game reserves to be established in Africa in 1895. Further moves to protect wildlife also took place in 1944 with the addition of False Bay Park to the protected areas, and in 1975 South Africa signed the international RAMSAR Convention to protect wetlands. It was then that the Greater St Lucia Wetland region was declared. More recently, land was recovered by the park in 1987 when the Eastern Shores State Forest was returned to the Natal Parks Board. Conservation measures have continued in the last decade, and many conservation initiatives were introduced when St Lucia won World Heritage status in 1999. One of the most important of these has been the controversial national ban on beach driving in February 2002, enraging many South African 4WD owners. Species have also been reintroduced, including cheetah and elephant.

In spite of these measures to protect St Lucia, the survival of the lake system has been under constant threat since the turn of the 20th century. One of the most intractable problems has been the effect of agriculture on the lake's water supply: land reclamation, drainage canals, the diversion of the Umfolozi River and the damming of the Hluhluwe River for irrigation have all contributed to the silting up of the lake. In the 1960s salinity levels increased to such an extent during a series of droughts that the water in the lake system was twice as salty as sea water, killing numerous plants, fish and crocodiles. A further problem was that of the vast pine plantations in the region that were first planted in 1954. The thirsty pines consumed a huge amount of water, but an ambitious reclamation plan was put in place in 1999. As of July 2005, the pine tracts have been removed, and it is hoped that indigenous trees will once again flourish in the area, attracting more wildlife. However, a continuing drought has dramatically reduced the level of water in some areas, notably Charter's Creek, False Bay and Fanies Island. The three KZN Wildlife camps in these places are no longer open to the public and boat trips cannot be operated on the low water. Recently the drought has become so severe, that by October 2007 the St Lucia rivermouth had become completely silted up, closing off access to the sea.

Wildlife

On the land Fringing the park's 155-km coastline are vegetated sand dunes exceeding 180 m in height and estimated to be over 30,000 years old. These are the second highest vegetated dunes in the world, after Fraser Island in Australia.

The Mkhuze, Mzinene, Hluhluwe and Nyalazi rivers flow into the northern end of the lake system. The lakes are shallow and interspersed with islands and reedbeds and reach a maximum of 3 m in depth although large areas are only up to 1-m deep. A narrow channel connects the lakes to the estuary and the sea, and the lake's shores are bounded by papyrus, reeds, mangrove and forest swamps. The other inland areas in the park are grasslands with zones of thornveld, coastal and dune forest. Depending on where you are in the park, there are chances of seeing elephant, buffalo, kudu, waterbuck, rare black rhinos and leopards.

St Lucia

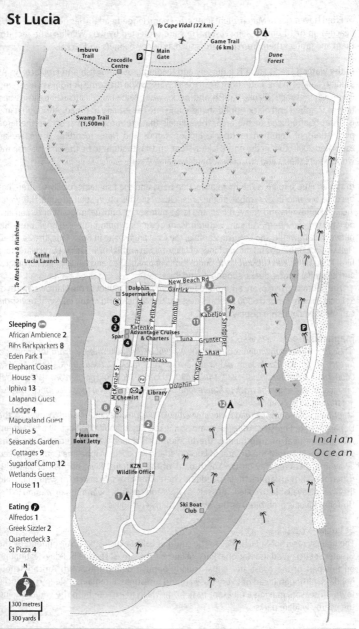

To Cape Vidal (32 km)

Imbuvu Trail

Main Gate

Crocodile Centre

Game Trail (6 km)

Dune Forest

Swamp Trail (1,500m)

To Mtubatuba & Hluhluwe

Santa Lucia Launch

New Beach Rd

Garrick

Dolphin Supermarket

Flamingo

Pelikaan

Hornbill

Kabeljou

Sandpiper

Katenkel

Spar

Advantage Cruises & Charters

Tuna

Grunter

Shad

Kingfisher

Steenbrass

McKenzie St

Dolphin

Chemist

Library

Pleasure Boat Jetty

KZN Wildlife Office

Ski Boat Club

Indian Ocean

Sleeping
African Ambience **2**
Bibs Backpackers **8**
Eden Park **1**
Elephant Coast House **3**
Iphiva **13**
Lalapanzi Guest Lodge **4**
Maputaland Guest House **5**
Seasands Garden Cottages **9**
Sugarloaf Camp **12**
Wetlands Guest House **11**

Eating
Alfredos **1**
Greek Sizzler **2**
Quarterdeck **3**
St Pizza **4**

N

300 metres
300 yards

From November to March, giant leatherback and loggerhead turtles nest on the park's beaches up to 10 times each season. They are protected by KZN Wildlife who monitor them and protect them from predators such as honey badgers and jackals.

In the water Lake St Lucia is a nursery and feeding ground for fish and crustaceans. As salinity changes in the water from fresh to salt water, so do the corresponding ecosystems. Fresh water attracts tilapia, catfish and ducks while saltier water attracts pelicans and herons. Zambezi and black-tipped sharks come into the estuary to breed. Although game is being reintroduced to the area, the animals that are most often seen are the large populations of common reedbuck, hippopotamus and Nile crocodile. There are an estimated 2000 crocs in the entire lake system, and it is thought to be the only place in the world where sharks and crocodiles share the same water.

In the air The birdlife is the main attraction here, and the fish eagle, easily spotted, has become the unofficial symbol of the area. Other species often seen around the water include kingfishers and weaverbirds, and large numbers of unusual migrant birds can also be spotted. Southern African waterbirds migrate depending on regional droughts between Bangweulu and Kafue in Zambia, the Okavango Delta in Botswana, the Zambezi Delta in Mozambique and the wetlands of Maputaland and St Lucia. The St Lucia waters are high in nutrients and support large populations of pinkbacked and white pelicans, greater and lesser flamingos, ducks, spoonbills and ibises.

The pelicans arrive every autumn to feed on migrating mullet in the Narrows, north of St Lucia Village. Around 6000 pelicans nest at the northern end of the lake where visitors can see their courtship displays.

Maphelana → Colour map 5, A3.
① *Head east from Kwambonambe to the Kwambonambi Lighthouse, from where it is a further 50 km to Maphelana along a narrow sand track. Oct-Mar 0600-1900, Apr-Sep 0600-1800; office daily 0800-1230, 1400-1630, T035-5901407. R20 per person. 4WD vehicles are recommended for the track to Maphelana but vehicles with high road clearance can also get through in dry weather.*
Maphelana National Park was established in 1897, but was later handed over to the Department of Forestry. After the campaign waged by the Wildlife Society of Southern Africa, the threat of strip-mining the titanium-rich dunes was averted. It is now the southernmost part of the Greater St Lucia Wetland Park. The Maphelana Camp is tucked away in a sheltered bay on the south bank of the Umfolozi River and is popular with fishermen who can launch their speedboats here. There is a safe beach for swimming and licences are available to collect mussels, oysters and crayfish. Swimming or wading in the Umfolozi River is prohibited as there are too many crocodiles.

St Lucia → Colour map 5, A3.
The holiday resort of St Lucia lies to the south of Lake St Lucia and is surrounded by the Greater St Lucia Wetland National Park. St Lucia is the largest seaside holiday destination on this part of the coast and is particularly popular during the South African school holidays. Although it can get very busy around Christmas, it remains a sleepy provincial town off season, making a pleasant base from which to explore both the wetlands and the nearby wildlife parks.

Many visitors come for a day trip, to explore the narrow reaches of the estuary leading up to the lake. Boats leave regularly from the jetty at the far end of McKenzie Street, usually seating around 20 people and taking a two-hour tour upriver. These provide an excellent introduction to the wetlands, with chances of seeing large pods of hippo and crocodile, and prolific birdlife.

Ins and outs The end of the R618 leads directly into the centre of the resort on McKenzie Street, which is lined with supermarkets, banks, restaurants, handicraft shops and boat charter companies. Continuing down past the end of McKenzie Street, the road leads to the large KZN Wildlife office to the left, and the jetty from which river cruises leave to the right.

The best source is **Advantage Cruises and Charters** ① *McKenzie St, close to the Spar, T035-5901259, www.advantagetours.co.za, daily 0700-1900*, a booking agent for all local activities and accommodation. St Lucia is the main tourist centre in this part of Zululand and is a good base to stock up on supplies before staying in self-catering accommodation either in the Greater St Lucia Wetland or in game reserves at Hluhluwe-Imfolozi and Mkuzi. For information on the Greater St Lucia Wetland Park, see page 531.

Beaches
The beaches lying to the east of St Lucia are large swathes of pristine white sand backed by dune forest, which stretch all the way to Cape Vidal. Visitors swim here at their own risk as there are dangerous currents, no shark nets and no lifeguards. Swimming is prohibited in the estuary and within 100 m of the river mouth as the strong unpredictable currents, sharks and crocodiles make it too dangerous.

St Lucia Public Resort and Estuary national parks
These areas directly surround St Lucia village. There is a 12-km network of self-guided trails, which start in the area near the Crocodile Centre (see below). As the trails extend from the Indian Ocean to the estuary they cross several different habitats such as dune forest, grasslands, mangroves and swamps. The trail leading from the Crocodile Centre to the estuary takes you to some good hippo-viewing riverside spots. The grasslands to the north of the village are a source of ncema grass, traditionally used by Zulus to make sleeping and sitting mats. The cutting season starts on 1 May when thousands of people come for the annual harvest.

The **Crocodile Centre** ① *T035-5901386, Mon-Fri 0800-1600, Sat 0830-1700, Sun 0900-1600, crocodile feeding Sat 1500, R20*, is next to the entrance gate to Cape Vidal, where a small display highlights the important role crocodiles play in the ecosystem of the park. The Nile, long snouted and dwarf crocodiles that are kept here in pens are all endangered in the wild and are part of an international breeding programme to protect them. KZN Wildlife routinely releases Nile crocodiles back into Lake St Lucia. The curio shop here is one of the best in St Lucia with a good selection of books and leaflets on the area. The tea garden serves light lunches.

Cape Vidal
① *32 km north of St Lucia, T035-5909012. Gates Oct-Mar 0500-1900, Apr-Sep 0600-1800; office daily 0800-1230, 1400-1630. R20 per person, R35 per vehicle. Only 100 vehicles per day are allowed past the gate at Cape Vidal; the speed limit in the park is 40 kph. Beach driving is not allowed.*

Cape Vidal makes an easy and pleasant day trip from St Lucia. A road heads north from the park gates (near the crocodile centre), passing through an area that was until recently pine forest but is now returning to indigenous wilderness. Elephants were recently reintroduced here, and the area is also home to kudu and cheetah.

Mission Rocks is 16 km from St Lucia, signposted off the dirt road. Snorkelling and scuba diving are allowed here but there are no facilities so it is essential to bring your own equipment. The rock pools here are full of life and are best seen at low tide.

Cape Vidal is an area of vegetated dunes along what must be one of the most spectacular beaches in KwaZulu Natal. The sand is pure white and the Indian Ocean is warm and inviting; the rocks just off the beach are teeming with tropical fish and the shallow water is safe to snorkel in. Thanks to the daily limit of cars into the reserve, the beach is never crowded even at the busiest of times. The camp has facilities for launching powerboats and is popular for game fishing, but as Cape Vidal marks the beginning of a marine reserve that stretches north to the Mozambique border, anglers require permits and many fish are on a tag and release system.

Exploring the park

Mount Tabor is the starting point for the three-day Mziki Trail ① *T033-8451000, or T035-590002 (local office), www.kznwildlife.com, advance booking essential*, operated by KZN Wildlife. Hikers sleep at the self-catering Mount Tabor base camp, which is reached by foot from Mission Rocks (2 km), and go out on three full-day hikes accompanied by armed game guides. Each day, a different loop is completed: the 10-km South Coast Loop passes through dune forest before reaching the sea at Rangers Rocks. From here the trail returns along the coastline to Mission Rocks before heading back to Mount Tabor through dune forest. Kudu are often seen on this trail. The 10-km Mfazana Pan Loop crosses the road to Cape Vidal and heads for the hides at Mfazana Pan, from where it turns north through grassland to the shore of Lake St Lucia. At 18 km, the North Coast Loop is the longest day hike. It heads north along Mount Tabor Ridge to Bokkie Valley and then returns along the coast past Bat's Cave and on to Mount Tabor. Note: Ticks and mosquitoes can be a problem on the trail.

Western shores

There are three reserves on the western shores of Lake St Lucia. However, a continuing drought has dramatically reduced the level of water in this area, and these reserves have been closed to visitors for some time. The KZN Wildlife camps are no longer open to the public and boat trips cannot be operated on the low water. Check with the KZN Wildlife office in St Lucia for updates. Access is via the N2 north of St Lucia. Charter's Creek is 20 km north of Mtubatuba on the N2; take the signposted turning 18 km to Charter's Creek, the last 6 km are on a dirt road. For Fanies Island, follow the signs to Charter's Creek from the N2; before reaching Charter's Creek, take the signposted turning north for 13 km. For False Bay, take the turning from the N2 to Hluhluwe village; the road continues 15 km to the park.

Zululand listings

Sleeping

Gingindhlovu and around p523
E Amatigulu Tented Camp, Amatigulu
Nature Reserve, KZN Wildlife, T033 8451000,
www.kznwildlife.com. 6 2-bed tents are
connected by wooden walkways. They have
proper beds on raised wooden platforms
overlooking the sea, a shared ablution block,
dining area, and fully equipped kitchen with
gas stoves, fridge and freezer; there is no shop
here so bring all your own food and supplies.

Eshowe and inland p524
A Protea Simunye Zulu Lodge,
T035-4503111, www.proteahotels.com.
You must be at the trading post by 1530,
from where you travel for 1 hr on horseback,
donkey or ox wagon (disabled guests can
request a 4WD transfer). The lodge is simple
and traditional with rooms in thatched
stone huts and open-air rock baths lit by
candles and oil lamps. In the evening,
music, singing and dancing is performed
by local people. Rates include all meals,
guides and demonstrations.
B Protea Shakaland, T035-4600912,
www.shakaland.com. If you are staying the
night the Shaka experience continues in the
adjacent Protea hotel, where Zulu dancers
escort you to your beehive-shaped hut.
The evenings are spent sampling the local
brew *tshwala* around the campfire while
being entertained with dancing and story
telling. The en suite huts are huge and have
all mod cons.

D Amble Inn, 116 Main St, Eshowe,
T035-4741300, ambleinn@corpdial.co.za.
Friendly guesthouse with 11 comfortable
rooms overlooking a pool. The dining room
offers hearty English meals like roast beef
and Yorkshire pudding or steak and kidney
pie for lunch and dinner.
D Kwabhekithunga/Stewarts Farm, 36 km
from Eshowe on the R34 towards Empangeni,
T035-4600929, www.stewartsfarm.com.
Rather than having been built especially for
tourists like many similar Zulu 'experiences'
in the area, this village is the real home of
Chief Mbhangucuza Fakude, his 4 brothers
and their extended families. Accommodation
is in Zulu beehive-shaped huts, all en suite,
with bright and colourful interiors and
electricity. Bar and swimming pool on site.
For an extra R165 per person, visitors are
treated to a 'cultural experience' – Zulu
dancing and singing, and a taste of Zulu
food and home-brewed beer. Pre-booking
is essential. Recommended for a feel of real
Zulu life.
E-F Zululand Backpackers, 38 Main St,
T035-4744919, www.eshowe.com. At the
back of the **George Hotel**. Dorms, kitchen,
showers, double rooms, camping possible,
M-Net TV, pool table, internet, swimming
pool, close to shops and banks, Baz Bus
stop. Has an excellent reputation for
organizing local tours, such as visits to
traditional Zulu weddings, mountain bikes
available for hire. Recommended.

Mtunzini and around p526
C Trade Winds, 12 Hely Hutchinson Rd,
T035-3402266, www.tradewindscountry
inn.co.za. Well-established, small town
hotel with 26 rooms, a/c, TV, restaurant,
swimming pool and à la carte restaurant.
D Highfield Country Home, 7 km from
town off the N2, however, you must get
to it from Mtunzini on the old Durban road,
T035-3401731. 5 double rooms with lovely
Victorian bathrooms, TV, meals on request,

pool, set in a beautiful farmhouse in 4 ha of parklands, sea views, ask for Willie or Sarco. International visitors return here year after year. Recommended.

B-C Mtunzini Forest Lodge, off Valley Dr, T035-3685642, www.goodersonva cations.com/mtunzinilodge.html. 22 self-catering beach chalets set in attractive dune forest right by the beach, sleeping up to 6 people in rustic log cabins. Swimming pool for guests' use; meals available in the **Twitchers Restaurant**, open Tue-Sat.

D-F Umlalazi Nature Reserve, KZN Wildlife, T033-8451000, www.kznwildlife.com. The camp has 13 self-catering 2-bedroom log cabins with DSTV, and 50 camping and caravan sites, all with braais, coin operated washing machines, swimming pool. Located in coastal dune forest a short walk to the beach.

E-F Xaxaza Caravan Park, at the top of town, T035-3401843, www.xaxaza.caravan parks.com. Standard caravan park with decent facilities, including simple self-catering cabins, need to bring own bedding, electrical points, clean ablutions, shop, games room and pool, a significant distance from the beach.

Empangeni and around p526

There is little accommodation in the town itself, and it doesn't make a very pleasant stop over; head along the R34 inland instead.

L Thula Thula, Thula Thula Private Game Reserve, T035-7928322, www.thula thula.com. Family-run exclusive safari lodge with 7 luxury thatched chalets decorated in an ethnic style, set on rolling lawns and surrounded by forests ringing with bird calls. Rates are all-inclusive of meals and game drives, and the excellent French food is served in an outside boma, with tables sets around a fire. Guests can also relax in the large, thatched bar area, overlooking the pool. Recommended.

Richards Bay p527

C The Ridge – Jacks Corner, 1 Jack's Corner, T035-7534312, www.jackscorner.co.za.

A good choice if you're passing through Richards Bay, this upmarket guesthouse has 14 tasteful rooms set around a pool, with views of the ocean and harbour. Restaurant and bar on site.

Hluhluwe-Imfolozi Game Reserve
p527, map p528

All reservations through **KZN Wildlife**, T033-8451000, www.kznwildlife.com. The lodges are only available for single group bookings. Codes refer to the price for 2 people when the unit is full.

A Masinda Lodge, Imfolozi sector. Luxury 6-bed self-catering lodge, lounge and dining room with Zulu decor, there's a resident cook. Beautiful setting with good views of the bush.

A Mtwazi Lodge, Hluhluwe sector. Original thatched house which was home to the park's first warden. 3 double bedrooms, comfortable lounge, dining room, cook (bring food) and a game guard.

A Nselweni, Imfolozi sector. A wonderfully atmospheric reed and thatch bush lodge raised on stilts just above the floodplain of Mfolozi River. 4 2-bed units, shared ablutions, lounge, dining area, fully equipped kitchen. Must be booked as a single unit and cooks will prepare meals, but guests must bring all their own food and drinks.

A-C Mpila Camp, Imfolozi sector. Centrally situated in the heart of Imfolozi, Mpila Camp commands magnificent views over the wilderness area to the east and the Msaseni Hills to the west. 12 1-bed self-catering thatched cottages, 2 self-contained 3-bed cottages (cook on hand to prepare food supplied by guests), 6 self-catering chalets sleeping up to 5. Also has a luxury tented camp with 9 units of walk-in tents (self-catering). The shop stocks basic provisions and petrol station.

A-D Hilltop Camp, Hluhluwe sector. The main camp was refurbished a few years ago and offers 4 types of accommodation. At the top end are 20 **2-bed chalets (A)** with 2 bedrooms, 2 bathrooms and fully equipped kitchen; slightly cheaper are the 7 **2-bed**

chalets (**B**), with fully equipped kitchen, and the 20 2-bed rest huts (not self-catering) with fridge and kettle. The cheapest options are the 20 **2-bed rest huts** (**C**), with communal kitchen and ablution block. This is the largest and most accessible of the camps and has a fabulous hilltop location, with sweeping views over much of the park and parts of Swaziland. Although this doesn't have the exclusivity of the smaller bush camps, the central lounge, restaurant, bar, pool and veranda are welcome at the end of the day. Game drives and guided walks can be arranged here.

Private lodges and camps
L2 Gqoyeni Bush Lodge, Imfolozi sector. 8-bed bush lodge, 4 thatched cottages, each with 2 bedrooms, on stilts connected by raised wooden walkways to the living area with lounge, dining area and kitchen, the camp has its own viewing platform overlooking the Mfolozi River where there are good chances of seeing crocodiles, lions and elephants in the summer. Must be booked as one unit, bring own food but in residence are a cook and a ranger for bush walks.
L2 Hlathikhulu, Imfolozi sector. 8-bed bush camp, rustic decor, lovely setting overlooking the Black Mfolozi. 4 2 bed en suite chalets, a central lounging area and kitchen linked by wooden boardwalks, must be booked as one unit, cook and game guide.
L2 Muntulu Bush Camp, Hluhluwe sector. 4 2-bed units in this rustic bush lodge, linked by wooden walkway to a central lounge and dining area, all overlooking the Hluhluwe River, verandas. Cooks are on hand to prepare meals, but guests must bring all food. There is also a game ranger on site.
L2 Munyawaneni, Hluhluwe sector. 8-bed bush lodge on the banks of the Hluhluwe River in a good area for seeing the elephant and nyala that come to drink at the secluded waterhole that can be seen from each of the 4 en suite rooms. Boardwalks link the accommodation units to a central lounge and kitchen. Again, cooks can prepare meals but guests must bring food.

Hluhluwe *p529*
L Hluhluwe River Lodge, 15 km from Hluhluwe village off the road to False Bay Park, T035-5620246, www.hluhluwe.co.za. 8 double A-frame thatched chalets with great views and swimming pool. Also has 2 family chalets and 2 luxury honeymoon chalets, with open bath area and private viewing deck. Central lodge houses a dining area, bar, lounge, curio shop and library. Rates are fully inclusive of meals and a game drive. Recommended.
AL Gazebo Safari Lodge, a short drive from Hluhluwe village, off the road to False Bay, T035-5621066, www.gazebo.co.za. 12 double en suite rooms, TV, a/c, verandas with stunning views of the bush. Restaurant, bar, lounge, beautiful swimming pool and deck, boma area where meals are served in summer, game drives to nearby reserves.
AL Zulu Nyala, 15 km on the Mzinene Rd, T035-5620177, www.zulunyala.com. Set within a private game reserve, 53 twin a/c rooms, restaurant, 2 bars, curio shop, pool, tennis, clay-pigeon shooting. Also 10 luxury 'Hemmingway'-style tents in the extensive gardens. Also on this reserve is the **Heritage Hotel**, set in a lovely 1940s colonial home.
A Hluhluwe Hotel, 104 Bush Rd, T035-5624000, www.hluhluwehotel.co.za. 75 a/c rooms, TV, tennis, swimming pool and volleyball, smart modern hotel decorated with African motifs, 2 restaurants serving an à la carte menu or a buffet, occasional performances of Zulu dancing in the evenings around the pool, can organize safaris to the local parks.
B Bushlands Game Lodge, T035-5620144, www.goodersonvacations.com/bushlands.html. 20 luxurious a/c self-catering wooden cabins sleeping 6 with rich decor set in lush gardens overlooking the swimming pool. Boardwalks lit by flaming lanterns in the evening link the cabins to the central eating boma and

lounge. If not self-catering, meals in the restaurant must be pre-booked.

C Sand Forest Lodge, 10 km from Hluhluwe village off False Bay Rd, T035-5622509, www.sandforest.co.za. A quality game farm within an ancient sand forest. 4 a/c self-catering cottages, en suite double room, kitchenette, veranda overlooks a neat lawn with acacia trees; variety of simpler self-catering log cabins on stilts in the forest with separate kitchen. Central bar, swimming pool and thatched lapa. Game walks and drives with resident guide plus visits to Zulu villages. Good value and peaceful setup.

F Isinkwe Backpackers, look out for the 'Bushlands' turning on the N2, 40 km north of the St Lucia/Mtubatuba turning, the lodge is a further 2 km down this road, T035-5622258, www.isinkwe.co.za. The Baz Bus stops here. A neat hostel with 40 beds in dorms, double rooms and camping. Swimming pool and a bar area for star gazing. Rustic set-up, has done much to create employment for local people. Great home-made meals served up most nights, or self-catering in the kitchen. Laundry. Well-organized day trips in a 4WD to all the local sights and transfers to Sodwana Bay.

Maphelana p534

C Maphelana Camp, KZN Wildlife, T033-8451000, www.kznwildlife.com. 10 5-bed log cabins, self-catering, with kitchen, bathroom, dining room and lounge. The cabins are set on a large forested dune with views over a large beach and the sea.

Camping

Maphelana Camp, 45 sites, ablution blocks. Electricity is restricted to generator times. Basic supplies are available at the camp site; petrol is not available. Campsite reservations T035-5901407.

St Lucia p534, map p533

Accommodation is cheap by international standards, however, there is almost always a shortage of beds so book well in advance.

B Seasands Garden Cottages, 135 Hornbill St, T035-5901082, www.seasands.co.za. Fairly large hotel, offering a mix of B&B rooms and self-catering cottages set in tropical gardens. Attracts groups and some conferences, but remains a popular choice. Restaurant, swimming pool and extensive gardens.

C African Ambience, 124 Pelikaan St, T035-5901212, www.africanambience.com. Delightful new guesthouse in a quiet thatched house a few blocks from the centre. Bright and airy TV-free rooms have chunky wooden furniture and ethnic fabrics, with huge beds and attractive bathrooms. Downstairs rooms have private terraces, and there is a garden with a swimming pool and fish ponds. An excellent, peaceful choice. Recommended.

C Elephant Coast House, corner of Garrick and Kingfisher streets, T035-5901888, www.elephantcoastbnb.co.za. 5 spacious rooms with balconies overlooking a large garden (where hippos sometimes come to graze) with a small fenced-off terrace and pool. Rooms are large and sunny, with tiled floors and vaguely ethnic decor. Friendly service, big breakfasts served in the large dining area, TV lounge, secure parking. Recommended.

C Lalapanzi Guest Lodge, 7 Sandpiper St, T035-5901167, www.lalapanzi.co.za. 6 large B&B double rooms with en suite facilities and fridge full of cool drinks. TV lounge, swimming pool, lush tropical garden full of birds, secure off-street parking.

C Wendy's Country Lodge, Riverview, just off the R618 in Mtubatuba, 10 km west of St Lucia, T035-5500407, www.wendybnb.co.za. Well outside town, but in an excellent location for access both to St Lucia and Hluhluwe-Imfolozi. Family-run guesthouse surrounded by tropical gardens, with spacious double rooms filled with quirky and antique furniture, and Victorian-style bathrooms. Good food served in the little restaurant. Range of activities organized, from game drives and fishing to tours of the wetlands. Very friendly and welcoming. Recommended.

C Wetlands Guest House, 20 Kingfisher St, T/F035-5901098, www.stluciawetlands.com. Family-run B&B set in a quiet street close to the centre. 6 large a/c rooms with en suite bathroom, 1 family unit, with high ceilings and wood floors which help keep things cool in the summer. Guest lounge with bar and TV. Self-catering flat also available. Large swimming pool with child protection fence.
D Maputaland Guest House, 1 Kabeljou St, T/F035-5901041, www.maputaland.com. 5 rooms, TV lounge, B&B, swimming pool set in a large tropical garden in a quiet suburb away from the main drag. Recommended. Wide selection of wildlife tours organized from here. German speaking.
E-F Bibs Backpackers, 310 McKenzie St, T035-5901056, www.bibs.co.za. Small dorms, double rooms, twins, self-catering chalets and camping. Great kitchen and self-catering area, Spar shop next door for supplies, evening meals on request. Braai area, rock swimming pool, relaxing gardens with hammock and bar area, Zulu dancing on Sat nights, email/internet access. Well-organized guided day trips to Hluhluwe and other local sights. Free transfer to beach, beach fires at night. On the Baz Bus route.

Camping

There are 3 **KZN Wildlife** campsites on the edge of town, reservations T035-5901340. Each has a shop selling a wide range of guides and curios and a restaurant.
Eden Park, in a small forest to the south of town, 20 sites, ablution block.
Iphiva, near the Crocodile Centre, 88 sites, ablution blocks and laundry facilities.
Sugarloaf Camp, close to the beach and estuary, 92 sites, swimming pool, ablution blocks, laundry facilities.

Cape Vidal p535

The small shop at Cape Vidal has a couple of narrow shelves stocked with food. Petrol and firewood are also on sale in the camp. If you are staying overnight stock up in St Lucia.

B-D Cape Vidal Camp, KZN Wildlife, T033-8451000, www.kznwildlife.com. 5- to 20-bed log cabins, all are self-catering with fully equipped kitchens, dining rooms, terraces and bathrooms. These represent great value for a group. All the cabins are set under trees on the dunes 200 m from the beach.

Camping

Cape Vidal Camp, T035-5909012. 50 sites set among the pines. Shared ablution blocks, power points and an area for cleaning fish. It gets overcrowded with fishermen here during the high season. The minimum charge of R300 per day is expensive by local standards and there are better options closer to St Lucia town.

🍴 Eating

Decent restaurants in this area are limited to the hotels. If you find yourself in St Lucia there is a wider choice.

Richards Bay p527

🍴🍴🍴 **The Grill Fish**, Tuzi Gazi Waterfront, T035-7880110. Offers views of the harbour and quality seafood, including excellent grills and a decent winelist.

Hluhluwe-Imfolozi Game Reserve
p527, map p528

There is a good restaurant at **Hilltop Camp** in the Hluhluwe sector, serving full English breakfasts, buffet meals, light snacks and braais, open until 2100. The tables on the shady outdoor terrace are in a superb setting overlooking the reserve; the game burgers are highly recommended.

St Lucia p534, map p533

🍴🍴 **Alfredos**, McKenzie St, T035-5901150. Good Italian food at this cheap and cheerful set-up, with occasional live music and tables inside and out. Fun, easy-going atmosphere.

†† The Greek Sizzler, 37 McKenzie St, T035-5901554. Hugely popular local restaurant serving steaks, seafood and a couple of Greek specials at tables spilling out on to the pavement. Friendly Greek management.

†† Quarterdeck, McKenzie St, T035-5901116. Great wooden deck overlooking the road, with a large (more beery) interior. Good selection of fresh grilled seafood, as well as burgers and salads. Popular cocktail bar downstairs.

† St Pizza, 13 McKenzie St, T035-5901048. Ever-expanding pizza joint with wooden tables strung out on a large deck over-looking the street. As well as good thin-crust pizzas, the seafood specials are filling. Wide choice of wines and beers, and a good atmosphere in the evenings.

O Shopping

Richards Bay p527
There are a number of shopping malls in the centre of town, the largest of which is the **Boardwalk**, where facilities include banks, chemists, supermarkets, restaurants, a wide range of shops, a cinema and a branch of **Rennies Travel** (Thomas Cook agent, foreign exchange).

Hluhluwe-Imfolozi Game Reserve
p527, map p528
In the Imfolozi sector there are souvenir shops selling gifts and books on natural history at Masinda and Mpila Camps. Otherwise there are no shops in the reserve so it is necessary to bring all your own food and other supplies; the nearest shop is in Mtubatuba. Petrol is sold at Mpila Camp.

In the Hluhluwe sector there is a curio shop at **Hilltop Camp** and a small supermarket, but it only has limited basic supplies. Petrol and oil are on sale.

Hluhluwe p529
Ilala Weavers, Thembalethu Craft Village, T035-5620630, is a quality handicraft shop selling traditional basketwork and beadwork, decorated with geometric patterns.

St Lucia p534, map p533
There is a large, modern **Spar** on the main street – McKenzie St – which sells a good range of supplies. In season, women often peddle fresh tropical fruit from stalls along this street.

Cape Vidal p535
There is a small shop selling a good range of wildlife identification books, T-shirts, souvenirs and limited supplies of food.

▲ Activities and tours

Eshowe and inland p524
Tour operators
Zululand Eco-adventures, based at Zululand Backpackers, T035-4744919, www.eshowe.com. Run by Graham Chennells, a registered guide involved in community projects for many years. Unusual cultural tours of the surrounding countryside moving from village to village, no shows are visited, see contemporary traditional life as it is. Interesting projects include the **Eshowe Skills Centre**, a papermaking project, and the **Rotary Classroom Project** (the building of 2000 classrooms in the region). Graham is the former mayor of Eshowe who has intimate knowledge of the Zulu people. Highly recommended for more of an insight into Zulu traditions than the usual all-singing all-dancing tourist traps.

Hluhluwe-Imfolozi Game Reserve
p527, map p528
Night drives, R200, and game walks, R175, can be booked through the camp office. There are 3 self-guided walking trails and daily guided walks with a game guard from Mpila camp lasting 2-3 hrs. No children under 13.

Zululand Adventures, T035-5500243, www.zululand-adventures.com. Morning and afternoon game drives run by the cheery Gavin to Hluhluwe-Imfolozi Game Reserve, including lunch or sundowners. Good on history of the park and very knowledgeable and enthusiastic about the area. Also offers day-long fishing trips off the coast.

Hluhluwe p529
Dinizulu Safaris, T035-5620025, www.dinizulu.co.za. An established family outfit with excellent knowledge of Zululand and its parks, full- and half-day guided game drives in 4WD open vehicles to Hluhluwe-Imfolozi and Mkhuze game reserves.
Isinkwe Tours & Safaris, at **Isinkwe Backpackers**, T035-5622258, www.isinkwe.co.za. Tours in open-top 4WDs to Hluhluwe Imfolozi, St Lucia and Mkhuze, including breakfast and a braai lunch. Good value.

St Lucia p534, map p533
Advantage Charters, T035-5901259, www.advantagetours.co.za. A wide choice of boat rides, including 2-hr estuary trips, costing from R130. Whale-watching trips run Jun-Nov when humpback, mink and occasional southern right whales travel along the coast heading for the warmer breeding waters of Mozambique. Expect to pay around R500, 80% of which is refundable if no whales are spotted. If you don't have a car, this is a good-value tour operator for day trips to Cape Vidal and deep-sea fishing.
Santa Lucia, T035-5901340, www.kznwildlife.com. 80-seater double-storey launch with a bar departs from the jetty next to the bridge at 0830, 1030 and 1430, R90. The tour lasts for 90 mins and travels up the estuary past thick banks of vegetation as far as the Narrows. There is a good chance of seeing hippo and waterfowl. Migrating mullet are often seen leaping out of the water during the autumn when they move from the lake into the sea.

⊖ Transport

Empangeni and around p526
Greyhound, T083-9159000 (in South Africa), T011-2768550 (from overseas), www.greyhound.co.za. Coaches depart from the museum in Turnbull St, towards **Durban**, **Johannesburg** and **Pretoria**.

Richards Bay p527
Air
There is a small airport at the northern edge of town, 5 km from the centre. **SAA**, T011-9781111, www.flysaa.com, has daily flights to **Johannesburg**.

Bus
Greyhound, T083-9159000 (in South Africa), T011-2768550 (from overseas), www.greyhound.co.za, has regular coaches to **Durban**, **Pretoria** and **Johannesburg**.

Car hire
All offices at the airport: **Avis**, T035-7896555, **Budget**, T035-7860986, **Imperial**, T035-7860896, **Hertz**, T035-7861201.

Taxi
Zululand Taxis, T035-6682108.

St Lucia p534, map p533
Passengers using the **Baz Bus** can be dropped off at **Bib's Backpackers** on Mackenzie St.

⊕ Directory

Richards Bay p527
Banks Ned Bank and Standard Bank are both on Bullion Blvd. **Medical services** Central Pharmacy T035-7893910. The Bay Hospital, Krugerrand CBD, T035-7806111.

St Lucia p534, map p533
Banks First National Bank, T035-5901008, and Standard Bank, T035-5901044, are on McKenzie St.

Maputaland

Named after the Maputa River, which flows through southern Mozambique, Maputaland covers an area of 9000 sq km stretching north from Lake St Lucia to the Mozambique border and east from the Indian Ocean to the Lebombo Mountains. One of South Africa's least developed regions, Maputaland has preserved a traditional African atmosphere. The land is unsuitable for intensive modern agriculture and small farmsteads and fishing communites dot the landscape.

The climate varies from being tropical in the north to subtropical in the south, and this has created a fascinatingly diverse range of ecosystems, from the forested Lebombo Mountains at 700 m to the low-lying expanses of the coastal plain. Maputaland's features include Lake Sibaya – South Africa's largest freshwater lake – as well as mangrove swamps, coral reefs, dune forest, riverine forest and savannah. And seeing Maputaland's last wild elephants from a Land Rover in Tembe or diving on the reefs at Sodwana Bay are among South Africa's ultimate wilderness experiences. ▸▸ *For listings, see pages 553-556.*

Ins and outs

Getting there Maputaland is well connected by road on the N2 highway. By car it is only a three-hour drive from Durban or six hours from Johannesburg. Leave the N2 at the Hluhluwe exit, and follow the Lower Mkuzi Road (R22), which runs along the southern boundary of Mkhuze Game Reserve and passes a number of luxury private game lodges. This tarred road continues on to Mbazwana and Sodwana Bay (90 km) (see page 547) and then on to Kosi Bay (see page 550) and the border with Mozambique at Ponta Do Ouro. (see box, page 549).

From Mkhuze there is a dirt road heading south parallel to the N2 which leads to the turning to **Mkhuze Game Reserve** (20 km). There is also an alternative northern route on dirt roads from Mkhuze to Sodwana Bay (120 km), passing through Ubombo, Tshongwe and Mbazwana. The drive to Mkhuze passes through sisal plantations before entering a beautiful rustic area. The road winds through gently rounded hills dotted with aloes and acacias. Donkeys and cows graze on the meadows at the side of the road and wander about freely. The road is in good condition but after rain it is crossed by numerous streams. Mkhuze has a supermarket, bank and petrol station.

A further 10 km along the N2 from Mkhuze is the exit for **Jozini** (the N2 continues north towards Lavumisa, 40 km, on the frontier with Swaziland). Jozini is the last place of any size before the reserves in northern Maputaland; it is a good idea to fill up on petrol and buy any last minute supplies while you are here. The tarred road east from Jozini crosses the Lebombo Mountains and the Maputaland coastal plain and is an alternative to the R22 if you are coming from the north.

Passengers using the **Baz Bus**, T021-4392323, www.bazbus.com, are dropped off and picked up at the **Ghost Mountain Inn** (see Sleeping, page 553). ▸▸ *For further details, see Transport, page 556.*

Mkhuze Game Reserve ◉ ▸▸ *pp553-556.*

① *Clearly signposted from the N2, 335 km from Durban and 145 km from Richards Bay, T035-5739004, Oct-Mar 0500-1900, Apr-Sep 0600-1800, office daily 0800-1630. R35 per person, plus R35 per vehicle.*

The reserve, established in 1912 and covering an area of 40,000 ha, has a flat and dry landscape of open grasslands, dense forests, coastal dunes and pans. The area to the north is tropical whereas the southern part of the reserve is more temperate. The protected area conserves a representative cross-section of the Maputaland ecosystem. Mkhuze is not visited as often as Hluhluwe-Imfolozi (see page 527) as there are not as many rhino, but it offers opportunities to go on guided bush walks and see some of Maputaland's more unusual animals.

There is some frozen food for sale in the curio shop and a selection of books on natural history and postcards. It's also a good place to pick up some informative leaflets on birds, trees, walks and drives. There's petrol is for sale at the entrance gate. Reservations for camping sites should be made here.

Maputaland game reserves

Sleeping
Ghost Mountain Inn **1**
Kosi Bay Lodge **14**
Kosi Forest Lodge **2**
Lake Nhlange Camp **15**
Mantuma **9**

Mkuze Falls Private Game Reserve **16**
Ndumo Camp **3**
Nhlonhlela **10**
Pakamisa Private Game Reserve **17**
Rocktail Bay Lodge **4**
Sodwana Bay Camp **12**

Sodwana Bay Lodge **5**
Tembe Elephant Lodge **6**
Thonga Beach Lodge **13**
White Elephant Lodge **7**

Maputaland turtles

Five species of turtle can be found off the Maputaland coast but the loggerhead and the leatherback turtles are the only ones to breed here. The turtles arrive between October and February migrating vast distances from as far afield as Madagascar, Kenya and the Cape. There are two theories as to how the turtles return to the beaches where they were born after spending at least 15 years at sea. One proposes that the turtles are guided by the earth's magnetic fields, while the other holds that they use their sense of smell to find the right beach.

After mating offshore the female turtles, who can weigh up to 900 kg, struggle through the surf and up the beach to lay their eggs. Egg laying takes place at night and after digging a hole in the beach the female will lay around 100 eggs. She then covers the nest with sand and returns to the sea.

Incubation takes around 60 days, the tiny turtles then hatch together and dig their way to the surface. Few hatchlings live to become adults and the threat of being eaten by predators begins immediately with ghost crabs and jackals waiting to catch them before they can reach the sea. About one turtle in every 500 will survive.

The Maputaland Marine Reserve has played a vital role in rescuing the loggerhead and the leatherback from extinction. The beaches along this coast are an important breeding area and years of protection have finally resulted in increasing the numbers of turtles returning each year to breed.

Some of the lodges north of Sodwana Bay offer turtle-watching tips. In St Lucia, KZN Wildlife has granted a single concession to **Shaka Barker Tours**, 4 Hornbill St, T035-5901162, www.shakabarker.co.za, who run night time trips to see the turtles laying at Leven Point, which is normally a restricted area. It's not uncommon to see crocodiles and snakes, as well as turtles, on the beach. This is a very special wildlife experience conducted in an eco-friendly way and highly recommended. The tour departs at 1830 and returns at 0300 the following morning. A minimum of two people are required and advance booking is essential. The cost is R1450, which includes supper and night drives in search of genets, leopard, bush babies, chameleons and hippos.

Wildlife

Mkhuze is an excellent place to see some of Maputaland's big game. Elephant, giraffe, blue wildebeest, eland, kudu, black and white rhino, cheetah, leopard and hyena are all present in the reserve. It is also one of the best places to see the shy nyala antelope – nearly 8000 live here. As part of the Mozambique coastal plain, Mkhuze attracts many tropical birds often seen further north. Over 450 species have been recorded here, representing 7% of the world's total number of species. Look out for Neergard's sunbird, the yellowspotted nicator and the African broadbill. Many aquatic birds visit the pans here during the summer when you can see woolly necked storks, herons, flamingos, pink-backed and white pelicans, ibises, spoonbills and jacanas from the hides overlooking the pans. You may also spot hippo and crocodile.

Exploring the reserve

A 100-km network of roads crosses the reserve, passing through areas of thick bush which are not ideal for game viewing; the grasslands, however, are more open and animals are easier to see. The best game-viewing areas are the **Loop Road**, the **Nsumo Pan** and the **airstrip**.

There are four game-viewing hides next to the Kubube, Kumasinga, Kwamalibala and Kumahlala pans. The viewing here is excellent and you can watch the game coming down to drink. There are car parks nearby where you can leave your car and walk to the hides.

Sodwana Bay ☺▲☺ ▶ pp553-556. Colour map 5, A3.

ⓘ *Entrance gates open 24 hrs, T035-5710051; R20.*

Sodwana's is South Africa's premier scuba diving destinations – and is the site of the world's southernmost tropical reefs. Eighty percent of South Africa's 1200 species of fish can be found in the waters off Sodwana; ragged-toothed and whale sharks, humpback whales, black marlin and turtles are some of the major attractions. Diving has become so popular here that over 100,000 dives a year are made on these reefs.

Ins and outs

Getting there Sodwana Bay is 350 km from Durban and is well signposted from the N2, approaching from the south on the N2 take the Ngwenya/Sodwana Bay exit. The road is tarred and goes through **Mbazwana** en route to Sodwana Bay (80 km). This small village has mushroomed in recent years. There is a colourful market selling fruit and handicrafts, as well as a petrol station and ATM. It is 15 km from here to Sodwana Bay along a tar road.

From the N2 in the north take the turning to Jozini and Mbazwana. Follow the dirt road to Sodwana Bay (120 km), passing through Ubombo, Tshongwe and Mbazwana, which can be tackled without a 4WD.

Best time to visit Sodwana is popular with visitors all year round. Divers prefer April to September, whereas fishermen tend to congregate here in November and December. December and January are the best times to see the turtles laying their eggs. Sodwana gets very crowded during the school holidays when the accommodation is fully booked months in advance.

Diving

The coral reefs at Sodwana lie just offshore and teem with colourful tropical fish. Among some of the more unusual sightings are the loggerhead, leatherback and hawksbill turtles, honeycomb moray eels, dolphins, whale sharks, stingrays, humpback whales and black marlins. **Two Mile Reef** is very popular with divers. It is 1.5 km long and nearly 1 km wide, with depths ranging from 9 m to 34 m. There are numerous dive sites to explore here and anemones, triggerfish, sponges and fan-shaped gorgoniums can be seen in this area of overhangs and caves. The dives at **Five Mile Reef** and **Seven Mile Reef** are at around 22 m, and both are renowned for their corals. Access to Five Mile Reef is limited, but it is worth trying to get on a dive to see this protected area with its delicate miniature Staghorn Coral Gardens. **Nine Mile Reef** is only open for a limited number of dives and is well known for its soft corals. There are some large caves which can shelter pyjama sharks. Depths range from 5 m to 24 m. ▶ *For more detailed dive facts and recommendations, see Essentials, page 22.*

The closest snorkelling site to Sodwana is on **Quarter Mile Reef**, 500 m off Jesser Point. Further south are **Algae Reef** (5 km) and **Adams Reef** (10 km). These are shallow rocky reefs with good visibility inhabited by tiny tropical fish.

Lake Sibaya → *Colour map 2, C6.*
ⓘ *This is an endemic low-risk malaria area.*

North of **Mbazwana** the R22 has been newly tarred all the way to the Mozambique border at Ponta do Ouro (see box, page 549) and provides access to the remote northern coastal reserves. An alternative dirt track heads from Mbazwana towards the coast to **Manzengwenya** but this route can only be negotiated with a 4WD. Lake Sibaya, 20 km north of Sodwana, is the largest freshwater lake in South Africa and was previously connected to the sea. The lake is now surrounded by swampy reed beds and patches of forest which provide varied habitats for the many species of birds which can be found here. A long strip of thickly forested dunes runs between the Indian Ocean and the lake. Tropical birdlife is Lake Sibaya's main attraction and kingfishers, cormorants and fish eagles are often seen, as are the lake's hippos and crocodiles.

Lala Neck, Rocktail Bay and Black Rock

Continuing north past the forest station of **Manzengwenya** there is a dirt track running parallel to the coast which leads to three secluded beach beaches: **Lala Neck** (8 km), **Rocktail Bay** (12 km) and **Black Rock** (20 km). These are renowned for being among the ultimate game fishing sites in South Africa. **Lala Neck** and **Black Rock** have clear waters that offer spectacular opportunities for snorkelling and diving, with good chances of seeing turtles and sharks as well as hundreds of colourful tropical fish. There are no facilities here (other than one upmarket place to stay) but there is a day entry fee of R20 per person.

Ndumo Game Reserve ⬤ ▸▸ *pp553-556. Colour map 2, C6.*

ⓘ *Park gates Apr-Sep 0600-1800, Oct-Mar 0500-1900; office daily 0800-1200, 1300-1600. R35 per person, plus R35 per vehicle. Shop sells beer, wine, soft drinks but no food.*

Ndumo is a low-lying and humid tropical floodplain renowned for its magnificent birdlife and large numbers of crocodiles and hippos. This is one of the wildest and most beautiful reserves in South Africa and its verdant wetlands have been compared with the Okavango Delta. The area had been heavily hunted since the 1850s. Early hunters left records of having seen large herds of game here, but within 50 years a huge proportion of them had been shot. One of the species which has recovered well is the nyala which was hunted here by Courtney Selous. He visited this region at the turn of the last century to capture nyala for London Zoo.

Ins and outs

Getting there and around From Jozini the road heads directly north to Ndumo. The reserve is 14 km beyond the village of Ndumo on a rough dirt road and lies along the border of Mozambique. The roads are in good condition and visitors can drive around the reserve in their own cars or travel by Land Rover with a guide. There are five game viewing hides to stop at and a leaflet is available for a self-guided car trail.

Wildlife

The reserve was initially established in 1924 to protect the hippos which lived here. As human activity has decreased the animal population of the park has increased dramatically. Some species have been reintroduced and the varied flora of the reserve,

To Mozambique via Ponta do Ouro

The R22 is tarred all the way to the border but on the Mozambique side it is soft sand and a 4WD is required. However, there is the option of parking a vehicle safely at the border and pre-arrange for the Mozambique lodges south of Maputo to come and pick you up.

Border opening hours The border post is small but open daily 0800-1700.

Customs and immigration Mozambique visas are available, payable in South African rand or US dollars.

which includes numerous pans and reedbeds interspersed with patches of riverine forest and mixed woodland, provides habitats for many different species.

The pans at Banzi and Nyamithi are fascinating areas to experience the atmosphere of an African tropical swamp. There are many waterbirds to look out for on the pans including some rare tropical species at the southern limit of their habitats. Thousands of birds congregate here in the evenings and it is possible to see flocks of flamingos, geese, pelicans and storks.

Buffalo are occasionally seen in the swampy areas of the reserve, but nyala, hippo and crocodiles are present in large numbers. The vegetation in the rest of the reserve is quite thick and makes game viewing difficult. Black and white rhino, leopard and suni antelope thrive in these thickets but they are very rarely seen. A good way to see Ndumo is on one of the tours organized by the reserve. It is possible to go on five different guided walks with a game ranger.

Tembe Elephant Park ● ➤ pp553-556. Colour map 2, C6.

ⓘ 72 km from Jozini. Park gates Apr-Sep 0600-1800, Oct-Mar 0500-1900; office daily 0700-1600. R35 per person, plus R35 vehicle.

The reserve was established in 1983 to protect this area's elephant population, which had declined to just 130. They used to migrate over the border into Mozambique but suffered greatly at the hands of poachers; scars left by poachers can still be seen on some of the older elephants. This herd is reckoned to be the only indigenous elephants in KwaZulu Natal. The 30,000-ha protected area at Tembe is a vast impenetrable wilderness of sand forest, thick bush and the Muzi Swamp. This is a very special place to visit, but you will need to plan well in advance, given the strict access controls.

Ins and outs

Getting there Tembe lies on the border with Mozambique between Ndumo Game Reserve and Kosi Bay. It is 72 km from Jozini and although the road is tarred as far as the entrance to the park, the roads inside are so rough that only 4WDs are allowed in. If you are staying at the luxury lodge (the only accommodation within the park), you can leave your car at the gate and arrange for a 4WD transfer.

Wildlife

In addition to overnight visitors staying in the lodge, only a further five groups of day visitors in a 4WD are allowed into the park each day. Each group is accompanied by a park ranger and there are good chances of seeing Tembe's abundant game and birdlife. Some

Elephants crossing

Ndumo Game Reserve and Tembe Elephant Park are now part of the Ndumo-Tembe-Futi Transfrontier Conservation Area (commonly known as the Futi Corridor). This will eventually conserve 79,500 ha of elephant habitat and link the two parks with Maputo Special Reserve, also known as Maputo Elephant Reserve, over the border in Mozambique. In 1986 the South African Defence Force erected an electrified fence between South Africa and Mozambique due to the civil war across the border. This blocked a natural elephant migration path. By removing fences in the trans-frontier conservation area, the elephants' range has expanded. The approximate number of elephants in this area is 1350-1500 in Tembe, 600 in Ndumo, and 250 in Maputo Special Reserve.

of the more common species to be seen include giraffe, elephant, waterbuck, zebra, nyala and buffalo. Lion have been introduced to the park, now making it home to the Big Five. If you are lucky you may see the small, shy, suni antelope and a leopard. There are two hides in the reserve: one at Ponweni by Muzi swamp, this overlooks an elephant crossing point; the second overlooks Mahlasela Pan. There is also a self-guided walk within the Ngobazane enclosure area.

Kosi Bay Nature Reserve ● ▸▸ pp553-556. Colour map 2, C6.

ⓘ *96 km from Jozini. Park gates open Apr-Sep, 0600-2000, Oct-Mar 0500-2000; office daily 0700-1600. R20 per person, R15 per vehicle.*

Kosi Bay is one of South Africa's favourite wilderness destinations. The protected area is over 25 km long and consists of four lakes separated from the sea by a long strip of forest-covered dunes. Lakes Amanzimnyama, Nhlange, Mpungwini and Sifungwe are part of a fascinating tropical wetland environment. Lake Amanzimnyama is a freshwater lake with darkened water due to decomposing plants. The shores of the lakes are bordered with reedbeds, ferns, swamp figs and umdoni trees. Five species of mangrove thrive in the estuary. Kosi Bay is home to South Africa's only remaining estuarine hunter-gatherer tribe, the Tembe-Thonga, whose traditional fishing traps you can see across the estuary.

Ins and outs

Getting there and around From Jozini head north as if going to Ndumo but stay on the road through the villages of Sihangwana and Ngwanase, from where the entrance gate to Kosi is around 10 km to the north. Alternatively, take the R22 north from Mbazwana and Sodwana Bay. There is a rough dirt road leading to the park and access to Kosi Mouth itself is through deep sand for which a 4WD is needed. The nearest petrol station and supermarket are at Kwangwanase.

Best time to visit The tropical climate here can be debilitatingly hot and humid. The best time to visit is in August and September, which are the coolest months and tend not to be so humid.

Wildlife

The lakes are inhabited by hippos and crocodiles, which can be seen basking in the sun around Lake Amanzimnyama. There are no large mammals here but you are likely to see

To Swaziland via Golela

Just after the Pongola Nature Reserve is Golela and the border with Swaziland. From here it is possible to head north into Swaziland through **Lavumisa**. This is not a very interesting place and most people pass straight through. The alternative route into Swaziland is to head west into Mpumalanga along the N2 towards **Piet Retief**.

Border opening hours Daily 0700-2200.

Customs and immigration You will need a valid passport.

Facilities Fuel and snacks are available here and there is a basic hotel.

Public transport Continuing on into Swaziland is relatively easy as this is one of the busiest crossings into Swaziland, with many local buses plying the route between Lavumisa and Manzini.

Vehicle formalities If you are driving a hired car, make sure you get a letter from your car hire firm confirming that you may take the car out of South Africa.

samango and vervet monkeys. The tropical climate is a boon to reptiles and two species of monitor lizard, the Rock and the Nile, are often seen. Many of the snakes which live here are poisonous. The gaboon adder, boomslang, green mamba and forest cobras are all found here.

Many aquatic birds are attracted to the lakes and over 200 species have been spotted here. Rarities include the palmnut vulture and Pel's fishing owl.

The research station at Bhanga Nek has been tagging turtles and protecting nesting sites since 1963. Leatherback and loggerhead turtles arrive on these beaches after lengthy journeys from as far away as Madagascar and the Cape.

Exploring the reserve

A four-day trail, recently taken over by the local community, can be booked on T035-5920234. The trail is 34 km long and is probably the best way to see the Kosi Bay Nature Reserve. Hikers are accompanied by a guide who leads the group through the entire ecosystem. The distances covered every day are quite short so this gives ample time to relax and enjoy the atmosphere of the lakes. The trail is very popular and can be fully booked up to six months in advance, a maximum of 10 people are allowed on each trail. More information can be found at www.kznwildlife.com.

Northwest along the N2 ● ⤻ pp553-556.

Returning to the N2 via Jozini, the highway heads northwest towards Pongola and Swaziland. The Pongola Dam can be seen lying to the east with the Lebombo Mountains in the background. The entrance to the Pongola Nature Reserve is clearly signposted off the N2.

Pongola Nature Reserve → Colour map 2, C5.

① *The reserve is accessed from the right of the N2 approximately 25 km before the town of Pongola. Take the Golela turn-off to Swaziland for 10 km. At Golela take the road turning right and follow this road to the main entrance gate. Park gates open summer 0500-1900, winter 0600-1800. R20 per person, plus R20 per vehicle.*

This large area of bush surrounding the dam has been declared a biosphere reserve and large game was reintroduced some years ago. These include white rhino, elephant, giraffe, blue wildebeest and zebra that now live alongside resident nyala, kudu, impala, suni antelope, reedbuck and warthog. The dam itself has significant populations of hippo and crocodile, and the elusive tiger fish that lures fishermen every year for the annual tiger-fishing competition. The landscape is rolling grasslands interspersed with acacias and patches of thick bush. There is a beautiful stretch of lush riverine woodland along the Pongola River and the dam itself attracts thousands of aquatic birds during the winter months (probably the best time to visit as the tracks within the reserve become impassable after rain in the summer months). Interestingly, this was the site of the first game reserve in Africa, proclaimed by Paul Kruger in 1894, which comprised 17,400 ha of farmland between Swaziland, the Lebombo Mountains and the Pongola River. The Anglo-Boer War doomed the existence of the reserve but the Pongola Nature Reserve was reinstated in 1964.

Itala Game Reserve ● ►► pp553-556. Colour map 5, A2.

ⓘ 74 km east of Pongola, 400 km north of Durban and 500 km from Johannesburg, T034-9832540. Park gates Oct-Mar 0500-1900, Apr-Sep 0600-1800; Reception office at Ntshondwe Camp, daily 0700-1930; R35 per person, plus R30 per vehicle.

The R69 heads west off the N2 at Candova. The gravel road goes as far as Magudu. From there the R69 is tarred leading to the Ithala Game Reserve. This section of the R69 is a fascinating drive through rural Zululand, passing through low-lying grasslands and cattle-ranching country. In November and December, after the rains, the countryside is green and lush and rich in birdlife. Many private game reserves and farms have opened over recent years, stocking their land with game bought at the annual game auctions that occur in the area. Ithala reserve was established in 1972 after the Natal Parks Board began buying farms on the land lying between the top of the escarpment at Louwsburg and the Pongola River Valley. After years of overgrazing the land had seriously deteriorated and very little wildlife remained. In the last 30 years Ithala has been transformed into one of KwaZulu Natal's most spectacular reserves.

Ins and outs

Getting there From Durban, travel north on the N2 as far as Pongola. From here take the R66 and then the R69 for 73 km and the park entrance is near the village of Louwsburg. From Gauteng the easiest route is via the N2 to Pongola, though the park can also be approached via Vryheid from the Battlefield region.

Getting around There is a network of dirt roads looping around the reserve which offer good game viewing by car. Large herds of grazers are often seen on the grasslands. Near the airstrip look out for white rhino and tsessebe and particularly cheetah, which favour grass airstrips because of their openness. There are also some self-guided walking trails passing through forest.

Best time to visit The climate is warm all year round but it can get cold in the evenings from May to August when there are occasional frosts. Most of the rain falls in the summer months of November, December and January.

Safety The rivers at Thalu and Mbiso camps are not infected with bilharzia and are safe for swimming.

Wildlife and vegetation

The reserve's landscapes are mostly large areas of low-lying grasslands at 400 m rising up through steep-sided forested valleys to granite cliffs at 1450 m. The streams in these mountains flow down into the Pongola River. The steep terrain has created several different ecosystems from deep narrow valleys and boulder outcrops to cliff faces, with an interesting diversity of wildlife. Twenty new species have been reintroduced into the reserve including a herd of young elephant and the only herd of tsessebe in Natal. Animals commonly seen include eland, giraffe, kudu, blue wildebeest and zebra. The following animals are also present here but are rarely seen: cheetah, white rhino, elephant, klipspringer, leopard, nyala and black rhino. For visitors wanting to see the park on foot, guided day hikes (as well as self-guided trails) can be booked at reception (see details, above).

Some 320 species of bird have been recorded here, including black eagle, bathawk, bald ibis, martial eagle and brown-necked parrot. Some interesting plants to look out for in season are the flowering aloes trees, unmistakable in June and July when they come into bloom. Their large orange flowers are an important source of nectar at this time of year and they attract birds and insects.

⦿ Maputaland listings

Hotel and guesthouse prices
L over US$300 **AL** US$220-300 **A** US$150-220
B US$100-150 **C** US$75-100 **D** US$35-75
E US$15-35 **F** under US$15
Private game reserves
L4 over US$900 **L3** US$550-900
L2 US$450-550 **L1** US$300-500
Restaurant prices
⛾⛾⛾ over US$30 **⛾⛾** US$15-30 **⛾** under US$15
See pages 46-51 for further information.

⦿ Sleeping

Mkhuze Game Reserve *p544*

The prices for the following are for the whole lodge or cottage; when split among a group, they are quite good value. Reservations: **KZN Wildlife**, T033-8451000, www.kznwildlife.com. Camping is booked directly, T035-5730001.
AL Nhlonhlela. This luxury 8-bed bush lodge looks out over the fever trees and Nhlonhlela Pan. There is a central lounge and kitchen where a cook will prepare your meals and there's a game guard for guided bush walks.
A Ghost Mountain Inn, T035-5731025-7, www.ghostmountaininn.co.za. Next to the northern entrance to Mkhuze. 52 rooms,

a/c, stylish decor, TV, restaurant, spa and swimming pool. Good-value safari packages. The inn also owns **Moyeni Lodge**, a remote self-catering lodge sleeping up to 8, very private, set up in the mountains with impressive views.
B-D Mantuma. The main camp with a variety of cottages, including 2 7-bed cottages with 3 bedrooms, 2 bathrooms and fully equipped kitchen; 5 4-bed en suite bungalows with 2 bedrooms and fully equipped kitchen; 4 3-bed en suite chalets with fully equipped kitchen; 10 2-bed and 3 3-bed tents raised on a wooden deck with en suite bathrooms and communal open-plan kitchen; 6 3-bed rest huts with communal kitchen and ablution block. This is the largest camp, the buildings are set among natural gardens and are not fenced off from the reserve so game does sometimes wander through. There is also a pool and a shop; game drives and guided walks can be arranged.

Camping

Campsite 1 km from the main gate, 9 km from Mantuma, can accommodate 60 people, ablution blocks with hot and cold water.

Sodwana Bay p547

The supermarket sells petrol and oil and stocks bread, tinned food and beach gear. Freezer drawers are available for hire and should be booked in advance, but at R30 for 24 hrs they are expensive.

B Sodwana Bay Camp, KZN Wildlife, T033-8451000, www.kznwildlife.com. 10 8-bed and 10 5-bed self-catering fully equipped log cabins, some recently renovated.

B Sodwana Bay Camp, T035-5716000, www.sodwanadiving.co.za. Accommodation is in 20 twin-bedded reed and thatch huts on stilts overlooking woodland, restaurant serving seafood (what else) bar, pool, game-fishing trips available. The lodge offers a number of all-inclusive diving package deals plus a full range of PADI courses, with a fully equipped dive shop and learning pool.

E-F Gwalagwala is a large campsite with 413 basic sites in the main section which can become very crowded, plus 33 luxury sites with their own water and electricity supplies. Camping is booked directly T035-5710051/3.

Heading north from Mbazwana p548
Private lodges and camps

L3 Thonga Beach Lodge, on the coast 6 km from Lake Sibaya, T035-4756000, www.isibindiafrica.co.za. New super luxury lodge with 24 spacious a/c thatched suites with stone bathrooms, reed walls, large open windows, built on stilts in the forest, each very private, bar and restaurant with ocean views, rates inclusive of meals. Activities include turtle tracking, kayaking on Lake Sibaya, diving and snorkelling. The lodge is set in one of the most isolated stretches of the Coastal Forest Reserve and is the ideal place for a tropical beach holiday. It lies on the strip of forested dunes between Lake Sibaya and the sea, and a path connecting the camp to the beach passes through thick tropical forest rich in birdlife. Lying just offshore is a fascinating area of rarely visited coral reefs and rock pools, but it's only possible to visit here in a 4WD. Guests can leave their 2WD cars at a cashew nut factory approx 40 km north of Mbazwana and the lodge will collect them by 4WD.

L2 Rocktail Bay Lodge, 12 km north of Manzengwenya along a dirt track running parallel with the beach, www.rocktailbay.com. A luxury bush camp with 11 A-frame chalets set on stilts among dunes and coastal forest a few hundred metres from the beach and the Indian Ocean. A wide range of activities available including birdwatching, diving, snorkelling, swimming, fishing and 4WD trips to nearby beaches and Lake Sibaya. The highlight of a stay here is a night-time search for egg-laying turtles on the beach just below the lodge. Access is by 4WD only. Same arrangement as above for pickups at the cashew nut factory. Reservations through **Wilderness Safaris**, Johannesburg, T011-8830747, www.wilderness-safaris.com.

Ndumo Game Reserve p548

D Ndumo Camp, KZN Wildlife, T033-8451000, www.kznwildlife.com. 7 2-bed rest huts, with a/c and private verandas. Lovely setting overlooking the Pongola floodplain, surrounded by tropical vegetation. Well-equipped kitchen, swimming pool. Cook on hand to prepare meals (but guests must bring their own food). Game drives can be arranged from here.

Camping

8 sites near the hutted camp, with kitchen and ablution block, T035-5910058.

Tembe Elephant Park p549

L Tembe Elephant Lodge, T031-2670144, www.tembe.co.za. The bush camp consists of upmarket tents raised on wooden platforms tucked away in secluded areas. There are hot showers with glass walls that look out over the bush, small pool with thatched roof and relaxing veranda. Rates include meals and game drives, which are also available to day visitors by prior arrangement.

Kosi Bay Nature Reserve *p550*
L Kosi Forest Lodge, reservations
T035-5929239, www.isibindiafrica.co.za.
Luxury all-inclusive safari camp within the
reserve. 16-bed lodge, with individual reed
and thatch suites, beautiful hardwood
floors, open-air bathrooms, very secluded –
popular with honeymooners. Excellent
restaurant, bar, swimming pool. Beautiful
setting, range of activities on offer including
turtle-watching trips, canoeing and diving.
Non-4WD drivers can park cars at the Total
garage in KwaNgwanase and prearrange
a 4WD pickup by the lodge.
A-C Kosi Bay Lodge, 500 m from the lake,
500 m from the bay itself outside the reserve,
T035-5929561, www.kosibaylodge.co.za.
Restaurant, swimming pool, pub,
self-catering also an option, in A-frame
chalets with communal ablution block or
2-bed reed en suite huts. The lodge runs
trips to the eastern shore of the lake from
where you can hike 5 km to the beautiful
beaches. One of the cheaper options in the
region. Normal cars can reach here, only the
last 3 km are dirt road.
C-D Lake Nhlange Camp, KZN Wildlife,
T033-8451000, www.kznwildlife.com.
There are 3 thatched cabins here with
either 6, 5 or 2 beds. All 3 are fully equipped
for self-catering.

Camping
15 pitches with electricity points and
an ablution block among the trees near
Lake Nhlange, T035-5920236.

Northwest along the N2 *p551*
C Pongola Country Lodge, 14 Jan Mielie
St, Pongola, T034-4131352,
www.pongolacountrylodge.co.za. Hardly
a country lodge as it's next to an industrial
area in the village but pleasant enough
inside. 62 individually decorated rooms,
some on the small side, en suite, DSTV, a/c,
phone, parking outside of the rooms, pool,
extensive gardens, restaurant, bar.

D-F Pongola Caravan Park, 219 Hans Meyer
St, PO Box 539, Pongola, T034-4131789.
9 self-catering chalets, TV, a/c, shady and
grassed caravan and camping sites, all sites
have electric points, spotless ablution block,
mini-golf course, small kiosk with basic
camping supplies, ideal base for exploring
the region as well as Swaziland.

Camping
Pongola Nature Reserve, T034-4351012.
20 basic sites next to the dam, ablution block,
cold water only.

Private lodges and camps
L4 Mkuze Falls Private Game Reserve,
near the village of Mahlangasi, access off the
R66, T034-4141018, www.mkuzefalls.com.
Super luxury in 8 thatched chalets with
private plunge pool and open-air showers,
1 safari suite, or 5 en suite tents with a/c,
mosquito nets, all accommodation has
fantastic views of the waterfall on the
Mkhuze River, personal attentive service,
all-inclusive with meals and game drives.
The reserve is home to the Big Five.
L3 White Elephant Lodge, next to the
dam Pongola Nature Reserve, T034-4132489,
www.whiteelephant.co.za. A luxurious,
all-inclusive 5-star game lodge. The 8
elegant safari tents have a colonial theme
and en suite open-air baths. Lots of
activities on offer, including game drives,
guided mountain biking, boat cruises,
tiger fishing, rhino walks and short flights
in a 6-seater plane.
L1 Pakamisa Private Game Reserve, off
the R66, T034-4133559, www.pakamisa.co.za.
2500-ha estate that is home to several
species of antelope, giraffe and zebra, with
8 spacious luxury rooms designed in a
Spanish villa style with private balconies,
terrace restaurant overlooking the Pakamisa
Mountains, dinners 'out bush' can be
arranged, horse riding, game drives and
walks, clay pigeon shooting, swimming
pool. Rates are all inclusive.

Ithala Game Reserve *p552*
Reservations through **KZN Wildlife**,
T033-8451000, www.kznwildlife.com.
A Ntshondwe Lodge. Sleeps 6 in 3 luxurious
en suite double bedrooms, small plunge pool,
viewing deck, self-catering but with a cook.
Ingeniously camouflaged in a jumble of
boulders and flowering plants and trees.
Game drives and walks are available.
C-D Ntshondwe Camp. 25 2-bed and 12
4-bed self-catering chalets, with fully
equipped kitchens, a lounge and dining
room. Also 28 2-bed en suite units with no
cooking facilities. There's a shop, restaurant
serving meals and takeaways, bar and a
pool. The camp shop sells limited tinned
and dried food, wildlife books and charcoal
and petrol is on sale next to the main gates.
The nearest shop is in Louwsburg (5 km).

Bush camps
The camps are all self-catering but are
supplied with bedding and have a fully
equipped kitchen; the lodges are thatched
and built from natural materials. The camps
are set by themselves in the bush and guests
can game watch from the comfort of their
verandas in front of the huts or go on a game
walk accompanied by a guard. Price codes
refer to the price for 2 people although the
bush camps are only available for single
group bookings.
B Mbizo. Sleeps 8 in 2 lodges with a shared
lounge, kitchen and viewing deck. Overlooks
the rapids on the Mbizo River.
B Mhlangeni. Sleeps 10 in 2 lodges, and
is set in a rocky area overlooking the Ncence
River well away from the busiest areas of the
park and is renowned for its game viewing.
A central open-plan lounge and kitchen with
its own sundeck provide wonderful views.
B Thalu. 4-bed camp with kitchen, lounge
and viewing deck on the banks of the
Thalu River.

Camping
Campsite, Main camp, T034-9832540.
Ablution block with 1 toilet and cold
showers only. Maximum 20, tents only,
caravans not permitted. Animals can
be seen wandering around and it's a
great place for wilderness camping.

▲ Activities and tours

Sodwana Bay *p547*
Coral Divers, T033-3456531,
www.coraldivers.co.za, is consistently
recommended. PADI courses from open
water to dive master and include dorm
accommodation, equipment but no meals
or park entry fees. Open water courses start
from R2350. It has its own backpacker resort
at Sodwana with bar, restaurant, deck, pool,
TV room and internet access, and will pick
you up from Hluhluwe for an extra R100.
Ghost Mountain Inn, T035-5731025,
www.ghostmountaininn.co.za, offers a
range of all-inclusive safari tours in the
area, ranging from 1-5 days.

⊖ Transport

Sodwana Bay *p547*
This is a relatively remote part of the coast
and until recently it was only accessible to
people with 4WDs. Now many of the roads
have been tarred, it's possible to get to the
coastal reserves in a normal car, or at least
get part way there, park, and arrange 4WD
transfers to the lodges. See individual
listings for details.

The **Baz Bus**, T021-4392323,
www.bazbus.com, drops passengers off
at the Isinkwe Backpackers near **Hluhluwe**
on its way north to **Swaziland**.

Contents

Footprint features

Gauteng

At a glance

Getting around Buses and Baz Bus on major routes, car hire, tours start and finish in Johannesburg.

Time required 2-4 days.

Weather Cold, dry and sunny in winter, summer thunder showers.

When not to go Good all year.

Loud, brash and rich, Johannesburg has long been both the bane and lifeblood of South Africa. Since its sudden birth in 1886 when a hapless Aussie discovered gold on the highveld, it has dominated the country, morphing from a rough and debauched frontier town into a financial metropolis with a good deal of debauchery still imbedded in its fabric. Built on a high plateau surrounded by the world's richest gold mines, Johannesburg dominates Gauteng. The high-rise city centre is surrounded by some 600 suburbs: to the north lie the realms of the wealthy and white, while in the southwest is the vast township of Soweto. Although the city has suffered from much-publicized high crime rates, it is now dusting off its dodgy reputation and drawing back visitors for the first time in over a decade. Crime busting regeneration programmes have seen areas like run-down Newtown transformed and filled with restaurants and shops, while recent additions include some of South Africa's finest cutting-edge museums, including the Apartheid Museum. The northern suburbs are an enclave of posh boutiques, good restaurants and sophisti-cated nightlife, while Soweto now attracts more tourists than Kruger National Park.

Fifty kilometres to the north is the capital of the state, Pretoria. Although connected by an almost unbroken ribbon of development, the two cities couldn't be more different. Pretoria is staid and conservative, with wide streets lined with jacaranda trees which bloom a ladylike purple in spring. The centre feels peaceful and orderly, with attractive sandstone buildings and large, tidy parks. Pretoria has long been a centre of Afrikanerdom, best summed up by the sombre Voortrekker Monument. But its conservative feel has mellowed of late, with a lively student population and the influx of a multi-lingual diplomatic community.

Neither Johannesburg nor Pretoria merit more than a couple of days' exploration; if you're on a tight schedule, a day or two will cover the major sights and give you time to explore the excellent shopping and dining opportunities, some of the best in Africa. However, it is the area's history and its excellent museums which give a real feel for the country's troubled past – and for the shape of its future.

Arriving by air

OR Tambo International Airport ① *Kempton Park, T011-9216262, www.airports.co.za,* is 24 km from the city centre and 35 km from the northern suburbs on the R24, roughly halfway between Johannesburg and Pretoria. Both cities can be reached by car in 30 minutes. There are two terminals, one catering for international flights and the other for domestic flights. The terminals are next to each other, and passengers have to walk between the two (along a safe pavement), taking about five minutes, but a new building is being constructed to connect the two. The airport has been undergoing steady redevelopment in recent years and is now a slick complex, and one of the most important hubs for air travel in the southern hemisphere. The airport had a name change in 2006 to honour late anti-Apartheid activist Oliver Reginald Tambo.

To check the status of a flight, send an SMS to T35007 with the flight number, in reply to which you'll receive up-to-date flight details.

Facilities for international passengers include food courts, some decent shops and several banks. **Rennie's/Thomas Cook** and **American Express** branches are open 0530-2130 and there are a number of ATMs. In international arrivals, there is a cell phone and South African SIM card hire counter and a post office. Note that the airport post office can put post on the next flight to Europe for a small fee, in addition to the cost of postage. This is as close to overnight delivery you can get apart from sending via a courier service. The duty-free shops in international departures are extensive and the terminal now resembles a typical South African shopping mall. **Lock-up Luggage**, T011-3902064, can provide 24-hour secure luggage storage as well as curio wrapping and packaging service.

Opposite the two terminals is the **Parkade Centre**, a multi-storey car park and site of all car hire offices (see Transport, page 586) and shuttle bus companies. **Magic Bus** ① *T011-5480822, www.magicbus.co.za,* and **Airport Link** ① *T011-7922017, www.airportlink.co.za,* drop off at the major hotels in Johannesburg and Pretoria. Metered taxis can be found outside the main terminal building but tend to be more expensive than the shuttle services and drivers often do not know the way without direction.

All the hotels located within the environs of the airport offer a free pickup shuttle service, and a drop-off service for a nominal fee. Opposite the main terminal building are a series of hotel bus stops where the hotel shuttles come and go, but at quieter times of the day you may need to phone the hotel to tell them you are waiting. Some backpacker hostels also offer free pickups, so phone ahead to check.

● *Johannesburg Airport is served by almost 60 airlines, more than 17 million passengers pass through each year, and it employs 18,000 people. With a growth rate in passenger traffic of 10% per annum, it has overtaken Cairo and Dubai airports.*

Best time to visit

The area on which Johannesburg and Pretoria are located is known as the highveld, a high plateau with an average altitude of over 1500 m. The weather here can be extreme.

Arriving at night

Johannesburg International Airport is open 24 hours but most flights from Europe arrive in the early morning. If you do happen to arrive at night, you will find the airport perfectly safe, some restaurants and shops stay open and banking hours are until 2130. There are also ATMs.

Shuttle buses will collect you at any time though it is worth arranging this in advance, as the shuttle desks at the airport close at night. The same is true for the car hire companies. There are several hotels within a few kilometres of the airport that will collect you for free if you phone ahead.

Summer, from October to March, can get very hot, with most of the yearly rainfall, characterized by spectacular electric storms. Temperatures drop in winter, and during June and July frosts are common. Johannesburg also suffers from unpleasant yellow-tinged hazes before the arrival of the first rains in summer, when strong winds blow loose particles from the mine workings into the atmosphere.

Tourist information

The **Gauteng Tourism Authority** ① *1 Central Pl, corner of Jeppe and Henry Nxumalo streets, Newtown, T011-6391600, www.visitgauteng.net,* is responsible for information for the whole province. It's a fairly new office with only has a small selection of maps and brochures, but its staff are very helpful and will advise you on sites and attractions. **Johannesburg Tourism Company** ① *Grosvenor Corner, 195 Jan Smuts Av, Parktown, T011-2140700, www.joburgtourism.co.za,* is a rather odd set-up, with limited information in the walk-in office but a good website. The **City Council** ① *www.joburg.org.za,* also has tourist information on its excellent website, which covers every aspect of the city. For information on Pretoria contact the **Tshwane Tourism Information Bureau** ① *Old Nederlandsche Bank Building, Church Sq, T012-3581430, www.tshwane.gov.za.*

Johannesburg

→ Phone code: 011. Colour map 2, C2.

Johannesburg is the largest financial, commercial and industrial centre in South Africa. Barely over 100 years old, the discovery of gold transformed this deserted heartland into a vast urban sprawl and made it one of the wealthiest cities in the world. The gold rush brought in settlers from all over the world creating a multiracial and cosmopolitan city, but Apartheid changed all that. Forced relocations altered the fabric of Johannesburg, creating deep divisions in society that still remain evident today. Despite Apartheid's demise, Johannesburg is still mostly segregated, albeit no longer by legal requisite. The city centre and neighbouring suburbs, such as Hillbrow, are largely home to the urban black population, a condensed area of overcrowded high-rise flats where poverty and crime is rife. Soweto is a vast, sprawling township of government housing and informal settlements, home to the majority of Johannesburg's black commuters. Most white residents, on the other hand, live in the leafy and affluent northern suburbs.

But things are changing. Soweto has become a city in its own right, with new affluent suburbs and a fast-growing middle class, while a breed of wealthy, successful black people – known locally as 'Buppies' (Black Upwardly-mobile People) – have moved into what were until recently the reserves of rich whites. The notorious city centre, meanwhile, is undergoing extensive regeneration programmes, with streets being cleaned up and closed-circuit cameras deterring casual criminals. But while crime rates have dropped considerably, safety remains an issue, with most visitors, like most well-off locals, confining themselves to the safe suburbs and numerous shopping malls.
▶▶ For listings, see pages 576-587.

Ins and outs

Getting there

For detailed information on Johannesburg International Airport, see Arriving by air, page 560. The **railway station** and the **main bus terminal** are at the Park City Transit Centre. ▶▶ *For further details, see Transport, page 585.*

Getting around

Although public transport is improving in the city, it is still advisable to stick to private transport, hire cars and metered taxis. Locals rely mainly on minibus taxis, thousands of which ply the centre throughout the day, but these are not recommended for visitors due to high accident rates and issues of crime. The new **metrobuses** ① *T011-8335538, www.mbus.co.za*, are a far safer option, running along 100 routes in and around the city from 0600 to 1900. Tickets run on zones; the central zone is by the bus terminus in Gandhi Square (formerly Vaderbijl Square) at the corner of Main and Rissik streets where there is an information office. A single tickets costs from R3.80. If you hire a car, plan your route before setting out and always carry a map – the system of one-way streets and snaking highways can be utterly bewildering. The **Gautrain**, a new high-speed rail link between Johannesburg and Pretoria via the airport and Midrand is presently under construction and should be completed by 2009.

Orientation

The once-prosperous central business district is today a hectic muddle of abandoned office blocks, market stalls and concrete flyovers. Crime remains a problem here and most businesses have moved out to the safer northern suburbs, although recent regeneration projects are starting to draw back investment. A visit to the city centre is well worthwhile for an insight into how Johannesburg has developed over the decades, although it is recommended that you go on an organized tour.

Johannesburg's affluent suburbs are in the northern part of the city. Clustered around the main freeway to Pretoria, the M1, they feel far removed from the hectic bustle of the centre. These are the safest areas in town and home to most of the city's tourist accommodation.

1 Greater Johannesburg

➡ Johannesburg maps
1 Greater Johannesburg, page 563
2 Johannesburg centre, page 566
3 Sandton, page 570
4 Rosebank to Hyde Park, page 571
5 Soweto, page 573

Sleeping 😴
Westcliff 1

2 km
2 miles

The largest of Johannesburg's suburbs feels very different. The infamous township of **Soweto** lies southwest of the city, named because of its location – South West Township. Soweto is linked to the city by a number of freeways that carry hundreds of thousands of commuters to the city centre and northern suburbs each day. Adjoining Soweto to the south, are smaller townships where other communities were relocated during Apartheid; coloured people were forced to move to **Eldorado Park**, and Indians were moved to **Lenasia**.

Tourist information

Gauteng Tourism Authority ① *1 Central Pl, corner of Jeppe and Henry Nxumalo streets, Newtown, T011-6391600, www.visitgauteng.net, Mon-Fri 0800-1700*, is the main source of information in the city centre. There are also kiosks in the Mall of Rosebank at the **African Craft Market** ① *T011-3272000, daily 0900-1800*, **Sandton City Mall** ① *T011-7849596, daily 0900-1800* and **OR Tambo International Airport** ① *T011-3903614, daily 0600-2200*. All have a selection of maps and brochures and can help with accommodation. **Johannesburg Tourism Company** ① *Grosvenor Corner, 195 Jan Smuts Av, Parktown, T011-2140700, www.joburgtourism.co.za, Mon-Fri 0800-1700, Sat 0900-1300*, has limited information but an excellent website.

◗ *Johannesburg is a city full of trees, there are over six million on pavements, in parks and private residences. The city resembles a rainforest on pictures taken from satellites, making it one of the greenest urban areas in the world.*

Background

The city centre of Johannesburg is surrounded by some 600 suburbs covering approximately 500 sq km. The population of greater Johannesburg is roughly 3.2 million excluding Soweto. As it is almost impossible to estimate the population of Soweto due to the constant arrival of people from rural areas and illegal immigrants looking for work, the population of greater Johannesburg including Soweto is put at somewhere between six and eight million.

Much of Johannesburg's fabric was formed by the actions of the Apartheid regime from the mid-1950s. The thriving multi-racial conurbation (see page 568) was changed dramatically with the advent of the Group Areas Act, which forcibly relocated the city's black population from the centre to specially built townships outside town, such as Soweto. The most infamous forced removal was the bulldozing of an area to the west of Johannesburg called Sophiatown. This was an area of slum housing near to the city centre and was home to a diverse population of Africans, coloureds and 'poor whites'. During the 1940s and 1950s there was a huge outburst of a new African urban culture in Sophiatown, based mainly on the influence of American jazz musicians. This cultural explosion attracted bohemian whites and a huge number of African writers, journalists and politicians. To the Apartheid planners, the area stood for everything they opposed. In the mid-1950s the entire population was removed and the bulldozers were sent in. A new white suburb was built over the ruins and, in a gesture that was crass even by the standards of Apartheid, they named the new suburb Triomf – Afrikaans for 'triumph'. In 2006, the name was changed back to Sophiatown.

Since the mid-1980s this forced movement of Africans from the city centre to the townships has been reversed. The breakdown of influx controls led to the rapid growth of the African population of Johannesburg city centre, especially in Hillbrow, which has one

24 hours in Johannesburg

Start the day with a sumptuous breakfast at Fourno's Bakery. It's a great place to watch Jo'burg's high-fliers conduct power breakfasts over fashionable coffees.

Set off on a mind-expanding morning tour of Soweto, South Africa's oldest and most famous township. Drop in at Mandela's former home which is now a museum; drink a cool Castle lager in a *shebeen*; and visit the memorials and museums dedicated to the struggle against Apartheid.

Lunch at Rosebank Mall before hitting the shops. Jo'burger's love their shopping malls and Rosebank has an excellent African Craft Market and a lively rooftop flea market on a Sunday.

In the afternoon drive out to the Lion Park, where you can get close to lions and play with some cubs, then go to the Lesedi Cultural Village. After the two-hour tour of four authentic African villages recreated from the Xhosa, Zulu, Pedi and Sotho tribes, enjoy traditional dancing from over 60 performers around a large fire and dinner of game meat such as impala or crocodile.

Crack open a good bottle of South African wine at the stylish Blues Room in Sandton, one of the best jazz and blues venues in Gauteng, before heading to Melville, Jo'burg's happening nightlife district – two streets of bars, restaurants and late night lounges where people go to be seen.

---

of Africa's highest population densities. Since the end of Apartheid this trend has continued and has been bolstered by the arrival of new immigrants from outside South Africa's borders. Tens of thousands of Nigerians, Congolese and Zimbabweans have flooded, often illegally, into the centre, suburbs and townships. The population has mushroomed in the last decade, with a growth of around 23% since 1996.

The inner city has suffered from soaring crime rates in the last two decades, although much is being done to reverse the trend. While the mid-1990s saw much of central Johannesburg being deserted, with business and offices moving out to the northern suburbs, and the city being tagged as the murder capital of the world, the local government has clamped down in recent years. Massive raids on apartment blocks in Hillbrow have ousted thousands of illegal immigrants. An extensive network of CCTV cameras, a huge new Metro police force and numerous regeneration projects have made the centre far safer. Improved border security arrangements with neighbouring countries have blocked the traffic in stolen cars to other African countries, and the rate of carjackings has been reduced considerably. According to one study street crime in general has dropped dramatically, and you're just as likely to be a victim of violent crime in the Cape as in Johannesburg. The first of the regenerated areas was Newtown, where the streets were pedestrianized and the Mary Fitzgerald Square upgraded; the area is now filled with restaurants and shops and is attracting businesses back to the centre, including the new Gauteng tourism office. This is acting as a model for other parts of town, and it's hoped that the centre will once again become as safe as it once was.

Improved security is drawing back visitors, but its sensible to take common-sense precautions. Johannesburg is still not yet a city which can be casually explored on foot, and the best way of seeing the sights is on a guided tour.

City centre

The **Newtown** area, once the cultural heart of Johannesburg, has once again, after years of deterioration, become a popular spot with locals. A huge regeneration project, which saw the introduction of closed-circuit cameras, a police presence and the revamping of Mary Fitzgerald Square into a smart cobbled square, has transformed the area. Shops and cafés have moved in, and this is the site of the new **Gauteng Tourism Authority** office, see page 564. Unlike the rest of the city centre, it is safe to wander around the square and the facilities lining it including the Market Theatre, Museum Africa and Newtown Park. There is safe parking on the eastern part of Mary Fitzgerald Square, just

2 Johannesburg centre

200 metres
200 yards

Sleeping ⊜	Eating 🍴	Bars & clubs 🍸
Sunnyside Park 1	Gramadoelas 1	Bassline 3
	Moyo 1	Kippies 2

in front of the Museum Africa, and behind at the back of the Market Theatre. Newtown can now be accessed from Braamfontein in the north by the new Nelson Mandela Bridge that spans over 40 railway lines.

The **Museum Africa** ① *Old Market Building, 121 Bree St, T011-8335624, Tue-Sun 0900-1700, free,* is one of the city's major museums, but despite its reputation it is rather run down and disappointing. Housed in the city's former fruit and vegetable market, it attempts to explain the black experience of living in Johannesburg. There are displays on the struggle for democracy and on life in the goldmines and the townships, with mock-ups of an informal settlement. On the second floor is a gallery dedicated to San rock art and the most popular gallery is called 'Tried for Treason', with some interesting original editions of newspapers dating from treason trials in the 1960s, although the displays pale in comparison to those of the Apartheid Museum (see page 569). Perhaps most rewarding is the ground floor gallery, with changing temporary exhibitions, including some excellent photography shows. There is a small café and gift shop by the entrance.

The **Market Theatre Complex**, next to Museum Africa, is the main hub of the area's regeneration. As well as the theatre, there is the **Market Theatre Mall** (a series of small craft shops), and a couple of popular restaurants and bars, with stalls strung along the street selling Zulu beadwork, jewellery and crafts. At weekends, the market expands into Mary Fitzgerald Square, which also holds special events and occasional live music. In one corner is a giant TV screen that shows important sports matches. The theatre itself is one of the best and most established in Gauteng (see page 582).

The **KwaZulu Muti Museum of Man and Science** ① *corner of Diagonal (14) and President St, T011-8364470, Mon-Fri 0730-1700, Sat 0730-1300.* This isn't actually a museum but a *muti* shop which has been on this site since 1897. *Muti* is a form of witchcraft practised exclusively by witch doctors, and this shop is crammed with products used in traditional herbal medicine and magic. The ingredients on sale include leaves, seeds and bark, as well as more specialized items like monkey skulls, dried crocodiles and ostrich feet.

South African Breweries' (SAB) **World of Beer** ① *15 President St, T011-8364900, www.worldofbeer.co.za, Tue-Sat 1000-1800, R25 including 2 complimentary beers, pub lunches available,* will appeal to anyone who enjoys the golden nectar. SAB dominate the African beer industry and control many local breweries throughout southern and eastern Africa and now owns Miller Lite in the US. Their flagship lager, Castle, is probably now the most popular beer between Cape Town and Cairo. The 90-minute tour covers the brewing process, a greenhouse that nurtures ingredients, and a variety of mock-up bars from a township *shebeen* to a honky-tonk pub from Johannesburg's mining camps.

Further east between Marshall and Commissioner streets, Gandhi Square is the main terminus for the Metrobuses in the city centre. Built in 1893 as Government Square, it was renamed after Mahatma Gandhi in 1999 and was completely refurbished in 2002. Gandhi came to Johannesburg in 1902 and worked as a lawyer and civil rights activist (see page 474). There's a statue of him in his lawyer's robes and carrying a law book and there are plaques around the square telling the history of his time in South Africa. To the south of the square is a line of shops and restaurants and the entrance to a new shopping mall that leads through to Marshall Street.

To get a feel for why locals call it the Manhattan of Africa, head to the **Top of Africa** ① *Carlton Tower, daily 0900-1700, R7.* Amidst the hectic highrises and run-down office blocks in the centre of town, the soaring Carlton Tower is a popular stop-off for tours. The lift whisks visitors up to the 50th floor, from where a glass-fronted lookout deck is wrapped around the building. The views are astounding, the glittering grid of skyscrapers

City of gold

The high plateau on which Johannesburg was built was originally an arid place inhabited by a few Boer farmers grazing cattle and cultivating maize and wheat. This harsh and isolated landscape was transformed after the discovery of gold in 1886. During the 1880s, prospectors began arriving in the Eastern Transvaal attracted by reports of gold in Barberton and the mountains of the Eastern Drakensberg. George Harrison arrived from the Cape and travelled north to look at an abandoned gold mine on a farm in the Witwatersrand. He was employed to build a farmhouse at Langlaagte but in his free time he continued his search for gold. He discovered Main Reef in March 1886 and travelled to Pretoria to register his claim. Within weeks hordes of prospectors and fortune hunters began to arrive and officials of the Pretoria government were quickly sent to inspect the diggings and to lay out plans for a town.

Johannesburg expanded at a phenomenal rate and within three years had become the largest town in the eastern Transvaal. Confidence in Johannesburg's future was so great that traders in other regions of South Africa dismantled their wood and corrugated-iron buildings and transported the component parts to reassemble them in the new boom town. *The Star* newspaper relocated to Johannesburg from Grahamstown and transported its printing press across the veld by ox wagon. The gold rush attracted people from all over the world and Johannesburg became a cosmopolitan town where vast fortunes could be made overnight. Gambling dens, brothels and riotous canteens lined the streets and hundreds of ox-drawn wagons arrived daily to deliver food, drink and building supplies.

The mines expanded as new technologies opened up the deeper deposits of gold and Johannesburg was gradually transformed from being a gold rush boom town to being a large modern industrial city.

tapering out to an endless urban sprawl. There are good views of Gandhi Square from here, too, as well as the few remaining historical buildings left in the centre, such as City Hall (1915) and the post office (1897). There is a little curio shop and a café.

To the north of the centre is **Constitution Hill** ① *1 Kotze St, Braamfontein, T011-2745300, www.constitutionhill.org.za, Mon-Fri 0900-1700, Sat-Sun 0900-1200, R22, the complex is completely wheelchair accessible*, the site of the notorious Old Fort Prison Complex. Opened in 2004, this is one of Johannesburg's newest tourist attractions and, in a similar way to the Apartheid Museum, it uses multimedia tools to display its exhibits. Known as Number Four, the old prison, which only closed in the 1980s, was known for holding hundreds of blacks in appalling overcrowded conditions; most had been arrested for not carrying their pass books. Illustrious prisoners include Nelson Mandela, Mahatma Gandhi and many of the leading anti-Apartheid activists. You can wander around the complex yourself or there are regular tours, which include a video about Mandela's time here, a tour of the women's gaol and a photo exhibition of ex-inmates and wardens. You can still see graffiti on the backs of the cell doors and the giant pots that prisoners ate simple porridge from. South Africa's Constitutional Court has recently been built here and some of the old bricks from the old prison were used in the new court to demonstrate the injustice of the past being used towards justice in the future. The site is seen as an important symbol of the changes that the country has witnessed since 1994, and it's another of the city's excellent contemporary museums.

Not far from Constitution Hill at the top of Rissik Street, is the Miner's Monument. The bronze statue of three giant miners in shorts, hard hats and gum boots holding a giant drill was erected by the Chamber of Mines in 1964. The Civic Theatre is just to the north of here (see page 582).

Outside the city centre

Twenty years ago, few people would have believed that the **Apartheid Museum** ⓘ *next to Gold Reef City, T011-3904700, www.apartheidmuseum.org, Tue-Sun 1000-1700, entry R25,* could ever exist. Today, this is the most critically acclaimed museum in the country and an excellent insight to what South Africa – past and present – is all about. This extraordinarily powerful museum was officially opened by Nelson Mandela in April 2002 and is the city's leading tourist attraction. The museum is divided into 'spaces' which follow the birth of Apartheid to the present day. When paying your entry fee you are issued with a random white or non-white ticket that takes you through two different entry points to symbolize segregation. The building itself has an innovative design to reflect the cold subject of Apartheid – harsh concrete, raw brick, steel bars and barbed wire.

The museum begins with a 15-minute video, taking you briefly through Voortrekker history to the Afrikaner government of 1948 which implemented Apartheid. The 'spaces' are dedicated to the rise of nationalism in 1948, pass laws, segregation, the first response from townships such as Sharpeville and Langa, the forced removals and the implementation of the Group Areas Act. From here, exhibits cover the rise of Black Consciousness, the student uprisings in Soweto in 1976, and political prisoners and executions.

The reforms during the 1980s and 1990s are well documented including President FW DeKlerk's un-banning of political parties, Mandela's release, the 1994 election, sanction lifting, and the new constitution. One of the most interesting 'spaces' is the House of Bondage, named after a book of photographs published in 1967 by Ernest Cole and banned in South Africa at the time. A white photographer, he managed to class himself as coloured in order to go into the townships and take the pictures. The black and white photographs are both tragic and beautiful. The exhibitions effectively use multimedia, such as television screens, recorded interviews and news footage, all providing a startlingly clear picture of the harshness and tragedy of the Apartheid years. Allow at least three or four hours for a visit.

The **Johannesburg Zoo** ⓘ *Jan Smuts Av, Parktown, T011-6462000, www.jhbzoo.org.za, daily 0830-1730, last ticket 1600, R36,* has over 400 different species of birds and animals set in an area of parkland and gardens. Covering 54 ha of spacious enclosures surrounded by moats and trees, the zoo is home to over 2000 animals from 355 species. The only polar bears in Africa can be found in the zoo. The ponds attract free-ranging aquatic birds, which come here to breed. All the enclosures have been upgraded and the night tours to see the nocturnal animals are fun, ending with marshmallows and hot chocolate around a bonfire. There is a small restaurant here for light meals and drinks.

Near the Johannesburg Zoo is the **South African National Museum of Military History** ⓘ *20 Erlswold Way, Saxonwold, T011-6465513, www.militarymuseum.co.za, daily 0900-1630, R20,* which has exhibits on the role South African forces played in the Second World War including artillery pieces, aircraft and tanks. There is a more up-to-date section illustrating the war in Angola with displays of modern armaments including captured Soviet tanks and French Mirage fighter planes. *CASSPIRS*, the armoured personnel carriers used by security forces in the townships during black uprisings against Apartheid are on display.

Origins Centre ① *Wits University, Braamfontein, which can be accessed from both Bertha St and Yale Rd on the east and west of the university respectively, T011-7174700, www.originscentre.co.za, daily 0900-1700, R45, children R25.* This is another of Johannesburg's excellent new attractions which was opened in 2006 by President Mbeki in a chocolate brown building on the campus of Wits University. Wits's Rock Art Research Institute has over the last few decades been very much involved in the archaeological sites to the northwest of the city in the Cradle of Humankind (see page 575) and all the guides at the centre are required to complete a course with the institute. The museum covers archaeological and genetic materials relating to the origins of humankind. There are displays of tools made by early man that show how they were made, as well as their spiritual significance. There are also displays of examples of South Africa's ancient rock paintings and engravings, and their supposed meanings, with a large portion of the display dedicated to the beliefs and art of the San (Bushmen), which the centre claims to be the planet's oldest inhabitants. There's a film of the San retreating into their spiritual world through trance which is both vivid and a little disturbing. The final exhibit focuses on how genetic testing can contribute to understanding our ancestry and visitors can add their own DNA to a world database. There's a café and good shop selling books and DVDs and some crafts.

③ Sandton

➡**Johannesburg maps**
1 Greater Johannesburg, page 563
2 Johannesburg centre, page 566
3 Sandton, page 570
4 Rosebank to Hyde Park, page 571
5 Soweto, page 573

Sleeping 🛏
Michaelangelo 1
Quatermain 3
Sandton Hilton 2
Tladi Lodge 4

Eating 🍴
Browns of Rivonia 4
Butcher Shop & Grill 2
Grassroots 3
Pappas on the Square 5

Bars & clubs 🍸
Blues Room 1

500 metres
500 yards

④ Rosebank to Hyde Park

Sleeping

Backpackers Ritz **8**
Grace **1**
Melrose Arch **3**
Protea Wanderers **2**
Saxon **6**

Eating

Cranks **1**
Fourno's Bakery **4**
Grillhouse **5**

Linger Longer **12**
Melville Grill **7**
Moyo **2**
Nino's **6**
Osteria Tre Nonni **14**
Sahib's **11**
Soi **9**
Suan Thai **15**
Wombles **3**

➡ **Johannesburg maps**
1 Greater Johannesburg,
  page 563
2 Johannesburg centre,
  page 566
3 Sandton, page 570
4 Rosebank to Hyde Park,
  page 571
5 Soweto, page 573

200 metres
200 yards

Gold Reef City ① *Northern Parkway, Ormonde, T011-2486800, www.goldreefcity.co.za, Tue-Sun 0930-1700, R170, children R70, theme park rides, R110, R60, family combination tickets available, casino open 24 hrs*, is built on the site of one of Johannesburg's gold mining areas, but today has developed into a garish theme park with rides, amusement arcades and a gaudy casino. Of greater interest are the original miners' cottages, the gold-pouring demonstration and the tour of the gold mine. The tour drops to a depth of about 220 m, taking you down No 14 Shaft, one of the richest deposits of gold in its day.

Northern suburbs

The hills to the north of the city centre are criss-crossed by wide avenues, lined with posh shopping malls and large houses with well-tended gardens. Here, homes are surrounded by high walls, topped with razor wire and guarded by dogs and armed response units. **Rosebank**, a few kilometres north of the city, and **Sandton**, further north off the M1 to Pretoria, are the most popular areas. To the east of Rosebank are the fashionable suburbs of **Melville**, one of the few places in Johannesburg with a street restaurant and bar scene, as well as **Parkhurst** and **Parktown**.

Soweto

① *It's recommended you only visit Soweto on a guided tour; see Activities and tours, page 584, for further details.*

The most popular excursion from Johannesburg is to the (in)famous township of Soweto, lying 13 km southwest of Johannesburg city centre. It covers 135 sq km and is home to around one million people, Soweto has mushroomed into a city in its own right. Short for South West Township, people first moved here in 1904 from Sophiatown where there was an outbreak of plague. The township increased in size dramatically in the 1950s and 1960s when black peoples were forced to relocate from the city centre into designated areas outside the city. Since then, the population has soared, bolstered by immigrants from rural areas, as well as from Nigeria, Mozambique, Zimbabwe and other African countries.

Despite its reputation, Soweto feels remarkably ordinary. Large areas are given over to tidy rows of affluent suburban houses. Like in any other South African city, there are districts and suburbs and shopping centres. The streets are well maintained, there are banks and golf courses and the giant FNB Soccer City, which is currently going under an overhaul for the 2010 Football World Cup. Yellow commuter trains trundle to Johannesburg and Mercedes cruise between smart homes with well-tended gardens and satellite dishes. Soweto allegedly has the highest concentration of millionaires in the country and one of the most successful BMW dealerships. The flip-side, much like in any other city in the country, is that there are also areas of squatter camps and informal housing, where unemployment is as high as 90%. Rudimentary two-roomed government-built houses make up the majority of township homes, and many still don't have basic amenities such as running water, electricity and sanitation. For every 7000 people who live in these areas, there are approximately 90 toilets and five taps, and houses sleep up to 10 people. The government has pledged to improve the situation, but efforts are hampered by an estimated influx of 20,000 people who flood into Soweto every month, fleeing rural poverty and desperate for jobs. And signs of Soweto's troubled history are everywhere. Two cooling towers, which once spewed out smoke while producing electricity for Johannesburg's white suburbs, still dominate the skyline; Soweto, meanwhile, had no electricity until 1986.

Most tours of Soweto take in a handful of important historical sites. The new **Soweto Tourism Information office (STIC)** ① *T011-9453111, www.sowetotourism.com*, is located in the Walter Sisulu Square of Independence in Kliptown. This square is at the site where the Freedom Charter, calling for equality for all, was presented by the ANC to a mass gathering of people in 1955. The square, which used to be called Freedom Square, was renamed after one of the delegates, Walter Sisulu, when he died in 2003. The authorities broke up the illegal gathering but the charter was adopted as a guiding document, and it remains the cornerstone of ANC policy to this day and is seen by many as the foundation of South Africa's 1996 Constitution. Back in 1955 it was just a dusty patch of land, but since 2003 it has been redeveloped as a tourist attraction and is now an attractive paved square housing a number of monuments. A four-star hotel is presently being built and a Kliptown museum is in the pipeline.

The **Baragwanath Hospital**, which claims to be the largest hospital in the world, with over 5000 beds and 20,000 employees is usually the first sight to be pointed out on a tour of Soweto. It is estimated that half of Soweto's residents were born here and it also attracts unfortunate attention for its large proportion of AIDS patients and victims of street violence. All tours take in the excellent **Hector Pieterson Museum** ① *Khumalo and Pela streets, Orlando West, 1011-5360611, 1000-1700, R15*. This modern museum stands two blocks away from where 13-year-old Hector Pierterson was shot dead by riot police during a school demonstration on 16 June 1976. The children had been demonstrating about the use of Afrikaans as the dominant language in education, before the police opened fire and killed more than 170 students. This event, captured on camera in an image that shocked the world, sparked the final 10-year battle against Apartheid causing townships across the country to rise up in bitter revolt. (The incident is now known as the Soweto Uprising and the 16 June is a public holiday, Youth Day.) Outside the museum is a memorial to Hector, marked by the iconic image of his body being carried by a friend with

5 Soweto

→ Johannesburg maps
1 Greater Johannesburg, page 563
2 Johannesburg centre, page 566
3 Sandton, page 570
4 Rosebank to Hyde Park, page 571
5 Soweto, page 573

1 km
1 mile

Hector's wailing 17-year-old sister running alongside. Inside, the museum is similar to the Apartheid Museum, using multimedia exhibits, films, newspapers, personal accounts and photographs to piece together what happened on and around that date. There is an excellent museum bookshop with dozens of interesting books on South Africa.

A few blocks away is **Vilakazi Street**, the only street in the world to have been home to two Nobel Peace Prize winners, Nelson Mandela and Desmond Tutu. The home where Nelson and Winnie Mandela lived before he was incarcerated is today a small museum. It is a diminutive three-roomed house, regularly rebuilt after attacks from the South African Defence Forces. Visitors are led through the small living room and into the bedroom, with its odd fur-covered bed. The house is crammed with pro-Winnie propaganda (she suffered a fall from grace in the mid-1990s after numerous incidents of corruption and violence). She originally opened the house as a museum and there are famous stories of her selling bottles of Mandela soil from the garden, but it's now in the hands of the Soweto Trust. Guides reverently point out the few personal belongings left by Mandela, including three pairs of his shoes. Further down the road is the home of Archbishop Desmond Tutu, hidden behind high walls. Next door is a good restaurant, **Sakhumuzi**, often visited by tour groups, but it's also a drinking hole popular with well-heeled Sowetans.

Also worth visiting is **Regina Mundi**, to the southwest, off Potchefstroom Street, the largest church in Soweto, and an important site of demonstrations in the 1980s. You can still see bullet holes in the ceiling, a lasting testament to shots fired by police. Old photos of government attacks are pasted outside, and, if you're lucky, you'll catch the choir practising inside.

🌙 *On his release from prison, Mandela insisted on moving back into his house in Soweto, but eventually its small size and the difficulty of keeping it secure put too much of a strain on him and he moved out of the township.*

Around Johannesburg

Lesedi Cultural Village ① *on the R512, 12 km north of Lanseria Airport, T012-2051394, www.lesedi.com, tours at 1130 and 1630, R295 per person including lunch or dinner*, is an easy day-trip from Johannesburg or Pretoria. Four African villages have been recreated from the Xhosa, Zulu, Pedi, and Sotho tribes and there are two tours daily (each lasting three hours). These include an audio-visual presentation on all aspects of tribal life of the 11 ethnic groups that live in South Africa, as well as music, singing and traditional dancing from over 60 performers around a large fire in an amphitheatre. The morning tour includes lunch and the afternoon tour includes a dinner of game meat such as impala or crocodile. Lesedi is the Sotho word for 'light'. For those who wish to extend the experience, the **Protea Hotel Lesedi** (www.proteahotels.com) is part of the cultural village and provides en suite accommodation in traditional bomas or rondavels decorated with Ndebele crafts.

The **Lion Park** ① *30 mins' drive from Johannesburg on the Old Pretoria– Krugersdorp road, T011-6919905, www.lion-park.com, Mon-Fri 0830-1700, Sat-Sun 0830-1800, R85, children R55, restaurant and curio shop*, en route to Lesedi (see above), is worth a stop for the excellent photo opportunities. There are over 80 lions kept in the park including many cubs and a rare pride of white lions. Although they are bred in captivity, they are well cared for and have ample room in the drive-through enclosures. The lions are accustomed to vehicles and don't think twice about strolling right up to a car. Keep windows at least half closed. Other animals kept here include hyenas, cheetah and a variety of antelope. Walks and close encounters with cubs are on offer.

Approximately 40 km to the northwest of Johannesburg is a region dubbed the **Cradle of Humankind** ① *www.cradleofhumankind.co.za*, thanks to thousands of humanoid and animal fossils being unearthed over recent decades. It holds some of the world's most important archaeological sites, revealing over 40% of all hominid fossils ever discovered and has overtaken Tanzania's Olduvai Gorge in significance. The 470 sq km area was declared a UNESCO World Heritage Site in 1999.

Maropeng ① *7 km from the Sterkfontein Caves (see below) on the R24, T011-6683200, www.discover-yourself.co.za, 0900-1700, last boat ride 1600, R80, R45 children,* meaning 'returning to the place of origin' in the setswana language is a new interactive museum that tells the story of the creation of our world and the evolution of man over a four billion-year period. Opened by President Mbeki in 2005, it's another of Johannesburg's excellent new cutting-edge museums that uses computer wizardry and multimedia displays. The entrance has been built as a grassy burial mound, while the exit is a sleek structure of modern glass and concrete and the journey from one to the other takes the visitor from the birth of planet earth to where we are at today. The first experience is a boat ride through a tunnel of erupting volcanoes, icebergs, an eye of a storm and swirling gases that made up the planet. It's rather magical and the sounds and temperatures are lifelike but be warned, it may frighten very small children. Once off the boat the series of exhibits start from how the earth was formed, early life forms and the emergence of man, and go through to cover topics on how man has changed the environment, such as population explosion, use of the earth's resources and global appetite. Towards the end is a large display of photographs of people's faces from all over the world and a mesmerizing series of images of man's achievements are flashed on a giant screen covering everything from man inventing the wheel to landing on the moon. Allow at least two to three hours for the experience and there are three restaurants on site.

Off the N14 from Randburg towards Hartbeetspoort Dam are **Sterkfontein Caves** ① *T011-9566342, www.sterkfontein-caves.co.za, Tue-Sun 0900-1600, guided tours run every 30 mins, R35.* Although the dolomite hill holding the caves was discovered in the late 19th century, it was not until 1936 that the most important find was made, the first adult skull of the ape-man Australopithecus africanus – 'Mrs Ples' for short. The skull is estimated to be over 2.6 million years old, and was found by Dr Robert Broom. Even older hominid remains have been found here since. The caves consist of six chambers connected by passages. Tours begin in the impressive multimedia visitor centre, which includes comprehensive exhibitions on our ancestors, with displays of life-sized hominid replicas and a large amphitheatre. Tours then pass through the six caves, taking in the archaeological sites. There is a craft market and a choice of restaurants on site.

The **Walter Sisulu Botanical Gardens** ① *T011-9581750, www.sanbi.org, daily 0800-1700, exit closes 1800, R18,* is a pleasant place to visit for a quiet stroll away from the bustle of the city. The gardens are planted with oaks, cherry trees and a mixture of exotic and indigenous plants. The nursery, with over 2500 species of succulent plants, is a fascinating area and the nearby ponds attract birds, including yellowbilled ducks, Egyptian geese and crested grebes. The gardens are a 30-minute drive from the city centre on the banks of the Emmarentia Dam in Roodepoort (take the Beyers Naude exit off the N1 and follow the R564).

Hotel and guesthouse prices
L over US$300 AL US$220-300 A US$150-220
B US$100-150 C US$75-100 D US$35-75
E US$15-35 F under US$15
Restaurant prices
♥♥♥ over US$30 ♥♥ US$15-30 ♥ under US$15
See pages 46-51 for further information.

⦿ Sleeping

Most of the city's best hotels are in the safe areas of Sandton, Rosebank, Parkhurst and Melville. Accommodation tends to be pricey; there's a wide selection of luxury hotels, but little in the lower price bracket other than the odd hostel.

Alternatively, there are mid-range options from the City Lodge group and there are dozens of **City Lodges**, **Road Lodges** and **Town Lodges** all over Johannesburg; www.citylodge.co.za. These are all identical, purpose-built, modern, functional blocks with comfortable rooms TV and internet and car parks in the **C-D** range. They hardly need individual descriptions. Check out the website for locations, and if you can't get a room at your first choice the staff at each will try and get you into the nearest one.

Township B&Bs are mushrooming in Soweto and many have opened their doors near to the sights in Orlando West. Visit the website of the **Soweto Bed & Breakfast Association**, www.sowetobedand breakfast.co.za. Most are spare double rooms in people's houses where you are likely to become friendly with the hosts.

Near the airport
There are several airport hotels within a few kilometres, all providing free pickups. The closest are:
A Airport Sun Intercontinental, T011-9615400, www.southernsun.com. This smart 5-star hotel is conveniently located directly opposite the terminal buildings. You can push your trolley from the airport into your room, there's flight arrival and departure TV information throughout the hotel. Gym and beauty salon available for passengers on long waits between flights.
B City Lodge, Sandvale Rd, Edenvale, T011-3921750, www.citylodge.co.za. Modern, well-run hotel for the business traveller, restaurant, pool, 4 km from the airport.
C-D Africa Centre, 65 Sunny Rd, Lakefield-Benoni, T011-8944857, www.africacentre lodge.co.za. Double, single and dorm rooms. Shared kitchen, meals available, garden with pool, sauna and jacuzzi, Wi-Fi, travel services and airport pick-up.
D-E Purple Palms Travel Lodge, 1 Boom-pieper Av, Birch Acres, T011-3934393,

www.purplepalms.co.za. Owned by the same couple as North South Backpackers in Pretoria, this lodge is 10 km from the airport and offers free pickups and transfers. Dorms, doubles and twin rooms, bar area, swimming pool, lapa area, kitchen and meals available. Well run with a good travel centre.
E-F Airport Backpackers, 3 Mohawk St, Rhodesfield, Kempton Park, T011-3940485, www.airportbackpackers.co.za. Only 2 km from the airport close to the end of the runway, so planes fly low overhead. Dorms, double rooms and camping. Internet, swimming pool, free airport pickup and drop off, free basic breakfast. Festival Mall nearby, but little else to do in area.

Northern suburbs *p572, maps p570 and p571*
L The Grace, 54 Bath Av, Rosebank, T011-7807200, www.thegrace.co.za. Beautiful luxury hotel set right next to Rosebank Mall (with a convenient passage connecting to it). Large rooms spread over 9 floors, some with great city views, decorated in country-style fabrics, with pretty pale-green colour themes, dark wood and colonial prints on the walls. Excellent restaurant, popular for brunch, serving contemporary South African cuisine, plus good extras such as complimentary tea and cakes in the afternoon. Business centre with free internet access, spa, stunning rooftop pool, and efficient friendly service. Recommended.
L Melrose Arch, Melrose Arch, T011-2146666, www.africanpridehotels.com. A trendy addition to the northern suburbs, with stylish rooms, lots of chrome, bare-brick walls and flat-screen TVs, mood-enhancing lighting, designer furniture. Smart bar and superb **March Restaurant** for gourmet food. The location is overlooking the attractive square in the Melrose Arch gated development, with its many upmarket shops and restaurants just a safe stroll away.
L The Michelangelo, 135 West St, Nelson Mandela Sq, T011-2827000, www.legacy hotels.co.za. 242 super-luxury rooms, including a variety of giant suites, residents' lounge, restaurants, bar, heated swimming pool,

fitness centre, one of the best luxury options of Sandton, which has contributed to the area becoming one of the smartest centres of Johannesburg. Plenty of restaurants and shops in the lovely Nelson Mandela Sq.
L Saxon, 36 Saxon Rd, Sandhurst, T011-2926000, www.thesaxon.com. Voted the 'World's Leading Boutique Hotel' every year since it opened in 2000. 26 suites including one named after Nelson Mandela, who spent 7 months here working on his book *Long Walk to Freedom*. Set in 2 ha of beautifully tended grounds, gigantic heated swimming pools, state of the art gym, spa, restaurant, 2 wine cellars. Expensive by South African standards, the cheapest suite is R5000.
L Westcliff, 67 Jan Smuts Av, Westcliff, near Johannesburg Zoo, T011-4816000, www.west cliff.co.za. A bright pink Mediterranean-style hillside village on a 3 ha estate, with 106 a/c rooms and 14 suites, 2 heated swimming pools, floodlit tennis court with resident coach, gym, health spa, old-fashioned charm in the cigar bar and restaurant, great views of the northern suburbs and zoo.
AL Sandton Hilton, 138 Rivonia Rd, Sandton, T011-3221888, www.hilton.com. Big business hotel with 329 luxury rooms, including the latest Hilton feature – a separate executive floor with its own lounge-cum-club room where business folk can breakfast and snack throughout the day. 2 restaurants, bar, health club, swimming pool, tennis court, extensive conference facilities, all set in a beautiful landscaped garden, close to smart shopping malls in Sandton.
A A Room with a View, 1 Tolip St, corner of 4th Av, Melville, T011-4825435, www.aroom withaview.co.za. As the name would suggest, beautiful views over leafy Melville from this delightful hotel. 13 rooms in 2 buildings; those in the newer building, designed to look like an Italian villa, have bare-brick walls, soaring ceilings and stylish, colourful furnishings, as well as huge beds, slate-tiled bathrooms and private balconies. Those in the older house have carved wooden bed frames and polished wooden floors.

Legendary breakfasts, pleasant pool and very friendly service. Highly recommended.

A Quatermain Inn, 137 West Road South, Morningside, Sandton, T011-2900900, www.quatermain.co.za. Home-from-home in the heart of Sandton, 114 spacious luxury rooms set in manicured indigenous gardens with oak trees and swimming pool, comfortable lounge, gym and bar.

B Protea Wanderers, corner of Corlett Dr and Rudd Rd, Illovo, T011-7705500, www.proteahotels.com. Directly opposite Wanderers cricket stadium. Quality hi-tec modern hotel, but lacking in character. 230 rooms have individual office station with faux African and sporting motifs, and sound proofing. Pleasant pool area except for the traffic noise from the busy road below.

B Sunnyside Park, Prince of Wales Terr, Parktown, T011-6437226, www.legacy hotels.co.za. 104 rooms, restaurant, swimming pool, converted Victorian mansion declared a national monument, with new annexes set in picturesque gardens; an unusual find and close to the city. Decent restaurant. Pleasant old-fashioned atmosphere but not great service.

B Tladi Lodge, 1 David St, Sandton, T011-7849240, www.tladilodge.co.za. Attractive and spacious 10 rooms and 2 suites with contemporary furnishings, under-floor heating, set in low thatched buildings in extensive gardens, pool, red-brick terraces, a peaceful spot with easy access to Sandton and an alternative to the big hotels.

D-F Backpackers Ritz, 1A North Rd, Dunkeld West, T011-3257125, www.backpackers-ritz.co.za. One of Johannesburg's best-established long-running hostels. Large house in a secure neighbourhood with garden and swimming pool. Dorms, double rooms, travel desk, Soweto and city tours, internet access, individual safes plus long-term baggage storage, helpful place to start your visit. Meals available. Close to shops and entertainment at Hyde Park and Rosebank, all in a safe suburb, 30 mins from airport, free pickup, call before leaving home. Recommended.

❷ Eating

Johannesburg *p562, maps p566, 570 and p571*
Many of Johannesburg's restaurants and bars are within the confines of a shopping mall. However, thanks to good architecture, in the most part you will not be aware that you are eating in a mall. This is especially true of the 19 restaurants lining Nelson Mandela Sq, which is an atmospheric place to eat out with twinkly lights in the trees and a large statue of a smiling Mandela looking over the outside tables. Another mall hotspot is the square at Melrose Arch off Corlett Dr in Melrose not far from the Wanderer's Cricket Stadium. This is currently the place to be seen in the evening. The best area in town for lively streetside restaurants and bars is the suburb of **Melville**, in the northern suburbs off the M1. The streets around 7th St are lined with popular bars, fashionable restaurants and kooky cafés. Most appealing is the fact that its safe to park and wander around here, even at night. Other smaller streetside restaurant districts include the Gleneagles roundabout in Greenside, 4th Av in Parkhurst and 7th Av in Parktown North.

There are few specific vegetarian restaurants in Jo'burg (see **Grassroots**, below), but most menus offer a range of meat-free dishes.

ΨΨΨ Browns of Rivonia, 21 Wessels St, Rivonia, T011-8037533, www.browns.co.za. Mon-Sat. Meals served in the courtyard of an old farm house, expensive but extensive menu includes roast lamb, salmon timbale, mustard sirloin and crêpes. Impressive wine list with some 40,000 bottles in the cellar.

ΨΨΨ Carnivore, 69 Drift Blvd, Muldersdrift, 30 mins' drive (approx 30 km) from Johannesburg centre on the N14, some hotels and back packers arrange transport out here, T011-9573132. This has become something of an institution and is the ultimate 'African' eating experience. Rustic decor, zebra-skin chairs and a large central fire pit characterizes the interior. Meals consist of eat-as-much-as-you-can, with slabs of game carved off Masaai spears onto cast-iron plates. There's a choice of at least 10 different types of meat every

Jo'burg's Chinatown

Johannesburg's Chinatown is a vibey strip of neon-lit Chinese supermarkets and restaurants in a less than salubrious part of the city located on Derrick Avenue, Cyrildene, just east of Observatory. To get there you'll need to rely on a good-natured taxi driver or someone who knows Jo'burg well. From the northern suburbs it involves a drive through Hillbrow and along the notorious Rockey Street, before it turns into Observatory Street and follows through to Cyrildene. Once at Chinatown, there are car guards and vehicles are looked after safely for a tip. On each side of Derrick Street are restaurants, dumpling shops, noodle bars, teashops, Chinese greengrocers and general dealers, herbalists, beauty salons and video-rental shops. Walk up and down until you find a restaurant that takes your liking or one that's not already full. Most are small eateries with formica top tables,

plastic chairs, fluorescent lights, take away counters, unbelievably kitsch decorations on the walls, and sometimes dead duck-lings hanging in the window. Some only seat several people at a time whereas others have the luxury of four or five tables. Regional dishes include Szechuan, Shanghai, Hong Kong and Taiwanese; and there's sushi, Mongolian and Korean for good measure. The food is delicious and you won't get more authentic Chinese dishes elsewhere in South Africa. Few menus are written in English, and it's best to order a selection of dishes to share. Drink Chinese beer or tea, or bring your own wine. The most delightful aspect of this eating experience is the bill: hardly any of the staff speak English and they simply write the total down on the paper tablecloth or a napkin, only cash is accepted and it's ridiculously cheap. Arrive early, most kitchens close at 2100.

day, which usually includes ostrich, croco-dile, warthog as well as beef and pork. If vegetarians can bear it, they actually have a good choice, including *aviyal*, a mix of vegetables cooked in spicy coconut sauce.

Daruma, Sandton Sun/Towers Hotel, T011-7805157/9. Formal Japanese restaurant that serves some of the best sushi in town. The food is presented delicately in a low-key stylish modern dining room, hung with Japanese art. Extensive menu, fairly pricey.

Gramadoelas, Market Theatre Complex, Bree St, Newtown, T011-8386960, www.grama doelas.co.za. Mon-Fri lunch and dinner, Sat dinner only. One of the best places to get a full overview of Southern African dishes is at this long-standing favourite, set in the renovated Market Theatre Complex. The faux-ramshackle decor adds to the atmosphere, and there are tables outside in summer. Starters include fried *mopani* worms served in peri-peri sauce, and to follow you can try *sosaties* (spicy kebabs),

bobotie (sweet and spicy ground beef pie), or a range of dishes from further afield such as Morocco or Ethiopia. A delicious desert is the sticky malva pudding, or *melktert* (milk tart). This is also the place to try home-brewed sorghum beer or *mageu* (fermented milk).

Linger Longer, 58 Wierda Rd, Wierda Valley, Sandton, T011-8840465. Mon-Fri lunch and dinner, Sat dinner only. One of Johannesburg's top restaurants and something of an institution – it's been going for 45 years – serving an imaginative mix of old-fashioned and contemporary cooking, from seafood casserole to lemon pepper filet. Attractive homely setting.

Melville Grill, corner of 3rd Av and 7th St, Melville, T011-7262890, www.melville grill.com. Mon-Sat lunch and dinner. Slick, upmarket steakhouse, serving the best steaks in the city. The interior has low lighting and wooden floors, white tablecloths and red walls. Different cuts and prices are chalked up on the walls, and the menu includes details such as how long a cut was aged and whether the meat is free range. Simple salad starters and a couple of fish and poultry choices, followed by warm chocolate brownies. Good, unpretentious service. Recommended.

Ψ Moyo, Melrose Sq Melrose Arch, T0861-006696, www.moyo.co.za. Popular new chain of upmarket African-themed restaurants appearing around South Africa. This outlet is in chi-chi Melrose Arch, and is spread over 3 floors, with rustic, candlelit ethno-fashionable decor, and pan-African cuisine, including good Moroccan tagines. Live music in the evenings. There are also branches in Newtown, next to **Gramadoelas** and in the Zoo Lake Park near the Johannesburg Zoo.

Ψ Osteria Tre Nonni, 9 Grafton Av, Craighall, T011-3270095. Tue-Sun lunch, Tue-Sat dinner. Expensive but sophisticated north Italian cuisine, home-made pasta, fresh seafood, best tiger prawns in the city, rich creamy sauces, reservations recommended.

Ψ Butcher Shop & Grill, Nelson Mandela Sq, Sandton City Mall, T011-7848676/7. Mon-Sat 1200-2245, Sun 1200-2145. This award-winning steakhouse is a top-quality restaurant and shouldn't be missed by meat-lovers. The **Butcher Shop** is famous for its aged steaks, and although there are a few outlets around the country now, this is the original and gets through 5 tons of steak each week. The menu is, obviously, focused on steak and other grills: when available, there's a specially aged T-bone which is cut to order. There's also a selection of seafood, and a good range of starters and desserts, but literally nothing for vegetarians other than a couple of salads.

Ψ Café Flo, 116 Greenway Rd, Greenside, T011-6466817. Mon-Sat 1200-1430, 1830-2200. Pavement dining in this little cult restaurant. A young, fashionable crowd come here for Flo's imaginative home-cooked meals, including a delicious lamb and aubergine pizza and malva pudding with custard. The connected **Ova Flo** has also opened next door for breakfasts.

Ψ Cranks, Shop 162, Rosebank Mall, next to the African Craft Market, T011-8803442. Delicious Vietnamese and Thai dishes are served in this eccentric Asian eatery, well situated in the popular Rosebank mall. The decor is in itself worth a visit, with Barbie and Ken dolls dangling from the ceiling in compromising positions. Freshly prepared Thai, including green chicken curry and pad thai, and some spicy Vietnamese dishes. Asian beer plus Thai schnapps and soothing herbal teas. Live blues performed Sat and Sun.

Ψ Grillhouse, The Firs, Oxford Rd, Rosebank, T011-8803945. Popular for its melt-in-the-mouth fillets and succulent sauces. Exposed brick and green leather furniture, excellent service and a lively atmosphere. Opposite and under the same ownership is **Katzy's** late night piano bar and cigar lounge, which has live music most nights and is fast making its way onto Jo'burg's nightlife circuit. Vast selection of Cognacs and malt whiskies. You would never know you're in a shopping mall.

Ψ Pappas on the Square, Nelson Mandela Sq, Sandton City Mall, T011-8849991. Open 0930-2330. Authentic Greek themed restaurant with plate breaking, Greek wine and a fun atmosphere, the chef once cooked for Christina Onassis. Share a mezze or try the *kleftiko* (lamb shank). One of the many restaurants overlooking the lovely square.

Ψ Primi Piatti, Upper Level, The Zone, Rosebank Mall, T011-4470300, Melrose Sq, Melrose Arch, T011-6841648, www.primi-piatti.com. Stylish Italian chain found in 8 locations, though the hippest are at Rosebank and Melrose Arch, with colourful, industrial-style decor and lively staff. Huge portions of imaginative pasta, excellent wood-fired pizzas and big salads. **Primi Studio**, attached, is a lounge bar with big comfy sofas and music, perfect for relaxing after a meal.

Ψ Soi, corner of 7th and 3rd Av, Melville, T011-7265775. Open 1200-1415, 1800-2200. Excellent Thai and Vietnamese cuisine in this low-lit restaurant. Wide selection of curries, pad thai noodles and interesting dishes like 'angry duck' – perfect for those with fiery tastes. Fashionable, friendly serving staff, stylish, understated decor and a chatty crowd make this one of the best places on the Melville drag. Recommended.

Suan Thai, corner of 3rd Av and 7th St, Melville, T011-7827801. Another Melville quality restaurant, authentic Thai cooked dishes including great curry (try the duck and prawn), tom yam soup and Mozambican crab. Good vegetarian options. Mango and coconut ice cream for dessert, live jazz some Sun evenings.

Wombles, 17 3rd St, Parktown North, T011-8802470, www.wombles.co.za. Closed Sat lunch and Sun. A relative newcomer, Wombles has been going for nearly 25 years – first in Zimbabwe, then in Australia and now in Johannesburg and has fast gained an excellent reputation for its matured steaks. The setting is attractive colonial style, with dark wood tables, high-backed chairs and white linen table cloths. It's a simple menu, with traditional starters like grilled mushrooms, or chicken liver salad, followed by a choice of cuts and sauces. There's also a fair choice of poultry, fish and even a couple of vegetarian dishes. Service is friendly and relaxed.

Grassroots, Village Walk mall, Sandton, T011-8836020. Healthy eating from this shopping mall restaurant, serving only vegetarian and vegan dishes, and fully organic. Pastas, salads, bagels and cakes that lean towards the fruity, nutty, leafy and grainy type of cuisine. Pumpkin and leek soup and hash browns are recommended.

Sahib's, 83 4th St, Melville, T011-4826671. Open 1000-1500, 1700-2200. Simple, cheap and slightly run-down curry house, but refreshingly unpretentious, with a wide range of bunny chows, roti wraps, tandoori grill, and biryanis, and lots to tempt vegetarians. Good-value buffet lunches at weekends.

Cafés

Fourno's Bakery, Dunkeld West Centre, Jan Smuts Av, T011-3252110. Mon-Fri 0700-1800, Sat-Sun 0700-1400. Cheap eats with a number of branches around the city. The bakers work through the night to provide a huge range of fresh pastries, cakes, croissants, quiches and pies. Big breakfasts, coffee, simple lunches, very popular at the weekend.

Nino's, 22 Cradock Av, Rosebank, T011-4474758. Daily 0700-1800. Large, open, street-side eating area, reasonably priced coffee and build-your-own panini sandwich bar, opposite the Rosebank craft market, a good place to start the day with a fat 3-egg omelette.

Bars and clubs

Johannesburg p562, maps p566, 570 and p571
Entertainment listings are published in the weekly *Mail and Guardian*, with a 'Gig of the Week' review and online listings at www.mg.co.za.

Bassline, 10 Henry Nxumalo St, Newtown, T011-8309145, www.bassline.co.za. Established and popular South African jazz venue that's recently moved from Melville into Newtown's old red-brick Music Hall and now has a capacity of 1000 and regularly hosts South Africa's top jazz, hip-hop and kwaito artists. Tickets through **Computicket**; www.computicket.com. Cover charge varies. Outside is a lovely statue of a soulful bare-footed singer leaning into a microphone. You can sit on the seat next to her for a photo.

Blues Room, Village Walk, Sandton, T011-7845527, www.bluesroom.co.za. Tue-Sat 1900-late. One of the best jazz and blues venues in Gauteng, this is a stylish basement bar and restaurant, catering for music lovers who are after a decent meal. There's live music on every night and the pace picks up later on when diners take to the floor for a dance. The American-style dishes are named after blues legends.

Catz Pyjamas, corner of 3rd and Main streets, Melville, T011-7268596. Jo'burg's original 24-hr bistro and cocktail bar, rather shabby these days with a funky atmosphere (avoid the food though). It's open throughout the day but pretty lackluster – the atmosphere really only picks up late in the evening, carrying on until the early hours.

Cool Runnings, 27a, 4th Av, Melville, T011-4824786. The popular Jamaican-themed chain of bars/clubs comes into its own at this Melville branch, which is one of the most popular bars around. There's loud music every night, when a young crowd gathers to work its way through the extensive cocktail list. There are occasional drumming sessions held in the bar.

Jolly Roger, 10, 4th Av, Parkhurst, T011-4423954. Landmark pub on the main stretch in popular Parkhurst, with an excellent balcony perfect for watching the area's stylish locals swan up and down 4th Av. Good draught beer and pizza specials, plus live music at weekends.

Kippies, corner of Carr and Quinn streets, Newtown, T011-8331805. Revamped legendary jazz venue in Newtown, famous for its township jazz and serving light meals.

Monsoon Lagoon, at **Emperor's Palace Casino**, Jones Rd, next to the airport, T011-9281000, www.monsoonlagoon.co.za, Wed-Sat 2100-late. One of Jo'burg's biggest and brashest clubs is this huge special events venue, regularly hosting TV and fashion parties. It's an upmarket mainstream club (over 23s only) covering several floors with a number of dance floors, bars and lounges. It's lavish and totally over the top – great for a big night out.

Ratz, 7th St, Melville, T011-7262019. 1700-late. Friendly drinking hole with a couple of sofas and high tables dotted around in front of the wooden bar. Gets packed on Fri nights, and serves decent cocktails, but is more of a low-key beer joint for students.

Xai Xai, 9b 7th St, Melville. Super-trendy lounge bar with a Mozambique theme. Great cocktails, low-level sofas, good-looking punters and chilled music make this a relaxing and stylish setting for a few pre-dinner drinks.

🌐 Entertainment

Johannesburg *p562, maps p566, 570 and p571*
Computicket, T011-3408000, www.compu ticket.com. A central booking agency for tickets to the cinema, theatre, concerts, sports events and city tours. Note that international credit cards are not accepted online or over the phone; you can pay by international credit card at kiosks, located in most of the large shopping malls. If you're heading to one of the downtown theatres, its best to travel by taxi and pre-order one for after the show. The Market Theatre area is safe, but don't wander away from Mary Fitzgerald Sq.

Cinema
All the latest Hollywood, European and home-grown releases can be seen at multi-screen cinemas in shopping malls and casinos. Check local newspapers for listings. They are run by **Nu Metro**, T011-3254257, www.numetro.co.za, or **Ster-Kine Kor**, T011-4457700, www.sterkinekor.co.za.

Theatre
Civic Theatre, Loveday St, Braamfontein, T011-8776800, www.showbusiness.co.za. Modern theatre complex with 3 auditoriums, frequent performances of South African plays, visiting international musicals, ballets and classical orchestras.

Gold Reef City, Northern Parkway, Ormonde, T011-2485168, www.goldreefcity.co.za. The 300-seat **Globe Theatre** shows cabaret and comedy.

Liberty Theatre on the Square, Nelson Mandela Sq, Sandton City Mall, T011-8838606. Plays and occasional lunchtime concerts.

Market Theatre, 56 Margaret Mcingana St, Newtown, T011-8321614, www.market theatre.co.za. 3 auditoriums, famous for its community theatre and controversial political plays during the 1980s. The recommended **Moyo** and **Gramadoelas** restaurants are here.

Montecasino, corner of William Nicol Dr and Witkoppen Rd, Fourways, T011-5111818, www.montecasinotheatre.co.za. 2 theatres in the casino and entertainment complex, one of which was specifically built to stage South Africa's version of the **Lion King** musical.

O Shopping

Johannesburg *p562, maps p566, 570 and p571*

African art

Art Africa, 62 Tyrone Av, Parkview, T011-4862052. Mon-Fri 0900-1800, Sat 0900-1500. Great place to pick up inexpensive gifts, strong emphasis on recycled art products. Some of the most interesting pieces include flowers made from recycled plastic, and baskets woven from telephone wire. There are also some genuinely rare antiques from across Africa.

African Craft Market of Rosebank, Cradock Av, Rosebank, T011-8802906, www.craft. co.za. 0900-1800. The former street traders of this area have now been housed in one ethnic-inspired building in the centre of the popular Mall of Rosebank. Curios from all over Africa are for sale at over 140 stalls. Credit cards are accepted and shipping can be arranged. It's a lively spot, with street performers and musicians, and on Thu evenings African food is served and there's a dance show.

Kim Sacks Gallery, 153 Jan Smuts Av, Parkwood, T011-4475804. Mon-Sat 0800-1700. A selection of quality ethnic art from all over Africa is on show in this gallery, housed in a lovely old home and regarded as one of the top galleries in the city. There is a good range of contemporary South African pieces, including prints, sculptures, beadwork, and ceramics.

Camera equipment

Kameraz, Rosebank Mews, Oxford Rd, Rosebank, T011-8802885, www.kameraz. co.za. Mon-Fri 0800-1700, Sat 0800-1400. One of the largest dealers in new and second-hand camera equipment in Gauteng. New and used accessories and lenses, and specialists in insurance claims. On the first Sun of every even month they hold a flea market of second-hand equipment, and on the first Sun of every odd month, an exhibition and sale of work from local photographers.

Camping and hiking equipment

Cape Union Mart, Hyde Park Mall, Jan Smuts Av, T011-3255038, www.capeunionmart.co.za, and 14 other branches in Johannesburg's various shopping malls, plus one at the airport. Excellent shop selling outdoor equipment, practical clothing, backpacks, mosquito nets, and a great range of walking shoes.

Gold

Scoin Shop, U24a, Sandton City Mall, T011-7848551, www.sagoldcoin.com. Mon-Fri 0830-1630. Krugerrands, South Africa's famous gold coins, can be bought here as an investment or souvenir. It also produces collector's coins such as the Mandela Medallion.

Shopping malls

Johannesburg has an abundance of vast, modern shopping malls filled with shops, restaurants, cinemas and bars. There are over 20 malls around the city, some of which are so enormous and extravagant that they are worth visiting in their own right. In most, the shops open 0900-1800, while the restaurants and cinemas stay open until 2200 or 2300.

Hyde Park, Jan Smuts Av, Hyde Park, T011-3254340. Luxury shopping aimed at ladies who lunch. Also has cinemas, and the excellent **Exclusive Books** has an outlet here.

The Mall of Rosebank, corner of Cradock and Baker streets, Rosebank, T011-7885530. One of the more pleasant malls with a large open-air plaza lined with cafés, ideal for sitting in the sun and watching people go by. Flea market on the roof every Sun selling crafts and snacks. Also home to the excellent **African Craft Market** (see box, page 565). At the time of writing the mall's layout was changing to incorporate the new line and station for the Gautrain, currently under construction.

Sandton City Mall, corner of Sandton Dr and Rivonia Rd (attached to Nelson Mandela Sq by a walkway), T011-8832011. Massive double-storey mall featuring all of South Africa's chain stores, cinemas, African art galleries and hypermarkets. The opulent Nelson Mandela

Sq has international exclusive stores and fashionable restaurants around an attractive piazza-style square, which is now home to a formidable 6-m bronze statue of the great man himself. His shoes are 1 m across and children can sit on them.

▲▲ Activities and tours

Johannesburg p562, maps p566, 570 and p571
Cricket
Wanderers' Stadium, Corlett Dr, Illovo, T011-3401500 information, T011-3401509 tickets, www.wanderers.co.za. This is one of South Africa's premier cricket grounds and regular international matches are played here in season.

Football
FNB Stadium, Nasvec Rd, Ormonde. More popularly called Soccer City, it is the largest of Johannesburg's stadiums and home of the South African Football Association. This will be the venue of the opening match and the final of the 2010 FIFA World Cup (see box on page 875) and the whole of Soweto is euphoric these will be played on their door step. It is currently undergoing a complete upgrade and should reopen in 2009.

Golf
There are over 40 golf courses around Johannesburg and several of South Africa's top courses are open to visitors midweek.
Glendower Club, Marais Rd, Bedford View, T011-4531013, www.glendower.co.za. Beautiful location in a bird sanctuary, tough course with 85 bunkers, 20 mins from the city centre.
Houghton Golf Club, 2nd Av, Lower Houghton, T011-7287337, www.houghton.co.za. One of the country's top courses; many major tournaments are held here including the South African Open.
Royal Johannesburg and Kensington Golf Club, Fairway Av, Linksfield North, T011-6403021. Visitors Mon-Fri 0700-1300.

Century-old club with 2 courses, East and West. South African Open held on the East Course, 30 mins from the city centre.
Wanderers Golf Club, Rudd Rd, Illovo, T011-4473311, www.wanderersgolf club.co.za. One of the oldest courses in South Africa, quite challenging, hosts the South African PGA Championship, next to the cricket ground, just north of Rosebank.

Rugby
Ellis Park, Staib St, Doornfontein, T011-4028644, www.ellispark.co.za. This is the home of the Gauteng Strikers and the Cats, and matches are played regularly during the season. The stadium seats 50,000 spectators and it can be a rowdy day out, with fans bringing their braais and beers with them. It's also home to Kaizer Chiefs soccer club, and will be a venue for the 2010 FIFA World Cup.

Tour operators
There are dozens of tour operators in Johannesburg that offer a range of half- and full-day tours. Most use minibuses, have registered guides and pick up from all hotels. Expect to pay in the region of R300-350 for a half-day tour.
A Taste of Africa, www.tasteofafrica.co.za. A full range of day tours including all the museums and interactive Soweto tours; even offers horse and cart rides in Soweto. Recommended.
Emthunzini Tours, T011-9850085, www.emthunzini.com. Soweto-based operator, making this a good choice for township tours. Also has full-day trips which include the Apartheid Museum and city centre, plus longer tours out of the city.
Jimmy's Face to Face Tours, T011-3316109, www.face2face.co.za. One of the original Soweto tour operators, with a focus on climbing out of the minibuses and meeting local people. Good for exploring on foot.
JMT Tours, T011-9806038, www.jmt tours.co.za. Half-day Soweto tours, trips to Lesedi, Sun City, and longer grips to Kruger.

Karabo Tours, T011-3257125, www.backpackers-ritz.co.za. Based at the Backpackers Ritz but will pick up from all northern suburb hotels, affordable in-depth Soweto tours, plus historic Pretoria tours, Gold Reef City, Lion Park and comprehensive Johannesburg city tours.

Lords Travel & Tours, T011-7915494, www.lordstravel.co.za. Range of set and tailor-made city tours to Soweto, Sterkfontein Caves, Botanical Gardens, Lion Park and Lesedi; further afield packages to Pilanesberg and Sun City and Kruger.

⊖ Transport

Johannesburg *p562, maps p566, 570 and p571*
Air
OR Tambo International Airport is southern African's biggest transport hub and one of the largest airports in the world, with numerous daily flights connecting to all major cities domestically and internationally.

South African Airways (SAA) has countless daily flights run in conjunction with its subsidiary, **SA Airlink**, covering the entire country. **Comair/British Airways** has several daily flights to all major cities.

Mango has daily flights from Johannesburg to **Cape Town**, **Durban** and **Bloemfontein**.

Nationwide has daily flights to **Cape Town**, **Durban**, **George**, **Port Elizabeth** and **Kruger**.

Kulula flies to **Cape Town**, **Durban**, **George** and **Port Elizabeth**.

One Time flies to **Cape Town**, **Durban**, **George**, **Port Elizabeth** and **Bloemfontein**.

Airline offices Air Botswana, T011-4476078. **Air France**, T086-1340340. **Air Malawi**, T011-3901211. **Air Namibia**, T011-3902876. **Air Tanzania**, T011-6161870. **Air Zimbabwe**, T011-9701687. **British Airways**, T011-4418400. **Cathay Pacific**, T011-3940905. **Comair/British Airways**, T0860-435922, www.britishairways.com. **Delta Airlines**, T011-9786770. **Egypt Air**, T011-8804547. **Emirates**, T011-3901215.

Ethiopian Airlines, T011-6167624. **Kenya Airways**, T011-2345747. **KLM**, T011-9616700. **Kulula**, T0861-585852, www.kulula.com. **Lufthansa**, T011-3250870. **Mango**, T0861-162646 (in South Africa), www.flymango.com. **Malaysia Airways**, T011-8809614. **Nationwide**, T0861-737737, www.flynationwide.co.za. **One Time**, T0861-345345, www.1time.co.za. **Singapore Airlines**, T011-8808560. **South African Airways** (SAA), central reservations T011-9781111, www.flysaa.com. **Virgin Atlantic**, T011 3403400.

Bus
Local Magic Bus, T011-5480822, www.magicbus.co.za and **Airport Link Shuttle**, T011-7922017, www.airport link.co.za, run shuttle services to the major hotels in Johannesburg and Pretoria.

Long distance Translux, Intercape, Greyhound, and all the smaller bus companies depart from and arrive at the Park City Transit Centre, which is also where the railway station is, in central Johannesburg. The surrounding area has long had a bad reputation for muggings. Although crime levels have dropped in the area, be extra vigilant in and around the terminal and don't go wandering outside with a backpack. Many of the buses depart and arrive late at night or early in the morning, so make sure you have pre-arranged a pickup with your hotel or one of the shuttle companies (see above).

All the bus companies listed below have frequent departures between Johannesburg and Pretoria throughout the day (1 hr). You cannot pre-book this short journey, but it is never a problem to get a standby ticket; expect to pay around R150.

The 3 main coach companies cover routes from Johannesburg across the country and some services go as far as Malawi. Full timetables can be found on the websites and tickets can be booked online.

Bus companies Translux, T0861-589282 (in South Africa), T011-774333 (from overseas), www.translux.co.za. **Intercape**, T0861-287287 (in South Africa), T012-3804400 (from overseas), www.intercape.co.za. **Greyhound**, T083-9159000 (in South Africa), T011-2768550 (from overseas), www.greyhound.co.za.

The **Baz Bus**, reservations T021-4392323, www.bazbus.com, is the best option for backpackers. See Essentials, page 41 for full details of the service.

Car hire
Phone the toll-free numbers for nearest branch. **Avis**, T0861-021111, www.avis.co.za. **Budget**, T0861-016622, www.budget.co.za. **Imperial/Europcar**, T0800-011344, www.europcar.co.za, www.imperialcarrental.co.za. **Hertz**, T0861-600136, www.hertz.co.za.

Taxi
Some of the malls have taxi ranks outside. **Maxi Taxi Cabs**, T011-6481212. **Rose Taxis**, T011-4039625/4030000, www.rosetaxis.com.

Train
Local Local Metrorail trains run between Johannesburg and Pretoria every 30 mins, but it is best avoided due to problems of crime. The **Gautrain**, a new high-speed rail link between Johannesburg and **Pretoria** via the airport and Midrand is currently being built and should be completed by 2009.

Long distance The railway station is in the Park City Transit Centre. Central reservations, T086-0008888, www.spoornet.co.za. Even though rail travel is relatively slow, the train service is popular and seats should be reserved well in advance. There are services (usually Mon, Tue, Thu, Fri and Sun) to **East London**, **Musina**, **Komatipoort**, **Cape Town** via **Bloemfontien**, **Durban** and **Port Elizabeth**.

Directory

Johannesburg *p562, maps p566, 570 and p571*
Banks
American Express, Sandton City Mall, T011-2944444; 33 Bath Av, Rosebank, T011-8808382; Hyde Park Mall, T011-3254424. **Rennies Travel**, and all the banks have branches in the larger shopping malls.

Embassies and consulates
Although there are some consulates in Johannesburg, for any passport or consular queries, you'll have to go to the embassies in Pretoria (see page 599).

Immigration
Dept of Home Affairs, President St, T011-8363228, www.home-affairs.pwv.gov.za. Mon-Fri 0730-1600. Visa extensions willtake 10 working days. You will need to produce an onward ticket and proof of funds.

Medical services
Sandton Medi-Clinic (private), corner of Peter Pl and Hendrik Verwoerd Dr, Bryanston, T011-7092000, www.sandtonmc.co.za. **Rosebank Clinic** (private), 14 Sturdee Av, Rosebank, T011-3280500. **Netcare 911**, T082-911, 24-hr medical services and ambulances. **Netcare Travel Clinic**, Morningside Close Office Park, 222 Rivonia Rd, Morningside, Sandton, T011-8020059, www.travelclinic.co.za. Mon-Fri 0730-1800, Sat 0830-1300. Useful stop to update vaccinations and pick up anti-malarials.

Internet
All the shopping malls have internet cafés; you will also be able to access the internet in most hostels and hotels and increasingly free Wi-Fi is available in coffee shops and other public places including the airport.

Post office
Main post office, T012-4017902 customer services, www.sapo.co.za (store locater on the website). Again found in all shopping malls.

Pretoria

→ Phone code: 012. Colour map 2, B2. Altitude: 1363 m.

The name Pretoria was given to the new settlement by Marthinus Wessel Pretorius, in memory of his father, Andries Pretorius, who had led the Voortrekkers in the bloody massacre of the Zulus at Blood River. Today it is the administrative capital of South Africa and the third largest city in the country. Despite being almost joined to Johannesburg 56 km to the south by a band of green-belt towns, the atmosphere of each city couldn't be more different. While Johannesburg was built on gold and industry, Pretoria's was founded on the Voortrekker period of South Africa's turbulent past and retains a rather stern, bureaucratic atmosphere – albeit softened by a large student population. While it is safer than Johannesburg, downtown Pretoria, like most major cities in South Africa, has gone through a transformation in recent years. With the demise of Apartheid, black South Africans are again permitted to live and work freely within the city centre, and it has much more of an African feel about it. ▶▶ For listings, see pages 595 600.

Ins and outs

Getting there

The centre of Pretoria is about 45 km from OR Tambo International Airport. The easiest way to travel to and from the airport is to take an airport shuttle service. There is a Metro commuter train service between Pretoria and Johannesburg but high crime levels means you should avoid it. Intercape, Greyhound and Translux have several departures between the two cities per day. The new high-speed **Gautrain** will link up Pretoria, Johannesburg and the airport, and is currently under construction.▶▶ *For further details, see Transport, page 598.*

Getting around

Most of Pretoria's sights lie in the surrounding hills. While there is a good local bus service, it does not connect between the various monuments in the city's suburbs. The easiest

Greater Pretoria

➡️Pretoria maps
1 Greater Pretoria, page 587
2 Central Pretoria, page 590
3 Hatfield & Hillcrest, page 592

Sleeping
Alpine House **2**
Battiss-Zeederberg Guest House **1**
Elegant Lodge **2**

Eating
Cynthia's **3**
La Madeleine **4**

way to appreciate the city sights is either on a guided tour or with a hire car. During the day, taking a municipal bus that runs between the centre and suburbs is a safe and cheap way of getting about town. **Church Street** is Pretoria's main through road, running from east to west, and at 26 km long is considered to be one of the world's longest streets. From the city centre it leads east to **Arcadia** where many of the embassies and the Union Buildings are located. To the south of here is **Sunnyside**, which until recently was home to most hotels and nightlife. However, the area has suffered a decline in recent years, with increasing crime rates. Many restaurants, hotels and backpacker hostels have relocated to the safer suburbs of **Hatfield** and **Brooklyn** a few kilometres further east where the colleges, universities and sports stadiums are located. Both are attractive suburbs, dotted with parks and gardens, and streets lined with Pretoria's distinctive jacaranda trees.

Best time to visit
Pretoria has a pleasant climate with warm to hot summers and mild sunny winters. In winter the daily temperature averages 19°C, the days are still and the skies are clear and cloud-free. In the evening it can get cool. The average annual rainfall is 741 mm, usually falling between November and March. The best time to visit is during the spring when the city is transformed by 60,000 flowering jacaranda trees, covering the parks and gardens in a mauve blanket.

Tourist information
The **Tshwane Tourism Information Bureau** ① *Church Sq, T012-3581430, www.tshwane.gov.za, Mon-Fri 0800-1600*, is in the Old Netherlands Bank Building. While there isn't the usual desk and helpful staff found in most local tourist offices, this bureau does produce a couple of useful maps, highlighting the major sights in the city.

The Pretoria office of **South Africa National Parks** (SANParks) ① *643 Leyds St, Muckleneuk, reservations T012-4265000, www.sanparks.org*, is the head office and handles all bookings for accommodation and special long-distance hikes such as the Otter Trail in Tsitsikamma National Park.

Background
From the outset, Pretoria has been closely involved with political upheaval in South Africa, culminating in the inauguration of President Nelson Mandela at the Union Buildings on 10 May 1994. In August 1854, work began on building a church right by today's Church Square – this was to be the beginnings of the town. The first streets were laid out by Andries du Toit, a self-taught surveyor, while the first suburb was known as Arcadia, which was developed by Stephanus Meintjes who in turn was commemorated by naming the hillock nearby, Meintjeskop.

During the 1860s, as the city was steadily growing, Marthinus Pretorius, who had been made president of the republic, tried to unite the Orange Free State with the Transvaal. He failed, resigned as president and was replaced by the Reverand Thomas François Burgers in 1870. Under Burgers, the city developed and schools and parks were built, but the political problems remained unresolved. The British eventually annexed the Transvaal in April 1877, and their first action was to establish a garrison which in turn attracted a large number of immigrants. New buildings were erected and the fortunes of the city began to look more promising. However, during the Transvaal War of Independence, the British withdrew and the city was taken over by the dominant Paul Kruger who was to cause countless problems once gold had been discovered.

At the end of the Anglo-Boer War, Pretoria was named as the capital of the British colony, and under such conditions it continued to prosper so that when the Union of South Africa was created in 1910, Pretoria was made the administrative capital of the new state. Shortly afterwards, the Union Buildings were constructed to house the new government. The growth of the town was now closely related to the expanding civil service and its status as an important city was assured. The city has remained a centre for government and today most overseas diplomats are based in Pretoria. The city is also headquarters of the defence forces and home to the University of South Africa (UNISA). Today it has over 125,000 students throughout the world and is regarded as one of the largest correspondence universities in the world.

Like Johannesburg, Pretoria has large township areas to the northwest and northeast of the city. The greater Pretoria area covers over 1600 sq km and the population is estimated at 1.9 million. The metropolitan council has reorganized itself to unite the previously segregated areas under one council administration. The greater area is now called Tshwane, which means 'we are the same'. Technically this is the new name for Pretoria but, like other regional name changes in South Africa, it will be some time before this is widely recognized and the name change is still under debate.

Sights

Pretoria's sights are spread between the city centre, the Church Square area and the suburbs, and can easily be seen in a day. Most popular is the controversial Voortrekker Monument, although there are also a couple of decent museums and historical buildings worth visiting. The other major attractions are the glitzy distractions of Sun City, a couple of hours' drive away and often visited as a day trip. Johannesburg and its outlying attractions such as Soweto and Walter Sisulu Botanical Gardens are dealt with in the Johannesburg section (see page 574) but are easily accessed from Pretoria.

City centre

The oldest buildings in Pretoria are clustered around Church Square, once a Voortrekker marketplace. Today it is the heart of the city and is a popular meeting spot for locals, with suited businessmen stopping on the grass for lunch and hawkers selling roasted mealies to passers by. A rather unattractive statue of a grim-faced, grizzled Paul Kruger stands in the middle, surrounded by fluttering flocks of pigeons and flanked with important late 19th-century banks and government offices. The most interesting of these is the **Palace of Justice**, where Nelson Mandela and other leaders of the ANC were tried during the notorious Treason Trials of 1963-1964. On the southwest side, the Raadsall, or parliament, and the Old Netherlands Bank building, which now houses the tourist office.

The **Transvaal Museum** ⓘ *Paul Kruger St, T012-3227632, www.nfi.org.za, daily 0800-1600, R10*, is a typically dusty natural history museum. It was founded in 1892 and moved into its current premises in 1912. Today, the museum serves as a research and documentation centre for the fauna of southern Africa, one of the leading centres for zoological research in the country. The displays, focusing on geology and stuffed animals, are spread over a series of halls, including the Austin Roberts Bird Hall, which showcases the varied birdlife of southern Africa, and a collection of semi-precious stones. More interesting, perhaps, is the fact that the world-renowned hominid fossil, 'Mrs Ples' (*Australopithecus africanus transvaalensis*), is kept here, although sadly the public doesn't

➡ **Pretoria maps**
1 Greater Pretoria, page 587
2 **Central Pretoria, page 590**
3 Hatfield & Hillcrest, page 592

Snake Park
Pretoria Zoo

Boom

Bloed

De Waal

Turner
Brown
Ford

Strubben

To ❶ & Union Buildings

Shepherd

Pinsloo

Proes

Shepherd

Vermeulen

To Miriammen Temple

Bosman

Palace of Justice

Groote Kerk

Church Square

First National

Ned Bank

Sammy Marks Square

Airport Shuttle

Reserve Bank

Church

Lilian Ngoyi Square

Taxis

State Theatre

ABSA

To ❹ Sunnyside, Arcadia, Muckleneuk & Mpumalanga (Kruger

Parliament

Bureau

Standard

Nelson Mandela Dr

Sanlam Centre

Cinema

Schoeman

ABSA

St Albans's Cathedral

Skinner

VD Byl

Skinner

To African Window

Volksteen

To ❷ & Pretoria Art Museum

Visagie

City Hall

Pretorius Square

Transvaal Museum

Burgers Park

To ❹ ❺, Sunnyside & Arcadia

Paul Kruger

Minnaar

Burgers Park

Minnaar

Nelson Mandela

Van Boeschoten

Jacob Maré

Melrose House

Rissik

Hoop

Christina

Scheiding

Taxis

Greyhound, Translux & Intercape

Loop

Rhodes

Berea Park

Railway

Gerard Moerdyk

Joubert

Walker

To ❺

N

| 200 metres |
| 200 yards |

Sleeping 🛏
224 **4**
Arcadia **3**

Court Classique **2**
That's It **5**
Whistletree Lodge **1**

Eating 🍴
Café Riche **1**
Oriental Palace **2**

have access to her. Opposite the museum is **City Hall**, dating from 1935, a grand building fronted by broad square, with a fountain and a statue of Andries Pretorius on horseback.

The **Treaty of Vereeniging** ending the Anglo-Boer War (1899-1902) was signed in **Melrose House** ① *275 Jacob Maré St, T012-3222805, www.melrosehouse.co.za, Tue-Sun 1000-1700, R9, small café in the converted stables*, on 31 May 1902, between the British High Command and Boer Republican Forces. The house was originally built in 1886 for George Heys, who made his fortune from trade and a stagecoach service to the Transvaal. It is regarded as one of the finest examples of Victorian domestic architecture in South Africa; marble columns, stained-glass windows and mosaic floors all help create a feeling of serene style and wealth. The house was restored after being bombed by right-wingers in 1990. Today the grounds are used for classical concerts.

Kruger House Museum ① *Church St West, T012-3321266, daily 0830-1700, R16*, is where President Kruger lived between 1884-1901. Now a museum, it displays a fairly diverting collection of his possessions, as well as objects relating to the Anglo-Boer War. At the back of the house is the state coach and his private railway carriage.

Pretoria Zoo ① *corner of Paul Kruger and Boom streets, the entrance is on Boom St, T012-3283265, www.zoo.ac.za, 0800-1730, R36, children R22*, now known officially as the National Zoological Gardens, is heavily involved in research and conservation. Covering 80 ha, with 6 km of walkways and just over 2500 species, it is South Africa's largest and best-designed zoo and is surprisingly spacious. It is home to the only koala bear to be born in Africa. Golf buggies are available for hire to get around.

Difficult to miss if you are walking about in the centre of town, the sprawling **Lilian Ngoyi Square** was known until 2006 as Strijdom Square and used to be dominated by a massive bust of JG Strijdom, covered by a curved concrete roof. The roof, considered something of an architectural feat, collapsed on 31 May 2001, 40 years to the day from when it was built. Strijdom was prime minister between 1954 and 1958 when the government started to place heavy restrictions on the ANC and banned the Communist Party – his statue doesn't seem to be missed much today. In 1956, Lilian Ngoyi led a march of 20,000 women from the square to the Union Buildings to demonstrate against obligatory carrying of pass books. The square was renamed after her on Women's Day 2006, the 50th anniversary of the march. It is flanked by the tall ABSA Bank building and the State Theatre, and remains a popular meeting place at lunchtime.

Burgers Park ① *between Van der Walt and Andries streets, winter 0600-1800, summer 0600-2200*, is the most central of Pretoria's city parks. This fine Victorian park was first laid out as a botanical garden in the early 1870s, and is today a popular meeting place where visitors relax in the shade of rubber trees, palms and jacarandas. The 'florarium' houses a collection of exotic plants in contrasting environments, from subtropical flowers to succulents from the Karoo and Kalahari regions. Elsewhere in the garden is a statue of remembrance for the officers of the South African Scottish Regiment who were killed during the First World War.

African Window ① *149 Visagie St, between Bosman and Schubart streets, T012-3246082, daily 0900-1700, free*, promotes itself as a centre of 'living' culture. There are good temporary exhibitions as well as displays on San rock art and information on the history and development of the Hananwa people from the Blue Mountain before the arrival of the first Europeans in Africa. The main entrance hall contains a curio shop and restaurant.

Sunnyside and Arcadia

Pretoria Art Museum ⓘ *Arcadia Park, T021-3441807, Tue-Sun 1000-1700, guided tours, www.pretoriaartmuseum.co.za, R6,* houses a fine collection of South African art as well as a selection of run-of-the-mill 17th-century Dutch paintings. The collection includes works by Pierneef, Frans Oerder and Anton van Wouw. It also houses interesting temporary exhibitions, including photography. Teas and light meals are available.

The magnificent red sandstone complex of the **Union Buildings** ⓘ *Church St, Arcadia, T012-3005200,* sits proudly on top of Meintjeskop overlooking the city centre. This is the administrative headquarters of the South African President, most famous for being the site of Nelson Mandela's speech after his inauguration as president on 10 May 1994, when

③ Hatfield & Hillcrest

➡Pretoria maps
1 Greater Pretoria, page 587
2 Central Pretoria, page 590
3 Hatfield & Hillcrest, page 592

Sleeping 🛏
La Maison 2
Mutsago Guesthouse 3
North South Backpackers 7
Pretoria Backpackers 6
Protea Hatfield Apartments 4

Eating 🍴
Café Bugatti 1
Cuban Café 8
Mozarellas 6
Wangthai 5

Bars & clubs 🍸
Cool Runnings 2
Keg & Hound 3
Drop Zone 4
Tings an' Times 7

200 metres
200 yards

the grounds in front of the building where packed with thousands of well-wishers. The building, designed by Herbert Baker, who also designed St George's Cathedral and Rhodes Memorial in Cape Town, was completed in 1913. Baker went on to help Edwin Lutyens in the planning of New Delhi, India. (The Union Buildings in Pretoria influenced his designs for the new Government Secretariat and the Imperial Legislative Assembly). The formal gardens below the buildings are pleasant to walk about, but the best reason for coming here is for the city view. Look out for the statues of South Africa's famous generals: Botha, on horseback, Hertzog and Smuts. Also found on the hill is the Pretoria War Memorial, Delville Wood Memorial and the Garden of Remembrance.

Pretoria's suburbs

Miriammen Temple ① *follow the N4, Proes St, from the city centre for 2 km, turn right into 7 St, daily all day*, is a pleasant reminder of the importance of the Indian population in South Africa. The temple is one of the oldest (1905) buildings in Pretoria. The imposing *gopuram*, or tower, is a 12.5-m-high layered structure of brightly painted gods, goddesses and demons interspersed with white layers of stones. The temple is devoted to Miriammen, the Hindu goddess of infectious diseases such as smallpox. You are free to enter most areas but remember to remove your shoes.

South of the city is the looming granite hulk of the **Voortrekker Monument** ① *south of the city, just off the R28, T012-3266770, www.voortrekkermon.org.za, daily 0800-1700 winter 0800-1800 summer, R35 pp, R30 car*, a controversial Afrikaner memorial. The monument, a 40-m cube, was completed in 1949 after 11 years of work. It is a sombre and unattractive structure, a windowless block dominating the landscape, but one of particular significance to Afrikaners. It was built to commemorate the Great Trek of the 1830s, when the Afrikaners struck inland from the Cape with just their ox wagons and little idea of the trials that lay ahead of them. Inside is the cavernous Hall of Heroes, guarded by a carved head of a buffalo above the entrance (thought to be the most dangerous animal in Africa). Around the walls 27 marble friezes depict both the trek and scenes from the Zulu wars, including a seriously suspect portrayal of the Battle of Blood River (see page 847), where the Afrikaners are shown as brave soldiers and the Zulus as cowardly savages. The monument was, until recently, the site of a huge annual celebration on 16 December, the date of the battle (known as the Day of the Covenant). At exactly midday on this date a ray of sunlight falls onto a large slab of stone in the centre of the basement (rather like a tomb), spotlighting the carved words: "Ons Vir Jou, Suid Afrika" (We are for you, South Africa). The fact that this date celebrated the bloody massacre of Zulus proved, unsurprisingly, hugely controversial, and after the end of Apartheid, this national holiday was renamed the Day of Reconciliation. Today, the celebrations are very low key indeed. For impressive views of the surrounding countryside and to the city, take the lift to the viewing area around the roof. In the basement are some displays of life during the Great Trek. Outside, the surrounding wall recreates the circular laager of 64 ox-wagons that can be seen at the site of the battlefield.

Located significantly on a hill opposite the Voortrekker Monument, **Freedom Park** ① *entrance off Potgieter St, across from Pretoria Central Prison, T012-3610021, www.freedompark.org.za*, is currently being built to commemorate the country's political history and to celebrate its cultural and natural heritage. Once completed the 52-ha site will comprise a museum and garden of remembrance, with statues and sculptures to honour ordinary South Africans who contributed to the country's development. Its mission is to be a testament to the truth and reconciliation process that occurred at the end of Apartheid. Completion is expected in 2009.

The best reason for coming to **Klapperkop Fort** ① *off the R28 on J Rissik Dr, daily 0800-1700, small entry fee*, is to enjoy the excellent views from this high vantage point. You can walk around the battlements but the rest of the fort is closed to the public. A separate building houses a **museum** on South Africa's military history. There is an old steam locomotive in the car park, plus a couple of tanks in the grounds. The fort was built to guard the southern entrance to the town, but no resistance was put up when the British entered the town in May 1900.

Pretoria, known as the Garden City, is well known for its parks and gardens and the city takes much pride in its magnificent open space. To the east of the city centre towards the N1, **Springbok Park**, between Schoeman Street and Nelson Mandela Drive in Hatfield, has a much more informal layout. This park was declared a national monument in 1979. It was first planted in 1905 when WH Lanham was planning the suburb of Hatfield. A stream flows through the grounds and there are some fine trees from different regions of the country.

Like Springbok Park, **Venning Park** is found between Schoeman Street and Nelson Mandela Drive, but slightly closer to the centre of town. It is a neatly planned garden known for its immaculate rose beds. An avenue of palm trees ends beside a pleasant tea garden and restaurant; the park is close to the diplomatic enclave and many families come here at weekends.

Jan Celliers Park, on the corner of Wenning and Broderick streets, west of Queen Wilhelmina Road in Groenkloof, is also known as **Protea Park**. It is the furthest park from the city centre, is on a natural slope and is made up of rock gardens, mixed borders, groups of trees and a water garden; two ponds are linked by a series of 14 small waterfalls. Aside from being a relaxing spot for a wander, the park is worth visiting if you are keen on wild flowers and wish to see some of South Africa's indigenous flora close up.

Pretoria listings

Hotel and guesthouse prices
L over US$300 AL US$220-300 A US$150-220
B US$100-150 C US$75-100 D US$35-75
E US$15-35 F under US$15
Restaurant prices
††† over US$30 †† US$15-30 † under US$15
See pages 46-51 for further information.

Sleeping

Pretoria *maps p587, p590 and p592*
As in many South African cities, most of
the best accommodation is found in
Pretoria's suburbs.

AL Whistletree Lodge, 1267 Whistletree
Dr, Queenswood, T012-3339915/6,
www.whistletree.co.za. Award-winning
guesthouse close to the Union Buildings.
12 en suite rooms elegantly decorated,
private balconies, attractive lounge with
traditional, sumptuous furniture, and high
ceilings, landscaped gardens and pool,
tennis court, sauna, cocktail bar, dinner
and snacks on request, no children
under 12. Popular with diplomats.

A Court Classique, corner of Schoeman
and Beckett streets, Arcadia, T012-3444420,
www.courtclassique.co.za. Practical choice
in the suburb of Arcadia, range of suites
aimed at families or business travellers, all
are spacious, en suite and have kitchenettes,
set around landscaped patios with water
features, swimming pool, restaurant bar
and conference centre. Within walking
distance of Loftus Stadium.

B Elegant Lodge, 83 Atterbury Rd,
Menlo Park, T012-3466460,
www.elegantlodge.co.za. Attractive
business hotel with easy access to the
N1 and Menlyn Park Mall. 16 a/c rooms,
comfortable furnishings, en suite, TV,
internet line, small pleasant restaurant,
escape the traffic on the main road in
the pretty courtyards.

B La Maison, 235 Hilda St, Hatfield,
T012-4304341, www.lamaison.co.za.

6 large en suite bedrooms, old-fashioned
decor, grand white Victorian mansion,
close to many diplomatic missions,
restaurant is highly regarded lush gardens,
swimming pool, roof-top terrace.

B Protea Hatfield Apartments, 1080
Prospect St, Hatfield, T012-3626105,
www.proteahotels.com. 28 en suite suites,
TV, a/c, pleasant decor, pool area, bar,
great location in the throng of shops
and restaurants of Hatfield.

B-C Mutsago Guesthouse, 327 Festival St,
Hatfield, T012-4307193, www.mutsago.co.za.
Smart 2-storey home surrounded by lush
tropical gardens, good-sized pool with
deck chairs set around it. 14 rooms with
an African theme, murals painted on the
walls depicting Zulu homesteads, African-
print fabrics on the beds, all en suite,
TV and minibar.

C Alpine House, 552 Atterbury Rd, Menlo
Park, T012-8110169, www.alpinehouse.co.za.
5 self-catering units, open-plan kitchen,
private lounge with DSTV, undercover
parking, tasteful contemporary decor,
stylish furniture, bleached wooden floors
and framed artwork. B&B available.

C Arcadia, 515 Proes St, T012-3269311,
www.arcadiahotel.co.za. 139 a/c rooms
with TV, quality city centre hotel, clean,
well managed and aimed at business
travellers and tour groups. Restaurant, bar,
coffee shop, lounge, gym, undercover
parking, part of the **Arcadia** shopping
complex, close to embassies and a short
walk to the Union Buildings.

C Battiss-Zeederberg Guest House,
3 Fook Island, 92 20th Street, Menlo Park,
T/F012-4607318, http://battiss.co.za.
Guesthouse set in original home of the
artist Walter Battiss, and much of his
character is still evident around the house –
his murals remain on the walls and the
floors as a reminder of his love for San
paintings. 4 double rooms with lofty
ceilings, shiny wood floors and large

French windows opening on to a leafy courtyard, en suite, TV, fans, kitchenette. You'll need your own car to get into town, but it's a short drive from the N1 and Menlyn Park shopping mall (see Greater Pretoria map, page 587).

D That's It, 5 Brecher St, Clydesdale, T012-3443404, www.thatsit.co.za. Neat B&B set in a family home in a quiet suburb. 4 simple and pleasant rooms, whitewashed walls and blue-and-white fabrics, thatched lapa in the tropical gardens, swimming pool, TV lounge, useful location if you need to apply for visas at one of the nearby foreign embassies.

D Hotel 224, corner of Schoeman and Leyds St, T012-4405281, www.hotel224.com. Huge concrete block offering 224 single and double a/c rooms, rooms are dated and on the small side, DSTV, video channel, restaurant, bar, secure parking, short walk from the Union Buildings.

D-F North South Backpackers, 355 Glynn St, Hatfield, T012-3620989, www.northsouthbackpackers.com. Clean and airy lodge with well-tended gardens and spotless pool within a few mins' walk of the shops and restaurants at Hatfield Sq. Doubles and dorms, bar with fireplace, pool table, helpful with booking tours. Will pick up from Johannesburg airport if arranged in advance.

D-F Pretoria Backpackers, 425 Farenden Rd, Clydesdale, T012-3439754, www.pretoriabackpackers.net. The oldest backpacker hostel in town, relocated and thoroughly renovated a few years ago. 2 houses around the corner from each other, 2 small dorms, several very comfortable doubles in garden huts or in the main house, 1 family unit sleeping 4, stylishly decorated with a guesthouse feel, lovely tropical gardens with fish ponds and gazebos, pool, travel desk. Organize local tours of Pretoria, Sun City/Pilanesberg, Lesedi Cultural Village. Will collect from Johannesburg airport. Staff will accompany guests to football and rugby matches at Loftus Stadium. Recommended.

⊙ Eating

Pretoria maps p590 and p592
In a city as spread out as Pretoria, the restaurants tend to be found in or near the large shopping malls (see Shopping, page 598). The city centre has plenty of sandwich bars and fast-food outlets serving office workers during the day, but few places to eat in at night. The best places to go in the evening are **Hatfield** and **Brooklyn**.

₮₮₮ Cynthia's, Maroelana Centre, near **Pretoria Country Club**, in the Maroelana Centre, in the southern suburbs off the N1, phone for directions, T012-4603220. Open 1800-2200. Popular local restaurant, rural feel to decor and menu, traditional meat dishes such as roasted lamb shank and chateaubriand, some seafood and game. Extensive wine list.

₮₮₮ La Madeleine, 122 Priory Rd, Lynnwood Ridge (from the N1 go east on the M6, then left into Camelia Av and left again into Priory Rd), T012-3613667. Dinner Tue-Sat 1900-2200, lunch only on Fri 1200-1400. Long-standing top restaurant, running for over 30 years. Fine cuisine and a pleasant, airy setting, classical French cuisine, dishes including Provençal lamb and confit of duck, award-winning wine list. Reservations recommended.

₮₮ Cuban Café, 129 Duxbury Rd, Hillcrest, T012-3621800, www.cubacafe.co.za. 0900-late. Located in a converted old post office, this has a formal restaurant, a cocktail bar and an upstairs cigar lounge, with contemporary earthy decor. Cuban fare such as *espetadas* and *arapas* (filled cornmeal pancakes) plus seafood platters, steaks and good crunchy salads.

₮₮ Oriental Palace, Colosseum Hotel, 410 Schoeman St, Arcadia, T012-3222195. Authentic Indian restaurant, chefs from Pakistan and north India who prepare genuine curries, good tikka and tandoori, delicious and great-value dhal, tandoori breads and kulfi. Everything halaal, no alcohol.

Wangthai, 281 Middle St, Brooklyn, T012-3466230. Open 1200-1430, 1800-2130. Authentic and elegant Thai restaurant, huge menu, lots of choice for vegetarians, not cheap but excellent food, sister restaurant in prestigious Nelson Mandela Sq in Jo'burg.

Mozzarellas, Hatfield Sq, Hatfield, T012-3626464. Good-value Italian pizza and pasta, tables spilling from the brightly painted interior onto lively Hatfield Sq, popular with students, good selection of pasta and decent pizzas, plus seafood and steaks.

Cafés

Café Bugatti, Burnett St, Hatfield. Popular spot, especially with the brunch crowd on Sun mornings. Alfresco tables plus a bar and restaurant inside. Great sharing platters, breakfasts and brunch, plus light meals, friendly service.

Café Riche, Church Sq (southwest corner), T012-3283173. Open 0600-2400. Restored historical building, feels like a Parisian café, great views over the square, range of breakfasts, light meals and late night dinners, thought to be the oldest café in Pretoria. Atmospheric spot.

Cool Runnings, Burnett St, Hatfield, T012-3620100. Open 1100-late. One of the chain of bar-cum-restaurants that attract a young studenty crowd, loud and raucous evenings, live reggae music on Sun. Always busy at the weekend, garish cocktails and imported beers.

Drop Zone, 141 Burnett St, Hatfield Sq. Stylish late-night cocktail bar, music has a chilled vibe, over 21s, more popular with young professionals than the usual student crowd, happy hour every day 2000-2100.

Hillside Tavern, 320 Hillside Rd, Lynnwood, T012-3481402. Closed Sat lunch. Pub and steak restaurant, substantial bar with wide choice of beers and ciders, revamped to look like a traditional English country pub.

Keg & Hound, 1077 Arcadia St, Hatfield. Good choice of imported beers, plus a snack menu. Popular pub atmosphere among the local university students, late nights at the weekend.

Tings an' Times, 21 Arcadia St, Arcadia, T012-4303176. Recently moved to bigger premises, this bar is popular for live music, can get very crowded, best to arrive mid-evening to guarantee a table, great cocktails, Middle Eastern and vegetarian meals including filled pitas, fun place.

🌓 Bars and clubs

Pretoria *maps p587, p590 and p592*
Again, by far the best areas to head for in the evening and at weekends are **Hatfield** and **Brooklyn**, both to the east of the town centre. Ask the taxi to take you to Hatfield Sq, from where there are dozens of places to explore within a short walk of each other.

Boston Tea Party, Menlyn Park, T012-3653625. Tue-Sat 1800-late. This is a large conference centre during the day, but at night it transforms into a popular venue with a mix of live music, comedy, and dancing with DJs spinning records. Impressive place holding up to 1000 revellers.

☺ Entertainment

Pretoria *maps p587, p590 and p592*
Computicket, T083-9158000, www.computicket.com. Advance booking for all events, has kiosks in Hatfield Plaza and Menlyn Park malls.

Cinema

Drive-in, on the rooftop of the shopping mall, Menlyn Park, T012-3488766. Showings nightly at 1930 and 2130. If you don't have your own car, you can hire a renovated original Chevvy or Chrysler convertible.

IMAX, Menlyn Park, T012-3488766. Giant screen with wrap-around sound, showing wildlife and landscape films.

NuMetro, at Menlyn Park, T012-3681301, 15 screens; and at Hatfield Plaza, T012-3625898, www.numetro.co.za.

O Shopping

Pretoria *maps p587, p590 and p592*
Most of Pretoria's shopping is limited to its large shopping malls: **Brooklyn Mall**, 338 Bronkhorst St, New Muckleneuk, T012-3461063; **Hatfield Plaza**, Park St, Hatfield. A lively flea market is held here at the weekend; **The Tramshed**, corner of Van der Walt and Schoeman streets, though avoid this area after dark; **Sanlam Centre**, Andries St, in the town centre.
Menlyn Park, Atterbury Rd, Menlo Park, clearly seen from the N1, T012-3488766, www.menlynpark.co.za. Pretoria's premier mall for 'shopper-tainment', with 300 shops and restaurants, 15-screen cinema, IMAX theatre, bowling alley, and unique drive-in cinema. Its architectural focal point is its large tent-like roof that can be seen from far away.

▲▲ Activities and tours

Pretoria *maps p587, p590 and p592*
Cricket
Supersport Stadium, formerly Centurion Park, 23 km from the centre of town, off the R21 to Johannesburg, enquiries 012-6631005, www.titans.co.za, tickets from www.computicket.com. The ground where international matches for Pretoria are now played is 23 km from the centre of town, off the R21 to Johannesburg. The ground, home to the Nashua Titans cricket team, is a modern circular stadium dominated by a huge single grandstand. The rest of the boundary is made up of grass banks which are great fun for picnics and braais.

Rugby
Pretoria is the home town for the **Vodacom Bulls**, T012-3444011, www.thebulls.co.za, tickets from www.computicket.com.
Loftus Versveld Rugby Stadium, Kirkness St, Sunnyside, is the main rugby stadium and is also the venue for occasional football matches and rock concerts.

Tour operators
Apart from city tours, the most popular day trips from Pretoria are to **Sun City**, **Pilanesberg National Park** and the **Gold Mines**. Expect to pay in the region of R350 per person for a half-day tour of the city, which takes in the major sights such as the Voortrekker Monument and Union Buildings. The tour operators listed under Johannesburg do city tours of Pretoria and can pick up from accommodation in Pretoria.
Rennies Travel, 15 Sanlam Centre, T012-3202240. National chain, all purpose travel agent plus Thomas Cook bureau de change, useful for reconfirming flights.
Ulysses, T012-6634941, www.ulysses.co.za. Daily city tours and trips to Pilanesberg, Sun City and Cullinan Diamond Mine.

⊖ Transport

Pretoria *maps p587, p590 and p592*
Exercise caution about the bus stand and train station as muggings have occurred in this area. Pretoria is 500 km to the Zimbabwe border (**Beitbridge**), 474 km to **Bloemfontein**, 1492 km to **Cape Town**, 688 km to **Durban**, 1060 km to **East London**, 1078 km to **Harare** (Zimbabwe), 58 km to **Johannesburg**, 530 km to **Kimberley**, 1406 km to **Knysna**, and 1133 km to **Port Elizabeth**.

Air

See page 585 for flight details for OR Tambo International Airport. **Magic Bus**, T011-5480822, www.magicbus.co.za, and **Airport Link Shuttle**, T011-7922017, www.airportlink.co.za, both drop off at the major hotels in Johannesburg and Pretoria.

Bus

Local Municipal buses run between the city centre and the suburbs. Timetables are available in chemists and from the service information office in Church Sq, T012-3080839. **Translux**, **Greyhound**, and **Intercape** buses run between Pretoria and Johannesburg (1 hr). Although they are long-distance coaches, there are several departures throughout the day. They cannot be pre-booked but seats are always available; expect to pay around R150 standby. You can then connect with other buses or trains at Johannesburg's Park City terminus.

Long distance The bus stand is to the left of the railway station (as you face it) in the 1928 Building. **Translux**, **Intercape** and **Greyhound** all have an office here, open during normal office hours. There are departures to destinations to all over the country from Pretoria, though on some southern routes, you have to swap on to another bus in Johannesburg. Full timetables can be found on the websites and tickets can be booked online. **Baz Bus** is the only budget transport for backpackers which will pick up and drop off at hostels in Pretoria. See page 41 for details of the service.

Bus companies Baz Bus, T021-4392323, www.bazbus.com. **Greyhound**, T083-9159000 (in South Africa), T011-2768550 (from overseas), www.greyhound.co.za. **Intercape**, T0861-287287 (in South Africa), T012-3804400 (from overseas), www.intercape.co.za. **Translux**, T0861-589282 (in South Africa), T011-774333 (from overseas), www.translux.co.za.

Car hire

Phone the toll-free numbers for the nearest branch.

Car hire

Phone the toll-free numbers for nearest branch. **Avis**, T0861-021111, www.avis.co.za. **Budget**, T0861-016622, www.budget.co.za. **Hertz**, T0861-600136, www.hertz.co.za. **Imperial/Europcar**, T0800-011344, www.europcar.co.za, www.imperialcarrental.co.za.

Taxi

Taxis in front of the railway station, on Prinsloo opposite the tourist office, and on Church St by Lilian Ngoyi Sq. **Rixi Taxi**, T012-3258072.

Train

Long distance Pretoria is on the Johannesburg–Musina route. All the other long-distance trains depart from Johannesburg. There is a booking office to the right in the main railway station building. **Central Reservations**, T086-0008888, www.spoornet.co.za.

Directory

Pretoria *maps p587, p590 and p592*
Banks American Express, 306 Brooklyn Mall, Bronkhorst St, T012-3463580; **Rennies Travel**, agents for Thomas Cook, Sanlam Centre, corner of Andries and Pretorius streets, T012-3202240. There are **Rennies Travel** and **American Express** bureaux de change at Johannesburg International Airport, daily 0500-2100. All banks have outlets in the many shopping malls dotted about the suburbs and have foreign exchange facilities where you can cash TCs and change money or withdraw money from your credit card at an ATM. **Embassies and consulates** Australia, T012-4236000. **Belgium**, T012-4403201. **Botswana**, T012-4309640. **Canada**, T012-4223000.

Denmark, T012-4309340. **Finland**, T012-3430275. **France**, T012-4251600. **Germany**, T012-4278900. **Ireland**, T012-3425062. **Israel**, T012-4703500. **Japan**, T012-4521500. **Lesotho**, T012-4607648. **Malawi**, T012-3420146. **Mozambique**, T012-4010300. **Namibia**, T012-4819100. **Netherlands**, T012-4244500. **Swaziland**, T012-3441910. **UK**, T012-4217500. **USA**, T012-3414000. **Zambia**, T012-3261854. **Zimbabwe**, T012-3425125. **Immigration** Dept of **Home Affairs**, corner of Maggs and Petroleum streets, Waltloo, T012-8108911, www.home-affairs.pwv.gov.za, Mon-Fri 0730-1600. Visa extensions will take 10 working days. You will need to produce an onward ticket and proof of funds.

Internet There are numerous internet cafés in all the malls, an in and around Hatfield Sq. Most backpacker hostels and hotels offer internet access. **Medical services** Wilgers Hospital, Denneboom Rd, Lynnewood Ridge, T012-8070019; **Zuid-Afrikaans Hospital**, (private) 255 Bourke St, Muckleneuk, T012-2430300. **Vaccinations:** Netcare Travel Clinic, 213 Middelberg St, Muckleneuk, T012-4216805, www.travelclinic.co.za.

Contents

Footprint features

At a glance

⊖ **Getting around** Buses and Baz
Bus to Nelspruit, car hire, tours
start and finish in Johannesburg.

◉ **Time required** 4-6 days for
Kruger and Panorama Region.

☀ **Weather** Chilly but sunny in
winter, some humidity and
showers in summer.

✖ **When not to go** Christmas
and Easter South African
school holidays.

Mpumalanga, the 'place of the rising sun', is one of South Africa's most popular tourist destinations, thanks almost entirely to the magnificent Kruger National Park. Despite being completely geared towards tourism – and receiving a staggering one million visitors every year – there are few places in Africa offering such excellent game viewing. It's a vast area, roughly the same size as Wales and with a bewildering variety of habitats. While it's entirely possible to see the Big Five in one afternoon, a longer stay allows visitors to fully appreciate the wilderness of the park – and to escape to its less-visited corners. Fringing the national park are large private reserves where game wanders unrestricted by fences; also here are some of the world's most luxurious safari lodges.

The rest of the province is understandably eclipsed by Kruger, but the area west of the park is well worth a detour. The forests and waterfalls of the Eastern Drakensberg make a pleasant change from the heat of the Lowveld. This mountainous area is dotted with quiet agricultural towns, clustered along the top of the spectacular Blyde River Canyon, the third largest in the world, and a handful of viewpoints open up stunning vistas to the Lowveld shimmering to the horizon. Further into the mountains is the historical gold-mining town of Pilgrim's Rest, a string of restored miners' cottages nestling in a quiet valley. The gold-rush story continues in the Victorian town of Barberton, set in the hills close to Swaziland.

Ins and outs

Getting there

Kruger Mpumalanga International Airport (KMIA) is 25 km from the centre of Nelspruit towards Kruger, 10 km from the Maputo corridor (N4) and a short drive from Kruger's Numbi and Malelane gates. The airport is served by national airlines as well as a number of small private charter companies flying visitors into the private game reserves.

▶▶ *For further details, see Ins and outs, page 605, and Transport, page 616.*

Getting around

The two main areas of interest in Mpumalanga are the Kruger National Park and the eastern Drakensberg, or Panorama Region, famous for the Blyde River Canyon. The public transport network doesn't link the towns and sights effectively, so the best way to visit the more isolated beauty spots is to hire a car, and it's possible to do a leisurely circuit in two or three days. For budget travellers, the **Baz Bus** picks up and drops off at backpacker hostels in Nelspruit. From here it is possible to arrange pickups by other hostels and there are many tour operators to choose from who run inexpensive two- to three-day tours combining Kruger and the Panorama region. Alternatively, a number of affordable tours run from Johannesburg, see page 584.

Malaria

Visitors to this region must take a malaria prophylactic. Look at a map and imagine a straight line running from Nelspruit in the south directly north to the border with Zimbabwe in the Northern Province. Anywhere to the right or east of this line is an endemic malarial area. Kruger National Park is regarded as medium risk, especially during and just after the rainy season when there is a lot of free-standing water. Advice is available from the very useful Kruger malaria hotline, T082-2341800 (mob).

Tourist information

Mpumalanga Tourism Authority ① *T013-7527001, www.mpumalanga.com, Mon-Fri 0800-1630*, is the regional office. It is located next door to the Mpumalanga Parks Board. They publish a useful regional guide and have numerous leaflets on the surrounding area, and they can make bookings and give advice on Kruger. To get there, head 5 km west of Nelspruit on the N4 (turn off at the Shell Halls Gateway service station).

Landscape

The **Lowveld** is the strip of land which extends eastwards from the foot of the Drakensberg escarpment to the border with Mozambique. It begins below the foothills of Swaziland and stretches as far north as the Blyde River Canyon and the border with the Limpopo Province. Most of the region is a low-lying humid plain, crossed by many small rivers and broken up with ridges of hills, none of which rise above 600 m.

Kruger National Park is a classic Lowveld region with its rolling savannah plains, acacia trees and herds of slowly moving game. There is superb game viewing to the west of Kruger, which is where most of the luxury private game reserves can be found. These lodges are administered separately, but now form part of what is termed as the Greater Kruger National Park thanks to the removal of fences between private reserves and the park itself.

There are several irrigation schemes along the rivers which flow eastwards off the escarpment into Kruger. The actual land under cultivation isn't large, but this is an important area for growing tropical fruit. The plantations, a major source of employment, produce bananas, avocados, mangoes, lychees and citrus fruits. Throughout the year, stalls line the roads in the area selling off fresh produce.

Nelspruit and around

→ *Phone code: 013. Colour map 2, B5. Altitude: 716 m.*
Nelspruit developed around the railway when the line between Pretoria and Lourenço Marques (now Maputo) was completed in 1891. Briefly the capital of the Transvaal Republic after Paul Kruger abandoned Pretoria in 1900 during the Boer War, Nelspruit is now the industrial centre of the Lowveld and a processing point for the fruit, tobacco and beef farms of the surrounding region. The town has a sleepy, tropical feel with broad, modern streets lined with acacias, bougainvillea and jacaranda trees. Although there's little to keep you here, most visitors to the region pass through at some point. ►► *For listings, see pages 612-617 For places north of Nelspruit, see pages 646-660.*

Ins and outs

Getting there Nelspruit has good transport links, with an important international airport and good train and bus links. There are great facilities here for tourists planning trips to Swaziland, the Panorama region and Kruger National Park, as well as across the border to Mozambique (there is a daily train service between Pretoria/Johannesburg and Komatipoort, the border post with Mozambique). The **Baz Bus** runs from Johannesburg, Pretoria and Swaziland. **Greyhound**, **Intercape** and **Translux** all operate services from Johannesburg and Pretoria to Maputo in Mozambique, which stop in Nelspruit. ►► *For further details, see Transport, page 616.*

Getting around Nelspruit has excellent road links to Mpumalanga's major tourist attractions. The nearest entrance gates to Kruger are less than 80 km away on the N4 (east), and the R40 through White River (north), and a day trip to see the southern sector of the park is quite feasible. The gold rush town of Barberton is 43 km to the south on the R40, and a visit here could be combined with a day trip over the border to Swaziland. The mountain villages of Sabie and Graskop are equally accessible and make a pleasant change from the heat of the Lowveld. All these places have an excellent range of accommodation and there is little reason to stay in the centre of town. The shopping centres in town are convenient for stocking up on food and equipment before setting off to stay in self-catering accommodation in Kruger.

Orientation Nelspruit has grown rapidly in recent years and it has a prosperous air with a new sprawl of well-off suburbs surrounding the city centre. New business parks and a number of shopping malls have been built in the area, especially along the road to White River. As a consequence, Nelspruit has extended its municipality by joining with neighbouring White River and Hazyview to form the Mbombela Municipal Region (meaning, appropriately, 'a lot of people put together in a small space'). Mbombela is now the provincial capital of Mpumalanga Province. The Mbombela Stadium is currently being built 8 km north of Nelspruit for the 2010 FIFA Football World Cup.

Tourist information **Lowveld Tourism Association** ① *Crossing Centre, at the junction of the N4 and the R40, just west of the centre, T013-7551988, www.lowveldinfo.com, Mon-Fri 0800-1700, Sat 0800-1300,* is the main tourist office for the entire region. It can organize car hire, safaris, game drives and accommodation in Kruger.

From Gauteng to Nelspruit

The journey east along the N4 from Gauteng crosses a bland, sprawling area of cattle ranching country, broken up by industrial towns like Witbank and Middleberg. There's little to break the monotony of the drive, other than a couple of looming coal-fired power stations. At **Machadodorp** the views improve; the road starts to drop into the Elands River Valley and the vista opens up over the Lowveld, passing through the towns of **Waterval Boven** and **Waterval Onder**. This is a beautiful stretch of road with high cliffs on either side. Dotted along the valley are a number of country hotels and motels which catch the holiday traffic en route to Kruger Park and Mozambique.

Nelspruit

Sleeping 🛏	Orion Promenade 4	Eating 🍴
Bavaria 1	Palms Guest House 12	Brewer's Feast 2
Funky Monkey	Roost 10	Chez Vincent 7
Backpackers 15	Safubi River Lodge 7	Costa do Sol 5
Jörns 16	Shandon Lodge 13	Ku's 3
La Roca 11	Sheppard Boutique 6	Le Gourmet 4
Loerie's Call 14	Sun Lodge 5	O'Hagen's 6
Mercure Inn 8	Utopia in Africa 17	Pappa's Pizzeria 1
Nelspruit Backpackers &		Parillo's 8
Mbombela Safaris 3		

Lowveld National Botanical Gardens

ⓘ *1 km north of Nelspruit on the R40. T013-7525531, www.sanbi.org. Daily 0800-1800. R15.*

The Lowveld National Botanical Gardens are relatively small but have a very important and rare collection of plants, and there are a number of trails you can follow. The visitor centre has interesting information on the flora and fauna of the area, as well as an attached nursery and bookshop. If you turn left after entering the gardens you will see a boardwalk which takes you through a 3-ha **Tropical Rainforest**. At the far end of the path is an open area of marshland which is good birdwatching country.

At the other end of the gardens is the **Cycad Collection**, the largest of its kind in Africa, and the **Riverside Trail** – a 1-km walk along the banks of the Crocodile River, with a bridge linking the two sides. The well-illustrated guide that accompanies the trail identifies over 130 plants and shrubs that were typical of what was once a wilderness around Nelspruit. This is also home to a rare and shy bird, the African finfoot, but you will have to walk very quietly to have any chance of spotting it. The trail takes about an hour but is steep and uneven in parts.

Croc River Enviro Park

ⓘ *North of town, off the R40 towards White River, T013-7525511, www.enviropark.co.za. Daily 0800-1700; handling demonstrations on Sat-Sun and South African school holidays at 1100 and 1500. R45, R25 children.*

Like so many other crocodile parks in southern Africa, this one claims to be the largest of its type in the whole continent. It's certainly attracted quite a bit of investment, and has developed into an exciting attraction (especially for children). The reptiles are on show in a variety of houses, each with a different environment, rather like the greenhouses in a botanical garden. The turtle pond, crocodile pool and fishpond are linked by a cascading waterway. Inside the tropical house is a 9-m waterfall and an aquarium with some dwarf crocodiles from Central America. The reptile gallery houses 88 indigenous and exotic species. Visitors can view two snake pits from the safety of an elevated walkway. There is also a desert house with a realistic desert landscape.

Sudwala Caves

ⓘ *36 km northwest of Nelspruit, follow the N4 westwards, turn onto the R539 (towards Sabie) after 30 km and follow the signs for the caves, T013-7334152, www.sudwalacaves.co.za. A 90-min tour departs every 30 mins 0830-1630. R40, children R20.*

The entrance to the caves is on a forested hillside in the Houtbosloop Valley. Only the first 2.5 km of the cave system has been explored and it is thought that the passages could lead much further into the mountains. A tour explores the first 600 m of the cave system, where the stalactites and stalagmites are lit by coloured spotlights. The rock formations have been given biblical names, such as Lot's wife, Devil's pulpit and the weeping Madonna. One of the most interesting formations is the Gong, which resonates through the cave chambers when struck. Keen cavers can organize a special visit to the Crystal Chamber on the first Saturday of each month, which takes five hours and must be booked in advance; no children or large people.

Towards Komatipoort and Mozambique ⊝❶▲⊖❶ ➤ pp612-617.

The N4 heads east from Nelspruit to Komatipoort (104 km), past the villages of Kaapmuiden, Malelane and Hectorspruit. The road follows the Crocodile River Valley through an area of fruit plantations at the bottom edge of Kruger National Park. This valley is one of the hottest areas of South Africa with year-round temperatures averaging between 25 and 30°C.

Malelane → *Phone code: 013. Colour map 2, B5.*

A dusty town with a sprawling shopping centre, Malelane is the hub of a sugarcane- and fruit-growing area. There's not much to the town itself but thanks to its proximity to Kruger there are a number of excellent game lodges along the Crocodile River around this region. Indeed, it's common for buffalo and elephant to cross the river here and graze in people's gardens. The R570 continues north through the village to the entrance to Kruger Park at Malelane Gate. Information is available at the **Kruger Park South Tourism Association** ① *Daph's Leather Shop, Spar Mall, T013-7901193, www.malelane.co.za*. It's a helpful private office with a collection of brochures and will book local accommodation.

The Matsamo/Jeppes Reef border crossing into **Swaziland** (open 0800-2000), is 38 km south of Malelane on the R570.

Komatipoort → *Altitude: 137 m. Phone code: 013. Colour map 2, B5. 104 km from Nelspruit.*

Komatipoort is the last town in South Africa before the main road enters Mozambique at Lebombo. In the early days, it was just a campsite by the river crossing but as soon as the railway arrived in 1890, it quickly developed into a permanent settlement. Travelling from Lourenço Marques (today Maputo), this was the only place where the railway could pass through the Lebombo Mountains. The Nkhomati Accord was signed here in March 1984 between Samora Machel, President of Mozambique and PW Botha, Prime Minister of South Africa. The accord intended to promote peace and co-operation between the two countries but met with limited success as Mozambique, along with the rest of Africa, was still a staunch opponent to the Apartheid regime and supported sanctions. Not far from here on the Komati flats is the **Machel Memorial** which is a national monument marking the site where President Samora Machel tragically died in a plane crash in 1986. Joaquim Chissano succeeded him and his widow Graca Machel went on to marry Nelson Mandela a few years later.

Today, the town is an important marshalling yard for the railways and a popular centre for supplies for visitors to Kruger National Park (**Crocodile Gate** is only 9 km away). Lying at the foot of the Lebombo Mountains at the confluence of the Komati and Crocodile rivers and little over 60 km from the Indian Ocean, the climate here is tropical and humid, with high summer temperatures and rainfall. Fortunately, the streets are shaded by poinciana and jacaranda trees, which provide essential shade. There are supermarkets in the town centre along Rissik Street.

☾ *Mahatma Gandhi was imprisoned in Komatipoort in 1907, before escaping to the coast (see box, Mahatma Gandhi in South Africa, page 474).*

Footprint Mini Atlas
South Africa

NAMIBIA

BOTSWANA

ZIMBABWE

MOZAMBIQUE

LIMPOPO

Polokwane ○

Mmabatho ○

PRETORIA □

MPUMALANGA

Nelspruit ○

Johannesburg ○

GAUTENG

MBABANE □

SWAZILAND

NORTH WEST PROVINCE

Upington ○

Kimberley ○

FREE STATE

KWAZULU NATAL

Springbok ○

NORTHERN CAPE

Bloemfontein ○

MASERU □

LESOTHO

Durban ○

Atlantic Ocean

EASTERN CAPE

East London ○

WESTERN CAPE

Cape Town ○

George ○

Nelson Mandela Bay ○

Indian Ocean

Altitude in metres		Main roads
	3000	Minor roads
	2000	Tracks
	1500	Railways
	1000	
	500	
	200	
	0	

N

200 km
200 miles

Neighbouring Country

Map 1

A

BOTSWANA

Kgalagadi
Transfrontier
Park

Nossob

Kgalagadi
Transfrontier
Park

Nossob

Makap

Molopo

M
N
Re

B

Mata Mata

Vorsters

Auob

Tshabong

McCarthy's Rest

R380

Seve

Twee Rivieren   Two Riviers

Middelputs
border post

Aansluit

Rietfontein

Hakskeenpan

Molopo

Van Zylsrus

Andriesvale

Askham   Staansaam

R31

Black
Rock

Cramond

Sonstraal

Hota

Koranna berg

Tswalu Kalahari
Reserve

Gordonia

Obobogorap

Kalahar

C

Noenieput

K

Sishen Ir
Ore Min

Olifantshoek

To Keetmanshoop   Nakop

R360

3

Ariamsvlei

Green Kalahari

N8

Spitskop
Nature Reserve

2

N14

3

Postma

Lutzputz

1

Map 3

Sendelingsdrift

NAMIBIA

Ai-Ais/Richtersveld
Transfrontier Park

Kuboes

Alexander Bay

Eksteenfontein

Noordoewer

Viooolsdrif

Gariep (Orange)

Onseep

Lekkersing

Henkries

Goodhouse

Pella

A

Pofadd

Aggeneys

Annenous Pass

Steinkopf

Sonop

Port Nolloth

R382

Concordia

N14

Nababeep

Okiep

Diepvlei

Springbok

Goegap
Nature Reserve

Grootmis

R355

Kleinsee

Komaggas
Wildeperdhoek
Pass

R358

Gamoep

N7

Kamieskroon

Vaalputs

Platbakkies

Hondeklipbaai

Karkams
Namaqua
National Park

N a m a k w a

Wallekraal

Garies

B

Kliprand

Nariep

Groenriviersmond

Loeriesfont

Kotzesrus

Bitterfontein

6

Sout

Atlantic Ocean

Nuwerus

Komkans

Niewoudtvi

Vanrhyns
Pass

Lutzville

Vanrhynsdorp

R27

Papendorp

Vredendal

Krakadouw Mountains

Strandfontein

Klawer

Doring Bay

Trawal

Olifants

Pakhuis
Pass

N

Lambert's Bay

Graafwater

Clanwilliam

Wupper

30 km

Wadrif Salt Pan

R364

Jakkals

Clanwilliam
Dam

30 miles

Leipoldtville

Algeria

Cederber
Wilderne
Area

C

Elands Bay
Baboon Point

R365

Verlorenvlei

Cederbe

Redelinghuys

Piekenierskloof Pass

Citrusdal

Rocherpan
Nature Reserve

Aurora

Hot
Springs

Shell Bay
Point

St
Helena
Bay

Velddrif

Piketberg Mountains

Eendekuil

R3

Paternoster
Cape
Columbine

R399

Groot Berg

R399

Piketberg

Porterv

Vredenburg

Hopefield

Moorreesburg

R44

Saldanha
Saldanha Bay
Postberg
Reserve

Langebaan

*West Coast
National
Park*

R45

Swartland

Gydo P
Winterhoekb
Tulbagh

1

2

Map 8

Atlantic Ocean

Indian Ocean

① ② ③

N

20 km
20 miles

A
B
C

West Coast National Park
Tienie Versveld Reserve
Yzerfontein
Dassen Island
Bok Point
Bay
Swartland
Darling
Mamre
Moorreesburg
Riebeek West
Riebeek Kasteel
Malmesbury
Philadelphia
Melkbosstrand
Bloubergstrand
Robben Island
Table Bay
Camps Bay
Cape Town
Milnerton
Parow
Fish Hoek
Kommetjie
Hout Bay
Silvermine Nature Reserve
Simon's Town
Cape of Good Hope Nature Reserve
Cape Point
False Bay
Muizenberg
Strand
Gordon's Bay
Somerset West
Stellenbosch
Wellington
Paarl
Franschhoek
Pringle Bay
Rooiels
Betty's Bay
Cape Hangklip
Kleinmond
Hawston
Onrus
Hermanus
Walker Bay Nature Reserve
Stanford
Gansbaai
De Kelders
Danger Point
Dyer Island
Pearly Beach
Franskraal
Quoin Point
Die Dam
Grootbos Nature Reserve
Wolvengat
Elim
Napier
Bredasdorp Mountains
Salmonsdam Nature Reserve
Bredasdorp
Overberg
Caledon
Shaw's Pass
Bot River
Botrivier
Grabouw
Elgin
Villiersdorp
Theewaterskloof Dam
Genadendal
Greyton
Riviersonderend
Riviersonderend
Boesmanskloof Trail
McGregor
Robertson
Ashton
Montagu
Bonnievale
Swellendam
Bontebok National Park
Marloth Nature Reserve
Tradouw Pass
Suurbraak
Barrydale
Heidelberg
Witsand
Port Beaufort
Malgas
Infanta
Cape Infanta
St Sebastian Bay
Breede
Ouplaas
De Hoop Nature Reserve
Waenhuiskrans
(Arniston)
De Mond Nature Reserve
Struisbaai
L'Agulhas
Cape Agulhas
Agulhas National Park
Soetendal Vlei
Sandbaai
Grootvadersbosch Nature Reserve
Grootvadersbosch
Uitvlugt
Riversdale
Still Bay
Albertinia
Jongensfontein
Langeberg Mountains
Langeberg
Garcia Pass
Langberg
Seven Weeks Poort
Calitzdorp
Van Wyksdorp
Ladismith
Vlieland
Rooinek
Matjiesfontein
Anysberg Nature Reserve
Touws River
Touws
Witberge
Witteberg
De Doorns
Hex River Valley
Aquila Private Game Reserve
Hex River Dam
Hattentorskloof
Worcester
De Dooms
Ceres
Prince Alfred Hamlet
Gydo Pass
Michell's Pass
Voëlvlei Dam
Tulbagh
Winterhoekberg
Wolseley
Hermon
Botha
Rawsonville
Breede River Valley
Brandvlei Dam
Loke Marais
Bainskloof
Huguenot Toll Tunnel
Sir Lowry's Pass
Kogelberg Nature Reserve
Hottentots Holland Nature Reserve
Viljoens Pass
Groenland Mountains

R27
R315
R45
R307
R302
R44
N2
R310
R316
R43
R326
R60
R62
R317
R318
R324
R322
N1
R43
R303
R323

Distance chart

	Bloemfontein	Cape Town	Durban	East London	George	Johannesburg	Kimberley	Nelson Mandela Bay	Nelspruit	Polokwane
Cape Town	1004									
Durban	634	1753								
East London	584	1079	674							
George	773	438	1319	645						
Johannesburg	398	1402	588	982	1171					
Kimberley	177	962	811	780	762	472				
Nelson Mandela Bay	677	769	984	310	335	1075	743			
Nelspruit	757	1762	707	1226	1530	355	827	1434		
Polokwane	727	1736	929	1323	1499	331	798	1393	315	
Pretoria	456	1460	646	1040	1229	58	530	322	273	1133

Distances in kilometres

Map symbols

- □ Capital city
- ○ Other city, town
- International border
- Regional border
- ⊖ Customs
- Contours (approx)
- ▲ Mountain, volcano
- Mountain pass
- Escarpment
- Glacier
- Salt flat
- Rocks
- Seasonal marshland
- Beach, sandbank
- Waterfall
- Reef
- Motorway
- Main road
- Minor road
- Track
- Footpath
- Railway
- Railway with station
- ✈ Airport
- Bus station
- Ⓜ Metro station

- - - - - Cable car
- Funicular
- Ferry
- Pedestrianized street
- ⊃ ⊂ Tunnel
- One way street
- Steps
- Bridge
- Fortified wall
- Park, garden, stadium
- Sleeping
- Eating
- Bars & clubs
- Building
- Sight
- Cathedral, church
- Chinese temple
- Hindu temple
- Meru
- Mosque
- Stupa
- Synagogue
- Tourist office
- Museum
- Post office
- Police

- Ⓢ Bank
- @ Internet
- ♪ Telephone
- Market
- Medical services
- Ⓟ Parking
- Petrol
- Golf
- Archaeological site
- National park, wildlife reserve
- Viewing point
- Campsite
- Refuge, lodge
- Castle, fort
- Diving
- Deciduous, coniferous, palm trees
- Hide
- Vineyard, winery
- Distillery
- Shipwreck
- Historic battlefield
- Detail map
- Related map

Index

To Mozambique via Komatipoort/Lebombo

The South African border post is at Lebombo, 3 km out of town. There is a viewpoint on a hill by the border from where one can look into Mozambique, striking for the rolls of barbed wire that stretch along either side of the border to prevent people crossing illegally. There is a new toll road between Nelspruit and Maputo; the journey between the two cities takes around 2½ hours. Komatipoort is 96 km from Maputo.
Border opening hours Daily 0600-2200.
Customs and immigration Most visitors require visas for Mozambique; these are issued at the border, US$25 or R170. South African passport holders do not need a visa.
Vehicle formalities Note that most hire car firms do not allow vehicles into Mozambique. If you are in your own vehicle, you will need a carnet de passages and will need to purchase third-party insurance at the border.

Barberton 😊😊🏔️😊😊 ⮕ pp612-617. Colour map 2, C5.

→ Phone code: 013.
This quiet colonial town, 43 km from Nelspruit, is a pleasant place to spend a day or two, and offers a surprising amount to do and see, including a couple of community projects and several museums. The Swaziland border is only 43 km away. It has an interesting gold mining past and, unlike the gold mining town of Pilgrim's Rest near Sabie, which is completely devoted to tourism, the old corrugated-iron roofed mining buildings in Barberton are very much part of the working commercial town. **Lone Tree Hill**, on the outskirts of Barberton, is one of the most popular hang-gliding centres in South Africa. It is set in the De Kaap Valley where some of the oldest sedimentary rock formations in the world have been found (4200 million years). The Makhonjwa Mountains around Barberton are covered in grasslands and woods and are an extension of the southern Drakensberg.

The road into Barberton passes the Emjindini township before entering the quiet, wealthy, garden suburbs on the edge of town. An old, abandoned mining centre, suitably named Eureka City, is tucked up in the hills at the back of the working Sheba mine (visits can be arranged in a 4WD vehicle). The main sights in town are all within walking distance and the hiking trails start from the edge of town.

Ins and outs
Tourist information **Barberton Information Bureau** ⓘ *Market Sq, T013-7128800, www.barberton.info, Mon-Fri 0800-1300, 1400-1630, Sat 0830-1200*, is a friendly and helpful office with good information on tours and accommodation in the area. Check here for up-to-date information on excursions to Swaziland.

Background
The De Kaap Valley was originally known as the 'Valley of Death' due to the many prospectors who had died here of malaria. Barberton is famous for being the site of one of South Africa's first large-scale gold rushes. Pioneer Reef was discovered in 1883 by 'French Bob' and by 1886 over 4000 claims were being worked in the valley. Barberton became a wild frontier town of corrugated iron shacks, gambling dens and whisky bars.

The town soon developed into a wealthy hub. South Africa's first gold stock exchange opened here in 1887 and many of Barberton's most attractive colonial buildings were erected during the gold rush. Unfortunately, the gold rush only lasted a few years – the stock market crashed after too many speculators were sold shares in bogus companies and investors lost fortunes in the Transvaal and Britain. By the outbreak of the Boer War, Barberton had been virtually abandoned by the miners who had moved on to Witwatersrand. However, in recent years the industry has been revived and four gold mines operate within the area: Sheba, Fairview, New Consort, and Agnes, providing employment for much of the local community.

> ☽ In the 19th century Cockney Liz, a notorious prostitute and resident of Barberton, would dance on a snooker table every night whilst being auctioned off to the highest bidder.

Barberton

Sleeping 🛏
Barberton Chalets & Caravan Park 6
Digger's Retreat 5
Fountain Baths 1
Kloofhuis 3
Phoenix 2
William George 4

Eating 🍴
Old Rock Café 1
Victoria Tea Garden 2

Sights

The historical sites within the town have been clearly mapped out by Barberton's tourism initiative as the **Heritage Walk**, and are all within walking distance of Market Square. Pick up a map at the tourist office. The walk starts from the Barberton Museum and ends at the Steam Locomotive. The sights have been listed below in order of the walk. Only Belhaven House Museum and Stopforth House Museum have an entry fee, R10 per person, but you only need pay once to cover entrance at both.

Barberton Museum ① *36 Pilgrim St, 1013-7124280, daily 0900-1600*, is the town's local history museum with displays on geology, mining and cultural history of the area, including some displays on Swazi history. **The Blockhouse** ① *on the corner of Lee Rd and Judge St*, is a small fort built in 1901 during the Boer War as part of the defence of Barberton. It is made from wood and corrugated iron and is one of the earliest examples of its kind. **Belhaven Museum** ① *Lee Rd, 1000-1200, 1400-1500*, is a large, early Edwardian mansion built in 1904 and set in mature gardens. The interior is decorated with period furniture and gives an interesting insight into the comfortable lifestyles of Barberton's middle class. **Fernlea House** ① *Lee Rd, Mon-Fri 0900-1300, 1400-1600*, was built in the 1890s from wood and iron. The house is in a beautiful setting at the bottom of a wooded valley on the edge of Barberton. It is decorated with period furniture and has displays on Barberton's famous botanists.

The walk passes **Rimer's Creek**, the site where, on 24 June 1884, David Wilson the mining commissioner, broke a bottle of gin over a rock to christen the new town of Barberton. At the time, Rimer's Creek was a popular recreational spot for the townsfolk, particularly on Wednesdays when it was frequented by the barmaids of the town.

To the west, **Stopforth House** ① *18 Bowness St, 1000-1200, 1400-1500*, belonged to James Stopforth, a baker and a general dealer, and was built in 1886. The Stopforth family lived here until 1983.

The **De Kaap Stock Exchange** on Pilgrim Street was built in 1887. All that remains of the original structure is the façade, which has been declared a national monument. The **Lewis and Marks Building**, also on Pilgrim Street and completed in 1887, was Barberton's first two-storey building and housed the **Bank of Africa**. In later years, the iron veranda was removed and a third storey added. Close by, **Market Square**, is a quiet place shaded by trees with whitewashed colonial buildings on all four sides.

Heading north, the walk continues to President Square and the town hall. In front is a statue of **Jock of the Bushveld**, the faithful dog of Percy Fitzpatrick during his days as a transport rider. The **steam locomotive** on General Street, by the entrance to the caravan park, dates to 1899 and used to run between Barberton and Kaapmuiden.

An **aerial cableway** crosses town and is clearly visible climbing the mountains that border Swaziland. It was built in 1938 to transport asbestos 20 km over mountainous terrain from the Havelock mine in Swaziland to the railhead in Barberton. Until 2002, it was still in use taking coal, transported to Barberton from Witbank, back to Swaziland on the return journey to fuel the mine. Today, it hangs rather forlornly over Barberton.

There are two other short local walking trails starting from the centre of town; the **Rose Creek Walk** and the **Fortuna Trail** (2 km). The Fortuna Trail starts on Crown Street and passes through a 500-m tunnel, which is part of an old mine. There is no lighting inside the tunnel so bring a torch.

Nelspruit and around listings

Hotel and guesthouse prices
L over US$300 AL US$220-300 A US$150-220
B US$100-150 C US$75-100 D US$35-75
E US$15-35 F under US$15
Restaurant prices
ⅲ over US$30 ⅱ US$15-30 ⅰ under US$15
See pages 46-51 for further information.

Sleeping

Nelspruit *p605, map p606*

A Sheppard Boutique Hotel,
23 Sheppard Dr, T013-7523394,
www.sheppardboutique.co.za. A relative
newcomer and the only luxury offering
in town. Tastefully decorated suites with
large beds, antique furnishings, stylish
prints, and low-key lighting. Elegant,
old-fashioned lounge and dining room
filled with antiques and serving good
South African cuisine. Swimming pool
and tennis courts.

B La Roca, 56 van Wyk St, T013-7526628,
www.laroca.co.za. Recently refurbished
guesthouse with 9 rooms, each with a
private balcony or patio with views across
the Lowveld, stylish decor and stone
bathrooms, TV, bar fridge, ceiling fans,
lounge, lovely swimming pool surrounded
by boulders, will collect from town centre
and airport.

B Mercure Inn, corner of Graniet St and
N4, T013-7414222, www.mercure.com.
Part of a successful quality French chain.
104 luxury self-catering, single-storey units,
TV, a/c, airport transfers, large conference
facilities. Spacious lounge and bar, attractive
pool area (harps on a bit about having
the largest pool in Nelspruit). Good quality,
with the benefit of having self-catering
facilities. Good deals on the website if
booking online.

B Orion Hotel Promenade, Louis Trichardt
St, T013-7533000, www.oriongroup.co.za.
A smart hotel in a Spanish-style hacienda,
71 a/c rooms with en suite bathrooms,

TV, non-smoking room available. Restaurant,
bar, terrace overlooks a small pool, tastefully
designed interior, secure parking, but
suffers from a lack of recreational space.
Many of the mainline buses stop here.

B The Roost, 21c Koraalboom St, T013-
7411419, www.roostguestlodge.co.za.
Spacious old house with 8 smart double
rooms and en suite bathrooms, TV,
M-Net, overhead fans, swimming pool,
set apart from the main house, conference
facilities, secure parking, plenty of
atmosphere. Recommended.

C Jörns, 62 Hunter St, T013-7441894,
www.jorns.co.za. Large guesthouse run
by a German couple, 9 comfortable rooms,
all en suite and some with corner bath in
the bedroom. Lounge, bar, swimming pool
with beautiful views over the Lowveld, koi
fishpond in the tropical garden.

C The Loerie's Call, 2 Du Preez St,
T013-7441251, www.loeriescall.co.za.
Boutique-style guesthouse with 10
spacious double rooms with en suite
bathroom, minibar, all set in a in separate
modern building, private terrace with
views across the Crocodile River Valley,
non-smoking room, TV, laundry service,
B&B, swimming pool, gardens.

C Shandon Lodge, 1 Saturn St, quite a
distance from the town centre, follow
Ferreira St out of town, T013-7449934,
www.shandon.co.za. Fine colonial-style
house on a hilltop suburb, 5 mins' drive
from town. Each room opens up onto
a shaded veranda running around the
house, with views over the small pool
and terrace overlooking the countryside.
7 large double rooms with en suite shower,
country-style decor, separate seating
area, M-Net TV, tea and coffee facilities
with home-made biscuits. Pleasant bar,
meals on request, huge breakfasts served
in the cool dining room. Friendly, family-
run with lots of advice on the area.
Recommended.

C Utopia in Africa, 6 Daleen St, T013-7457714, www.utopiainafrica.com. B&B in a stylish house in quiet suburb. Open-plan layout with thatched roof and 5 large, sunny bedrooms, stylishly furnished, all en suite with balconies. Full English breakfasts served, elevated pool with views of a nearby nature reserve, secure parking, no children under 8.

D Bavaria, 45 Zebrina Cres, T013-7411703, norman.rigo@iburst.co.za.co.za. Homely guesthouse set in a converted home surrounded by tropical gardens, in a quiet suburb just west of town. 9 en suite luxury rooms with bright, African-themed decor, all rooms have M-Net TV, tea and coffee facilities and work stations. Breakfasts served in bright breakfast room overlooking garden. Pool, bar, laundry, car hire can be arranged.

D Palms Guest House, 25 van Wijk St, T013-7554374, thepalmsnelspruit@absamail.co.za. 3 double rooms, 3 single rooms all with en suite bathroom, TV, M-Net, lounge areas, B&B, all meals available on request, swimming pool, sauna, gardens, secure parking, comfortable and relaxing.

D-F Safubi River Lodge, 45 Graniet St, 2 km from the city centre, T013-7413253, www.safubi.co.za. Self-catering chalets, with fully equipped kitchen, bathroom, lounge, TV, secure parking, braai in the garden, set in 16 ha of bushveld on the banks of the Gladdespruit River. Also a 40-site camping and caravan park. Large peaceful and secure, swimming pool plus communal kitchens for self-catering and coffee shop serving breakfast and light meals. Good value.

E-F Funky Monkey Backpackers, 102 van Wyk St, T013-7441310, www.funkymonkeys.co.za. Dorms, double rooms and camping, with rooms spread through a spacious house adorned with bright artwork. Swimming pool and pool table, fully licensed bar. Can organize trips to Kruger or Blyde River Canyon.

E-F Nelspruit Backpackers, 9 Andries Pretorius St, T013-7412237, www.nelback.co.za. Mix of dorms and double rooms in a good location next to a nature reserve. Kitchen, laundry, bar, pool table, swimming pool, close to restaurants and pubs in the Sunpark Centre. Free pickup service from town, on the Baz Bus route. Excellent base from which to explore the area. Day trips to Blyde River Canyon and Kruger, see Tour operators, page 616, for details.

E-F Sun Lodge, 7 de Villiers St, T013-7411857, www.sunlodge.co.za. Garden chalet plus double room in main house, dorms, pool set in colourful lush gardens, close to shops and restaurants. This used to be a guesthouse but with the addition of a dorm room is reinventing itself as a backpackers, on the Baz Bus route.

Malelane p608

L Serenity Forest Eco Reserve, T013-7902000, www.serenitylodge.co.za. While most of the lodges in this region are on the fringes of Kruger and the Crocodile River, this lodge is in an unusual location in a patch of rainforest high up in the hills in the opposite direction, 12 km off the R570 toward the Jeppe's Reef border with Swaziland. 2 camps of luxury thatched chalets overlooking the trees, en suite, private verandas overlooking the butterfly-filled forest, all linked by walkways in the trees. Unusual sunken bar. Hiking and 4WD trails through forest, no children under 16, rates include dinner and afternoon tea. Beautiful spot that combines visits to Kruger with somewhere a little different to stay. Recommended.

C Thanda-Nani Game Lodge, the turning is 11 km east of Malelane, clearly signposted on the left of the N4, T013-7924543, www.thandanani.com. 6500-ha private luxury game farm with 10 a/c stylish double rooms with en suite bathrooms, set in thatched rondavels. Lounge and dining area set under an open thatched area, attractive pool, game drives with chance of seeing range of wildlife including black and white rhino and a fairly tame herd of zebra that wander through the grounds. Enjoyable and good-value variation on the full-on Kruger experience.

C-D Selati 103 Guest Cottages, 103 Selati Cres, in a suburb north of town, T013-7900978, www.selati103.co.za. 9 garden cottages, self-catering or B&B, colourful decor, TV, large swimming pool, comfortable option before entering Kruger Park.

D Bezuidenhout Guest House, in a quiet suburb north of town, T013-7900728, www.bezuidenhoutbnb.co.za. 8 smart rooms in double B&B rooms, each with a/c, fridge, TV and en suite bathroom, thatched house in pleasant gardens, swimming pool, dinner on request.

Komatipoort p608

C Tree's Too, 11 Furley St, T013-7908262, www.treestoo.com. 8 large, spotless a/c en suite rooms under thatch, all with separate entrance and set in lush tropical gardens under palm trees. Lounge, pleasant pool area, small **Gecko's** restaurant serving breakfast, lunch and dinner. English-owned. Recommended.

Barberton p609, map p610

C Fountain Baths, 48 Pilgrim St, T013-7122707. Mix of B&B double rooms and self-catering units sleeping 2-4, simple decor with wooden floors, garden with swimming pool, peaceful setting edging on to the hills. The house was originally built in 1884 as a bath house for miners.

C Kloofhuis, 1 Kloof St, T013-7124268, www.kloofhuis.co.za. Central location just behind Belhaven House, a short walk from the tourist office. Fine Victorian home with wrap-around veranda. 4 rooms, doubles and twins, en suite or shared bathroom. Homely setting, floral decor, relaxing place to stay.

D Digger's Retreat, 14 km out of town, signposted just off the R38 to Kaapmuiden, T013-7199681, diggersretreat@mweb.co.za. 18 double rooms or thatched rondavels.

À la carte restaurant, **Old Gold Rush** pub with themed decor, swimming pool. Hiking, birdwatching and 4WD trips can be arranged.

D Phoenix Hotel, 20 Pilgrim St, T013-7124211, www.thephoenixhotel.co.za. Historical town hotel dating from the gold rush; apparently Paul Kruger was entertained here after meetings with the miners. The hotel was so popular in its day that on occasions guests had to sleep on or under the billiards table. Today it's looking rather dated, with lots of chintz and swirly carpets. A/c, bar lunches and à la carte restaurant, 3 pool tables, **Jocks Tavern** is a lively bar.

D William George House, 1 Bok St, T/F013-7125886, wilgohouse@telkomsa.net. Pretty colonial house with 50 m of covered veranda. 9 double en suite rooms, TV, minibar, pool, B&B but choice of early breakfast or takeaway brunch, evening meals on request,

D-F Barberton Chalets & Caravan Park, General St, T013-7123323, www.barberton chalets.co.za. Self-catering chalets sleeping up to 6, serviced daily, caravan spots and campsite set in the neatly maintained shady gardens with a swimming pool, tea garden, shop and laundrette.

● Eating

Nelspruit p605, map p606
The centre of town gets very quiet at night, with just a handful of restaurants open for evening meals.

♦♦ **Chez Vincent**, 56 Ferreira St, T013-7441146. Fri-Sat 1800-2030. Weekend dinner venue in an informal restaurant with modern paintings on the wall, bistro-style menu, good calamari and prawns, small but well-selected winelist.

♦♦ **Costa do Sol**, ABSA Sq, Paul Kruger St, T013-7526382. Mon-Sat 1100-2200. Well-established restaurant set in a mall, specializing in Mozambique seafood that arrives fresh from the coast daily, Italian and Portuguese dishes, pizzas and pastas, seafood platters; best known for their giant prawns; good winelist that includes some Portuguese wines.

† Le Gourmet, 24 Branders St, T013-7551941. Wed-Fri lunch and dinner; Tue and Sat lunch only. Provincial French-style cuisine in intimate surroundings and pretty garden, excellent wine list, menu changes weekly.

† Brewer's Feast, on the corner of the N4, T013-7414674. Cheap and cheerful roadside restaurant open all day and well into the night serving truck drivers and passing tourists, budget takeaway meals. Huge menu, and bargain breakfasts.

† Ku's, Sunpark Mall, corner of General Dan Pienaar and Piet Retief streets, T013-7413989. Economically priced Chinese dishes, takeaway service close to some of the backpackers and other budget accommodation, and **O'Hagen's** pub, so popular for a cheap night out.

† O'Hagen's, Sunpark Mall, corner of General Dan Pienaar and Piet Retief streets, T013-7413584. Good Irish theme pub chain, wide selection of imported beers, open-air terrace and music, standard pub meals.

† Pappa's Pizzeria, 56 Brown St, T013-7551660. Simple wooden chalet-style building serving wood-fired pizzas which are a little on the small side, but the selection of delicious pastas is a good bet. Friendly service, enjoyable wooden deck and live acoustic music in the evenings.

† Parillo's, Crossing Centre, N4, T013-7527680. Mon-Sat 0900-2200, Sun 0900-1500. Good affordable family steak restaurant in the mall, T-bones, fillets, rumps and ribs and a carvery at Sun lunch, children's portions, fish and salads for non-meat eaters.

Malelane *p608*

††† Crockafellas, 150 m before Malelane Gate into Kruger, T013-7903415. A thatched boma overlooking a small lake with

7 crocodiles; you can watch them from the wooden deck, 500 g T-bones are a speciality, also has a curio shop, popular with tour groups.

Komatipoort *p608*

This small town is well-known for its seafood, which arrives daily from Mozambique.

††† Tambarina, 57 7937988 St, T013-7937988. A fun restaurant decorated in bright colours with a lovely courtyard shaded by mango trees and serving good Portuguese cuisine and seafood. If you can't make it to the coast, the meals here are the next best thing. Guests from **Crocodile Bridge** camp in Kruger Park often dine here, bookings essential.

††† The Border Country Inn, T013-7937328. A hotel restaurant 1 km from the border, pleasant outdoor setting on a leafy terrace (watch the mosquitoes at night), indifferent service, but excellent prawns and calamari and there's some alternative African dishes on the menu, from Kenya and Zimbabwe, for example.

Barberton *p609, map p610*

† Old Rock Café, 73 de Villiers St, T013-7123477. Open 1300-late. Family pub and grill with large-screen TV, gets very busy during big games. Standard pub menu with range of steaks and burgers, some seafood and salads.

† Victoria Tea Garden, Market Sq, T013-7124985. Charming open-air café under a white gazebo serving toasted sandwiches, juice and light snacks, open until late afternoon. Close to the tourist office, a good place to start the Heritage Walk around town.

O Shopping

Nelspruit *p605, map p606*

Crossing Centre, at the junction of the N4 and the R40, just west of the centre. A variety of shops and banks, including a **Woolworths** food shop and a **Clicks** pharmacy.

Riverside Mall, 5 km out of town on the White River road. A wider selection than the Crossing Centre and proudly boasting to be the largest shopping centre in Mpumalanga, with a variety of shops, restaurants and a **Nu Metro** 8-screen cinema. Next door is the **Emnotweni Casino**.

Barberton *p609, map p610*
Umjindi Jewellery Project, is an initiative by the municipality to teach young people from disadvantaged communities jewellery design and manufacture. The gallery is next to the museum, where there's also a coffee shop.

▲ Activities and tours

Nelspruit *p605, map p606*
Green Rhino, T013-7511952, www.greenrhino.co.za. National adventure operator. Tours from 2-4 days throughout the region.
Mbombela Safaris, Nelspruit Backpackers, 9 Andries Pretorius St, T013-7412237, www.nelback.co.za. Will pick up from anywhere in Nelspruit if you are staying elsewhere. 2-day/1-night Kruger tour, from R900 per person, longer tours available, free night's stay at the backpackers if you book a Mbombela safari.
Place of Rock, T013-7515319, www.placeofrock.co.za. Wide range of day and overnight trips to Kruger, the Panorama region and elsewhere, for a variety of budgets.
Travel agent Harvey World Travel, Riverside Mall, T/F031-7570883. Reliable national chain of general travel agents, flight sales.
Vula Tours, T031-7412826, www.vulatours.co.za. Affordable day trips to Kruger, the Panorama region and Sudwala Caves.

Malelane *p608*
Zozi's, T013-7788849, T072-3609701 (mob). An enterprising and entertaining local female guide who runs tours of the Matsulu township on the edge of Kruger. The site of the village was originally inside the park's boundary, but in 1968 the fences were removed and people were relocated from neighbouring farms to form the Matsulu community. Today, it's not uncommon to have an elephant stride through the village. Zozi shows you around in a taxi, and visits include a *shebeen* (pub), a hairdresser's where the art of African plaiting is demonstrated, a witch doctor who will 'throw the bones', and a school. This excellent tour not only gives insight into African rural life, but also shows how the local people manage to live alongside the animals. Great fun and highly recommended. A 3-hr tour costs in the region of R400, less per person for groups.

⊖ Transport

Nelspruit *p605, map p606*
Air
Nationwide has flights to **Cape Town** and **Johannesburg**. SAA has flights to **Johannesburg, Cape Town** and **Durban**.
 Airline offices Nationwide, T0861-737737, www.flynationwide.co.za. SAA, T011-9781111, ww2.flysaa.com.

Bus
Baz Bus has services towards **Johannesburg, Pretoria** and **Swaziland**. **Greyhound** has buses to **Pretoria, Johannesburg, Durban** and **Maputo** in Mozambique. **Translux** runs buses to **Pretoria, Johannesburg** and **Maputo**.
 Bus companies Baz Bus, T021-4392323, www.bazbus.com. **Greyhound**, T083-915000, www.greyhound.co.za. **Translux**, T0861-589282, www.translux.co.za

Car hire

All offices are at the **Kruger Mpumalanga International Airport** terminal building, 25 km from Nelspruit: **Avis**, T013-7501015, www.avis.co.za; **Budget**, T013-7511774, www.budget.co.za; **Hertz**, T013-7509150, www.hertz.co.za; **Imperial**, T013-7502871, www.imperialcarrental.co.za.

Rail

The **Komati Express** between **Pretoria/Johannesburg** and **Komatipoort** (border post with Mozambique) stops daily in Nelspruit, T0860-008888, www.spoornet.co.za.

Taxi

City Bug, T013-7533392, www.citybug.co.za. Taxi service and does intercity transfers on request and picks up from Kruger Mpumalanga International Airport.

Komatipoort p608
Bus

The buses between **Pretoria/Johannesburg** and **Maputo** stop at the border post.

Rail

The **Komati Express** is the daily service running between **Pretoria/Johannesburg** and **Komatipoort**, T0860 008888, www.spoornet.co.za. The train connects with a shuttle minibus service to the border. There is a railway from the border to **Maputo** but it is currently under repair. Minibuses can be found on the Mozambique side of the border for Maputo.

Barberton p609, map p610

There is no public transport to Barberton. Without a car, the only (expensive) option is take a taxi from Nelspruit.

⊙ Directory

Nelspruit p605, map p606

Banks American Express, Riverside Mall, T013-7570400. There are branches of all other banks in the Riverside Mall and the Crossing Centre. **Internet Alpha Internet Café**, Riverside Mall. **Consulates Mozambique Consulate**, 43 Brown St, T013-7527396, Mon-Fri 0830-1500. Visas take 3 days but can be issued on the same day or within 24 hrs for an extra fee, you will need to bring 2 passport-size photos and then fill in the application form at the embassy. Expect to pay in the region of US$15 but double this for same day issue. Alternatively visas are now issued at all Mozambique borders, costing R170 or US$25. South African passport-holders no longer need visas. **Medical services Chemist**, after hours, T013-7525721. **Medi Clinic**, 1 Louise St, T013-7590500.

Komatipoort p608

Banks First National, Rissik St, open for foreign exchange. **FX Bureau de Change**, at the Komati Oasis service station just before the border, T031-7907457, Mon-Sat 0700-1700, Sun 0700-1300.

Kruger National Park → Colour map 2, B5.

Kruger Park is the king of South African game parks and one of the best game-viewing areas in all of Africa. The figures speak for themselves: 507 bird species, 114 reptiles, 49 fish, 34 amphibians, 147 mammal and over 23,000 plant species have been recorded here. The region itself is enormous, extending from the Crocodile River in the south to the Limpopo in the north, from the wooded foothills of the eastern escarpment to the humid plains of the lowveld. It certainly fulfils most visitors' fantasies of seeing magnificent herds of game roaming across acacia-studded stretches of savannah and, of course, is home to the Big Five. The park is 60 km wide and over 350 km long, conserving 21,497 sq km, an area the size of Wales or Israel. Despite its size, it is very well developed, with a good network covering 2600 km of roads and numerous camps, making a Kruger safari relatively hassle free.

Don't expect to have the park to yourself, however. Kruger receives over one million visitors a year and the park camps cater for up to 5000 visitors a day. Nevertheless, despite the huge number of people passing through, Kruger has managed to maintain its wild atmosphere. Only 5% of the park is affected by the activities of the visitors and only a few areas in the south come close to the overcrowding seen in East Africa's game parks.

While much of the park is designed for self-driving and self-catering, it is also possible to stay in an ever-expanding choice of top-end private reserves, which are popular with first-time visitors as all game drives are led by rangers, so you can leave the animal-spotting to the experts. The fences that once split Kruger from the private reserves have now all come down, so game can roam freely between the national park and private concessions. Moreover, the fences between the countries bordering South Africa have also come down in the last few years: the demolition of fences between Kruger and Mozambique's Limpopo National Park and Zimbabwe's Gonarezhou have created the Great Limpopo Transfrontier Park – a conservation area straddling a staggering 35,000 sq km. ▸▸ For details of the private game reserves along the park's western boundary, see pages 637-640. For listings, see pages 641-645.

Ins and outs

Getting there and around

Air SAA flies between Johannesburg and Kruger Mpumalanga International Airport, Phalaborwa Airport and Eastgate Airport. **Kruger Mpumalanga International Airport** is the largest airport in the area, located 22 km from Nelspruit. **Phalaborwa Airport** is just outside the park and within easy reach of many of the entry gates, while the **Eastgate Airport**, at Hoedspruit, is close to Orpen Gate. Some of the luxury game lodges also have their own landing strips for chartered flights.

Road Most people arrive in Kruger by road, either on a tour or in their own vehicle. There are nine entry gates and numerous options of approach. Which area you end up staying in will depend to a large extent on where you are coming from. Petrol is available at all the camps during office hours, and the mark-up on litre prices is not as unreasonable as you'd expect (although note that credit cards aren't accepted). There is a speed limit of 50 kph on the surfaced roads in the park. **Kruger Emergency Road Services** is based at Skukuza, T013-7354152. The service is not equipped to do any major repairs, but if you break down within the park they will tow you to the nearest garage outside the park.

Kruger National Park opening times

National Park gates		Camp gates	
January	0530-1830	January	0430-1830
February	0530-1830	February	0530-1830
March	0530-1800	March	0530-1800
April	0600-1800	April	0600-1800
May-July	0630-1730	May-July	0630-1730
August	0600-1800	August	0600-1800
September	0600-1800	September	0600-1800
October	0530-1800	October	0530-1800
November	0530-1830	November	0430-1830
December	0530-1830	December	0430-1830

Orientation The information provided in the following section is intended as a guide for the whole of the national park. Given its huge size, many visitors to Kruger concentrate on one area of the park on each visit. Unless you are staying for more than a couple of nights, it is impossible to combine effective game viewing and visit all the areas. For the purposes of this guide, the park has been divided into three areas: Southern, Central and Northern, with a description of each of the different camps within these areas.

Best time to visit

Each season has its advantages. The park looks its best after the summer rains when the new shoots and lush vegetation provide a surplus of food for the grazers. Migratory birds are attracted and display their colourful breeding plumage, and this is a good time to see courtship rituals and nesting. The animals look their best thanks to their good diet, and mammals give birth to their young. The disadvantages of summer are that the thick foliage and tall grasses make it harder to spot animals and daytime temperatures can rise to a sweltering 40°C; afternoon rains are also common.

The winter months are good for game viewing because the dry weather forces animals to congregate around waterholes and there is less foliage for them to hide in. However, the animals tend not to be in their best condition. The winter months of June, July and August are more comfortable with daytime temperatures of around 30°C, but nights can be surprisingly cold at this time of year with temperatures at times dropping to 0°C. This is a good time of year to visit the northern areas of the park which can be unbearably hot in the summer.

Kruger is at its most crowded during the South African school holidays (see page 34). Accommodation within the park will be completely full and the heavy traffic on the roads can detract from the wilderness experience.

Cost

Conservation fees are R132 per adult per day, and R66 per child under 12. South Africans get a substantial discount. If you're planning to stay for several days it may be worth investing in a Wild Card (see page 25).

Malaria

The park is in an endemic malaria area. Take anti-malarial medication and use insect repellent. Malaria hotline, T082-2341800.

Major James Stevenson-Hamilton

James Stevenson-Hamilton, Kruger's first game warden, was appointed at the end of the Boer War. He established his headquarters of Sabie Bridge at the end of the railway on the branch line from Komatipoort to the Sabie River. He began his work with two other rangers and spent years patrolling the reserve on horseback and on foot. His main duties were to encourage a healthy game population and to rid the park of poachers. However, his deep love of the African bush inspired him to campaign to increase the size of the park and to ensure the continued protection of the wildlife within its borders. His philosophy was that man's attempts to manage the park only interfered with natural processes. He believed that all the creatures within the park deserved to live regardless of temporary effects and that the balance of nature would always be preserved. James was known as Skukuza, a Shangaan name meaning either "he who sweeps clean" or "he who turns everything upside down", by his staff at Kruger National Park. He retired in 1946 after working in Kruger for 44 years.

Arriving

Most of the camps are at least an hour's drive from the nearest entrance gate so always make sure you arrive in time to get to the camp. At the park gate, your reservation will usually be checked before you are allowed in, especially during the busy periods when all the accommodation, including campsites, gets booked up. You could be fined if you arrive at the camp gate after it has closed. **Camp receptions** are open daily April to June 0800-1800; March, September and October 0800-1830; November to February 0800-1900.

Background

The first area of what was to become Kruger National Park was officially protected in 1898 by President Kruger when he established the Sabie River Game Reserve. This consisted of what is now the southern sector of Kruger, the area extending between the Crocodile and the Sabie rivers. The area's early inhabitants were San and the Baphalaborwa tribes, who had little impact on the region's wildlife but did leave their mark in cave paintings throughout the area.

The game reserve was established to protect wildlife from the threat of 'biltong hunters' who were visiting the lowveld in ever increasing numbers during the dry season. Hunters had already slaughtered vast herds of animals throughout South Africa and this was an early attempt to preserve an undisturbed wilderness. A single police sergeant at Komatipoort was given the daunting task of protecting the entire area from poachers.

It was re-proclaimed by the British in 1903, increasing the size of the park with both the Shingwedzi Game Reserve, the area between the Letaba and the Luvuvhu rivers, and the 5000 sq km of unworked ranches between the Sabi and the Letaba rivers. The new area under protection covered roughly the same area as Kruger does today. However, numerous factions threatened the survival of the park: hunters wanted access to the park, soldiers returning from the First World War expected land for sheep farming; prospectors looking for gold, coal and copper wanted mining rights; and South Africa's vets were campaigning for a mass slaughter of wildlife to prevent the possible spread of tsetse fly.

The seeds of creating a self-financing national park open to visitors were unwittingly sown by South African Railways when they opened a new tour running from Pretoria to Lorenço Marques (today Maputo) which stopped in the reserve for game rangers to take visitors into the bush. The first tourists arrived in 1923 and the visits became such a popular feature of the holiday that park visits were used as publicity by the railways. Public support for a national park empowered the conservationist lobby and public access was finally allowed in 1926.

The first cars arrived in 1927 and were able to travel by road through Sabi Bridge between the Olifants and Crocodile rivers. Visitors were expected to fend for themselves and made their own thorn bush camps to stay in. The animals reacted well to visitors in cars as long as they stayed inside them, but night driving was stopped almost immediately as too many animals were being killed. The first camp was built for tourists at Pretoriuskop after the chaos of the early years when tourists had been known to spend the night in trees hiding from predators.

By 1946, 38,000 tourists a year were visiting Kruger and in 1947 Princess Elizabeth and Princess Margaret visited the park on their royal tour of South Africa where they stayed in the first luxury lodges. The publicity surrounding the tour ensured that a visit to Kruger became a fixture on every tourist's trip to South Africa. By 1955 over 100,000 people were visiting each year.

The land area available to the park's wildlife has increased considerably in the last two decades. In 1994 the game fences between the private reserves on Kruger's western border were taken down, allowing animals to roam freely in an extra 2000 sq km of bush. Even more significantly, 2001 saw the removal of the fences between the international borders, creating the Greater Limpopo Transfrontier Conservation Area. This now incorporates Parque Nacional do Limpopo in Mozambique and Gonarezhou National Park in Zimbabwe, forming one of the largest conservation areas in Africa. The Mozambique section of the park can now be accessed from the Giriyondo border gate.

Staying in the park

Kruger has 14 main rest camps, five bushveld camps, two bush lodges and three satellite camps, owned and managed by South African National Parks (SANParks), head office in Pretoria. Although there is a choice in the type of accommodation available, all the room rates are very reasonable. There are also now a handful of private luxury lodges within Kruger run by concessionaires and not SANParks, such as Tinga Private Lodge and Jock Safari Lodge. The SANParks website, www.sanparks.org, has excellent information on all the lodges within Kruger. If you're looking for luxury, the private game reserves adjoining Kruger offer some of the finest camps in Africa. ▸▸ *For details of private reserves outside the park, see pages 637-645.*

Reservations

The direct line for each camp is included with the description of the camp. This number can only be used for making a last-minute booking, up to 48 hours prior to arrival. All other bookings should be made through **SANParks** ⓘ *T012-4289111, www.sanparks.org.* Once you are in the park it is always worth calling a day ahead or in the early morning to see if there have been any cancellations. The camp receptions will also be able to change your reservations to another camp if there is availability.

Driving into Mozambique via Giriyondo

The Mozambique section of the park can now be accessed from the Giriyondo border gate, situated 45 km northeast of Letaba on the eastern boundary of Kruger Park. There is a limit of 250 cars per day and they must be 4WD vehicles or have reasonable ground clearance as the roads on the Mozambique side are still being developed.

Border opening times October-March 0800-1600 and April-September 0800-1500.

Customs and immigration Entry is R50 per person plus R50 per vehicle. South African passport holders do not need a visa; foreign visitors can get visas at the border.

Facilities On the Mozambique side facilities remain very basic, although there have been a few new initiatives including a self-drive 4WD eco-trail, the **Machampane wilderness trail** (with a new luxury bush lodge) and **Massingir hiking trail**, for hikers willing to carry their food in and rubbish out. In addition to this there is a national parks campsite approximately 50 km from the border post. Bookings for the trails and camp can be made through either **SANParks**, www.sanparks.org, or **Transfrontier Trails do Limpopo**, www.dolimpopo.co.za. This website has full details of activities and access on the Mozambique side.

Main public camps

The majority of overnight visitors stay in one of the 12 main public camps in the park at **Berg-en-Dal**, **Crocodile Bridge**, **Lower Sabie**, **Pretoriuskop**, **Skukuza**, **Letaba**, **Mopani**, **Olifants**, **Orpen**, **Satara**, **Shingwedzi** and **Punda Maria**. Most of the accommodation is in the form of chalets or cottages, which can sleep between two and 12. If you are self-catering, you'll have the choice between a separate fully equipped kitchen, a kitchenette or the use of a communal kitchen. The units with just a kitchenette do not have any cutlery or crockery. All accommodation comes with a refrigerator, bedding and towels. If in doubt, always check when booking exactly what you will be getting. More precise details of the choices are listed under the separate entry for each of the camps.

Some of the older camps feel a little outdated, but the grounds are universally clean and well-kept. The facilities from one camp to the next vary but in most cases they include a shop selling basic self-catering supplies, a petrol pump, a restaurant or cafeteria, laundrette, toilets and hot showers, braai areas with seating, public telephones and an office with information on the other camps. During the school holidays, the atmosphere in the larger camps can feel like holiday camps, and you can easily forget you are in the middle of a game reserve.

Campsites

Although most of the main public camps have a separate area for caravans, tents and camper vans, there are two separate campsites at **Maroela** and **Balule**. The only facilities here are washblocks and communal kitchen facilities – there are no power points. Camping costs R120 per site for two people, with your own tent (R40 per extra person).

Bush lodges

Bush lodges offer secluded luxury accommodation and are smaller and more remote than public camps, without facilities such as shops, restaurants, or petrol stations.

These camps are ideal for a large group of friends, since the whole camp has to be taken with each booking. The two bush lodges are **Boulders**, which sleeps 12, and **Roodewal**, sleeping 19. Reservations should be made well in advance as they offer exceptionally good value if the maximum number of people stay in the camp. The camps are located away from the main public camps but are close enough for visits to the shops for supplies. Although they are privately owned, all bookings are dealt with by **SANParks**.

Bushveld camps
The five bushveld camps at **Biyamiti**, **Shimuwini**, **Talamati**, **Bateleur** and **Sirheni** are smaller and offer more of a wilderness experience than the main camps, but they also have far fewer facilities. Staying in these camps is one of the best ways to experience Kruger, but it does involve a degree of advanced planning. The chalets are all self-catering with fully equipped kitchens; bedding and towels are provided, and each chalet can sleep up to four people.

Eating
The camp restaurants are open daily for breakfast (0700-0900), lunch (1200-1400) and dinner (1800-2100). Some of the camps also have a bar. At small camps, or when there are fewer guests, you will be asked to order your evening meal in advance.

Shopping
Camp shops are open daily April to June 0800-1800; March, September and October 0800-1830; and November to February 0800-1900. The closer you are to Skukuza (the largest camp), the fresher the produce stocked in camp shops. Most shops stock firewood and braai lighters, bread, frozen meat, tinned vegetables, jams, biscuits, beer, wines, spirits, cool drinks, books and a few curio items. If you don't have a cool box in your car and you are self-catering, it is still possible to buy all you need for a meal from the shops each day.

Other facilities
Some of the camps have **swimming pools** for residents, a good option if you choose to base yourself at a camp for several days in summer and want to relax during the midday heat. Camping areas have **laundry blocks** and hot, clean **showers**. The **communal kitchens** have power points, instant boiling water machines, electric rings and a sink. It is your responsibility to clean up after yourself. Always secure rubbish to minimize the risk of baboons raiding the bins. There is a **bank** with ATM and an internet café at Skukuza.

Wildlife, activities and tours

Wildlife management
Although Kruger appears impressively wild, many aspects of the ecosystem are carefully monitored and controlled by the park authorities. Windpumps, for example, have been built at waterholes in dry areas so that game congregates in large numbers, and a number of species have been reintroduced. White rhinos were first reintroduced in 1961; the programme has been so successful that there are now over 2000 in the park. Black rhino were reintroduced in 1971, 40 years after they had last been seen here. Other animals which have been re-established include tsessebe and roan.

The 'Magnificent Seven'

The herds of elephant that roam around Kruger, migrating from east to west, are one of the park's biggest attractions. The population was estimated at 12,000 in 2007, having grown substantially from the 986 elephants found during an aerial census of 1959.

Elephants have voracious appetites and will eat bark, fruit, leaves and roots. The damage caused by feeding elephants is easy to spot and they have played an important role in the creation of the African landscape. However, too many elephants feeding in a restricted area can cause serious damage to trees and shrubs.

The air-conditioned **Letaba Elephant Hall** at Letaba camp in central Kruger has an amazing exhibition devoted to elephants. A small theatre shows wildlife videos and a large hall has displays related to the life cycle of the elephant.

The most impressive section of the museum, however, focuses on the 'Magnificent Seven'. These were Kruger's finest elephants who became famous for their exceptionally large tusks. The skulls and tusks are on display, accompanied by a photo of the elephant and a map showing each animal's range.

Game viewing

Kruger is, of course, home to the Big Five: lion, elephant, buffalo, black rhino and leopard. The highest concentrations and variety of game are around **Lower Sabie**, **Satara** and **Skukuza**. The best times for game viewing are after dawn and just before dusk, as animals tend to rest during the heat of the day.

There is a network of tarred and dirt roads linking the camps and looping through the best game-viewing areas. They are only open to the public during daylight hours and are subject to speed limits, which are monitored by radar. Game viewing takes time and it is best to drive below 20 kph to maximize your chances of spotting animals. Although there is a temptation to head for the most isolated dirt tracks and to neglect the tarred roads, this can be a mistake as cars are quieter on tarred roads and the animals living near them are more used to traffic. The run-off from tarred roads also makes the vegetation greener and attracts more animals. Driving around Kruger can be very tiring, so it's a good idea to visit one of the get-out points (marked on park maps) and to spend time game viewing at a waterhole.

Kruger shops sell a wide choice of identification guides. Their own publications, including the map, travel guide and the comprehensive *Find it* guide are an excellent introduction to the geology, history, vegetation and wildlife of Kruger.

Game drives

A guided tour with a game ranger can increase your chance of game spotting and provides a deeper understanding of the wilderness. Most camps offer guided day and night drives. Both are very popular and should be booked in advance at camp reception as soon as you arrive. A drive costs from R160-220 per person, depending on the camp and time of day. Night drives are an added attraction as private vehicles are not allowed outside the camps after sundown. These usually depart around 1700. Make sure you have warm clothing as temperatures drop in the evenings. The drives finish in time for guests to have an evening meal at the camp restaurant. Some camps also offer a late drive after dinner, departing at 2030 and lasting for up to three hours.

Guided walks and mountain biking

A number of camps offer two- or three-hour walks in the morning or afternoon accompanied by an armed game ranger from around R245 per person. Groups are kept small – up to eight people – and the rangers are trained in field guiding. These provide an excellent way of getting close to smaller animals and are a thrilling way of exploring the bush.

Wilderness trails

A relatively new initiative consists of a series of seven wilderness trails, offering three-day guided walking safaris. Seeing the park on foot is the most exciting way to experience the wilderness, and places on the hiking trails are booked up months in advance. A maximum of eight people go on each trail and they are accompanied by an armed ranger. Hikers spend every night at the same rustic bush camp and go out on day walks. Food, water bottles, sleeping bags, rucksacks and cutlery are all provided.

The wilderness trails last for two days and three nights, and cost R2350 per person, no children under 12. For reservations contact **South African National Parks (SANParks)** offices; bookings can be made up to a year ahead and places fill up quickly. The best time of year for hiking is from March to July when the weather is dry and daytime temperatures are cooler.

Bushman Trail This is a good area for seeing white rhino and wild dogs and the walks also visit nearby San paintings. The camp is in an area of mountain bushveld, southwest of Kruger in an isolated valley surrounded by koppies. Hikers stay in thatched bush huts. Hikers check in at Berg-en-Dal which is an hour's drive by Land Rover from the camp.

Napi Trail Passes through a variety of habitats following the banks of the Biyamiti River through thick riverine bush and crossing through mixed woodlands. This is a good area for seeing both the black and white rhinos, duiker, jackal, kudu and giraffe. Hikers check in at Pretoriuskop.

Metsi-Metsi Trail The camp is in an area of mountain bushveld near the N'waswitsontso River. The trail also visits areas of marula savannah where many plains animals are seen. Hikers check in at Skukuza.

Nyalaland Trail Passes through a vast expanse of mopane scrub, dotted with baobabs, aloes and koppies. The wildlife here is unique to this sector of the park and nyala are often seen. The birdlife here is spectacular. The hutted camp is shaded by kuduberry trees next to the Madzaringwe Stream. Hikers check in at Punda Maria.

Olifants Trail Crosses through a region of classic African plains. It is excellent for seeing large herds of buffalo, wildebeest and zebra. The hutted camp overlooks the Olifants River and is 1½ hours by Land Rover to Letaba. Hikers check in at Letaba.

Sweni Trail Southeast of Satara overlooking the Sweni River and crossing through knobthorn and marula savannah where large herds of buffalo, wildebeest and zebra can be seen. The interesting species to spot are cheetah, lion, kudu, sable and steenbok. Hikers check in at Satara.

Wolhuter Trail Passes through lowveld savannah where it is possible to see some of the rare species such as lions, cheetah, black and white rhino, roan, sable and wild dog. The trail is named after the park ranger Harry Wolhuter, who killed a lion with his knife in 1903. The bush camp has wooden huts and is near the Mlambane River. Hikers check in at Berg-en-Dal.

Tours

Organized tours of Kruger are widely available throughout South Africa and can be booked in all major cities. The variety of tours on offer can be baffling, so it is a good idea to shop around. Prices vary according to the quality of accommodation, the length of the tour, additional destinations, and whether you travel by minibus, open-air game vehicle or air-conditioned coach. There are dozens of companies offering tours; the tourist offices at Nelspruit (see pages 604 and 606) have a list of operators. ▶▶ *See also Activities and tours, page 645.*

Camps in southern Kruger

The greatest concentrations of game and most of Kruger's large camps are in southern Kruger and many visitors only ever see this section of the park. The landscape here is far more varied than the rest of the park and therefore supports a wider range of animals.

Ins and outs

The entrance gates at **Crocodile Bridge** and **Malelane** are on the southern boundary of the park and are clearly signposted from the N4 running between Nelspruit and Komatipoort. The entrance gates at Numbi, Paul Kruger and **Phabeni** are on the southwestern boundary. **Numbi Gate** is signposted off the R538 between Nelspruit and Hazyview; **Paul Kruger Gate** is on the R536 from Hazyview.

Berg-En-Dal

ⓘ *12 km to Malelane Gate, T013-7356106 for last-minute reservations (maximum 48 hrs before arrival).*

This large, modern camp has a rather austere, institutional feel to it. It is set in a hilly landscape, wooded with acacias, marulas and jackalberry overlooking the Matjulu Dam. **Facilities** include a swimming pool, in-camp trail, environmental centre showing wildlife films, petrol station, camp shop, restaurant, telephones and laundrette; open to day visitors. The camp accommodates 300 guests when full and offers day walks and day and night game drives. The **cottages (A)** at this camp are slightly larger than at the other camps and sleep six to eight people. There are also three-bed **bungalows (C)** and 74 **camping** and caravan sites with ablution blocks and kitchen units.

Biyamiti

ⓘ *26 km to Crocodile Gate, 45 km to Malelane, T013-7356171 for reservations (maximum 48 hrs before arrival).*

This bushveld camp is in the far south of Kruger on the banks of the Mbiyamiti River set in an area of crocodile thorn thicket. The camp sleeps 70 people in 15 one- or two-bed **cottages (B-C)** with kitchen. Day walks and night drives can be booked at reception.

Crocodile Bridge

ⓘ *34 km to Lower Sabie, 175 km to Orpen, 125 km to Pretoriuskop, 127 km to Satara, 77 km to Skukuza, T013-7356012 for reservations (maximum 48 hrs before arrival).*

This small camp is next to the park's southern gate set in acacia woodland. There is a hippo pool on the dirt road to Malelane where elephant and other animals come to drink. The camp has 20 two- or three-bed **self-catering chalets (C)**, plus eight **safari tents (D)**, one of which is wheelchair accessible, and two **camping** and caravan sites, with ablution block and kitchen units. Facilities include a petrol station, camp shop, cafeteria, telephones, laundrette; open to day visitors. Night drives and game walks can be booked at reception; day drives are open to people staying outside the park.

① Kruger Park southern sector

➡**Kruger Park maps**
1 Kruger Park southern sector, page 627
2 Kruger Park central sector, page 630
3 Kruger Park northern sector, page 634

Sleeping ⊝	Jock Safari Lodge **6**	Rhino Post Lodge **3**
Berg-En-Dal **1**	Lower Sabie **7**	Skukuza **12**
Biyamiti Bushveld Camp **2**	Malelane **8**	Tinga Private Game Lodge **5**
Crocodile Bridge **4**	Pretoriuskop **11**	

Lower Sabie
① 113 km to Berg-en-Dal, 141 km to Orpen, 53 km to Paul Kruger Gate, 213 km to Phalaborwa, 90 km to Pretoriuskop, 342 km to Punda Maria, 93 km to Satara, 43 km to Skukuza, T013-7356056 for last-minute reservations (maximum 48 hrs before arrival).

The region around Lower Sabie is part of a classic African savannah landscape, with grasslands, umbrella thorn and round-leaf teak stretching off into the distance. This is one of the best regions for seeing game, particularly rhino. Game is attracted here by water at the Mlondosi and Nhlanganzwani dams and the camp overlooks the Sabie River. The accommodation here is impersonal but the camp itself is fairly peaceful. Facilities include the **Ingwe Restaurant**, a bar, shop, petrol station, laundrette, phones and swimming pool. Day walks and night drives can be booked at reception.

Accommodation is provided in large four-, five- or seven-bed **cottages (A-B)** with two bathrooms and a kitchen; two- or three-bed **chalets (C)** with bathroom, fridge and hot-plate; two-bed **rondavels (C)** with bathroom and fridge; two-bed **huts (D)**, with bathroom and fridge; small, two-bed **cottages (C)** with a/c, fridge, veranda, ablution block; one-bed **safari tents (D)** with ablution block; one-bed **huts (E)** with a/c, fridge and ablution block; plus **camping** and caravan sites, with ablution blocks and kitchen facilities.

Malelane
① Check in at Berg-en-Dal.

Malelane is a luxury satellite camp to Berg-en-Dal, set in a rugged area of mountain bushveld on the banks of the Crocodile River on the southern boundary of the park. It has five luxury three- and four-bed **cottages (C)**, with bathroom and solar-powered communal kitchen unit, plus **camping** and caravan sites with ablution block and kitchen unit.

Pretoriuskop
① Near Numbi Gate, 92 km to Berg-en-Dal, 125 km to Crocodile Bridge, 90 km to Lower Sabie, 184 km to Orpen, 140 km to Satara, 49 km to Skukuza, T013-7355128 for last-minute reservations (maximum 48 hrs before arrival).

This is the oldest camp in Kruger and is also the third largest, with a fairly institutional feel. The game drives around Pretoriuskop pass through marula woodland and tall grassland, with good game-viewing areas to the north along the Sabie River and to the south along the Voortrekker Road, which follows the original wagon route through the veld. Rhino are often seen close to Numbi Gate. More animals congregate in this area in the summer than in the winter but it is always a rewarding area for game. Facilities include a restaurant, cafeteria, swimming pool made out of natural rock, petrol station, shop, laundry; day walks and night drives can be booked at reception. It is also possible to join a night drive at Numbi Gate if you are staying outside the park in the Hazyview Area.

There are 142 sleeping units: six-, eight- and nine-bed guest **cottages (A)**, with two bathrooms and a kitchen; four-bed **cottages (B)** with one bathroom and a kitchen; two- to four-bed **bungalows (C-D)** with bathroom, fridge and hot plate; two-, three-, five- and six-bed **huts (D)** with a/c, fridge and ablution block, plus 45 **camping** and caravan sites with ablution blocks and kitchen units.

Skukuza

ⓘ *72 km to Berg-en-Dal, 77 km to Crocodile Bridge, 43 km to Lower Sabie, 137 km to Orpen, 213 km to Phalaborwa, 49 km to Pretoriuskop, 342 km to Punda Maria, 93 km to Satara, T013-7354152 for last-minute reservations (maximum 48 hrs before arrival).*

Located on the south bank of the Sabie River, Skukuza is Kruger's largest camp and the administrative centre of the park. The camp has grown to such an extent that it resembles a small town and you can forget that you're surrounded by a national park. In spite of all the development, Skukuza is still at the centre of Kruger's prime game-viewing area and is a good base for game drives. The road heading northeast towards Satara has high concentrations of game and this region is said have one of the densest concentrations of lion in Africa – and the densest population of cars in Kruger.

Facilities here cater to almost every need and include a supermarket, petrol station, car wash, two restaurants, bank, post office, telephones, internet café, two swimming pools, doctor and laundrette. There is also an open-air cinema showing wildlife videos in the evenings, a good information centre and library, and a small nursery selling indigenous plants including baobabs. Day walks and night drives can be booked at reception and there's a nine-hole golf course. **Kruger Emergency Road Services** is also based here.

Skukuza accommodates over 1000 people in four-, six- and eight-bed **cottages (AL)**, with two bathrooms and kitchen; two-, three- and four-bed **cottages (B)** with one bathroom and kitchen; two-bed **chalets (C)** with one bathroom and kitchen; three-bed **chalets (C)** with bathroom, fridge and hot-plate; three-bed **bungalows (C)**, with bathroom and fridge; two- and four-bed **safari tents (D)** with ablution block, kitchen units, plus 80 **camping** and caravan sites, ablution blocks and kitchen units.

Camps in central Kruger

The central area of Kruger is quieter than the south. There are large areas of flat mopane woodland inhabited by herds of buffalo, elephant, wildebeest and zebra. The camp at Olifants is in a spectacular location.

Ins and outs

Orpen Gate and **Phalaborwa Gate** are on the western boundary. Orpen Gate is on the R531 from Acornhoek and Phalaborwa is on the R71 route from Polokwane and Tzaneen.

Balule

ⓘ *11 km from Olifants where visitors must check in. T013-7356606 for last-minute reservations (maximum 48 hrs before arrival).*

Balule is on the banks of the Olifants River and is one of Kruger's wildest camps. It is little more than a patch of cleared bush surrounded by an electrified chain-link fence; visitors can see animals wandering by only metres away. There are six three-bed **huts (D)**, with an ablution block but no electricity, though there are gas stoves and lanterns are provided, and 15 basic caravan and **camping** sites, with ablution block and braai sites; firewood is on sale here. The smell of barbecued meat attracts hyenas who patrol the fence all night in search of scraps (but don't under any circumstances feed them).

Boulders

ⓘ *54 km to Letaba, 31 km to Mopani, 54 km to Phalaborwa Gate; check in at Mopani, the camp must be booked as a single unit, maximum 12.*

To Shingwedzi

Mooiplas
Picnic Spot

2

(497m)

Giriyonda
Border Post

Kaleka

Makhadzi
Picnic Spot

MOZAMBIQUE

11

Longwe
(480m)

3

Engelhardt
Dam

Letaba

To R71 & Phalaborwa Airport

Masorini
Picnic Spot

Phalaborwa
Gate

Olifants

7

1

Nsumaneni
(367m)

➡ **Kruger Park maps**
1 Kruger Park southern sector,
   page 627
2 **Kruger Park central sector,
   page 630**
3 Kruger Park northern sector,
   page 634

Shisakashanghondzo

Timbavati
Picnic Spot

Tim bavati

10

Nwanetsi
Picnic Spot

4
8 **14**

To Acornhoek ◀ Orpen
Gate

Muzandzeni
Picnic Spot

Sweni

6

13

Baobab Tree ◀ *To Skukuza*

N

Sleeping 🛏	Orpen **8**	Talamati Bushveld
Balule **1**	Satara **10**	Camp **13**
Boulders **2**	Shimuwini Bushveld	Tamboti **14**
Letaba **3**	Camp **11**	
Maroela **4**	Singita Lebombo **6**	
Mopani **5**	Singita Sweni **6**	
Olifants **7**		

10 km
10 miles

This unfenced private camp is in an area of acacia, knobthorn and mopane woodland. The camp blends in beautifully with its environment and is set amongst massive granite boulders. The four thatched **bungalows (AL)** are raised on stilts and have a veranda from which to observe the wildlife wandering through the camp. Each sleeps three people and has a communal kitchen and solar power.

Letaba

ⓘ *234 km to Berg-en-Dal, 117 km to Orpen, 51 km to Phalaborwa, 176 km to Punda Maria, 69 km to Satara, 162 km to Skukuza, T013-7356636 for last-minute reservations (maximum 48 hrs before arrival).*

Letaba is one of the larger public camps in central Kruger and is a pleasant, neatly laid-out camp on the banks of the Letaba River. The restaurant is in a magnificent setting for watching the game come down to drink. Some interesting species can be seen here, most notably the large herds of elephant, but the list also includes cheetah, lion, ostrich, roan, sable, steenbok and tsessebe. There is good game viewing to the east of Letaba along the river and at Engelhardt Dam. The two hills rising in the distance to the east of the dam are Longwe, 480 m, and Mhala, 465 m. They are flanked by some beautiful round-leaf teak woodland and baobabs. Middelvlei windmill is 20 km north of Letaba on the H1-6 and provides the only source of water for miles around. Facilities include a mini supermarket, good restaurant, swimming pool, laundrette, petrol station, museum with exhibits on Kruger's elephants (see box, page 624), TV lounge showing wildlife films and Kruger Emergency Road Services. There is a short nature trail around the camp and day walks and night drives can be booked at reception.

Accommodation is available in six-, eight- and nine-bed **cottages (AL)** with two bath rooms and kitchen; two- and three-bed **chalets (C)** with bathroom, fridge and hot plate; three-bed **bungalows (D)** with bathroom and fridge; four-bed **huts (D)** with a/c, fridge and veranda; four-bed **safari tents (D)** with ablution blocks and kitchen units, plus a large, shadeless **campsite**, with 35 camping and caravan sites with ablution blocks and kitchen units.

Maroela and Tamboti satellite camps

ⓘ *Check in at Orpen Gate, 4 km.*

These are both satellite camps to Orpen. Maroela large camp ground is on the south bank of the Timbavati River, and has 20 camping and caravan sites, ablution blocks and kitchen units. There are no other facilities here, but there is a shop at Orpen Gate where you check in and where you can also arrange day walks and night drives. Not far from Maroela, Tamboti (C-D) is a tented camp on the banks of the Timbavati River, offering accommodation in 35 furnished safari tents for two to four people, either fully equipped or sharing communal kitchen, ablutions and eating boma. This is the ideal spot for people looking for a complete bush experience without having to bring all the equipment. There is no restaurant or shop.

Mopani

ⓘ *281 km to Berg-en-Dal, 47 km to Letaba, 86 km to Olifants, 74 km to Phalaborwa Gate, 258 km to Punda Maria, 209 km to Skukuza, T013-7356535 for last-minute reservations (maximum 48 hrs before arrival).*

This is one of Kruger's largest public camps set on a rocky hill overlooking the Pioneer Dam. It is only a few kilometres south of the Tropic of Capricorn, set on a seemingly endless plain of mopane shrub. The accommodation at Mopani has been made from

The Olifant hermit

During the 1940s a hermit lived naked by the Olifants River for five years. He made his home in enlarged aardvark holes and lived off fruit and game. The park authorities left him in peace, partly because there were not enough people to catch him – he could run and hide too well through the bush – and partly because he wasn't causing any trouble.

However, he was eventually caught, after he began stealing equipment from the rangers. A group of them tracked him to his shelter and surprised him late one night while he was sleeping next to his fire. The hermit escaped but the rangers recovered the knives, pots and pans that he had stolen.

Finally, an anti-poaching patrol caught up with him after surprising him on the banks of the Olifants River. He stumbled whilst trying to escape and the rangers grabbed him and tied him up. He was prosecuted for poaching and committed to a lunatic asylum.

natural materials and is more pleasant and spacious than some of the older camps. Choose from an eight-bed **cottage** (**AL**); six-bed **cottages** (**B**) with kitchen, or two- and three-bed **bungalows** (**C**) with kitchen. Facilities include swimming pool, nature trail, petrol station, shop, restaurant, bar overlooking the dam, cafeteria, laundrette; night drives can be booked at reception.

Olifants
ⓘ *219 km to Berg-en-Dal, 147 km to Lower Sabie, 102 km to Orpen, 158 km to Paul Kruger Gate, 83 km to Phalaborwa Gate, 212 km to Punda Maria, 147 km to Skukuza, T013-7356606 for last-minute reservations (maximum 48 hrs before arrival).*

This peaceful camp is in a spectacular setting high on a hill overlooking fever trees and wild figs lining the banks of the Olifants River. The game drives in the immediate area pass through flat mopane woodland in the north and a hilly area of rocks and woodland in the south where klipspringer are often seen. Olifants is one of Kruger's most attractive camps, blending into the surrounding woodland. Facilities include a restaurant, shop, information centre, wildlife films, petrol, laundrette, open to day visitors; night drives can be booked through reception. This is the only camp in Kruger offering guided mountain biking trails. A thatched veranda perched on the edge of the camp looks down into the river valley and is a superb place for game viewing. The thatched accommodation, shaded by large old sycamores and sausage trees, encompasses eight-bed **cottages** (**AL**); four-bed **cottages** (**B**) with kitchen; two-bed **chalets** (**C**) with kitchen or bathroom, fridge and hot plate and three- or two-bed **bungalows** (**D**) with bathroom and fridge.

Orpen
ⓘ *Just beyond Orpen Gate, T013-7356355 for last-minute reservations (maximum 48 hrs before arrival).*

Orpen is a small camp past the entrance gate on the western central plains, set amongst acacias, marulas and aloes. The road passing along the Timbavati River offers a chance of seeing game and the area around the camp is known as a good place to see leopard, lion and cheetah. There are six-bed **cottages** (**B**) with bathroom and three-bed **huts** (**C**) with ablution block. A communal cooking area is available for all the accommodation. Facilities include a petrol station, camp shop, and day walks and night drives can be booked at reception.

Satara

ⓘ *15 km from Berg-en-Dal, 127 km from Crocodile Bridge, 69 km from Letaba, 93 km from Lower Sabie, 48 km from Orpen, 104 km from Paul Kruger Gate, 140 km from Pretoriuskop, 245 km from Punda Maria, 93 km from Skukuza, T013-7356306 for reservations (maximum 48 hrs before arrival).*

Satara, Kruger's second-largest camp looks rather like a motorway service station in the middle of the bush, although the institutional atmosphere of the accommodation is softened by its trees and lawns. Satara is set in the flat grasslands of the eastern region, which attract large herds of wildebeest, buffalo, kudu, impala, zebra and elephant. There is good game viewing on the road to Orpen.

Accommodation is available in guest **cottages (AL-A)** sleeping six, eight or nine, with one or two bathrooms and kitchen; two- or three-bed **bungalows (C)** with bathroom, fridge and hot plate; and on 74 **camping** and caravan sites, with ablution blocks, kitchen units. Facilities include petrol station, car wash, Kruger Emergency Road Service, camp shop, cafeteria, restaurant, laundry, swimming pool, day walks and night drives can be booked at reception.

Shimuwini

ⓘ *66 km to Letaba, 118 km to Olifants, 52 km to Phalaborwa, T013-7356683 for reservations (maximum 48 hrs before arrival).*

This bushveld camp is set in a region of bushwillow and mopane woodland, with less of a concentration of wildlife, compared to the south of Kruger. However, this is still an interesting wilderness area with a good variety of wildlife. The private access road leading to Shimuwini follows the Letaba River where elephant can sometimes be seen bathing and the riverine forest around the camp is good for birdwatching.

The camp overlooks the Shimuwini Dam. Visitors to the camp have private access to the dam which is surrounded by giant sycamore trees. There is a hide here from which to see crocodiles, hippo, waterbuck and waterbirds. The camp consists of a row of four- and six-bed thatched **cottages (B)** with kitchen and veranda, some have additional outside showers, shaded by appleleaf trees and acacias. The camp can accommodate up to 70 visitors and offers day and night game drives.

Talamati

ⓘ *30 km to Orpen Gate, T013-7356343 for reservations (maximum 48 hrs before arrival).*

This rustic bushveld camp is set on the banks of the Nwaswitsonto River which is normally dry. The grassland and acacia woodland along the western boundary attract kudu, giraffe, sable and white rhino. Klipspringer can be seen on the rocky outcrops. There are two hides in the camp for game viewing and birdwatching. The camp accommodates 80 visitors in two-, four- and six-bed **cottages (B)**, with bathroom and kitchen, and offers day and night game drives.

Camps in northern Kruger

This is a dry and remote region that is rarely visited by tourists. As there is no year-round water supply, there isn't the same density of animals as in the south of Kruger, but the area does support animals unique to this part of Kruger, including Sharpe's grysbok, tsessebe, sable and nyala.

The **Luvuvhu River** offers some of the best wildlife viewing in the area. The river banks are lined with ironwood, ebony and sycamore fig – huge pythons thrive in the thick forests, and some of the largest crocodiles in Kruger can be seen in the Luvuvhu River. The bridge over the Luvuvhu is an excellent spot for birdwatchers after heavy rains. Many birds are attracted to the fruit trees, and some of the more unusual species which can be seen here are the Cape parrot, Basra reed warbler, tropical boubou and yellow-bellied

3 **Kruger Park northern sector**

➡ Kruger Park maps
1 Kruger Park southern sector, page 627
2 Kruger Park central sector, page 630
3 **Kruger Park northern sector**, page 634

Sleeping 🛏
Bateleur Bushveld Camp 1

Pafuri Camp 2
Punda Maria 3

Shingwedzi 4
Sirheni 5

sunbird. There are also two interesting raptors here, Ayre's eagle and Dickinson's kestrel. A good location is the picnic site at Mooiplaas between Letaba and Shingwedzi, which overlooks a waterhole on the Tsende River where game can be seen.

Close to the Luvuvhu River, in the northern corner of Kruger Park, is the late Iron Age site of **Thulamela**. This is an important archaeological site that has forced people to reconsider their understanding and interpretation of the local regional history. Sidney Miller was responsible for the excavation project, which was sponsored by the Gold Fields Foundation. Aside from clearing all the vegetation and collecting items such as spearheads, pots, beads, bracelets and harpoons, the team embarked upon an ambitious project of rebuilding some of the stone walls, which had originally been built over 400 years ago. The whole site lies on the top of a sub-plateau which is reached after a steep 25-minute climb. It is estimated that more than 1500 people lived here. The stone enclosure was a royal palace, which, during its heyday in the Khami period, was an important commercial centre of a powerful agro-pastoral kingdom. Evidence collected at Thulamela points towards a thriving metal-working community producing spearheads and hoe blades in iron, as well as more delicate items from copper and gold. Guided walking tours to Thulamela depart from the Pafuri picnic spot twice daily. Bookings can be made at Sirheni, Shingwedzi, Punda Maria and Pafuri Gates.

To the east, **Gumbandevu Hill** used to be a traditional centre for rain makers, where offerings of livestock and snuff were given in return for rain. The sounds of a goat being sacrificed at the base of the hill helped to summon the spirits that made rain. The hill is still thought to be haunted and is always greener than the surrounding area.

Ins and outs

Punda Maria Gate and **Pafuri Gate** are in the far north of the park. Punda Maria Gate is on the R524 and can be reached from Makhado/Louis Trichardt. Pafuri Gate is in the far north and can be reached on the R525 from Venda.

Bateleur

ⓘ *37 km to Shingwedzi, T013-7356843 for last-minute reservations (maximum 48 hrs before arrival).*

Bateleur is an isolated bushveld camp surrounded by a vast area of mopane and acacia woodland with the Phonda Hills (400 m) lying to the north. Visitors to the camp have exclusive access to the two nearby dams, Rooibosrand and Silverfish, both of which are good areas for game watching, especially for sable and nyala. There is a viewing platform nearby overlooking a waterhole which is best seen after the rains. The camp is solar powered and accommodates up to 34 visitors in four- and six-bed **cottages** (B) with kitchens. Day and night game drives are available.

Shingwedzi

ⓘ *37 km to Bateleur, 71 km from Punda Maria, T013-7356806 for last-minute reservations (maximum 48 hrs before arrival).*

This is the most northerly large camp in the national park. Brick units are arranged in a large circle, looking in on an open area, which has no grass, just a shady area of short mopane trees. The best game viewing in this area is around Kanniedood Dam and the riverine forest along the banks of the Shingwedzi. Many animals from the surrounding areas come here for water. There is a bird hide south of the camp on the S134 overlooking the river.

The railway lions

The entrance gate to Sabi Sand at Newington used to be the site of a layby on the Selati railway line, and the graves of the construction workers who died of malaria or were killed by wild animals can still be seen here. This area is known for its lions. When the railway was still running, the threat to passengers waiting for trains was so serious that they were provided with ladders by the railway company so that they could climb to safety in the trees, where the lions couldn't reach them.

Accommodation comprises one four-bed **cottage** (**AL**) with kitchen; two-bed **chalets** (**B-C**) with bathroom and fridge or kitchen; two-bed **bungalows** (**C**) with bathroom and fridge; three-bed **huts** (**D**), with fridge, veranda, ablution blocks and kitchen facilities. Facilities include a restaurant, cafeteria, shop, petrol, information centre, swimming pool and laundrette. Night drives and guided walks can be booked at reception. The restaurant has a pleasant outside terrace where one can sit during the day and look out over the Shingwedzi River. The **campsite** is well away from the cottages and chalets. It has plenty of space, but there is limited shade and virtually no grass.

Punda Maria

① *8 km from the Punda Maria Gate, 415 km from Berg-en-Dal, 176 km from Letaba, 130 km from Mopani, 201 km from Phalaborwa Gate, 71 km from Shingwedzi, 342 km from Skukuza, T013-7356873 for last-minute reservations (maximum 48 hrs before arrival).*

This peaceful camp, hidden by dense woodland, is the northernmost large public camp in Kruger and by far the most pleasant. It is situated in a unique area of sandveld dotted with baobabs, white seringa and pod mahogany. There are spectacular views of the surrounding landscapes from the top of Dzundzwini (600 m) and good game viewing near the camp on the Mahonie Loop and up by the Witsand windmill. Look out for nyala and kudu. The game drive north to Pafuri passes through mopane shrubveld inhabited by roan, sable and tsessebe. The bridge over the Luvuvhu River is a top place for birdwatchers, where many species of bird are attracted to the fruit trees along the banks of the river. This is the only area in the park where you can see and enjoy Mopani Forest. The short Paradise Flycatcher nature trail loops around the camp.

Accommodation is available in four-bed **cottages** (**B**) with kitchen; two-bed **chalets** (**C**) with kitchen – some of the chalets date from the 1930s but are still adequately comfortable; two-bed **bungalows** (**D**) with bathroom, fridge, ablution block and communal kitchen, plus a camping and caravan park, with ablution block, braai sites and communal kitchen. Note that this is a small camp and is often fully booked at weekends. Facilities include restaurant, bar, shop and petrol. The food in the restaurant is better than other camps, but meals must be ordered in advance.

🌙 *Punda Maria was named after the zebra that Captain JJ Coetzer saw when he first arrived here; he mistakenly believed 'punda maria' to be the Swahili word for zebra. In fact, it's 'punda milia', but the first name has stuck.*

Sirheni

ⓘ *28 km to Shingwezi, 48 km to Punda Maria, T013-7356860 for reservations (maximum 48 hrs before arrival).*

This is a bushveld camp overlooking Sirheni Dam, surrounded by mopane and acacia woodlands. This region is better known for birdwatching than game viewing and, although game is present, it is not found in the same concentrations as in southern Kruger. The road approaching the camp from the south on the S66 passes through the alluvial plains and riverine forest of the Mphongolo River, inhabited by leopard, nyala and waterbuck. It is signposted off the H1-7. The camp accommodates up to 80 visitors in four- and six-bed **cottages** (**B-C**) with kitchen, and offers day and night bush drives.

Private game reserves ● ▸▸ *pp641-645.*

The reserves fringing the western border of Kruger offer some of the most exclusive game viewing in the world. Here you have the chance of seeing the Big Five and exploring the natural environment of Kruger from the comfort of a private 4WD, with the promise of luxury accommodation and superb cuisine at the end of your game drive. Each lodge has its own secluded setting, providing an enjoyable 'in the wild' experience. But the biggest advantage of staying in the private reserves are the excellent game guides, who provide a fantastic introduction to the bush — usually with far better game-spotting skills, too, which means you'll see much more than if you were self-driving.

Ins and outs

Access to the lodges is straightforward. Guests are collected from either **Phalaborwa Airport**, **Eastgate Airport** at Hoedspruit, or **Kruger Mpumalanga International Airport** near Nelspruit (scheduled flights or charter flights are usually included in packages) and driven by safari vehicle to the lodge. Alternatively, a charter by light aircraft will take you directly to those lodges that have a private airstrip, or you can drive yourself – it takes around six hours from Johannesburg.

Reserves

There are now numerous private reserves, each holding countless game lodges. The best-known private reserves include **Klaserie**, **Timbavati**, **Thornybush**, **Mala Mala**, and **Sabi Sabi**, which together form the largest private game area in the world. The first three are in Limpopo, but are included here together with the Mpumalanga reserves. Within these reserves are several smaller reserves, which have been incorporated into a single wilderness area; some still retain their original name which can be a bit confusing. For example, **Idube Game Reserve** and **Londolozi Game Reserve** are now both part of the much larger Sabi Sand Game Reserve. In the last decade, the fences between all these reserves have been removed, including, most significantly, the western Kruger National Park fence. This development has helped, in part, to restore natural east-west migration routes and has created the **Greater Kruger National Park**. Despite a confusing range of names for reserves and camps, they all now fall into this greater area.

Game viewing

Game viewing is, of course, the main activity in all the lodges. Days normally begin with an early-morning game drive, returning in mid- to late-morning for breakfast. Guests can then either choose to go on a game walk or relax by the pool before lunch. When the

Luxury bush camps & safari lodges

10 km

10 miles

worst of the day's heat has passed, the vehicles set off on another game drive, returning for dinner. Optional night drives are usually also available.

Game viewing can vary from lodge to lodge, depending on how many vehicles patrol an area and, of course, how much effort the rangers put into showing visitors around. Nevertheless, game viewing is always dependent on luck, and staying in a five-star private game lodge does not mean that you will be guaranteed better animal sightings than if you were travelling around Kruger in a hire car and staying in a SANParks campsite. The benefits, however, are that you will have a personal and knowledgeable guide, and you're unlikely to come across many other tourists.

Lodges

Most guests spend between two and three days at a lodge to get the most out of game viewing. Prices vary considerably, and can range from fairly expensive, old fashioned lodges, to full-on luxury living, with extravagant accommodation, sumptuous cuisine and a variety of extras such as butler service. Most lodges are fairly luxurious, however, and in between outings you can appreciate the full extent of your surroundings: most camps have platforms overlooking a waterhole or a river, there are usually comfortable lounge areas, libraries of books and magazines about wildlife, and most lodges have swimming pools. Recent additions to some camps include gyms, spas and conference facilities.

Special deals are often available, and it is worth looking out for fly drive packages and discounts out of peak season. The daily cost of staying at a lodge can vary from R2000 to R8000 for two people sharing, though rates can soar to over R25,000; prices include all meals, game walks and game drives. Reservations should be made well in advance because, despite high prices, the most popular lodges get fully booked very quickly.
▶▶ For further information, see Sleeping, page 641.

Timbavati Game Reserve

Timbavati extends from Orpen to the region just south of the Olifants River. As well as large herds of elephant, giraffe, blue wildebeest, zebra and impala, this area is known for its white lions, although these have largely become assimilated in to the larger lion population. Open savannah, riverine forest, acacia, marula and mopane woodlands support a tremendous variety of wildlife including 350 species of bird. The reserve was created in the 1950s from a group of privately owned farms where hunting was banned. Game, such as cheetah, sable and white rhino, was reintroduced to re-establish populations which were originally present in this area. You can get to the lodges in the northern part of the reserve via the turning 7 km south of Hoedspruit off the R40. The nearest airport is Eastgate, although many of the lodges have private airstrips. Camps in the southern areas are accessed by the turning 9 km north of Klaserie at Kapama, off the R40. ▶▶ There are 13 luxury lodges and camps dotted about the reserve, www.timbavati.co.za.

Kapama Private Game Reserve

Kapama Private Game Reserve is one with the easiest to access as it's right next to Eastgate airport near Hoedspruit in Limpopo Province. The reserve covers approximately 13,000 ha of prime big game territory, with three luxury lodges within its borders. A highlight here are the elephant-back safaris offered at Camp Jabulani, the first operation of its kind in South Africa following a successful programme at Victoria Falls in Zimbabwe. Twelve fully trained African elephants arrived at Kapama in early 2002, after being relocated from Zimbabwe. Guests are seated on canvas-covered saddles positioned behind an experienced elephant handler. From this vantage point, you are able to view game from a close proximity as the elephants move silently and in a single file through the bush. The reserve also offers game drives, clay pigeon shooting, bush walks, birdwatching from a bird hide on the banks of a large dam, sundowner cruises, traditional dancing, hot-air ballooning and quad biking. All the activities are exclusively for the guests at the luxury lodges within the reserve. ▸▸ *There are three luxury lodges in the reserve, www.kapama.co.za.*

Thornybush Nature Reserve
Thornybush started life as a private farm sharing a border with Timbavati. It was converted into a private game reserve of 11,500 ha and is now part of the Greater Kruger National Park. There are eight game lodges here. The main entrance is 9 km north of Klaserie off the R40; look out for the signs for Kapama and the Hoedspruit Cheetah project. The nearest airport is Eastgate at Hoedspruit.

Mala Mala Game Reserve
Mala Mala was one of the first private reserves to identify and cater for the top end of the luxury market. It has three camps (www.malamala.com), with an excellent reputation for combining luxury service and game viewing; rates for the main camp start at over R7000 per person. Guests have exclusive access to over 50 km of riverfront along the Sand River, offering some of the best game viewing in South Africa thanks to the fact that this is a perennial river. Seeing the Big Five is a central part of the Mala Mala experience and guests get a certificate to authenticate their sightings.

The camps in the south of the reserve are approached from the R536, the Hazyview to Skukuza road. For the lodges to the north, turn off the R40 about 15 km north of Hazyview. It is at least a further 50 km to the accommodation.

Sabi Sabi Game Reserve
Sabi Sabi Private Game Reserve is a relatively small area of land in the extreme south of the block of contiguous reserves which stretch all the way from the Olifants River to the Sabie River. To get there, follow the R536 from Hazyview to Skukuza, turn off at Glano. Although it is now part of the Greater Kruger National Park, the collection of private lodges and camps in Sabi Sabi couldn't be more different than the Skukuza camp across the Sabie River. Sabi Sabi has an excellent reputation by virtue of being the only private reserve on the perennial Sabie River. ▸▸ *Sabi Sabi is home to four of the most fashionable lodges, www.sabisabi.com.*

Sabi Sand Game Reserve
Sabi Sand has the highest density of lodges and game-viewing vehicles and is slightly more crowded than Timbavati or Thornybush. However, the Sand River has water all year round, which does attract large numbers of game. The reserve was established in 1934 by the owners of farms in this area but the first lodge wasn't opened to the public until 1962. The quality of the game viewing here is superior to that of Kruger and the rangers are extremely knowledgeable about the wildlife and don't just concentrate on the Big Five. Some of the most famous private concessions are within Sabi Sand, including Londolozi and Ulusaba. The game-viewing experience here is intended to give visitors a deeper understanding of the wilderness. To reach the reserve, turn off the R40 about 15 km north of Hazyview; this is the same road for Mala Mala Game Reserve. It is at least a further 50 km to the accommodation. ▸▸ *There are no fewer than 19 lodges in the reserve, www.sabisand.co.za.*

Kruger National Park listings

Hotel and guesthouse prices
L over US$300   AL US$220-300   A US$150-220
B US$100-150   C US$75-100   D US$35-75
E US$15-35   F under US$15
Private game reserves
L4 over US$900   L3 US$550-900
L2 US$450-550   L1 US$300-500
Restaurant prices
††† over US$30   †† US$15-30   † under US$15
See pages 46-51 for further information.

Sleeping

For SANParks accommodation within the different sections of Kruger, see pages 621 and 626-637. There are far too many lodges in the private game reserves to list in full, but below is a selection – be sure to shop around while choosing where to stay. Most reserves have good websites.

Timbavati Game Reserve *p639, map p638*
L4 King's Camp, T013-7554408, www.kings camp.com. An exclusive camp which enjoys easy access with Johannesburg via Eastgate Airport. 10 luxury en-suite, a/c thatched suites, with minibar and outdoor showers, lounge-dining room, bar, swimming pool, gym, game-viewing platform and deck overlooking a very active waterhole. After a night drive guests enjoy dinner in the *boma*, wine cellar, or out bush under canvas.
L4 Tanda Tula, part of the Constantia Uitsig group in Cape Town, T021-7946500, www.uitsig.co.za. Set in an area of thick acacia woodland, is not ideal country for seeing the Big Five but you will see some of the more unusual animals. This is one of the oldest lodges and with only 16 guests offers a more personal service. The accommodation consists of thatched bungalows and luxury East African safari tents furnished with wicker furniture and Victorian bathrooms. The bar on the veranda overlooks the swimming pool and a waterhole. In the evenings, weather permitting, barbecued dinners are held in the dried-up river bed in front of the camp.

L3 Motswari, T011-4631990, www.mot swari.co.za. One of the smaller luxury camps, located in the northern region of Timbavati, with exclusive access to a large area. Game viewing can be from a jeep, on foot or at hides over-looking waterholes. Lodge facilities include a traditional open-air *boma*, a spacious lounge and bar overlooking a beautiful dam, an art gallery exhibiting original wildlife art, a fully equipped conference room and a refreshing swimming pool. The lodge accommodates 30 guests in 15 luxury en suite bungalows. All bedrooms have a/c and overhead fans, with magnificent bush and river views from the beds.
L3 Ngala, T011-8094300, www.ccafrica.com. Ngala is a long-running favourite amongst the area's luxury lodges. The lodge is on the Timbavati Flood Plain, a region known for its herds of elephant and prides of lion. Visitors in this part of the reserve experience 2 contrasting ecosystems; the open savannah grasslands, and the magnificent mopane woodlands. The range of habitat means that the birdlife in this area is particularly interesting and varied. The 20 a/c thatched cottages, filled with antique furnishings, and the luxury Safari Suite with its own lounge, dining area, swimming pool, and private Land Rover, are all set in an area of mopane woodland overlooking a waterhole. Meals are served on the open decking area overlooking the waterhole, or in a lantern-lit lapa area. The food here is particularly good, and the game rangers very knowledgeable. Recommended.
L3 Umlani Bush Camp, T012-3464028, www.umlani.com. Accommodates 16 guests in en suite reed and thatch rondavels with open-air showers. This is a lowveld area where kudu, nyala, giraffe, elephant, lion and white rhino can be seen. Game drives are run during the day and in the evenings but the emphasis is on the game walks. There is a treehouse overlooking a waterhole which is good for birdwatching. No electricity and the whole camp is lit atmospherically by candles and oil lamps.

L1 Gomo Gomo Game Lodge, T013-7523954, www.gomogomo.co.za. A relatively simple bush camp, one of the less expensive options around. Here the emphasis is very much on the bush and the wildlife, rather than the luxury and the food and drink. A friendly camp where guests enjoy traditional South African fare under the open sky. There are 5 thatched rondavels with en suite bathrooms and 4 luxury tents, the gardens are an interesting collection of aloes and other indigenous plants and a swimming pool. Game drives and bush walks included.

Kapama Game Reserve *p639, map p638*
L4 Camp Jabulani, T012-4605605, www.camp jabulani.com. Relatively new camp offering guests opulent accommodation and elephant-back safaris. They use 13 fully grown elephants, which were relocated from Zimbabwe following a threat to their safety during election time. 6 stylish suites, with private decks and splash pools, butler service, open showers, fireplaces, fashionable fusion food spread over several courses, spa.
L2 Buffalo Camp, T012-3680600, www.kapama.co.za. Built on the theme of an East African safari camp of bygone days, 8 luxury canvas tents, each sleeping 2 guests, set on stilts in the upper reaches of tall trees, overlooking a seasonal river. Each tent is interconnected to other tents by wooden walkways high above a sandy river bed. Dining is in an outside boma around a fire, and there's a pool. New in 2008 is a wellness centre with lap pool, gym and spa.
L2 Kapama Lodge, T012-3680600, www.kapama.co.za, 20 luxurious thatched chalets set in indigenous gardens. Winding timber walkways link the reception area, conference room, lounge, library and dining room. The tea deck is a relaxing venue for watching an abundance of birds in the balmy evening, while the lounge offers a warm, cosy welcome on cool winter evenings. A good option for families and offers extra activities for small children while parents go on game drives.

Thornybush Nature Reserve *p640, map p638*
L4 Thornybush Game Lodge, T011-8837918, www.thornybush.co.za. The largest lodge in the reserve but you can still enjoy a relaxing and private time in the bush here. The lodge has 18 a/c rooms and 2 family suites with outdoor showers, the bar and the *boma* are a popular feature beside the Monwana River. Discuss with the camp rangers how you would most like to enjoy your game viewing; night drives, bush walks and morning drives are all possible and there are children's activities, swimming pool and spa.
L1 Kwa Mbili Game Lodge, T015-7932773, www.kwambili.com. A pleasant small lodge that offers comparatively cheap accommo dation. Game drives in open vehicles or bush walks are on offer, all in the company of experienced game rangers and trackers. The lodge has a choice of thatched chalets or safari tents, all with en suite bath rooms and simple decor. Meals are served around a camp fire or on the open veranda where there is also a bar and a lounge area, plus a swimming pool.

Mala Mala Game Reserve *p640, map p638*
There are 3 camps to choose from, each with its own character. No children under 12 at **Mala Mala Main Camp** or at **Sable Camp**; no under 16s at **Rattray's**. Reservations: T011-4422267, www.malamala.com.
L4 Mala Mala Main Camp. The accommo-dation consists of 18 ochre-coloured thatched rondavels, extremely spacious, each with his and hers bathrooms, a/c, heating, and minibar, 1 room for wheelchair users. Lounge area is decorated with elephant tusks, hunting rifles, spears and African memorabilia. The whole camp is set in a shady wood beside the river; good meals served. Swimming pool.
L4 Rattray's. Original farmhouse dating from the 1920s when the area was a cattle ranch belonging to Harry Kirkman. Kirkman was one of Kruger's first game rangers and the house is decorated with early photos, hunting rifles and old maps of the Transvaal. Appealing colonial atmosphere, 8 luxury suites each with private veranda and plunge pool, antique

furnishings, satellite TV and internet access. Swimming pool, gym and massage room.

L4 Sable Camp. In the southern corner of the reserve, away from the **Main Camp**, is the most intimate of the 3 camps. Just 5 luxury suites, and one 2-bedroom suite, colonial theme, beautiful setting overlooking the Sabie River. Deck and swimming pool with views, meals served outdoors. Excellent game viewing from here – the camp is very close to Kruger Park headquarters at Skukuza.

Sabi Sabi Game Reserve *p640, map p638*
The 4 lodges have won multiple 'Best Game Lodge in Southern Africa' awards. Rates are as high as R12,000 per person per night. Reservations: T011-4833939, www.sabisabi.com.

L4 Bush Lodge. Overlooking a water hole amongst trees on the banks of the Msuthlu River, 20 a/c thatched chalets and 5 luxury suites, ethnic decor, swimming pool, spa, meals served in open-air boma. The main building is decorated with African art and animal trophies.

L4 Earth Lodge. Set on the banks of the Sabie River, this innovative lodge feels like an ultra-trendy boutique hotel set deep in the African bush. The design cuts into the earth, which means that the lodge is virtually invisible, with smooth stone and grass-covered roofs blending into the surroundings. 13 suites with stylish decor of muted colours and natural materials, private plunge pool, glass-fronted bathrooms and butler. Bar area made up of the roots of trees, and meals are served in an open-air *boma* cut into the ground.

L4 Little Bush Camp. The newest addition with only 6 thatched suites decorated with contemporary African art, outdoor showers, private viewing decks, the camp is linked by wooden boardwalks, meals are taken outside under the arms of giant trees, guests can use spa facilities at the **Bush Lodge**.

L4 Selati Lodge. 8 stone and thatch chalets, colonial and steam train theme, antiques and 4-poster beds. The camp is lit with oil lamps at night, but there's electricity for ceiling fans and a/c. Meals served on a deck next to the pool or in a boma or farmhouse-style kitchen.

Sabi Sand Game Reserve *p640, map p638*
Several of the private concerns have more than one camp, providing you with a choice in style as well as price. The camps have been grouped under their collective names.

Londolozi

Along with Mala Mala, Londolozi is one of the best-known and most exclusive luxury game lodges in the region. The highlight of a game drive here is the opportunity to see leopards (in Londolozi these normally elusive creatures are used to game viewing vehicles). There is an emphasis on finding the Big Five, but the rangers here are also willing to spend time searching for other animals. Londolozi operates 5 camps along the banks of the Sand River. The Life Centre offers a spa, yoga and gym to guests of all the lodges. Reservations, T011-2806640, www.londolozi.co.za

L4 Founders Camp. 5 chalets and 1 suite secluded in dense riverine forest overlooking the Sand River. The a/c chalets with their wooden decks feature a personal bar and the suite has a stone-laid outdoor shower. Charming and intimate, the dining area at Founders Camp overlooks the Sand River, with a walkway leading to a thatched viewing deck where guests can relax while game and bird viewing. The boma is adjacent to the camp's swimming pool. There is a covered sitting area, with a well-stocked drinks cabinet.

L4 Pioneer Camp. Sitting on a gentle rise in the landscape with elevated views of the reserve and breathtaking river views, the camp consists of 3 suites and 3 chalets all of which are furnished in classic safari style. The suites have a fireplace, and all have a personal bar, and en suite bathrooms with baths and indoor and outdoor showers. The intimate guest area provides a unique interactive experience with the kitchen, sitting and dining areas all being open plan. The camp has a swimming pool and boma where evening meals are enjoyed under the stars.

L4 Tree Camp. One of the best game lodges in Africa. 6 thatched chalets each with en suite facilities and private view platforms high in the trees above the Sand River. The furniture is made from old railway sleepers of beautifully polished hardwoods and the beds are made from leather, giving the camp a luxurious but ethnic feel. It is set amongst the rocks in a patch of riverine forest and has a platform on stilts over the river. No children under 16.

L4 Varty Camp. 10 luxurious chalets on the site of an old hunting camp built in 1926. All have private plunge pools and wooden decks, earthy decor. Bathrooms have capacious tubs with uninterrupted views of the surrounding bush. The camp has a well-stocked wine cellar, a library (with internet), historical photographs of the reserve, spacious deck which incorporates an ancient ebony tree with views of the Sand River, and there is a large swimming pool.

Ulusaba

Owned by Sir Richard Branson, Ulusaba has 2 camps, the **Safari Lodge** and the more expensive **Rock Lodge**. Both are hugely expensive and offer game drives and bush walks. Pampering is available for guests in the Aroma Boma beauty spa. Splash pools are presently being added to some of the suites. Reservations: T011-3254405, www.ulusaba.com.

L4 Rock Lodge. In an extraordinary setting on a koppie 200 m above the reserve. The views are spectacular. Pathways lead down the rock face to a veranda from where you can see the animals coming to drink at the Ulusaba dam. 10 spacious a/c rooms with en suite bathrooms and colourful furnishings; there is a rock pool surrounded by a sundeck, and meals are served on the deck.

L4 Safari Lodge. 10 thatched chalets built on elevated wooden platforms shaded by wild fig trees. Some of them can only be reached by rope swing bridges. Each chalet has an outside shower, and there is also a rock pool above the river where guests can swim.

Singita

This luxury operator runs 4 lodges that are generally regarded as some of the finest and most expensive in South Africa (they have won the Condé Nast Traveller Best Hotel award for

several years running (rates are over R15,000 per couple per night). The company has also won the Fair Trade in Tourism stamp. Reservations: T021-6833424, www.singita.com.

L4 Singita Boulders. Impressive lodge built of curving thatch and stone moulded into the rock. Set on the banks of the Sands River. Luxurious suites, stone theme, natural decor and cool, neutral colours, beautiful views from the beds. Spa, sun deck, swimming pool, attractive lounge, meals served on deck.

L4 Singita Ebony. Suites nestling in the shade of jackleberry trees on the banks of the Sand River. Stunning decor, spacious suites with a mix of antiques and splashes of vibrant colour, open-plan bathrooms, plunge pools and private decks. Super-stylish lounge area, excellent meals served outdoors on deck. Gym and beauty spa.

Kruger Park concessions *p621, map p627*
Several concessions have been granted to private camps within the boundaries of the Kruger National Park. The safari experience at these is similar to the private reserves and rates include game drives, bush walks and all meals and, if you don't have your own vehicle, transfers from the nearest airport can be arranged. The first 2 are part of Singita (see above) and are close to one another on the banks of the Sweni River near the border with Mozambique, 64 km from Orpen Gate.

L4 Singita Lebombo, on the banks of the Sweni River near the Mozambique border, 64 km from Orpen Gate. A modern and stylish lodge built of glass, steel and stone. Fashionable alternative to the usual colonial or ethnic themes, the suites, linked by walkways, have sleek decks, designer furniture, infinity pool with white loungers and bar area.

L4 Singita Sweni, near **Singita Lebombo**. Smallest of the Singita lodges, with just 6 suites built on stilts. Decor is dark wood, ethnic fabrics and earthenware with splashes of bright lime. Attractive suites tucked way in the trees with views over the bush, stylish dining room with floor-to-ceiling windows and views over the river.

L4 Tinga Private Game Lodge, 8 km from Paul Kruger Gate, T013-7358400, www.tinga. co.za. 2 luxurious lodges close together set under jackelberry trees overlooking the game-rich Sabie River, each with 9 vast suites with plunge pools, double showers, enormous baths, separate lounges, DSTV, DVD players, huge windows with uninterrupted views of the bush, superb food and a wellness centre, library and lounge, walks on offer to a nearby hippo pool as well as the regular game drives.

L3 Jock Safari Lodge, southeast of the park, 35 km from Malelane Gate, T041-4071000, www.jocksafarilodge.com. The camp is in an area of mixed woodland between Malelane and Skukuza. This used to be a national park camp and was the first to be turned over to private hands. The 12 cottages have been refurbished to the highest standard and are decorated with prints of the original illustrations from the novel, *Jock of the Bushveld*. Each has its own private viewing deck and outside showers overlooking the Mitomeni and Biyamiti rivers. Rock swimming pool.

L2 Pafuri Camp, close to the Pafuri Gate, Wilderness Safaris, reservations T011-8071800, www.pafuri.com. This concession is in the extreme north of Kruger between the Limpopo and Luvuvhu rivers and is excellent for bird-watching, the area was proclaimed a RAMSAR site in 2007. The camp sits under giant ebony trees and overlooks the Luvuvhu River, 20 tents on raised platforms under thatch, some sleep families of 4, outdoor shower, game viewing deck, eating boma, plunge pool, children's activities to learn about the bush.

L2 Rhino Post Lodge and Rhino Walking Safaris, a 12,000-ha concession 10 km north-east of Skukuza, T011-4671886, www.rws.co.za. 8 elegant suites on the banks of the Mutlumuvi River, free-standing baths and outdoor showers, swimming pool with deck overlooking a water hole, as well as game drives, offers walking safaris and dinner in the bush accompanied by an armed guard.

▲ Activities and tours

Tour operators

Bundu Safaris, T011-6750767, www.bundu safaris.co.za. Budget backpacker camping tours. 4- to 8-day overland tours including Kruger; they have their own camp in the park from where is possible to go game walking.
Mozaic Travel, Maputo, T+258-2132788, www.mozaictravel.com. Tours through to the Mozambique side of the park, overnighting in a new luxury camp on the Machampane River.
Spurwing, T011-9572222, www.spurwing tourism.com. Luxury tours using 4WDs and top-end lodges, Kruger and Panorama region.
Viva Safaris, T011-4768842, www.viva safaris.com. 3- to 5-day budget and camping tours, owns its own lodges, range of accommo-dation, also has walking safaris and fly-ins.
Wildlife Safaris, Randburg 2125, Johannes-burg, T011-7914238, www.wildlifesafaris.com. 3- to 5 day overland safaris from Johannesburg with mid-range prices and accommodation in Kruger Park. Knowledgeable and friendly guides. Recommended.

Panorama region

The road north of Nelspruit gradually climbs up into the eastern Drakensberg, generally referred to as the Panorama region. The region is dotted with small towns, popular with local tourists who come for the craft shops and restaurants, but the main reason for a visit is the spectacular Blyde River Canyon, the third largest canyon in the world. The mountains provide blessed relief from the heat on the plains of the Lowveld. ▸▸ *For listings, see pages 654-660.*

Panorama region

Sleeping
Chestnut Country Lodge **3**   Misty Mountain Chalets **5**
Hulala Lakeside Lodge **4**

White River → *Phone code: 013. Colour map 2, B5. Altitude: 800 m.*

This small country town is at the centre of a citrus fruit-growing area; fresh local produce includes macadamia nuts, pecans, cashews, avocados, lychees and mangoes. The first settlers here were Boer cattle ranchers who arrived in the 1880s, at the end of the Anglo-Boer War a settlement was created to accommodate a new farming community made up of newly demobilized soldiers. There's little in the town itself, although the Motor Museum and Orange Winery attract a fair share of South Africa tourists. **Lowveld Tourist information** ⓘ *T013-7501073, www.lowveld.info,* has a small helpful office on the Hazyview road, at Casterbridge Farm.

The **History and Vintage Car Museum** ⓘ *Casterbridge Farm, 2 km from town on the Hazyview road, T013-7502196, daily 0900-1630, R20,* has small displays on local history, but more impressive is the collection of over 60 vintage cars. One of the most remarkable cars on display is a 1912 Willy's Overland, which was purchased by a Mr Brandt in 1924. Legend has it that he parked his beloved car in a room in his house and, presumably in an eccentric effort to preserve it, bricked up all the doors and the windows. Many years later, after his death, Mr Brandt's grandson unearthed the vehicle and it was restored in 1997. Also at the farm is a shopping centre.

In the heart of the Nutcracker Valley, a short distance from White River, **Rottcher Wineries** ⓘ *T013-7513884, Mon-Fri 0800-1700, Sat and Sun 0800-1500; tours 1000 and 1400,* incorporates a nursery, macadamia nut farm and nut factory, as well as the orange winery, which produces a range of orange liquors. For children there is a riding school offering pony and horse rides each day.

Hazyview → *Phone code: 013. Colour map 2, B5. 58 km from Nelspruit.*

Hazyview lies on the banks of the Sabie River in the hot lowveld country on the southwestern border of Kruger, surrounded by banana plantations. The town is a convenient stop on the way to Kruger, and is only 16 km to Numbi Gate and 10 km to Phabeni Gate. There is a wide range of accommodation from caravan parks to luxury private game reserves, useful if you'd rather not stay in the park itself. Information is available from **Big 5 Reservations** ⓘ *Perry's Bridge Trading Post, Main Rd, T013-7378191, www.big5country.co.za, Mon-Sat 0800-1700, Sun 0800-1300,* which acts as an agent for a range of tour operators in the region.

Sabie → *Phone code: 013. Colour map 2, B4/5. Altitude: 1020 m.*

Once a gold-mining town, Sabie has little left to show of its glistening age and is now a prosaic timber-processing centre. Nevertheless, it has a pretty setting, ringed by mountains, pine and eucalyptus plantations, and it attracts a fair number of visitors who flock to its main road, lined with pleasant craft and coffee shops.

Prospectors first found gold in the region during the 1870s, but it wasn't until 1895 that gold was discovered at Sabie. The land here belonged to a big game hunter named Glynn who found the gold while on a picnic at Lower Sabie Falls. Glynn and his friends began shooting at a row of empty bottles on an outcrop of rock – the bullets chipped away at the rock revealing flecks of sparkling gold. This led to an influx of fortune hunters who came and camped on the banks of the Sabie River. In the process, many indigenous forests were chopped down to meet the demand for mine props and firewood. Fortunately, the far-sighted mine manager, Joseph Brook Shires, realized that man-made forests were necessary and planted the first trees in 1876. Planting continued into the next century, creating forestry jobs during the 1930s depression.

Today, Sabie lies in one of the largest man-made forests in the world. Driving around this region, the roads pass through endless tracts of neat rows of trees – impressive, but only a very few remaining patches of indigenous forest remain. Tourist information is available from **Sabie Information** ① *Sabie Market Sq, T013-7641177, www.sabie.co.za, Mon-Fro 0800-1630, Sat 0900-1300.*

The **Forestry Museum** ① *Ford St, T013-7641058, www.komatiecotourism.co.za, Mon-Fri 0800-1630, Sat 0800-1200, R10,* has displays on the development of South Africa's plantations and the timber industry, including an interesting cross-section of a 250-year-old yellow-wood tree, which highlights aspects of South African history on its rings. The museum is also home to a satellite office of **Komatiland Forestry,** T013-7641392, which has information on hiking and mountain bike trails in the region.

Mac Mac Falls and **Mac Mac Pools** ① *R5 per person,* 11 km from Sabie on the road to Graskop, are 65 m high. Over 1000 miners rushed to the falls in 1873 after gold was discovered above the falls. Originally there was a single fall, but in their eagerness to get to gold, some miners tried to divert the waterfall's flow and an over-enthusiastic application of dynamite created the second fall. The name of Mac Mac Falls originates from the large numbers of Scottish miners who came here. The tourist office has leaflets on day hikes which visit these and other local waterfalls: **Bonnet Falls**, **Maria Shires Falls** and **Forest Falls**. These are signposted off the road to Graskop. There is a turning before Graskop onto the R533 to Pilgrim's Rest.

Sabie

Sleeping
Hillwatering Country House **5**

Jock Sabie Lodge **2**
Misty Mountain Chalets **1**
Villa Ticino **4**
Woodsman, Restaurant & Woodsman Centre **6**

Eating ⓐ
Wild Fig Tree **1**

200 metres
200 yards

N

Lydenburg → *Phone code: 013. Colour map 2, B4. Altitude: 1469 m.*

This quiet agricultural and mining town is a typically unexceptional town in the central region of Mpumalanga. The descent from **Long Tom Pass** west to Lydenburg opens up vistas of rolling grasslands, cattle ranches and wheat-growing country stretching out into the distance. Approaching from the south, the town is

Lydenburg Heads

The Lydenburg Heads are a collection of seven clay heads that date back to AD 590. They are unique pieces in the history of South African art and some of the earliest sculptures of the human form. The clay heads have only ever been found in this region and it is thought that they may have been used in initiation ceremonies.

The heads were first discovered in 1957 by Ludwig von Bezig on a farm near Lydenburg. Ludwig was 10 years old when he found the pieces of pottery but it wasn't until five years later that he became interested in archaeology. He returned to the farm several times between 1962 and 1966, where he found the pieces of the broken heads. When they were reconstructed he had seven heads of different sizes, one of which had the snout of an animal.

The heads on display in the Lydenburg Museum are replicas of the originals, now in the South African Museum in Cape Town.

often described as the gateway to the Lowveld. On the other side of Long Tom Pass you are over the escarpment formed by the Drakensberg, which marks the boundary between the Highveld and the Lowveld. Information is available from **Lydenburg Information Centre** ① *at the museum T013-2352213, www.lydenburg.org.* **Note** Beware of fog at the top of Long Tom Pass and, in the winter months, note that the pass is sometimes blocked by snow.

Lydenburg Museum ① *1 km from town on the R37, T013-2352121, Mon-Fri 0800-1300, 1400-1600, Sat and Sun 0800-1700, small entry fee,* is fascinating, with well-presented displays on the history of the Lydenburg region from the Stone Age to the present. It is famous for being the first home of the **Lydenburg Heads** (see box, above), and has displays illustrating South African history before the arrival of the Voortrekkers. This is the best local museum in the region, and superior to most local history museums in the country. The museum also distils its own *mampoer* – a local brew similar to brandy or schnapps – ask for a taster.

Several short hiking trails lead from the museum into the adjoining 2200-ha **Gustav Klingbiel Nature Reserve**, where you have the opportunity to view some small antelope and a vulture's restaurant. Staff at the museum can direct you to some Iron Age sites and the remains of some early trenches from the Boer War.

Pilgrim's Rest ●❼❽▲» *pp654-660. Colour map 2, B4.*

Pilgrim's Rest, a tiny mining town dating from the late 19th century, has been totally reconstructed as a living museum to preserve a fascinating part of South Africa's cultural heritage. It's a pretty spot: lining the main street, a row of miners' cottages with their corrugated-iron roofs and wooden walls nestles in a lush, leafy and utterly quiet valley. It's easy to imagine how it must have once looked, with a magistrate's court, church, local newspaper and schoolhouse. However, it's all almost too perfect, and the artificial atmosphere is exacerbated by the coachloads of tourists that pitch up throughout the day. Many of the reconstructed cottages today house gift shops and cafés, and a large craft market is held at the entrance to the village. The best time to see Pilgrim's Rest is early in the morning or in the late afternoon after the day-trippers have gone and the locals creep back onto the streets and into the bars. Although most of the buildings are strung out along one long street, the settlement has a very clear division between Uptown and Downtown, but both now attract tourists.

Background

The history of Pilgrim's Rest is a fascinating tale of gold fever in southern Africa during the late 19th century, as prospectors opened up new areas in search of a fortune. The town was named by one of the first prospectors, William Trafford, because he believed that his wandering days in search of gold had finally ended and yelled out "the pilgrim is at rest!". The first gold was found by Alec 'Wheelbarrow' Patterson, in a fertile valley then known as Lone Peach Tree Creek, in September 1873. Once Trafford announced that he had also found gold, the newspapers quickly spread the word and by the end of the year more than 1500 prospectors had pitched their tents along the creek. Life was far from easy for these fortune seekers, who slept on grass mattresses in makeshift tents, often sick with malaria and exposure, in a place where lawlessness and violence was rife.

Although some of the best finds were made in 1875, the region continued to produce gold until 1972, when the last mine was closed. In 1881, a financier, David Benjamin, formed the Transvaal Gold Exploration and Land Company, which effectively ran the gold fields until they were closed. Although there were poor years there were also some bountiful periods: in the 1890s a particularly rich reef – the Theta Reef – was discovered, which yielded more than five million ounces of gold over a period of 50 years. In 1986 Pilgrim's Rest was declared a National Monument and restoration of the old mining buildings began.

Pilgrim's Rest

To ③④⑤, Robber's Pass & Lydenburg

To Blyde River Canyon & Alanglade Period House Museum

Blyde

Caravan Park ▲

DOWNTOWN

⑤

Transvaal Gold Mining Estates

Main

②

③

①

Historic Cemetery

Dresden Store & House Museum 🏛

④

✉

Pilgrim's Rest Museum
🛈 🏛

Pilgrim's Creek

Pol

Old PO

Pilgrim's & Sabie News

Print House

P

Town Hall

Masonic Lodge

UPTOWN

R533

Diggings Site Museum 🏛

N

To Graskop (16 km)

200 metres
200 yards

Sleeping 🛏
Crystal Springs
Mountain Lodge **3**
District Six
Miners' Cottages **1**
Inn on Robber's Pass **5**

Mount Sheba **4**
Royal **2**

Eating 🍴
Jubilee Potters
& Coffee Shop **2**
Pilgrim's Pantry **3**
Scott's Café **4**
The Vine **5**

Sights

Historical displays and exhibits on gold-panning techniques can be found at the **Pilgrim's Rest Tourist Information Centre and Museum** ⓘ *Main St, T013-7681060, www.pilgrims-rest.co.za, daily 0900-1245, 1345-1630*. There are three other small village museums, housed in old miner's cottages, within walking distance.

The **Diggings Site Museum** ⓘ *daily tours 1000, 1100, 1200, 1400 and 1500 with gold-panning demonstration, R10, tickets from the tourist office*, is at the top of Uptown where the coaches park. A visit here helps visitors to gain an insight into the lives of the diggers and prospectors during the gold rush at the end of the 19th century, before the first gold mining company took control of the town. Gold panning is demonstrated and visitors can have a go themselves.

The **Alanglade Period House Museum** ⓘ *guided tours only, daily 1100 and 1400, R20, tickets from the tourist office*, is north of the village on the Mpumalanga escarpment. Built in 1915, the house is typically early 20th century and was the official mine manager's residence for Pilgrim's Rest up until 1972. Today it is furnished with Edwardian, art nouveau and art deco pieces.

Robber's Pass

Robber's Pass is 9 km from Pilgrim's Rest on the R533 and rises 650 m in only 9 km. Gold bullion and mail from Pilgrim's Rest was taken to the commercial banks in Lydenburg by coach twice a week via the pass north of town. The first major robbery took place here when two masked gunmen on horseback held up the stagecoach and made off with £10,000 worth of gold bullion. The second robbery in 1912 was not as successful. The armed robber was Tommy Dennison, a local barber, who carried out the crime and returned to Pilgrim's Rest to celebrate. He was soon arrested and spent five years in jail in Pretoria. On his release he returned and went into business at the Highwayman's Garage.

Graskop ⊖🅱🅾⚠🅲 ›› *pp654-660. Colour map 2, B5.*

→ *Phone code: 013.*

This small town lies just south of the Blyde River Canyon, but despite having a large selection of holiday accommodation, restaurants and craft shops, it remains surprisingly quiet and makes a peaceful base from which to explore the region. Miners arrived here during the 1880s and established a camp, but modern Graskop is surrounded by forestry plantations and is an important centre of the timber industry. Today Graskop attracts fame as being home of the South African stuffed pancake – the famous **Harrie's** restaurant started it all, and the stuffed sweet and savoury pancakes are renowned throughout the country. Local residents have capitalized on this reputation, and there is now a line of pancake houses along the main street.

Information is available in the private **information office** ⓘ *Louis Trichardt St, T013-7671866, www.graskop.co.za, daily 0800-1700* or the **Graskop Tourism Office** ⓘ *Spar Centre, T013-7671833, www.wildaventures.co.za*.

Graskop is 1000 m higher than the Lowveld at the bottom of the escarpment and temperatures here are normally up to 8°C cooler; night-time temperatures in winter often go below 0°C and even in summer a sweater can be useful. This is also one of the wettest regions in South Africa but most of the rain falls during torrential thunderstorms in the summer months. This is the best time of year to see the waterfalls; the force of the water crashing into the pools below is spectacular.

Around Graskop

The road east goes over **Kowyn's Pass** a few kilometres from Graskop. Before descending towards the Lowveld it passes **Graskop Gorge**, where adrenaline junkies try out the **Big Swing** (see Activities and tours, page 659), and there are views looking up to **God's Window** (see page 653). This is a fruit-growing area of mangoes and lychees, which are sold at stalls on the side of the road in season.

Jock of the Bushveld Trail is an 8-km circular trail starting from within **Graskop Holiday Resort**. Along the trail you will pass a magnificent 500-year-old bearded yellowwood tree as well as several eroded sandstone formations mentioned in the story of *Jock of the Bushveld*; the walk can be completed in three hours.

Berlin Falls and **Lisbon Falls** are further north on the R532 heading straight out of Graskop. Berlin Falls are 45 m high, and the water cascades into a circular pool surrounded by forest. At 92 m, Lisbon Falls are the highest in the area, and the river is separated into three streams as it plunges into the pool below.

Blyde River Canyon ● ▸▸ pp654-660. Colour map 2, B5.

The Blyde River Canyon is the third largest in the world after the Grand Canyon in the USA and Fish River Canyon in Namibia. It is the product of the Blyde River, which tumbles down from the Drakensberg escarpment to the Lowveld over a series of waterfalls and cascades that spill into the **Blydespoort Dam** at the bottom. Blyde means 'river of joy', and the river was so named after Hendrik Potgieter and his party returned safely from Delagoa Bay (Mozambique) in 1844. Voortrekkers, who had stayed behind at their camp, first named the river Treur River ('river of mourning'), under the mistaken impression that the party had been killed, so when Pogieter returned, they had to rename it.

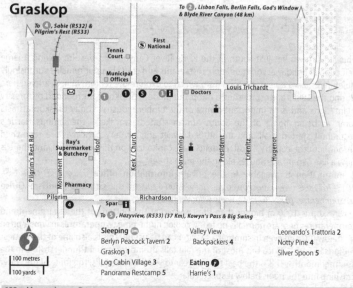

Graskop

To ② , Lisbon Falls, Berlin Falls, God's Window & Blyde River Canyon (48 km)

To ④ , Sabie (R532) & Pilgrim's Rest (R533)

First National ⑤

Tennis Court

Municipal Offices

Louis Trichardt

Doctors

Pilgrim's Rest Rd

Ray's Supermarket & Butchery

Pharmacy

Monument

Hoof

Kerk / Church

Oorwinning

President

Erlentz

Hugenot

Pilgrim

Spar

Richardson

To ⑤ , Hazyview, (R533) (37 Km), Kowyn's Pass & Big Swing

N

100 metres
100 yards

Sleeping ●
Berlyn Peacock Tavern 2
Graskop 1
Log Cabin Village 3
Panorama Restcamp 5

Valley View Backpackers 4

Eating ●
Harrie's 1

Leonardo's Trattoria 2
Notty Pine 4
Silver Spoon 5

The winding canyon is 26 km in length and is joined by the similarly spectacular 11 km **Ohrigstad Canyon** near Swadini. The 27,000 ha **Blyde River Canyon Nature Reserve** extends from God's Window down to the far side of the Blyde River dam. The canyon drops down 750 m, and for most of its length it is inaccessible. There are no roads crossing the reserve or linking the top and bottom of the canyon, but there are some short walking trails, and a number of view points snake off the along the R532 and overlook the Canyon and Lowveld beyond. Do take the time to drive down to the viewpoints, as you can't see much of the spectacular canyon if you stick to the R532.

Viewpoints

The most famous of the viewpoints is **God's Window**, right on the edge of the escarpment overlooking an almost sheer 300-m drop into the tangle of forest below. The views through the heat haze stretch over the Lowveld as far as Kruger. At the top of the hill there is a tiny patch of rainforest, which survives in the micro-climate on the very tip of the ridge. At 1730 m, **Wonder View** is the highest viewpoint accessible from the road and **Pinnacle Rock** is a 30-m-high quartzite 'needle' that rises dramatically out of the fern-clad ravine. From here it is possible to see the tops of the eight waterfalls that take the Blyde River down 450 m in a series of cascades to the dam.

The most developed viewpoint is at **Bourke's Luck Potholes**, an unusual series of rock formation resembling Swiss cheese. The smooth rock has been moulded and formed by the swirling action of whirlpools where the Treur and the Blyde rivers meet, creating spectacular dips, hollows and holes. The name 'Bourke's Luck' comes from Tom Bourke, a prospector who worked a claim here in the vain belief that he would find gold. There is a **visitor centre and kiosk** ① *daily 0700-1700, R44, serving snacks and light meals.* The visitor centre includes an eco-awareness exhibition outlining the geological history of the area. From here, a wood walkway winds around and over the potholes. A short drive further north, the viewpoint at the **Three Rondavels** is by far the most dramatic. At the car park by the walkway is a small craft market and some toilets. From here, a walkway leads out onto the lip of the canyon, with the vast cleft in the rock opening out in front of you, and **Blydespoort Dam** shimmering intensely blue at the bottom. The Three Rondavels easily recognized as the three circular rocky peaks opposite, capped with grass and vegetation and looking distinctly like thatched African rondavel huts.

North into Limpopo

The R532 continues north from the top of the canyon until it joins the R36 and the road descends through the **Strijdom Tunnel** and north to Hoedspruit and Phalaborwa. **Echo Caves** ① *T013-2380015, www.echocaves.co.za, daily 0830-1630, 45-mins guided tours R35,* are on the R36 continuing south to **Ohrigstad**. The caves extend 2 km into the mountain and are known for the echoes produced when the stalactites are tapped. Many human bones have been found inside, proving that at one time they were inhabited. A tour takes 45 minutes, and there are lights and rails throughout the caves, although you might have to crawl to get to the further reaches of the caves, such as the spectacular Crystal Palace cave.

You could easily spend a few days exploring the lower section of the **Blyde River Canyon Nature Reserve** around the dam on the Limpopo side of the Strijdom Tunnel. Once you have passed through the tunnel the road quickly descends and you will immediately notice the rise in temperature. You can either continue to Hoedspruit and into Kruger Park via Phalaborwa or Orpen Gates, or take the R36 to Tzaneen, where another region awaits you. ▶▶ *For further details, see the Limpopo chapter, pages 661-690.*

Panorama region listings

Hotel and guesthouse prices
L over US$300   AL US$220-300   A US$150-220
B US$100-150   C US$75-100   D US$35-75
E US$15-35   F under US$15
Restaurant prices
₸₸₸ over US$30   ₸₸ US$15-30   ₸ under US$15
See pages 46-51 for further information.

Sleeping

White River *p647*

AL Hulala Lakeside Lodge, 22 km from White River on the R40 towards Hazyview, T013-7641893, www.hulala.co.za. Situated on a peninsula in a lake that gives the feeling of being on an island, this lodge has 25 luxury suites, private lounge, fireplace, TV, secluded patios overlooking the garden or lake, fine dining in the restaurant, pool, 2 bars. Choice of canoes, rowing boats, specially adapted boats for anglers, or the nightly sundowner cruise. A romantic setting, recommended for couples. The completely secluded honeymoon suite has its own pool.

B Balcony Manor, 51 Frank Townsend St, T013-7512024, www.balcony.co.za. 2 double a/c rooms with en suite bathroom, TV, non-smoking, 2 suites, all set in a fine old 2-storey house with an elegant upstairs balcony, a mix of modern fittings with antique furnishings, old fashioned and comfortable. Each room has its own character, mature gardens, swimming pool, very ornate.

B Greenway Woods, T013-7511094, www.greenway.co.za. 35 self-catering chalets set in the beautiful countryside focussed on a championship golf course, with swimming pool. Each chalet has 3 bedrooms, 2 bathrooms, a/c, DSTV, open fireplace in the lounge, a popular conference venue, swimming pool, mountain bikes for hire, restaurant and bar. Prices depend on how many people share a chalet.

C iGwalagwala, 5 km to the south of town off the R40, T013-7501723, www.igwalagwala.co.za. 5 garden suites, each with own entrance and private terrace, simple decor with cool tiled floors, 2 self-catering units, large swimming pool. Good breakfasts served. *iGwalagwala* means purple-crested loerie; these are sometimes spotted in the beautiful mature gardens.

C Karula, Old Plaston Rd, 1 km from town centre, T013-7512277, www.karulahotel.co.za. 46 double rooms with en suite bathroom, TV, restaurant, bar, swimming pool, tennis, billiard room, a slightly dated, old-fashioned hotel but nevertheless it is popular and has an excellent local reputation. Rates include set dinner.

C Linga Longa, Karee Cres, T013-7511942, www.lingalongabb.co.za. 8 elegantly decorated bedrooms with private entrances and fan or a/c, TV, bar fridge, lovely verandas, pool and jacuzzi in tropical gardens.

Hazyview *p647*

B Hippo Hollow Country Estate, 3 km from Hazyview off the R40 en route to Paul Kruger Gate, T013-7376628, www.hippohollow.co.za. A selection of 37 semi-self-catering thatched cottages with private balconies overlooking the Sabie River populated with hippos. Stylish, understated decor, large bathrooms, each has a gas braai, kitchenette and kettle. Also has 26 en suite hotel rooms, good restaurant, bar, curio shop, 2 swimming pools. Watch the hippos on the lawn at night. Kruger game drives can be arranged for those without a car.

B Rissington Inn, 2 km from Hazyview on the R40 White River road, T013-7377700, www.rissington.co.za. 17 comfortable en suite cottages, some with outside showers, Victorian baths and private verandas overlooking the countryside. Neat gardens, views of the river, swimming pool. Best known for its good à la carte restaurant that is also open to non-guests, pub and outside eating on the veranda, great breakfasts and brunch, good vegetarian dishes. Recommended.

B-C Chestnut Country Lodge, 11 km out of Hazyview off the R40 to White River and Nelspruit, T013-7378195, www.chestnut lodge.co.za. A comfortable rural retreat with 13 individually designed double rooms with en suite facilities, simple decor, TV, each with a private patio, all set on a 48-ha farm. Evening meals available on request. Swimming pool with deck where sun-downers are served, homely lounge with reference library bar. 15 mins' drive from Numbi Gate. Off-season special deals.
F Kruger Park Backpackers, junction of R40 and the road leading to Numbi Gate, T013-7377224, www.krugerparkback packers.co.za. Dorms and doubles set in Zulu huts, en suite bathrooms, painted in bright tribal designs, lounge, bar, pool table, swimming pool, meals using home-grown organic produce, camping available. Kruger and Drakensberg tours are organized from here. Will collect Baz Bus passengers from Nelspruit at no extra charge if you book one of their tours.

Sabie *p647, map p648*
B Misty Mountain Chalets, 24 km from Sabie, at Long Tom Pass on the R532, T013-7643377, www.mistymountain.co.za. 27 self-catering or B&B chalets sleeping 2-6 in a beautiful mountain setting, all linked to a cosy pub and restaurant, veranda with small infinity pool and stunning views, the endangered blue swallow nests on the site.
C Hillwatering Country House, 50 Marula St, T013-7641421, www.hillwatering.co.za. Country house set in a beautiful garden on the outskirts of Sabie, 5 en suite rooms with private terraces and mountain views, simple, homely decor, breakfast is served outside in summer, or packed as a picnic if on an early start into Kruger, other meals on request.
C Jock Sabie Lodge, off Main St, T013-7642178, www.jock.co.za. 2.5 ha of attractive lawns, with wide choice of accommodation including self-catering log cabins with 2 bedrooms, 11 en suite hotel rooms, backpackers dorm (**E**) sleeping 40.

Restaurant, bar, pool, wheelchair friendly, very popular with South African families.
C Villa Ticino, Louis Trichardt St, T013-7642598, www.villaticino.co.za. German-owned guesthouse with 5 double rooms with en suite bathroom, B&B, outdated decor but comfortable, TV lounge, swimming pool, non-smoking, no children under 14, pleasant gardens with a superb view across the valley and forests, central, next door to **Wild Fig Tree** restaurant.
D The Woodsman, next door to the restaurant and bookshop of the same name, 94 Main St, T013-7642204, www.thewoodsman.co.za. 12 suites set in an uninspiring block, but very comfortable inside with dark wood furniture, en suite bathrooms, TV, tea- and coffee-making facilities. Restaurant and pub serving Greek Cypriot dishes, with pleasant deck overlooking the valley, underground parking, walking distance to restaurants and shops.

Lydenburg *p648*
D-E Laske Nakke, 2 km on the Dullstroom road, T013-2352886, www.laskenakke.co.za. Self-catering chalets or budget en suite B&B rooms, camping and caravan park, 2 pools, bar, simple restaurant. Don't be put off by the sad-looking concrete blocks, the good-value rooms are fine inside.

Pilgrim's Rest *p649, map p650*
A Mount Sheba, 19 km from Pilgrim's Rest off the R533, T013-7681241, www.forever sa.co.za. Set in the Mount Sheba Nature Reserve. 25 double rooms with en suite bathrooms, lounge with fireplace and DSTV, **Potted Owl** pub, **Chandelier** restaurant, a luxury retreat high up in the hills, excellent birdwatching. Rates include dinner and breakfast. Cheaper rates in the low season.
B Inn on Robber's Pass, 17 km above Pilgrim's Rest on the R533 heading towards Lydenburg, T013-7681491. 4 self-catering cottages plus 6 double rooms with en suite bathrooms in the converted stables, restaurant with a long gleaming wooden

bar and fireplace which is put to good use during the winter, rates include dinner if not self-catering, trout dams for fishing, excellent quiet rural retreat, no children under 14.

C Crystal Springs Mountain Lodge, T013-7685000, www.grc-resorts.co.za. A holiday resort high up in the hills off the R533 north of Pilgrim's Rest, large number of luxurious self-catering chalets set in 5000 ha of mountain bushveld, plus larger lodges sleeping up to 8, popular **Pointer's Rest** restaurant, bush *boma* braais, a full range of sporting activities including hiking, tennis, squash, birdwatching, health spa, gym, game drives, indoor and out-door heated swimming pools. An all-round resort in a convenient location to explore the region, rates drop considerably off-season but it can be very cold here in winter.

C The Royal, Main St, Uppertown, T013-7681100, www.pilgrimsrest.org.za/royal.htm. The original Royal Hotel is over 100 years old and dates from the time of the gold rush; it has been thoroughly restored with period-style corrugated-iron roof and wooden walls. 50 rooms set around courtyards, decorated with reproduction antique furniture, floral fabrics, open-plan bathrooms and claw-foot baths, very rickety brass beds. Also has rooms in cottages spread around the village. Great restaurant serving excellent traditional buffets, popular with tour groups, also has the historical **Church Bar** filled with Victorian memorabilia. Good choice in a great central location, but let down by unfriendly service.

D District Six Miners' Cottages, T013-7681211. The cottages are on the hill above Pilgrim's Rest, 7 self-catering cottages with 4 or 6 beds, the cottages were built in 1920 and are decorated in the original style with brass bedsteads and period furniture. The best-value budget accommodation in the area, book in advance.

Graskop *p651, map p652*

B-C Graskop Hotel, Hoof St, T/F013-7671244, www.graskophotel.co.za. An excellent recently renovated hotel in the centre of town, with a range of rooms at

different prices, decorated with an attractive mixture of modern and African furniture (from the shop next door), contemporary feel, the 'artist's' rooms have funky splashes of colour and modern art on the walls. Great main restaurant, worth making a detour to eat here, bar with large fireplace, swimming pool in the gardens.

C Berlyn Peacock Tavern, Berlin Waterfalls, T031-7671085, www.peacocktavern.co.za. A fine old house in the country with 5 double rooms, en suite bathrooms and private verandas, non-smoking room, dining room, bar, comfortable lounge, swimming pool, nearby hikes and horse riding, emphasis is on peace and privacy, no young children.

D Log Cabin Village, Louis Trichardt St, T013-7671974, www.logcabin.co.za. 8 wooden self-catering cabins with 1 or 2 bedrooms, comfortably furnished, TV, well-equipped kitchen, small private garden with swimming pool, situated on the main road right in the middle of town. Good for families, and must be booked in advance during local school holidays.

D-E Panorama Restcamp, on the road to Kowyn's Pass, T013-7671091, www.panorama restcamp.co.za. Holiday resort overlooking the Blyde River Canyon and has a selection of very basic self-catering chalets and camping sites with a kitchen block, kiosk selling provisions, TV and pool room, the highlight here is the amazing rock swimming pool perched on the edge of the escarpment.

E-F Valley View Backpackers, 47 De Lange St, T013-7671112, www.yebo-afrika.nl. Located on the west of the village, this backpacker place offers good dorms, comfortable doubles in self-catering rondavels and apartments, plus space for camping. Also arranges a wide variety of activities in the area and has mountain bike rentals. Kitchen, TV room with DVD player.

Blyde River Canyon *p652, map p646*
There is a wide range of accommodation around Hoedspruit in Limpopo.
For further details, see page 688.

D-E Forever Resorts Blyde Canyon,
T013-7698005, www.foreversa.co.za. Huge
family resort in a great setting, with 93
self-catering chalets, campsite, youth hostel,
restaurant, shop selling provisions, bar,
swimming pool, golf course, view points.
This is a very popular family resort that
gets packed during school holidays.

⊘ Eating

White River p647
₩ **Injabula Boma**, Greenway Woods Hotel,
T013-7511094. African-themed restaurant set
in a luxury hotel in a lovely setting, with a
price tag to match. Good range of dishes
and South African wine list, but can be
overrun with conference delegates.
₩ **Salt**, in the Bagdad Centre across the road
from Casterbridge Farm, T013-7511555.
Tue-Sun 1200-1430, Tue-Sat 1830-2130.
Modern open-plan restaurant, some tables
outside beneath bougainvillea, the chefs
work in an open kitchen, excellent if not
pretentious fusion food, blue cheese, Cajun
chicken and liquorice salad for example,
the apricot glazed duck is delicious.
₩ **Ten Green Bottles**, Casterbridge Farm,
2 km out of town towards Hazyview,
T013-7501097. Open 0900 late. Mixed
menu in pleasant, atmospheric converted
farm building, located in a smartly renovated
series of courtyards filled with posh food
shops and boutiques and an arty theatre.
Good daily specials on the blackboard; try
the famous Maputo sandwich – fresh
Mozambique prawns and home-made
bread – or local stuffed trout with avocado.
Pretty outside terrace or candlelit interior.

Hazyview p647
Most restaurants are located in the hotels.
₩ **Ant & Elephant**, 6 km from Hazyview on
the R536 to Sabie, T013-7378172. Mon-Sat
0700-2100. Worth stopping just to enjoy the
wonderful gardens among mango and
lychee plantations. Good breakfasts, and

a sophisticated evening menu of T-bone
steaks, seafood chowder, venison and
good pan-fried calamari and prawns.
₩ **Summerfields Kitchen**, 4 km on the R536
to Sabie, T013-7376500. Gourmet restaurant
at an upmarket spa, open for breakfast, light
lunches and formal dinners. Perfectly presented
dishes with all the trimmings, and the likes of
crème brûlée and pavlova for dessert.

Sabie p647, map p648
₩ **The Wild Fig Tree**, Main St, T013-7642239.
Open 0800-2100. Quality restaurant serving
light lunches and more ambitious meals in
the evening, choice of cool interior or shaded
veranda. Fresh trout, guinea fowl, crocodile,
warthog and some delicious home-made
desserts, good choice for vegetarians.
Attached curio shop full of overpriced but
good quality items.
₩ **The Woodsman**, 94 Main St,
T013-7642015, www.thewoodsman.co.za.
Open daily, smart restaurant and bar on the
outskirts of town attached to a B&B and craft
centre, emphasis on Greek food and wine,
try the *stifadho* (a rich stew made from beef,
onions, red wine and spices), local trout and
steaks also available, sit outside on the terrace
for a few beers in the evening.

Lydenburg p648
₩ **Vroutjies Coffee Shop**, corner of
Voortrekker and Rensburg streets,
T013-2353016. Mon-Sat 0700-1700. Coffee
shop in a historic building, a refuelling stop
on the way through town for sandwiches,
cakes, breakfasts, burgers, quiches and
baked potatoes with fillings.

Pilgrim's Rest p649, map p650
₩ **Inn on Robber's Pass**, 17 km from
Pilgrim's Rest on the R533, T013-7681491.
Meals made from fresh farm produce are
served in the dining room or on the open
veranda overlooking the mountains. A rare
opportunity for vegetarians to enjoy good
imaginative dishes. Recommended. Also
has overnight rooms, see Sleeping, above.

The Vine, Main St, Downtown, T013-7681080. Old world pub-cum-restaurant with small **Ladies Bar**, very popular and typical of the town, filled with tour groups during the day, hearty steaks and other typical local fare such as bobotie, ostrich-neck *potje*, and oxtail and samp.

Jubilee Potters & Coffee Shop, Main St, Downtown, T013-7681151. Open 0900-1900, early closing Tue. Burgers and salads along with coffee, cakes and Blyde River trout.

Pilgrim's Pantry, Main St, Downtown, T013-7681129. Local baker also acts as a coffee shop and handicraft shop. The pancakes make for a pleasant light lunch, home-made jams, mustards, and pickles.

Scott's Café, Main St, Uppertown, T013-7681061. Open 0900-1800. Salads and hot dishes, quality country cooking using local fruit and vegetables, afternoon teas with scones and fresh cream, also an art gallery.

Graskop p651, map p652
Most restaurants only open for lunch off season.
Leonardo's Trattoria, Louis Trichardt St, T013-7671078. Mon-Sat 0900-2100, Sun 1000-1500. Family-run Italian restaurant on the main drag, serving standard pizzas and wide selection of pasta dishes, average quality meals but one of the few places open in the evening.

Notty Pine, 3 Pilgrim St, T013-7671030. Lunch and dinner, sophisticated set-up and smart atmosphere, try the delicious freshly grilled trout – pan-fried and filled with sautéed onions and mushrooms is the best, in winter there is a lovely central fireplace, one of the best restaurants in the area.

Harrie's, Louis Trichardt St, T013-7671273. Open 0800-1730. Wide selection of pancakes, with sweet and savoury fillings including a good chicken and mushroom or spicy butternut, and a mouth-watering banana and caramel. Also serves salads and other snacks. This is the original pancake house that somehow established a countrywide reputation; consequently pancake houses have opened up all over town.

The Silver Spoon, corner of Louis Trichardt and Kerk streets, T013-7611039. Open 0700-1900. More of those pancakes, also has huge burgers, salads and famous black forest gateau that's made from a German recipe, and hosts art shows. Pleasant deck overlooking the street or cosy interior in winter with a roaring fire.

☻ Festivals and events

Pilgrim's Rest *p649, map p650*
Sep The **South African Gold Panning Championships** are held annually in Pilgrim's Rest, www.sagoldpanning.co.za, and attract about 700 participants. The World Gold Panning Championship was held here in 2005. Anyone can enter, including small children and there's also a parade, a wheelbarrow race, and a pub crawl up and down the main street.

O Shopping

Throughout the Panorama region are curio markets in the car parks of the waterfalls and viewpoints.

White River *p647*
Casterbridge Farm, www.casterbridge.co.za, 2 km from White River on the R40 to Hazyview. Daily 0830-1800, restaurants later. Upmarket group of boutiques set in converted farm buildings. Railway sleeper furniture, leather goods, art, ceramics, **Ten Green Bottles** restaurant (see above), bookshop, the **Barnyard Theatre** and cinema, and **Frederick & Co** who bake gourmet biscuits including macaroons and gingerbread men.

Bagdad Centre, across the road from **Casterbridge Farm**. Daily 0830-1800, restaurants later. A small shopping centre selling African handicrafts, furniture, safari clothes and books, and home to trendy **Salt** restaurant (see above). Nursery sells

bonsais grown from indigenous trees.
Delicatessen sells home-made jams,
cheeses, chocolates, fresh trout, soups,
pies and ready-made frozen meals – good
place to stock up on provisions en route
to self-catering accommodation in Kruger.
The indigenous African butterfly sanctuary
is worth a look.

Hazyview p647

Marula Market, 5 mins from Hazyview
on the R535 to Graskop. Open 0900-1700,
tea garden open until 1600. Traditional
market set in the Shangana Cultural Village,
with a good range of curios including
clay pots, wooden sculptures and
contemporary metalwork.
Perry's Bridge Trading Post, Main St.
This group of shops include the Trading
post curio shop with some good-value
African crafts as well as maps, books and
gifts. There's also an internet café here.

Sabie p647, map p648

The Bookcase, Woodsman Centre,
Main St, T013-7642014. One of the best
second-hand bookshops in South Africa,
stuffed with collectors' items. The African
section is particularly good with turn-of-
the-20th-century volumes on the great
explorers and once-controversial titles
from the 1950s and 1960s on the rise of
Apartheid. A number of books that were
banned in South Africa during the
Apartheid years have resurfaced in
this shop.
Mphozeni, Woodsman Centre, Main St.
Large selection of African arts and crafts,
jewellery and fabrics.

Graskop p651, map p652

Africa Silks, Louis Trichardt St, T013-
7671655. Fine selection of hand-woven
silk products, including hand-dyed
scarves, clothes, cushion covers and
bedspreads. Also has outlets in Pilgrim's
Rest and Hoedspruit.

▲▲ Activities and tours

Panorama region *p646, map p646*
For a the most comprehensive choice of
adventure activities in the Panorama region,
contact **Big 5 Reservations**, in Hazyview,
T013-7378191, www.big5country.com.
See also page 647.

Adrenaline activities

Big Swing & Foefie Slide, Graskop
Gorge, Graskop, T072-2238155,
bigswing@mweb.co.za. Open 0900-1700,
weather permitting, R285 or R420 tandem,
which includes the Foefie Slide, or slide
on its own R60. Similar to a bungee jump,
but with more of an outward swing on the
descent. The free fall is 68 m and lasts 3 secs.
Once the bungee cord has reached its
optimum length, you are lowered down
into the rainforest at the bottom of the
gorge, before a 10-min walk back to the
top. The 131 m Foefie Slide goes across
the gorge at a height of 80 m.

Horse riding

Ponieskrantz Stables, Pilgrim's Rest,
T013-7681465, www.pilgrimsreststables.co.za.
A variety of horse-riding trips ranging from
2 hrs to 2 days. There are also some
self-catering bungalows on site.

Mountain biking

Increasingly popular in the forests around
Sabie. 13 km, 22 km and 45 km guided and
self-guided trails have been marked out by
the forestry department, **SAFCOL**, including
challenging ascents and downhill runs over
loose shale and eroded gullies.
The Bike Doc, corner of Louis Trichardt and
Main streets, Sabie, T013-7642123,
ghoeks@iafrica.com. Bikes for hire, R100
per day.
Valley View Backpackers, 47 De Lange St,
Graskop, T013-7671112, www.yebo-afrika.nl,
rents mountain bikes for R160 for a full day
with maps, helmets and basic first-aid kits.

Scenic flights

The Blyde River Canyon region and the Sabie Valley look even more impressive from the air. **Helicopter** trips from 15 mins to 1 hr fly right into the canyon and dip down to the various waterfalls in the region. It's an exhilarating experience but prices are steep, from R9000-10,000 for 4 people. Early morning (1-hr) **balloon** rides float wherever the wind maybe going over the Sabie Valley, R2100 per person, and **microlight** flights from Hazyview take in Graskop, God's Window, and the Sabie River, from R900 per person. Reservations and details from **Big 5 Reservations** (see above and page 647).

Whitewater rafting

The tamest rafting routes are on the lower **Blyde River** – 3 km of mild rapids – or the **Sabie River** – 3-hr trips through well-wooded banks. A day on the **Olifants River** takes you over grade II-III rapids and the odd grade IV rapid that can be avoided if you walk around. Arguably the best river action in South Africa is at the northern section of the **Blyde River**, 8 km of intense rapids with the occasional grade V, which can also be walked around. A 5-km ferry trip on the Blydepoort Dam is usually included on this day trip. For adrenaline junkies, day or multi-day trips on Blyde River and Olifants River offer a combination of exciting rapids and gentle paddles through some spectacular scenery, over-night in either riverside bush camps, local accommodation or a combination of both. Check that operators are members of the **South African River Association** (SARA). Tourist offices can supply further information.
Hardy Ventures, T013-7511693, www.hardy venture.com. A wide choice of whitewater rafting and canoeing trips on a choice of 3 rivers, suited to all ages and experience.

Induna Adventures, T015-7378308, www.indunaadventures.com. Olifants and Sabie River rafting, including overnight trips staying at a camp on the banks of the Olifants River.

⊖ Transport

Panorama region *p646, map p646*
White River is 20 km from **Nelspruit** on the R40. The entrance to Kruger Park via **Numbi Gate** (35 km), is signposted off the R538 heading north towards **Hazyview** (40 km); the entrance at Paul Kruger Gate is on the R536. The R40 continues north into Limpopo Province to **Acornhoek** (56 km), **Orpen Gate** (100 km), and the private game reserves on Kruger's western boundary. The R536 climbs up from the lowveld around Hazyview onto the edge of the Drakensberg escarpment at Sabie. **Sabie** is 34 km west of Hazyview on the R536. **Graskop** is 24 km west of Hazyview on the R535. **Lydenburg** lies 66 km from the N4 on an important route that takes traffic from the Highveld down to the Lowveld.

ⓘ Directory

Hazyview *p647*
Internet Perry's Bridge Trading Post, Main St.

Sabie *p647, map p648*
Medical services Hospital, T013-7641222.

Graskop *p651, map p652*
Banks First National Bank Kerk St.
Medical services Chemist, T013-7671055, open all hours.

Contents

Footprint features

Limpopo

At a glance

◉ **Getting around** Buses only
on N1, car hire.

◉ **Time required** 3-6 days, can
be visited from Kruger.

☀ **Weather** Good all year round,
hot December and January.

✖ **When not to go** Good all year.

MOZAMBIQUE

ZIMBABWE

Kruger National Park

Kruger National Park

★ Don't miss ...

1 Birdwatching in Nylsvley Nature Reserve, page 666.
2 Magoebaskloof Mountains in spring, page 681.
3 The Trading Post, page 689.
4 Golf in Phalaborwa, page 690.

Crooks Corner

Pafuri Gate

Madangani

Nwanedi National Park

Punda Maria Gate

Beitbridge

Musina

Tshipise

Venda

Madandi

Soutpansberg

Verwoerd Tunnels

Makhado/ Louis Trichardt

Giyani

Thohoyandou

Phalaborwa Gate

Hans Merensky Nature Reserve

Gravelotte

Hoedspruit

Orpen Gate

Paul Kruger Gate

Phabeni Gate

Klaserie

Eastern Drakensberg

Phalaborwa

Hazyview

Pontdrif

Limpopo

Mapungubwe National Park

Bridgewater

Gregory

Alldays

Oorwinning

Zoutpansberg

Catlow

Vivo

Dendron

Soekmekaar

Duiwelskloof

Modjadji Cycad Reserve

Tzaneen

Magoebaskloof

Big Baobab Tree

Haenertsburg

Drakensberg

Graskop

Sabie

Pilgrim's Rest

Blyde River Canyon

Strijdom Tunnel

Ohrigstad

Lydenburg

Burgersfort

Erts

Mooihoek

Woolbergber Wilderness

LIMPOPO

Polokwane

Percy Fyfe Nature Reserve

Mahwelereng

Mokopane

Strydpoort Berge

Roedtan

Springbok Flats

Hlogotlou

Marble Hall

Groblersdal

Baltimore

Setateng

Marken

Mogalakwena

Melkrivier

Vaalwater

Modimolle/ Nylstroom

Nylsvley Nature Reserve

Mabula

Holme Park

Radium

Tom Burke

Palala

Lapalala Wilderness Area

Mogol

Mokolo Dam

Matlabas

Thabazimbi

Marakele National Park

Waterberge

Leeupoort

Mabula

Bela-bela/ Warmbaths

Borakalalo Game Reserve

Klipvoor Dam

Limpopo

Ellisras

Stockpoort

Buffelsdrifthek

Spanwerk

Sentrum

Mokolo

BOTSWANA

Ngotwane

Derdepoort

N

30 km

30 miles

Few foreign visitors see much of Limpopo, formerly the Northern Province, unless travelling to the northern reaches of Kruger National Park which makes up a chunk of the eastern side of the province (and is covered in the Mpumalanga chapter). Many, however, pass through Limpopo on the Great North Road, the thoroughfare linking South Africa with the rest of the continent via its neighbours: Zimbabwe and Botswana. The importance of this route has defined development in the region but the province offers plenty more than the service stations and dusty towns dotting the highway. As well as Kruger, Limpopo has over 50 nature reserves and countless private game farms that sustain intricate African eco-systems. While much of the countryside is dry bushveld, the mountains around Makhado/Louis Trichardt and Tzaneen are green and lush, forming some of the most important agricultural districts in South Africa. The Drakensberg Escarpment is a beautiful forested area and, within the Magoebaskloof range, there are spectacular waterfalls and patches of indigenous forest, providing excellent hiking territory. Further south is a region promoted as the 'Valley of the Olifants', an area rich in wildlife and with an interesting history. To the north, the landscape opens up into dry plains dotted with tubby boabab trees, home to the fascinating Venda people, famous for their wood carvings.

Zebra-drawn mail coach

A weekly mail-coach service between Pretoria and Pietersburg was introduced by the Zeederberg Coach Company in 1890 and was later extended north into Rhodesia (Zimbabwe). The coaches seated 12 passengers inside and two on top, together with the driver, co-driver and luggage. Trips by coach could be hazardous and drivers had to negotiate mountain passes, swollen rivers, muddy tracks and attacks by wild animals and highwaymen. In order to deal with the problem of the tsetse fly, which causes sleeping sickness in horses, the company trained a team of zebras to pull the coaches on the eastern leg of the run through Limpopo. Although the training was fairly successful, the zebras lacked the stamina of horses and the practice was later discontinued.

Ins and outs

Getting around

On leaving Pretoria, the N1 passes through the **Springbok Flats**, a featureless plain between Bela-Bela and Mokopane. Before the road reaches the provincial capital, **Polokwane**, it runs parallel to the Waterberg plateau, an area which in recent years has seen the development of many private game reserves for hunting and game viewing. The route to the east of Polokwane on the R71 will take you through the green and fertile **Magoebaskloof Mountains**, before continuing on to either Phalaborwa and central Kruger, or the lowveld region of the Limpopo Province. Continuing north of Polokwane on the N1, the country is flat, typical bushveld country where the principal activity is cattle ranching, but as you approach **Makhado/Louis Trichardt** the impressive **Soutpansberg Mountains** dominate the horizon and straddle the N1.

From Makhado/Louis Trichardt most visitors will be faced with the choice of two routes: to turn off the N1 and head east through **Venda** to the northern camps in Kruger; or to continue over the mountains to **Musina** and **Zimbabwe**. The Great North Road cuts through Wyllie's Port and the two Hendrik Verwoerd tunnels in order to cross the Soutpansberg. On the northern side of the mountains the landscape quickly changes; much of the country is in rain shadow from the Soutpansberg and the temperatures are significantly warmer. As you approach Musina, look out for groups of the distinctive baobab tree, a popular sight in these parts. From Musina it is only 12 km to the border at Beitbridge. ▸▸ *For further details, see Transport, pages 679 and 690.*

Tourist information

The **Limpopo Tourism Board** ① *corner of Grobler and Kerk streets, Polokwane, T015-2907300, www.golimpopo.com*, is responsible for promoting tourism in the whole province. It produces a good brochure, map and guides to accommodation and activities. The tourist board also produces a self-drive route booklet, which includes the popular **African Ivory Route** ① *T015-2953025, www.africanivoryroute.co.za*, a 4WD driving and camping route which covers most of the Limpopo Province from the far north of Kruger National Park to the remote game farms towards the Botswana border.

Up the Great North Road

The N1, sometimes referred to as the Great North Road, is the only direct route linking South Africa with Zimbabwe and, in effect, the rest of Africa. Between Pretoria and the Zimbabwe border, the road passes through four regional centres, which are linked by bus and train. However, these towns have few local attractions, and you really need a car to explore the countryside on either side of the N1 to fully appreciate Limpopo Province. ▸▸ *For listings, see pages 676-680.*

Bela-Bela/Warmbaths ⬤🅟🅖🅢⬤ ▸▸ *pp676-680. Colour map 2, B2.*

→ *Phone code: 014.*

This resort town only exists because of the natural hot springs 'discovered' in the 1860s by Jan Grobler and Carl van Heerden whilst hunting in the region. Previously known as Warmbaths, the new name comes from the Tswana *Biela bela*, 'the water that boils on its own'. The 50°C springs bubble out of the earth at about 22,000 litres per hour and are rich in sodium chloride, calcium carbonate and are also slightly radioactive. Less than an hour's drive from Pretoria, a staggering two million people visit Bela-Bela each year. The mild climate during the winter months ensures an average of 286 sunny days a year. The principal springs now lie engulfed within the massive Forever Resort (see page 676), where visitors can enrol in a variety of treatments at the spa.

Sights

There is very little of interest in town, and there's no point stopping unless you're here to take the waters. If you do stay overnight, the most popular attraction is the **Carousel Entertainment World**, 56 km from Bela-Bela on the N1 (free shuttle bus from town at weekends), a 24-hour gambling and entertainment complex on a bleak section of the highway. Otherwise, the **Thaba Kwena Crocodile Farm** ⓘ *T014-7365059, daily 0900-1600, feeding Sat 1500, R15*, has over 20,000 crocs. **Bela-Bela Tourism Association** ⓘ *corner of Old Pretoria and Voortrekker streets, Waterfront development, T014-7363694, www.belabelatourism.co.za, Mon-Fri 0800-1700; Sat and Sun 0900-1200*, is a useful municipal office that can book local accommodation. Ask here about the choice of game farms in the area, offering game drives and meals. There are also a number of shops and restaurants in the Waterfront development and a petting farm for kids.

Modimolle/Nylstroom and around ⬤🅜🅐⬤ ▸▸ *pp676-680. Colour map 2, B2.*

→ *Phone code 014.*

Modimolle, meaning 'place of the spirits', is the commercial centre of the Waterberg region with a small centre shaded by jacaranda and poinciana trees. Grapes, watermelons and peaches are the principal sources of income, and stalls sell boxes of fruit at the roadside after the harvests. A grape festival is held here in January. The NTK is the largest agricultural cooperative society in the Limpopo Province, where you can see nuts being sorted and peanut butter being made.

Sights

The main attraction in the area is **Nylsvley Nature Reserve**, one of the finest birdwatching spots in South Africa. Being a quiet rural centre, Modimolle itself has little in the way of sites, although it does boast a surprising number of distinguished previous residents, including Gerhard Moerdijik, the architect that designed the Voortrekker Monument in Pretoria, and South Africa's fifth prime minister (1954-1958), JG Strijdom, who lived here while he was a member of parliament for the Waterberg constituency. His house, **Strijdom House** ① *Church St, Tue-Sat 0900-1300, 1400-1700, Sun 1400-1700*, is a national monument and a museum about his life. The **Hervormde Kerk** on Calvyn Street, is also a national monument, built in 1889.

Nylsvley Nature Reserve

① *20 km out of town towards Naboomspruit. Daily 0600-1800, R10, information can be found on the Friends of Nylsvley website, www.nylsvley.co.za.*

The Nyl River (see box, above) rises in the hills near Modimolle and eventually spills into the Limpopo. For much of its journey, the river meanders back and forth, forming a marshy floodplain that is the largest and best conserved in South Africa. The floodplain reaches 6 km in width and extends for nearly 70 km between Middlefontein and Moordriftan. It is an important wetland ecosystem, which attracts up to 80,000 breeding birds during the rains. Consequently, this is a hugely popular birdwatching destination; it's not unheard of to see 200 of the 420 recorded species on a single day. It's home to the biggest concentration of water birds in the southern hemisphere, with species numbering just over 100, and 37 red-data species, including the critically endangered bittern. Up to 80,000 wetland birds are attracted to the area at any one time. The reserve is listed as a RAMSAR site, an internationally important habitat for waterfowl. A birdwatching festival and bird census are held here each year. Visitors are allowed to walk or ride bikes on tracks through the reserve and there are a number of bird hides, from which you may also spot eland, tsessbe, kudu, waterbuck, reedbuck, zebra, and giraffe. Even if birdwatching isn't your thing, this is a beautiful environment.

Mokopane/ and around ⬤🅵🅹🅧🅾 ▸▸ *pp676-680. Colour map 2, B3.*

➔ *Phone code: 015.*

Mokopane is a busy centre for the surrounding agricultural area. Peanuts, cotton, wheat and oranges are major crops; the Zebediela Citrus Estate, 55 km to the southeast, is the largest citrus farm in the country and was handed back to its original owners, the Bjatladi community, in 2003. It is a modern town with few attractions, although it does have an interesting past. In 1854 the local chief, Makapan, hid in caves in the Makapan Valley with his people to escape from the Voortrekker commandos. During the siege, which lasted from 25 October to 21 November, the Boer leader Piet Potgieter was killed by the warriors of Makapan; over 1500 of the warriors and their families died from starvation during the siege. After these events, the local town changed its name from Vredenburg to Pieter Potgietersrus and, in 1935, it became Potgietersrus. In 2002 it was renamed Mokopane after the Ndebele chief.

Sights

If you find yourself in the area with time to spare then the **Arend Dieperink Museum** ① *Voortrekker Rd, T015-4912244, Mon-Fri 0800-1630, small entry fee*, is a cut above the average provincial collection. It has displays on the Sotho and the early settlers of the Transvaal, as well as dinosaur fossils and a reproduction of the *Australopithecus africanus* skull found in the **Makapan's Caves**, part of an excellent palaeontological display. The **Mogalakwena Bushveld Tourism** ① *Voortrekker Rd, T015-4918458, www.potgietersrus-mokopane.com, Mon-Fri 0900-1630*, organize tours of the caves, which are 15 km north of the town (see page 667).

Around Mokopane

The **Game Breeding Centre** ① *1 km north of town on the N1 to Polokwane, T015-4914314, Mon-Fri 0800-1600, Sat and Sun 0800-1800, small entry fee*, is part of the National Zoological Gardens of Pretoria and breeds rare species such as cheetah, roan antelope, black rhino and pygmy hippo from West Africa. These are then taken to Pretoria in order to expand the national zoo's breeding programmes. It is a member of the World Zoo Organisation, which focuses on the breeding of exotic, indigenous and endangered wildlife. A network of roads run throughout the 1500-ha area of bushveld but dense vegetation makes game viewing difficult. At the entrance is a pleasant picnic area and small aviary. Guided tours and game drives can be organized from reception.

Fifteen kilometres northwest of Mokopane on the R518 to Marken are the **Ana Trees**, a clump of apiesdoring trees *Acacia albida* under which David Livingstone camped on one of his journeys. The biggest tree has a circumference of 6 m; they are considered a botanical rarity in this area.

Percy Fyfe Nature Reserve is an important reserve about 35 km northeast of Mokopane. Percy Fyfe was a local farmer who, in 1933, bought a few head of blesbok from the Orange Free State to try and introduce the species to the region. After he donated the farm to the state in 1954 it has been used as a sanctuary to breed threatened antelope. Roan, sable and tsessebe have all been successfully bred here and then reintroduced to parts of the Waterberg range. Addo buffalo have recently been introduced. There is a simple campsite here for overnight visitors.

Mokopane

To Percy Fyfe Nature Reserve, Makapan's Caves (19 km) & Polokwane

Game Breeding Centre

To Marken, Glen Alpine Dam & Ana Trees

Sussex
Pretorius
De Klerk
Van Heerden
Potgieter
Caltex
Shell
CNA
Retief
Standard
Van Riebeeck
Arend
Dieperink
Museum
ABSA
Kruger
Caltex
Pretorius
Voor
Ruiter
Thabo Mbeki Dr
Hooge
Rabe
Foutie

To Pretoria (R101/N1)

N

Sleeping 😴	Eating 🍴
Oasis Lodge **1**	KFC **2**
Orinoco **2**	Nando's **3**
Protea Park **3**	Spur **4**

400 metres
400 yards

Makapan's Caves

① *19 km north of Mokopane in the Makapan's Valley. Visits by guided tour only, information from Mogalakwena Bushveld Tourism Association T015-4918458.*

The caves of the Makapan's Valley are a unique archaeological site: nowhere else in the world is there such an extensive and complete record of hominid occupation. They provide a record of occupation from australopithecine times through the Stone and Iron Ages right up to the present day – over 3.3 million years.

In 1925 the first archaeological finds were made by Professor Raymond Dart. Following his discoveries, a local teacher from Pietersburg, Mr Eitzman, sent Professor Dart a collection of rocks he had found near some lime kilns close to the caves. After close examination Dart realized they had stumbled across an important site and in 1936 the caves were declared a national monument, later becoming a National Heritage Site. In total there are seven caves plus a couple of other sites all of which have yielded thousands of bones and artefacts – the Cave of Hearths, Hyaena Cave, Rainbow Cave, Historic Cave, Buffalo Cave, Ficus Cave and Peppercorn's Cave.

Polokwane ●❼▲●❻ ›› pp676-680. Colour map 2, B3.

→ Phone code: 015. Altitude: 1312 m.

Formerly known as Pietersburg, the capital of Limpopo Province is a sprawling, low-rise town built on a grid system. It was founded in 1884 by Voortrekker Commandant-General Pieter Joubert as the main agricultural and industrial centre for the thinly populated province. The town is located in a shallow hollow surrounded by level grass plains, a rather dull setting, but making a practical base nevertheless. Polokwane offers alternative routes to Kruger: one via Makhado/Louis Trichardt to the northernmost entrance at Punda Maria, and the other through the beautiful Magoebaskloof to Phalaborwa.

Ins and outs

Tourist information The **Limpopo Tourism Board** ① *corner of Grobler and Kerk streets, T015-2907300, www.golimpopo.com, Mon-Fri 0800-1630,* is responsible for promoting tourism in the whole province. It has little information on the city itself, but produces a useful brochure on the province.

Best time to visit The town enjoys a very pleasant climate; the summer temperatures are moderated by the altitude and in winter the average temperature is 20°C. Rainfall varies between 400-600 mm and falls during the summer months.

Polokwane

Sleeping ●
African Roots **1**
Cycad Guest House **4**
Landmark Lodge **2**
Plumtree Lodge **3**

Eating ❼
Falcon Rock Spur **2**

Greek 'n' Chef **1**
La Villa Italiana **3**
The Restaurant **4**

City centre

As the regional capital, the city has grown rapidly in recent years and is by far the largest centre between Pretoria and Harare in Zimbabwe. If you have spent a few days in the surrounding countryside it can come as quite a shock as you drive into the busy centre with its wide tree-lined roads, traffic jams and tall buildings.

The first stop for most visitors is likely to be the 'Irish House', home to the **Polokwane Museum** ⓘ *corner of Thabo Mbeki and Market streets, T015-2902183, Mon-Fri 0800-1600, Sat 0900-1200, Sun 1500-1700, free.* The history of the building is as interesting as the collection it houses. The building is a prefabricated steel structure from Germany which was imported by Aug Julius Möschke after his shop had been destroyed by a fire in 1906. It is a classic example of late Victorian architecture with wrought-iron decorations topped by a fine clock tower and weather vane. During the First World War, Möschke was interned and on his return to Pietersburg he found his business to be bankrupt and was forced to sell the shop to James Albert Jones in 1920. It was Jones who named the building the Irish House and over the years it grew into a very successful local fashion shop, which imported the latest quality materials from Europe. The museum itself traces the history of the region from the Stone Age to modern times; it is a well-presented display in a spacious and airy building.

On the other side of Thabo Mbeki St from the Irish House, in the gardens which form the civic square, you will find the **Hugh Exton Photographic Museum** ⓘ *T015 2902186, Mon-Fri 0900-1530, Sun 1100-1300, free,* housed in the town's first Dutch Reformed Church, dating from 1890. This is a superb collection of prints and over 23,000 glass negatives, tracing the first 50 years of Pietersburg – few towns have such a record of their past. Hugh Exton was a local photographer who had a studio in Pietersburg.

North of the Civic Centre on Jorrissen Street is the library, which houses the **Polokwane Art Museum** ⓘ *T015-2902177, Mon-Fri 0900-1600, Sat 0900-1200, free.* This has a fine collection of South African modern art and sculptures from Jacobus Botes's collection. Although lacking in funding and with poor labelling, the collection is interesting.

Around Polokwane

Polokwane Bird Sanctuary ⓘ *T015-2902331, daily 0700-1700, R12, entry on foot only,* is an award-winning sanctuary set around a couple of lakes in the acacia bush. There are numerous hides all around the lakes for spotting the more than 280 bird species that have been recorded here. The sanctuary is 4 km north of town along Market Street, on the R521 to Dendron; the turn-off is on the right-hand side just after crossing the Sand River, and is diagonally across from a petrol station.

For the chance to see larger wildlife, and just on the edge of town, visit **Polokwane Game Reserve** ⓘ *T015-2902331, daily 0700-1630, R20, R15 car,* one of the largest municipal game reserves in South Africa. You can walk or drive around the 3200-ha reserve and view 21 species of game, including white rhino, tsessebe and sable antelope. There are several hides and view points along the streams, which flow through the reserve. Game drives can be arranged and night drives run on Friday evenings during the summer; phone for details. There is also a 20-km trail, with overnight accommodation. Bird species include grey-backed camaroptera, yellow-bellied greenbul, terrestrial brownbul, yellow-breasted apalis and many other warbler species, which can be seen in the summer months.

One of the most significant modern-day landmarks in this region is the **Zion City** at Moria, 30 km from Polokwane on the R71 towards Haenertsburg. Although there is nothing much for the visitor to see here, this is the seat of the Zion Christian Church, an entirely black denomination that has the largest following of any denomination in Southern Africa. During Easter weekend each year, up to one million followers congregate here from all over South Africa and Zimbabwe for mass worship, when they traditionally wear white robes. It's extraordinary to see such staggering numbers of people in the Polokwane region.

Routes east and north of Polokwane

If you are not heading for Zimbabwe or the northern camps in Kruger National Park, an interesting alternative route out of Polokwane is to take the R71 to **Tzaneen** (95 km) and **Phalaborwa** (see page 674). Once in Tzaneen it is possible to take R40 south through the game farm region of the Lowveld to either the **Blyde River Canyon** in Mpumalanga (see page 652) or central Kruger's Orpen Gate (see page 632).

The N1, meanwhile, continues north to **Makhado/Louis Trichardt**. This section of the road has been upgraded to a dual carriageway, although the onward stretch from Makhado/Louis Trichardt to the Zimbabwe border is still single carriageway. About 61 km from Polokwane the N1 crosses the **Tropic of Capricorn**.

Makhado/Louis Trichardt and the Soutpansberg ●❶▲❺❻
↠ *pp676-680. Colour map 2, A4.*

→ *Phone code: 015. Altitude: 984 m.*

The name of this town is still undecided. Along with other towns in Limpopo Province, Louis Trichardt was renamed **Makhado** in 2003, after the Venda King Makhado who ruled in the region from the mid-1800s until his death in 1887. He played a role in resisting settlement in the area by the Boers. However, there was local rejection to the new name, and it was claimed less than 1% of the town's population had been consulted on the change. A residents' association applied to Pretoria's High Court in 2005 to have the name overturned. They were rejected but rather astonishingly appealed in South Africa's Supreme Court and won, and the name was changed back to Louis Trichardt in 2007. It is expected to be renamed Makhado again, but only after proper consultancy procedures involving all the residents have taken place.

It's another important agricultural centre, where tea, coffee, timber and sub-tropical fruits are the main crops. The world-renowned Elim Hospital is 25 km southeast of Makhado/Louis Trichardt on the Gyani Road. There's not much to see in town itself – it's a sleepy backwater that trucks rumble through on the N1 – but to the north and west is the sandstone **Soutpansberg** mountain range, which stretches for about 130 km and reaches 1753 m at its highest point, known as Lejume. It takes its name from the salt-pan and brine spring at the western end of the range. These hills have played an important role in the early history of the region and now offer good wilderness hikes. Dotted along the high plateau are traditional Venda villages.

Many of the valleys and lakes in the Soutpansberg are considered sacred – the best known of these are the Phiphidi Falls and Guvhukuvhu Pool, Lwamomdo Hill, Lake Fundudzi and the Thathe Vondo Forest. These sights are difficult to find and you should enlist the services of a registered guide if you wish to visit them. This will also help ensure that you approach and treat the sights sensitively. A self-drive route, taking in the area's arts and crafts highlights, begins in Makhado – information is available from the **Soutpansberg Tourist Office** ⓘ *corner of Songozwi St and the N1, T015-5160040, www.tourismsoutpansberg.co.za, Mon-Fri 0900-1700, Sat 0800-1300.*

Background

The town was named after Louis Trichardt, the Voortrekker leader who set up camp near here in May 1836. He had travelled up to the Soutpansberg with another group of Voortrekkers under Hans Van Rensburg. After arguments between the two groups, Hans Van Rensburg led his people east in search of a route to Lourenço Marques (today's Maputo in Mozambique). They disappeared into the wilderness and were never heard from again. Louis Trichardt remained in the area for a year before following Hans Van Rensburg east. This was one of the classic journeys of the Voortrekkers, taking seven months to reach Lourenço Marques. It took them two and a half months to get down the Drakensberg escarpment and by the end of their trek, 27 of the original 53 Boers had died. Louis Trichardt and his wife survived the journey but both died of malaria soon after. After his death other Voortrekkers settled in the area as ivory hunters but left after Chief Makhado (after whom the town is now named) and his vhaVenda people defeated them in 1867. Only in 1898 did the Zuid-Afrikaansche Republiek take control of the region.

Manavhela Ben Lavin Nature Reserve

① T015-5164534, daily 0600-1900, R30. To get there, follow the N1, 8 km south of the town, and look out for the Fort Edward Rd, the reserve is 5 km along this road.

The Manavhela Ben Lavin Nature Reserve is a protected area of indigenous woodland with 18 km of walking trails, mountain biking trails and hides. The reserve is a good place for

Makhado/Louis Trichardt

To Hanglip Forest

To Vivo & Alldays

To 4 5 & Zimbabwe

500 metres
500 yards

N

To Tzaneen (R71), Polokwane, Pretoria (N1),
Manavhela Ben Lavin Nature Reserve

To Thohoyandou & Punda Maria
(Kruger National Park)

Sleeping
Bergwater 1
Clouds End 5
Inn on Louis Trichardt 4

Lutombo 3
Makhado Caravan Park 2
Shiluvari Lakeside Lodge
& Wood Owl Restaurant 6

Eating
Café d'Art 2

birdwatching and has giraffes, wildebeest and other game indigenous to the area. There are also some interesting archaeological sites, which have been dated to around AD 1250. Hikers and bikers are provided with a booklet that helps interpret the environment. There are some new overnight huts along the hiking trail (see Sleeping page 678), which are fully furnished. When exploring the park on foot always remember to look out for wild animals.

Hanglip Forest Reserve
ⓘ 3 km west of town, signposted off the N1, R10.
The Hanglip Forest Reserve is an area of indigenous forest around the base of the Hanglip, a wall of rock rising 1719 m. The top of the cliffs are some of the highest points of the Soutpansberg. From the picnic site is a 20 min circular trail which is excellent for birdwatching in the forest. The **Soutpansberg Hike**, a 21-km, three-day walk and overnight accommodation is in huts. Although this is a circular route all hikers must walk in the same direction and only 30 people are allowed on the trail at any one time. For further details contact **Komatiland Forestry**, a subsidiary of the **Department of Forestry** (SAFCOL) ⓘ T013-7542724, www.komatiecotourism.co.za, which has information on the trial, and issues permits. Listen out for the resident scaly-throated honeyguides in the picnic site.

Beyond Makhado
The N1 continues to the north winding through wooded valleys. After 21 km the highway passes through the Soutpansberg, via the **Verwoerd Tunnels**. The R524 heads east from town through **Thohoyandou**, the former capital of the Venda homeland, to Punda Maria Camp (140 km), one of the most northerly camps in **Kruger National Park** (see page 618).

Venda ▶▶ Colour map 2, A4/5.

You are only likely to pass through this former homeland region if you are heading to the northern camps of Kruger from Makhado on the R524 or from Polokwane or Tzaneen on the R81. The area has more in common with rural Tanzania or Kenya than with most areas of South Africa. Unlike Bophuthatswana in North West Province, which the Apartheid government proclaimed a black homeland simply because they had no use for the inadequate land, Venda is fertile and green and produces tea, bananas and mangoes. Despite this, and efforts made by the current government, the infrastructure is still poor, the roads are badly maintained, and families survive on subsistence hand-to-mouth farming.

Background
The culture of the vhaVenda is steeped in the belief of the spirit world, and there are many important sacred, and private, sites in the region. Originally from Zimbabwe, it is thought that the vhaVenda people migrated here at the beginning of 18th century. They are regarded as some of the finest artists in South Africa, and are particularly renowned for their drum making and pottery.

Thoyoyandou and around
Thoyoyandou is the former capital of the independent homeland and is the commercial and administrative centre for the district. Its name means 'head of the elephant' in tshiVenda. The town has an energetic African feel to it: business, schooling and life in general is conducted outdoors, the people are astoundingly friendly, and local produce is sold at stalls along roadsides.

The upside-down tree

The baobab tree (*Adansonia digitata*) is the undisputed king of the African savannah and grows throughout east and southern Africa. The trees reach to about 25 m in height, with trunk diameters of up to 10 m, and live for thousands of years. They are noted for storing water inside their swollen trunk, with the capacity to hold up to 120,000 litres of water to endure harsh drought conditions. This giant tree, with its enormous girth and unmistakable appearance, is surrounded by legend. One story suggests that the tree's root-like branches are a result of the gods, in a frivolous mood, planting the tree upside down. Another legend has it that if you drink water in which you have soaked baobab seeds, you can wade across a crocodile-infested river and get to the other side unharmed. However, few people seem willing to test this theory.

Musina ◐◗◔◕ ▸ *pp676-680. Colour map 2, A4.*

→ *Phone code: 015.*

Musina is the northernmost town in South Africa and is the frontier town with Zimbabwe. It is your last chance to buy South African products before crossing the border at Beitbridge, 12 km to the north at the end of the N1, which has been expanded to a newly built double-lane highway on this short stretch. The town started life as a camp, set up around the copper mines that opened in 1905, though these closed down decades ago. The main street is lined with shops, banks, petrol stations and fast food outlets all catering to the steady stream of traffic to and from the border. It's not an especially attractive town, and is increasingly being dwarfed by large hastily built townships that are home to Zimbabweans who have managed to cross the border. Although there's little of interest in town, it makes a reasonable base from which to explore Venda to the east, Mapungubwe National Park to the west and there is also a good road across to the northern camps of Kruger via Tshipise.

Mapungubwe National Park → *Colour map 2, A3.*

ⓘ *Gates, 0600-1800, office 0800-1600, T015-5342014, R60.*

Mapungubwe is the country's youngest and northernmost national park, developed on the South African side of the confluence of the Shashe and Limpopo rivers. At the confluence itself is a picnic site with a view over the point where South Africa, Zimbabwe and Botswana meet. The park forms part of what will become the Limpopo-Shashe Transfrontier Conservation Area, covering the corner of the province which borders Zimbabwe and Botswana. It protects important San rock art sites, but is best known for **Mapungubwe Hill**, which researchers believe was the site of the first capital of the ancient kingdom of Great Zimbabwe between AD 900 and 1300. Gold and silver artefacts have been unearthed here, including the famous Golden Rhino, as well as items of Arab, Chinese, Indonesian and Indian origin – indicated important trading routes – many of which are on display at the University of Pretoria. Mapungubwe is the earliest evidence of Africa's Iron Age and was awarded World Heritage status in 2003. The park now covers 28,000 ha of arid bush and tufted grassveld dotted with acacia thorn and giant baobab trees. It's home to a variety of wildlife, including black and white rhino, elephant, kudu, zebra, eland, waterbuck, gemsbok, giraffe and baboon. Although predators such as lion, cheetah, hyena and leopard

To Zimbabwe via Beitbridge

In view of the current political climate in Zimbabwe, it is recommended that all visitors refer to the British Foreign and Commonwealth Office website, www.fco.org, for up-to-date travel advice before attempting to enter Zimbabwe. Do not state your occupation to Zimbabwe custom officials as that of journalist or any other media-related job.

Border opening hours 24 hours. Considering the problems in Zimbabwe (see box, page 675) formalities at the border can be very slow – the process can take several hours and it gets very hot here during the summer.

Customs and immigration Visa requirements for Zimbabwe change frequently but most nationals do need a visa and they can be issued at the border post. Costs vary from US$30 to US$55 depending on nationality. Entry visas are valid for a maximum of 90 days.

Facilities There is a duty-free shop on the South African side, selling a limited range of cigarettes and spirits, and a VAT refund office (see page 55), but expect a long wait.

Public transport Expect to pay no more than R10 for a ride from Musina to the border post in a minibus taxi. Once you have negotiated the South African side, you will either have to walk or hitch across the bridge over the Limpopo River. Minibus taxis to **Bulawayo, Masvingo** and **Harare** can be found waiting on the other side of Zimbabwe immigration, but due to the lack of fuel in Zimbabwe, these services cannot be relied on. There are mainline bus services that operate between Johannesburg or Pretoria and Bulawayo or Harare and in theory the total bus journey on both these routes is around 18 hours. However, expect long delays as all Zimbabwean bus passengers are searched thoroughly and there can be lengthy vehicle queues on both sides of the border.

Vehicle formalities At present, most hired cars from South Africa are not allowed into Zimbabwe. For those that are, **third-party insurance** is required by law for all vehicles entering Zimbabwe. Short-term policies can be bought at the border. Visitors from overseas countries must have an English translation of their **licence** plus a photograph. Tourists in private vehicles must also have a **vehicle registration certificate** and will normally be granted a temporary **import permit** free of charge, provided the vehicle is licensed in its home country and has the appropriate number plates. People travelling in their own vehicle on a **carnet** must get it stamped when exiting South Africa and entering Zimbabwe, as Zimbabwe is not part of the South African Development Community (SADC), the shared customs agreement that covers South Africa, Namibia and Botswana.

Be wary of petty thieves, especially on the Zimbabwe side. Lock everything up and make sure anything on the outside of the vehicle is tied down. Do not under any circumstances accept help from touts in the car park who offer to sell relevant forms or 'look after' your car; all forms are available free of charge inside the border control building, and official uniformed security guards patrol the car park.

Africa's Rio Grande

The Limpopo River marks the 300-km border between South Africa and Zimbabwe, and Beitbridge is the only border post. In recent years the river has been likened to the Rio Grande, the river that marks the border between the US and Mexico, over which thousands of Mexicans try to cross illegally in search of a better life in the US. Because of the present dire political and economic situation in Zimbabwe, several thousand Zimbabwean people attempt to cross this border every week. Some cross legally through Beitbridge to shop in South Africa, and return again with much-needed provisions. But, in a desperate attempt to escape from poverty and unemployment, most cross the (crocodile-infested) Limpopo River illegally, and then need to get through the three walls of fortified fencing on the South African side.

If they don't get stopped, they often make it down to Gauteng to live in relative anonymity in the townships, though these are routinely raided for illegal immigrants. There is now an International Organisation for Migration Support Centre at Beitbridge, established by a Belgium NGO concerned with the humane treatment of migrants. Those caught crossing the border illegally are now sent here, where they are fed and provided with transport back to Bulawayo, the first sizeable town in Zimbabwe. However, from there many people immediately head south to try their luck at crossing the border again. No one knows for sure how many Zimbabweans have successfully made it into South Africa since the crisis began, but estimates have been put as high as 3-5 million. It goes without saying that there's a heavy police presence in the region.

are present, they are rarely sighted. Pythons and black mambas, on the other hand, are common. Birders can tick off 400 species, including kori bustard, tropical boubou and Pel's fishing owl. There are four camps within the park, all accessible by normal car.

Ins and outs

Getting there and around The park is 68 km due west from Musina on the R572. It can also be reached from the east via the R521, an alternative route from Polokwane. Facilities are still being developed in the park, but at present a series of rough roads pass through a variety of terrains, offering a range of wildlife viewing opportunities. Of these, 35 km are suitable for normal cars while another 100 km are open to 4WDs, so make sure you pick up a map at reception. There are a handful of hides overlooking pans and dams, and an interpretive centre is being built at the main entrance gate. One of the highlights of the park is its hiking trails: **Vhembe Trails** operates much like the wilderness trails in Kruger, with guests venturing out on guided day hikes from a main base camp. There are also a couple of 4WD routes going through rugged hilly terrain, including the **Tshugulu Eco Route** which covers 45 km, with a game hide en route.

Malaria This is a malarial area, so take prophylactics. There are, as yet, no shops or petrol available in the park, so stock up in Musina before you visit.

Best time to visit This region gets on average just 10 days of rain a year and summer temperatures can reach 45°C.

Up the Great North Road

Hotel and guesthouse prices
L over US$300 AL US$220-300 A US$150-220
B US$100-150 C US$75-100 D US$35-75
E US$15-35 F under US$15
Restaurant prices
♥♥♥ over US$30 ♥♥ US$15-30 ♥ under US$15
See pages 46-51 for further information.

Sleeping

Bela-Bela p665

AL Mabula Game Lodge, 35 km from Bela-Bela off the Thabazimbi–Rooiberg Rd, T014-7347000, www.mabula.com. 47 luxury self-catering and full-board double rooms, with restaurant, swimming pool, squash, tennis, gym, sauna, bush walks, game drives, horseback trails, luxury game farm with excellent facilities, recommended for a longer break. Also has timeshares. Day visitors are welcomed for game drives and lunch.

C Villa Palmeira, 9 Knoppiesdoring Av, T014-7362558, www.villapalmeira.co.za. 13 en suite rooms in this comfortable guesthouse in a quiet suburb 2 km from the springs. En suite a/c rooms, DSTV, internet access, set in a thatched villa surrounded by well-tended sub-tropical gardens. B&B, other meals on request, pool in garden, thatched lapa with braai.

C-E Forever Resorts Warmbaths, T014-7368500, www.foreversa.co.za. This resort contains the main Bela-Bela springs and is so vast that guests are required to wear plastic identity bracelets at all times. The caravan park alone extends for a couple of kilometres to the edge of the town. Chalets and log cabins, 124 in total, surround 3 man-made dams, and there's a standard 45-room hotel at the entrance gate. A selection of restaurants and bars, mineral pools, spa and hydro with a full range of beauty treatments, horseriding, squash, tennis, cable water ski circuit, water slides, go-karts, quad bikes, fishing. Advance booking is essential. Day visitors permitted until 1700.

Modimolle and around p665

C Shangri-La, Eerstebewood Rd, midway between Bela-Bela and Modimolle on the R101 on a bushveld farm, T014-7181600, www.shangri-la.co.za. Part of the **Protea** group. Geared towards conferences, but with decent accommodation in 42 thatched cottages, with en suite bathroom, spacious and tastefully decorated. Pool, restaurant, bar, tennis courts, all set in lush gardens with views of the Waterberg.

Camping

F Nylsvley Nature Reserve, T015-2889000, simple campsite with 80 spaces in a beautiful setting within the nature reserve.

Mokopane p666, map p667

C Protea Park, 1 Beitel St, T015-4913101, www.thepark.co.za. 125 a/c double rooms with en suite bathroom, non-smoking rooms, TV MNet, lounge, restaurant, bar, laundry service, swimming pool set in garden in the middle of the complex with a few decorative palms, regular quality Protea hotel.

D Oasis Lodge, 1 Thabo Mbeki Dr, T015-4914124, www.oasishotel.co.za. Simple double rooms with en suite bathroom, ceiling fans, cool tiled floors, DSTV, conference facilities, Wi-Fi, restaurant, laundry service, shady garden.

D Orinoco, 66 Ruiter St, T015-4915891, www.orinoco.co.za. Local 2-star hotel, a/c double rooms with M-Net TV, restaurant, sports bar, both popular with local Afrikaners, swimming pool, some economy rooms sleeping 4.

Polokwane p668, map p668

Don't go out of your way to make Polokwane an overnight stop. With 1 or 2 exceptions, accommodation is aimed at the business traveller and, while being perfectly functional, is also unremarkable.

B African Roots, 58a Devenish St, T015-2970113, www.africanroots.info. Attractive converted farmhouse dating from 1928 with wrap-around veranda, owned by artists so the rooms have an interesting mix of antique furnishings and contemporary art, 21 en suite a/c garden rooms, lounge and bar, deck overlooking swimming pool. Recommended.

C Cycad Guest House, corner Schoeman and Suid streets, T015-2912123, www.cycad guesthouse.co.za. Red-brick block of modern a/c rooms, DSTV, internet, fridge, secure parking, conference facilities, business orientated so cheaper rates at the weekend.

C Landmark Lodge, next to the N1 Shell Ultra City just south of town, T015-2557255, www.proteahotels.com. Part of the **Protea** chain. 80 a/c functional rooms, aimed at business travellers, TV, pool, bar, restaurant, buffet breakfast, Wi-Fi. Standard business hotel but conveniently located.

C Plumtree Lodge, 138 Marshall St, T015-2956153/4, www.plumtree.co.za. 14 double rooms in a modern house, with cool terracotta floors, en suite bath or shower, separate lounge area with sofas, a desk and TV, motel-style parking. Palm-shaded pool surrounded by sun loungers, breakfast is served in a bright dining room. The staff are friendly and helpful. Gets booked up quickly.

Camping

D-E Polokwane Game Reserve, 5 km out of town along Dorp St, T015-2902331. Reserve with 60 sites for caravans and tents, 12 rondavels, self-catering, clean ablution block, electric points, laundry.

Makhado/Louis Trichardt and the Soutpansberg *p670, map p671*

B Inn on Louis Trichardt, 11 km north of Makhado on N1, T015-5177020, www.inn-on-louistrichardt.co.za. The tranquil setting makes this guesthouse a popular choice, great views of the Soutpansberg Mountains from its thatched rondavels, dotted around tended gardens. 18 rondavels have enormous beds, en suite bathrooms, TV and phone. Swimming pool in the garden, rates include dinner and breakfast served on the terrace restaurant, also has a bar and tea rooms. Recommended.

B Shiluvari Lakeside Lodge, off the R578 to Elim, T015-5563406, www.shiluvari.com. A peaceful country lodge located in the Albasini Conservancy, 23 km from Makhado, with 60 ha of grounds, ideal for birdwatching, fishing and hiking. Spacious thatched double rooms and chalets overlooking a dam, attractive decor, cool tiled floors, mosquito nets over beds, separate seating area with wicker furniture. Full-board rates available, **Wood Owl** restaurant and pub with fireplace is well regarded, swimming pool, Fair Trade curio shop. Boat trips organized during the day and at sunset on the dam. Recommended.

C Clouds End, N1 north out of town, T015-5177021, cloudsend@mweb.co.za. 38 double rooms, a/c, en suite, TV, all in a variety of blocks dotted about the hillside, restaurant serves good 5-course dinners, bar and spacious lounge with large open fireplace, essential in the winter months, swimming pool, floodlit tennis court, extensive grounds, even a cricket pitch. A popular hotel though old fashioned – think 1970s chintz. Rates are for dinner, bed and breakfast, excellent service, probably the best value in town.

D Bergwater Hotel, 5 Rissik St, T015-5160262, bergho2@mweb.co.za. 24 double a/c rooms with en suite bathroom, a/c, DSTV, à la carte restaurant favoured by the locals, 2 bars, lounge, swimming pool, conference facilities, a whitewashed double-storey building overlooking a pond on edge of town.

D Lutombo, 141 Anderson St, T015-5160850, www.lutombo.co.za. 3 homely rooms with en suite bathroom, non-smoking, TV lounge, all meals available on request, gardens, swimming pool, good value B&B.

D-F Manavhela Ben Lavin Nature Reserve, T015-5164534. Range of thatched self-catering chalets and huts, plus 30 campsites, caravan park, electric points and lighting, plenty of shade, spotless ablution block. Also has permanent tents, with en suite bathrooms and attached kitchen, sleeping 4.

F Makhado Caravan Park, T015-5193025, www.makhado.caravanparks.com. Excellent caravan site which has won national prizes. In the middle of town next to the Indigenous Tree Park, 120 sites with electric points, hot water, plenty of shade under towering trees, lovely setting next to a meandering stream with 2 dams, although mosquitoes can be a problem. Walking distance from restaurants and pubs, peaceful most of the year but can get very busy in school holidays.

Musina p673
B-C Musina Lodge, 9-13 Limpopo Av, T015-5343352, www.musina-lodge.co.za. Good standard of 13 spacious rooms set in tropical gardens with an enormous baobab tree, a/c, DVD players and TV, internet, modern interiors, private terraces, cosy bar, good restaurant.
C-E Forever Resorts Tshipise, 37 km from Musina, 105 km from Kruger's Pafuri Gate on the R508 or R525, T015-5390634, www.foreversa.co.za. Family resort conveniently situated en route to Kruger. Tennis, swimming pools, horse riding, hiking, mini-golf, hot springs, laundry, shops and restaurants on site. 96 a/c self-catering rondavels, TV, braai area, large camping and caravan park with shared ablutions. Summer temperatures are regularly over 40° C.
D Bushmen Inn, 43 Irwin St, T015-5340243, www.bushmen.co.za. 3 non-smoking a/c B&B rooms in a modern house, fridge, DSTV, thatched lapa in the garden, swimming pool, dinner on request.
D-F Baobab Caravan Park, on the left as you approach town from Makhado/Louis Trichardt, T015-5343504. Tent and caravan sites, some self-catering chalets, electric points, laundry, well-grassed and shaded. A greatly improved site since the management passed from the municipality into private hands.

● Eating

Bela-Bela p665
❡ **O'Hagans**, in the Waterfront development close to the tourist office, T014-7365068. Successful nationwide chain with attractive setting in the Waterfront development, outdoor tables. Interior filled with mock Irish touches, menu is Irish-style pub fare. Small choice, with steaks and schnitzels, steak and ale pie and sausages and mash. Good range of local and imported beers.
❡ **Tocoma Spur**, in the **Aventura Resort**. A reliable steakhouse chain found in most small towns throughout South Africa. Steaks, burgers and average salad bar.

Modimolle and around p665
❡❡ **Mattaniah**, 111 Thabo Mbeki Dr, T014-7174802. Mon-Sat 0900-1700, Sun 1200-1700. Daytime restaurant on the outskirts of Modimolle with a wide sunny veranda, good range of steaks and sauces, fish including kingklip and trout, and surf 'n' turf combos.

Mokopane p666, map p667
The restaurant scene here is limited to the standard chain outlets found throughout the country: **KFC**, **Nando's**, and **Spur**, are all on Thabo Mbeki Dr. Otherwise head to the restaurant and pub in the **Orinoco Hotel**.

Polokwane p668, map p668
Polokwane has a couple of excellent restaurant choices which make a welcome change from the usual chains. Most standard restaurants are in the Savannah Mall on Grobler St, away from the centre.
❡❡❡ **The Restaurant**, 50 Dorp St, just out of the centre, T015-2911918. Mon-Sat 1000-1600, 1800-2200. By far the best restaurant in town, if not in the entire province. Lengthy menu offering selection of salads, steaks, venison and a delicious prawn curry. Good wine list, too, and pleasant wooden deck spreading out from the fine old building. Recommended.
❡❡ **Greek 'n' Chef**, Savannah Centre, T015-2960662. Mon-Sat lunch and dinner, Sun lunch only. Good Mediterranean cuisine, including pasta, risotto and meze platters, plus a couple of Moroccan dishes like couscous and lamb tagine. Makes a pleasant change from the usual steak and burger menus.
❡❡ **La Villa Italiana**, Savannah Centre, T015-2960857. Open 1100-2300.

Long-standing family-run restaurant, serving an excellent selection of pasta dishes (penne with prawns in white wine is the best) huge range of pizzas and substantial mains such as roast lamb. Relaxed, friendly atmosphere.
†† Falcon Rock Spur, Savannah Centre, T015-2961991. Hugely popular outlet of the steakhouse chain set in the basement of the mall. Stick to the steaks; the burgers aren't great. Standard salad bar.

Makhado/Louis Trichardt and the Soutpansberg *p670, map p671*
††† Wood Owl, Shiluvari Lakeside Lodge, off the R578 to Elim, T015-5563406, www.shilu vari.com. Open 1200-1500, 1830-2030. Hotel restaurant with an excellent local reputation. Smart à la carte menu, using local produce such as Venda maize bread and beef. Delicious specials, beef with mustard mash or sweet potato soup, good choice of desserts, and the decor is from the Fair Trade shop attached.
†† Café d'Art, 129 Krogh St, T015-5165760. Open 1000-2100. Central family-run restaurant, sin attractive old house and serving traditional South African food, including good T-bone steaks, light lunches such as soup or quiche, great desserts or afternoon tea and cakes. All the baking is done on the premises.

Musina *p673*
The only restaurants in town are either in the hotels or the standard chains, such as **Buffalo Ridge Spur**, on Main St, which serves the usual choice of ribs, steaks and fried chicken.

⊛ Festivals and events

Bela-Bela *p665*
May The town hosts an annual **Tourism Festival**, with a wide range of stalls, events and special offers.

Mokopane *p666, map p667*
Oct If in the area around this time, look out for the **Biltong Festival**, when a whole range of game biltong can be tried and bought.

▲▲ Activities and tours

Makhado/Louis Trichardt and the Soutpansberg *p670, map p671*
Face Afrika Tours, Lommies Emporium Building, 104 Burger St, T015-5162076; faceafrika@mweb.co.za. Good for a complete tour of the region. Expert local knowledge. Recommended. Owner-manager Chris Olivier is a formidable character and a member of the Limpopo Tourism Board.
Kuvona Cultural Tours, T015-5563512, www.kuvona.com. Tours to the tribal sacred sites, traditional ceremonies, and villages in the Soutpansberg and Venda. Community development through tourism.
Saddles Horse Trails, based at the Lalapanzi Hotel 28 km south of Makhado on the N1, T072-5165455. Horse trails in the Soutpansberg Mountain, suitable for novices, overnight at bush camps, swim bareback with the horses.

⊖ Transport

Bela-Bela *p665*
Train
Spoornet, Central reservations T0860-008888, www.spoornet.co.za. Trains run between **Johannesburg** and **Musina** (11 hrs) via Polokwane and Makhado.

Modimolle and around *p665*
Bus
Greyhound, T083-9159000, www.greyhound.co.za. Coaches depart from the Engen Garage for **Bulawayo** and **Harare** (Zimbabwe); **Pretoria** (2 hrs) and **Johannesburg** (3 hrs).

Mokopane *p666, map p667*
Bus
Greyhound runs coaches to **Bulawayo** and **Harare** (Zimbabwe) and **Johannesburg**. **Translux** runs coaches to **Bulawayo** and **Harare** (Zimbabwe), **Johannesburg** and **Pretoria** (3 hrs).

Bus companies Greyhound, T083-9159000, www.greyhound.co.za. **Translux**, T0861-589282, www.translux.co.za.

Train

T086-000888, www.spoornet.co.za. Trains run between **Johannesburg** and **Musina** via Polokwane and Makhado.

Polokwane *p668, map p668*
Air

Gateway Airport is 5 km north of the city centre off the N1, information T015-2880122. **SAA**, T011-9781111, www.flysaa.com, operate daily flights between Polokwane and **Johannesburg**.

Bus

Greyhound coaches depart from Shell Ultra City on the outskirts of town, to **Bulawayo**, **Harare** (Zimbabwe), **Pretoria** and **Johannesburg**. **Translux** coaches depart from Thabo Mbeki St, to **Bulawayo**, **Harare**, **Pretoria** and **Johannesburg** (4 hrs).

 Bus companies Greyhound, T083-9159000, www.greyhound.co.za. **Translux**, T0861-589282, www.translux.co.za.

Car hire

The following companies are located at Gateway Airport. **Budget** T015-2880169; **Hertz** T015-2889900; **Imperial** T015-2880097.

Train

Spoornet, T086-000888, www.spoornet.co.za, runs trains to **Johannesburg** and **Musina**.

Makhado/Louis Trichardt and the Soutpansberg *p670, map p671*
Bus

Coaches depart from Safari Motors, Caltex garage in Baobab St close to the tourist office. **Greyhound** runs coaches to **Bulawayo**, **Harare** (Zimbabwe), **Pretoria** (5½ hrs) and **Johannesburg** (6½ hrs). **Translux** runs coaches to **Bulawayo**, **Harare**, **Pretoria** (5 hrs) and **Johannesburg** (6 hrs).

 Bus companies Greyhound, T083-9159000, www.greyhound.co.za. **Translux**, T0861-589282, www.translux.co.za.

Train

Spoornet, T086-0008888, www.spoor net.co.za. Trains to **Musina** and **Johannesburg** (11 hrs).

Musina *p673*
Bus

Greyhound runs coaches to **Bulawayo**, **Harare** (Zimbabwe), **Pretoria** (7 hrs) and **Johannesburg** (8 hrs). **Translux** runs coaches to **Bulawayo**, **Harare**, **Pretoria** and **Johannesburg** (7 hrs).

 Bus companies Greyhound, T083-9159000, www.greyhound.co.za. **Translux**, T0861-589282, www.translux.co.za.

Train

T086-0008888, www.spoornet.co.za. Trains to **Johannesburg** via Makhado, Polokwane and Mokopane.

● Directory

Polokwane *p668, map p668*
Internet Vodashop in the Savannah Centre, T015-2963907, Mon-Sat. **Medical services** Medi Clinic, corner of Thabo Mbeki and Burger streets, T015-2903600. **Pharmacy**, daily 0800-2000, T015-2955737.

Makhado/Louis Trichardt and the Soutpansberg *p670, map p670*
Banks Standard, ABSA and First National are on Krogh St, at Nos 93, 98 and 295.

Musina *p673*
Banks First National, Main Rd. Standard, corner of Main Rd and Emery St. **Bureau de change**, Main Rd next to the PO, T015-5343412, daily 0700-1700. There are also bureaux de change at the service station just before the Zimbabwe border. **Medical services** Medical Centre, T015-5340557.

East of the Great North Road

→ *Colour map 2, A4.*

While the area north towards Zimbabwe seems largely flat and featureless, venturing off the main north-south route leads to more varied landscapes and interesting sights. This is especially true of the region around the agricultural centre of Tzaneen, surrounded by tea plantations, lush mountains and fruit farms. Turning off the N1 at Polokwane onto the R71 towards Tzaneen, the landscape changes dramatically after around 30 km, from dusty scrubland dotted with acacias and untidy villages, to forest-covered hills. This craggy range, swathed in indigenous forests and peppered with waterfalls and dams, is known as the Magoebaskloof. ▸▸ *For listings, see pages 686-690.*

Ins and outs

Getting there and around The best way of exploring the area is by car; there is no public transport in the region. SA Airlink flies between Johannesburg and **Phalaborwa Kruger Park Gateway Airport**, T015-7815823, on the edge of Phalaborwa, 2 km from the entrance to Kruger National Park. ▸▸ *For further details, see Transport, page 690.*

The Magoebaskloof ●●❶❸ ▸▸ *pp686-690. Colour map 2, B4.*

→ *Phone code: 015.*

One of the best times of the year to explore this mountainous area is in spring, when the tropical valleys burst into a riot of colour. The area is best known for its cherry blossoms, and a small cherry blossom festival takes place here every year. The valleys are also famed for their orchids (over 200 species have been recorded here), and during December and January you can see bright pink and mauve 'pride of India' trees. Many of the country hotels in the area get fully booked at this time of year, as this is the most popular time for walking. Birdlife is prolific and includes knysna and purple crested louries, several species of eagle, and the rare black-fronted bush shrike. The lower slopes are cultivated with tea and banana plantations and gum tree forests, creating the effect of a rolling green patchwork quilt.

Before the region was peacefully settled, it witnessed a bloody feud between the Transvaal government and the Tlou tribe of the chief Makgoba. In 1894 the followers of Makgoba retreated into the forests refusing to pay government taxes. The European soldiers were unable to dislodge the force and it took a group of Swazi warriors, working for the government, to defeat Makgoba. The warriors beheaded Makgoba to prove to the government that they had killed him, and the mountains were named after him.

Towards Tzaneen

The small village of **Haenertsburg** is the principal centre at the western end of the mountains. There are a handful of tea gardens and craft shops in town, and Market Square is dominated by a display of over 400 species of trees from each of the five continents laid out in five rings, much like the Olympic Games logo. Information and accommodation bookings are available from **Magoebaskloof Tourism** ① *Rissik St, behind the Atholl Arms, T015-2764972, www.magoebaskloof.com, Mon-Fri 0800-1700, Sat and Sun 0830-1200.* From Haenertsburg you are faced with the choice of two possible routes to Tzaneen. The R71 continues past Ebenezer Dam and winds through the beautiful, forested

Magoebaskloof Valley; the other option is to follow the R528 along the less scenic George's Valley.

Magoebaskloof Hiking Trail

The Magoebaskloof Hiking Trail has a variety of sections, ranging from two- to five-day hikes, with six huts for overnighting. The trail is considered tough and should only be attempted by seasoned hikers. Permits must be obtained from **Komatiland** Forestry ⓘ *T013-7542724, www.komatiecotourism.co.za*, a subsidiary of the Forestry Department (SAFCOL), as each section has restrictions on the minimum and a maximum number of hikers. The website has detailed trail information, with information on overnight huts.

Tzaneen and around ⊖❷❸❶ ›› *pp686-690. Colour map 2, A/B4.*

→ *Phone code: 015.*

Tzaneen lies at the centre of a prosperous agricultural region on the eastern side of the Magoebaskloof Mountains. After the scrubby dryness of surrounding areas, this region seems gloriously green and fertile, with verdant banana plantations and sweet-smelling orange groves creating a tropical setting. Although the town itself is little more than a busy grid of chain stores and petrol stations ringed by quiet suburbs, the abundance of the area's soil is apparent in the numerous stalls selling tropical fruits – this is, in fact, South Africa's biggest producer of avocados, mangoes and tomatoes. **Limpopo Tourism and Parks Board** ⓘ *T051-3073582, www.golimpopo.com, Mon-Fri 0800-1700*, is on the R71, on the right-hand side as you approach town from the Phalaborwa and Kruger National Park. It's a very helpful office with a wealth of information on the area.

Background

Although it is now the largest town in Limpopo after Polokwane, Tzaneen is a relatively young town, which only became a permanent settlement when the Selati Railway arrived in 1912. There are several versions of how the town was named. One theory suggests that the name comes from the very old Bantu word, *Tsaneng*, used to refer to the people in this area. The change in spelling is explained by the first German settlers transcribing the sound 'ts' as 'tz' when they wrote down the Bantu word.

Sights

Do not be deceived by its unassuming appearance, the **Tzaneen Museum** ⓘ *Agatha St, T015-3072425, Mon-Fri 0900-1600 (donate generously for the upkeep of the building)*, is one of the best provincial museums in South Africa and deserves far greater recognition and resources. The displays are a private collection of ethnological artefacts put together by Jurgen Witt. Crammed into three small rooms is an impressive and absorbing selection of pottery, carvings, drums and beadwork from the regional Tsonga and Venda peoples. The enthusiastic staff lead visitors around the displays, explaining certain items and providing a fascinating overview of this priceless muddle of a collection.

Modjadji Cycad Reserve → *Colour map 2, A4.*

ⓘ *32 km north of Tzaneen on the R36, daily 0830-1600, R20 per car, R10 per person.*

Modjadji Cycad Reserve is the home of the Rain Queen, the hereditary female monarch of the Lobedu people, who has reigned since the 16th century. The last queen, the sixth

Queen Makobo, died of AIDS in June 2005 at the age of 27. Traditionally the Rain Queen never marries, and her sexual partners are chosen by the Royal Council so that all of her children will have blue blood. Because Makobo's daughter, who was only born in 2005, was fathered by a commoner, the traditionalists are not likely to accept her as the rightful heiress to the Rain Queen crown. Consequently there are worries that the 400-year-old Rain Queen dynasty may be coming to an end. No new Rain Queen has been chosen since Makobo died. That aside, the position of Rain Queen remains of huge importance in the area. Legend maintains that she has the power to produce rain, which is traditionally very important in this fertile region. Her powers seem to have had considerable success: the 12,000 cycads in the reserve stand at over 13 m high (normal growth in other areas is around 5-8 m tall). This particular species of fern, *Encephalartos transvenosus*, is thought to be billions of years old and has been protected for four centuries by the Modjadji Rain Queen. The reserve at the top of a steep hill protects these plants and surrounds the royal village. There are a few trails within the reserve, a picnic site and an information centre.

Magoebaskloof & Tzaneen

Sleeping
Cheerio Trout Fishing Lodge **2**
Coach House &
  Zeederburg Restaurant **3**

Glenshiel **5**
Magoebaskloof **1**
Magoebaskloof Ruskamp **6**
Tzaneen Country Lodge **4**

Hans Merensky Nature Reserve → *Colour map 2, A4.*
ⓘ *68 km east of Tzaneen, on the R529 towards Giyani, T015-2889000, R10.*

Hans Merensky Nature Reserve is on the southern banks of the Great Letaba River and was founded in 1954 to protect various species of lowveld antelope, in particular roan and sable. The natural vegetation is described as mopane lowveld and there is a chance of viewing giraffe, bushbuck, zebra, impala, duiker, impala, tsessebe and blue wildebeest. There are leopard but they remain elusive. There are four species of poisonous snake in the reserve: puff adder, Mozambique spitting cobra, black mamba and boomslang. There's a 32-km network of roads. Most people visit here while staying at the Eiland Resort (see Sleeping, page 687), which is in the reserve.

Sunland Nursery
ⓘ *68 km north of Tzaneen, just off the R526, signposted off the main road, T015-3099039, www.bigbaobabco.za.*

The Sunland Nursery is home to what claims to the world's largest boabab tree, with an impressive 46.8 m circumference. It is said to be over 6000 years old, and the owners have built a bar into the hollow areas in part of the trunk and reputedly it can hold 60 people. A couple of self-catering chalets and quadbikes are for hire.

East of Tzaneen ☺▲☺◐ ▸▸ *pp686-690.*

There are two possible routes east and south of Tzaneen: the R71 leads to Gravelotte, Phalaborwa (111 km) and the entrance to Kruger National Park at Phalaborwa Gate; the R36 heads south towards Hoedspruit (120 km), the Drakensberg escarpment and Kruger's Orpen Gate. Both routes pass through the region known as the **Valley of the Olifants**, an area filled with private game reserves providing an attractively wild drive if you're passing through. If not entering Kruger, the route continues to the **Blyde River Canyon** in Mpumalanga, see page 652.

Phalaborwa → *Phone code: 015. Colour map 2, B5. Altitude: 450 m.*

This quiet Afrikaner town is only 2 km from Kruger's Phalaborwa Gate and is a convenient base from which to visit Kruger, although it's a rather dull choice compared to the reserves and camps nearby. South Africa's Amarula cream liqueur is distilled here, and you can visit the **distillery** ⓘ *T015-7817766, www.amarula.com, Mon-Fri 0900-1600, Sat 0900-1200,* for tasting and tours. It's a young town, established since 1958, when open-cast mining for minerals and copper began here. The mine is considered to be the widest man-made hole in Africa at almost 2 km wide and 890 m deep. It currently produces some 28,000 tons of copper ore daily. Information is available from the **Phalaborwa Tourism Centre** ⓘ *Hendrick van Eck St, near the Spar, T015-7813620, www.phalaborwa.org.za.*

Hoedspruit and around ☺❶◐☺ ▸▸ *pp686-690. Colour map 2, B5.*
→ *Phone code: 015.*

Hoedspruit is Afrikaans for 'hat creek', and the place acquired its name when, after a long trek over the mountains into the heat of the Lowveld, one of the Voortrekkers removed his hat, threw it into the cool waters of the Sandspruit River and decided to stay. Today, the town has barely expanded beyond its string of shops, banks and petrol station, and remains a sleepy outpost surrounded by game-rich country, loomed over by the Drakensberg escarpment. At the very south of Limpopo in the lowveld region, Hoedspruit is close to both the private game reserves around Kruger (see page 637), and the Panorama region of Mpumalanga (see pages 646-660). There is little of interest to keep you in town itself; the main attractions and accommodation options are along the R531 towards Blyde River Canyon.

Bombyx Mori Silk Farm

① *23 km south of Hoedspruit on the R531, T015-795556, www.silkcompany.co.za. Mon-Sat 0900-1600, Sun in summer only 1100-1400; 5 daily tours. R20.*

Skilled women weavers from the local community show visitors the intricate methods of commercial silk farming and weaving at this farm. The cultivated silk, a soft creamy colour, is produced from the cocoons of the Bombyx Mori silkworm, and the farm shop sells a wide range of products: silk scarves, blankets, silk-filled duvets and cushions, and there is a kiosk and tea garden.

Hoedspruit Endangered Species Centre

① *23 km south of Hoedspruit on the R531, T015-7931633, www.wildlifecentre.co.za. Daily 0800-1700; 2-hr tours depart hourly 0800-1600. R100, elephant riding R900. Curio shop and tea garden.*

This project conducts essential research on endangered species, in particular cheetah. There are daily standard tours lasting two hours, which begin with an informative video about the plight of endangered species, before viewing cheetah, African wild dog, ground hornbills, and the 'vulture restaurant', where wild vultures come to feed. Around 80 cheetah can be seen. The extended tour, which runs twice daily for three hours, also includes a visit to a breeding and rehabilitation camp for rhino and the rare Barbary lion. Booking is advised for both tours as many local school groups visit the centre. The new activity here is elephant riding, and there are 13 elephants on the adjacent Kapama Game Reserve.

Moholoholo Rehabilitation Centre

① *T015-7955236, www.moholoholo.co.za. Mon-Sat 0930 and 1500. R80.*

Moholoholo is a rehabilitation centre for abandoned, injured and poisoned wildlife. Animals are brought here from all over South Africa and, once healthy enough, are reintroduced into their natural environment. There are a number of big birds such as raptors and vultures, many of which are injured from flying into power lines. Another important function of the centre is breeding and they have successfully bred and released into the wild the endangered crowned eagle, serval and many other species.

Khamai Reptile Park

① *33 km south of Hoedspruit on the R531, T015-7955203. Daily 0800-1700. R25.*

This impressive reptile park was established 25 years ago by Donald Strydom, one of Africa's leading snake specialists, as a refuge and platform for understanding reptiles. There are numerous enclosures holding a wide variety of snakes, lizards, tortoises and crocodiles, and Donald's staff provide a good understanding of how many snakes are needlessly killed by farmers in South Africa. For an extra fee you can have a photo taken with a python wrapped over your shoulders. The park also offers a free service to people with phobias of snakes and spiders.

⊙ East of the Great North Road listings

⊙ Sleeping

Magoebaskloof *p681, map p683*
There is a range of accommodation options in the 2 valleys; if you are not staying in the more expensive hotels they are still worth visiting for lunch or afternoon tea.
A Glenshiel, 2 km from Haenertsburg on the R71, T015-2764335, www.glenshiel.co.za. 15 luxury suites in a country lodge, each with an open fireplace and TV. The lodge is well known for its excellent cuisine. Tennis, swimming pool, trout fishing, delightful gardens, walking trails, good service. Worth trying to bargain on the price out of season.
B Magoebaskloof Hotel, off the R71, approximately 26 km from Tzaneen, T015-2765400, www.magoebaskloof.co.za. Recently rebuilt leisure hotel with range of self-catering units, double rooms and family rooms, all with en suite bathroom, disabled access, and some with fabulous valley views. À la carte restaurant and café, pub showing big-screen sport, squash, swimming and the Samango monkey project, with viewing platforms to watch the monkeys in their natural habitat. Popular with weekending groups from Gauteng. Wide choice of walks available from here.
B-C Cheerio Trout Fishing Lodge, at the Cheerio Nursery off the R71, T015-2761804, www.cheerio.co.za. Self-catering chalets or B&B in pretty rondavels, sleeping 2-5. Swimming pool and tennis court. Perfect setting with fine views across the valley. Trout fishing offered in 3 dams. The nursery here is the site of the annual cherry blossom festival.

D Magoebaskloof Ruskamp, 25 km from Tzaneen on the R71, T015-3054142, www.magoebaskloofruskamp.co.za. Long-established resort with a cluster of 27 rondavels perched high up on the R71 where it climbs over a winding pass; gets a bit chilly at night. Self-catering or smaller B&B units, TV, heater, pool, sub-tropical gardens, good restaurant with a fantastic terrace overlooking the valley, but availability on the menu a bit hit and miss depending on how many people are staying.

Tzaneen *p682*
Most of the accommodation options are around Tzaneen, on the road from Phalaborwa.
AL Coach House, T015-3068000, www.coachhouse.co.za. Hidden away in the forests south of Tzaneen, close to the Agatha Forest Reserve, delightful country hotel with mountain views and colourful gardens with a swimming pool, beauty spa on site. 39 cosy bedrooms with en suite bathrooms, DSTV, and little touches like mohair blankets on the beds and home-made biscuits and fruit laid out each day. Some have log fires. Much of the fresh produce served in the restaurant is grown within the grounds, and it is possible to hire mountain bikes or walk on marked trails in the forest straight from the hotel. Excellent restaurant and they have a dedicated kitchen for making nougat, biscuits and brittle (www.nougat.co.za).
B Tzaneen Country Lodge, 17 km from Tzaneen on the R71 from Phalaborwa, T015-3043290, www.tznlodge.co.za. 25 a/c functional rooms, DSTV, bar, large, pretty gardens. Facilities include the Earth Spa that offers treatment/accommodation packages, farmyard with animals that kids can stroke, outside restaurant that serves pub lunches and good pancakes, plus fancier evening meals. Popular wedding venue.

Hans Merensky Nature Reserve *p684*

C-F Eiland Spa & Eco Park, Hans Merensky
Nature Reserve, 68 km east of Tzaneen
T015-3868000, www.eiland.co.za.This a
huge resort with 103 self-catering a/c
thatched rondavels with TV, sleeping 2-6,
250-stand caravan and camping park with
electric points, restaurant, bar, swimming
pool, sauna, mineral pools, horse riding,
water park, beauty spa, gym, mini-golf,
and tennis. Full-on family resort with
entertainment programs, aimed at the
local market and overrun in school holidays.

Phalaborwa *p684*

Being so close to Kruger, this town has a wide
range of accommodation options, although
it's still preferable to stay closer to the wildlife
in the park

A Hans Merensky Estate, just out of town, at
the Kruger end, off Koper Rd, T015-7813931,
www.hansmerensky.com. Marketed as a golf
and wildlife resort, with 30 self-catering a/c
chalets in a long, low, thatched building
overlooking a golf course where game
from Kruger casually wanders around, and
14 hotel rooms surrounding the swimming
pool. Clubhouse has a restaurant and bar.
A Tulani Safari Lodge, on the R40 to Mica,
T015-7815414, www.tulanisafarilodge.co.za.
Set in the Balule Nature Reserve on the
western border of Kruger. 37 chalets with mix
of ethnic and modern decor, a/c, restaurant,
bar, swimming pool, tennis, hiking trails,
open bush drives into Kruger. Rates
include breakfast and dinner.
B Ingwe Park, 3 km out of town on the
Tzaneen road, T015-7813776, www.ingwe
park.com. This relaxed and fun bush lodge
is set in a restored old miners' camp with
comfortable, self-contained bungalows,
each with TV and kitchen. Swimming pool,
hiking and day tours into Kruger.
B Sefapane Lodge, corner of Copper
and Essenhout streets, T015-7806700,
www.sefapane.co.za. 31 upmarket, thatched,
self-catering chalets in a large indigenous
garden. Braai boma, restaurant, swimming

pool with a sunken bar. They have a 'meet
and greet' desk at the airport, fly-in packages
available, day trips to Kruger and other
regional tours. If you don't have a car this is
a good mid-range option. Also offers beach
time in Mozambique, check out the website
for packages.
C Steyn's Cottage, 67 Bosvlier St,
T015-7810836, steyncot@lantic.net. 15 a/c
double rooms with en suite bathroom, TV,
elegant lounge filled with fine antiques,
rooms overlook a neat garden and
swimming pool, excellent service, one
of the best mid-range options. The **La
Werna** restaurant is next door.
C-D Raintree Cottage, 1 Essenhout St,
T015-7810995, www.raintreecottage.co.za.
8 a/c en suite rooms with attractive
Victorian-style decor and TV. B&B with
attached tea garden, swimming pool,
close to park gates, evening meals on
request, friendly hosts.
D Daan & Zena, 15 Birkenhead St,
T015-7816049, www.daanzena.co.za.
21 funky units, individually decorated en suite
double rooms, self-catering units and budget
rooms all decorated with whacky furniture
and bright colours, with M-Net TV, a/c and
tea- and coffee-making facilities. Swimming
pool, colourful lounge, secure parking.
Friendly set-up. Recommended.
D-F Elephant Walk, 30 Anna Scheepers Av,
T015-7815860, www.accommodation
phalaborwa.com. A welcome backpacker
place close to Kruger Park which also offers
good-value game-viewing trips into Kruger
Park. Choice of 10-bed dorm, 4 attractive en
suite B&B double rooms, or camping in the
shady garden with separate ablution block.
Fully equipped kitchen, laundry, meals on
request, braai, swimming pool.
D-F Lantana Lodge, corner of Kiaat and
Hall streets, T015-7815191, lantanalodge@
intekom.co.za. Well-appointed self-catering
units with, a/c, DSTV, plus small, cheaper log
cabins aimed at backpackers. Also has
camping space. Good restaurant, garden bar,
swimming pool. Can arrange tours of Kruger.

Hoedspruit *p684*

The accommodation listed below is at the bottom of Blyde River Canyon close to Hoedspruit. For accommodation at the top of the canyon, refer to the Mpumalanga chapter, page 656. All are situated within 1 hr's drive of Kruger's Orpen Gate.

A-D Moholoholo Mountain View Camp, from Hoedspruit, turn off the R531 towards the bottom of the Blyde River Canyon Nature Reserve, opposite **Blyde River Canyon Lodge**, T/F015-7955684, www.moholoholo.co.za. A 4000-ha private reserve with wild lion, rhino and hippo and a range of accommodation to suit most budgets. 19 simple, reed-wall, self-catering chalets, dining boma over-looks a waterhole, or 10 upmarket thatched chalets where the price includes all meals and game activities. Game walks with a ranger, night drives, an educational bush experience.

B Blyde River Canyon Lodge, 28 km from Hoedspruit, turn off the R531 towards the bottom of the Blyde River Canyon Nature Reserve and **Aventura Swadini**, T015-7955305, www.blyderivercanyonlodge.com. A very intimate and individual lodge, 6 double thatched rooms with verandas, bar, pool, excellent cuisine. The building is constructed from natural materials, beautiful grounds, which the owners have gone to great lengths to keep totally indigenous, zebra, warthog, and a blue wildebeest wander across the lawns and through the car park. Recommended.

C Blue Cottages Country House, 37 km from Hoedspruit on the R527 towards Blyde River Canyon, T015-7955114, www.countryhouse.co.za. 5 bungalows and 2 suites, set in a beautiful bush garden, swimming pool, each unit is decorated with unique pieces of artwork and African antiques from the attached **Monsoon Gallery**, home-cooked breakfast and dinner is served on the verandas. The owner, has been instrumental in promoting the lowveld and central Kruger region as a world-recognized biosphere. Recommended.

C-E Forever Resorts Swadini, at the very base of Blyde River Canyon off the R531, adjacent to the Blyde River Nature Reserve and dam, T015-7955141, www.forever sa.co.za. Award-winning resort in a stunning location. 78 chalets, 180 camping/caravan stands, shops, restaurants, swimming pools, tennis, mini-golf, lots of hikes and a pleasant drive to viewpoints in the reserve, boat rides on the dam. As the crow flies, there is another Forever Resort, **Blyde Canyon** only a few kilometres away at the top of the canyon (see the Blyde River Canyon section in the Mpumalanga chapter), but they are actually over 100 km apart by road.

❶ Eating

Magoebaskloof *p681, map p683*

🍴 **Iron Crown Pub and Grill**, in front of the tourist office in Haenertsburg on Rissik St, T015-2764755. Tue-Sat 1000-late, Sun 0900-1500. Friendly, atmospheric pub, big-screen TV for sports, hearty country fare, good steaks and sauces, schnitzels and fish and chips, Sun set lunch.

🍴 **Picasso's**, a prominent wood cabin just off the main road through Haenertsburg, T015-2764724, closes at 1630. Comfortable restaurant and curio shop with a good choice of light meals. The pancakes are a speciality, but also on offer are more substantial dishes like beef stew or chicken casserole. Great local grilled trout, too. Resident African grey parrot. Internet access.

🍴 **Pot & Plow**, 8 km out of town on the Tzaneen Rd. Closed evenings. Popular roadside restaurant and bar, good for lunch, decent home-made pies and tasty salads, also sells a few curios and home-made preserves.

Tzaneen *p682, map p*

The town features the usual steakhouse chains such as **Spur** and **Steers**. The best restaurants are in the country hotels, and during the day there are a number of roadside tea gardens which serve snack lunches.

Zeederburg, The Coach House, T015-3068000, 14 km from town. 1230-1400, 1930-2100. One of the finest restaurants in the region set in this top-class lodge. Colonial decor, professional service. Good local produce, including smoked trout, and delicious mains, plus some decent veggie options. Huge wine list, laden dessert trolley and famous for their home-made nougat.

Ashley's Cafe, 30 Agatha St, T015-3077270. Mon-Sat 0730-2100, Sun lunch only. Best restaurant in town, offering great breakfasts, coffees, salads and sandwiches at lunchtime, and larger meals in the evenings, including a good pepper-crusted fillet steak, plus a decent cocktail menu. Pleasant balcony overlooking gardens.

Letaba Junction, 28 km from Tzaneen on the R71 to Gravelotte, just before Letsitele, T015-2451693. Mon-Sat 1000-late. Country restaurant decorated with local art with a pub and deck overlooking the Letaba River which is home to hippo and crocodile. Grills, fish, seafood, large portions, attached gift shop, a popular wedding venue.

Phalaborwa p684

La Werna, 67 Busvlier St, T015-7810836. The best restaurant in town is this smart diner next to **Steyn's Cottage**. Meals are served by candlelight. There's an enjoyable selection of meat and poultry dishes, plus good local ingredients like trout. Beautifully decorated intimate dining room, booking advised. Recommended.

Sefepane Lodge, Copper Rd, T015-7806700. Daily until 2100. Smart lodge restaurant with indoor ethnic dining room and pleasant outdoor boma lit by lanterns and candles. Good South African fare such as lamb *potjies* or bobotie, plus venison specials such as springbok. The boma is popular with tour groups; buffets served.

Hoedspruit p684

Mad Dogz Café, on the R527, east of the junction of the R527 and R36, T015-7955425, by the entrance for the **Blue Cottages** on the main road. Open 0730-1630. The food here is some of the best you'll find in the region, and this makes for a great lunchtime stop-off en route to Kruger National Park. Big, wholesome breakfasts, excellent lunches using fusion dishes, Creole chicken, spicy Thai beef and Cape Malay bobotie. The setting is lovely, with brightly painted tables clustered under thatched roofs, surrounded by lush tropical vegetation. Recommended.

The Trading Post, 26 km from Hoedspruit via Klaserie on the R531, T015-7955219, tradingpost@mweb.co.za. 0800-late. An attractive and unusual restaurant and pub owned by a friendly ex-game ranger and his French wife. A happy combination of the traditional South African way of cooking and the French social way of eating. Each table has an built-in gas braai, and you cook your meat to your liking. Game platters including strips of warthog and crocodile meat are available, as are ready-prepared meat dishes, salads, and pizzas

The Cotton Club, 23 km from Hoedspruit on the R531, at the Bombyz Mori Silk Farm, T015-7955682. Open 0800-1630. Set in an attractive thatched building in landscaped gardens, serves light meals such as sandwiches, salads and quiches, main courses include ostrich kebabs, pies and burgers, or opt for tea and cake in the afternoon.

☻ Festivals and events

Magoebaskloof p681, map p683
Sep The **Spring Cherry and Azalea Blossom Festival**, **Craft Fair** and **Orchid Exhibition** take place around Haenertsburg. The flowers transform entire valleys into blankets of colour.

O Shopping

Hoedspruit p684
Monsoon Gallery, next door to the **Mad Dogz Café** (see above), www.mansoon gallery.com. Tasteful gallery selling fine African art, jewellery, cloth and antiques, plus some contemporary pieces. All the packing and shipping can be arranged from here. There is also a shop here selling items produced at the **Bombyx Mori Silk Farm** (see page 685).

▲ Activities and tours

Phalaborwa p684
Golf
Hans Merensky Country Club, T015-7813931, www.hansmerensky.com. Based around an 18-hole PGA championship golf course. Golfers negotiate wildlife on the greens while they play; watch out for the hippos on the 17th hole. Also has accommodation. Call in advance. The best times early morning or late afternoon.

Tour operators
Jumbo River Safaris, T015-7816168, www.riversafaris.co.za. Organizes a fun 3-hr boat trip on the Olifants River for ever-popular sundowners. Always a good chance of seeing game and colourful water birds. Also arranges longer Kruger safaris.

⊖ Transport

Phalaborwa p684
Air
Phalaborwa Kruger Park Gateway Airport, 2 km from town centre and entrance to Kruger Park, T015-7815823, has a fabulous design. The baggage reclaim is under a thatched roof, the seats in the waiting area are rocks and the drinking fountain spouts from a tree stump. **SAA**, T011-9781111, www.flysaa.com, operates daily flights between Phalaborwa and **Johannesburg** (1 hr).

Car hire
Budget T015-7815404, www.budget.co.za, and **Imperial** T015-7810376, www.imperial carrental.co.za, are at the airport.

Hoedspruit p684
Air
Eastgate Airport is 7 km from Hoedspruit on the road to the Timbavati Game Reserve, T015-7933681. **SAA**, T011-9781111, www.flysaa.com, operates daily flights between Eastgate and **Johannesburg** (1 hr 15 min). It is also used by charter companies for guest of the luxury lodges in private reserves.

❶ Directory

Tzaneen p682
Internet Procom Internet Café, 18 Peace St, T015-3074836, a short distance from the commercial centre; follow the one-way street towards the swimming pool, Mon-Sat. **Medical services** Chemist, T015-3073790. Medi Clinic, Wolkberg Av, T015-3068500, www.tzaneenmc.co.za.

Phalaborwa p684
Internet Net-o-Mania, T015-7817812, Phalaborwa Mall, Palm St, not open evenings or Sun. **Medical services** Chemist, 24-hr, T015-7811805. **Hospital**, Grosvenor Cres, T015-7853511.

Contents

Footprint features

North West Province

At a glance

⊜ **Getting around** Buses on major routes, car hire, tours start and finish in Johannesburg.

◉ **Time required** 2-5 days for major sights.

☀ **Weather** Mostly dry, sunny and hot, chilly nights in winter.

✕ **When not to go** Avoid Sun City on public holidays.

★ **Don't miss...**

1 Mafikeng Museum, page 696.

2 Spot the Big Five in Madikwe, page 697.

3 Magaliesberg Mountains, pages 707 and 708.

4 Sun City, page 709.

5 Animal spotting in Pilanesberg National Park, page 710.

North West Province is known first and foremost (for better or worse) as the home of Sun City, a huge entertainment complex and one-time gambling haven which was once the most visited site in South Africa. It remains hugely popular, and is the most likely reason for visitors to venture into this dry and stark state.

Much of North West Province is visually unremarkable, made up of flat Kalahari grasslands and dotted with lonely farming communities which were some of the most important agricultural centres in the 19th century. This was once the Western Transvaal, one of the areas where the Voortrekkers settled at the end of the Great Trek, and towns such as Mafikeng and Rustenburg have a fascinating history.

Gambling and history aside, the best reason for visiting is the region's excellent game parks, all at a malaria-free altitude of 1000-2000 m. The well-publicized Pilanesberg National Park is easily accessible, lying incongruously close to Sun City, while Madikwe Game Reserve is one of the finest parks in the country, offering excellent accommodation and the chance of seeing the Big Five just a few hours from Johannesburg and Pretoria.

A more low-key attraction and a big draw for locals are the Magaliesberg Mountains, less than one hour's drive from Pretoria. Although made up by a fairly bland series of bush-covered hills, they are filled with wild hiking trails and dotted with comfortable holiday resorts. Further west are numerous private game farms, which provide an insight into life in the bushveld on the edge of the Kalahari.

Ins and outs

Getting around

The North West Province can really only be visited by car. Public transport is virtually non-existent and very few mainline buses run services to this region. Driving, however, isn't a terribly pleasant experience and involves covering long distances through isolated farmland. Plan journeys so that you arrive at your destination before dark as goats, cows, stray dogs and antelope are a hazard on the roads at night, and be careful not to fall asleep at the wheel. It's also a good idea to fill up with petrol whenever you can, as there are some big distances between service stations. Be sure to carry a mobile phone in case of breakdown. The emergency number from mobiles is 112.

Tourist Information

North West Parks and Tourism Board ⓘ *Heritage House, Cookes Lake, 30/31 Nelson Mandela Dr, Mafikeng, T018-3971500, Mon-Fri 0800-1640, www.tourismnorthwest.co.za,* is responsible for promoting tourism throughout the province. Contact them in advance for maps and useful brochures they have on the little-known parks.

Western region

The western region of the province is a largely empty expanse of rough scrub given over to huge game farms and remote hamlets. This empty corner of South Africa holds little of interest, and the arrival of visitors can stir up quite a bit of interest amongst the sleepy inhabitants of the ancient farming communities dotted around the region. Most visitors to the area are actually just passing through en route to Botswana, where things liven up again over the border. The largest settlement of note is scruffy Mmabatho, a modern and featureless town, and neighbouring Mafikeng, which despite having a chequered history doesn't warrant much distraction. The highlight of this region is undoubtedly the Mudikwe Game Reserve, one of South Africa's best-kept secrets. ▸▸ *For listings, see pages 700-702.*

Mafikeng and Mmabatho ⊜❼⊙⊜ ▸▸ *pp700-702. Colour map 1, B6.*

Mmabatho is a modern town created in 1977. Before the free elections were held in South Africa and the new political boundaries came into effect, **Mafikeng** was in the old Western Transvaal and Mmabatho was the capital of the homeland known as Bophuthatswana and was the site of several government buildings. When the North West Province was created, it was decided to keep Mmabatho on as the regional capital. However, there has been a gradual shift of power back to the principal town in the region, Rustenburg. Mmabatho remains a relatively modern and rather garish concrete sprawl, and although the majority of government offices are still here there remains an air of artificiality and incompleteness. Dusty open ground between isolated buildings waits for the city to grow around it, and the poverty of the former homeland of Bophuthatswana remains evident. The whole town is dominated by a sports stadium of Olympic proportions that seats 70,000, which is in itself quite an impressive architectural specimen. Its other claim to fame, rather bizarrely, is that of being home to a state-of-the-art recording studio where the soundtrack to *The Lion King* was recorded. But the most likely reason for visiting here is to have a quick look around the historic town of

Mafikeng, another hot and dusty commercial centre on the highveld, but one with an interesting early history, and plenty of buildings that help tell its story. Having said that, neither town warrant a specific journey, and they act mainly as stop-off points to the Ramatlabama border of Botswana, 25 km away.

Ins and outs → *Phone code: 018. Altitude 1278 m.*
Getting around There are regular minibus taxis running between Mafikeng railway station and **Mega City** shopping centre in Mmabatho.

Tourist information There are several different sources of tourist information in the two towns. For local and regional information call in at the **North West Parks and Tourism Board** ① *Heritage House, Cookes Lake, 30/31 Nelson Mandela Dr, Mafikeng, T018-3971500, Mon-Fri 0800-1640, www.tourismnorthwest.co.za* The Mafikeng Museum (see page 696) is also a useful source of information.

Background
Mafikeng was founded as a British administrative centre in 1885, when Sir Charles Warren was sent with a military force to occupy and bring peace to this frontier territory. Only 20 km away was the Goshen Republic, an independent state created by a group of European mercenaries who had been given farms by the local Rolong tribe. The name of the new settlement came from the Tswana *maFikeng*, 'place of boulders'. The surrounding territory became known as British Bechuanaland, with Mafikeng as the centre for the local farmers, traders and hunters. At the time this was still very much frontier territory, occupied by a rough crowd and policed by the tough Bechuanaland Border Police.

On 14 October 1899, a Boer force under the command of General JP Snyman besieged the town, and so started the period of events that was to put the town on the map. The Siege of Mafeking lasted 217 days until 17 May 1900, when the town was relieved by a combined force of Rhodesian troops from the north and Imperial troops from the south. At the time, the siege captured the imagination of the British public in England – the Anglo-Boer War was the first war to be reported in such detail, with pictures, cartoons and newspaper articles. It was during the siege that the British commander, Colonel RSS Baden-Powell, made his name and conceived the idea for the Boy Scout movement (see box, page 696).

Baden-Powell proved himself to be very competent in organizing the defences, but in later years was criticized for his treatment of the black troops. One of his well-documented ideas was to place life-size dummies in observation posts around the town. The Boer commander, General Cronje believed that he was pinning down a large British force planned for the invasion of the Western Transvaal. Mafeking was, in fact, an insignificant centre but it became an important focal point and when the siege had been lifted, the Boer resolve seemed to weaken and the towns of Ladysmith and Kimberley were relieved soon after.

After the war, Mafikeng returned to the life of a sleepy border town. Up until 1965 it was the centre for the British administration of the Bechuanaland Protectorate. This was a fairly unusual set-up where the government for one state, Bechuanaland, was in fact located in a foreign country, South Africa. In 1965 the government moved to Gaborone and on 30 September 1966 Botswana became an independent republic, led by Sir Seretse Khama. Today the town is the centre for the local cattle industry. Although the relics from the Boer War are interesting, the town does not attract many tourists and is well off the beaten track.

Siege of Mafikeng

During the long days of the seven-month Siege of Mafikeng (which lasted from 13 October 1899 to 17 May 1900), the English schoolboys in this colonial town started to become undisciplined – especially when their school closed because of the daily bombardment of the town by artillery shells. The commander of the town's British forces, Colonel Baden-Powell, whose small force was having difficulty defending the town, had an idea. He organized boys, aged between nine and 15 years, into a disciplined Siege Cadet Corps and put them to non-combat use. Their tasks included carrying supplies and messages between the front line and command posts, delivering post within the town, assisting the aged, and acting as observers for the regular soldiers. They were given uniforms and bicycles, and sport and military drills all played a part in fostering self-discipline and responsibility. Despite the dangers there was only one casualty during the siege among the cadets, that of nine-year-old Frankie Brown, who was killed by an exploding shell; his grave can be seen in Mafikeng cemetery. Baden-Powell went on to found the Boy Scout movement at Brownsea in southern England in 1907. He said of the boys of Mafikeng, "These lads proved by their achievements that, if trusted, boys can be relied upon to act as men when needed."

The impact of the war between Britons and Boers on the majority of the southern African population is also often forgotten. Neither side made much use of African soldiers directly, though a great many were employed (or forced to work) as porters, transport handlers and messengers. Nevertheless, they were inevitably caught up in the war and a great many were killed, either directly or as a result of disease and starvation, and many more had their livelihoods destroyed.

Sights

The **Mafikeng Museum** ① *corner of Martin and Robinson streets, Mafikeng, T018-3816102, Mon-Fri 0800-1600, Sat 0900-1230,* has an excellent series of displays relating to the Siege of Mafeking, as well as some informative exhibits which trace the history of the region along with the culture of the indigenous peoples. **Mafikeng Cemetery** contains the graves of British servicemen, the Town Guard and South African troops. The most prominent grave is that of Andrew Beauchamp-Proctor, South Africa's most highly decorated First World War airman. **Kanon Kopje** is the site of a fort on the southern banks of the Molopo River built during a conflict between the Goshen Republic and the Barolong Boo Tshidi. The fort has been restored along with some cannon and guns and there are panoramic views out over Mafikeng.

The **Mafikeng Game Reserve** ① *T018-3815611, 0700-1800, R15,* lies at the edge of town, though the entrance is 10 km out on the Zeerust road. The reserve, covering 4600 ha of open Kalahari grassland and acacia thorn scrub, contains large populations of plains game, buffalo, and giraffe and is a good place to try and see white rhino. There are various tracks through the reserve, dotted with picnic sites, and the main circuit takes only two hours.

 Minchin's law office on the southwest corner of Market Square was built in 1890 and is where Baden-Powell directed operations from a lookout tower on the roof during the siege.

North of Mmabatho ⚫⚫ ⟩⟩ pp700-702.

Botsalano Game Reserve → Colour map 1, B6.

ⓘ Follow the R52 Ramatlabama border road north from Mmabatho for 30 km (the park is signposted), T018-3862433, Apr-Aug 0800-1700, Sep-Mar 0600-1800, R15, car R5. Hunting is still permitted in the reserve and between Apr and Aug it may well be closed.

Like many of the game reserves in the North West Province, this is a little-known park in beautiful countryside, stocked with a good range of wild animals. The 5800-ha reserve is set in typical Kalahari country – open grasslands with patches of acacia and karee woodlands. It is well known locally for its successful breeding of white rhino. You can also hope to see gemsbok, eland, springbok, steenbok, giraffe, jackal, hartebeest, zebra, kudu, duiker, warthog and impala. Hiking is allowed and there are several waterholes and dams which are ideal spots for game viewing.

Zeerust → Colour map 1, B6. Altitude 1187 m.

Zeerust is a small centre for the local sheep and cattle industry, with little of interest in the town, although it does serve as a useful overnight stop between Gauteng and Gaborone. The commercial centre is along **Church Street**, where you will find banks to change money, supermarkets and snack bars at the 24-hour petrol stations. Among these is a Woolworths with a food hall, a godsend in these remote parts.

Madikwe Game Reserve ⚫ ⟩⟩ pp700-702. Colour map 1, A6.

Madikwe is the fourth largest game reserve in South Africa. Although the reserve lies entirely within South Africa, it is only 35 km from the Botswana capital, Gaborone. The northern limits of the park are marked by the international border, while the southern limits coincide with the Dwarsberg Mountains. Most of the park sits between the main road to Botswana and the Marico River to the east. Covering over 60,000 ha, it has the second largest elephant population and it lies in a malaria-free zone. At present the park is not open to day visitors on a casual basis, but they are allowed into the reserve if they pre-book through one of the lodges for a game drive, which usually includes lunch. For overnight visitors, Madikwe offers excellent accommodation and activities and there are now 21 lodges within the reserve.

🌙 There are fewer cheetah in South Africa than spots on a single animal. Cheetah are found in Madakwi, Pilanesberg and Kruger national parks, some breeding centres and zoos, a number of private game reserves and on farmland mainly in the northern regions of the country.

Ins and outs

Getting there If you are driving from Gauteng, take the N4 west through Magalies, Swartruggens. At Zeerust turn right onto the R49 following signs to Gaborone. After about 100 km, just before the border crossing, turn right onto a sand road for 12 km to the Tau Gate. There are other gates at Derdepoort and Abjaterskop. Visitors should establish entry points before arrival; gates are opened by arrangement for pre-booked visitors. Entrance fees are included in the rates for the lodges. Madikwe Charters ⓘ T011-8054888, www.madikwecharter.com, flies daily to and from the reserve and Johannesburg (50 minutes). The lodges pick up from the Madikwe airstrip. ⟩⟩ For more information visit www.madikwe-game-reserve.co.za.

Best time to visit Most of the rain falls during the summer between November and March. Up to 600 mm is expected in the south, but as you move across the plains northwards, the annual rainfall averages about 100 mm less. In summer it can get very hot during the day – this is not ideal weather for walking. During winter it is dry but gets very cold at night.

Wildlife

One of the great features of the reserve is its diverse geology which has resulted in a broad mix of habitats suitable for a wide range of animals. In the northern part of the reserve the land is a level savannah plain. Running across the middle of the park and, in effect, dividing it in two, is the **Tweedepoort Escarpment**. Above the escarpment is an undulating plateau covered with dense vegetation, a marked contrast to the grasslands below. At the southern edge is a more extensive range of rocky mountains, the **Dwarsberg Range**. These are similar in appearance to the Magaliesberg but have been severely eroded over the years, the highest point being only 1228 m. The final distinct environment is provided by the perennial **Marico River** along the eastern boundary, where an aquatic and well-vegetated environment exists.

When the area was being prepared for inclusion within a game reserve, only a few of the indigenous species had survived the years of hunting and farming, as well as an outbreak of *rinderpest*. Back in 1836 the hunter William Cornwallis came across the first known sable in the Marico Valley and wrote of large herds of elephant and prides of lion

Madikwe Game Reserve

BOTZWANA

To Derdepoort Gate

Wildebeest Kop (1215m)

Dithabaneng (1069m)

To Botswana

Tshwene Tshwene (1328m)

Watertower

Old Mafeking Rd

Airstrip

Tswasa Gate

Wonderboom Gate

Tweedepoort Escarpment

Phiri Koppie (1147m)

Abjaterskop Gate

To Zeerust

Old Mafeking Rd

Molatedi Gate

Dwarsberg Range

N

2 km
2 miles

Sleeping
Etali Safari Lodge **1**
Jaci's Safari Lodge **4**

Jaci's Tree Lodge **5**
Mateya Safari Lodge **2**
Mosetlha Bush Camp **6**

Tau Game Lodge **3**

Crossing into Botswana

The most commonly used border crossings between the North West Province and Botswana is **Pioneer Gate** (24 hours), 56 km northwest of Zeerust, the route most of the haulage trucks take along on the N4 between Pretoria and Gaborone, and part of the Great Kalahari Highway that stretches all the way to Walvis Bay in Namibia. **Tlokweng Gate** (6000-2200), next to Madikwe Game Reserve and 101 km north of Zeerust on the R49, is an alternative crossing and links with Botswana's main A1 highway between Gaborone and Francistown. The **Ramatlabama** (0600-2000) border post is on the R503, 26 km north of Mafikeng, which is more convenient if coming from the Cape or interior of South Africa. Around 70 km west of Mafikeng is the **Makgobistad** border post which, despite being more remote on a minor road, is open 24 hours so is an alternative to Ramatlabama if crossing at night.

Customs and immigration All the borders are easy to cross and formalities at customs and immigration are quick and courteous.

Facilities There are bureaux de change at the border where you can change rand into Botswana pula, as well as small duty-free shops (mostly booze and cigarettes) and a VAT refund desk (see page 55).

Public transport Intercape buses use the Pioneer Gate border post on the service between Pretoria and Gaborone – the Botswana capital is only 102 km north of the border.

Vehicle formalities If you are in a hire car, ensure that you have documentation from the car rental company that allows you to take a car out of South Africa. Botswana is part of the Southern Africa Development Community (SADC) customs agreement so if you are in your own car travelling on a carnet, you do not need to produce your carnet here and won't need to until you reach Zimbabwe or Zambia which are outside SADC. You simply fill out the car's details in a book. On the Botswana side you will have to pay for temporary third-party insurance but this costs very little.

frightening the local farmers. In 1991, Operation Phoenix was launched – one of the largest game translocation programmes in the world. By 1996 more than 10,000 animals from 28 species had been successfully released into the reserve.

Animals now present in the park include elephant, zebra, lion, buffalo, white rhino, spotted hyena, wild dog, steenbok, duiker, kudu, leopard and cheetah. Visitors are able to view these animals during game drives or on morning walks with a guide and experienced tracker. A special feature of the reserve is the introduction of community projects, which is allowing local communities to benefit from, and contribute to, the ecological management of the reserve. Another project planned for the future is the development of the Heritage Park conservation corridor that will join Madikwe with Pilanesberg. This proposed conservation estate will allow greater migration for the animals, creating a prime ecotourism destination. It's expected to take 20 years to achieve.

South of Mmabatho ›› *Colour map 1, B5.*

After leaving Mafikeng, the R27 leads southwest across a large expanse of unremarkable savannah broken only by the occasional stands of acacia trees. For most of the year this is a hot and dusty region, in desperate need of rain. Most of the country is given over to farming cattle, maize and groundnuts. **Stella**, 181 km from Mafikeng, is the largest settlement between Mafikeng and Vryburg. This is a typical, quiet farming centre where nothing much seems to be going on when you drive through. However, every October the town wakes up for the national **Cattle and Beef Festival** which attracts farmers from all over the country.

Vryburg ⬤🅿️🅰️🅾️ ▶ pp700-702. Colour map 1, C5.

No matter which direction you approach from, the size of Vryburg often takes visitors by surprise, appearing as it does in the middle of a vast area of flat dry savannah. This is an important cattle centre where an auction is held every Friday. From Vryburg, the N14 continues 126 km to Kuruman in the Northern Cape (see page 755).

Background

The early history of Vryburg is interesting in so far as it provides a vivid picture of life along the frontier of the British empire. Before the arrival of any organized form of authority in the region, there was a protracted war between the Tlapin people of Chief Mankwarane and the Koranna Khoikhoi, led by David Massouw. In an effort to win the conflict, Massouw offered farms to a collection of European mercenaries as their share of the loot and eventually 416 farms were given away. Shortly afterwards, in August 1883, the ex-mercenaries proclaimed their block of farms to be a new (short-lived) independent republic, which would be known as Stellaland. The capital of this new republic was Vryburg, the 'town of freedom'.

Sights

Leon Taljaardt Nature Reserve ① Apr-Aug 0700-1500, Sep-Mar 0700-1800, small entrance fee, 5 km from the town centre, to the left off the Botswana road, is the municipal game reserve. It's a small, pleasant reserve stocked with a mix of plains game including black and blue wildebeest, eland, gemsbok, impala, red hartebeest, Burchell's and mountain zebra and waterbuck.

◉ Central region listings

Hotel and guesthouse prices
L over US$300 AL US$220-300 A US$150-220
B US$100-150 C US$75-100 D US$35-75
E US$15-35 F under US$15
Private game reserves
L4 over US$900 L3 US$550-900
L2 US$450-550 L1 US$300-500
Restaurant prices
♦♦♦ over US$30 ♦♦ US$15-30 ♦ under US$15
See pages 46-51 for further information.

⬤ Sleeping

Mafikeng and Mmabatho p694
A Mmabatho Tusk, Nelson Mandela Dr, Mmabatho, T018-3891839, www.tusk-resorts.co.za. Upmarket hotel complex with several restaurants, swimming pool, 18-hole golf course and casino. Once an important gambling centre when gaming was illegal in the rest of South Africa, but it now looks some what out of place next to the dusty townships.
C Buffalo Park Lodge, 59 Molopo St, corner of Botha and Molopo streets, Mafikeng, T018-3812159, www.buffalolodge.co.za. Modern guesthouse with 20 simply decorated rooms, mix of double and twin rooms, all with DSTV, en suite, very popular bar and restaurant, home-cooked meals and a good Sun lunch.
C Ferns, 12 Cook St, Mafikeng, T018-3815971, www.ferns.co.za. A modern quality guesthouse with 24 double rooms with pleasant decor, a/c, en suite bathroom or shower, TV. Guest lounge, bar, laundry service, swimming pool, secure parking.

Good value. The smart restaurant is probably one of the better places to eat at in town.

C-D Getaway Lodge, corner Tillard and Baden Powell streets, Mafikeng, T018-3811150, www.travellodge.co.za. Friendly guesthouse in a good, central location. 33 en suite rooms with TV, fridge, good reasonably priced restaurant and relaxing gardens. Very welcoming staff who can advise on what to do in the area. Also run 2 other similar lodges in Mafikeng, which jointly offer conference facilities.

Botsalano Game Reserve *p697*
Reservations T083-66527896 (mobile), mafgr@mweb.co.za

E Mogobe Tented Camp, 4 tents with 2 beds in each, bedding supplied, there is a fully equipped kitchen. The camp is in a typical shady thicket overlooking Mogobe Dam, in a central position.

F Campsite, next to the main entrance gate, open campsite and picnic area with basic amenities.

Zeerust *p697*
D Marico Bushveld B&B, 5 President St, T018-6423545. Pretty B&B with 9 en suite rooms, TV, bar, secure motel style parking, evening meals on request.

D-F Abjaterskop, Rustenburg Rd, T018-6422008, abjaters@qds.co.za. Mix of guestrooms and rondavels set in gardens, this is the most comfortable and friendly option in town despite looking very dated. 19 a/c rooms, with en suite bathroom and DSTV, camping and caravan site and much cheaper accommodation in 10 simple rondavels with showers round the back. Restaurant, bar serving home-distilled peach schnapps, lounge, swimming pool, gardens, secure parking, rates include breakfast.

Madikwe Game Reserve *p697, map p698*
Private lodges and camps
Madikwe is a low-density tourism facility and the luxury lodges are built as far away as possible from each other. There are at present 21 lodges run under various concessions; below are a selection. Rates include all meals and game activities. A full list of lodges can be found at www.madikwe-game-reserve.co.za.

L4 Etali Safari Lodge, T012-3460124, www.etalisafari.co.za. 8 luxury a/c thatched chalets joined by wooden boardwalks, rooms are a blend of contemporary earth colours and crisp white linen, each with a deck and outdoor jacuzzi, the main lodge has a pool, outdoor gym, pampering in the Wellness Centre, or beauty therapists will give guests a massage on their private sun deck after a day of game driving, outside eating around a fire, cuisine is African and Asian using organic vegetables.

L4 Jaci's Safari Lodge and **Jaci's Tree Lodge**, T014-7789900, www.madikwe.com. Both lodges regularly win awards. The **Safari Lodge** has 8 large thatched suites with gauze walls, double-poster beds, handcrafted stone baths, outside shower, private plunge pool, viewing deck, personal safari guide for all game drives, walks, and information. The **Tree Lodge** comprises 8 treehouses on stilts up to 4 m from the ground, built in the arms of giant leadwood or tambotie trees, outdoor jungle shower and stone bath, private decks, linked by raised boardwalks, central outside *boma* for eating, set on a circular candlelit table around a fire.

L4 Mateya Safari Lodge, T014-7789200, www.mateyasafari.com. 5 enormous, super-luxurious, thatched suites, en suite bathrooms and open-air showers, each with its own pool and deck with views of the plains and a waterhole below. The lodge is decorated with a valuable African art collection with pieces from as far away as Cameroon and Ghana, the library has 3500 books, the wine cellar has 7000 bottles, and there are 40 staff to look after the whims of only 10 guests.

L3 Tau Game Lodge, T011-13144350, www.taugamelodge.co.za. 30 luxury chalets with en suite bathrooms, private wooden view/sun deck, swimming pool, not as luxurious and a bit more crowded than some of the lodges but very comfortable nevertheless. The chalets are arranged in an arc looking out onto a large seasonal waterhole, allowing good game viewing. Also has a conference centre.

L1 Mosetlha Bushcamp, T011-4449345, www.thebushcamp.com. Good-value alternative to the luxury camps. Offers rustic accommodation in an unfenced camp without electricity. 9 simple, raised wooden cabins with oil lamps, shared outdoor safari showers, bush food cooked over an open fire. The camp is in the middle of the park close to the Tswene Tswene Hills, game drives or guided walks are available twice a day, the guides are exceptionally good. Friendly and well run.

Vryburg *p700*
C International, 43 Market St, T053-9272235, www.internationalhotel.co.za. 40 a/c rooms with en suite bathrooms, TV, M-Net, restaurant, popular local pub, swimming pool. Average and outdated.
D Lockerbie Lodge, Vry St behind the International, T053-9272302, www.locker bielodge.co.za. 29 doubles with en suite bathroom, comfortable lounge with an open fire for winter, self-catering kitchen, pool. This hotel, now a listed historical building, was established in 1890 and was used by Cecil Rhodes.

🍴 Eating

Mafikeng and Mmabatho *p694*
Apart from the obligatory ⅋ **Spur**, found in most of South Africa's small towns, there are very few eating options in either town. Unusually, however, most of the guesthouses have their own decent, à la carte restaurants, which are reasonably priced and open to non-residents. These are where local people go out to eat.

Vryburg *p700*
Vryburg has the usual range of chain steakhouses and little else; vegetarians may struggle to find something to eat. The pub in the **International Hotel** is the best bet.

🛍 Shopping

Mafikeng and Mmabatho *p694*
Mega City is a modern shopping centre close to the parliament buildings in Mmabatho. This obviously once had grand ambitions of being a typical modern South African mall, but is far too big for the number of shops required for the region. Many units within the mall stand empty. Outside the main entrance is a small selection of Botswana curio sellers with some marula, mopane and ebony carvings.

🚌 Transport

Mafikeng and Mmabatho *p694*
It's 217 km to **Gaborone**, 287 km to **Johannesburg**, 320 km to **Kimberley**, 200 km to **Rustenburg**, 156 km to **Vryburg**, 70 km to **Zeerust**. Public transport is almost non-existent and there are no scheduled flights, buses or trains; you will need a car to explore this region.

Zeerust *p697*
Bus
Intercape, T0861-287287, www.intercape.co.za, buses stop daily on the route between **Johannesburg** and **Gaborone**.

🚌 Transport

Vryburg *p700*
It's 250 km to **Botswana** (Bray), 420 km to **Johannesburg**, 212 km to **Kimberley**, 156 km to **Mafikeng**, 400 km to **Upington**.

Eastern region

The eastern region of the province gets the lion's share of visitors, thanks to the extravagant attractions of Sun City and the excellent Pilanesberg National Park, where stocks of game readily stand to attention for camera-toting safari enthusiasts. Surrounding the historic town of Rustenburg are the gently rolling Magaliesberg Mountains, which, thanks to their proximity to the urban sprawl of Pretoria and Johannesburg, are a popular weekend retreat offering a number of good country hotels and nature reserves. It's a scenic region for sports and outdoor pursuits and the mountains are ideal for hiking. ›› *For listings, see pages 712-716.*

Pretoria to Botswana

The N4, which heads westwards from Pretoria, is a toll road and therefore avoided by most local traffic, which sticks to an alternative route via the R27. The N4 has been upgraded and most of the tract between Gauteng and Botswana is well maintained tar broken up by frequent toll gates. This road is part of the Trans-Kalahari Highway which links Pretoria with Walvis Bay in Namibia.

Hartbeespoort Dam → *Colour map 2, C2. Altitude 1200 m.*

The proximity of Johannesburg and Pretoria (35 km) has made this dam in the Magaliesberg Mountains a popular watersports resort and weekend retreat. Around the shoreline are marinas and large private homes overlooking the lake. For information contact the **Hartbeespoort Dam Information Shop** ① *Damdoryn crossroads next to the curio market, T012-2531567, www.hartbeespoortdam.com, Tue-Sun 1000-1700.*

The dam was built in 1923 in a narrow gorge where the Crocodile River cuts through the Magaliesberg Mountains. There are two major canals which conduct water away from the dam into a series of smaller canals that irrigate the farmlands around Brits. The old main road from Pretoria runs through the village of **Schoemansville** on the north shore of the lake before crossing the dam wall and continuing to Rustenburg and Sun City. There is a **Snake and Animal Park** ① *T012-2531162, daily, 0800-1700, R50*, which remains a popular attraction for visiting families from Gauteng, but alongside the collection of reptiles are chimpanzees, panthers and Bengal tigers, making it unpleasant and zoo-like. Boat trips on the dam leave hourly. Also here is the **Hartbeespoort Dam Cableway** ① *on the R513 towards Pretoria, T012-2531706, R30, Mon-Fri 1000-1530, Sat and Sun 1000-1700*, a 2.3-km link to one of the highest points of the Magaliesberg Mountains.

Once over the dam wall from Schoemansville, the road reaches the Damdoryn crossroads where the tourist office and a large curio market are located. From here, 2 km along the R104 is the **Elephant Sanctuary** ① *T012-2580423, www.elephantsanctuary.co.za*, daily programmes start at 0800, 1000 and 1400, starting from R325, which is the sister operation to the elephant sanctuary on the Garden Route. Guests can interact with the six tame elephants and ride them. Check out the website for programmes, some of which include lunch or dinner. There's luxury accommodation (**L**) and overnight guests can 'brush down' the elephants first thing in the morning.

Brits → *Colour map 2, B2.*

Brits is a medium-sized industrial centre surrounded by highly productive farmlands irrigated from the Hartbeespoort Dam. It is also, incidentally, the sole source in Africa of the production of optical fibres. However, most visitors steam past Brits on their way west and are only likely to pass through town if heading north to the little-known Borakalalo Game Reserve (see below), one of several excellent reserves tucked away in the province. The **De Wildt Cheetah Centre** ① *T012-5041921, www.dewildt.org.za, R180, extra R100 for photograph with a cheetah, 3-hr tours Tue, Thu, Sat and Sun at 0830 and 1330; booking ahead is essential*, is an important breeding centre and is famous for being the first such place where a cheetah was successfully born in captivity. Other species include wild dog, brown hyena and vultures. The tour begins with a talk about the centre and the genetics of cheetahs, followed by a game drive around the spacious enclosures.

Borakalalo Game Reserve ● ▸ *pp712-716. Colour map 2, B2.*

① *T012-7291008, Apr-Aug 0600-1900, Sep-Mar 0500-2000, R15, car R10.*

This is a pleasant nature reserve north of Pretoria, primarily known for the excellent fishing in the Klipvoor Dam (permits are issued at the gate). The reserve surrounds the dam and the area on the northern shore has been restocked with a variety of wild animals so that visitors have a choice of hiking, game viewing and fishing. There is a small shop at the main gate.

Ins and outs

Getting there From Brits, take the R512 and then the right turning signposted Lethlabile. After Lethlabile follow the signs for Jericho. At Jericho take a right at the T-junction and then the first left signposted Legonyane. The reserve is signposted along this road. There is no petrol available here, so fill up in advance.

Best time to visit The reserve receives most of its rain during the summer months, October to April; the summer temperatures range from a very hot 37°C to an average 20°C in the evening. During winter it can get very cold at night.

Wildlife

At 13,000 ha this was, for a time, the second largest national park in the former Bophuthatswana. It is closer to Pretoria than Pilanesberg National Park, yet it receives far fewer visitors. Since the reserve was proclaimed in 1984, there has been a complete restocking programme in order to replace the animals that once roamed the plains: white rhino, buffalo, giraffe, zebra, eland, elephant, hippo, buffalo, nyala, leopard, crocodile, jackal, tsessebe, gemsbok and roan antelope. There are over 350 species of bird in the park – enough to keep any keen ornithologist happy. Several sturdy hides have been built where you can enjoy viewing the wildlife without being stuck inside a car.

The Moretele River flows through the park which encompasses the 800-ha **Klipvoor Dam**. The dam contains carp, bream and barbel. To the southwest of the dam is the game-viewing area, where 50 km of gravel roads have been cut through the open savannah woodland. There is also another small dam, **Sefudi Dam**, where animals may be seen drinking.

Hiking trails

One of the most rewarding experiences in the park is to follow one of the self-guided walks through the riverine forest along the banks of the Moretele River. These vary from 1-4 km in distance. Guides are available for the longer walks, which are usually made in the early morning and last up to three hours.

→ *Phone code 014. Altitude 1160 m.*

Rustenburg, or 'castle of rest', is one of the oldest towns in the region and was an important centre under the Transvaal Republic. Today, much of its old charm has disappeared and it is little more than a scruffy, sprawling crossroads between Gauteng, Sun City and Pilanesburg. Nevertheless, its proximity to Johannesburg and Pretoria on the one hand, and the Magaliesberg Mountains and the Kgaswane (Rustenburg) Mountain Reserve on the other, means that hotels are often full and it's a good idea to book in advance.

Ins and outs

Getting around The only bus that stops in Rustenburg is the regular **Intercape** service that runs between Pretoria and Gaborone in Botswana. There is little in the way of public transport, and a hire car is essential for exploring the area. If you're heading to Sun City, Pilanesberg or Madikwe, it's best to head straight through.

Tourist information **Rustenburg Tourism Information and Development Centre** ⓘ *corner of Nelson Mandela Dr and Kloof St, T014-5970904, on the outskirts of town, visible when approaching from the Pretoria side on the N4, Mon-Fri 0800-1630, Sat 0800-1200*, is staffed by a friendly and enthusiastic team (take their accommodation recommendations with a pinch of salt). The office also has some useful maps and leaflets for the **Magalies Meander**, www.magaliesmeander.co.za, a self-drive route through the mountains. It's a satellite office for the **North West Parks and Tourism Board** so they can provide information on the whole region.

Background

The first white settlers were a group of burghers who had followed the Voortrekker leader Andries Pretorius from the Cape. Among the first Voortrekkers to start farming on the northern slopes of the fertile Magaliesberg in the mid-1800s were AH Potgieter and Casper Kruger, the father of the future president of the Transvaal, Paul Kruger.

During the short existence of the Boer Republic, Rustenburg was the capital before the government moved to Pretoria. On 16 March 1852, the town was the scene of the reconciliation between Andries Pretorius and Hendrik Potgieter, two of the leaders of the splintered Voortrekkers' Great Trek. This was an important step within the republic, as Pretorius had gone to the Orange Free State and Potgieter to the Eastern Transvaal and Mozambique. Reconciling their differences helped unify the two states (Orange Free and Transvaal) as a strong force against the British.

Sights

Despite being the third oldest town in the region and an important historic settling point for the Voortrekkers, there is very little of historical interest within Rustenburg. Two exceptions are **Hervormde Church Square**, which was the site of the reconciliation between Andries Pretorius and Hendrik Potgieter, and the **Statue of a Voortrekker Girl** in Plein Street opposite the Hervormde Church. The candle in the girl's hand represents the introduction of Christianity to the area.

Around Rustenburg

Paul Kruger Country House Museum ⓘ *18 km northwest of Rustenburg, off the R565 towards Sun City, look out for a left turning just after Phokeng, T014-5733218,*

Rustenburg, the Magaliesberg & Sun City

Pilanesberg National Park ▲

Sun City

Kwa Maritane Gate

▲ To Thabazimbi & Northern Province

R510

Tsitsing

Wevedeen

Boekenhoutfontein & Paul Kruger's House

Phokeng

R565

To Mafikeng, Botswana &

Bosspoort Dam

Besspruit

Kane

R510

To Brits & Pretoria ▶

R27

Thlabane

Rustenburg

Ultra City

Waterfall Mall

R30

Kroondal

Marikana

R52

Kgaswane (Rustenburg) Mountain Reserve

To Koster & Lichtenburg

To Brits & Pretoria ▶

R27

Buffelspoort

Olifantsnek Dam

R30   R24

To Derby, Koster & Klerksdorp

To 13, Magaliesberg & Krugersdorp

To Magaliesberg ▼

N

4 km

4 miles

Sleeping
Ananda Country Lodge 1
Hunter's Rest 4
Kedar Lodge 5
Montana Guest Farm 6

Mountain Sanctuary Park 7
Mount Grace 13
Revel In 2
Road Lodge 12
Sundown Ranch 10

Wigwam 11

www.rali.co.za, daily 1000-1600, R25, is at Boekenhoutfontein, the farm where Paul Kruger lived as an obscure farmer before he became the president of the Transvaal Republic from 1883 until the end of the Anglo-Boer War. Four buildings have been preserved and restored as museums to the life of Paul Kruger and the earliest farmers in the Transvaal. The oldest building is a cottage built in 1841 by the first owner of Boekenhoutfontein, a single-storey building with a thatched roof and stone patio out front. When Paul Kruger moved here in 1863, he built a new thatched homestead for his family, known as the 'Pioneer House'. To its right stands the main homestead, a double-storey stone house built in 1872 in typical Eastern-Cape style. It contains many of Kruger's possessions along with an assortment of period furniture from other homes. The fourth house, built for Kruger's son Pieter, dates from 1892.

Of the original 500-ha farm, 32 ha have been kept as part of the museum. The gardens have been partially restored and visitors are free to stroll around looking at the birds and plants; picnic areas have been laid out. The old **Rustenburg Museum** has moved here and has a small but interesting collection of local historical items. The statue of Paul Kruger which used to stand in front of the information office in Rustenburg has also been moved to Boekenhoutfontein. Sculpted in bronze by a French artist, Jean Archand, the statue was discovered in Paris in 1919 by General Louis Botha and General Jan Smuts. It is of the president sitting grumpily in his armchair during his last days in exile in France.

Magaliesberg Mountains ⊜❼▲ ≫ *pp712-716. Colour map 2, C1.*

The Magaliesberg are a range of flat-topped quartzite mountains which extend roughly from Pretoria to just beyond Rustenburg. In 1977 the area was declared a Natural Heritage Site, and the entire area is one of the most visited in South Africa. Much of the mountains have been parcelled off into private resorts, but there remain some pockets of indigenous landscapes, notably in the excellent Pilanesberg Park and Kgaswane (Rustenburg) Mountain Reserve.

Ins and outs

Getting around To explore the Magaliesberg take the R30 shortly before entering Rustenburg from Pretoria. This road leads up into the mountains to **Olifantsnek**, a gap in the Magaliesberg created by the Hex River. There are plenty of hotels and resorts along this road.

Background

When the first white hunters came to the region they named the hills the 'Cashan Mountains', a corruption of Khashane, the name of the local chief. They were renamed by the Voortrekkers who called the range after another local leader, Mohale, but whose name they misspelled as Magalie.

The region witnessed a number of bloody battles during the 19th century. The first major conflicts were between Mzilikazi, leader of the Ndebele, and the local peoples when he arrived here from modern-day KwaZulu Natal. A few decades later, the mountains were the scene of several important battles during the Anglo-Boer War. One of these was the Battle of Nooitgedacht on 13 December 1900, in which the British forces suffered their heaviest defeat since their arrival in July 1900. Three hundred men were killed and a similar number taken prisoner, and the Boers managed to seize 70 full wagons, 200 tents, ammunition, 300 mules, some cattle and over 400 horses. The gorge where the battle took place is just off the R560 close to Hekpoort.

Wildlife and vegetation

The range is about 160 km long, reaching 1852 m at its highest point – which is actually no more than 400 m above the surrounding countryside. The difference in elevation is, however, sufficient to ensure that the hills receive a relatively high rainfall and are far greener than the plains, with some remaining stands of forest. Most of the wild animals that once lived in the hills have long since been hunted out. An exception can be found on the ledges on the south-facing cliff faces, which are important nesting sites for the endangered Cape vulture. The north-facing slopes are no more than a gentle climb, cut by mountain streams and leafy gorges. The range forms the natural divide between the cool highveld to the south and the warm bushveld to the north.

Kgaswane (Rustenburg) Mountain Reserve ⬤

▸▸ *pp712-716. Colour map 2, B/C1.*

ⓘ *T014-5332050, Sep-Mar 0530-1900, Apr-Aug 0600-1830, R15 per person, R10 per car.*
This popular mountain reserve stretches along the summit and the northern slopes of the Magaliesberg range, 400 m above Rustenburg, providing excellent hiking territory. The reserve is an important recreational area for visitors from Johannesburg and Pretoria, just over 100 km away, and school buses are a regular sight. Because it is so close to the large cities, the number of visitors is tightly controlled and anyone wishing to camp or enjoy the longer hiking trails needs to book well in advance.

Ins and outs

From the centre of Rustenburg, follow Wolmarans Street (from the junction with Van Staden by the municipal offices) through the residential suburbs to the very end where it then curves to the left and becomes Boekenhout Road. Follow this road out of town until you come to a T-junction, turn left (the right is signposted to the **Ananda Hotel**). Shortly after passing Rustenburg Kloof, just before the entrance gates to the **Orion Safari Lodge**, is a right turn to the main gates of the reserve. The reserve is not clearly signposted in the centre of town.

Wildlife

The land was originally part of Rietvallei farm, which belonged to President Paul Kruger. The reserve was proclaimed in 1967 after the council had been given the land by one of Kruger's descendants. In 1981 the nature reserve was extended to include an adjoining farm to the east and today the total area protected is 4257 ha. From the top of the reserve you can see the flat bushveld to the south, while the ridge of the mountains disappears east towards the Hartbeespoort Dam and Pretoria.

Some of the species of antelope found here include grey duiker, klipspringer, mountain reedbuck, impala, oribi, waterbuck, steenbuck, kudu, zebra and red hartebeest. Jackal, leopard, hyena and caracal are also known to live in the mountains. There are also raptors which live high up along the rocky cliff faces. Scops owl, martial eagles and black eagles can be viewed along with an important breeding colony of the endangered Cape vulture.

Hiking

There are currently three marked hiking trails in the reserve. Two of the trails are open for day visitors; the third trail requires spending a couple of nights in the reserve. For information on the trails, visit www.tourismnorthwest.co.za/kgaswane. Detailed maps are available at the reserve office.

Sun City ●● ⇢ pp712-716. Colour map 2, B1.

Tucked between dusty plains and rolling bushveld is the surreal highrise, neon-lit resort of Sun City, one of the most-visited sights in the country. Much like Las Vegas in the US, the resort was built around gambling and today comprises a vast complex of four hotels, linked by a skytrain, and extravagant recreational facilities, including a fake sandy lagoon and a constructed tropical rainforest. The result is both staggeringly impressive and laughably tacky – all good fun if you take it with a pinch of salt.

Ins and outs

Getting there Follow Nelson Mandela Street straight out of Rustenburg, past the golf course to your left, and then take the right turning on the R565, signposted Phokeng and Sun City. Shortly before Sun City is a left turn for Pilanesberg National Park. The entrance to Sun City is just after a large shopping mall by the staff housing complex. There is an entrance fee for day visitors, R70 per person, part of which is redeemable in tokens to spend inside, R130 including entrance to the Valley of the Waves. The **Welcome Centre** ⓘ *T014-5571544, daily 0800-2000*, is in the middle of the complex and is a good place to start and pick up a map. The free skytrain runs throughout the complex, and shuttle buses run to and from the car park. Day visitors can join a tour of The Palace of the Lost City, costing R60.

The complex has four hotels, numerous restaurants and fast-food outlets, two golf courses, a water park, a man-made rainforest, a crocodile park, an aviary, a lake offering watersports, a cultural centre, casino and the Superbowl, a large entertainment hall which in recent years has hosted the likes of Black Eyed Peas and Westlife.

Background

The first part of the complex was opened in 1979, when the central features were the **Sun City Hotel** and a golf course designed by Gary Player. Much of the appeal of Sun City was its gambling licence: the hotel was in the homeland of Bophuthatswana where gambling was legal, unlike in the rest of South Africa at that time. Wealthy whites travelled to what were then the designated black homelands to gamble, and like many other casino resorts from the Apartheid era, the contrasts between the luxury of the resorts and the impoverished areas around them were (and, to some extent, still are) stark.

In the same year Pilanesberg National Park opened. A year later the second phase was complete – the 284-room **Sun City Cabanas** opened, aimed at families. In 1980 the famous **Sun City Million Dollar Golf Challenge** was founded, and over the years this has attracted most of the world's top golfers. In 1984 the third hotel was opened, the five-star **Cascades**, surrounded by waterfalls, streams and a tract of forest. In 1992 came the icing on the cake: the **Lost City** and the **Valley of the Waves** (see Sights and activities, below).

With the change in gambling laws, visitor numbers dropped sharply in the 1990s, but these have crept up again as the focus has switched from gambling to family entertainment, golf and conferences. Although it's far removed from the culture and landscapes that draw most tourists to South Africa, Sun City's glitz and garishness is fascinating and well worth a day's visit.

Sights and activities

The complex focuses on the newest and most excessive addition to the Sun City stable, the **Palace of the Lost City**, a magnificent hotel completed in 1992. The vaguely Moorish construction is characterized by soaring dome-capped towers ringed by prancing statues of antelope; you can only actually reach the hotel if you're staying there, but regular tours are held for day visitors. Below the hotel is the **Valley of the Waves**, reached by a bridge that trembles and spouts steam during mock earthquakes (every 30 minutes). This stunning artificial sandy lagoon, complete with desert island and palm-lined soft white sand, has a wave machine capable of creating metre-high waves. Day visitors have to pay extra to enter the Valley of the Waves, accessed from the entertainments centre, but this doesn't seem to put anyone off – the beach gets completely packed at weekends, with noisy music pumping out of loudspeakers and every large wave bringing forth a yell of jubilation from the crowds. Smaller swimming pools dotted around the lagoon are quieter.

A welcome retreat lies around the hotel and lagoon, the impressive 25-ha **man-made forest**. Remarkably lush and quiet, the forest was originally made up of 1.6 million plants, trees and shrubs, and the rainforest component includes three layers with creepers and orchids growing in the canopy. Although the moulded cement rocks and perfectly pruned paths give it a distinctly Disney feel, the plants have attracted prolific birdlife and the walking trails, lasting up to 1½ hours, allow a real sense of isolation from the resort.

Elsewhere, an abundance of activities is available to guests. There are two 18-hole golf courses, including the Gary Player course, home to the annual **Nedbank Golf Challenge**, one of the world's great championships with a prize of US$2 million. At **Waterworld**, guests can try parasailing, waterskiing and jetskiing. There is a horse-riding centre, tennis, mini-golf, squash, a gym and spa, mountain biking trails, jogging routes, 10-pin bowling and numerous swimming pools (the more peaceful of which are located in the hotels).

Close to the entrance is **Kwena Gardens Crocodile Sanctuary** with over 7000 crocs, including the three biggest captive Nile crocodiles in the world. Nearby is the **Cultural Village**, where guests are shown around mock-ups of villages of eight tribal groups, with dancing and singing displays and a Shebeen serving pan-African cuisine. There's also an aviary, a bird of prey centre, several cinemas, a casino, a vast hall filled with slot machines, and countless restaurants and bars.

Pilanesberg National Park ⊜▲▲ ▶▶ *pp712-716. Colour map 2, B1.*

① *T014-5555354, www.pilanesberg-game-reserve.co.za, Nov-Feb 0530-1900, Mar-Apr 0600-1830, May-Aug 0630-1800, Sep-Oct 0600-1830, R20 per person, R15 per car. This is a malaria-free zone.*

This is the fourth largest national park in South Africa, and was created in 1979 to complement the new luxury development being built at Sun City. The two have been closely linked ever since.

Ins and outs

Follow directions for Sun City and take the R565 from Rustenburg. Alternatively, follow the R510 from Rustenburg and after 51 km take a left turn, follow this road for a further 5 km past a couple of factories and take a right turn by the petrol station. The entrance to **Pilanesberg National Park** and Manyane Camp is just on the left. Pretoria is about 140 km from the park. It can be visited as a long day trip from Pretoria or Johannesburg, but most visitors stay at least one night in the region and combine a trip to Pilanesberg with Sun City. Visitors to Sun City can book on one of the numerous two-hour game drives that leave the Welcome Centre throughout the day.

Background and sights

The area earmarked for the park in the 1970s was home to a large number of Tswana people, but these were either coerced into leaving or forcibly removed – a hugely controversial move, but one that was not reported at the time. On a more positive note, the area's reintroduction of game has been heralded as a huge success. This complex and ambitious project was known as Operation Genesis. The animals came from all over southern Africa: elephant and buffalo from Addo Elephant National Park, black and white rhino from the Natal Parks Board, eland from Namibia, Burchell's zebra and waterbuck from the Transvaal and red hartebeest from the Northern Cape and Namibia. As a transition zone between the Kalahari sandveld and the bushveld, it was also the natural habitat for a number of rare species already in existence, including brown hyena, Cape hunting dog and sable antelope. As you drive around the 55,000-ha reserve you now have a good chance of seeing all the large animals including rhino, elephant, lion, cheetah, buffalo and the occasional leopard. More than 8000 animals have now been successfully introduced.

The park encompasses the caldera of an extinct volcano, which is geographically similar to the Ngorongoro Conservation Area in Tanzania. The crater is surrounded by three concentric rings of hills and in the centre is a lake, **Mankwe Dam**, where you can see crocodile and hippo. The hills are broken up with wooded valleys, which gradually give way to open savannah grasslands. This variety of habitat is ideal for wild animals and it is a rewarding birdwatching

Pilanesberg National Park

To Botswana

NORTH WEST PROVINCE

Sleeping 🛌
Bakgatla Resort **1**
Bakubung Lodge **2**

Kwa Maritane **3**
Manyane Resort **4**
Tshukudu Game Lodge **5**

5 km
5 miles

environment where over 340 species have been recorded, some of which are extremely rare. A number of walk-in viewing hides have been constructed. Excellent tar and gravel roads traverse the park and maps and game check lists are available at each of the four gates: Manyane, Bakgatla, Bakubung and Kwa Maritane – the last one being the closest to Sun City.

◉ Eastern region listings

Hotel and guesthouse prices
L over US$300 **AL** US$220-300 **A** US$150-220
B US$100-150 **C** US$75-100 **D** US$35-75
E US$15-35 **F** under US$15
Private game reserves
L4 over US$900 **L3** US$550-900
L2 US$450-550 **L1** US$300-500
Restaurant prices
††† over US$30 †† US$15-30 † under US$15
See pages 46-51 for further information.

◎ Sleeping

Hartbeespoort Dam p703
B-C Berg & Dam, 90 Scott St, T012-2530522, www.bergdam.co.za. 3 linked modern guesthouses, with a choice of B&B, self-catering or semi-self-catering (ie rooms with microwaves). All come with TV, en suite, spacious rooms, a/c and heating. Pretty gardens, secure parking, meals on request, welcoming staff. Great choice but very popular, often booked up months in advance. Recommended.
C-E The Ring Oxwagon Inn, T012-2591506, www.thering.co.za. 6 chalets attached to historical, restored and furnished ox-wagons, sleeping up to 6 (double beds in the wagons), en suite bathroom, homely restaurant, swimming pool, cheaper beds available in a backpackers' dorm built out of an old double-decker bus, situated high up in the hills with nice views and hiking trails.
D Squires on the Dam, 1 Scott St, opposite the snake and animal park, T012-2531001, www.squiresonthedam.co.za. A simple set of 7 rooms attached to the **Squires on the Dam** restaurant. Plain, but comfortable en suite motel rooms with Mnet TV.

Borakalalo Game Reserve p704
For reservations contact T012-2520131, www.borakalalo.co.za.
D Moretele Camp, 2 camps of semi-permanent tents with basic furnishings, including gas lamps and fridge. Self-catering facilities and shared ablution blocks, bring everything you need with you including towels, and all eating and cooking utensils.
D Phudufudu Safari Camp, tented camp, 10 upmarket tents, fully self-catering. Set in a secluded corner, shaded by large trees, shared ablution block, central dining area and lounge overlooking a small waterhole, fully equipped kitchen with freezer, plunge pool.
F Campsite, a basic, rustic camp beside the dam, primarily used by anglers, camping sites have a braai area and a water tap, the central washblock is made from reeds, hot water and clean washing and toilet facilities, the camp has no electricity or fridges.

Rustenburg p705, map p706
Most of the local hotels are located beyond the built-up area towards the Magaliesberg Mountains. Within town, the choice is fairly dire. Far more attractive are the fine country resort hotels in the Magaliesberg range, or the (albeit pricey) hotels in Sun City and Pilanesberg National Park.
A Kedar Lodge, 20 km from Rustenburg towards Sun City on the R565, T014-5733218, www.rali.co.za. A peaceful group of cottages next to the historic farm of President Kruger, with 27 en suite double rooms, open log fires, plunge pools, rustic stone shower rooms. Zebra and ostrich within the grounds, small restaurant and bar, new addition is a beauty spa. Fishing trips can be organized from here.
C Sundown Ranch, 33 km from Rustenburg centre, on the R565, T014-5731000,

www.sundownlionpark.com. 10 km from Sun City and Pilanesberg National Park. 101 double hotel rooms set within 1600 ha of grounds, 2 restaurants, swimming pool in a pleasant palm courtyard, outdoor bar, tennis courts, squash, bowls, horse trails and a lion park, where visitors can play with lion cubs.

D Bergsig Lodge, 9 Fourth Av, T014-5974844, www.bergsiglodge.co.za. Friendly B&B with handful of double rooms and a couple of singles with en suite facilities, ceiling fans, TV lounge, M-Net, separate entrance, braai area, swimming pool, well-kept garden with shady corners, central location, secure parking, dinner available. Well-run and good value.

D Road Lodge, on the N4, corner Howick and Magaliesburg roads, T014-5373088, www.roadlodge.co.za. Standard functional modern block favoured by business travellers, 90 rooms, TV, same price for 1-3 people, breakfast available in the lobby.

E Revel In, 38 km west of Rustenburg off the N4 towards Swartruggens, turn right at Bokfontien and travel up a dirt road for 6.5 km, T072-2257182, www.revelin.co.za. A hostel and campsite set on a beautiful remote farm. Hiking trails to natural springs, bar with a reggae feel, stone-and-thatch rustic bungalows, some with sunken baths made from rock, open fires, a bunkhouse with 16 dorm beds, also has some treehouses (bring bedding), home-made furniture, pool, self-catering kitchen. The owner is promoting this place as an outdoor music festival venue to compete with Rustlers Valley in the Free State. Several festivals are held throughout the year and draw revellers from the big cities. At other times you might have the place to yourself.

Magaliesberg Mountains *p707, map p706*

L Mount Grace, approaching Magaliesberg village on the R24 towards Johannesburg, T014-5775600, www.grace.co.za. 80 double rooms with en suite bathrooms, rooms are in a variety of thatched cottages set in 4 ha of beautiful gardens with lakes and waterfalls, swimming pool, tennis, library. Excellent food. Sumptuous spa with set of hydro pools,

natural stone walls and thatch roof, most treatments, such as massages, scrubs, hand and foot grooming, are conducted outside beneath olive trees. Spa and restaurant open to non-guests. Recommended.

A Hunter's Rest, 14 km from Rustenburg on the R30, T014-5378300, www.huntersrest.co.za. 91 spacious rooms with private patio, arranged up the side of the hill; a bit of a hike from the furthest room to the restaurant. Bar serves a good range of imported beers and has an English pub feel, large swimming pool, well-kept garden, curio shop, huge range of activities including tennis, sauna, squash, fitness centre, horse riding and 9-hole golf course. Good for families.

C Ananda Country Lodge, 8 km from Rustenburg, T014-5973875, www.anandahotel.co.za. 68 hotel rooms, thatched chalets and a shady campsite, all set in the lee of the Magaliesberg, restaurant, bar, 3 swimming pools, tennis courts, bowls, squash, golf nearby, though often overrun with conference delegates.

C Wigwam Holiday Hotel, 14 km from Rustenburg centre, T014-5378000, www.wigwam.co.za. Mix of large a/c rooms or one of 7 rather hideous 'wigwam' units which sleep up to 5. Restaurant, bar, neat colourful gardens, large holiday resort that can sleep up to 270, recreational facilities include: 2 swimming pools, 4 tennis courts, 9-hole golf course, squash court, games room, mini-golf and a choice of hikes behind the complex.

D Montana Guest Farm, T014-5340113, www.montanagf.co.za. 8 self-catering chalets, some with thatched roofs, well-equipped kitchens, surrounded by the natural woodlands of the Magaliesberg, swimming pool, pub and games room, no restaurant, bring all your own food, a small and friendly retreat with some excellent local hikes.

D-F Mountain Sanctuary Park, T014-5340114, www.mountain-sanctuary.co.za. A private nature reserve in the mountains 35 km from Rustenburg. Simple rest camp, visitor numbers are controlled and there are strict regulations to preserve and maintain this mountain wilderness, so early booking is advised even for day visits. Accommodation consists of self-catering chalets, fully equipped and furnished (but bring your own bedding, towels, soap and food), caravans for 2-4 people, and a shady campsite. Stunning pool built from natural stone on the lip of the valley, offering fantastic views. Guests have access to over 1000 ha of hiking country. Horse trails offered.

Kgaswane (Rustenburg) Mountain Reserve p708
E Hiking Huts, reservations T014-5332050. 4 huts sleeping 4, between the 2 bedrooms is a communal seating and dining area. Meals have to be cooked by wood fire over a braai, cooking pots, buckets to collect water and 2 lamps are provided. There is also a veld toilet close by. During the winter months you'll need a sleeping bag.

Sun City p709, map p706
The whole complex is part of the **Sun International Group**, central reservations T011-7807800, www.suninternational.com. The rooms aren't cheap, but are of a very high standard. The hotels listed below must be booked through central reservations. Off-season packages are sometimes available.
L The Cascades has the best of both worlds: it has 5-star amenities but is neither over the top nor overrun with families. The 242 a/c rooms have been renovated in muted colours, with dark wood furniture and olive and beige fabrics. M-Net TV, minibar, stylish bathrooms, 24-hr room service. All rooms face the forest and pools with thrashing waterfalls and tinkling streams. Auditorium seating 6000. **The Peninsula** is a smart international restaurant with a weekend buffet. **The Santorini** is a Greek and seafood restaurant overlooking the pool. There are 2 bars, **Vistas** and **Grotto**.
L The Palace of the Lost City, is the central point of the complex and is both impossibly kitschy and beautifully lavish. 338 a/c rooms spread across a string of airy courtyards, each

overlooking fountains and sculptures of game. The entrance is marked by a super-sized sculpture of cheetahs hunting, surrounded by lakes and tinkling fountains. The lobby is a palatial hall lined with vast columns, leading to a variety of restaurants and elegant bars. It's all totally over the top, and has attracted so many goggling visitors that only guests are now allowed entry, unless you're on a pre-paid tour. **Villa del Palazzo**, with classic northern Italian cuisine, is an excellent restaurant overlooking the pools; **Crystal Court** has gourmet cuisine, live piano music and is surrounded by jungle (smart dress code); elsewhere in the hotel there are 3 bars and a poolside snack bar and bar; there is a selection of shops, a beauty spa, and a heated swimming pool.
L Sun City, the original hotel, was refurbished in 2007. 341 a/c rooms overlooking the swimming pool and lush lawns; plenty of choice on the restaurant front: **The Harlequin**, à la carte, in the casino, casual dress; **The Calabash**, carvery and salad bar; **Sun Terrace**, fast food during the day, formal restaurant at night; 2 cocktail bars.
AL Sun City Cabanas, 144 standard cabanas for 2 people; 236 family cabanas which can accommodate 4, all are fully a/c, TV, en suite bathrooms. The cottages are set in neat gardens close to a lake and Waterworld, with a kid's petting farmyard and adventure playground in the grounds. This is the best-value option available, and has families firmly in mind. **Morula** restaurant serves steaks and grills; **Palm Terrace** is an informal carvery; **Famous Butcher's Grill** has more of those steaks and is a vegetarian's nightmare; **Pool Bar** serves snacks during the day.

Pilanesberg National Park p710, map p711
These 2 camps are run by **Golden Leopard Resorts**, T014-5551000, www.goldenleopard.co.za.
AL-B Bakgatla Resort, at the northwest of the park close to the Bakgatla Gate. 58 self-catering chalets, sleeping a maximum of 5 people, all are a/c and are fitted with a

kitchen, en suite bathroom, lounge area plus a private patio and braai area. At the centre of the complex is a large swimming pool, picnic site and kiosk. There is also a limited number of caravan and campsites available (**E**). The campsites have a central kiosk plus a small bar. **AL-B Manyane Resort**, 300 m from the Manyane Gate. 60 2- to 6-bed self-catering thatched chalets with kitchen, lounge, bathroom, braai, couple of swimming pools among the chalets. Behind the chalets is a caravan and campsite (**E**), electric points, clean washblocks and shade trees. Central restaurant block open for all meals, bar, central swimming pool, children's play area. The camp is in open savannah grasslands with a few trees dotted about. Can get very busy during school holidays. There is a day visitors' complex with a shop, picnic area, swimming pool, a couple of walk-in aviaries, a 4WD track, walking trails, and mini-golf.

Private lodges and camps

There are several camps within the park operated by different concessionaries, but advance booking is essential. Except for self-catering, rates include meals and game drives. The following 3 lodges are part of the **Legacy Hotels Group**, central reservations T011-8066888, www.legacyhotels.co.za.
L4 Tshukudu Game Lodge, in the middle of the park on the slope of a steep rock outcrop. Small lodge, 6 stone thatched chalets built into the rock, slate floors, wicker furniture and a fireplace, beds on an elevated platform, sunken double bath with a view, lounge area with bar fridge, books and magazines. Chalets are linked to the main lodge by a steep, winding stone staircase. From the top you have clear views across the park and a floodlit waterhole, restaurant, bar, swimming pool. Rates include meals, game drives and transfers to the lodge from the other lodges near the gates where you can park.
L1 Bakubung Lodge, on the edge of the park, 10 km from Sun City. Large complex, 75 rooms, 66 self-catering chalets, restaurant, bar, curio shop, tennis court, swimming pool,

game drives and hikes are extra, there are superb views of the surrounding bush and a waterhole with resident hippos, a free shuttle runs to Sun City every couple of hours.
L1 Kwa Maritane, a smart bush lodge with 90 a/c rooms and 54 self-catering chalets, each with a TV, high thatched ceilings, and a private veranda. Restaurant, outdoor braai. Nearby waterhole with underground hide reached via a 180-m tunnel from the lodge. Game drives and guided walks, 2 swimming pools, floodlit tennis courts, table tennis, sauna, gym. There is a free shuttle to Sun City.

Eating

Rustenburg *p705, map p706*
There is little choice in the town centre and most restaurants are in the shopping centre area of the **Waterfall Mall** on the edge of town on the R30; here there's a predictable range of pasta, steak and fast-food joints. Otherwise, there are some fine restaurants in the Magaliesburg Mountain resorts and hotels.

Shopping

Hartbeespoort Dam

At the junction after crossing the Hartbees poort Dam on the R514 from Schoemansville is an enormous open-air curio market and the **Welwitschia Country Market**, T083-3028085, www.countrymarket.co.za, Tue-Sun 0900-1700. Here are over 40 shops in prefabricated sheds arranged in lanes, selling crafts, clothes, snacks, furniture, toys and all manor of other things aimed at day tippers from the cities. There are also 2 open-air restaurants and a mini kids' fairground.

Activities and tours

Magaliesberg Mountains *p707, map p706*
Most of the holiday resorts are equipped with a complete range of sports facilities, including

golf courses, tennis courts and gyms. Pick up a map for the **Magalies Meander**, www.magaliesmeander.co.za, or the **Crocodile Ramble**, www.theramble.co.za, at the tourist office in Rustenburg, which both list craft shops, accommodation, sports, and restaurants within the region.

Balloon rides
Bill Harrop's Original Balloon Safaris, T011-7053201, www.balloon.co.za. 1-hr early-morning flights over the Magaliesberg followed by a champagne breakfast, R2115, minimum 2.

Hiking
Hiking remains the most popular pastime in the region and each of the resorts have their own hiking trails, some of which lead further up into the mountains. Maps and permits are available from the resorts.

Pilanesberg National Park p710, map p711
Safaris
You'll get the most out of a visit to the park by going on a guided tour, as the rangers are in constant radio contact and monitor the movements of the Big Five. If you are visiting Sun City on a day trip and do not have your own transport, 2-hr guided tours leave frequently from the **Welcome Centre**.
Mankwe Safaris, based at Pilanesberg's Manyane Gate, T014-5557056, www.mankwesafaris.co.za. Runs 2½-hr game drives in the morning, afternoon and at night, around R220 per person, plus 3-hr walking trails, R250 per person, minimum 5 and maximum 8 in a group.
Pilanesberg Elephant Back Safaris, T014-5525020, www.pilanesberg elephantback.co.za. 5 elephants that can carry 2 riders plus the guide. Silently travelling through the bush on elephant back is a unique game-viewing experience. The ride is about 1 hr but the whole excursion lasts

2-3 hrs, interaction with the elephants is encouraged. Pickups from Sun City's Welcome Centre. R1090. Similar set-up in Kruger, page 645.

⊖ Transport

Rustenburg p705, map p706
It's 48 km to **Sun City** via R27 and R565, 200 km to **Mafikeng**, 130 km to **Zeerust**, 105 km to **Pretoria**, 112 km to **Johannesburg**.

Bus
Intercape, central reservations T0861-287287, www.intercape.co.za, buses stop here en route between **Gaborone** and **Pretoria**.

Sun City p709, map p706
Air
Pilanesberg International Airport, 10 km from Sun City, close to Kwa Maritane Gate, T014-5521261, www.airports.co.za. Built to serve the luxury resorts and upgraded a few years ago to an international airport for flights from neighbouring countries. Buses connect with Sun City. There are currently no scheduled flights, but there are daily charter flights from **Johannesburg** and **Cape Town**.

Car hire
Avis, Sun City, T014-5521501, www.avis.co.za. **Imperial**, airport, T014-5521767, www.imperialcarrental.co.za.

ⓘ Directory

Rustenburg p705, map p706
Emergencies Police T10111.
Internet Vodacom Store, in the Waterfall Shopping Mall, at the far end of the mall.
Medical services Ambulance T10177. Peglerae (private) Hospital 173 Beyers Naude Dr, T014-5977200.

Contents

Footprint features

At a glance

☺ **Getting around** Buses only on the N1, car hire.

◉ **Time required** 3-5 days for major sights.

☼ **Weather** Hot summers, cool winters with snow on the highlands.

✖ **When not to go** Good all year round.

Don't miss ...

★ 1 De Oude Kraal, page 726.

2 Arts and crafts in Clarens, page 730.

3 Golden Gate Highlands National Park, page 731.

4 Horse riding in the Maluti Mountains, page 738.

5 Whitewater rafting on the Ash River, page 738.

Between the Vaal River to the north and the Gariep (Orange) River to the south lies an undulating plateau and sparsely populated prairie land known as Free State. In the latter half of the 19th century the region was an independent Boer Republic governed by the Voortrekkers who had left the British Cape Colony in the 1830s. During this brief period of independence, Bloemfontein developed into a fine modern capital with many grand sandstone buildings. But the discovery of diamonds at Jagersfontein and Kimberley, along with gold in the second independent Boer Republic of the time, led to the outbreak of the Anglo-Boer War on 11 October 1899, a fact that has left its mark on the province.

While there is not much to see in the arid farmlands to the west of Bloemfontein, the Maluti Mountains in the eastern Free State hold many surprises. The scenery is spectacular as it rises to meet the lands of Lesotho, scattered with dams, mountain rivers and nature reserves, and connected by pretty rural villages with a wide range of accommodation choices and activities. At the centre of this area lies the spectacular Golden Gate Highlands National Park, where, even during the summer months, the hills can sometimes be covered with snow.

Ins and outs

Getting there and around

Bloemfontein is one of South Africa's most central transport hubs for buses, flights and trains, so you will not have any trouble getting to the Free State's capital. Getting around this part of South Africa is another matter, however, and you will need a car to explore it properly. The general flow of traffic is between the Cape and Johannesburg along the N1 but there are several contrasting routes you can take from Bloemfontein.

The **N1 north** takes you across the veld to Johannesburg; most of the countryside is flat and scattered with ugly mine dumps. There is little to stop for between here and Gauteng. The **N1 south** passes by the early settler towns of the **Xhariep** region before entering the **Great Karoo**. There is a long way to go before you reach the first fertile valleys of the Cape. The **N8** to the east goes to the higher lands of Lesotho and what are known as the **Eastern Highlands**. The countryside here is the most spectacular in Free State and this is the main road to Maseru (140 km), the capital of Lesotho. **Thaba 'Nchu** is a huge township that used not to be signposted from the main road during Apartheid; the lands around here were once part of the quasi-independent homeland known as Bophuthatswana, but it is all Free State today. Finally a short trip to the west along the N8 takes you to the mining town of **Kimberley**; further west the road skirts the fringes of the Kalahari en route to Namibia.

Bloemfontein

→ *Phone code: 051. Colour map 4, B3. Altitude: 1392 m.*

With one million residents, the provincial capital of the Free State is the sixth biggest city in South Africa and the country's judicial capital; the Court of Appeal sits here. The city is located on the highveld plains surrounded by a group of flat-topped hillocks. It has warm, wet summers and cold, dry winters. The surrounding countryside is very fertile and an important farming region, maize being the principal crop. The city centre is an interesting mix of modern tower blocks built during the 1960s and 1970s with the State's mineral wealth, and a core of fine sandstone buildings dating from the late 19th century when Bloemfontein was the capital of the small independent Orange Free State Republic. Its location right in the centre of South Africa, makes it is an important transport centre, and a popular overnight spot for motorists driving between Gauteng and the Cape. Like much of the Free State it has yet to figure on the tourist map, though fans of Lord of the Rings should note that JRR Tolkien was born here in 1892, moving to England when he was four years old. Despite its interesting history, modern Bloemfontein has few visitor attractions, although it is a pleasant enough place to spend a couple of days. ▸▸ *For listings, see pages 725-728.*

Ins and outs

Getting there **Bloemfontein Airport** ① *T051-4332901, www.airports.co.za*, is 10 km east of the city centre, off the N8, the Thaba Nchu road. Taxis are available for transfers. Three different long-distance **trains** stop in Bloemfontein each week, it is thus possible to travel to all the major towns in South Africa. While the train is very comfortable it is much slower than the bus, for example the journey from Cape Town takes 20 hours by train, but only 11 hours by bus. Check timings carefully if you plan on changing bus or train in Bloemfontein. **Buses** starting their journey from here tend to leave at a convenient hour, but those stopping to pick up and drop off can pass through in the middle of the night or very early in the morning. **Greyhound**, **Intercape** and **Translux** buses depart from and stop at the Tourist Centre on Park Road. ▶ *For further details, see Transport, page 728.*

Tourist information The **Tourist Centre** ⓘ *60 Park Rd, T051-4058489, www.bloemfontein.co.za, Mon-Fri 0800-1615, Sat 0800-1200*, is helpful and the staff are knowledgeable and keen to promote Bloemfontein as a tourist destination. **Motheo District Municipality Tourism** ⓘ *next to the Tourist Centre, T051-4471362, www.motheo.co.za, Mon-Fri 0730-1600*, has a range of leaflets covering most of the province including the Xhariep. It has a good selection of information on the Free State, strong supporters of cultural and community-based tourism projects and arranges township tours.

Bloemfontein

Sleeping 🛏
City Lodge **8**
Garden Court
  Bloemfontein **9**
Haldon House **12**
Halevy Heritage **2**
Hobbit House **5**

Lepel-le Garden Unit **3**
Naval Hill Backpackers **4**
Protea Bloemfontein **1**
Resting Place **11**

Eating 🍴
Beef Baron **1**

De Oude Kraal **6**
Die Keller **3**
Jazz Time Café **4**
Margaritas **7**
Primi Piatta **2**
Workshop Roadside Café **5**

Background

There are several theories about the name Bloemfontein, but the accepted version is that the wife of Johannes Nicolaas Brits, one of the first settlers in the area who started to farm here in 1840, planted some flowers around the fountain which was used by everyone travelling across the central plains.

In 1846 the Governor of the Cape Colony, Sir Peregrine Maitland, made a treaty with the Griqua chief, Adam Kok, whereby the land between the Riet and Modder rivers was opened to European settlement. Major Henry Warden, the British resident in Griqua territory, was instructed to move to the location to co-ordinate the new settlers. He chose Bloemfontein farm and Brits received £37.10 in compensation, followed by £50 a few years later and a farm in Harrismith, which he also named Bloemfontein.

In 1848 Sir Harry Smith visited the new settlement and proclaimed the territory between the Orange and Vaal rivers as British, calling it the Orange River Sovereignty, with Bloemfontein as its capital. Queen's Fort was built and the town slowly started to take shape. By 1853, Church Square and Market Square (now Hoffman Square) had been laid out. However, the surrounding countryside was still full of wild animals, which meant that travellers and farmers were in danger of attacks from lions, leopards and wild dogs. The British Government had decided the territory was hardly fit for habitation and not worth the trouble of maintaining. In 1854 the Bloemfontein Convention was signed, giving independence to the land between the Orange and Vaal rivers, and the British soldiers marched out of the town.

Josias Hoffman was the first President of the Republic of the Orange Free State and a *volksraad* (people's council) was elected to sit in the simple *raadsaal* (council chamber). This first council chamber can still be seen in St George's Street. President Johannes Brand followed him in 1863, under whom the town enjoyed 25 years of stable and prosperous independence when some fine government buildings were built. In 1890 the railway link with the Cape was finally completed and the town prospered further, though in 1904 there was a disastrous flood that cut the city in half and destroyed many buildings.

The discovery of diamonds at Jagersfontein and Kimberley along with gold, quickly led to the British wanting to re-establish control over these two regions. The Anglo-Boer War broke out and President Steyn of the Orange Free State sided with the South African Republic. When the British forces approached the town in March 1900 the Boer forces retreated to save the citizens and historic buildings. After the war was over, Bloemfontein became the capital of the Orange River Colony. In 1910, with the creation of the Union of South Africa, Bloemfontein aspired to be the country's capital; as it was it became the judicial capital, and remains so today.

Sights

① *The Tourist Centre produces a useful map showing 'The Rose Walk through Bloemfontein', which covers the major historical sites and takes about 1½ hrs.*

Most buildings of note are within easy walking distance of each other along President Brand Street. Many of these grand sandstone buildings date from the second half of the 19th century when Bloemfontein was the capital of the small – in terms of population – Orange Free State Republic. (It is not possible to go inside all of them because some are still in use today.) On the corner of President Brand and Charles streets is the **Appeal Court** ① *T051-4472631, by appointment only*. Although Bloemfontein was designated as the seat of the Appeal Court with the advent of the Union in 1910, this building was only completed in 1929. It was built in a free-Roman style with corrugated Italian tiles on the roof and window ledges. Above the main entrance the helmet of Faith and the torches of Truth are portrayed.

Standing opposite is the neoclassical, Doric-columned **Fourth Raadsaal** (Council Chamber) ① *T051-4478899, by appointment only*, with its domed tower. This was the last home of the *volksraad* (council) in the days of the independent republic and is now the seat of the Provincial Council. The impressive building was designed by L Canning and was completed in 1893. Inside, the original coat of arms of the Free State carved out of wood hangs behind the seat of the chairman, and the busts of six presidents are arranged around the chamber walls.

East of here is the **National Museum** ① *36 Aliwal St, T051-4479609, www.nasmus.co.za. Mon-Fri 0800-1700, Sat 1000-1700, Sun 1200-1730, R5.* It has the usual collection of natural history exhibits including a number of interesting dinosaur skeletons and a live snake park, as well as rooms dedicated to Bloemfontein's history and a mock-up early-19th-century street with dummies of various traders and families. The museum also has a café.

On the corner of President Brand and Maitland streets, is the **Old Government Building**, now the **National Afrikaans Literature Museum** ① *Mon-Fri 0800-1215, 1300-1600, Sat 0900-1200, T051-4054711*, an important collection of Afrikaans literature, and original manuscripts by leading poets and novelists. The original single storey building had a high clock tower and was built by Richard Wocke in 1875 to house a government office. A second storey was added and then in 1906 an extension designed by Herbert Baker was built at the back. Baker created the present form after a serious fire in 1908.

On President Brand Street is the **Jubileum** building. It was built in the late 1920s by boys from a local orphanage to provide a venue for reading and refreshments for young Afrikaners. A variety of entertainments were staged here, including concerts and art exhibitions, as well as political rallies.

Opposite the fire station is the **Supreme Court** ① *corner of President Brand and Fontein streets, T051 4478837, by appointment only*. This seat of the Provincial Law Court was built in 1909 at a cost of £60,000. It is a stately and vast court building where many famous cases have been tried in recent years.

Across the river is the **Old Presidency** ① *corner of President Brand and St George's streets, T051-4480949, Tue-Fri 1000-1200, 1300-1600, Sat-Sun 1300-1700, free*. This was home to the last three state presidents before the British invasion, and it occupies the site where Brits erected his original farm buildings and where Major Warden built his first residence in 1846. It has now been converted into a concert hall and a museum depicting the lives of the presidents. The original stables at the back have been converted into a coffee shop.

Just around the corner is the **First Raadsaal** (Council Chamber) ① *St George's St, Mon-Fri 1015-1500, Sat-Sun 1400-1700, small entrance fee*. This is a typical pioneers' building with a thatched roof, beaten dung floor and long white mud walls. It was opened in 1849 as the Government Schoolhouse, but was also used as a church and council chamber. After the creation of the Orange Free State Republic, the inauguration ceremonies for the first two presidents, Josias Hoffman and Jacobus Boshof, were held here. The *volksraad*, or people's council, met here until 1856, hence the name First Raadsaal. In 1877 the building was given to the town to be used as a museum.

On Church Street, the **Twin-towered Church**, which was fully restored in 1985, is on the site of the first small church built in 1849. Inaugurated in 1880, the church played a major role as the venue for the inauguration ceremonies for the last three state presidents, JH Brand, FW Reitz and MT Steyn. In 1935 the western tower collapsed and the other tower was removed, only for residents then to complain that the absence of spires spoilt the church's appearance; so in 1942 the two spires were re-erected.

In **Hertzog Square**, outside the City Hall, is a memorial and statue of General Hertzog. He became Prime Minister of South Africa in 1929 and again in 1934. A founder member of the Afrikaans-supporting, right-wing National Party in 1914, he introduced much of the legislation against non-whites.

The **National Women's Memorial and Anglo-Boer War Museum** ① *Monument Rd, T051-4470079, www.anglo-boer.co.za, Mon-Fri 0800-1630, Sat 1000-1700, Sun 1400-1700, small entry fee*, are 2 km south of the city centre. The memorial is an obelisk, 36.5 m high, built of sandstone from Kroonstad and resting at the foot of two *koppies* on the outskirts of Bloemfontein on Monument Rd. On each side of the column is a bronze bas-relief depicting scenes from the suffering of women and children during the Anglo-Boer War. The monument was unveiled on 16 December 1913 to commemorate the 26,370 women and children who died in concentration camps as a result of the Anglo-Boer War. (In a niche at the foot of the memorial are the ashes of Emily Hobhouse, a British woman who campaigned against the harsh conditions in the concentration camps.) The museum tells the story of the Anglo-Boer War, with extensive background information on the discovery of gold on the Witwatersrand and displays of the British and Boer campaigns.

Naval Hill was once outside the city, but is now almost completely engulfed by the expanding suburbs. The panoramic views of the city are worth the drive. At the top of this hill are the **Franklin Game Reserve**, the **Observatory Theatre** and a **White Horse**. The White Horse was laid out by soldiers during the Anglo-Boer War as a landmark for returning horsemen. There are eland, hartebeest and springbok in the reserve, and it is not uncommon to get very close to giraffe in the car park of the Observatory Theatre where they seek out shade.

South of the centre is the **Queen's Fort**, or **Military Museum** ① *Church St, T051-4475478, Mon-Fri 0800-1600, free*. Following his victory over the Boers at the battle of Boomplaats, Sir Harry Smith decided to build a new fort on a more strategically situated hill, named after Queen Victoria. For the first 30 years of the Free State Republic it was left to fall into a state of disrepair. In 1879, Captain FW Albrecht was appointed to oversee the complete rebuilding of the fort and mounted four iron nine-pounder guns. During the Second Anglo-Boer War it was occupied by British troops and at the end of the war it was given to the South African Constabulary. After housing a military headquarters the building is now a museum.

Free State National Botanical Garden ① *Rayton Rd, off Dan Pienaar Dr, R702, T051-4363612, www.sanbi.org, daily 0800-1800, R10*, covers 70 ha on the outskirts of Bloemfontein and spans a valley between picturesque dolerite koppies. Its natural vegetation comprises tall grassland and woodland, dominated by magnificent wild olive and karee trees and is home to about 400 species of plants. From November to March most of the plants in the garden are in full leaf; from March to June the colourful autumn shades dominate. There are pleasant walks through the gardens and up to the koppies and there's a birdhide, restaurant and visitor centre. Two new demonstration gardens are being developed; one on plants with medicinal properties, and the other to show water-wise gardening techniques.

Township tours

ⓘ *Township tours are playing an increasingly important role in the South African tourism industry, creating jobs for local communities.*

While Bloemfontein has important 'white' historical sites, the nearby townships also have significance relating to the birth of the ANC and the legacy of the struggle. To see how life is lived in these places is interesting in its own right, and tours visit cultural and art centres, *shebeens* (pubs), dance demonstrations, traditional restaurants, jazz clubs, and the various historical sites. There are three major townships outside Bloemfontein.

Within the city limits, **Mangaung** was where the ANC was founded in 1912. **Botshabelo**, meaning 'place of refugees', is 60 km from Bloemfontein on the N8. Estimated to be the second largest in the country after Soweto, it was established when blacks were forcibly removed from the Orange Free State towns. The vision of Pretoria during the Apartheid era was to develop Botshabelo into a so called 'Golden City' for the Sotho and Xhosa people, and rapid Apartheid planning at the time made it the fastest-growing urban centre in South Africa. Beyond Botshabelo, 65 km from Bloemfontein, **Thaba 'Nchu** was originally settled by Voortrekkers and later by Chief Moroka, the founder of the Barolong tribe and an important member of the early ANC. There is a rich Tswana culture here, particularly in the villages, which are still governed by chiefs and traditional courts. ▸▸ *For further details, see Tour operators, page 727.*

⦿ Bloemfontein listings

Hotel and guesthouse prices
L over US$300   AL US$220-300   A US$150-220
B US$100-150   C US$75-100   D US$35-75
E US$15-35   F under US$15
Restaurant prices
⍾⍾⍾ over US$30   ⍾⍾ US$15-30   ⍾ under US$15
See pages 46-51 for further information.

⦿ Sleeping

Bloemfontein *p720, map p721*
As Bloemfontein is an overnight stop for traffic between Jo'burg and Cape Town, there is a vast range of accommodation here. Look out for signs as you drive into town from the N1. The tourist centre has a full list.

B Garden Court Bloemfontein, (this is a Holiday Inn which has been rebranded) corner of Nelson Mandela Dr and Melville Dr, T051-4441253, www.southernsun.com. 147 a/c rooms, smoking and non-smoking, set around an open courtyard, restaurant, bar, swimming pool, disabled facilities, secure parking, comfortable if not predictable hotel on the outskirts of the city.

B Halevy Heritage Hotel, corner of Markgraaff and Charles streets, T051-4030600, www.halevyheritage.com. Very stylish, historic building dating from 1893, now completely refurbished with Victorian and Edwardian decor and reopened in 2004, 21 elegant rooms with all the mod cons, 2 bars, quality restaurant and cosy courtyard.

B Hobbit House, 19 President Steyn Av, T051-4470663, www.hobbit.co.za. 12 double en suite rooms with fluffy towels and duck-down duvets in a superior renovated boutique hotel dating from 1925 and obviously named after Tolkien's creation, full of period furnishings. Bar fashioned out of a tree, gourmet food in the restaurant served on china and silver-ware, after a day of exploring the city on foot the neat garden and swimming pool are a welcome sight. A special touch is a glass of sherry and chocolate at bedtime. Recommended.

C City Lodge, corner of Nelson Mandela St and Parfitt Av, T051-4442974, www.city lodge.co.za. 50 doubles, 102 singles, a/c, good-value town hotel geared for the business traveller, hence lots of small, single rooms, option of non-smoking, evening bar, pay extra for breakfast which is served in lobby lounge, small swimming pool. Rooms tend to suffer from traffic noise when you open windows.

C Lepel-le Garden Unit, 14 Usmar St, T082-6713137, lventer22@polka.co.za. The name means 'to lie like spoons'. A cosy, peaceful poolside cottage, self-catering for 4 people, in a quiet suburb, private entrance, TV, the owner manages the tourist office so you'll be in good hands. Recommended.

C Protea Hotel Bloemfontein, Sanlam Plaza, East Burger St, T051-4038000, www.protea hotels.com. 113 a/c rooms, TV, restaurant, bar, shops, secure parking, swimming pool, the principal hotel in the city centre, full quota of facilities but lacking in charm.

D Glen Country Lodge, 20 km north of Bloemfontein on the N1, T051-8612042, www.glencountrylodge.co.za. An alternative to city accommodation for drivers, 12 thatched chalets with bathrooms and kitchenettes, nestled amongst acacia trees, breakfast and dinner on request, swimming pool, lovely spot in the bush with sweeping lawns.

D Haldon House, Japie Spesery Lane, Kwaggafontein, 3 km west of the city, T051-5233607, www.haldon.co.za. 8 en suite double rooms with TV, most have a separate entrance. This is a fine house set in a mature estate with a swimming pool and a large shady veranda. Evening meals can be arranged. Short drive from city centre. Recommended.

D The Resting Place, 50 Scholtz St, T051-5225008. A total of 23 units set around the garden or pool, doubles and family rooms, some with DSTV, microwave, a/c, safe, jet bath and Turkish bath, also self-catering chalets, breakfast on request, spacious and secure central guesthouse, children and wheelchair friendly.

E-F Naval Hill Backpackers, Delville Rd, north of the centre, follow West Burger St towards Naval Hill and Franklin Reserve, T051-4307266, info@navalhillback packers.co.za. Regular users of backpackers will appreciate the different building; here the set-up has been created in an old water pump station dating from 1896. Dorms in ingenious corrugated-iron shacks within the old building, camping in the large grounds, 1 double private room with bush shower, large lounge and unusual underground eating area with pizza oven.

❷ Eating

There are more than 20 restaurants and cafés in the Loch Logan Waterfront. See Shopping, below.

Bloemfontein *p720, map p721*

❤❤❤ De Oude Kraal, 35 km out of town, off the N1 to Cape Town, T051-5640733, www.oudekraal.co.za. Open 0730-2130. Something a bit special, so despite its remote location booking is essential. Famous for its typical South African food, such as *boerekos*, formal 6-course dinners, fine wines, and cigars in a wonderful setting in a restored farmhouse. This restaurant is a favourite of South Africa's *Eat Out* magazine. Also offers 8 spacious garden rooms and 2 suites (**B**) each with its own bathroom and fireplace. Recommended.

❤❤ Beef Baron, 22 Second Av, Westdene, T051-4474290. Tue-Fri 1200-1430, 1830-late, Sat dinner only, Sun lunch only. Well-established steakhouse, good Karoo lamb as well as mature steaks and wide range of sauces, friendly service, good wine list, wooden deck for alfresco dining.

❤❤ Butcher's Brothers Steakhouse and Deli, Loch Logan Waterfront, T051-4301253. Open 1000-2200. Quality steakhouse with excellent cuts of beef also available from the deli along with olives and home-made pasta, excellent though expensive wine list, quick service.

❤❤ Catch 22, Mimosa Mall, T051-4446877. Open 1030-2300. Good and fresh seafood, despite the distance from the sea; try the seafood paella or casserole, or snails in garlic sauce, pleasant decor and friendly staff.

† Die Keller, 149 Zastron St, Westdene, T051-4487840. Open 1100-late. Good-value restaurant and cellar bar, beer on tap, giant TV screen, fun atmosphere at the weekend.

† Jazz Time Café, Loch Logan Waterfront, T051-4305727. Open 1200-2400. Huge cocktail bar, outside terrace, excellent music, jazz, blues, big band, hubble-bubble pipes, extensive menu, try the *Zivas*, a Yemeni dough with a savoury filling, folded and toasted, a great place for an evening out.

† Margaritas, Bays Village, 59 Milner Rd, Bayswater, T051-4363729. Tue-Sat 1200-1430, 1830-2230, Sun 1200-1430. A good choice of fresh seafood and steaks, try the well-matured rump with creamy biltong and brandy sauce, extensive wine list, or snacks at the English pub-style bar.

† Primi Piatta, Loch Logan Waterfront, T051-4487662. Open 0900-2200. Modern funky decor with walls lined with coloured bottles and an open kitchen, leans towards Italian but a long menu of breakfasts, daily specials, pizza, pasta and snacks. Good service from staff in orange overalls.

† Workshop Roadside Café, 109 President Reitz St, Westdene, T051-4472761. Open 1000-late. Café with a giant TV screen, packed solid when there's a rugby match on, good value for the budget-minded.

● Bars and clubs

Bloemfontein *p720, map p721*
There high number of students in Bloemfontein mean there is also a large club scene. As in any city, clubs go in and out of favour quickly and often change names or move location. For the latest information ask the waiters at the **Jazz Time Café** (see above).

● Shopping

Bloemfontein *p720, map p721*
Loch Logan Waterfront, 1st Av.
An attractive shopping mall next to a lake and dam in Kings Park. Some of Bloemfontein's trendiest restaurants and bars are scattered along the board-walk on the water's edge and there is a 6-screen cinema. It's currently being extended to a 4-storey mall to incorporate most of South Africa's chain stores, and is already home to **Kloppers**, a large department store. Strangely, department stores are not common in South Africa. An arts and crafts market is held here on the first Sat of every month.

Mimosa Mall, corner of Nelson Mandela and Parfitt streets. A standard South African mall with the usual facilities, banks, food court, 4-screen **Ster-Kinekor** cinema, 2 internet cafés, American Express office.

▲ Activities and tours

Bloemfontein *p720, map p721*
Cricket
International cricket matches are played at the **Goodyear Park Stadium** which is part of the complex of excellent sports facilities to the west of the city centre close to the tourist office. It has been renamed Springbok Park, but it is mostly referred to by its old name. The cricket ground is a fun, small stadium, which has yet to be spoilt by towering modern stands. Here fans can still lounge around or cook up a braai on grass banks as the game unfolds in front of them, a cool beer in hand. Tickets through **Compu ticket**, www.computicket.com, and contact the **Free State Cricket Union's**, T051-4475715, www.fscu.co.za, for fixtures.

Football and rugby

Free State Stadium, is next door to the cricket ground in Kings Park, and is a neat modern stadium where international football and rugby matches are played. It's currently in the throes of being upgraded for the 2010 FIFA Football World Cup when it will accommodate 40,000.

Tours

A full-day tour visits all 3 townships, while a half-day tour visits 1 or 2, which can be combined with a half-day city tour. Contact **Motheo District Municipality Tourism** (see page 721).

⊖ Transport

Bloemfontein *p720, map p721*
It's 1000 km to **Cape Town**; 415 km to **Johannesburg**; 186 km to **Kimberley**; 157 km to **Maseru**.

Air

Airport information, T051-4072240, www.airports.co.za. **Mango** has flights between **Cape Town** and Bloemfontein. **One Time** has flights to and from **Cape Town** and **Durban**. **SAA** has flights to and from **Johannesburg**, **Cape Town**, **Durban** and **Port Elizabeth**.

Airline offices Mango, T0861-162646 (in South Africa), T011-3591222 (from overseas), ww5.flymango.com. **One Time**, T0861-345345 (in South Africa), T011-9288000 (from overseas), www.1time.co.za. **SAA**, T011-9781111, ww2.flysaa.com.

Bus

Intercape, **Greyhound** and **Translux** have offices in the tourist centre on Park Rd where the buses stop and run daily services to just about all the other large cities including **Cape Town**, **Durban**, **Johannesburg**, and **Port Elizabeth**. Big Sky Coaches runs a service to **Upington**, in the Northern Cape Province, Fri at 1400 from the tourist centre; this service returns from Upington on Sun at 1300.

Bus companies Big Sky Coaches, T051-5233620, www.bigskycoaches.co.za. **Intercape**, T00861-287287, www.inter cape.co.za, **Greyhound**, T083-9159000, www.greyhound.co.za, and **Translux**, T0861-589282, www.translux.co.za.

Car hire

Avis, airport, T051-4332331, and Gysie Pienaar Motors, Nelson Mandela St, T051-4476185, www.avis.co.za; **Budget**, airport, T051-4331178, www.budget.co.za; **Imperial**, airport T051-4333511; **Sasol Garage**, President Boshoff St, T051-4484530, www.imperialcarrental.co.za.

Taxi

Silver Leaf Taxis, at the tourist centre T051-4302005, for airport transfers.

Train

Part of the original station building from 1890 still remains. Information T051-4082941, reservations T0860-008888, www.spoor net.co.za, timetables and fares are published on the website. Bloemfontein is connected to most major cities, there are services to **Port Elizabeth**, **Johannesburg**, **East London**, **Kimberley** and **Cape Town**.

⊙ Directory

Bloemfontein *p720, map p721*
Banks All the main branches are within the Mimosa Mall, corner of Nelson Mandela and Parfitt streets. **Medical services Chemist** and **MediClinic**, corner of Parfitt and Keller streets, T051-4046666, www.bloemfonteinmc.co.za.

Eastern Highlands

The countryside neighbouring the Lesotho border, dominated by sandstone outcrops and eroded river valleys, is the most dramatic and interesting in the Free State. The hills once provided shelter for the early San hunters who lived in the region and there are some fine examples of cave paintings as a record of this past. (You will need guidance from the local tourist offices to find and see the art.) The region looks its best in the spring when the cherry orchards are in blossom. During winter there can be heavy snowfalls in the mountains. The highlands are perfect hiking country and ideal for pony trekking and there are some great accommodation options on farms and in secluded valleys. Running parallel to the Lesotho border, the R26 passes through all the towns of note in this region.
▶▶ *For listings, see pages 734-738.*

Ladybrand ●◐ ▶▶ *pp734-738. Colour map 4, B4.*

→ *Phone code: 051.*

A pleasant country town surrounded by a sandstone ridge full of San paintings and hidden caves, Ladybrand is the closest South African town to the Lesotho capital, Maseru (15 km). Along with Ficksburg, the town was founded in 1867 after the war between the Boers and the Basothos, to help guarantee peace in the Conquered Territory. It was named after Lady Catharina Brand, the mother of President Brand of the Orange Free State Republic. Sandstone from this area was used to build the Union Building in Pretoria. The small **Catharina Brand Museum** ① *17 Church St, Tue-Sat 0900-1200, 1400-1600, Sat 0900-1200*, has an interesting feature on the **Lesotho Highlands Water Project** (see page 807), as well as some exhibits on bushmen and early administration of the Lesotho border.

Ins and outs

Maloti Route Tourism Office ① *Catharina Brand Museum, T051-9245131, www.malotiroute.co.za, Mon-Fri 0800-1700.* The Maloti Route covers the Free State's Eastern Highlands, parts of the Eastern Cape and Lesotho, so this enthusiastic tourist office is well worth going out of your way for if you are planning to travel in any of these regions. They can provide an excellent booklet and map.

Sights

There are two major **San rock painting** sites nearby that can be visited with a guide from the tourist office. One of 12 San art national monuments in the country, it is thought that they are the most concentrated San paintings in South Africa, ranging from 250 to 5000 years old. At **Modderpoort**, 15 km to the north, there is a unique cave church dating from 1869. It was built by the Anglican Society of St Augustine, a small group of monks. You can visit by prior arrangement, T051-9243318.

Ficksburg ●◐◐ ▶▶ *pp734-738. Colour map 4, A/B5.*

→ *Phone code: 051. Altitude: 1629 m.*

Named after Commandant-General Johan Fick, a hero of the Basotho wars, the town was founded in 1867 to occupy what was known as the Conquered Territory after the Basotho war. Its role was to prevent cattle rustlers coming over from Lesotho and to strengthen general control over the area. Interestingly, cattle rustling still occasionally occurs in this region. A **cherry festival**, is held here during the third week of November each year, when you can indulge in cherry liqueur, maraschino, schnapps, and brandied cherries in syrup. These days the small town has important trade links with Lesotho, but otherwise it is only worth visiting for basic supplies and for the **tourist office** ① *96 McCabe St, T051-9332130, www.ficksburg.org.za*, which has an exhibition on the **Lesotho Highlands Water Project** (see also page 807). A small **museum** ① *Mon-Fri 1000-1200, 1400-1600*, commemorates the (not very interesting) life of General Fick.

Rustler's Valley was a popular destination to the north of Ficksburg in the foothills of the Witteberge Mountains, which had become famous as one of South Africa's premier festival sites. Unfortunately, a fire destroyed the lodge and the whole valley in September 2007. It will remain to be seen if the site is resurrected in the future.

Fouriesburg to Clarens ●→ *pp734-738. Colour map 5, A5.*

→ *Phone code: 058.*

Fouriesburg is a small, untidy town 12 km from the **Caledonspoort** border post with Lesotho. Founded in 1892, it was named after Christoffel Fourie, the local farmer who originally owned the land. For a few months during the **Anglo-Boer War**, the town was the last seat of the Orange Free State's republican government and a stronghold of the Boer forces. As a consequence it was almost destroyed by the British army.

About 2 km south of Fouriesburg is the **Meiringskloof Nature Park** ① *T058-2230067, www.meiringskloof.co.za, R20 per car, R10 per person*. Within the park are overnight chalets and a campsite and short walks among the cliffs where there is a large open cave, 'holkrans', once used as a hide-out during the Anglo-Boer War. For visitors with a head for heights there is a chain ladder which goes up a steep cliff face to a dam supplying water to Fouriesburg.

North of Fouriesburg

Travelling north from Fouriesburg there is a choice of two routes; 45 km direct to Bethlehem on the R26, or a much more interesting route, the R711 to Clarens, which also provides the opportunity to visit the Golden Gate Highlands National Park (see page 731).

Surrender Hill is 7 km before Clarens on the R711. The name reminds the Boers of their most devastating defeat during the Anglo-Boer War, when on 29 July 1900, 4314 Free State soldiers under General Prinsloo were cornered in the mountains and surrendered to the British. Most were sent to India as prisoners of war.

Clarens ●●●▲→ *pp734-738. Colour map 4, A5.*

→ *Phone code: 058.*

This village was named after the Swiss resort on the shore of Lake Geneva where President Paul Kruger died in 1904. The settlement was only laid out in 1912 and has no historical past to explore but the relaxed feel of the place makes it the ideal spot to use as a base to explore the highlands. Tourism has taken over in this tiny, pretty village and a number of galleries, craft shops, and tea rooms surround a grassed square with a few sandstone buildings and large trees. The grasslands which dominate the sandstone slopes are known for their large variety of wild flowers in the summer months. It is the closest village to the Golden Gate Highlands National Park when approaching from the west. The natural beauty of the area has attracted a number of artists to the region.

There are five quite well-preserved **cave paintings** on a farm called Schaapplaats, 20 minutes' walk from town. To visit these paintings, call in at the local tourist office, **Clarens Destinations** ① *Market St, T058-2561542, www.clarenstourism.co.za, daily 0900-1300, 1400-1700*, who will phone ahead to let the farm owners know you are coming. Clarens is a small community and the staff in this office are helpful, local booking agents for accommodation and activities, and know all the local artists and craftspeople. It's worth a stop if you are considering buying quality pieces.

Around Clarens

From Clarens, head towards Golden Gate Highlands National Park, to **Basotho Cultural Village** ① *10 km before the park gate on the right, T058-7210300, Mon-Fri 0900-1600, Sat-Sun 0900-1700, entry and 30-min guided tour R25*. It is a worthwhile stop and offers an insight into the lives of the Basotho people who have similar traditions to those people living over the border in Lesotho. Guided tours take you around a scattering of *bomas* and huts where traditional craft-making is demonstrated, local beer can be sampled, and a lively band and dancers provide entertainment. The village also has tea gardens, a curio shop and art gallery.

On the Bethlehem road, 8 km from Clarens, there's a viewpoint over the Ash River outfall, a new surge of water created by the Lesotho Highlands Water Project.

Golden Gate National Park ● ▶ *pp734-738. Colour map 4, A5.*

A small (11,600-ha) national park on the edge of the Drakensberg and Maluti Mountains, the Golden Gate Highlands National Park is set in an area of massive sandstone rock formations. The eroded valleys have produced some spectacular shapes, with caves, cliffs and green grasslands against a backdrop of golden rocks. This is a particularly special place at sunset when the colours of the rocks are at their most intense. The Caledon River rises in these mountains. It is a popular park given its proximity to Johannesburg (three hours by car). The principal attractions are the hiking opportunities, the climbing and the spectacular rock formations. The Rhebok Hiking Trail is also in the park, see below.

Ins and outs

Getting there The common approach is the main road from Clarens (15 km), which is surfaced all the way through the park. As you enter the park and approach the offices the road passes through a narrow valley with giant cliffs which give the name 'Golden Gate'. The sun shining on the oxides in the sandstone produces a brilliant golden hue to the cliff face.

Tourist information A public road runs through the middle of the park so day visitors do not have to pay an entrance fee. Overnight visitors, R60, children R30. All enquiries can be dealt with at the **Glen Reenan Camp reception** ① *T058-2550000*. Fuel is available at Glen Reenen, 0700-1730. **Glen Reenen Shop** ① *daily, winter 0730-1700, summer 0700-1730*, stocks limited groceries, beer and wine, firewood and a few fresh items, maps and curios.

Climate The typical climate is cool rainy summers and cold winters with a high chance of snow. There is heavy snowfall on the high peaks while the valleys and surrounds remain untouched. Do not hike without suitable protective clothing in the winter. The park receives over 800 mm of rain annually so it is lush and green nearly all year.

Bread basket

About 90% of the Free State is used for agriculture with about two million hectares under cultivation for crops. Of these, about 100,000 are irrigated. The Free State is aptly referred to as the 'bread basket' of South Africa, producing about 40% of the total maize production of South Africa, 50% of wheat, 80% of sorghum, 33% of potatoes, 18% of red meat, 30% of groundnuts and 15% of wool. Around 11,500 commercial farmers are farming on some 50,000 farms in the province. The other big earner is mining and the Free State produces about one third of South Africa's gold. It also has large deposits of coal, and produces approximately 80% of South Africa's bentonite (a sort of clay that used in the building trade). The mining industry is also the biggest net supplier of jobs in the province, employing approximately 22% of the labour force.

Wildlife

You are unlikely to see many wild animals from the car, but once you get into the wooded valleys and the quiet hills you may well see black wildebeest, Burchell's zebra, mountain reedbuck, blesbok, eland and grey rhebok. The larger raptors favour the high rocky cliffs; look out for the bearded vulture, jackal buzzard, bald ibis and black eagle.

Rhebok Hiking Trail

ⓘ *The trail has to be booked in advance through one of the SANParks offices or online, www.sanparks.org, bookings open 13 months in advance.*

This popular two-day hike covers a total distance of 30 km. The path starts from the campsite at Glen Reenen and it is about 16 km to the overnight Rhebok Hut; look out for the San cave near the start of the trail. On the second day you will cover 14 km, but this includes the ascent of Generaalskop (2837 m). This is the highest point in the Free State and has views to match. On hot sunny days, the waterfall and Langtoon Dam are welcome sights near the end of the second day. The trail ends back at Glen Reenen, so you can look forward to hot showers at the end of some strenuous walking. Do not walk alone, a minimum of four people is ideal in this terrain. There are plenty of shorter day walks that have been marked out; some will take you to a peak top and back, others enable you to explore wooded kloofs. Keep an eye out for game at all times. ⏵ *For horse riding and other activities in the area, see page 738.*

Bethlehem ●❶❷❸ ⏵ *pp734-738. Colour map 4, A5.*

➔ *Phone code: 058.*

The town was founded in 1864 on a farm known as Pretoriuskloof. It is the principal town of the Eastern Free State, an important wheat-growing area and one of South Africa's biggest exporters of roses. It is also where South Africa's national hot-air balloon race is held in May each year. A prominent local church minister, FP Naude, gave the settlement its name, reflecting the fact that the first settlers found that wheat flourished in the fertile Jordan Valley. It is a large town with a good range of restaurants and accommodation, but there is little here for the visitor apart from some fine examples of early sandstone buildings. The Dihlabeng Municipality **tourist office** ⓘ *9 Muller St, T058-3035732, www.dihlabeng.org.za, Mon-Sat 0830-1300, 1400-1600*, has a good range of brochures including a map of the Sandstone Walking Tour which takes you around the old buildings and lasts about 1½ hours.

The **Museum of Cultural History** ① *in the former Nazareth Mission Church at the top end of Muller St, T058-3033477, Fri 1000-1230, 1430-1700*, has a collection depicting the region's local history, with an early steam locomotive in the grounds.

Harrismith ◉❼ ▸▸ *pp734-738. Colour map 4, A6.*

→ *Phone code: 058.*

Most visitors pass Harrismith on the N3 en route to Durban. The town is dominated by a long flat mountain, the **Platberg**, 2377 m. Each year on 10 October a race is run up the mountain and along the top for 5 km before returning to the town. The origin of the race is very much part of local history. At the end of the Anglo Boer War a Major John Belcher from the British Army referred to the mountain as 'that little hill of yours'. He was immediately bet that he could not run to the top in less than an hour. He duly won the bet, and the race, along with a trophy, was born.

The town was named after the British Governor Sir Harry Smith and nearby Ladysmith is named after his Spanish wife. The growth of the settlement was influenced by the discovery of diamonds at Barkly West and Kimberley in the 1860s, and gold on the Witwatersrand in 1886. Before the railway was built from the coast, at least 50 wagons a day used to stop over in the town.

Today it is still a popular stop for travellers between Gauteng and Durban, either overnight or for a break in one of the many service stations off the N3. Information is available from the **tourist office** ① *Southey St, T058-6223525, Mon-Fri 0800-1630, Sat 0930-1230*.

Around Harrismith

Sterkfontein Dam Nature Reserve, set in the foothills of the Drakensberg, 23 km from Harrismith, covers an area of more than 7000 ha with a 104-km shoreline and is one of the largest in South Africa. Most visitors come here for watersports and fishing. Hiking is possible and there are good opportunities for viewing raptors, and an interesting vulture 'restaurant' that attracts Cape and bearded vultures. The entrance is off the R74 between Harrismith and Bergville. For those staying overnight at the reserve's resort, day trips can easily be made from here to the Northern Drakensberg (see page 498).

⊚ Eastern Highlands listings

⊜ Sleeping

Ladybrand p729

C Cranberry Cottage, 37 Beeton St, T051-9242290, www.cranberry cottage.co.za. Smart award-winning B&B in a restored Victorian country house with additional rooms in the original ticket office and waiting rooms of Ladybrand Railway Station decorated with railway memorabilia and antiques. 24 en suite double rooms with DSTV and kettles, some with fireplaces, swimming pool, gym and beauty spa. Gourmet dinners are served on the patio or in the candlelit dining room. If you're not staying, the **Duck Pond** restaurant is still worth a visit on the way through the village. Recommended.

C My Housy, 17a Prinsloo St. T051-9241010, www.myhousy.co.za. A well run B&B with 7 double and 1 family room with en suite bathroom, TV, heaters for winter and private entrance, peaceful garden, all individually decorated thanks to one of the owners being an artist, very stylish breakfasts, think stacked omelettes garnished with asparagus spears and flower petals.

D Arbutus Lodge, 19 Prinsloo St, T/F051-9242258, arbutuslodge@lbrand.com. 4 doubles, 1 garden self-catering cottage in the former stables, historic sandstone house that is a national monument, B&B with high ceilings and antique furnishings, garden full of flowers, neat veranda.

Ficksburg p729

Apart from the dreary **Highland Hotel**, which isn't recommended, there's a limited choice in town, but there are a couple of good rural retreats.

B Franshoek Polo Lodge, take the Fouriesburg Rd 9 km, turn left on to a dirt road, the S385 for 18 km, T/F051-9332828, www.franshoek.co.za. A comfortable rural lodge, 10 rooms, some with wrought-iron beds, thatched restaurant with cosy log fires, swimming pool. Plenty of emphasis on outdoor pursuits, including polo, rock climbing, abseiling, trout fishing, swimming pool, limited numbers, intimate atmosphere. The chef here also offers Thai cookery courses. Rates are full board.

C Bella Rosa, 21 Bloem St, T/F051-9332623, bellarosa@telkomsa.net. 11 elegant suites make up this quality B&B set in a sandstone Victorian town house. Start the day with a delicious breakfast overlooking the mature gardens. A quiet and comfortable home decorated with antiques, pub and wine cellar with roaring fire, dinner on request, no young children.

D Green Acorn, 7 Fontein St, T051-9332746, www.greenacorn.co.za. Comfortable guesthouse centrally situated in Ficksburg, quiet and tranquil. 10 rooms with private entrances in the house and in pretty garden cottages, light and airy furnishings.

D Hoekfontein Oxwagon Camp, 10 km to the south of Ficksburg on the R26 is a turning onto a gravel road, follow signs for 15 km, T/F051-9333915, oxwagon@ telkomsa.net. Accommodation in original ox wagons arranged in a semi-circle around a central eating and lounge boma. Double beds in the wagons themselves under white starched canvas roofs, also some rondavels, shared ablution block and self-catering kitchen, tractor rides, visits to San rock art and abseiling on the neighbouring cliffs. Recommended.

Fouriesburg to Clarens p/30

C Fouriesburg Country Inn, 17 Reitz St, T058-2230207, www.fouriesburgcountry inn.co.za. 22 rooms, the only hotel in town, the façades have been taken from the old railway buildings, a comfortable, quiet overnight stop, small rooms opening onto sheltered veranda overlooking the church, a pleasant touch is being able to go into the original sandstone wine cellar and choose your wine before dinner. Restaurant offers a selection of mixed grills and salads, and rates include breakfast and dinner.

C-E Meiringskloof Nature Park, 2 km south of Fouriesburg, follow Fleck St out of town, T058-2230067, www.meiringskloof.co.za. Simple self-catering stone chalets and basic campsite with braai pits and power points in a beautiful kloof surrounded by sandstone cliffs with open caves, thick indigenous bush and abundant bird life. Swimming pool, horse riding, 4WD trails, a number of short hikes, kiosk selling basic groceries, popular with families.

D-F Shumba Valley Farm, 9 km south of Fouriesburg towards Ficksburg, turn off at the S293 for 3 km, T058-2230277, www.shumbavalleyfarm.co.za. A mixture of accommodation in B&B en suite rooms, self-catering caravans or cottages, some in converted stables, or camping, cosy lounge and pub. Farm retreat with lots of activities, quad biking, hiking, excellent horse trails from 1 hr for beginners to 5-day excursions into the mountains for experienced riders sleeping out under the stars with the horses.

Clarens p730

The tourist office will fax or email a complete list of accommodation.

B Cranford Inn, 19 Larola St, T/F058-2561358. Modern red-brick hotel with 24 comfortable rooms, private patios, fresh flowers, TV, hot-water bottles, heating, restaurant and bar.

C Maluti Mountain Lodge, Steil St, T058-2561422, www.malutilodge.co.za. 20 en suite double rooms, 4 family rondavels, with heating and M-Net TV, set in neat gardens,

good country cooking, fun atmosphere in the **Duck & Hound** pub, swimming pool.

C-F Bokpoort, signposted 5 km out of Clarens on road to Golden Gate, T/F058-2561181, www.bokpoort.co.za. A 3-km dirt road winds up into the hills onto a ridge where the farms and stables are laid out. There are 8 B&B chalets and 2 8-bed hikers' huts and camping, the shower block has plenty of hot water when the wood fires are burning, simple dining room and bar. Well known for their excellent horse-riding safaris from 2 hrs to 10 days in the Maluti Mountains, when you are treated to some superb countryside and real South African breakfasts. A 2-day ride takes you to the snowline in winter. Recommended for keen riders.

D Patcham Place, 262 Church St, T/F058-2561017, www.clarenstourism.co.za/patchamplace. 5 double or twin rooms with en suite facilities in a timber cottage and good mountain views, TV, each has a private balcony and separate entrance, but share a kitchen and lounge. Electric blankets and heaters serve as a reminder as to how cold it can get in this area during the winter months.

D The Thistle Stop, 58 Le Roux St, T/F058-2581003. A neat town house B&B, lounge area where tea, coffee and rusks are available, also a family self-catering cottage sleeping 4, electric blankets and heaters are available in the winter months.

D-F Clarens Inn, Van Reenen St, T058-2561199. Family cottage sleeping 6 plus a dorm (no bedding) with communal kitchen with microwave, fridge, stove and coffee machine, and some space for tents. Good value, pretty spot, central location.

Golden Gate Highlands National Park p731

All accommodation is booked through **SANParks**, T012-4289111, www.sanparks.org.

B Highlands Mountain Retreat, 7 km from Glen Reenen off the Oribi Loop road (2200 m above sea level), **SANParks**, T058-2550012. This new camp has 8 double and family log cabins with kitchen, braai, TV and fireplace (pretty essential most nights), some with

disabled access. Check in is at Glen Reenen where you will be given a map and directions. The last kilometre to the camp is quite steep, but manageable in a normal car.
B-C Brandwag Hotel, beside the main road that runs through the park, T058-2551000. Refurbished large hotel with rooms for up to 4, with bathroom and TV; in the grounds are 4-bed chalets, with bathroom, kitchenette, fridge, TV and braai facilities. The restaurant has excellent views, bar serves pub lunches, kiosk does takeaways. Professional set up and from your room you have an unimpeded view of the mountains, but unfortunately no effort was made to blend the complex into the otherwise uninterrupted scenery and it really shouldn't have been built in 1965 in such a naturally beautiful spot.
C-E Glen Reenen Camp, beside the main road that runs through the park. It is always worth calling the park reception direct on T058-2550000 to check for late availability, reception hours, winter 0730-1700, summer 0700-1730. If you arrive outside these hours the nightwatchman can give keys to pre-booked guests but cannot check you in without a prior booking. There are 2 types of self-catering hut, each has shower, fridge, cooking utensils, 1 type has a TV, 2 single beds and a double bed in the loft, the other has 3 single beds in 1 room. Some have fireplaces. All accommodation has been recently refurbished and the old staff houses have been turned into 10 2-bed units. Across the road is the campsite which has plenty of shade and is beside a mountain stream, kitchen, electric points in shower block, swimming pool, a peaceful setting in a narrow, steep-sided valley. Be warned it can get far too cold for camping in the winter. Some recognized hikes start from here; you can pick up a map at the shop.
E Rhebok Hut, overnight hut on the Rhebok Hiking Trail. 3 bedrooms with 6 bunks and mattresses, coal stove, paraffin cooker, basic utensils in the kitchen, cold showers, toilets, bring a sleeping bag and food.

Bethlehem *p732*
B-C Fisant, Bokmakierie and Hoephoep Guest House, 8-10 Thoi Oosthuyse St, T058-3037144, www.fisant.co.za. Smart modern houses on the outskirts of town, 7 double rooms and 9 family units with en suite bathroom, some with kitchenettes for self-catering, non-smoking room available, buffet breakfasts, TV, laundry, peaceful garden, undercover parking, German spoken, well run and good value.
D Bread House, 14 President Vorster St, T058-3034329, www.breadhouse.co.za. 6 modern double rooms with en suite bathroom, DSTV, under-carpet heating, electric blankets, homely guest lounge with fireplace, braai area, swimming pool, pool table, excellent value.
D Die Nes, 3 van Raalte St, T058-3034073, www.dienesguesthouse.co.za. 4 double rooms with en suite bathroom, bar fridge, TV. A smart B&B decorated in strong primary colours, bright, fresh and hospitable. Lower rates at the weekend.
D Park Hotel, 23 Muller St, T/F058-3035191. 15 double rooms, 27 single rooms, all a/c and with TV, cheaper family and double rooms in old block, the new part is built around a leafy atrium. Restaurant, bar, swimming pool, secure parking, one of the best in town.
D-F Loch Athlone Holiday Resort, 3 km on the Fouriesburg road, T058-3034981. Popular family resort beside Loch Athlone, a large lake created by damming the Jordan River. Good-value rooms out of season, but very busy during school holidays, space for 200 caravans! Self-catering chalets, restaurant, bar, TV room, laundry, tennis, mini-golf, swimming pool, all watersports available on the dam, from pedal boats to power boats.

Harrismith and around *p733*
C Harrismith Inn, McKechnie Rd, T058-6221011, www.africanskyhotels.com. 119 a/c en suite modern rooms in a 2-storey block surrounding a swimming pool, restaurant offering buffet meals, **Harry's Bar**, business orientated but a comfortable overnight stop.

C Shady Pines, 67 Stuart St, T058-6223020, www.shadypines.co.za. Comfortable and hospitable guesthouse in a restored house built in 1880, wooden floors, some 4-poster beds, white linen, spacious gardens, 7 en suite rooms and 2 self-catering units, home cooked meals available, tiny chapel in the grounds for weddings.

C-E Eagle Mountain Game Lodge, 21 km northeast of Harrismith on the R722 to Verkykerskop, T058-6230235, www.eaglemountain.co.za. 5 simple self-catering log cabins and chalets sleeping up to 6, tent sites and caravan stands, all with plenty of privacy, all set on a private 1000-ha reserve with the usual collection of antelope, which roam freely among the guest rondavels.

🍴 Eating

Ladybrand *p729*

❚❚❚ Cranberry Cottage, 37 Beeton St, T051-9242290. If you're not staying at this guesthouse phone ahead to book dinner, 3-course set dinners, generous portions, country cooking, some game and duck dishes, extensive winelist.

❚❚❚ Impero Romano, 11 Church St, T051-9241184. A surprising find for a small town this Italian restaurant comes complete with pillars and statues. The wide range of pizzas and pasta is actually cooked by an Italian.

Ficksburg *p729*

❚ The Bottling Co, Piet Retief St, T051-9332404. Mon-Sat. Pub and restaurant with good choice of beer, steak, chicken and fish.

Clarens *p730*

❚ Artist's Café, Windmill Centre, Main Rd, T058-2561404. Open daily for milkshakes, pies, cakes, waffles, pastries, light meals, sandwiches made from fresh bread, jungle gym in the garden for kids.

❚ Café Moulin, Windmill Centre, Main St, T082-6901382. Thu-Tue 0800-1700. Country cooking, light meals, salads and quiches, home-made bread and preserves, chicken pies and South African traditional .

❚ Street Café, T058-2561064. Daily 0800-late. Snack meals like pizza and shwarmas and afternoon teas, steaks, fish and pasta in the evening, open-air veranda, pub open late.

Bethlehem *p732*

❚❚❚ O'Hagens, 8 Theron St, T058-3030919. 1100-late. Good-value pub/restaurant chain, English pub decor, varied menu, large portions, the very hungry can try the foot-long pies.

❚❚❚ Park Grill, in the Park Hotel, see Sleeping page 736. Has an extensive menu including good healthy stir-frys and steaks and sauces, but slow service and gloomy dark wood interior.

Harrismith *p733*

❚❚❚ Princess & Frog, 17 Vowe St, T058-6222476. Tue-Sat 1000-late. Unusual for the area, a cosy double-storey Victorian house, fine French cuisine, a limit of 12 people so advance booking essential.

🛍 Shopping

Clarens *p730*

For a small village Clarens has no fewer than 18 galleries and craft shops, so its just a case of browsing around. For sale are local handicrafts and jewellery, various paintings by local artists, antiques, ceramics and decorations and furniture from as far away as Malaysia. As Clarens is a popular day tripping destination, all are open at the weekends.
Art & Wine Gallery on Main, Main St, T058-2561298, www.artandwine.co.za. Sells wines from Stellenbosch and exhibits paintings, sculptures, ceramics and glassware.
Clarens Meander Shops, next to the Caltex garage as you approach town, has several craft shops and galleries, a farm stall selling

home-made treats, ATMs and a café. Also here is an information office for the **Lesotho Highlands Water Project**, www.lhwp.org.ls.

▲ Activities and tours

Clarens *p730*
Golf
There is presently an 18-hole golf and trout fishing estate being laid out in the lee of the Rooiberg Hills, the **Clarens Golf and Trout Estate**, T058-2561171, www.theclarens.co.za, which should be operational by the time you read this and will accept guest players.

Horse riding
Bokpoort, T/F058-2561181, www.bokpoort.co.za (see Sleeping). The most exciting horse trails in the region. Standard route lasts for 2 days, with a night at a deserted homestead in the Maluti Mountains, the larger the group the better the value. Shorter rides also available and the Basotho ponies are suitable for young children.

Quad biking
Sethuthuthu Tours, (the name means motorbike in Sesotho), T058-2561569, or book at the tourist office. Quad-bike tours from 1 hr to a full day on guided trails connecting local farms. These trails are not for the thrill seeker as the pace is quite slow, but there are some great views over the Free State and Maluti Mountains.

Whitewater rafting
Outrageous Adventures, T083-4859654, www.outrageousadventures.co.za. Since the opening of the Katse Dam in Lesotho, part of the mammoth Lesotho Highlands Water Project to increase the feed of many of South Africa's rivers, **Clarens Ash River** has experienced a surge of extra water from the new Trans Caledon Transfer Tunnel. The water exits the tunnel at 54 cu m per second and a series of rapids has developed on the river; some grade III-IV. This company offers full-day whitewater rafting runs for R580 per person including lunch and drinks and transfers to and from Clarens. This is now considered one of the best runs in the country.

Golden Gate Highlands National Park *p731*
Horse riding
There are stables outside the park at Gladstone, 3 km from the Glen Reenan towards Clarens, T058-2250951. Although the owners will tell you that anyone can go on these rides they are not suitable for totally inexperienced people as the horses will occasionally break into a gallop. There are plenty of horses and it is not necessary to book, just turn up around 1000, though to be certain of a ride phone ahead. Rides cost about R50 per hr.

⊙ Transport

Bethlehem *p732*
Bus
Translux, www.translux.co.za, and **Greyhound**, www.greyhound.co.za, buses stop at the Wimpy on Church St. Bethlehem is on the **Bloemfontein–Durban** route. For **Johannesburg** and **Cape Town** there are connections in Bloemfontein.

Train
There is a weekly service between **Cape Town** and **Durban** that stops in Bethlehem. **Spoornet**, T0860-008888, www.spoornet.co.za, timetables and fares are published on the website.

Contents

Footprint features

Northern Cape

At a glance

◒ **Getting around** Buses only on
N7 and N14, car hire, tours from
Cape Town during spring flower
season.

◉ **Time required** 3-5 days for
major sites, 1 week for Kgalagadi
Transfrontier Park.

☼ **Weather** Mostly dry, sunny
and hot.

⊗ **When not to go** Desert regions
get very cold on winter nights.

BOTSWANA

NAMIBIA

NORTH WEST PROVINCE

Nossob

Molopo Nature Reserve

Kgalagadi Transfrontier Park

Mata Mata

Vorstershoop

Setlagole

Twee Rivieren

Rietfontein

Askham

Van Zylsrus

Black Rock
Hotazel

Vryburg

Lykso

Sonstraal

R41

Kalahari

Noenieput

Tswalu Kalahari Reserve

Kathu

Kuruman

Wonderwerk Cave

NORTHERN CAPE

N14

Ariamsvlei

Nakop

Barkly West

Ai-Ais Richtersveld Transfrontier Park

Kuboes

N8

Upington

Witsand Nature Reserve

Kimberley

Augrabies Falls National Park

Keimoes

Cannon Island (Kanoneiland)

Magersfontein

Mokala National Park

Alexander Bay

Vioolsdrif

Kakamas

Pella

Pofadder

Kenhardt

N10

Prieska

Copperton

Petrusburg

Krankuil

Steinkopf

Gariep (Orange)

Port Nolloth

Springbok

Geegap Nature Reserve

Gamoep

Grootvloer

Verneuk Pan

Van Wyksuki

Sodium

Namaqua National Park

Kamieskroon

Brandvlei

Vosburg

Bristown

Colesberg

Kliprand

Sakrivier

Carnarvon

De Aar

N1

Nariep

Niewoudtville

Williston

Loxton

N12

Richmond

Atlantic Ocean

Vanrhynsdorp

Middlepos

Fraserburg

Three Sisters

N9

Doring Bay

Lambert's Bay

Beaufort West

Graaff-Reinet

Aberdeen

Velddrif

Saldanha

Porterville

Hottentotskloof

Dwyka

Die Hel

Rietbron

WESTERN CAPE

Willowmore

Yzerfontein

N7

Ceres

Touws River

Calitzdorp

N2

Herold

Cape Town

Stellenbosch

Riviersonderend

N2

Mossel Bay

Betty's Bay

Napier

Albertinia

Struisbaai

Indian Ocean

N

100 km

100 miles

The Northern Cape is South Africa's largest province, although it is home to fewer than a million people. It is also one of the most beautiful areas of the country but, compared to other provinces, it remains tourist-free. Much of this has to do with the sheer harshness of the area: this is where the rock-strewn semi-desert of Namakwa (Namaqualand) merges with the rolling red dunes of the Kalahari, where cruel heat pounds the parched wilderness for much of the year. But it is this sun-bleached emptiness and inaccessibility that gives the area its stark beauty, endless shimmering plains and hazy saltpans providing it with a real sense of isolation.

The state can be divided into three distinct regions: Namakwa in the west; the Kalahari to the north of the Gariep River; and the Karoo to the south. Despite the pervasive arid conditions, it is an area of excellent game viewing, with the magnificent Kgalagadi Transfrontier Park offering one of the finest national park experiences in Africa. In spring, Namakwa becomes the main attraction, as the valleys are transformed into carpets of vibrant colour as desert flowers explode from the earth with the first rains. The Gariep River – formerly the Orange – runs through much of the state; it was recently been given its Nama name, meaning 'great river'. It thunders over the surreal Augrabies Falls, the fifth largest in the world, and offers superb whitewater rafting. Lastly, this is diamond country, and the key town of Kimberley has a rich history and a number of sights, not least the colossal diamond mines themselves.

Ins and outs

Getting around

The Northern Cape is not well served by public transport and long-distance buses only run along the N7, the route from Cape Town to Namibia. To explore the remote settlements of the Kalahari, Namakwa (Namaqualand) or the Kgalagadi Transfrontier Park, you'll need a car and should be prepared for some challenging driving. Distances are vast, fuel needs careful attention and you need to plan your journey carefully to reach your destination before dark, as animals on the road make driving at night dangerous. Breakdowns can be a problem in remote regions, so it's useful to carry a mobile phone, and, in some areas, a 4WD is advised.

4WD driving is hugely popular in South Africa but 4WD companies are loathe to rent their vehicles to complete novices. Consider doing a one-day 4WD course in your home country before your arrival in South Africa. Alternatively, if you don't want to self-drive there are tours on offer from the regional centres.

Best time to visit

Although summer can be oppressively hot, winter has pleasant daytime temperatures but frost at night; the best times to visit are the more moderate seasons of spring or autumn.

Tourist information

Northern Cape Tourism Authority ① *15 Dalham Rd, Belgravia, Kimberley, T053-8331434, www.northerncape.org.za*, is responsible for regional information and produces some excellent literature which they can post you.

Kimberley

→ *Phone code: 053. Colour map 4, A2.*

Kimberley, the capital of the Northern Cape, has a fascinating history and it is en route to some of the most beautiful and unspoilt wild country in South Africa – yet it is rarely visited by tourists. It is known first and foremost for its diamonds, and the flat land surrounding the town is pockmarked with mines. No longer the fortune-seeker's frontier town, Kimberley is today a bustling commercial centre with a surprising number of interesting sights. The climate is one of hot summers, with sporadic raging thunderstorms which account for most of the annual rainfall. The winters are warm but with cold nights and morning frosts. ►► *For listings, see pages 752-754.*

Ins and outs

Getting there The airport is 10 km south of the town centre. There are daily flights to Cape Town and Johannesburg. Mainline trains stop in Kimberley daily on the Pretoria/Johannesburg–Cape Town route. **Greyhound**, **Intercape** and **Translux** buses to Cape Town, Pretoria and Johannesburg start and finish their journey outside the Tourist Information Centre in Bultfontein Street. All through services stop at the Shell Ultra City on the Transvaal Road (N12) in the northern suburbs. ►► *For further details, see Transport, page 754.*

Getting around A subtle reminder of Kimberley's past is the irregular street pattern, which more or less runs true to the mud tracks which once criss-crossed the land between the tented camps and diamond diggings.

Tourist information **Diamond Fields Tourist Information Centre** ① *corner of Bultfontein and Lyndhurst streets, T053-8327298, www.kimberley.co.za, Mon-Fri 0800-1700, Sat 0800-1200*, has a list of local SATOUR registered guides for tours of the town, the surrounding region and the Kimberley Mine Museum. Staff can also organize a night-time ghost tour, which includes a visit to the spot where a former librarian committed suicide. It is reputed that his ghost is responsible for regularly rearranging the books in the Africana Library. For self-guided walks, pick up one of the useful maps of the Belgravia Historical Walk and the Great Kimberley North Walk, which take in most of the sights. For regional information, visit the **Northern Cape Tourism Authority** (see Tourist information, above).

Background

The early history of Kimberley is also the tale of the discovery of diamonds, a definitive turning point in the history of the country. The first significant find was in 1866 on a farm called De Kalk, owned by Daniel Jacobs, near modern-day Hopetown. Jacobs' children gave a stone to their neighbour, Schalk van Niekerk. He in turn gave it to a trader, John O'Reilly, and asked him to find out the value of the stone. The stone ended up in Grahamstown in the hands of Dr Guyborn Atherstone, who found it to be a diamond of 21.25 carats, worth R1000 and later named *Eureka*. In 1869 Schalk van Niekerk bartered for a larger stone from a Griqua shepherd; news soon spread of this stone and public interest began to grow. It came to be known as *The Star of Africa* and, in 1974 was sold in Geneva for over half a million US dollars.

In 1869 the search for diamonds was divided between two areas: the wet diggings along the Vaal River; and the dry diggings on two farms some 40 km to the south. The Vaal River diggings attracted most prospectors, as the heat and drought of summer made conditions very tough on the farms at Bultfontein and Dorstfontein. In December 1870 the future of the region was finally determined when the children of Adriaan van Wyk found diamonds near their farm, Dorstfontein. The area was immediately overrun by diamond-diggers and their equipment, including a party from Colesberg led by Fletwood Rawstone, known as the Red Caps. One night a servant appeared at his master's tent with a handful of diamonds. He had found them on the slopes of a hill on the nearby farm of Vooruitzicht, owned by the brothers Diederick and Nicolaas Johannes de Beer. The hill was named Colesberg Kopje and, within just a few months, 50,000 diggers had turned the hill into a hole. Living conditions were very tough, and supplies expensive. In 1873 the name 'New Rush' was changed to Kimberley in honour of the Earl of Kimberley, British Secretary of State for the Colonies. A twin town grew up around the Bultfontein and Du Toit's pan mines, called Beaconsfield, named after Benjamin Disraeli, the Earl of Beaconsfield. In 1912 the two towns amalgamated to become a city.

As the mines delved deeper, it became clear that individual claims would have to merge; there was simply no way of keeping them separate. At one point, there were 1600 separate claims at the Kimberley mine (now known as the Big Hole; see page 745). In addition to the problems of mining logistics, the price of diamonds started falling because of over production. It was at this point that Cecil John Rhodes (see page 746) and his partner, Charles Dunell Rudd, entered the scene. Together they began buying up claims in the De Beers mine and, in 1880, they founded the De Beers Mining Company. As Rhodes and Rudd expanded their operation, they came up against a man with similar ideas, Barney Barnato. The ensuing infamous power struggle was only resolved when Rhodes gave Barnato a colossal pay-off for his Kimberley Central Mining Company. The

Big Hole stopped producing diamonds in 1914 but three mines remain productive today: Dutoitspan, Bultfontein and Wesselton.

Sights

Most of Kimberley's attractions are in some way connected to the diamond industry. Although there are some elegant Victorian buildings in town, there is far less evidence of the diamond wealth here than one might expect. Indeed, Kimberley was little more than a rough frontier settlement for most of its history, with most of the diamond wealth making its way back to the more civilized and comfortable surroundings of the Cape. Nevertheless, it is thought that in the 1890s more millionaires met together under the roof of the **Kimberley Club** ① *T053-8324224, private visits can be arranged*, than anywhere else in the world. Past members include Cecil Rhodes, and Ernest and Harry Oppenheimer. The club still stands in Du Toitspan Road close to the Africana Library, and the 1891 building is now a national monument. Also on Du Toitspan Road is a **statue of Cecil Rhodes** astride his horse with a map of Africa on his lap, while just south of here, opposite the Civic Centre, are the **Oppenheimer Memorial Gardens** and the **Diggers Fountain**. This is a memorial to Sir Ernest Oppenheimer, mining magnet and erstwhile Mayor of Kimberley, featuring a fountain and a statue of five miners holding up a sieve, surrounded by a rose garden.

Kimberley

Sleeping 🛏
Carrington Lodge 12
Cecil John Rhodes
  Guest House 2
Edgerton House 11
Estate 4

Garden Court Kimberley 6
Great Batch Guest House
  & Backpackers 1
Gum Tree Lodge 9
Milner House 7
Protea Diamond Lodge 3

Eating 🍴
George & Dragon 1
Halfway House 5
Old Diggers Inn 7
Star of the West 4
Umberto's 6

Big Hole: big statistics

The Big Hole is the largest hand-dug hole on earth. It has a surface area of 17 ha and a perimeter of 1.6 km. Before the consolidation of diggings, 50,000 men dug here night and day, and for several kilometres around Kimberley you could hear the dull noise of tapping and machinery. The diggers reached 400 m down before it became impossible to mine as a group of individuals. In 1889 De Beers sunk the first shaft, extending the hole to a depth of 800 m. By August 1914, when the mine was closed, the shafts were 1100 m deep.

It is estimated that between 22 and 28 million tonnes of earth were removed to create the Big Hole. All this labour resulted in the recovery of 14.5 million carats: only 2722 kg of diamonds or less than three metric tonnes. Today, water fills the hole to a depth of over 600 m.

The suburb of **Belgravia** (see page 748) has a fine collection of Victorian houses but the rest of the city centre is made up of dull modern shops and office blocks. (There are some early pictures of the town centre at the **Kimberley Mine Museum**, along with a display on the siege of Kimberley; see page 746). Today, the town's skyline is dominated by the **Telkom Tower** and the **De Beers** headquarters, an ugly tinted-glass building. More interesting is the equally unattractive **Harry Oppenheimer House**, near the Civic Centre. This is the main diamond sorting centre in South Africa, which was designed to allow in optimum natural light by which to judge the stones.

The pale yellow and white, Corinthian-style **City Hall** was built in 1899. From here, you can catch a **tram** (daily 0900-1600, on the hour every hour, R7), to the Kimberley Mine Museum. Trams played an important role in the history of public transport in Kimberley. The first passenger tramway, pulled by mule, was opened in June 1887 to bring labour from the Beaconsfield township to Kimberley. Today, the restored model in Kimberley, dating from the early 1900s, is the only working tram in South Africa.

Africana Library

① *Du Toitspan Rd, T053-8306247. Mon-Fri 0800-1245, 1330-1630.*

The Africana Library is a major research centre and a rewarding place to visit for those with a particular interest in local history. There is a wealth of archive material on the diamond industry, missionary work in the region and early SeTswana books. Two of its most famous books are Dr Moffat's copy of his 1829 translation of the Old Testament into SeTswana, the first bible to be printed in Africa, and a first edition of Schedel's *Nuremburg Chronicle*, 1493.

William Humphreys Art Gallery

① *Jan Smuts Blvd, in the Civic Centre complex, T053-8311724, www.whag.co.za. Mon-Fri 0800-1645, Sat 1000-1645, Sun 1400-1645. Small entry fee.*

This gallery houses one of the most important art collections in South Africa, with fine examples of 16th- and 17th-century art by British and Flemish Old Masters. More interesting is the newer collection of contemporary South African art. There are works by South African impressionists, an excellent graphics and prints display and a few individual treasures, such as the Irma Stern portraits. Also of interest is the rock engravings collection, tracing ancient San engravings dating back to 12,000 BC with photographs and actual examples.

Cecil John Rhodes

Cecil Rhodes was perhaps the ultimate British imperialist and he played a central role in the history of southern Africa in the years after the discovery of diamonds at Kimberley.

He was born in the English town of Bishops Stortford in 1853 and was sent to Natal at the age of 17 to work on his brother's farm and to recuperate from bouts of tuberculosis. He was not, however, suited to farming life and soon set off for the new diamond sites at Kimberley. From humble beginnings he began to prosper, slowly buying up shares in diamond-buying concerns and through other schemes related to the diggings. With the money he earned from these businesses, he went back to England in 1872 to study for a degree at Oxford. The contacts he made while at Oxford put him in an advantageous position in Kimberley and he was able to utilize British capital in his programme of gaining control of all the diamond mining activities. In 1880 Rhodes founded the De Beers Diamond Mining Company and continued to expand his commercial interests.

When diamonds were first discovered, plots were sold cheaply to the first digger to lay claim to the site but, very quickly, and especially as the diggings became deeper, one or two individuals and companies managed to buy up all the shares and monopolize the buying and selling of diamonds. By the end of the 1880s, there were only really two players left in the game: Cecil Rhodes and Barney Barnato. In 1888, with the backing of British capital, Rhodes eventually bought out Barnato – with one cheque for the sum of £5,338,650.

As befits a grand imperialist, Rhodes combined his hugely successful business career with a career in politics. He was first elected to the Cape parliament, as member for Barkly West, in 1880, and soon gained a reputation as an ardent supporter of British interests in South Africa and the expansion of British rule to the whole of southern Africa. In 1890 he became the colony's Prime Minister and continued to advocate British imperial expansion into remaining African-controlled areas, such as Pondoland. This expansionism was driven partly by jingoistic pride in Britain but mainly by his commercial ambitions.

Despite Rhodes' commercial genius he had made a serious miscalculation when

Kimberley Mine Museum and the Big Hole

ⓘ *Entrance on Tucker St, T053-8304417. Daily 0830-1700; 1-hr guided tours run throughout the day. Last tour 1600. R55, R30 children, family of four package R145. Shops and restaurants.*
Sitting alongside the Big Hole, this fascinating museum went under a major R52 million revamp and extension in 2006. Now guided tours take in all the components and begin with a short film that tells the full Kimberley diamond story. The **Old Mining Town** is made up of a collection of 40 original and model buildings dating from the late 19th century, that have been arranged to form a muddle of streets, with sound effects such as singing or snatches of conversation playing inside the shops. Each shop or office is furnished with items dating from the early days of Kimberley, and the overall result is very effective. There are a number of professions on show, including Dr JM Osborne's dental surgery, R Bodley & Son Undertakers, Barney Barnato's Boxing Academy, EHW Awty, a well-known watchmaker, the Standard Bank and A Ciring, the Pawnbroker – the window display includes objects that have never been redeemed. One of the most impressive items is the original De Beers Directors' Private Pullman Railway Coach, a very plush carriage

gold was first discovered on the Witwatersrand. Taking the advice of an American prospector who told him that the gold was not even worth getting off a horse for, Rhodes decided to sit out the initial rush to buy up the best goldfields. By the time the true worth of the new reef was apparent, Rhodes was too late to make an economic killing, though he did become involved with deep-level mining activities. Frustrated by missing a golden opportunity, Rhodes began to look to the lands further to the north, beyond the Limpopo River. Gold had been mined in these areas for centuries in small-scale mines. In 1888 Rhodes sent his Kimberley business partner, Charles Dunell Rudd, to secure from Lobengula, the leader of the Ndebele, mineral rights in the area they controlled. Armed with the mineral concession, he was able to secure agreement from London to set up a 'charter company' (the South Africa Company), which would not only prospect for minerals in the area but also be granted ownership of all the land and run all the administration. In 1890 Rhodes sent out a 'Pioneer Column' to lay claim to the area. Their dreams of huge gold reserves

proved illusory but the country was still rich in minerals and many of the pioneers indulged in the settlers' favourite activity of land speculation.

With the failure to find a second Witwatersrand, Rhodes turned his attention back to his investments in the Transvaal. Rhodes' annoyance with President Kruger's constraints on non-Boer residents led him to make one of his worst political mistakes in backing the ill-fated Jameson Raid. This failed attempt to topple Kruger's government led to a serious breach in relations between Rhodes and Afrikaners in the Cape. He was forced to resign as Prime Minister and take a less public role in the Charter Company in Rhodesia.

At the outbreak of the Anglo-Boer War, Rhodes was staying at his house in Kimberley, where he remained throughout the siege (see page 749). His health was poor throughout much of his life and the harsh conditions during the siege did not help. He died in his Muizenberg cottage outside Cape Town in 1902; his body was transported by train and gun carriage to be buried in the Matopo Hills in present-day Zimbabwe.

complete with a dining table, laid with silverware and cut-glass decanters, and luxurious leather chairs. Another highlight is Sir Davis Harris' ballroom, an ingenious structure built in 1901. It is constructed entirely out of corrugated iron, with stamped steel walls made to look like smart wallpaper, fake skirting boards and metal stucco on the ceilings.

The new and very impressive 90 m-long viewing platform over the **Big Hole** (see also page 745) looks a bit like half a suspension bridge, and it sticks out over the rim of the hole so you can look down and see the murky green lake at the bottom. It is an astounding sight when you remember that only a fraction of the hole lies above the water level, and that every piece of earth and rock was removed by hand. The viewing platform is 30 x 30 ft in size – the exact size of a 19th-century mining claim.

The **Underground Mine Experience** is a mock-up of a 19th-century mine shaft, where visitors can experience the heat and dust and hear trembling dynamite blasts. Inside the **Exhibition Centre** are examples of the first machines used in the diamond-mining industry, and early photographs of the diggings as the Big Hole gradually started to take shape, providing a vivid impression of life during the heady days of the boom. In the art gallery is a set of De Beers-commissioned watercolours depicting Victorian life in Kimberley. Equipment used to process diamonds can be seen in the Pulsator Building, where you can try your hand at sorting and selecting diamonds. The **Real Diamond Display** is more of a bank vault than a hall, and contains a collection of uncut stones, including the *616 diamond* (at 616 carats, it's the world's largest octahedron uncut diamond), and *Eureka*, the first diamond found on the banks of the Orange River in 1864 by curious children.

Belgravia

Just to the east of the city centre is the residential suburb of Belgravia where many of the wealthy mines people built grand Victorian houses. There is a 2-km historical walk through the suburb, which takes you past most of the old buildings, and a map is available from the tourist office. The majority can only be appreciated from the outside, as they remain in private hands, but the best of the buildings open to the public are **Rudd House** ① *5-7 Loch Rd*, and **Dunluce** ① *10 Lodge Rd*. Both are national monuments and have been fully restored. They are kept closed for security reasons but they can be viewed on weekdays by prior arrangement with the McGregor Museum (see below). The first owner of Dunluce was Gustav Bonus of Dunluce, who instructed the architect to design a house fit for a member of the Diamond Syndicate. He was not disappointed; when the house was completed in 1897 it perfectly reflected the prosperity of the period. Unfortunately, it was badly damaged during the Siege of Kimberley in 1899 by a shell from the Boers' infamous 'Long Tom' gun.

Also in Belgravia is the **Duggan-Cronin Gallery** ① *T053-8392700, Mon-Sat 1000-1300, 1400-1700, Sun 1400-1700, donation,* set back on Edgerton Road. The basis of this collection is a series of 8000 ethnographic photographs taken between 1919 and 1939 by Alfred Martin Duggan-Cronin, a De Beers' nightwatchman with an interest in photography.

McGregor Museum

① *2 Edgerton Rd, entrance from Atlas St, T053-8420099, www.museumsnc.co.za, Mon-Sat 0900-1700, Sun 1400-1700. Small entrance fee. Café and museum shop.*

The history of this building is worth mentioning in addition to the collection inside. The original house was built by Rhodes to serve as a hotel and a health spa, since the pure dry climate of Kimberley was thought to be healthy. During the siege of Kimberley, Rhodes lived in two rooms on the ground floor. These now form part of the museum and are furnished as he had them; note the austere surroundings preferred by Rhodes. During the next period of use, the building was converted into the very elegant **Hotel Belgrave**. One of the rooms upstairs has been furnished as it would have been in the 1920s. As the diamond industry fell into decline, the wealthy customers disappeared and the hotel was forced to close. In 1933 it was taken over by the Sisters of the Holy Family and turned into a school and convent. Forty years later the McGregor Museum moved its displays and offices here.

The collection is a mix of objects depicting the history of Kimberley and the northern region, and standard displays of natural history. While the latter are of little interest, the displays relating to Kimberley are reasonably absorbing.

Galeshewe

① *For tours of Galeshewe, contact the tourist office.*

Kimberley was the first town in South Africa to establish 'locations' for housing non-white mine labourers on its outskirts. Galeshewe, the resulting township, rose significantly in

Siege of Kimberley

During the Anglo-Boer War, Kimberley was besieged by some 4000 Boer soldiers between 15 October 1899 and 16 February 1900. Hemmed inside the town were 500 British troops under Colonel Kekewich and about 50,000 civilians including the town's most famous resident, Cecil Rhodes, whose capture was a particularly enticing prospect for the Boers. However, they were never able to break through some carefully mounted British defences, as the surrounding countryside made an attack difficult.

The Boers, therefore, had to content themselves with trying to starve the town into surrender. Nevertheless, the extensive stores owned by De Beers Diamond Mining Company meant that the town did not suffer from food shortages to the same extent as Ladysmith or Mafeking, and Kekewich prudently passed a military law that all food prices were to remain at pre-siege levels. The town's inhabitants did suffer, though, and inevitably the African population suffered the most. There were widespread reports of scurvy and very high rates of infant mortality. By the end of the siege horse meat was the main item on many menus.

Rhodes, nearing the end of his life, put the full resources of De Beers into defending the town. This included manufacturing ammunition in the mine's workshops and, most impressively, a big gun, inevitably nicknamed 'Long Cecil', that could return fire on the Boer siege guns. The mine tower was also invaluable as a lookout post. This lookout also proved invaluable as an early-warning post for incoming shells. The system undoubtedly saved many lives – though the shelling did take a heavy toll.

Relations between Colonel Kekewich and Rhodes were very poor. Rhodes wanted the town relieved and could not understand why a large British army located just 20 miles away at Modder River was unable to break through and relieve them. To the ire of Kekewich he managed to get out to the South African and British press increasingly critical statements about the performance of the British military. In February 1900 Rhodes threatened to call a public meeting, at which Kekewich was convinced he would call for Kimberley to surrender, unless they were given specific information about plans to relieve the town. Kekewich was determined that the meeting should not take place so, instead, Rhodes and 12 other leading citizens demanded that Kekewich send a message to the British Commander-in-Chief, General Roberts, calling for their immediate relief. When Kekewich refused, the two of them almost resorted to a fist fight.

Relief was not far off, however. General Roberts' arrival at Modder River with reinforcements had revitalized the British efforts. A bold plan of attack was developed. The British cavalry completely outflanked General Cronje's Boer forces, unblocking the main advance and allowing Roberts to relieve Kimberley. With this attack the whole impetus of the war turned against the Boers. On 16 February Kimberley was at last relieved and Cecil Rhodes (and many London stockbrokers) were able to celebrate.

importance during the struggle against Apartheid, and was second only to Soweto as a centre of political activism. It was home to **Robert Sobukwe**, the leader of the Pan African Congress (PAC), who spent the last days of his life under house arrest in Galeshewe, following his imprisonment on Robben Island.

Pioneers of Aviation Museum
① *General van der Spuy Dr, 4 km from the airport, T053-8392700. Mon-Fri 1000-1530, Sur,*
1400-1700. Small entrance fee.
On the site of South Africa's first flying school, this museum comprises a reconstructed
hangar and a replica of the biplane used in the early days of flight training. The flying
school was set up here in 1913 and the graduates went on to become the first pilots of the
newly formed South African Aviation Corps, which in turn saw its first action over Walvis
Bay in May 1915.

Around Kimberley

Kamfers Dam
Kamfers Dam is 5 km out of town on the N12 towards Johannesburg, partially hidden
from the road by the raised railway line. This is a natural heritage site and an important
area for greater and lesser flamingos; just driving past the dam allows views of the carpet
of pink created by the resident flamingos. Sadly, the waters are under threat from
continual agricultural pollution, and it has been predicted that the flamingos may soon
disappear from here. Look out for a gravel track leading from the road under the railway
line, where there is a small parking area.

Magersfontein Battlefield → *Colour map 4, B2.*
① *32 km from Kimberley; follow the new road to Bloemfontein and follow signs for Modder*
River, T053-8337115. Daily 0800-1500. Small entry fee. Tea room and museum.
On 11 December 1899 one of the most famous battles of the Anglo-Boer War took place
here. The British force, under the command of Lieutenant-General Lord Methuen, was
defeated by a Boer force under General Piet Cronje while attempting to come to the aid of
besieged Kimberley (see page 749). This was the first appearance of trench warfare and
the first major defeat suffered by the British: in the first encounter 239 British soldiers
were killed and 663 wounded. The Boer trenches can still be seen from the hilltop. There
are nine memorials commemorating the dead, including a Celtic cross in memory of the
Highland Regiment, a granite memorial to the Scandinavians who fought with the Boers,
and a marble cross in memory of the Guards Brigade.

Routes west from Kimberley

Wildebeest Kuil Rock Art Centre and Nooitgedacht
① *www.museumsnc.co.za, Mon-Fri 1000-1700, Sat and Sun 1100-1600, R10.*
Both these are open-air sites displaying glacial geological rock formations, which have
been covered in ancient San rock engravings, thought to be 1500 years old. At the
Wildebeest Kuil Rock Art Centre ① *16 km from Kimberley on the R31 towards Barkly West,*
T053-8337069, there is a visitor centre with shop and tearoom, an auditorium showing a
short film about the rock art and an 800-m walking trail. At **Nooitgedacht** ① *24 km from*
Kimberley on the same road, T082-2224777, display boards and a boardwalk have been
developed. At both sites there is the opportunity to meet the local community of Xun and
Khwe San people who were granted 1200 ha of land under the Land Reform Programme.
The communities share this land, from where they produce traditional and progressive
arts and crafts.

Mokala National Park

South Africa's newest national park was proclaimed in June 2007. The name means 'camel thorn' in Setswana and aptly describes the 19,611 ha region of dry savannah dotted with acacia trees. It's roughly 80 km southwest of Kimberley. Take the N12 towards Cape Town and after 57 km, at the Heuningneskloof Crossing, turn right, then drive 21 km along a gravel road to the park turn-off. Mokala was created as a home for animals relocated from the former Vaalbos National Park closer to Kimberley, which was de-proclaimed after a successful land claim made by local people. Some 863 animals were moved, including five white rhinos and 141 buffalo, and other species

such as giraffe, red hartebeest, blue wildebeest, tsessebe, gemsbok, zebra, springbok and eland. While the park is officially open and two camps have been built by SANParks, these are only presently available to conference groups and it won't be fully operational for the general public until roads and other facilities have been developed (although a campsite may be up and running by the time you read this). Future developments include a network of roads for game driving and self-catering camps, which will offer day and night game drives, and possibly horse trails and mountain biking as there are no predators in the park as yet. Check with SANParks for progress; www.sanparks.org.

Barkly West → *Phone code: 053. Colour map 4, A2.*

The R31 passes through Barkly West, 32 km from Kimberley en route to Kuruman. The first site of the diamond rush in South Africa, the town is named after Sir Henry Barkly, Governor of the Cape when diamonds were discovered here. This is also the town Cecil Rhodes represented when he was first elected to the Cape parliament.

Today, the town is tatty and run down, and you may still see prospectors using manual methods to work their claims along the **Vaal River**. In 1869, the first diamond-digging area, known as **Klipdrift**, drew thousands of prospectors to the river. The following year the diggers at Canteen Kopje took the unexpected step of establishing the independent Republic of Klipdrift. In 1871 the Cape government decided to annex the territory to keep it out of the hands of the Transvaal government. On the north bank of the Vaal River is the steel-girdered **Barkly Bridge**, which was the first bridge to span the river in 1885. The restored tollhouse serves as the local **museum** ① *daily 0900-1700, small entry fee*, with a limited display on geology and archaeology. The old **pump house**, a few metres from the bridge, is now a pub.

Wonderwerk Cave

① *Signposted 42 km before Kuruman, T082-8327226. Book in advance and then stop at the homestead to collect a key. Small entry fee. Small display centre and toilets.*
Wonderwerk Cave is an important archaeological site on a private farm, set back from the road in the Kuruman Hills. The main attraction is some rock paintings and the evidence of early human habitation. The display contains interesting background material on the prehistory of the region. The cave has been extensively examined by the Kimberley museum; most of the floor has been divided into squares for research purposes and archaeologists are often at work here. It stretches back 140 m into the hillside, with a level path leading into it. The rock paintings are near the entrance. The grandparents of the current owners (and their 11 children) lived in the cave when they first settled in the region and started farming. Allow one hour for a visit.

⊙ Kimberley listings

⊙ Sleeping

Kimberley *p742, map p744*

A-B Edgerton House, 5 Edgerton Rd, T053-8311150, www.edgertonhouse.co.za. Historic house built in 1901 with pressed ceilings, wooden floors, fireplaces, plenty of antiques, 11 a/c double rooms with en suite bathroom, some with free-standing tubs and gold-plated fittings, TV, all meals available, swimming pool, gardens, secure parking, a relatively large guesthouse with home comforts. Nelson Mandela has stayed here.

B The Estate Private Hotel, 7 Lodge Rd, T053-8322668, www.theestate.co.za. Luxury hotel set in a house built for Sir Ernest Oppenheimer's wife as a wedding present in 1907. 7 en suite rooms, grand furnishings such as gilt mirrors and wing-back chairs, gardens with pool, superb **Butler's** restaurant offering gourmet food (see Eating), close to sights.

C Cecil John Rhodes Guest House, 138 Du Toitspan Rd, T053-8302500, www.ceciljohnrhodes.co.za. Luxurious old-style guesthouse set in converted house built in 1895 that is a national monument. 7 comfortable rooms, en suite bathrooms, a/c, TV, shady tea garden, friendly management, attached tea garden, dinner on request. Recommended.

C Garden Court Kimberley, 120 Du Toitspan Rd, T053-8331751, www.southernsun.com. Bland but comfortable hotel with 135 a/c rooms in a concrete block. Disabled access.

Restaurant is an attached franchise steakhouse. Bar, swimming pool, sauna.

C Milner House, 31 Milner St, T053-8316405, www.milnerhouse.co.za. Well-run guesthouse in a good location in Belgravia, 6 luxurious double rooms with fans, en suite bathroom, TV, phone, swimming pool, large gardens, log fires in the winter evenings, good breakfasts, internet access, an excellent B&B.

C Protea Hotel Diamond Lodge, 124 Du Toitspan Rd, T053-8311281, www.protea hotels.com. 34 large a/c modern rooms, with 2 double beds, minibar, Mnet TV, restaurant, bar, swimming pool, good service, airport pickup by arrangement.

D Carrington Lodge, 60 Carrington Rd, T053-8316448, www.carringtonlodge.co.za. A comfortable guesthouse with 16 en suite rooms with TV, ceiling fans and minibar. Spacious gardens with pool, hearty cooked breakfasts served in the pretty dining room, secure parking, central location.

D-F Gum Tree Lodge, Old Bloemfontein Rd (R64), 4 km from town, T053-8328577, www.gumtreelodge.com. Large complex on 5 ha with 150 beds in dorms and doubles with communal kitchen, some self-contained flats, lounge, **Old Diggers** restaurant and bar next door, shop, TV room, swimming pool, probably the best option for budget travellers, quiet but inconvenient for the sights.

E-F Great Batch Guest House and Backpackers, 3 Edgerton Rd, T053-8321113. New backpackers set up in an original mining mansion, good central location in Belgravia and on the historic walk route, a mixture of doubles, self-catering flats, with or without bathrooms but all with DSTV and kettle, and dorms sleeping 20, pool, central thatched lapa, bar, kitchen. Communal areas are decorated with antiques and mining memorabilia. Reports welcome.

🍴 Eating

Kimberley *p742, map p744*

Kimberley is better served by pubs and bars than restaurants. There are the usual fast-food outlets by the taxi stand behind the City Hall, including **King Pie**, **Steer's** and **Captain Do Regos**. There are also the standard chain steak restaurants, and a number of bars and restaurants in the **Flamingo Casino** complex just out of town on the Jo'burg road.

↑↑↑ Butler's, in the **Estate Private Hotel**, 7 Lodge Rd, T053 8331038, www.theestate.co.za. 1600-2200. Gourmet, formal and intimate restaurant with sweeping drapes, starched white linen and silverware. Inventive menu that mixes flavours such as springbok carpaccio with rose petal ice cream or fillet steak with chilli and chocolate sauce. Reservations essential.

↑↑ George & Dragon, 187 Du Toitspan Rd, T053-8332075. Daily 1100-late. Popular English-style theme pub serving decent meals and beer on tap, varied menu from steaks to their famous foot-long pies. Part of a chain that is slightly more upmarket than most bars. Good for lunch and stays open until 0200 if the demand is there.

↑↑ Halfway House, Du Toitspan Rd, T053-8316324. Mon-Sat 1030-0200. Historical pub with bizarre drive-in section, claiming to be where Cecil Rhodes used to ride in to sip a quick beer while still on his horse. Good atmosphere, late opening, simple pub meals, can get very busy at weekends.

↑↑ Star of the West, North Circular Rd, T053-8326463. Open 1000-late. The oldest pub in South Africa, dating from 1873. It was originally a corrugated-iron shack were thirsty miners paid tuppence for a beer and a halfpenny for a glass of wine. Bit of a tourist trap but characterful, with a long wooden bar. Tram to the Mine Museum stops outside across the road (on request). Enjoy a cool beer and a pub lunch before visiting the Big Hole.

↑↑ Umberto's, 229 Du Toitspan Rd, T053-8325741. Mon-Sat 1200-1430,

1800-late. Excellent Italian restaurant just next to the **Halfway House**. Superb pizza and home-made pasta dishes, some 260 items on the menu, meat and fish a little more expensive, traditional red and white checked tablecloths and friendly service. Recommended.

↑ Old Diggers Inn, next to the **Gum Tree Lodge**, T053-8328577. Large restaurant frequented by backpackers staying next door, open all day for good-value meals, hearty portions, busy bar.

⛰ Activities and tours

Kimberley *p742, map p744*
Birdwatching

Kimberley is less known for its birds than its Big Hole but there are a number of sites around the town that are excellent for birdwatching. There are up to 20,000 flamingos on the **Kamfers Dam** (see page 750), and 50 pairs of African white-backed vultures can be spotted on the De Beers' Dronfield Farm a few kilometres north of the city. During summer European bee-eaters breed in the suburb of West End, and saltpans and rivers in the region support populations of waterbirds and raptors.

Cricket

International matches are played at the **De Beers Diamond Oval**, Dickenson Av, Cassandra, enquiries T053-8332601, tickets from Computicket, www.computicket.com. Watching a game here makes a pleasant change from the large stadiums found in the cities. The atmosphere is very relaxed and if you're lucky you may meet the players in the club bar. During the domestic season, Kimberley is home to Griqualand West.

Tour operators
Diamond Tours Unlimited, T053-8614983, www.diamondtours.co.za. Half- and full-day tours of local diamond-mining sites including Barkly West, 35 km northwest of Kimberley,

where old prospectors still pan by hand. Also tours to bushman rock art and battlefields.

Whitewater rafting
River rafting is not what you might expect looking out over the dry, flat countryside around Kimberley but to the south flows the **Gariep (Orange)**, one of South Africa's largest rivers. It is possible to raft the rapids between Hopetown, on the N12, and Douglas. The river flows through beautiful dolerite hills past old farms and orchards. **Aquarush**, Hopetown, 120 km south of Kimberley, can organize trips from Kimberley, T083-5861795 (mob), www.aquarush.co.za.

⊖ Transport

Kimberley *p742, map p744*
It's 485 km to **Johannesburg**, 979 km to **Cape Town**, 238 km to **Kuruman**, 401 km to **Upington**.

Air
The airport is 10 km south of the town centre, T053-8511032, www.airports.co.za. **SAA**, T011-9781111, ww2.flysaa.com, operates 5 flights a day between Kimberley and **Johannesburg**.

Bus
Buses depart from outside the Tourist Information Centre on Bultfontein Rd. There are daily services to **Cape Town** (13 hrs), **Johannesburg** and **Pretoria** (6½ hrs). All services also stop at the Shell Ultra City on the N12, 6 km from the centre of town. The local booking agent for buses is **Tickets for Africa** at the Tourist Information Centre on Bultfontein Rd, T053-8326040.
　　Bus companies Greyhound, T083-9159000, www.greyhound.co.za. **Intercape**, T0861-287287,

www.intercape.co.za. **Translux**, T086-1589282, www.translux.co.za.

Car hire
All the companies are based at the airport and are open throughout the day during the week, but only when flights arrive over the weekend. If you want to take a vehicle over the border to Namibia make sure you mention this. **Avis**, T053-8511082, www.avis.co.za. **Budget**, T053-8511182, www.budget.co.za. **Hertz**, T053-8302200, www.hertz.co.za. **Imperial**, T053-8511131, www.imperialcarrental.co.za.

Taxi
AA Taxis, T053-8614015. The main rank is behind the City Hall.

Train
For steam enthusiasts there is a collection of locomotives in perfect condition in the Beaconsfield Marshalling Yards to the south of the city centre, visits by appointment only T053-8383131. The railway station is on Florence Rd, T053-8382709. There are daily trains to Cape Town and Johannesburg/Pretoria, **Spoornet**, T053-8382631, central reservations T0860-008888, www.spoornet.co.za.

⊙ Directory

Kimberley *p742, map p744*
Banks Standard Bank, 10 Old Main St. ABSA, 69 Du Toitspan Rd. **Internet Small World Net Café**, 42 Sidney St, T053-8313484. **Medical services Medi-Clinic Private Hospital**, 177 Du Toitspan Rd, T053-8381111, www.kimberleymc.co.za.

The Kalahari

The Kalahari, like all great deserts, evokes images of vast lapis skies, shimmering horizons and cruel heat. The name Kalahari is derived from Kgalagadi, the San term for 'place without water'. It is at once enthralling and intimidating, begging to be explored but overwhelming in its sheer size and harshness. The landscape is semi-desert – rolling red sand dunes, salt pans, dry river beds and endless scrub – stretching from the Gariep (Orange) River to northern Botswana and west into Namibia. Despite the arid conditions, the Kalahari supports some of the best game viewing in South Africa, in the magnificent Kgalagadi Transfrontier Park. But the main draw of the Kalahari is its vast open spaces and the true wilderness of the desert; even today, travelling here evokes a real sense of adventure. For more information on the Kalahari visit www.roaringkalahari.co.za. ➤ *For listings, see pages 765-770.*

Ins and outs

Getting around Kuruman is the principal town in this part of the Kalahari. If you plan to travel north from here, make sure you stock up on all supplies and check the condition of your car, especially water, oil and fuel levels. The R31 north is one of only two routes to the Kgalagadi Transfrontier Park. The only other road into the park is from Upington. Each route involves stretches on gravel, although much of the road between Upington and Askam is now tarred. Note that driving on loose gravel and sand can be dangerous and these are not the best conditions in which to break down. Do not be tempted to drive too fast if the roads are empty and straight. If you have an accident you could be waiting a long time for help.

Climate As a desert, the Kalahari region is known for its extreme temperatures. Rainfall in the region is only 50 mm annually and usually arrives in dramatic but brief thunderstorms during summer. Temperatures in the northern Kalahari and along the Gariep (Orange) River often reach above 40°C during the summer, while, on winter nights, they can drop as low as 6°C – a consideration if camping.

Kuruman ●❼▲➌❻ ➤ pp765-770. Colour map 1, C4.

→ *Phone code: 053.*

This isolated northern town has two reasons for being on the tourist map: the Moffat family and their mission station; and a natural spring known as The Eye. Neither take up much time and the town itself is scruffy and unappealing, so half a day here should be more than enough on your way through. However, Kuruman is an important regional centre, so it's a good place to stock up on fuel and supplies.

Ins and outs

The **tourist office** ① *Voortrekker St, T053-7121001, www.kurumankalahari.co.za,* is in an old cottage next to The Eye. This is, in fact, the old Drostdy House, once home to the local magistrate. Part of the building is given over to a tea room that serves light lunches and tea and coffee throughout the day. Birdwatchers can pick up a map and an identification list for the northern Kalahari Raptor Route. More than 50 species, 35 of which are resident, have been recorded in the region.

The Eye

ⓘ *Main St, T053-7121095. Daylight hours. Minimal entrance fee. Small café.*

The Eye, or 'die oog' in Afrikaans, is an amazing spring which has continuously produced almost 20 million litres of fresh water per day, with little variance between the wet and the dry season. It was the presence of this water and the resultant river that made settlement possible in this area. The site was proclaimed a national monument in 1992. There is little to see of the spring, save for a wet, moss-covered rock, but the gardens around the clear pond are a popular and attractive picnic spot – the pond is full of large goldfish, fattened by breadcrumbs. The enormous willow trees were planted by the first magistrate in 1881. Unfortunately the grounds are not quite as peaceful as they might appear: there is a constant background noise of buried pumping equipment. The gardens around town rely on the spring water, which is fed into two 7-km-long irrigation channels, giving Kuruman the feel of an oasis during the dry season when the surrounding farmlands are burnt brown.

There is an 11-km **hiking trail** that starts at The Eye, crosses the golf course, goes through some local villages and ends at another small natural spring to the west of Kuruman. Ask the tourist office for a map.

Moffat Mission

ⓘ *5 km north of town on Moffat Lane; follow Voortrekker St out of town past the police station, T053-7121352. No public transport. Daily 0800-1700; allow at least 2 hrs. Small entrance fee.*

Under the guidance of Robert Moffat (see page 758), the Kuruman Mission Station became one of the best-known missions in Africa. Today it is run by the United Congregational Church of Southern Africa, and the complex is an atmospheric and fascinating place. This was the first house that Livingstone lived in when he came to Africa.

The first building you come to is the **stable**, with a few portraits on the walls and an early wagon used by the mission. Turning left out of the stable, you find yourself walking parallel to a **furrow** that Moffat had dug to bring water from The Eye, 5 km away (see page 755). Across the furrow is a small garden created by Mary Moffat; it was here that explorer David Livingstone proposed to the Moffats' daughter, after she had nursed him back to health following an attack by a lion. Opposite the garden is the **Moffat Homestead**, built in 1824 and fully restored in the 1980s. Inside, the main room has a few objects on display but, overall, it is disappointing. The kitchen has been turned into a tea room and curio shop. Just beyond the homestead is the original **Mission Church**, for many years the largest building in the interior of South Africa. Despite having only nine converts when he designed the T-shaped church, Moffat planned for it to seat 800 people. The stone walls stood for seven years before timber of sufficient length could be found for the roof. Moffat found the trees on one of his journeys 350 km away in the Marico Valley. The building still has a thatch roof, dung floor and wooden pews, and the acoustics are surprisingly good.

The final building of note is the **school classroom**; inside are the original wooden school benches and desks. The room is now home to the original press Moffat used to print the Tswana Bible, the first bible to be printed in Africa. The press was also used to print school books and publications for the church.

Northwest from Kuruman 🚌 ▸▸ pp765-770.

Hotazel and Black Rock → Phone code: 053.
Travelling on the R31 from Kuruman allows you to explore more of the Kalahari region. This is a good road but it is only surfaced as far north as Hotazel, 61 km; 25 km further north is Black Rock. These are nothing more than searingly hot dorps but both are important manganese ore-mining centres. Oddly enough, both these centres have sports clubs with tennis and squash courts, golf, even bowls, built for the miners but they can be used by visitors for a small fee, and it's not a bad idea to stop for a swim after a hot drive. From Hotazel, follow the signs for Sonstraal and Van Zylsrus, 105 km.

Tswalu Kalahari Reserve
ⓘ off the R31 between Hotazel and Sonstraal, www.tswalu.com.
Tswalu is a magnificent 100,000-ha reserve created by the late Stephen Boler. Over US$7 million was spent in establishing the enterprise, reputedly South Africa's largest private reserve. Today it is owned by the Oppenheimer family.

At the foot of the Korannaberg mountains, this is a region of stunning red sand dunes and typical savannah dotted with acacia trees. The park has been well stocked with wildlife, including lion, buffalo, three types of zebra, red hartebeest, blue and black wildebeest, giraffe, gemsbok, kudu and impala. A breeding programme for the rare desert black rhino has been set up and, from just eight that were introduced from Namibia in 1995, the population now stands at 19. The head count for large game has risen from 5000 to 14,000 in the last decade, so conservation in this region has been incredibly successful. You can explore the reserve on game walks, by 4WD or on horseback. The only places to stay are in the two five-star lodges. Generally, guests arrive by the reserve's private plane from Johannesburg or Cape Town. ▸▸ For further details, see Sleeping, page 765.

Van Zylsrus to Kgalagadi Transfrontier Park
Van Zylsrus is a typical Kalahari town: one dusty street is lined with a few shops and a tea garden, fittingly called The Oasis, but other than that there is little of interest. From Van Zylsrus the road follows the dry course of the Kuruman River as far as **Askham**. At this point the route combines with the road from Upington, and just one (gravel) road leads a further 75 km to the gates of the Kgalagadi Transfrontier Park. After a long and dusty drive, the national park camp at **Twee Rivieren** is a welcome sight, especially the swimming pool. The total distance from Kuruman to the park gates is 385 km and from Upington 275 km. These are undeniably tiring journeys but allow you to experience the vast southern fringes of the Kalahari Desert.

Southwest from Kuruman 🚌 ▸▸ pp765-770.

From Kuruman the N14 runs 263 km southwest to Upington via Kathu and Olifantshoek. The only reason for stopping en route is to refuel and buy something to eat and drink, unless you wish to marvel at an opencast mine in the midst of a beautiful and fragile environment.

Kalahari Raptor Rehabilitation Centre
ⓘ 19 km from Kuruman, on the Upington road. Look out for a side road, the D3340 on the right, signposted Ulster; the farm is a further 12 km from here, T053-7123576, www.raptor.co.za. By appointment only. Small entrance fee.

Robert Moffat

Robert Moffat is known in southern Africa for two reasons, first for translating the Bible into Tswana and secondly for his association with David Livingstone, the great Victorian explorer of the region. Moffat was born at Ormiston in Scotland into a poor family; he left school at the age of 11 and then worked as a gardener for 10 years – hardly a background to prepare him for 50 years of scholarly work in remotest Africa. After a brief theological training he was accepted by the London Missionary Society on 30 September 1816. His first posting was to Namaqualand where he immediately made a name for himself by converting an outlaw called Jager Afrikaner. In 1819 he married Mary Smith, his employer's daughter, in St George's Church in Cape Town. The first days of their marriage were spent in a wagon crossing the Karoo to Kuruman.

In 1824 Moffat persuaded the missionaries to move to the present site, which he considered to be far more suitable because of the abundant water supply, and the fertile level land was ideal for farming. It took four years to build the Moffat Homestead and a house for his colleague, Robert Hamilton. Fine materials were used and neat gardens were laid out. They wanted to show what Christianity could do. The homestead is still standing today and is the oldest building north of the Orange River.

An important part of a missionary's work was teaching. And it was when Moffat was confronted with a class "of Batswanas, Hottentots, two Bushmen and two Mantatees", that he realized the problem of language. The next 40 years of his life were dominated by translation and printing. He was the first person to print the language of the Matabele people, on his press in Kuruman, and so laid the foundations for their modern education system. His greatest feat was the translation of the Bible into Tswana. In 1857 he printed 1000 copies despite a whole range of problems. He then had to teach the Tswana people to read their own language. It was both the first time the Bible had been printed anywhere in Africa, and the first time it had been produced in a previously unwritten African tongue.

It was beyond the capacity of the Kuruman press to print the New Testament, and Moffat could find no one in South Africa to help, so the couple had no choice but to return to England, only to find out that they were famous. This helped them to raise vital funds and to get the printing done but, after three years away, they both yearned for Africa. The Moffats worked in Kuruman until 1870, when the Missionary Society persuaded them to return to England. Mary died within six months of their return but Robert Moffat continued to work for the LMS. He died 13 years later on 9 August 1883. In 1983 a bronze bust of Moffat was moved from Brixton, London, to Kuruman to mark the centenary of his death.

This privately owned centre has a wealth of information on raptors and a chance to see the rehabilitation work on injured birds, most of which get hurt from flying into power lines. Staff can advise on the best areas for birdwatching in the Kalahari. There is also a small selection of rescued and hand-raised mammals, such as young impalas, meerkats and bat-eared foxes. Accommodation is available in one double thatched self-catering chalet.

Just off the main road (N14), this modern settlement has grown up entirely around the mining industry, first started in 1972. This is the location of **Sishen Iron Ore Mine** ① *guided tours are usually held on the first Sat of the month; contact T083-6605336*, a massive scar in the earth and the largest single pit opencast mine in the world. It's roughly 12 km long and 1.5 km wide, and over 28 million tonnes of iron ore is extracted each year, employing 3200 people. Everything associated with the mine is giant – the trucks that move the ore look oversized, and can carry over 170 metric tonnes. The mine is connected to Saldanha ore terminal on the west coast by a single railway line which you can see in the vicinity of Elands Bay and Velddrif. For a small fee visitors are welcome at the mine's 18-hole golf club, T053-7233288, with clubhouse and bar, and at the adjoining recreation club, which has a swimming pool and squash and tennis courts.

Upington ⊜❼▲⊜❻ ➤➤ *pp765-770. Colour map 3, A5.*

Despite Upington's attractive setting on the banks of the Gariep (Orange) River, it is a bland and modern town with searing summer temperatures and little in the way of sights. It is, however, the largest town in the region, making it a welcome stop for those who've been off the beaten track for a while. It is a major service centre, with all the usual South African shops and high-street chains, and, as such, it is an excellent place to restock your supplies. As a major entry point to the Kalahari, Upington is also a good spot to organize trips to the Kgalagadi Transfrontier Park and Augrabies Falls National Park, and it is also en route, via the Ariamsvlei/Nakop border crossing, to the Fish River Canyon in Namibia to the west on the N8.

Ins and outs

Getting there There are daily flights from Cape Town and Johannesburg, and buses from Cape Town via Clanwilliam, Johannesburg and Pretoria. There is a train station but no South African passenger trains stop here and it's only used for freight. However, Namibia's railway company, **Transnamib Starline Passenger Services**, runs a service from Upington in South Africa to Windhoek twice a week. ➤➤ *For further details, see Transport, page 769.*

Tourist information Upington Tourist Office ① *Kalahari Oranje Museum, Schröder St, T054-3326064, www.upington.co.za, www.upington.com, www.greenkalahari.co.za, Mon-Fri 0800-1730, Sat 0900-1200.* This office has a good selection of brochures on the Kalahari area.

Background

The origin of the town is rather more disreputable than one might expect. In the mid-19th century the northern reaches of the Cape Colony were home to a colourful variety of outlaws and rustlers; there were no settlements, making it impossible for the police to track people into the uncharted wilderness. By 1879 the Cape government had had enough and founded a small settlement on the Gariep (Orange) River to try and exercise some control over the area. In 1884 Sir Thomas Upington, the new Prime Minister of the colony, visited the settlement, which was renamed in his honour.

The fortunes of the new settlement and the subsequent development of the district, can be attributed to the pioneering work of two men, the Reverend Christiaan Schröder and Johann 'Japie' Lutz. Together they built the first irrigation canal, constructed a pump

on the river and started a pontoon ferry. After the Anglo-Boer War, Lutz built canals a
Kakamas, Marchand and Onseepkans. These irrigated areas now produce cotton, lucerne
vegetables, grapes and sultanas. Today the **SA Dried Fruit Cooperative** and the **Garie**
(Orange) River Wine Cellars Cooperative are responsible for handling most of the
agricultural produce in the region. Another famous resident was Scotty Smith, a
legendary rogue and Robin Hood of the Northern Cape, who stole and gave to the poor
He died in Upington in 1918 during a flu epidemic and his grave is in the local cemetery.

Sights

The main building of the **Kalahari Oranje Museum** ① *Schröder St, overlooking the roa*
bridge, T054-3311373, Mon-Fri 0800-1700, free, is the restored manse where the Reverend
Schröder lived in the 1870s. This houses a collection of Victorian furniture and household
objects. Look out for item No 20, a fine old compendium of games. The doorways are a
very low on account of the Reverend Schröder being somewhat vertically challenged

Upington

To Airport, Spitskop Nature Reserve;
Kgalagadi Transfrontier Park
& Namibia - (N10)

Gariep (Orange) River

To Groblershoop & Kimberley

200 metres
200 yards

Sleeping
Affinity Guest House **1**
Africa River Lodge **3**
Eiland Holiday Resort **2**
Libby's Lodge **4**
Le Must River Manor **5**

Le Must River Residence **6**
Protea Upington **10**
River City Inn **8**

Eating
Arabesque **1**

Le Must **2**
O'Hagan's **3**
Saddles **4**
Sakkie se Arkie **5**

inside the church are some odd bits and pieces from Upington's past. They are poorly displayed, although worth seeking out are the photographs of Augrabies Falls in 1957 when they were dry. The building also houses the town tourist office. Outside is a statue of a bronze donkey working a horsemill.

Around Upington

Upington is the nearest town to **Augrabies Falls National Park**, a visit to which is possible in a day trip (see page 772). The highlight of the Northern Cape, the **Kgalagadi Transfrontier Park** is also relatively near, lying 250 km to the north (see page 761), but you'll definitely need a few days to fully appreciate the park.

More than 1000 ha of grapes and 8000 ha of sultanas are cultivated along the Gariep (Orange) River. Upington is a convenient centre for trying some of the wines produced on the vineyards in the region by the **Gariep (Orange) River Wine Cellars Cooperative** ① T054-33/8800, www.owk.co.za. You can visit the cooperative shop in Upington's industrial area; ask at the town tourist office for more information. The grapes originate from several hundred wineries along the Gariep (Orange) River and produce an extensive range of wines, from dry whites to dessert wines.

Witsand Nature Reserve ① *200 km from Upington off the N14 towards Kuruman, information and bookings T053-3131061, www.witsandkalahari.co.za, gate hours daily 0800-1800, R20, R10 children*, is a popular day or overnight trip from Upington. A beautiful area of desert landscape, its highlight is a collection of white sand dunes set incongruously on the typical red sand of the Kalahari. The dunes are up to 60 m high and stretch for 9 km, making them an impressive sight. The reserve is also home to the well-known 'Brulsand', the phenomenon of roaring sand dunes, thought to be caused by shifting sand lacking the usual red coating of iron oxide, plus the dry air. There is a comfortable resort, visitors can walk freely around the reserve, and there is a 4WD trail. There is also a concealed bird-hide dug into the ground, allowing an eye-level view of a waterhole; if you're lucky you might spot the pygmy falcon which is Africa's smallest raptor. Dune boarding is a new activity here, and boards as well as bicycles can be hired from the information centre.

Closer to town, about 13 km north of Upington off the R360, en route to the Kgalagadi Transfrontier Park (follow Swartmodder Street past the swimming pool), is the **Spitskop Nature Reserve** ① *information and bookings, T054-3321336*. The 5000-ha reserve makes for a pleasant day trip and acts as a good introduction to the flora and fauna that lie further north. Here you can view a variety of wildlife commonly found throughout the Kalahari region, including springbok, eland, zebra and gemsbok. In the centre of the reserve is a *koppie* with an observation platform and telescope. There are hiking trails throughout the reserve, the staff at reception will point you in the right direction, or you can explore the reserve in your own car.

Kgalagadi Transfrontier Park ● ›› pp765-770. Colour map 1, B1.

① *Twee Rivieren is the only entrance on the South African side, T054-5612000. Gate/office/shop hours vary: Jan and Feb 0600-1930, Mar 0630-1900, Apr and Aug 0700-1830, May 0700-1800, Jun and Jul 0730-1800, Sep 0630-1830, Oct 0600-1900, Nov and Dec 0530-1930. Daily conservation entrance fee R120, children R60, also covers your vehicle (South Africans pay reduced rates).*

Although probably one of the least visited national parks in the country, the Kgalagadi Transfrontier Park has some of the finest game viewing in Africa. It is remote and relatively undeveloped, with uncomfortably high summer temperatures, but few visitors begrudge

the hot dusty roads once they've glimpsed their first lion. The roads follow the scrubb
valleys of two seasonal rivers, the Auob and Nossob, and cut across red sand dunes typica
of the Kalahari.

Ins and outs

Getting there From Upington, the first 190 km is an excellent tarred road followed b
61 km of badly corrugated gravel; allow at least 3½ hours to the park gates. Petrol i
available at Noenieput and Andriesvale. From Kuruman, it is 385 km to the park gates, vi
Hotazel, Sonstraal and Van Zylsrus (see page 757).

Best time to visit This is an arid region with less than 200 m of rainfall a year, fallin
between the summer months of January and April. In the summer it gets very hot and yo
should carry at least 10 litres of drinking water in your vehicle. The best months ar
February to May, but most of the accommodation is fully booked during these month
especially at weekends and around Easter. Camping is usually possible, although the mai
camp, Twee Rivieren, is likely to be very busy. Camping in winter requires warm sleepin
bags as temperatures fall below zero. Always check the availability of rooms in advance
this is the end of the road and even space for tents gets fully booked. If you plan to visi
during the main season, pre-book your accommodation before your arrival in South Africa

Malaria Kgalagadi is free from malaria.

Park information The three main rest camps – **Twee Rivieren**, **Nossob** and **Mata Mata**
have shops which stock basic groceries but none stock fresh vegetables. Meat and brea
are available at Twee Rivieren, which also has a restaurant and swimming pool. Petrol i
available at all the camps; electricity is provided by generators (220V) and is available in th
early morning and evening (1700-2300). From each camp guided day walks and nigh
drives are available and can be booked at reception. There are also six unfenced wildernes
camps: **Gharagab**, **Kielie Krankie**, **Urikaruus**, **Kalahari Tented Camp**, **Bitterpan** an
Grootkolk, none of which have shops or other facilities.

Due to the remoteness of the region a close record is kept of your movements and yo
have to sign in and out of every camp. There is a curfew on returning to the camps in th
evening; if you do not make it back to the gates on time, you will be fined. When drivin
here you have to remember that distances are vast and you may well be delaye
considerably by game viewing so some careful planning on driving times is needed. Note
too, that some tracks are one-way only (see map below). Without stops, it takes 2½ hour
to drive between Twee Riveren and Mata Mata (and Kalahari Tented Camp which is 3 km
from Mata Mata); Twee Riveren to Nossob, 3½ hours; Twee Riveren to Grootkolk, si
hours; Twee Riveren to Kieliekrankie, 1½ hours; Twee Riveren to Urikaruus, two hour
Nossob to Grootkolk, 2½ hours; Nossob to Bitterpan, 2½ hours; Nossob to Gharagab, fou
hours; Nossob to Bitterpan, 2½ hours; Bitterpan to Mata Mata, two hours.

Although the park authorities and the Upington tourist office insist that 4WDs are nc
necessary, saloon vehicles can be uncomfortable on the gravel roads and prone to fla
tyres. If you don't have a 4WD vehicle, be sure that your car is in good condition and ca
deal with several days on gravel. Although Twee Rivieren has a car workshop, there is n
system in place to cope with breakdowns. In the event of a breakdown, stay in the car an
wait for passing cars to assist you. You will have to make your way back to Twee Rivieren
from where a mechanic can drive out to your car. You should never leave the gravel road

It is illegal to drive off road and it's easy to get stuck in the soft sand. The nearest place to rent a 4WD is in Upington and many operators also hire out camping equipment too. **Note** All routes on the Botswana side of the park are strictly 4WD and must be travelled in a convoy of at least two vehicles. **Note** Remember there is no mobile phone reception in the park in the event of an emergency.

Background

The area was proclaimed a national park on 3 July 1931 as part of a progressive initiative to combat the problem of poachers. Known until a few years ago as the Kalahari Gemsbok National Park, the area was adjacent to the Gemsbok National Park in Botswana. On 7 April 1999 the two parks were formally merged into a single ecological unit, now known as the Kgalagadi Transfrontier Park.

Kgalagadi Transfrontier Park

Sleeping		Kalahari Tented Camp **3**	Nossob **6**
Bitterpan **1**		Kieliekrankie **9**	Twee Rivieren **7**
Gharagab **8**		Mata Mata **4**	Urikaruus **10**
Grootkolk **2**		Molopo Kalahari Lodge **5**	!Xaus Lodge **11**

To Namibia and Botswana via Kgalagadi Transfrontier Park

To Namibia There is now direct access from Namibia, through the **Mata Mata** border gate which opened in October 2007. Alternative access from Namibia is via the **Aroab/Rietfontein** border (0800-1630) to the south of the park.

To Botswana There are gates between the South Africa and Botswana sides. Visitors wishing to visit the Botswana side do not need a passport as long as entry and exit is made through the same gate. However, if you are entering the park in one country and exiting through the other, than you will need a passport. There are border posts at **Twee Rivieren** on the South African side and at **Two Rivers** on the Botswana side of the park, daily 0700-1600.

The first camp for tourists was built in 1940 near the confluence of the Auob and Nossob rivers. Most of the game viewing is along these riverbeds where the vegetation is concentrated. Thanks to the aridity of the region, vegetation remains sparse and mostly close to the ground, which is why game viewing is so good here. The rivers rarely flow but rainwater collects in the bed under the sand, which is sufficient for grasses and plants to survive. Both rivers were once thundering waterways, evident in the great width of the valleys in some areas. Between the two rivers stretch mighty red sand dunes, aligned from north to south and covered with yellow grass following good rains. These are fossil dunes, and their red tint is produced by an iron oxide coating on the white grains of sand. Between the 20-m-high dunes are level valleys known as streets. Two roads cross the dunes; do not venture off them as you will get stuck in sand.

Near Mata Mata camp, look out for signs of past settlement; a couple of families lived here during the First World War to watch over the waterholes in case the Germans invaded from Namibia. The Germans did enter South Africa, but by a different route, and the families were forgotten for several years after the war ended.

Wildlife

The park is famous for its predators, particularly the dark-maned Kalahari lion which can sometimes be spotted lazing in the shade of trees found along the river beds. Other predators to look out for include cheetah, wild dog, spotted hyena, bat-eared fox, black backed jackal and the honey badger. Leopard are, as always, elusive but are seen relatively regularly in the park. The park's prize antelope is the gemsbok, a beautiful creature with a dark glossy coat, strong frame and characteristic long, straight horns. You should also see giraffe, red hartebeest, Burchell's zebra and huge herds of wildebeest and springbok. Try to spot meerkats too. These energetic mongoose-like animals can be seen at dawn and dusk scurrying round their burrows in search of food. Look out for the windmills which pump the boreholes – these waterholes are usually frequented by some form of wildlife.

The birdlife, too, is impressive. Over 200 species have been recorded in the park. The best viewing months are between February and May, especially if the rains have been good. The park is known for its variety of raptors, which prey upon the smaller mammals. Look out for tawny eagle, martial eagle, chanting goshawk, white-backed vulture and eagle owl. Other birds include Burchell's courser, Namaqua sandgrouse, the Kalahari robin and the pink billed lark. You also frequently see pairs of secretary birds strutting along the dry riverbeds.

The Kalahari listings

Hotel and guesthouse prices
L over US$300 **AL** US$220-300 **A** US$150-220
B US$100-150 **C** US$75-100 **D** US$35-75
E US$15-35 **F** under US$15
Private game reserves
L4 over US$900 **L3** US$550-900
L2 US$450-550 **L1** US$300-500
Restaurant prices
⑪ over US$30 ⑪ US$15-30 ⑪ under US$15
See pages 46-51 for further information.

Sleeping

Kuruman *p755*

C Eldorado Motel, Main St, T053-7122191.
Bland 1960s roadside motel on the outskirts
of town, 60 a/c refurbished rooms in 4 blocks
arranged around swimming pool, large airy
dining room with plenty of light, quiet but
overpriced, more suited to business travellers.

C Riverfield, 12 Seodin Rd, T/F053-7120003,
www.riverfield.co.za. Modern house set in
large well-kept gardens, 12 en suite doubles
or family rooms, TV, lounge, braai area at
the back, swimming pool, self-service bar,
good breakfasts.

C Oude Werf Lodge, Winkel St,
T053-7120117, www.oudewerf-lodge.co.za.
17 comfortable a/c en suite rooms, 1 sleeping
4, DSTV, bar, restaurant, tables outside under
acacia trees, motel-style parking, friendly set up.

Tswalu Kalahari Reserve *p757*
Private lodges and camps

L4 Tswalu Lodge. T053-7819234,
www.tswalu.com. Part of the **Relais &
Chateaux** luxury hotel group. Top-notch
luxury lodge, 12 beautifully appointed stone
cottages with private decks, outdoor showers
with views of the Kalahari, swimming pool,
library. Excellent service and meals, beauty
spa, swimming pool. Rates include all meals,
game drives and horse riding. Air transfers
from Cape Town or Johannesburg can be
arranged in the private jet. At over R8000
per couple per night this is a serious
extravagance but a wonderful experience.

Southwest from Kuruman *p757*

C Khai Appel Resort (formerly known as
Gamagara Lodge), Hendrik van Eck St,
Kathu, T053-7232261, www.gamagara.co.za.
1-bedroom chalets and 2- or 3-bedroom
park homes, fully equipped for self-catering.
Swimming pool with slide. Also grassy
campsite (**E**) with power points and braais.
All set next to a peaceful dam, horse riding
and fishing can be arranged.

C-F Red Sands Country Lodge, 15 km from
Kuruman, along the N14 towards Upington,
T082-8014414, www.redsands.co.za. Located
on a private game farm in the hills above
town that is home to several species of
antelope. Selection of B&B double rooms,
fully equipped self-catering chalets, camping
and caravan sites, swimming pool with slide,
restaurant. Gets busy during school holidays.

Upington *p759, map p760*

**B-C Le Must River Residence and Le Must
River Manor**, 14 Butler St and 12 Murray Av,
T054-3323971, www.lemustupington.com.
2 elegant guesthouses set in mock Cape
Dutch buildings overlooking the river. In total,
18 double rooms with en suite facilities, TV,
heating and a/c, crisp white linen on the beds.
The houses are filled with South African art and
antiques and a large selection of books and
music. The **Residence** is a 5-star guesthouse,
while the **Manor** is a 3-star. Recommended.

C Affinity Guest House, 4 Butler St, T054-
3312101, www.affinityguesthouse.co.za.
25 en suite rooms, all a/c with TV and fridge,
in a bright pink building. Secure parking,
swimming pool, good views of the river
from the spacious garden, can arrange
boat cruises. Good value. Recommended.

C Africa River Lodge, T054-3311846,
www.africariverlodge.co.za. 10 individually
decorated en suite rooms and 2 self-catering
family cottages arranged around attractive
lawns under palms, antiques, fresh flowers,
some 4-poster beds, meals on request, pool,
relaxing and peaceful riverside spot.

C Protea Hotel Upington, 24 Schröder St, T054-3378400, www.proteahotels.com. A well-run hotel, with 56 clean and spacious a/c rooms some with river view, TV. 4-bed rooms are good value. Pool at back in secluded grounds overlooking the river. Attached is a standard steak restaurant, the **Totem Creek Spur**. Ask about weekend specials. If you are heading for the national parks ask here about 4WD hire.

C River City Inn, Scott and Park streets, T/F054-3311971. A newish mid-range hotel in the centre of town popular with business travellers. 29 a/c rooms, TV, bar and braai area, small gym, breakfast area but no restaurant.

D Libby's Lodge, 140 Schröder St, T054-3322661, www.upington.co.za/libbys_lodge. Peaceful B&B in the town centre, 7 a/c en suite rooms with private garden verandas and 3 family self-catering flats sleeping 3-5, TV, swimming pool, braai, covered parking.

D-E Eiland Holiday Resort, T/F054-3340286, corp@kharahais.gov.za. Good location on a large island opposite the town, a mix of 58 self-catering chalets and rondavels, good value for 4 people, campsite has plenty of large trees and grass, well kept, clean, electric points, swimming pool, restaurant, shop, telephones, a well-run municipal campsite. Has what is claimed to be the longest palm avenue (1041 m) in the southern hemisphere. The 200 palms were planted in 1935 and the avenue is a national monument. Recommended. Sundowner cruises on the river depart from here whenever there is sufficient demand.

Around Upington *p761*

C Witsand Nature Reserve, see page 761, T053-3131061, www.witsandkalahari.co.za. 10 comfortable self-catering chalets with 3 bedrooms, all a/c, 1 bathroom, safari decor, one has disabled facilities. Small shop with basic groceries and curios, 2 swimming pools, full board packages. Also a **campsite** (**E**) with basic facilities, ablution block and electricity points.

C-E Monate Lodge, Spitskop Nature Reserve (see page 761), T054-3321336, www.spitskopmonate.com. 6 self-catering, a/c **chalets** (**C**) with 3 beds, and 43 **camp-sites** (**F**) with electricity points, swimming pool and braais.

Kgalagadi Transfrontier Park *p761, map p763*

There are 3 main camps in the park: **Twee Rivieren**, the main camp at the entrance gate; **Mata Mata**, a more remote camp on the Namibian border; and **Nossob**, on the Botswana border. At each main camp there is a mix of self-catering cottages plus a campsite with washing and braai facilities. There are no electric points in the campsites, but lighting is provided by generator until 2300. Check in is from 1200 but all rooms must be vacated by 0900. Reservations through **SANParks** in Pretoria, T012-4289111, www.sanparks.org, Mon-Fri. You can also contact the park direct, T054-5612000; credit card bookings are accepted over the telephone. Wheelchair bound visitors are accommodated in nearly all the camps; enquire with SANParks.

Six new, upmarket wilderness camps have opened. Unlike the main camps, these are not fenced but a ranger is on duty at all times. If the park is full there are several options just outside (see below).

On the Botswana side there are campsites at **Polentswa**, **Rooiputs** and **Two Rivers**. Bookings are made through the **Botswana Parks Authority**, PO Box 131, Gaborone, T+267(0)3-9180774, dwnp@gov.bw.

L2 !Xaus Lodge, 94 km from Twee Rivierene, central reservations T021-4265111, www.xauslodge.co.za. A new initiative between SANParks and the local Khomani San bushmen) and Mier communities that live on the fringes of the park. 12 upmarket en suite thatched chalets, perched on stilts decorated with Bushmen art, overlooking the Klein Skrij Pan and a waterhole, splash pool. A typical day begins with an early-morning walk in the sand dunes with a bushman tracker to follow animal spoor, a visit to the cultural village where bushman women make traditional beads and tell spiritual stories, an afternoon game drive, followed by dinner, including traditional dishes, in the thatched boma. An interactive experience that the bushmen benefit from financially. Reports welcome.

Twee Rivieren

The biggest of the camps with 31 units in total. Accommodation and administrative buildings are lined up on a sandy slope. A shop sells groceries, meat, bread, wine, beer and souvenirs. There is also a takeaway selling snacks, a bar with TV, a swimming pool and an overpriced (and frankly awful) restaurant. Self-catering is a far better option. Night drives and guided walks can be arranged at the information centre.

C Chalets, self-contained thatched cottages with a/c, sleeping 6, shower, fully equipped kitchen, no oven but hot plate and braai area.

D Cottages, sleep 3 (2 adults and 1 child on a sleeper bed) or 4; one has wheelchair access, kitchenette and a/c.

E Campsite, dusty site but with good prefabricated shade, some trees, plus good ablutions including a laundry but no cooking facilities other than braais. Swimming pool. Can be very busy with noisy families.

Mata Mata

118 km from the entrance gate, allow at least 2½ hrs travelling time. This road is one of the most beautiful in the park with some of the best game-viewing opportunities. The camp has a small shop selling groceries and firewood. Electricity is generated from 0500 for a few hours, and again 1700-2300.

C Chalets, self-contained chalets sleeping up to 6 in 2 bedrooms, with extra beds in dining room, shower, kitchen, no oven, braai area.

D Huts, 1 double room, shower, kitchen, no oven, hot plate and braai area.

D Park Homes, sleep 3 or 5 but cramped, kitchenette, shower.

E Campsite, sandy plots in front of the chalets, little shade but fantastic setting, good ablution facilities, braai areas.

Nossob

152 km from the entrance gate, allow at least 3½ hrs travelling time; the first sign of the camp is a pair of white gates and a few battered trees beside the white buildings. This is the most remote camp, with the least facilities, and probably provides the best opportunity of hearing lions roar at night. The camp has recently been refurbished and there is now a predator information centre where you can organize guided game walks and night drives.

B Guesthouse, 2 units attached by a connecting door, sleeping 8 or 2 groups of 4. Each has 2 bedrooms, bathroom, dining room, lounge, fully equipped kitchen, enclosed veranda, good value for a group.

C Cottages, sleep 4 or 6, 2 bedrooms, 2 bathrooms, dining room, kitchen with gas stove and fridge.

D Chalets, sleep 2 or 4 in 1 or 2 bedrooms, bathroom, kitchen with hotplate and fridge.

E Campsite, ablution block and braai pits, the whole camp overlooks a broad section of the riverbed and a waterhole.

Wilderness camps

C Bitterpan. Situated in the dunes, about 3 hrs from Nossob but accessible by 4WD only along sand roads. Accommodation in stilted huts sleeping 2, with en suite bathroom, built with natural materials. Walkways link the 4 huts to a communal kitchen/entertainment/braai area. There is also a 6-m-high tower allowing excellent views out over the dunes. Electricity is solar-powered.

C Gharagab, 100 km north of Nossob. 4 log cabins sleeping 2, kitchen, shower, braai, solar power, bring your own drinking water and firewood, strictly 4WD access.

C Grootkolk, 100 km north of Nossob, this new camp is again set in red sand dunes but is more basic. 4 simple en suite chalets sleeping 2, built out of sandbags and canvas. There is a communal kitchen with fridge and hotplates, plus a braai, solar-power.

C Kalahari Tented Camp, 3 km from Mata Mata, 15 fully equipped spacious tents with kitchen and bathroom, sleeping 2-4, swimming pool, overlooks a waterhole in the Auob riverbed.

C Kieliekrankie, 37 km north of Twee Rivieren. 4 dune cabins, with 2 single beds, shower, kitchen, fridge, braai, solar power, bring your own drinking water and firewood.

C Urikaruus, 72 km north of Twee Rivieren. Units sleeping 2 built on stilts, kitchen, fridge, shower, braai, solar power, bring your own drinking water and firewood.

Outside the park

During peak season park accommodation is fully booked for weeks on end. There are several other accommodation options en route to Twee Rivieren, but these are also likely to be booked up at peak times.

B-F Molopo Kalahari Lodge, 15 km from Askham, on the gravel road to the park (50 km), T054-5110008, www.molopo lodge.co.za. Well-run lodge on the edge of the park, 22 en suite rondavels, 4 family self-catering chalets, and campsite set in dusty grounds, large restaurant, bar, TV lounge, swimming pool. Rates are very reasonable and children under 6 go free (including breakfast). The last stop before the park, has its own petrol station and limited supplies of oil, tyres and tubes, plus a liquor store that sells ice. Recommended.

C-D Rooipan Guest House, T082-4151579 (mob). Old farmhouse which has been converted into a guesthouse and tea room. Swimming pool, braai area. Evening meals on request, specializes in South African dishes. Located midway between Upington and the Kgalagadi Transfrontier Park. Ask about the 2-hr hiking trail.

C-F Klipkolk Lodge, Opstaan, T072-1596726 (mob), bott@upington.co.za. A simple B&B sleeping 12 with attached tea room camp site set on a typical Kalahari farm. Evening meals available on request. 13 km to the border post at Rietfontein. Follow the R360 from Upington, take the R31 turning. Run by Gertuida and Hendrik who can organize tours by donkey cart to meet the local Mier people.

C-F Kalahari Trails Nature Reserve, 10 km east of Askham, on the R31 to Van Zylsrus, T054-5110140, www.kalahari-trails.co.za. Combination of simple guesthouse rooms sleeping 2-3, some with en suite, a self-catering chalet sleeping 6, permanent tents under thatch for 2, campsites with shade. All accommodation is self-catering in the large shared fully equipped kitchen, dining room, lounge with fireplace, shop selling meat and firewood.

🍴 Eating

Kuruman *p755*

Eating is limited in Kuruman, though there are branches of **Spur**, **Wimpy** and **KFC** on Main St. The food is good at the **Red Sands Country Lodge**, 15 km from town, so if you are staying there, stay put for dinner. There's also a small coffee shop at The Eye. For those self-catering, **Pick 'n Pay** supermarket is on Beare St and **Spar** is on Main St.

🍴 **Kalahari Pub**, 63 Main Rd, T053-7121271. Mon-Sat 1000-late, Sun 1100-late. Pub and grill serving predictable meals, steaks, burgers, ribs and the like, and South African standard starters – crumbed mushrooms and chicken livers.

Upington *p759, map p760*

All South African small towns have the standard and unimaginative steakhouse chain restaurants; Upington must feature every single one of them. **Saddles** is on Market St and **Spur** is in the Protea Hotel Upington. For coffee try the **Pick 'n Pay** shopping mall and, for a late night drink, try **Scotty's Bar**, also at the Protea Hotel Upington.

🍴🍴 **Le Must**, 11 Schröder St, T054-3323971. Sun-Fri 1200-1500, daily 1800-2200. By far the best restaurant in town and one of the best in the Northern Cape – Mandela, Mbeki and FW De Klerk have eaten here. Book ahead. Not to be confused with **Le Must** accommodation in Upington – the 2 have recently gone under separate management despite the same

name. Sophisticated decor, tables overlooking the riverbank, well-prepared dishes,
good service, interesting local wine list priced
with overseas visitors in mind. If you've been
out in the desert for a few days, this is the
place to treat yourself. Intriguing items on
the menu include biltong bobotie with
sultana compote. Recommended. It's a must!
♥♥ **Dros**, Pick 'n Pay Centre, Le Roux St,
T054-3313331. Open 0900-2200. Another
chain with mock wine cellar decor but
relatively good and varied food, steaks, grills,
pizza, aimed at families.
♥♥ **Desert Casino & Restaurant**, Upington
Golf Course, 7 km on the Kuruman road N14,
T054-3384100, www.desert palace.co.za.
1000-0200. New casino complex with an
Italian-themed restaurant and bar serving
pizza and pasta and 145 slot machines.
♥♥ **O'Hagan's**, 20 Schröder St, T054-3312005.
Open 1100-late. Irish theme pub and
restaurant, usual steak, pasta and pies, big
portions and good selection of beers.
♥ **Arabesque Coffee Shop**, 24 Scott St, T054-
3313412. Mon-Tue 0800-1700, Wed-Sat 0800-
late, Sun 0900-1600. Brightly decorated café
with internet access and small garden, serving
breakfasts, tea and cake, simple meals in the
evening like lasagne, smoothies and shakes.
♥ **Sakkie se Arkie**, T082-5645447 (mob).
Sundowner cruise with a braai on an
attractive double-storey pontoon departing
from the **Eiland Holiday Resort**. If you're not
staying here, enquire at reception.

▲ Activities and tours

Kuruman *p755*
Golf
Kuruman Country Club, T053-7321242,
9-hole course. Also tennis, squash and bowls.

Upington *p759, map p760*
Tour operators
Trips into the Kalahari are not cheap, as 4WDs
are essential and all equipment and
provisions (including water) has to be taken

along. This requires quite a bit of organization, but the rewards are well worth it. Expect
to pay in the region of R3000 per person for
a 2-night/3-day guided camping tour. These
operators can also organize tours to the the
Ai-Ais/Richtersveld Transfrontier Park.
Kalahari Safaris, 3 Oranje St, T054-3325653,
www.kalaharisafaris.co.za. Budget tours
including 3- to 5-day trips to the Kgalagadi
Transfrontier Park, 1-day trip to Augrabies
Falls, rafting on the Gariep (Orange) River
and trips to Witsand and Spitskop nature
reserves. Pieter really knows and loves
the area, making him a great guide.
Consistently recommended by readers.
Kalahari Tours & Travel, T054-3380375,
www.kalahari-tours.co.za. Well organized
and established local operator organizing a
range of tours into the Kalahari, including
to the Kgalagadi Transfrontier Park,
Augrabies and Namakwa (Namaqualand).

⊙ Transport

Kuruman *p755*
It's 238 km to **Kimberley**, 263 km
to **Upington**.

Bus
Intercape, reservations T0861-287287,
www.intercape.co.za. Buses leave daily from
the Leach petrol station on the main road for
Johannesburg and **Pretoria** (7½ hrs), and
Upington (3 hrs).

Upington *p759, map p760*
It's 804 km to **Johannesburg**, 894 km to
Cape Town, 401 km to **Kimberley**, 263 km
to **Kuruman**, 374 km to **Springbok**, 120 km
to **Augrabies Falls National Park**, 80 km
to **Kakamas**, 50 km to **Keimoes**.

Air
The town airport, T054-3377900, www.air
ports.co.za, has one of the longest runways
in southern Africa. **SAA**, T011-9781111,
ww2.flysaa.com, has 1 flight a day between

Upington and **Cape Town** and 2 flights a day between Upington and **Johannesburg**. These are very useful services if your time is short and you wish to visit the magnificent Kgalagadi Tranfrontier Park – you can fly in, hire a car at the airport and be in the park by the end of the day.

Bus

Intercape coaches arrive/depart from their town office in Lutz St, which is a short walk from the Protea hotels. Buses run daily to/from **Cape Town** (10 hrs), via **Springbok** (5 hrs) and **Clanwilliam** (7 hrs); to/from **Johannesburg** and **Pretoria** (10 hrs) via **Kuruman** (3 hrs), and to/from **Windhoek** in Namibia (12 hrs). **Big Sky Coaches** runs a service to **Bloemfontein**, in the Free State, on Sun at 1300 from the Protea Hotel Upington. From Bloemfontein it leaves on Fri at 1400 from the tourist centre.

   Bus companies Intercape, T0861-287287, www.intercape.co.za. **Big Sky Coaches**, T051-5233620, www.bigskycoaches.co.za.

Car and 4WD hire

Car hire is available at the airport: **Avis**, T054-3324746-7, www.avis.co.za; **Hertz**, T054-3373613; 56 Le Roux St, T054-3373600; www.hertz.co.za; and **National**, T054-3321089, www.nationalcar.co.za.

   If you want to hire a 4WD there are several local companies in Upington catering specifically for the wilderness regions of the Northern Cape, some also hire out camping equipment such as roof-top tents and fridges. Expect to pay in the region of R900 per day, although some packages have additional kilometre costs, which can make it very expensive; it's definitely worth shopping around. Also ask about emergency back-up. Some firms will allow you to take the vehicle into Botswana and Namibia, too. Try **Kalahari 4x4**, 66 Scott St, T054-3323098, www.kalahari4x4hire.co.za; **Kgalagadi 4x4**, T054-3377133, www.kgalagadi4x4.com;

or **Desert 4x4**, 26 Swartmodder Av, T054-3321560, desert4x4@upington.co.za.

Train

There is a service of sorts between Upington and **Windhoek** in Namibia run by **Transnamib Starline Passenger Services**, T+264 (0)61-2982032, www.transnamib.com.na. However, as Namibia's trains are primarily used for freight, it is slow going with a lot of stops. Despite this, the passenger compartments are comfortable with airline-like seats, videos and vending machines for drinks and snacks. There are often delays but, in theory, the service departs Upington on Thu and Sun at 0500 and arrives in Windhoek the following morning at 0700. In the other direction the train departs Windhoek on Wed and Sat at 1940 and arrives in Upington the following day at 2130 with a lengthy stop at Keetmanshoop en route. (**Intercape Mainliner** bus takes 12 hrs to do the same route, compared to around 24 hrs on the train.)

⊙ Directory

Kuruman *p755*
Banks First National and ABSA Bank, Beare St. **Standard Bank**, Voortrekker St. **Emergencies** Police, Voortrekker St, T10111. **Tow-in-Service** (24 hrs), T053-7122551, after hours, T083-2598537. **Medical services** Hospital, Main St, T053-7128100. **Post office** School St.

Upington *p759, map p760*
Banks First National and ABSA have branches in Schröder St, close to the hotels. **Emergencies** Police, Schröder St, opposite the camel and rider statue, T10111. **Internet** Café de Net, in the Pick 'n Pay Centre. **Medical services** Ambulance, T10177. Hospital, T054-3386100. **Medi Clinic Private Hospital**, corner 4th Av and Du Toit St, T054-3388900.

West towards Namakwa and Springbok

Driving across the Northern Cape between Upington and Springbok, stop for a moment and look out over the endless horizons and stillness of the desert. Here one gets a real sense of how large South Africa is, pausing in countryside that has barely changed in thousands of years. Although stark and deserted, the emptiness has a certain beauty. The first part of the journey is particularly striking as the road follows the Gariep (Orange) River, with its band of lush vegetation along either bank. The highlight in this region is a visit to the dramatic waterfall in Augrabies Falls National Park. Once in Springbok, you will have arrived in Namakwa (Namaqualand), the name given to the arid northwest corner of the Northern Cape, starting in the south at the Doorn River bridge near Klawer and extending north to the Namibian border. The area is best known for its magnificent wild flowers, which transform the barren, rocky countryside every spring. The regional centre is Springbok, the most viable base for exploring the area. ▸▸ For listings, see pages 780-784.

Cannon Island (Kanoneiland) → *Phone code: 054. Colour map 3, A5.*

Between Upington and Keimoes there is a choice of two roads along the banks of the Gariep (Orange) River. The main road follows the northern bank, but if you take the southern road you can stop off at Cannon Island (Kanoneiland). This is the largest island on the river, 14 km long and 3 km at its widest point. These days, 1700 ha out of a total area of 2500 ha are irrigated. Before the Cape government had managed to establish control over the region, the island was a stronghold for Korana tribes who harassed the early sheep farmers. The island was named after a terrible incident when the Korana tried to fire a cannon made from the hollowed-out trunk of a quiver tree – when the smoke cleared, six of them lay dead amongst the debris.

Keimoes → *Phone code: 054. Colour map 3, A5.*

Keimoes is the local farming centre at the junction with the R27, the main road south across the Karoo to Calvinia. This is the quickest route to Cape Town but it means missing out Namakwa. The name in Afrikaans means 'mouse nest' so presumably the settlement once had a problem with mice. Look out for the Persian waterwheel in the centre of town, still in use on an irrigation canal. A short 4-km drive from the centre takes you to **Tierberg Nature Reserve**, a municipal reserve covering some 160 ha which is notable for aloes and succulents. Most of the flowers are in bloom between August and September.

Kakamas → *Phone code: 054. Colour map 3, A4.*

The second most important farming centre along this stretch of the Gariep (Orange) River is Kakamas. The settlement was founded in 1893 by the Cape Parliament, as a centre for the Dutch Reformed Church to establish a colony for poor farmers who had lost everything following periods of drought and an outbreak of *rinderpest*. For tourist information contact the **Kalahari Gateway Hotel** ① *19 Voortrekker Rd, T054-4310838, www.kalaharigateway.co.za*.

Most of the town is strung out along the main road which runs parallel to the southern canal. The canal is one of several fed by the **Neus Weir** which irrigate the surrounding vineyards and fruit farms. The wier is 936 m long and was the first cylindrical weir with a smooth overflow to be built in South Africa. Driving along Voortrekker Road in the town centre, look out for the set of fine, giant **waterwheels**. These nine wheels were built by a local farmer, Piet Burger, to help lift water from the canals into his fields. They are still in use today and considerably more economical to operate than modern lifting methods such as pumps. Along the route of the northern irrigation canal are a couple of **water tunnels**. One tunnel is 97 m long; the second is an incredible 172 m, and both are 2 m high and 3-4 m wide. They were built in 1889-1901 by Cornish tin miners.

Pofadder and around → *Phone code: 054. Colour map 3, A3.*

The road to Springbok runs through the dusty town of Pofadder which is a small *dorp* (village) lying on a particularly arid stretch of road; were it not for a small natural spring it would never have come into being. There is little more here than a cluster of ramshackle houses, a petrol station, a general store and bottle shop. It is only worth a mention as it is one of the most remote settlements in the country and is the butt of much South African humour. For those South Africans who admit they have been to Pofadder, it's as good as saying that they have been to the ends of the earth. Pofadder is not actually named after the venomous snake, but after Klaas Pofadder, a cattle rustler, who based himself here during the 1860s.

To the north of here is the settlement of **Pella**, founded by the London Missionary Society in 1814, and named after the village which provided refuge for Christians in Macedonia. In 1878 the running of the station was taken over by the Catholic church. Of particular interest is the original **mission church** which has been consecrated as a cathedral. It was designed and built by Father LM Simon and Father Leo Wolf – neither had any experience or knowledge of building, so they used an encyclopaedia for reference. The cathedral comes as a welcome cool refuge, standing in a neat walled garden fringed with date palms.

Augrabies Falls National Park ●❼▲ ›› *pp780-784. Colour map 3, A4.*

ⓘ *T054-4529200. Gates 0700-1830. Office 0700-1900, R60.*

The remote location of the Augrabies Falls park has saved it from mass development, and it remains one of the highlights of the north. The main reason for coming here is to see the huge waterfall, although the surrounding landscape is equally impressive: a bizarre moonscape of moulded rock formations, surrounded by shimmering semi-desert. There is good hiking here, and the Gariep (Orange) River above and below the falls has some excellent whitewater rafting. ›› *For further details, see Activities and tours, page 784.*

Ins and outs

Getting there There is only one route into the park, the R359. From Upington, take the N14 and turn off at Alheit. From Springbok, there is a left turning before you reach Alheit. All are clearly signposted. The park is 120 km from Upington and 304 km from Springbok.

Best time to visit March to October is the best time to visit. This area has a typical arid climate, with very hot summer days. Rain falls in autumn and, in winter, conditions are ideal for walking, although it gets very cold at night.

Tourist information There is a large shop stocking a selection of groceries including meat and a few fresh vegetables, plus beer and wine; open office hours. In the same building there is a restaurant with views of the falls. Petrol is available by the entrance and there are pay phones (cards only) by the reception desk.

Landscape and wildlife

The park was created in 1966 to protect the waterfall and conserve the surrounding area, a unique ecosystem of riverine and desert environments. The landscape is typical of the arid north, seemingly barren but rich in wild plants and with a growing population of small mammals. It was extended in 1973 but not without some controversy. Around the small settlement of Riemvasmak to the northeast of the park, the residents were forcibly removed as part of Apartheid's Group Areas Act and to extend the park. The community was displaced, with the Xhosa resettled in Cape Town and the Nama people sent to South West Africa (now Namibia). However 74,000 ha of land to the northeast of the park was returned to the community in 1995 and many people have now returned to the area to live.

The impressive **waterfall** is the sixth largest in the world. Above the falls, the Gariep (Orange) River passes over a series of impressive cataracts, dropping about 100 m. From here the main channel passes over a 56-m drop into a narrow gorge of steep, smooth rock, the water churning below. There are a number of viewpoints along the southern side of the gorge. Thanks to the slippery surface of the rock and the number of over-curious visitors who slid to their deaths, the edge of the gorge is today lined with a small fence. Following heavy rains, a number of smaller waterfalls drop into the main gorge along the sides of the main falls – a tremendous sight, but fairly rare.

Walking along the cliffs above the river, you pass a number of unusual **plants** that have adapted to the harsh desert environment. Some of the more notable trees include the quiver tree, camel thorn, tree fuschia and the wild olive; there are some informative displays by reception. There is also a fair range of **wildlife**, including klipspringer, eland, kudu, gemsbok and springbok, although these all tend to be elusive. You are more likely to see ground squirrels foraging between the rocks. A good time of day to visit is around sunset, when the swallows flitting through the gorge are slowly replaced by small bats which stream from cracks in the rock faces surrounding the falls.

Augrabies Falls National Park

1 km / 1 mile		
Sleeping 😴	Fish Eagle **2**	**Eating** 🍴
Augrabies Falls **1**	Mountain **3**	Shibula **1**

Hiking

There is a popular three-day, 40-km hiking trail, the **Klipspringer Trail**, which is open 1 April to 30 September but is often booked up during local school holidays (see Sleeping, page 780, for details of overnight huts). There are also several one-hour hikes which you don't have to book, each leading to a scenic point close to the camp. The walk to **Arrow Point** is perhaps the best, with superb views downstream. You need to wear shoes with a good grip, but the walk does not involve any climbing. **Note** There are some dangerous spots at the edge of the gorge. Take care when approaching it, especially if you are with small children.

Game drives

There are several short game drives from the campsite; ask at reception for a map. The gravel roads take you to Echo Corner, Oranjekom, Ararat and Moon Rock. The only game you're likely to see is klipspringer and eland, but the birdlife is very rewarding, as is the unusual desert plantlife. The park also organizes guided night drives in an open 4WD, which may be a better way of learning about the flora and fauna found in the park. These can be booked at reception.

Springbok and around 🏢🏨🏢🔺🏢🏢 ➤ pp780-784. Phone code: 027. Colour map 3, B2.

The capital of Namakwa is set in a narrow valley surrounded by the Klein Koperberge (Small Copper Mountains) and hemmed in by koppies littered with rough butter-coloured rocks. It is a modern town with little of interest within its confines, but it has an important position, straddling the N7, and is a good base from which to explore the countryside north to the Namibian border and west to the Atlantic coast. The town is quiet for most of the year but is totally transformed when the spring wild flowers start to bloom.

Namakwa Tourism Information ⓘ *Voortrekker St, on the left as you enter town, T027-7128035, www.namakwa-dm.gov.za, Mon-Fri 0800-1615; during the flower season also Sat and Sun 0830-1600,* is the main office for the Namakwa region. The staff are very knowledgeable and have a good selection of pamphlets and maps on the region, but the office sometimes closes completely out of season.

Sights

In the past, the fortunes of the town were closely linked with the **copper industry**. In 1852 the first copper mine started production; this was the first commercial mining operation of any type in South Africa. Despite several other discoveries further north, Springbok was able to develop into an important regional centre because of its abundant supply of drinking water from a spring, a rare and valuable commodity in the region before dams and pipelines were built. There is a small town **museum** ⓘ *Van der Stel St, T027-7188100 Mon, Wed and Fri 0830-1530,* outlining local history, housed in what was once a synagogue.

Goegap Nature Reserve ➔ Colour map 3, B2.
ⓘ *From the centre of Springbok, pass under the N7 and turn right; just before the airport, take a left turn; it is 15 km to the gates. T027-7189906. Daily 0800-1600. Small entrance fee per car and per person. Visitor centre and café.*

Named after the Nama word for waterhole, this popular little reserve has a well-known aloe collection, a couple of mountain-bike trails and a 4WD route. The local O'Okiep Copper Company donated the area to the government in 1960 to establish a reserve to help protect the wild flowers of the region. The park has since been added to, including the opening of the **Hester Malan Wild Flower Garden** in 1966, which displays over 100 different species of aloes and succulents, and sells plants and seeds; it's a beautiful spot in August and September. The reserve is a mix of granite koppies and dry valleys, with a good cross-section of typical Namakwa vegetation. Although the area looks parched and barren, it supports a surprisingly varied ecology – 581 plant species have been recorded in the reserve. Like much of the area, the park becomes carpeted with wild flowers after the rains, making it very popular during spring.

Visitors can drive a 17-km loop which wends into the hills, offering opportunities to see game and birdlife – the most common species are gemsbok, mountain zebra, springbok, klipspringer, duiker and steenbok. The longer 4WD route can only be visited by booking a trip through the reserve office. The route travels through more remote and dramatic corners of the reserve and lasts for three hours. There are also two hiking trails, 6 km and 12 km long, and when the flowers are in full bloom the walks allow visitors to gain some height, providing excellent views of the colourful carpets below. During the summer temperatures soar; it is unwise to go walking in these conditions.

Springbok

To Ai-Ais Richtersveld National Park & Namibia

To Upington

To Springbok Airport & Goegap Nature Reserve

To Vanrhynsdorp & Cape Town

To Cape Town

200 metres
200 yards

Sleeping
Annie's Cottage 1
Masonic 2
Okiep Country 7
Old Mill Lodge 3

Springbok 5
Springbok Caravan Park 8
Springbok Lodge 6

Eating
BJ's Steakhouse 2
Carne Casa 3
Melboschkuil 5
Titbits 6

Namakwa flowers

Namaqualand, now referred to as Namakwa, the 'land of the Nama people', is a scorched area of semi-desert which, for much of the year, holds little more than shimmering dust and rock-strewn mountains. However, following the spring rains the ground explodes in a riot of colour, literally carpeting the region with wild flowers. The Namakwa flowers have become a major tourist attraction and, in spring, the still valleys and sleepy towns are transformed into busy visitor hubs.

Nevertheless, the very nature of the attraction – the flowers appear in different locations from year to year – prevents the flower-viewing industry from getting too over the top. Under normal conditions, rains are expected in July and August; the further north you travel, the less rain the land receives. The occurrence and distribution of the wild flowers is determined by the interaction between temperature, light, and the timing and intensity of rainfall. As climatic factors vary from year to year, so too does the composition of the vegetation. A late frost or intense sand-storm can cause a sudden end to the flower season in an area, while in the mountains, some blooms last until the end of October.

Over 4000 species have been discovered, the most common of which is the **orange and black gousblom**, a large daisy. These flowers look their best when they occupy a valley floor, forming a stunning carpet of orange. On the mountainsides or rocky hills you will see **mesembryanthemums**, commonly known as vygies or sour figs. Their blossoms can be pink, scarlet, blue or yellow. Closer to Springbok are **quiver trees** (*Aloe dichotoma*), the tree from which the San made their quivers. This is a slow-growing plant which reaches a height of 7 m when fully grown. Another interesting plant to look out for is the **halfmens** (*Pachypodium namaquanum*), a strange-looking succulent which has a long spine with a clump of leaves at the top; some specimens are thought to be several hundred years old. These are usually seen along the Gariep (Orange) River and on isolated granite koppies.

Springbok to Namibia ☺ ⏩ *pp780-784. Colour map 3, A1.*

➔ *Phone code: 027.*

The N7 continues directly north of Springbok for 118 km to the border with Namibia. The unremarkable and untidy settlement of **Okiep**, 8 km north of Springbok, lays claim to having once been the world's richest copper mine, before production ceased in 1918. From the late 1880s miners from the tin mines in Cornwall arrived to help establish the mines and share their expert knowledge. Today the Cornish pump house, containing a steam engine that used to pump water from the mine, and the smokestack next to it, are evidence of the only Cornish mining techniques found in the southern hemisphere. The N7 continues north to **Steinkopf** which marks the junction with the R382 that goes to Port Nolloth, Alexander Bay and the Ai-Ais/Richtersveld Transfrontier Park (see page 777).

Port Nolloth ➔ *Phone code: 027. Colour map 3, A1.*

ⓘ *Information can also be found at www.portnolloth.org.za.*

Port Nolloth is an odd little town on the windswept west coast. It is an important fishing centre but, more interestingly, it is renowned for attracting fortune-seekers who trade (often illegally) in diamonds. The town was established as a harbour and railway junction for the copper industry in 1854, but it proved too shallow for the bulk-ore carriers and the trade moved north to Alexander Bay. These days it has developed into a small holiday centre – the only one on this stretch of the coast – with crayfishing and diamonds supplementing local income. The town is split into two sections, Port Nolloth being the business and fishing sector, and **McDougalls Bay**, 4 km to the south, the holiday resort. The local fishing fleets are not permitted to fish off the coast at McDougalls Bay, which is reserved for angling and crayfish diving for visitors. The beaches have a certain wild, windswept beauty to them, although the long stretches of sun-bleached sand can appear rather bleak at times and it often gets misty along the coast. Don't be deceived by the calm sea; it's very cold all year round.

Alexander Bay → *Phone code: 027, Colour map 3, A1.*

The diamond industry becomes more apparent further north in Alexander Bay, by the Namibian border. Diamonds were first found here in 1925, and today the town is run by the mining company Alexkor Ltd. Alexander Bay was closed to visitors until a few years ago; today visitors can take part in diamond mine tours, although most people come here for easy access to the Ai-Ais/Richtersveld Transfrontier Park (see below). The Gariep (Orange) River estuary has been awarded RAMSAR status as an important wetland habitat for birds; more than 200 species have been recorded in the region.

If you wish to explore the diamond region, contact **Alexkor Ltd** ① *Alexander Bay, T027-8311330, www.alexkor.co.za, or www.coastofdiamonds.co.za*. Tours run on Thursday 0800-1230; book a week in advance as you need to supply copies of your passport; no children under 16; the price depends on the size of the group. The tour starts at the town museum and goes into the mining region to visit the workshops and mining blocks, harbour area, as well as an oyster farm and seal colony. The **museum** ① *Mon-Fri 1000-1400*, has exhibits on the history of the region's diamond industry and a video of the mine. Alexkor also runs the local **tourist information office** ① *in the museum, T027-8311330, www.diamondcoast.co.za*.

Ai-Ais/Richtersveld Transfrontier Conservation Park ⊙▲ ₩ pp780-784 *Colour map 3, A1.*

The magnificent Ai-Ais/Richtersveld Transfrontier Conservation Park covers some of the most remote and starkly beautiful scenery in Namakwa. The park is isolated and inaccessible and the terrain is rough – much of it can only be reached by 4WD. Richtersveld was proclaimed a national park in 1991. The northern boundary was the Gariep (Orange) River and the international border with Namibia. However, after much negotiation, the Richtersveld is now part of a transfrontier park, joining it with Namibia's Ai-Ais Hot Springs and Fish River Canyon over the border.

The park encompasses a mountainous desert, seemingly barren but full of sturdy succulents, many of them endemic. These, coupled with the surreal rugged terrain, are the principal attractions of the park. Some of the most visible plants include the kokerboom (quiver) and halfmens trees, while hidden in the mountains are hundreds of different succulents. None of the larger mammals are able to survive in such a hostile environment, but you may come across klipspringer, grey rhebok, steenbok, duiker and mountain zebra; consider yourself very fortunate if you see leopard, jackal, brown hyena or caracal. Swimming and fishing (with a permit) are allowed in the Gariep (Orange) River, but you always need to be wary of the current.

To Namibia via Vioolsdrif

The N7 continues to the Vioolsdrif border with Namibia where there is a bridge over the Gariep (Orange) River. This is the major border between South Africa and Namibia.

Customs and immigration The border crossing (open 24 hours) is pretty straightforward and, although there is a lot of traffic, formalities at customs and immigration are quick and courteous.

Facilities There is a VAT refund desk at the border (see page 55). It is worth noting that the Namibian dollar is interchangeable with the South African Rand and both are accepted throughout Namibia, so you do not need to change money.

Vehicle formalities Vehicles are likely to be searched. You are not permitted to take firewood across the border. If you are in a hire car, ensure that you have documentation from the rental company that allows you to take a car out of South Africa. Namibia is part of the Southern Africa Development Community (SADC) customs agreement so if you are in your own car travelling on a carnet, you do not need to get it signed here, and you won't need to until you reach Zimbabwe or Zambia which are outside the SADC. You simply fill out the car's details in a book. On the Namibia side you will have to pay for temporary third-party insurance but this costs very little.

Into Namibia **Noordoewer** is the first town in Namibia, 1 km beyond the border, and has a petrol station, a small shop and one hotel: the **Orange River Lodge**, which has a bar and restaurant; you can also camp here. Beyond Noordoewer, it is 350 km to the next major town – **Keetmanshoop**. If you want to explore the Ai-Ais Hot Springs and Fish River Canyon before you get here then you need to stock up on provisions in South Africa; the **Spar** in Springbok is the best bet.

Ins and outs

Getting there The easiest route is to drive north from Springbok on the N7 to Steinkopf (49 km). Take the Port Nolloth turning and follow the R382 to the coast via Annenous Pass. In Port Nolloth take the coast road north towards Alexander Bay. The park is signposted from Alexander Bay. It is a further 93 km of gravel along the Gariep (Orange) River, curving back inland to the park's office at Sendelingsdrift (see below). Those coming from Namibia can take the road from Vioolsdrift, via Kotzehoop, through spectacular scenery to Eksteenfontein and then on to Sendelingsdrift.

Getting around None of the routes within the reserve are suitable for normal cars; a 4WD is essential. Due to its remoteness, it is not possible to visit the park on a day trip and it is recommended that you don't go alone, so try to group up with other vehicles. Those in single vehicles have to sign an agreement to report back to the office on departure. Fuel is available at reception at Sendelingsdrift, though not unleaded. The nearest unleaded fuel available is in Alexander Bay. Entry permits are issued here. Visitors must arrive before 1600 in order to reach the designated campsites before dark. Keep clear of all 'no entry' signs, most of which denote mining and security areas. At Sendelingsdrift, a pontoon has been established to ferry people and vehicles across the Gariep (Orange) River to the Namibian side of the park. This has a carrying capacity for two fully loaded double-cab 4WD vehicles. For now it's only used by mining personnel, and will only be operational for the public once border officials have been put in place, which they may happen by the time you read this; check with SANParks.

Transfrontier conservation area

Since 2003, the Richtersveld National Park in South Africa, and Fish River Canyon, Ai-Ais Hot Springs and the Hunsberg Conservation Area in Namibia, are all part of the Ai-Ais/Richtersveld Transfrontier Conservation Park. This is the first such park between Namibia and South Africa. The ultimate aim is to link the Ai-Ais/Richtersveld Transfrontier Conservation Park with the newly proclaimed Sperrgebiet National Park along Namibia's coast and then to the Lona National Park in Angola.

The park currently covers 6045 sq km and spans some of the most spectacular desert scenery in southern Africa. The park is managed jointly by SANParks and the Namibian Ministry of Environment and Tourism, is and sponsored by the Peace Parks Foundation (www.peaceparks.org), which promotes sustainable development, conservation and political stability across the region.

By taking down fences, original migration routes for the game are re-established and park authorities from neighbouring countries are encouraged to work as a team. Other transfrontier parks include the Kgalagadi Transfrontier Park, between South Africa and Botswana, and the Great Limpopo Transfrontier Park between South Africa, Zimbabwe and Mozambique where the fences along Kruger National Park and the international borders have been removed. There are others in the pipeline throughout southern Africa.

Best time to visit Visits in the spring and autumn avoid the climatic extremes. The region receives virtually no rainfall in the east, while the western margin is frequently covered by coastal fog known as the *malmokkie*. In summer the daytime temperatures can exceed 50°C, so this is definitely a time to avoid the area. Three hiking trails are open from 1 April to 30 September: **Vensterval Trail** (four days, three nights); **Lelieshoek-Oemsberg Trail** (three days, two nights) and the **Kodaspiek Trail** (two days, one night). Conditions are tough and for experienced hikers only. It is also possible to walk a little in the vicinity of the campsites.

Tourist information The **park office** ① *Sendelingsdrift, 330 km from Springbok, T027-8311506, www.sanparks.org, gate hours 0700-1800, office hours 0800-1600, R80, children R40 per day,* strictly controls visitor numbers; always call in advance. There is a small general store (weekdays only), selling cool drinks and basic provisions. The nearest shops are at Kuboes and Alexander Bay. Petrol and diesel are also available in the latter. Fresh drinking water is only available at Sendelingsdrift; make sure you have containers which can hold up to 20 litres. The park authorities advise visitors to bring gas stoves for cooking, rather than campfires, as there can be strong winds at the end of the day. All rubbish must be removed from the park so ensure you have rubbish bags. There is no mobile phone reception in the park, but if you have international roaming you can call from a few spots around Sendelingsdrift.

Springbok to Cape Town ● ›› *pp780-784.*

As you travel south from Springbok, the N7 winds through rugged granite scenery. There are no settlements of note until you reach Van Rhynsdorp. After 66 km the road passes the small settlement of **Kamieskroon**, which has little more than a petrol station, a shop, a few houses and a couple of places to stay. During the spring many visitors stop in this area to admire the wild flowers.

Continuing south on the N7 there is little of interest until you are past Van Rhynsdorp and enter the **Olifants River Valley**. From here you can explore the West Coast fishing villages (see page 186) or the beautiful Cederberg Mountains (see page 203). Cape Town (495 km) can easily be reached in a single day.

Namaqua National Park → Colour map 3, B2.

ⓘ T027-6721948. Daily 0800-1700 during the flower season when the park can get very crowded; the best time is 1030-1600. Outside the flower season, there is little to see. R60, children R30. The information centre has a shop, tea room and toilets (only open in season). Formerly known as the Skilpad Wildflower Reserve, the 1000-ha Namaqua National Park has some of the best flower displays in the region. The reserve is being incorporated into a larger 60,000-ha area designed to protect its unique and fragile ecosystem. Lying to the west of the N7 highway between Garies and Kharkams, it covers the area between the Spoeg and Groen rivers, allowing for the protection of the Atlantic seaboard marine ecosystems as well as the associated estuaries.

Its fine flowers have much to do with the park's location, set on the first ridge of hills in from the coast, which ensures that it receives the first rains of the season. Even in poor years, the displays here are better than in most areas. Visitors can expect to see various bulb species: *babianas*, *lapeirousias* and *romuleas*, plus duikerwortel (*Grielum humifusum*) and orange mountain daisies (*Ursinia cakilefolia*).

Access is via a gravel road, heading north and then west from the **Kamieskroon Hotel**. The entrance is 17 km from the N7. From here, a 5-km gravel road winds in a loop around the hill, which, during the flower season, is a carpet of orange. Visitors can either walk around the park or ride a mountain bike. There is also a slight chance of seeing some wildlife: klipspringer, steenbok, duiker and black-backed jackal. The park is home to the world's smallest tortoise, the Namaqua Speckled Padloper.

◉ West towards Namakwa and Springbok listings

⊜ Sleeping

Kakamas p771

C Kalahari Gateway Hotel, Voortrekker St, T054-4310838, www.kalaharigateway.co.za. 25 a/c rooms, restaurant, 2 bars, swimming pool in pleasant palm setting, comfortable, good-value hotel. Very enthusiastic about the region and can advise on local activities.
C Vergelegen, from Upington the farm is located just before Kakamas before crossing

the Gariep River, T054-4310976, www.augrabiesfalls.co.za. 10 comfortable rooms with a/c and heating, some have internet access, swimming pool, superb restaurant that has been rated by the South African magazine *Eat Out*, try the unusual biltong and peppadew soup, also has a farm stall and tea garden so well worth a stop even if not staying.

Pofadder and around p772

C-D Pofadder Hotel, Voortrekker St, T/F054-9330063, www.pofadderhotel.co.za. Squat, orange building on the main street, 23 basic rooms, restaurant with hot buffet in the evening, lively bar, swimming pool, secure parking, the only hotel in town. Also has 5 newly built a/c self-catering chalets sleeping 4.

Augrabies Falls National Park *p772, map p773*

Reservations through **SANParks**, Pretoria, T012-4289111, www.sanparks.org, Mon-Fri. Bookings can also be made in person at the offices in Cape Town and Durban (see page 48). For reservations under 48 hrs prior to your arrival contact reception directly, T054-4529200; credit card bookings are accepted over the telephone.

Next to the falls

Check-in is from 1200, but all rooms must be vacated by 0900. The cottages and campsite are well spaced out and private. There are 3 small swimming pools, ideal for hot summer days when temperatures can rise above 40°C. The campsite is located at the far end of the complex from the office. In between are a mix of 2, 3 and 4-bed cottages. These are self-catering, but many guests choose to eat in the restaurant in the evening. Overall the park's accommodation here is good, and while the campsite can get crowded, it is in a beautiful setting. The shop and restaurant are in the main reception centre.

C Cottages. All 59 cottages have a/c and fully equipped, clean, comfortable units with views towards gorge, typical parks style, good value for 4 people.

D Campsite. Not all of the 40 pitches have electricity, grass patches are preserved for recreational use, which means you have to pitch your tent in the dust. The best shady spots get occupied quickly. The kitchen block has electric hot plates, a laundry and an ironing room.

Klipspringer Trail

E Fish Eagle and **Mountain** are both overnight stone huts. Each sleeps 12 and is fitted with bunks, mattresses, toilets, drinking water, firewood and simple cooking utensils. There are no showers or lamps. Hikers must carry their own food, cooking pots, sleeping bag and light. Numbers are limited so it is always advisable to book in advance. The trail is closed mid-Oct to end Mar due to high temperatures.

Springbok *p774, map p775*

At present there are insufficient hotel rooms to cope with the peak seasonal demand. During spring, Aug-Oct, you should reserve well in advance. If you are unable to find a room, try to join a tour to the region; there are plenty advertised in Cape Town.

A Naries Namakwa Retreat, 27 km west of Springbok on the R355, which has been newly tarred, reservations T021-9304564, www.naries.co.za. An isolated and peaceful country retreat with good food and service, accommodation is in 5 en suite rooms in the main manor house, 3 Namakwa Mountain Suites in domed units designed to look like giant boulders, or a self-catering unit sleeping 4, decor is stylish in muted browns and creams, swimming pool.

B Annie's Cottage, 4 King St, T/T027-7121451, www.springbokinfo.com. Finely restored old farmhouse with immaculate polished floors and comfortable furnishings. 11 en suite double rooms, one in the attic and 2 with kitchenettes, neat and mature gardens with 40-year-old jacaranda trees, swimming pool, secure off-street parking. Annie can also organize stays on farms in the surrounding area. Recommended.

C Masonic Hotel, 3 Van Riebeeck St, T027-7121505, www.namaqualand flowers.co.za/masonic_hotel.html. 26 a/c en suite rooms, TV, restaurant, bar, homely rooms, plenty of character, retains much of the original 1940s decor, helpful and friendly management. Some of the rooms are next door in a renovated Victorian cottage.

C Old Mill Lodge, 69 Van Riebeeck St, T027-7181705, www.oldmilllodge.com. 11 a/c stylish en suite rooms with queen-size bed, duck-down duvets, electric blankets, TV, bar, lounge and braai area, a comfortable B&B option.

C Springbok Hotel, 87 van Riebeeck St, T027-7121161, www.namaqualandflowers. co.za/springbok_hotel.html. The main hotel in town, an old building but comfortable and clean, central setting, 28 rooms, most a/c, bar with pool table, à la carte restaurant, serves buffet dinners during flower season, popular with coach groups.

C-D Springbok Lodge, Voortrekker St, T027-7121321, www.springboklodge.com. 45 rooms of various formats, most of the houses in neighbouring streets are outbuildings belonging to the lodge, look out for the deep yellow paintwork, some are double rooms, others are self-catering flats. A bizarre local institution run by Jopie Kotze, who spends his day at reception watching all the goings-on of his mini empire. The reception area is also an information centre, newsagent and curio shop, with an interesting semi-precious stone display and some old photographs on historic Springbok. In the middle of all this is the restaurant (see Eating, page 783). This popular lodge has a prime central location and is good value when compared with the larger hotels.

F Springbok Caravan Park, 2 km from town centre, on the opposite side of the N7, on the left off the road to Goegap Nature Reserve, T027-7181584. Small with 1 chalet and 2 caravans, limited shade, few power points, coin-operated washing machine, kitchen, swimming pool, small shop.

Springbok to Namibia *p776*

C-D Okiep Country Hotel, 120 km south of the border with Namibia and 8 km north of Springbok on the N7, T27-7441000, www.okiep.co.za. Pleasant en suite rooms with DSTV, parking and good country cooking in the restaurant and bar. Cheaper en suite rooms are in another building across the road. A good overnight stop en route to Namibia.

D Bedrock Lodge, 2 Beach Rd, Port Nolloth, T027-8518865, www.bedrocklodge.co.za. An attractive collection of simple restored fisherman's cottages with tin roofs and corrugated-iron walls, yellowwood floors, cottage-style decor, MNet TV, fully equipped for self-catering for 2-6.

D Scotia Inn Hotel, Beach Rd, Port Nolloth, T027-8518353, scotiainn@telkomsa.net. Modern single and double en suite rooms in a neat brick block, cheaper rooms with shared

bathroom. Restaurant, bar, swimming pool surrounded by pleasant patio, secure parking.

F Fiddler's Creek, just before the border, by the police station, is a track to the left that follows the banks of the Gariep (Orange) River, 12 km from Viooolsdrift border, T027-7618953, www.bushwhacked.co.za. Beautiful shady camping on the river, hot/cold showers in reed huts, tents and sleeping bags can be hired, boma for buffet meals, great little rustic bar next to the river. Also the home of **Bush whacked**, a tour operator offering full-, half-day or overnight canoeing trips on the Gariep, a very relaxing way to explore the scenery. A very popular New Year's Eve party is held here each year, attracting revellers and bands from Cape Town, followed by a spot of canoeing on New Year's Day. Recommended. There are similar set-ups on the Namibian side of the river – see *Footprint Namibia*.

D-F McDougall's Bay Caravan Park, 4 km south of Port Nolloth, T027-8511110. A delightful clutch of self-catering cottages and chalets right on the beachfront, and some sheltered sites for camping and caravans, beautiful clean beach to walk along. This area is well known for lobster and crayfish, so enjoy a delicious seafood braai while staying here.

Ai-Ais/Richtersveld Transfrontier Conservation Park *p777*

Reservations through **SANParks**, T012-4289111, www.sanparks.org, or through the offices in Cape Town and Durban (see page 48). For late availability contact reception direct, T027-8311506.

D Tatasberg and Ganakouriep Wilderness Camps. The former is near the river and the latter is in the south of the park. Both have 4 2-bed self-catering units with hot showers, lighting, fridges, gas stoves and a there's a caretaker. Bring your own drinking water.

D-E Sendelingsdrift Restcamp. New rest camp at the park gate with 10 chalets, 4-bed and 6-bed units, each with a/c, fridge and stoves. Porches have views over the Gariep (Orange) River. 12 campsites with shared ablutions (cold showers). Swimming pool.

E Camping. There are 4 designated sites in the park: **Potjiespram**, **De Hoop**, **Richtersberg** (all close to the river) and **Kokerboomkloof** to the southeast of the park. Do not sleep on the bare ground, as there are many scorpions in the park, and heavy dew in the mornings. Kokerboomkloof only has toilets, each of the other sites has toilets and cold showers. You must bring everything you might need with you, including containers to carry drinking and cooking water. 4WDs and all the necessary camping equipment can be hired in Upington (see Activities and tours, page 769) but it is strongly advised that you have experience in driving 4WDs (see Ins and outs, page 742).

Springbok to Cape Town p779
D-F Kamieskroon Hotel, Kamieskroon, T027-6721614, www.kamieskroonhotel.com. Well run family hotel and handy for the Namaqua National Park which is just 17 km away. 25 rooms plus a caravan and camping park and 5 self-catering apartments, rates include breakfast and dinner, tasty country meals. Good source of information and has an excellent reputation for its photographic courses during the flower season.

🍴 Eating

Augrabies Falls National Park p772, map p773
🍴 Shibula, at the park entrance. Open 1200-1400, 1800-2200. A surprisingly smart dining room given the location, with a choice of pricey continental dishes. Last orders are at 2030. Next to the restaurant is the cosy **Gariep** ladies bar, while downstairs is a cafeteria for drinks and light meals during the day.

Springbok p774, map p775
The hotels all have restaurants and there are a few fast-food options along Voortrekker St and by the petrol stations.
🍴 BJ's Steakhouse, Hospital St, T027-7122701. Open 1800-late. Basement

restaurant with spaghetti western theme, generous portions, German dishes, boozy bar, pleasant change to hotel food. Recommended.
🍴 Carne Casa, Voortrekker St, just before the **Springbok Lodge**, T027-7181475. Mon-Sat. New steak-house with a vague Portuguese theme, pleasant outdoor seating, excellent steaks, chicken dishes, schnitzels and seafood.
🍴 Melboschkuil, Voortrekker St, T027-7181789. Mon-Fri 0800-1700, Sat 0800-1300. Attractive, brightly painted restaurant in an old town house with a pleasant outdoor deck, serves a range of snacks, pasta dishes, some vegetarian options, good wine list. Attached is a curio and information shop with internet café.
🍴 Springbok Lodge, Voortrekker St, T027-7121321. Part of the reception area and the curio shop is the hotel restaurant, interesting photos of the region on the walls, popular – most residents seem to eat here. Good selection and generous portions but bland food. Laid-back and slow service, settle for breakfast here and have a more hearty meal elsewhere in the evenings.
🍴 Titbits, Voortrekker St, T027-7181455. A friendly pizzeria with excellent stone-baked pizzas, also a range of other dishes such as pasta and steaks, breezy outdoor seating overlooking the main road.

🛍 Shopping

Springbok p774, map p775
Springbok has all of South Africa's main high street shops and supermarkets. Most are within walking distance of the car park below the small koppie in the centre of town. **CNA Books**, Van der Stel St, stock glossy coffee-table books showing the flowers at their best. If you are self-catering or heading towards Namibia, the large **Spar**, on the outskirts of town is probably the biggest and best supermarket in the Northern Cape and a good stop for provisions, charcoal and ice. The deli counter and bakery are especially good. Remember that there are no shops for

a long distance on the Namibian side of the border. All overland trucks do a big shop at the Springbok Spar before entering Namibia.

▲ Activities and tours

Augrabies Falls National Park p772, map p773
Canoeing and rafting
An excellent way of experiencing the gorge at Augrabies is by rafting its rapids. The most popular stretch is the **Augrabies Rush**, an 8-km section of grade II-III rapids pulling out 300 m above the falls. Longer 2- to 5-day trails involve rafting some excellent rapids as well as calmer stretches in 2-man inflatables. The park also organizes the **Gariep 3-in-1 Adventure**. This involves descending into the gorge, canoeing for 3 km and then hiking the 4 km out of the gorge. The final 11 km back to the rest camp is completed by mountain bike. The river is still relatively uncommercial, which means that you're unlikely to see anyone on the longer trails. For more details, contact the **Kalahari Adventure Centre**, T054-4510218, www.kalahari.co.za, prices start at around R400 for the 3-hr Augrabies Rush. The centre also offers a range of rafting and back-road tours to the **Kgalagadi Transfrontier Park**. Recommended. Check their website.

Ai-Ais/Richtersveld Transfrontier Conservation Park p777
Canoeing and rafting
Many Cape Town companies offer multi-day canoe trips on the Gariep (Orange) River through the Ai-Ais/Richtersveld Transfrontier Park in 2-man inflatable or fibreglass canoes. This is a wonderful experience. The trips pass amazing rock formations and each night is spent on the riverbank under the stars, with meals cooked over an open fire. Rapids are grades II-III. A guide boat carries all equipment but you will need a sleeping bag, sleeping mat, torch, cutlery, a plate and a cup. You will also need your passport as some nights are spent on the Namibian side.

Amanzi Trails, Cape Town, T021-5591573, www.amanzitrails.co.za. 4- to 5-day trips either catered or self-catering. You just need to bring food and drink for the self-catering option as they provide equipment such as cool boxes, kettles and braai grids.
Umkulu, Cape Town, T021-8537952, www.umkulu.co.za. 60-80 km, 4- to 6-day fully catered rafting and canoeing trips, with return transport from Cape Town included or meet them at their Vioolsdrift base camp, which has secure parking, lock-up storage, showers and a bar. The guides have years of experience on the river and come highly recommended.
Wildthing Adventures, Cape Town, T021-5561917, www.wildthing.co.za. 4- to 5-day trips, fully catered, except drinks.

⊖ Transport

Springbok p774, map p775
It's 1274 km to **Johannesburg**, 554 km to **Cape Town**, 374 km to **Upington**, 401 km to **Lamberts Bay**, 256 km to **Van Rhynsdorp**, 239 km to **Ai-Ais** (Namibia), 941 km to **Windhoek** (Namibia).

Air
There is a small airfield close to Goegap Nature Reserve but it is only used by charter airlines en route to Namibia.

Bus
Intercape, central reservations, T0861-287287, www.intercape.co.za. Buses depart daily from the **Springbok Lodge** to **Cape Town** (8½ hrs) and **Windhoek** (12 hrs).

⊙ Directory

Springbok p774, map p775
Banks Standard, Voortrekker St. ABSA, Van der Stel St. **Internet** Melkboschkuil, Voortrekker St, has speedy internet access, Mon-Fri 0800-1700, Sat 0800-1300.

Contents

Footprint features

Lesotho

At a glance

⊖ **Getting around** Poor local buses, car hire.

◉ **Time required** 3-7 days, longer if hiking.

☀ **Weather** Best in October and November and March-May.

✖ **When not to go** Roads deteriorate in wet summers and snowy winters.

★Don't miss ...
1 Thaba Bosiu, page 794.
2 Maletsunyane Falls, page 795.
3 The road to Katse Dam, page 804.
4 Morija Arts and Cultural Festival, page 808.
5 Pony trekking from Malealea Lodge, page 811.

Lesotho, the 'Kingdom in the Sky', is a tiny, proudly independent country completely surrounded by South Africa. Its nickname is apt – not one of its 30,000 sq km lies below 1000 m and many of its peaks reach as high as 3480 m. It is dominated by the Maluti Mountains, which cover three-quarters of the country, with the dramatic Drakensberg escarpment forming the eastern side and the border with KwaZulu Natal. This region of lofty landscapes has been declared the Maluti Drakensberg Transfrontier Park. To the west the land flattens out somewhat into what is known as the Lowlands. Here are most of the kingdom's towns, the small capital of Maseru, the richest agricultural land and it is where the majority of the population lives.

Lesotho's mountain scenery is markedly different from any of South Africa's landscapes: the mountains are more rugged, the lower slopes drier and the villages maintain a traditional subsistence lifestyle. Tourism is still in its infancy here, and heading even a little off the beaten track will allow a fascinating insight into time-honoured Lesotho customs. Herder boys roam the mountains and farmers travel on horseback, wrapped in traditional blankets. The country's lack of fences also provides excellent hiking conditions, while trekking with mountain ponies opens up some of the most remote areas of the country.

Maseru → *Colour map 4, B4.*

Maseru must be one of the world's sleepiest capital cities – though, in comparison with the rest of the country, life here seems almost frantic. The city centre straggles along the Clarendon River, with most of the shops, offices, hotels and restaurants strung along one long central street, called Kingsway. Even this main road is surprisingly quiet, however, with the languid pace of life broken only by beeping minibus taxis. Although largely modern and unremarkable with very few sights, it is a pleasant enough place for a wander and a good spot to soak up the vibrant feel of an African town. The Basotho people are outstandingly friendly, and it's not uncommon for people to approach you in the street simply to ask how you are and where you come from. During the day safety isn't an issue, but it's best to avoid wandering around after dark, particularly around the eastern end of Kingsway. Approaching from the rural farmland on the South African side, the city centre appears unexpectedly and even the newer tower blocks look pretty behind the numerous trees of the more affluent suburbs above

Maseru

Sleeping 🛏
Anglican Mission
  Training Centre **6**

Foothills Guest House **7**
Lancer's Inn **1**
Lesotho Sun **2**

Maseru Sun **3**
Mpilo Lodge **5**
Victoria **4**

the river. In the other direction, the city sprawls for miles of poorer, often unplanned, suburbs.
▶▶ *For listings, see pages 790-793.*

▶▶ *For listings, see pages 790-793.*

Ins and outs

Getting there

Moshoeshoe I International Airport ⓘ *T22350777*, is 21 km south of Maseru along the Main South Road. There are buses or taxis to most centres in Lesotho. Long-distance buses depart from the **bus station** about 500 m along the Main South Road from Cathedral Circle. The main bus and taxi station is on and around Market Street one block from Cathedral Circle where buses for the towns in the Lowveld depart, and from where taxis depart randomly to all centres in the country. ▶▶ *For further details, see Transport, page 792.*

Getting around

The city is easily navigated on foot but if you're in a car, there is parking outside the shopping centres, in a guarded carpark behind the Besotho Hat building, and in front of the tourist office. A fairly constant stream of minibus taxis moves up and down Kingsway from Cathedral Circle down to the border post. The two main roads out of Maseru both start at the Cathedral Circle; Main Road North (A1)and Main South Road (A2).

Tourist information

The **Tourist Information Centre** ⓘ *Basotho Shield building, central Kingsway (opposite the Basotho Hat building; both are hard to miss thanks to their huge thatched roofs), T22312427, www.ltdc.org.ls*, is extremely helpful and welcoming, with a wide range of leaflets on accommodation, national parks and tour operators. They also produce a useful official brochure, with information and addresses on sights and accommodation. The staff can assist with advice on road conditions and the best routes around the country. If you are crossing into the country through Maseru Bridge, drop in at the **Moloti Tourist Office** in Ladybrand which also covers Lesotho in its jurisdiction. (See Free State chapter, page 729, for details.)

Note Lesotho phone numbers are given as they should be dialled within Lesotho; South African numbers as they should be dialled within South Africa. Other numbers are shown with their international code. See also page 74.

Background

Maseru was founded in 1869 when Lesotho's second colonial leader, Commandant JH Bowker, sited his headquarters at this strategically important site overlooking a good fording point on the Clarendon. Shortly afterwards the first traders were also established on the site now occupied by the Lancer's Inn. In the early years the city grew only very slowly and up to independence in 1966 the city centre underwent few changes. The main street was only tarred when King George VI visited in 1947 (when it was also renamed Kingsway) and by the mid-1960s there were still no buildings over two storeys.

Since the 1960s the city has grown rapidly, both in terms of population and urban development. Along central Kingsway there are modern office and shopping buildings holding the same high street shops as you'll find in urban South Africa.

Sights

There are very few sights worth visiting. There is nothing of architectural significance, though a couple of buildings are interesting for historical reasons. In front of **Lancer's Inn**, on Central Kingsway, is **St John's Church**. Built in 1912 the small church's interior has a number of inscriptions to some of Maseru's more important past residents.

Behind the Lesotho **National Bank Tower** is a park, which houses a statue of **Moshoeshoe I**, the founder of the Basotho nation. It was unveiled in 1976 to mark 10 years of independence. To the north of Kingsway and along Constitution and Parliament roads there are many of the main government departments, mostly in colonial sandstone one-storey buildings.

The **parliament** building is at the far end of Parliament Road and is a fairly impressive modern structure in well-maintained grounds. This is due to move premises when the new parliament is built on the hill behind the Lesotho Sun, which is being funded by the Chinese.

◉ Maseru listings

Hotel and guesthouse prices
L over US$300 AL US$220-300 A US$150-220
B US$100-150 C US$75-100 D US$35-75
E US$15-35 F under US$15
Restaurant prices
🍴🍴🍴 over US$30 🍴🍴 US$15-30 🍴 under US$15
See pages 46-51 for further information.

● Sleeping

For a capital city, Maseru has very few hotels, or indeed eating and drinking venues.

A Lesotho Sun, off Nightingale Rd, behind Queen Elizabeth Hospital, T22313111, www.suninternational.com. The most luxurious hotel in Lesotho, on a hilltop setting overlooking town. Large, modern, with 192 a/c rooms with satellite TV, great city views, simple bathrooms and comfortable brown and faux-African decor. There are 2 popular bars, an attached casino, 2 good restaurants, gym, massage room, outdoor swimming pool with a pleasant terrace, and a shopping arcade with internet café. Transfers to and from the airport available.

A Maseru Sun, 12 Orpen Rd, T22312434, www.suninternational.com. The other luxury choice in town, also part of the Sun International Chain, smaller than the **Lesotho Sun**, but modern with 115 a/c rooms, all with South African TV and good standard decor. Restaurant, 2 bars, gym, sauna, swimming pool, tennis courts, internet facilities at the office next to the front gate. Small casino with slot machines attached.

C Hotel Victoria, central Kingsway, T22313687. Housed in a modern, plain multi-storey tower in the centre of town. Comfortable, contemporary rooms with a/c, TV. Popular, if slightly dreary, restaurant serving international dishes, bar. Good central location, popular with business travellers.

C Lancer's Inn, central Kingsway, T22312114. Historical hotel bang in the centre of town, with 21 rooms, some self-catering, and a few cosy en suite rondavels in the garden. 2 popular bars, gym, decent restaurant, bakery, bottle store, swimming pool, relaxed atmosphere. It was upgraded a few years ago, as it was totally looted during the 1998 riots.

C-D Mpilo Lodge, Maluti Rd, off Kingsway, T22317800, mpilo@ilesotho.com. Family-run guesthouse on the western outskirts of town, a low-key alternative. 15 spacious en suite rooms, with satellite TV and telephones, simple tiled floors and vaguely African theme. Restaurant and bar with views over the golf course and mountains.

D Foothills Guesthouse, 121 Maluti Rd, T58706566, melvin@xsinet.co.za. Small friendly guesthouse in a colonial sandstone building in leafy Maseru West where many government people live. B&B, old fashioned tired decor but spacious en suite rooms, DSTV in lounge, braai area and secure parking.

F Anglican Mission Training Centre, Assissi Rd, T22322046. One of the few places in town offering backpacker accommodation, with rather bare twin rooms with shared bathrooms. Usually used by church groups.

❶ Eating

Various international chains are springing up around town, including a **Steers**, opposite the post office, a **KFC**, just north of Cathedral Circle, and a **Nando's**, not far from the border. There are street vendors all along Kingsway

and around the taxi station during the day selling the staple Basotho meal of stiff maize porridge (pap) and stew, or roasted maize.

₸₸₸ Lehaha Grill, Lesotho Sun Hotel, Nightingale Rd, T22313111. Daily 1830-2330. The main à la carte restaurant in the basement of the hotel, popular with Maseru's richer residents. Rather grand, if slightly faded decor, but very friendly service and decent meals, including Lesotho trout and traditional stewed oxtail, and a good choice of South African wine. Reservations necessary at weekends and public holidays. Recommended.

₸₸ China Dragon, also at the **Lesotho Sun Hotel**, see above, daily 1830-2230. Authentic Chinese restaurant with Oriental chefs, red and white decor, long menu with a good choice for vegetarians, the buffet on Wed night is good value.

₸₸ The Regal, next door to the Basotho Hat craft shop, T22313930. Vaguely oriental decor in this international restaurant, serving good-value lunches (chicken with chips or pap, plus toasted sandwiches) and (British-style) Indian curries and grills in the evenings. Very friendly service, and excellent coffee served all day.

₸₸ Rendezvous, Lancer's Inn, Kingsway, T22312114. Popular restaurant, with chandeliers and a vaguely African theme, serving standard international cuisine including some African and French dishes. Some outside seating in the beer garden. King Letsie III regularly dines here.

₸ China Garden, LNDC shopping centre, closed Sun, T22313915. Reasonable Chinese food, catering in part for the city's burgeoning Chinese populations. Central location, service is notoriously slow but the food isn't bad, cheaper takeaways available. Popular early evening bar attached.

❶ Bars and clubs

The few bars are attached to big hotels or to restaurants. The small public bar at **Lancer's Inn** is often referred to as the alternative

Parliament; it is frequented by a regular clientele of (male) civil servants, teachers and lecturers from the National University. The lounge bar has a more relaxed atmosphere, especially for women, and there are a couple of pool tables; ignore the sign that says the bar is for hotel residents only – everybody else does. The terrace of the first-floor bar at the **Hotel Victoria** is ideal for watching the world go by on Kingsway. The casino at the **Lesotho Sun Hotel** is popular with guests, and the basement bar is a busy meeting spot for well-heeled locals.

Good Times Café, LNDC Shopping Centre, T22317705. Mon-Sat. The only non-hotel bar that also serves food (†). Surprisingly modern decor for Maseru with chrome and suede sofas and a big screen TV for sports. Busy at weekends, but weeknights are very quiet, more popular for lunch.

O Shopping

Central Maseru has various outlets of South African chain stores and supermarkets, including **Shoprite**, in the LNDC Shopping Centre on Kingsway, and another branch near the Cathedral Circle, which are useful stops if you are self-catering. The main hotels all have craft or curio shops but these tend to be overpriced. The best craft shop is the **Basotho Hat**, opposite the tourist office, T22322523, Mon-Sat 0800-1700, although even here the selection of local crafts is basic. The best buys include mohair blankets, woven baskets, and the traditional wicker Basotho hats. In the industrial area to the north of town on Raboshabane Rd is the **Maseru Tapestries and Mats** workshop, T22311773, which is operated by a group of women weavers who produce colourful mohair tapestries of animal and village scenes as well as geometric patterns. Mohair, woollen, sheepskin and leather products can be bought from a handful of other workshops around Maseru – look out for signs by the road as you drive out of town.

One of these is **Seithati Weavers**, 7 km out of town on Main South Rd, T22313975, www.villageweavers.co.ls. This cooperative of 14 women makes a range of mohair, rugs, tapestries, bags and shawls; you can watch them at work in the workshop or browse in the shop. One of their tapestries decorates the lobby of the **Lesotho Sun Hotel**.

▲ Activities and tours

The **Tourist Information Centre** recommend local guides to take you to areas of scenic, historic or artistic interest around Maseru, although most of these areas are easily explored alone. The **Sun** hotels also organize tours. **Harvey World Travel**, next to the Hotel Victoria on Kingsway, T22323706, www.harveyworld.oc.za, is a branch of a quality South African travel agency, and useful for booking inter national flights and South African mainline buses.

⊖ Transport

Air
There is an airport departure tax of M20 for all international flights. **South African Airways** (SAA), central reservations T011-9781111, www.flysaa.com, operates the route between Moshoeshoe I International Airport and Johannesburg's OR Tambo International Airport. There are 5 flights per day Mon-Fri, 4 on Sat and 3 on Sun. Flying time is 1 hr 15 mins. Expect to pay around R800-900 one way.

Bus
Long-distance buses, run by **Lesotho Freight and Bus Services**, T22313535, running to **Thaba Tseka** (7 hrs), **Semonkong** (6 hrs), Linakaneng (9 hrs), and **Qacha's Nek** (11 hrs) depart from the main bus terminal about 500 m along the Main South Rd from Cathedral Circle. Buses to **Mokhotlong** (8 hrs) depart from next to the Feida Supermarket (also known as Chen Si). The longer journeys depart at 0630.

Car hire

Avis, Lesotho Sun Hotel, T22320087, and at Moshoeshoe I International Airport, T22350328, www.avis.co.za. **Budget**, Maseru Sun Hotel, T22316344, www.budget.co.za, can arrange pickup and drop-off at the airport. **Imperial Car Rental**, T22350292, www.imperial carrental.co.za, rents 4WDs for reasonable rates, with pickups and drop-offs at the airport.

Taxis

There have been reports of muggings in the area around the Cathedral Circle and bus and taxi terminals. Avoid the area after dark.

Local Minibus taxis depart from the maze of streets around Market St just north of the Cathedral Circle. There is a regular stream of minibus taxis up and down Kingsway from Cathedral Circle down to the Border Post. Minibus taxis will take you off their set route for a negotiable price as long as they do not have other passengers. For conventional taxis try **Moonlight Telephone Taxis**, T22312605, or **Luxury Telephone Taxis**, T22326211.

Long distance Most taxis going south depart from the **New Taxi Rank** on Moshoeshoe Rd behind the Shoprite Supermarket, about 300 m north of Cathedral Circle, while those heading east and north go from the **Old Taxi Rank**, 200 m to the east of here. Taxis heading towards **Bloemfontein** and **Ficksburg** in South Africa leave from the South African side of Maseru Bridge border post.

✆ Directory

Banks

The **Lesotho Bank**, **Nedbank** and **Standard Bank** are all on central Kingsway, Mon-Fri 0830-1530, Sat 0830-1200. The best and quickest place for foreign exchange is the Standard Bank, in the Lesotho Bank Tower, which also has an ATM.

Embassies and consulates

South Africa (High Commission), 10th floor, Lesotho Bank Centre, Kingsway, T22315758. **USA**, 254 Kingsway, T22312666, http://maseru. usembassy.gov. Most other countries deal with Lesotho from their embassies in South Africa.

Emergencies

Police Constitution Rd, between Lerotholi and Palace roads, T22317262.

Internet

Data Kare, in the LNDC Shopping Centre, Kingsway, daily 0800-2100; **Leo Internet Services**, by the Basotho Hat, Mon-Fri 0800-1700. There is also an internet café in the Lesotho Sun. Expect to pay around R25 per hr.

Medical services

Maseru Private Hospital, Thetsane Rd, T22313260. **Queen Elizabeth Hospital**, Kingsway, T22312501. Reasonably well equipped and staffed, but patients with serious illness or injuries will be transported to a South African hospital.

Cathedral Pharmacy, Main North Rd, near Cathedral Circle, T22324351. **MHS Pharmacy**, in the LNDC Shopping Centre, Kingsway, T22325189. There are no after-hours pharmacies in Lesotho; in an emergency you will have to go to a hospital.

Post office

New Post Office Building, Kingsway opposite Steers, Mon-Fri 0800-1630, Sat 0800-1200.

Telephone

You can send and receive faxes at the main post office. Local and international telephone calls can be made from the phone boxes outside or from the public phone shop in the LNDC Shopping Centre. The main hotels will make international connections but these are expensive. Mobile phones work well in Maseru, but don't expect to get much coverage away from the capital although services are improving all the time. Local Sim and top up cards are available to buy everywhere.

Maseru to Semonkong

There are three main routes out of Maseru: the well-maintained Main North Road that runs along Lesotho's narrow lowland strip; the Main South Road through the farming towns of the wider lowland strip; and the road from Maseru branching off to Semonkong in the central mountains or Thaba Tseka in the east (see page 804). Beyond Roma, the road climbs into the eastern side of the Thabo Pusoa Mountains, part of the Lesotho Highlands, and ends at Semonkong. This dramatic drive passes through beautiful mountain scenery and a string of traditional Lesotho villages, with very different lifestyles from those of Maseru's city streets. ▶▶ *For listings, see pages 796-797.*

Thaba Bosiu → *Colour map 4, B4.*

Thaba Bosiu, 20 km outside Maseru, was the mountain stronghold of the founder of the Basotho nation, Chief Moshoeshoe. It is an isolated and steep-sided mountain with a large flat plateau at the top. From this secure defensive position Moshoeshoe was able to launch raids against his neighbours before retreating to safety. He, and many other important Basotho (including King Moshoeshoe II who died in 1996 in a car accident), are buried at the mountain's summit. There are remnants of Moshoeshoe's village and his restored two-roomed house. Also here on a protruding rock is a chiselled out footprint left by Maleleka, one of Moshoeshoe's sons. The story goes that he was forbidden to marry the girl he loved because she was below his rank, so lamenting the loss of his loved one, he carved the footprint as an epitaph before throwing himself off the mountain to his death. Thaba Bosiu means 'mountain at night' and legend has it that what is a hill during the day becomes a mountain at night. Today regarded as a national monument, it has earned recognition as a UNESCO World Heritage Site for its importance to the Lesotho people.

There are a number of pathways up the mountain but visitors usually use the steep Rafutho's Pass. The defensive wall built by Moshoeshoe's men when they first arrived at the mountain can still be seen. The views are lovely, and nearby is **Qiloane**, a strangely nipple-shaped mountain, the shape of which is supposed to have inspired the Basotho Hat.

Tour guides can be found at the car park and small visitor centre between 0800-1700, T58883504, at the base of the mountain; most are fairly knowledgeable and will give visitors a fascinating (if not always completely accurate) account of the role of the Thaba Bosiu stronghold and much of Lesotho's early history. The tours usually take about two hours in total and the price will depend on your skills of negotiation. There is talk of a cultural village being developed at the site.

Roma → *Colour map 4, B5.*

Roma is 31 km east of Maseru along the road to Semonkong. It is the principal centre of the Roman Catholic Church in Lesotho, hence the Italian sounding name, and was founded in 1862 when Mosheshwe granted the land to Father Joseph Gerard, a French pioneer missionary. It is the site of the National University of Lesotho and a large number of churches, presbyteries and schools. The town itself is little more than a few houses scattered around these institutions in a pretty, wooded valley at the foothills of the Maluti. The University was founded in 1945 by the Catholic Church. It became part of the combined university of Botswana, Lesotho and Swaziland in the 1960s until that institution collapsed and it was brought under the sole control of the Lesotho Ministry of

Sesotho greetings

Greetings are very important in Sesotho culture. It is considered very rude if you do not formally greet people before addressing them and, except on busy town streets, people will expect you to greet them if you are passing them on a street or path. A simple 'hello' – 'lumela' – will suffice.

Remember not to take photographs of any Royal building or the airport, and naturally always ask first if you want to photograph people.

Education. The entrance to the University is on the left as you enter the town from Maseru. Few of the University buildings are of any historical interest but the campus is green and well maintained and visitors are welcome to wander around.

> *Pope John Paul II visited Roma in 1988 to posthumously beatify Father Joseph Gerard, who died in Roma in 1914.*

Semonkong and around ⊕❶❷▲⊖ ›› pp796-797. Colour map 4, B5.

From Roma to Semonkong (85 km) the road climbs into the central mountains and the scenery becomes more dramatic, passing through tiny villages and past Lesotho horsemen in their gum boots and blankets. The tar road turns to gravel at **Moitsupeli**, 19 km beyond Roma, after which it continues to climb through **Ramabanta** (access point for the excellent **Trading Post Adventures** lodge) and into the Thabo Putsoa Mountains, peaking at 2000 m. Under normal conditions, the journey from Maseru to Semonkong (120 km) is about four hours – a 4WD is vital in winter or if it's wet. Alternatively there are two daily buses that takes about six hours and leave Maseru at 1000 and 1400. **Semonkong** is at the end of the road and is a small town that historically had a reputation for being a secret hideout of outlaws.

Maletsunyane Falls

Semonkong is of interest mainly because of the nearby **Maletsunyane Falls** which are the highest single drop falls in southern Africa. They are also referred to as the **Semonkong Falls**, Semonkong means 'place of smoke', or the **Lebinhan Falls** after Father Francois Le Binhan, the first European to see them in 1881. They can be visited on a hike or pony trek from **Semonkong Lodge** or on a pony trek from **Malealea Lodge**. Though the volume of water is usually small, the falls are very impressive and drop 192 m (twice the drop of the Victoria Falls, though a fraction of the width) into a huge gorge that winds through the mountains for many kilometres. Part of the attraction is that there are absolutely no tourist facilities around the falls. They are about 4 km south of Semonkong; it is possible to drive part of the way but the walk from Semonkong is easy. They are best seen during the late rainy season when they are full. At the end of very dry periods they are often reduced to little more than a trickle and occasionally in winter they freeze, forming spectacular ice pinnacles.

Ketane Falls

Very few people have seen the pristine Ketane Falls which drop 122 m as they are in one of the highest and most remote regions of Lesotho, midway between Semonkong and Malealea (see page 808). From Semonkong it's possible to reach them in a day's hike or to drive (by 4WD only) to the tiny village of Ha Bati, 5 km from the falls, and hike the rest of the way. From both Semonkong and Malealea lodges the option is to get to the falls by horseback, overnight from Semonkong and four days from Malealea. This is stunning mountain scenery and you are unlikely to see other people, except for the occasional herd boy.

◉ Maseru to Semongkong listings

Hotel and guesthouse prices
L over US$300 AL US$220-300 A US$150-220
B US$100-150 C US$75-100 D US$35-75
E US$15-35 F under US$15
Restaurant prices
♔♔♔ over US$30 ♔♔ US$15-30 ♔ under US$15
See pages 46-51 for further information.

◉ Sleeping

Thaba Bosiu p794

D Mmelesi Lodge, near the bottom of the main path, T52500007. Has a restaurant serving basic dishes and a rather plush bar, with a few comfortable en suite rondavels set in pretty gardens out the back. Heaters are provided in winter. Avoid if there is a government conference on, but at other times you are likely to have the place to yourself.

Roma p794

C-E Trading Post Guest House, signposted off the main street, T22340202, www.tradingpost.co.za. Offers a mix of luxury rondavels and more basic back-packer accommodation in an original sandstone trading post building built in 1903, plus camping in the well-tended gardens. Breakfast is available and other meals by prior arrangement, self-catering facilities, small swimming pool. Also owns the excellent Trading Post in Ramabanta (see below). Ashley and Jennifer Thorn are experts on the area and can organize short pony treks to the surrounding hills above Roma. Recommended.
F Roma Roman Catholic Mission, T22340224, also known as Christ the King. Has dorms, doubles and singles in basic austere accommodation. The mission is behind the large Catholic Church on

the right about 1 km further on from the University entrance.

Semonkong and around p795

C-F Trading Post Adventures, signposted from the centre of the village of Ramabanta, T22340202, www.tradingpost.co.za. Stunning location in a trading post dating from 1939, with wide-reaching mountain views. Luxurious and stylishly decorated rondavels, looking straight onto the mountains, or more basic en suite rooms in the old stables. Delicious meals served in the candle lit dining room. Huge range of activities on offer, from short walks, to pony treks, 4WD routes, dirt-bike tracks and overnight stays in a nearby village. Run by the affable and hugely knowledgeable Rosemary. Highly recommended.
D-F Semonkong Lodge, T27006037, T62021021 (mob), www.placeofsmoke.co.ls. This popular lodge offers a handful of thatched en suite huts, with African decor and log fires, plus simpler rooms in the house, a dorm and camping space. Excellent meals served in the restaurant, bar, well-equipped communal kitchen, braai fire pits and gas braai, plenty of hot water (unless pipes freeze in which case boiling water is provided from the kitchen), pool table. There is broad range of outdoor activities on offer.

◉ Eating

Roma p794

♔ Speak Easy, opposite University entrance. Restaurant and bar with a limited but fairly cheap menu. The bar has a wide variety of alcoholic drinks, is popular in the evening and a good place to meet students or staff of the university.

University dining room. It is also possible to eat lunch at the university, which serves one, usually tasty, dish a day.

Semonkong and around *p795*
There is a restaurant in **Semonkong Lodge**, and a couple of bars near the main bus stop that serve up alcohol and basic meals.

▲ Activities and tours

Semonkong and around *p795*
Semonkong Lodge, T27006037, T62021021 (mob), www.placeofsmoke.co.ls. Offers pony trekking packages from 1-5 days. Overnight rides are quite strenuous and involve 6-7 hrs riding each day but they can be attempted by novices. Accommodation is in Basotho huts with cooking equipment. Pack horses are also available for hire to hikers. A recent initiative is the world's highest commercial abseil, a 204-m drop down Maletsunyane Falls. This takes place over 2 days with training on 25 m cliffs the first day, followed by the spectacular drop at the falls the following morning.
Trading Post Adventures, T2234020, www.tradingpost.co.za. Offers a wide range of activities from short self-guided walks, crossing the valley and passing through villages, to longer pony treks with a local Basotho guide. 4WD trails are opening up in the wilder reaches of the mountains. Overnight stays in villages can be arranged, as well as singing performances from local children. Recommended.

⊖ Transport

Thaba Bosiu *p794*
Taxi
There are frequent minibus taxis to and from Thaba Bosiu directly from **Maseru** along a

good tarred road. If you are arriving from **Roma** or the Semonkong road, taxis and the twice-daily bus from **Semonkong** will drop you off at the junction with the Thaba Bosiu Rd, from where it is fairly easy to pick up a connecting taxi. The main hotels in Maseru organize frequent half-day trips to the mountain, though it is just as easy and cheaper to go under your own steam.

Roma *p794*
Bus
The buses between **Maseru** and **Semonkong** passes through Roma in the afternoon.

Taxi
Taxis to and from **Maseru** leave throughout the day, but stop at sunset. This is the last place to buy fuel if you are driving to **Semonkong**, a further 83 km away.

Semonkong and around *p795*
Bus
The gravel road to Semonkong is fairly good except for the last 10 km or so. There are 2 daily buses to and from **Maseru** leaving at 1000 and 1400, and the journey takes about 6 hrs. If you just miss the bus in Maseru, it is worth catching a taxi to Roma, which will inevitably overtake the slow-moving buses. If you miss the daily bus at the Semonkong end, ask about lifts at the bar next to the bus stop.

❶ Directory

Roma *p794*
Banks **Lesotho Bank**, opposite the main University entrance. Will make foreign transactions, open Mon-Fri 0900-1300.

North from Maseru

The main route north out of Maseru is along the well-maintained Main North Road that runs along Lesotho's narrow lowland strip. The countryside on either side of the route is fairly heavily populated, dotted with affluent villages and banded by terraced fields, with good views across to the mountains. Commonly referred to as the 'Roof of Africa', these northern mountains are the highest and harshest in southern Africa. The high mountain peaks have a stark beauty, desolate and empty bar the odd herd boy during summer, and cloaked in snow every winter. There is one main road that runs across the area, from Butha-Buthe to Sani Pass, known for being the highest road in all of Africa. Upgraded to tar, the 200 km stretch between Butha-Buthe and Mokhotlong has opened up the entire region to visitors, but remember, in winter this road may well be blocked by snow. ▶▶ *For listings, see pages 801-803.*

Teyateyaneng → *Colour map 4, B5.*

The ramshackle town of Teyateyaneng, 'TY' as it is referred to, was founded as an administrative centre by the British colonial authorities in 1886. Teyateyaneng, meaning 'the place of quick sands', takes its name from the quicksand in the river that runs past the town occasionally sucking in hapless cattle. TY is well known as a handicraft centre and this is the primary reason most people visit the town. Traditional Sesotho goods tend to be cheaper here than in Maseru and there are well-established centres that are run to ensure that profits return to the artists and not middlemen (see details under Shopping). Having said that, don't expect slick shops or smart complexes; here, goods are sold in run-down cement blocks by the roadside.

Ha Maketa

A half-hour's drive or minibus ride southeast from Teyateyaneng on a good tarred road brings you to the village of Ha Maketa. The reason to come here and a worthy distraction off the Main North Road is the **Kome Caves**, a collection of cave dwellings under an overhang of rock where people have lived since the 19th century. The seven residences, rounded mud-built domes with semi-circular doorways, have been recently restored and declared a National Monument. Were they covered in grass, they would not be too dissimilar to the Hobbit houses of Hobberton. There's a small visitor centre and you can park in the village and enlist local children to take you along the path for the half hour walk.

Leribe (Hlotse) → *Colour map 4, B5.*

Back on the Main North Road, Hlotse is the administrative centre of Leribe district (and is often also known simply as Leribe). Founded in 1876, it was an important town in the 1880 Gun War. Still to be seen today are the remains of a British fort and a primitive statue of a kneeling British soldier. The Anglican Church dates from 1877 and is the oldest building in town. About 8 km north on the old Butha-Buthe road, in the Subeng stream about 400 m downstream from the bridge, are three- and five-toed dinosaur tracks estimated to be 108-200 million years old. Ask for directions in the village.

Butha-Buthe is the northernmost town in the lowlands, and not too far from the Caledonspoort border post, which is open daily 0800-1600. From here you can either continue north into South Africa or turn east onto the mountain road. Butha-Buthe gets its name from the mountain that dominates the town; the name means 'place of lying down' or 'place of security' and it is here that Moshoeshoe had his first mountain stronghold. Towering above the town, this is the main attraction. The walk to the top is fairly strenuous but is worth it for the fine views across the town and surrounding countryside. The town itself is a busy centre with a number of supermarkets where people from the highlands come every few weeks to stock up on provisions. A large suburb known as Likileng has been constructed to provide accommodation for the workforce engaged on the tunnelling and hydropower components of the Lesotho Highlands Water Project.

From Butha-Buthe the mountain road begins in earnest and this is the original 'Roof of Africa' motor rally route that takes place annually at the beginning of summer. About 25 km from Butha-Buthe is the small **Muela Dam**, and a short tar road leads up to a lookout point on the right of the Main North Road. This is another component of the Lesotho Highlands Water Project, and although you can't see it, the newly opened underground Muela Hydroelectric Power Station here now provides the majority of Lesotho with power. Water is transferred to Muela from Katse Dam by way of a 45 km long tunnel which has a diameter of 4 km. It then flows though Muela's power station before emptying into a second tunnel 37 km through the mountains to the Ash River near Clarens in South Africa's Free State. The Ash is a tributary of the Vaal River that leads to Vaal Dam in Gauteng, which provides all the thirsty province's water. There's a visitor centre at Muela and there are plans to turn some of the construction buildings into a lodge. For more information contact the Lesotho Highlands Water Project office in Butha-Buthe, T22913206, www.lhwp.org.ls.

Another 5 km beyond Muela is the **Liphofung Cave Cultural and Historical Site** ⓘ *T22913206, www.lhwp.org.ls, daily 0830-1630, R15*. This cultural centre is another Lesotho Highlands Water Project initiative and includes three traditional Basotho huts, a small museum, and a pathway and boardwalk leading to some San rock paintings dotted under and around a large overhang of rock. More significant for the Basotho is it was once a hideout of the young Moshoeshoe I. Local guides accompany visitors and explain the significance of the art. The curio **shop** sells high standard local handicrafts and you can camp here or stay overnight in a couple of basic rondavels.

Moteng Pass

Travelling northeast, spending much of the journey over 2500 m, this tightly twisting road climbs up gradients of over 35% to the scenic **Moteng Pass** (2840 m) 68 km before Oxbow. The summit offers excellent views of the authentic Basotho homesteads in the valley below.

Oxbow → Colour map 4, A5.

Oxbow has the last petrol stop until Mokhotlong and is also the centre of the Lesotho ski industry – as you'd expect, the industry isn't exactly booming, but there's a fairly new 1 km ski slope and a beginners area 11 km beyond Oxbow in a valley below the Mahlasela Pass (3220 m), which has a T-bar ski lift and smaller rope lift, and a snow-making machine. Operations are run by **Afri-Ski**, T086-1754754 (South Africa), www.afriski.net, and the ski season is generally from the beginning of June to the end of August, though the lodge is open all year round and offers other activities such as hiking. This is a new Austrian run outfit who have built some comfortable self-catering chalets at the site as well as a shop for renting out equipment and they can arrange tuition.

Tlaeeng Pass
The road between Oxbow and Mokhotlong (114 km; approximately three hours) snakes and twists higher until almost at the halfway point it reaches the **Tlaeeng Pass**. The summit of the highest road in Africa is 3275 m above sea level. As you can imagine, the views here are truly outstanding, and the drive offers undulating mountain scenery and clean crisp air. About 40 km after the pass the road starts to climb down towards Mokhotlong.

Mokhotlong → Colour map 4, B6. Population: 75,000.
Mokhotlong Town or Camp is one of Lesotho's remotest towns and is the administrative and economic centre of the northern mountain area. The town's name means 'the place of the bald ibis', and these birds can still be seen along the river and in the surrounding valleys. The town was established as a police post in 1905 and grew as a trading centre supplied by pack ponies coming over the Drakensberg from KwaZulu Natal. Until 1947 when radio contact was established with Maseru, it had no connections with the rest of the country and until the 1950s it had no road connection with the outside world. Despite the arrival of the tarred road, in winter, Mokhotlong can still be cut off for many weeks by snow.

There is little of great interest in the town itself, but it retains something of an isolated outpost atmosphere. Sheep and goats are still shorn by hand in the surrounding sheds. An interesting sight is the Basotho in their striking blankets, hitching their horses outside and entering the modern computerized bank to do their banking. This is also the logical place from which to start exploring the remote valleys and high mountains of this area. The main supply stores are either near the bank or next to the airfield. There is a petrol station opposite the bank.

Sani Pass → Colour map 4, B6.
About 5 km south of Mokhotlong is the turn off to Sani Pass (60 km), which is a rough gravel road that should only be attempted by 4WD and can be blocked by snow in winter. It is a torturously steep, cork-screwing road and is the only pass from the northern mountains into South Africa. The views across the mountains of KwaZulu Natal are awe inspiring. The Sani Pass was originally a bridle track for pack horses and was opened to vehicular transport in the 1950s, there are currently plans to tar it on the South African side. About 12 km from Sani Pass is the highest mountain in southern Africa, Thabana-Ntlenyana (3482 m). The name means 'pretty little mountain', hardly a fitting name for what is the 2nd tallest mountain in Africa after Kilimanjaro. There are some beautiful walks in this rugged area; for details of hikes see page 512 and for details of approaching the Sani Pass from the South African side see page 511.

Hotel and guesthouse prices
L over US$300 AL US$220-300 A US$150-220
B US$100-150 C US$75-100 D US$35-75
E US$15-35 F under US$15
Restaurant prices
††† over US$30 †† US$15 30 † under US$15
See pages 46-51 for further information.

◉ Sleeping

Teyateyaneng p798

D Blue Mountain Inn, signposted from Main North Rd, T22500362. The only hotel in town is in an ugly red-brick block just outside the centre, with a simple bar and restaurant (serving pizza) and 43 fairly basic but comfortable rooms with TV. Pleasant gardens and friendly staff, secure parking.

D Palace Hotel, 15 km south of TY and 25 km north of Maseru on Main North Rd, T58861905. A modern motel popular as a conference location for businesses from Maseru, but in a pleasant rural setting. Rooms have big beds, decent bathrooms, TV, phone and communal balconies (ensure doors are locked at all times). The restaurant and bar serves the usual meat and chicken with chips, rice or pap, and there's a nightclub next door that gets very noisy at the weekends.

Leribe (Hlotse) p798

D Leribe, town centre, T22400559. Dilapidated exterior but pleasant enough inside. 33 en suite rooms with TV, in either a motel-style terrace or rondavels in the pretty garden, 2 bars, both busy at the weekends. Restaurant serves standard grills, steak and trout.

F Anglican Mission, will sometimes allow visitors to camp in their grounds, no charge but leave a donation.

Butha-Buthe p799

D Crocodile Inn, in the southern suburbs of town, signposted from main road, T22460223. Local hangout (more for its heaving 2 bars than its rooms), with 29 run-down but clean rooms with en suite bathrooms and TV. Restaurant serves standard Basotho food. Pool table, secure parking, camping allowed.

F Butha-Buthe Youth Hostel, about 3.5 km outside town past St Paul's Roman Catholic Mission, turn off Main North Rd at the village of **Ha Sechele**, then ask directions, T22461832. Also known as **Mr Ramakatane's Home Hostel**, the owner has turned part of his house into a hostel that provides accommodation for the nearby World Vision Vocational School. The female dorm sleeps 6, the male dorm sleeps 10, campsite, basic facilities, communal kitchen, borehole water, gas cookers, lights, and heaters are used. Friendly set up but is only accessible by 4WD or on foot and you need to bring your own food. Staying here gives one a good insight into village life in the Lowlands.

Oxbow p799

B New Oxbow Lodge, T051-9332247 (South Africa), www.oxbow.co.za. 32 cosy en suite chalets, either in doubles or family rooms, set in a mix of Alpine and thatched Lesotho buildings. Licensed restaurant, great bar overlooking the river, log fires in the lounge. Camping allowed in grounds, natural rock pool for swimming, skiing equipment, pony trekking, 4WD routes, guides and trout fishing arranged, popular especially when there is snow which attracts curious South Africans, so make reservations in advance. Rates include breakfast and dinner.

B-D Afri-Ski, 11 km from Oxbow before the Mahlasela Pass, T086-1754754 (South Africa), www.afriski.net. A range of brand new Alpine-style, double storey wooden self-catering chalets sleeping 2, 4 or 8, plus a bunk room for backpackers. Contemporary decor, fireplaces, all set on the hillside near the ski slope, communal lounge with pool table, small shared kitchen. Skis and snowboards can be hired from the shop.

Mokhotlong p800

C Senqu Hotel, on left-hand side of road as you enter town from the west, T22920330. Standard small-town hotel with 10 poky but clean en suite rooms, better are the 8 new rooms in brick blocks with tin roofs, which have heating and DSTV. Restaurant with the usual standard meat and chicken, bar and public lounge. Nothing special, but probably the best bet in town.

D-F Molumong Guest House, 15 km from Mokhotlong on the Thaba Tseka Rd, T083-2543323 (South Africa mob), molumong@mweb.co.za. An old colonial trading post homestead, high on the mountainside affording great views. Dorms, doubles with bedding, camping and fully equipped kitchen, no electricity. Gas and candles are used, basic supplies are available, and a bottle store is close by. It's best to bring own food and drinks. There is no signpost to the lodge from the road, but 'Molumong' is painted on the roof. Confusingly, it is not in Molumong village, but in upper Rafalotsane village. Pony trekking can be arranged.

Sani Pass p800

There are several options on the South African side at the bottom of the pass, including the **Sani Pass Hotel** and **Sani Lodge**, see page 518.

C-E Sani Top Chalet, top of the pass, next to the Lesotho border post, T033-7021158 or T082-7151131 (mob), www.sanitop chalet.co.za. A combination of double rooms in the main building or in stone en suite rondavels out back, plus backpacker rooms with dorms and shared bathrooms in a converted store in the nearby village – bring warm bedding for these. You can camp but you'll need thermals. The hotel has a licensed pub (the highest in Africa) and dining room warmed by roaring wood fires, overlooking the dramatic road below. Fantastic hiking and pony trekking to some awesome viewpoints along the escarpment. When it does snow it is possible to hire skis from the hotel.

❶ Eating

Teyateyaneng p798
The **Blue Mountain Inn** has a decent standard restaurant and bar, and there are numerous (very) basic cafés and bars around the main road junction of the Main North Rd.

Leribe (Hlotse) p798
There is little to be found in town other than a handful of basic cafés scattered around town serving pap and stew.

Butha-Buthe p799
There are a number of small, cheap eateries on the main road near the bus stop or you can get a basic meal at the **Crocodile Inn**.

Mokhotlong p800
The **Senqu Hotel** has a reasonable restaurant with a fairly varied menu. There are a large number of small eating and drinking houses and street vendors along the main street, selling mutton stew and pap or the delicious local brown bread with a hot sauce. The **Sunshine Bar**, is the busiest in town thanks to its satellite television, which draws in highland horsemen in droves.

❍ Shopping

Teyateyaneng p798
Helang Basali Handicrafts, Main North Rd to the south of town centre, T22501546, is run by a local mission and sells reasonably priced rugs, blankets, tapestries and other handicrafts from a run-down shop next to the road. **Setsoto Design**, opposite **Blue Mountain Inn**, T58086312. Lesotho's oldest and finest weaving company where visitors can watch women weaving. A great selection of wall hangings and carpets, all hand-woven with homespun mohair, are for sale in the show room. Be wary of paying with credit cards, however, as we've had reports of card fraud here. **Hatooa Mose Moasali showroom**, on the right coming into town, T58086312, meaning

a woman must stand up and work hard', a women's weaving cooperative that produces wall hangings.

Leribe (Hlotse) p798

Leribe Craft Centre, T22400323, northern outskirts of town, sells mohair blankets, ponchos, scarves, baskets, hats and beadwork.

⊕ Transport

There's a daily bus run by the **Lesotho Freight and Bus Services** from **Maseru** to **Mokhotlong** that departs Maseru at 0630 and takes about 8 hrs and stops in all the towns on the Main North Rd as well as **Oxbow**.

Teyateyaneng p798

There are frequent taxis, leaving from near the main junction along the Main North Rd. If you are going to **Leribe** (**Hlotse**) it is usually necessary to change taxis at the junction for **Maputsoe** where most turn off the Main North Rd for the Ficksburg border crossing. There are plenty of petrol stations in the town centre.

Leribe (Hlotse) p798
Taxi

Taxis to **Butha-Buthe** leave throughout the day from the south end of the main street. Taxis towards **Teyateyaneng** and **Maseru** leave from the same area, though passengers usually have to change at **Maputsoe** (where the approach road to the Ficksburg border crossing turns off from the Main North Rd).

Butha-Buthe p799
Bus

The bus towards **Oxbow** and **Mokhotlong** leaves from the far side of the petrol station near the main junction and usually gets to Butha-Buthe from Maseru about 0900. This is a steep road so your nerves need to be up to it.

Taxi

Taxis heading towards **Leribe Maseru** and the **Caledonspoort** border leave from the

end of the main street. Taxis to **Ficksburg** and **Fouriesburg** can be found on the South African side of the border. This is the last place to get fuel before Oxbow, 68 km away.

Oxbow p799
Bus and taxi

The daily bus and 2-3 taxis a day operate between **Butha-Buthe** and **Mokhotlong**, and stop at Oxbow.

Mokhotlong p800
Car

The road from Mokhotlong to **Sani Pass** (60 km) is very poor and should only be attempted by 4WDs. It is a spectacular road that winds over the Black Mountain Pass (3240 m) then down to the Sani Flats and Sani Top village. There are only taxis if the weather and the state of the road is good enough so travellers without their own transport will have to hitch a lift over the Sani Pass.

Bus

There is a daily bus to and from **Maseru**, and the lowland towns departing about 0800 from outside the **Pep** store on the main street. There are also a couple of much faster, taxis that do the route to **Butha-Buthe**.

ⓓ Directory

Teyateyaneng p798
Banks The main banks have branches in the town centre, near the **Blue Mountain Inn**.

Mokhotlong p800
Banks Lesotho Bank on the north side of the main street, slow foreign exchange transactions. **Emergencies** The Lesotho Mounted Police is at the east end of the main street, near the large radio mast. **Post office** Next to the police station and LTC Office. **Telephone** Local and international calls can be made from the LTC Office.

Central mountains

The central mountain areas are the most accessible highland regions from Maseru. The new dams built here as part of the Lesotho Highlands Water Project have created excellent tar roads, opening up the region to tourists. This is the best area to visit for a glimpse of mountain life if you lack the time to travel in the more challenging areas to the north and the less accessible areas to the south. ▶▶ *For listings, see page 806.*

Mohale Dam

The Mohale Dam, part of the Lesotho Highlands Water Project (see box, page 805), is accessed along the A3. The irregular-shaped lake made by the dam is stunning and the drive is beautiful, passing through untouched swathes of mountains east of the usual tourist route. The road passes through the small town of Nazareth and dips down before climbing up to Bushmen's Pass at 2263 m, offering beautiful views towards the highlands. From here, you dip down into a series of winding valleys, dotted with homesteads, to a police check point. Do not under any circumstances pass the 'Stop' sign here without permission: the bored officers have been known to root for bribes for the tiniest breach of the rules. Also look out for the rather aggressive herd boys, who run into the road to try and sell lumps of quartz and cutting from rare aloes (it is illegal to buy the latter). The road then continues up to the wonderfully named **God Help Me Pass**, at 2281 m and past the **Basotho Pony Trekking Centre** (T22312318), which offers a range of treks in the area. Continue on over **Blue Mountain Pass**, and you'll catch your first glimpse of the impressive dam, mirroring the peaks around it. At the village of Likalaneng there's a small **visitor centre** ① *T22936217, 0800-1700*, from where you can organize a tour of the 165-m-tall dam wall. A lodge has recently opened with expansive views of the dam. From here, the road turns to gravel and continues over the mountains to Thaba-Tseka, which peaks at the steep Mokhoabong Pass (2860 m).

Thaba Tseka → *Colour map 4, B5.*

This new town was established in 1980 as the administrative centre for a new mountain district. There have been a large number of aid projects established in and around Thaba Tseka and there are, therefore, a disproportionate number of government and aid organization offices in the town. There is little of interest in the town itself, although it is a place through which most visitors to the central mountains will pass. The advent of the **Lesotho Highlands Water Project** has had considerable impact on Thaba Tseka. Apart form a good gravel road linkage, the project sponsored a skills training centre to enable inhabitants to acquire expertise that would help them find jobs with project contractors.

Katse Dam ●● ▶▶ *p806. Colour map 4, B5.*

The new road from Leribe (Hlotse) to the Katse Dam (121 km) is an impressive feat of engineering. The drive from Hlotse to the visitors' centre at Katse Dam takes about three to four hours but allow more time for stops at the top of the mountain passes to take in the sweeping views. What used to be the roughest track in the country is now smooth tar though there are some very steep ascents and sheer drops to the side of the road. Bearded vultures and other unusual montane birds can often be seen from the pass summits and this region is also home to the ice rat, a rodent that is endemic to Lesotho.

Lesotho Highlands Water Project

The massive Lesotho Highlands Water Project, one of the biggest of its kind in the world, is currently under construction with final completion expected in the 2020s. The project has received major funding from South Africa, which maintains a large degree of control over its administration, although eventually it will provide the whole of Lesotho with electricity; the hydroelectrical power plant at Muela is already up and running.

The first phase of the project, completed in 1997, was the construction at Katse of a huge dam which pumps water into the South African river system to help meet the demand of thirsty mines and industry in Gauteng. The second phase, the construction of the Mohole Dam further upstream, was completed in 2003; by early 2006 it had finally filled up, and has doubled the water supply to South Africa by way of a transfer tunnel that feeds the Ash River in South Africa's Free State.

The Lesotho Highlands Development Authority (LHDA) has stressed tourism development as a major part of the project. It has established new national reserves, including Ts'ehlanyane National Park and the Bokong Nature Reserve, both north of the Katse Dam. As a result of the new roads and infrastructure put in place for the construction of the dams, the previously difficult-to-access central mountain area of Lesotho has opened up and new lodges and facilities are being established. The dams themselves, surrounded by stunning mountain vistas, have become tourist attractions in their own right. For more information and updates, visit www.lhwp.org.ls.

and only lives above 2000 m. The highest point is the **Mafika-Lisiu Pass** (3090 m), where there is a carpark and viewpoint and the visitors' centre for the **Bokong Nature Reserve** (see below).

From the pass, the road drops down to the northern end of the Katse Dam and passes the **Intake Tower** which marks the beginning of the tunnel that takes water through to Muela Dam and then ultimately Gauteng. It then crosses the impressive 465 m long and 85 m high **Malibamatso Bridge** at the northern end of the dam before climbing again to 2600 m over the **Laitsoka Pass** and 2500 m over the **Nkaobee Pass** before dropping to below the dam wall where the growing settlement of Katse is located. The dam itself is the highest in Africa, and the second largest after Lake Volta Akosombo Dam in Ghana. It is an impressive structure and can hold over two billion cubic litres of water. The dam wall is 185 m high and 60 m thick and curves inward to such an extent that when looking down from the top, the bottom of the dam wall is invisible – an odd experience. As you enter Katse you will see the modern yellow building with a blue roof of the Lesotho Highlands Water Project **visitor centre** ① *T22910377, Mon-Fri 0800-1200, 1300-1600, Sat-Sun 0800-1200, M10*, from where popular tours into the dam wall take place at 0900 and 1400. The centre also has displays on the dam's construction, with a video and models of how water will be moved around when all five dams are completed in the 2020s. Nearby is the **Katse Alpine Botanical Gardens** ① *T229100311, M5*, which was created to replant some of the indigenous flora that was disrupted in the construction of the dam, especially orchids and the spiral aloe, the latter being Lesotho's national flower. There are three water features, a medicinal plant garden, an area of succulents and a short wild flower walking trail.

Bokong Nature Reserve → *Colour map 4, B5.*
ⓘ *T22913206, www.lhwp.org.es. Daily sunrise to sunset, M5.*

Bokong Nature Reserve covers 1970 ha and straddles the main road from Hlotse to Katse Dam at the 3000 m high Mafika Lisiu Pass. It claims to be one of the highest nature reserves in Africa and there are some outstanding views across the highlands. There is an **information centre** ⓘ *daily 0800-1700*, perched on the edge of a 100-m cliff, which features exhibits on the ecology of the highlands, information on the 39 km overnight hiking trail to Ts'ehlanyane National Park and the network of shorter trails, and pony trekking. At this alpine altitude the reserve is of course not exactly full of animals, other than colonies of the ice rat, the occasional hardy rhebuck and a number of raptors including the bearded vulture. However, the scenery is tremendous, with extensive wetlands at the source of the Bokong River and vast heath covered plateaus. In winter the Lepaqoa Waterfall freezes into a column of ice.

Ts'ehlanyane National Park
ⓘ *T22913206, www.lhwp.org.es. 24 hrs. M15, car M5.*

Ts'ehlanyane National Park covers some 5600 ha, and lies at the junction of the Ts'ehlanyane and the Holomo rivers on the western range of the Maluti mountains. To get there take the gravel road which leaves the Main North Road 3 km south of Butha-Buthe. The 32-km road parallels the Hlotse River along a very picturesque valley until it reaches the park entrance. In the park are extensive tracts of woodlands and it's full of rivers and streams bordered by bamboo and montane fynbos. Again there are very few animals but it's a haven for butterflies and birds. Developments in the park include picnic areas, overnight trails with accommodation huts, and a series of walks and trails of varying length, as well as pony rides.

◉ Central mountains listings

● Sleeping

Mohale Dam
C Mohale Lodge, Likalaneng, T22936432, www.oriongroup.co.za. Comfortable mid-range option managed by the Orion hotel group. 69 en suite rooms in red brick blocks with good views of the dam, with swimming pool, tennis and squash courts, à la carte restaurant, bar. Good option for eating if you've driving past too. Can arrange pony trekking.

D-F Mirakabei Lodge, a few kilometres beyond Likalaneng at the settlement of Mirakabei, T63062650. Attractive country lodge with 6 rustic double en suite thatched rondavels, a dorm with 10 beds and camping, shared bathroom with hot water. Meals available, bar with TV, self-catering kitchen, all set in pretty gardens on the Senqunyane River. They may be able to loan out fishing tackle.

Thaba Tseka *p804*
D Mountain Star Hotel, T22900415. Scruffy and unappealing hotel with simple en suite rooms with TV and phone, popular with local business men. Friendly service and the only option in town, also has restaurant and bar.

Katse Dam *p804*
Campers should enquire at the Lesotho Highlands Water Project visitor centre about where to camp.

C Katse Lodge, Katse village, T22910202, www.oriongroup.co.za. Recently taken over by the Orion hotel group, this is a sprawling ex-construction worker settlement in stone clad buildings with red tin roofs that has been transformed into tourist accommodation. 40 basic en suite rooms with stunning views over the dam, good restaurant, pool, tennis and squash courts.

🍴 Eating

Thaba Tseka p804

There are a couple of basic options and numerous small, cheap eating and drinking places in the older section of town on the north side of the stream.

🚌 Transport

Thaba Tseka p804

There are 3 roads into Thaba Tseka: from Leribe (Hlotse) via the Katse Dam (tarred as far as the dam followed by good gravel); a gravel road from Mokhotlong; and a decent gravel road from Maseru, tarred for about the first 50 km out of Maseru. This last one is a beautiful route through the mountains, crossing the lowlands before ascending the first range of the Maluti Mountains via Bushman's Pass (2268 m). It is commonly known as the Mountain Rd simply because it

was the first road into the mountains that could be negotiated by a saloon car.

There are 3 daily **Lesotho Freight and Bus Services** buses to and from **Maseru** leaving at 0830, 0900 and 0930 from the main bus terminal, which take 7 hrs. These stop in Likalaneng for the Mohale Dam. Minibus taxis run to and from **Katse Dam**, from where there are buses and taxis to **Leribe** (**Hlotse**). There is no public transport to **Mokhotlong** and this is a very difficult road, which should only be attempted with a 4WD and in good weather. Another basic gravel road (4WDs only) runs south to the Selabathebe National Park. There are no roads from Thaba Tseka to Semonkong though it's possible to hike.

Katse Dam p804

The tar stops at Katse but the road that continues to Thaba Tseka (45 km) is good gravel. From Katse there are taxis to and from **Thaba Tseka**, from where there are buses and taxis to **Maseru** that follow the mountain road. While most of this route is tarred, to do this circuit in your own vehicle, it is recommended you have a vehicle with high clearance. The untarred stretch between Thaba Tseka and Marakabei is difficult going over the steep Mokhoabong Pass (2860 m). There are also buses and taxis from Katse to **Leribe** (**Hlotse**) where again you can hook up with a bus to **Maseru** via Main North Rd.

South from Maseru

The main route south from Maseru runs along the southern lowland strip. This is one of the main farming regions, but it tends to be a drier area than further north. There are a number of important urban centres along the route connected by tar roads, so it's easy to get around, although none of them could be considered tourist attractions.

The southern mountain area is dominated by the Senqu River Valley that winds through the area. The majestic river meanders through rugged mountain scenery and past steep cliffs but the water level has been reduced considerably as all the dams of the Lesotho Highlands Water Project are being completed. The mountain road from Moyeni (Quthing) in the Lowveld is tarred until just past Mphaki, passing through beautiful highland terrain. From here the road is gravel until Whitehill, where it becomes tarred again as far as Qacha's Nek. This stretch can, in fine weather, be managed in an ordinary vehicle, but you'll need a 4WD to get to the Sehlabathebe National Park. ▶▶ *For listings, see pages 811-814.*

Morija/Matsieng → *Colour map 4, B4.*

Morija is the site of Lesotho's oldest church and a well-run museum. The French Protestant missionaries who established the church named the town after Mount Moriah in Palestine. Lesotho's first printing press was established here and the village is still an important centre for culture, theology and printing. Books in more than 50 languages have been printed here for export to other African countries. The **Morija Museum** ⓘ *T22360308, www.morijafest.com/museum, Mon-Fri 0800-1700, Sun 1200-1700, small entry fee*, has a number of important historic and prehistoric exhibits and a well organized archive of personal and church papers. There is a large fossil collection and a good display on the dinosaur relics found throughout the country, and there are some of Moshoeshoe's personal belongings on display, including his china tea set. It's all a bit jumbled but the staff are very helpful. There is a delightful tea shop in the grounds serving tea, cold drinks, and snacks. The annual **Morija Arts and Cultural Festival** (contact the museum or visit www.morijafest.com for information) takes place here in the first week of April, and includes concerts, traditional dance, choirs, food and craft fairs. This is the only event of its kind in Lesotho's so it's worth making an effort to get here if you are in the country at the time.

About 7 km from Morija is the royal family's country home, **Matsieng**. The royal court met at Matsieng more or less throughout the colonial period and, in theory, all decisions taken by the colonial authorities in Maseru had to be agreed to by the monarch. Though the village is of great historical interest there is not a great deal to see or anywhere to stay.

Malealea → *Colour map 4, B4.*

South from Morija the road continues to Mafeteng. About 10 km south of Morija the B40 turns off the Main South Road to the left and follows through to Malealea about 32 km away. In the spring the sides of the the road are covered in flowering mountain plants. Apart from the last 7 km, the road is tarred and fine for a normal car, though take care going over the Gates of Paradise in wet weather, which is 6 km before the lodge. This is an escarpment that opens out to a broad panorama over the plains below where there's a plaque on the rock to the right of the road that says 'Wayfarer pause and look upon a gateway to Paradise' – words uttered by Mervyn Bosworth-Smith, the founder of the Malealea trading post in the early 1900s. Today it's a popular pony trekking and hiking centre in the foothills of the Thaba Putsoa range, 85 km south of Maseru, and is probably the best place to stay to experience what Lesotho is all about. Here there are San rock paintings, isolated waterfalls, rock pools and peaceful hikes and treks in the surrounding mountains.

Mafeteng → *Colour map 4, B4.*

Mafeteng is 36 km south on the Main South Road from Morija. It is the main commercial and administrative centre for the southern lowlands. The town is a 15-minute drive from Van Rooyens border post (open 0600-2200) so this will be the first place you get to if crossing from Wepner in South Africa's Free State. There are pleasant views from the town across the lowlands towards the Thaba-Putsoa range of mountains. The town suffered considerably during Lesotho's 1998 riots. The **British War Memorial**, erected in memory of members of the Cape Mounted Rifles who died during the Gun War of 1880, is located near St John's Primary School on the road from Mafeteng towards the Van Rooyens border post.

Mohales Hoek → *Colour map 4, B4.*

This is a pleasant town named after King Moeshoeshoe's younger half-brother. There are San cave paintings in the cliffs beside the Main South Road as you enter town from the north, but they are difficult to get to. There are also paintings in various caves about 10 km from the Main South Road up the Maphutseng Valley. Although there is nothing to see in town, the most interesting story behind this region are the **Cannibal Caves**, 2 km south near the Agricultural Training Farm. Found throughout Lesotho, they are a reminder of *lifaqane*, 'the terrible time', when in the 1820s roving bands of warriors fleeing the Zulu attackers prevented farmers from growing crops, and people resorted to cannibalism to survive.

Moyeni (Quthing) ⬤⬤⬤⬤ ➤➤ *pp811-814. Colour map 4, B5.*

Moyeni ('place of the wind') is the administrative centre of Quthing district (the town itself is often also called Quthing – 'Ou' means river in San). It was established as an administrative centre by the British in 1877 but was abandoned three years later during the Gun War, and later rebuilt. It straddles one main street running uphill from the Main South Road. The town is in the far south of the lowlands at the point where the Senqu (Orange) River leaves the mountains and winds out across the flatter central South African plateau.

Sights

There are a couple of good sets of **dinosaur footprints** on the riverbank on the northern outskirts of Moyeni. There are also some dinosaur footprints further up the **Qomoqomong Valley** though they are hard to find without a guide. The Qomoqomong Valley is also the home to some of the best preserved **San cave paintings** in Lesotho; follow the small road east out of Moyeni towards the village of Qomoqomong (where the road ends), the caves are in the hills to the southwest. **Masitise Cave House**, T89794167, www.morijafest.com/masitise, about 5 km to the west of Moyeni near Masitise Primary School. The cave house, which was renovated and turned into a small museum, has five rooms and was home to the Reverand DF Ellenberger and his family who established a mission in the area in the late 19th century. This is now a national monument, and there are displays of objects from that time in the house.

Mount Moorosi → Colour map 4, B5.

About 40 km beyond Moyeni (Quthing) towards Qacha's Nek is Mount Moorosi and the village of the same name. This is an important historical site. In the mid-19th century it was the home of the Chief of the Baphuthi clan (Moorosi), who carried out numerous raids against white settlers in nearby areas. After the British made Moyeni the district capital in 1877, they tried to subdue Moorosi by taking his son captive, but Moorosi resisted and managed to free his son. The British then spent over two years trying to eliminate the threat of Moorosi, eventually succeeding in capturing his mountain stronghold and massacring him and about 500 of his followers, including many children. Near to the village is **Letsie Lake**, a reeded wetlands area that attracts waterbirds. A wildlife conservation project has been set up here involving the local people in the protection of the bearded vulture.

Qacha's Nek → Colour map 4, B5.

This border town at the southeastern corner of Lesotho is on the only road pass from the southern mountain area into South Africa's Eastern Cape. Its location means that, unlike most of the country, there are residents from a number of southern African ethnic groups and visitors are as likely to hear Xhosa being spoken in the street as Sesotho. Until 1970, Qacha's Nek had no direct road communication with the rest of Lesotho, and depended on the town of Matatiele in the Eastern Cape for supplies. This linkage was particularly important, given that Matatiele had a rail link by which migrant workers could travel to the South African mines. Qacha, meaning hideaway, was the name of a local 19th-century chief who was apparently able to disappear into the mountains for months at a time. The British established an administrative centre at the location in 1888 in an attempt to maintain control of this region which had a reputation for lawlessness. This is one of the few regions of Lesotho that is heavily forested and of particular interest are the giant California redwood trees, which exceed 25 m and are over 60 years old. Interestingly, the government hospital here is used exclusively to treat tuberculosis patients.

Sehlabathebe National Park ⬤ ›› pp811-814. Colour map 4, B6.

This national park is isolated, inaccessible and rugged – but these are the main reasons for coming here. The park is situated in the far east of Lesotho on the border with South Africa and has more than 6500 ha of sub-alpine grasslands, with an average elevation of 2400 m. It has some breathtaking landscape with sandstone overhangs and rock features, mountain streams, natural pools, waterfalls, and 65 San rock art sites, some of which are accessible by foot or pony. At time of writing, the Maloti Drakensberg Transfrontier Project, a joint environmental management initiative between Lesotho and South Africa, announced that they plan on bringing down the boundaries between Sehlabathebe and the uKhahlamba-Drakensberg national parks. This will effectively create a transfrontier park, and is likely to improve the park's infrastructure. For now, facilities are limited and the park is only really popular with South Africa 4WD owners and trout fishermen.

There is little large game within the park, except for the occasional hardy eland or baboon but there is plenty of birdlife, including the rare bearded vulture and black eagle. There is excellent trout fishing and the park is also home to the water lily of the Sehlabathebe and the tiny Maluti minnow, a flower and fish both thought to be extinct

Sotho: what's in a name?

Lesotho is one of the few countries in Africa in which the vast majority of people belong to the same ethnic ('tribal') group: the Basotho. Many people in South Africa will talk about 'the Sotho' but in Lesotho you will rarely hear the phrase; rather people will use the word 'Basotho', meaning 'the Sotho people'. The singular of Basotho is Mosotho, Sesotho is the language spoken by the Basotho and Lesotho means the place, or home, of the Basotho. Today there are as many Basotho living in South Africa as in Lesotho.

for many years. The park was gazetted in 1970; the prime minister of the time, Leabua Jonathan, loved trout fishing, which may explain the park's existence. The park lodge used to be called Jonathan's Lodge, and when he stayed all the other guests had to leave. There are stables here and guided pony treks and hikes can be arranged.

Ins and outs

Getting there There are two routes into the park: one via Sehlabathebe village and one across the border from South Africa. Access to Sehlabathebe village is either from Qacha's Nek about 100 km to the southwest, or from Thaba Tseka about 120 km to the northwest. Both roads are difficult and a 4WD is essential, but the route from Thaba Tseka is especially challenging. The route from South Africa is possible on foot or horse only; the path crosses the border at Nkonkoana Gate (open 0800-1600) and then heads down to the South African border post at Bushman's Nek which is 38 km from Underberg in KwaZulu Natal. Sehlabathebe Lodge is a 10 km walk or ride from Bushman's Nek. There are no border facilities here on the Lesotho side but there is a small office on the South African side, next to which is a basic campsite and a hikers hut run by KZN Wildlife.

◉ South from Maseru listings

◉ Sleeping

Morija p808

D Morija Guesthouse, perched on a hill right at the top of the village behind the museum, T63065093, www.morijaguesthouses.com. An attractive sandstone and thatch house with outstanding views of the Maluti Mountains (on a clear day you can see for 45 km), and a veranda and pretty gardens. The main house sleeps 14 in 5 bedrooms with shared bathroom, kitchen and lounge, while several smaller, ethnic-themed rondavels in the garden sleep 2. Meals on request. The lodge can organize pony trekking and overnight stays in local villages and several easy hikes start here, too. Stunning spot. Recommended.

Malealea p808

D-F Malealea Lodge, reservations South Africa, T082-5524215 (mob), www.malealea.com. A collection of en suite rooms, and comfortable thatched Basotho huts, plus en suite rooms in the old farmhouse and dorms in forest huts, built around old trading post, established in 1905. Communal kitchens for self-catering, or great meals served on request. Camping allowed in grounds, honesty bar, general store, beautiful setting. Owners Mick, Di and Glenn are active in supporting community projects in the area, and introduced pony trekking for tourists here and treks last from 1 hr to 6 days. They also offer hiking, and visits to villages. Recommended for an all-round Lesotho experience.

Mafeteng p809
C Golden Hotel, to the right of the road as it enters the town from Maseru, T22700566. Plain brick block with comfortable but small en suite rooms. Lounge with DSTV, bar with plastic tables and pool table, restaurant serving standard meat dishes and surprisingly good pizzas.
D Mafeteng Hotel, town centre, T58855555. 27 en suite rooms or cottages with satellite TV, swimming pool set around the odd looking main building, which resembles an air traffic control tower. Restaurant and 3 bars. The whole set-up is run-down and shabby and can get noisy at weekends when the bars and the Las Vegas disco in the hotel grounds fill up.

Mohales Hoek p809
C Hotel Mount Maluti, north of the town centre, T22785224, www.hotel mountmaluti.co.za. One of the oldest hotels in Lesotho, 34 en suite rooms with TV and heating and colourful, if rather dark, decor, plus camping. Restaurant has a good vegetarian choice (rare in Lesotho), bars, tennis courts, swimming pool, nice gardens, one of the country's better small town hotels, run by Danny and Anne who are very helpful in organizing activities. Reservations recommended.

Moyeni p809
There are a couple of run-down hotels in town, where things barely function, so you're better off staying in Mohales Hoek and visiting here on a day trip.

Mount Moorosi p810
There is no official accommodation in Mount Moorosi, but, as elsewhere in Lesotho, it should be possible to find somewhere to stay by simply asking around. Camping is possible throughout the valley, but always ask permission before pitching a tent.

Qacha's Nek p810
C-D Nthatuoa Hotel, near the airfield, T22950260. A little faded with an intermittent water supply but has a variety of tidy en suite rooms set in a series of blocks of varying size and price. Good restaurant with high ceilings and ancient chandeliers, bar. Rates include an excellent breakfast. Can arrange pony treks or trout fishing, camping in grounds.
D-F Letloepe Lodge, 4 km before the border, T22950383, www.letloepelodge.co.ls. String of neat thatched rondavels housing en suite rooms, some with small kitchenettes and TV, dorms, plus camping, restaurant serving basic meals, run by the friendly Moletsane family who can organize pony trekking and boat trips on the Senqu River.
F St Joseph's Mission, in a wooded valley to the north of the town centre. Visitors may camp in the grounds or stay in one of the outbuildings.

Sehlabathebe National Park p810
E-F Sehlabathebe Lodge, approximately 10 km from the entrance gate and visitor centre, reservations, Ministry of Tourism, Environment and Culture, Post Office Building, Maseru, T22311767, www.maloti.org.ls. Note that the park will be undergoing changes as part of the Maloti Drakensberg Transfrontier Project and there are plans to build 15 self-contained, self-catering chalets to be run by a private operator. For now, accommodation is in a 14-bed lodge in 5 very basic rooms with communal showers, toilets and kitchen, a little faded but clean. Bedding, eating and cooking equipment provided, horse riding available. Camping is allowed anywhere but you have to buy a permit from the park office.

There is no food available and very little in Sehlabathebe village, so bring your own supplies. Payment can only be made in cash.

🍴 Eating

Mafeteng *p809*
Other than the restaurants in the **Mafeteng** and **Golden** hotels, there are a large number of street vendors in the town centre and some cafés in the area just to the south. There is a popular open-air restaurant and a **KFC** near the taxi terminal.

Mohales Hoek *p809*
There are few places to eat other than the **Hotel Mount Maluti** restaurant. There are a couple of cafés and street vendors on Mafoso Rd.

Moyeni *p809*
The **Orange River Hotel** has the town's only restaurant though there are numerous street vendors and cafés around the taxi terminal in lower Moyeni. There are a number of popular and noisy bars in lower Moyeni.

Mount Moroosi *p810*
You can get takeaways at the Mitchell Brothers' Trading Store which serves as the village's main petrol station and general store.

Qacha's Nek *p810*
The **Nthatuoa Hotel** dining room has a varied menu and a good reputation. There are a number of smaller cafés selling cheap and filling meals near the bus and taxi terminal.

🏃 Activities and tours

Malealea *p808*
Malealea Lodge, T082-5524215, www.malealea.com. Mike and Di Jones, who were born in Lesotho, can organize pony treks (no experience necessary), hikes or 4WD tours to all the local sites from 1 hr to 6 days.

These include day treks to the Botsoela Waterfalls and Pitseng Gorge and rock pools plus overnight treks to the Ribaneng (2 days), Ketane (4 days) and Maletsunyane waterfalls (4 days), the 3 highest in Lesotho. Expect to pay in the region of M260 per person per day on the overnight pony trekking trips and M145 for a 2-3 hr trek, and slightly less on the guided hikes.

The horses and huts used for overnight accommodation on the trails are hired from local Basotho, who also act as guides. The huts are equipped with mattresses, gas cooker, cooking and eating utensils and a bucket of water. Remember to bring a torch and candles. Mike and Di can also arrange informal performances by the village youth choir, accompanied by home-made instruments, and visits to local villages. All activities can be arranged as soon as you get to the lodge.

🚌 Transport

Morija *p808*
There are frequent buses and taxis to and from **Maseru**, **Mafeteng** and **Mohale's Hoek**.

Malealea *p808*

Bus
There is a daily mid-morning bus between **Malealea** and **Mafeteng**. If travelling from **Maseru**, you can intercept the bus at Motsekuoa where the B40 turns off from the Main South Rd (about 10 km south of Morija). If travelling from **Mohales Hoek** or if you miss the bus at Motsekuoa you can catch one of the taxis going along the road marked B40 on most maps (though not on signposts).

Taxi
Some taxis go all the way to **Malealea Lodge**. If none of these are running get dropped off at the Malealea turning (about 25 km from the Main South Rd) and walk or hitchhike the last 7 km.

Mafeteng p809

There are buses and taxis to and from **Maseru** via **Morija**, and to and from **Mohales Hoek** and **Moyeni**. This is also the place to pick up public transport to **Malealea Lodge**, and there is a daily bus that leaves mid morning and the occasional taxi.

Mohales Hoek p809

Taxis leave from either side of Mafoso Rd. People hitchhiking south may find it easier to get a lift if they first get a taxi about 4 km out of town to the turn off to the **Makhaleen Bridge** border post. The road over the border is now tarred but on the South African side the road to Zastron in Free State reverts to a good gravel road.

Moyeni p809

Frequent buses and taxis towards **Maseru** via **Mohales Hoek** leave from near the petrol station in lower Moyeni. There is 1 bus a day to **Qacha's Nek** that leaves at around 0630 and takes about 8 hrs, and frequent taxis to the nearby border post **Tele Bridge** 21 km away.

Mount Moorosi p810
Road

This is the last place to get fuel before Qacha's Nek, 130 km. The road towards Qacha's Nek is now mostly tarred; the gravel has been improved in recent years and is passable in a saloon car (but check locally in wet weather).

There are fairly frequent taxis running the route between **Moyeni** and **Mount Moorosi** and the daily bus between **Maseru** and **Qacha's Nek** passes through the town.

Qacha's Nek p810
Air

Given Qacha's Nek's distance from the main towns, air travel is a popular form of transport and the airfield has a tarred runway and is relatively busy. There are no scheduled flights but it is possible to pay for a seat on one of the many charter flights that operate between here and **Maseru**, weather permitting. Ask at the airfield for information.

Car

The drive to Qacha's Nek border post is steep and winding, but can be accessed in a saloon car (but check locally if the weather is wet). Visitors without their own transport wanting to cross into **South Africa** will have to walk across the border and then hitchhike.

Taxi

There are daily taxis between Qacha's Nek and **Moyeni** that depart from outside the Shell petrol station and a daily bus from **Maseru** that departs from there at 0630 and takes 10 hrs.

❶ Directory

Mafeteng p809
Banks Standard Bank and the Lesotho Bank have branches in the town centre.

Mohales Hoek p809
Banks Standard Bank is on Mafoso Rd and Lesotho Bank is on Maluti Ring Rd near the post office.

Moyeni p809
Banks There is a branch of Lesotho Bank in upper Moyeni.

Qacha's Nek p810
Banks There is a branch of Lesotho Bank on the western outskirts of town.

Contents

Swaziland

Essentials

⬤ **Getting around** Baz Bus, car
hire, poor local buses.

◉ **Time required** 3-5 days.

◐ **Weather** Mostly warm and
sunny, summer thunderstorms.

⊗ **When not to go** Good all year.

Nelspruit

Malelane

SOUTH AFRICA

MPUMALANGA

Jambi

Barberton

Matsamo

Hhohho

Jeppe's Reef

Phophonyane Falls

Rocklands

Sihoye

Mananga

Namaacha

Lomahasha

Bulembu/ Josefsdal

Havelock Mine

Pigg's Peak

Sand River Reservoir

Tshaneni

Maguga Dam

Komati

Mhlume

Mhjoli Dam

Shewula Nature Reserve

Malolotja Nature Reserve

Forbes Reef

Mission Falls

Simunye

Mlawula

Ngwenya/ Oshoek

Motjane

Sibebe Rock

Black Mbuluzi

Mliba

Hlane Royal National Park

Mlawula Nature Reserve

Mhlumeni

MBABANE

Luve

Highveld

Ezulwini

Middleveld

Mhlambanyatsi

Milwane Sanctuary Lobamba

Manzini

Helehele

Siteki

Mantenga Falls

Malkerns

Matshapa

Lowveld

Bhunya

Loyengo

Sidvokodvo

Siphofaneni

Mkhaya Game Reserve

Usutu

Sandlane/ Nerston

Mankayane

Ngwempsi Hiking Trail

Singceni

Big Bend

Mahlangatja Hills

Mkhondvo

Singceni Mountains

Grand Valley

Sitobela

Gege

Hlatikulu

Maloma

Nsoko

Ingawaruma

Piet Retief

Mbulungwane

Cecil Macks Pass

Mahamba

Nhlangano

Mhlotsheni

Ngwavuma

Commondale

Salitje

Lavumisa

Golela

KWAZULU NATAL

Pongola

Pongola Dam

Pongola Nature Reserve

Itala Game Reserve

Candover

Jozini

Louwsburg

MOZAMBIQUE

Lebombo Mountains

N

10 km
10 miles

With an area of just over 17,000 sq km (less than the Kruger National Park), Swaziland may be the smallest country in the southern hemisphere but it has myriad African landscapes, all of which can be seen from the top of Mlembe (1862 m), a mountain on the country's western border. Swaziland was plundered by European gold prospectors in the 19th century but, unlike South Africa, huge fortunes were never really made here and even throughout the colonial period, the government was more or less left in the hands of the royal family. Following independence in 1968, Swaziland has remained one of only three monarchies left in Africa, and is the only absolute monarchy on the continent

On the whole, Swaziland is an accessible country to visit; it has moderate temperatures all year round, you can travel between the highveld and the lowveld in a day, and none of the major sights are more than a two-hour drive away. The tourist industry developed during the Apartheid years, when South African tourists left their puritanical regime to visit Swaziland's casinos and nightclubs. Unfortunately, as a consequence, the country developed a reputation for seedy sex and gambling holidays, but since the change of government in South Africa, this market has, thankfully, plummeted. Thanks to a handful of pioneering conservationists, effective anti-poaching initiatives and substantial animal restocking, Swaziland's game parks have improved dramatically in recent years. It's also a good destination for adventurers, with an effective backpackers' set-up and a number of adventure activities on offer. The Swazi people are friendly and expert craft makers, producing a wealth of high-quality African curios. Compared to South Africa, Swaziland is a country where tribal values, craftsmanship and royal loyalty have withstood the test of encroaching modernization.

Mbabane and around

→ *Colour map 2, C5. Altitude: 1250 m.*

Mbabane is a small modern town built on the site of a trading station on the busy route between Mozambique and the Transvaal. After the Boer War the British established their administrative headquarters here and the town grew up around them. Over the last few decades, development has been in the form of a disorganized collection of unattractive concrete blocks and a snarled traffic system, broken up by modern shopping malls. It remains a small town, however, and the main business district is spread over a small grid of busy streets in the centre of town. ▸▸ *For listings, see pages 823-826.*

Ins and outs

Getting there and around There are buses from Mbabane to all major centres in Swaziland, though they may only run a couple of times per day on each route – arrive early at the bus station. Minibus taxis run regular short routes, but the vehicles are generally of poor standard, making them dangerous. Do not use them. The **Baz Bus** (see page 41) includes Swaziland on its route between Durban and Johannesburg and Pretoria and drops off and picks up at the backpacker hostels. ▸▸ *For further details, see Transport page 826.*

Tourist information The **Swaziland Information Office** ① *Swazi Plaza, T4042531, www.welcometoswaziland.com, Mon-Fri 0800-1700, Sat 0830-1230,* is an extremely helpful office with a wide range of information on hotels, nature reserves and tour operators. It also produces a useful map and annual brochure, covering the whole country.

Sights

Mbabane is a cluster of concrete shopping malls at the bottom of a hill, surrounded by ring roads and the highway that leads to the nearby Ezulwini Valley. There isn't much to do here and it's the valley itself that holds the best of the Swazi attractions, but the **Swazi market** near the central roundabout is worth a quick look for its excellent display of fresh produce. Piled in high pyramids on wooden stalls are mangoes, tomatoes, cabbages, pineapples and avocados. You can engage in some good-humoured bartering with the Swazi women. There are also a few curios, although you'll get better value in the rural areas where these items are

Mbabane

Sleeping 🛏
City Inn **1**
Kapola Guest House **3**
Khula Golden Guest House **4**
Mountain Inn **2**

Eating 🍴
Finesse **6**
La Casserole **3**
Mediterranean **1**

The world's most dangerous road?

The road to Manzini and the Ezulwini Valley from Mbabane has to be one of the world's most dramatic roads. It is very straight and alarmingly steep. Before the completion of a double-lane highway, which involved whole sides of the mountain being blasted away, this road was little more than a narrow track going straight down a cliff face. All other traffic had to get out of the way if the royal family's motorcade was going up or down

between Mbabane and the Royal Palace in the Ezulwini Valley. It once made a listing in the Guinness Book of World Records as having the highest car accident rate in the world. The father of Ted Reilly (the man who was instrumental in reintroducing wildlife into Swaziland's parks), owned the first car in Swaziland, a Model T Ford. This road was so steep for the rudimentary car that the only way he could get back up to the top was in reverse.

made. Mbabane also has a selection of South African chain supermarkets, which are useful for stocking up.

Ezulwini Valley ⬤🅟🅕🅒🅞▲↦ *pp823-826. Colour map 2, C5.*

Clearly signposted from Mbabane, the Ezulwini Valley (the Valley of Heaven) is the centre of Swaziland's tourist industry. The tourist route follows the old main road through Ezulwini. Take the fly-off at the bottom of Malagwane Hill. In the daytime there are superb views as you leave the highveld and drop into the middleveld. The valley itself has no real centre, but every few hundred metres you will pass a smart hotel, craft shop or restaurant. The 30 km long valley ends at Lobamba, the Royal Village of the King.

Lobamba

At the eastern end of the Ezulwini Valley before the airport is the royal village of Lobamba, set amongst typical open bush countryside. This is where the present king, King Mswati III, lives and from where he rules Swaziland with his Queen Mother or Ndlovukazi, meaning 'she-elephant'. Every August the king gets to add to his growing stable of wives at the **Umhlanga (Reed) Dance** when virgins perform in front of the 'she-elephant' and the King picks out his next wife – an honour she cannot refuse. The custom has attracted increasing criticism over the years, notably in 2003 when the King's choice was not supported by the bride's family. Nevertheless, it is an astounding event, where hundreds of young women from across the country congregate and dance bare-breasted in front of a congregation of royalty, subjects and curious tourists.

All of the royal buildings are closed to the public, but the **Somhlolo National Stadium** is the venue for major celebrations, including sports events, musical shows and royal events such as the annual independence celebrations and the Reed Dance. On no account try to take any photographs of the Lozitha Palace or the Embo State Palace. The parliament buildings are open to visitors but the effort to gain admittance is not worth the tour.

Of much greater interest is the **National Museum** ① *T4161481, Mon-Fri 0800-1300, 1400-1545, Sat and Sun 1000-1300, 1400-1545, E20*, which has some excellent displays relating to Swazi life throughout history, with old photographs, traditional dress and Stone Age implements. If you wish to find out more ask for a guided tour, well worth it for an insight into local life and customs. Opposite the museum is a memorial to King

Sobhuza II and a small museum depicting his life. The showroom houses his three rather splendid royal black limousines. His statue stands under a domed cover with open arches and an immaculate white tiled floor.

Mlilwane Wildlife Sanctuary ⊜ ↠ pp823-826.

Mlilwane is one of the most popular of Swaziland's nature reserves and covers a varied landscape of highveld and lowveld along a section of the Ezulwini Valley. It is a peaceful and beautiful reserve, allowing a wide range of activities, from self-guided walking to mountain biking, with a good chance of getting very close to wildlife. The land which now makes up the sanctuary was originally used as farmland and for tin mining. The hydraulic sluicing used to mine the tin with high pressure water jets had caused massive damage to the landscape leaving it scarred with ravines. The mine operators had simply abandoned the land after the mine closed, leaving a wasteland of slag heaps and open excavations behind.

The land has been extensively regenerated into a wildlife sanctuary, and it is now possible to see a wide variety of bird and animal species, including: hippo, giraffe, crocodile, eland, zebra, blue wildebeest, kudu, nyala, klipspringer, waterbuck, impala, steenbuck, duiker, warthog, suni antelope, oribi, many species of waterfowl and purple-crested lourie, the brilliantly coloured national bird of Swaziland. For more information visit www.biggameparks.org.

Ins and outs

Getting there The reserve is signposted just past the Caltex service station at Lobamba. Turn right and travel 4 km to Sangweni Gate at eSitjeni. Gates are open 24 hours allowing guests staying in the reserve to visit the nightlife, casinos and restaurants in the Ezulwini Valley. Entry is E25 per person, which covers the whole length of your stay within the sanctuary. The Interpretorium in the rest camp and the

Ezulwini Valley to Manzini

Sleeping ⊜ Ezulwini Sun 1
Forester's Arms 8
Gables 12

Happy Valley 2
Legends 10
Lugogo Sun 5
Malandela's 11

Mantenga Lodge 3
Mountain Inn
& Friar Tuck's
Restaurant 4

Sangweni Gate complex offer interesting information on nature conservation in Swaziland, including anti-poaching efforts.

Sights

There are over 100 km of dirt roads, with some marked for 4WD vehicles only. As there are no predators in the park, the wildlife is quite relaxed, enabling close viewing. Alternatives for exploring the sanctuary include guided horse rides, open 4WD game drives, guided mountain-bike rides, and an extensive system of self-guided walking trails including the Macobane, Sondzela, Hippo and Mhlambanyatsi Trails. The 8-km **Macobane Trail** offers an easy gradient and particularly spectacular views of the Ezulwini Valley as it winds its way along the contours of an old aqueduct on the Nyonyane Mountain (1136 m). All activities can be booked through the activity centre at the main camp. For all activities a minimum of two people is necessary.

Mantenga Nature Reserve

ⓘ *T4161151, www.sntc.org.sz. E25.*

Close to the Mantenga Lodge is an area of outstanding beauty and mature patches of forest between the main road and the Mantenga Falls. The Little Usutu River flows through the area and the well-known waterfalls are about a 2-km walk away. There is an authentic cultural village, and picnic spots and walking trails have been marked out.

Mantenga Cultural Village

ⓘ *Daily tours 0830-1800, dance shows 1115 and 1515, E45.*

Every aspect of this 'show' village is based upon traditional methods and materials. This is exactly how a medium-sized Swazi homestead would have looked 100 years ago. There are 16 beehive-shaped huts built from local materials, laid out in a plan that can be seen throughout rural Swaziland. The huts form a semicircle partly surrounded by a cattle kraal. The focal point is a larger hut, the 'great hut', and the kraal. This is a polygamous homestead – each wife has her own circle of huts for cooking, making beer and sleeping in. Slightly separate are the huts for unmarried mature boys and girls and for married sons.

The whole complex is brought to life by traditional dance performances and songs as the guides show visitors around. You will also see food being prepared, clothes and household objects being made. The **Village Café** is a great place for a sundowner (see Eating, page 825).

Manzini

University

To Sidvokodvo

✈ Matsapha

To Sidvokodvo

To Usuthu & Mankayane

Timbali Lodge &   Swaziland Backpackers **7**
  Boma Restaurant **9**   Tum's George **13**
Royal Swazi Sun **5**
Sondzela Backpackers **6**

Mantenga Craft Centre

① *T4161136, daily 0830-1700.*

Swaziland is an excellent place to buy curios, with a wider selection and lower prices than in South Africa. The Mantenga Foundation was formed in 1974 to retail the finished works of local artists in the Mantenga Craft Centre. From the outset, the project has been managed on the basis of long-term self-sufficiency. The centre stocks an excellent range of jewellery, crafts, clothes, gold and silver, screen prints, leather goods, ceramics, rugs and carvings. There is also a coffee shop and snack bar and a small tourist information desk with a selection of brochures. **Swazi Trails** are also based here. See Tour operators, page 70.

Malkerns Valley

About 5 km beyond the National Museum is a right turning for Malkerns, M18. This makes for an enjoyable circuit from Mbabane which can easily be covered on a day trip, although most people choose to stay overnight in Mlilwane Wildlife Sanctuary (see page 824). This is the ideal place to discover a more typical Swazi lifestyle than you encounter along the Ezulwini Valley. One kilometre from the junction towards Malkerns is a cluster of roadside shops and farmstalls. **Swazi Candles** ① *T5283219, www.swazicandles.com, 0900-1700*, is one of the best known shops in the country, producing interesting candles in a variety of designs and colours. A newer addition is the **House on Fire**, a stylish complex which includes the **Malendela** restaurant, an internet café, a live music venue and a bed and breakfast (see page 824). Also here is **Baobab Batik** and **Gone Rural**, which sells stylish, contemporary woven goods in bright colours.

Bhunya and around

The road south from Malkerns towards Bhunya (26 km) is tarred, and for part of the route it follows the Great Usutu River, passing rolling farmlands; be careful of groups of schoolchildren and cattle straying into the road. As the road climbs up into the highlands, the forest closes in and it can get quite cool out of the sunlight. The factory town of Bhunya is the centre of the local timber industry – the local pulp mill is responsible for much of the local pollution. From Bhunya there is a choice of two routes. The road to the South African border (34 km) at **Sandlane/Nerston** (daily 0800-1800) crosses the Lusutfu River and then climbs steeply for 2 km into the coniferous plantations. This is the **Usutu Forest** a man-made plantation which extends for over 65,000 ha. All along this road are numerous lookout towers protecting Swaziland's forests. The second road out of Bhunya heads north towards **Mhlambanyatsi** and Mbabane.

Mbabane and around listings

Hotel and guesthouse prices
L over US$300 AL US$220-300 A US$150-220
B US$100-150 C US$75-100 D US$35-75
E US$15-35 F under US$15
Restaurant prices
₸₸₸ over US$30 ₸₸ US$15-30 ₸ under US$15
See pages 46-51 for further information.

● Sleeping

Mbabane *p818, map p818*
B Mountain Inn, 4 km out of town on
the road to Ezulwini Valley, T4042781,
www.mountaininn.sz. 60 smart, comfortable
rooms, en suite bathrooms, telephone, TV,
swimming pool and neat lawns, **Friar Tuck**
à la carte restaurant, balconies have
commanding views over the mountains
and valley. Offers a range of excursions
and rents out mountain bikes.
C City Inn, Gwamile St, city centre, T4042406,
cityinn@realnet.co.sz. 22 rooms, en suite
bathroom, some a/c, DSTV, laundry service,
Pablo's restaurant and **Caribbean Coffee
Shop**. Big difference between the new rooms
and the originals in the old part of the hotel.
Advisable to look at the room on offer before
making your mind up.
C Kapola Guest House, Malagwane Hill,
T4048266, www.kapola_eden.co.sz, phone
Annette for directions, 6 km in a suburb
to the west of town. 6 en suite rooms,
comfortable decor, TV lounge, breakfast
buffet, lovely forest scenery, secure parking.
C Khula Golden Guest House, Moba St,
well signposted from Gwamile St, 3 km from
town in an upmarket suburb, T4045095,
thecastle@realnet.co.sz. B&B rooms or
self-catering units, swimming pool, braai
areas, secure parking in lock-up garages,
nice views over the city.

Ezulwini Valley *p819, map p820*
L Royal Swazi Sun, T4165000, www.suninter
national.com. 149 a/c rooms, TV, bar,
restaurant, gym, sauna, spa, swimming pool,
bowls, squash, tennis, horse riding, 18-hole
golf course, **Planter's** colonial-themed
restaurant, casino. Every room has
magnificent views of the valley and
mountains, probably the most luxurious
hotel in Swaziland, an amazing contrast
to life in the rest of the country.
A Ezulwini Sun, T411550, www.suninter
national.com. 60 a/c rooms, TV, **Valley Blues**
restaurant, coffee shop, swimming pool,
sauna, tennis, horse riding, volleyball, casino
next door, ghastly Caribbean decor.
A Lugogo Sun, in the grounds of the **Royal
Swazi**, T4164000, www.suninternational.com.
202 a/c rooms, **Ilanga restaurant**, bar, a large
establishment aimed at families, caters for
conferences and large tour groups, 'pub
night' on Wed has a live band – popular with
ex-pats and locals from all over the country.
C Happy Valley Motel, T4161061,
happyvalley@africaonline.co.sz. Good value
and lots going on, next door to the **Why
Not Disco**, and **If Not Go-Go Bar**. There are
several restaurants, bars and nightclubs in
and around the hotel so it's the place to go
if you want to live it up, probably not suitable
for children though. 57 a/c rooms with fridge,
TV, in a simple concrete block around a pool,
rates include breakfast and entry to the disco
and the Royal Swazi Casino, ask for special
3-day weekend specials.
C Mantenga Lodge, T4161049,
www.mantengalodge.com. 38 en suite
double rooms with satellite TV, à la carte
restaurant with wide outdoor terrace, lively
bar, swimming pool, sauna, hidden amongst
the trees this is a pleasant country hotel next
to the **Mantenga Craft Centre** and in the
Mantenga Nature Reserve, with easy access
to the Mlilwane Wildlife Sanctuary.
C-F Timbali Lodge & Boma Restaurant,
T4161156, www.timbali.co.sz. 24 nicely
decorated en suite rooms, fridge, TV, and
3 self-catering family cottages, popular for
conferences. Also has campsite covering
1.5 ha with 30 terraced sites and is well

grassed and shady. Pool, dinner is served in a boma braais or a variety of *potjies*.

Mlilwane Wildlife Sanctuary *p820, map p820*
Reservations for all through **Big Game Parks**, T5283944/3, www.biggameparks.org.
AL Reilly's Rock Hilltop Lodge, or 'kaGogo', 3 km from the Main Camp. This is an exclusive 6-room period guesthouse and 4-bed family cottage, brimming with antiques and local history, en suite facilities, set in a lush tract of botanical gardens with fabulous views of the game sanctuary. Rates include entry, dinner, bed and breakfast. This is the original home of Ted Reilly's father and the main house dates back 100 years. Recommended.
D-F Main Camp, a mixture of stone cottages, thatched rondavels and traditional domed Swazi thatched huts known as the Beehive Village, many are en suite, or there's a neat ablution block, camping ground under the shade of eucalyptus trees, self-catering facilities, bedding provided. **Note** If you are self-catering, watch your food – the local warthogs don't think twice about foraging in tents or kitchen huts. **Hippo Haunt** restaurant with a lovely deck overlooking a hippo pool. Warthogs, ostriches and impalas frequently wander through the grounds. Swimming pool. Traditional dancing team, made up of park staff, performs on a nightly basis in The iNkhundla, a boma in the Main Camp.
E-F Sondzela Backpackers, 15 mins' walk from the main camp. Excellent backpackers in a stunning setting overlooking the Nyonyane Mountains, in the centre of the reserve. Spotless dorms, twins and doubles in the large main house, plus very comfortable and spacious thatched rondavels sleeping up to 4, with shared ablutions. Camping, tents and bedding can be hired, pool, volleyball court, bar with pool table. Great meals served around a roaring fire, shop selling basic food, ATM machine. Travel desk can arrange a wide choice of tours in the area, making this a great choice for people without their own transport. **Baz Bus** stop. Excellent value, good fun and in a beautiful setting – one of the best budget options in the country. Highly recommended.

Mantenga Nature Reserve *p821*
D Mantenga Tented Camp, T4161151, www.sntc.org.sz. 20 en suite tents on stilts with hard-cover roofs climbing up the mountain, some with views of the river. Game is present, sandy paths lead to the **Village Restaurant** in the reserve.

Malkerns Valley *p822*
A-B Forester's Arms, 12 km out of Bhunya, T4674177, www.forestersarms.co.za. Delightful hotel set in the cool Great Usuthu highlands with a number of pretty waterfalls and surrounded by forest in its own colourful garden. 30 en suite rooms, colourful decor, restaurant which serves excellent meals and caters for vegetarians, cosy pub with log fire, it's less than 40 km away from the Nerston/Sandlane border so people from South Africa come here for the famous Sunday lunch, and occasional Swazi dancing performed in the evenings. Swimming pool, sauna, trout and bass fishing in the local dams, tennis and squash courts, hiking, horse riding from their own stables, mountain bikes for hire. Rates include dinner, bed and breakfast.
C Malandela's, Malkerns Rd, T5283448, malandelas@africaonline.co.sz. New set-up, attached to an excellent restaurant and the House on Fire venue. Set in quiet gardens, pool, 8 stylish en suite double rooms and 2 family units, Afro-chic decor, family-run, friendly staff, great addition to the area. Recommended.
E Swaziland Backpackers, near the turn-off to Malkerns Rd, T5282038, swazilandback packers@realnet.co.sz. Dorms, doubles, camping, internet and laundry facilities. The main house has a comfy lounge, pretty gardens with pool, jacuzzi and hammocks, communal kitchen for self-catering or meals provided with advance notice. Range of tours on offer, including free hikes in the area. The Baz Bus stays overnight here on the route between Durban and Johannesburg.

🍴 Eating

Mbabane *p818, map p818*

🍴 La Casserole, Omni Centre, Gwamile St, T4046426. Open 0900-late. Smart restaurant serving German and international cuisine, fully licenced, pizza oven, afternoon teas, outside patio, relaxed, charming atmosphere.

🍴 Finesse, New Mall, T4045936. Mon-Sat 1100-late. French-owned à la carte restaurant with a seasonal menu, excellent seafood such as lobster with vanilla sauce or oriental prawns and Mozambique chicken.

🍴 Friar Tuck's, **Mountain Inn**, T4042781. Open 1200-1400, 1900-2200. Good quality hotel restaurant in a somewhat dark vaulted cellar, also has pleasant outside tables on the patio overlooking the pool with great views, filling buffet lunches, and à la carte evening menu.

🍴 The Mediterranean, Gwamile St, T4043212. Mon-Sat 0930-late, Sun 1630-late. Despite the name, this serves Indian cuisine, excellent and cheap curries, seafood including superb prawns, snacks, fully licensed, good South African and Portuguese wines, takeaway service, all food is halal, good choice for vegetarians. Also has a bar with large-screen TV for sports.

Ezulwini Valley *p819, map p820*

🍴 Calabash, close to **Timbali Lodge**, T4161187. Delicious German, Swiss and Austrian meals and seafood, Becks beer on draught, lovely wooden wine cellar where you can choose a bottle, a very popular venue, one of Swaziland's top à la carte restaurants, booking advised.

🍴 Malandela's, T5283115. Excellent restaurant in a stylish setting, surrounded by gardens, pleasant shady deck, great menu, fusion food mixing African and European dishes. Also has a popular pub and is attached to the **House on Fire** live music venue.

🍴 Sirloin Steakhouse and **Bella Vista Pizzeria**, in the **Happy Valley Motel**, T4161061. Mon-Sat until 0200. Both serve hearty, good-value portions, good atmosphere, booth seating.

🍴 Village Café, Mantenga Nature Reserve. Open all day for breakfast, lunch and dinner, plus teas and coffees. Specializing in dishes such as stroganoff made from game meat and peri-peri chicken livers, there's late bar, and it's a great place for a sundowner on the wooden deck. Also has weekly braais at the waterfalls.

🍴 Woodlands, between **Royal Swazi Sun** and **The Gables** mall, T4163466. Smart addition to the valley, airy dining room serving good international cuisine, open 1100-late, popular Sun buffets.

🍴 Kanimambo, in the Gables mall, T4163549. Tue-Sun 1200-1900. Day-time restaurant in the confines of a mall serving Portuguese and continental cuisine including good peri-peri chicken.

🎭 Entertainment

Ezulwini Valley *p819, map p820*

House on Fire, Malkerns Rd, T5282100, www.house-on-fire.com. Excellent new venue which has quickly become the country's leading spot for live music. Open air, extravagant, funky decor including colourful, mirrored mosaics, surreal statues, moulded seating area around circular stage. Rock music and live jazz on most nights.

Why Not Disco & Night Club and **If Not Go-Go Bar** (adult cabaret), T4161061. Swaziland institution that has been going for decades, at the weekends bands perform here, all very tacky but fun. Open nightly except Sun at 2200, live bands/cabaret acts at 2345 and 0100.

🛍 Shopping

Mbabane *p818, map p818*

Crafts and curios

African Fantasy, the Mall in Mbabane, the Mantenga Craft Centre and The Gables,

Ezulwini Valley, T4040205. A wide selection of curios. Look out for Swazi candles, made in the Malkerns Valley.
Swazi Market, Msunduza Rd, at the end of Gwamile St. A full range of curios from all over the country, although you will have to haggle for the best bargains. The fruit and vegetable market is here too and is an excellent place to buy fresh guavas, mangoes, lychees and other tropical fruits.

Shopping malls
Swazi Plaza, **The Mall** and **New Mall**, are all within walking distance of each other on OK Link Rd. They are large, covered, modern malls with department stores, banks, pharmacies, travel agents, cafés and restaurants. There's a Shoprite at Swazi Plaza and a Spar at the Mall.

Ezulwini Valley p819, map p820
The main road passing through the valley is lined with craft stalls selling a good range of handmade curios. See also page 822 for details of the **Mantenga Craft Centre** and page 822 for craft shops in the Malkerns Valley. **The Gables** is a modern shopping mall.

▲ Activities and tours

Ezulwini Valley p819, map p820
Royal Swazi Spa, T4161164, hugely popular resort, mainly for the intriguingly named 'cuddle puddle', a swimming pool fed by a hot natural mineral spring. Housed in dome-shaped buildings modelled on a Swazi village, there are 2 large saunas, 2 indoor hot mineral pools, cold plunge pools, whirl and bubble bath, an aromatherapy steam-tube. Also has a gym.

Tour operators
Swazi Trails, Mantenga Craft Centre, Ezulwini Valley, T4162180; T011-7041975 (South Africa), www.swazitrails.co.sz, is a leading countrywide tour operator that specializes in Swaziland culture, wildlife and adventure

tours, including caving, whitewater rafting and hiking. The new activity is an 8-km quad-bike trail in the Ezulwini Valley. All the guides are local Swazis with excellent local knowledge. Swazi Trails also manages an excellent community tourism initiative and part of the fee you pay goes to the local Mphaphati community.

⊖ Transport

Mbabane p818, map p818
Bus
The South African **Baz Bus**, T021-4392323, www.bazbus.com, includes Swaziland on its route 3 times a week.

Car hire
Avis and **Imperial** have desks at Matsapha Airport near Manzini (see page 833). **Affordable Car Hire**, Swazi Plaza, T4049136, affordable@posix.co.za. It is also possible to drive South African hire cars as long as you have a covering letter from the company you hired the car from, so remember to mention this when you hire it.

⊕ Directory

Mbabane p818, map p818
Embassies and consulates Most countries deal with consular services for Swaziland through their embassies or high commissions in Pretoria (see page 599). **Germany**, Dhlan'ubeka House, Tin and Mhlonhlo streets, T404 3174. **Mozambique**, Gwamile St, T4043700. **Portugal**, Portuguese Club, OK Rd, T4046780. **South Africa**, 2nd floor, New Mall, Dr Sishayi Rd, T4044651; **US**, 2350 Mbabane Place, T4042445, www.swaziland.usembassy.gov.
Emergencies Police, T4042221, emergency T999. **Medical services** **Mbabane Clinic** (private), St Michael St, T4042423. **Mbabane Government Hospital**, Usutu Rd, T4042111.

Central and southern Swaziland

The central and southern regions of Swaziland are home to the country's now healthy populations of big game including rhino, elephant, lion and cheetah. Big Game Parks manage the Hlane Royal National Park and Mkhaya Game Reserve where game drives and other activities are on offer. Meanwhile there's good hiking in the Lebombo Mountains in the smaller private nature reserves. ➤➤ *For Sleeping, Eating and other listings, see pages 832-833.*

Manzini ●❶❷ ➤➤ *pp832-833. Colour map 2, C5.*

Manzini and its outlying districts comprises of Swaziland's largest urban population. The town is an industrial centre with a brewery, a meat-processing plant and electronics factories that attract commuter labourers from outlying areas. The industrial atmosphere is not particularly pleasant and there is little of interest for the visitor. The **market** ① *corner of Mhlakuvane St and Mancishane Rd, Thu*, brings the local farming communities into town once a week and is worth a browse. This is one of the busiest local markets in Swaziland, selling fresh fruit and vegetables, clothes, a good selection of curios and freshly cooked snacks. The **Bhunu Mall** on Ngwane Street and **The Hub** on Mhlakuzane Street are Manzini's newest shopping centres. Tiger-City on Villiers Street is a small complex where the cinema and a couple of restaurants are located.

Background
The first trading station was opened here in 1885 and was originally run from a tent. The plot was later sold on to Alfred Bremer who built a hotel and a shop. Manzini was originally known as Bremersdorp after Alfred Bremer, but it was renamed Manzini after the Boers burnt the settlement to the ground during the Anglo Boer War. The administrative centre then moved to Mbabane. In 1894, while Swaziland was being administrated by a temporary government composed of representatives of the Transvaal, the British government and the king, the headquarters were in the local hotel.

Hlane Royal National Park ● ➤➤ *pp832-833. Colour map 2, C5.*

① *T5283943, www.biggameparks.org. Park gates close at sunset, notify in advance if you think your arrival will be after dark. E25 per person.*

Formerly a royal hunting ground, Hlane was declared a protected area in 1967 by King Sobhuza II. Covering 30,000 ha, this is the kingdom's largest protected area. Following heavy poaching in the 1960s, the park has been restocked by **Big Game Parks**, with wildlife from neighbouring countries as well as species propagated at Mkhaya Game Reserve. A number of predators have been reintroduced and the park now has healthy numbers of lion, cheetah and leopard. Other game includes elephant, white rhino, herds of wildebeest, and zebra, kudu, steenbuck, bushbuck, giraffe, impala, hyena and jackal. In the past, poaching was such a serious problem that the rhino had to have their horns removed for their own protection. Hlane supports the densest population of raptors in the kingdom, with vultures in particular being very visible at kills and waterholes. The nesting density for the white-backed vulture is the highest in the whole of Africa, and the most southerly nesting colony of marabou stork is found here. Birdlife in and around the two camps is prolific.

Ted Reilly and wildlife conservation in Swaziland

Like the rest of Africa, Swaziland used to teem with game before the Europeans arrived in the mid-1800s with guns, modern farming methods and medical knowledge. Morality went downhill, the human population flourished and the need for space meant that the wildlife was doomed. This was followed by other problems. The cattle plague, *rinderpest*, reached Swaziland by 1896, wiping out not only cattle but many antelope which led to the death by starvation of many predators. During the 1930s the so-called 'wildebeest scourge' led to one of the most shocking episodes in the history of wildlife conservation. A great number of wildebeest entered Swaziland following a migratory route, as they had for centuries. Their invasion of farmland led to them being declared vermin and they were exterminated by any possible means. Whole herds were wiped out by machine guns and drinking water was poisoned, the latter undoubtedly causing the deaths of many other animals and birds. By 1960, most of Swaziland's remaining game had been decimated by uncontrolled hunting, poaching and by rapid commercial and agricultural development. The preservation of the few wild animals that survived, and the reintroduction of species that had become extinct, was largely due to the efforts of two men – the late King Sobhuza II and Ted Reilly, founder of Mlilwane Wildlife Sanctuary. In 1963, Reilly turned the family farm in the Ezulwini Valley into a game reserve, planted indigenous trees, created wetland habitat, and began a game restocking programme. Meanwhile the king asked Reilly to help stamp out poaching in the royal reserve of Hlane, and for three decades Reilly embarked on a near-military campaign to eradicate poaching in Swaziland. In 1967, Sobhuza declared Hlane a protected national park and it was restocked with wildlife from neighbouring countries. The Reilly family then donated Mlilwane to a non-profit-making trust in 1969 and it has since grown to 10 times it original size. All of Swazi's parks are now home to substantial numbers of game and at least some of the country again looks like it did 150 years ago. Without Ted Reilly and King Sobhuza II, the Swaziland game reserves would simply not exist. Today the Reilly family still live at Mlilwane where they manage Big Game Parks. Ted's daughter, Anne, contributed information to this book.

Ins and outs

Getting there The park is 67 km from Manzini towards Simunye, where the main road bisects the park. Turn left into the Ngongoni Gate, where all arrivals must report.

Sights

The western area of the park is linked with a network of roads which the visitor can use for game viewing. The area around the **Black Mbuluzi River** attracts animals during the dry winter season. Close to Ndlovu camp is an **Endangered Species area**, where elephant and rhino have been concentrated for security reasons. The **Mahlindza waterhole**, with its hippo, crocodile and waterbird population, is one of the most peaceful picnic sites in the country. A wide range of activities are offer in the park include guided walks, guided mountain biking, horse riding trails, full-day Land Rover tours with lunch, and two-hour game drives (day or night). There are two camps in the park (see page 832), or you can visit on a guided day trip 1000-1600, which includes game drives and lunch. These can all be booked at the park office, or through Big Game Parks, where you can also pick up a guide to accompany you in your own car to a nearby Swazi village 20 km from the park gates.

Simunye ⊜𝟕 ➤ pp832-833. Colour map 2, C5.

Simunye is a small town that is quite unusual in that the centre lies behind the boom gate of the Royal Swazi Sugar Corporation that owns the surrounding sugar plantations. There is nothing much here but it is a stop-off en route to Hlane, Mlawula and the border with Mozambique at Lomahasha/Namaacha. The main road to Simunye coming north skirts Hlane Game Sanctuary and there are amusing if sobering signposts warning cyclists and pedestrians to beware of lion and elephant.

Mlawula Nature Reserve ⊜ ➤ pp832-833. Colour map 2, C5.

① *Reservations: National Trust Commission, T4161151, www.sntc.org.sz. Daily entrance charge E25.*
Mlawula is signposted after Simunye and Hlane. The nature reserve covers an area extending from the Lebombo Mountains down to the lowveld and is part of the greater Lubombo Conservancy. The Siphiso Valley and the Mbuluzi Gorge are good areas for game viewing on hiking trails or game drives.

Ins and outs
Best time to visit Summers are hot and humid with high rainfall, the winters are warm and dry although they can be cold at night with the occasional frost. The best time for birdwatching is between September and October.

Sights
This is a region of amazing and varied scenery ranging from Lebombo Mountain forest to dry thorn savanna and coastal thickets. The reserve is criss-crossed with 33 m of rough roads for self-guided tours. Over 1000 species of plant have been identified here although this region is best known for its birdlife: 350 species have been recorded including African fin foot, crested guinea fowl and yellow spotted nicator, and facilities include the vulture feeding area and the bird hide. The **Mbuluzi Gorge** is an excellent area for birdwatching but the road is not always in good condition. The game likely to be seen in the reserve includes kudu, oribi, mountain reedbuck, samango monkeys, and Sharpe's grysbok, but sadly there are no longer any rhino. Early traces of *homo sapiens* dating back 100,000 years have been found in the riverbeds of the Mbuluzi and Mlawula rivers, good places to spot crocodiles. Many of the animals which are protected here are particularly difficult to spot and include rare species of reptile and amphibian. The interesting plantlife includes the rare Lebombo ironwood and the *encephalartos umeluziensis*, a cycad that only grows in the deep mountain valleys of the reserve. Visitors to the reserve are encouraged to hike on the network of trails, which pass through beautiful gorges, pools, waterfalls and rapids with views over Mozambique from the top of the escarpment. There is a leaflet on the trails and the reserve available from the camp shop where you can also pick up a guide to go with you.

To South Africa via Lavumisa → *Colour map 2, C5.*

Lavumisa is a busy border post which most travellers pass through on their way to Big Bend or into KwaZulu Natal. There is one main street lined with snack bars and petrol stations.

Border opening hours 0700-2200.

Public transport The bus station is on the main street and buses regularly depart for Big Bend, Manzini and Mbabane.

Shewula Nature Reserve ● ▸▸ *pp832-833.*

① *T6051160, www.shewulacamp.com.*

The community-owned Shewula Nature Reserve just north of Mlawula is also part of the Lebombo Conservancy, straddling the 500-m high Lebombo Mountains on the border with Mozambique and covering an escarpment of ancient ironwood mountain forest stretching down the Mbuluzi River. The views from the **Shewula Mountain Camp**, which is literally perched on top of a mountain, are incredible – on a clear day the high-rise blocks of Maputo can be seen to the east, and there is an uninterrupted 100-km view across Swaziland.

Ins and outs

The Shewula turning is 10 km south of the Lomahasha/Namaacha border with Mozambique. The camp is a further 30-minute drive from here. Apart from during heavy rains (December to February) it is accessible by ordinary saloon cars. When the road is too muddy, it is possible to leave your vehicle at the chief's office in the village, and be transported in a 4WD.

Manzini to Mahamba ● ▸▸ *pp832-833.*

Grand Valley

The drive down through Grand Valley passes through beautiful mountain scenery with cliff faces rising above the Mkhondvo River and forests on either side of the road. The MR9 passes through the village of **Hlatikulu** before reaching Nhlangano. The weather here is often misty with drizzle, which for many is a welcome relief after the hot and humid plains.

Nhlangano → *Colour map 2, C5.*

Nhlangano means 'meeting place' and was named to commemorate when King Sobhuza II met King George VI here in 1947. This used to be a popular resort with South African tourists who crossed the border to gamble and watch films which were banned at home. Since the end of Apartheid, the number of South African visitors has fallen sharply. There is a small shopping centre in town and a market. Buses depart from the station next to the mall to Manzini, Mahamba and Lavumisa.

Mahamba border post

The MR9 continues south to the border at Mahamba, daily 0700-2200. The routes into South Africa from here lead to Piet Retief in Mpumalanga.

Mkhaya Game Reserve → Colour map 2, C5.
ⓘ Access by prior reservation only, T5283943, www.biggameparks.org.

This small reserve, one of the best places in southern Africa to see black rhino, is Swaziland's most exclusive reserve, set in an area of acacia lowveld southeast of Manzini. Mkhaya was established as a game reserve in 1979 to protect the Nguni breed of long-horned cattle from extinction that today graze among the zebra and wildebeest, but it has expanded over the years to include other endangered species such as black rhino, roan and sable antelope, tsessebe, white rhino, and elephant. In 1995 the park received six black rhino from South Africa, a project funded, rather oddly, by the Taiwanese Government, and during 1997 the first two baby elephant to be born in Swaziland in 100 years were born at Mkhaya. At present the only large cat you might see is the leopard. The birdlife here is interesting and there are chances of seeing a good number of raptors including bateleur, booted, martial and tawny eagles. The summers here are very hot and humid with potentially heavy thunderstorms, while in winter the climate is warm during the day and cool at night.

Ins and outs Travelling from Mbabane and Ezulwini Valley go through Manzini; 8 km after Manzini take a right turn and continue towards Big Bend. The reserve is signposted to the left after about 11 km. If you are approaching from Durban via the Lavumisa border follow the road to Big Bend and then Siphofaneni. The turning is on the right, 22 km after Big Bend. All visitors are met at the locked gates by a ranger. This is a private reserve and guests must arrange to arrive at either 1000 and 1600 when the rangers will pick you up. Cars are parked at the gate. Mkhaya is a private reserve and it can be visited by prior reservation as an overnight visitor staying at the tented safari camp. Open-top Land Rover game drives are the main activity, with the opportunity to take guided bush walks, all promising close contact with a variety of big game. Rates include all activities. Day visitors can pre-arrange to meet guides at the gate at 1000 for game drives and lunch and are returned to their cars at 1600.

Big Bend → Colour map 2, C5.
Big Bend is named after the loop of the Lusutfu River that passes by the town. The land around Big Bend is covered in sugar plantations and the Ubombo Ranches sugarmill in town is the area's main processing centre. The terrain here is very similar to South Africa's northern KwaZulu Natal, which is only 50 km to the south. The town is a quiet, neatly laid out settlement with a small shopping centre and craft centre, **Emoya Crafts**, which sells crafts from all over Swaziland – ethnic clothing, glassware, candles, cotton rugs, place mats, tablecloths, batiks, baskets and ethnic jewellery.

Nisela Safaris
ⓘ T3030318, www.niselasafaris.co.za. Day visitors E10, for game drives and walks there needs to be a minimum of 6 people.

Nisela Safaris is a fairly new private game lodge development nestled at the foot of the Lebombo Mountains, near the village of Nsoko, 30 km south from Big Bend on the road to the Lavumisa border, which is a further 20 km. This is a small private reserve where game including lion, wilderbeest, giraffe, and zebra have been introduced; existing populations of nyala, red and grey duiker, jackal, bushbuck, reedbuck and steenbok are also present. Day visitors can pre-book game drives and there are also a number of hand-reared lion cubs to visit near the entrance gate where there is also a reptile park, coffee shop and curio stall.

Central and southern Swaziland

Hotel and guesthouse prices
L over US$300 **AL** US$220-300 **A** US$150-220
B US$100-150 **C** US$75-100 **D** US$35-75
E US$15-35 **F** under US$15
Restaurant prices
††† over US$30 †† US$15-30 † under US$15
See pages 46-51 for further information.

● Sleeping

Manzini p827

B Tum's George Hotel, corner of Ngwane and Du Toit streets, T5052260, www.tgh.sz. 53 a/c comfortable rooms with DSTV, buffets and set menus in the main dining room, à la carte menu in **St Georges Pub & Lounge**, generous Sun lunch around the swimming pool, conference facilities, secure parking.

Hlane Royal National Park p827

Reservations: T5283943, www.biggame parks.org. Traditional dance performances, open-air bar and restaurant at Ndlovu but in Bhubesi visitors must be fully self-sufficient.
C-D Bhubesi Camp, 6 self-catering stone cottages, 2 bedrooms, bathroom, kitchenette, bedding and towels, electricity, a beautiful setting overlooking the Umbuluzana River.
C-F Ndlovu Camp, 14 en suite rondavels sleeping 2; 7 en suite thatched family cottages sleeping up to 8. Bedding, towels, cutlery and crockery provided, hot outside showers. No electricity, paraffin lanterns provide light, fridges are gas powered and cooking is over an open fire, a camp assistant will help with this and he keeps the fire going all day, you just need to bring food, or eat at the camp restaurant. Next to a waterhole. A small shop sells some provisions and curios; game activities can be organized. There are few simple camping sites nearby, with an ablution block at Ndlovu Camp.

Simunye p829

C-D Simunye Country Club, once through the boom gate turn right (15-min drive to Mozambique, and 30 mins to South African

borders), T3134758, www.visit swazi.com. Owned by the Royal Swazi Sugar Corporation. There's a variety of cheap single rooms, self-catering houses and flats. Pool, very good restaurant, 3 bars, one serving pizza and filled wraps, TV lounge. Tennis, squash and gym available for a nominal fee. Accommodation is nothing special but facilities are good.

Mlawula Nature Reserve p829

Reservations: T4161151, www.sntc.org.sz.
C-F Mapelepele, self-catering cottage sleeping 4. Nearby campsite on the banks of the usually dry Sipisi stream with an ablution block and cooking facilities, firewood available.
D Tented camp, 4 tents sleeping 2, each with braai area, communal lounge and kitchen, bring all your own food. The highlight here is the position of the tents, perched on the edge of a sheer cliff with outstanding views and the outside bathrooms have a boiler heated by fire and a galvanized bath tub hidden in a cleft of rock on the cliff edge.

Shewula Nature Reserve p830

E-F Shewula Mountain Camp, T6051160, www.shewulacamp.com. Beautiful hilltop setting, community-owned, 4 huts sleeping up to 6, camping ground, shared ablution block and kitchen, no electricity, but there are gas stoves and fridge, paraffin lamps, hot showers. Bedding is not supplied so you will need a sleeping bag. Traditional meals can be ordered, prepared by local families. Activities include guided nature walks, swimming in the river, cultural tours around the villages.

Manzini to Mahamba p830

C Phumula Guesthouse, 10 km before the Mahamba border post, T2079099, www.phu mulaguesthouse.co.za. Farm guesthouse not far from Nhlangano with 11 comfortable rooms in modern garden units, DSTV, ceiling fans and electric blankets, some with patios, bass fishing can be arranged in the farm dam, 3-course candlelit dinners on request.

Mkhaya Game Reserve p831
Access by prior reservation only, T5283943, www.biggameparks.org. Rates include entry, 3 meals and 3 guided game-viewing trips.
L Stone Camp, 12 self-contained stone and thatched cottages sleeping 3-5 shaded by hardwood forest, thatched summerhouse, meals, prepared by the camp staff, are served with South African wines. One of Swaziland's most comfortable game-viewing experiences.

Big Bend p831
D The New Bend Inn, on a hill to the south of town, T3636855. 25 a/c plain but adequate en suite rooms with TV, à la carte restaurant, indoor and outdoor bars, swimming pool, snooker, gets very lively at the weekends.

Nisela Safaris p831
Reservations T3030318, www.niselasafaris.co.za.
C Game Lodge, 5 luxury thatched rooms sleeping 2-4. The pool, bar, and restaurant here is used by guests in all the facilities.
C Rondavels, 7 a/c rondavels sleeping 4 with mezzanine floor and spacious bathrooms.
D Guest House, 10 rooms in a very pleasant colonial house, B&B, en suite, a/c and ceiling fans, attractive lawns surrounding the house.
D-E Overland Camp, 2 4-bed rustic self-catering chalets, 16 km into the bush on a dirt road, only accessible by 4WD.
E Beehive Village, traditional Swazi grass huts with twin beds, shared ablution block and kitchen. There's also a campsite.

🍴 Eating

Manzini p827
† Fontana di Trevi Pizzeria, The Hub, corner of Villiers and Mhlakuvane streets, T5053608. Mon-Thu and Sun 1000-1800, Fri-Sat 1000-2200. Standard coffee shop and good-value pizzas and pasta dishes throughout the day.
† Gil Vicente, Martin St, Ilanga Centre, T5053874. Tue-Sun 0830-2400. Good-value Portuguese dishes (good peri-peri chicken) in the boring environs of a shopping centre.

Simunye p831
†† Simunye Club Restaurant, Simunye Country Club, T3134758, www.visitswazi.com. Has a popular family restaurant, à la carte menu and carvery lunches on weekdays, pizzas, braais every Fri evening, seating on terrace.

Big Bend p831
†† Lismore, Lismore Lodge, T6366080. Open 0700-2300. Small restaurant specializing in seafood from Mozambique, also has good mountain trout, and Portuguese dishes including a full charcoal-grilled chicken to share.

⊖ Transport

Manzini p821
Air
Matsapha International Airport, T5186192, also referred to as Manzini International Airport, is 8 km from Manzini. There is an airport departure tax, E50. There are buses and minibus taxis going to Manzini and Mbabane. **Swazi Express** has daily flights between Swaziland and **Johannesburg** and weekday flights linking **Swaziland** with **Maputo** and **Vilanculos** (Mozambique) and **Durban**. **South African Airways** has at least 4 daily flights to and from **Jo'burg**.

Airline offices South African Airways (SAA), reservations South Africa, T011-9781111, ww2.flysaa.co.za. **Swazi Express**, 15186840, T031-4081115 (South Africa), www.flyswazi.com.

Bus
Buses and minibus taxis leave from the bus station on Louw St to **Mbabane**, **Big Bend**, **Lavumisa**, **Nhlangano** and **Mahamba**.

Car hire
There are offices at the airport for **Avis**, T5186266, www.avis.co.za, and **Imperial**, T5184393, www.imperialcarrental.co.za.

Big Bend p831
Buses to **Manzini**, **Mbabane** and **Lavumisa**.

Northern districts

The only settlement of note between Mbabane and South Africa is Motjane, where the MR1 branches north to Malolotja Nature Reserve and Pigg's Peak. There are a couple of good places to stay in this region. ►► *For Sleeping, Eating and other listings, see page 836.*

Mbabane to South Africa ● ►► *p836.*

Motjana and around
Motjane is a good centre for curio items. **Ngwenya Glass** ① *5 km before the border, T4424053, www.ngwenyaglass.co.sz, 0830-1730,* and attached coffee shop is a popular stop-off for coach parties. All the items for sale are made from 100% recycled glass, and you can watch glass blowers do their thing. A kilometre or so on the road behind the glass factory is **Endlotane Studios** ① *T4424940, www.endlotane.net,* which sells a varied collection of crafts from mohair tapestries to rugs, wall hangings, paintings, woodcrafts and pottery.

The border with South Africa is west of Motjane at **Ngwenya/Oshoek** ① *23 km from Mbabane, daily 0700-2200.* **Tourist information** ① *T4424206,* is available here. Close to the border post are numerous curio stalls, worth a glance if you are leaving Swaziland. Buses to the capital and the rest of the country depart from Ngwenya.

The road north from Motjane is the MR1; 9 km along this road is the small **Hawane Nature Reserve** and dam. As the surfaced road heads north it passes through the small settlement of **Forbes Reef**. A general store is the centre of activity here, hidden close by are the remains of a long-abandoned gold mine.

Hawane Nature Reserve Reserve
① *T4161151, www.sntc.org.sz.*
Established in 1978, this small nature reserve protects an area of wetlands along the Mbuluzi river. When the Hawane Dam was built in 1988, the reserve was extended to protect the area's water supply. The main reason for coming here is for the excellent birdwatching, with many rare species being attracted by the river and dam. Look out for the endangered red hot poker plant, which can be found here. There is a good birdwatching trail set out in the park. Other activities include horseback trails, available from the **Hawane Resort** (see page 836).

Malolotja Nature Reserve ● ►► *p836. Colour map 2, C5.*

Malolotja is a wild region of mountains and forest along the northwestern border with Mpumalanga, offering the country's finest hiking with challenging landscapes and altitudes rising from 615 m to 1800 m. Mgwayiza, Ngwenya (1829 m) and Silotfwane (1680 m) are three of Swaziland's highest peaks and local hikes cross deep forested ravines, high plateaux and grasslands dotted with waterfalls. Archaeological remains show that this region has been inhabited for thousands of years and the site of the world's oldest mine, thought to be 43,000 years old, is within the park. The diggings were used to excavate red and black earth, possibly for use as pigments.

Ins and outs

Getting there From the MR3 there is a turning at Motjane on to the MR1 heading north to Pigg's Peak. The turning into the reserve, easily identified by the collection of curio sellers (look out for the fine soapstone sculptures), is 7 km from the junction of the two roads and the park gates are a further 18 km from the MR1. Be wary of traffic along this road; there are a few precipitous drops and the buses tend to drive down in the middle of the road.

Best time to visit The weather can change suddenly with rain and fog closing in without warning. The summers here are hot and humid with heavy rains. Winter is warm and dry but the nights can be bitterly cold with occasional frost.

Wildlife

There is a chance of seeing blesbok, klipspringer, oribi, zebra and both blue and black wildebeest, and surplus game from other reserves is gradually being introduced. Rare plants here include aloes, Barberton and Kaapasche Hoop cycads, proteas, orchids and fever trees. The small herbarium at the main camp has a good collection of unusual plants. Malolotja is an excellent area for birdwatching, and over 280 species have been recorded here. There is a breeding colony of the rare bald ibis at the **Malolotja Falls** which drop an impressive 90 m into the Nkomati River. This is also a site for breeding blue swallows and the blue crane. There is a 25-km network of gravel roads for self-guided game drives but the best way to see the park is on foot by going on one of the many hiking trails. The longest is 7 km and leads up to the 95-m Malolotja Falls. Maps for the overnight hiking trails, information brochures and wildlife lists are all available from the Malolotja camp office.

Further north ⬤ ➤ p836.

Pigg's Peak → Colour map 2, C5.

The MR1 continues north and on the right is the new Maguga Dam, some 12 km south of Pigg's Peak. A joint venture with South Africa, the Komati River was damned in 2002 and has now formed a picturesque lake surrounded by green hills. There's an alternative Maguga Dam loop road to Pigg's Peak, that veers off 26 km north of Motjane, which offers view points. Pigg's Peak is a small, straggling town was named after William Pigg, a French gold prospector who came here in 1884. There was a working gold mine here until 1954, although no great fortunes were ever recovered. There's nothing here to warrant a stop, other than to stock up on cool drinks and petrol. From Pigg's Peak, the MR20 dirt road, heads west to the border post at **Bulembu/Josefsdal** (daily 0800-1600).

Phophonyane Nature Reserve

Look out for a signpost for Phophonyane Lodge and Reserve about 15 km after Pigg's Peak. This is one of the most beautiful and relatively unspoilt patches of Swazi countryside, including dense riverine forest, home to small mammals such as duiker, bushbuck and the clawless otter. A number of 4WD and walking trails have been set out, including to the **Phophonyane Falls** – some of the best known falls in Swaziland. An artificial swimming pool has been created in the rocks just below the lower Phophonyane Falls. There is another scenic route north on a tarred road through Rocklands and Hhohho to the border post at **Matsamo/Jeppe's Reef** to Barberton in South Africa (daily 0800-2000).

Northern districts listings

Hotel and guesthouse prices
L over US$300 **AL** US$220-300 **A** US$150-220
B US$100-150 **C** US$75-100 **D** US$35-75
E US$15-35 **F** under US$15
Restaurant prices
††† over US$30 †† US$15-30 † under US$15
See pages 46-51 for further information.

◓ Sleeping

Mbabane to South Africa *p834*
C-F Hawane Resort, 9 km from Ngwenya/
Oshoek border post and 2 km south of
Malolotja, T4424744, www.hawane.co.sz.
23 luxury chalets, intriguing mix of traditional
Swazi and contemporary architecture, stylish
decor with splashes of bright colour. Also
22 backpacker beds arranged in twin units
in a converted barn. Excellent restaurant
serving fusion cuisine in a stylish open-plan
dining room. Also has a bright lounge area,
swimming pool, sauna and outside bar.
The whole set-up is on the banks of the
Hawana Dam which is good for birdwatching and safe for swimming and the
Hawane Stables can organize horse and
pony treks in the surrounding countryside.
An excellent set-up for all budgets.
E-F Sobantu Guest Farm, 26 km north of
Motjane look out for the turning to Maguga
Dam, the farm is 6 km on this dirt road,
T6053954, www.swaziplace.com/sobantu.
A backpacker place with basic doubles,
dormitories and camping space, nice
farmland views, bar, kitchen (you can buy
organic vegetables), or meals provided,
short hikes through the farm or borrow
the mountain bike, swimming in the
dam or nearby rock pools. Will pick up
from Pigg's Peak or Mbabane.

Malotja Nature Reserve *p834*
Reservations: T4161151, www.sntc.org.sz.
D Log cabins, 13 self-catering cabins,
sleeping up to 6, fully equipped, set in
a beautiful mountain location.

Camping
The main site has room for 15 tents
or caravans, an ablution block and a
communal cooking area, firewood
available. There are very basic campsites
along the hiking trails but you will need
to be totally self-sufficient, and as no fires
are allowed outside the main campsite,
a portable cooker is essential.

Phophonyane Nature Reserve *p835*
C Phophonyane Lodge, 3km off the
MR1, T4371429, www.phophonyane.co.sz.
Designed for peace and privacy, 23 guests
sleep in luxury cottages and tented camps,
perched on stilts for fabulous private
balconies. Some units are self-catering.
Good à la carte restaurant, **Driftwood** bar
has a prime location on a balcony
overlooking the river. Recommended.

Pigg's Peak *p835*
B Orion Pigg's Peak, 10 km northeast of
Pigg's Peak, T4371104, www.oriongroup.co.za.
103 upmarket rooms set in a vast unattractive
block but in a beautiful setting, en suite
bathrooms, TV, telephone, great views of
the deeply forested Phophonyane Valley
from every balcony, 2 restaurants, 4 bars,
nightclub, swimming pool with pool bar,
tennis courts, squash courts, bowls, horse
stables, gym, sauna, casino, live
entertainment most nights, set in
beautiful highlands.

Contents

Footprint features

Background

History

South Africa

History, and not just modern history, is often a very contentious issue in South Africa. During the Apartheid era, schoolchildren, both black and white, were taught a particularly lopsided version of the country's history. Since the end of Apartheid there have, of course, been massive moves towards rewriting the history books, but it remains a field of conflict between left and right. Not all the myths, or misconceptions, come from racist Apartheid historians and we will try to be even-handed in our approach. However, we start with one of the most important myths taught by Apartheid historians: that Europeans arrived at the Cape at just about the same time as African people were crossing the Limpopo River and migrating into present-day South Africa. It is one of the easier myths to dismiss.

Early humans in South Africa

South Africa is actually home to some of the oldest fossil human remains in the world. Three million-year-old fossil remains of an early human-like species *Australopithecus africanus*, have been discovered at a number of sites on the highveld. The exact way in which the evolution of the early human-like species into modern human took place is a matter of considerable debate amongst archaeologists. Whatever the exact timing and process of this evolution, by one million years ago a species that looked and behaved very much like modern humans, called *Homo erectus*, ranged far and wide across Asia, Africa and Europe. Within the last 100,000 years some of these groups seem to have developed still further into *Homo sapiens*, or modern humans. According to some archaeologists the earliest fossil remains anywhere in the world of modern man come from Klasies River mouth in Eastern Cape and Border Cave on the KwaZulu Natal border. They are dated as being more than 50,000 years old.

As elsewhere in the world, early humans in southern Africa were hunter-gatherers. They had stone tools to help with basic tasks. At first these tended to be large and multi-purpose but over time they became increasingly specialized and usually smaller. Early humans tended to live in small nomadic groups and their activities were largely dependent upon the particular environment they occupied. It is often assumed that the life of hunter-gatherers is necessarily harsh with very little leisure time, but anthropological studies of present-day hunter-gatherers indicates that this is probably not the case.

The Khoi and the San The fossil evidence of early humans in present-day South Africa confirms that the Apartheid myth of an unpopulated land is indeed simply fiction. However, Apartheid historians were too sophisticated in telling their particular stories to be put off by the presence of a few fossils. The argument was not so much that the land was totally empty when Europeans arrived but that it was not populated by the ancestors of the present-day African population of South Africa. The fossil remains, according to this argument, were of the ancestors of a totally separate race of people who were killed by the ancestors of the present-day African population as they migrated south.

Physical anthropologists working early in the 20th century believed that all humans fell into a small number of distinct race groups that had evolved independently from early human-like species. The Khoi and San people of southern Africa, called Hottentots or Bushmen by European settlers, were believed to have been one of these totally distinct race groups and to be the direct descendants of the early humans whose fossils are found across South Africa. More recent scientific studies, especially studies of the gene pools of present-day populations, indicate that this was not the case. While Khoi and San people may look racially distinct from other African peoples, they share many of the same genes (as do Europeans with Africans and so on). However, the perception that Khoi and San people were very different from other human groups and stuck in some sort of stone-age past where little ever changed, has lived on. While Khoi and San technologies had remained relatively unsophisticated, political units small and populations sparse, it is wrong to think that when Europeans first arrived at the tip of Africa they somehow encountered primitive stone-age people. These communities had changed and adapted over time and had long established trading contacts with other groups in southern Africa.

Up until about 20,000 years ago, the ancestors of the Khoi and San people were all hunter-gatherers living in small egalitarian communities of about 20 to 30 people. They were nomadic and moved with the herds of wild game as they undertook seasonal migrations. Their tools were made out of stone, water was stored in ostrich egg shells rather than pottery and they lived in caves or simple tents. As they were nomadic they had few personal possessions and there was no concept of personal possession of land or wealth. They spoke a series of similar languages distinctive for the large number of clicks and whistling noises included in their speech.

Given their lifestyle, few of their remains have been discovered by archaeologists, with one notable exception: their famous and beautiful cave paintings. These are found throughout southern Africa and usually depict hunting expeditions or the trance dances through which the San believed they could communicate with their dead ancestors. These paintings were at first monochrome but over time some artists began to experiment with colour. The contents also changed over time with later paintings showing domesticated animals, especially cattle and, after the arrival of Europeans, people holding guns.

Around 20,000 years ago some of these hunter-gatherer communities underwent a huge and relatively rapid change that was to have far reaching effects on their lifestyles. At this time a number of groups, probably sited in present-day northern Botswana, acquired domesticated livestock. The first livestock they had were fat-tailed sheep. These were probably originally domesticated in North Africa and the Middle East and the southern African hunter-gatherers traded for them with the Sudanic tribes who then occupied much of eastern Africa. Later they were able to acquire cattle from Bantu groups who migrated from the forest margins of West Africa into East and southern Africa.

The arrival of domesticated livestock radically altered the social relations within hunter-gatherer communities. With livestock came the concept of ownership of property and it was possible for one or two individuals to amass wealth and prestige. The people who acquired cattle also became more politically powerful and formed into larger groups under one or two chiefs. These groups, who became known as the Khoi, migrated south from present-day Botswana and occupied the coast zone of the Cape region from the Fish River right round to Namibia. The interior was occupied by San hunter-gatherers who maintained the smaller social units and a more egalitarian society. There was a large degree of interchange between these two peoples. The San hunters often raided the livestock herds of the Khoi, especially if these herds had displaced the wild animals upon which they relied and there is some evidence that the Khoi had San working for them as servants. There was also probably a large flow of people backwards and forwards between the two categories – If San acquired livestock they could become Khoi and if Khoi fell on hard times and lost all their cattle they could end up as San.

Arrival of the Bantu speakers There was also contact between the Khoi and San and other African peoples living in southern Africa. Apartheid history was right when it taught that these other African peoples had migrated into southern Africa from the north but got the dates wrong by some 1000 years. These newer arrivals, the ancestors of the vast majority of South Africa's present-day population, spoke a group of languages known as the Bantu group of languages. The people themselves are sometimes called Bantu people but this word is now associated with the racist institutions of the 1960s that used the name.

Bantu-speaking peoples began migrating into present-day South Africa about the period 500 AD, bringing with them new technologies, especially iron smelting and new domesticated livestock. The migration was not one big trek southwards but a whole series of small movements by groups of individuals setting off in search of new pastures and looking to establish new villages. Where they came into contact with San and Khoi groups occupying good pasture they tended to displace them, pushing them into the more marginal desert and mountain areas. Some groups occupied the highveld areas whilst others spread out along the fertile coastal strip that was later to become KwaZulu Natal and the Eastern Cape. The peoples who settled along the coastal strip were known as **Nguni** and were the ancestors of the present-day Zulu and Xhosa people, whilst those who settled on the highveld were eventually to become the Sotho, Tswana and other related people. When the Bantu speakers came up against organized and established coastal Khoi groups in the area between the Fish and Sundays rivers, in present-day Eastern Cape, and the drier interior Karoo and Kalahari areas on the highveld, the migration came to a halt.

Like the Khoi these newer arrivals were essentially herders and cattle were the mainstay of their economy. But they were also keen agriculturists and raised crops of millet, sorghum and other cereals and vegetables. In good rainfall years any surplus was exchanged for cattle with other people not so fortunate and in bad years cattle could in turn be exchanged for cereals. The Bantu-speaking peoples tended to form larger and more politically organized groups with clear hierarchical structures. In the dry interior they tended to form large villages around regular water supplies, whilst on the better-watered coastal strip they tended to live in more isolated homesteads. Iron smelting was an important activity and iron goods were traded over long-distance exchange networks. In present-day Zimbabwe some Bantu-speaking peoples were especially successful with smelting gold and this was traded with Arabs along the east African coast and later with Europeans.

There is a good deal of trading contact between the Bantu speakers and the Khoi. The Khoi were particularly keen to get hold of iron which they used in their tools, as well as *dagga* (marijuana), which they enjoyed eating or drinking in tea and which did not grow well in the dry Cape. Both Khoi, San and Bantu speakers only started smoking *dagga* after being introduced to pipes by Europeans. This large degree of contact is reflected in the fact that some Bantu speakers incorporated the Khoi-San clicks into their language – today these clicks can be heard in both Xhosa and Zulu. There was also a degree, small but significant, of intermarrying between the Khoi and Bantu-speakers, the Xhosa in particular.

Arrival of the Europeans
Dutch, Khoi and slave society at the Cape The first Europeans to make contact with these three different social groups in southern Africa were Portuguese sailors attempting to find routes to the spice islands of Asia. For many years the Portuguese had been

pushing further and further south along Africa's western coastline and in 1487 a ship captained by Bartholomeu Dias made it around the Cape of Good Hope and sailed up the eastern coast of southern Africa as far as Algoa Bay. Ten years later another Portuguese sailor, Vasco da Gama, rounded the Cape and continued up the continent's eastern coast before heading further east, eventually to India. Over the next 200 years increasing numbers of Portuguese traders and their Dutch and British competitors began to make the journey to the east via the Cape of Good Hope. Though they occasionally stopped for fresh water and supplies in some of the more sheltered Cape bays and river mouths, the Portuguese usually tried to give a wide berth to the territory that is now South Africa. Apart from the treacherous coastline they also often encountered a hostile reception from the local inhabitants. Instead the Portuguese had trading and supply posts in present-day Angola and Mozambique where they were able to both resupply their ships on the way to their eastern empire and capture slaves to send to their American colonies.

The Dutch were the first European trading power to set up a permanent settlement in South Africa. In 1652 the powerful **Dutch East India Company** built a fort and established a supply station under the command of Jan Van Riebeeck on a site that later became Cape Town. The idea was that this was to be simply a point where passing Dutch ships could drop in to get fresh supplies and to rest sick members of their crew. The company did not envisage the settlement growing into a larger community and at first, every inhabitant was a company servant. This situation soon altered, however, when the company decided that it would allow a group of servants who had worked out their contracts to settle close by as independent farmers and supply the post with their produce. Prior to this decision all fresh supplies had been either delivered by sea or brought from the Khoi groups living in and around the Cape Peninsula. These independent settlers were known as burghers and their number was soon increased by the freeing of more servants and the arrival of new settlers from Holland and, after 1685, Huguenots fleeing French anti-protestant legislation.

With the advent of free burghers, the size of the settlement began to increase and some farmers moved out into outlying districts. This brought them into increased conflict with Khoi herders. There were a series of small skirmishes which the Dutch, with their superior weapons, easily won and the Khoi found themselves displaced from more and more land and their herds of cattle diminished. Under these circumstances some began to work for the burghers on their farms, theoretically as free labourers but in effect as little more than slaves. In this early expansion and subjection of the Khoi the seeds of a whole long history of dispossession of the established population of South Africa are apparent. As the settler farming areas expanded they came into contact with San groups whom they systematically slaughtered in revenge for their raids on settler livestock. European and Asian diseases, especially smallpox, also killed many more San and Khoi and by the end of the 18th century they had almost all been either absorbed into the settler economy as servants, pushed into the most marginal mountain and desert areas, such as the Kalahari, or exterminated.

As the settlers moved further to the east and north they encountered environments less conducive to settled agriculture and more suited to pastoralism. Many settlers adopted a life as semi-nomadic trekboers living exclusively by trading their livestock and the products of hunting with the settled colonists in the western Cape. As they moved east they also began to come into contact with Bantu-speaking Africans, in particular the Xhosa in what is now the Eastern Cape. Trading relations were established between the settlers and Xhosa and some Xhosa also came to work on settler farms in return for guns and other European imports. As well as trade, however, the settlers and Xhosa also interacted through warfare. Cattle raiding was especially common and some historians also argue that settlers also indulged in widespread slave raiding (see Mfecane section for more details about this). These battles were, however, inconclusive and a fluid and unstable boundary between the trekboers and Xhosa persisted for many years.

The other factor that began to alter the original function of the settlement was the arrival, in 1658, of a group of slaves captured from the Portuguese in Angola. The company had originally intended that there would be no slaves at the settlement but the company servants and free burghers soon became accustomed to avoiding the hardest and most menial manual tasks and demanded that they be supplied with more slaves. Unlike in the Americas most of these slaves did not come from West Africa but from Asia and Madagascar. They tended not to be owned in large numbers on huge plantations but in small groups, often less than 10, by individual farmers. The balance between the slave and free population of the Cape remained much more even than in West Indian and South American colonies.

There was, however, always a big gender imbalance in both the settler and slave populations, with far more men than women. Sexual encounters between slave owners and their female slaves, or Khoi servants, were frequent and a number of slave owners married freed slaves. Apartheid history taught that the present-day coloured population are the descendants of slaves and passing sailors, but even a cursory reading of the contemporary Dutch and other European reports of the settlement show that it it is probably more accurate to see the present-day Afrikaner and coloured population as having the same ancestry. Another fact about the present-day coloured population that is seldom recognized is that they are frequently the direct descendants of original Khoi inhabitants of the area. This is especially so in the Eastern and Northern Cape, where there was never a large slave population and certainly no sailors.

A number of slaves managed to escape from their captivity and joined up with still independent groups of Khoi and miscellaneous European and mixed-race adventurers beyond the frontiers of the Dutch colony. Here they formed new and unusual political groupings who often existed by raiding both European settlers and African groups in the interior. The best-known of these bands were the so-called **Griquas**. With European horses and guns they became an important political force in the South African interior right through until the mid-19th century.

Arrival of the British During the 18th century Dutch economic and political power began to wane. Just as the Dutch had superseded the Portuguese they were themselves challenged by the rising power of the British. In 1795 the British sailed into False Bay and annexed the Dutch colony (The Battle of Muizenberg). The British were concerned that the French, with whom they were fighting in Europe, would take over the strategic port. In a general peace settlement of 1803 the colony was returned to the Dutch but in 1806 the British reconquered the territory and their sovereignty was finally accepted by other European powers in the peace settlement of 1816.

The British were only really interested in the Cape as a staging post and strategic port to protect trade with their new Asian empire. The colony was not profitable and neither the British government nor business took much interest in the new possession. There were, however, two important events in the early years of British rule that were to have crucial impacts on the subsequent history of South Africa.

The first factor was the British authorities' concern over persistent and inconclusive fighting along the colony's eastern frontier with the Xhosa. Some Xhosa groups had taken advantage of the instability in the colony to re-establish themselves to the west of the

Fish River. The British decided that the only way to stop the persistent battles was to push the Xhosa back across the Fish River and establish a secure and clear frontier. During the first years of their rule they cleared the Xhosa occupying this area and tried to ban trekboers from having any contact with them. It was decided that what was needed was a group of permanent settlers on new farms in the area from which the Xhosa had been cleared in order to keep them apart from the trekboers.

In 1820 the British parliament agreed to release £50,000 to transport settlers from Britain to occupy this area. The money was used to send out 4000 settlers, with an additional 1000 paying their own passage to the region. These people became known as the 1820 Settlers and formed the nucleus of the subsequent British settler community. Though the British authorities had intended that they should become farmers and hence occupy the disputed territory, most of the settlers were from urban artisan backgrounds and few had the skills or inclination necessary to become successful cultivators in the difficult and unfamiliar environment of the Eastern Cape. Most of them quickly gravitated towards the small towns, especially Port Elizabeth and Grahamstown, where they used their previous experience to become traders or skilled artisans. Their presence introduced an important new element to the equation, not least cultural, and 1820 Settler attitudes towards things such as the freedom of the press and towards the proper role of government played an important part in shaping 19th-century Cape settler society.

It soon became apparent that the British attempts to create a permanent border between the Xhosa and settlers had failed and cattle raiding backwards and forwards across the border continued. The Xhosa tried on numerous occasions to reclaim their land, occupied now by the settlers, but these attempts always failed, despite many initial successes. The Frontier Wars between Xhosa and settler continued for the next half century with Xhosa independence and land occupation being progressively eroded until their remaining areas (which became known as Transkei), were eventually incorporated into the Cape Colony.

The other fundamental change that British rule brought about was the ending of the slave trade and then the total banning of slavery. The peripheral role of South Africa in the British colonial empire and the dispersed nature of its slave population meant that it was seldom considered in debates about slavery, which instead concentrated on the massive slave plantations of the West Indies. Nevertheless, when the British parliament eventually decided to call an end to the institution that many felt was both inhumane and, more importantly, not beneficial to the empire's economy, it was also banned in South Africa. In 1834 slaves throughout the British Empire were officially emancipated, though they were to remain with their owners as apprentices until 1838. Slave owners were also offered compensation of one third of the value of their slaves. Though emancipation provided some slaves with new opportunities, in reality many of them continued to live very similar lives, carrying out the same heavy manual labour, under extremely harsh conditions, on the same Cape farms.

Nevertheless, many of the original Dutch settlers were extremely unhappy about the emancipation of slaves. To make things worse the British government, after extensive lobbying by British missionaries working in South Africa, also prevented them from introducing legislation aimed at tying both freed slaves and Khoi servants to individual farms as indentured labourers. The Dutch settlers had already been annoyed by the way their extremely loose system of administration had been reformed by the British, making it more difficult for individual farmers to impose their own law on their particular district. Many trekboers in the eastern districts also felt that the British were not quick enough in coming to their support when they had cattle raided by Xhosa groups to the east. Now they were not only losing a large proportion of their 'property' (slaves) but were being prevented from making sure they had a captive (cheap) labour supply. Though they were offered compensation at one third of the value of their slaves this had to be claimed in London. Many slave owners, therefore, sold their compensation rights to agents at usually about one fifth of the slave's value.

In response to these complaints a number of Dutch settlers decided that they would set out with their families and servants in search of new land beyond the British colonial boundaries. Between 1835 and 1840 around 5000 people left the Cape colony and headed east in a movement that later became known as the **Great Trek**. It tended to be the trekboers from the eastern areas, who had fewer possessions and little investment in established farms who took part in this movement. The settlers taking part in the trek became known as *voortrekers* and their experiences beyond the colonial frontiers became fertile ground for 20th-century Afrikaner nationalism. One thing not often celebrated in the national myths that grew up around the Great Trek is that accompanying the treks were a large number of Khoi servants and a small number of freed slaves still economically and socially bound to their masters/patrons.

African States and the mfecane

The area the voortrekers were entering into was the home of numerous Bantu-speaking African chiefdoms, but at the very time they made their appearance on the scene these political groupings were undergoing unprecedented political upheaval. The causes and indeed the very nature of this upheaval is a matter of considerable debate amongst historians and for once this is not a debate between Apartheid historians and their opponents. Rather the debate is between those who believe that the turmoil was caused by wholly internal African political manoeuvrers and those who believe that external parties, especially slave raiders from Mozambique and the Cape, were to blame. Inevitably the truth is probably somewhere between the two. External factors, such as the presence of European traders interested in products such as ivory, may have lead to increased competition amongst African chiefdoms for lucrative resources, but the dynamics of the upheaval probably had more to do with internal African state formation. On balance, the evidence used by those who argue for a basically internal dynamic to the process seems to be stronger than those arguing the opposite.

Prior to the early 19th century African political units tended to be small and loyalty fluid. If there was disagreement within a chiefdom one section would simply set off and establish a new village in a new area. In the early 19th century, however, new larger and more strictly organized African political groupings (something closer to European nations), were formed. The epicentre of this new process of state formation was between the Tugela and Pongola rivers in present-day northern KwaZulu Natal and involved one of the best-known pre-colonial African personalities: Shaka Zulu.

Before the rise of Shaka, the Zulu clan had been just one of a large number of small political groups amongst the northern Nguni people in the coastal strip below the Drakensberg escarpment. At the time of Shaka's birth there were two powerful chiefdoms in the area, the Ndwandwe and the Mthethwa, who clashed repeatedly and with unprecedented ferocity. Shaka, an illegitimate son of the head of the Zulu clan, joined the army of the Mthethwa and proved to be a highly successful warrior and quickly rose through the ranks. When his father died and with the support of the chief of the Mthethwa, he managed to overcome all his half-brothers' claims to lead the Zulu clan.

With Shaka as their chief, the Zulus were transformed into a very powerful political and military force. When the chief of the Mthethwa was killed by the Ndwandwe, Shaka was able to reunite the larger chieftainship under his Zulu clan. Unlike previous chiefs who had been willing to make loose alliances with other groups, Shaka ensured that everyone who came under his leadership expressed loyalty to the Zulu alone. He vigorously enforced a rule that his followers had to follow only Zulu cultural and religious practices and speak only the Zulu dialect.

By the process of incorporating surrounding smaller groups Shaka quickly forged a very powerful Zulu state. He took on and decisively beat the Ndwandwe and then set about raiding all surrounding chiefdoms for cattle and grain. His *impis*, organized regiments of full-time soldiers, were a new innovation amongst the Bantu speakers, as was their method of attack, which involved using short spears that were thrown or thrust from close quarters.

During the 1820s the Zulu *impis* became increasingly predatory, whilst at home Shaka's reign became even more autocratic and his punishment of any sign of opposition truly terrible. This lead to an era of unprecedented disruption, fighting and suffering known in the Nguni areas as the *mfecane* and on the highveld as the *difaqane*.

Shaka's reign of terror eventually came to an end in 1828 when he was assassinated by Dingane, one of his half brothers. Dingane continued many of the same domestic and external policies as Shaka, though with less vigour and skill but the Zulu chiefdom maintained its position as the most powerful African state in southern Africa until its eventual defeat by the British Imperial forces in 1879.

The *mfecane* had caused havoc across southeastern Africa. People's crops and cattle had been destroyed and starvation was widespread. The population of the southern highveld was decimated and survivors existed mainly in small, frightened bands. A number of larger political groups had arisen out of the chaos, such as the Zulu, the Ndebele, the Sotho, the Swazi and the Pedi, all of whom to some extent regarded large portions of highveld as either belonging to them or falling within their sphere of influence but none of them really occupied the area. This was the arena into which the voortrekers made their unexpected arrival in the late 1830s.

European expansion

The voortrekers were by no means a unified movement. In fact there were numerous splits and some of the leaders were not on speaking terms. In the early years there were a number of small autonomous communities established by the voortrekers, but these often failed because of a poor location or challenges from nearby African states. Over time, however, two separate republics were established, the Orange Free State and the Transvaal. In the 1850s the British recognized these two states' sovereignty over most of the South African highveld to the east of the Orange River. However, this was not exactly the location to establish their republics that the voortrekers had hoped for.

After leaving the Cape Colony one of the groups of voortrekers turned south and crossed the Drakensberg in search of a site for the new republic with access to the sea. In so doing they entered into the Zulu kingdom's domain. The Zulu king did not trust these new arrivals, especially as he had heard they had inflicted a defeat on the Ndebele and the Zulu killed the voortrekers leader when he came to negotiate a deal to be given land. A few months later, in the Battle of Blood River, the voortrekers extracted a terrible revenge and carved out a space for themselves south of the Tugela River. Their plans for a new republic with access to the sea were scuppered, however, when the British set up a new colony based at a site that became Durban and created the new colony of Natal.

The Natal colony was not willing to challenge the might of the Zulu kingdom to the north of the Tugela until 1879, so for many years the two separate entities existed side-by-side. During this time the Zulu kingdom was an inward-looking entity and the Natal colonists were unable to attract many Zulu labourers to work on the sugar plantations they established in the area. They therefore turned to India as a source of labour following the lead of West Indian plantation owners who had imported indentured Indian servants as a replacement labour force for the newly emancipated slaves. These indentured Indian labourers were followed by free Indian merchants and together the two groups make up the ancestry of the present-day Indian population based in Natal.

On the highveld the Boer Republics also appropriated land from African polities. The Sotho lost much of their territory in a long series of wars with the Orange Free State and eventually turned to the British for protection. A similar chain of events led to the declaration of the Bechuanaland Protectorate (present-day Botswana). Through the 19th century the Boer Republics on the highveld gradually defeated all the independent African states, the last one, the Venda, fell in 1898. The defeated African populations usually managed to maintain access to at least some land. These areas were later exclusively reserved for African occupation after it was realized that if all the land was appropriated the colonies and republics would have to find space for large numbers of African people.

Whilst voortrekers may have lodged claims to certain farms they invariably contained resident African populations. More often than not the Boers were happy to leave the African population in place and simply collect rent, either in the form of produce or labour. Later on in the century this created tensions when some landowners wanted to set up proper productive farms and had trouble getting enough labour. They often looked across at the neighbours' farms and saw a potential labour force simply getting on with its own peasant farming activities. They therefore lobbied for legislation outlawing what they described as kaffir farming. This was to become a more important issue after the 1870s when an unexpected event was to transform the South African economy and produce a new market for agricultural goods.

Mineral revolution

Despite the machinations on and beyond their frontiers the two colonies remained very much a backwater of the British empire. Wool exports from the Karoo and wine from the Western Cape created some commercial interest but other colonial possession held greater promise. But this was all to change in 1867 when alluvial diamonds were discovered near the confluence of the Harts and Vaal rivers. The flurry of interest and activity that this discovery created were just petering out when a larger outcrop of diamonds were discovered at a dry digging nearby. By 1872 20,000 Europeans and a larger number of Africans and coloureds had converged on the site that soon revealed itself as the world's richest diamond pipe and grew to become the world's diamond capital, Kimberley. At first there were numerous small individual plots at the mines but these soon became concentrated into the hands of one or two companies who bought up the claims from small entities. Eventually total control of the mines rested in the hands of Cecil Rhodes' DeBeers Consolidated Mines.

In 1886 there was a further mineral discovery in South Africa; this time it was gold on the Witwatersrand in the Transvaal Republic. Miners from across the world rushed to the new reef and capitalists were quick to make sure they got a slice of the pie. The deep level and relatively poor grade of the ore meant that it was only large capitalist organizations that could secure the investment necessary to succeed and, just as at Kimberley, mine ownership was quickly consolidated into a few hands. The main town on the Rand, Johannesburg, grew rapidly from nothing to about 75,000 white residents and many more Africans by the turn of the 20th century.

These mineral discoveries fundamentally altered South African society. It was at the mines that many of the features that dominated life in 20th-century South Africa first came into existence, in particular the pass laws, the migrant labour system, the compounds and the colour bar. The deep-level diggings and the complicated process of extraction from poor gold ores meant that production expenses were high and, as the gold price was fixed internationally, the one way mining companies could ensure high profits was to hold down or reduce labour costs. The diamond mines at Kimberley provided the model of how this was to be done.

At first all labour at Kimberley was able to demand a high wage, but as the number of companies were rationalized there were fewer and fewer opportunities. White labourers began to realize that they were losing out to cheaper African labourers and pressurized the government to reduce this competition. Whilst government was unwilling to institute too overtly racist legislation, they did introduce a pass law that required all Africans present in the town to carry a pass signed either by a magistrate or a mine owner showing that they had legitimate employment. This legislation was aimed at preventing large numbers of Africans arriving at Kimberley in hope of jobs and hence pushing down wage rates.

The mines' owners, however, wanted to keep wages as low as possible and therefore to substitute more expensive white labour with cheaper African labour. The solution to this problem lay in the migrant labour system, where only male Africans came to the mines leaving their families at home on the reserves. The DeBeers mining company had quickly introduced a system whereby all African labour had to live in a single compound above the mine from which they were prohibited to leave for the duration of their contract. The official reason was that this was to prevent diamond thefts, but there were also many other advantages for the employers. As the compounds were only to house single male African labourers the company did not have to pay adequate wages to support the miner's family, who usually remained in the reserves and farmed to meet their own subsistence needs. Furthermore the mine owners could be assured of economies of scales in buying in provisions and therefore were able to feed African labourers on the site. If Africans had to buy their own food they would have needed higher wages. At first DeBeers wanted to introduce a compound system for white labourers, but because they had a political voice they were able to resist these plans.

For white labour the migrant labour system meant that they were being squeezed out of the job market by cheaper African labour. The mining companies were always nervous that white and African labour would unite, especially as many of the white labourers were experienced trade union activists. Over time there developed a sort of tacit agreement between white labour and capitalists that in exchange for the political support of labour, the capitalists would introduce a colour bar that reserved the more skilled and better paid jobs for whites only. At times this arrangement broke down, especially in the years after the First World War, but on the whole white labour never rocked the boat.

While capitalists on the Rand were able to develop a labour system that ensured wages were kept low, they were not always able to secure African labour in the quantities they required. They were, therefore, always pressurizing the respective governments to introduce policies to push more African men out of the reserves. They also went to great lengths to get labour from wherever it was available, including beyond the borders of South Africa as far away as Malawi. The mine owners also decided to co-operate with one another to keep wages low and formed a Witwatersrand Native Labour Association that was to look after all recruitment of African labour. When mine owners experienced a particular shortage of labour early in the 20th century, they recruited 63,000 Chinese labourers on fixed contracts who undermined the wage levels demanded by Africans. Once the wage rate had been forced down, the Chinese labourers were simply repatriated.

One reason the capitalists felt that Africans were not entering the labour market in the numbers they required was the success that African peasant farmers were having at this time. African farmers were the first to react to the new markets created by the mines at Kimberley and on the Rand and, using new farming techniques learnt from missionaries, they increased their grain output tremendously. Many of the successful African peasant farmers lived in the reserves, but others had managed to buy or rent land outside these areas. White farmers were not usually able to cope with the competition these new African peasants presented and lobbied government for support. This was forthcoming in the form of subsidies, soft loans and technical advice and after the turn of the last century these African peasant farmers began to lose out against their white competitors. In 1913 legislation was introduced that made it impossible for Africans to buy or rent land in many 'white' areas. The depression of the 1930s was the final nail in the coffin for many peasant farmers and after that date very few struggled on. Today it seems hard to believe that there was once a highly successful African peasant class, outperforming their white neighbours, and that it was deliberately ruined by government action. The success of African farmers at this time was ignored by all school history textbooks during the Apartheid era and even today few South Africans, black or white, know that African farmers were at one time much more successful than their white competitors.

Anglo-Boer War

When diamonds were discovered at Kimberley it was not quite clear who had sovereignty over the area, with a Tswana chiefdom, the Orange Free State, the Transvaal Republic and the Griquas all claiming the area. Britain pressurized the rival claimants to undergo a process of arbitration under their direction. At the arbitration it was decided that the Griqua's claim was strongest, but the British immediately offered the Griqua leader substantial compensation if he agreed that the territory should be administered by the British. Not surprisingly, the Orange Free State, which had the strongest claim out of the two republics, was annoyed by this sleight of hand, especially as the British soon incorporated the area into the Cape Colony, but there was little they could do about it.

The Rand, on the other hand, was clearly within the Transvaal Republic. The British had annexed the Transvaal in 1877 but after a brief Boer uprising they handed control back. They must have regretted the decision when gold was discovered just five years later. The government of the Republic was primarily concerned with looking after the interests of its richer Boers, the vast majority of whom were farmers. They were a little unsure about how to treat the new mining economy. On the one hand the extra revenue from taxing the operations was clearly to be welcomed, whilst on the other they were nervous about the implications of having a large number of new immigrants, known by them as uitlanders, or foreigners, in their midst. They therefore introduced legislation restricting the franchise to white adult male naturalized citizens who had lived in the Republic for at least 14 years.

While most uitlanders were too busy trying to make their fortune to worry about politics, they did complain about the inefficiency of the Transvaal government in meeting the conditions necessary for an efficient capitalist system. British Imperialist forces were keen to get their hands on the Republic and in 1895 tried to manipulate uitlander dissatisfaction in a plot to overthrow the Transvaal government. In 1895, with the backing of the Colonial Office in London, Cecil Rhodes, then Prime Minister of the Cape Colony, tried to organize a committee of leading uitlanders to seize control of Johannesburg and declare a new government. Rhodes also arranged for a column of British police, under the control of his old friend Leander Starr Jameson, based in the Bechuanaland Protectorate, to come to their assistance. The plot, later known as the Jameson Raid, was a fiasco. The uitlander committee in Johannesburg bickered amongst themselves and did not command any mass following. Realizing this, Rhodes called off the proposed intervention by Jameson's force, but Jameson ignored his command and entered the Transvaal. When the committee learnt of this, they did belatedly declare that they had taken over Johannesburg but even in the process of doing so they entered into negotiations with the Transvaal Republic and came to an agreement. Jameson's column, therefore, had no crisis in which to intervene and were simply met and arrested by a Transvaal commando. This embarrassing incident marked the end of Rhodes' political career and helped to alienate British and Afrikaners across South Africa.

Despite the failures of the Jameson Raid the British were still keen to gain control of the Transvaal. Just four years after, Britain mounted a far better equipped, more sustained and ultimately successful bid to gain control of the whole of South Africa; the Anglo-Boer (or South African) War of 1899 to 1902. There is some disagreement among historians about the underlying cause of the war. Afrikaner Nationalist historians tend to view it simply as an example of British Imperial expressionism. Some historians of the British Empire, on the other hand, argue that it was more to do with British strategic concerns; they were worried that the Transvaal Republic could inspire Afrikaners in the Cape to rebel against the British who would, therefore, lose control of ports such as Simon's Town which were vital for protecting her sea routes. Most historians, however, see gold as being the key. The British were, not surprisingly, keen to control the world's largest supply of gold and make sure their investment in the mines was profitable.

During the late 1890s the Colonial Office in London and the British High Commissioner in the Cape both lobbied for direct British military intervention to overthrow the Transvaal and the Orange Free State Republics. The situation grew more and more tense and in September 1899 Britain sent a large party of British soldiers to reinforce their troops. Sensing that Britain was about to invade the Transvaal, the Orange Free State decided to strike before the reinforcements arrived and on 11 October 1899 declared war on Britain in an attempt to preserve their independence. Deciding that attack was the best form of defence, they invaded both the Cape and Natal colonies.

At first the Boer Republics had great success and achieved victories in both northern Natal and the northeastern Cape. They drove back British forces and laid siege to Ladysmith, Kimberley and Mafikeng. They were, however, unable to advance much further in either colony and the general uprising of Afrikaners in the Cape that they had hoped for never materialized. Initially they held off British attempts to relieve the three towns, but with the arrival of huge numbers of British troops the fortunes changed. During 1900 the British set off on a triumphant and unstoppable advance on Pretoria and Paul Kruger, the president of the Transvaal Republic, escaped into exile via the Portuguese colony of Mozambique.

British victory seemed secure, but a number of die-hard Boers had other ideas. For the next two years they indulged in a continuous and, for the British, exceptionally frustrating, guerrilla war. The British were unable to capture the small bands of highly skilled Boer commandos so set about instituting a scorched earth policy to deny the guerrillas any help from local populations. Large numbers of Boers from areas with a guerrilla presence were placed in concentration camps to prevent them from supplying the commandos in the field with provisions. Though it was by no means a deliberate policy of the British, poor administration meant that food and medical supplies in the camps often ran out and many Boers, including many women and children, died of disease or starvation. Memories of the British scorched earth policy were often revived by Afrikaner politicians throughout the 20th century, though they conveniently forgot that the Boers tended to use very similar techniques in their battles against African chiefdoms. Also forgotten is the British policy of rounding up any African workers on Boer farms and placing them in similar concentration camps during the war.

Peace and union The British scorched earth policy and the sheer hopelessness of their situation eventually lead many Boers to abandon the fight and return to their farms. The remaining guerrilla bands, who became known as the bitterenders, eventually surrendered to the British under the Treaty of Vereening in April 1902. The British were keen to ensure that the two defeated Boer republics were fully incorporated into a unified South Africa and therefore agreed a number of concessions for the defeated army. One of the key issues that the British were willing to concede was that any discussion of political rights for Africans be delayed until some unspecified future date.

The British hoped that after the war they would be able to substantially Anglicize the country by enforcing English as an official language and encouraging mass immigration from Britain. This policy proved to be a failure but they were successful in encouraging the four territories to agree to Union just seven years after the end of the war. One of the key sticking points in discussions over Union was the issue of African voting rights. In the Cape Africans and coloureds had the right to vote as long as they owned above a set value in property. While this excluded most Africans it did give at least some an opportunity to vote and therefore a political voice, however weak. Natal also had a property qualification but the figure was set so high for Africans that only a handful ever managed to vote. The other two Boer republics had never allowed Africans any political rights whatsoever. During the discussions over Union, which only Natal had reservations about, it was decided that the issue of voter representation for Africans would be side-stepped by entrenching a constitutional clause maintaining the pre-Union franchise arrangements in each of the four territories. With this issue solved and agreement on things such as dual official languages (English and Dutch), all sides agreed on the Act of Union, which was passed by the British Houses of Parliament in 1909 and the Union of South Africa came into being in 1910.

The rise of nationalism

First stirrings of African nationalism The Act of Union, and particularly the entrenchment of the Boer republics' voting arrangements, felt like a powerful slap in the face for very many Africans. Most Africans had supported the British during the Anglo-Boer War and had assumed that their loyalty would be recognized in the post-war settlement. Though Africans in the Cape had their voting rights entrenched in the Constitution they feared that the Cape government's willingness (with British backing) to placate the two northern former republics was a very bad omen. This proved all too correct; in 1935 they had their voting rights removed by an Act which amended the Constitution.

In the early 20th century African political opposition to racist policies tended to be exceptionally moderate. During the 19th century there had been small but steady growth of the African educated middle class. They were mostly educated in mission schools, were committed Christians and employed as teachers or government clerks. They tended to look to London for support and were especially concerned about preserving their voting rights. Not surprisingly these early African political leaders were dismayed about the proposals for Union and sent a delegation to London to try to urge the British House of Commons to amend the Act. Despite receiving some support from Labour politicians they failed in this venture. In 1912 a group of African leaders called for a national convention for all African political groups in the country. This gathering in Bloemfontein marked the formation of a more organized phase in African opposition to racist legislation and lead to the South African Native National Congress, later renamed the **African National Congress**.

Despite the formation of a national opposition organization, African protest still tended to be extremely moderate. Many African leaders placed a special emphasis on education as a means to achieving political recognition. Many still believed in the old Cape liberal ideology of 'equal rights for all civilized men' and went to great lengths to prove just how civilized they were. London remained the Mecca for these early leaders and the most common form of protest was appeals to the Imperial authorities.

Over the next few decades, however, there were also a number of shorter lived, more radical, opposition movements. The most successful of these was the Industrial and Commercial Union (ICU) established by the very colourful figure, Clements Kadalie. The ICU spread rapidly through South Africa in the 1920s and was especially successful amongst farm workers. It demanded fairer wages for African workers and full political rights for all. The organization of the ICU left much to be desired, however, and just as quickly as it grew it subsided.

After the First World War a few white communists also made attempts to forge links between the white union movements and African workers. Though there were many influential Africans who came up through these Communist Party links the movement was never able to reach out to a wide range of Africans, especially Africans in the rural areas. The Party also suffered from numerous internal splits, often caused by contradictory statements coming from the international Communist leadership and from continual harassment from the police. White Unionists also resisted the attempts to form a non-racial movement and in 1922 the South African Labour Party, which represented the interests of white working-class voters, entered into an election pact with the Afrikaner nationalists in the National Party.

While the 1920s had seen a great deal of protest from African peoples, especially from the ICU, the 1930s were a period of relative quiet. The international depression also affected the South African economy and many Africans found themselves unemployed or on low wages. To make matters worse the early years of the decade also saw one of the worst ever droughts, ruining the residual African farming economy in the reserves. Under these circumstances political protest seemed to be secondary to the tough job of simply surviving. During the Second World War, however, there was an upswing of African protest culminating in a series of protest movements amongst squatters outside Johannesburg and a massive African mineworkers strike. After the war African protest entered a more radical phase as younger leaders came to the forefront.

Rise of Afrikaner nationalism It is a common misconception that Afrikaner nationalist sentiments existed right from the arrival of Van Riebeeck and that the 'Afrikaner spirit' somehow grew out of the harsh conditions of the frontier. This is a misconception that has often been fuelled by Afrikaner nationalists' versions of history. The reality is very different and, whilst Afrikaners have used the imagery of the Great Trek to help create a sense of nationalism, it was by no means an event in which all Afrikaners took part.

Class divisions were strong among both the descendants of the original settlers who remained in the Cape and those who migrated to the north. The established richer Western Cape farmers looked down both on the people who migrated to the new Republics and their poorer neighbours. Because of these deep-rooted divisions it is not really correct to talk about Afrikaners as a single category prior to the 20th century, when there were potent political forces that led to increased collective nationalism. It is, therefore, somewhat of an anachronism to talk about *Afrikaners*, which simply means African in Dutch, prior to the 20th century. In the Western Cape it is possible to see an earlier sense of Afrikaner nationalism, but this might more accurately be called a Dutch settler identity, whilst in the two Republics the sense of nationalism was firmly tied up with an extremely local (agricultural) identity, hence the use of the term Boer, which simply means farmer in Dutch.

In the 19th century the Afrikaans language, later to become a potent symbol of Afrikaner nationalism, was regarded by the more élite settlers as a bit of an embarrassment. Because the language had developed out of a mixture between Dutch and the various languages spoken by the Khoi and slaves, it was regarded as a rather low form of dialect and its association with coloured servants was apparently the common description of a language known as kitchen Dutch. There had been one attempt to raise the profile of Afrikaans in the 1870s but it had not spread much beyond the movement's base in Paarl. During the negotiations over Union, Boer leaders were not arguing for Afrikaans to be a dual official language, they were arguing for Dutch. At the very time these negotiations were taking place, however, there was a second attempt to gain respectability for the Afrikaans language. The political climate was much more conducive to the movement and it quickly spread throughout the Cape and the two former Boer Republics.

The ravages of the war and the development of mechanized agriculture meant that many poorer Afrikaner tenant farmers were being forced off the land in the early decades of this century. They migrated to the new towns in search of work, but had few skills to offer and often ended up poor and unemployed. Their plight, often labelled 'the poor white problem', was a continual worry for Afrikaner politicians. They were especially fearful that their marginal position in the new towns was pushing them into closer contact with the growing band of African urban poor. The 'poor white problem' was a key motivation behind the deepening of segregationist policies in the urban areas, designed to keep black and white apart. During the first half of the century the nitty-gritty of segregation tended to be largely left up to local authorities to implement, with central government simply providing the legislative framework for local regulations. Nevertheless, in almost every town residential segregation and pass laws strictly regulated the daily lives of Africans.

The 'poor white problem' was also an important force behind the development of Afrikaner nationalism. As poorer Afrikaners moved to the towns they became immersed in a very different working-class culture to the one they had experienced in the countryside. The Afrikaner leaders realized that if these new urban residents became part of this new urban culture they may well lose much of their separate Afrikaner identity and the Afrikaner politicians would find their support base undermined. They therefore decided that they needed to create a stronger sense of Afrikaner nationalism that would incorporate all Afrikaners, rich and poor. Historical events, such as the Great Trek, were deliberately resurrected and celebrated, the Afrikaans language was encouraged and, crucially, the Afrikaner leaders developed exclusively Afrikaner economic institutions that deliberately helped Afrikaner small businesses.

Afrikaner politics

Despite the deliberate fostering of Afrikaner nationalism the Afrikaner leadership was constantly fighting amongst itself and political parties frequently split and reformed. One of the key issues of disagreement was over the relationship between the new Union and the British Empire. After Union the British asked an ex-Boer General, Louis Botha to form the first government. He, and his close ally and successor General Jan Smuts, both strongly believed that the Afrikaners should strive to have good relations with the Imperial government and unite English and Dutch/Afrikaans-speaking white South Africans. Their **South Africa Party**, built on a coalition between the Transvaal and Cape ruling parties easily won the first election, but another important ex-Boer General, Hertzog, felt that they were too keen on maintaining good relations with the British government and formed a rival **National Party**. At first the National Party only had support in Hertzog's home province, the Orange Free State, but later he was joined by DF Malan, an ardent anti-British Afrikaner from the Cape province.

The First World War caused a further and more vicious split in Afrikaner ranks. A number of important generals resisted Botha's strong support for Britain in the war and his commitment to send South African troops to Europe. Their attempted coup failed and Botha quickly put the rebellion down, but the issue resurfaced again and again over the next few decades. A strike by white miners in 1922, which grew into a mini revolt as workers seized power in Johannesburg, was dealt with in a similar fashion by Botha's successor, Smuts. This time, however, white workers were able to gain a measure of revenge: in 1924 their support was crucial in electing a coalition Labour/Nationalist government.

Under Hertzog, Afrikaner nationalist sentiment was given an important boost by the replacement of Dutch by Afrikaans as one of the two official languages. In 1934 there even seemed a chance of forging a united Afrikaner leadership when Hertzog and Smuts joined together under a new United Party banner during the crisis caused by the great depression. This, however, was not to be, as Malan led a breakaway group to form a new 'Purified' National Party. The decision whether or not to join the Second World War caused a further split and Hertzog resigned as Prime Minister to join Malan in opposition, in so doing creating yet another version of the National Party – this time the Herenigde (Reunited) National Party. Smuts, the ardent supporter of close ties with Britain, became the new Prime Minister and took South Africa into the war. He won an election in 1943 on the back of a wave of pro-British feeling and his international reputation grew and grew. After the war, however, he found his popularity at home waning. The economic boom caused by the war had lead to massive African urban migration and the National Party was able to use this to stir up fear amongst white, especially Afrikaner, voters. In 1948 they voted in Malan's Nationalists on an election platform promising a new ideology of Apartheid.

The Apartheid programme

What exactly was meant by Apartheid was not exactly clear in 1948; and the full programme of legislation was only really finalized in the mid-1950s. In fact the real beauty of the concept in 1948 was that it meant different things to different sections of the white voting population. The word simply means 'apart', and as such can be seen as simply a refinement of segregationist ideas that had dominated in the first half of the century. Despite the image of Apartheid created by many popularist historians and journalists, it was by no means or exclusively Afrikaner Ideology. Indeed the roots of the idea can be traced back to English-speaking liberals in the early years of the century.

There was a distinct group of white South Africans who were very concerned about the plight of Africans and saw the solution as being total separation of the two races. They believed that rapid urbanization was destroying the basis of African culture and that they needed to be protected from the evils of white urban civilization. This ideology was tied up with ideas of both paternalism – that whites should be like parents to child-like Africans – and ideas of Social Darwinism, that different races were at different points along an evolutionary scale. In the middle decades of the century these ideas began to be considered by a group of Afrikaner intellectuals who saw the total separation of the races as being the only way in which whites could maintain political power over South Africa. They began to argue that if Africans were allowed to take part in the white capitalist economy they could rightly expect to be given political rights, so the solution was to keep them in a totally separate political and economic sphere where they could exercise their own rights.

This political philosophy was obviously not at all popular amongst white factory owners and farmers who relied upon cheap African labour to run their business. To these people Apartheid should be simply a way of maintaining a cheap supply of African labour with few employment or political rights that would allow the demand of higher wages. There was, therefore, a clear conflict between the ideology of Apartheid as expressed by Afrikaner intellectuals and the wishes of the average Afrikaner voter. During the early 1950s this conflict was solved by the nationalists stating that their long-term aim was the total separation of races, but in the meantime they had to be practical and recognize the economic reality that white industry relied upon African labour.

Apartheid became in essence a way of ensuring a continual supply of cheap African labour whilst denying Africans any political rights. Legislation such as the Group Areas Act tightened previous segregation regulations and the government set about a massive national campaign to remove Africans from urban areas or squatter camps close to urban centres. Africans living in vibrant urban communities such as Sophiatown in Johannesburg found their homes bulldozed as they were ordered out. Those without passes were returned to the reserves, now restyled as homelands, whilst those with rights to reside in urban areas were removed to distant townships such as Soweto. Segregation of all amenities was also tightened and there became no areas of African life where the state did not intervene. In the countryside, Africans who had retained access to land either as freeholders or tenant farmers, in areas that were labelled 'black spots', were also forcibly removed to the homelands.

African opposition Africans did not take these new assaults lying down, and the 1950s saw an unprecedented display of African political opposition to the white state. The ANC was revitalized and radicalized by the rise of a group of young militant activists, including Nelson Mandela, who had joined the ANC's Youth League in the 1940s. The organization saw that their attempts to appear moderate had not done them any favours and they could clearly not rely upon Britain to look after their interests. In 1952 the ANC launched a Defiance Campaign that used Gandhian tactics of peaceful resistance to the new Apartheid legislation. The ANC, in alliance with Indians, coloureds and a few radical whites, took the lead in deliberately breaking racist laws and offering themselves up for arrest. These peaceful protests were often met with violence from the police and many ANC members were harshly treated after arrest. Though the campaign failed, the ANC's membership mushroomed in its aftermath.

The National Party met this increased opposition with new legislation that firstly banned the South African Communist Party and then increased restrictions on the ANC and other political organizations. The banning of the Communist Party meant that many Communists now looked to the ANC as their main political organization. Some within the ANC were worried about the increased prominence of communists within the organization, especially as they tended to have very strong links with white communists, many of whom joined a newly formed white organization called the Congress of Democrats. These people were also concerned about the developing alliances with Indian and coloured organizations and wanted to maintain the ANC as an exclusively African organization. Uniting under the slogan "Africa for the Africans", they formed a splinter group within the ANC and finally broke off to form a rival Pan African Congress (PAC) under Robert Sobukwe.

Apartheid policies also made themselves felt in the homelands where the government introduced 'betterment' policies designed to shore up the faltering subsistence economy in the areas which provided food for the families of migrant workers and for the workers themselves when unemployed. The plans consisted of regulations to consolidate small plots of land and setting aside areas for farming and areas for grazing. A crucial element of the plans was the compulsory culling of African cattle when there were deemed to be too many head of livestock on grazing land. This was really the first time that the white state had intervened in the daily lives of Africans living in the reserves and many resented the fact that there was now no area of their life free from the control of the racist authorities. The compulsory culling regulations were especially resented and when the government tried to implement them there was violent resistance in a number of areas. These outbreaks were inevitably dealt with extremely harshly.

A number of urban areas also experienced bouts of violence, with African protesters displaying their frustration through rioting. In response to the growing protest the government moved to break the ANC-led alliance and put 156 of its leaders on trial for treason. The mammoth trial lasted from 1956 to 1960, eventually resulting in their acquittal. Despite the acquittal it was important in diverting the accuseds' energy away from organizing opposition. Furthermore, by the time the trial was over it had also been overtaken by other events.

In late 1959 the newly formed PAC decided to launch a massive anti-pass law campaign. The pass laws were one of the most hated Apartheid policies as they strictly controlled African mobility and were also used by the police as an excuse to stop and search any African. Their campaign was to start on 21 March 1960, in order to pre-empt an ANC led campaign due to start on 31 March 1960. The PAC called on all African men to leave their passes at home and present themselves for arrest at the nearest police station. They believed that the prison system would be swamped and the pass laws would have to be revoked. One of the main areas of PAC activity on the morning of 21 March was the southern Transvaal. At Evaton and Vanderbijlpark police stations large crowds were dispersed by police baton charges and low flying jets, but at Sharpville the crowd stayed put when they were buzzed by the jets. At 1315 there was a small scuffle and a small section of the wire fence surrounding the police station was knocked over. The police later claimed they were under extreme danger and were being stoned but this is denied by almost all eyewitness accounts. What is clear, however, is that the police suddenly opened fire on the crowd with machine guns. The terrified crowd ran for cover but the police continued to fire on the fleeing protesters. Most of the 69 dead and 180 wounded were shot in the back.

Moves towards armed resistance The Sharpville Massacre marked a turning point in African political opposition to Apartheid. As news of the killings spread around the country

Africans rioted and refused to go to work. In Cape Town there was a series of huge marches from the townships into the city centre which created panic amongst the white residents and police. The march leaders were, however, insistent that they passed off peacefully and had negotiations with the local police chief to ensure this was the case. They were rewarded with arrest and the Cape Town townships also erupted into rioting. A nationwide state of emergency was declared and the police arrested thousands of political activists from across the country. Strikers were beaten and township food supplies cut off to force people back to work. Both the ANC and PAC were banned and many of their leaders thrown into prison under new security legislation that meant they could be held without being charged. Over the next few months the unprecedented harshness of the police action broke the back of the widespread resistance. It also convinced many ANC and PAC members that non-violent action meant nothing if it was met by police brutality.

The leadership of both the PAC and ANC were concerned that they were about to lose control of their rank-and-file members unless they modified their position on the use of violence. The ANC leadership decided that it would establish an organized armed wing, named Umkhonto we Sizwe (Spear of the Nation), to carry out sabotage attacks on economic targets and not to threaten human lives. During an 18-month period from December 1961 the organization carried out a total of 200 attacks on targets such as post offices, government buildings, electricity sub-stations and railway lines. Despite the official policy on not putting human lives at risk a number of Umkhonto we Sizwe activists did attack policemen and collaborators. The organization was effectively neutralized by the security police in July 1963 when its headquarters at Lilliesleaf Farm in Rivonia were discovered and a number of crucial documents were unearthed. The majority of the organization's leadership, including Nelson Mandela, Walter Sisulu and Govan Mbeki, were arrested and sentenced to life imprisonment.

The PAC leadership had more ambitious and less well-organized plans for armed struggle. The PAC's armed wing, Poqo (meaning 'standing alone'), attempted to organize a general armed uprising to overthrow the white government once and for all. The leadership had little control over the individual cells and was unable to coordinate the armed attacks. One cell did organize an attack by some 250 men armed with makeshift weapons on the police station and prison in Paarl, but the attack failed against a police force armed with guns, and instead they attacked nearby houses, killing two people. There was also an isolated attack which killed five unarmed whites asleep in a car in the Transkei. Plans for a general uprising were effectively crushed when Potlako Leballo, one of the organization's founders and then resident in the British colony of Lesotho, stupidly boasted of the plans. As a result the PAC headquarters were raided by the British authorities and Poqo membership lists were handed over to the South Africans. Hundreds of people were arrested in a huge police operation and the PAC was effectively smashed. Despite its short-lived publicity and success, the organization was unable to reorganize effectively in exile and it was never again able to compete with the ANC for the leadership of South Africa's disposed African population.

1960s: the darkest days With the ANC and PAC banned and their leaders either in prison or exile, political opposition by Africans to the Apartheid state was muted in the 1960s. The 'separate development' policies of the nationalists began to be applied with more rigour and economic opportunities for Africans became even more constrained. The winds of change may have been sweeping across the rest of Africa but for most South Africans the 1960s represented the darkest days.

The newly declared Republic appeared confident and strong and the National Party was able to gain support from all sections of the white electorate, English-speaking as well as Afrikaans. The economy boomed and quickly recovered from the financial crash in the aftermath of Sharpville. International capital was attracted back by exceptionally good rates of return on investment and by the promise of cheap and non-unionized African labour. Germany and France were particularly keen on grabbing a piece of the pie and began to invest heavily in South African industry for the first time. In response to this new investment the South African economy rapidly diversified and actively sought out new export markets. The South African government played an active role in the economic boom and channelled investment into state-run enterprises including, significantly, the arms industry. The National Party also set about promoting Afrikaners within the civil service and state-run industry. Over this period the economic divide between English and Afrikaans-speaking white South Africans significantly narrowed.

The economic divide between white and black, however, widened. Whilst wages in manufacturing for whites increased, Africans found theirs held down. With organized opposition smashed, the government set about fully implementing its Apartheid policies. Forced removals increased as the government set about dividing the country into clear white, Indian, coloured and African zones. The official policy was that all Africans should live within the homelands though the presence of large townships like Soweto made this policy look unlikely. Nevertheless Africans living in cities such as Pretoria with homeland areas within daily commuting distance (in reality huge distances), found themselves removed to new townships within the homeland. On occasions the government also altered the borders of homelands so that townships on the outskirts of cities were absorbed into a new administrative structure. Forced removals and natural population growth meant that the populations of the homelands increased rapidly and though these areas were officially rural, their population densities were closer to urban areas.

Apart from the insidious change of name there were important differences between the previous reserve system and the homelands. The Apartheid government attempted to allocate each and every African to one of eight tribes and then allocated them to a homeland. This proved very difficult, partly because many Africans, especially those who were long-term residents in urban areas, did not identify themselves as belonging to a particular tribe and partly because, as the history of pre-colonial African groups discussed above indicates, tribal identity was often fluid and somewhat confused. Many people resisted attempts to define them as belonging to one of eight hard and fast categories and the government tacitly admitted this problem when it increased the number of possible tribes to which people could be allocated to 10.

Under the Apartheid system all Africans were supposed to express their political rights through the homeland administration. The government established totally separate bureaucracies in each homeland and then began a process of encouraging the areas to become increasingly autonomous. A number of African leaders saw that they could gain power and economic wealth through the new system and actively collaborated with the Apartheid state.

During the 1970s the South African government encouraged the homeland administrations to become independent states. They argued that this was a process that would allow Africans to enjoy full political rights in their own area. The first homeland to take independence was Transkei in 1976 and over the next five years Ciskei, Bophuthatswana and Venda followed suit. Transkei was at least a more or less unified block of land with a long coastline, but the other three were divided into numerous small blocks totally surrounded by South Africa. Their independence was never recognized by any country other than the Republic of South Africa: and they even refused to recognize each other's independence! The borders of Bophuthatswana were so complicated that neither South Africa's nor the homeland government were ever quite sure exactly where they were. Indeed just before independence the borders had to be altered when it was discovered that the South African embassy to Bophuthatswana was not actually inside the homeland. Though homeland independence was a farce it had great significance for the South Africans labelled as belonging to that particular tribe. They were now considered foreigners in the land of their birth.

The developing Apartheid programme had not just material effects on the African population but also psychological. In the late 1950s and early 1960s many African people felt that the overthrow of the racist white state was imminent. But the Apartheid state had managed to break African opposition and for almost a decade renewed resistance seemed impossible. The effects on many Africans' morale was not surprisingly extremely bad.

Union and student opposition In the early 1970s South Africa entered a new era of opposition to Apartheid, but this time not led by organized political groups such as the ANC and PAC but by the trade unions. During the 1960s there had been very little labour unrest; only about 2000 workers went on strike each year. Then in early 1973 there was suddenly a huge rise in strike activity and in the first three months of the year there were 160 strikes involving something like 61,000 workers. The epicentre for the strike activity was Durban but they quickly spread to other areas such as East London and then on to the Rand. These strikes were unusually successful in gaining the workers' demands; almost always this was for increased wages to reflect the recent sharp rises in the inflation rate. One reason they were surprisingly successful was that the workers refused to elect leaders to enter into negotiations with their employers; rather they simply published their demands and then struck for short periods, usually staying in the vicinity of the factory. This meant that the employers had no target on which to aim reprisals and the police could not be called in to arrest strike leaders.

The early 1970s also saw the rise of a more vocal African student protest movement. This was spearheaded by the South Africa Students Organization (SASO), which had broken away from the white-dominated National Union of South African Students in 1968, under the leadership of Steve Biko. SASO had a Black Consciousness ideology which stressed the need for all black people in South Africa, Africans, Indians and coloureds, to free themselves from the mental oppression that taught them white people were somehow innately superior to blacks. SASO took this message out into the country at large and played particular attention to spreading the ideology amongst school pupils.

With the example of the striking workers before them and a Black Consciousness message in their minds school pupils began to rebel against an education system designed to make them fit only for un-skilled and semi-skilled occupations. The immediate issue around which they organized their protest was the new rules enforcing the Afrikaans language as a medium of instruction. On the 16 June 1976 a Soweto school pupils' committee organized a mass march to deliver their complaints to the local authorities. This peaceful march was met with a violent response and the police shot two of the pupils. At first the pupils fled but then many turned and started throwing stones at the police. They then went on a rampage throughout the township destroying every symbol of their oppression that they could get to, including the government-run beer halls which many pupils felt bought off their fathers' opposition to state oppression with cheap beer. The **Soweto Uprising**, as the incident soon became known, marked an important turning point in the history of opposition to Apartheid: from 16 June 1976 onwards there was constant and violent unrest across South Africa, lead by school pupils but gaining widespread support.

Rioting erupted around the country when news of the Soweto Uprising spread. The government was hard pressed to stop the unrest spreading beyond the townships but in a nationwide clampdown they eventually managed to quieten some of the protest. The SASO and school pupil leaders found themselves under arrest or harassed by the police. Many of the young people involved in the uprising escaped across the border.

ANC re-enters the scene Though the ANC had not been involved in the organization of the school pupils' protest, their underground cells, which had been carefully and quietly organizing in the early 1970s, it did help channel escaping pupils towards the guerrilla training camps they had set up in countries like Tanzania, Algeria and the newly independent Angola. The ANC benefited greatly from this new arrival of activists and managed effectively to amalgamate them into their organization. The ANC had made better use of their time in exile than the PAC, who suffered from poor organization and internal splits. Many of the pupils were ideologically closer to the PAC but they nevertheless ended up in ANC camps. In recent years these camps have been revealed to have often been pretty brutal places and people who disagreed with the camps' leaders were sometimes dealt with extremely harshly.

Despite the government crackdown, protests continued and a generalized culture of resistance was fostered. The ANC made use of this new climate of opposition to begin to reinfiltrate South Africa. In the late 1970s they began a new campaign of sabotage, but now there was less care to avoid civilian casualties and the ANC released a statement saying they were at war with the Apartheid state and, whilst their attacks were aimed at Apartheid and economic targets, they could not promise that civilians would not be caught up in the struggle. A number of Unkhonto cells seemed to ignore these commands and bombs were set off in shopping centres and similar locations.

The ANC quickly regained legitimacy amongst Africans, many of whom had been disillusioned with the organization during its long dormant period. Black Consciousness organizations, smashed apart by the police after the Soweto Uprising, lost support to the ANC, though it could be argued that the movement had achieved its aim of increasing African pride. In August 1983 there was a large gathering of 575 community, church and similar non-governmental organizations which resulted in the formation of the United Democratic Front (UDF) which spearheaded protest throughout the 1980s. The government argued that the organization was simply a front for the ANC. This was an exaggeration but it is true that the UDF did have strong links with the ANC and that they regarded it as the government in exile and the imprisoned Mandela as the legitimate president of the country.

'Total onslaught' and destabilization The Apartheid state was not only coming under attack from internal protest but from international criticism of the Pretoria regime. The ANC in exile had managed to foster anti-Apartheid groups in Europe and North America that began to put pressure on their governments to institute economic sanctions against South Africa. Most Commonwealth governments supported these sanctions and also instituted sporting and cultural sanctions on South Africa. The anti-Apartheid movement also started campaigns detailing the working conditions inside branches of multi-national companies in South Africa and asking individuals to boycott companies with large investments in South Africa. Despite the resistance of Margaret Thatcher and Ronald Reagan, during the 1980s these campaigns began to take effect and a number of important companies withdrew from South Africa.

This international isolation of Pretoria added to their gradual geopolitical isolation in southern Africa during the 1970s. Up until the mid-1970s South Africa had been surrounded either by states run by white settler régimes or by small states that rarely criticized their actions. However, independence for Angola and Mozambique in 1976 and Zimbabwe in 1980 changed all that. Now South Africa had hostile, left-wing, neighbours right on its doorstep, and even the previously compliant weaker states, such as Lesotho, began actively to oppose the Apartheid state. White South Africa felt increasingly vulnerable and the government argued that they were now facing a 'total onslaught' led by communists that were intent on bringing them down.

The Apartheid government reacted to this 'total onslaught' with a careful mixture of economic, diplomatic and military foreign policy designed to neutralize the threat. The exact mix of the different elements varied in each country and over time. In Angola, for example, intervention was in the form of a direct military invasion designed to overthrow the communist government. When the invasion faltered they concentrated on supplying an armed opposition movement and therefore helped to fuel a bloody civil war that has gone on more or less ever since. In Mozambique they also intervened militarily, but this time through another opposition organization that had originally been set up by Ian Smith's settler régime in Rhodesia/Zimbabwe. They encouraged their clients in Mozambique to blow up railways and pipelines running from Zimbabwe to their nearest ports. With these out of action, Zimbabwe and other landlocked central African states were forced to continue trading with South Africa in order to get access to the sea. This, in turn, gave the South Africans an important economic hold over the countries to the north.

Across the region South African guerrilla troops carried out occasional raids designed both to knock out ANC camps and to keep their neighbours in political and economic turmoil and therefore as less effective opponents. South Africa's proxy war with the rest of the region caused a huge amount of suffering to very many people, especially in Mozambique and Angola. Though these states did receive some international support the international media tended to concentrate more on events unfurling in the South African townships than on these regional events.

Reform or revolution?

In the mid-1980s South Africa's townships, simmering since the Soweto Uprising, exploded into violence. The primary target of the violence were Africans who had taken jobs as administrators in the 'homelands' or townships and African policemen. Many had their families killed and their houses burnt down and a new and horrendous form of execution was invented, called 'necklacing'. This involved placing a car tyre full of petrol over the victim's torso and then setting fire to it. The police reacted violently to unrest in the townships and shot, arrested and beat many protesters. Bus boycotts, strikes and 'stay aways', were frequent and often met with violence by the police.

Violence became endemic to the townships and there was a fine line between political violence and general crime. Many of the young ANC supporting comrades decided that they should take the law into their own hands and kangaroo courts were frequent occurrences. Older Africans sometimes found it hard to take orders from the youngsters and inter-generational battles broke out on a number of occasions, most violently at

Crossroads squatter camp on the outskirts of Cape Town. The violence was fanned by massive new flows of illegal migrants into the towns. The government was unable to cope with the new influx of people and eventually was forced into the withdrawal of the hated pass laws. The growth of squatter camps was spectacular and no sooner had the government removed squatters from one site than they appeared somewhere else. During the 1970s wage increases in established industry had been generous, partly reflecting the move towards a more capital intensive economy and partly a result of the strikes. The downside of this was massive and endemic unemployment, especially among the young. A whole generation of young people missed all their formal education because of their involvement in 'the struggle' and their chances of employment were extremely remote. Inevitably this fuelled the violence and crime.

The worst violence took place in the townships surrounding Pietermaritzburg and Durban. These areas were within the KwaZulu 'homeland' run by Gatsha Buthelezi. Originally Buthelezi had been an ANC supporter and had even received the organization's (reserved) blessing in the establishment of a Zulu cultural organization called Inkatha. The organization, however, began to act much more like a political party and ran the KwaZulu 'homeland' administration. When ANC supporters began to challenge the 'homelands' authority this lead to violent clashes as the two organizations vied for control of the townships. This conflict has continued until the present and has involved numerous atrocities committed by both sides.

By the late 1980s the South African state had more or less lost control of large portions of the townships. The unrest and international sanctions were hitting the economy hard and South African businesses were feeling the pinch. While the state security apparatus was strengthened and numerous crackdowns were attempted, the government, fearing revolution, also undertook a programme of reform.

To some extent this programme had begun in the 1970s but it was accelerated in the early 1980s under the presidency of PW Botha. One strand of the reform process was to pull coloureds and Indians into the political process under a new tri-cameral parliament. Under a new constitution there were to be three houses in the parliament, one for white voters, one for coloureds and one for Indians. Most coloureds and Indians saw this move as an attempt to drive a wedge between them and the African population and refused to vote for the new parliament. The National Party's reform policy also lead to a new split in Afrikaner ranks and the creation of a new, more right-wing, Conservative Party. Over the 1980s the new Party was to attract more and more Afrikaner support and the National Party became increasingly reliant upon English-speaking supporters.

Botha also set about dismantling some of the segregationist policies, in particular the 'petty Apartheid' legislation that divided up facilities such as beaches. These did very little to assuage the unrest in the townships and were probably more to do with creating an international impression of reform to hold off further sanctions. Under these circumstances the National Party began to do the unthinkable and sat down to negotiate with the ANC. Business leaders were the first South African establishment figures to talk with the ANC in exile, in September 1985. With sanctions and unrest big business was being squeezed hard and Apartheid was no longer making them good profits as it had in the 1960s. The business leaders were therefore keen for a political settlement, but were obviously nervous about the intentions of an ANC strongly influenced by communist ideology. South African ministers and eventually Botha himself met with Mandela, offering him his freedom if he repudiated the use of violence as a weapon in the fight against Apartheid. Mandela refused the offer and for a time it seemed further reform was impossible.

The late 1980s, however, saw a crucial shift in the global political scene that opened up an important window to allow a negotiated settlement. The unexpected collapse of the Soviet block suddenly made Botha's image of a 'total onslaught' seem meaningless and the ANC was no longer seen by whites as a front for Soviet-backed communist expansion into South Africa. These changes coincided with a change in leadership of the National Party and the replacement of Botha with FW de Klerk. Even though de Klerk had been regarded as a conservative he soon made it clear he was embarking on a bold new policy. The ANC was unbanned, Mandela and other political leaders were released and the process of negotiating a settlement got underway.

Lesotho

As the history of Lesotho is so tied up in that of South Africa, you should also refer to pages 838-862.

The rise of the Basotho state

The roots of modern-day Lesotho were in an era of intense political upheaval known to the Basotho as the *difaqane* (and the Zulu and Xhosa as the *mfecane*). The exact causes of the *difaqane* are a subject of considerable debate (see page 845) but what is clear is that out of this intense upheaval a new and powerful Basotho state was forged under the influential ruler Moshoeshoe. Before this time there had not been such a thing as a Basotho state, but simply a set of clans speaking similar dialects and with similar cultural practices. These clans formed constantly shifting sets of loose alliances and rivalries and their fortunes tended to wax and wane over time.

During the early 19th century these clans came under attack from highly organized and militarily ruthless Zulu and Ndebele armies (*impis*). Instead of uniting against these new enemies most clans ended up attacking their neighbours in an attempt to raid back cattle and grain lost to the *impis*. Moshoeshoe, chief of the insignificant Koena clan, however, had a more sophisticated approach. He carefully sued for peace with all the more powerful clans or marauding *impis* with whom he came into contact and would send them tribute gifts of cattle. At the same time he attacked and stole the cattle of weaker clans and then invited them to join with him in a new alliance. Using this strategy, Moshoeshoe was able to build up the power and influence of the Koena clan, especially after moving his headquarters to the strong defensive position at Thaba Boisiu. Soon his influence spread over the whole of the southern highveld with his chiefdom centred on the fertile Clarendon Valley. Unlike Shaka and Dingane, kings of the Zulu, Moshoeshoe did not insist that all his followers give up their previous clan identity and indeed his new Basotho state was more an alliance of a number of different clans than a united and centralized kingdom.

Wars with the Free State

During the 1830s, two new forces entered into the Basotho sphere from the south and west: Voortrekkers leaving the Cape Colony in search of new territory (see page 845); and missionaries looking for converts. These groups offered both threats and opportunities for the new Basotho state. The first missionaries to arrive in Lesotho were French Protestants. Moshoeshoe was keen to have them in Lesotho, partially because he wanted to learn more about the powerful Europeans impinging more and more on his state and partially to help him gain access to European guns. Their presence also presented a threat, however, as the converts' loyalty could sometimes be divided.

Chief Moshoeshoe and Thaba Bosiu

Chief Moshoeshoe, often regarded as the founder of the Basotho nation, was born in about 1786 at Menkhoaneng in the north of present-day Lesotho. Though he was later to become one of the most powerful chiefs in southern Africa, he was by birth no more than a village headman. According to oral tradition, however, even as a young man he had dreams of becoming a great chief. Fearing that his short temper and over-weening ambition would lead him into trouble, Moshoeshoe's father sent him for instruction from the famous chief Mohlomi. Mohlomi impressed on the young Moshoeshoe the need for a ruler to gain loyalty from his followers not just through violence but by ensuring they were materially reliant upon his protection.

Moshoeshoe learnt his lessons well and realized that control of large numbers of cattle was the key to political power. With many cattle he could afford the brideprice needed to marry many wives (eventually over 40) and therefore bind other lineages and clans to his own, and by lending some of his cattle to his supporters he was able to make them materially reliant upon his power. So Moshoeshoe set about building up his herds by both careful management and raiding his neighbours. His reputation soon grew and with his followers he broke away from his previous clan to establish a new chieftainship on Butha-Buthe.

Through a careful strategic balance of making alliances with stronger chiefs and attacking weaker ones (and raiding their cattle), Moshoeshoe soon built up his power base. He never went into any battle he could risk losing and often managed to buy off enemies with gifts of cattle – sometimes raiding the same herds back if his rival fell upon hard times. Nevertheless the interior of South Africa in the early 19th century was a violent and complex political world and Moshoeshoe came under increasing military pressure from nearby chiefs. Realizing Butha-Buthe was not easy to defend Moshoeshoe sent out his brother to find a new stronghold. He returned with news of a larger flat-topped mountain with plenty of water resources two days' journey to the south.

In June 1824 Moshoeshoe and his followers set off on the dangerous trek to their new headquarters. Despite coming under attack during the move and losing Moshoeshoe's grandfather to a band of cannibals, he and his followers managed to secure themselves in their new stronghold. From this new position Moshoeshoe was able to extend his power and controlled the whole of the Clarendon Valley and a large number of followers.

Later in his reign he came under intense pressure from the new Boer republics and lost much of his kingdom, eventually turning to the British for protection. Nevertheless, this remarkable leader had managed to build a powerful and unified kingdom during a time of intense strife and continual conflict out of an initial handful of followers. He died at Thaba Bosiu in 1870.

A more obvious threat came from the Voortrekkers. They wanted land and, unlike other new African arrivals, were unwilling to show allegiance to a Basotho state. With their guns and wagons they were a powerful military force and over the next 30 years slowly gained more and more control over areas formerly belonging to the Basotho. By the end of the 1860s the Basotho had lost half of their best arable land in the Clarendon Valley to the new Voortrekker Free State republic. But despite this major setback the Voortrekkers also provided the Basotho with an opportunity. Most were unable or unwilling to survive by farming, instead relying on hunting, trading and land speculating as their economic mainstay. They, therefore, had to buy food, especially grain, and the Basotho were able to provide them with it. Using new techniques, often learnt from the missionaries, and the new grain crop maize, brought by Europeans from the Americas, the Basotho developed a thriving agricultural economy. They soon began to trade not just with the Voortrekkers but also further afield, especially with the eastern districts of the Cape Colony. In exchange for grain the Basotho bought new European goods, especially guns.

Moshoeshoe realized, however, that their booming economy did not make them immune to attack from the Free State and he decided to turn to the British for help. At first the British refused to become involved but over time they began to realize that it was in their interests to have peace between the Boers and Basotho. In 1868, with Voortrekker commandos laying siege to Thaba Bosiu and burning acres of the Basotho's maize, the British declared Lesotho a British Protectorate. At a peace convention the following year the boundaries of Lesotho, or 'Basutoland' as the British named the area, were firmly established. The Basotho had lost huge swathes of their territory to the Free State but British protection did allow them to maintain a degree of political independence. This was more or less the last big political manoeuvre by Moshoeshoe, who died just two years later.

British Protection and the Gun War

At first the sole concern of the British was to maintain peace along the new boundaries, but that changed when administration was handed over from direct British rule to rule by the Cape Colony. The Cape Colony began to intervene in a more direct way in the government of the country. Chiefs found their powers reduced and everybody found themselves subject to a new hut tax. Not surprisingly, many Basotho were unhappy about these new arrangements. There were also tensions between the new Paramount Chief Letsie and his two brothers and also between the main Koena lineage and other clans who had been integrated into the Basotho state. One of these clans, the Phuti in southern Lesotho, refused to recognize the authority of the local Cape magistrate. When the magistrate tried to arrest the son of the Phuti's chief, Moorosi, open conflict broke out. To the disgust of many Basotho, Letsie sided with the Cape Colony and assisted in putting down the rebellion. In November 1879 after months of fighting the Cape forces finally stormed Moorosi's stronghold, slaughtering him and many of his people.

The following year there was another, more serious, outbreak of fighting. The immediate cause was the attempts by the Cape Colony to enforce a general policy of disarming all Basotho. For most Basotho, already unhappy about the way they were being administered and worried about rumours that the south of the country would be opened to white settlement, this was too much. The so-called Gun War of 1880-1881 saw the Cape forces verging on the brink of outright defeat and there were numerous bloody battles. Not all chiefs agreed with the war, however, and Letsie himself never publicly supported the attacks on the Cape authorities. Fighting broke out, especially in the north, between elements in favour of the war and those against it. Peace only returned when the British agreed to suspend the policy of enforced disarmament and agree that administration should be taken away from the Cape Colony and returned to rule from London.

Colonial era

The return to British rule also saw a return to the much less interventionist policy, and the country was basically administered through the chiefs, not white magistrates. The British continued with the policy right through until the 1930s and there were few significant political developments. Economically and socially, however, the country changed drastically. The early years of British rule saw the agricultural economy continue to thrive, especially as the new diamond mines at Kimberley gave the Basotho a new and profitable market to serve. Over time, however, these markets became less and less lucrative. The arrival of railways meant that Basotho farmers had to compete with cheap imported grain from places like the USA and Canada. And as time went on, white farmers were also providing more and more competition, especially after they began to receive vast quantities of state subsidies and other assistance. The agricultural economy began to falter and during the first decades of the 20th century the country no longer managed to produce enough food for export and indeed became a major importer. Part of the problem was also the migrant labour system that the Basotho found themselves tied into. Basotho men began to travel to the mines to earn wages to buy European goods and to pay taxes, but as the agricultural economy faltered it became more important for simple survival. This created a vicious cycle, as more Basotho men went to the mines there were fewer of them to help their wives with agriculture which, as a consequence, became less productive.

The early decades of the 20th century also saw the growth of a small but important educated class within Lesotho. They resented the continued political power of the chiefs and, through their Progressive Association, lobbied the British to introduce a more democratic system of administration. Another more radical political organization also began to make a mark. Known as Lekhotla la Bafo (Council of Commoners) this group was highly critical of both the British and of the chiefs, who they claimed were corrupt, and conniving with the British to impoverish the Basotho nation. While criticizing the chiefs for their individual actions they strongly supported the institution of chieftainship and advocated a return to pre-colonial systems of government.

One of the key reasons the British never bothered to intervene (and certainly not invest any money) in Lesotho was their belief that the country would at some stage be incorporated into the rest of South Africa. Over time, however, this eventuality became less and less likely, especially with the enactment of increasingly racist segregation legislation in South Africa. The British colonial authorities realized that transferring the country's administration to South Africa would not only encounter stiff opposition in Lesotho but also from the increasing number of people in Britain criticizing the South African government. From the mid 1930s and especially after 1945 the British colonial authorities, therefore, began to take a more active interest in the internal affairs of Lesotho, and even began to invest some capital into development schemes for the country.

The Progressive Association lobbied the British hard for the introduction of a more democratic government, believing that they, the educated élite, should be the country's natural leaders not the chiefs. Starting in the late 1930s, the British started to reform the system of government. These reforms at first had the effect of increasing the power of a few of the most important chiefs, to the detriment of some of the less important ones. This was one of the major causes of an outbreak of 'medicine murders' in which people were killed in order to use parts of their bodies in 'medicines' believed to bring power or protection. A number of the most important chiefs were implicated in these murders, which were seen by many as further proof that the chiefs were incapable of running the country. From the mid-1950s onwards new reforms led to a decrease in all chiefs' political powers and the gradual handing over of the national administration to the developing political parties.

The first of these new political parties was the Basutoland Congress Party (BCP). The BCP had many of its roots in the Lekhotla la Bafo organization and strong links with the ANC in South Africa, especially with the 'Africanist' wing of the ANC who later split to form the PAC (see pages 855-868). Not unlike *Lekhotla la Bafo*, which withered away as the BCP grew, the BCP did not call for a return to 'traditional' Basotho political systems but for a new democratic and independent nation. One of the key elements of its platform was strong criticism of the racist South African regime. This stance was opposed by some more conservative elements within the organization and they split to form a rival Basutoland National Party (BNP). The BNP was more traditional in outlook and received substantial support from the Catholic Church. The first elections in the country were held in 1960 to elect members to District Councils who then sent representatives to the National Council. These elections returned BCP candidates around the country, but the turnout was extremely low and women had still not been granted suffrage.

The British colonial authorities entered into wide-ranging discussions with the members of the National Council about writing a new national constitution under which the country would be granted its independence. After numerous wranglings a new constitution, based on the Westminster model, was produced. There would be a directly elected lower house from which the prime minister and cabinet would be chosen and an appointed upper house (Senate) consisting of the most important chiefs. The Senate's powers were limited to delaying legislation. Much to the dismay of the new and young incumbent, Moshoeshoe II, the monarch was to be no more than a ceremonial Head of State. Under this new constitutional framework elections were held in 1965 to form the government to take Lesotho to independence. To the surprise of many these were won by a tiny majority by the BNP. Their leader, Leabua Jonathan, therefore became the country's first Prime Minister and on 4 October 1966 Lesotho became an independent country.

Independence

Most Basotho had high expectations for this new system of government; expectation which the BNP proved incapable of fulfilling. The civil service was dominated by BCP members and the BNP was unwilling to work with them and instead relied on many expatriate workers, including a number from South Africa. The BNP's inability to deliver once in power helped the BCP regroup and in the 1970 elections they won a clear majority, maintaining their urban powerbase and managing to gain widespread support in the mountains as well. To the surprise of just about everyone Leabua Jonathan refused to hand over power, declared a state of emergency and arrested hundreds of BCP supporters. At first it looked as if he would have to come to an agreement with the BCP especially when Britain suspended all aid to Lesotho but as the crisis dragged on and Britain and other countries resumed their aid programmes the BNP's position became stronger.

Under pressure from Britain the BCP split, with some moderates entering into a new national assembly appointed by Jonathan to write a new constitution and others turning to more radical methods. An attempted counter-coup by elements of the BCP in January 1974 was a fiasco and the BNP tightened their grip on power. BCP civil servants were purged and activists arrested or sent into exile. Jonathan concentrated more and more power into his hands and developed many of the state security policies of other dictators. His attitude towards South Africa, however, shifted somewhat unexpectedly. From having been an advocate of close and cordial relations with the Apartheid regime he began to be more and more outspoken in his opposition. He developed close links with the ANC, who were offered support within Lesotho. This stance in turn brought him into confrontation with South Africa and led to attempts by South Africa to destabilize his regime. On the other hand the changed stance gave him increased legitimacy in the eyes of the international community and the government benefited from a generous influx of development aid.

The BCP, meanwhile, tried to build on its links with the PAC and some of their members received guerrilla training at camps in Libya. Elements within the South African security apparatus actively courted members of the BCP and offered them assistance in their attempts to wage a guerrilla war against Jonathan's regime. Some BCP members seemed willing to drink from this poison chalice and during much of the 1980s the country suffered a very low-level guerrilla war. Some members of the military were very unhappy with the situation and in 1986 the South Africans managed to toppled Jonathan's government.

At first the new government was a coalition between the military and Moshoeshoe II. Though they promised to hold new elections, things moved very slowly and if anything the new regime was more corrupt than the previous one. Relations soon broke down between the military and Moshoeshoe II, who went into exile. In the early 1990s the military government began to make arrangements for new elections, with the process being spurred on by outbreaks of rioting and by the negotiation process across the border in South Africa. These long-awaited elections finally took place in March 1993 and the BCP won a huge majority and every single seat in the national Parliament. Twenty-three years after being denied his position the leader of the BCP, Ntsu Mokhehle, at last became Prime Minister.

Swaziland

The precolonial history of Swaziland started with the Dlamini clan in the late 16th century when they migrated south settling in the region around what is now Delagoa Bay. Around two centuries later, in 1750, Ngwane III migrated to what is now Swaziland. The land was a well-watered mountain area with fertile soils and good pastures for raising cattle. The mountainous territory also offered good protection from Zulu raids.

By the 19th century, Swaziland had become a major power in the region controlling a much larger area than it does today. Europeans arrived in 1836, and called the place Swaziland after the leader at the time Mswasi II. After gold was discovered at Pigg's Peak and Forbes' Reef, large numbers foreigners were attracted to the area and pressure for land concessions increased. The 'concession rush' occurred during the reign of Mbandeni when speculators believed there was about to be a great boom in Swaziland. Five hundred concessions were eventually granted on which the king received a payment. When the gold rush ended without any great results most of the concessionaires left the country.

The Transvaal administered Swaziland from 1894 to 1903. After the Anglo Boer War the British took control of the country leaving the traditional forms of government in the hands of the royal family. One of the major problems was that most of the land had been granted to foreigners in concessions. The Swazis believed that the concessions were only temporary but a government commission recognized the concessions as valid as long as the rents continued to be paid. In 1907 a third of the land under concession was expropriated to give the Swazis somewhere to live. Sobhuza II, the grandson of Mbandeni, became king in 1921 and spent his resources on regaining the land for the Swazi nation. Over 60% of the land has now been bought back from the concession holders.

Political activity in modern Swaziland began in the 1960s with the formation of the Swaziland Progressive Party by younger educated Swazis. The party later split into three factions of which the Ngwane National Liberatory Congress (NNLC) became the most influential. Swazi royalists formed the Imbokodvo National Movement in 1964. They formed an alliance with the European Advisory Council which had been established to look after the interests of European farmers and miners. The elections held before independence in 1964 were won by Imbokodvo who controlled all the seats.

Modern Southern Africa

South Africa

Politics

Constitution South Africa's first democratic constitution was passed by the Constitutional Assembly in May 1996, the 1994 elections being held under an interim version. After ratification by the Supreme Court most of it passed into law, while some elements were returned to the Constitutional Assembly for reconsideration. The Constitutional Assembly is made up of both Houses of Parliament sitting together and constitutional provision needs to be passed by a two-thirds majority. The bi-cameral Parliament consists of a directly elected lower house (the National Assembly) and an upper house (the Senate) appointed by provincial assemblies. The National Assembly is elected via a system of proportional representation. The President is elected by members of the National Assembly and chooses his cabinet from those members.

Parliament sits in Cape Town and government ministries are in Pretoria. This geographical division dates from the Act of Union in 1910 as a way of balancing power between the two former British colonies and the two former Boer republics. This division has been criticized in recent years as government representatives have to waste time and money travelling backwards and forwards to opposite ends of the country. There are moves to relocate Parliament in Pretoria, though this will require a change in the constitution and would be strongly opposed by delegates from the Western Cape.

Significant powers are devolved to the nine provincial administrations. Provincial assemblies are also elected via proportional representation and in turn they elect members to the Senate who are specifically charged with looking after provincial interests against the power of central Government.

Provincial governments have significant scope over things such as regional planning, investment policies, social services and education. Provincial leaders are, therefore, powerful political figures and a number of politicians of national standing have decided to serve as provincial representatives rather than seek election to Parliament.

1994 elections

The African National Congress (ANC), together with its alliance partners, the South African Communist Party (SACP) and the Congress of South African Trade Unions (Cosatu) won the national vote in South Africa's first democratic elections in April 1994 by a huge majority. They gained 63% of the total vote giving them 252 seats in the National Assembly. The only other parties to win significant numbers of votes were the National Party (NP) (20.5%) and Inkharta Freedom Party (IFP) (10.8%). The ANC's victory was based upon widespread support from the majority African population throughout the country. The only area in which its support amongst Africans was threatened was in KwaZulu Natal where the IFP received significant support from rural Zulu speakers. The IFP were unable to convert their popularity in their political heartland to any other parts of the country. The NP received widespread support from the white population and, more surprisingly, from a majority of coloured voters in the Western Cape.

Four other parties managed to secure seats, though with tiny proportions of the total vote. The Freedom Front (FF), an alliance of right-wing Afrikaner Nationalists, won nine seats with a 2.3% share of the vote, coming mainly from working-class Afrikaners fearful of the new political dispensation. The Democratic Party (DP), traditionally the party of liberal English-speaking white South Africans, were unable to expand their attraction and won a paltry 1.7% of the vote. The Pan African Congress (PAC) fared particularly badly; an organization which in the 1950s had seriously challenged the ANC's position as the most popular political organization amongst the African population received only 1.2% of the national vote, giving them just five seats. The remaining two seats were won by a newly formed political organization called the African Christian Democratic Party (ACDP) which called for the enactment of policies in line with the gospels.

In line with the interim Constitution, the leader of the ANC, Nelson Mandela, was duly elected President and set about choosing his cabinet. The constitution stated that any party who gained more than 20% of the vote was eligible to have its leader instated as a Deputy President. Mandela, therefore had two deputy presidents, Thabo Mbeki from the ANC and FW de Klerk, the leader of the NP. The selection of Thabo Mbeki as Deputy President effectively marked him as Mandela's likely successor. All other parties were invited to join the ANC in a Government of National Unity (GNU). Despite the continued antagonism between the ANC and IFP, Mongosuthu Buthelezi was given the important post of Minister of Home Affairs. A number of cabinet posts were also filled by delegates from the NP. The only party to stay out of the GNU were the DP who felt they could have more of an impact as the official opposition.

The elections for provincial assemblies resulted in the ANC winning control of seven out of the nine provinces. In a number of provinces they won huge majorities: 80% of the vote in the Free State, 83% in Mpumalanga, 85% in the Eastern Cape, 87% in North West Province, and a staggering 95% in Northern Province. Though many of these areas are associated with hardline Afrikaner nationalism it has to be born in mind that the vast majority of the population in these areas are poor, rural Africans who solidly support the ANC.

In the more populous provinces of Gauteng and KwaZulu Natal, the ANC fared less well. In KwaZulu Natal the ANC were beaten into second place by the IFP who won just over half of the votes. In Gauteng the ANC still won an impressive overall majority of 58%, but they lost seats to the NP (24%) who gained the support of the urban middle-class whites and to smaller parties such as the FF and DP. Three seats in Gauteng also went to the IFP: their only seats outside KwaZulu Natal.

In the Western and Northern Cape the NP did better than many people had expected. Their 40% in the Northern Cape was still substantially behind the ANC's 50% but in the Western Cape they managed to gain 55% to the ANC's 33%. In both these provinces the NP vote was based upon widespread support amongst coloured voters who feared an ANC government would put the interests of Africans ahead of their own. The irony of the only NP election victory being built on the back of coloured voters is quintessentially South African!

Politics since the 1994 election

The GNU's first task was to set about ratifying the interim constitution. Debate on some issues was intense. Labour rights proved to be a bone of contention between the NP and ANC while the ANC and IFP frequently clashed over the division of power between central government and the provinces. Despite their official position as part of the GNU and Buthelezi's cabinet seat the IFP boycotted much of the debate on the constitution on the grounds that the ANC had gone back on a pre-election promise to allow international mediation on the issue of KwaZulu Natal ceding from the rest of the country. Nevertheless by May 1996 all the clauses of the new constitution had been agreed and the Constitutional Assembly voted to ratify the new constitution. With the new constitution in place De Klerk announced that the NP would be leaving the GNU to become the official opposition and try to rebuild itself in order to fight the next national elections due in 1999. The NP ministers selected in 1994 left the cabinet in June 1996 and were replaced by members of the ANC. No new Deputy President was selected; effectively increasing the power of Thabo Mbeki. The IFP remained within the GNU.

In the aftermath of the election the most pressing political problem was the continuation of violence in KwaZulu Natal between supporters of the ANC and supporters of the IFP. Unprovoked attacks, revenge killings and political intrigue all continued to haunt the townships and villages of the province. Peace talks between the leaderships of the provincial parties and high-level discussions between Mandela and Buthelezi were frequently called off and when they did take place made no impact on the rate of violence. Local elections for new unitary local government structures took place throughout the country in mid-1995 but were frequently delayed in KwaZulu Natal because of the violence and allegations over fraudulent electoral rolls. The elections did eventually take place, about one year after the rest of the country and marked the beginnings of a period of significantly reduced levels of violence in the province. Buthelezi and the IFP continue to be primarily interested in provincial issues, though Buthelezi's reputation nationally has somewhat improved from its dire position in 1995 to 1996. The local elections in KwaZulu Natal indicate that the IFP has continued to command widespread support in the rural areas, though the urban townships returned ANC local governments by big majorities.

Mandela commanded huge popular support amongst the African population and won the backing of many of South Africa's white population as well. Mbeki lacked the same mass popularity, but was seen as having aa good grasp of the major issues and is credited with being a key player in bringing peace to KwaZulu Natal. Mandela's punishing international schedule meant that Mbeki was left with many of the domestic political chores, especially dealing with the ANC's internal problems. His position as Mandela's successor left him vulnerable to accusations of manipulating internal ANC politics to strenthen his position over some of his colleagues. This was particularly the case with the easing out of Cyril Ramaphosa, who had led the ANC negotiating team during initial negotiations with the NP. Prior to the election he was seen by many as Mandela's likely successor and his decision to leave politics and join a commercial company was seen as evidence that his leadership ambitions had been frustrated.

The ANC has had its fair share of internal wranglings. In 1995 the most serious of these was over the role of Winnie Mandela (or since her divorce, Winnie Madikizela-Mandela). Since mid-1995, she has experienced a spectacular fall from grace. She was sacked from her cabinet position in 1995, and was divorced by Nelson Mandela the following year. She has faced a series of charges and convictions, including for her role in the kidnapping and murder of a 14-year-old anti-Apartheid activist; she received a six-year prison sentence, which was reduced to a fine. In 2003 she was found guilty of 43 counts of fraud and 25 of theft. Although she again managed to walk away from a prison sentence, she resigned from her positions as a Member of Parliament and President of the ANC Women's League. It seemed Madikizela-Mandela's lifestyle had finally caught up with her.

Provincial ANC governments have also had their share of problems. The Free State party was subject to a bitter split during 1996 between the then provincial premier Patrick Lekota and his Finance executive, who was investigated for corruption. The national ANC leadership stepped into the battle and redeployed Lekota as a member of the National Assembly. In the midlands region of KwaZulu Natal the local ANC leader, Sifiso Nkabinde, was expelled after he was accused of having been an informer during the Apartheid era.

He has since joined Holomise's National Consultative Forum and accused the ANC of fostering violence and stockpiling weapons in the region. The Eastern Cape ANC has also had more than its fair share of problems and the national executive have intervened on more than one occasion.

The NP has very little success in repositioning itself as a non-racial centrist party. Its efforts to change its image have not been helped by the continual unearthing of more and more horror stories from the Apartheid years. Particularly damaging to the NP are the stories about covert actions taking place right up to the evening of the 1994 elections, a time when the party had supposedly thrown off its old ways and embraced democracy. The Steyn Report into the actions of the Third Force includes many disturbing allegations, including reports that SADF operatives initiated the spate of train massacres that took place on the Witwatersrand in the run up to the 1994 election. Other allegations in the report included reports that the SADF used chemical bombs against Frelimo troops in Mozambique in the late 1980s and that they stockpiled weapons in game reserves in countries as far away as Kenya.

Other reports of atrocities have come out of the hearings of the Truth and Reconciliation Commission (TRC) chaired by Desmond Tutu. These hearings were intended to be a process of national healing, but many of the wounds revealed look more like running sores. Reports of Apartheid-era death camps in the South African countryside resulted in the media putting huge pressure on De Klerk to say exactly what he, and other senior NP members, knew about. Instead De Klerk went on the offensive, denying any knowledge of the camps and attacking the TRC for being 'political'. His image was tarnished by both the allegations and his reaction: his claims that ANC members had attacked his fundamental human rights by saying they did not believe his denials made him look petty, especially in the context of the gross human rights violations being continually reported in the TRC.

De Klerk also dithered over restructuring the NP. There were originally two basic visions for the party's future within the organizations. Firstly a more conservative wing, centred around the hard-line Western Cape Premier Hernus Kriel, wanted to develop the NP as the 'party of minorities' and look to maintain control of Western Cape and perhaps make in-roads in the Northern Cape and KwaZulu Natal. They argued that this approach might leave the party in constant opposition nationally but that it would allow them to retain control of at least one province. The other vision, associated with a more liberal section of the party, centred around former secretary general Roelf Meyer, wanted radically to restructure the party, looking for support amongst the African population and sought to challenge the ANC for national power. De Klerk's attempt to accommodate both visions proved to be untenable and in mid-1997 he appeared to opt for the first. Meyer was first dismissed as secretary general and then he had his task team (trying to find viable African NP leaders) disbanded.

Not surprisingly, Meyer left the party and formed an alternative organization known as the New Movement Process. He took a number of members of the Gauteng Provincial Assembly (his home province) with him to the new organization. There was some speculation at the time that he might team up with Holomise's National Consultative Forum or the Democratic Party.

In June 1999 Nelson Mandela passed the mantle of power over to his long time deputy Thabo Mbeki. In the national elections the ANC won a large victory despite a widespread feeling that they had still to deliver on promises they made when they first came to power in 1994. Although there was some violence associated with the elections it was a great triumph for the country on a continent which has so rarely witnessed fair and peaceful democratic elections.

The outcome of the election showed that people still saw the ANC as the only party capable of providing for their needs. Mbeki was always going to find Mandela a hard act to follow. He surrounded himself with a cabinet of loyal supporters, and he is regarded as an efficient if not dynamic party leader. Keeping the ANC-SACP-Cosatu alliance intact has been one of Mbeki's biggest challenges. Following the 1999 election, relations between the ANC and its alliance partners became increasingly strained over the issues of privatization, the neo-liberal growth, employment and redistribution (Gear) policy, and the government's approach to dealing with HIV/AIDS. Much to Mbeki's embarrassment, Cosatu timed a two-day general strike against privatization to coincide with the International Conference on Racism in Durban during August-September 2001. Cosatu also publicly supported a court challenge to the Government's AIDS policy by the HIV/AIDS NGO, Treatment Action Campaign. However, by February 2002 there were signs of rapprochement between the government and Cosatu, and rumours of a split were premature, although Cosatu has continued to criticize the government's AIDS policy.

Thabo Mbeki has been keen to see South Africa expand its scope of activity in regional and international affairs. Infused with Mbeki's vision for an African Renaissance, South Africa has been a driving force behind restructuring the Southern African Development Community (SADC), establishing the new African Union, and developing the New Partnership for Africa's Development (Nepad). South Africa has also been involved in efforts to solve a number of conflicts and political crises on the continent, such as the long-running war in the DRC; former president Nelson Mandela has led efforts to bring an end to political instability in Burundi. South Africa has become an articulate advocate for Third World interests and has helped to reinvigorate the Non-Aligned Movement. South Africa is usually careful to balance the concerns of smaller countries with those of the broader international community. After September 11 for example, the country voiced its opposition to terrorism, but demurred from supporting US military action. South Africa also courted controversy by declaring the contentious 2002 Zimbabwean elections free and fair, but Mbeki ultimately decided, along with the leaders of Australia and Nigeria, to recommend Zimbabwe's suspension from the Commonwealth. However, Mbeki's continued refusal to openly criticize Robert Mugabe's regime – preferring instead to stick to 'quiet diplomacy' – has attracted condemnation.

Mbeki's views on AIDS cast a shadow over the first four years of his presidency. Going against the weight of medical opinion, he questioned the link between HIV and AIDS, and the effectiveness of anti-retroviral drugs. The Department of Health's refusal to provide anti-AIDS drugs to pregnant women and rape survivors angered AIDS activists and drew widespread criticism of the government. However, the Treatment Action Campaign won a High Court case against the Department of Health in 2001, forcing it to provide the anti-retroviral drug Nevirapine to all HIV-positive pregnant women. In November 2003, the cabinet voted to provide anti-retroviral drug across the board.

The 1999 election did not dramatically alter South Africa's political landscape, except for some growth in support for the Democratic Party (DP). The DP's line on crime and tough talk from its leader, Tony Leon, won it a substantial proportion of the white vote. In an effort to unite opposition to the government in the lead up to the 2000 local elections, the DP joined forces with the NP, under the new guidance of Marthinus van Schalkwyk to form the Democratic Alliance. The Alliance was however short-lived and fell apart following in-fighting about the party's administration in the Western Cape. Van Schalkwyk became the leader of what was then known as the New National Party (NNP), and continued to develop his organization as a 'party of minorities'. Efforts to expand the NNP's profile

2010 FIFA World Cup

South Africa is in the throes of preparing for the FIFA World Cup from 11 June to 11 July 2010, in which 64 matches will be played. This is the first time the prestigious football tournament has been held on African soil and a record 204 out of FIFA's 208 member countries entered the qualifying tournament. As host nation, South Africa automatically qualifies, and in total Africa will have six teams competing. Ten stadiums are in the process of being built or upgraded. **Johannesburg**: Soccer City, being upgraded (capacity 94,700), is the principal stadium and will host the opening ceremony, the final and most of the important matches. Ellis Park Stadium, being upgraded (60,000), will host five first-round matches, a second-round match and a quarter-final. **Durban**: Moses Mabidha Stadium, being built on the site of the demolished Kings Park Soccer Stadium (70,000), will host five first-round and one second-round match, as well as one of the semi-finals. **Cape Town**: Green Point Stadium, being built on the demolished old one (68,000), will host

eight matches, including a semi-final. **Tshwane/Pretoria**: Loftus Versfeld Stadium, being upgraded (52,000), matches to be announced. **Nelson Mandela Bay/Port Elizabeth**: Nelson Mandela Bay Stadium, being built (50,000), will host seven matches, including one of the semi-finals. **Bloemfontein**: Free State Stadium, being upgraded (48,000), will host five first-round and one second-round match. **Polokwane**: Peter Mokaba Stadium, being built on the demolished old one (45,000), will host three first-round matches and be used as a practice stadium. **Nelspruit**: Mbombela Stadium, being built (43,000), will host four first-round matches. **Rustenburg**: Royal Bafokeng Stadium (40,000) will host five first-round and one second-round match.

FIFA requires all the stadiums to be ready for the 2009 FIFA Confederations Cup, one year before the World Cup, and the total cost of the finished stadiums is expected to be in the region of R8.4 billion. Visit www.fifa.com or www.southafrica2010.org for progress.

beyond the Western Cape were unsuccessful and in 2004 it was announced the he was to become a member of the ANC, and that the NNP would be disbanded in 2006.

April 2004 saw the latest set of general elections, which the ANC, led by Thabo Mbeki, won in a characteristic landslide, gaininig 69.7% of votes. Theoretically, this proportion would allow them to change the constitution, but they have pledged not to. The main opposition party, the Democratic Alliance, won an increased share of the votes (thought to be largely thanks to former supporters of the NNP switching allegiances). The NNP, meanwhile, won just 1.7% of the votes. The elections were particularly notable as 2004 marked South Africa's decade of democracy. Van Schalkwyk was appointed minister of Environmental Affairs and Tourism, and in 2006, following March's local elections, the NNP finally folded.

The final term of office for Mbeki expires in 2009, but there is growing speculation over his successor as it is not clear who will stand or who the likely victor will be. One possible candidate is Deputy President Jacob Zuma who faced both rape and corruption charges in 2006 but was proved not guilty and has since been voted president of the ANC.

Economy

South Africa is often referred to as being a First and Third World economy within one country. While it is true that parts of South African society are extremely rich and the majority are extremely poor this situation is not actually that different from many other countries classified as Third World (or developing or South countries). The well-off sections of society are bigger than in other African countries but they are not dissimilar in size and wealth to countries such as Brazil or Argentina. The overall per capita levels of wealth in South Africa are also pretty much similar to these Latin American economies (referred to as the Higher Middle Income nations in World Bank league tables).

Structure of the economy The economy is dominated by the industries exploiting the country's extremely rich mineral resources. The mineral sector of the economy accounts for something like two-thirds of export earnings, though it employs less than 10% of the labour force. Apart from the gold and diamonds for which the country is famous it also produces a range of other mineral products, including platinum and chromium (of which it is the major world producer). The country lacks oil, though it does have some reserves of natural gas. The scarcity of oil was a key issue in the Apartheid days, hence the conversion of coal into oil by SASOL.

Agricultural production also continues to make a significant contribution to the economy, especially if you add the food preparation secondary industries based on primary agricultural products. Almost one-third of the workforce is in agriculture, though employment in this sector is characterized by extremely low wages and seasonal unemployment. The agricultural base is very diverse and in non-drought years, the country is a net food exporter.

The manufacturing sector of the economy has tended to suffer from low productivity levels, meaning that South Africa has found it difficult to break into lucrative export markets. The southern African regional market, where South Africa does have an advantage, is constrained by low levels of consumption and is, in any case, already pretty much saturated with South African goods. The most important local manufacturing sectors include automobile assembly, machinery, textiles, iron and steel, chemicals and fertilizers.

Recent economic developments The ANC came to power in 1994 with the economy in a mess. Throughout much of the 1980s and early 1990s the economy had grown slower than population growth rates and in some years had contracted in absolute terms. Inflation rates were high, the rand was slipping against the major currencies, investment rates were low, productivity was low and unemployment rates were extremely high. Much of this was due to global isolation which had led the country down an economic dead end. Growth was low because of the limitations of the domestic market and the inaccessibility of export markets, difficulties in obtaining technology due to sanctions and an unskilled labour force due to the poor state of African education. Probably the only area in which South Africa was better placed than comparable economies was in the level of external debt: sanctions by international banks and finance organizations had prevented the government from borrowing heavily. Despite its stated objectives of reducing poverty, increasing equality and providing basic social services for all, the new ANC government also signalled its intentions to ensure macro-economic stability. The first post-Apartheid Minister of Finance, Derek Keys, was appointed from outside party politics and the subsequent budgets did not include the heavy public borrowing and increased taxation that many observers predicted before the election. Macro-economically the economy has been a qualified success. Economic growth rates have been running at around 3-4% per annum, inflation has been controlled and deficit spending and public borrowing have only risen slowly. The rand has continued to slip on the international currency markets, though not as catastrophically as might have been expected when currency dealing and profit repatriation legislation were revoked. A significant development for South Africa's export industries was the signing of the EU-South Africa Trade, Development and Co-operation Agreement (TDCA) in October 1999. The benefits of increased access to European markets for South African goods have become immediately apparent; South Africa's trade surplus with the EU increased four-fold between 1999 and 2005. Since 1999 the economy has experienced uninterrupted growth, and it grew 4.9% a year in 2006 and 2007. With an investment and construction boom, growth of up to 5.1% in 2008 and 5.4% in 2009 are expected as preparations for the 2010 FIFA Football World Cup gather momentum.

The major problem area for the economy has been unemployment. Despite the fact that the economy is growing there are still more young people entering the employment market than there are new jobs being created. Although the number of jobs being created is increasing, the growth in the population means that South Africa's unemployment rate remains stubbornly high. In September 2007, the unemployment rate was put at 25.6%.

In terms of meeting its objectives to provide basic social services for all, the government's record has been mixed. Some ministries have performed well while others barely seem to have got programmes off the ground. The much-vaulted Reconstruction and Development Programme collapsed under its own weight and its functions were parcelled out to various government agencies. The provision of clean drinking water and rural electrification programmes have both been making steady progress and in 2007 two new gas-fired power stations were commissioned in the Western Cape. Provision of new housing to meet the huge urban backlog, on the other hand, is far slower. International development organizations have shown a huge amount of interest in the country and there have been some significant flows of new capital into the country from these sources.

The ANC government is beginning to show signs of reassessing the growth, employment and redistribution policy (Gear), which was criticized by trade unions as being a 'home-grown structural adjustment programme'. The 2001 budget showed a significant increase in public expenditure on social services. This may be an acknowledgment that Gear has not delivered the expected levels of economic growth. Ultimately, it is HIV/AIDS that may have the greatest impact on South Africa's economic future; a recent study predicts that by 2010, the disease may have shrunk the South African economy by between 17% and 20%. Mining and manufacturing, the two largest segments of the South Africa economy, are estimated to be effected the most by HIV/AIDS, with absenteeism due to ill health driving down profits.

The tourism sector has been highlighted as a significant area of revenue for South Africa, with expected steady growth towards the 2010 FIFA World Cup. Although the country has been hampered by its reputation for high crime rates, positive developments in the centre of Johannesburg and Cape Town have reassured many visitors. The contribution from tourism to the GDP has grown from 4.6% in 1993 to 8.3% in 2006. The record-breaking 8.4 million tourists who visited South Africa in 2006 are in turn responsible for almost one million jobs and bringing in some R66 billion to the economy annually.

Lesotho

Politics

With the March 1993 election Lesotho returned to a system of parliamentary democracy, suspended in 1970 after Chief Jonathan refused to hand over power to the Basotho Congress Party. The current Prime Minister is Pakalitha Mosisili, who chairs a Cabinet made up of members of Parliament. In addition to the main elected legislative lower house there is an upper house, with the power to delay and comment upon legislation, made up of the most senior chiefs and a number of appointed members. The monarch again fulfils the largely ceremonial role of Head-of-State, with a limited political role.

Despite sweeping the board in the 1993 election the Basotho Congress Party (BCP) failed to build on its strong political position. Many people in the country felt that after so many years in the wilderness the BCP came to power with surprisingly few new policies in the pipeline. Periodic political unrest has continued despite the advent of democratic elections. The first of these turmoils was in August 1994 when King Letsie III (who had succeeded his father, Moshoeshoe II, when he was exiled in November 1990) dismissed the BCP government. Though the exact links between this royal coup and the military and the opposition BNP are a little hazy it is clear that Letsie III was not acting on his own. His excuse for declaring the suspension of the government was the allegation that the leader of the BCP, Ntsu Mokhehle, had entered into talks with neighbouring heads of government to deploy a peace-keeping force because of his fears about political interference from the military. In the ensuing political unrest a number of people were shot dead and many more injured when the police and the military broke up demonstrations against Letsie's actions. Mokhehle and the BCP refused to acknowledge that the head-of-state had dismissed their government and, after direct involvement from regional heads-of-government, Letsie III eventually backed down and reinstated the elected government.

Another element in this confused political situation was that Letsie III wanted to abdicate in favour of his father, Moshoeshoe II. Moshoeshoe II had returned to Lesotho shortly before the return to democracy, but had not taken over the throne. Moshoeshoe had fairly wide domestic support and was respected by many individuals in the international development community because of his pronouncements on human rights while in exile in the early 1990s (although some of his actions while in coalition with the first military government painted a slightly different picture). This popularity explained the reason why the BCP were not altogether keen on seeing him reinstated as King, despite Letsie's actions in August 1994. Nevertheless, in February 1995, after another bout of intense political activity, Letsie did abdicate in favour of his father. Moshoeshoe II's reign on the throne proved to be short-lived, on the 16 January 1996 he was killed in a car accident.

The BCP itself has been plagued by internal political wranglings, which came to a surprising climax in June 1997. Soon after the BCP came to power two tendencies emerged within the party: one became known as the Pressure Group and the other as Majelathoko. The Pressure Group, who saw themselves as more progressive, were led by Molapo Qhobela, whilst the more conservative faction organized itself around Prime Minister Mokhehle. The division became wider when Mokhehle sidelined Qhobela in both government and the party.

In retaliation, the Pressure Group attempted to remove Mokhehle from his position as leader of the BCP, a move that under the 'Westminster system' of government would have also forced him to stand down as Prime Minister. In mid-1997 the Pressure Group seemed to be on the verge of winning this political battle when Mokhehle totally outflanked them

1998 riots and the torching of the Basotho Hat

The only blip in Maseru's history happened in 1998, when the results of the general election sparked a dispute. After the election, the Lesotho Congress of Democrats party claimed almost all the seats. This led to claims of vote rigging by the opposition who called for fresh elections. The government refused and the opposition began a long-running protest. The Southern African Development Community (SADC) became involved in mediation, but with the military becoming restive, Prime Minister Mosisili appealed to SADC to send in troops to prevent a military coup. South African troops entered Lesotho in September 1998 and confusion spread throughout the country as most people did not know exactly what was going on and were under the mistaken impression that South Africa was invading Lesotho. In response, there were widespread riots and the South African shops in Maseru and some of the other larger towns were looted and a large number of commercial buildings burnt down. In Maseru, one of these included the landmark Basotho Hat. The South African troops quickly restored order and promptly left the country.

with a cunning political move. While Mokhehle knew there was a good chance that the party as a whole would vote against him he also calculated that he had the support of the majority of BCP members of Parliament. He therefore resigned from the BCP, registered a new political party (the Lesotho Congress of Democrats) – with him as leader, and managed to persuade 40 of the 63 elected BCP parliamentarians to join him in the new party. After a vote of confidence, his position as Prime Minister and a Lesotho Congress of Democrats (LDC) government were both confirmed, and the BCP became the official opposition party. While this move was unprecedented, it did not appear to be unconstitutional.

The opposition parties tried to restructure and reposition themselves to contend the 1998 general elections, which were won by the LDC under new leader Pakalitha Mosisili. Although the elections were deemed free and fair by international observers, opposition parties rejected the results, and protests intensified. This culminated in a violent demonstration outside the royal palace in August 1998. In September, junior members of the armed services mutinied, and, to prevent a full military coup, Prime Minister Mosisili appealed to the Southern African Development Community (SADC) to intervene and restore stability. A military force of South African and Botswana troops, entered the country in September and encountered stiff resistance from the Lesotho Defence Force. Confusion spread throughout the country and there followed a period of intense unrest, with widespread looting and destruction of property. The South African shops in Maseru were looted and a large number of commercial buildings burnt down. Eventually South African and Botswana forces restored order and quelled the mutiny, and a long process of mediation began.

An interim council was established to prepare a new electoral system, under which elections are now processed. SADC troops left Lesotho in May 2000. Given Apartheid-era tensions, South Africa was uneasy about deploying troops in Lesotho, but the SADC intervention was ultimately successful in helping to maintain political stability. South Africa has set about improving relations with its neighbour, and is keen to emphasize Lesotho's sovereign equality. In 2001 the foreign ministers of Lesotho and South Africa met to begin mapping out a new relationship for the two countries. Elections in Lesotho in 2002 passed peacefully. The ruling LDC swept to victory and there were no signs of the instability that had followed the elections four years earlier. The LDC again comfortably won elections again in February 2007.

Swaziland

Swaziland became independent in 1968, and although the constitution guaranteed a parliamentary system when the NNLC won three seats in the 1972 election, the Swazi royal family dissolved parliament and banned all political parties. Since then political opponents have regularly been imprisoned and until 1993 attempts to reintroduce a parliamentary constitution failed. The government is now headed by the king, who is assisted by the prime minister; there are two legislative houses, the Senate and the House of Assembly. Non-party elections were held in September and October 1993, and the power of the king has been slightly reduced.

A Constitutional Review Commission was appointed by King Mswati in 1996 and while Swazis were promised that the new constitution would contain a bill of rights, it was assumed that power would remain in the hands of the king. Labour unions, banned political parties and human rights organizations boycotted the commission's work, arguing that it was un-democratic and open to manipulation by the authorities. In the absence of formal political opposition, the labour movement and the media have led the call for democratization.

The Swaziland Federation of Trade Unions represents 83,000 people out of a total population of 1 million. Tensions between the government and the pro-democracy movement reached boiling point in 2000/2001. Protest meetings were moved to neighbouring South Africa after they were banned by Prime Minister Sibusiso Dlamini. Leaders of the trade union movement were put on trial for organizing a strike, restrictions were placed on the media, and the independence of the judiciary was effectively ended. Internal opposition and a threat by the US to take away Swaziland's trade privileges however pressured Mswati into lifting these restrictions in July 2001. The king has been heavily criticized for his excessive spending, notably in 2002 when he spent US$45 million on a luxury jet, during a period of terrible drought and famine in the country. Tensions between Royalists and pro-democracy campaigners continue to fluctuate considerably; in 2006, the king was once again under international fire for imprisoning dozens of his opponents, and in 2007 thousands demonstrated on the streets of Manzini demanding democratic reform. For the time being, Swaziland remains Africa's last absolute monarchy.

As with the rest of southern Africa, Swaziland has one of the world's highest rates of HIV/AIDS infection – thought to be second only to that of Botswana. Infection rates now stand at an estimated 38%. Anti-retrovirals were introduced in 2003, but the disease is still surrounded by taboo, which is both hindering effective education about transmission, and preventing people from seeking treatment. Life expectancy in the country has now dropped from 51 (mid-1990s) to 39 (2006).

Economy

Swaziland is virtually surrounded by South Africa and is dependent on this market for much of its external trade. It is a prosperous country with iron, coal and asbestos mines. Much of the higher western mountainous regions have been planted with timber plantations, whilst the central and eastern lowveld regions are dedicated to cotton, tobacco, citrus fruits, sugar cane and cattle ranching. Subsistence farming is the main occupation for the majority of Swazis and much of the landscape is devoted to small scale agricultural plots and cattle pastures. One of the largest foreign direct investments in Swaziland in years came in 2000 when a Taiwanese firm opened a textile factory which employed thousands of workers. Swaziland is one of the few countries that has diplomatic relations with Taiwan.

Culture

South Africa

Population distribution

Figures from South Africa's 2001 census show the total population to be around 48.8 million, a considerably growth from 1996, when the population was estimated to be around 38 million.

The two most populous provinces are KwaZulu Natal and Gauteng. KwaZulu Natal contains a major urban area, Durban, but higher rainfall figures also means that the KwaZulu Natal countryside is able to support a greater population density than other rural areas of the country. The legacy of Apartheid means that former homeland areas have much higher population densities than other rural areas: the scattered fragments of what was the homeland of KwaZulu Natal stretch across the province and account for much of the region's 7.7 million people.

Gauteng, the country's smallest province in area (1.4% of the total), contains 19% of the total population, the vast majority of whom are urban residents living in the towns and cities around Johannesburg.

The Eastern Cape's 5.9 million people are less urbanized. Though the province contains a major city, Nelson Mandela Bay (Port Elizabeth), many of its people live in the area that used to comprise the homelands of Transkei and Ciskei.

The Western Cape, by contrast, never contained any homeland areas. Its 4.1 million people mainly live in and around Cape Town though there is also a significant population of farmworkers and residents of small rural towns and villages.

The next four provinces in terms of population size, Northern Province, North West, Mpumalanga and the Free State, all have their population divided between smaller industrial centres, sparsely populated white rural areas and densely populated fragments of former homelands.

Finally, the Northern Cape, the largest province in area (361,830 sq km), has a tiny population of just 700,000 people widely dispersed across this semi-arid region.

Ethnic groups

South Africa's population is a true melting pot, with numerous races, religions, ethnicities and cultures which can be somewhat bewildering for visitors. While many people today resent being classified in terms or race and ethnicity – it was, after all, racial classifications which denied the majority of the population many of its basic human rights for many years – it is impossible to discuss modern South Africa without touching on these terms.

The Apartheid system recognized four major population groups (races) in the country: African, Asian, coloured and white (the terminology has changed over time). Despite the avowed non-racial nature of the present South African state, this fourfold classification remains profoundly important to South African life. This does not mean, however, that everyone fits neatly into these four categories: during the Apartheid era, huge numbers of people had their race altered by official decree. This could have profound impacts and often resulted in people being evicted from their homes and their children thrown out of schools. Within each of the four racial categories it is possible to make further sub-divisions on the basis of home language, tribe and geography – these sub-divisions (especially tribe) are even more fluid and open to debate than the fourfold racial classification.

African The African population makes up around 75% of South Africa's total population. The terminology used to describe this section of the population has changed over the years: in the 19th and early 20th century they tended to be referred to as 'natives' while in the 1960s the Apartheid authorities adopted the term 'Bantu'. Both these names have strong connotations of racism. The word Bantu simply comes from the Zulu and Xhosa words for people but it is resented by most South Africans because of its connection to the Apartheid institutions who adopted it in the 1960s, especially in the field of education. Today it is only acceptable to use the term when discussing languages; the Bantu group of languages includes all the African languages spoken in South Africa and related Bantu languages are spoken as far away as Somalia.

The Apartheid system also designated the African population on the basis of tribe. This was not as straightforward as it might seem. Many Africans, especially those living in urban areas and those who were long-term residents on white farms, had only weak links with any tribal authority and often did not describe themselves in terms of their tribal background. Under the Apartheid system every African was allocated to one of nine different tribes, each with a designated tribal authority and a homeland. This classification system lead to many complaints and many people claimed that they did not belong to any of the tribes or that their clan constituted a separate tribe – originally there were eight designated tribes but complaints of this nature lead to the creation of a ninth.

In terms of population, the biggest African tribal group is the Zulu. The majority of Zulus live in KwaZulu Natal or in the industrial centres of Gauteng. Rural Zulus probably have the greatest ethnic identity out of the entire African population and this has been fuelled by the IFP calls for more autonomy for KwaZulu Natal. The second biggest ethnic group is the Xhosa. Under the Apartheid system they were ascribed two separate homelands: the Ciskie and Transkie, now incorporated into Eastern Cape. There is a large Xhosa population in Cape Town and on the farms of the Western Cape. Many of the ANC's leaders are Xhosa from the Eastern Cape, reflecting the area's long history of resistance politics and the education provided in the large number of mission schools in the region. These two groups together account for about 40% of the African population.

There are three ethnic groups in the country who are closely related to the populations of three neighbouring countries dominated by people of that tribe: the Tswana (Botswana), the Swazi (Swaziland) and the Southern Sotho (Lesotho). These three and the other four ethnic groups, the Shangana or Tsonga, the Ndebele, the Venda and the Northern Sotho have their populations dispersed in the previous homeland areas or mixed together in the towns and cities of the highveld.

Each one of the nine ethnic groups has an official language. Many of these are more or less mutually intelligible. The major distinction is between the Nguni languages (Xhosa, Zulu, Swazi and Ndebele) and those closely related to SeSotho and SeTswana. There are distinctive cultural activities associated with each ethnic group, though these usually only come into play at times like weddings and funerals. In the urban areas, where the majority of Africans live, many of these ethnic tribal customs have been replaced by generic amalgams of different practices. Similarly a distinctive urban African language containing words from all the languages plus English and Afrikaans has evolved in the urban areas.

White South Africa's white population accounts for something like 13% of the total. It can be sub-divided into two main groups on the basis of home language: English speakers and Afrikaans-speaking people. The ancestors of English-speaking white South Africans first arrived in the country in 1820 and since then there has been a steady stream of new immigrants. The first English settlers to arrive were concentrated in the Eastern Cape but today they are to be found in every town and city. They tend to be more urbanized and more metropolitan in outlook than the Afrikaners, though this is a generalization that does not always match up to reality.

The Afrikaner population are descended from the original Dutch and Huguenot settlers who came with the Dutch East India Company. The word Afrikaner simply means African in Dutch. They account for just over half of the white population. They have a reputation for being conservative, rural and more racist than the English-speaking population. In reality the vast majority live in town and you can very often only tell the difference between an English-speaking and Afrikaans-speaking white South African by their surnames.

There are a number of other smaller communities of white South Africans, including a Jewish community descended from early 20th-century immigrants from eastern Europe and a Portuguese community, many of whom came to South Africa from Mozambique and Angola in the 1970s.

Asian South Africa has a small Asian population, accounting for about 3% of the total. It is descended from two main groups: indentured labourers brought to the sugar cane farms of Natal in the 19th century and a number of traders and their families who followed the indentured labourers. The vast majority of the Asian population are originally from South Asia and they are also often referred to as Indian. The majority of Asians still live in KwaZulu Natal though there are small Asian communities in most towns and cities across the country, especially in Gauteng. About 70% of the Asian population are Hindu and 20% Muslim. Almost all Asians speak English as their home language.

Coloured This is probably the most contentious of the four basic racial categories used in South Africa. In some ways the coloured category just represents the rest lumped together into one group. There is a distinctive coloured cultural identity – though by no means all people classified as coloured during Apartheid would subscribe to it. Under Apartheid about 9% of the population was classified as coloured. The coloured population is concentrated in the Western Cape. Many of them are descended from slaves brought to work on the farms of the Cape during the era of rule by the Dutch East India Company and from slave owners and other white settlers. There are also many coloured people who are descended from the pre-colonial San and Khoi populations of the Cape. This is especially so in the Northern and Eastern Cape which never had large slave populations. Some coloured people, especially the 200,000-strong Malay community in Cape Town, have retained elements of their pre-slavery culture, including Islam.

On the whole, the coloured community is very closely linked (both culturally and through descent) with the Afrikaner community. About 80% of the coloured population speak Afrikaans as their home language: it surprises many visitors to discover that coloured Afrikaans speakers outnumber white Afrikaans speakers. In post-Apartheid South Africa the links between the coloured and Afrikaner communities have been increasingly stressed by people on both sides.

Music and dance
Most visitors will be familiar with the most famous of South African sounds, the rousing vocal harmony of Ladysmith Black Mambazo, made internationally famous by Paul Simon's *Graceland* album. It doesn't end there, though: the country has produced an incredible

variety of music – little surprise given its immense range of cultures and influences. In fact, the key to understanding South African music is in realizing where it comes from. Be it the adaptation of Dutch instruments in the 17th century by Indonesian slaves, or the mutation of 1990s house music into township Kwaito, home-grown and foreign sounds mingle to produce a singularly South African sound. And like so much of South African culture, music is inextricably linked with the political upheavals of the last century.

Vocal harmony is the oldest music tradition in South Africa, with its roots in communal dances accompanied by elaborate call-and-response patterns. This movement, defined as gospel acapella (and known as Isicathamiya in Zulu), has long been popular in South Africa, but it was the band Ladysmith Black Mambazo who first propelled it into the international arena. The beginnings for the group were not easy; at their first concert in Soweto in the 1980s, they received the princely sum of R5.28 each. The band, however, became an instant hit and, when Paul Simon invited them to sing on his *Graceland* album, they were thrust into the international limelight, and they remain the most popular South African band of all time. Made up of 10 male singers, including the charismatic front-man, lead singer and original founder Joseph Shabalala, the band continue to tour, and have now recorded over 40 albums.

However, few musical styles have been as influential as jazz, something of a harmonious hotbed since emerging from the Johannesburg slums in the 1920s. Today, the jazz scene is once again flourishing following a turbulent few decades when many of the biggest jazz stars left South Africa under Apartheid, and is now best experienced at the Cape Town International Jazz Festival, held every March in Cape Town. Many of the godfathers of Cape Jazz, including Abdullah Ibrahim (previously known as Dollar Brand) and Hugh Masekela can be seen performing during the three-day festival, while newcomers, using a range of influences from the harmonica of migrant west African miners, to the clubbing beats of drum 'n' bass, are also making a bit impact. Every year the South African acts are complemented by the latest international recruits.

If music is the very heartbeat of this country, then dance also features as an integral part of life for many South Africans. In KwaZula Natal tourists can be treated to a traditional Zulu ceremony, while the talented *Gumboots* dance company have toured the world with their unforgettable mix of music, dance and showmanship.

Western music is hugely popular with young South Africans, and both Durban and Cape Town have significant live rock scenes. A number of home-grown talents such as rock band Just Jinger have recently made it onto the national arena, but the most popular white musician remains Johnny Clegg. In the 1970s, Clegg began performing traditional Zulu material with Sipho Mchunu, and later added a mix of Western rock to form the band Juluka. Clegg remains something of a South African legend, and still draws thousands of fans when he performs. Known affectionately as the 'White Zulu', Clegg challenged the racial boundaries manifest in music under Apartheid, and blazed a cross-over trail which survives to this day. Although popular mainly amongst (liberal) white people, his tours are sell-outs and he remains a big influence on the music scene.

Kwaito The fastest-moving force in music today is undoubtedly Kwaito, the sound of young, black Johannesburg. The style is resolutely urban, drawing on American and British house music, with slow, deep beats and electronic melodies overlaid with chanted *tsotsi* (township gangster) slang. Born from 1980s pop-influenced dance music known as bubblegum, Kwaito has a darker, edgier feel, carrying with it an unmistakable association with gangster culture. But despite its underground roots and reflection of a despondent

Natonal dress of Lesotho

As the Basotho are one of the few African ethnic groups living in a mountainous environment, they have had to make adaptations to their living conditions. The Basotho blanket is one example. Most people in the rural areas wear colourful blankets attached at the shoulder with giant pins to form a sort of coat to provide warmth and keep the rain off. These are usually worn with well-patched gumboots, essential in the cool mountain climate. However, neither garment is produced locally

and both the gumboots and blankets are imported from South Africa.

Originally, people wore clothing made from animal hides, but in 1860 European traders presented Moshoshoe with a blanket and, a decade later, demand for these blankets was insatiable. In those days the blankets were imported from the textile regions of England around Leicester and Coventry and in fact, many of the trading stores and centres in today's Lesotho started out selling blankets.

township youth, Kwaito has become the country's definitive youth sound, led by top record label Kalawa Jazzmee and stars like Mandoza and Zola. Ubiquitous in the clubs of young black urbanites, it is also now popular in designer nightclubs – until relatively recently the reserve of the white and wealthy.

Lesotho

Lesotho's population, of just under two million, is made up almost exclusively of Basotho people, and Sesotho is the language spoken by the vast majority. There are a few Xhosa speakers in Qacha's Nek district and a handful of Asian and European settlers in the lowland towns. One of the key reasons why there are few non-Basotho settlers in Lesotho is that (officially) all land is owned communally 'by the nation'. Unofficially there is a market in land but it is very difficult for a non-Basotho to own or even lease land.

Population density in the lowlands is very high and the urban sprawl around Maseru merges into neighbouring towns and villages. In contrast the population in the mountain regions is very low and concentrated into the valleys. The high mountain tops are more or less uninhabited with the exception of the occasional herd boy. Over 80% of the population is rural, though the high density of population sometimes makes the rural/urban distinction a little hazy.

The vast majority of **Basotho**, over 80%, would classify themselves as Christians. The Catholic church is the largest and richest church in the country. In the past it received generous external funding, especially from Quebec, and indeed many of its priests were French Canadian. This has, however, dried up and efforts have been made to localize all the clergy. The Catholic Church was strongly associated with the establishment of the BNP and, though many priests were uneasy with the stance, it rarely voiced opposition to the autocratic regime of Chief Jonathan. The largest Protestant church, the Lesotho Evangelical Church (LEC), has received far less external funding and is much poorer, though its position as the first major autonomous church in Lesotho has given it prestige and strong local support. It was the first major church to ordain women and a growing number of its trainee clergy are female. The LEC frequently criticized the actions of Chief Jonathan and in return its leaders were persecuted by the government and many forced into exile. The Anglican church is also well represented in Lesotho and, as it is a diocese of the South African Anglican structure, it has good external contacts. There are also a large number of smaller churches and spiritualist movements which are receiving growing support, such as the Methodists, Pentacostalists, Zionists and Seventh Day Adventists. Whatever the specific church, Christianity plays an important part in the lives of most Basotho and the church is a focal point of many communal activities.

As in all societies, however, Christianity in Lesotho co-exists with other (sometimes contrary) beliefs and rituals. Many Basotho continue to include some elements of 'ancestor worship' in their religious practice and there is a strong belief in the power of witchcraft. Initiation ceremonies, including circumcision lodges for young men, still exist in many areas of Lesotho, indeed there is some evidence they have made something of a comeback in recent years.

One of Lesotho's biggest modern-day challenges is HIV/AIDS. The country has the third highest infection rate of HIV/AIDS in the world, with a prevalence rate of around 29%. The UN estimates that this rate is likely to increase to 36%, with a dramatic drop in national life expectancy. As in South Africa, the Lesotho government has been slow to recognize the scale of the crisis, although it now has a programme of education, counselling and treatment. In late 2005, it introduced the world's first HIV/AIDS testing project for the entire population (see page 61), which it hopes will reduce the stigma associated the HIV/AIDS and its treatment.

Swaziland

This is a traditional African society preserving many long-standing ceremonies and customs. The *Umhlanga* dance, for example, is celebrated every two years at Loamba where the nation's young girls dance and sing in homage to the Queen Mother.

Land and environment

South Africa

South Africa is a big country with an extremely diverse physical environment. The country's total land area amounts to 1,219,912 sq km (1,267,462 sq km including Swaziland and Lesotho). Contained within this land area are a wide mix of environments, ranging from tropical moist forest, through high mountains, rolling grasslands and temperate woodlands to sparsely vegetated areas of semi-desert. South Africa's natural scenery is world famous and rightly so. There are some amazingly beautiful areas which can take the breath away from even the most world-weary traveller. The wild and empty beaches of the south coast, the panoramic views of the Drakensberg Mountains, the wide open spaces of the Karoo and many other stunning landscapes can all leave a lasting impression.

There are also, however, some big areas of undistinguished natural scenery and the impacts of both industrialization and Apartheid have also had their toll. This is obviously worth bearing in mind when you are planning a holiday, especially if you are only going to be there for a short period of time. If your primary interest is in South Africa's natural beauty read the following sections carefully before planning your route.

Landscape

South Africa's physical geography is dominated by one feature: a massive escarpment that runs right around the subcontinent dividing a thin coastal strip from a huge inland plateau. This escarpment is clearest in the east, where it is marked by the spectacular Drakensberg Mountains, running in an arc from the Eastern Cape round to northern Mpumalanga. To the west the escarpment is confused by a jumble of beautiful mountain chains (the Cape Folded Mountains), such as the Cederberg, the Tsitsikamma, the Swartberg and the Hottentot-Hollands. The inland plateau, usually known as the highveld, is a relatively flat plain sloping gently down towards the west and north. This plain is, however, broken up by numerous geological features, resulting in isolated steep sided hills or longer chains of higher ground.

This interior plateau forms the southernmost tip of the massive Africa continental plateau which stretches as far north as Ethiopia. This plateau was part of the ancient landmass of Pangaea (c200 million years ago), which split in two to form Gondwanaland in the southern hemisphere and Laurasia in the north. Gondwanaland later broke up to form the continents of South America, Australasia and Africa, around 135 million years ago. As it is made up of an old continental plate many of South Africa's rocks are very old and some rocks found in the Limpopo valley, Northern Province, rank with the oldest yet discovered anywhere in the world.

Other areas, such as the Witwatersrand and Barberton complexes, are also made up of ancient Precambrian rocks, about 3000 million years old. This contrasts with rock formations in places such as the Western Cape coast which were only formed in the past 250,000 years, during the Quaternary era. Most of the country is, however, made up of sandstone and slates laid down in the Carboniferous to Jurassic periods (when Pangaea began to break up). These are commonly referred to as the Karoo sequence of rocks. The eastern portions of the Karoo sequence have been covered by an intrusion of basalt. This harder layer of rock has protected the softer Karoo sandstones from erosion and stands out as a highland area, especially in Lesotho.

The Karoo sequence is particularly rich in fossil remains. Contained in the sandstones and shales are the remains of many reptilian creatures who lived in the low-lying areas of swamps and shallow lakes. Some of these fossils have been crucial to scientists' attempts to reconstruct the way in which reptiles evolved into mammals. The best places to look for fossils is along the sides of the many steep-sided hills or koppies that dominate the Karoo landscape. The best fossils are usually found in the dull red shales, which erode easily to reveal the fossil remains.

Climate

Over most of South Africa rain falls during the southern hemisphere summer months (November to March). Rainfall tends to be in the form of intense cloud bursts, often accompanied by thunderstorms, though there can also be periods of longer rainfall. During the summer months warm and wet easterly winds sweep in from over the Indian Ocean. As these winds flow over the southeastern coast and the Drakensberg they drop much of their moisture, making these areas the wettest parts of the country with annual totals over 1000 mm. Over the highveld the moisture-bearing winds trigger rain showers and thunderstorms. In the east of the highveld these tend to be more regular but towards the west, especially in the Northern Cape, they are infrequent. Here average annual rainfall figures are usually below 200 mm per annum. The summer rains never reach the western coast of the Northern Cape province and rainfall levels here can be as low as 20 mm per annum. South Africa is, on the whole, a very dry country, with something like 30% of the land area receiving below 250 mm a year on average. Rain may be unpopular with visitors but it is almost always welcomed by South Africans.

The only part of the country where the major rainfall does not come from summer easterlies is the Western Cape and the extreme west of Northern Cape province. Here most rain falls during the winter months as depressions over the southern Atlantic sweep north and east bringing with them frontal systems and cool rains. Late in the winter and early spring an occasional winter storm will travel further north than usual and bring with it much needed rain to the arid northwestern coastal belt. Apart from these occasional storms this area receives its moisture from mists that roll in from the cold Atlantic during the summer months.

The winter weather systems can also sometimes skirt up along the southern coast bringing rain and even snow to the Eastern Cape, Lesotho and KwaZulu Natal. Snowfalls tend to be minor and confined to light dustings of the highest peaks, though there are occasionally significant falls of a few inches or more.

This seasonal pattern is also highly variable from year to year. This variability tends to be most pronounced in the lowest rainfall areas: here there can be some years where the rains fail entirely. The exact reasons for this variability are a matter of considerable academic debate. There does appear to be a cycle of wet and dry years in South Africa over a period of about four to eight years. This cycle is related to a frequent, but irregular, event known as the El Niño, in which ocean and air currents in the South Pacific are reversed. This, in turn, triggers changes in the circulation of air around the southern hemisphere and results in weaker easterlies and drought in South Africa. The weather system is, however, extremely complex and involves the interaction of global and local variables, so predicting exactly how something like El Niño will affect South African rainfall is impossible with any degree of accuracy. Global warming may also be further complicating the already complex weather systems. Beyond short-range forecasting all that meteorologists can predict with any degree of accuracy is that the climate is very unpredictable.

Temperatures vary according to season, altitude and distance from the moderating influence of the oceans. During the summer months the inland plateau tends to heat up considerably, especially if the rains fail. The highest daytime temperatures are to be found in the lower-lying semi-desert areas of the Northern Cape and the lowveld regions of Mpumulanga. On the highveld temperatures can also soar in summer, though they tend to be moderated by the higher altitudes. Fortunately in these inland regions the evenings tend to be significantly cooler, especially under clear skies. Travelling at night or in the early morning is a sensible and popular option in these regions during summer. The coastal fringes of Natal are also hot and sticky in summer and don't expect too much relief at night. The most pleasant area of the country during the summer months is the Western Cape, with hot but often breezy days and comfortable evenings.

During the winter the Western Cape can get very chilly, with frequent blustery storms and heavy rain. On the highveld and in the Karoo stable high pressure systems result in clear skies, warm days and cold nights. It is a combination many visitors find very comfortable especially for travelling long distances. In the highest areas of the Drakensberg winter temperatures can plummet to way below freezing at night: the best time to visit these areas is during the autumn or spring. The Natal coast remains warm throughout the year, especially in the northern subtropical areas near the Mozambique border. Winter is a good time to visit the lowveld game parks: the drier conditions make it easier to spot wildlife, especially around water holes.

Vegetation

There are a number of different ways of categorizing South Africa's vegetational zones, which are sometimes called biomes or ecozones. All these categorizations are simplifications of complex and dynamic patterns of vegetation and rarely are there clear boundaries between the different zones. Even without the influence of humans this pattern has constantly shifted with long-term trends in climate: when you add in millenniums of human impacts, mapping a set pattern of different biomes becomes an extremely difficult task.

One vegetational zone that is not difficult to classify as distinctive is the fynbos of the Western Cape. Although fynbos covers only a relatively small area it comprises one of the earth's six separate floral kingdoms. The other five floral kingdoms cover huge areas such as most of the northern hemisphere or the whole of Australia. The Cape floral kingdom is both the smallest and the richest floral kingdom in the world, with the highest known concentration of plant species per unit area. There are over 7700 different plant species within the fynbos biome and of these over 5000 are endemic to the Western Cape (ie they do not occur naturally anywhere else). The 470 sq km of the Cape Peninsula is home to 2256 different plant species – more than the whole of the UK, an area 5000 times bigger! The 60 sq km of Table Mountain alone supports 1470 species. The richness of the fynbos is well demonstrated by its ericas or heaths, of which there are over 600 different species. There are just 26 in the rest of the world. Not surprisingly the Western Cape is a magnet for plant enthusiasts.

The word fynbos comes from the Dutch for fine-leaved plants. Almost all of the woody plants have small leaves (microphyllous) which are hard, tough and leathery (sclerophyllous). True grasses are also relatively rare and as much as 5% of the biome is covered by Cape reeds (of the *Restionaceae* family). Most of the plants that fill the niches usually taken up by grasses have small, thin (ericoid) leaves. Additionally, the fynbos biome contains proteas, ericas and members of seven plant families found nowhere else in the world. These include the king protea, South Africa's national flower, the beautiful red disa, symbol of the Cape Province and the popular garden plants, pelargoniums, commonly known as geraniums. The largest family in number of species is *Asteraceae* (daisy family), with just under 1000 species, of which more than 600 are endemic. Fynbos is very rich in bulbous plants (geophytes) and many species from the family *Iridaceae* have become household names such as babiana, freesia, gladiolus, iris, moraea, sporaxis and watsonia.

As many of the endemic fynbos species have amazingly small ranges (sometimes as small as a football field), they are extremely vulnerable to extinction. One small housing project, for example, could wipe out a whole species. Given this and the fact that the Western Cape has fairly dense human population, it is not surprising that many of South Africa's threatened and rare plants are found in the fynbos. Almost 500 species are classified as rare, threatened or endangered. Fynbos species tend to grow fairly slowly. This is because they are in a winter rainfall region so during the summer months there is not enough water available and during the winter low temperatures restrict plant growth. The hot dry summer months also make fire a common occurrence in the biome. The fynbos plants are well adapted to fire and the biome is adapted to quickly re-establishing itself after naturally occurring burns. If fire is totally restricted fynbos often loses out to plant species from surrounding biomes. If fires are too frequent, however, the fynbos plants do not have time to re-establish themselves and this can lead to local extermination of species.

Soils under fynbos tend to be extremely infertile, due partially to the chemical make-up of the underlying rocks and partially to heavy leaching that has occurred over long periods. The nutrient-poor soils produce plants that are also low in nutrients and therefore of low feeding potential for grazing animals. This means that there is a relatively low density and diversity of mammals and birds in the fynbos biome.

The western coast of South Africa also has a large number of endemic plant species. This area, stretching north into Namibia, has extremely low and erratic rainfall and the plant life reflects this. Many of the plants in this region are succulents and about 200 of these are classified as rare or endangered. When rains do come to the area there is a dramatic transformation of the vegetation. Hundreds of flowering plants lying dormant during the long dry periods burst into bloom covering the whole of the landscape in a carpet of brightly coloured flowers. This is a spectacular annual event and attracts many visitors to the region every spring, but as the flowers are reliant upon unpredictable rainfall it is impossible to say exactly when and where they will appear. The rains are expected in the spring, and once the first blooms start to appear a 'Flower Hotline' can be called for the latest information, see page 888 for full details. After a brief period of flowering the plants drop their seeds which then lie dormant until the next rainfall event.

The inland plateau of the Cape is dominated by Karoo types of vegetation. This is made up mainly from low-lying shrubs and succulents, though in good rainfall years grasses can also make an appearance. There tends to be a lot of open soil between the shrubs so much of the region takes on the red tinge of the underlying soils and this can lead to some wonderful sunsets and sunrises. The low density of vegetation also makes fires a less common occurrence than in better-watered regions. There are occasional areas of green alongside streams and rivers and these are the only places you will see trees in the biome.

The northern highveld areas (along the Botswana border) and the lowveld areas of Northern Province, Mpumalanga and Swaziland, by contrast, have a fair number of trees. This is the classic savanna formation: areas of grassland interspersed with occasional trees. In the highveld areas the vegetation is dominated by thorny acacia woodland, often referred to as bushveld. In valley bottoms and in lowveld areas the vegetation is often dominated by mopane, which can tolerate the extremes of waterlogging and drying encountered on heavy soils. This region tends to have fertile soils and grasses have a high nutrition content. They are, therefore, heavily populated by grazing animals (both wild and domestic). The major wildlife viewing areas fall within this biome.

The remaining highveld, the KwaZulu Natal midlands, Lesotho and the inland areas of Eastern Cape are taken up by grasslands with few naturally occurring trees. The grasses grow vigorously during the hot and wet summer months and then remain dormant during the dry, cold winter. The grasslands are often divided into two different categories: sweet and sour veld. Sweetveld occurs in the areas with lower rainfall figures (400-600 mm per annum), especially on heavier clay soils. It tends to be more nutritious than the sour velds and is therefore popular for grazing, especially during the summer months. Sourveld tends to occur in the areas with rainfall above 600 mm per annum. Greater availability of water means that sourveld grasses grow rapidly, though they tend to have a lower nutritional content. Both these veld types intermingle and it is hard to draw a clear distinction between the two. The division between the Karoo and grassland areas is also hazy. During dry spells and in areas which have been overgrazed, Karoo-type shrubs expand into the grasslands while in wetter years or if grazing pressure is reduced they will retreat. On the highveld much of this grassland has been converted to agriculture or covered with factories, roads and cities.

The densely populated narrow coast strip of the Eastern Cape and KwaZulu Natal was once heavily wooded. The closed canopy subtropical forests of KwaZulu Natal can still be found in a few isolated patches but most of the area has been converted to agriculture. In the Eastern Cape the evergreen temperate forest has also been largely cut down, though some small patches are left around Knysna. The forests here give some idea of what the environment would have been like before the arrival of Europeans with commercial logging: there are some beautiful trees such as the stinkwood, Cape chestnut, yellowwood and the white and red alder. In total, indigenous closed canopy woodland accounts for only 1% of South Africa's land area, with a similar amount under commercial plantations (many of these on the Drakensberg escarpment in Mpumalanga).

Urban and rural environments

Any description of the South African landscape that leaves out the impact of humans would not give a visitor any real idea about what the place actually looks like. Though Apartheid has now come to an end its legacy is often apparent in the South African landscape and the pattern of South African cities and towns. For many years some of the most striking features of Apartheid social engineering, such as the huge rural slums that sprang up around the country, were never shown on official maps. Visitors were often shocked to suddenly encounter a massive area of slum housing way out in the countryside which they could not find on their road maps and which did not appear on any road signs. Official maps and guides are now slowly catching up with reality but the landscape itself will take much longer to transform.

Agriculture While large areas of South Africa are given over to wildlife or wilderness areas most of the countryside is dominated by farming. The nature of the country's agricultural sector, therefore, has a huge impact on the landscape. The pattern of agriculture in South Africa is determined by two major factors: the physical environment and the legacy of Apartheid. Low and variable rainfall figures make arable farming an extremely risky business and only about 10% of the country is covered by arable crops. Maize is the country's staple crop. It is mainly grown in the Free State, the southern and eastern portions of North West, the western portions of Mpumalanga and those parts of Gauteng not covered by towns and industry. These areas comprise some of the least eventful countryside in South Africa. Maize and other grain crops, such as sorghum or millet, are also grown in the Eastern Cape and KwaZulu Natal. In these wetter areas the constraining factor is often not availability of water, but of sufficient flat land to plough amongst the broken topography. The most rewarding landscapes for a tourist are inevitably very different from the most rewarding landscapes for a farmer.

Other arable crops include wheat, grown mostly in the Western Cape, and sugar cane, grown mostly in KwaZulu Natal. The Western Cape is also well known for its vineyards and fruits, such as peaches and nectarines. The lowveld areas of Mpumalanga and Northern Province are also major fruit growing areas.

The majority of the countryside is, however, given over to extensive grazing land. This accounts for something like 65% of the country's total land area, the vast majority of this given over to large enclosures of naturally occurring veld plants rather than improved and carefully managed paddocks. The wetter areas in the east, where grasses dominate over woodier Karoo shrubs, are given over mainly to cattle. The rolling hills of the KwaZulu Natal Midlands are particularly good cattle-rearing country: well watered but with sufficiently cool evenings and winters to kill off disease-bearing insects that flourish in the more tropical coastal fringes and the lowveld regions. Further west, especially in the Karoo, livestock rearing is dominated by sheep and in the very driest areas by goats.

This pattern of agriculture is confused, however, by the legacy of Apartheid. Until very recently African farmers were not allowed to own or buy land outside certain prescribed areas. These areas, known as the homelands, comprised only 13% of the country and were supposed to provide land for an African population comprising 75% of the total. In these areas the population density is high and plots of land for agriculture are very small. Most of these plots are unproductive and yields from agricultural crops very low. Grazing in these areas is on common land owned by the local community. Though individual herds tend to be small the total animal population is high and includes a mixture of goats, sheep and cattle. As the grazing land is unfenced and communal herds will be looked after by a shepherd – usually a teenage boy – livestock will most probably be brought back to the village at night where they are kraaled to stop them wandering and to reduce the risk of theft.

This contrasts with the white farming areas where farms tend to be huge. Arable agriculture is highly mechanized and produces huge yields. Some farms, such as the fruit-growing areas, employ large numbers of seasonal labour but on the whole the number of people employed permanently on each farm is not high. On the white farms livestock are grazed in large fenced paddocks at a lower density than on the former homeland areas. Except on the dairy farms, livestock are only checked up on periodically.

These different patterns of farming produce very different-looking landscapes. The former homeland areas are more densely populated with small plots of unhealthy-looking maize interspersed amongst scattered homesteads. The grazing areas often look barren, especially towards the end of the winter dry season when all available forage has been eaten by livestock. The white farming areas, on the other hand, have large fields of arable crops or huge areas of grazing land. On the grazing land there will tend to be more vegetation available to the livestock, though in drought years these areas can also look pretty barren. It is unusual to see many people in the fields and paddocks of the white farming areas.

Though the restrictions on buying or renting land have now been lifted this pattern will remain for many years. Some African farmers who were evicted from white farming areas during the Apartheid era have been resettled on their original farms, but this process is very slow and the geography of agriculture is unlikely to change significantly in the conceivable future.

Living in the city South Africa's urban geography has been largely shaped by segregation: this pattern is now changing rapidly but the legacy of residential segregation will be apparent for a very long time to come. Under the Group Areas Act different areas of each city were reserved for one of the four major population groups (white, Indian, coloured or African). Prior to the passing of the Group Areas Act in 1950 most cities and towns were already segregated to an extent. The pattern of segregation was complicated however and there were in most cities a number of areas in which the different population groups intermingled. Under the Group Areas Act the government attempted to consolidate this pattern of segregation into bigger, clearly defined blocks of land and to do away with any areas where there was a mixture of the different races. This process continued right through to the mid-1980s. The urban environment that this system created is distinctive.

Prior to the Group Areas Act much of the poorer urban population lived in slum areas near the central business areas of industrial centres. These areas were home to large numbers of Africans, Indians and coloureds and a few 'poor whites'. Under the Group Areas Act these slum areas were knocked down and new housing for whites was built in their place. The African, Indian and coloured populations were moved to new, racially segregated, planned settlements on the outskirts of cities, known as townships. These areas tend to be some distance from the city centre and are divided from the white suburbs by areas of unoccupied land. There are often only one or two access routes into the township and the streets are wide and straight: both factors were deliberately intended to make the control of unrest and protest easier to handle. The best known of these township areas is the vast residential area called Soweto, which originally stood for South Western Townships, on the outskirts of Johannesburg.

The vast majority of Africans living in urban areas still live in these townships. They tend to be made up of large areas of small uniform houses with few local urban amenities. Many of the roads in township areas are not tarred, rubbish is strewn across the streets and air pollution is horrendous. In recent years there have been a proliferation of squatter camps within the townships on areas of open ground and many of the residential plots include not just the original house but a large number of additional shacks. These townships contrast sharply with the suburbs reserved for white populations during the Apartheid years. Houses in these areas are usually large, streets are clean and often tree-lined. The fear of crime means that in areas like Johannesburg's northern suburbs many of these houses look like mini-forts.

This pattern of residential segregation will remain for many years to come. A few rich Africans, coloureds and Indians have moved into formerly all white suburbs, but on the whole these middle-class groups tend to live in small richer enclaves in the townships. The major change in the pattern of residential segregation over the past decade or so has been the rebirth of inner city African housing, resulting in areas such as Hillbrow in Johannesburg.

Industry and infrastructure Not surprisingly the pattern of industry and infrastructure has also been affected by Apartheid. Obviously industrial development has been influenced by matters such as the proximity to raw materials, but industrial development planning has also had an influence. The main industrial centre is Gauteng where the South African industrial revolution was centred around the gold mines on the Wit watersrand. Other important industrial centres are in the major coastal port cities of Cape Town, Nelson Mandela Bay (Port Elizabeth) and Durban and around secondary mining centres in the Free State and Mpumalanga.

During the Apartheid years some efforts were made to decentralize industrialization in order to provide jobs for the African population in areas closer to the homelands. The idea was to try to prevent rural to urban migration amongst the African population and to foster the plan of overall segregation. On the whole these decentralization policies were unsuccessful, though a number of labour-intensive industries, such as garment manufacturers, did relocate to the borders of homeland areas to take advantage of the low wages prevalent in these areas of high unemployment.

Infrastructural development tends to reflect the pattern of racial segregation. The major cities and the smaller towns and villages of the former white rural areas are well served by roads, railways and other economic infrastructure. The former homeland areas tend to be badly served by roads and railways and other infrastructure, such as piped water, is also lacking. This pattern will again take many years to rectify completely, but nevertheless spending on infrastructure continues to grow steadily.

Lesotho

Landscape

Lesotho is a small country of 30,350 sq km totally surrounded by South Africa. The country is made up of a thin lowland strip along the Clarendon River valley in the west and a high mountain plateau cut into by numerous deep valleys. The lowland strip is in reality part of the great central plateau of southern Africa and hence the lowest altitude in Lesotho is over 300 m above sea level – the highest 'low point' in the world.

The vast majority of the country's rivers drain south and east. The headwaters of the famous Orange River (known as the Senqu in Lesotho) are in the far northwest of the country and its deeply incised valley runs diagonally across the mountain area, eventually flowing into South Africa across the southeastern border. Water is one of the few resources Lesotho has in abundance and, given the growing constraints of water shortages on South Africa's economy, it is a resource that is becoming increasingly valuable. The headwaters of a number of tributaries of the Senqu River are currently being developed in the massive Lesotho Highlands Water Project to allow water to be transferred to economically important South African river systems. Phase one of the scheme was successfully completed in 1996 when the massive Katse Dam was opened. The huge weight generated by filling up the dam triggered a number of minor local earth tremors, but these problems now seem to have been overcome. The Mohole dam was operational by 2004. The transfer of water from these dams to South Africa by way of tunnels now earns a substantial foreign income for the country. Lesotho has few other natural resources. Some diamonds have been discovered but not in profitable quantities and there is little hope of any lucrative mineral deposits.

With the exception of a few willows and fruit trees in sheltered kloofs and government sponsored woodlots, Lesotho is treeless. The lowlands and mountain valleys are planted with maize and, in the higher areas, wheat. The vast majority of the country is given over to communal grazing: the mountain grasses are considered to be some of the best sheep pasture in southern Africa.

Wildlife

Lesotho's large mammalian fauna has been decimated by hunting and displaced by agriculture. If you are very lucky you may see an eland in Sehlabathebe National Park or perhaps the occasional baboon or jackal, but there is none of the large game generally associated with southern Africa. There are, however, a number of interesting and unusual bird species, such as the bald ibis, found particularly in Mokhotlong district. The natural flora is dominated by grasses.

Swaziland

Landscape

The **Highlands** in the northwest are Swaziland's most important economic region with extensive forestry plantations and mining development. This is the coolest region of the country where the mountains, forests and streams of Malolotja and Pigg's Peak attract many visitors. The road descending through the Ezulwini Valley from Mbabane to Manzini is Swaziland's most popular region for tourists. The **Middleveld** runs through the centre of the country and is the major agricultural region covered in rolling grasslands. The **Lowveld** is a hot dry region of typical African savanna where pineapples and sugarcane are cultivated. Hlane National Park is a good example of this landscape. The **Lebombu** region is part of the escarpment rising up to 600 m which runs from Maputaland through the eastern boundaries of Swaziland and on into Mpumalanga. This is the least populated area with only two notable settlements at Big Bend and Siteki.

Game and nature reserves

The game reserves in Swaziland are rather overwhelmed by Kruger which is only a short drive away. However, the private game reserve at **Mkhaya** is one of the best places in Africa to see black rhino and **Malolotja** offers some challenging opportunities for hikers. Malolotja is a wilderness area developed for hikers with only the most basic facilities. The amazing mountain scenery is a relatively undiscovered, top hiking area, where a good network of trails has been developed. The Mbuluzi Gorge in **Mlawula Nature Reserve** is a little-visited region with over 300 recorded species of birds and a new network of hiking trails.

Books

Literature

South Africa has produced internationally recognized and award-winning novelists. Probably the best known is **John Coetzee**, whose novels include *Dusklands*, In the *Heart of the Country*, *Waiting for the Barbarians*, *Life & Times of Michael K* (winner of the 1983 Booker Prize), *Age of Iron, Foe* and *The Master of Petersburg*. He won the Booker Prize again in 1999 for his novel, *Disgrace*, and won the Nobel Prize for Literature in 2003, only the fourth African author to do so and the second South African after Nadine Gordimer. His style is stark and intellectual, but surprisingly accessible. He is one of the most brilliant commentators on the effects of Apartheid.

Another award-winning South African novelist is **Nadine Gordimer**. Her novels include *A Guest of Honour, The Conservationist* (winner of the 1974 Booker Prize), *Burger's Daughter, July's People, A Sport of Nature, My Son's Story, None to Accompany Me* and *Get a Life*. Her beautifully written work tends to concentrate on the way wider political/social events impact on individual lives, and she won the 1991 Noble Prize for Literature.

Bessie Head is a widely respected South African author, though much of her work is set in Botswana where she was exiled in 1964. She wrote 3 novels – *When Rain Clouds Gather*, *Maru* and the semi-autobiographical *A Question of Power*, a collection of short stories *The Collection of Treasures*, and *The Village of the Rain-wind*, a portrait of the Botswanan village, Serowe, where she lived and eventually died at the age of just 49.

Andre Brink is another internationally recognized author who has published in both English and Afrikaans. His novels in English include *A Chain of Voices, The Ambassador, Looking on Darkness, Rumours of Rain, An Act of Terror* and *A Dry White Season* (made into a Hollywood film). Like Coetzee he has published extensively on literary criticism as well as his own fiction.

Tom Sharpe, an Englishman who lived in South Africa throughout the 1950s, represents a very different literary genre. His novels *Riotous Assembly* and *Indecent Exposure* are both hilarious and the absurd situations and characters he conjures up seem eminently believable in the South African context.

Another novelist representing a previous generation is **Alan Paton**, internationally recognized (though some find him sentimental) for his novel *Cry the Beloved Country*, but he also published *Too Late the Phalarope* and *Ah, But Your Land is Beautiful* and a collection of short stories *Debbie Go Home*.

Olive Schreiner's *The Story of an African Farm* is another well-known South African novel. When it was first published in 1883 (under the pseudonym Ralph Iron) it received notoriety for its feminist and anti-racist message. **Rider Haggard** covered very different topics. His hugely popular novels *King Solomon's Mines* and *She* have a romantic theme with an African setting and remain popular today. More recently **John van de Ruit**'s 2006 novel *Spud* has taken South Africa by storm and quickly became a bestseller. It's set in 1990, the year Nelson Mandela was released and Spud Milton's first year at an élite boys-only private boarding school. This humorous book follows the adventures of the young adolescent.

The majority of the internationally recognized South African novelists described above are white. This does not mean that there is not a tradition of novel writing amongst South Africa's African, coloured and Indian populations. The two earliest African novelists in the country were **RRR Dhlomo**, who wrote *An African Tragedy* (1928) and **Sol Plaatje**, who wrote *Mhudi*, completed in 1917 but not published until 1930.

There has also been a strong emergence of modern black creative writing since the end of Apartheid. Perhaps the most important black writer today is **Zakes Mda**, who for many years worked as a playwright and poet before turning his hand to novels. His first two novels, *She Plays with Darkness* and *Ways of Dying*, place contemporary politics in the context of family and community in modern-day South Africa. *The Heart of Redness* won the Commonwealth prize and interlaces the present with the story of Nongqawuse, a princess who brought ruin to the Xhosa people. A young author who made a significant impact before tragically committing suicide in 2005 was **K Sello Duiker**. His novels *Thirteen Cents* and *The Quiet Violence* explore, respectively, street kids in Cape Town and the life of an ostracized gay student. An insight to the physical and moral decay of life in Hillbrow is provided by the critically acclaimed **Phaswane Mpe** in *Our Hillbrow*. Far from enjoying the freedoms allowed by democracy, the book depicts the native black South Africans facing the new challenges of poverty, unemployment and HIV/AIDS. He died in 2004, of an unknown illness, presumed to be HIV related.

Autobiography and political writing

The autobiography that has received most attention is **Nelson Mandela**'s *Long Walk to Freedom* (London, Abacus, 1995), a fascinating insight into the struggle. A number of other ANC leaders have also published autobiographies, including a posthumous publication by **Joe Slovo**, *Slovo: the unfinished autobiography* (Ocean Press, 1997). Autobiographies tracing the lives of less famous South Africans include **Ezekiel Mphahlele**'s *Down Second Avenue* (Johannesburg, Picador Africa, 2004), **Bloke Modisane**'s *Blame me on History* (London, Penguin, 1990), and the highly recommended *Call me Woman* by **Ellen Kuzwayo** (Johannesburg, Picador Press, 2004). There have also been collections of political speeches, articles and other writing by major political figures such as **Steve Biko**'s *I Write what I Like* (edited by Aelred Stubbs, Edinburgh, Heinemann, 1987). Others have published diaries written while in prison, such as **Albie Sachs**'s *The Jail Diary of Albie Sachs* (London, Paladin, 1990). Another interesting diary is **Sol Plaatje**'s *Mafeking Diary: a Black Man's View of a White Man's War* (edited by John L Comaroff, Johannesburg, Southern Book Publishers, 1989).

History and biography

Recommended biographies include: **Peter Alexander**'s biography of the South African novelist and well-known liberal Alan Paton, *Alan Paton* (Oxford, OUP, 1994), **William Hancock**'s biography of Jan Smuts, *The Sanguine Years, 1870-1919* and *The Fields of Force 1919-1950* (Cambridge, CUP, 1962 and 1968); **Richard Mendelsohn**'s biography of the businessman Sammy Marks, *Sammy Marks* (Cape Town, David Philip, 1991); **Antony Thomas**' book on Cecil Rhodes, *Rhodes: The Face for Africa* (Johannesburg, Jonathan Ball, 1996); **Donald Woods**' book on Steve Biko, *Biko* – the basis for the film *Cry Freedom* (London, Paddington Press, 1978); **Ruth First**'s biography of the novelist, feminist and anti-racism campaigner *Olive Schreiner* (London, Women's Press, 1989); and finally **Brian Willan** on Sol Plaatje, the novelist and early African nationalist, *Sol Plaatje: South African Nationalist 1876-1932* (London, Heinemann, 1984). Biography tends to be associated with the lives of 'great men'; one that is not is **Charles Van Onselen**'s *The Seed is Mine: the Life of Kas Maine, a South African Sharecropper, 1894-1985* (Oxford, James Curry, 1996) – it is a long book but fascinating and highly recommended. **Allister Sparks**' *Beyond the Miracle* (University of Chicago Press, 2004), charters the country's first decade of democracy, giving a balanced view of the governments successes and failures. **Antjie Krog**'s *Country* of My Skull (Three Rivers Press, 2000), an national bestseller, is written by the head of the SABC reporting team during the Truth and Reconciliation Commission, providing an often harrowing picture of how the commission affected those involved. **Greg Marinovich** and **Joao Silva**'s *The Bang Bang Club* (Arrow Books Ltd, 2001), looks at South Africa's press corps, particularly photographers, as they covered the violence in South Africa during the final years of Apartheid.

Natural history and environment

Good guides to game parks and wildlife include: **Jean Dorst** and **Pierre Dandelot**, *A Field Guide to the Larger Mammals of Africa* (London, Collins); **Gordon Maclean Roberts'** *Birds of South Africa* (Cape Town, CTP)(considered the best and has been published since 1940); **Kenneth Newman**'s *Newman's Birds of Southern Africa* (Struik Publishers, 2002); and **Braam and Piet van Wyk**, *Field Guide to the Trees of Southern Africa* (Cape Town, Struik, 1991).

Footnotes

Glossary

Braai Outside barbeque, usually a metal grill where you light your own fire underneath with wood or coals.

Dorp Literally meaning 'town', although usually refers to a small urban centre with just a collection of houses and a few farmers wandering around.

Jol A slang word derived from the Cape dialect which can refer to anything from a nice picnic to an all-night rave.

Lapa Thatched shelter, usually without walls, for entertaining, especially when braaiing.

Kraal Traditional African hut for living in, usually thatched with mud or stone walls.

Kopjie A hill or outcrop of rocks, which are usually balanced on top of each other and a common feature on wide open plains.

Potjiekos Three-legged cast-iron pots used for cooking over coals.

Bakkie A pickup car.

Biltong Dried meat to chew on as a snack, similar to beef jerky, often spiced.

Boerwors Spicy beef or game sausage popular for braaiing.

Robot South African term for traffic lights.

Shebeen Township pub.

Sesotho phrases

Hello *Lumela*

How are you? *U phela joang?*

I am fine *Ke phela hantle*

What is your name? *Lebitso la hau u mang?*

My name is… *Lebitso la ka ke…*

Where do you come from? *U tsoa kae?*

I come from… *Ke tsoa…*

May I have some water *Ke kopa metsi*

May I have food *Ke kopa lijo*

What is the price? *Ke bokae?*

Stay well *Sala hantle (salang hantle* – plural)

Thank you *Kea leboha*

Siswati

Hello *Sawubona*

How are you? *Kunjani?*

Goodbye (stay well) *Sala kahle*

Thank you *Ngiyabonga*

Yes *yebo*

No *cha*

Index → *Entries in bold refer to maps.*

Advertisers' index

Acknowledgements

Lizzie would like to thank the various tourism offices, bureaus and associations that cover just about every *dorp* (village) in South Africa as well as the regional and national tourism associations who are doing such an outstanding job at promoting South African to a worldwide audience. Thanks also to all friends in the tourism industry from backpacker's hostels to tour operators who constantly keep me updated with what's new to do and see in South Africa. Readers that wrote in with updates and helpful suggestions include Johan and Essie M, Carol and James Watson, Lars Elle, Michael Anderson, John Hicks, Colman Chamberlain, Michael Mattle, Barbara Squires, Amanda Sebestyen, Pat Horsler, Robert van der Bruggen, Rosemary Goodman, John Summerhayes, Adam Furse, David Hamburger, Anne O'Neill and Danousia Anthony.

    Thanks also to William Gray, Robert Joseph and Caroline Sylge authors of Footprint's *Travel with Kids, Wine Travel Guide to the World* and *Body & Soul escapes*, for contributing to the front colour section of this guide.

Credits

Footprint credits
Editor: Felicity Laughton
Map editor: Sarah Sorensen
Picture editor: Kassia Gawronski

Managing Director: Andy Riddle
Publisher: Patrick Dawson
Editorial: Alan Murphy, Nicola Gibbs,
Sara Chare, Ria Gane, Jen Haddington
Cartography: Robert Lunn, Kevin Feeney,
Emma Bryers
Cover design: Robert Lunn
Design: Mytton Williams
Sales and marketing: Zoë Jackson,
Hannah Bonnell
Advertising sales manager: Renu Sibal
Finance and administration: Elizabeth
Taylor

Photography credits
Front cover: Johan Swanepoel/Shutterstock
Back cover: Sean Nel/Shutterstock

Wildlife colour section: NATUREPL (Karl
Ammann, Ingo Arndt, Peter Blackwell, Nigel
Bean, John Cancalosi, Philippe Clement,
Richard Du Toit, Laurent Geslin, Tony Heald,
Eliot Lyons, Pete Oxford, Andrew Parkinson,
Constantinos Petrinos, T J Rich, Jose B Ruiz,
Francois Savigny, Anup Shah, Mike Wilkes)

Manufactured in India by Nutech
Photolithographers, Delhi
Pulp from sustainable forests

Footprint feedback
We try as hard as we can to make each Footprint
guide as up to date as possible but, of course,
things always change. If you want to let us know
about your experiences
– good, bad or ugly – then don't delay, go
to **www.footprintbooks.com** and send in
your comments.

Publishing information
Footprint South Africa
9th edition
© Footprint Handbooks Ltd
September 2008

ISBN 978 1 906098 19 3
CIP DATA: A catalogue record for this book
is available from the British Library

® Footprint Handbooks and the Footprint
mark are a registered trademark of Footprint
Handbooks Ltd

Published by Footprint
6 Riverside Court
Lower Bristol Road
Bath BA2 3DZ, UK
T +44 (0)1225 469141
F +44 (0)1225 469461
discover@footprintbooks.com
www.footprintbooks.com

Distributed in the USA by Globe Pequot Press,
Guilford, Connecticut